DICTIO...
FAITHS &
FOLKLORE

A SUPERSTITION OF THE MONTH OF DECEMBER.

On Christmas Eve it is reputed in some districts that cocks crow all night, and thus scare away evil spirits for future days.

DICTIONARY OF
FAITHS &
FOLKLORE
BELIEFS, SUPERSTITIONS
AND POPULAR CUSTOMS

W. C. HAZLITT

Dictionary of Faiths and Folklore

First published in 1905 by
Reeves and Turner, London.

This edition published in 1995 by Bracken Books, an imprint of
Studio Editions Ltd, Princess House, 50 Eastcastle Street,
London W1N 7AP, England

ISBN 1 85891 251 2
Printed and bound in Guernsey by
The Guernsey Press Co Ltd

PREFACE.

It is very rarely indeed that a book on Popular Antiquities or any other analogous topic so commends itself to the public, and so maintains its rank and estimation, as to continue to be the recognised source of reference in successive editions during more than a century and a half.

The present work, from its first appearance under the auspices of the Rev. Henry Bourne in 1725, and under the title of *Antiquitates Vulgares*, has so largely and essentially partaken of the anecdotal character, and so much depends on detail, not only for the confirmation of statements, but for the maintenance of interest, that an Editor, whatever he may do in the withdrawal of positive redundancies, is scarcely able to emulate the judicial conciseness of Buckle in his *History of Civilization* or the rhetorical and imposing periods of Macaulay. A compiler of a picture of Ancient Manners and Opinions on a documentary and lexicographical principle or basis, besides a bare statement of facts, has, as it were, to call witnesses, and record their depositions for the benefit of the reader. His personal views and experience are apt to be of service in chief measure in the choice of authorities and in the arrangement of evidence. Much of the charm in a book of the present class must necessarily lie in more or less copious and varied illustration, and its value and use would be impaired by lending to it the character of a summary or digest. The reader in this case prefers to form his own conclusions, and to linger over descriptive passages.

JOHN BRAND, as Secretary to the London Society of Antiquaries, and as a zealous collector of old and curious books during a long series of years, while such things remained within the reach of persons of moderate resources, enjoyed the opportunity of selecting extracts illustrative of the subject, which he had made his own in the character of successor to the author of *Antiquitates Vulgares;* and so far as an amplified republication of Bourne went, he lived to bring out in 1777 a more complete edition, yet on the same narrow and imperfect lines. During the latter years of his life, however, he proceeded to accumulate material for an undertaking on a larger and more comprehensive scale, and at the time of his death was in possession of a large body of MSS. collectanea of unequal value, eventually secured by a firm of publishers, and placed for editorial purposes in the hands of Sir Henry Ellis, of the British Museum. Ellis found, no doubt, amid the pressure of official work, considerable difficulty in reducing the whole to anything like method and form; but he accomplished what he could, and presented the world with the result in two large quarto volumes in 1813.

When I in 1869 entered on an examination of this text, I was disposed to exercise a free hand in every way; but I remember that I was dissuaded from going so far as my own feeling prompted me by the idea on the part of some of my advisers that to interfere with the work of such eminent antiquaries too drastically was little less than sacrilege. I have only once regretted the course, which I actually took thirty-five years ago—and that is ever since.

As material Brand's extracts had, and have, their undoubted worth, nor is the text of Ellis much more than rough copy; but it was found requisite on the former occasion to rearrange and collate the whole, and in once more re-editing the volumes on a new principle certain matter, from the discovery of better information and other causes, proved superfluous or undesirable.

The sectional arrangement, which has hitherto prevailed in regard to the book, unavoidably interfered with its use as a ready means of acquiring the desired particulars about any given subject, more especially as it constituted one of the exigencies of such a method to repeat in substance, even in the laboriously revised text of 1870, certain statements and, which was yet more inconvenient, to make it necessary for the referrer to collect the full detail, of which he might be in search, from two or three divisions of the three-volume work, under which they were perhaps not inappropriately ranged.

The new plan has been one of Disintegration and Redistribution, and will have, it is trusted, the effect of bringing more promptly and handily within reach the details connected with the enormous number of subjects, with which the Dictionary deals. At the same time, an excess in the way of subdivisions of matter or entries has been, so far as possible, avoided, as such a course has a necessary tendency to scatter references up and down the volume, and to interfere with the view of a subject in all its bearings.

By reason of the new lexicographical form, which the *Popular Antiquities* takes, a very considerable body of additional matter has been introduced from a wide variety of sources, sometimes, in justice to those authorities, in an abbreviated form with a reference. But, as a rule, the accounts of customs and other topics, where they occurred in the Editor's Brand of 1870, were already more copious and satisfactory. Nothing, however, has been taken from other works, unless it was directly connected with the subject-matter of the present undertaking.

In the edition of 1870 I thought it desirable to intersperse occasional quotations and extracts from modern sources, in order to shew the survival of customs and beliefs, and this feature has now been considerably developed, as it seemed of importance and interest as establishing the two-sided aspect of these matters in a large number of instances and the fact, not always realized, that we have not yet, after all these centuries and in the face of our boasted education and enlightenment, outlived the prejudices of our ancestors.

Numerous cross-references will be observed to the Glossary of Nares, 1859, the Dictionary of Halliwell, 1860, and Davis's *Supplementary Glossary*, 1881. The Editor did not see the utility of repeating or borrowing information elsewhere so readily accessible, and in some cases of a glossarial character rather than cognate to the immediate object. The value of this class of entry lies in its collateral service as a sort of index to the body of facts or statements readable elsewhere.

Two other publications by the present writer run on very parallel lines : his edition of Blount's *Jocular Tenures*, 1874, and of Ray's *Proverbs* (second and improved edition), 1882. Many collateral illustrations of the topics embraced in the volume before us occur in those two works, to which I must frequently content myself with directing the reader.

Since the first recension of the archæological labours of Blount, Bourne, Brand, and Ellis was published by me, the critical and comparative study of Popular Mythology has, under the auspices of the Folk-Lore Society, been elevated into a science. It was impracticable, even had it been expedient and proper, to incorporate with these pages facts and opinions based on this higher and deeper view of the topics before me, and my volume has to recommend itself to attention and favour mainly as a repository, more or less methodically assorted, of all the substantive information, which it has been in my power to collect and to reduce, in this second essay, to a reformed system.

There may be said perhaps to be three periods or stages of development in the case of our national popular archæology : 1. the early school of lexicography and writing, when philology and etymology were very imperfectly understood : 2. the age of the more modern antiquaries and glossarists when this study was placed on a very improved footing, but was still limited to superficial or *prima facie* evidence: and 3. the quite recent Folk-Lore movement, when in all these matters a latent sense is sought and *sometimes* found.

Whatever view may be taken of a large proportion of the obsolete or moribund usages and superstitions, of which the following pages attempt to constitute a record, it is certain that on two broad and solid grounds they deserve and demand commemoration. For in the first place they very importantly illustrate the writings and policy of our ancestors alike in their absolute and in their relative aspects, and secondly they render it more possible for us to judge the amount and degree of progress in knowledge and culture, which have been attained in the intervening time, and of which we are in actual enjoyment.

It is quite a moot question indeed, if not something more, whether the stricter scientific platform will ever extinguish or indeed seriously affect the public interest in this class of antiquities as described in the ordinary fashion on more or less uncultured lines.

In reference to some of the authorities quoted it may be desirable to meet the allegation that they are too slight and untrustworthy, by pointing out that for the immediate and special purpose, authenticity and *bona fides* being presumed and granted, the minor popular writers are precisely the class of witnesses and vouchers, which we require to assist us in elucidating the statements and views of those of a higher reach.

The authors quoted naturally and necessarily often belong to the school brought up side by side with the notions and beliefs, of which I am treating, and in not a few cases were partakers of them. It is necessary, however, to guard against accepting secondary or unscientific testimony for more than it is in its nature worth, and it is on that account that I have endeavoured, so far as it lay in my power, to arrange the text of this recension agreeably to the principle of proportion or degree of contributory weight.

The governing aim has been to accumulate and arrange to the best advantage and in the most convenient shape as large a body as possible of real or supposed matters of fact on all branches of the subject, with which I deal; and in re-editing the 1870 book, to adapt it to an improved state of knowledge, I trust I have been fairly successful.

It is to be remarked that the moral and conclusion derived from a perusal of the following pages are not perhaps likely to be of a very flattering nature, so far as regards either the opinions and intelligence of former ages or their educational progress. Amid a vast amount of material and detail, which can hardly fail to prove entertaining and valuable, there is much, too much, even as we draw near to our own epoch, which bespeaks a prevalence of low mental development arising, no doubt, in great measure from a faulty system of teaching both in a secular and clerical direction. Modern principles of instruction will gradually extinguish most, if not all, of the foolish prejudices and superstitions recorded here, and while it will be an unquestionable blessing, that such a change should occur, it also seems desirable that we should possess in a tolerably complete shape the means of comparison between the Older and the Newer Life of this Empire.

It is hardly too much to say that, in scrutinizing many of the headings in the Dictionary, the average reader may have to reflect, before he is assured that the views or accounts contained under them refer to the country known as Great Britain; yet how many of these customs and corruptions yet survive!

W. C. H.

Barnes Common, Surrey,
September, 1904.

NATIONAL FAITHS
AND POPULAR CUSTOMS.

Abbot of Bon Accord. — The Aberdeen name for the *Lord of Misrule*.

Abbot of Unreason. — The Scotish name for the *Lord of Misrule*, q.v. In Scotland, where the Reformation took a more severe and gloomy turn than in England, the *Abbot of Unreason*, as he was called, with other festive characters, was thought worthy to be suppressed by the Legislature as early as 1555. Jamieson seems to have thought, however, that the abolition of these sports was due rather to the excesses perpetrated in connection with them than to the Reformation. Perhaps this may be considered almost as a distinction without a difference.

Abingdon, Berks.—For a custom after the election of a mayor here, see the *Gentleman's Magazine* for Dec., 1782.

Abraham-Men, itinerant beggars, who ranged town and country after the Dissolution of Monasteries and the absence of any other system of p r-relief. There is some illustration of this subject in *Hazlitt's Popular Poetry*, 1864-6, iv, 17 *et. se.*, in Harman's *Caveat*, 1567, &c., Compare *Tom of Bedlam*.

Advertisements and Bills. — The Poster for a wide variety of purposes is known to have been in use in England, nc less than in France and Germany, at an early period, and shared with the Cry and Proclamation the function of notifying approaching events or official ordinances. Hazlitt's *Shakespear: The Man and the Writer,* 2nd ed. 1903, pp. 102-3. This method of notification also prevailed toward the latter end of the reign of Elizabeth in respect to theatrical performances, which were announced on advertisements affixed to conspicuous places; but the modern play-bill was a much later comer. There is an Elizabethan broadside recently discovered among some old MSS., setting forth the particulars of a tilting match at Westminster, to be held in honour and vindication of a certain lady, whose beauty and accomplishments the challenger was prepared to defend against all opponents. Hazlitt's *Collections and Notes*, 1903, v. *Gallophisus.*

Adventurer.—A partner in a voyage of discovery or colonization. *Adventurers on return* were persons who lent money before they started on one of these enterprizes, on condition that they should receive so much profit, if they returned home.

Admiral of the Blue, a sobriquet for a tapster, from his blue apron. Compare, as to the blue apron, Hazlitt's *Garden Literature,* 1887, pp. 9-10. The gardener and fruit-grower, however, still cling to blue paper, as a material for covering their baskets of produce.

Adoption.—Several of our sovereigns adopted children offered to them, and then contributed toward their maintenance, but did not necessarily, or indeed usually, remove them from their parents' roof. Very numerous illustrations of this custom might be afforded. In the "Privy Purse Expenses of Elizabeth of York," May, 1502, we have, for instance, this entry: "Item the xijth day of May to Mawde Hamond for keping of hire child *geven* to *the Quene* for half a yere ended at Estre last past. . . . viijs."

Æpiornis or **Epiornis.** — An extinct bird of Madagascar, of which an egg was discovered in an alluvial deposit in 1850, by M. d'Abbadie. It is said to be 13 or 14 inches long, and to have six times the capacity of that of the ostrich. The Epiornis seems to be identifiable with the *Roc* or *Rukh*, which is mentioned by Marco Polo. But it is doubtful whether this enormous creature really exceeded in size the great apteryx or moa of New Zealand, also extinct. A specimen of the egg was sold in London (November, 1899) for £44, described as about a yard in circumference, a foot in length, and of the capacity of 150 hens' eggs. Compare *Roc.*

Aërolites, the modern name and view given to the mediæval and ancient fire-balls, firedrakes, *dracones volantes,* thunderbolts, &c. Their nature is at present generally better understood, although we have yet to learn their exact origin. A very intelligent writer says, speaking of the matter of falling stars : " Amongst our selves, when any such matter is found in the fields, the very countrey-men cry it fell from Heav'n and the starres, and as I remember call it the *Spittle of the Starres.*" He adds : " An Ignis fatuus has been found fallen down in a slippery viscous substance full of white spots. They stay upon military ensigns and spears; because such are apt to stop and be tenacious of them. In the summer and hot regions they are more frequent, because the good concoction produces fatnesse." *White's Peripatetical Institutions,* 1656, p. 148. Compare *Fire-drake.* In an official account of Bendothey, co. Perth, written in 1797, it is said : "The substance called shot stars is nothing else than frosted potatoes. A night of hard frost, in the end of autumn, in which those meteors called fallen stars are seen, reduces the potatoe to the consistence of a jelly or soft pulp having no resemblance to a potato, except when parts of the skin of the potato adhere below undissolved. This pulp remains soft and fluid, when all things else in Nature are consolidated by frost : for which reason it is greedily taken up by crows and other fowls when no other sustenance is to be had, so that it is often found by man in the actual circumstance of having fallen from above, having its parts scattered and dispersed by the fall, according to the law of falling bodies. This has given rise to the name and vulgar opinion concerning it." *Stat. Acc. of Scotl.*, xix., 351.

Ætites.—The *Ætites*, or Eagle Stone, was regarded as a charm of singular use to parturient women. Lemnius says : "It makes women that are slippery able to conceive, being bound to the wrist of the left arm, by which from the heart towards the Ring Finger, next to the little Finger, an artery runs : and if all the time the woman is great with child, this jewel be worn on those parts, it strengthens the child, and there is no fear of abortior or miscarrying."—*Occult Miracles of Nature*, 1658. p. 270. Lemnius tells us elsewhere, that "the jewel called Ætites, found in an eagle's nest, that has rings with little stones within it, being applied to the thigh of one that is in labour, makes a speedy and easy delivery; which thing I have found true by experiment." Lupton speaks of "*Ætites*, called the Eagle's stone, tyed to the left arm or side; it brings this benefit to women with child, that they shall not be delivered before their time : besides that, it brings love between the man and the wife: and if a woman have a painfull travail in the birth of her child, this stone tyed to her thigh, brings an easy and light birth." Elsewhere he says: "Let the woman that travels with her child, (is in labour) be girded with the skin that a serpent or snake casts off, and then she will quickly be delivered."

Agatha's Letters, St.—Bishop Pilkington observes : "They be superstitious that put holiness in *S. Agathes Letters* for burning houses, thorne bushes for lightnings." *Burnynge of Paules Church* in 1561, 88, 1563, I. 8 and G. i.

Afternoon Music. — In Brooke's "Epithalamium," inserted in *England's Helicon*, 1614, we read :
"Now whiles slow Howres doe feed the Times delay,

Confus'd Discourse, *with Musicke mixt among*,
Fills up the Semy-circle of the Day."
In the margin opposite is put "*Afternoone Musicke*."

Agnes Day or **Eve, St.**—(Jan. 21.) St. Agnes was a Roman virgin and martyr, who suffered in the tenth persecution under the Emperor Diocletian, A.D. 306. In the office for St. Agnes' Day in the "Missale ad usum Sarum," 1554, this passage occurs : "Hec est Virgo sapiens quam Dominus *vigilantem invenit*," The Gospel is the parable of the Virgins. The "Portiforium ad usum Sarum" declares that Agnes was the daughter of immaculate parents. — *Cujus mater Virgo est, cujus pater fœminam nescit*, and that she was so deeply versed in magic, that it was said that Christ was her spouse. The festival of St. Agnes was not observed with much rigour in Germany in the time of Naogeorgus; but he describes the celebration at Rome on this anniversary as very solemn. It was customary to offer two lambs in remembrance of the legend at the high altar; these were taken by the priest and kept till shearing time, when their fleeces were used for palls. The same practice was noticed by Jephson the traveller in Italy in 1794. The life of this Saint was written by L. Sherling (*i.e.*, Daniel Pratt), in prose and verse, and printed in 1677. On the eve of her day many kinds of divination are practised by virgins to discover their future husbands. It is called fasting St. Agnes' Fast. The following lines of Ben Jonson allude to this :

"And on sweet St. Agnes' night
Please you with the promis'd sight,
Some of husbands, some of lovers,
Which an empty dream discovers."

She was condemned to be debauched in the public stews before her execution; but her virginity was miraculously preserved by lightning and thunder from Heaven. About eight days after her execution, her parents going to lament and pray at her tomb, they saw a vision of angels, among whom was their daughter, and a lamb standing by her as white as snow, on which account it is that in every graphic representation of her there is a lamb pictured by her side.

Burton, in his "Anatomy," also speaks of this sort of divination, and Aubrey, in his "Miscellanies," directs that "Upon St. Agnes' Night you take a row of pins, and pull out every one, one after another, saying a Pater Noster, sticking a pin in your sleeve, and you will dream of him or her you shall marry." This anniversary is known in connection with the celebrated poem by Keats. In the bishopric of Durham, the country people have the following address in use:

" Fair St. Agnes, play thy part,
And send to me my own sweetheart,
Not in his best nor worst array,
But in the clothes he wears every day :
That to-morrow I may him ken,
From among all other men."

I have observed that in Cornwall, where
we should speak of St. Agnes, they say *St.
Anne*, as if the two names, if not persons,
were the same. Yet females are sometimes
christened *Agnes Anne*.

Agues.—Aubrey furnishes an infallible receipt for the cure of an ague : Write
this following spell on parchment, and
wear it about your neck. It must be writ
triangularly :

> ABRACADABRA
> ABRACADABR
> ABRACADAB
> ABRACADA
> ABRACAD
> ABRACA
> ABRAC
> ABRA
> ABR
> AB
> A

With this the writer affirms that one at
Wells in Somersetshire had cured above a
hundred of the disease. He gives another
specific for the same purpose a little further on : " Gather cinquefoil in a good aspect of ♃ to the ☾ and let the moone be in
the mid-heaven, if you can, and take
—— of the powder of it in white
wine. If it be not thus gathered
according to the rules of astrology,
it hath little or no virtue in it."
Other superstitious cures follow for the
thrush, the toothache, the jaundice, bleeding, &c.—*Miscellanies*, ed. 1857, 133, 134,
137, where farther information may be
found. Blagrave prescribes a cure of
agues by a certain writing which the
patient weareth, as follows : " When Jesus
went up to the Cross to be crucified, the
Jews asked Him, saying, Art thou afraid?
or hast thou the ague? Jesus answered
and said, I am not afraid, neither have I
the ague. *All those which bear the name
of Jesus about them shall not be afraid,
nor yet have the ague.* Amen, sweet Jesus,
Amen, sweet Jehovah, Amen." He adds :
" I have known many who have been cured
of the ague by this writing only worn
about them ; and I had the receipt from
one whose daughter was cured thereby,
who had the ague upon her two years."
To this charact, then, may be given, on the
joint authority of the old woman and our
doctor, " *Probatum est*." — *Astrological
Practice d'Physic*, p. 135. In Ashmole's
Diary, 11 April, 1681, is preserved the following curious incident : " I took early in
the morning a good dose of elixir, and
hung three spiders about my neck, and
they drove my ague away. Deo Gratias !"

Ashmole was a judicial astrologer, and the
patron of the renowned Mr. Lilly. *Par
nobile fratrum.* In Pope's Memoirs of P.
P. Clerk of the Parish, is the following :—
" The next chapter relates how he discovered a thief with a Bible and key, and
experimented verses of the Psalms that
had cured agues." Douce notes that, in
his day, it was usual with many persons
about Exeter, who had the ague, " to visit
at dead of night the nearest cross road five
different times, and there bury a new-laid
egg. The visit is paid about an hour before the cold fit is expected ; and they are
persuaded that with the egg they shall
bury the ague. If the experiment fail,
(and the agitation it occasions may often
render it successful) they attribute it to
some unlucky accident that may have be-
fallen them on the way. In the execution
of this matter they observe the strictest
silence, taking care not to speak to any
one, whom they may happen to meet.—
Gentleman's Magazine, 1787, p. 719. I
shall here note another remedy against the
ague mentioned as above, viz., by breaking a salted cake of bran and giving it to
a dog, when the fit comes on, by which
means they suppose the malady to be
transferred from them to the animal."
Compare *St. Germanus.*

Aldate, St.—Hearne, in his *Diary*,
informs us that this personage was a
bishop of Gloucester, living in the time of
Hengist, whom he slew ; and a part of Oxford is still named after him. But his existence is questionable. *Diary*, 1869, ii.,
285.

Ale.—*Ale*, or *eale*, A.-S. (a form not yet
obsolete) seems to be considered as significant in the present connection of nothing,
more or less, than a merry-making. " That
ALE is *festival* appears from its sense in
composition," says Warton ; " as amongst
others, in the words Leet-ale, Lamb-ale,
Whitsun-ale, Clerk-ale, and Church-ale.
Leet-ale, in some parts of England, signifies the dinner at a court-leet of a manor
for the jury and customary tenants. Lamb-
ale is still used at the village of Kirtling-
ton in Oxfordshire, for an annual feast or
celebrity at lamb-shearing. Clerk-ale occurs in Aubrey's ' History of Wiltshire,'
printed in 1847. Church-ale was a feast
celebrated for the repair of the church, or
in honour of the church saint. In Dods-
worth's Manuscripts, there is an old indenture, made before the Reformation, which
not only shews the design of the Church-
ale, but explains this particular use and
application of the word ale. . . But Mr.
Astle had a curious record about 1575,
which proves the Bride-ale synonymous
with the Weddyn-ale.* . . . . Among
Bishop Tanner's MSS. additions to Cowel's
' Law Glossary,' in the Bodleian Library,
is the following note from his own collec-

tions : 'A.D. 1468. Prior Cant. et Commissarii visitationem fecerunt (Diocesi Cant. vacante per mortem archipiscopi) et ibi publicatum erat, quod potationes factæ in ecclesiis, vulgariter dictæ Yelealys, vel Bredealys, non essent ulterius in usu sub pœna excommunicationis majoris.' ". For Scot-ales, give-ales, leet-ales, bride-ales, clerk-ales, &c., see " Archæol," vol. xii. p. 11-77. In the MSS. Papers of Aubrey, under date of 1678, it is said that " in the Easter Holidays, was the Clerk's ale for his private benefit and the solace of the neighbourhood." " Antiquarian Repertory." No. 26. Mr. Denne, in his " Account of stone figures carved on the porch of Chalk Church," ("Archæol." vol. xii. p. 12,) says: " the Clerks' ale was the method taken by the Clerks of parishes to collect more readily their dues ." In the *Church Times* about twenty years ago, appeared the following account of the matter by Mr. Pope, which may be considered worth preservation :— " We read of Scotales and give-ales, appellations thought to be used synonymously ; but their meanings are distinct. Scotales, as the word imports, were maintained by contribution of those resorting to them. Thus the tenants of South Malling in Essex, which belonged to the Archibishop of Canterbury. were at keeping of a court to entertain the lord or his bailiff with a feast, or an ale, and the stated quotas toward the charge were. that a man should pay 3½d. for himself and his wife, and a widow 1¼d. In Terring, Sussex, it was the custom to make up a Scot-ale of sixteen pence halfpenny, and allow out of each sixpence three halfpence to find drink for the bailiff. There were also feasts in which the prefix Scot was omitted, and instead thereof, leet-ale, bride - ale, clerk - ale, and Church - ale, To the first contributed all the residents the second was defrayed by the relatives of the happy pair, who were too poor to buy a wedding dinner. The Clerk's-ale was at Easter, and was the method taken to enable clerks of parishes to collect the more readily their due. (Aubrey's Hist., Wilts). From an old indenture, before the Reformation, is seen the design for a church-ale. " The parishioners of Elveston and Okebrook (Derbyshire) agree jointly to brew four ales, and every ale of one quarter of malt betwixt this and the feast of St. John the Baptist next coming. That every inhabitant of Okebrook be there. That every husband and his wife shall pay twopence, and every cottager one penny, and all profits and advantages shall be and remain to the use of the church of Elveston. And the inhabitants of Elveston shall brew eight ales betwixt this and the said feast of St. John, at which feasts or ales the inhabitants of Okebrook shall

come and pay as before rehearsed." These different contributions were mostly, in a greater or less degree, compulsory. But the giveales were the legacies of individuals and differed from the Scotales in that they were entirely gratuitous; though some might be in addition to a common giveale before established in the parish. The history of Kent gives many instances in the parishes of Hoo, Snodland, Cowling, Wateringbury, and others, *e.g.*,: — " St. Mary's, Hoo, Test. Will Hammond, ' Also I will that specially my feoffees and exors. see that the Yeovale of St. James's be kept for ever, as it hath bin here aforetime.' " Hoo, Alhallows, Test. John Devell. ' Allsoe I will that the geavalle of Alhalows in Hoo have one acre of land after my wife's decease to maintain it withall, called Pilchland, and that it be done after the custom of olde time." At Cowling, Test. Tho. Love and Tho. Tomys. " I will that my wife Joane shall have house and my daur [? daywere] land to keep or doe a yevall on St. James's day, to which yevall I bind it (the land) whosoever have it without end." Giveales differ also materially from Scotales in their having been blended with notions of a superstitious tendency ; for the bequest was often to the light or altar of a saint, with directions to sing masses at the obit, trental, or anniversary of the testator's death. Lands were settled for the perpetual payment of the legacies thus appropriated. The parish of St. John, Thanet. is possessed of 15 acres acquired by a legacy bequeathed for a giveale by Ethelred Banen in 1513, who willed that " such a yearle yeovale should be maintayned while the world endureth." It was evident that a man in high glee over " a stoup of strong liquor " was not an unusual sight within the precincts of a church. At St. Mary's, Chalk, near Gravesend, William May, in his will, 1512, gave, *inter alia*, To every godchild he had in Kent 6 bushels of barley ; if 4 of them could bear him to the church 6d. each: his executors to buy 2 new torches for his burial, 2d. each to men to bear them. That his wife make every year for his soull an obit in bread 6 bushels of wheat, in drink 10 bushels of malt, in cheese 20d., to give poor people for the health of his soull. His wife to continue the obit before rehearsed for evermore, These give-ales on obsequies, as on dedications, allowed great freedom in sports, dissolute dances in churches and churchyards, and this is particularly instanced in the churchyard of St. Mary, Chalk. " The porch has a grotesque carving in the portrait of a jester grasping a jug, while his principal is exercising his talents as a posture maker, and two other faces appear on whom the sculptor seems to have bestowed such an indelible smirk, that in spite of corrosion by time and weather, to the almost loss of features, the smile is yet visible. In the centre is a niche formerly occupied by the figure of the Blessed Virgin. The whole subject is doubtless intended to realise a feast in the precincts of the church on the dedication carried on whilst a private Mass was being performed at the altar." (*Archæologia*, 1794). At many other churches grotesque figures are mixed up with sacred subjects. At St. Mary's Church, Chalk, her statue was demolished by the iconoclasts of the 17th century; although possibly there might not be at that time a parishioner aggrieved, or in whose mind the image would have excited an idolatrous propensity. But the grotesque figures escaped the hammers of those pious reformers, whose tender feelings were not hurt with the view of a toper and hideous contortionist carved on the front of a house of prayer, notwithstanding, in their own conceits, they held purer doctrines, were sanctimonious in their devotions and stricter in their morals than other men. Compare *Whitsuntide*.

Ale-House.—Ale-houses are at present licensed to deal in tobacco; but it was not so from the beginning; for so great an incentive was it thought to drunkenness, that it was strictly forbidden to be taken in any ale-house in the time of James I. There is an ale-house licence extant, which was perhaps *circâ* 1630 granted by six Kentish justices of the peace: at the bottom the following item occurs: "Item, you shall not utter, nor willingly suffer to be uttered, drunke, or taken, any tobacco within your house, celler, or other place thereunto belonging." See Hazlitt's *Bibl. Coll.*, General Index, 1893. v. *Alehouse*, and Lemon's *Cat. of the Soc. of Antiquaries' Broadsides*, 1866.

Ale-Stake, or Bush.—The former term is found in very early use, as in 1375 the Mayor and Aldermen of London imposed restrictions on the extent to which alestakes might project over the highway. Riley's *Memorials*, 1868, p. 386. Bansley, in his "Treatise on the Pride and Abuse of Women," *circâ* 1550, says:

" For lyke as the jolye ale house
 Is alwayes knowen by the good ale stake,
So are proud Jelots sone perceeved to
 By theyr proude foly, and wanton gate."

Comp. *Bush.*

Allhallow Even, *vulgarly Hall E'en* or *Nutcrack Night*. Hallow Even is the vigil of All Saints' Day, which is on the first of November. In the Roman Calendar I find under November 1: " The feast of *Old Fools* is removed to this day." This was also known as Soulemass Day, or corruptly, *Salmes Day*, which latter form occurs in the " Plumpton Correspondence," under 1502. Comp. *Hallowe'en.*

All Fours.—A game at cards, said in the *Compleat Gamester*, 1680, to be very much played in Kent. But in the time of Queen Anne it appears from Chatto (*Facts and Speculations*, 1848, p. 166), to have shared with Put, Cribbage, and Lanterloo the favour of the lower orders. Comp. Davis, *Suppl. Glossary*, 1881, p. 11. (ii.) A sport for the amusement of children, where a grown-up person goes *a quatre pattes*, and allows a child to ride on his back. Masson, in his *Napoléon et les Femmes*, describes that great man doing this to please his nephew, the future Emperor.

All-Hallows..—See *Hallowe'en* and *Hallowmass.*

All-Hid. — See Levins' *Manipulus*, 1570, p. 293. In *Love's Labour Lost*, written, before 1598, iv., 3, this is called " An infant play." In *Hamlet, Act* iv., sc. ii., the Prince of Denmark says: " . . . The King is a thing," upon which Guilderstein rejoins, " A thing, my lord?" whereupon Hamlet adds: " Of nothing. Bring me to him. Hide, fox, and all after." This is supposed to be an allusion to the sport called *All Hid.* Steevens tells us that it is alluded to in Decker's " Satiromastix:" " Our unhandsome-faced poet does play at bo-peep with your Grace, and cries *All-hid* as boys do." In " A Curtaine Lecture," 1637, p. 206, is the following passage: " A sport called *All-hid*, which is a mere children's pastime."

All in the Well, a juvenile game described by Halliwell (*Dict.* 1860, in v.) as played in Newcastle and the neighbourhood.

All Saints. — See *Hallow-e'en* and *Hallowmass.*

Alsatia, a popular name for Whitefriars, while it enjoyed the privilege of a sanctuary. Shadwell's *Squire of Alsatia*, Scott's *Fortunes of Nigel*, and Ainsworth's *Whitefriars*, illustrate this point.

Altar.—Selden remarks: " The way of coming into our great churches was anciently at the west door, that Men might see the Altar, and all the Church before them; the other Doors were but posterns." *Table Talk*, ed. 1860, p. 131. Moresin tells us that altars in Papal Rome were placed toward the east, in imitation of ancient and heathen Rome. *Papatus*, 117. Thus we read in Virgil's Eleventh Æneid :

" Illia ad surgentem conversi lumina
 Solem
Dant fruges manibus salsas."

Comp. *Bowing.*

Ambassador. — A trick to duck some ignorant fellow or landsman, frequently played on board ships in the warm latitudes. It is thus managed: a large tub is filled with water, and two stools placed on each side of it. Over the whole is thrown a tarpaulin, or old sail: this is kept tight by two persons, who are to represent the King and Queen of a foreign country and are seated on the stools. The person intended to be ducked plays the Ambassador, and after repeating a ridiculous speech dictated by him, is led in great form up to the throne, and seated between the King and Queen, who rising suddenly as soon as he is seated, he falls backward into the water.

Ampoule, St.—See *Graal.*

Amulets.—There appears to be some ground for supposing that the most ancient amulets, sentences from Scripture, originated in the usage of burying portions of the sacred writings with holy men. A paper on the subject is printed in the *Antiquary* for 1896. Burton has the following passage: "Amulets, and things to be borne about, I find prescribed, taxed by some, approved by others: looke for them in Mizaldus, Porta, Albertus, &c. A ring made of the hoofe of an asse's right fore-foot carried about, &c. I say with Renodeus they are not altogether to be rejected. Piony doth help epilepsies. Pretious stones, most diseases. A wolf's dung carried about helps the cholick. A spider, an ague. &c. . . . Such medicines are to be exploded that consist of words, characters, spells and charms, which can do no good at all, but out of a strong conceit, as Pomponatius proves, or the Divel's policy that is the first founder and teacher of them." *Anatomy,* 1621, 476. Among Mr. Cockayne's "Saxon Leechdoms," there are some, as it may be supposed, for *bewitched* persons, in the form of amulets held to be efficacious. One is as follows: "Against every evil rune lay, and one full of elvish tricks, write for the bewitched man this writing in Greek, alfa, omega, Ivesum, Beronike [Veronica]." Another is: "Take a bramble apple, and lupins, and pulegium, pound them, then sift them, put them in a pouch, lay them under the altar, sing nine masses over them, put the dust into milk, drip thrice some holy water upon them, administer this in drink at three hours, at nine in the morning. etc." From the middle ages gems and rings have been regarded and employed as amulets and charms. The belief in their virtues, which were numerous and varied, was fostered by the churches, and a rich store has descended to our times. The gems bearing the effigy or figure of Pegasus or Bellerophon was held to confer courage, and was prized by soldiers. Those engraved with Andromeda reconciled differences between men and women. The image of Mercury rendered the possessor wise and persuasive, and so on. Roach Smith's

Richborough, 1850, p. 90-92. The ruby was supposed to be an amulet against poison, plague, sadness, evil thoughts, and wicked spirits; and, most wonderful of all, it warned its wearer of evil by becoming black or obscure. Brahman traditions describe the abode of the gods as lighted by enormous rubies and emeralds. The magical properties of the sapphire are rated as high as those of the ruby. It was sacred to Apollo, and was worn by the inquirer of the oracle at his shrine. During the Middle Ages it continued in high estimation, because it was supposed to prevent evil and impure thoughts. and it was worn by priests on account of its power to preserve the chastity of the wearer. St. Jerome affirmed that it procures favour with princes, pacifies enemies, and obtains freedom from captivity; but one of the most remarkable properties ascribed to it was the power to kill any venomous reptile that was put into the same glass with it. *H. B. Wheatley.* The turquoise was believed to be a protection from falls, and the amethyst against intoxication. Jasper cured madness, and agate was an antidote to the poison of scorpions and spiders, besides being beneficial to the eyes. Lemnius remarks, "So coral, piony, misseltoe, drive away the falling sicknesse, either hung about the neck or drank with wine. Rosmary purgeth houses, and a branch of this, hung at the entrance of houses, drives away devils and contagions of the plague, as also ricinus, commonly called Palma Christi, because the leaves are like a hand opened wide. Corall bound to the neck takes off turbulent dreams and allays the nightly fears of children. Other jewells drive away hobgoblins, witches, nightmares, and other evill spirits, if we will believe the monuments of the Antients." — *Occult Secrets of Nature,* 1658, p. 270. But coins with the effigies of saints, such as the gold *angels,* and the *George noble,* or the touch-pieces in gold and silver, in the English series, were also credited with the power of guardianship against sickness and casualties. The George noble. with its legend taken from a hymn by Prudentius *Tali Dicata Signo Mens Fluctuare Nequit,* was supposed to protect the wearer who suspended it round his neck, against accidents in riding; and perhaps the peculiar rarity of the half noble of this type may indicate its more general uses for the purpose aforesaid. A curious gold florin, with the Madonna and Child on reverse. struck by one of the Dukes of Gueldres, is still preserved in the original gold box, and is supposed to have been carried on the person as a charm. Hazlitt's *Coins of Europe.* 1893, p. 200. In cases of trepanning for epilepsy, the portions excised were formerly employed as amulets against the disease. Hering has the following: "Perceiving many in this citie to weare about their necks, upon the region of the heart, certaine placents or amulets, (as preservatives against the pestilence), confected with arsenicke, my opinion is that they are so farre from effecting any good in that kinde, as a preservative, that they are very dangerous and hurtfull, if not pernitious, to those that weare them."—*Preservative against the Pestilence*, 1625, sign. B. 2 *verso*. Cotta inserts "A merrie historie of an approved famous spell for sore eyes. By many honest testimonies, it was a long time worne as a jewell about many necks, written in paper and enclosed in silke, never failing to do soveraigne good when all other helps were helplesse. No sight might dare to reade or open. At length a curious mind, while the patient slept, by stealth ripped open the mystical cover, and found the powerful characters Latin: ' Diabolus effodiat tibi oculos, impleat foramina stercoribus.' " — *Short Discoverie*, 1612, p. 49. In Wiltshire, a lemon stuck with pins, and in Lincolnshire the heart of an animal similarly treated, were, so lately as 1856, treated as amulets against witchcraft. — *Notes and Queries*, 2nd S., i., 331, 415. It was a supposed remedy against witchcraft to put some of the bewitched person's water, with a quantity of pins, needles, and nails into a bottle, cork them up and set them before the fire, in order to confine the spirit: but this sometimes did not prove sufficient, as it would often force the cork out with a loud noise, like that of a pistol, and cast the contents of the bottle to a considerable height. In one of the Essays of Montaigne, where he refers to the marriage of Madame de Gurson, we see that the fear of a spell being cast upon the couple, when they had retired to their chamber, was met, when the company had assembled in the room, and the bride and bridegroom had partaken of the spiced wine, by Jacques Pelletier producing his amulet, which defeated the enchantment. Douce has given wood engravings of several Roman amulets: these were intended against fascination in general, but more particularly against that of the evil eye. Such, he observes, are still used in Spain by women and children, precisely in the same manner as formerly among the Romans.--*Illustr. of Shakespear*, 1807, i., 493. Mungo Park, in his Travels, speaking of "certain charms or amulets called Saphies, which the negroes constantly wear about them," says: "These saphies are prayers or sentences from the Koran, which the Mahometan priests write on scraps of paper and sell to the natives, who suppose them to possess extraordinary virtues. Some wear them to guard

against the attack of snakes and alligators: on such an occasion the saphie is enclosed in a snake or alligator's skin, and tied round the ancle. Others have recourse to them in time of war, to protect their persons from hostile attacks: but the general use of these amulets is to prevent or cure bodily diseases, to preserve from hunger and thirst, and conciliate the favour of superior powers." He informs us in another place, that his landlord requested him to give him a lock of his hair to make a saphie, as he said he had been told it would give to the possessor all the knowledge of white men. Another person desired him to write a saphie · Mr. Park furnished him with one containing the Lord's Prayer. He gave away several others. These saphies appear to have corresponded with the " chartes of health," mentioned in some of our own early writers. The same, speaking of a Mahometan negro who, with the ceremonial part of that religion, retained all his ancient superstition, says that, "in the midst of a dark wood he made a sign for the company to stop, and, taking hold of an hollow piece of bamboo that hung as an amulet round his neck, whistled very loud three times; this, he said, was to ascertain what success would attend the journey. He then dismounted, laid his spear across the road, and, having said a number of short prayers, concluded with three loud whistles; after which he listened for some time as if in expectation of an answer, and receiving none, said, the company might proceed without fear, as there was no danger. — See *Caracts, Charms, Magic*, &c

Anagram. — An anagram has been defined to be " a divination by names, called by the ancients Onomantia. The Greeks referre this invention to Lycophron, who was one of those they called the Seven Starres or Pleiades; afterwards (as witnesses Eustachius) there were divers Greek wits that disported themselves herein, as he which turned Atlas for his heavy burthen in supporting Heaven, into *Talas*, that is, wretched. Some will maintain, that each man's fortune is written in his name, which they call anagramatism or metragramatism: poetical liberty will not blush to use E. for Æ., V. for W., S. for Z. That amorous youth did very queintly sure, (resolving a mysterious expression of his love to Rose Hill) when in the border of a painted cloth he caused to be painted as rudely as he had devised grossly, a rose, a hill, an eye, a loaf, and a well, that is if you spell it, ' I love Rose Hill well.' " Worcester, in his "Dictionary," gives a somewhat more satisfactory account of the meaning of the word and thing. " An Anagram," he says, " is a word or sentence of apt significance, formed by transposing the letters of another word or sentence *Est vir qui adest*, formed from Pilate's question *Quid est Veritas?*" Mr. Wheatley's monograph "Of Anagrams," 1862, should also be consulted, as well as the Editor's extensive *Additions* in the *Antiquary*.

Ancients.—The governing body at Gray's Inn corresponding to the Benchers of the two Temples and Lincoln's Inn.

Andrew's Day, St. — (November 30). The patron saint of Scotland. The legend of St. Andrew, with that of St. Veronica, in Anglo-Saxon, has been edited for the Cambridge Antiquarian Society (8vo. series) by Mr. Goodwin. A Life of St. Andrew, from a MS. in the Bibliothéque Imperiale at Paris, is given in "Chronicles of the Picts and Scots," 1867. It is a mere summary or sketch. A second and more lengthy narrative, from Harl. MS., 4628, occurs in the same volume. The reduction to nudity in this case must not be supposed to have been intended (primarily, at least) as an act of indecency, but rather as a relict of paganism. The ancients, our own Saxon forefathers not excepted, seem to have made an absence of clothing in some instances part of their religious rites, and the same idea was found by early travellers prevailing among the inhabitants of the American continent.—See *Ourselves in Relation to a Deity and a Church*, by the present Editor. 1897, pp. 92, 97. Luther says, that on the evening of the Feast of St. Andrew, the young maidens in his country strip themselves naked; and, in order to learn what sort of husbands they shall have, they recite a prayer.—*Colloquia Mensalia*, part i. p. 232. The prayer was: "Deus Deus meus, O Sancte Andrea, effice ut bonum pium acquiram virum: hodie mihi ostende qualis sit cui me in uxorem ducere debet." Naogeorgus probably alludes to the observances noticed above as to nudity, when he says:

"To Andrew all the lovers and the lustie wooers come,
Beleeving, through his ayde, and certain ceremonies done,
(While as to him they presentes bring, and conjure all the night.)
To have good lucke, and to obtaine their chiefe and sweete delight."

We read, that many of the opulent citizens of Edinburgh resort to Dudingston parish, about a mile distant, in the summer months to solace themselves over one of the ancient homely dishes of Scotland, for which the place has been long celebrated. The use of singed sheeps' head boiled or baked, so frequent in this village, is supposed to have arisen from the practice of slaughtering the sheep fed on the neighbouring hill for the market, removing the carcases to the town, and leaving the head, &c., to be consumed in the place. Singed sheeps' heads are borne in the procession before the Scots in London on St. Andrew's Day. Hasted, speaking of the parish of Easling, says, that, "On St. Andrew's Day, Nov. 30, there is yearly a diverson called squirril-hunting in this and the neighbouring parishes, when the labourers and lower kind of people, assembling together, form a lawless rabble, and being accoutred with guns, poles, clubs, and other such weapons spend the greatest part of the day in parading through the woods and grounds, with loud shoutings; and, under the pretence of demolishing the squirrils, some few of which they kill, they destroy numbers of hares, pheasants, partridges, and in short whatever comes in their way, breaking down the hedges, and doing much other mischief, and in the evening betaking themselves to the alehouses, finish their career there, as is usual with such sort of gentry."—"Hist. of Kent," folio ed. vol. ii. p. 757. At Stratton, in Cornwall, on this anniversary, at a very early hour a number of youths pass through the different parts of the town to the accompaniment of the blowing of a remarkably unmelodious horn, the fearful strumming of tin pans, &c., driving out, presumably, any evil spirits which haunt the place—greed, fraud, drunkenness, gluttony, and their companions. The hand-bell ringers follow, gently inviting more acceptable spirits—content, fair play, temperance, chastity, and others. After a suitable pause, the church bells ring out, in peals of eight, a hearty welcome to these latter.

Andrew's Well, St. — Martin, speaking of the Isle of Lewis, says that, "St. Andrews' Well, in the village of Shadar, is by the vulgar natives made a test to know if a sick person will die of the distemper he labours under. They send one with a wooden dish, to bring some of the water to the patient, and if the dish, which is then laid softly upon the surface of the water, turn round sun-ways, they conclude that the patient will recover of that distemper; but if otherwise, that he will die." — *Western Islands of Scotland*, p. 7. In a French version of the romance of *Bevis of Hampton* there is an allusion to the pilgrimage on foot to St. Andrew's Well as of equal efficacy to that to Mont St. Michel in Brittany for the removal of certain physical troubles. This was St. Andrew's, in Fifeshire. Michel, *Les Ecossais en France*, 1862, ii., 498.

Angelica. — See Nares, *Glossary*, 1859, in v.

Angels or **Genii.** — Bourne says: " The Egyptians believed that every man had three angels attending him: the Pythagoreans, that every man had two; the Romans, that there was a good and evil genius."—Butler's "Angel bad or tutelar." "Every man," says Sheridan in his notes to "Persius," (2d. edit. 1739, p. 28) "was supposed by the ancients at his birth to have two Genii, as messengers between the gods and him. They were supposed to be private monitors, who by their insinuations disposed us either to good or evil actions; they were also supposed to be not only reporters of our crimes in this life, but registers of them against our trial in the next, whence they had the name of Manes given them." Few are ignorant that Apollo and Minerva presided over Athens, Bacchus and Hercules over Bœotian Thebes, Juno over Carthage, Venus over Cyprus and Paphos, Apollo over Rhodes: Mars was the tutelar god of Rome, as Neptune of Tænarus; Diana presided over Crete, &c., &c. St. Peter succeeded to Mars at the revolution of the religious Creed of Rome. He now presides over the castle of St. Angelo, as Mars did over the the ancient Capitol. Hereupon Symmachus, Against the Christians, says: "The divine Being has distributed various Guardians to cities, and that as souls are communicated to infants at their birth, so particular genii are assigned to particular societies of men." Moresin tells us that Papal Rome, in imitation of this tenet of Gentilism, has fabricated such kinds of genii for guardians and defenders of cities and people. Thus she has assigned St. Andrew to Scotland, St. George to England, St. Denis to France, St. Egidius to Edinburgh, St. Nicholas to Aberdeen. Popery has in many respects closely copied the heathen mythology. She has the supreme being for Jupiter, she has substituted angels for genii, and the souls of saints for heroes, retaining all kinds of dæmons. Against these pests she has carefully provided her antidotes. She exorcises them out of waters, she rids the air of them by ringing her hallowed bells, &c. The Romanists have similarly assigned tutelar gods to each member of the body: as, for instance, the arms were under the guardianship of Juno, the breast, of Neptune, the waist, of Mars, the reins, of Venus; and so on." The following extract from "Curiosities, or the Cabinet of Nature," by Robert Basset, 1637, p. 228, informs us of a very singular office assigned by ancient superstition to the good Genii of Infants. The book is by way of question and answer: " Q. Wherefore is it that the childe cryes when the absent nurses brests doe pricke and ake?" ' A. That by dayly experience is found to be so, so that by that the nurse is hastened home to the infant to supply the defect: and the reason is that either at that very instant that the infant hath finished its concoction, the breasts are replenished, and, for want of drawing, the milke paines the breast, as it is seen likewise in milch cattell: or rather the good genius of the infant seemeth by that means to sollicite or trouble the nurse in the infants behalfe: which reason seemeth the more firme and probable, because sometimes sooner, sometimes later, the child cryeth, neither is the state of nurse and infant alwayes the same." The Negroes believe that the concerns of the world are committed by the Almighty to the superintendence and direction of subordinate spirits, over whom they suppose that certain magical ceremonies have great influence. A white fowl suspended to the branch of a particular tree, a snake's head, or a few handsful of fruit, are offerings to deprecate the favour of these tutelary agents.

Aneling.—Among the articles of expense at the funeral of Sir John Rudstone, Mayor of London, 1531, given by Strutt, we find the following charges: "Item to the priests at his ennelling, 9s. 0d.: to poor folke in almys, £1 5s. 0d.: 22 days to 6 poor folke. 2s. 0d.: 26 days to a poore folke, 8d." *Ennelling* is the extreme unction. Comp. Nares, *Glossary,* 1859, in v.

Anne's Well, near Nottingham, St.—Deering says: "By a custom time beyond memory, the Mayor and Aldermen of Nottingham and their wives have been used on Monday in Easter week, morning prayers ended, to march from the town to St. Anne's Well, having the town waits to play before them, and attended by all the Clothing and their wives, *i.e.,* such as have been Sheriffs, and ever after wear scarlet gowns, together with the officers of the town, and many other burgesses and gentlemen," &c.— *Hist. of Nottingham,* 125.

Anthony of Egypt or Thebes, St. — This eminent man, sometimes called *The Great,* has been occasionally confounded with his namesake of Padua, and the error appears to be of old standing, as there are early representations, where the Egyptian saint is exhibited with a firebrand in his hand, with flames beneath him, and a black hog, the symbol of gluttony and sensuality, under his feet, so that he may have been regarded as the archenemy of the qualities characteristic of the animal, rather than as the patron or protector of it. In the "Memoirs of Arthur Wilson," the historian and dramatist, written by himself, the erysipelas is called St. Anthony's fire, and such continues to be its common or vulgar name;

it has received certain others; *Ignis sacer, rual des artus, ergot*, &c., and it was not unknown to the ancients. In the Cleveland country, the disease, instead of St. Anthony's fire, is known as Wildfire. The alleged reason was that the people of Dauphiny, cured by the saint of this complaint, gave it his name; but the real fact seems to be, that the disease sprang from his penury and physical under-nourishment, and that the sufferers in this province were apt to be cured by being received into the Abbey of St. Antoine at Vienne, where they were properly fed. Sir John Bramston notes the death of his daughter-in-law Elizabeth Mountford, 9th December, 1689, and describes this complaint, to which she seems to have suc-cumbed. "She had been very ill," he says, "with a distemper called St. An-thonie's fier, her eyes, nose, face, and head swelled vastly; at length it took her tongue and throat."—*Autobiography*, p. 348.

A writer in the *Globe* newspaper, March 6th, 1899, observes: "One of the most picturesque customs in Mexico is that of blessing animals, called the bless-ings of San Antonio. The poorer class take their domestic animals of all kinds, dogs, cats, parrots, sheep, horses, burros, &c., to be sprinkled with holy water, and to receive through the priest St. An-thony's blessing. It is the custom of the common class to clean and bedeck their animals specially for this blessing. Dogs are gaily decorated with ribbons tied around their necks. Sheep are washed thoroughly until their fleece is as white as snow, and then taken to the father to be blessed. The beaks of the parrots are gilded. Horses and burros are adorned with garlands.

Anthony of Padua, St., *Abbot and Confessor.* — Riley furnishes the sub-stance of the oath exacted in 1311, 4. Ed-ward III., from the Renter as to the swine of the House of St. Anthony or An-tonine, whereby that official was re-strained from making the privilege en-joyed by such animals a cover for begging or alms, and from putting bells round their necks, or suffering others to do so in regard to their property to the extent of his power. *Memorials of London Life*, 1868, p. 83. Davis, *Suppl. Glossary*, 1881, p. 19. The exemption from the ordinary regulations in regard to vagrant swine also prevailed in mediæval times with perhaps greater latitude. Hazlitt's *Venetian Republic*, 1900, ii., 352. Bale, in his "Kynge Johan," says: "Lete Saynt Antoynes hogge be had in some regarde." There is an early notice of the legend of St. An-thony and the pigs to be found in the "Book of Days" under January 17. In

"The World of Wonders," translated from Stephanus, p. 57, is the following translation of an epigram:

"Once fed'st thou, Anthony, an heard of swine,
And now an heard of monkes thou feed'st still;
For wit and gut alike both charges bin:
Both loven filth alike: both like to fill
Their greedy paunch alike. Nor was that kind
More bestly, sottish, swinish, then this last.
All else agrees: one fault I onely find,
Thou fedest not thy monkes with oaken mast."

The author mentions before persons "who runne up and downe the country, crying, "Have you anything to bestow upon my lord S. Anthonies swine?"

Apostle Spoons.—It was anciently the custom for the sponsors at christenings to offer gilt spoons as presents to the child: these spoons were called Apostle spoons, because the figures of the twelve Apostles were chased or carved on the tops of the handles. Opulent sponsors gave the whole twelve. Those in middling cir-cumstances gave four; and the poorer sort contented themselves with the gift of one, exhibiting the figure of any saint in hon-our of whom the child received its name. It is in allusion to this custom that when Cranmer professes to be unworthy of being sponsor to the young Princess, Shake-spear makes the King reply, "Come, come, my lord, you'd spare your spoons." In the year 1560, we find entered in the books of the Stationers' Company: "A spoyne, the gyfte of Master Reginold Wolfe, all gylte, with the pycture of St. John." Ben Jonson also, in his "Bar-tholomew Fair," mentions spoons of this kind: "And all this for the hope of a couple of Apostle spoons and a cup to eat caudle in." So, in Middleton's "Chaste Maid in Cheapside," 1630: "Second Gos-sip: What has he given her? What is it, Gossip?—Third Gossip: A faire high-standing cup and two great postle spoons, one of them gilt." Again, in Davenant's "Wits," 1636:

"My pendants, carcanets, and rings,
My christening caudle-cup and spoons,
Are dissolved into that lump."

Again, in the "Noble Gentleman," by Beaumont and Fletcher:

"I'll be a gossip. Bewford,
I have an odd Apostle spoon."

Shipman, in his "Gossips," is pleasant on the failure of the custom of giving Apostle spoons, &c., at christenings:

" Especially since Gossips now
Eat more at christenings than bestow.
Formerly, when they us'd to troul
Gilt bowls of sack, they gave the bowl ;
Two spoons at least ; an use ill kept ;
'Tis well now if our own be left."

Comp. Nares, *Glossary*, 1859, and Halliwell's *Dict.*, 1860, in vv.

Apparitions. — " The Chylde of
Bristowe," the romances of " Sir Amadas " and " The Avowynge of King
Arthur," Shakespear's " Hamlet," the
ballad of " William and Margaret," Dryden's " Cymon and Iphigenia " (a very
ancient fiction in a comparatively modern
dress), may be mentioned in passing, as
fair samples of the various shapes which
the inhabitants of the Land of Shadows
have taken from time to time at the bidding of poets, playwrights, novelists, and
balladmongers. Scott has sufficiently demonstrated, in his " Letters on Demonology and Witchcraft," that the appearance of spectres to persons in their sleep,
and even otherwise, can in most cases be
explained on the most common-place
medical principles, and originates in mental illusions engendered by undue indulgence or constitutional debility. A great
deal of learning in connection with our
popular superstitions generally is in that
work most entertainingly conveyed to us ;
but I do not feel that I should be rendering any substantial service by transplant-
ing thence to these pages detached
passages illustrative of the immediate
subject. The " Letters " should be read
in their full integrity, for they are
among the most admirable things Scott
has left. In connection with the subject
of apparitions, may be cited the visions of
the Holy Maid of Kent, and the vision of
John Darley, a Carthusian monk. The history of the former is perhaps too familiar
to need any recapitulation here. Darley
relates that, as he was atending upon the
death-bed of Father Raby, in the year
1534, he said to the expiring man : " Good
Father Raby, if the dead can visit the
living, I beseech you to pay a visit to me
by and by : " and Raby answered, " Yes,"
immediately after which he drew his last
breath. But on the same afternoon about
five o'clock, as Darley was meditating in
his cell, the departed man suddenly appeared to him in a monk's habit, and said
to him, " Why do you not follow our
father?" " And I replied," Darley tellse
us, " ' Why ? ' He said, ' Because he is a
martyr in heaven next to the angels.'
Then I said," says Darley : " 'Where are all
our other fathers who did like him ?' He answered and said ' They are all pretty well,
but not as well as he is.' And then I asked
him how he was, and he said
' Pretty well.' And I said, ' Father,

shall I pray for you ? ' To which he
replied, ' I am as well as need be, but
prayer is at all times good,' and with
these words he vanished." On the following Saturday, at five o'clock in the morning, Father Raby reappeared, having this
time a long white beard and a white staff
in his hand. " Whereupon, says Darley,
" I was afraid, but he, leaning on his
staff, said to me, ' I am sorry that I did
not live to become a martyr ;' and I answered, that I thought he was as well as
though he had been a martyr. But he
said, ' Nay, for my Lord of Rochester and
our father were next to the angels.' I
asked ' What else ? ' He replied, ' The
angels of peace lamented and mourned un-
ceasingly' ; and again he vanished." The
" Lord of Rochester " was, of course,
Bishop Fisher. A curious and interesting
account of the pretended visions of Elizabeth Barton, whose case excited so strong
a sensation in the reign of Henry VIII.,
will be found in Mr. Thomas Wright's
Collection of Original Letters. On the
Suppression of the Monasteries, 1843. In
" The Death of Robert Earl of Hunting-
ton," 1601, Matilda feels the man who has
been sent by King John to poison her and
the abbess, and says :

" Are ye not fiends, but mortal bodies,
    then ?"

The author of the popular ballad of " William and Margaret " (quoted in the
" Knight of the Burning Pestle," 1613),
in describing Margaret's ghost, says :

" Her face was like an April morn,
    Clad in a wintry cloud ;
And clay-cold was her lily hand,
    That held her sable shroud."

In Aubrey's Miscellanies, 1696, there
is the well-known tradition of Lady
Diana Rich, daughter of the Earl of Holland, beholding her own apparition, as
she walked in her father's garden at Kensington, in the day-time, shortly before
her death, and of her sister experiencing
the same thing prior to her decease. The
former lady was in bad health at the time,
a fact which may partly account for the
circumstance. It may be recollected that
at an abbey not far from the residence of
Sir Roger de Coverley was an elm walk,
where one of the footmen of Sir Roger saw
a black horse without a head, and accordingly the butler was against anyone going
there after sunset. In this legend have
we the germ of Captain Mayne Reade's
Headless Horseman? Gay has left us a
pretty tale of an apparition. The golden
mark being found in bed is indeed after
the indelicate manner of Swift, or rather
is another instance of the obligation of our
more modern writers to the ancient story-
books), but yet is one of those happy

strokes that rival the felicity of that dash of the sponge which (as Pliny tells us) hit off so well the expression of the froth in Protogenes' dog. It is impossible not to envy the author the conception of a thought which we know not whether to call more comical or more pointedly satirical. Comp. *Ghosts, Spirits,* &c.

Apollonia's Day, St. (Feb 9.)— In the *Comedy of Calisto and Melibœa,* circâ 1520, in Hazlitt's Dodsley, i. :

" It is for a prayer mestres my de-
　　mandyng,
That is sayd ye haue of Seynt Appolyne
For the toth ake wher of this man is in
　　pyne."

In the *Conflict of Conscience,* by N. Woodes, 1581, this " virgin and martyr," it is said, should be invoked in cases of toothache.

Apple-Howling.—In several counties the custom of apple-howling (or Yuling), to which Herrick refers in his " Hesperides," is still in observance. A troop of boys go round the orchards in Sussex, Devonshire, and other parts, and forming a ring about the trees, they repeat these doggerel lines :

" Stand fast root, bear well top,
Pray God send us a good howling crop ;
Every twig, apples big :
Every bough, apples enou ;
Hats full, caps full,
Full quarter sacks full."

Hasted says : " There is an odd custom used in these parts, about Keston and Wickham, in Rogation Week ; at which time a number of young men meet together for the purpose, and with a most hideous noise run into the orchards, and incircling each tree, pronounce these words :

" Stand fast root ; bear well top ;
God send us a youling sop,
Every twig apple big,
Every bough apple enow."

For which incantation the confused rabble expect a gratuity in money or drink, which is no less welcome : but if they are disappointed of both, they with great solemnity anathematize the owners and trees with altogether as significant a curse. " It seems highly probable that this custom has arisen from the ancient one of perambulation among the heathens, when they made prayers to the gods for the use and blessing of the fruits coming up, with thanksgiving for those of the preceding year ; and as the heathens supplicated Eolus, god of the winds, for his favourable blasts, so in this custom they still retain his name with a very small variation : this ceremony is called Youling, and the word is often used in their invo-

cations." Comp. *Twelfth Day, Wassail* and *Yule.*

Appleton-Thorn. — Mr. Wilbraham, in his " Cheshire Glossary," 1826, says : " At Appleton, Cheshire, it was the custom at the time of the wake to clip and adorn an old hawthorn which till very lately stood in the middle of the town. This ceremony is called the Bawming (dressing) of Appleton Thorn."

April Fools.—Maurice, speaking of " the First of April, or the ancient Feast of the Vernal Equinox, equally observed in India and Britain," tells us : " The first of April was anciently observed in Britain as a high and general festival, in which an unbounded hilarity reigned through every order of its inhabitants ; for the sun, at that period of the year, entering into the sign Aries, the New Year, and with it the season of rural sports, and vernal delight, was then supposed to have commenced. The proof of the great antiquity of the observance of this annual festival, as well as the probability of its original establishment in an Asiatic region, arises from the evidence of facts afforded us by astronomy. Although the reformation of the year by the Julian and Gregorian Calendars, and the adaptation of the period of its commencement to a different and far nobler system of theology, have occasioned the festival sports, anciently celebrated in this country on the first of April, to have long since ceased : and although the changes occasioned, during a long lapse of years, by the shifting of the Equinoctial points, have in Asia itself been productive of important astronomical alterations, as to the exact era of the commencement of the year ; yet on both continents some very remarkable traits of the jocundity which then reigned, remain even to these distant times. Of those preserved in Britain, none of the least remarkable or ludicrous is that relic of its pristine pleasantry, the general practice of making April-Fools, as it is called, on the first day of the month ; but this Colonel Pearce proves to have been an immemorial custom among the Hindoos, at a celebrated festival holden about the same period in India, which is called 'the Huli Festival.' During the Huli, when mirth and festivity reign among the Hindoos of every class, one subject of diversion is to send people on errands and expeditions that are to end in disappointment, and raise a laugh at the expense of the person sent. The Huli is always in March, and the last day is the general holiday. I have never yet heard any account of the origin of this English custom : but it is unquestionably very ancient, and is still kept up even in great towns, though less in them than in the country. With us, it is chiefly confined to the lower class of people; but in India high and low join in it; and the late Suraja Doulah, I am told, was very fond of making Huli Fools, though he was a Mussulman of the highest rank. They carry the joke here so far, as to send letters, making appointments in the name of persons who, it is known, must be absent from their house at the time fixed upon; and the laugh is always in proportion to the trouble given.' The least inquiry into the ancient customs of Persia, or the minutest acquaintance with the general astronomical mythology of Asia, would have taught Colonel Pearce that the boundless hilarity and jocund sports prevalent on the first day of April in England, and during the Huli Festival of India, have their origin in the ancient practice of celebrating, with festival rites the period of the Vernal Equinox, or the day when the new year of Persia anciently began." *Ind. Antiq.*, vi., 71. Cambridge tells us that the first day of April was a day held in esteem among the alchemists, because Basilius Valentinus was born on it. In the North of England persons thus imposed upon are called " April gowks." A gouk or gowk is properly a cuckoo, and is used here metaphorically in vulgar language for a fool. The cuckoo is indeed everywhere a name of contempt. *Gauch*, in the Teutonic, is rendered *stultus*, fool, whence also our Northern word, a goke or a gawky. In Scotland, upon April Fool Day, they have a custom of " hunting the gowk," as it is termed. This is done by sending silly people upon fools' errands from place to place by means of a letter, in which is written:

"On the first day of April
Hunt the Gowk another mile."

A custom, says " the Spectator," prevails everywhere among us on the first of April, when everybody strives to make as many fools as he can. The wit chiefly consists in sending persons on what are called " sleeveless errands, for the " History of Eve's Mother," for " pigeon's milk," with similar ridiculous absurdities. He takes no notice of the rise of this singular kind of anniversary. But Dr. Pegge, in the " Gentleman's Magazine " for 1766, has a tolerably plausible conjecture that the first of April ceremonies may be deducible from the old New Year's Day rejoicings. New Year's Day formerly falling on the 25th March, the first of April would have been the octaves on which the proceedings may have terminated with some such mummeries as these. A writer in one of the papers, under date of April 1, 1792, advances a similar theory, not aware

that he had been anticipated. In " The Parson's Wedding," the Captain says: " Death! you might have left word where you went, and not put me to hunt like Tom Fool." So, in Defoe's " Memoirs of the late Mr. Duncan Campbel," 1732, p. 163: " I had my labour for my pains; or, according to a silly custom in fashion among the vulgar, was made an April-Fool of, the person who had engaged me to take these pains never meeting me." In the " British Apollo," 1708, is the following query: — " Whence proceeds the custom of making April Fools? Answer. — It may not improperly be derived from a memorable transaction happening between the Romans and Sabines, mentioned by Dionysius, which was thus: the Romans, about the infancy of the city, wanting wives, and finding they could not obtain the neighbouring women by their peaceable addresses, resolved to make use of a stratagem; and accordingly Romulus instituted certain games, to be performed in the beginning of April (according to the Roman Calendar), in honour of Neptune. Upon notice thereof, the bordering inhabitants, with their whole families, flocked to Rome to see this mighty celebration, where the Romans seized upon a great number of the Sabine virgins, and ravished them, which imposition we suppose may be the foundation of this foolish custom." This solution is ridiculed in No. 18 of the same work as follows:

" Ye witty sparks, who make pretence
To answer questions with good sense,
How comes it that your monthly Phœbus
Is made a fool by Dionysius?
For had the Sabines, as they came,
Departed with their virgin fame,
The Romans had been styl'd dull tools,
And they, poor girls! been April Fools.
Therefore, if this ben't out of season,
Pray think, and give a better reason."

Poor Robin, in his " Almanack for 1760," alludes to All Fools' Day, and to the practice of sending persons " to dance Moll Dixon's round," and winds up with the query—Which is the greatest fool, the man that went, or he that sent him? The following verses are hardly perhaps worth quoting:

" While April morn her Folly's throne exalts:
While Dob calls Nell, and laughs because she halts;
While Nell meets Tom, and says his tail is loose,
Then laughs in turn, and calls poor Thomas goose;

Let us, my Muse, thro' Folly's harvest
range,
And glean some Moral into Wisdom's
grange,
Verses on several Occasions, 1782, p. 50

Hone, in his *Every Day Book*, of course
mentions this custom, and illustrates it by
the urchin pointing out to an old gentleman that his handkerchief is falling out of
his tail-pocket. The French, too, have
their All-Fools' Day, and call the person
imposed upon "an April Fish," *Poisson
d'Avril*. Minshew renders the expression,
"Poisson d'Avril," a young bawd; a page
turned pandar; a mackerell; which is thus
explained by Bellingen: "Je sçay que la
plus part du monde ignorant cette raison,
l'attribue à une autre cause, & que par-
ceque les marchands de chair humaine, ou
courtiers de Venus, sont deputez a faire
de messages d'Amour & courent de part
et d'autre pour faire leur infame traffic;
on prend aussy plaisir à faire courir ceux
qu'on choisit á ce jour-lá pour objet de
raillerie, comme si on leur vouloit faire
exercer ce mestier honteux." *Ibid.* He
then confesses his ignorance why the
month of April is selected for this purpose,
unless, says he, "on account of its being
the season for catching mackerell, or that
men, awaking from the torpidity of the
winter season, are particularly influenced
by the passions, which, suddenly breaking
forth from a long slumber, excite them to
the pursuit of their wonted pleasures."
This may perhaps account for the origin
of the word "macquereau" in its obscene
sense. Leroux, "Dictionnaire Comique,"
tom. 1., p. 70, quotes the following:—

"Et si n'y a ne danger ne peril
Mais j'en feray votre poisson d'Avril."

Poesies de Pierre Michault. Goujet, Bib-
lioth. Franç. tom. ix., p. 351. The Festival of Fools at Paris, held on this day,
continued for two hundred and forty
years, when every kind of absurdity and
indecency was committed. This was probably a legacy from Pagan times, when,
according to the authorities presently
cited, the Calends of January were set
apart by all the early Christians for a
species of loose festival. Conf. "Monta-
cut. Orig. Eccles." pars prior, p. 128.
"Maeri Hiero-lexicon," p. 156; "Joannes
Boemus Aubanus," p. 265 (all quoted by
Brand). One of the Popes prohibited these
unholy rites on pain of anathema, as appears from a Mass inserted in some of the
old missals, "ad prohibendum ab Idolis."
The French appear to have had an
analogous usage on another occasion:
envoit au Temple les Gens un peu
"A la Saint Simon et St. Jude on
simple demander de Nefles (Medlars)
a fin de les attraper & faire noircir

par des Valets."—*Sauval Antiq. de Paris,*
vol. ii., p. 617.—Douce. The Quirinalia
were observed in honour of Romulus on
the 11th of the kal. of March; that is, the
19th of February. "Why do they call
the Quirinalia the Feast of Fools? Either
because they allowed this day (as Juba
tell us) to those who could not ascertain
their own tribes, or because they permitted those who had missed the celebration of the Fornacalia in their proper
tribes, along with the rest of the people,
either out of negligence, absence, or ignorance, to hold their festival apart on this
day." Plu. Quæst. Rom.; Opera, cum
Xylandri notis, fol. Franc. 1599, tom. ii.,
p. 285. The translation was communicated to Mr. Brand by the Rev. W. Walter, of Christ's College, Cambridge. The
custom of making fools on the 1st of April
prevails among the Swedes and Spaniards.
In Toreen's "Voyage to China," he says:
"We set sail on the 1st of April, and the
wind made April Fools of us, for we were
forced to return before Shagen, and to
anchor at Riswopol." For a similar
practice at Venice see Hazlitt's *Venetian
Republic*, 1900, ii., 793.

Apprentices.—We are to infer that
it was anciently usual for apprentices to
collect presents at Christmas in the form
of what we call Christmas-boxes, for Aubrey, speaking of an earthern pot dug up
in Wiltshire in 1654, tells us that it
resembled an apprentice's earthern
Christmas - box. — *Miscellanies*, ed. 1857,
p. 212. In "Pleasant Remarks on
the Humours of Mankind," we read:
"'Tis common in England for Prentices,
when they are out of their time, to make
an entertainment, and call it the Burial of
their Wives." This remains a common
expression.

Arbor Judæ.—See *Elder.*

Archery.—With the history of this
exercise as a military art we have no concern here. Fitzstephen, who wrote in the
reign of Henry II., notices it among the
summer pastimes of the London youth:
and the repeated statutes from the 13th
to the 16th century, enforcing the use of
the bow, usually ordered the leisure time
upon holidays to be passed in its exercise. Sir T. Elyot, in his "Governor,"
1531, terms shooting with or in a long
bow "principall of all other exercises,"
and he adds, "in mine opinion, none may
bee compared with shooting in the long
bowe, & that for sundry vtilities, yt come
theroff, wherein it incomparably excelleth
all other exercise. For in drawing of a
bowe, easy and congruent to his strength,
he that shooteth, doth moderately exercise his armes, and the other part of his
body: and if his bowe be bigger, he must
adde too more strength wherin is no lesse

valiant exercise then in any other. In shooting at buttes, or broade arrowe markes, is a mediocritie of exercise of the lower partes of the bodye and legges, by going a little distaunce a measurable pase. At couers or pryckes, it is at his pleasure that shoteth, howe faste or softly he listeth to goo, and yet is the praise of the shooter, neyther more ne lesse, for as farre or nigh the marke is his arrow, whan he goeth softly, as when he runneth." No one requires to be told, that a few years after the appearance of Elyot's "Governor," the learned Ascham devoted an entire treatise to this peculiarly national subject. His "Toxophilus" was published in 1545, and is still justly celebrated and admired. The regulations connected with the practice of archery constantly underwent alteration or modification. The common "Abridgement of the Statutes" contains much highly curious matter under this, as under other heads. It is sufficiently remarkable that by the Act, 12 Edw. IV. c. 2 (1472), each Venetian merchant, importing wine into England, was required to give in with each butt "four good bowstaves," under the penalty of a fine of 6s. 8d. for each default. This demand was enlarged, 1 Richard III. c. 11, in the case, at any rate, of Malvoisin or Tyre wine, with every butt of which ten bowstaves were to be reckoned in, under pain of 13s. 4d. By 19 Hen. VII. c. 2, all bowstaves of the length of six feet and a half were admitted into England free of duty. The price of a bow, by 22 Edw. IV. c. 4, was not to exceed 3s. 4d. under pain of 20s. fine to the seller. In the Robin Hood collection, printed in Hazlitt's *Tales and Legends*, 1892, p. 312, there is an account of a shooting at Nottingham. under the greenwood shade, to which all the bowmen of the North were freely invited to repair, and the prize to the winner was a silver arrow, feathered with gold. Robin won the award. We are to regard this narrative of a fourteenth century incident as one edited by a late-fifteenth century writer, namely the compiler of the *Little Gest*. By 6 Hen. VIII. cap. 13, it was ordered: "That non Shote in any crosebow nor handgon excepte he haue possessyons to the yerely valew of ccc. marke or els lycence from hensforth by the kynges placard vnder payne of .x li. ye one halfe to the kynge and the other halfe to hym that wyll sew for it / and ye forfetour of the same crosbow or handgonne to hym that wyll sease hit by accyon of det / and yt non kepe any crosebowe or hand gonne in his house on payne of iprisonment & of forfetour to the kynge .x li . . . prouydyd alway that this acte extend not to crosebow makers / nor to dwellers i wallyd townes within vii. myle of the see / and other holders on

the see costes or marchis for agayns Scotlad / kepyng crosebows for theyr defence / nor to no marchautes hauyng crosebowes & handgonnys to sel only / nor to non host loggyng any ma bryngyng them in to his house, but the forfetur to be onely vpon the brynger." Among the Churchwardens' accounts of St. Laurence Parish, Reading, 1549, is the following entry:— "Paid to Will'm Watlynton, for that the p'ishe was indetted to hym for makyng of the Butts, xxxvis." Ibid. St. Mary's Parish, 1566: "Itm. for the makyng of the Buttes, viijs." Ibid. 1622: "Paid to two laborers to playne the grounde where the Buttes should be. vs. vjd." 1629: "Paid towards the butts mending, ijs. vjd." Among the accounts of St. Giles's Parish, 1566, we have: "Itm. for carrying of turfes for the buttes, xvjd." 1605: "Three labourers, two days work aboute turfes for the butts, iiijs." "Carrying ix. load of turfes for the butts, ijs." "For two pieces of timber to fasten on the railes of the buttes, iiijd." 1621: "The parishioners did agree that the Churchwardens and Constables should sett up a payre of buttes called shooting butts, in such place as they should think most convenient in St. Giles Parish, which butts cost xivs. xjd." Wood, in his "Bowman's Glory," 1682, has republished some of the statutes relating to archery; but the earliest which he gives is of the 29 Hen. VIII. A remarkably curious tract is printed by Wood in the same volume, called "A Remembrance of the Worthy Show and Shooting of the Duke of Shoreditch (a man named Barlow, whom Henry VIII. jocularly so entitled) and his Associates, &c., 1583." Queen Elizabeth was fond of this sport, and indulged in it, as Henry Machyn the Diarist informs us, during her visit to Lord Arundel at Nonsuch, in the autumn of 1559. "The v day of August," says Machyn, "the Queens grace removyd from Eltham unto Non-shyche, my lord of Arundells, and ther her grace had as gret chere evere nyght and bankettes. . . . . as ever was sene. . . . . On monday the Quens grace stod at her standyng in the further park, and there was corse after—." Upon which Mr. Nichols quotes Hunter's "New Illustrations of Shakespeare," to show that shooting with the cross-bow was a favourite amusement then and afterward among ladies of rank. But this fact had been already sufficiently demonstrated by Strutt, who has shown that in England women excelled and delighted in the use of the common bow and cross-bow from a very early date. "In the sixteenth century we meet with heavy complaints." says Strutt, "respecting the disuse of the long-bow, and especially in the vicinity of London." Stow informs us that before his time it had been customary at Bartholomew-tide for the Lord Mayor, with the Sheriffs and Aldermen, to go into the fields at Finsbury, where the citizens were assembled, and shoot at the standard with broad and flight arrows for games: and this exercise was continued for several days: but in his time it was practised only one afternoon, three or four days after the festival of Saint Bartholomew. Stow died in 1605. After the reign of Chas. I., archery appears to have fallen into disrepute. Davenant, in a mock poem, entitled "The long Vacation in London," describes the attorneys and proctors as making matches in Finsbury Fields:

"With Loynes in canvas bow-case tied, Where arrows stick with mickle pride; Like ghosts of Adam Bell and Clymme; Sol sets for fear they'll shoot at him!"

A correspondent of the "Gentleman's Magazine" for August, 1731, notices the ancient custom among the Harrow boys, of shooting annually for a silver arrow of the value of £3; this diversion, he states, was the gift of the founder of the school, John Lyon, Esq. About 1753, a society of archers appears to have been established in the Metropolis, who erected targets on the same spot during the Easter and Whitsun holidays, when the best shooter was styled captain, and the second lieutenant for the ensuing year. Of the original members of this society, there were only two remaining when Barrington published his Observations on the Statutes in the "Archæologia." It is now incorporated in the Archers' Division of the Artillery Company. In the latter half of the 18th century, the taste remained dormant; in the earlier part of the next one the Toxophilite Society started at Old Brompton, Robert Cruikshank being one of the members; and of late years the movement has exhibited symptoms of new vitality, and archery-clubs are established in almost every part of the country. The bow, however, has ceased for ever to be a weapon of offence. It has been resigned entirely to the ladies, who form themselves into Toxophilite associations. Archery forms one of the subjects of a series of papers on our Sports and Pastimes, contributed to the *Antiquary*.

Arches, Court of, the original Consistory Court of the see of Canterbury, held in Bow Church, or St. Mary *De Arcubus*. See Nares, *Glossary*, in v.

Arles, earnest money, given to servants at hiring as a retainer. See Halliwell in v.

Armorial Bearings in Inns.— See Pegge's *Curialia*, 1818, p. 349.

Arthur, King. — "A game used at sea, when nearing the Line, or in a hot latitude. It is performed thus: a man who is to represent King Arthur, ridiculously dressed, having a large wig, made out of oakum, or some old swabs, is seated on the side, or over a large vessel of water. Every person in his turn is to be ceremoniously introduced to him, and to pour a bucket of water over him, crying. Hail, King Arthur! If, during this ceremony, the person introduced laughs or smiles, (to which his Majesty endeavours to excite him, by all sorts of ridiculous gesticulations), he changes place with, and then becomes King Arthur, till relieved by some brother tar, who has as little command over his muscles as himself."— *Arthur O'Bradley.* See Nares, Glossary, 1859, in v.

Arthur O'Bradley..—See Nares, Glossary, 1859, in v.

Arthur's Show.—A sort of dramatic spectacle presented before Queen Elizabeth at Mile-End Green, in 1587-8. See Black's *History of the Leathersellers' Company.* 1871, p. 65, and Hazlitt's Monograph on Shakespear, second edition, 1903.

Arvals. — In the North of England, at funerals, a particular sort of loaf, called arvel - bread, is distributed among the poor.—Brockett, *N.C. Gloss.*, 1825, p. 7. Mr. Atkinson notices a special kind of bread formerly made at Whitby, for use at the arval-suppers; he describes it as "a thin, light, sweet cake." It has occurred to me that the game of hot cockles, of which Aubrey has left us a tolerably good description, originated in the practice of kneading one of these funeral loaves, as the rhyme with which the girls used to accompany the supposed moulding of cockle-bread, begins—

"My dame is sick and gonne to bed, And Ile go mould my cockle-bread—"

And it is not an unreasonable supposition that, in course of time, the reason of the thing was lost, and the practice degenerated into a stupid and indelicate female sport. At the funeral of John Bagford, 1716, Mr. Clifton, a vintner, gave four bottles of sack to be drunk by the guests. Moresin, *Papatus*, tells us that in England in his time they were so profuse on this occasion, that it cost less to portion off a daughter, than to bury a dead wife. These burial feasts are still kept up in the North of England, and are there called arvals or avvils. The bread distributed on these occasions is called arvil bread. The custom seems borrowed from the ancients, amongst whom many examples of it are collected by Hornman.— *De miraculis Mortuorum*, c. 36. This word occurs in "The Praise of Yorkshire Ale":

"Come, bring my jerkin, Tibb, I'll to
    the Avril,
Yon man's ded seny scoun, it makes me
    marvill."
—P. 58.

Hutchinson thus mentions the Arval
Dinner : " On the decease of any person possessed of valuable effects, the
friends and neighbours of the family
are invited to dinner on the day of
interment, which is called the arthel
or arvel dinner. Arthel is a British
word, and is frequently more correctly
written arddelw. In Wales it is written
arddel, and signifies, according to
Dr. Davies' Dictionary, *asserere*, to
avouch. This custom seems of very distant antiquity, and was a solemn festival,
made at the time of publicly exposing the
corps, to exculpate the heir and those entitled to the possessions of the deceased,
from fines and mulets to the Lord of the
Manor, and from all accusation of having
used violence : so that the persons then
convoked might avouch that the person
died fairly and without suffering any personal injury. The dead were thus exhibited by antient nations, and perhaps the
custom was introduced here by the
Romans.—*Northumberland*, ii. 20. Compare *Funeral Customs.*

These funeral entertainments are of
very old date. Cecrops is said to have instituted them for the purpose of renewing
decayed friendship amongst old friends,
&c.

Ascension Eve. — By his will.
proved in December, 1527, John Cole, of
Thelnetham, Suffolk, directed that a certain farm-rent should be applied yearly
to the purpose of providing " a busshell
and halffe of malte to be browne and a
hushelle of whete to be baked to fynde a
drinkinge upon Ascension Even everlast-
inge for ye parishe of Thelnetham to
drinke at the crosse of Trappetes."

Ascension Day.—It was a general
custom formerly, and is still [1903] observed in some country parishes, to go
round the bounds and limits of the parish,
on one of the three days before Holy Thursday, or the Feast of our Lord's Ascension,
when the minister, accompanied by his
churchwardens and parishioners, were
wont to deprecate the vengeance of God,
beg a blessing on the fruits of the earth,
and preserve the rights and properties of
the parish. It is the custom in many villages in the neighbourhood of Exeter to
' hail the Lamb,' upon Ascension morn.
That the figure of a lamb actually appears
in the east upon this morning is the popular persuasion : and so deeply is it rooted,
that it hath frequently resisted (even in
intelligent minds) the force of the strongest argument. The following supersti-

tion relating to this day is found in Scot's
" Discovery of Witchcraft," 1584 : " In
some countries they run out of the doors
in time of tempest, blessing themselves
with a cheese, whereupon was a cross
made with a rope's-end upon Ascension
Day."—" Item, to hang an egg laid on
Ascension day in the roof of the house,
preserveth the same from all hurts."
" Yesterday being Ascension Day, work
was entirely suspended at Lord Penrhyn's
extensive slate quarries near Bangor. The
cessation of work is not due to any religious regard for the day, but is attributable
to a superstition, which has long lingered
in the district, that if work is continued
an accident is inevitable. Some years ago
the management succeeded in overcoming
this feeling and in inducing the men to
work. But each year there was a serious
accident, and now all the men keep at a
distance from the quarries on Ascension
Day."—*Times*, April 11, 1888. Ascension
Day is thus described in Googe's Naogeorgus, 1570 : —

" Then comes the day when Christ as-
    cended to his fathers seate,
Which day they also celebrate, with store
    of drink and meate.
Then every man some birde must eate, I
    know not to what ende,
And after dinner all to Church they come,
    and there attende.
The blocke that on the aultar still till then
    was seene to stande,
Is drawne vp hie aboue the roofe, by ropes
    and force of hande :
The Priests aboute it rounde do stande,
    and chaunte it to the skie.
For all these mens religion great in sing-
    ing most doth lie.
Then out of hande the dreadfull shape of
    Sathan downe they throw
Oft times, with fire burning bright, and
    dasht asunder tho,
The boyes with greedie eyes do watch, and
    on him straight they fall
And beate him sore with rods, and breake
    him into peeces small.
This done, the wafers downe doe cast, and
    singing Cakes the while,
With Papers rounde amongst them put,
    the children to beguile.
With laughter great are all things done :
    and from the beames they let
Great streames of water downe to fall, on
    whom they meane to wet.
And thus this solemne holiday, and hye
    renowned feast,
And all their whole deuotion here is ended
    with a ieast."
The unique Venetian pageant, La Sensa,
commenced on this day, and lasted a fort-
night. It was a fair, where every descrip-
tion of property, including pictures by
Titian and Tintoretto, were offered for

sale. Its attractions were as multifarious as those at Nijny Novgorod, and more elegant and refined.—Hazlitt's *Venetian Republic*, 1900, ii., 355, 756.

Ash.—Gilbert White, writing at the end of the eighteenth century, informs us that "In a farm yard near the middle of this village (Selborne) stands, at this day, a row of pollard-ashes, which by the seams and long cicatrices down their sides, manifestly shew that in former times they have been cleft asunder. These trees, when young and flexible, were severed and held open by wedges, while ruptured children, stripped naked, were pushed through the apertures, under a persuasion that by such a process the poor babes would be cured of their infirmity. As soon as the operation was over, the tree, in the suffering part, was plastered with loam, and carefully swathed up. If the parts coalesced, and folded together, as usually fell out, where the feat was performed with any adroitness at all, the party was cured ; but, where the cleft continued to gape, the operation, it was supposed, would prove ineffectual. Having occasion to enlarge my garden not long since, I cut down two or three such trees, one of which did not grow together. We have several persons now living in the village, who in their childhood were supposed to be healed by this superstitious ceremony, derived down perhaps from our Saxon ancestors, who practiced it before their conversion to Christianity. At the south corner of the Plestor or area, near the Church, there stood, about twenty years ago, a very old grotesque hollow pollard-ash, which for ages had been looked upon with no small veneration as a shrew-ash. Now a shrew-ash is an ash whose twigs or branches, when gently applied to the limbs of cattle, will immediately relieve the pains which a beast suffers from the running of a shrew mouse over the part affected : for it is supposed that a shrew-mouse is of so baneful and deleterious a nature, that wherever it creeps over a beast, be it horse, cow or sheep, the suffering animal is afflicted with cruel anguish, and threatened with the loss of the use of the limb. Against this accident, to which they were continually liable, our provident fore-fathers always kept a shrew-ash at hand, which, when once medicated, would maintain its virtue for ever. A shrew-ash was made thus : (for a similar practice see Plot's Staffordshire) : Into the body of the tree a deep hole was bored with an auger, and a poor devoted shrew-mouse was thrust in alive, and plugged in, no doubt, with several quaint incantations long since forgotten. As the ceremonies necessary for such a consideration are no longer understood, all succession is at an end, and no such tree is known to subsist in the manor or hundred. As to that on the Plestor, 'the late Vicar stubb'd and burnt it,' when he was Way-warden, regardless of the remonstrances of the by-standers, who interceded in vain for its preservation, urging its power and efficacy, and alledging that it had been

'Religione patrum multos servata annos.'"

The sap of the ash, a powerful astringent, was formerly given to the Highland children, not only as a medicine, but because it was supposed to be efficacious as a preservative against witchcraft and its allied influences. The ash itself was thought to be possessed of certain virtues by the herd-boys of the same district, who entertained an idea, that they might throw a stick of it at their cattle without injury. Comp. *Charms.*

Ash Wednesday.—Durandus, in his "Rationale" tells us, Lent was counted to begin on that which is now the first Sunday in Lent, and to end on Easter Eve ; which time, saith he, containing forty-two days, if you take out of them the six Sundays (on which it was counted not lawful at any time of the year to fast), then there will remain only thirty-six days : and, therefore, that the number of days which Christ fasted might be perfected, Pope Gregory added to Lent four days of the week before-going, viz. that which we now call Ash Wednesday, and the three days following it. So that we see the first observation of Lent began from a superstitious, unwarrantable, and indeed profane, conceit of imitating our Saviour's miraculous abstinence. Lent is so called from the time of the year wherein it is observed : Lent in the Saxon language signifying Spring, being now used to signify the Spring-Fast, which always begins so that it may end at Easter to remind us of our Saviour's sufferings, which ended at his Resurrection. Ash Wednesday is in some places called "Pulver Wednesday," that is, *Dies pulveris.* The word Lentron, for Lent, occurs more than once in the edition of the "Regiam Majestatem," 1609. Sir H. Ellis mentions that Lenten-tide for spring, when the days lengthen, occurs in the Saxon "Heptateuch," 1698. Exod. xxxiv. 18. There is a curious clause in one of the Romish Casuists concerning the keeping of Lent ; it is "that beggars which are ready to affamish for want, may in Lent time eat what they can get." This, which is the first day of Lent, *Caput Jejunii*, is called Ash Wednesday, as we read in the Festa Anglo-Romana, p. 19, from the ancient ceremony of blessing ashes on that day, and therewith the priest signeth the people on the forehead, in the form of a cross. The ashes used this day in the Church of Rome, are made of the palms blessed the Palm Sunday before. In the "Festyvall," 1511, fol. 15, it is said : "Ye shall begyn your faste upon Ashe Wednesdaye. That daye must ye come to holy chirche and take ashes of the Preestes hondes, and thynke on the wordes well that he sayeth over your hedes, (*Memento, homo, quia cinis es; et in cinerem reverteris*), have mynde thou man, of ashes thou art comen, and to ashes thou shalte tourne agayne." In a convocation held in the time of Henry the Eighth, mentioned in Fuller's "Church History," p. 222, "Giving of ashes on Ash Wednesday, to put in remembrance every Christian man in the beginning of Lent and Pennance, that he is but ashes and earth, and thereto shall return &c., is reserved with some other rites and ceremonies, which survived the shock that at that remarkable era almost overthrew the whole pile of Catholic superstitions. In a proclamation, dated 26th Feb. 30 Henry VIII., we read : "On Ashe Wenisday it shall be declared, that these ashes be gyven, to put every Christian man in remembraunce of penaunce, at the begynnynge of Lent, and that he is but erthe and ashes." On the 9th March, 1550-1, a proclamation was published against the use of flesh on "ymberyng days," as well as in Lent, &c. "Mannerlye to take theyr ashes devoutly," is among the Roman Catholic customs censured by John Bale in his "Declaration of Bonner's Articles," 1554, signat. D 4 verso, as is, ibid. D 2 verso, "to conjure ashes." In "The Doctrine of the Masse Book," 1554, fig. B 3 verso, we find translated the form of "The hallowing of the ashes." The Masse Book saith, that upon Ash-Wedensdaye, when the prieste hath absolved the people, &c., then must there be made a blessynge of the ashes, by the Prieste, being turned towards the East. In the first prayer is this passage : "Vouchsafe to blesse and sanctifie these ashes, which because of humilitie and of holy religion for the clensyng out of our trespaces, thou hast appointed us to cary upon our heades after the manner of the Ninivites." And after directions to sprinkle the ashes with holy water, and another prayer, this Rubric is added : "Then let them distribute the ashes upon the heades of the Clarckes and of the lay people : the worthier persons makyng a sygne of the Crosse with the ashes, saying thus : 'Memento, homo, quod cinis,' &c." In Bp. Bonner's "Injunctions," 1555, signat. A 1 verso, we read, "that the hallowed ashes gyven by the Priest to the people upon Ashe Wednisdaye, is to put the people in remembrance of penance at the begynnynge of Lent, and that their bodies ar but earth,

dust, and ashes." In Howes's edition of Stow's "Annales," 1631, 1547 - 8, occurs : "The Wednesday following, commonly called Ash Wednesday, the use of giving ashes in the Church was also left throughout the whole Citie of London." Lord North, in his "Forest of Varieties," 1645, p. 165, in allusion to this custom, styles one of his essays, "My Ashewednesday Ashes." The ancient discipline of sackcloth and ashes, on Ash Wednesday, is at present supplied in our Church by reading publicly on this day the curses denounced against impenitent sinners, when the people are directed to repeat an Amen at the end of each malediction. Enlightened as we now think ourselves there are many who consider the general avowal of the justice of God's wrath against impenitent sinners as cursing their neighbours : consequently, like good Christians, they keep away from church on the occasion.

"The peasantry of France," says the *Morning Chronicle*, March 10th, 1791, "distinguish Ash Wednesday in a very singular manner. They carry an effigy of a similar description to our Guy Faux round the adjacent villages, and collect money for his funeral, as this day, according to their creed, is the death of good living. After sundry absurd mummeries, the corpse is deposited in the earth." This may possibly be a relic of the same usage. Armstrong, in his "History of Minorca," says, "During the carnival, the ladies amuse themselves in throwing oranges at their lovers : and he who has received one of these on his eye, or has a tooth beat out by it, is convinced, from that moment, that he is a high favourite with the fair one who has done him so much honour. Sometimes a good hand-full of flour is thrown full in one's eyes, which gives the utmost satisfaction, and is a favour that is quickly followed by others of a less trifling nature."—"We well know that the holydays of the antient Romans were, like these carnivals, a mixture of devotion and debauchery." — "This time of festivity is sacred to pleasure, and it is sinful to exercise their calling until Lent arrives, with the two curses of these people, abstinence and labour, in its train." Aubanus tells us of a custom in Franconia on Ash Wednesday, when such young women, he says, as have frequented the dances throughout the year are gathered together by young men, and, instead of horses, are yoked to a plough, upon which a piper sits and plays : in this maner they are dragged into some river or pool. He suspects this to have been a kind of self-enjoined voluntary penance for not having abstained from their favourite diversion on holidays, contrary to the injunctions of the Church.

Ashton Fagot.—At Lidiard Lawrence, between Bishop's Lidiard and Stokegomer, Somersetshire, it has been a custom at Christmas to burn what is known as the Ashton Fagot, perhaps a designation or name derived from Long Ashton in the same county. A quart of cyder was originally provided for those—a limited company—who witnessed the ceremony, as the fagot, in reality a bundle of sticks hooped together, disappeared in the flames, the hoops successively bursting with the heat. The cyder seems to have developed into a carouse at the local inn, and as lately as 1902, one of the spectators was brought before the magistrates for disorderly conduct, and the Bench pronounced the custom a bad one. It has the aspect of being a form of the Yule-log.

Ass.—There is a superstition remaining among the vulgar concerning the ass, that the marks on the shoulders of that useful and much injured animal were given to it as memorials that our Saviour rode upon an ass. "The Asse," says Sir Thomas Browne, "having a peculiar mark of a Crosse made by a black list down his back, and another athwart, or at right angles down his shoulders, common opinion ascribes this figure unto a peculiar signation : Since that beast had the honour to bear our Saviour on his back." In the "Athenæum," about forty years ago, appeared the following:—"The popular belief as to the origin of the mark across the back of the ass is mentioned by Sir Thomas Browne, in his 'Vulgar Errors,' and from whatever cause it may have arisen it is certain that the hairs taken from the part of the animal so marked are held in high estimation as a cure for the hooping-cough. In this metropolis, at least so lately as 1842, an elderly lady advised a friend who had a child dangerously ill with that complaint, to procure three such hairs, and hang them round the neck of the sufferer in a muslin bag. It was added that the animal from whom the hairs are taken for this purpose is never worth anything afterwards, and, consequently, great difficulty would be experienced in procuring them ; and, further, that it was essential to the success of the charm that the sex of the animal, from whom the hairs were to be procured, should be the contrary to that of the party to be cured by them."

Assumption of the Virgin Mary (August 15). — Naogeorgus describes the consecration of the herbs on this festival by the priests of Germany, and laments the nourishment of popular ignorance and prejudice by such means, as the herbs when blessed or sanctified were held to be efficacious in witchcraft and magic, and if cast into the fire, to afford protection from malignant influences: "far otherwise," as the writer says truly enough, "than nature of the Worde of God doth tell."—*Pop. Kingdom,* by Barnaby Googe, 1570, p. 55. Bishop Hall, in his *Triumphs of Rome,* p. 58, also tells us, "that upon this day it was customary to implore blessings upon herbs, plants, roots, and fruits."

Aston, Birmingham.—A writer in the "Gentleman's Magazine" for February, 1795, gave the following account of a custom which took place annually on the 24th of December, at the house of a gentleman residing at Aston juxta Birmingham : "As soon as supper is over, a table is set in the hall. On it is placed a brown loaf, with twenty silver threepences stuck on the top of it, a tankard of ale, with pipes and tobacco: and the two oldest servants have chairs behind it, to sit as judges if they please. The steward brings the servants, both men and women, by one at a time, covered with a winnow-sheet, and lays their right hand on the loaf, exposing no other part of the body. The oldest of the two judges guesses at the person, by naming a name, then the younger judge, and lastly the oldest again. If they hit upon the right name, the steward leads the person back again ; but, if they do not, he takes off the winnow-sheet, and the person receives a threepence, makes a low obeisance to the judges, but speaks not a word. When the second servant was brought, the younger judge guessed first and third ; and this they did alternately till all the money was given away. Whatever servant had not slept in the house the preceding night forfeited his right to the money. No account is given of the origin of this strange custom, but it has been practiced ever since the family lived there. When the money is gone, the servants have full liberty to drink, dance, sing, and go to bed when they please." Can this be what Aubrey, in a passage elsewhere quoted from his "Natural History of Wiltshire," calls the sport of "Cob-loaf stealing?"

Astrologer. — Fuller has this passage : "Lord, hereafter I will admire thee more and fear astrologers lesse : not affrighted with their doleful predictions of dearth and drought, collected from the Collections of the planets. Must the earth, of necessity be sad, because some ill-natured starr is sullen? As if the grass could not grow without asking it leave. Whereas thy power, which made herbs before the stars, can preserve them without their propitious, yea, against their malignant aspects." *Good thoughts in Bad Times,* ed. 1669, p. 37. A prose writer of the same period observes : "Surely all astrologers are Erra Pater's disciples, and the Divil's professors, telling their opinions in spurious ænigmatical doubtful tearmes, like the Oracle at Delphos. What a blind dotage and shamelesse impudence is in these men, who pretend to know more than saints and angels? Can they read other men's fates by those glorious characters the starres, being ignorant of their owne? Qui sibi nescius, cui præscius? Thracias the sooth-sayer, in the nine years drought of Egypt, came to Busiris the Tyrant and told him that Jupiter's wrath might bee expiated by sacrificing the blood of a stranger: the Tyrant asked him whether he was a stranger: he told him he was,

> "Thou, quoth Busiris, shalt that stranger bee,
> Whose blood shall wet our soyle by Destinie."

If all were served so, we should have none that would relye so confidently on the falshood of their Ephemerides, and in some manner shake off all divine providence, making themselves equal to God, between whom and man the greatest difference is taken away, if man should foreknow future events. — Browne's *Map of the Microcosme*, 1646, sign. D 8 *verso.* Sir Aston Cokain, in his *Poems*, 1658, has a quip for the astrologers:

To Astrologers.

Your Industry to you the Art hath given
To have great knowledge in th' outside of Heaven:
Beware lest you abuse that Art, and sin,
And therfore never visit it within."

The quack astrologer has been thus portrayed: "First, he gravely inquires the business, and by subtle questions pumps out certain particulars which he treasures up in his memory; next, he consults his old rusty clock, which has got a trick of lying as fast as its master, and amuses you for a quarter of an hour with scrawling out the all-revealing figure, and placing the planets in their respective pues; all which being dispatch'd you must lay down your money on his book, as you do the wedding fees to the parson at the delivery of the ring: for 'tis a fundamental axiome in his art, that, without crossing his hand with silver no scheme can be radical: then he begins to tell you back your own tale in other language, and you take that for divination which is but repetition. . His groundless guesses he calls resolves, and compels the stars (like Knights o' th' Post) to depose things they know no more than the man i' the moon: as if Hell were accessory to all the cheating tricks Hell inspires him with. . . . He impairs God's universal monarchy, by making the stars sole keepers of the liberties of the sublunary world, and, not content they should domineer over naturals, will needs promote their tyranny in things artificial, too, asserting that all manufactures re-

ceive good or ill fortunes and qualities from some particular radix, and therefore elects a time for stuing of pruins, and chuses a pisspot by its horoscope. Nothing pusles him more than fatal necessity: he is loth to deny it, yet dares not justify it, and therefore prudently banishes it from his theory, but hugs it in his practice, yet knows not how to avoid the horns of that excellent dilemma, propounded by a most ingenious modern Poet:

> "If fate be not, how shall we ought fore-see,
> Or how shall we avoid it, if it be?
> If by free-will in our own paths we move,
> How are we bounded by decrees above?' "

—*Character of a Quack Astrologer.* 1675. He, we are told, " offers, for five pieces, to give you home with you a talisman against flies; a sigil to make you fortunate at gaming; and a spell that shall as certainly preserve you from being rob'd for the future; a sympathetical powder for the violent pains of the toothache." *Ibid.* sign. C. *verso.* Some years ago, a periodical entitled *The Astrologer* was set up in London, for the purpose of casting the horoscopes of correspondents, and furnishing intelligence connected with astrology. Its success was great; but in fact that very success it was, which killed it. The pressure of applicants was so enormous, it is said, that the post brought the letters for the editor in sacks, and the undertaking had to be given up. It is difiuclt to say when the belief in divination by the stars will be extinguished or expire: at present that belief is entertained by a numerous body of people, educated and uneducated, whose enthusiasm and credulity remain unabated. Henry, speaking of astrology, tells us, " Nor did this passion for penetrating into futurity prevail only among the common people, but also among persons of the highest rank and greatest learning. All our kings, and many of our earls and great barons had their astrologers, who resided in their families, and were consulted by them in all undertakings of great importance. Of this," he says, " we meet with a very curious example in the account given by Matthew Paris of the marriage of Frederick Emperor of Germany and Isabella sister of Henry III. A.D. 1235. The great man kept these to cast the horoscopes of his children, discover the success of his designs, and the public events that were to happen." "Their predictions," he adds, " were couched in very general and artful terms."—*History of Great Britain*, iii., 515, and iv., 577. " Nocte vero prima qua concubit Imperator cum ea, noluit eam carnaliter cognoscere, donec competens hora ab astrologis ei nunciaretur." M.

Paris, p. 285, ad ann. 1235. **Bishop Hall** says:—

"Thou damned mock-art, and thou brain-
　　sick tale
Of old astrologie"—
"Some doting gossip 'mongst the Chaldee
　　wives
Did to the credulous world thee first
　　derive:
And superstition nurs'd thee ever sence,
And publisht in profounder arts pretence:
That now, who pares his nailes, or libs his
　　swine,
But he must first take counsell of the
　　signe."

—*Virgidemiarum*, lib., ii., sat. 7. Astrology is ridiculed in a masterly manner
in *King Lear*, 1608. Mason mentions in
his list of the then prevailing superstitions: "erecting of a figure to tell of
stolne goods. Philip Henslowe has a
receipt "To know wher a thinge is that
is stolne:—Take vergine waxe and write
upon yt ✠ Jasper ✠ Melchisor ✠ Balthasar ✠ and put yt under his head to
whome the good partayneth, and he
shall knowe in his sleape wher the
thinge is become." — *Diary*, ed., 1845.
Johnson speaking of *Hudibras*, says:
"Astrology, however, against which
so much of the satire is directed,
was not more the folly of the
Puritans than of others. It had at that
time a very extensive dominion. Its predictions raised hopes and fears in minds
which ought to have rejected it with contempt. In hazardous undertakings care
was taken to begin under the influence
of a propitious planet; and, when the
King was prisoner in Carisbrook Castle an
astrologer was consulted as to what hour
would be found most favourable to an
escape." "Astrology," says "a person
of honour," "imagines to read in the constellations, as in a large book, every thing
that shall come to pass here below, and
figuring to itself admirable rencounters
from the aspects and conjunctions of the
planets, it draws from thence consequences as remote from truth as the stars
themselves are from the earth. I confess
I have ever esteemed this science vain and
ridiculous: for indeed it must be either
true or false: if true, that which it predicts is infallible and inevitable, and consequently unuseful to be foreknown. But,
if it is false, as it may easily be evinced
to be, would not a man of sense be blamed
to apply his mind to and lose his time
in, the study thereof? It ought to be the
occupation of a shallow Braine, that feeds
itself with chimerical fancies, or of an
impostor who makes a mystery of every
thing which he understands not, for to
deceive women and credulous people.—
Courtier's Calling, 1675, p. 241. Agrippa
exposes astrology as the mother of heresy,

and adds: "Besides this same fortune-
telling astrology not only the best of
moral philosophers explode, but also
Moses, Isaias, Job, Jeremiah, and all the
other prophets of the ancient law: and
among the Catholick writers, St. Austin
condemns it to be utterly expelled and
banish'd out of the territories of Christianity. St. Hierome argues the same to
be a kind of idolatry. Basil and Cyprian
laugh at it as most contemptible. Chry-
sostome, Eusebius, and Lactantius utterly
condemn it. Gregory, Ambrose, and Se-
verianus inveigh against it. The Council
of Toledo utterly abandon and prohibit it.
In the Synod of Martinus and by Gregory
the younger and Alexander III. it
was anathematized and punished by the
civil laws of the Emperors. Among the
ancient Romans it was prohibited by
Tiberius, Vitellius, Diocletian, Constan-
tine, Gratian, Valentinian, and Theodosius, ejected also, and punish'd. By Justinian made a capital crime, as may appear in his Codex."—*Vanity of Sciences*,
p 98. He pleasantly observes of astrologers, that "undertaking to tell all people
most obscure and hidden secrets abroad,
they at the same time know not what happens in their own houses and in their own
chambers. Even such an astrologer as
Henry More laught at them in his epigram:

"The Stars, ethereal bard, to thee shine
　　clear,
And all our future fates thou mak'st
　　appear.
But that thy wife is common all men know,
Yet what all see, theres not a star doth
　　show.
Saturn is blinde, or some long journey
　　gone,
Not able to discern an infant from a stone.
The moon is fair, and as she's fair she's
　　chast,
And wont behold thy wife so leudly em-
　　brac't,
Europa Jove, Mars Venus, she Mars
　　courts,
With Daphne Sol, with Hirce Hermes
　　sports.
Thus while the stars their wanton love
　　pursue,
No wonder, Cuckold, they'll not tell thee
　　true."

It appears that figures were often erected
concerning the voyages of ships from London to Newcastle, &c.—Gadbury's *Nauti-
cum Astrologicum*, 1710, pp. 93, 123, &c.
We are told in one place that the prediction was verified; the ship, though not
lost, had been in great danger thereof,
having unhappily run aground at Newcastle, sprung a shroud, and wholly lost
her keel. In another, there is a figure
given of a ship that set-sail from London

towards Newcastle, Aug. 27, 11 p.m., 1669. This proved a fortunate voyage. "As indeed," saith Gadbury, "under so auspicious a position of Heaven it had been strange if she had missed so to have done; for herein you see Jupiter in the ascendant in sextile aspect of the sun; and the moon, who is Lady of the Horoscope, and Governess of the Hour in which she weighed anchor, is applying ad Trinum Veneris. She returned to London again very well laden, in three weeks time, to the great content as well as advantage of the owner." I have to observe here that the shipowners in the Newcastle trade are now much wiser than to throw away money on such fooleries, and, with much greater propriety, when things augur ill, apply to the assurance office, in preference to that of the diviner or fortune-teller.

Dallaway tells us that astrology was a favourite folly with the Turks. "Ulugh-bey," he says, "amongst very numerous treatises is most esteemed. He remarks the 13th, 14th, and 15th of each month as the most fortunate; the Ruznameh has likewise its three unlucky days, to which little attention is paid by the better sort. The Sultan retains his chief astrologer, who is consulted by the Council on state emergencies. When the treaty of peace was signed at Kainargi in 1774, he was directed to name the hour most propitious for that ceremony. The Vizier's Court swarms with such impostors It was asserted that they foretold the great fire at Constantinople in 1782. There was likewise an insurrection of the janissaries which they did not foretel, but their credit was saved by the same word bearing two interpretations of *Insurrection* and *Fire*. It may now be considered rather as a state expedient to consult the astrologer, that the enthusiasm of the army may be fed and subordination maintained by the prognostication of victory.— *Tour to Constantinople*, p. 390.

There are even literary gentlemen who seeks counsel of their astrologer before they undertake a new venture, and when they desire to know the most propitious time for publication. A lady informed the present writer that, before she was married, she consulted Professor Wilson, of the Caledonian Road, who asked her the hour of her birth and other questions, and after elaborate calculations mentioned certain circumstances which were untrue. He then made a second experiment, placing her nativity half an hour later, and then related some matters which had really occurred to her, and others which had not, and never did—particularly, that she would have plenty of money.

Astrology, Judicial, or Astronomy.

—In "Dives and Pauper," 1493, Signat. ε 2, we meet with the following: "Or take hede to the Judicial of Astronomy—or dyvyne a mans lyf or deth by nombres and by the Spere of Pyctagorus, or make any dyvyning therby, or by Songuary or Sompnarye, the Boke of Dremes, or by the boke that is clepid the Apostles lottis." The author adds: "And alle that use any manner wichecraft or any misbileve, that all suche forsaken the feyth of holy Churche and their Cristendome, and bicome Goddes enmyes and greve God full grevously and falle into dampnacion withouten ende, but they amende theym the soner." Zouch says, mentioning Queen Mary's reign: "Judicial astrology was much in use long after this time. Its predictions were received with reverential awe; and men, even of the most enlightened understandings, were inclined to believe that the conjunctions and oppositions of the planets had no little influence in the affairs of the world. Even the excellent Joseph Mede disdained not to apply himself to the study of astrology."— Ed. of *Walton's Lives*, 1796, p. 131.

Auctions.

—The earliest Roman auctions were held *sub hastâ*, to indicate that the proceedings were carried on under public or official authority.—Smith's *Dict. of Gr. and Rom. Antiq.* 2nd ed., v. *Hasta*. During the middle ages, and down to comparatively modern times, the auctioneer continued to be known as the *subhastator*, and an auction as the *Asta*. —Lacroix, *Mœurs et Usages*, 1872. p. 337. But the trumpet and bell also came into use, as well as the crier. At Venice, in the fourteenth century, we find the bell and the cry (*campanella* and *incanto*), and there it was said that a sale was held by the bell, as in England in the 17th century the parallel expression was "to sell at the candle." Among the Anglo-Saxons time-candles appear to have been known. The Venetians, in the case at all events of official or Government sales, required guarantees for the payment of the money offered by the highest bidder.— Hazlitt's *Venetian Republic*, 1900, ii., p. 355. The system of selling by inch of candle is still retained at Broadway, Dorsetshire, when the annual lease of a meadow is sold in this way. The biddings started at £3. and the candle expired at £8 4s. 0d.—*Daily Mail*, Jan. 10. 1903. Comp. Davis. *Suppl. Glossary*, 1881, p. 100. A Dutch Auction has become a mere phrase rather than an usage. It signifies the practice of quoting an upset price, and descending by bids, until a customer occurs, whose maximum has been reached.

Augrim Stones.

—Counters formerly used in arithmetic. See Halliwell in v.

Avenor.—From Fr. *avoine*, the person who, in great towns, formerly had the superintendence of the horse-meat. See Halliwell in v.

Babies in the Eyes. See Nares, *Glossary*, 1859, in v. In Braithwaite's "Two Lancashire Lovers," 1640, p. 19, in Camillus' speech to Doriclea, in the Lancashire dialect, he tells her, in order to gain her affections, " We han store of goodly cattell; my mother, though shee bee a vixon, shee will blenke blithly on you for my cause; and we will ga to the dawnes and slubber up a sillibub; and I will looke babbies in your eyes, and picke silly-cornes out of your toes: and we will han a whiskin at every rush-bearing, a wassel cup at Yule, a seed-cake at Fastens, and a lusty cheese-cake at our sheepe-wash; and will not aw this done bravely, Jantlewoman?" In her answer to this clown's addresses, she observes, among other passages, " What know you but I may prove untoward, and that will bring your mother to her grave; make you, pretty babe, put finger ith' eye, and turne the door quite off the hinges." The above romance is said to have been founded on a true history; the costume appears to be very accurate and appropriate.

Bachelor's Buttons.—There is a rustic species of divination by bachelor's buttons, a plant so called. There was an ancient custom, says Grey, amongst the country fellows, of trying whether they should succeed with their mistresses by carrying the bachelor's buttons, a plant of the lychnis kind, whose flowers resemble also a button in form, in their pockets: and they judged of their good or bad success by their growing or not growing there. *Notes on Shakespear*, i., 108. Bachelor's buttons are described as having been worn also by the young women, and that too under their aprons. " Thereby I saw the batchelors butons, whose vertue is to make wanton maidens weepe, when they have worne it forty weekes under their aporns for a favour."—Greene's *Quip*, 1592, reprint *Collier*, p. 10.

Backgammon.—See *Tables*.

Badger-in-the-Bag. — In the tale of *Pwyll Prince of Dyved*, in the *Mabinogion*, an account is furnished of the alleged circumstances under which this game was first played, where Rhiannon persuades Gnawl, the son of Clud, to put his feet into the bag to tread down the food within, and he finds himself overhead in it, whereupon all present kicked the bag with their foot, or struck it with a staff. Every one as he came in asked, " What game are you playing at thus?" " The game of Badger-in-the-Bag," said they. And then was the game of Badger-in-the-Bag first played ." Ed. 1877, p. 350.

Badger-the-Bear.—A rough game played by boys, and described by Halliwell in v.

Bagatelle. — A well-known game played with one black and eight coloured or white balls, and a cue and mallet, and somewhat following the lines of billiards, but without pockets in the table. It is said to have been well established in 1827. Its origin is uncertain, but it is said not to be French, although the name is so. It is played with variations.

Baker's Clem.—At Cambridge the bakers have an annual supper, which is called " The Bakers' Clem." A correspondent of "Notes and Queries" (Cuthbert Bede) testifies to its celebration in 1863.

Baker's Dozen. — Originally a *Devil's Dozen*. Comp. Nares, *Glossary*, 1859, in v., and see *Numbers*.

Ballad - Monger. — Braithwaite, describing a ballad-monger, in his *Whimzies*, 1631, writes : By this time they (his ballads) are cashiered the City, and must now ride poast for the countrey: where they are no lesse admir'd than a gyant in a pageant : till at last they grow so common there too, as every poore milk-maid can chant and chirpe it under her cow, which she useth as an harmlesse charme to make her let downe her milke."

Ball-Money. — See *Nuptial Usages*.

Ball. — In the *Odyssey*, Nausicaa, daughter of the King of Phœacia, is represented playing at this game with her handmaidens; and there are Greek coins where a girl is seen engaged in the same sport. At a period posterior to Homer, it was known as Phœninda. Sophocles the tragedian, in his play of *Nausicaa*, distinguished himself in the performance by his skill at the game. Playing at ball, as early as the fourteenth century, is denounced by a bishop of London as one of the ways in which the precincts of St. Paul's Church, London, were then desecrated (1385); and this disorderly and licentious condition of affairs continued during centuries. There used to be a practice of rolling a ball down the table after dinner; it is thought that this was, when a match had been recently played, where the ball was used, and the victorious party, to whom it belonged, thus exhibited it as a trophy.

Balloon.—This was played with an inflated ball of leather, which was struck by the arm, the latter being protected by a bracer of wood. In " Eastward Hoe," 1605, Sir Pretonel Flash is represented as having a match at balloon with my lord Whackham for four crowns. Donne also mentions it :

" 'Tis ten a clock and past; all whom the
    mues,
Baloun, tennis, diet, or the stewes

Had all the morning held, now the second
Time made ready, that day, in flocks are
found."

And in a writer of somewhat later date
it is coupled with several other diversions
of the period: "also Riding the Great
Horse, Running at a ring, Tilts and Tour-
naments, are noble exercises as well as
healthy, and becoming his (the gentleman's) grandeur. In like manner, Balon,
Quintan, Stop-Ball, Pitching of a Bar,
Casting of a Weight, are healthy and laudable." — *The Gentleman's Companion*,
1676, p. 136-7. Randolph, in his eclogue
on the revival of the Cotswold Games by
Dover, seems to speak of balloon as a sort
of football. The whole passage is curious:

"Colin, I once the famous Spain did see,
A nation famous for her gravity.
Yet there a hundred knights on warlike
    steeds
Did skirmish out a fight arm'd but with
    reeds;
At which a thousand ladies' eyes did gaze,
Yet 'twas no better than our prison-base.
What is the barriers but a worthy way
Of our more downright sport, the cudgel-
    play?
—*Works*, 1875, 621.

Balls, Three.—The three blue balls
prefixed to the doors and windows of
pawnbrokers' shops, (by the vulgar humorously enough said to indicate that it is
two to one that the things pledged are
ever redeemed) were in reality the arms of
the Medici family, a branch of whom, with
many other Lombard houses, settled in
London at an early date, and concen-
trated themselves chiefly in a quarter
which was called after them Lombard
street. But in the Medici cognizance
there are six balls. On a Brabantine coin
anterior to the rise of the Medici appear
nine balls.

Ballock.—See Halliwell in v.

Bally-bleeze. — Speaking of the
Cleveland word Bally-bleeze (a bonfire),
in his Glossary of that dialect, 1868, Mr.
Atkinson remarks: "It need scarcely be
added that any assumption of an etymological connection between the name Baal
and this word bally-bleeze must be groundless. Even in the Gaelic form *baltein*,
while *tein* is equivalent to our bleeze, Dan.
blysse, Sw. *blosse*, &c., I doubt if *bal* be
radically distinct from E. *bale*, Sw. *bal*,
&c. In other words, I do not for a moment
suppose the worship of Baal, any more
than that of Balder, or Apollo, or Phœbus, considered as persons with distinct
ethnic names, was intended in these bale-
fires. It was the worship of the Sun-god
simply, and his name not even hinted at
in that of the fire-rites involved."

Banbury Cross.—Halliwell, in his
Nursery Rhymes, prints two versions of

"Ride a Cock-horse," but does not give
the following. which was often repeated to
the present Editor, while he was on his
nurse's or mother's knee, with an action
suited to the words:

'Ride a cock-horse
To Banbury-Cross,
To see an old woman
Ride on a white horse.
Rings on her fingers,
And bells on her toes,
And she shall have music
Wherever she goes."

Which appears to indicate some custom incidental to Banbury Mop or Michaelmas
Statute Fair, where perhaps some female
character on horseback was one of the performers in a procession or sport. The suggestion is offered, that there was some
local imitation of the Godiva pageant.

Banks's Horse.—See Halliwell in
v. At Hereford Midsummer Fair, in 1640,
there was, it seems, a fellow, a second
Bankes, who exhibited a dancing horse;
for in the account book of Mrs. Joyce
Jeffries under this year occurs a payment
to him.—*Archæologia*, xxxvii.

Banns. — The following account of
this subject is derived from the information of my friend Mr. Yeowell: *Notes and
Queries*, 4th S. i., 149-50. "We learn
from Tertullian, *Ad Uxorem*, De Pudici-
tiâ, c. 4, that the Church, in the primitive
ages, was forewarned of marriages. The
earliest existing canonical enactment on
the subject, in the English Church, is that
in the 11th canon of the synod of Westminster or London, A.D. 1200, which en-
acts that 'no marriage shall be contracted
without banns thrice published in the
church, unless by the special authority of
the bishop.' Wilkins' *Concilia*, i., 507.
It is supposed by some that the practice
was introduced into France as early as the
ninth century; and it is certain that Odo,
Bishop of Paris, ordered it in 1176. The
council of Lateran, in 1215, prescribed it
to the whole Latin Church. Before publishing the banns, it was the custom for
the curate anciently to affiance the two
persons to be married in the name of the
Blessed Trinity; and the banns were sometimes published at vespers, as well as during the time of mass. In the early ballad
of *Robin Hood and Allen a Dale* we have a
curious reference to the banns, where the
bishop says, in answer to Robin:

"That shall not be, the bishop he said:
For thy word shall not stand;
They shall be three times askt in the
    church,
As the law is of our land."

Banyan Day..—See Davis, *Suppl.
Glossary*, 1881, in v.

Barbara, St.—(December 4). Although Nicholas, in his "Chronology of

History," on the authority of Arundel MS. 155, seems to indicate the existence of two saints of this name, I doubt if he is not in the present case making two persons out of one, and if St. Barbara of Heliopolis in Egypt, who is mentioned in the "Anniversary Calendar" as martyred in A.D. 306, and whose life is in the "Golden Legend," as well as in a separate biography printed by Julian Notary in 1518, where she is styled virgin and martyr, is not, in reality, the only canonized lady of this name. It was formerly the usage at York to preach a sermon in St. William's Chapel on St. Barbara's Day, and Davies, in his "Extracts from the Municipal Records of York," 1843, mentions a payment of two shillings to a Bachelor of Divinity for this purpose in 18 Edw. IV. "In time of thunder," remarks Aubrey (1678), "they invoke St. Barbara. So Chaucer, speaking of the great hostess, says that her guests would cry St. Barbara, when she let off her gun."

Barbers. — The sign of a barber's shop being singular, has attracted much notice. It is generally distinguished by a long pole, with coloured bandages depicted on it, instead of a sign. The true intention of that party-coloured staff, it is explained correctly in the "Antiquarian Repertory, was to shew that the master of the shop practiced surgery, and could breathe a vein as well as mow a beard : such a staff being to this day, by every village practitioner, put into the hand of a patient undergoing the operations of phlebotomy. The white band, which encompasses the staff, was meant to represent the fillet thus elegantly twined about it. In confirmation of this opinion the reader may be referred to the cut of the barber's shop in Comenii "Orbis pictus," where the patient under phlebotomy is represented with a pole or staff in his hand. And that this is a very ancient practice appears from an illumination in a missal of the time of Edward I. I find the following odd passage in Gayton : "The barber hath a long pole elevated ; and at the end of it a labell, wherein is in a fair text hand written this word Money. Now the pole signifies itself, which joined to the written word makes Pole-money. There's the rebus, that Cut-bert is nobody without Pole-money. — *Festivous Notes*, 1654, p. 111. Lord Thurlow in his speech for postponing the farther reading of the Surgeons' Incorporation Bill, July 17th, 1797, to that day three months, in the House of Peers, stated "that by a statute still in force, the barbers and surgeons were each to use a pole. The barbers were to have theirs blue and white, striped, with no other appendage ; but the surgeons', which was the same in other respects, was likewise to have a galley-pot and a red rag to denote the particular nature of their vocation."

Stephanus ridicules the "grosse ignorance" of the barbers : "This puts me in minde of a barber who after he had cupped me (as the physician had prescribed) to turn away a catarrhe, asked me if I would be sacrificed. Sacrificed? said I. Did the Phisition tell you any such thing? No (quoth he) but I have sacrificed many, who have bene the better for it. Then musing a little with myself I told him, Surely, Sir, you mistake yourself, you mean scarified. O Sir, by your favour (quoth he) I have ever heard it called sacrificing, and as for scarifying I never heard of it before. In a word I could by no means perswade him, but that it was the barber's office to sacrifice men. Since which time I never saw any man in a barber's hands, but that sacrificing barber came to my mind." — *World of Wonders*, transl. by R. C., 1607, p. 125. Rowlands, in his "Pair of Spy-Knaues," 1619, describes the humours of "A Fanatical Knaue," and pictures him giving directions to his servant :

"First to my barber, at his bason signe,
Bid him be heere to-morrow about nine."

As to the barber's chair and basin, see Nares, *Glossary*, 1859, in v., and under *Basin*, where it is shown that barbers' basins were hired by the mob, when any infamous person was carted, in order, by beating them ahead of the procession, to draw the attention of spectators. "The Barbers' Chaire," says Gabriel Harvey, in the *Trimming of Thomas Nash*, 1597, "*is* the verie Royall-Exchange of newes, barbers the head of all trades." He adds, a little farther on : "if they be happie, whom pleasure, profit, and honor make attaine to happiness. . . . if at home and happie, then barbers with great facilitie at worke, they are in pleasing conference ; if idle, they pass that time in life-delighting musique." The beating down the barbers' basins on Shrove Tuesday, I have not found elsewhere than in Fennor's *Pasquils Palinodia*, 1619 :—

"It was the day of all deys in the yeare,
That unto Bacchus hath his dedication,
When mad-brained prentices, that no men feare,
O'erthrow the dens of bawdie recreation :
When tylors, cobblers, plaist'rers, smiths, and masons
And every rogue will beat down Barbers' basons,
Whereat Don Constable in wrath appeares,
And runs away with his stout halbardiers.

"It was the day whereon both rich and
  poore
Are chiefly feasted with the self-same
  dish,
When every paunch, till it can hold no
  more,
Is fritter-fill'd, as well as heart can wish;
And every man and maide doe take their
  turne,
And tosse their pancakes up for feare they
  burne,
And all the kitchen doth with laughter
  sound,
To see the pancakes fall upon the ground.

"It was the day when every kitchen
  reekes,
And hungry bellies keepe a Jubile,
When flesh doth bid adieu for divers
  weekes,
And leaves old ling to be his deputie.
It was the day when Pullen goe to block,
And every spit is fill'd with bellie timber,
When cocks are cudgel'd down with many
  a knock,
And hens are thrasht to make them
  short and tender;
When country wenches play with stoole
  and ball,
And run at barly breake untill they fall."

The subsequent is from Greene's "Quip
for an upstart Courtier," 1592: "Barber,
. . . when you come to poore Cloth-
breeches, you either cut his beard at your
own pleasure, or else, in disdaine, aske
him if he will be trimd with Christs cut,
round like the half of a Holland cheese,
mocking both Christ and us." In "Wits,
Fits, and Francis," 1595, we read: "A
gentleman gave a gentlewoman a fine
twisted bracelet of silke and golde, and
seeing it the next day upon another gentle-
womans wrist, said it was like a Barber's
girdle soon slipt from one side to
another." Steevens remarks: "It was
formerly part of a barber's occupation to pick the teeth and ears. So
in the "Trimming of Thomas Nashe,
Gentleman," 1597, Gabriel Harvey
says to his antagonist, who taunted
him (Harvey) with being the son of
a barber: "for thoughe (as I am a
cirurgian) I could pick your teeth for the
other stinkinge breath, yet this I durst
not meddle with"; and in Herod and
Antipater," 1622, Tryphon the barber
enters with a case of instruments, to each
of which he addresses himself separately:

"Toothpick, dear tooth-pick: ear-pick,
  both of you
Have been her sweet companions!" &c.

Austin, in his poem entitled *Urania*, 1629,
seems to suggest that barbers sold books—
at all events popular ones; for, speaking
of a volume of amatory or satirical productions, he writes that in either case:

"— this would take,
Eu'n like Tobacco, each Barbours shop
  would make
A sale of it ——."

Gay, in his fable of the goat without a
beard, thus describes a barber's shop:

"His pole with pewter basons hung
Black rotten teeth in order strung,
Rang'd cups, that in the window stood,
Lin'd with red rags to look like blood,
Did well his threefold trade explain,
Who shav'd, drew teeth, and breath'd a
  vein."

In the *British Apollo*, 1708, there is a
solution of the custom of combining the
two trades of barber and surgeon, which
has, perhaps, more humour than weight:

"In antient Rome, when men lov'd
  fighting,
And wounds and scars took much de-
  light in,
Man-menders then had noble pay,
Which we call surgeons to this day.
'Twas order'd that a huge long pole,
With bason deck'd, should grace the hole
To guide the wounded, who unlopt
Could walk, on stumps the others hopt:—
But, when they ended all their wars,
And men grew out of love with scars,
Their trade decaying; to keep swimming,
They joyn'd the other trade of trimming;
And on their poles to publish either
Thus twisted both their trades together."

In the North of England, within living
memory, the two callings of barber and
bookseller were occasionally united. Although it does not strictly belong to the
province of popular antiquities, it may be
useful to refer to the paper in Pegge's
Curialia, 1818, "on the Barber for the
King's most High and Dread Person."
There used to be in barbers' shops, hung
up against the wall, a thrift-box, into
which each customer was supposed to put
a trifle. Comp. *Curfew*.

Barguest, The or **Great Dog-
fiend.**—In Beaumont and Fletcher's
Thierry and Theodoret, i., 1, we have:—

"—— Let night-dogs tear me,
And goblins ride me in my sleep to jelly,
Ere I forsake my sphere."

In the North of England ghost is pronounced "guest." This appears to be an
offshoot or side-growth of the Nature-cult
prevalent among the Romans, and after
them among the Spaniards (*Current
Notes*, August, 1856, p. 72), and the word
barguest is evidently synonymous with the
Celtic baarge, which is still used for a sow
(the Roman *numen porcinum*), by the
peasantry of Exmoor. The streets of Newcastle-upon-Tyne were formerly, according to vulgar tradition, haunted by a
nightly guest, which appeared in the

shape of a mastiff dog, &c., and terrified such as were afraid of shadows. This word is a corruption of the Anglo-Saxon ᚱᚨᚾ, *spiritus, anima*. Brand heard, when a boy, many stories concerning it. The bar-guest is the "Rongeur d'Os" of Norman folk-lore, and the boggart of Lancashire, both great dog-spirits, which prowl about in the night time, dragging heavy chains behind them. The authors of "Lancashire Folk Lore," 1867, say: "Near Blakeley, in Lancashire, is a romantic spot, still known as the 'Boggart Hole,' the position of which may seem to militate somewhat against Drake's etymology of Barguest—burh, a town, and gast, a ghost, that is, a spirit haunting towns. The fact is, however, that this derivation is not at all likely to be correct on other grounds, for the Lancashire and Yorkshire boggart or barguest was, from all the evidence we have, an ubiquitous goblin, who did not restrict himself to any particular localities." The appearance of the barguest is still considered in Lancashire a "certain death sign," and "has obtained the local names of Trash and Skriker," say the authors of "Lancashire Folk Lore." This dog-spirit may be the malignant influence referred to under the name of Fray-bug, in a curious extract from a letter of Master Saunders to his wife, 1555, printed in the "Dialect of Craven," 1828. Under the name of boggle this incubus or spirit is introduced into the "Flyting Betwixt Montgomery and Polwart," written about 1580. Sir Patrick Hume of Polwart is made to say to Montgomery:

"Leaue boggles, brownies, gyr-carlings, and gaists;
Dastard, thou daffes, that with such divilrie mels."

Perhaps the Cleveland beeagle (a scarecrow), the Whitby beagle (the same), and the other Yorkshire forms boggle, bogle, or bogill (same as bogie?) boc, beggar, bull beggar, are merely varieties of the boggart or barguest.

Gibbon says, in reference to Hunniades, Regent of Hungary, 1441-52, "By the Turks, who employed his name to frighten their perverse children, he was constantly denominated Jancus-Lam, or the Wicked. See farther, Lucas, *Studies in Nidderdale*, pp. 145, *et seqq*; and Davis, *Suppl. Glossary*, 1881, p. 39, and comp. *Richard Coeur de Lion*.

Barley-break. — Jamieson, in his "Etymological Dictionary," calls this "A game generally played by young people in a corn-yard. Hence called Barlabracks about the stacks, S. B." (*i.e.* in the North of Scotland.) "One stack is fixed on as the dule or goal: and one person is appointed to catch the rest of the company

who run out from the dule. He does not leave it till they are all out of his sight. Then he sets off to catch them. Any one, who is taken, cannot run out again with his former associates, being accounted a prisoner, but is obliged to assist his captor in pursuing the rest. When all are taken, the game is finished; and he, who was first taken, is bound to act as catcher in the next game. This innocent sport seems to be almost entirely forgotten in the South of S. It is also falling into desuetude in the North." The following description of Barley Break, written by Sir Philip Sidney, is taken from the Song of Lamon in the "Arcadia," where he relates the passion of Claius and Strephon for the beautiful Urania, and shews the English practice:—

—"She went abroad, thereby,
At barley brake her sweet, swift foot to try.
 *   *   *   *   *
A field they goe, where many lookers be.
 *   *   *   *   *
Then couples three be streight allotted there,
They of both ends, the middle two doe flie:
The two that in mid-place Hell called were,
Must striue with waiting foot and watching eye,
To catch of them, and them to Hell to beare,
That they, as well as they Hell may supplye;
Like some which seeke to salue their blotted name
With others blot, till all doe taste of shame.

There may you see, soon as the middle two
Doe coupled towards either couple make,
They false and fearfull do their hands vndoe;
Brother his brother, friend doth friend forsake,
Heeding himselfe, cares not how Fellow doe,
But if a stranger mutuall helpe doth take:
As periur'd cowards in aduersitie,
With sight of feare from friends to fremb'd doe flie."

Another description of the sport occurs in *Barley-breake, or a Warning for Wantons*, 1607:
"To barley-breake they roundly then 'gan fall:
Raimon, Euphema had unto his mate:
For by a lot he won her from them all:
Wherefore young Streton doth his fortune hate.

But yet ere long he ran and caught her out,

And on the backe a gentle fall he gaue her.
It is a fault which iealous eyes spie out,
A maide to kisse before her iealous father.

Old Elpin smiles, but yet he frets within,
Euphema saith, she was vniusly cast,
She striues, he holds, his hand goes out,
and in:
She cries, Away, and yet she holds him
fast.

Till sentence giuen by another maid,
That she was caught, according to the law:
The voice whereof this ciuill quarrell staid,
And to his make each lusty lad 'gan draw.

Euphema now with Streton is in hell:
(For so the middle roome is alwaies cald)
He would for euer, if he might, there
dwell:
He holds it blisse with her to be inthrald.

The other run, and in their running
change:
Streton 'gan catch, and then let goe his
hold,
Euphema, like a Doe, doth swiftly range,
Yet taketh none, although full well she
could.

And winkes on Streton, he on her 'gan
smile,
And faine would whisper something in
her eare.
She knew his mind, and bid him vse a wile,
As she ran by him, so that none did heare.

Some other pastimes then they would
begin;
And to locke hands one doth them all
assummon.
Varietie is good in euery thing,
Excepting onely Gods and earthly
women."

Drayton introduces fairies playing at
this:

" At barly-breake they play
Merrily all the day,
At night themselues they lay
Vpon the soft leaues—"

This was perhaps rather a stretch of poetic
licence. Suckling also has given the following description of this pastime with
allegorical personages:

" Love, Reason, Hate did once bespeak
Three mates to play at barley-break.
Love Folly took, and Reason Fancy;
And Hate consorts with Pride, so dance
they;
Love coupled last, and so it fell
That Love and Folly were in Hell.

The break; and Love would Reason
meet,
But Hate was nimbler on her feet;
Fancy looks for Pride, and thither
Hies, and they two hug together:
Yet this new coupling still doth tell
That Love and Folly were in Hell.

The rest do break again, and Pride
Hath now got Reason on her side;
Hate and Fancy meet, and stand
Untouch'd by Love in Folly's hand;
Folly was dull, but Love ran well,
So Love and Folly were in Hell."

Barly-break is several times alluded to in
Massinger's Plays. The subsequent is
from Herrick, p. 34:

" *Barly-Break;* or, *Last in Hell.*
We two are last in hell: what may we
feare
To be tormented, or kept pris'ners here:
Alas, if kissing be of plagues the worst,
We'll wish, in hell we had been last and
first."

Comp. Nares, *Glossary*, 1859, in v. *Barli-
break.*

Barnabas, St.—In the Churchwardens' account of St. Mary at Hill,
London, 17 and 19 Edward IV., the following entry occurs: " For Rose-garlondis
and woodrove garlondis on St. Barnebes'
Daye, xjd." And, under the year 1486:
" Item, for two doss' di bocse garlands for
prestes and clerks on Saynt Barnabe daye,
js. xd." Under 1512 occurs: "Recd. of
the gadryng of the Maydens on St. Barnabas' Day, vi. s. viijd." And among the
disbursements of 1512 we have: "Rose-
garlands and lavender, St. Barnarbas, i.s.
vjd." In the same accounts, for 1509, i.s.
the following: "For bred, wine, and ale,
for the singers of the King's Chapel, and
for the clarks of this town, on St. Barnabas, i.s. iijd." Collinson, speaking of
Glastonbury, tells us, that, " besides the
Holy Thorn, there grew in the Abbey
Church-yard, on the north side of St.
Joseph's Chapel, a miraculous walnut tree,
which never budded forth before the feast
of St. Barnabas, viz. the eleventh of June,
and on that very day shot forth leaves,
and flourished like its usual species. This
tree is gone, and in the place thereof
stands a very fine walnut tree of the common sort. It is strange to say how much
this tree was sought after by the credulous; and, though not an uncommon walnut, Queen Anne, King James, and many
of the nobility of the realm, even when the
times of monkish superstition had ceased,
gave large sums of money for small cuttings from the original." The original
tree was mentioned in the metrical Life of
Joseph of Arimathea, 1520:

" Great meruaylles men may se at
Glastonbury
One of a walnot tree that there doth
stande
In the holy grounde called the semetery
Hard by ye place where Kynge Arthur
was foude
South fro Iosephs Chapell it is walled
in roude

It bereth no leaues tyll the day of Saynt
    Barnabe,
And than that tree that standeth in the
    grounde
Sproteth his leaues as fayre as any other
    tree."

And Manningham, in his *Diary*, May 2,
1602, speaking of Glastonbury, says:
"There is a walnut-tree which hath no
leaues before Barnabies Day in June, and
then it begins to bud, and after becomes
as forward as any other." The diarist
was indebted for this piece of intelligence
to a friend. According to the old style,
this was Midsummer Day, and hence came
the proverb:

"Barnaby bright, Barnaby bright
The longest day and the shortest night."

Barnaby bright is the popular name of
the lady-bird in some localities, probably
from this insect being seen more about St.
Barnabas' Day than at any other. For
two other curious particulars relative to
this day the reader may be referred to the
"Book of Days (June 11)."

Barnacles. — Suaverius refers to
barnacles in his MS. Diary (1535), giving
an account of English and Scotish
customs, &c. : There are trees (he
says) in Scotland from which birds
are produced: he is told it is undoubtedly true; those birds which fall
from the trees into water become animated, but those which fall to the ground
do not; the figures of birds are found in
the heart of the wood of the trees and on
the root: the birds themselves (which are
very delicate eating) do not generate.
"There are," (says Gerarde, in his
"Herbal," edit. 1597, p. 1391) "in the
North parts of Scotland certaine trees,
whereon do grow shell-fishes, &c., &c.,
which, falling into the water, do become
fowls, whom we call Barnakles, in the
North of England Brant Geese, and in
Lincolnshire Tree Geese," &c. It seems
hardly conceivable that so gross an error
in natural history could so long have prevailed, as that the barnacle, a well known
kind of shell-fish, which is found sticking
on the bottom of ships, should when
broken off become a species of goose. Yet
old writers of the first credit in other respects have fallen into this mistaken and
ridiculous notion : and we find no less an
authority than Holinshed gravely declaring that with his own eyes he saw the
feathers of these barnacles "hang out of
the shell at least two inches."

"That Scottish barnacle, if I might
    choose,
That of a worme doth waxe a winged
    goose."
                          Hall's *Virgid.* iv. 2.

" —— Like your Scotch barnacle, now
    a block,
Instantly a worm, and presently a great
    goose."
                  Marston's *Malcontent*, 1604.

"My meal hath done. Avoided for the
    nonce :
I wrong the devil should I lick their
    bones.
That fall is his; for when the Scots
    decease,
Hell, like their nation, feeds on
    barnacles.
A Scot, when from the gallows-tree got
    loose,
Drops into Styx, and turns a Scotland
    goose."
                  Cleveland's *Rebel Scot*, 1647.

The best account of these mythical
creatures is to be found in Drayton's
Polyolbion, Song xxvii.

Barnwell Fair. — The reputation of
this Fair does not seem to have been very
good in Heywood's time, for in his "If
you know not me," &c., 1605, that writer
makes Hobson say :

"Bones a me, knave, thou'rt welcome.
    What's the news
At bawdy Barnwell, and at Stourbridge
    fair?"

The place was so called, says the editor of
"England's Gazeteer," 1751, (enlarged
from Adams' "Index Villaris," 1690),
"from the wells of children or bearns, because they used to meet here for sport on
St. John's Eve; so that it came at last to
be what is now called Midsummer Fair."
It is to be concluded that the deplorable
fire which, in 1727, committed dreadful
havoc among the spectators at a puppet-
show in a barn, happened at this season.
The scene of one of Scogin's jests is laid
at Barnwell Fair.

Barring Out. — See *Bromfield* and
Eton. But the usage does not seem to
have been limited to these places.

Bartholomew Baby. —— In describing "a zealous brother," Braithwaite
says: "No season through all the yeere
accounts hee more subject to abhomina-
tion than Bartholomew faire : their drums,
hobbihorses, rattles, babies, iewtrumps,
nay pigs and all, are wholly Iudaicall."
The roasted pigs at St. Bartholomew's
Fair are also noticed in "Poor Robin's
Almanack" for 1677. "Poor Robin" for
1695 has this passage: "It also tells farmers what manner of wife they shall
choose, not one trickt up with ribbens and
knots like a Bartholomew Baby, for such
an one will prove a Holy-day wife, all
play and no work,

And he who with such kind of wife is
    sped,
Better to have one made of ginger-
    bread."
        —*Whimzies*, 1631, p. 300.

In Nabbes's "Totenham Court," 1638, p.
47, is the following: "I have pack't her
up in't, like a Bartholomew-babie in a
boxe. I warrant you for hurting her."

**Bartholomew, St., the
Apostle.**—(August 24).

[⁴ "Ða wæs ſe eahtoða dæg þæs kalendes
Septembres, þe man au þa tid wurðað Sæ
Bartholomei þæs apoſtoles, þa ſe eadiga mer
Guðlac com to pære foreſprecenan ſtowe, to
Cruwlande."—*Anglo-Saxon Verſion of the Life
of St. Guthlac*, ed. Goodwin, p. 22-4.]

Gough mentions an ancient custom at
Croyland Abbey, of giving little knives to
all comers on St. Bartholomew's Day.
This abuse, he says, "was abolished by
Abbot John de Wisbech, in the time of
Edward the Fourth, exempting both the
abbot and convent from a great and need-
less expence. This custom originated in
allusion to the knife, wherewith St. Bartholomew was flayed. Three of these knives
were quartered with three of the whips so
much used by St. Guthlac in one coat
borne by this house. Mr. Hunter had
great numbers of them, of different sizes,
found at different times in the ruins of the
abbey and in the river. We have engraved
three from drawings in the Minute Books
of the Spalding Society, in whose drawers
one is still preserved. These are adopted
as the device of a town-piece, called the
'Poores Halfepeny of Croyland,' 1670."—
History of Croyland Abbey, p. 73. In
Stephens' "Essayes and Characters,"
1615. we read: "Like a booksellers shoppe
on Bartholomew Day at London: the stalls
of which are so adorn'd with Bibles and
Prayer-bookes, that almost nothing is left
within, but heathen knowledge."

Bartholomew Fair.—In a tract
entitled, "Bartholomew Faire or variety
of fancies," 1641, occurs this account:
"Bartholomew Faire begins on the twenty-
fourth day of August, and is then of so
vast an extent, that it is contained in no
less than four several parishes, namely
Christ Church, Great and Little St. Bar-
tholomewes, and St. Sepulchres. Hither
resort people of all sorts and conditions.
Christ Church cloisters are now hung full
of pictures. It is remarkable and worth
your observation to beholde and heare
the strange sights and confused noise in
the faire. Here, a knave in a fooles coate,
with a trumpet sounding, or on a drumme
beating, invites you to see his puppets:
there, a rogue like a wild woodman. or in
an antick shape like an Incubus, desires
your company to view his motion: on the
other side, hocus pocus, with three yards

of tape, or ribbin, in's hand, showing his
art of legerdemaine, to the admiration and
astonishment of a company of cocko-
loaches. Amongst these, you shall see a
gray goose-cap, (as wise as the rest), with
a what do ye lacke, in his mouth, stand in
his boothe, shaking a rattle, or scraping
on a fiddle, with which children are so
taken, that they presentlie cry out for
these fopperies: and all these together
make such a distracted noise, that you
would thinck Babell were not comparable
to it. Here there are also your gamesters
in action: some turning of a whimsey,
others throwing for pewter who can
quickly dissolve a round shilling into a
three halfepeny saucer. Long Lane at
this time looks very faire, and puts out her
best cloaths, with the wrong side outward,
so turn'd for their better turning off:
and Cloth Faire is now in great request:
well fare the alehouses therein, yet better
may a man fare, (but at a dearer rate)
in the Pig-Market, alias Pasty-Nooke, or
Pye-Corner, where pigges are al houres of
the day on the stalls piping hot, and would
cry (if they could speak), 'come eate me.'
The fat greasy hostesse in these houses instructs Nick Froth, her tapster, to aske
a shilling more for a pig's head of a
woman big with child, in regard of her
longing. than of another ordinary cumer.
Some of your cutpurses are in fee with
cheating costermongers, who have a trick,
now and then, to throw downe a basket of
refuge peares, which prove choake-peares
to those that shall loose their Hats or
Cloakes in striving who shall gather
fastest.

Now farewell to the Faire: you who are
    wise,
Preserve your purses, whilst you please
    your eyes."

The pickpockets and cutpurses did not
spare anyone. In "A Caveat for Cut-
purses," a ballad of the time of Charles
I., there is the following illustration:
"The players do tell you, in Bartholomew
    Faire,
What secret consumptions and rascals
    you are;
For one of their actors, it seems had the
    fate
By some of your trade to be fleeced of
    late."

Gayton says in his *Art of Longevity*, 1659,
p. 3:
    —"(As if there were not Pigg enough)
Old Bartholomew with purgatory fire,
Destropes the Babe of many a doubtfull
    Sire."

And speaking of plums, he adds:
"If eaten as we use at Barthol'mew tide,
Hand over head, that's without care or
    guide,
There is a patient sure."

Pepys, under date of August 25, 1663, says: "It seems this Lord Mayor (Sir John Robinson) begins again an old custome, that upon the three first days of Bartholomew Fayre, the first, there is a match of wrestling, which was done, and the Lord Mayor there and the Aldermen in Moorfields yesterday: second day, shooting; and to-morrow hunting. And this officer of course is to perform this ceremony of riding through the City. I think to proclaim or challenge any to shoot. It seems that the people of the fayre cry out upon it, as a great hindrance to them." Sir John Bramston, in his *Autobiography*, p. 315, under the date of 1688, refers to the annual custom by which the Lord Mayor proclaimed St. Bartholomew Fair on that Saint's Eve, and riding past Newgate was accustomed to receive from the keeper or governor a cup of sack. In *Wit and Drollery*, 1682, p. 227, we have:

"Now London Mayor, in Saddle new:
Rides into fair of Bartholomew:
He twirles his Chain, and looketh big,
As he would fright the head of Pig:
Which gaping lies on greasy stall —"

Ladies were fond of attending Bartholomew Fair. In a little work printed in 1688, it is observed: "Some women are for merry-meetings, as Bessus was for duck; they are ingaged in a Circle of Idleness, where they turn round for the whole year, without the interruption of a serious hour, they know all the players names & are intimately acquainted with all the booths in Bartholomew Fair.— *The Lady's New Year's Gift, or Advice to a Daughter*, p. 187. In 1711, an attempt was made without success to extend the duration of the fair to fourteen days, and a tract was published and specially addressed by the author to the civic authorities, to oppose and denounce the project. It is said, on the authority of Mrs. Piozzi, that, during a whole year, Andrew Johnson, the doctor's uncle, kept the ring here, where the boxing and wrestling took place, and was not once beaten. Perhaps his nephew inherited from him his burly appearance. In *Current Notes* for February, 1851, are some memoranda by Theodore Hook, from a copy of Ackermann's *Microcosm of London*, in one of which he notes the occupation of the site of Bartholomew Fair by *Billingsgate Market*. Charles Lamb, in one of his letters to Coleridge, speaks of the Wordsworths being in town, and of his having been their guide over the Fair, in September, 1802. Rimbault, in his "Book of Songs and Ballads," 1851, has printed from rare musical works two or three ballads illustrative of the old usages and scenes at Bartholomew Fair. The entertainments appear, from all accounts, to have been of the most various description, with a view, doubtless, to the satisfaction of every taste. The puppet-shows and drolls included St. George and the Dragon, Guy of Warwick, Judith and Holofernes, Robin Hood (an opera), the Quaker's Opera, Susanna and the Elders, Dives and Lazarus, Punchinello, The Devil and the Pope, and the Whore of Babylon. The character of the performances at Bartholomew Fair, a little later on, seems to have been singularly heterogeneous; for Strutt quotes a bill of the beginning of the eighteenth century, which announces that, "at Heatly's booth, over against the Cross Daggers, will be presented a little opera, called The old creation of the world, newly reviv'd, with the addition of the glorious battle obtained over the French and Spaniards by his Grace the Duke of Marlborough." During the reign of George II., the class of entertainment changed somewhat, if we are to judge from the contents of the "Stroler's Pacquet Opened," 1741, which purports to be a collection of the drolls played at Southwark and other fairs at that time. These pieces, sufficiently contemptible in their construction, were, in most cases, formed out of old dramas. Down to the year 1854 it was customary for the representative of the Merchant Taylors' Gild to proceed to Cloth Fair, which immediately joined Bartholomew Fair, and test the measures used for selling cloth there by the Company's silver yard. This very ancient practice expired with the institution. Hazlitt's *Livery Companies of London*, 1892, p. 280, where a facsimile of the yard is engraved. For a more particular account of this fair the reader may be referred to *Memoirs of Bartholomew Fair*, by the late Professor Morley, 8v., 1859, with illustrations by Fairholt. Also see Hone's *Every Day Book*, i., 1572. *Robin Hood* and the *Quaker's Opera* were printed in 1730 and 1728 respectively with the music.

Basil.—In the second part of the *Secrets of Alexis of Piedmont*, translated by W. Warde, 1563, there is this entry: "*To make that a woman shall eate of nothing that is set vpon the table.* "Take a little grene Basil, & when men bring the dishes to the table, pvt it vnderneth them, yt the woman perceiue it not: for men saye that she will eate of none of that which is in the dishe where vnder the Basill lieth." The family of aromatic plants, so-called, has long been recognized among the Hindoos as of virtue in protection from malaria, like the Australian eucalyptus, and from the attack of the mosquito, and their great or supposed efficacy in either case was naturally very important in tropical regions unprovided with other safeguards from contagion with masses of decayed animal and vegetable refuse.

Basilisk.—See *Cockatrice.*

Basset.—In a MS. song purporting to proceed from a lady of honour in Queen Flizabeth's days, the supposed speaker, enumerating her virtues and claims to respectful remembrance, says:

> "I never bought cantharides,
>   Ingredient good in Passett,
> Nor ever stript me to my stayes
>   To play ye Punt att Bassett."

Sir Samuel Tuke, in the *Adventures of Five Hours,* 1671, an adaptation from Calderon, speaks of the chairmen as engaged *a las pintas,* the same game as this, where Diego is made to say:

> They are deeply engaged
> A *las pintas,* and will not leave their
>   game,
> They swear, for all the dons in Seville.
> —Hazlitt's Dodsley, xv. 265.

Bastard.—A species of wine. Compare examples from old writers in Nares, *Glossary,* 1859, in v.

Bats.—Willsford supplies this item of intelligence: "Bats, or flying mice, come out of their holes quickly after sunset, and sporting themselves in the open air, premonstrates fair and calm weather." *Nature's Secrets,* 1658, p. 134. Compare *Weather Omens.*

Battledore or **Shuttle-cock.**— It is as old as the fourteenth century. Skelton has the expression, "Not worth a shyttle cocke." Strutt, in his "Sports and Pastimes," illustrates it by a drawing of that period lent to him by Douce. Manningham, in his Diary, Feb. 1602-3, notes: "The play at shuttlecocke is become soe much in request at Court, that the making shuttlecocks is almost growne to a trade in London." Manningham relates an odd anecdote in connection about Lady Effingham. Armin, in the "Two Maids of More-Clacke," 1609, says: "To play at shuttlecock methinkes is the game now." It was a favourite amusement with Prince Henry, who died in 1612. In his "Horæ Vacivæ," 1646, Hall observes: "Shittle-Cock requires a nimble armc, with a quick and waking eye; 'twere fit for students, and not so vehement as that waving of a stoole, so commended by Lessius." A somewhat similar amusement is mentioned in the *Journal of the Asiatic Society* for 1835, as followed in Bengal. The game is now known as Battledore and Shuttlecock, and is almost exclusively a juvenile recreation, though it is sometimes played by grown-up persons in the country on wet indoor days. Stevenson, in his *Twelve Months,* 1661, under October, says: "The Shuttle-cock and Battledore is a good house exercise,

and occupies the Lady before she be drest."

Battle Royal.—See *Cock-Fighting.*

Bawdry.—Wallis, in his essays on the Privileges of the University of Oxford," printed in "Collectanea Curiosa," notices that by a charter of 37 Hen. VI. the Chancellor had the power of banishing to a distance of not more than ten miles all whores, and of imprisoning them if they returned. The subsequent extract from a proclamation of Henry VIII., April 13, year 37, will be thought curious: "Furthermore his Majesty straightlie chargeth and commandeth that all such Householders as, under the name of Baudes, have kept the notable and marked Houses, and knowne Hosteries, for the said evill disposed persons, that is to saie, such Householders as do inhabite the Houses whited and painted, with Signes on the front, for a token of the said Houses, shal avoyd with bagge and baggage, before the feast of Easter next comyng, upon paino of like punishment, at the Kings Majesties will and pleasure." The punishment for this offence was riding in a cart through the parish where it was committed, and sometimes through the adjoining ones also, with a paper attached to the back or front of the dress, descriptive of the particulars, and a basin ringing before them to draw the attention of the people to their disgrace. Occasionally the culprit went on horseback. The examples given by Stowe and others of this class of chastisement are not only very numerous; but we cannot fail to be struck by the great frequency of cases, where parents were guilty of the crime towards their own offspring, and of the respectable position of many of those who were implicated. The publication of the delinquency on a sheet of paper pinned to the person was common to many other crimes, such as perjury, &c., but then it seems to have been more usually fixed over the culprit's head. In 1560-1 a woman who had sold fish contrary to law, was led about London on horseback by the beadle of Bridewell with a garland on her head, strung with these fish, and others hanging from the saddle, both before and behind her. In Strype's edition of Stow, 1720, Book i. p. 258, we read, that in the year 1555, "An ill woman, who kept the Greyhound in Westminster, was carted about the city, and the Abbot's servant (bearing her good will) took her out of the cart, as it seems, before she had finisht her punishment, who was presently whipped at the same cart's tail for his pains." In 1556, "were carted two men and three women. One of these men was a bawd, for bringing women to strangers. One of the women kept the Bell in Gracechurch

Bull beside London-stone; both bawds and whores." In 1559, "The wife of Henry Glyn, goldsmith, was carted about London for "being bawd to her own daughter." It is remarked with much probability in a Note upon Dekker's "Honest Whore," that it was formerly a custom for the Peace-officers to make search after women of ill-fame on Shrove-Tuesday, and to confine them during the season of Lent. So, Sensuality says in Nabbes' masque of "Microcosmus," act 5: "But now welcome a Cart or a Shrove-Tuesday's tragedy." Overbury, in his "Characters," speaking of "a *Maquerela*, in plaine English, a bawde," says: "Nothing daunts her so much as the approach of Shrove-Tuesday." *Ibid.*, speaking of "a roaring boy," he observes, that "he is a supervisor of brothels, and in them is a more unlawful reformer of vice than prentices on Shrove-Tuesday." In Dekker's play of "Match Me in London," Bilbo says, "I'll beate down the doore, and put him in mind of Shrove-Tuesday, the fatall day for doores to be broke open." The punishment of people of evil fame at this season seems to have been one of the chief sports of the apprentices. In a *Satyre against Separatists*, 1642, we read:

"— — The Prentises—for they
Who, if upon Shrove-Tuesday, or May-Day,
Beat an old Bawd or fright poor Whores they could,
Thought themselves greater than their Founder Lud, . . .
They'r mounted high, contemn the humble play.
Of Trap or Football on a Holiday
In Finesbury-fieldes—"

Bay-Tree. — Parkinson writes: "The Bay-leaves are necessary both for civil uses and for physic, yea, both for the sick and for the sound, both for the living and for the dead. It serveth to adorne the House of God as well as man — to crowne or encircle, as with a garland, the heads of the living, and to sticke and decke forth the bodies of the dead: so that, from the cradle to the grave, we have still use of it, we have still need of it." *Paradisus Terrestris*, 1629, p. 426. In "A strange Metamorphosis of Man," &c., 1634, it is observed, that "hee (the Bay) is fit for halls and stately roomes, where if there be a wedding kept, or such like feast, he will be sure to take a place more eminent then the rest. He is a notable smell-feast, and is so good a fellow in them, that almost it is no feast without him. He is a great companion with the Rosemary, who is as good a gossip in all feasts as he is a trencher-man." Among death omens the withering of bay trees was, according to

Shakespear, reckoned one. Thus in Richard II.:
"'Tis thought the King is dead; we will not stay.
The bay trees in our country are all wither'd—"
Upon which Steevens observes that "Some of these prodigies are found in Holinshed, 'In this yeare, in a manner throughout all the realme of England, old Baie Trees withered, &c.'" This we also learn from Lupton, "Neyther falling syeknes, neyther devyll, will infest or hurt one in that place whereas a bay tree is. The Romaynes calle it the Plant of the good Angell," &c. Sir Thomas Browne observes that the Christian custom of decking the coffin with bay is a most elegant emblem. It is said that this tree, when seemingly dead, will revive from the root, and its dry leaves resume their wonted verdure. William Browne, in a sonnet to Cœlia, evidently alludes to some ancient love-omen or portent, still current in his time, in connexion with the rind of the laurel:

"Fair Laurell, that the onelye witnes art
To that discourse, which vnderneath thy shade
Our griefe swolne brests did lovinglie impart
With vowes as true as ere Religion made:
If (forced by our sighs) the flame shall fly
Of our kinde love, and get within thy rind,
Be warye, gentle Baye, & shrieke not bye,
When thou dost such vnusuall feruor finde."
Hazlitt's edit. ii., 288.

Beadsmen.—See *Blue-Gowns*.
Beans, Religious use of.—The choosing of a person King or Queen by a bean found in a piece of a divided cake, was formerly a common Christmas gambol at the English and Scotish Courts, and in both English Universities. "Mos inolevit et viget apud plurimas nationes, ut in profesto Epiphaniæ, seu trium Regum, in quaque familia seu alia Societate, sorte vel alio fortuito modo eligant sibi Regem, et convivantes unà ac genialiter viventes, bibente rege, acclamant: Rex, bibit, bibit Rex, indicta multa qui non clamaverit." See the "Sylva Sermonum jucundissimorum," 8vo. Bas. 1568, pp. 73, 246.— *Douce.* In Ben Jonson's "Masque of Christmas," the character of Baby-Cake is attended by "an Usher bearing a great cake with a bean and a pease." These beans, it should seem from the following passage in Burton's "Anatomy of Melancholy" were hallowed. He is enumerat-

ing Popish superstitions: "Their Breviaries, Bulles, hallowed beans, Exorcisms, Pictures, curious Crosses, Fables, and Bables." Democritus to the Reader, p. 29. edit. fol. Oxf. 1632. Bale, in his "Yet a Course at the Romysh Foxe," &c. Signat. L. 11, attributes to Pope Euticianus, "the blessynge of Benes upon the Aultar."

In the "Anniversary Calendar," there is an amusing extract from Teonge's "Diary" (1676), giving an account of a cake they made on board his ship off the Morea. He (Teonge) says: "The cake was cut into several pieces, and all put into a napkin, out of which every one took his piece, as out of a lottery, then each piece was broken to see what was in it, which caused much laughter to see our lieutenant prove the cuckold." Probably the piece which contained the bean is referred to. In "A World of Wonders," 1607, a translation by R. C from H. Stephanus, "Apologie d'Herodote," there are some curious extracts from the "Quadragesimale Spirituale," 1565. Thus, chap. 2: "After the sallad (eaten in Lent at the first service) we eate fried Beanes, by which we understand confession. When we would have beanes well sodden, we lay them in steepe, for otherwise they will never seeth kindly. Therefore, if we purpose to amend our faults, it is not sufficient barely to confesse them at all adventure, but we must let our confession lie in steepe in the water of Meditation." "And a little after: We do not use to seeth ten or twelve beanes together, but as many as we mean to eate: no more must we let our confession steepe, that is, meditate, upon ten or twelve sinnes onely, neither for ten or twelve dayes, but upon all the sinnes that ever we committed, even from our birth, if it were possible to remember them." Chap. 3: "Strained Pease (Madames) are not to be forgotten. You know how to handle them so well, that they will be delicate and pleasant to the tast. By these strained pease our allegorizing flute pipeth nothing else but true contrition of heart." "River-water, which continually moveth, runneth, and floweth, is very good for the seething of pease. We must (I say) have contrition for our sins and take the running water, that is, the teares of the heart, which must runne and come even into the eyes." The soft beans are much to our purpose: why soft, but for the purpose of eating? Thus our peas on this occasion are steeped in water. In the "Roman Calendar," I find it observed on this day, that "a dole is made of soft beans." I can hardly entertain a doubt but that our custom is derived hence. It was usual amongst the Romanists to give away beans in the doles at funerals: it was also a rite in the funeral ceremonies of heathen Rome. Why we have substituted peas I know not, unless it was because they are a pulse somewhat fitter to be eaten at this season of the year. They are given away in a kind of dole at this day. Our popish ancestors celebrated (as it were by anticipation) the funeral of our Lord on Care Sunday, with many superstitious usages, of which this only, it should seem, has travelled down to us. Durandus tells us, that on Passion Sunday "the Church began her public grief, remembering the mystery of the Cross, the vinegar, the gall, the reed, the spear," &c. Among the "Cries of Paris," a poem composed by Guillaume de Villeneuve in the thirteenth century, and printed at the end of the poem printed by Barbazan, *Ordene de Chevalerie,* beans for Twelfth Day are mentioned: "Gastel à feve orrois crier." There is a very curious account in Le Roux, *Dictionnaire Comique,* tom. ii., p 431, of the French ceremony of the "Roi de la Feve," which explains Jordaen's fine picture of "Le Roi boit." Bufalde de Verville "Palais des Curieux," edit. 1612, p. 90. See also Pasquier, Recherches de la France, p. 375. To the account given by Le Roux of the French way of choosing King and Queen, may be added, that in Normandy they place a child under the table, which is covered in such a manner with the cloth that he cannot see what he is doing; and when the cake is divided, one of the company, taking up the first piece, cries out, "Fabe Domini pour qui?" The child answers, "Pour le bon Dieu:" and in this manner the pieces are allotted to the company. If the bean be found in the piece for the "bon Dieu," the King is chosen by drawing long or short straws. Whoever gets the bean chooses the King or Queen, according as it happens to be man or woman. Urquhart of Cromarty says, ("Discovery of a most exquisite jewel, &c." 1651, p. 237): "Verily, I think they make use of Kings—as the French on the Epiphany-day use their Roy de la fehve, or King of the Bean; whom after they have honoured with drinking of his health, and shouting aloud "Le Roy boit, Le Roy boit," they make pay for all the reckoning; not leaving him sometimes one peny, rather than that the exorbitancie of their debosh should not be satisfied to the full." And elsewhere (Stephanus, World of Wonders, transl. by R. C. p. 189), we read of a Curate, "who having taken his preparations over evening, when all men cry (as the manner is) the King drinketh, chanting his Masse the next morning, fell asleep in his Memento; and when he awoke, added with a loud voice, The King drinketh."

There is a great deal of learning

in Erasmus's Adages concerning the religious use of beans, which were thought to belong to the dead. An observation which he gives us of Pliny, concerning Pythagoras's interdiction of this pulse, is highly remarkable. It is "that beans contain the souls of the dead." For which cause also they were used in the Parentalia. Plutarch also, he tells us, held that pulse to be of the highest efficacy for invoking the manes. Ridiculous and absurd as these superstitions may appear, it is yet certain that our Carlings deduce their origin thence. Erasmi Adag. in "A fabis abstineto, Edit. fol. Aurel. Allob. 1606, p. 1906; and Spencer "De Legibus Hebræorum," lib. i. p. 1154. But the latter seems to have thought that the reason for the Pythagorean doctrine was the use of beans and other vegetables at funeral repasts, and their consequent pollution. In the Lemura, which was observed the 9th of May, every other night for three times, to pacify the ghosts of the dead, the Romans threw beans on the fire of the altar to drive them out of their houses. There were several religious uses of pulse, particularly beans, among the Romans. Hence Pliny says, "in eâdem peculiaris Religio." Thus in Ovid's "Fasti," B. v. l. 435, where he is describing some superstitious rites for appeasing the dead:

"Quumque manus puras fontana pro-
    luit unda;
Vertitur, et nigras accipit ore fabas.
Aversusque jacit: sed dum jacit, Hæc-
    ego mitto
His, inquit, redimo meque meosque
    fabis."

Thus also in Book ii. l. 575:
"Tum cantata ligat cum fusco licia
    plumbo:
Et septem nigras versat in ore fabas."

Bear the Bell, To.—A writer in the "Gentleman's Magazine" says: "A bell was a common prize: a little golden bell was the reward of victory in 1607 at the races near York; whence came the proverb for success of any kind, 'to bear away the bell.'" Lord North alludes to this custom:

"Jockey and his horse were by their
    Master sent
To put in for the Bell——
Thus right, and each to other fitted
    well,
They are to run, and cannot misse the
    Bell."

Forest of Varieties, 1645, p. 175. Another old writer remarks: "Whoever bears the bell away, yet they will ever carry the clapper." *Paradoxical Assertions*, by R. H., 1664, p. 4.

Bear-Baiting.—Bear-baiting appears anciently to have been one of the Christmas sports with our nobility. "Our nobility," says Pennant, in the "Zoology," "also kept their bear-ward. Twenty shillings was the annual reward of that officer from his lord, the fifth Earl of Northumberland, 'when he comyth to my Lorde in Cristmas, with his Lordshippes beestes for making of his Lordschip pastyme the said twelve days.'" Gilpin, in his "Life of Cranmer," tells us: "Bear baiting, brutal as it was, was by no means an amusement of the lower people only. An odd incident furnishes us with the proof of this. An important controversial manuscript was sent by Archbishop Cranmer across the Thames. The person entrusted bade his waterman keep off from the tumult occasioned by baiting a bear on the river before the King; he rowed however too near, and the persecuted animal overset the boat by trying to board it. The manuscript, lost in the confusion, floated away, and fell into the hands of a priest, who, by being told that it belonged to a Privy Counsellor, was terrified from making use of it, which might have been fatal to the head of the Reformed Party." In a Proclamation "to avoyd the abhominable place called the Stewes," dated April 13, 37 Hen. 8, we read as follows: "Finallie to th' intent all resort should be eschued to the said place, the Kings Majestie straightlie chargeth and comaundeth that from the feast of Easter next ensuing, there shall noe beare-baiting be used in that Rowe, or in any place on that side the Bridge called London Bridge, whereby the accustomed assemblies may be in that place clearly abolished and extinct, upon like paine as well to them that keepe the beares and dogges, whych have byn used to that purpose, as to all such as will resort to see the same." Accompanying Lily the grammarian's *Antibossicon*, an attack on Whittinton the grammarian, printed in 1521, is a woodcut, three times repeated, of a bear worried by six dogs. Maitland, in his *Early Printed Books at Lambeth*, 1843, pp. 316-18, has done his best to explain the allegory and the origin of the terms. In Laneham's "Letter from Kenilworth," 1575, we have the following curious picture of a bear-baiting, in a letter to Mr. Martin, a mercer of London:—

"Well, syr, the Bearz wear brought foorth intoo the Coourt, the dogs set too them, too argu the points eeuen face to face; they had learned counsell allso a both partz: what may they be coounted parciall that are retaind but to a syde? I ween no. Very feers both ton and toother & eager in argument: if the dog in pleadyng woold pluk the bear by the throte, the bear with trauers woold claw him again by the skalp; confess & a list, but a voyd a coold not that waz bound too the bar: And hiz coounsell toldd him that it coold bee too him no pollecy in pleading. Thearfore thus with fending and proouing, with plucking and tugging, skratting and byting, by plain tooth & nayll a to side & toother, such exspés of blood & leather waz thear between them, az a moonths licking I ween wyl not recoouer; and yet remain az far oout az euer they wear.

"It was a Sport very pleazaunt of theez beastz; to see the bear with his pink nyez leering after hiz enmiez approoch, the nimbleness & wayt of ye dog to take hiz auauntage, and the fors & experiens of the bear agayn to auoyd the assauts: if he war bitten in one place, hoow he woold pynch in an oother to get free: that if he wear taken onez, then what shyft, with byting, with clawyng, with rooring, tossing & tumbling, he woold woork to wynd hym self from them: and when he waz lose, to shake his earz twyse or thryse wyth the blud and the slauer aboout his fiznamy, waz a matter of a goodly releef." In Vaughan's "Golden Grove," 1600, we are told: "Famous is that example which chanced neere London, A.D. 1583, on the 13th Daye of Januarie being Sunday, at Paris Garden, where there met together (as they were wont) an infinite number of people to see the beare-bayting, without any regard to that high Day. But, in the middest of their sports, all che scaffolds and galleries sodainely fell downe, in such wise that two hundred persons were crushed well nigh to death, besides eight that were killed forthwith." In *The Merry Wives of Windsor*, Shakepear makes Slender speak of a bear-baiting as "meat and drink" to him, while Anne Page says she is afeard of it. In "The Life of the reverend Father Bennet of Canfilde," Douay, 1623, p. 11, is the following passage: "Even Sunday is a day designed for beare bayting and even the howre of theyre (the Protestants) service is allotted to it, and indeede the tyme is as well spent at the one as at the other." R. R. was at least an honest Catholic: he does not content himself with equivocal glances at the erroneous Creed, but speaks out plainly.

Bear's Cubs.—Thomas Vaughan, otherwise *Eugenius Philalethes*, observes: "I shall here gainsay that gross opinion, that the whelps of bears are, at first littering, without all form or fashion, and nothing but a little congealed blood on lump of flesh, which afterwards the dam shapeth by licking, yet is the truth most evidently otherwise, as by the eye-witenss of Joachimus Rheticus, Gesner and others, it hath been proved. And herein, as in many other fabulous narrations of this nature (in which experience checks report) may be justly put that of Lucretius thus rendered by Vaughan:—

" ' What can more certain be than sense Discerning truth from false pretence.' "

Brief Natural History, 1669, p. 87. Browne places this among his "Vulgar Errors;" but Ross, in his "Medicus Medicatus," affirms that "the bears send forth their young ones deformed and unshaped to the sight, by reason of the thick membrane in which they are wrapt, which also is covered over with so mucous and flegmatick matter, which the dam contracts in the winter time, lying in hollow caves, without motion, that to the eye it looks like an unformed lump. This mucosity is licked away by the dam, and the membrane broken, and so that which before seemed to be informed, appears now in its right shape. This is all that the antients meant, as appears by Aristotle, who says that in some manner the young Bear is for a while rude and without shape."

Beaulieu, Witch of. — See *Mary Dore.*

Beaver.—"The Bever," observes Vaughan, "being hunted and in danger to be taken, biteth off his stones, knowing that for them his life only is sought, and so often escapeth: hence some have derived his name, Castor, *a castrando seipsum;* and upon this supposition the Egyptians in their hierogliphics, when they will signify a man that hurteth himself, they picture a bever biting off his own stones, though Alciat in his emblems turns it to a contrary purpose, teaching us by that example to give away our purse to theeves, rather than our lives, and by our wealth to redeem our danger. But this relation touching the bever is undoubtedly false, as both by sense and experience, and the testimony of Dioscorides, lib. iii. cap. 13, is manifested. First, because their stones are very small, and so placed in their bodies as are a bore's, and therefore impossible for the bever himself to touch or come by them: and secondly, they cleave so fast unto their back, that they cannot be taken away, but the beast must of necessity lose his life, and consequently most ridiculous is their narration who likewise affirm that when he is hunted, having formerly bitten off his stones, he standeth upright, and sheweth the hunters that he hath none for them, and therefore his death cannot profit them, by means whereof they are averted, and seek for another."—*Brief Natural History*, p. 89. An early essayist refers to this belief without seeming to question the accuracy of it. "The beauer, when hee heares the houndes, he knows for what they hunt, and immediately to secure his skinne, he biteth of his stones. Nature hath taught both it and vs how to preserve ourselves—." —Tuvill's *Essays*, 1609, I. 3 *verso*.

Bed.—Ady says: "It appeareth still among common silly country people, how they had learned charms by tradition from Popish times, for curing cattel, men, women, and children; for churning of butter, for baking their bread, and many other occasions; one or two whereof I will rehearse only, for brevity. An old woman in Essex, who was living in my time, she had also lived in Queen Maries time, had learned thence many Popish charms, one whereof was this; every night when she lay down to sleep she charmed her bed, saying:

'Matthew, Mark, Luke, and John,
The bed be blest that I lye on;'

and this would she repeat three times, reposing great confidence therein, because (as she said) she had been taught it, when she was a young maid, by the Church-men of those times. — *Candle in the Dark*, 1659, p. 58. This idea may have had its germ in St. John's Gospel, xx., 12. In Cornwall, an experiment was once made on some poor, who were coaxed with great difficulty into confessing what they said the last thing before they got into bed, and it was a varied and extended form of the above, namely:

"Matthew, Mark, Luke, and John,
Bless the bed that I lie on.
Four Angels around my bed.
One to foot, and one to head,
And two to carry me when I'm dead."

Bede's-Well.—About a mile to the west of Jarrow (near Newcastle-upon-Tyne), there is a well still called Bede's Well, to which, as late as the year 1740, it was a prevailing custom to bring children troubled with any disease or infirmity; a crooked pin was put in, and the well laved dry between each dipping. My informant has seen twenty children brought together on a Sunday, to be dipped in this well, at which also, on Midsummer Eve, there was a great resort of neighbouring people, with bonfires, music, &c.—Brand's *Newcastle*, ii., 54.

Bedfellow.—Men used formerly to sleep together, even those of rank, as Henry V. and Lord Scroop, and it was so abroad. We find Charles VIII. of France and the Duke of Orleans occupying the same bed. See Hazlitt's *Venetian Republic*, 1900, ii., 43. Compare an interesting note in Nares, 1859 in v., Halliwell's *Dict.*, 1860, in v. and *Span Counter, infrâ*.

Bedlamer.—Bedlamer was a name for a Fool. He used to carry a horn. Quære, if thence the expression "hornmad." See Braithwaite's "Boulster Lecture," 1640, p. 242. Comp. *Tom of Bedlam*.

Bedlam Beggars.—See Halliwell in v.

Beer. — "A booke howe to brewe all sortes of beere,' was licensed at Stationers' Hall in 1591, but is not at present known. See Hazlitt's *Bibl. Coll.* Gen. Index, *Beer, Gallobelgicus, Wine, and Y - Worth*. Three halfpenny beer and single beer are mentioned in the Churchwardens' and Chamberlain's Accounts of Kingston, Surrey, 24 Hen. VII., and provided for the entertainment at the King-Game and Robin Hood. A kilderkin of each cost together 2s. 4d. The term *Doctor Double Ale* is applied to a dissolute person in a poem printed by Hazlitt (*Popular Poetry*, iii., 296, *et seqq.*) The subjoined passage seems to be nothing more than an alliteration intended to convey a complete devotion to beer—he wants nothing but the ale-tap and toast, till he is laid under the turf:

"Call me the sonne of Beere, and then confine
Me to the tap, the tost, the turfe; let wine
Ne'er shine upon me."

Hesperides, 1648, p. 87. Comp. Halliwell's *Dict.* in v. Putting a cold iron bar upon the barrels, to preserve the beer from being soured by thunder, has been noticed in another section. This is particularly practiced in Kent and Herefordshire.

Bees.—A vulgar prejudice prevails in many places of England that when bees remove or go away from their hives, the owner of them will die soon after. A clergyman in Devonshire informed Mr. Brand, about 1790, that when a Devonian makes a purchase of bees, the payment is never made in money, but in things, corn for instance, to the value of the sum agreed upon. And the bees are never removed but on a Good Friday. In "The Living Librarie," translated by John Molle, 1621, we read: "Who would beleeve without superstition (if experience did not make it credible), that most commonly all the bees die in their hives if the master or mistress of the house chance to die, except the hives be presently removed into some other place. And yet I know this hath hapned to folke no way stained with superstition." Hilman observes, respecting bees: "The tinkling after them with a warming pan, frying pan, or kettle, is of good use to let the neighbours know you have a swarm in the air, which you claim wherever it lights; but I believe of very little purpose to the reclaiming the bees, who are thought to delight in no noise but their own."—*Tusser Redivivus,* 1710, ed. 1744, p. 42. I found the follow- in the "Argus," a London newspaper, Sept. 13, 1790: "A superstitious custom prevails at every funeral in Devonshire, of turning round the beehives that be- longed to the deceased, if he had any, and that at the moment the corpse is carry- ing out of the house. At a funeral some time since at Cullompton, of a rich old farmer, a laughable circumstance of this sort occurred : for just as the corpse was placed in the herse, and the horsemen, to a large number, were drawn up in order for the procession of the funeral, a person called out, 'Turn the bees,' when a ser- vant who had no knowledge of such a custom, instead of turning the hives about, lifted them up, and then laid them down on their sides. The bees, thus hastily invaded, instantly attacked and fastened on the horses and their riders. It was in vain they galloped off, the bees as precipitately followed, and left their stings as marks of their indignation. A general confusion took place, attended with loss of hats, wigs, &c., and the corpse during the conflict was left unattended; nor was it till after a considerable time that the funeral attendants could be ral- lied, in order to proceed to the interment of their deceased friend." The necessity of inviting bees to the funeral of their late owner, having previously apprised them of his decease, and of clothing the hive in mourning, is a very common and familiar superstition still, or at least very recently, cherished in many parts of Eng- land. The correspondents of "Notes and Queries" have contributed to assemble very numerous examples of its existence. The bees are thought to have a presci- ence of the death of their master; but formal notice of the event, and a summons or request to serve his successor, are thought to be essential to the preservation and welfare of the insects.

Beggar my Neighbour. — A well-known simple game at cards, where the two players divide the pack, and the winner is the one, who succeeds in getting the majority of court cards, especially knaves. Whether Taylor, the water-poet, intended the allusion to it in his *Motto,* 1621, seriously, he cites it there. And see Davis, *Suppl. Glossary,* 1881, in v.

Beggar's Bush Fair.—This was a fair held at Rye in Sussex on St. Bartholo- mew's Day, by virtue of a charter granted in 1290 by Edward I. It was not origi- nally appointed for that date, but was altered to it in 1305; the mayor used to be chosen on the same anniversary. Beg-

gar's Bush lay just above the hospital grounds; the fair was limited to stalls kept by small pedlars, and has been long discontinued. While it lasted the lord of the manor of Brede claimed, through his steward, a trifling fee from each stall- keeper by way of nominal rent; but he ceased to attend in consequence of having been once roughly handled, and driven out of the place. A ring which, so late as 1878, was still to be seen in a field near the King's Head Inn, was the last memento of the practice of bull-baiting, formerly usual on this occasion. The last bull-baiting is said to have been about 1808. It seems very probable that Beau- mont and Fletcher's play of *Beggar's Bush,* printed in the folio of 1647, but acted as early as 1622, was so called from the locality near Rye, as Fletcher was a Rye man.

Beggar's Clack-Dish. — The beggars, it is observable, two or three centuries ago, used to proclaim their want by a wooden dish with a moveable cover, which they clacked, to shew that their vessel was empty. This appears from a passage quoted on another occasion by Grey. Grey's assertion may be supported by the following passage in Middleton's "Family of Love," 1608 :—

> "*Ger.* —can you think I get my living by a bell and a clack-dish?
> *Dryfat.* By a bell and a clack-dish? How's that?
> *Ger.* Why, by begging, Sir," &c.

And by a stage direction in the second part of Heywood's "Edward IV." 1600: "Enter Mrs. Blague, poorly drest, beg- ging with her basket and clap-dish."

Belfry.—Election of a mayor there. See *Brightlingsea.*

Bell, Book, and Candle. — The solemn form of excommunication under the Romish Church.—See Nares, 1859, in v.

Bell Corn.—A small perquisite be- longing to the clerk of certain par- ishes in North Wales. Pennant's *White- ford and Holywell,* 1796, p. 100. It seems to have been connected with the service for ringing the Passing and other bells.

Bellman.—See Nares, *Glossary,* 1859, in v., where his function in blessing slee- pers as he passed their doors on his round, is noticed.

Bellman of the Dead.—Till the middle of the 18th century, a person called the Bell-man of the Dead went about the streets of Paris, dressed in a deacon's robe, ornamented with deaths' heads, bones, and tears, ringing a bell, and exclaiming, "Awake, you that sleep ! and pray to God for the dead !" This custom prevailed still longer in some of the provinces, where

they permitted even the trivial parody,
"Prenez vos femmes, embrassez-les."—
Voyageur à Paris, i., 71.

Bells.—It is well known that before
the present principles of horology were
established, a clock was nothing more than
a piece of striking machinery, moved first
by hydraulic pressure, and afterward by
the action of a bell. Hence in German,
Anglo-Saxon, French, and other languages
the same word stood, and still stands, for
a bell and for a clock. Hazlitt's *Venetian
Republic*, iv., 344-6. The ancients had
some sort of bells. I find the word "Tin-
tinnabula," which we usually render bells,
in Martial, Juvenal, and Suetonius. The
Romans appear to have been summoned
by these, of whatever size or form they
were, to their hot baths, and to the business of public places. In the account we
have of the gifts made by St. Dunstan to
Malmesbury Abbey, it appears that bells
were not very common in that age, for he
says the liberality of that prelate consisted chiefly in such things as were then
wonderful and strange in England, among
which he reckons the large bells and organs
he gave them. An old bell at Canterbury took twenty-four men to ring it; another required thirty-two men *ad sonan-
dum*. The noblest peal of ten bells, without exception, in England, whether tone
or tune be considered, is said to be in St.
Margaret's Church, Leicester. When a
full peal was rung, the ringers were paid
pulsare Classicum. Durandus tells us
that, "when any one is dying, bells must
be softly tolled, that the people may put
up their prayers: twice for a woman and
thrice for a man: if for a clergyman, as
many times as he had orders, and at the
conclusion a peal on all the bells, to distinguish the quality of the person for
whom the people are to put up their
prayers. A bell, too, must be rung
while the corpse is conducted to
church, and during the bringing it out of
the church to the grave." This seems to
account for a custom still preserved in the
North of England, of making numeral distinctions at the conclusion of this ceremony: *i.e.*, nine knells for a man, six for
a woman, and three for a child, which are
undoubtedly the vestiges of this ancient
injunction of popery.—*Rationale*, lib. i.,
c. 4. It appears from an account of Killin
parish, co. Perth, printed in the end of
the 18th century, in Sinclair's *Statistical
Account*, that at that time there was a
bell "belonging to the Chapel of St.
Fillan, that was in high reputation among
the votaries of that Saint in old Times.
It seems" (says the writer) "to be of some
mixed metal. It is about a foot high, and
of an oblong form. It usually lay on a

grave-stone in the Church-yard. When
mad people were brought to be dipped in
the Saint's Pool, it was necessary to perform certain ceremonies, in which there
was a mixture of Druidism and Popery.
After remaining all night in the Chapel,
bound with ropes, the bell was set upon
their head with great solemnity. It was
the popular opinion that, if stolen, it
would extricate itself out of the thief's
hands, and return home, ringing all the
way." It is added: "For some years
past this bell has been locked up, to prevent its being used for superstitious purposes. It is but justice to the Highlanders
to say that the dipping of mad people in
St. Fillan's pool and using the other ceremonies, was common to them with the
Lowlanders. "The origin of the bell,"
pursues the author of the above narrative,
"is to be referred to the most remote ages
of the Celtic Churches, whose ministers
spoke a dialect of that language. Ara
Trode, one of the most antient Icelandic
historians, tells us, in his second chapter,
that when the Norwegians first planted a
colony in Ireland, about the year 870, 'Eo
tempore erat Islandia silvis concreta, in
medio montium et littorum: tum erant
hic viri Christiani, quos Norwegi Papas
appellant: et illi peregre profecti sunt
ex eo quod nollent esse hic cum viris Eth-
nicis, et relinquebant post se Nolas et
Baculos: ex illo poterat discerni quod
essent viri Christiani.' Nola and Bajula
both signify handbells. Far in the 19th
century it is curious to meet with things
which astonished Giraldus, the most credulous of mortals, in the 12th. St. Fillan is
said to have died in 649. In the tenth
year of his reign, Robert the Bruce
granted the Church of Killin in Glendo-
chart, to the Abbey of Inchaffray, on condition that one of the canons should offici-
ate in the Kirk of Strathfillan." The bell
of St. Mura, or Muranus, which long belonged to the Abbey of Mabian, near Innis-
bowen, c. Donegal, founded in the 7th
century, during the reign of Abodle Slaine,
was said to have descended from Heaven,
ringing loudly, but that as it approached
the earth, the tongue detached itself, and
returned whence it came, till the bronze
object was deposited in some holy receptacle. This bell was regarded with peculiar veneration by the local peasantry, and
especially as a medium for mitigating the
pains of childbirth. It was eventually
sold to the late Lord Londesborough, and
is figured (the size of the original) in
Miscellanea Graphica, 1857, plate xxx.
See some curious particulars upon the
subject of bells in Spelman's "History of
Sacrilege," p. 284, *et seq*. I find the following monkish rhymes on bells in "A
Helpe to Discourse," edit. 1633, p. 63:

"En ego Campana, nunquam denuntio
  vana,
Laudo Deum verum, Plebem voco, con-
  grego Clerum,
Defunctos plango, vivos voco, fulmina
  frango,
Vox mea, vox vitæ, voco vos ad sacra
  venite.
Sanctos collaudo, tonitrua fugo, funera
  claudo,
Funera plango, fulgura frango, Sabbatha
  pango:
Excito lentos, dissipo ventos, paco cruen-
  tos."

Misson, in his "Travels," says: "Ringing
of bells is one of their great delights,
especially in the country. They have a
particular way of doing this; but their
chimes cannot be reckoned so much as of
the same kind with those of Holland and
the Low Countries." By the will of a
mercer of London, named Donne, deposited in the Hustings Court, the tenor
bell of Bow Church, Cheapside, used long
to be rung every day at six o'clock in the
morning and eight in the evening. Mr.
Tanswell has furnished the following extracts from the Churchwardens' Books of
Lambeth:—"1579. Payd for making the
great clapper to a smithie in White
Chapel, it waying xxxi. lb. et dim. at vid.
the pounde, 15s. 9d. 1598. Item, the olde
great belle that was broken in the time of
Roger Wynslo, Rychard Sharpe, and John
Lucas, churchwardens, in 1598, did contain in weighte xiiii. cwt. one quarter, and
xxii. lb. 1623. Payd for ryngynge when the
Prince came from Spain, 12s. 1630. June
27. To the ryngers the day the Prince was
baptized, 3s. 1633. October 15. Payd for
ryngynge on the Duke's birthday, 7s
1705. Ap. 10. Gave the ringers when the
siege of Gibraltar was raised, 15s."—*History of Lambeth*, p. 108. Du Cange
quotes an authority to shew that in the
time of Charles IV. of France, 1378, the
ringing of bells was recognized as a royal
salutation, and Kennett seems to establish that in this country it used, in the
fifteenth century at least, to be looked
upon as an affront to a bishop if the bells
were not set in motion on his approach to any town within his diocese.—*Continuator Nangii*, Anno 1378,
Kennett MS, A.D., 1444, quoted by
Ellis. In "Articles to be inquired of
within the Archdeaconry of Yorke (any
year till 1640), I find the following:
"Whether there be any within your
parish or chapelry that use to ring bells
superstitiously upon any abrogated holiday, or the eves thereof." The custom of
rejoicing with bells on high festivals,
Christmas Day, &c., is derived to us from
the times of popery. The ringing of bells
on the arrival of emperors, bishops, abbots, &c., at places under their own jurisdiction was also an old custom. Whence
we seem to have derived the modern compliment of welcoming persons of consequence by a cheerful peal. In the Churchwardens' Account of Waltham, 34 Hen.
VIII. there is this: "Item. paid for the
ringing at the Prince his coming, a
Penny." In similar accounts for St.
Laurence's Parish, Reading, is the following article under 1514. "It. payd for
a galon of ale, for the ryngers, at the
death of the Kyng of Scots, ijd." The rejoicing by ringing of bells at marriages of
any consequence, is every where common.
On the fifth bell at the church of Kendal
in Westmoreland is the following inscription, alluding to this usage:

"In Wedlock bands,
  All ye who join with hands
  Your hearts unite;
So shall our tuneful tongues combine
  To laud the nuptial rite."

Nicolson and Burn's *Westmoreland and
Cumberland*, i., 620. "I remember once
that in the dead time of the night there
came a country-fellow to my uncle in a
great haste, intreating him to give order
for knocking the bells, his wife being in
labour, (a thing usual in Spain), my good
curate then waked me out of a sound
sleep, saying, Rise, Pedro, instantly, and
ring the bells, for child-birth, quickly
quickly. I got up immediately, and as
fools have good memories, I retained the
words quickly, quickly, and knocked the
bells so nimbly, that the inhabitants of
the town really believed it had been for
fire."—*The Lucky Idiot*, transl. from Quevedo, 1734, p. 13. The small bells which
are seen in ancient representations of her-
mitages were most probably intended to
drive away evil spirits. On the ringing of
bells for this purpose, much may be collected from Magius "de Tintinnabulis."
Brand writes: "Durandus would have
thought it a prostitution of the sacred
utensils, had he heard them rung, as I
have often done, with the greatest impropriety, on winning a long main at
cock-fighting. He would, perhaps, have
talked in another strain, and have represented these aërial enemies as lending
their assistance to ring them. In 1461
is a charge in the Churchwardens' Accounts of Sandwich for bread and drink
for "ryngers in the gret Thunderyng."
In "The Burnynge of Paules Church in
London," 1561, we find enumerated,
among other Popish superstitions: "ringing the hallowed belle in great tempestes
of lightninges." Aubrey says: "At Paris
when it begins to thunder and lighten,
they do presently ring out the great bell
at the Abbey of St. Germain, which they
do believe makes it cease. The like was

wont to be done heretofore in Wiltshire. When it thundered and lightened, they did ring St. Adhelm's bell at Malmesbury Abbey. The curious do say that the ringing of bells exceedingly disturbs spirits." *Miscellanies*, p. 148. Our forefathers, however, did not entirely trust to the ringing of bells for the dispersion of tempests, for in 1313 a cross, full of reliques of divers saints, was set on St. Paul's steeple to preserve from all danger of tempests. In 1783, Frederic II. of Prussia prohibited the ringing of bells on such occasions.—*News-letter* of Nov. 3, 1783, cited by Brand.—Hering advises that "the bells in cities and townes be rung often, and the great ordnance discharged; thereby the aire is purified.— *Certain Rules for this time of Pestilential Observance*, 1625. In Googe's translation of Naogeorgus, we have the following lines on the subject :

"If that the thunder chaunce to rore, and
   stormie tempest shake,
A wonder is it not for to see the wretches
   how they quake,
Howe that no fayth at all they have, nor
   trust in any thing,
The Clarke doth all the bells forthwith at
   once in steeple ring :
With wond'rous sound and deeper farre,
   than he was wont before,
Till in the loftie heavens dark, the thunder bray no more.
For in these christned belles they thinke,
   doth lie such powre and might
As able is the tempest great, and
   storme to vanquish quight.
I sawe myself at Naumburg once, a towne
   in Toring coast.
A belle that with this title bolde hirself
   did proudly boast :
By name I Mary called am, with sound I
   put to flight
The thunder-crackes and hurtfull stormes,
   and every wicked spright.
Such things when as these belles can do,
   no wonder certainlie
It is, if that the Papistes to their tolling
   alwayes flie.
When haile, or any raging storme, or tempest comes in sight,
Or thunder boltes, or lightning fierce, that
   every place doth smight."

The popular rhyme of *Oranges and Lemons*, in connection with church bells is too well known for repetition; but we are told that there was in the eighteenth century a notice at Chiswick that from the music of the bells there could be made out "My dun cow has just calved." Sir Richard Phillips, *Walk from London to Kew*, 1817, p. 212. The bells of our early churches, as well as the general

fabrics, were under the supervision of the consistory court of the diocese. On the 24th October, 1617, the parochial authorities at Stratford-on-Avon were cited to appear at Worcester to answer a charge of having allowed the Church of the Holy Trinity and its bells to fall out of repair. *Extracts by J. O. Halliwell from the Vestry Book of the Church of the Holy Trinity*, 1865, p. 19.

The large kind of bells, now used in churches, are said to have been invented by Paulinus, Bishop of Nola, in Campania, whence the *Campana* of the lower Latinity, about the 400th year of the Christian æra. Two hundred years afterwards they appear to have been in general use in churches. Mr. Bingham, however, thinks this a vulgar error; and at the same time he informs us of an invention before bells of convening religious assemblies in monasteries : it was going by turns to every one's cell, and with the knock of a hammer calling the monks to church. This instrument was called the Night Signal and the Wakening Mallet. In many of the colleges at Oxford, the Bible-clerk knocks at every room door with a key to waken the students in the morning, before he begins to ring the chapel bell. A vestige, it should seem, of the ancient monastic custom. The Jews used trumpets for bells. The Turks do not permit the use of them at all : the Greek Church under their dominion still follows their old custom of using wooden boards, or iron plates full of holes, which they hold in their hands and knock with a hammer or mallet, to call the people together to church. Durandus tells us, "In festis quæ ad gratiam pertinent, Campanæ tumultuosius tinniunt et prolixius concrepant."—*Rationale*, lib. i. cap. 4, p. 12. At Venice and elsewhere, in the beginning of the fourteenth century, we find bells employed in lieu of clocks, and the hours of the day and night were divided and notified by this process. A decree of the Venetian Council of Ten in 1310, ordered, "that no person whosoever shall be suffered without special licence to walk abroad *after the third bell of the night*. Hazlitt's *Venetian Republic*, 1900, ii., 606. But this was part of an exceptional restriction, as it was during an acute political crisis.

China has been remarkably famous for its bells. Father Le Comte tells us, that at Pekin there are seven bells, each of which weighs one hundred and twenty thousand pounds. Comp. Ditchfield's *Old English Customs*, 1896, ch. xv.

Bells, Baptism of.—Bells were a great object of superstition among our ancestors; each of them was represented to have its peculiar name and virtues, and many are said to have retained great affection for the churches to which they belonged and where they were consecrated. When a bell was removed from its original and favourite situation, it was sometimes supposed to take a nightly trip to its old place of residence, unless exercised in the evening, and secured with a chain or rope.—Warner's *Hampshire*, ii., 162. In an Italian *Ordinale* of the fifteenth century, one of the miniatures represents the blessing of the bell by the bishop, or prelate, attended by his clergy, and by a person who wears a beard, and carries his cap in hand—apparently a lay attendant. The bell is laid on a cushion or ottoman and is apparently of large dimensions. The presiding dignitary holds the service-book before him, and reads from it the service, which follows in the text; he invokes the divine blessing on the water with which the bell is to be baptised. Egelrick, Abbot of Croyland, about the time of King Edgar, cast a ring of six bells, to all which he gave names, as Bartholomew, Bethlehem, Turketul, &c. The Historian tells us his predecessor Turketul had led the way in this fancy. The superstition is one which we find indicated in the "Beehive of the Romish Church," a compilation by George Gilpin, 1579, and which was followed in many other places at a later period, particularly at Winchester and at Christ-Church, Oxford. In the churchwardens' accounts of St. Laurence's Parish Reading, anno 14 Hen. VII., is the following article: "It. payed for halowing of the bell named Harry, vjs. viijd. and ovir that Sir Willm Symys, Richard Clech, and Maistres Smyth, beyng Godfaders and Godmoder at the Consecracyon of the same bell, and beryng all oth' costs to the Suffrygan." Coates, *Hist. of Reading*, i., 214. Pennant, speaking of St. Wenefride's Well, (in Flintshire), says: "A bell belonging to the Church was also christened in honour of her. I cannot learn the names of the gossips, who, as usual, were doubtless rich persons. On the ceremony they all laid hold of the rope; bestowed a name on the bell; and the priest, sprinkling it with holy water, baptized it in the name of the Father, &c., &c.; he then cloathed it with a fine garment. After this the gossips gave a grand feast, and made great presents, which the priest received in behalf of the bell. Thus blessed it was endowed with great powers, allayed (on being rung) all storms; diverted the thunder-bolt: drove away evil spirits. These consecrated bells were always inscribed." The inscription on that in question ran thus:

"Sancta Wenefreda, Deo hoc commendare memento,
Ut pietate sua nos servet ab hoste cruento."
And a little lower was another address:
"Protege prece pia quos convoco, Virgo Maria."

"The following ceremonies," observes Mr. Tanswell, "were formerly used at the baptism of bells:—1, the bell must be first baptized before it may be hung in the steeple; 2, the bell must be baptized by a bishop or his deputy; 3, in the baptism of the bell there is used holy water, oil, salt, cream, &c.; 4, the bell must have godfathers, and they must be persons of high rank; 5, the bell must be washed by the hand of a bishop; 6, the bell must be solemnly crossed by the bishop; 7, the bell must be anointed by the bishop: 8, the bell must be washed and anointed in the name of the Trinity; 9, at the baptism of the bell they pray literally for them. The following is part of the curious prayers used at the above ceremony:

"'Lord, grant that whatsoever this holy bell, thus washed and baptized and blessed, shall sound, all deceits of Satan, all danger of whirlwind, thunder and lightning, and tempests, may be driven away, and that devotion may increase in Christian men when they hear it. O Lord, pour upon it thy heavenly blessing, that when it sounds in thy people's ears they may adore thee; may their faith and devotion increase; the devil be afraid and tremble, and fly at the sound of it. O Lord, sanction it by thy Holy Spirit, that the fiery darts of the devil may be made to fly backwards at the sound thereof, that it may deliver us from the danger of wind, thunder, &c., and grant, Lord, that all that come to the church at the sound of it may be free from all temptations of the devil.'"—*History of Lambeth*, 1858, p. 105. In the *Diary* of the Abbé Legrix of Saintes, under 1781, we read:—January 4. After High Mass, the blessing of a bell. weighing about 6 cwt., took place. M Delaage, the Dean, performed the ceremony, at which all the Canons and the under-choir assisted. M. le Marquis de Monconseil and Madame la Comtesse de la Tour du Pin were *godfather and godmother.*—*Antiquary* for 1898, p. 268. The following is from the programme of the ceremony of the blessing of the new bells in St. Mary's Roman Catholic Church, Newport:—"The ancient and solemn rite of blessing bells is full of meaning, and very expressive. The Bishop, vested with mitre and crozier, begins by intoning the l. Psalm, 'Miserere mei Deus,' followed by the liii., lvi., lxvi., lxix., lxxxv. and cxxix. Psalms, which he recites aloud together with his clergy These psalms are expressive of confidence in obtaining the protection of Almighty God when invoked by prayer, and it is especially the object of the benediction service to ask of God to manifest his power against the spirits of wickedness, whenever these bells shall be sounded. The Bishop next proceeds to bless water, with which, according to apostolic tradition, salt is mingled; and with this water the bells are washed inside and out, and wiped afterwards with a linen cloth—hence, no doubt, has arisen the incorrect expression of baptism of bells. While this is being done, seven psalms of praise are recited, and then the bells are anointed, first with the oil used for the sick and dying, and afterwards with holy chrism, such as is used to anoint bishops, priests and kings. After anointing each bell the bishop prays:—'Grant, we beseech Thee, O Lord, that this vessel, moulded for Thy Church, be sanctified by the Holy Suirit, so that the faithful may by its tolling be invited to their reward. And when its melodious notes sound in the ears of the people, let their faith and devotion increase; let every snare of the enemy, rattling hail, rushing whirlwinds, &c.—be driven to a distance; let Thy mighty right hand lay the powers of the air low,' &c. When the bells have been blessed, the Bishop places a burning thurible with incense underneath each bell, whilst the lxxxxvi. Psalm is recited. The whole ceremony is concluded by a deacon chanting a portion of the holy Gospel." Baronius informs us that Pope John XIII., in 968, consecrated a very large new cast bell in the Lateran Church, and gave it the name of John. This would be almost contemporary with the case in England above-mentioned.

Ringing the bells backwards was anciently a practice to which the authorities of towns, &c., resorted as a sign of distress, or as an alarm to the people. Hazlitt's *Popular Poetry*, 1864-6, ii., 153, note. The custom has escaped the notice of our popular antiquaries. Cleveland, in his "Poems," 1669, employs the term metaphorically. It was also the usage in some districts of Italy, and in other parts of the Continent, to ring the church-bells backward, when a fire broke out, in order to summon assistance, as every one on such an occasion was formerly, and is indeed still, in many places (particularly in Switzerland and Sweden) bound to lend his aid. That the practice is of considerable antiquity may be inferred from the fact that it is mentioned in the "Gesta Romanorum," and in the old ballad-poem of "Adam Bel, Clym of the Clough," &c., when the outlaws came to Carlisle to release Cloudesley, it is said:

"There was many an oute horne in Carlyll blowen,
And the belles bacewarde did they ring."

Beltein.—In Sinclair's "Statis. Acc. of Scot." vol. iii. p. 105, the Minister of Loudoun in Ayrshire tells us: "The custom still remains amongst the herds and young people to kindle fires in the high grounds, in honour of Beltan. Beltan, which in Gaelic signifies Baal, or Bels Fire, was anciently the time of this solemnity. It is now kept on St Peter's Day. The minister of Callander in Perthshire reported in 1794, as follows: "The people of this district have two customs, which are fast wearing out, not only here, but all over the Highlands, and therefore ought to be taken notice of, while they remain. Upon the first day of May, which is called Beltan, or Bàl-tein-day, all the boys in a township or hamlet meet in the moors. They cut a table in the green sod, of a round figure, by casting a trench in the ground of such a circumference as to hold the whole company. They kindle a fire, and dress a repast of eggs and milk in the consistence of a custard. They knead a cake of oatmeal, which is toasted at the embers against a stone. After the custard is eaten up, they divide the cake into so many portions, as similar as possible to one another in size and shape, as there are persons in the company. They daub one of these portions all over with charcoal, until it be perfectly black. They put all the bits of the cake into a bonnet. Every one, blindfold, draws out a portion. He who holds the bonnet is entitled to the last bit. Whoever draws the black bit is the devoted person, who is to be sacrificed to Baal, whose favour they mean to implore, in rendering the year productive of the sustenance of man and beast. There is little doubt of these inhuman sacrifices having been once offered in this country as well as in the East, although they now pass from the act of sacrificing, and only compel the devoted person to leap three times through the flames; with which the ceremonies of the festival are closed." Sinclair's *Statis. Acc. of Scotland*, vol. xi. The minister of Logierait, in Perthshire, says: "On the first of May, O.S. a festival called Beltan is annually held here. It is chiefly celebrated by the cowherds, who assemble by scores in the fields to dress a dinner for themselves, of boiled milk and eggs. These dishes they eat with a sort of cakes baked for the occasion, and having small lumps, in the form of nipples, raised all over the surface, The cake might, perhaps, be an offering to some deity in the days of Druidism." Pennant's account of this rural sacrifice is more minute. He tells us that, on the first of May, in the Highlands of Scotland, the herdsmen of every village hold their bel-tein. "They cut a square trench in the ground, leaving the turf in the middle; on that they make a fire of wood, on which they dress a large caudle of eggs, butter, oatmeal, and milk, and bring, besides the ingredients of the caudle, plenty of beer and whisky: for each of the company must contribute something. The rites begin by spilling some of the caudle on the ground, by way of libation: on that, every one takes a cake of oatmeal, upon which are raised nine square knobs, each dedicated to some particular being, the supposed preserver of their flocks and herds, or to some particular animal, the real destroyer of them. Each person then turns his face to the fire, breaks off a knob, and, flinging it over his shoulders, says :—' This I give to thee, preserve thou my horses;' 'This to thee, preserve thou my sheep;' and so on. After that, they use the same ceremony to the noxious animals. 'This I give to thee, O fox! save thou my lambs'; 'this to thee, O hooded crow;' 'this to thee, eagle!' When the ceremony is over, they dine on the caudle; and, after the feast is finished, what is left is hid by two persons deputed for that purpose; but on the next Sunday they re-assemble, and finish the reliques of the first entertainment." Comp. *Ireland* and *St. John's Eve.*

Benchers.—The designation of the governing bodies or committees at Lincoln's Inn and the two Temples. At Gray's Inn they are termed Ancients, and at Clifford's Inn they were known as Rules. The Bench was originally and formerly, and is still by strict right, an elective assembly chosen from the whole constituency; but of recent years it has gradually and tacitly converted a merely temporary and fiduciary power into an absolute one, and spends the revenue of the Inn, and controls its hospitality without any reference to the Barristers' Table. It is a signal abuse and usurpation of long standing. which there might be a considerable difficulty in correcting or removing.

Bene (or Bean) House.—In the *Owl's Almanac,* 1618, mention is made of "a tapstering or *bene* house," evidently a place of common entertainment, and possibly the germ of the modern bean-feast, or workmen's holiday.

Benedictio Mensœ. — The grace before meat, as well as, though not so properly, that after it. Furnivall's *Babees Book; Antiquary* for January, 1895. In the latter place a knife, preserved at the Louvre, and belonging to the 16th century, bears the former upon it with the musical notation; the words are:

Quæ sumpturi benedicat trinus & unus, Amen. A very full account of the graces pronounced at the Oxford Colleges will be found in Hearne's *Diary,* 1869, Appendix V. Other forms are found in the printed collections (Hazlitt's *Bibl. Coll,* vv. *Graces* and *Seager*); and doubtless there were many no longer known.

Benedictio Panis. — The blessing on the consecrated bread used in the Communion; it is printed in the service-books for Salisbury and other uses, with the other forms of a similar character.

Benedictio Salis et Aquæ. — A form of prayer found in the Romish service-books, including those for English use. It is inferrible from the Durham Ritual that this blessing was pronounced when the salt was poured into the water, for the rubric is: "Hic mittatur sal in aquâ, Benedictio salis et Aquæ. Gratia Domini vobiscum." In the Durham Ritual (Surtees Society, 1840, pp. 97-104), a remarkable series of forms of benediction are given, dating from the ninth or tenth century. It seems to have been an ancient practice to bless objects of use and consumption under a variety of circumstances; and we here find: *Benedictio super vasa reperta in locis antiquis, Benedictio quorunlibet vasorum, Benedictio Arborum, Benedictio Pomorum, Benedictio Panis, Benedictio ad omnia quæ volueris, Benedictio Domus, Benedictio quando judicium exituri sunt homines, Exorcismus aquæ ad Furtum Requirendum, Benedictio Aquæ, Benedictio Vestium virginum,* and *Benedictio Lac et Mel.* This frequent and habitual resort to adjuration and prayer led to the introduction of the liturgical *Benedictional.*

Benediction-Posset.—See *Sack Posset.*

Benefit of Clergy.—This privilege was abolished by 7 & 8 Geo. IV. Before that time, it appears that a felon could plead benefit of clergy, and be saved by what was aptly enough termed the neckverse, which was very usually the *miserere mei* of Psalm 51, but was at the judge's discretion. At a period when capital punishment was inflicted on what would now be considered terribly slight grounds, such a means of evasion was perhaps not improperly connived at. In our old jest books, however, the practice was one of the themes selected for derision and satire. Machyn the diarist points to a provision in this obsolete usage, which I do not see noticed elsewhere. He tells us that, on the 8th March, 1559-60, an old man, who was a priest, was hanged for cutting a purse, "but," adds Machyn, "he was burnt in the hand afore, or elles ys boke would have saved hym." In the Year

Book of 30 Edward I. it seems to be intimated that, in order to claim benefit of clergy, a technical denial of the charge was then considered absolutely an essential condition.

Benski, or **The Fairy's Wife.**— See *Wraith*.

Beryl.—Aubrey, in his Miscellanies, 1696-1721, ed. 1857, pp. 1547, devotes a section to this subject, with an illustration of one of these mirrors. They were formerly used by magicians in their superstitious and diabolical operations. Delrio informs us that the Emperor Julian made use of a mirror for this purpose, and refers us to his life by Spartianus. *Disquis. Magicæ*, lib. iv., c. v. "Lilly," says Grose, "describes one of these berryls or crystals. It was as large as an orange, set in silver, with a cross at the top, and round about engraved the names of the angels, Raphael, Gabriel, and Uriel. A delineation of another is engraved in the frontispiece to Aubrey's Miscellanies. This mode of inquiry was practised by Dr. Dee, the celebrated mathematician. His speculator was named Kelly. From him, and others practising this art, we have a long muster-roll of the infernal host, their different natures, tempers, and appearances. Reginald Scot has given us a list of some of the chiefs of these devils or spirits. Aubrey's had the name of Gabriel, Uriel, Raphael, and Michael. "Another mode," Grose remarks, "of consulting spirits was by the berryl, by means of a speculator or seer, who, to have a complete sight, ought to be a pure virgin, a youth who had not known woman, or at least a person of irreproachable life, and purity of manners. The method of such consultation is this: the conjuror, having repeated the necessary charms and adjurations, with the Litany, or Invocation peculiar to the spirits or angels he wishes to call, (for every one has his particular form), the seer looks into a chrystal or berryl, wherein he will see the answer, represented either by types or figures: and sometimes, though very rarely, will hear the angels or spirits speak articulately. Their pronunciation is, as Lilly says, like the Irish, much in the throat." In Andrews's Continuation of Henry, we read: "The Conjurations of Dr. Dee having induced his familiar spirit to visit a kind of talisman, Kelly (a brother adventurer) was appointed to watch and describe his gestures." The stone used by these impostors was formerly in the Strawberry Hill collection. It appears to be a polished piece of cannel coal. To this Butler refers when he writes,

"Kelly did all his feats upon
The Devil's looking-glass, a stone."

I do not know whether this is the same stone which was in the possession of the late Mr. Henry Huth. The latter is said, at any rate, to have been Dr. Dee's. Did he employ it, when Queen Elizabeth came to Mortlake, to consult him? In Lodge's "Wits Miserie," 1596, in the Epistle to the Reader, are the following quaint allusions to sorcerers and magicians: "Buy therefore this chrystall, and you shall see them in their common appearance: and read these exorcisms advisedly, and you may be sure to conjure them without crossings; but if any man long for a familiar for false dice, a spirit to tell fortunes, a charme to heale diseased, this only booke can best fit him."

This species of divination has still its believers, and a case occurred about forty years ago, from which it transpired that the beryl or mirror was consulted by some among our contemporaries who ought to have been superior to so silly a superstition.

Betrothal.—See *Handfasting and Troth-Plight*.—Harl. MS. 980, cited by Strutt, states that, "by the Civil Law, whatsoever is given ex sponsalitia Largitate, betwixt them that are promised in marriage, hath a condition (for the most part silent) that it may be had again if marriage ensue not; but if the man should have had a kiss for his money, he should lose one half of that which he gave. Yet with the woman it is otherwise, for, kissing or not kissing, whatsover she gave, she may ask and have it again. However, this extends only to gloves, rings, bracelets, and such like small wares." To the betrothing contract under consideration must be referred, if I mistake not, and not to the marriage ceremony itself (to which latter, I own, however, the person who does not nicely discriminate betwixt them will be strongly tempted to incline) the well-known passage on this subject in the last scene of Shakespear's play of "Twelfth Night." The priest, who had been privy to all that had passed, is charged by Olivia to reveal the circumstances, which he does, reciting the ceremonies of joining the hands, kissing, and interchanging rings, as preliminaries which had taken place in the usual course. The same drama affords an example of the old English practice of lovers plighting their troth in the chantry, in the presence of their minister. It is where Olivia and Sebastian accompany the priest with this object in view. It appears to have been formerly a custom also for those who were betrothed to wear some flower as an external and conspicuous mark of their mutual engagement: the conceit of choosing such short-lived emblems of their plighted loves cannot be thought a very happy one. That such a custom, however, did certainly prevail, we have the testimony of Spenser:

"Bring coronations and sops in wine
Worn of paramours."

This passage is illustrated by the following extract from Gunning's "Reminiscences of Cambridge.": "The Dean (of St. Asaph), who appeared very desirous to clear up the matter, asked him, amongst other questions, if he had never made her any presents? He replied that he never had, but, recollecting himself, added, ' except a very choice bunch of flowers, which I brought from Chirk Castle.'" "This explains the whole matter," said the Dean; "in Wales, a man never sends a lady a bunch of flowers, but as a proposal of marriage, and the lady's acceptance of them is considered the ratification." This was in 1788. Fletcher the dramatist says:

"I knit this lady handfast, and with
     this hand
The heart that owes this hand, ever
     binding
By force of this initiating contract
Both heart and hand in love, faith,
     loyalty,
Estate, or what to them belongs."
     Wit at Several Weapons, act v. sc. i.

In "Witt's Recreations," 1640, the annexed passage belongs to a piece called "Abroad with the Maids"; it was written by Herrick:

"Next we will act how young men wooe;
And sigh, and kisse, as lovers do,
And talk of brides, and who shall make
That wedding-smock, this bridal-cake;
That dress, this sprig, that leafe, this
     vine;
That smooth and silken columbine.
This done, we'l draw lots, who shall buy
And guild the bayes and rosemary:
What posies for our wedding-rings;
What gloves we'l give and ribbanings."

Strutt, in his "Manners and Customs," has illustrated this by an extract from the old play of the "Widow." From this it also appears that no dry bargain would hold on such occasions. For on the Widow complaining that Ricardo had artfully drawn her into a verbal contract, she is asked by one of her suitors, "Stay, stay,—you broke no gold between you?" To which she answers, "We broke nothing, Sir." And, on his adding, "Nor drank to each other?" she replies "Not a drop, Sir." Whence he draws this conclusion: "that the contract cannot stand good in law." The latter part of the ceremony seems alluded to in the following passage in Middleton's "No Wit like a Woman's" (written before 1626):

"E'en when my lip touch'd the contracting cup."

Thiers quotes passages from three ritualistic works apposite to this portion of the nuptial process, as practised in France. *Rituel de Bordeaux,* 98-9. Both the Synodal Statutes of Sens, in 1524, and the Evreux Ritual (1621) refrained from prescribing betrothal, merely leaving it permissive and optional; and the same may be said of the Provincial Council of Rheims, in 1583; but all these authorities laid down the rule that, where the espousal was solemnized, the ceremony must take place openly and in the church.

Beverage, Beverege, or Beveridge, reward, consequence. 'Tis a word now in use for a refreshment between dinner and supper; and we use the word when any one pays for wearing new clothes, &c. Hearne's Glossary to Robert of Gloucester's Chronicle in v. It is at present employed in the general sense of any liquid refreshment.

Bible Omens.—The superstitious among the ancient Christians practised a kind of divination by opening the Old and New Testament. Gibbon speaks of Clovis who, "marching (A.D. 507) from Paris, as he proceeded with decent reverence through the holy diocese of Tours, consulted the shrine of St. Martin, the sanctuary and oracle of Gaul. His messengers were instructed to remark the words of the psalm which should happen to be chaunted at the precise moment when they entered the church. These words, most fortunately, expressed the valour and victory of the champions of heaven, and the application was easily transferred to the new Joshua, the new Gideon, who went forth to battle against the enemies of the Lord." He adds: "This mode of divination by accepting as an omen the first sacred words which in particular circumstances should be presented to the eye or ear, was derived from the Pagans, and the Psalter or Bible was substituted for the poems of Homer and Virgil. From the fourth to the fourteenth century, these *Sortes Sanctorum,* as they are styled, were repeatedly condemned by the decrees of councils, and repeatedly practised by Kings, Bishops, and Saints." Willis of Gloucester bears testimony to this point: "As I was to passe through the roome where my little grand-childe was set by her grandmother to read her morning's chapter, the 9th of Matthew's Gospell, just as I came in she was uttering these words in the second verse, ' Jesus said to the sicke of the palsie, Sonne, be of good comfort, thy sinnes are forgiven thee '; which words sorting so fitly with my case, whose whole left side is taken with that kind of disease, I stood at a stand at the uttering of them, and could not but conceive some joy and comfort in those blessed words, though by the childe's reading, as if the Lord by her had spoken them to myselfe, a paralytick and a sinner, as that Sicke man was," &c. This may be called a Bible omen. *Mount Tabor*, 1639, pp. 199-200. It appears that Arise Evans, in the time of the Commonwealth, used this species of divination by the Bible, and also that one of the Earls of Berkeley had recourse to the then prevailing superstition. His lordship's words are: "I being sick, and under some dejection of spirit, opening my Bible to see what place I could first light upon, which might administer comfort to me, casually I fixed upon the sixth of Hosea: the first three verses are these. [Here follows the quotation.] I am willing to decline superstition upon all occasions, yet think my self obliged to make this use of such a providential place of Scripture: First, by hearty repenting me of my sins past: Secondly, by sincere reformation for the time to come."—*Eccho to the Voice from Heaven*, 1652, p. 227. Martin, speaking of the Isle of Collonsay, says, that in confidence of curing the patient by it, the inhabitants had an antient custom of fanning the face of the sick with the leaves of the Bible. *Descr. of the West of Scotland*, 248. A correspondent of "Notes and Queries," in the number for October 19, 1861, states that he met with the custom of dipping into the Bible on New Year's Day before noon in the county of Oxford, and that it was believed that the tenor of the first passage which caught the eye of the dipper, was a prognostication of the person's good or bad luck for the year.

Bicker-rade, The.—This is a practice among reapers in some parts. A correspondent of Notes and Queries described it, so far as its indelicate character would allow, in the columns of that periodical in 1857. The writer seems to consider the custom as belonging chiefly to Berwickshire. At the harvest-dinner "each band-wun, consisting of six shearers and a bandster, had the use of a bicker (a small round wooden vessel, composed of staves or staps, and neatly bound with willow girths or girds); sometimes more than one bicker was used by the bandwun. After the dinner repast was finished, any of the men of the boun, who felt disposed to inflict on any female the bicker-rade, extende her upon her back on the ground and reclining upon her commenced a series of operations, which are too indelicate to be minutely described." It seems further, that resistance was useless, and that serious injuries were sometimes suffered by the victims of this barbarous process. It has probably become entirely obsolete by this time: it was nearly so forty years ago.

Bid-Ale.—There was an ancient custom called Bid-ale or Bidder-ale, from the Saxon word *biddan*, to pray or supplicate, when any honest man, decayed in his estate, was set up again by the liberal benevolence and contributions of friends at a feast, to which those friends were bid or invited. It was most used in the West of England, and in some counties called a help-ale. A writer in "The Gentleman's Magazine" for May, 1784, mentions this custom in some parts of South Wales, peculiar, he thinks, to that country, and still practised at the marriages of servants, tradesfolks, and little farmers, "Before the wedding an entertainment is provided, to which all the friends of each party are bid or invited, and to which none fail to bring or send some contribution, from a cow or calf down to half-a-crown or a shilling. An account of each is kept, and if the young couple do well, it is expected that they should give as much at any future bidding of their generous guests. I have frequently known of £50 being thus collected, and have heard of a bidding, which produced even a hundred." The *Cambrian Register*, 1796, p. 450, adds: "Some time previous to these weddings, where they mean to receive contributions, a herald with a crook or wand, adorned with ribbons, makes the circuit of the neighbourhood, and makes his 'bidding' or invitation in a prescribed form. The knight-errant cavalcade on horseback, the carrying off the bride, the rescue, the wordy war in rhythm between the parties, &c. which formerly formed a singular spectacle of mock contest at the celebration of nuptials, I believe to be now almost, if not altogether, laid aside every where through the Principality." The following is from the "Gentleman's Magazine" for 1789:—

"Bidding.—As we intend entering the nuptial state, we propose having a bidding on the occasion on Thursday the 20th day of September, instant, at our own house on the Parade: where the favour of your good company will be highly esteemed; and whatever benevolence you pleased to confer on us, shall be gratefully acknowledged and retaliated on a similar occasion by your most obedient humble servants, William Jones, Ann Davies; Caermarthen, Sept. 4, 1787. N.B.—The young man's father (Stephen Jones) and the young woman's aunt (Ann Williams) will be thankfull for all favours conferred on them that day." Another writer in the "Gentleman's Magazine" for 1784 mentions a similar custom in Scotland called Penny Weddings. In the *Penny Magazine* for January, 1835, an improved and more ambitious form of communication (among the humbler classes) to the friends of the parties, is given. A couple belonging to Caermarthenshire are represented as addressing a circular to guests as follows :—

"Carmarthenshire, February 1, 1834.

"Dear Friend,—We take this convenience to inform you that we confederate such a design as to enter under the sanction of matrimony on the 19th of February inst. And as we feel our hearts inclining to regard the ancient custom of our ancestors, *sef Hiliogaeth Gomer*, we intend to make a wedding-feast the same day at the respective habitation of our parent; we hereby most humbly invite your pleasing and most comfortable fellowship at either of which places; and whatever kindness your charitable hearts should then grant will be accepted with congratulation and most lovely acknowledgment, carefully recorded and returned with preparedness and joy, whenever a similar occasion overtake you, by your affectionate servants,

DAVID JOSHUA.
MARY WILLIAMS.

In this case the parents of both parties entertained; but in another example of 1830, belonging to Glamorganshire, the hospitality was limited to the bride's family. "Some of the Cumbrians," observes the compiler of the "Westmoreland and Cumberland Dialect," 1839, "particularly those who are in poor circumstances, have, on their entrance into the married state, what is called a bidding, or biddenwedding, over which a sort of master of the revels, called a birler, presides, and at which a pecuniary collection is made among the company for the purpose of setting the wedded pair forward in the world. It is always attended with music and dancing, and the fiddler, when the contributions begin, takes care to remind the assembly of their duties by notes imitative of the following couplet :

'Come, my friends, and freely offer;
Here's the bride who has no tocher (dowry).''

Bidding to Funerals.—From an early date it was customary among the gilds of the City of London to summon all the brethren to attend the obsequies of a departed member, and in more modern times a form of invitation on a small broadsheet, enclosed in a mourning border with the usual emblems of mortality was prepared and distributed. A facsimile of one of these notices is given in Hazlitt's *Livery Companies*, 1892. At South Shields, co. Durham, the bidders, *i.e.*, the inviters to a funeral never use the rapper of the door when they go about, but always knock with a key, which they

carry with them for that purpose. I know not whether this custom be retained any where else. The following form of inviting to burials by the public bellman of the town was, in Brand's time, in use at Hexham, Northumberland: "Blessed are the dead which die in the Lord. Joseph Dixon is departed, son of Christopher Dixon was. Their company is desired to-morrow at five o'clock, and at six he is to be bu—ri—ed. For him and all faithful people give God most hearty thanks." A writer in the *Penny Magazine* for 1837, in reference to Northumbrian manners and customs, says: "In many places it is usual to invite not only the friends, but also the neighbours of a deceased person to his funeral. This is done by bidders, dressed in black silk scarfs, going round formally. The bidders never used the rapper of the door, but always knocked with a key, which they carried with them for that purpose. In the town of Hexham, until within the last few years, the public bellman went round publicly to invite attendance at a deceased's funeral; on such occasions a notice somewhat similar to the following was used: 'Blessed are the dead which die in the Lord. John Robson is departed, son of Richard Robson that was. Company is desired to morrow at five o'clock, and at six he is to be buried. For him and all faithful people give God most hearty thanks." See *Funeral Customs.*

Bidding Prayer.—See Nares, *Glossary*, 1859, in v.

Billiards.—At what date this game was introduced into England is uncertain. It occurs in Spenser's *Mother Hubbard's Tale*, among his *Complaints*, 1591, and is named by Shakespear in *Antony and Cleopatra*, iii., v., where the Queen, referring to music, says: "Let it alone, let us to billiards." This drama was licensed in 1608. Even in the poet's day, *barring* was understood, as Mr. Symon points out. *Shakespear Quotation*, 1901, p. 49. The game is thus mentioned in the Book of Expenses of James Masters, Esq., of Yotes Court, Mereworth, co. Kent :—"December 21, 1661. For 4 yards & ¼ of Greene Cloath to cover my Billyard table at 10s. ye yard, 02. 05. 00." "Feb 12, 1661/2. For 2 Billyard Sticks, 2 balls, Ring & porch, 00. 18. 00." The *cannon* at billiards is taken to be a corruption of *carom*, itself an abbreviation of *carambole*, the French term for the red ball, which was neutral, and which was a form of the game formerly played with three balls it was the object of each of the two players to strike, as well as his adversary's. The name of this amusement is apparently derived from Fr. *bille*, for a ball, and hence *billard*. Cotton, in the *Compleat*

Gamester, 1676, refers to it in company with bowls, chess, cards, and dice. It is among the amusements described in a small volume entitled : "Games most in use in England. France and Spain," printed about 1710, and purporting to be regulated by the most experienced masters. The principal or largest monograph on the subject is that of Edwin Kentfield, of Brighton, folio, 1839, with a curious folding frontispiece and a series of diagrams, shewing the various stages of the game, and the modes of playing it in different places. Kentfield was himself a very expert hand, and was patronised by the then Duke of Devonshire, who, when he came to Brighton, used to play with him. It is said that Carter, at one time landlord of the Blue Posts, Brydges Street, Drury Lane, was a very successful player at this game from the length of his arms.

Bird of Paradise.

In *A Short Relation of the River Nile*, 1669, is is said : "The Bird of Paradise is found dead with her bill fixed in the ground, in an island joyning to the Maluccos not far from Macaca ; whence it comes thither, is unknown, though great diligence hath been imployed in the search, but without success. One of them dead came to my hands. I have seen many. The tayle is worn by children for a penashe, the feathers fine and subtile as a very thin cloud. The body not fleshy, resembling that of a thrush. The many and long feathers (of a pale invivid colour, nearer white than ash colour), which cover it, make it of great beauty. Report says of these birds, that they alwaies flie from their birth to their death, and are not discovered to have any feet. They live by flyes they catch in the ayr, where, their diet being slender, they take some little repose. They fly very high, and come falling down with their wings displayed. As to their generation, Nature is said to have made a hole in the back of the male, where the female laies her eggs, hatcheth her young, and feeds them till they are able to fly : great trouble and affection of the parent ! I set down what I have heard. This is certainly the bird so lively drawn in our maps." This beautiful creature is almost confined in its habitat to New Zealand and Southern Australia, once parts of the same continent. The account given above is of no value, except to shew the ignorance of the earlier travellers and naturalists. There are in fact several varieties. The *Paradisea apoda*, however, was not one of these, but merely a supposed footless genus, the specimens sent to Europe having lost their feet. This error produced a second, namely, that the bird was perpetually on the wing.

Bird and Fowl Augury.

These Fowl omens are probably derived to us from the Romans, at whose superstitions on this account Butler laughs :

"A flamm more senseless than the Rog'ry
Of old Aruspicy and Aug'ry,
That out of Garbages of Cattle
Presage'd th' events of truce or battel ;
From flight of birds or chickens pecking
Success of great'st attempts would reckon."

The ancient augurs foretold things to come by the chirping or singing of certain birds, the crow, the pye, the chough, &c. : hence perhaps the observation, frequent in the mouths of old women, that when the pie chatters we shall have strangers. Horace, in his "Ode to Galatea," has this thought :

"Teque nec lævus vetet ire picus,
Nec vaga cornix."

Pennant, speaking of the hoopoe, tells that the country people in Sweden look on the appearance of this bird as a presage of war : Facies armata videtur. And formerly the vulgar in our country esteemed it a forerunner of some calamity, which has probably occasioned its growing scarcity. The same writer tells us that the great auk, a species of penguin, is a bird observed by seamen never to wander beyond soundings, and according to its appearance they direct their measures, being then assured that land is not remote. Moresin and Gaule rank the unseasonable crowing of the cock among omens. As also the sudden fall of hens from the housetop. *Papatus*, 1594, p. 21 *Mag-Astromancer posed*, p. 181. Bartholomæus says of the crow : "Divynours tell, that she taketh hede of spienges and awaytynges, and teacheth and sheweth wayes, and warneth what shal fal. But it is ful unleful to beleve, that God sheweth his prevy Counsayle to Crowes as Isidore sayth. Amonge many divynacions divynours meane that crowes token reyne with gredynge and cryenge, as this verse metneth :

'Tum Cornix plena pluviam vocat improba voce.'"
that is to understonde,
'Nowe then the crowe calleth reyne with an eleynge voyce.'"

In the Earl of Northampton's "Defensative," 1583, signat. T 2 verso, we read : "The Flight of many crowes upon the left side of the campe, made the Romans very much afrayde of somme badde lucke : as if the great God Jupiter had nothing else to doo (sayd Carneades) but to dryve Jacke Dawes in a flocke together." Gaule particularizes among omens, "A crow lighting on the right hand or on the left."

Mag-Astromancer posed, p. 181. Another early author says: "If a crow fly but over the house and croak thrice, how do they fear, they, or some one else in the family shall die?" Ramsey's *Elminthologia*, 1668, p, 271. We are informed that "people prognosticate a great famine or mortality, when great flocks of jays and crows forsake the woods; because these melancholy birds, bearing the characters of Saturn the author of famine and mortality, have a very early perception of the bad disposition of that planet. *Athenian Oracle.* p 271. And Defoe writes: "Some will defer going abroad, tho' called by business of the greatest consequence, if, happening to look out of the window, they see a single crow." *Mem. of Duncan Campbel*, 60. Willsford has much to say on this branch of his subject: "Ravens and crows, when they do make a hoarse, hollow, and sorrowful noise, as if they sobbed, it presages foul weather approaching. Crows flocking together in great companies, or calling early in the morning with a full and clear voice, or at any time of the day gaping against the sun, foreshews hot and dry weather: but if at the brink of ponds they do wet their heads, or stalk into the water, or cry much towards the evening, are signs of rain." He adds: "The woodpecker's cry denotes wet. Buzards, or kites, when they do soar very high and much to lessening themselves, making many plains to and agin, foreshows hot weather, and that the lower region of the air is inflamed, which for coolnesse makes them ascend. Cranes soaring aloft, and quietly in the air, foreshows fair weather; but if they do make much noise, as consulting which way to go, it foreshows a storm that's neer at hand. Herons in the evening, flying up and down as if doubtful where to rest, presages some evill approaching weather." *Nature's Secrets*, 1658, p. 133. Pennant, speaking of the carrion crow, tells us Virgil says that its croakings foreboded rain. It was also thought a bird of bad omen, especially if it happened to be seen on the left hand.

"Ante sinistra cava monuisset ab ilice Cornix."

—*Zoology*, i. 220. In *Dives et Pauper*, ch. 46, we read: "Some bileve that yf the kyte or the puttock fle ovir the way afore them that they shuld fare wel that daye, for sumtyme they have farewele after that they see the puttock so fleynge; and soo they falle in wane by leve and thanke the puttocke of their welfare and nat God, but suche foles take none hede howe often men mete with the puttok so fleynge and yet they fare nevir the better: for there is no folk that mete so oft with the put-toke so fleynge as they that begge their mete from dore to dore." Hall in his "Characters," 1608, declares that in his time it was enough to induce the superstitious man to make his will, if a bittern flew over his head; but in these statements one may fairly suspect a tincture of hyperbole or exaggeration. Dr. Leyden observes of the magpie, that "it is, according to popular superstition, a bird of unlucky omen. Many an old woman would more willingly see the devil, who bodes no more ill luck than he brings, than a magpie perching on a neighbouring tree." Leyden also informs us that "in the South and West of Scotland, this bird is much detested, though not reckoned ominous. As it frequents solitary places, its haunts were frequently intruded upon by the fugitive Presbyterians, during the persecution which they suffered in the disgraceful and tyrannical reign of Charles II. and James II., when they were often discovered by the clamours of the lapwing." *Glossary to the Complaynt of Scotland*, 1801, vv. *Piett and Thriasneck*. The notes of the night-crow, or night-jar, have always been regarded as portentous, and significant of death in a household, where they are heard. Mary, Countess of Pembroke, in her poem on the passion, written perhaps about 1590, says:

"The night crowes songe, that soundeth nought but death."

And Shakespear himself alludes to the superstition. In the "Parlyament of Byrdes" (circâ 1550), the popular superstition relating to this creature is referred to by the Hawk:

"— The crowe hath no brayne, For to gyue counsell but of the rayne."

So, again, in "Tottel's Miscellany," 1557, one of the Uncertain Authors says:

"Thou dunghyll crowe that crokest agaynst the rayne, Home to thy hole."

The modern sailors pay respect to auguries in the same manner as Aristophanes in his *Aves*, line 597, tells us those of Greece did above two thousand years ago. Pennant farther observes, that the stormy petrol presages bad weather, and cautions the seamen of the approach of a tempest by collecting under the sterns of the ships. *Zoology*, i., 258; ii., 508, 554. Werenfels says: "If the superstitious man has a desire to know how many years he has to live, he will inquire of the cuckow." In 1609, Thomas Dekker printed his "Raven's Almanack," which expressly purported to be a prognostication of calamities in store for this kingdom; and in 1620 Rowlands produced his *Night Raven* with the following distich on the title:

"All those whose deeds doe shun the
      Light,
Are my companions in the night."

Gay, too, in his pastoral called "The Dirge," has noted this omen:

"The boding raven on her cottage sat,
And with hoarse croakings warn'd us
      of our fate."

Its being accounted unlucky to destroy swallows is probably a pagan relique. We read in Ælian that these birds were sacred to the penates or household gods of the ancients, and therefore were preserved. They were honoured anciently as the nuncios of the spring. The Rhodians are said to have had a solemn anniversary song to welcome in the swallow. Anacreon's Ode to that bird is well known.

The ancients were firm believers—as it is scarcely necessary to observe—in auguries derived from the flight of birds. Willsford speaks of the low flight of the swallow as indicative of rain; but this is doubtful (*Nature's Secrets*, 1658, p. 134). and Gaule, (*Mag-Astromancers posed*, 181) says that a swallow falling down the chimney was thought in his day to be an inauspicious symptom. The former observes generally that birds which frequent trees and bushes, "if they do fly often out, and make quick returns, expect some bad weather to follow soon after." Rosse, in allusion to the English Civil Wars in the seventeenth century, declares that these misfortunes were foretold by the appearance of unusual flights of birds, seen in the air fighting on opposite sides. *Arcana Microcosmi*, 1652, App. 219. It was considered a bad omen if a swallow died in one's hand, and from some remains of proverbial law it appears that a degree of sanctity, which it has since lost, was formerly attached to this bird. Every one must be familiar with the adage (of which there is more than one version, however):

"The martin and the swallow
Are God Almighty's birds to hollow";

where hollow is the old form of hallow, or keep holy. Parker, in his "Philomela," 1632, says, in allusion to the swallow:

"And if in any's hand she chance to
      dye,
'Tis counted ominous, I know not why."

There was also a belief that whoever stole a swallow's eggs, or a robin's or wren's young ones, would be punished by some domestic calamity. Lupton observes, that the peacock, by his loud and harsh clamour, prophesies and foretells rain, and the oftener they cry, the more rain is signified." Theophrastus and Mizaldus are cited:—"and Paracelsus saies, if a peacock cries more than usual, or out of his time, it foretells the death of some in that family to whom it doth belong."— *Notable Things*, 1579, ed. 1660, p. 311. Willsford enters into a somewhat elaborate catalogue of omens of this description. His words are these: "The offspring or aliance of the Capitolian Guard, when they do make a gaggling in the air more than usual, or seem to fight, being over greedy at their meat, expect then cold and winterely weather. Peacocks crying loud and shrill for their lost Io, does proclaim an approaching storm. Doves coming late home to their houses than they are accustomed to do, presages some evil weather approaching. Jack-daws, if they come late home from forraging, presages some cold or ill weather neer at hand, and likewise when they are seen much alone. Finally, that duck, mallards, and all water-fowls, when they bathe themselves much, prune their feathers, and flicker, or clap themselves with their wings, it is a sign of rain or wind. The same with cormorants and gulls. Sea-mews, early in the morning making a gaggling more than ordinary, foretoken stormy and blustering weather." This superstition was entertained in Scotland in the 18th century. A person writing from Holywood, co. Dumfries, about 1790, says: "During the whole year the sea gulls, commonly called in this parish sea-maws, occasionally come from the Solway Firth to this part of the country; their arrival seldom fails of being followed by a high wind and heavy rain, from the south-west, within twenty-four hours; and they return to the Firth again as soon as the storm begins to abate." *Nature's Secrets*, 1658, 132-4. The same notion appears to have prevailed in other parts. "The sea-gulls," says a writer from Arbilot, co. Forfar, "are considered as ominous. When they appear in the fields, a storm from the south-east generally follows; and when the storm begins to abate, they fly back to the shore." *Stat. Acc.*, i., 32. Such after all has always been, and is, pretty much the belief and experience all along our English coasts. We still attach credit to the symptoms of hard weather at sea, when the gulls fly landward, and are seen up the Thames. A traveller of the 18th century remarked that a bird, which he calls caldelia, appeared on the coasts of Corsica and Sardinia just before a storm, like the petrel with us. Smith's *Travels*, 1792, p. 11 Dallaway, when he visited the Bosphorus, was struck by the large flocks of sea-birds, like swallows, but, says he, "because they are never known to rest, they are called halcyons, and by the French *ames damnées*," which flew in a train from one sea to the other, and were looked upon as ominous by the inhabitants. It is held extremely portentous, says Grose, to kill a cricket, a ladybug, a swallow, martin, robin redbreast, or wren; perhaps from the idea of its being a breach of hospitality; all these birds and insects alike taking refuge in houses. Grose enumerates among unlucky things the killing of any of these birds or insects; and Park mentions that when he was a boy, he remembered a different version of a familiar distich:

"Tom Tit and Jenny Wren,
Were God Almighty's cock and hen."

Persons killing any of the above-mentioned birds or insects, or destroying their nests, will infallibly within the course of the year break a bone, or meet with some other dreadful misfortune. On the contrary, it is deemed lucky to have martins or swallows build their nests in the eaves of a house, or in the chimneys. Compare *Divination* and *Wren.*

Bishop in the Pan..—Tyndale, in his *Obedyence of a Christian Man*, 1528, p. 109, says: "When a thynge speadeth not well, we borrowe speach and saye the byshope hath blessed it, because that nothynge speadeth well that they medyll wythall. If the podech be burned to, or the meate ouer rosted, we saye the byshope hath put his fote in the pote, or the bishope hath played the coke, because the bishopes burn who they lust and whosouer displeaseth them." In Tusser's "Husbandry," under April, are the following lines:

"Blesse Cisley (good Mistress) that Bushop doth ban,
For burning the milke of hir cheese to the pan."

On which Hillman has the following note: "When the Bishop passed by (in former times) every one ran out to partake of his blessing, which he plentifully bestow'd as he went along: and those who left their milk upon the fire, might find it burnt to the pan when they came back, and perhaps ban or curse the Bishop as the occasion of it, as much or more than he had blessed them: hence it is likely it grew into a custom to curse the bishop when any such disaster happen'd, for which our author would have the mistress bless, *Anglice* correct, her servant, both for her negligence and unmanncrliness." Bishops were in Tusser's time still much in the habit of burning heretics.

Bishopping.—This is what is now generally known as Confirmation, a term which was not understood in early times. In the Privy Purse Expenses of the Princess Mary, under December, 1536, we have: "Itm Payed for the fascion of a Tablet geven to my lady Carowes (Carew's) Doughter beeng my ladyes goddoughter at the byshoppyng . . . . vjs." There is another and very different process, known technically as bishopping. In the printing business it used, before the introduction of the roller, to be the duty of the pressman to see to the bishopping of the balls, made of sheepskin attached to a stock, which are used to ink the type before printing. These balls, which are of considerable size, must be kept soft and moist to receive the ink, and this result is, or used to be, obtained by wrapping them after employment, against the following occasion, in a blanket dipped in urine. The practice was a sort of christening, and the term perhaps owed itself to the resentment of the printer at the old animosity of the episcopal order against the typographical art.

Bishops Stortford.—The following very extraordinary septennial custom at Bishops Stortford, Herts, and in the adjacent neighbourhood, on Old Michaelmas Day. I find in a London newspaper Oct. 18, 1787: "On the morning of this day, called Ganging Day, a great number of young men assemble in the fields, when a very active fellow it nominated the leader. This person they are bound to follow, who, for the sake of diversion, generally chooses the route through ponds, ditches, and places of difficult passage. Every person they meet is bumped, male or female; which is performed by two other persons taking them up by their arms, and swinging them against each other. The women in general keep at home for this period, except those of less scrupulous character, who, for the sake of partaking of a gallon of ale and a plumb-cake, which every landlord or publican is obliged to furnish the revellers with, generally spend the best part of the night in the fields, if the weather is fair; it being strictly according to ancient usage not to partake of the cheer any where else."

Bisley, Surrey.—See *St. John the Baptist's Well.*

Black Belly and Bawsy Brown.—See *Browny.*

Black Knight of Ashton. — See Hazlitt's *Proverbs*, 1882.

Black Monday. — Easter Monday, 1360, when the cold was so intense, that the English troops before Paris, under Edward III., suffered severely. The expression must have been subsequently employed in a somewhat vague sense, and among other uses, by schoolboys, as it was an usual day for returning from the holidays. Compare Nares, 1859, in v.

Black Veil.—Prior to the assumption of this in the Romish Church, the recluse goes through on an appointed day all the forms of ordinary marriage, the physical or fleshly husband excepted: she is attired in white satin, wears a wreath of flowers, receives a wedding ring, and presides at a breakfast, where there is bride-cake. During the day she receives her girl-friends, and all is gaiety. It is her final experience of the world and those whom she knows. She has already taken the white veil, which is regarded as the Betrothal, as distinguished from this —the wedding. The two services usually occupy an hour and a half to two hours.

Blank.—This is no doubt the same as *La Blanque* of the early French drama and poetry, and was a game of hazard, at which even the lower orders in both countries were fond of playing, and in which serious losses were sometimes incurred. In the *Interlude of Youth*, printed two or three times about 1550, there is the following highly curious enumeration :

Sir, I can teach you to play at the dice,
At the queen's game and at the Irish ;
The treygobet and the hazard also,
And many other games mo ;
Also at the cards I can teach you to play,
At the triump and one-and-thirty,
Post, pinion, and also aums-ace,
And at another they call dewce-ace.
Yet I can tell you more, and ye will con
   me thank,
Pink, and drink, and also at the blank,
And many sports mo.

Hazlitt's Dodsley, ii., 34-5. It is, as will appear, somewhat uncertain whether the writer intended to include blank among the games at cards or not, as he catalogues subject to the exigencies of rhyme.

Blaze's Day, St.—(February 3.) Hospinian describes this Saint as a Cappadocian Bishop who, in the persecution under Diocletian and Maximian, fled to a cavern and led the life of a hermit. He also followed the medical profession, and healed both men and animals. He was discovered, however, and cast into prison, from which, after enduring many tortures, he was led to the place of execution. After his martyrdom and canonization, candles were offered at his altar, which were said to possess the unusual property of curing diseases in human and other creatures. Minshew, in his "Dictionary," under the word Hock-tide, speaks of "St. Blaze his day, about Candlemas, when country women goe about and make good cheere, and if they find any of their neighbour women a spinning that day, they burn and make a blaze of fire of the distaffe, and thereof called S. Blaze his Day." Percy tells us "The anniversary of St. Blasius is

the 3rd of February, when it is still the custom in many parts of England to light up fires on the hills on St. Blayse night : a custom antiently taken up, perhaps for no better reason than the jingling resemblance of his name to the word Blaze." *Notes to Northumb. Household Book,* 1770, p. 333. Scot, in his "Discovery of Witchcraft," gives us a charm used in the Romish Church upon St. Blaze's Day that will fetch a thorn out of any place of one's body, a bone out of the throat, etc, to wit, "Call upon God and remember St. Blaze." The following is the account of St. Blaze in the "Popish Kingdome," fol. 47 b. :

> "Then followeth good Sir Blaze, who
>   doth a waxen candell give,
> And holy water to his men, whereby they
>   safely live.
> I divers barrels oft have seene, drawne
>   out of water cleare,
> Through one small blessed bone of this
>   same Martyr heare :
> And caryed thence to other townes and
>   cities farre away,
> Ech superstition doth require such earn-
>   est kinde of playe."

The following lines occur in an early MS. among Coles's MSS. in the British Museum :—

> "Imber si datur, Virgo dum purificatur,
> Inde notatur quod hyemps abinde
>   fugatur :
> Si sol det radium, frigis erit nimium."

A village in North Cornwall is called after this saint.

Blessing of Clouts.—The leaving of rags at wells was a singular species of popular superstition. Grose tells us that "Between the towns of Alten and Newton, near the foot of Rosberrye Toppinge there is a well dedicated to St. Oswald. The neighbours have an opinion that a shirt or shift taken off a sick person and thrown into that well, will show whether the person will recover or die ; for if it floated it denoted the recovery of the party ; if it sunk, there remained no hope of their life : and to reward the Saint for his intelligence, they tear off a rag of the shirt, and leave it hanging on the briars thereabouts ; where," says the writer, "I have seen such numbers as might have made a fayre rheme in a paper myll." Pennant tells us, "They visit the Well of Speye, in Scotland, for many distempers, and the Well of Drachaldy for as many, offering small pieces of money and bits of rags." Pinkerton, speaking of the River Fillan in the Vale of Strathfillan, says, "In this river is a pool consecrated by the antient superstition of the inhabitants of this country. The pool is formed by the eddying of the stream round a rock. Its waves were many years since consecrated by Fillan, one of the saints who converted the antient inhabitants of Caledonia from Paganism to the belief of Christianity. It has ever since been distinguished by his name, and esteemed of sovereign virtue in curing madness. About two hundred persons afflicted in this way are annually brought to try the benefits of its salutary influence. These patients are conducted by their friends, who first perform the ceremony of passing with them thrice through a neighbouring cairn; on this cairn they then deposit a simple offering of clothes, or perhaps a small bunch of heath. More precious offerings used once to be brought. The patient is then thrice immerged in the sacred pool. After the immersion, he is bound hand and foot, and left for the night in a chapel which stands near. If the maniac is found loose in the morning, good hopes are conceived of his full recovery. If he still remains bound, his cure is doubtful. It sometimes happens that death relieves him, during his confinement, from the troubles of life." Heron's *Journey through part of Scotland*, i., 282. In the "Statistical Account of Scotland," we read: — "A spring in the Moss of Melshach, Aberdeenshire, of the chalybeate kind, is still in great reputation among the common people. Its sanative qualities extend even to brutes. As this spring probably obtained vogue at first in days of ignorance and superstition, it would appear that it became customary to leave at the well part of the clothes of the sick and diseased, and harness of the cattle, as an offering of gratitude to the divinity who bestowed healing virtues on its waters. And now, even though the superstitious principle no longer exists, the accustomed offerings are still presented." (This was in or about 1794.) *Stat. Acc.* xiii., 76. We read " of a well called Craiguck, co. Ross, issuing from a rock near the shore of Bennetsfield, resorted to in the month of May by whimsical or superstitious persons, who, after drinking, commonly leave some threads or rags tied to a bush in the neighbourhood." *Stat. Acc. of Scotland*, xv., 613. Macaulay, speaking of a consecrated well in St. Kilda, called Tobirnimbuadh, or the spring of diverse virtues, says, that " near the fountain stood an altar, on which the distressed votaries laid down their oblations. Before they could touch sacred water with any prospect of success, it was their constant practice to address the Genius of the place with supplication and prayers. No one approached him with empty hands. But the devotees were abundantly frugal. The offerings presented by them were the poorest acknowledgments that could be made to a superior Being, from whom they had either hopes or fears. Shells and pebbles,

rags of linen or stuffs worn out, pins, needles, or rusty nails, were generally all the tribute that was paid; and sometimes, though rarely enough, copper coins of the smallest value. Among the heathens of Italy and other countries, every choice fountain was consecrated, and sacrifices were offered them, as well as to the deities that presided over them. *Hist. Acct.*

In the " Marriage of Wit and Wisdom," circâ 1570, Indulgence says to Wit:

" Well, yet before the goest, hold heare
　My blessing in a clout;
Well fare the mother at a neede,
　Stand to thy tackling stout."

The first allusion to this old belief and usage is, so far as I know, in John Heywoods " Dialogue," originally printed as early as 1546. The passage is as follows in the edition of 1562:

" Ye haue had of me all that I might make.
And be a man neuer so greedy to wyn,
He can haue no more of the foxe but the skyn.
Well (quoth he) if ye list to bring it out,
Ye can geue me your blessing in a clout
Ye can geue me your blessing in a clout."

Davies of Hereford seems to allude to the usage, where in his " Scourge of Folly," (1611), he gives the proverb:

" God-fathers oft give their blessings in a clout."

The only other example of this usage which I can find occurs in Lovelace:

" *To a Lady with Child that asked an old Shirt.*"
" And why an honour'd ragged shirt, that shows
Like tatter'd ensigns, all its bodies blows?
Should it be swathed in a vest so dire,
It were enough to set the child on fire.
But since to ladies 't hath a custome been
Linnen to send, that travail and lye in:
To the nine sempstresses, my former friends,
I su'd; but they had nought but shreds and ends.
At last, the jolli'st of the three times three,
Rent th' apron from her smock, and gave it me.
'Twas soft and gentle, subtly spun, no doubt;
Pardon my boldness, Madam; here's the Clout."

Bishop Hall, in his " Triumphs of Rome," ridicules a superstitious prayer of the

Popish Church for the blessing of clouts in the way of cure of diseases. Can it have originated thence? This absurd custom (observed Mr. Brand) is not extinct even at this day: I have formerly frequently observed shreds or bits of rag upon the bushes that overhang a well in the road to Benton, a village in the vicinity of Newcastle-upon-Tyne, which, from that circumstance, is now or was very lately called the Rag-Well. This name is undoubtedly of long standing: probably it has been visited for some disease or other, and these rag-offerings are the relics of the then prevailing popular superstition. It is not far from another holy spring at Jesmond, at the distance of about a mile from Newcastle. Pilgrimages to this well and chapel at Jesmond were so frequent, that one of the principal streets of the great commercial town aforesaid is supposed to have its name partly from having an inn in it, to which the pilgrims that flocked thither for the benefit of the supposed holy water used to resort. St. Mary's Well, in this village (Jesmond), which is said to have had as many steps down to it as there are Articles in the Creed, was lately inclosed by Mr. Coulson for a bathing place; which was no sooner done than the water left it. This occasioned strange whispers in the village and the adjacent places. The well was always esteemed of more sanctity than common wells, and therefore the failing of the water could be looked upon as nothing less than a just revenge for so great a profanation. But alas! the miracle's at an end, for the water returned a while ago in as great abundance as ever. Thus far Bourne. Brand's *Newcastle*, i., 339 and *Appendix*, 622.

Using rags as charms, it seems, was not confined to England or Europe, for I read the following passage in Hanway's "Travels into Persia," vol. i., p. 177: "After ten days' journey we arrived at a desolate caravanserai, where we found nothing but water. I observed a tree with a number of rags tied to the branches: these were so many charms, which passengers coming from Ghilan, a province remarkable for agues, had left there, in a fond expectation of leaving their disease also on the same spot." Mungo Park, in his "Travels," observes: "The company advanced as far as a large tree, called by the natives Neema Taba. It had a very singular appearance, being covered with innumerable rags or scraps of cloth, which persons travelling across the wilderness had at different times tied to its branches: a custom so generally followed, that no one passes it without hanging up something." Park followed the example, and suspended a handsome piece of cloth on one of the boughs."

Blindman's Buff. — This sport is found among the illuminations of the Missal, cited by Strutt in his "Manners and Customs." It is known to be an amusement with which the ancients were familiar. It is the Muinda and *Kollabismos* of the Greeks; and it is supposed to have originated in the traditional story of Polyphemus. Taylor, the water-poet, nevertheless, maintains in his *Great Eater of Kent*, 1630, that the invention was due to Gregory Dawson, an Englishman! See Levin's *Manipulus*, 1570, p. 293. Jamieson, in his Dictionary, gives us a very curious account of this game, which in Scotland appears to have been called belly-blind. In the Suio-Gothic it is called blind-hoc, i.e. blind goat; and, in German, blind kuhe, i.q. blind cow. The French call it *Clignemusset*, from *cligner*, to wink, and *mussé* hidden; also, *Colin-maillard*, equivalent to "Collin the buffon," and the old Greek *Kollabismos* is their *Capifolèt*.

"This game," says Jamieson, "is thus defined: Ludi genus qui hic quidem manibus expansis oculos suos tegit, ille vero postquam percussit, quærit num verberavit." Pollux ap. Scapul. It was also used among the Romans. But compare St. John's *Manners and Customs of Ancient Greece*, 1842, i., 149-50. Jamieson adds, under Blind Harie, (another name for Blindman's-buff in Scotland): "It may be observed that this sport in Isl. is designated kraekis-blinda. Verelius supposes that the Ostrogoths had introduced this game into Italy; where it is called *giuoco della cieca*, or the play of the blind." Chacke-blynd man and Jockie-blind man are other Scotish appellations for the same game. "We are told that the great Gustavus Adolphus, at the very time that he proved the scourge of the house of Austria, and when he was in the midst of his triumphs, used in private to amuse himself in playing at Blindman's Buff with his Colonels." "*Cela passoit*," says the *Dict. Trav.* v. *Colin Maillard, pour une galanterie admirable*." Day, in his *Humour out of Breath*, 1608, introduces one of his characters playing at the game, which one of them says that he learned when a student at Padua. A lady is told, when she is caught, that she must be hoodwinked or give a kiss to her captor as a ransom. Wodroephe, in his *Spared Hours of a Soldier*, 1623, says that it is "to winke and strike." Dr. Walker, in his *Paræmiologia*, 1672, gives the form "Blindman's buffet." Gay says concerning it:

"As once I play'd at Blindman's Buff, it hap't
About my eyes the towel thick was wrapt.

I miss'd the swains, and seiz'd on
    Blouzelind,
True speaks that antient proverb. 'Love
    is blind.' "

Blood-letting. — In the margin of
Harl. MS. 1772, fol. 115, verso, is written
the following caution in an early hand :
" Beware of letting blood, drinking, or
eating goose, on these three days, nono
k'lis Aprilis die lunis : intrante Augusto
die lunis xx : exeunte Decembris die
lunis." In the poem, " How the goode
Wife thaught hir Doughter," occurs the
line :

  " For aftir the wrenne hathe veynes,
    men schalle late hir blode "

which puzzled even Sir Frederic Madden. Edit. 1838. It seems almost to
refer to the hunting of the wren on St.
Stephen's Day (Dec. 26), when it was
deemed a propitious season for phlebotomy. In another (more modern) copy of
the poem, the line stands thus :

  " After the wren has vaines men may
    let blood—"

which has its signification, to be sure, but
it is a reading of doubtful genuineness.
Hazlitt's *Popular Poetry*, 1864, i., 187.
Among the " Receipts and disbursements
of the Canons of St. Mary, in Huntingdon," 1517, we have the following entry :
" Item, for letting our horses blede in
Chrystmasse weke, iiijd." Douce says the
practice of bleeding horses on St.
Stephen's Day is extremely ancient and
appears to have been brought into this
country by the Danes. In Tusser's " Husbandry," 1580, under December, are the
following lines :

  " Yer Christmas be passed, let horsse be
    let blood,
  For manie a purpose it doth them much
    good :
  The day of S. Steeven, old fathers did
    use,
  If that do mislike thee, some other day
    chuse."

On which is this note in " Tusser Redivivus," 1710 : " About Christmas is a very
proper time to bleed horses in, for then
they are commonly at house, then spring
comes on, the sun being now come back
from the winter solstice, and there are
three or four days of rest, and if it be upon
St. Stephen's Day, it is not the worse,
seeing there are with it three days of rest,
or at least two." The following is from
Copley's " Wits, Fits and Fancies, 1595 " :
" " On S. Stevens Day it is the custome
for all horses to be let bloud and drench'd.
A gentleman being (that morning) demaunded whether it pleased him to have
his horse let bloud and drencht, according

to the fashion? He answered with a poor
quibble on the well-known malady among
horses (the farcin or equine scrofula), No,
sirra, my horse is not diseased of the
fashions." Aubrey, in the " Remains of
Gentilisme," says: " On St. Stephen's
Day the farrier came constantly and
blouded all our cart-horses.

Hospinian quotes a notion from Naogeorgus that it is good to gallop
horses till they are all over in a
sweat, and then bleed them, on Stephen's Day, to prevent their having
any disorders for the ensuing year. Hospinian " De Orig. Fest. Christianor," foi.
160 :

  " Then followeth St. Stephens Day
    whereon doth every man
  His horses jaunt and course abrode, as
    swiftly as he can,
  Until they doe extreemely sweate, and
    than they let them blood,
  For this being done upon this day, they
    say doth do them good,
  And keepes them from all the maladies
    and sicknesse through the yeare,
  As if that Steven any time took charge
    of horses heare."

Googe's translation of Popish Kingdome,
fol. 45. Brand also quoted under this head
Hildebrandus " De Diebus Festis," SS.
Antiquitat. Epitome, p. 33.

Blood of Hales, The. — Perhaps to
the number of miraculous agencies to
which credit was given by our forefathers
may be added the holy blood of Christ in
Hales. This was a phial alleged to contain
some of the Saviour's blood, brought from
Palestine by Edmund, Earl of Cornwall,
and presented to the Cistercian brotherhood at Hales, Gloucestershire. There are
occasional allusions to this relic in our
household books, periodical oblations being
made to it, and Thomas Baker, of St.
John's College, Cambridge, states that
there was a short poetical narrative of the
prodigy, from the press of Wynkyn de
Worde. At the dissolution we find the
Abbot of Hales himself writing to Cromwell, and suggesting the demolition of the
shrine (worth, according to him, scarcely
£30 for the gold and silver about it), where
" the faynyd relycke called the Bloode "
was exhibited in order, as the abbot says,
that it may not " mynistre occasyon to any
weke person, loking thereupon, to abuse
his conscyens therewith ! " In a subsequent letter from Bishop Latimer to Cromwell the whole trick is laid bare. Ellis's
Orig. Letters, 3rd Series, iii., 249.

Latimer, in his seventh Lent sermon
before Edward VI., 1549, says : — " What
became of his blud that fell downe trowe
ye? Was the bloude of Hales of it (wo
worthe it). What ado was it to brynge

thys out of the Kynges heade, thys greate abhominacion of the bloud of hales could not be taken a great whyle out of his mynde. . . . . Vnpreacheynge Prelates haue bene the cause, that the bloud of Hales did so long blynd the Kynge."

Blood Portents, &c.—Scot, in his "Discovery," 1584, says. "I have heard by credible report, that the wound of a man murthered, renewing bleeding at the presence of a dear friend, or of a mortal enemy. Divers also write that if one pass by a murthered body (though unknown) he shall be stricken with fear, and feel in himself some alteration by nature." "Three loud and distinct knocks at the bed's head," says Grose, "of a sick person, or at the bed's head or door of any of his relations, is an omen of his death." King James, in his "Dæmonology," 1597, says, "In a secret murther, if the dead carkasse be at any time thereafter handled by the murtherer, it will gush out of blood, as if the blood were crying to Heaven for revenge of the murtherer." In the narrative by Sir Simonds D'Ewes of the Babb murder at Kingston, in Somersetshire, 1613, there is a reference to this common belief.

In the prose *Merlin* we get the incident of the supposed miraculous power of the blood of the child "born without father," to stay the destruction of King Vortiger's strong tower. This is to be regarded as an early example of the belief in charms, which was unquestionably far more ancient in this country than any existing records shew. In *Five Philosophical Questions Disputed*, 1650, one is : "Why dead bodies bleed in the presence of their murtherers," and the writer accounts for the phenomenon on scientific grounds, arising from the tendency of blood to liquefy after death by the heat generated by corruption. The air being heated by many persons coming about the body, is the same thing to it as motion is. 'Tis observed that dead bodies will bleed in a concourse of people, when murtherers are absent as well as present, yet legislators have thought fit to authorize it, and use this tryal as an argument at least, to frighten though 'tis no conclusive one to condemn them.". It was part of the system of witchcraft that drawing blood from a witch rendered her enchantments ineffectual. This curious doctrine is very fully investigated in Hathaway's Trial, published in the "State Trials." In Glanville's "Account of the Dæmon of Tedworth," speaking of a boy that was bewitched, he says, the "Boy drew towards Jane Brooks, the woman who had bewitched him, who was behind her two sisters, and put his hand upon her, which his father perceiving, immediately scratched her face and drew blood from her. The

youth then cry'd out that he was well." *Blow at Modern Sadducism*, 1668, p. 148. Compare *Witchcraft*. The following passage is in a tract by Arise Evans : "I had heard some say, that when a witch had power over one to afflict him, if he could but draw one drop of the witches blood, the witch would never after do him hurt." *Eccho to the Voice from Heaven*, 1652, p. 34. In the first part of "Henry the Sixth," act i. sc. 10, Talbot says to the Pucelle d'Orleans :

—" I'll have a bout with thee.
Devil or Devil's dam, I'll conjure thee,
Blood will I draw on thee, thou art a
   witch."

Thus also in Butler's "Hudibras" :

"Till drawing blood o' the dames like
   witches,
They're forthwith cur'd of their cap-
   riches."

And in Cleveland's "Rebel Scot : "

"Scots are like witches, do but whet
   your pen,
Scratch till the blood come, they'll not
   hurt you then."

Park here refers to a passage in Bastard's "Chrestoleros," 1598 :

"Phisition Lanio neuer will forsake,
His golden patiente while his head doth
   ake :
When he is dead, farewell, he comes not
   there.
He hath nor cause, nor courage to
   appeare.
He will not look vpon the face of death,
Nor bring the dead vnto her mother
   earth.
I will not say, but if he did the deede,
He must be absent lest the corpse
   should bleed."

This notion is illustrated by the ballad of "Young Redin : "

"O white, white were his wounds
   washen,
   As white as a linen clout ;
But as the traitor she came near,
   His wounds they gushed out."

Kinloch's *Ancient Scottish Ballads*, 1827, p. 1. And the Editor remarks, that he recollects "this ordeal having been practiced at Aberdeen about twenty years ago (this was written in 1827), on the occasion of the body of a pregnant woman having been found in the neighbouring canal." Blood flowed from her nostrils, it is said, directly the suspected murderer touched her ; but this proof, though accepted by the populace, was not thought conclusive by the lawyers. There is a pretty little anecdote, which may be regarded as an illustration of the present matter by the way in Copley's, *Wits, Fits, and Fancies,*

1595, ed. 1614, p. 85:—"A gentlewoman went to church so concealed, that shee thought no body could know her. It chanced that her louer met her, and knewe her, and spake vnto her: Sir (shee answered) you mistake me, how know yee me? All too well (reply'd the gentleman) for so soone as I met you, beholde my wounds fell fresh a bleeding: Oh heereof you onely are guilty."

The superstition still prevails in some parts of the country. At the Warwick Winter Assizes for 1867, John Davis, a maltster. formerly residing at Stratford-on-Avon, was charged with having wounded Jane Ward, and on this occasion the following extraordinary particulars were divulged. "The prisoner, with his family, up to the time of his arrest, had resided in Sheep-street, Stratford-upon-Avon, and they had laboured under an impression that the prosecutrix, who occupied an adjoining house, had bewitched them. In spite of the efforts of friends to the contrary, they persisted in the delusion, and frequently narrated, with singular circumstantiality, visits which had been paid them in the night time by spirits. Some of these, they stated, entered the dwelling by descending the chimney, and when they landed in the room they went through a variety of capers such as seizing the furniture, and pitching it about the apartment, pulling the clothes off the bed, and even tossing the inmates up into the air. One young girl, who was an invalid, and was obliged to recline upon the sofa, solemnly declared that a man and woman came down the chimney on one occasion, both being headless, and taking her by the body, cast her violently upon the ground, then tossed her up into the air, and performed similar feats with the sofa. The statement created so great a stir in the town that the police were called in to investigate the matter, and although they pointed to the accumulated dust around the feet of the sofa in proof that no such thing could have happened the prisoner and his family declared their firm belief that witches had been there, and the only way to break the spell was to draw blood from the body of the prosecutrix, who was suspected of having bewitched them. A day or two after, the prisoner rushed into the house occupied by Jane Ward the complainant, and inflicted a frightful gash in her cheek. He inflicted a wound half an inch in width and two and a half inches deep When he saw the blood flowing down her face, he exclaimed, 'There, you old witch, I can do anything with you now.' At the station, he said, in answer to the charge, 'Serve her right: she can do no more for me now. I have drawn first blood.'"

Blow-point.—Blow-point appears to have been a relatively advanced game. Procter, in his book "Of the Knowledge and Conducte of Warres," 1578, observes: "Lycurgus, the politique Prince, amonge his lawes and customes, which hee established theare (in Lacedæmon) ordayned that all spare tyme shoulde be expended in vertuous exercises, and principallye in the noble practyses of armes, to gett honour, and soueraynetye of the enemyes, cleane cuttinge of vnthriftye wastfull ryott, abandoninge delycate nycenesse, and banishinge idle, and chyldishe games, as commen cardplaye, cayles, coytes, slyde-bourde, bowles, and blowepoynt, which weare throwen oute of the commen-wealthe. From whence also bee dyscarded and expelled ianglers, iesters iuglers, puppetplayers, pypers, and suche like vnprofitable persons, in steade of which weare mayntayned menne of valure, frequentynge and exercisynge actiuitye of wrastelinge, dartynge, throwinge the barre, the sledge, vsinge the weapons of warre," &c. Marmion, in his "Antiquary," 1641, act i. says: "I have heard of a nobleman that has been drunk with a tinker, and a Magnifico that has plaid at Blow-point." Among the old proverbs is, "to leave boy's play, and fall to blowpoint." Hazlitt's *Proverbs*, 1882, p. 437. So, in "Lingua," 1607, act iii. sc. 2, Anamnestes introduces Memory as telling "how he plaid at Blowe-point with Jupiter when he was in his side-coats."

Blue Gowns, or Beadsmen, an order of privileged mendicants in Scotland, of which the latest trace did not expire till 1863. The first appellation was due to the distribution among these persons of a gown of blue cloth, to which were added a loaf of bread, a bottle of ale, and a leathern purse containing a penny for every year of the ruling sovereign's age; and annually a new beadsman or Blue Gown was elected. Each member of the body bore a pewter badge, on which were inscribed his name and the words *Past and Repast* The usage, which had had its origin in the ancient practice of vicarious prayer, resolved itself into a public charity, of which the sources were forgotten, and in 1833 sixty Beadsmen were on the roll. No appointments were made after that date, and the last survivor drew his allowance from the Exchequer at Edinburgh in May, 1863.

Boar's Head.—Holinshed says that, in the year 1170, upon the day of the young Prince's coronation, King Henry the Second "served his son at the table as sewer, bringing up the bore's head, with trumpets before it, according to the manner." It is probable that Chaucer alluded to the above custom in the following passage, in his Franklin's Tale:

"Janus sitteth by the fire with double
    berd,
And he drinketh of his bugle-horne the
    wine,
Before him standeth the brawne of the
    tusked swine."

Dugdale, speaking of the Christmas Day
Ceremonies in the Inner Temple, says:
"Service in the church ended, the gentlemen presently repair into the hall to
breakfast, with brawn, mustard, and
malmsey." At dinner, "at the first course
is served in a fair and large Bores Head,
upon a silver platter, with minstralsye."
Orig. Jurid., p. 155. Aubrey tells us (1678)
that, before the Civil Wars, it was customary in gentlemen's houses to bring in at
the first dish at Christmas a boar's head,
with a lemon in its mouth. Morant says
that the inhabitants of Horn Church, in
the Liberty of Havering, when they paid
the great tithes on Christmas Day, were
treated with a bull and brawn, and the
boar's head was wrestled for. The ceremony was long observed, as Hearne tells
us, at Queen's College, Oxford, with the
improvement that the boar's head was
neatly carved in wood. Ritson printed the
Carol sung in bringing in the head from
a collection published in 1521. *Ancient
Songs*, ed. 1877, p. 158. In later times the
words were greatly altered. In Dekker's
"Wonderful Yeare, 1603," signat. D 2,
our author, speaking of persons apprehen-
sive of catching the plague, says, "they,
went (most bitterly) miching and muffled
up and downe, with rue and wormewood
stuft into their eares and nosthrils, looking like so many bores heads stuck with
branches of rosemary, to be served in for
brawne at Christmas." In the "Gothamite Tales," 1630. No. 18 is an anecdote of
a Scot, who ordered of a carver a boar's
head for a sign to his inn at Gotham.
"Hee did come to a carver or a joyner,
saying in his mother tongue : I say, speake,
canst thou make me a bare-head? Yea,
said the carver. Then said the Scottish-
man : make me a bare-head anonst Youle,
and thouse have twenty pence for thy hire.
I will doe it, said the carver. On S. An-
drewes day before Christmas the which is
named Youle in Scotland (and in England
in the North), the Scottish man did come
to London for the boreshead to set it at
the doore for a signe." This is alluded to
in King's "Art of Cookery," p. 75 :

"At Christmas time—
Then if you wou'd send up the brawner's
    head,
Sweet rosemary and bays around it
    spread :
His foaming tusks let some large pippin
    grace,
Or, 'midst these thundring spears an
    orange place ;

Sauce, like himself, offensive to its foes,
The roguish mustard, dang'rous to the
    nose.
Sack, and the well-spic'd Hippocras the
    wine,
Wassail the bowl with antient ribbands
    fine,
Porridge with plumbs, and turkeys with
    the chine."

Boat-Show.—An annual ceremony
formerly practised at Cambridge, when the
College boats assembled at a certain point,
and were decorated with flags, flowers, &c.

Bodmin Riding..—The late Mr.
Thomas Quiller Couch of Bodmin, one
of our best informed Cornish antiquaries, permitted me, in 1870, to
introduce here a full account of this
little-understood subject, communicated
by him some years before to the "Journal of the Penzance Society" : "Whilst
the material remains of the past, with
which our county abounds, have occupied
many an able pen and pencil, the curious
memorials of old forms of faiths and modes
of life, hardly less ancient and fully as
interesting, have been singularly neglected
by the Cornish antiquary. Modified in
the course of their long descent, until but
faint traces of their origin and intention
remain, there is frequently enough left unaltered to shew that they are in their form
as old as those relics which the ever-during
granite has preserved to us. It is quite
time, however, that a record should be
made of them, since the rapid fluctuations
and changes of the last fifty years have
done more to alter and efface them than
many previous centuries of stagnation, or
of very gradual progress. I shall begin
with a festival of which the remembrance
lingers only among people past middle-age,
and which is never likely to be revived. It
was kept at Bodmin on the Sunday and
Monday after St. Thomas à Becket's Day,
July 7. A puncheon of beer having been
brewed in the previous October, and duly
bottled in anticipation of the time, two or
three young men were entrusted with the
chief management of the affair, and who
represented the wardens of Carew's church
ales, went round the town attended
by a band of drums and fifes or other instruments. The crier saluted each house
with : 'To the people of this house, a prosperous morning, long life, health, and a
merry riding !' The musicians then struck
up the Riding Tune, a quick and inspirit-
ing measure, said by some to be as old as
the feast itself. The householder was solicited to taste the riding ale, which was
carried round in baskets. A bottle was
usually taken in, and it was acknowledged
by such a sum as the means or humour of
the townsman permitted, to be spent on
the public festivities of the season. Next

morning, a procession was formed, (all who could afford to ride mounted on horse or ass), first to the Priory, to receive two large garlands of flowers fixed on staves, and then in due order through the principal streets to the town-end, where the games were formally opened. The sports, which lasted two days, were of the ordinary sort; wrestling, foot-racing, jumping in sacks, &c. It is worthy of remark that a second or inferior brewing, from the same wort, was drunk at a minor merry-making at Whitsuntide. The description of the ceremony has been obtained from those who took part in its latest celebration. No one who compares this account of the riding with Carew's description of Church-ales, can doubt that the two were originally identical in their meaning. That the custom of keeping Church-ales on a Sunday was a common one, appears from a sermon preached by William Kethe, at Blandford Forum, in 1570; and in which he tells us that his holyday 'the multitude call their revelyng day, which day is spent in bull-baitings, beare-baitings, bowlings, dicying,' &c. In the accounts which are preserved relative to the rebuilding of Bodmin parish church, 'the stewards of the Ridyng-Gild' are mentioned as contributors. In an order, dated Nov. 15, 1583, regulating the business of shoe-makers, (a class which seems for ages to have been more than usually numerous in Bodmin), it is directed by the Mayor and the masters of the occupation, 'that at the riding every master and journeyman shall give their attendance to the steward, and likewise bring him to the church, upon pain of 12d. for every master, and 6d. for every journeyman, for every such default, to the discretion of the masters of the occupation.' Polwhele gives an imperfect account of the Bodmin Riding. He is inclined to deduce it from the Floralia of Roman times; and he thinks that the Goddess Flora was, in later ages, superseded by St. Thomas of Canterbury, at whose shrine the garlands of flowers were presented. I have heard an opinion that the feast was in celebration of the restitution of St. Petrock's bones, which were stolen from the Priory of Bodmin in the year 1177, and carried to the Abbey of St. Mevennus in Brittany, but were restored at the powerful intercession of Henry II. Heath says, without giving any authority, that 'this carnival is said to be as old as the Saxons. Several attempts have been made to resuscitate this festival, but it is now hopelessly dead. I have a deprecatory pamphlet, dated 1825, entitled: 'A leter to a Friend, relative to the approaching games commonly called Bodmin riding.' At this bright season, when field and wood put on their gayest green, and even tongueless things seem full of praise and thankfulness, it is not strange that the heart of man should be moved to joy and thanksgiving, even though the gratitude due to the Giver of all good may often be misdirected. The feast of the Summer Solstice modified by circumstances of time and place, but almost universally observed, is probably as old as the gratitude which the season's profusion naturally inspires; so that, instead of deriving our midsummer games from the floral festivities of the Romans, we should more rightly consider them as similar in meaning and coeval in origin. I have heard some doubts expressed as to the antiquity of the Riding Tune (appended to this account); and I have asked the opinion of William Sandys, Esq., F.S.A., a well-known antiquary, and an excellent authority on such a subject. He says: 'It struck me as having a similarity to some tunes of the last century, or perhaps the end of the 17th, and of which there are examples in 'The Dancing Master,' of which so many editions were published, although now not common. The tune, therefore, does not appear to be of very high antiquity; but, at the same time, there is something about it which might induce one to suppose it might be founded on an older tune.' Mr. Sandys kindly submitted it to Mr. Chappell, author of the excellent work on the Popular Music of England; and his opinion on such a point is especially valuable. Mr. Chappell considers it not more than thirty or forty years old, and founded on 'The Fall of Paris.' 'But even if this were so,' says Mr. Sandys, 'The Fall of Paris' is founded on, and almost identical with, the celebrated French revolutionary air 'Ca ira,' which is more than seventy years old.' I have direct proof of its being in use at this festival for a century past. Heath (and almost all our guide-books follow him) makes the Bodmin Riding identical with the Halgaver Sports; but with insufficient reason. He says: " A carnival is kept every year, about the middle of July, on Halgaver Moor, near Bodmin, resorted to by thousands of people; the sports and pastimes of which were so well liked by King Charles II., when he touched there in his way to Scilly, that he became a brother of the jovial society.' The MM. Lysons doubt the story of Charles's participation in these games, since the time of the Prince's journey to Scilly does not accord with the period of the festival. I know of no author, besides Carew, who makes independent mention of the Halgaver sports, and, from the account in the Survey, it would seem that Halgaver was the scene of perennial jokes; nor is it anywhere said that its usages and immunities were confined to any season. The Bodmin Riding is evidently quite distinct; though proably, at a time of great merry-making in the neighbourhood of the Moor, the 'ungracious pranks' may have been more than usually rife. No remembrance of Halgaver Court exists among people now resident in the neighbourhood. "Now and then,' says Carew, 'they extend this merriment, to the prejudice of over-credulous people persuading them to fight with a dragon lurking in Halgaver, or to see some strange matter there, which concluded at last with a training them into the mire.' This also is an interesting illustration of the social life of our forefathers. It was a custom, which the existence of good parish maps now renders less necesary, on one of the days of Rogation week to make a yearly renewal of the ancient landmarks :

> 'Our fathers us'd in reverent processions
> (With zealous prayers and with praise-
>   ful cheere),
> To walke their parish-limits once a
>   yeare :
> And well-knowne marks (which sacri-
>   legious hands
> Now cut or breake) so bord'red out their
>   lands,
> That ev'ry one distinctly knew his own,
> And many brawles, now rife, were then
>   unknowne.''

"In this procession, when clergy and people went round to beat the bounds of the parish, praying here and there at certain wonted spots, (frequently marked by a cross), it was usual to drag round an effigy of a dragon, representing the Spirit of evil. The Dragon usually came to some ignominous end, and the place where he finished his career is still known in many places by the name of Dragon Rock, Dragon Well, Dragon Pit. An excavation called 'Dragon Pit' still exists on Halgaver Moor.''

The BODMIN "RIDING TUNE."

Boe Bullbagger.—See *Barguest* and *Bull-beggar*.

Bogane (Manx)..—See *Antiquary* for December, 1886.

Bo-Peep.—The best account of this child's amusement, which, however, grew into a proverb and an exclamation, is in Halliwell's *Popular Rhymes and Nursery Tales*, 1849, p. 109, *et seqq.* Compare Halliwell in v., *All-Hid* suprâ, and Davis, *Suppl. Glossary*, 1881. The fullest text is to be found. I think, in *Nursery Rhymes of England*, Percy Soc. ed. p. 75.

Boneshave.—The boneshave, a word perhaps nowhere used or understood in Devonshire but in the neighbourhood of Exmoor, means the sciatica ; and the Exmoorians, when affected therewith, use the following charm to be freed from it. The patient must lie upon his back on the bank of the river or brook of water, with a straight staff by his side between him and the water, and must have the following words repeated over him, viz. :

> Boneshave right,
> Boneshave straight,
> As the water runs by the stave
> Good for Boneshave.''

They are not to be persuaded but that this ridiculous form of words seldom fails to give them a perfect cure. *Exmoor Scolding*, p. 8, note.

Bonfire.—

Hickes defines a Bonefire to be a festive or triumphant fire. In the Islandic language, he says, *Baal* signifies a burning. In the Anglo-Saxon, Bael-ᵹᵹp, by a change of letters of the same organ, is made Baen-ᵹᵹp, whence our *Bonefire.*

In the Tinmouth MSS. cited so often in the History of Newcastle, "Boon-er," and "Boen-Harow," occur for ploughing and harrowing gratis, or by gift. There is a passage also, much to our purpose, in Ashton's Translation of Aubanus, p. 282:— ' Common fires (or as we call them heere in England bonefires.)'' I am therefore strongly inclined to think that bone-fire means a contribution fire, that is, a fire to

which everyone in the neighbourhood contributes a certain portion of materials. The contributed Ploughing Days in Northumberland are called "Bone-daags." See also a letter from Pegge in the "Gent. Mag." for 1774, p. 315.

The third Council of Constantinople, A.D. 680, by its 65th canon, has the following interdiction : — "Those bonfires that are kindled by certaine people on new moones before their shops and houses, over which also they use ridiculously and foolishly to leape, by a certaine antient custome, we command them from henceforth to cease. Whoever therefore shall doe any such thing; if he be a clergyman, let him be deposed; if a layman, let him be excommunicated. For, in the Fourth Book of the Kings, it is thus written : "And Manasseh built an altar to all the hoast of heaven, in the two courts of the Lord's house, and made his children to passe through the fire,' &c." Prynne observes upon this : "Bonefires therefore had their originall from this idolatrous custome, as this Generall Councell hath defined; therefore all Christians should avoid them." And the Synodus Francica under Pope Zachary, A.D. 742, inhibits "those sacrilegious fires which they call *Nedfri* (or bonefires), and all other observations of the Pagans whatsoever." Bourne tells us, that it was the custom in his time, in the North of England, chiefly in country villages, for old and young people to meet together and be merry over a large fire, which was made for that purpose in the open street. This, of whatever materials it consisted, was called a bonefire. In Newton's "Observations upon the Prophecies of Daniel and the Apocalypse of St. John," the author observes, that "the heathens were delighted with the festivals of their gods, and unwilling to part with those ceremonies; therefore Gregory, Bishop of Neo-Cæsarea in Pontus, to facilitate their conversion, instituted annual festivals to the saints and martyrs : hence the keeping of Christmas with ivy, feasting, plays, and sports, came in the room of the Bacchanalia and Saturnalia, the celebrating May Day with flowers, in the room of the Floralia; and the festivals to the Virgin Mary, John the Baptist, and divers of the Apostles, in the room of the solemnities at the entrance of the Sun into the Signs of the Zodiac in the old Julian Calendar."—*Gent. Mag.* for 1733, and *Antiq. of Cornwall*, p. 130. Leaping over the fires is mentioned among the superstitious rites used at the Palilia in Ovid's *Fasti*. The Palilia were feasts instituted in honour of Pales, the goddess of shepherds (though Varro makes Pales masculine), on the calends of May. In order to drive away wolves from the folds, and

distempers from the cattle, the shepherds on this day kindled several heaps of straw in their fields, which they leaped over. Borlase says sensibly : "Of the fires we kindle in many parts of England, at some stated times of the year, we know not certainly the rise, reason, or occasion; but they may probably be reckoned among the relicks of the Druid superstitious fires. In Cornwall the festival fires, called bonfires, are kindled on the eve of St. John Baptist and St. Peter's Day; and midsummer is thence, in the Cornish tongue, called 'Goluan,' which signifies both light and rejoicing. At these fires the Cornish attend with lighted torches, tarr'd and pitch'd at the end, and make their perambulations round their fires, and go from village to village carrying their torches before them, and this is certainly the remains of the Druid superstition, for 'faces præferre,' to carry lighted torches, was reckoned a kind of Gentilism ,and as such particularly prohibited by the Gallick Councils : they were in the eye of the law 'accensores facularum,' and thought to sacrifice to the devil, and to deserve capital punishment." Over and about this fire they frequently leap, and play at various games, such as running, wrestling, dancing, &c.; this, however, is generally confined to the younger sort; for the old ones, for the most part, sit by as spectators only of the vagaries of those who compose the

"Lasciva decentius ætas,"

and enjoy themselves over their bottle, which they do not quit till midnight, and sometimes till cock-crow the next morning.

In the play of "Sir Thomas More" (circâ 1590), Doll Williamson is made to say : "I, for we maye as well make bonefiers on Maye daye as at midsommer." "Leaping o'er a midsummer bonefire" is mentioned amongst other games in Tompson's "Garden of Delight," 1658. Torreblanca, in his "Demonology," has a passage, in which he tells us how the ancients were accustomed to pass their children of both sexes through the fire for the sake of securing them a prosperous and fortunate lot, and he adds that the Germans imitated this profane usage in their midsummer pyres in honour of the anniversary of St. John's Day. He, too, cites, among others, Ovid, where the poet says :—

"Certe ego transilii positas ter in ordine flammas."

Comp. *St. John's Eve* and *Midsummer*.

Books. — Books, by way of funeral tokens, used to be given away at the burials of the better sort in England. In my Collection of Portraits (notes Mr. Brand) I have one of John Bunyan, taken from before an old edition of his works, which I bought at Ware, in Hertfordshire. It is thus inscribed on the back in MS.: " Funeral Token in remembrance of Mr. Hen. Plomer, who departed this life Oct. 2, 1696, being 79 years of age, and is designed to put us that are alive in mind of our great change. Mr. Daniel Clerk the elder his book, Oct. 23, 1696." A writer in the "Athenian Oracle," considers that "a book would be far more convenient, more durable, and more valuable a present, than what are generally given, and more profitably preserve the memory of a deceased friend."

Boossenning.—See *Holy Wells.*

Booting. — Miss Baker, in her "Northamptonshire Glossary," 1854, describes this harvest usage of Booting, where any of the men has misconducted himself in the field. The culprit is brought up for trial at the harvest-home feast, and adjudged to be booted. The booting is also described by Clare the poet in his "Village Minstrel." A long form being placed in the kitchen, the good workers place themselves along it in a row, with their hands laid on each other's backs, so as to make a sort of bridge, over which the hog (so the delinquent is called, and there may be more than one) has to pass, running the gauntlet of a boot-legging, with which a fellow bastes him lustily as he scrambles over. The country people in Warwickshire use a sport at their harvest home, where one sits as a judge to try misdemeanors committed in harvest, and the punishment of the men is, to be laid on a bench and slapped on the breech with a pair of boots. This they call giving them the boots.

Borrowed or **Borrowing Days.** —There is a proverb: "April borrows three days of March, and they are ill." April is pronounced with an emphasis on the last syllable, so as to make a kind of jingling rhyme with "ill," the last word in the line. I have taken notice of this, because I find in the Roman Calendar the following observations on the 31st of March: "The rustic fable concerning the nature of the month. The rustic name of six days which shall follow in April, or may be the last in March." There is no doubt but that these observations in the Calendar, and our proverb, are derived from one common origin; but for want of more lights I am unable at present to trace them any farther. The Borrowed Days are common to many European countries, and M. Michel notices in his work on the Basques, that the idea prevails among that singular people. The Borrowing Days occur in "The Complaynt of Scotland." "There eftir i entrit in ane grene forest, to contempil the tendir zong frutes of grene treis, because the borial blastis of the thre

borouing dais of Marche hed chaissit the fragrant flureise of evyrie frut-tree far athourt the feildis."

" March said to Aperill,
I see three hogs upon a hill ;
But lend your three first days to me,
And I'll be bound to gar them die.
The first, it sall be wind and weet;
The next, it sall be snaw and sleet;
The third, it sall be sic a freeze
Sall gar the birds stick to the trees.
But when the Borrowed days were gane
The three silly hogs came hirplin hame."

The "Glossary" (in verbo) explains "Borrowing days, the three last days of March," and adds, "concerning the origin of the term, the following popular rhyme is often repeated:

" March borrowit fra Averill
Three days, and they were ill."

Speaking of the death of King James I., in 1625, at a time when a furious storm was raging along the Scotish coast, Chambers remarks : "This was long after remembered as the storm of the Borrowing Days. . . . It is a proverbial observation of the weather, which seems to be justified by fact, the bad weather being connected with the vernal equinox." *Domestic Annals of Scotland*, 2nd edit., i., 553. These days had not escaped the observation of Sir. T. Browne, who, however, gives no explanation. In the "Country Almanack" for 1676, among the "remarques upon April," are the following :

" No blust'ring blasts from March needs
April borrow :
His own oft proves enow to breed us
sorrow.
Yet if he weep (with us to sympathise),
His trickling tears will make us wipe our
eyes."

A clergyman in Devonshire informed Mr. Brand, about 1795, that the old farmers in his parish called the three first days of March "Blind Days," which were anciently considered as unlucky ones, and upon which no farmer would sow any seed. This superstition, however, was even then wearing out apace.

Bowed, or Crooked Money.— Bowed money appears anciently to have been sent as a token of love and affection from one relation to another. Thus we read in the "Third Part of Conny-Catching," by R. Greene, 1592, sign. b 2, verso : "Then taking fourth a bowed groat, and an olde pennie bowed, he gave it her as being sent from her uncle and aunt." In "The Country Wake," by Dogget, 1696, act v. sc. 1. Hob, who fancies he is dying, before he makes his last will and testimony, as he calls it, when his mother desires him to try to speak to Mary, "for she is thy wife, and no other," answers, "I know I'm sure to her—and I do own it before you all; I ask't her the question last Lammas, and at Allhollows'-tide we broke a piece of money; and if I had liv'd till last Sunday we had been ask'd in the church." Douce says:— "Analogous to the interchangement of rings seems the custom of breaking a piece of money." An example of this occurs in "Bateman's Tragedy," a well-known penny history, founded on Sampson's tragedy of the Vow Breaker," 1636, where the incident may be found. We find in *Hudibras* that the piece broken between the contracted lovers must have been a crooked one:

"Like Commendation Ninepence crook't, With to and from my Love it look't";

a circumstance confirmed also in "The Connoisseur," No. 56, with an additional custom, of giving locks of hair woven in a true lover's knot. "If, in the course of their amour, the mistress gives the dear man her hair wove in a true lover's knot, or breaks a crooken ninepence with him, she thinks herself assured of his inviolate fidelity." This "bent token" has not been overlooked by Gay:

"A ninepence bent, A token kind, to Bumkinet is sent."

A crooked sixpence is probably yet regarded as lucky.

Bowing *towards the Altar or Communion Table on Entering the Church.*—This custom, which was prevalent when Bourne wrote (*Antiq. Vulg.* ch. v.), he deduces from the ancient practice of the Church of worshipping towards the east. This, says he, they did that, by so worshipping they might lift up their minds to God, who is called the Light, and the Creator of Light, therefore turning, says St. Austin, our faces to the east, from whence the day springs, that we might be reminded of turning to a more excellent nature, namely the Lord. As also, that as man was driven out of Paradise, which is towards the east, he ought to look that way, which is an emblem of his desire to return thither. St. Damascen therefore tells us that because the Scripture says that God planted Paradise in Eden towards the east, where he placed the man which he had formed, whom he punished with banishment upon his transgression, and made him dwell over against Paradise in the western part, we therefore pray (says he) being in quest of our ancient country, and, as it were, panting after it, do worship God that way.

It is almost superfluou· to observe that bowing toward the altar is a vestige of the ancient Ceremonial Law. Concession must be made by every advo-

cate for manly and rational worship, that there is nothing more in the east, than in the belfry at the west end, or in the body of the church. We wonder, therefore, however this custom was retained by Protestants. The cringes and bowings of the Roman Catholics to the altar are in adoration of the corporal presence, their wafer God, whom their fancies have seated and enthroned in this quarter of the East. *Durandus Rat.* 226. One who has left a severe satire on the retainers of those forms and ceremonies that lean towards popish superstition, tells us: "If I were a Papist or Anthropo-morphite, who believes that God is enthroned in the East like a grave old King, I profess I would bow and cringe as well as any limber-ham of them all, and pay my adoration to that point of the compass (the East): but if men believe that the Holy One who inhabits Eternity, is also omnipresent, why do not they make correspondent ceremonies of adoration to every point of the compass?" Hickeringill's *Ceremony-Monger*, 15. "The maner of turnyng our faces to the Easte when wee praie, is taken of the old Ethnikes, whiche as Apuleius remembreth, used to loke Eastwarde and salute the sonne: we take it as a custom to put us in remembraunce that Christe is the sonne of Righteousnes, that discloseth all Secretes." Langley's Polydore Virgil, 1546, fol. 100, verso. Among the charges brought by Peter Smart, in 1628, against Bishop Cosin are the following: "Fifthly. He hath brought in a new custome of bowing the body downe to the ground before the altar (on which he hath set candlesticks, basons, and crosses, crucifixes, and tapers which stand ther for a dumb shew) as: hee hath taught and enjoyned all such as come neere the altar to cringe and bow unto it: he hath commanded the choresters to make low leggs unto it, when they goe to light the tapers that are on it in the winter nights; and in their returne from it, hee hath enjoined them to make low leggs unto it againe, going backwards with their faces towards the East, till they are out of the inclosure where they usually stand. Sixthly: Hee enjoynes them all that come to the Cathedrall Church to pray with their faces towards the East, scoulding and brawling with them, even in time of divine service, which refuse to do it, and bidding them either to pray towards the East, or to be packing out of the church, so devoted is hee to this Eastern superstition." *Vanitie and Downfall of Superstitiovs Popish Ceremonies*, 1628. This was re-printed in 1640. We are informed by Crofton that "The late Archbishop Laud was the first that ever framed a canon for bowing to, towards, or before the Communion Table." *Altar-Worship*,

1661, pp. 60, 116. This shrewd writer adds : " For which, reason will require some symbol of divine nature and presence. Its being an holy instrument of divine service, being of no more force for the altar, than for the tongs, or snuffers of the tabernacle, or Aaron's breeches under the law, or for surplices, organs, chalices, patens, and canonical coates and girdles, which are made instruments of holy service, by our altar-adorers ; and if on that reason they must be bowed unto, we shall abound in cringing not only in every church, but in every street. On Maundy Thursday, 1636, Mrs. Charnock, &c. went to see the King's Chapel, where they saw an altar, with tapers and other furniture on it, and a crucifix over it : and presently came Dr. Brown, one of his Majesties chaplaines, and his curate, into the Chappel, and turning themselves towards the altar, bowed three times ; and then performing some private devotion departed : and immediately came two seminarie priests and did as the doctor and his curate had done before them." *Altar-worship,* 1661, pp. 60, 116. In the " Lincoln Articles of Enquiry," 1641, the following occurs : " Do you know of any parson, vicar, or curate that hath introduced any offensive rites or ceremonies into the Church, not established by the lawes of the land ; as namely, that make three courtesies towards the Communion Table, that call the said table an altar, that enjoyne the people at their coming into the Church to bow towards the East, or towards the Communion-table ? " Mr. Brand tells us that he observed this practice in College Chapels at Oxford. But in 1813 Sir H. Ellis remarks : " The practice of bowing to the altar, the Editor believes, is now entirely left off at Oxford. That of turning to it at the repetition of the Creed is pretty generally retained, and certainly has its use, in contributing very often to recall the wandering thoughts of those who attend the Chapel service."

Mede tells us that whatever reverential guise, ceremony, or worship they used at their ingress into churches, in the ages next to the apostles (and some he believes they did) is wholly buried in silence and oblivion. The Jews used to bow themselves towards the mercy-seat. The Christians, after them, in the Greek and Oriental Churches, have, time out of mind, and without any known beginning, used to bow in like manner. They do it at this day. Gregory tells us, that the holy men of Jerusalem held a tradition generally received from the ancients that our Saviour himself was buried with his face and feet towards the east. Bourne quotes Bede as his authority for saying, " that as the holy women entered at the eastern part into the circular house hewn out in the rock, they saw the Angel sitting at the south part of the place, where the body of Jesus had lain, i.e., at his right hand : for undoubtedly his body, having its face upwards and the head to the west, must have its right hand to the south.' I find the following in " A Light Shining out of Darknes, or Occasional Queries," 1659, p. 26 : " This reason likewise the common people give for their being buryed with their feet towards the east, so that they may be in a fitter posture to meet the Sun of Righteousness when he shall appear with healing in his wings, viz. at the Resurrection." The subsequent remark is found at p. 30, " Whether it be not a pretty foundation for the Oxford doctors to stand booted and spurred in the Act ? because there is mention made in the Scripture of being shod with the preparation of the Gospel ? "

" 'Tis in the main allowed," says Selden, " that the heathens did, in general, look towards the East, when they prayed, even from the earliest ages of the World." Asplin's *Al Kibla,* 1728-31, quoted by Ellis. Comber says, " Some antient authors tell us that the old inhabitants of Attica buried thus before the days of Solon, who, as they report, convinced the Athenians that the Island of Salamis did of right belong to them by shewing them dead bodies looking that way, and sepulchres turned towards the east, as they used to bury." And the Scholiast upon Thucydides says it was the manner of all the Greeks to bury their dead thus. Again, it was used when they were baptized : they first turned their faces to the west, and so renounced the Devil, and then to the east, and made their covenant with Christ. Lastly, those of the ancient Church prayed that way, believing that our Saviour would come to judgment from that quarter of the heavens, St. Damascen asserting that when he ascended into Heaven, he was taken up eastward, and that his disciples worshipped him that way ; and therefore chiefly it was, that in the ancient Church they prayed with their faces to the east.

Bowing at the Name of Jesus.—Several arguments against this usage were published in a tract " by a learned author " in 1660. Both as regards bowing to the altar and in this other act, it is to be remarked that the conventional usage of women curtseying is a solecism.

Bowl or Bowling Alley.—A covered space for the game of bowls instead of a green. See Halliwell in v. Stevenson, in his *Twelve Months,* 1661, (taken from Breton's Fantasticks, 1626), says under July : " Bowling (however tearmed like cards and dice unlawfull) I am sure is an healthfull exercise, and good for the body, and hath been prescribed for a re-creation to great persons by the learned Physitians in which is a great deale of art and judgment to be seen especially in the expert bowler in choosing out his ground, ... whether it be in open wide places, or in Allies, and in this sport the choosing of the Bowles is not the least of the cunning belongs to it : your flat bowles being well for close Allies, your round byassed bowles for open ground of advantage, and your round bowles like a ball for green swarths that are plaine and levell." Braithwaite, in his "Rules for the Government of the house of an Earle," (circâ 1640) describes it as one of the duties of the gardener, "to make faire bowling alleys, well banked, and soaled ; which being well kepte in many howses are very profit-able to the gardiners."

The Bowling Green House was an old establishment under that name on Putney Heath, on the site of the residence of the younger Pitt. It is presumably the establishment to which John Locke alludes in his *Journal* under 1679, stating that during the whole summer several persons of quality might be seen bowling there two or three times a week. It was taken in 1693 by Edward Locket, keeper of an ordinary in White-hall, and had originally, no doubt, been a small and stealthy incroachment on the common, due to the negligence or complicity of the authorities. "The Bowling Green House at Putney," observes a writer in 1761, "is pleasantly situated, and affords a fine prospect. It is now turned into one of those fashionable summer breakfasting-places, which level all distinction, and mingle the sexes together in company." Marylebone and Islington were also formerly celebrated for their bowling greens, which were also found in the centre of the Metropolis, as we know it. Locke mentions Marylebone in 1679. One was attached to Shaver's Hall in the Haymarket. The reader may be referred to an interesting paper on bowling-greens in *Notes and Queries* for January 15, 1887. See also "A description of a Bowling Alley" in the "Compleat Gamester," 1674, and compare Nares, *Glossary*, 1859, in v. and under *Skittles*.

Half-Bowl.—What was termed the Half-Bowl is mentioned in a tract of 1580. "It was my chance," says the writer, "to be at John Crokes, where there is a bowling alley of the half bowle, whether doth repaire many merchants and sundry gentlemen, and in a chamber above divers were at play." The half-bowl was sufficiently celebrated to induce Francis Coules, the popular bookseller of Charles the First and Second's times, to adopt it as part of his sign, which formed a rather singular compound—"The Lamb and the Half-Bowl." In an edition of the "History of Tom a Lincoln," 1655, however, the imprint bears the latter only.

Bowls.—It is rather difficult to determine whether the game, which was to console the Princess of Hungary in her despondency, was the same as our bowls : if so, it was surely an indifferent prescription. In the "Squyr of Lowe Degre," the following passage is found :

> "An hundreth Knightes truly tolde,
> Shall play with bowles in alayes colde,
> Your disease to driue awaie."

A fair account of this diversion is given in Strutt's "Sports and Pastimes," and probably the best early one is in Taylor the Water-Poet's *Wit and Mirth*, 1629 : "This wise game of bowling," says he, "doth make the fathers surpasse their children in apish toyes and delicate dog-trickes. As first for the postures : first handle your bowle : secondly, aduance your bowle ; thirdly, charge your bowle : fourthly, ayme your bowle : fifthly, discharge your bowle : sixthly, plye your bowle : in which last posture of plying your bowle you shall perceiue many varieties and diuisions as wringing of the necke, lifting vp of the shoulders, clapping of the hands, lying downe of one side, running after the bowle, making long dutifull scrapes and legs (sometimes bareheaded), with entreating him to flee, flee, flee : and though hee the bowler bee a gentleman, yet there hee may meet with attendant rookes that sometimes will bee his betters six to four or two to one. . . . A bowler, although the allye or marke bee but thirty or forty paces, yet sometimes I haue heard the bowler cry, Rub, rub, rub, and sweare and lye that hee was gone an hundred miles, when the bowle hath beene short of the blocke two yards. The marke which they ayme at hath sundry names and epithites, as a blocke, a jacke, and a mistris." Perhaps the foregoing passage may serve to elucidate the rather obscure title (as it has been regarded) of Freeman's Epigrams," 1614 — "Rubbe and a Great Cast." Our ancestors pursued it with peculiar ardour and delight, and it is still a favourite amusement. Stow seems to say that, in his time, the open ground about London was being gradually built upon, and that the archers encroached upon the bowling alleys. Sir Nicholas Carew was playing at bowls with Henry VIII., when by some retort to an offensive remark by Henry, he gave umbrage to the latter, and was disgraced, and ultimately executed in 1539 on Tower Hill. In the Privy Purse Expenses of the Princess Mary, under April, 1538-9, there is a highly-curious entry :— "Itm. payd for a brekefaste loste at Bolling by my lady maryes gce.

. . . xs." It appears also from passages in "Wit at Several Weapons," and other dramas, that the small ball, which is now called the Jack, was sometimes known as the mistress."

It may be recollected that, in the feuds of the great families of Scotland in the sixteenth century, the murderer of George Drummond came upon him while he and his friends were playing at the game. See a letter in the *Antiquary* for January, 1886. While Charles I. was at Holmby in 1647, he frequented the bowling green at Althorp. One of the pleasanter traits in the personal history of Charles is the recourse of the King to the country seat of Mr. Richard Shute, a Turkey merchant, at Barking in Essex, for the purpose of playing with him at this game. Shute used to be called by his majesty *Satin* Shute, from the material of which his doublet was made. Sometimes one won, sometimes the other; but on one occasion Charles lost so frequently, that he gave up. His entertainer begged him to try another turn—another £1,000; but the King, laying his hand on his shoulder, said: "I must remember I have a wife and children to keep." In the story of *The King and a Poor Northern Man*, 1640, the latter, coming up to London to seek redress, does not believe that it is the King, whom they point out to him at the Court, playing at bowls in his shirt-sleeves. We have all heard how the poet Suckling, living at the same time:

"Prized black eyes and a lucky hit
At bowls above all the trophies of wit."

Charles's successor in the Stuart line, the merry monarch, is reported to have played at the same diversion with his select set for an East—a watch made by the early master of the craft so-named. A game at bowls or ninepins was formerly at least a favourite diversion for the rowing parties up the Thames between Putney and Teddington, and the riverside places of entertainment were usually provided with accommodation for this purpose.

Boxing. — Misson, in his *Travels in England*, toward the close of the 17th century, speaking of sports and diversions, says: "Anything that looks like fighting is delicious to an Englishman. If two little boys quarrel in the street, the passengers stop, make a ring round them in a moment and set them against one another, that they may come to fisticuffs. When 'tis come to a fight, each pulls off his neckcloth and his waistcoat, and gives them to hold to the standers-by; (some will strip themselves quite naked to their wastes;) then they begin to brandish their fists in the air; the blows are aim'd all at the face, they kick one another's shins, they tug one another by the hair, &c. He

that has got the other down, may give him one blow or two before he rises, but no more; and let the boy get up ever so often, the other is obliged to box him again as often as he requires it. During the fight the ring of by-standers encourage the combatants with great delight of heart, and never part them while they fight according to the rules: and these by-standers are not only other boys, porters, and rabble, but all sorts of men of fashion; some thrusting by the mob, that they may see plain, others getting upon stalls; and all would hire places if scaffolds could be built in a moment. The father and mother of the boys let them fight on as well as the rest, and hearten him that gives ground or has the worst. These combats are less frequent among grown men than children; but they are not rare. If a coachman has a dispute about his fare with a gentleman that has hired him, and the gentleman offers to fight him to decide the quarrel, the coachman consents with all his heart: the gentleman pulls off his sword, lays it in some shop, with his cane, gloves, and cravat, and boxes in the same manner as I have described above. If the coachman is soundly drubb'd, which happens almost always, (a gentleman seldom exposes himself to such a battle without he is sure he's strongest) that goes for payment; but if he is the beater, the beatée must pay the money about which they quarrell'd." Brand once saw the Duke of Grafton at fisticuffs, in the open street, with such a fellow, whom he lamb'd most horribly. It was in the very widest part of the Strand. The Duke was big and extremely robust. He had hid his Blue Ribband, before he took the coach, so that the coachman did not know him. Compare *Bartholomew Fair* for a curious anecdote of Dr. Johnson's uncle. "In France," adds Misson, "we punish such rascals with our cane, and sometimes with the flat of our sword: but in England this is never practis'd; they use neither sword nor stick against a man that is unarm'd: and if an unfortunate stranger (for an Englishman would never take it into his head) should draw his sword upon one that had none, he'd have a hundred people upon him in a moment, that would, perhaps, lay him so flat that he would hardly ever get up again till the Resurrection."

Boy-Bishop. — It is uncertain at what period the custom of electing boy bishops on St. Nicholas's Day commenced in England; but there is little doubt that after it had been established on the continent, it would soon be imported hither. The association of this saint with the rite was, of course, due to his patronage of children. Warton thought he found traces of the religious mockery of the boy bishop as early as 867 or 870, in the Greek Church. *H.E.P.*, by Hazlitt, 1871, ii., 228-32, where farther particulars may be found. The ceremony has been traced to Canterbury, Eton (1441), St. Paul's, London, Colchester, Norwich, Winchester (1380), Exeter, Salisbury, Wells, Westminster, Lambeth, York, Beverley, Rotherham, Newcastle-upon-Tyne, and to several places abroad; there can be little doubt that it was almost universal. Gregory thought that the boy bishop was peculiar to Salisbury, perhaps because he met with the usage in the Sarum service book, and Warton supposed that the custom was confined to collegiate churches. It seems to be thought that this character was originally known as *Episcopus Choristarum* merely. In the archives of Norwich, down to 1521, are sundry entries relevant to the expenses incurred here on this anniversary, and notices of moneys left to support the institution. Aubrey's *Letters, &c.*, 1813, i. 302-4. In the statutes of Salisbury Cathedral, enjoined anno 1319, Tit. 45, it is ordered that the boy bishop shall not make a feast. The boy bishop, as it should seem from the Register of the capitulary Acts of York Cathedral under the date 1367 was to be *corpore formosus*, or the election to be void; and as in the same church, under a regulation of 1390, every chorister was bound to possess "claram vocem puerilem," such a quality was as justly imperative in the *episcopus puerorum*. Hazlitt's Warton, 1871, iv., 237 The Boy Bishop at Salisbury is actually said to have had the power of disposing of such prebends there as happened to fall vacant during the days of his episcopacy.

Edward I., in the 28th year of his reign, being near Newcastle-upon-Tyne, gave forty shillings to the Boy-Bishop and his companions for singing before him on St. Nicholas's Eve. It was during the King's passage through Newcastle on this occasion that a boy-bishop said vespers before him in his chapel at Heton. It appears that at Canterbury in 1464 there was no election of a boy bishop in the Grammar-school owing to the default or negligence of the masters. *Liber Johannis Stone, monachi eccl. Cant. de Obitibus, &c. sui Cenobii* (1415-67), a MS. in the library of C. C. C. Camb. One of the original rules drawn up for the scholars of Dean Colet's Foundation, in 1510, was: "Your chylde shal, on Chyldermas Daye, wayte vpon the boy byshop at Paules, and offer there—.' In the Statutes of St. Paul's, 1518, the following clause occurs: "All these children shall every Childermas Daye come to Paulis Churche and hear the Childe Bishop sermon: and after be at the hygh masse, and each of them offer a 1d. to the Childe Bishop, and with them the Maisters and Surveyors of the Scole." A tract by Hugh Rhodes, one of the children of the chapel

under Henry VIII., appeared, according to Herbert, in 1555, containing, in thirty-six 6-line stanzas, the "Song of the Child-Bishop of St. Paul's," as it was sung before the queen at her manor of St. James in the Fields in her privy chamber on St. Nicholas's Day and Innocents' Day that year. It is described as a fulsome panegyric, in which the queen is compared to Judith, Esther, the Queen of Sheba, and the Virgin.

In cathedrals this Boy Bishop seems to have been elected from among the children of the choir. After his election, being completely apparelled in the episcopal vestments, with a mitre and crozier, he bore the title and state of a Bishop, and exacted ceremonial obedience from his fellows, who were dressed like priests. Strange as it may appear, they took possession of the Church, and, except mass, performed all the ceremonies and offices. Northumb. Housch. Book, ed. 1827, p. 439, for an 'Inventory of the Robes and Ornaments of a Boy or Bearn Bishop." In Hearne's "Liber Niger Scaccarii, 1728, vol. ii., pp. 674, 686, we find that Archbishop Rotheram bequeathed "a myter for the Barnebishop, of cloth of gold, with two knopps of silver gilt and enamyled." But in the ordinary churches the appointments were almost equally sumptuous and costly. The Churchwardens' accounts of St Mary at Hill, 10 Henry VI., mention two children's copes, also a mitre of cloth of gold, set with stones. In 1523, 2s. 8d. are charged for the Bishop's dinner and his company on St. Nicholas's Day in the same accounts at Lambeth. Even posterior to the Proclamation of 33 Henry VIII., in the St. Mary at Hill books, 1549, is: "For 12 oz. silver, being clasps of books and the Bishop's mitre, at vs. viijd. per oz. vjl. xvis. jd." These last were sold. In the "Inventory of Church Goods" belonging to the same parish, at the same time, we have: "Item, a mitre for a Bishop at St. Nicholas-tyde, garnished with silver, and enamyled, and perle, and counterfeit stone." Maskell pointed out that, from the services to be said by the Boy Bishop and his choristers, as laid down in the Sarum Processional, it appears that "not only upon the Innocents' or Childermas Day did the 'Episcopus Puerorum' claim his rights, and perform all the ecclesiastical duties of his temporary rank, except the mass, but from the feast of St. Nicholas to Innocents' Day, a period of nearly a month. Whence it does not seem so extraordinary, as it otherwise might, that during this time the Boy Bishop might die, in which case he would be buried with the due honours: and the tomb at Salisbury is explained." *Selected Centuries of Books*, 1843, pp. 15-16, *note*. On the eve of Innocents' Day, the Boy Bishop was to go in solemn procession with his fellows, to the altar of the Holy Trinity and All Saints, or (as the Pie directs) to the altar of Holy Innocents or Holy Trinity in their copes, and burning tapers in their hands. The Bishop beginning, and the other boys following: "Centum quadraginta quatuor," &c. Then the verse, "Hi emti sunt ex omnibus,' &c. and this was sung by three of the boys. Then all the boys sang the "Prosa sedentem in supernâ majestatis arce," &c. The Chorister Bishop, in the mean time, fumed the altar first, and then the image of the Holy Trinity. Then the Bishop said *modestâ voce* the verse "Lætamini," and the response was, "Et gloriamini," &c. Then the prayer which we yet retain : "Deus cujus hodierna die," &c. In their return from the altar Præcentor puerorum incipiat, &c., the chanter-chorister began "De Sancta Maria," &c. The response was "Felix namque," &c., et "sic processio," &c. The procession was made into the quire, by the west door, in such order that the dean and canons went foremost: the chaplains next : the Bishop, with his little Prebendaries, in the last and highest place. The Bishop took his seat, and the rest of the children disposed themselves upon each side of the quire, upon the uppermost ascent, the canons resident bearing the incense and the book : and the petit canons the tapers, according to the Rubrick. And from this hour to the full end of the next day's procession no clerk is accustomed (whatever his condition may be) to take place above his superiors. Then the Bishop on his seat said the verse : "Speciosus forma, &c. diffusa est gratia in labiis tuis," &c. Then the prayer, "Deus qui salutis æternæ," &c., "Pax vobis," &c. Then after the "Benedicamus Domino," the Bishop, sitting in his seat, gave the Benediction to the people in this manner: "Princeps Ecclesiæ Pastor ovilis cunctam plebam tuam benedicere digneris," &c. Then, turning towards the people, he sang or said : "Cum mansuetudine & charitate humiliate vos ad benedictionem" : the chorus answering, "Deo gratias." Then the cross-bearer delivered up the crozier to the Bishop again, *et tunc Episcopus puerorum primô signando se in fronte sic dicat,* "Adjutorium nostrum," &c. The chorus answering "Qui fecit Cœlum & Terram." Then, after some other like ceremonies performed, the Bishop began the Completorium or Complyn; and that done, he turned towards the quire, and said, "Adjutorium," &c., and then, last of all, he said, "Benedicat Vos omnipotens Deus, Pater, and Filius, & Spiritus Sanctus." All this was done with solemnity of celebration, and under pain of anathema to any that should interrupt or press upon these children. See

Gregory's Works, 1649, p. 114. The show of the Boy Bishop, rather on account of its levity and absurdity, than of its superstition, was formally abrogated by a Proclamation, July 22, 1542. But it had been interdicted abroad, a century before, by the Council of Basle, 1431, as appears from a citation in Prynne's "Histriomastix," 1633, and the later statutory prohibition was more or less disregarded in England. The conclusion of Henry VIII.'s Proclamation is : "And whereas heretofore dyvers and many superstitious and chyldysh observauncies have be used, and yet to this day are observed and kept, in many and sundry partes of this Realm, as upon Saint Nicholas, the Holie Innocents, and such like, children be strangelie decked and apparayled to counterfeit Priests, Bishops, and Women, and to be ledde with songes and dances from house to house, blessing the people, and gathering of money : and boyes do singe masse and preache in the pulpitt, with such other unfittinge and inconvenient usages, rather to the derysyon than anie true glorie of God, or honour of his sayntes. The Kynges Majestie wylleth and commaundeth that henceforth all such superstitious observations be left and clerely extinguished throwout all this Realme and Dominions." Bishop Tanner, in a letter to Hearne, says in allusion to the abuse of the ancient custom, that the choristers chose a bishop and waited on him in procession to several houses in the city, where the little rogues took great liberties. And Tanner traces to this circumstance the bye-name of St. Nicholas's Clerks conferred on them.

In Hall's "Triumphs of Rome" (Triumphs of Pleasure) he equally animadverts on the licence, which had crept into this Romish Observance, when he says, "What merry work it was here in the days of our holy fathers (and I know not whether, in some places, it may not be so still), that upon St. Nicholas, St. Katherine, St. Clement, and Holy Innocents' Day, children were wont to be arrayed in chimers, rochets, surplices, to counterfeit bishops and priests, and to be led, with songs and dances, from house to house, blessing the people, who stood girning in the way to expect that ridiculous benediction. Yea, that boys in that holy sport were wont to sing masses and to climb into the pulpit to preach (no doubt learnedly and edifyingly) to the simple auditory. And this was so really done, that in the cathedral church of Salisbury (unless it be lately defaced) there is a perfect monument of one of these Boy Bishops (who died in the time of his young pontificality) accoutred in his episcopal robes, still to be seen. Strype, however, in his "Memorials," speaking of the Boy

Bishop, among scholars, says: "I shall only remark that there might be this at least be said in favour of this old custom, that it gave a spirit to the children, and the hopes that they might at one time or other attain to the real mitre, and so made them mind their books."

With the Catholic Liturgy, all the pageantries of popery were restored to their ancient splendour by Queen Mary. Among these, the procession of the Boy Bishop was too popular a mummery to be overlooked. In Strype we read that, Nov. 13, 1554, an edict was issued by the Bishop of London to all the Clergy of his Diocese, to have a Boy Bishop in procession. In the same volume, however, we read, "The which was St. Nicholas Eve, at even-song time came a commandment that St. Nicholas should not go abroad nor about. But, notwithstanding, it seems, so much were the citizens taken with the mock of St. Nicholas, that is, a Boy Bishop, that there went about these St. Nicholases in divers parishes, as in St. Andrew's, Holborn, and St. Nicolas Olaves in Bread-street. The reason the procession of St. Nicolas was forbid, was, because the Cardinal had this St. Nicolas Day sent for all the Convocation, Bishops, and inferior Clergy, to come to him to Lambeth, there to be absolved from all their perjuries, schisms and heresies." In the accounts of St. Mary - at - Hill, London, 1554, is the following entry: "Paid for makyng the Bishops myter, with staff and lace that went to it, iiis. Paid for a boke for St. Nicholas, viijd." Strype says, that in 1556, on St. Nicholas' Even, "St. Nicholas, that is a boy habited like a bishop in pontificalibus, went abroad in most parts of London, singing after the old fashion, and was received with many ignorant but well-disposed people into their houses, and had as much good cheer as ever was wont to be had before, at least in many places." The Boy Bishop would naturally be put down again when Queen Elizabeth came to the crown: and yet, by Puttenham's account, it was exhibited in the country villages after her accession. Puttenham wrote his "Art of English Poesy" many years before it was published in 1589. He says: "Methinks this fellow speaks like Bishop Nicholas: for on St. Nicholas's night, commonly, the scholars of the country make them a bishop, who, like a foolish boy, goeth about blessing and preaching with such childish terms as make the people laugh at his foolish counterfeit speeches." The special service for Innocents' Day, in an early printed copy of it, is described as "In die innocentium sermo pro episcopo puerorum." It commences with the words: "Laudate, pueri, domi-

num, psalmo centesimo xii° et pro buius colacionis fundamento."

In the Posthumous Works of John Gregory, 1650, there is a monograph on this subject with three engravings; it is called: Episcopus Puerorum, In die Innocentium; or a Discoverie of an Antient Custom in the Church of Sarum, making an Anniversarie Bishop ameng the Choristers." In 12 Edward III., while the King was at Antwerp, the Boy-Bishop there received 13s. 6d. for singing before his majesty in his chamber. Hazlitt's Warton, 1871, ii., 229.

Aubanus tells us, that scholars on St. Nicholas's Day used to elect three out of their numbers, one of whom was to play the bishop, the other two the parts of Deacons. The Bishop was escorted by the rest of the boys, in solemn procession, to church, where with his mitre on, he presided during the time of divine worship: this ended, he and his deacons went about singing from door to door, and collected money, not begging it as alms, but demanding it as the Bishop's subsidy. On the eve of this day the boys were prevailed upon to fast, in order to persuade themselves that the little presents which were put that night for them into shoes (placed under the table for that purpose), were made them by St. Nicholas: and many of them kept the fast so rigorously on this account, that their friends, in order to prevent them from injuring their healths, were under the necessity of forcing them to take some sustenance. Bowle says, that in Spain formerly, on this commemoration-day, a chorister being placed with solemnity in the midst of the choir, upon a scaffold, there descended from the vaulting of the ceiling a cloud, which stopping, midway, opened. Two angels within it carried the mitre, and descended just so low as to place it on his head, ascending immediately in the same order in which they came down. This came to be an occasion of some irregularities; for till the day of the Innocents, he had a certain jurisdiction, and his prebendaries took secular offices, such as alguasils, catchpoles, dog-whippers and sweepers. From a paper in the St. James's Chronicle," for Nov. 16-18, 1797, it appears that at Zug, in Switzerland, the ceremonies of this day were suppressed in that year in consequence of the complaint addressed to the authorities against the exactions of the Boy Bishop and his attendants, who visited all the booths, &c., and demanded money.

Bragot Sunday.—In Lancashire, or some parts of it, a spiced ale, called Braget or Bragot, used to be drunk very largely on Palm Sunday, which was thence called Bragot Sunday.

Branks.—"They have an artifice at Newcastle under Lyme and Walsall," says Plot, "for correcting of scolds, which it does, too, so effectually and so very safely, that I look upon it as much to be preferred to the cucking stoole, which not only endangers the health of the party, but also gives the tongue liberty 'twixt every dipp; to neither of which this is at all liable : it being such a bridle for the tongue as not only quite deprives them of speech, but brings shame for the transgression and humility thereupon, before 'tis taken off : which being put upon the offender by order of the magistrate, and fastened with a padlock behind, she is led round the town by an officer, to her shame, nor is it taken off till after the party begins to shew all external signes imaginable of humiliation and amendment." *Staffordshire*, p. 389. In a plate annexed, he gives a representation of a pair of branks. They still preserve a pair in the Town Court at Newcastle-upon-Tyne, where the same custom once prevailed. Gardner's *England's Grievance*, 1656, and Brand's *History*, ii., 292. A fuller description of the brank occurs in Willis's "Current Notes" for May, 1854, where several engravings accompany and illustrate the letter-press. The writer says: It may be described as an iron skeleton helmet, having a gag of the same metal, that by being protruded into the mouth of an inveterate brawler, effectually branked that unruly member, the tongue. As an instrument of considerable antiquity at a time when the gag, the rack, and the axe were the *ratio ultima Romæ*, it has doubtless been employed, not unfrequently for purposes of great cruelty, though in most examples, the gag was not purposely designed to wound the mouth, but simply to restrain or press down the tongue. Several of these instruments are yet extant, though their use has now, thanks to more considerate civilization, become obsolete. . . . The earliest use of the brank in England is not antecedent to the reign of Charles." A curious variety of this old mode of penance is noticed in the same miscellany for October, 1854.

Brawl.—A dance introduced from France in or about the middle of the sixteenth century. See Halliwell in v.

Bread.—In Craven, in the West Riding of York, those who knead dough for baking are in the habit of making the sign of the cross, both when they knead or stiffen the material, and when they elt or moisten it with additional milk or milk and water, as a precaution against the sinister action of any witch or evil-eyed person at hand. Douce, in his interleaved copy of Brand's "Antiquities," pointed out that M. Thiers (in his *Traitè des Superstitions*) mentioned a belief as prevalent in France that bread baked on Christmas Eve would not turn mouldy.

Bread and Cheese Land.—Hasted, speaking of Biddenden, tells us that "twenty acres of land, called the Bread and Cheese Land, lying in five pieces, were given by persons unknown, the yearly rents to be distributed among the poor of this parish. This is yearly done on Easter Sunday, in the afternoon, in 600 cakes, each of which have the figures of two women impressed on them, and are given to all such as attend the church ; and 270 loaves, weighing three pounds and a half a-piece, to which latter is added one pound and a half of cheese, are given to the parishioners only at the same time. There is a vulgar tradition in these parts, that the figures on the cake represent the donors of this gift, being two women twins, who were joined together in their bodies, and lived together so till they were between twenty and thirty years of age. But this seems without foundation. The truth seems to be, that it was the gift of two maidens, of the name of Preston ; and that the print of the women on the cakes has taken place only within these fifty years, and was made to represent two poor widows, as the general objects of a charitable benefaction." "At Biddenden, Kent, yesterday, there was observed a curious Easter custom of distributing cakes bearing the impressed figures of the "Biddenden Maids." Their names were Eliza and Mary Chulkhurst, and they are said to have lived to the age of 34 years, when one died, and the other followed within six hours. They bequeathed land in the parish which produces about forty guineas a year, and from this the cost of the distribution is defrayed. The custom always attracts a very considerable number of visitors from the surrounding villages, and it is among these that the cakes, having a quaint representation of the maids, stamped with a boxwood die, are distributed, bread and cheese being given to the poor of the parish." *Globe*, April, 8 1890. There is a similar custom at Paddington, near London, where the gifts are thrown from the church steeple.

Breakfasting.—A Sussex custom. *Sussex Arch. Coll.*, xiv., 135.

Brival's, St.—At St. Briaval's, Gloucestershire, a very strange quasi-jocular custom formerly prevailed on Whit-Sunday. Several baskets full of bread and cheese, cut very small, were brought into church, and immediately after service were thrown by the churchwardens from the galleries among the congregation, who scrambled for them. The custom was kept up, and may be still, in order to secure to the poor of St. Briaval's and Havelfield the right of cutting and carrying wood from 3,000 acres of coppice in Hudknoll and the Meend. Every householder was assessed 2d. towards defraying the cost of the bread and cheese.

In 1687, the "Orders and Rules of the Court of St. Briavells in the Forest of Dean, in the County of Gloucester," were printed in a volume with similar regulations for the miners in the Forest.

Bridal Bed.—In the papal times no new-married couple could go to bed together till the bridal bed had been blessed. In a MS. cited by Blakeway, it is stated that "the pride of the clergy and the bigotry of the laity were such that new married couples were made to wait till midnight, after the marriage day, before they would pronounce a benediction, unless handsomely paid for it, and they durst not undress without it, on pain of excommunication." Blomefield's *Norfolk*, iv. 221.

Bride-Ale. — In Ihre's "Glossarium Suio-Gothicum," 1769, we read : v. *Brudskal*. Gifwa i Brudskálen dicitur de Erano vei munere collectitio, quod Sponsæ diæ Nuptiarum a Convivis in pateram mittitur, habito antea brevi Sermone a præsente Sacerdote. Nescio, an huc quicquam faciat Tributum illud, quod in Gallia Sponsæ dabatur Escuellatta dictum, et de quo Du-Fresne in Gloss. Lat." Ibid. v. *Jul* p. 1005 : "Hemkomol, *Convivium quod novi Conjuges in suis œdibus instruunt*." In the "Christen State of Matrimony," 1543, fol. 48, verso, we read : "When they come home from the church, then beginneth excess of eatyng and dryncking—and as much is waisted in one daye, as were sufficient for the two newe married folkes halfe a year to lyve upon." The following is from the Court Rolls of Hales-Owen Borough, Salop, of the 15th Elizabeth : — *Custom of Bride-Ale* : "Item, a payne is made that no person or persons that shall brewe any weddyn ale to sell, shall not brewe above twelve strike of mault at the most, and that the said persons so married shall not keep nor have above eight messe of persons at his dinner within the burrowe : and before his brydall daye he shall keep no unlawfull games in hys house, nor out of hys house, on pain of 20 shillings." In Harrison's "Description of Britain," it is remarked : "In feasting also the husbandmen do exceed after their manner, especially at bridales, &c., where it is incredible to tell what meat is consumed and spent ; ech one brings such a dish, or so manie with him, as his wife and he doo consult upon, but alwaies with this consideration, that the leefer friend shall have the better provision." Thus it appears that among persons of inferior rank a contribution was expressly made for the purpose of assisting the bridegroom and bride in their

new situation. This custom must have doubtless been often abused : it breathed, however, a great deal of philanthropy, and would naturally help to increase population by encouraging matrimony. This custom of making presents at weddings seems also to have prevailed amongst those of the higher order. From the account of the nuptials of the Lady Susan with Sir Philip Herbert, in the reign of James I. it appears that the presents of plate and other things given by noblemen were valued at £2,500, and that the king gave £500 for the bride's jointure. His majesty gave her away, and, as his manner was, archly observed on the occasion that "if he were unmarried he would not *give her*, but *keep her* for himself." Bride-ales are mentioned by Puttenham in his "Arte of Poesie" : "During the course of Queen Elizabeth's entertainments at Kenilworth Castle, in 1575, a bryde-ale was celebrated with a great variety of shews and sports." From a passage in Jonson's "Silent Woman," Andrews infers that it seems to have been a general custom to make presents to the married pair, in proportion to the gay appearance of their wedding. Newton, speaking of rushes, says "Herewith be made manie pretie imagined devises for bride-ales, and other solemnities as little baskets, hampers, paniers, pitchers, dishes, combes, brushes, stooles, chaires, purses with strings, girdles, and manie such other pretie, curious, and artificiall conceits, which at such times many do take the paines to make and hang up in the houses, as tokens of good-will to the new married bride : and after the solemnitie ended, to bestow abroad for bride-gifts or presents." In reference to the rose, he says : "At bride-ales the houses and chambers were woont to be strawed with these odoriferous and sweet herbes : to signifie that in wedlocke all pensive sullennes and lowring cheer, all wrangling strife, jarring, variance, and discorde, ought to be utterly excluded and abandoned ; and that in place thereof al mirth, pleasantnes, cheerfulnes, mildnes, quietnes, and love should be maintained, and that in matters passing betweene the husband and the wife all secresie should be used." Herbal from the Bible, 1587, p. 92. Compare *Bid-ale* and *Bride-Wain*.

Bride-Cake.—The connection between the bride-cake and wedding is strongly marked in the following custom still retained in Yorkshire, where the former is cut into little square pieces, thrown over the bridegroom's and bride's head, and then put through the ring. The cake is sometimes broken over the bride's head, and then thrown away among the crowd to be scrambled for.

This is noted by Aubanus in his description of the rites of marriage in his country and time. " Peractâ re divinâ Sponsa ad Sponsi domum deducitur, indeque Panis projicitur, qui a pueris certatim rapıtur," fol. 68. To break the cake over the head of the bride appears to have been sometimes usual in Drayton's time, for that writer, in his " Nimphidia, or the Court of Fairy," 1627, applies the custom, with the licence habitual to poets, to the fairy Tita :

" *Mertilla.* But coming back when she
    is wed,
Who breaks the cake above her head?
Claia. That shall Mertilla."

Thus Smollett, in his *Humphrey Clinker*, 1771 : " A cake being broken over the head of Mrs. Tabitha Lismahago, the fragments were distributed among the bystanders, according to the custom of the antient Britons, on the suppostion that every person who ate of this hallowed cake, should that night have a vision of the man or woman whom Heaven designed should be his or her wedded mate." In the North, slices of the bride-cake are put through the wedding ring : they are afterwards laid under pillows, at night, to cause young persons to dream of their lovers. Douce pointed out that this custom is not peculiar to the North of England, it seems to prevail generally. The pieces of the cake must be drawn nine times through the wedding ring. But it appears that the cake was not necessarily a wedding-cake. The " Spectator " observes also : " The writer resolved to try his fortune, fasted all day, and that he might be sure of dreaming upon something at night, procured an handsome slice of bride cake, which he placed very conveniently under his pillow." The " Connoisseur " says : " Cousin Debby was married a little while ago, and she sent me a piece of bride-cake to put under my pillow, and I had the sweetest dream : I thought we were going to be married together. The following occurs in the *Progress of Matrimony*, 1733 :

" But, Madam, as a present take
This little paper of bride-cake :
Fast any Friday in the year,
When Venus mounts the starry sphere,
Thrust this at night in pillowber,
In morning slumber you will seem
T' enjoy your lover in a dream."

In the " St. James's Chronicle," April 16-18, 1799, are some lines on the " Wedding Cake."

Bride-Cup.—This custom has its traces in Gentilism. It is of high antiquity, says Malone, for it subsisted among our Gothic ancestors. " Ingressus domum convivalem Sponsus cum pronubo suo, sumpto poculo, quod maritale vocant, ac

paucis a Pronubo de mutato vitæ genere prefatis, in signum constantiæ, virtutis, defensionis et tutelæ, propinat Sponsæ et simul Morgennaticam (Dotalitium ob virginitatem) promittit, quod ipsa grato animo recolens, pari ratione et modo, paulo post mutato in uxorium habitum operculo Capitis, ingressa, poculum, ut nostrates vocant, uxorium leviter delibans, amorem, fidem, diligentiam, et subjectionem promissum."—Stiernhook *De Jure Suecorum et Gothorum vetusto*, 1672, p. 163, quoted by Malone. In the Workes of John Heiwood, the following passage occurs :

" The drinke of my brydecup I should
    have forborne,
Till temperaunce had tempred the taste
    beforne.
I see now, and shall see while I am alive
Who wedth or he be wise shall die or he
    thrive."

Edit. 1576, sign. B. 4.

Bride Favours.—In " The Fifteen Comforts of Marriage," a conference is introduced, concerning bridal colours in dressing up the bridal bed by the bridemaids—not, say they, with yellow ribbands, these are the emblems of jealousy—not with " Fueille mort," that signifies fading love—but with true blue, that signifies constancy, and green denotes youth—put them both together, and there's youthful constancy. One proposed blew and black, that signifies constancy till death ; but that was objected to, as those colours will never match. Violet was proposed as signifying religion ; this was objected to as being too grave : and at last they concluded to mingle a gold tissue with grass-green, which latter signifies youthful jollity. For the bride's favours, top-knots, and garters, the bride proposed blew, gold-colour, popingay-green, and limon-colour—objected to, gold-colour signifying avarice—popingay-green, wantonness. The younger bridemaid proposed mixtures—flame-colour, flesh-colour, willow, and milk-white. The second and third were objected to, as flesh-colour signifies lasciviousness, and willow forsaken. It was settled that red signifies justice, and sea-green inconstancy. The milliner, at last, fixed the colours as follows : for the favours, blue, red, peach-colour, and orange-tawney : for the young ladies' top-knots, flame-colour, straw-colour, (signifying plenty), peach-colour, grass-green, and milk-white : and for the garters, a perfect yellow, signifying honour and joy. To this variety of colours in the bride favours used formerly, the following passage, wherein Lady Haughty addresses Morose, in Jonson's " Silent Woman," evidently alludes :

"Let us know your bride's colours and
    yours at least."

The bride favours have not been omitted in
"The Collier's Wedding":

"The blithsome, bucksome country
    maids,
With knots of ribbands at their heads,
And pinners flutt'ring in the wind,
That fan before and toss behind," &c.

And, speaking of the youth, with the
bridegroom, it says:

"Like streamers in the painted sky,
At every breast the favours fly."

Bride Knives.—Strange as it may
appear, it is however certain that knives
were formerly part of the accoutrements of
a bride. This perhaps will not be difficult
to account for, if we consider that it anciently formed part of the dress for women
to wear a knife or knives sheathed and suspended from their girdles: a finer and
more ornamented pair of which would very
naturally be either purchased or presented
on the occasion of a marriage. Among the
women's trinkets, about 1540, in the Four
P's of John Heywood, occur:

"Silke swathbonds, ribands, and sleeve-
    laces,
Girdles, knives, purses, and pin-cases."

From a passage in the "Raigne of Edward
the third," 1596, there appear to have
been two of them. So in the Lottery for
1601, No. xi. is:

"A Pair of Knives."
Fortune doth give these paire of knives
    to you,
To cut the thred of love if't be not
    true."

In Rowlands' "Well met, Gossip" (first
printed in 1602) the Widow says:

"For this you know, that all the wooing
    season,
Sutors with gifts continuall seeke to
    gaine
Their mistresse loue—"

The wife answers:

"That's very true——
In conscience I had twenty pair of gloues
When I was maid, giuen to that effect:
Garters, kniues, purses, girdles, store of
    rings,
And many a hundred dainty, pretty
    things."

A bride says to her jealous husband, in
Dekker's "Match me in London," 1631:

"See at my girdle hang my wedding
    knives!
With those dispatch me."

Bride-Laces.—These are noticed in
Laneham's *Letter from Kenilworth*, 1575.

In Jonson's *Tale of a Tub* Turf is introduced as saying: "We shall all ha' bride-
laces or points I zee." In the Lottery of
1601, the three following occur, in a list
of prizes for ladies: A dozen of points, a
scarfe, and a lace. Herrick, in his "Epithalamie on Sir Clipseby Crew and his
Lady," thus cautions the bridegroom's
men against offending the delicacy of the
new-married lady:

"We charge ye that no strife
(Farther than gentleness tends) get
    place
Among ye, striving for her lace:"

And it is observed, in the account
of the marriage of Jack of Newbury, that
his bride was led to church between two
sweet boys, "with bride-laces and rosemary tied about their silken sleeves." In
the second part of Dekker's "Honest
Whore," 1630, signat. K 3 verso, we read:
"Looke yee, doe you see the bride-laces
that I give at my wedding will serve to tye
rosemary to both your coffins when you
come from hanging." Heywood's *Woman
Killed with Kindness*, 1607, alludes to the
nosegays and bride-laces worn by the country lasses on this occasion in their hats.

Bridegroom Men.—These appear
anciently to have had the title of bride-
knights. "Paranymphi ejusmodi seu
Sponsi amici appellantur etiam
(Matt. ix. 15) filii thalami nuptialis; quâ
de re optimè vir præstantissimus Hugo
Grotius. Singulare habetur et apud nos
nomen ejusmodi eorum quos Bride-Knights
id est, Ministros Sponsalitios qui Sponsam
deducere solent, appellitamus." Seldeni
"Uxor Hebraica"; Opera, tom. iii. p.
638. He gives, ibid. a chapter "de Para-
nymphis Hebreorum Sponsi Amicis, in
utroque Fœdere dictis et in Novo Filiis
Thalami nuptialis." Those who led the
bride to church by the arms, as if committing an act of force, were always bachelors; Fletcher's "Scornful Lady," 1616,
(Dyce's B. and F. vol. iii. p. 16). But she
was to be conducted home by two married
persons. Polydore Vergil informs us that
a third married man, in coming home
from church, preceded the bride, bearing,
instead of a torch, a vessel cf silver or gold.
"In Anglia servatur ut duo pueri, velut
Paranymphi, id est, Auspices, qui olim pro
nuptiis celebrandis Auspicia capiebant,
nubentem ad Templum—et inde domum
duo viri deducant, et tertius loco facis
Vasculum aureum vel argenteum præ-
ferat." In "A Pleasant History of the
First Founders," we read: "At Rome the
manner was that two children should lead
the bride, and a third bear before her a
torch of white-thorn in honour of Ceres,
which custome was also observed here in
England, saving that, in place of the torch,
there was carried before the bride a bason

of gold or silver; a garland also of corn eares was set upon her head, or else she bare it on her hand, or, if that were omitted, wheat was scattered over her head in token of fruitfulness; as also before she came to bed to her husband, fire and water were given her, which, having power to purifie and cleanse, signified that thereby she should be chast and pure in her body. Moresin relates that to the bachelors and married men who led the bride to and from church, she was wont to present cloves for that service during the time of dinner. It was part of the bridegroom man's office to put him to bed to the bride, after having undressed him.

Bride Maids.—The use of bride maids at weddings appears as old as the time of the Anglo-Saxons: among whom, as Strutt informs us, "The bride was led by a matron, who was called the bride's woman, followed by a company of young maidens, who were called the bride's maids." The bride's maids and bridegroom men are both mentioned by the author of the "Convivial Antiquities" in his description of the rites of marriages in his country and time. "Antequam eatur ad Templum Jentaculum Sponsæ et invitatis apponitur, Serta atque Corollæ distribuuntur. Postea certo ordine Viri primum cum Sponso, deinde Puellæ cum Sponsa, in Templum procedunt." — *Antiquitat. Convivial*, fol. 68.

Bride-Stake.—Around this bridestake the guests were wont to dance as about a may-pole. Thus Jonson :

"With the phant'sies of hey-troll Troll about the bridal bowl, And divide the broad bride cake Round about the bride's stake."

Bride-Wain. — In Cumberland the Penny Wedding of the earlier Scots and the Bid-Ale of Wales had the appellation of a bride-wain, a term which will be best explained by the following extract from the Glossary, 1710, to Douglas's Virgil, v. Thig : "There was a custom in the Highlands and North of Scotland, where new married persons, who had no great stock, or others low in their fortune, brought carts and horses with them to the houses of their relations and Friends, and received from them corn, meal, wool, or whatever else they could get. The subsequent is extracted from the "Cumberland Packet," a newspaper :

"*Bride Wain.*

There let Hymen oft appear In saffron robe and taper clear, And pomp and feast and revelry, With mask and antient pageantry.

"George Hayton, who married Ann, the daughter of Joseph and Dinah Collin of Crossley Mill, purposes having a bride wain at his house at Crossley near Mary Port on Thursday, May 7th, next, (1789), where he will be happy to see his friends and wellwishers, for whose amusement there will be a saddle, two bridles, a pair of gands d'amour gloves, which whoever wins is sure to be married within the twelve months, a girdle (Ceinture de Venus) possessing qualities not to be described, and many other articles, sports, and pastimes, too numerous to mention, but which can never prove tedious in the exhibition, &c." A short time after a match is solemnized, the parties give notice as above, that on such a day they propose to have a bride-wain. In consequence of this, the whole neighbourhood for several miles round assemble at the bridegroom's house, and join in all the various pastimes of the country. This meeting resembles our wakes and fairs: and a plate or bowl is fixed in a convenient place, where each of the company contributes in proportion to his inclination and ability, and according to the degree of respect the parties are held in : and by this very laudable custom a worthy couple have frequently been benefited at setting out in life, with a supply of money of from ten to fourscore pounds. Eden, in "The State of the Poor," 1797, observes "The custom of a general feasting at weddings and christenings is still continued in many villages in Scotland, in Wales, and in Cumberland : Districts, which, as the refinements of legislation and manners are slow in reaching them, are most likely to exhibit vestiges of customs deduced from remote antiquity, or founded on the simple dictates of Nature : and indeed it is not singular, that marriages, births, christenings, housewarmings, &c., should be occasions in which people of all classes and all descriptions think it right to rejoice and make merry. In many parts of these districts of Great Britain as well as in Sweden and Denmark, all such institutions, now rendered venerable by long use, are religiously observed. It would be deemed ominous, if not impious, to be married, have a child born, &c., without something of a feast. And long may the custom last : for it neither leads to drunkenness and riot, nor is it costly ; as alas ! is so commonly the case in convivial meetings in more favoured regions. On all these occasions, the greatest part of the provisions is contributed by the neighbourhood : some furnishing the wheaten flour for the pastry ; others, barley or oats for bread or cakes ; some, poultry for pies ; some, milk for the frumenty ; some eggs ; some bacon ; and some, butter ; and, in short, every article necessary for a plentiful repast. Every neighbour, how high or low soever, makes it a point to contribute something. "At a daubing (which is the erection of a house of clay), or at a bride-wain, (which is the carrying of a bride home) in Cumberland, many hundreds of persons are thus brought together, and as it is the custom also, in the latter instance, to make presents of money, one or even two hundred pounds are said to have been sometimes collected. A deserving young couple are thus, by a public and unequivocal testimony of the goodwill of those who best know them, encouraged to persevere in the paths of propriety, and are also enabled to begin the world with some advantage. The birth of a child, also, instead of being thought or spoken of as bringing on the parents new and heavy burthens, is thus rendered, as it no doubt always ought to be, a comfort and a blessing: and in every sense an occasion of rejoicing." "I own," adds this honourable advocate in the cause of humanity, "I cannot figure to myself a more pleasing, or a more rational way of rendering sociableness and mirth subservient to prudence and virtue." Vol. i., p 598. In Cumberland, among the lower but not poorest, class, the entertainment consists of cold pies, furmety, and ale. "At the close of the day," says the author of the "Westmoreland and Cumberland Dialect," 1839, "the bride and bridegroom are placed in two chairs, in the open air or in a large barn, the bride with a pewter dish on her knee, half covered with a napkin: into this dish the company put their offerings, which occasionally amount to a considerable sum."

Bride's Pie.—The bride's pie should also be noticed as an important part of the wedding-feast, at least in some places or districts. It is thus referred to by Carr, in the "Dialect of Craven," 1828: "The bride's pie was so essential a dish on the dining-table, after the celebration of the marriage, that there was no prospect of happiness without it. This was always made round, with a very strong crust ornamented with various devices. In the middle of it was a fat laying hen, full of eggs, probably intended as an emblem of fecundity. It was also garnished with minced and sweet meats. It would have been deemed an act of neglect and rudeness, if any of the party omitted to partake of it." In the old song of "Arthur of Bradley," we read:

"And then did they foot it and toss it,
Till the cook had brought up the posset;
The bride-pye was brought forth,
A thing of mickle worth.
And so all, at the bed-side,
Took leave of Arthur and his bride."

Bridget, St. — (July 23). The "Roman Martyrology," 1627, observes under this date: "The departure out of this life of St. Bridget widdow, who, after many peregrinations made to holy places,

full of the Holy Ghost, finally reposed at Rome: whose body was after translated into Suevia. Her principal festivity is celebrated upon the seaventh of October." According to Porter's "Flowers of the Lives of the Saincts," 1632, p. 118, Brigitt's Day (Virgin of Kildare, in Ireland), was February the first. Her *Most Devout Prayers* were printed at Antwerp in 1659, See also Moore's "Diarium Historicum," 1590, p. 111, where we read under 23º, Julii, "Emortualis Dies S. Brigittæ Reg. Sueciæ, 1372." In the "Fifteen O's" the first O is introduced by a large woodcut representing a man crowned delivered out of purgatory by an angel, through the mediation of St. Bridget, who is kneeling at a small altar before him. Vallancey, speaking of Ceres, tells us: "Mr. Rollin thinks this deity was the same Queen of Heaven to whom the Jewish women burnt incense, poured out drink offerings, and made cakes for her with their own hands"; and adds: "This Pagan custom is still preserved in Ireland on the Eve of St. Bridget, and which was probably transposed to St. Bridget's Eve from the festival of a famed poetess of the same name in the time of Paganism. In an ancient glossary now before me she is described: 'Brigit, a poetess, the daughter of Dagha; a goddess of Ireland.' On St. Bridget's Eve every farmer's wife in Ireland makes a cake, called bairin-breac, the neighbours are invited, the madder of ale and the pipe go round, and the evening concludes with mirth and festivity."

Bridling Cast, The.—This seems to have been rather more common in Scotland than among the Southerners; it was the cup of drink offered to a visitor, at the gate, after mounting to depart. Skelton refers to it in the "Bowge of Courte," printed before 1500:

"What, loo, man, see here of dyce
a bale !
A brydelynge caste for that is in thy
male."

Weber says, in a note to his edition of Beaumont and Fletcher, "A bridling cast was probably similar to what is at present in Scotland, and particularly in the Highlands, called the door-drink, which is often administered after the guest is seated upon his horse, or while the horse is bridling." In Fletcher's "Scornful Lady," 1616, Young Loveless says:

"Let's have a bridling cast before you
go —
Fill's a new stoop."

It is more generally known as the stirrup-cup.

Brightlingsea, Essex. — "Yesterday the ancient custom of electing a mayor in the belfry of Brightlingsea

Church was observed, Mr. Miall Green, a yacht owner and resident of Kensington, being chosen for the second year in succession. The regalia, consisting of a truncheon and a handsome chain formed of gold models of oysters and silver models of sprats, was carried by a yacht captain. It was incidentally mentioned by the new mayor that according to an ancient statute the freedom of certain of the Cinque Ports, which included Brightlingsea, were entitled to wreck the house of any freeman who refused mayoral honours. *Daily Telegraph,* Tuesday, December 2, 1902.

Bring the Basket.—See *More Sacks to the Mill.*

Bromfield School.—Hutchinson tells us: "Till within the last twenty or thirty years, it had been a custom, time out of mind, for the scholars of the Free-School of Bromfield, about the beginning of Lent, or in the more expressive phraseology of the country, at Fasting's Even, to bar out the Master; i.e., to depose and exclude him from his school, and keep him out for three days. During the period of this expulsion, the doors of the citadel, the school, were strongly barricadoed within: and the boys, who defended it like a besieged city, were armed, in general, with bore-tree or elder pop-guns. The Master, meanwhile, made various efforts, both by force and stratagem, to regain his lost authority. If he succeeded, heavy tasks were imposed, and the business of the school was resumed and submitted to; but it more commonly happened that he was repulsed and defeated. After three days' siege, terms of capitulation were proposed by the Master and accepted by the boys. These terms were summed up in an old formula of Latin Leonine verses stipulating what hours and times should, for the year ensuing, be allotted to study, and what to relaxation and play. Securities were provided by each side for the due performance of these stipulations: and the paper was then solemnly signed by both Master and scholars. "One of the articles always stipulated for and granted, was, the privilege of immediately celebrating certain games of long standing; viz. a foot-ball match and a cock-fight. Captains, as they were called, were then chosen to manage and preside over these games: one from that part of the parish which lay to the westward of the school; the other from the east. Cocks and foot-ball players were sought for with great diligence. The party, whose cocks won the most battles, was victorious in the cock-pit; and the prize, a small silver bell, suspended to the button of the victor's hat, and worn for three successive Sundays. After the cock-fight was ended, the foot-ball was thrown down in the churchyard; and the point then to be contested, was,

which party could carry it to the house of his respective captain; to Dundraw, perhaps, or West-Newton, a distance of two or three miles: every inch of which ground was keenly disputed. All the honour accruing to the conqueror at foot-ball was that of possessing the ball. Details of these matches were the general topics of conversation among the villagers, and were dwelt on with hardly less satisfaction than their ancestors enjoyed in relating their feats in the Border Wars. "Our Bromfield sports were sometimes celebrated in indigenous songs: one verse only of one of them we happen to remember:

> "At Scales, great Tom Barwise gat the Ba' in his hand,
> And t' wives aw ran out, and shouted, and bann'd:
> Tom Cowan then pulch'd and flang him 'mang t' whins,
> And he bledder'd, Od-white-te, tou's broken my shins."

History of Cumberland, ii., 322. The writer thought this might be the basis of the (now obsolete) institution of the *Terræ Filius* at Oxford. It was a practice common to Eton.

Bromfield Sports.—Hutchinson, speaking of the parish of Bromfield, and a custom in the neighbourhood of Blencogo, tells us: — "On the common, to the east of that village, not far from Ware - Brig, near a pretty large rock of granite, called St. Cuthbert's Stane, is a fine copious spring of remarkably pure and sweet water, which (probably from its having been anciently dedicated to the same St. Cuthbert), is called Helly-Well, i.e. Haly or Holy Well. It formerly was the custom for the youth of all the neighbouring villages to assemble at this well early in the afternoon of the second Sunday in May, and there to join in a variety of rural sports. It was the village wake, and took place here, it is possible, when the keeping of wakes and fairs in the churchyard was discontinued. And it differed from the wakes of later times chiefly in this, that though it was a meeting entirely devoted to festivity and mirth, no strong drink of any kind was ever seen there; nor anything ever drank, but the beverage furnished by the Naiad of the place. A curate of the parish, about the year 1770, on the idea that it was a profanation of the Sabbath, saw fit to set his face against it; and having deservedly great influence in the parish, the meetings at Helly-Well have ever since been discontinued." *Cumberland,* ii., 323.

Broom.—An usage connected with marriage, and also with the broom, and of which the origin and significance do not appear to be very obvious, existed some years ago, it seems, in some parts of England. A man, when his wife left home for a short time, hung out a broom from one of the windows. Now a broom hung from the mast of a ship has a very different meaning from the one that must have been here intended—that the mistress of the establishment was away. An old woman in the Isle of Thanet adopted an odd method, so recently as 1850, of signifying her disapproval of her nephew's choice of a wife. She pronounced an anathema on the newly-married pair at the church-gate, procured a new broom, swept her house with it, and then hung it over the door. This was intended to be equivalent to cutting off with a shilling.

Broose.—Compare *Riding*.

Brougham, Westmoreland.— Every year, on the 2nd of April, the rector and churchwardens distribute the Countess of Pembroke's charity upon a stone tablet near the pillar, about two miles from Penrith. It and the pillar date from 1656, having been instituted and raised, the latter in the park at Whitfield, as a permanent memorial for the last parting of the Countess of Dorset, Pembroke, and Montgomery on that site with her mother, the Countess Dowager of Cumberland, April 2, 1616. The charity consists of a sum of £4 distributed here to the poor of Brougham. This custom was still observed in Beckwith the Elder's day; he died in 1799; and the monument is engraved in Pennant's *Journey to Alston Moor*, 1801.

Browny.—There were thought to have been a sort of domestic fairies, called *brownies*, who were extremely useful, and were said to have performed all sorts of domestic drudgery. The early Scotish poet, Dunbar, who died about 1515, in his *Dance of the Seven Deadly Sins*, speaks of two spirits called Black-Belly and Bawsy Brown. Warton thought it not unlikely that the latter might be identical with Brownie. "The spirit called Brownie," (says King James) "appeared like a rough man, and haunted divers houses without doing any evill, but doing as it were necessarie turnes up and downe the house; yet some were so blinded as to beleeve that their house was all the sonsier as they called it, that such spirits resorted there." *Demonology*, 127. Martin, speaking of the Shetland Isles, says : "It is not long since every family of any considerable substance in those Islands was haunted by a spirit they called Browny, which did several sorts of work : and this was the reason why they gave him offerings of the various products of the place. Thus some, when they churned their milk, or brewed, poured some milk and wort through the hole of a stone called Browny's Stone." He also says :— "A spirit by the country people called Browny, was

frequently seen in all the most considerable families in these Isles and North of Scotland, in the shape of a tall man : but within these twenty or thirty years past, he is seen but rarely." Speaking of three chapels in the Island of Valay, he says : "Below the chappels there is a flat thin stone, called Brownie's Stone, upon which the antient inhabitants offered a cow's milk every Sunday : but this custom is now quite abolished." *Western Islands*, p. 391. Johnson, in his *Tour to the Hebrides*, observes, that of Browny mentioned by Martin nothing has been heard for many years. Browny was a sturdy fairy who, if he was fed and kindly treated, would as they say do a great deal of work. They now pay him no wages, and are content to labour for themselves." We are told by Pinkerton that "The Brownie was a very obliging spirit, who used to come into houses by night, and for a dish of cream to perform lustily any piece of work that might remain to be done : sometimes he would work, and sometimes eat till he bursted : if old clothes were laid for him, he took them in great distress, and never more returned." Heron's *Journey*, 1799, ii., 227. Borlase informs us that in his time (a century since) the Cornish invoked a spirit whom they called Browny (a sort of Robin Goodfellow), when their bees began to swarm, thinking that "their crying Browny, Browny, will prevent their returning into their former hive, and make them pitch and form a new colony." *Antiquities of Cornwall*, 1769, p. 168. Milton, in a passage of his *Allegro*, seems to depict Browny rather than Robin Goodfellow :—

"Tells how the druging Goblin swet,
To earn his cream-bowl duly set,
When in one night 'ere glimpse of morn,
His shadowy flaile hath thresh'd the corn
That ten day-lab'rers could not end :
Then lays him down the lubbar-fiend,
And stretch'd out all the chimney's
length
Basks at the fire his hairy strength,
And crop-full out of doors he flings,
Ere the first cock his matin rings."

Buckler-Play.—The following order was made by the Government of James I. in 1609 : "That all plaies, bear-baitings, games, singing of ballads, buckler-play, or such like causes of assemblies of people be utterly prohibited, and the parties offending severely punished by any Alderman or Justice of the Peace." Misson says : "Within these few years you should often see a sort of gladiators marching thro' the streets, in their shirts to the waste, their sleeves tuck'd up, sword in hand, and preceded by a drum, to gather spectators. They gave so much a head to see the fight. which was with cutting swords, and a kind of buckler for defence. The edge of the sword was a little blunted, and the care of the prize-fighters was not so much to avoid wounding one another, as to avoid doing it dangerously; nevertheless, as they were obliged to fight, till some blood was shed, without which nobody would give a farthing for the show, they were sometimes forc'd to play a little ruffly. I once saw a much deeper and longer cut given than was intended. These fights are become very rare within these eight or ten years. Apprentices, and all boys of that degree, are never without their cudgels, with which they fight something like the fellows before-mention'd, only that the cudgel is nothing but a stick; and that a little wicker basket, which covers the handle of the stick, like the guard of a Spanish sword, serves the combatant instead of defensive arms."

Bug, Welsh *Bwg,* a goblin. We now use bugbear without much recollection, perhaps, of the etymology. Boggle-bo, says Coles, (now corruptly sounded Bugabow), signified "an ugly wide-mouthed picture carried about with May-games." It is perhaps nothing more than the diminutive of Bug, a terrifying object. *Lat. Dict.,* 1678, in v. In Mathew's Bible, Psalm xci., v. 5, is rendered, "Thou shalt not nede be afraied for any bugs by night," this is hence known as the *Bug Bible.* In the Hebrew it is "terror of the night"; a curious passage, evidently alluding to that horrible sensation the night-mare, which in all ages has been regarded as the operation of evil spirits. Compare Douce's *Illustr.,* i., 328. Boh, Warton tells us, was one of the most fierce and formidable of the Gothic Generals, and the son of Odin: the mention of whose name only was sufficient to spread an immediate panic among his enemies. The s me was the case with that of Narses among children. Compare *Richard-Cœur-de-Lion.*

Boe Bulbagger, as he is there called, in "Jacke of Dover, his Quest of Inquirie for the Veriest Foole in England," 1604, is mentioned as a sort of bogie or bugbear. Taylor the water-poet, in his "Great Eater of Kent," 1630, says of his hero, Nicholas Wood: ". . . he is a maine enemy to Ember weekes, he hates Lent worse than a butcher or a Puritan, and the name of Good Friday affrights him like a Bull-beggar." In Rowley's *Woman never Vext,* 1632, mine host says of his disorderly guests: "The bull-beggar comes when I show my head." Compare *Barguest.*

Bull-Baiting. — Fitzstephen mentions the baiting of bulls with dogs as a diversion of the London youths on holidays in his time. *Descr. of London, temp.* Henry II., apud *Antiq. Reper.* v., 1807, vol. i. Hentzner, who visited England in

Elizabeth's reign, says: "There is a place built in the form of a theatre, which serves for the baiting of bulls and bears; they are fastened behind, and then worried by great English bull-dogs; but not without great risk to the dogs, from the horns of the one and the teeth of the other: and it sometimes happens they are killed on the spot. Fresh ones are immediately supplied in the place of those that are wounded or tired. To this entertainment there often follows that of whipping a blinded bear, which is performed by five or six men, standing circularly, with whips, which they exercise upon him without any mercy, as he cannot escape from them because of his chain. He defends himself with all his force and skill, throwing down all who come within his reach, and are not active enough to get out of it, and tearing the whips out of their hands and breaking them. At these spectacles, and every where else, the English are constantly smoking tobacco." *Itinerary,* 1612, transl. 1757. When Robert Chamberlaine published in 1637 his *New Book of Mistakes,* there seems from the preface to have been a white bull at the Bear garden in Southwark, "who tosseth up Dogges," he says, "like Tennis-balles," and catching them again upon his hornes, makes them to garter their Legges with their owne guts." Misson, in his *Travels in England,* trans. by Ozell, 1734, describes bul-baiting as it was practised in the time of William III.

A considerable body of authentic testimony exists to shew that this apparently cruel amusement was due to a theory on the part of our ancestors, that the process rendered the flesh more tender, and some of the Leet Courts in England imposed a fine of 3s. 4d. on every butcher, who killed a bullock unbaited. Bull-rings were established for this purpose, and at Carlisle it is mentioned that the Butchers' Gild had charge of the chain used in the operation. *Antiquary* for April-May, 1893. We still deem a coursed hare, somewhat on the same principle, tenderer than a shot one. Bull-baiting was still carried on in the Midlands and in the North down to the second half of the nineteenth century; and the women enjoyed the sport as keenly as the men. At Leigh, near Preston, according to a story told me by a Leigh man, a fellow, in a room with his wife and a dog trained to this exercise, laid his head on a table; the dog rushed at his nose, the husband cried out from the pain, and would have got up, but, says the woman, 'lie still, man, he must draw blood, or he will be just ruined.' —Hazlitt's *Four Generations of a Literary Family,* 1897, ii., 296.

M. Michel, in "Le Pays Basque," 1857, traces back this diversion in that country to the year 1385. There is no want of material for the history of the sport on the other side of the Pyrenees subsequently to that date. Most of the Spanish princes appear to have encouraged it by their countenance and support.

At Stamford, in Lincolnshire, an annual sport used to be celebrated, called bull-running: of which the following account is taken from Butcher: "It is performed just the day six weeks before Christmas. The butchers of the town at their own charge against the time, provide the wildest bull they can get: this bull over night is had into some stable or barn belonging to the Alderman. The next morning proclamation is made by the common bellman of the town, round about the same, that each one shut up their shop-doors and gates, and that none, upon pain of imprisonment, offer to do any violence to strangers, for the preventing whereof (the town being a great thoroughfare and then being in Term Time) a guard is appointed for the passing of travellers through the same without hurt. That none have any iron upon their bull-clubs or other staff which they pursue the bull with. Which proclamation made, and the gates all shut up, the bull is turned out of the Alderman's house, and then hivie skivy, tag and rag, men, women, and children of all sorts and sizes, with all the dogs in the town promiscuously running after him with their bull-clubs spattering dirt in each other's faces, that one would think them to be so many Furies started out of Hell for the punishment of Cerberus, as when Theseus and Perillus conquered the place (as Ovid describes it):

Bull-Running.

"A ragged troop of boys and girls
    Do pellow him with stones:
With clubs, with whips, and many raps,
    They part his skin from bones."

And (which is the greater shame) I have seen both senatores majorum gentium and matrones de eodem gradu, following this bulling business." "I can say no more of it, but only to set forth the antiquity thereof, (as the tradition goes). William Earl of Warren, the first Lord of this town, in the time of King John, standing upon his castle-walls in Stamford, viewing the fair prospects of the river and meadow, under the same, saw two bulls a fighting for one cow; a butcher of the town, the owner of one of those bulls, with a great mastiff dog accidentally coming by, set his dog upon his own bull, who forced the same bull up into the town, which no sooner was come within the same but all the butchers' dogs, both great and small, follow'd in pursuit of the bull, which by this time made stark mad with the noise

of the people and the fierceness of the dogs, ran over man, woman, and child, that stood in the way; this caused all the butchers and others in the town to rise up as it were in a tumult, making such an hideous noise that the sound thereof came into the Castle unto the ears of Earl Warren, who presently thereupon mounted on horseback, rid into the town to see the business, which then appearing (to his humour) very delightful, he gave all those meadows in which the two bulls were at the first found fighting, (which we now call the Castle Meadows) perpetually as a common to the butchers of the town, (after the first grass is eaten) to keep their cattle in till the time of slaughter: upon this condition, that as upon that day on which this sport first began, which was (as I said before) that day six weeks before Christmas, the butchers of the town should from time to time yearly for ever, find a mad bull for the continuance of that sport." *Survey of Stamford*, 1775-76. In the "Antiquarian Repertory," an account is extracted from Plot of a similar bull-running at Tutbury, in Staffordshire, which occasioned much disorder annually, until it was abolished by the Duke of Devonshire, lay-prior of Tutbury, in the eighteenth century. This practice seems to have dated from ancient times, as it was usual, before the Dissolution, for the Prior of Tutbury to give the minstrels, who attended matins on the feast of the Assumption, a bull, if they would convey him on the side of the river Dove next the town or failing the bull, forty pence, of which a moiety went by custom to the lord of the feast. I believe that the practice of bull-running, and also of bull-baiting, is universally obsolete in this country, and has long been so.

Bull Week.—In Sheffield, this is the name given to the week before Christmas. The men work overtime, and often do not leave off till one or two in the morning, in order that they may earn money to spend in celebrating the great Christian festival. Their festive enjoyment chiefly consists in brutal drunkenness.

Bumpers.—Bumpers are of great antiquity. Paulus Warnefridus is cited in Du Cange's "Glossary," telling us in lib. v. "De Gestis Langobard." cap. 2, "Cumque ii qui diversi generis potiones ei a Rege deferebant, de verbo Regis eum rogarent, ut totam fialam biberet, ille in honorem Regis se totam bibere promittens, parum aquæ libabat de argenteo Calice." Vide Martial, lib. i. Ep. 72; lib. viii. 51, &c Comp. *Drinking Customs.*

Bundling used to be a widely diffused Welsh custom before marriage: the betrothed or engaged pair went to bed, or more frequently lay together in their clothes. It seems to have been intended as a method by which, without any detrimental result, the parties might form some idea of each other. It was by no means restricted to the lower orders. The mischievous consequences arising from such a practice are sufficiently obvious. It was formerly customary in Cumberland and Westmoreland, and produced similarly unfortunate and immoral consequences in the majority of cases. The usage was, however, growing obsolete there in 1839, when the author of the "W. and C. Dialect" wrote. According to a writer in the *Penny Magazine*, this practice was well known in Northumberland in or about 1830; but he does not seem to have heard that it was attended by very serious evils. It is not confined to this country. Such a practice was obviously prone to abuse, and more or less of mischief. But its localization seems to be an ill-founded hypothesis. Even among families of good position it is tacitly recognized and tolerated, and it was at the outset the product of the clothed state, where touch had to play the part of sight in the unclothed. It is a rigorous condition that no liberty is taken with the dress.

Burford.—Plot mentions a custom at Burford, in Oxfordshire (within memory) of making a dragon yearly, and carrying it up and down the town in great jollity on Midsummer Eve; to which, he says, not knowing for what reason, they added a giant. *Hist. of Oxfordshire*, p. 349. But a farther account of this usage may be found in Blount's *Tenures*, ed. Hazlitt, p. 49. The inhabitants of Burford formerly enjoyed the right of hunting deer in Whichwood Forest on Whitsunday. The Corporation still possesses the letter, directed to them in 1593, to stay the privilege for that year, and accept two bucks from the keepers in lieu thereof, without prejudice to the future.

Burial.—A paper on the Burial of the Britons forms part of his *Notes on Ancient Britain*, by W. Barnes, 1858. Strutt tells us, "that before the time of Christianity it was held unlawful to bury the dead within the cities, but they used to carry them out into the fields hard by, and there deposited them. Towards the end of the sixth century, Augustine obtained of King Ethelbert a Temple of Idols (where the King used to worship before his conversion) and made a burying place of it; but St. Cuthbert afterwards obtained leave to have yards made to the churches, proper for the reception of the dead." Comp. *Bidding, Deaths, Flowers, Gloves, Funeral Customs*, &c.

Burial Fees.—It is customary to give the clergy double fees where a person is buried not belonging to the parish.

Burlesque.—The antiquity of this practice is shown by the curious relics printed in *Reliquæ Antiquæ*, 1841-6, *et alibi*. At a very early date, the incantations of wizards and sorcerers appear to have been reduced to a burlesque sort of gibberish by those who either were unable to comprehend their meaning, or desired to ridicule their folly. See "Remains of Early Pop. Poetry of England," vol. i. p. 26 and vol. iv. p. 358. Dunbar, in his "Testament of Andro Kennedy," has parodied some of the rites which, in his day (he died about 1515), were observed at the interment of the dead. But the old Scotish Makar had less sympathy than the Southerners with this class of solemnity, for he belonged to a church, which treated the burial service lightly enough. Bishop Bale, writing in 1538, mentions the following burlesque charms:

"For the coughe take Judas Eare
Wth the parynge of a peare
And drynke them without feare
  If ye will have remedy:

Thre syppes are fore the hyckocke
And six more for the chyckocke
Thus, my prety pyckocke,
  Recover by and by.

If ye can not slepe but slumber,
Geve otes unto Saynt Uncumber
And beanes in a certen number
  Unto Saynt Blase and Saint Blythe.

Give onyons to Saynt Cutlake
And garlycke to Saynt Cyryake
If ye wyll shunne the heade ake:
  Ye shall have them at Quene hyth."

—*Comedy of Three Laws*, ed. 1562, sign. C 3 *verso*. And again:

"With blessynges of St. Germayne
I wyll me so determyne
That neyther fox nor vermyne
  Shall do my chyckens harme.
For your gese seke Saynt Legeared,
And for your duckes Saynt Leonarde,
For horse take Moyses yearde,
  There is no better charme.

Take me a napkyn folte
With the byas of a bolte
For the healyng of a colte
  No better thynge can be:
For lumpes and for bottes
Take me Saynt Wilfrides knottes,
And Holy Saynt Thomas Lottes,
  On my lyfe I warrande ye.

A dram of a shepes tyrdle,
And good Saynt Frances Gyrdle,
With the hamlet of a hyrdle,
  Are wholsom for the pyppe:

Besydes these charmes afore
I have feates many more
That kepe styll in store,
  Whom nowe I over hyppe."

So, in Heywood's Works, ed. 1598, sign.
C i. :

"I clawed her by the backe in way of a
  charme,
To do me not the more good, but the less
  harme."

In "Musarum Deliciæ," 1656, there is the
following incantation :

"—Or I to plague thee for thy sin,
Should draw a circle, and begin
To conjure, for I am, look to't,
An Oxford scholar, and can doe't.
Then with three sets of mops and mowes,
Seaven of odd words, and motley showes,
A thousand tricks that may be taken
From Faustus, Lambe, or Frier Bacon ;
I should begin."

Nash, in his 'Notes on Hudibras," says.
"Cato recommends the following as a
charm against sprains : 'Haut, haut, his-
ta, pista, vista.'" Andrews, the continuator of Henry, quoting Reginald Scot,
says : "The stories which our facetious
author relates of ridiculous charms which,
by the help of credulity, operated wonders,
are extremely laughable. In one of them
a poor woman is commemorated who cured
all diseases by muttering a certain form
of words over the party afflicted ; for which
service she always received one penny and
a loaf of bread. At length, terrified by
menaces of flames both in this world and
the next, she owned that her whole conjuration consisted in these potent lines,
which she always repeated in a low voice
near the head of her patient :

"Thy loaf in my hand,
  And thy penny in my purse,
Thou art never the better—
  And I am never the worse."

Melton tels us : "That a man may know
what's a clocke only by a ring and a silver
beaker." *Astrologestis*, 1620, p. 45. This
seems equally probable, with what we read
in Hudibras :

"And wisely tell what Hour o' th' Day
The clocke does strike by Algebra."

From Ravenscroft's *Deuteromelia*, 1609,
Dr. Rimbault has extracted the humorous
effusion of this class, entitled : *Martin said
to his Man,* where the second stanza runs :

I see a sheepe shearing corne,
  Fie ! man, fie !
I see a sheepe shearing corne,
  Who's the foole now ?
I see a sheepe shearing corne,
And a cuckold blow his horne ;
Thou hast well drunken, man,
  Who's the foole now ?

And the rest is in a similar strain. *A
Little Book of Songs and Ballads,* 1851,
pp. 115-17. See *Prevaricator*.

Burning the Dead Horse.—A
nautical ceremony performed with a
wooden horse suspended from the shrouds
on crossing the line. See a representation
of it in *Black and White,* January 9, 1892.
Its origin and meaning are explained on p.
36, and come from the prepayment of a
month's wages, which are usually squan-
dered on shore, so that a sailor works, as
he thinks, for nothing during what is
termed the Horse or first month, at the
conclusion of which this imaginary animal
is burnt, and Jack is really on his legs
again.

Burning Shame.—A custom said
to be peculiar to Newport, Isle of Wight.
See Mr. T. Nicholls's publication, 1812.

Burying Old Tom.—The labourers
in Herefordshire usually indulge in an extra glass or two on New Year's Eve, and
call this burying Old Tom. The festivities
usually include considerable uproar and
confusion, and the assistants at these peculiar funeral obsequies rarely quit the tavern parlour, till mine host makes a clear-
ance. They have some verses adapted for
the occasion, which they sing on their way
homeward through the streets, not always,
as it may be supposed, in the best time or
with the clearest accents. Mr. T. H. Pat-
tison communicated a copy to "Current
Notes" for January, 1856 :—

"I wish you a merry Christmas,
  And a happy New Year ;
A pocket full of money ,
  And a cellar full of beer ;
And a good fat pig,
  To serve you all the year.
Ladies and gentlemen sat by the fire,
Pity we, poor boys, out in the mire."

Bush.—There is a well known proverb,
"Good wine needs no bush" ; i.e. nothing
to point out where it is to be sold. Dickenson, in his "Greene in Conceipt," 1598,
has it : "Good wine needes no Ivie Bush."
The subsequent passage in Rowlands'
"Good Newes and Bad Newes," 1622,
seems to prove that anciently tavern keepers kept both a bush and a sign : a host is
speaking :

"I rather will take down my bush and
    sign
Then live by means of riotous expence."
In the same author's "Knave of Harts,"
1612, "the drunken knave exclaims :
"What claret's this ? the very worst in
    towne :
Your taverne-bush deserves a pulling
    downe."

In "England's Parnassus," 1600, the first
line of the address to the reader runs
thus : "I have no ivie out to sell my

wine " : and in Braithwaite's " Strappado for the Divell," 1615, there is a dedication to Bacchus, ' sole soveraigne of the Ivy-bush, prime founder of Red-Lettices," &c. In Dekker's " Wonderful Yeare," 1603, signat. F, we read : " Spied a bush at the ende of a pole (the auncient badge of a countrey ale - house)." Sir William Vaughan of Merioneth, in his " Golden Grove," 1600, says : " Like as an ivy-bush put forth at a vintrie, is not the cause of the wine, but, a signe that wine is to bee sold there ; so, likewise, if we see smoke appearing in a chimney, wee know that fire is there, albeit the smoke is not the cause of the fire." Elsewhere we find : " Nay if the house be not worth an ivie-bush, let him have his tooles about him ; nutmegs, rosemary, tobacco, with other the appurtenances, and he knowes how of puddle-ale to make a cup of English wine." In the preface to Braithwaite's *Laws of Drinking*, 1617, keeping a publichouse is called " the known trade of the ivy-bush, or red lettice." There is a wedding sermon by Whateley of Banbury, entitled, " A Bride - Bush," as is another preached to a newly - married couple at Œsen in Norfolk. See " Wedding Sermons," 12mo. Lond. 1732. Coles says : " Box and ivy last long green, and therefore vintners make their garlands thereof : though perhaps ivy is the rather used, because of the antipathy between it and wine." Poor Robin, in his *Perambulation from Saffion Walden to London*, 1678, says :

" Some alehouses upon the road I saw, And some with bushes shewing they wine did draw."

Nash, speaking of the head dresses of London ladies, says : " Even as angels are painted in church windowes, with glorious golden fronts, besette with sunne-beames, so beset they their foreheads on either side with glorious borrowed gleamy bushes ; which rightly interpreted, should signify beauty to sell, since a bush is not else hanged forth, but to invite men to buy. And in Italy, when they sette any beast to sale, they crowne his head with garlands and bedeck it with gaudy blossoms, as full as ever it may stick." *Christ's Teares over Jerusalem*, 1593, ed. 1613, p. 145.

Butter.—St. Hascka is said by her prayers to have made stinking butter sweet. See the Bollandists under January 26, as cited by Patrick in his " Devot. of the Romish Church," p. 37. Ady speaks of an old woman who came into an house when the maid was churning of butter, and having laboured long and could not make her butter come, the old woman told the maid what was wont to be done when she was a maid, and also in her mothers young time, that if it happened their butter would not come readily, they used a charm

to be said over it, whilst yet it was in beating, and it would come straight ways, and that was this :

" Come, butter, come, Come butter, come, Peter stands at the gate, Waiting for a buttered cake, Come, butter, come."

This, said the old woman, being said three times, will make your butter come, for it was taught my mother by a learned Church man in Queen Maries days, when as church men had more cunning, and could teach people many a trick, that our Ministers now a days know not." *Candle in the Dark*, 1659, p. 58. Jamieson, the editor of the *Scottish Ballads*, relates that when he was travelling on foot across the mountains from Fort Augustus to Fort Inverness, about the end of the 18th or beginning of the 19th century, he came to a dwelling, where the woman prepared the food to the accompaniment of song, and made him personally sing " like a mavis," to the bottle holding some cream, to make the butter come. She did the same in milking the cow, and searching in the hens' roost for some new-laid eggs.

Buzza, or **to Buzza One.**—I know nothing of the meaning of this word. I have been told that it is a college expression, and contains a threat, in the way of pleasantry, to black the person's face with a burnt cork, should he flinch or fail to empty the bottle. Possibly it may have been derived from the German " buzzen," *sordes auferre*, q.d. " Off with the lees at bottom." Grose explains this as signifying to challenge a person to pour out all the wine in the bottle into his glass, undertaking to drink it, should it prove more than the glass would hold. It is commonly said to one who hesitates to empty a bottle that is nearly out. To buzz a bottle of wine is usually understood in the sense of finishing it, which, if there is no more, is left to a guest.

Cakes and Salt were used in religious rites by the ancients. The Jews probably adopted their appropriation from the Egyptians : 'And if thou bring an oblation of a meat-offering baken in the oven, it shall be unleavened cakes of fine flour,' &c., *Levit.* ii. 4.—' With all thine offerings thou shalt offer salt.' "

Calendar.—There is a prevailing theory that the year was calculated prior to 1753 from the 25th of March, and only after that date from the 1st January. But, as a matter of fact, not only has wide diversity of practice existed everywhere in this respect, but even continues to do so, as well in Great Britain as abroad. Nicolas, *Chronology of History*, p. 40 *et seqq.* A writer from Sealby, near Scarborough,

Yorkshire, in a letter to the *Daily Graphic*, May 15, 1899, observes:—" In this part of England the new style has not yet been adopted in its entirety. With few exceptions rents become due and farms are entered or left on the 6th of April and 11th of October, called Lady Day and Michaelmas Day respectively. Midsummer Day is supposed to fall on the — July; and even in Scarborough and the larger towns of the district the 23rd of November is styled Martinmas. I know a few old inhabitants who firmly believe that May Day falls on the 13th of May."

Camp.—See *Football.*

Canaries.—A quick and lively dance. See Halliwell in v. and authorities cited by him.

Candlemas Bleeze. — Colonel Alexander Fergusson writes in *Notes and Queries*:—"My father, sometime Governor and Captain General of the colony of Sierra Leone, was born about 1804. As a very small child he attended a parish school in the 'Redgauntlet' country, hard by the Solway. It was then the custom, as I have been informed, on Candlemas Day for every scholar to carry, as an offering to the schoolmaster, a gift of peats, varying in number according to the distance to be traversed and the strength of the pupil. This duty was known by the name of the " Candlemas bleeze, (i.e., blaze)." Any one acquainted with the incomparable nature of the peats from the Lochar Moss —that terror to English troops and sanctuary for Border reivers—cut from a jetty soil as black as ink and smooth and soft as butter, and, when dried in the sun, the thin slices approaching coal in hardness, will understand what a welcome addition to the master's winter store of fuel was thus pleasantly provided. Probably this was about the last of an ancient custom; for in looking over, many years ago, some old accounts of the expenses connected with my father's education, there occurs an item of money paid to the schoolmaster "in lieu of the Candlemas bleeze." I have heard of a similar contribution being made to the parish schoolmaster in other parts of Scotland, where peat was not so common nor so good. It took the form of an offering of candles. I am sorry I can give no date for this latter instance of the survival of what was probably a custom dating from early Popish days."

Candlemas Day.—(February 2). The name is evidently derived from the candles, which are then carried in procession; it is otherwse known as the Purification of the Virgin. The word " Purification " itself carries in its original meaning the idea of cleansing by fire or light, and hither, rather perhaps than to Jesus Christ being the Spiritual Light, we ought to refer the connection of candles with this festival. The idea of celebrating the Purification of the Virgin on the same day strikes us as being an aftergrowth or graft, and was a piece of questionable clerical diplomacy, since it was apparently inconsistent with the Immaculate Conception. Fosbrooke (*British Monarchism*, i., 28) says: " The candles at the Purification were an exchange for the lustration of the Pagans, and candles were used " from the parable of the wise virgins."—' Alcuinus de divinis Officiis, p. 231. " This feast is called by the Greeks ὑπαπαντα, which signifies a meeting, because Simeon and Anna the prophetess met in the Temple at the presentation of our Saviour." L'Estrange's " Alliance of Divine Offices," p. 147. See Luke ii. In the " Roman Calendar," I find the subsequent observations on the 2nd of February, usually called Candlemas Day:

> " Torches are consecrated.
> Torches are given away for many days."
> " Feb. 2.   " Purificatio Virginis
>   Faces consecrantur.
>   Faces dantur multis diebus."

" To beare their candels soberly, and to offer them to the Saintes, not of God's makynge, but the carvers and paynters," is mentioned among the Roman Catholic customs censured by John Bale in his " Declaration of Bonners Articles," 1554, signat. D 4 b.; as is, Ibid. fol. 18 b. " to conjure candels." " There is a canon," says Bourne, " in the Council of Trullus, against those who baked a cake in honour of the Virgin's lying-in, in which it is decreed, that no such ceremony should be observed, because she suffered no pollution, and therefore needed no purification." Pope Sergius, says Becon, in his " Reliques of Rome," 1563, commanded that all the people "shuld go on procession on Candlemas Day, and carry candels about with them brenning in their hands in the year of our Lord 684." How this candle-burning on Candlemas Day came first up, the author of the *Festival* declareth in this manner: " Sometyme," saith he, " when the Romaines by great myght and royal power, conquered all the world, they were so proude, that they forgat God, and made them divers gods after their own lust. And so among all they had a god that they called Mars, that had been tofore a notable knight in battayle; and so they prayed to hym for help, and for that they would speed the better of this knight, the people prayed and did great worship to his mother, that was called Februa, after which woman much people have opinion that the moneth February is called. Wherefore the second daie of thys moneth is Candlemass Day. The Romaines this night went about the city of Rome with torches and candles brenning in worship of this woman Februa, for hope to have the more helpe and succoure of her sonne Mars. Then there was a Pope that was called Sergius, and when he saw Christian people draw to this false maumetry and untrue belief, he thought to undo this foule use and custom, and turn it onto Gods worship and our Ladys, and gave commandment that all Christian people should come to church and offer up a candle brennyng, in the worship that they did to this woman Februa, and do worship to our Lady and to her sonne our Lord Jesus Christ. So that now this feast is solemnly hallowed thorowe all Christendome. And every Christian man and woman of covenable age is bound to come to church and offer up their candles, as though they were bodily with our Lady hopyng for this reverence and worship, that they do to our Ladye, to have a great rewarde in Heaven." The Festyvall adds: "A candell is made of weke and wexe; so was Christ's soule hyd within the manhode: also the fyre betokeneth the Godhede: also it betokeneth our Ladyes moderhede and maydenhede, lyght with the fyre of love."

In Dunstan's "Concord of Monastic Rules" it is directed that, "on the Purification of the Virgin Mary the monks shall go in surplices to the Church for candles, which shall be consecrated, sprinkled with holy water, and censed by the Abbot.—Let every monk take a candle from the sacrist, and light it. Let a procession be made, thirds and Mass be celebrated, and the candles, after the offering, be offered to the priest." In some of the ancient illuminated calendars a woman holding a taper in each hand is represented in the month of February.

In a proclamation dated 26th of February, 30 Henry VIII., "concernyng Rites and Ceremonies to be used in due fourme in the Churche of England," we read as follows: "On Candlemas Daye it shall be declared, that the bearynge of candels is done in the memorie of Christe the spirituall lyghte, whom Simeon dyd prophecye as it is redde in the Churche that daye." The same had been declared by a decree of Convocation. Fuller's "Church History," p. 222. We read in Woodde's "Dialogue," cited more particularly under Palm Sunday, signat. d. 1, "Wherefore serveth holye candels? (Nicholas.) To light up in thunder, and to bless men when they lye a dying." See on this subject Dupre's "Conformity between ancient and modern ceremonies," p. 96, and Stopford's "Pagano-Papismus," p. 238. Moresin gives us his conjecture on the use of the candle upon this occasion: "It was an Egyptian hieroglyphic for Life,

meant to express here the ardent desire of having had the life of the deceased prolonged." *Papatus*, pp. 26 - 89. In the "Doctrine of the Masse Book," &c., 1554, signat. A 8, we find: "The hallowing of candles on Candlemas Day." The prayer. "O Lord Jesu Christ, ✠ blesse thou this creature of a waxen taper at our humble supplication, and, by the vertue of the holy crosse, poure thou into it an heavenly benediction; that as thou hast graunted it unto mans use for the expelling of darknes, it may receave such a strength and blessing, thorow the token of thy holy crosse, that in what places soever it be lighted or set, the Divil may avoid out of these habitacions, and tremble for feare, and fly away discouraged, and presume no more to unquiete them that serve thee, who with God," &c. There follow other prayers, in which occur these passages: "We humbly beseech thee, that thou wilt vouchsafe to ✠ to blesse and ✠ sanctifie these candels, prepared unto the uses of men, and health of bodies and soules, as wel on the land as in the waters." "Vouchsafe ✠ to blesse and sanctifye, and with the Candle of heavenly benediction, to lighten these tapers, which we thy servants taking in the honour of thy name (whan they are lighted) desire to beare, &c. "Here let the candles be sprinkled with holy water." Concluding with this rubrick: "When the halowyng of the candels is done, let the candles be lighted and distributed." Queen Mary, when princess, was a scrupulous observer of the custom of offering tapers, &c., peculiar to this day, as repeated entries in her "Privy Purse Expenses" testify, and in Bishop Bonner's "Injunctions," 1555, signat. A i. we read, "that bearyng of candels on Candlemasse Daie is doone in the memorie of our Saviour Jesu Christe, the spirituall lyght, of whom Saint Symeon dyd prophecie, as it is redde in the Church that day." This ceremony, however, had been previously forbidden in the metropolis: for in Stowe's "Chronicle," edit. 1631, p. 595, we read, "On the second of February, 1547-8, being the Feast of the Purification of our Lady, commonly called Candlemasse Day, the bearing of candles in the Church was left off throughout the whole citie of London," and, in fact, King Edward VI. had declared, by royal proclamation, that no man was to be subject to imprisonment for omitting the Popish ceremonies incidental to the day. At the end of Smart's "Vanitie and Downefall of superstitious Popish ceremonies," 1628, I find, in "a briefe but true historicall Narration of some notorious Acts and Speeches of Mr. John Cosens" (Bishop of Durham), the following: "Fourthly, on Candlemass Day last past, Mr. Cozens in renuing that Popish ceremonie of burning candles to the honour of our Ladye, busied himself from two of the clocke in the afternoone till foure, in climbing long ladders to stick up wax candles in the said Cathedral Church: the number of all the candles burnt that evening was two hundred and twenty, besides sixteen torches: sixty of those burning tapers and torches standing upon and near the high altar (as he calls it), where no man came nigh." Herrick, in his "Hesperides," has two or three passages illustrating curiously enough the usages peculiar to this season. In the "Country Almanack" for 1676, under February, we read—

"Foul weather is no news; hail, rain, and snow
Are now expected, and esteemed no woe;
Nay, 'tis an omen bad the yeomen say,
If Phœbus shews his face the second day."

Martin, in his "Description of the Western Islands," mentions an ancient custom observed on the second of February: "The mistress and servants of each family take a sheaf of oats and dress it up in women's apparel, put it in a large basket, and lay a wooden club by it, and this they call a Briid's Bed; and then the mistress and servants cry three times, "Briid is come, Briid is welcome." This they do just before going to bed, and when they rise in the morning they look among the ashes, expecting to see the impression of Briid's club there; which if they do, they reckon it a true presage of a good crop and prosperous year, and the contrary they take as an ill omen." There is a proverb:

"If Candlemas day be fair and bright,
Winter will have another flight;
If on Candlemas day it be shower and rain,
Winter is gone and will not come again."

Which appears to point to the deceptive character of a premature season. The heavy winds which visit us during February and March are sometimes called "Candlemas-eve winds." Hospinian's account of this festival is remarkbaly brief; but as Naogeorgus in Googe's paraphrase is a little more explicit, his account may be here inserted.

"Then comes the day wherein the Virgin offred Christ unto
The Father chiefe, as Moyses law commaunded hir to do.
Then numbers great of Tapers large, both men and women beare
To Church, being halowed there with pomp, and dreadful words to heare.
This done eche man his candell lightes where chiefest seemeth hee,
Whose taper greatest may be seene, and fortunat to bee;
Whose candell burneth cleare and bright a wondrous force and might

Doth in these candels lie, which if at any time they light,
They sure beleve that neyther storme or tempest dare abide,
Nor thunder in the skies be heard, nor any Devils spite,
Nor fearefull sprites that walke by night nor hurts of frost or haile."

Comp. *Candles, God's Sunday,* and *Wives' Feast-Day.*

Candle Omens.—In the "Knight of the Burning Pestle," 1613, in a sort of dirge, which Luce sings, there is this passage:

"Come, you whose loves are dead,
And whiles I sing,
Weep and wring
Every hand, and every head
Bind with cypress and sad yew;
Ribands black and candles blue
For him that was of men most true."

Melton says that "if a candel burne blew, it is a signe that there is a spirit in the house, or not farre from it." *Astrologaster,* 1620, p. 45. In "Ovid Travestie, 1673, the whimsical author makes Hero describe her alarm to her lover in consequence of an omen that she had seen in the candle:

"For last night late to tell you true
My candel as I sate burnt blew,
Which put poor me in horrid fright,
And expectation of black spright,
With sawcer eyes, and horns and tail."

But, in "A New Tricke to cheat the Divell," by Robert Davenport, 1639, the blue in the candle seems to be regarded as a portent of something different:

Constable. My watch is set, charge given and all in peace,
But by the burning of the candel blew,
Which I by chance espyed through the lanthorne,
And by the dropping of the Beadles nose, I smell a frost—"

Goldsmith, in his "Vicar of Wakefield," "speaking of the waking dreams of his hero's daughters, says, "The girls had their omens too, they saw rings in the candle." Willsford tells us: "If the flame of a candle, lamp, or any other fire does wave or wind itself, where there is no sensible or visible cause, expect some windy weather. When candles or lamps will not so readily kindle as at other times, it is a sign of wet weather neer at hand. When candles or lamps do sparkle and rise up with little fumes, or their wicks swell, with things on them (like mushrums) are all signs of ensuing wet weather." *Nature's Secrets,* 120. Boyle makes his 10th Meditation "upon a thief in a candle"—"which by its irregular way of making the flame blaze, melts down a good part of the tallow, and will soon spoil the rest, if the remains are not rescued by the removal of the Thief (as they call it) in the candle." *Occasional Reflections*, 1665, p. 218. The fungous parcels, as Browne calls them, about the wicks of candles are commonly thought to foretell strangers. See *Stranger*.

In the North, as well as in other parts of England, they are called letters at the candle, as if the forerunners of some strange news. These, says Browne, with his usual pedantry of style, which is so well atoned for by his good sense and learning, only indicate a moist and pluvious air, which hinders the avolation of the light and favillous particles, whereupon they settle upon the snast. That candles and lights, he observes also, burn blue and dim at the apparition of spirits, may be true, if the ambient air be full of sulphureous spirits, as it happens often in mines." The innkeepers and owners of brothels at Amsterdam are said to account these "fungous parcels" lucky, when they burn long and brilliant, in which case they suppose them to bring customers. But when they soon go out, they imagine the customers already under their roofs will presently depart. They call these puffs of the candle "good men." *Putanisme d'Amsterdam*, 1681, p. 92. A spark at the candle is held to import that the party opposite to it will shortly receive a letter.

Candle Rent.—A due or impost payable at Cambridge in ancient times. *Hist. of C. C. C.*, by Stokes, 1898, p. 29. But see Davies, *Suppl. Glossary*, 1881, p. 100, where the candle-rent seems to be satisfactorily explained.

Candle (Corpse), or Winding Sheet.—Corpse candles, says Grose, are very common appearances in the counties of Cardigan, Caermarthen, and Pembroke, and also in some other parts of Wales: they are called candles from their resemblance not to the body of the candle, but the fire; because that fire, says the honest Welchman, Mr. Davis, in a letter to Mr. Baxter, doth as much resemble material candle lights as eggs do eggs: saving that, in their journey, these candles are sometimes visible and sometimes disappear, especially if any one comes near to them, or in the way to meet them. On these occasions they vanish, but presently appear again behind the observer, and hold on their course. If a little candle is seen, of a pale bluish colour, then follows the corpse, either of an abortive, or some infant: if a larger one, then the corpse of some one come to age. If there be seen two, three, or more, of different sizes, some big, some small, then shall so many corpses pass together and of such ages or degrees. If two candles come from different places, and be seen to meet, the corpses will do the same; and if any of these candles be seen

to turn aside through some by-path leading to the church, the following corpse will be found to take exactly the same way. Sometimes these candles point out the places where persons shall sicken and die. They have also appeared on the bellies of pregnant women, previous to their delivery, and have predicted the drowning of persons passing a ford.

Candle (Religious Use of).—It appears from "Scogin's Jests," 1626, that in Henry the Eighth's time it was the custom to set two burning candles over the dead body. The passage is curious, as illustrative of more customs than one: "On Maundy-Thursday, Scogin said to his chamber-fellow, we wil make our maundy, and eate and drink with advantage. Be it, said the scholar. On Maundy-Thursday at night they made such cheere that the scholler was drunke. Scogin then pulled off all the schollers clothes, and laid him stark naked on the rushes, and set a forme over him, and spread a coverlet over it, and set up two tallow candles in candlesticks over him, one at his head, the other at his feet, and ran from chamber to chamber, and told the fellowes of that place that his chamber-fellow was dead: and they asked of Scogin if he died of the pestilence? Scogin said: no I pray you go up, and pray for his soule; and so they did. And when the scholler had slept his first sleepe, he began to turne himselfe, and cast down the forme and the candles. The fellowes of the house seeing that Scogin did run first out of the chamber, they and all that were in the chamber, one running and tumbling down on anothers neck, were afraid. The scholler, seeing them run so fast out of the chamber, followed them starke naked; and the fellowes seeing him runne after them like a ghost, some ran into their chambers, and some ran into one corner, and some into another. Scogin ran into the chamber to see that the candles should doe no harme, and at last fetcht up his chamber-fellow, which ran about naked like a madman, and brought him to bed; for which matter Scogin had rebuke." Hazlitt's *Old English Jestbooks*, ii., 55. In Herbert's "Country Parson," 1675, third impression, p. 157, he tells us, "Another old custom (he had been speaking of processions) there is, of saying, when light is brought in, God send us the light of Heaven; and the parson likes this very well. Light is a great blessing, and as great as food, for which we give thanks: and those that think this superstitious, neither know superstition nor themselves." The following is from Copley's "Wits, Fits and Fancies," 1595: "A gentlewoman in extremitie of labour sware that if it pleased God she might escape death for that once, she would never in all her life after hazard herselfe to the like daunger again; but being at last safely delivered, she then said to one of the midwives, ' So, now put out the holy candle, and keepe it till the next time." Comp. *Churching* and *Funeral Customs.*

Candles (Time).—There were no clocks in England in King Alfred's time. He is said by his biographer Asser, who is supposed to have died in 910, to have measured his time by wax candles, marked with circular lines to distinguish the hour.

Capon-Bell.—The following passage is in Dekker's "Strange Horse-Race," 1613. Speaking of "rich curmudgeons" lying sick, he says: "Their sonnes and heires cursing as fast (as the mothers pray) until the great capon-bell ring out." If this does not mean the passing bell, I cannot explain it.

Cappy-Hole. — This occurs, with other contemporary Scotish amusements, in the *Scotch Rogue*, 1722. It is also mentioned in the Notes to "Ancient Scotish Poems" from the Bannatyne MS. 1770, p. 251.

Cards, or the *Books of the Four Kings.* See Chatto's *Facts and Speculations on the History of Playing Cards*, 1848, Introductory Section. Cards seem to have evolved from chess, known in ancient times as *Chaturanga*, or the *Four Rajas*, which Edward I. learned to play in the Holy Land, and for which, in his wardrobe account, 8s. 5d. is delivered to him by Walter Sturton in 1278. The Arabians doubtless borrowed chess, if not cards, from India. Ducange cites card-playing as known to the modern Greeks in 1498; but it was familiar to Venice at a far earlier date, as in 1441 the Government of the Republic prohibited, on the prayer of the Painters' Gild, the importation of foreign cards, which paralysed the national trade. 1493 is the point of time fixed for their introduction into France in consequence of the necessity, after the King's seizure by sunstroke, for some amusement. This theory, however, is no doubt equally erroneous, since the cards described as being supplied to Charles VI. were evidently products belonging to a fairly advanced stage in the art, and, again, the French would have most probably received the idea from the Spanish Moors. The games alluded to in Benedictus Abbas, under the date 1190, did not include cards, which did not then exist in any shape, and were an accomplishment unknown to the ancient Greeks and Romans. But they may very well have played during the Crusades at various forms of dice. Cards are mentioned in the statute 11 Henry VII., c. 2 (1496). At a court held at Edgeware in 1551 two men were fined for playing at cards and draughts (*ad victas cartas et tabulas*),

which is a curious notice for so early a date, considering the presumed station of the offenders. Lysons' *Environs*, 1st edit., ii., 244. Richard Rice, in his *Invective*, 1579, has a curious passage on this subject: "Is the waie to attain godliness," he inquires, "by plaiyng, and sportyng, or resting of the wearie bones, with the bones of a paire of dice, or with a paire of cardes (otherwise nowe called the bookes of life) and though it be spoken but in iestyng, yet is it not altogether for naught, for the nature of some is to reste more in theim, and are more at quiete with the ace, kyng, queene, or varlet of spades, then thei can be with a spade to digge or delue honestly after Goddes preceptes for

CARD-PLAYING.
(*From an ancient MS.*)

their hiryng: yea, and delighte quietlier in the ace, king, queene, or varlette of the hartes, then thei dooe in the booke of life." Sir David Lyndsay, in his *Complaint*, enumerates cards among the amusements of the Scotish Court under James IV. and V., even of a bishop, and in 1503, when the former prince waited on his consort in the Castle of Newbattle, it is said: "The Kynge came prively to the said castell, and entred within the chamber with a small cumpany, whar he founde the quene playing at the cardes." Hazlitt's *Warton*, 1871, iii., 243. Warton, in a note to Lyndsay's Works, observes: "In our Author's tragedie of Cardinal Betoun, a soliloquy spoken by the cardinal, he is made to declare that he played with the

King (James IV.) for three thousand crowns of gold in one night, at cartis and dice." They (cards) are also mentioned in an old anonymous Scotish poem of Covetice. Dalrymple, *Anc. Scot. Poems*, 168. Lyndsay, in his *Satire of the Three Estates* (1535) makes the parson say that at various amusements, including *cartis*, he may above all others bear the prize. Cards were, from numerous references, in great vogue both in Scotland and on the Borders, even among the lower classes, in the sixteenth and seventeenth centuries. The stakes in the case of the humbler players were placks or hardheads, two coins of very small value in the old Scotish currency. Hall, of Cambridge, says: " For cardes, the philologie of them is not for an essay. A man's fancy would be sum'd up in cribbidge; gleeke requires a vigilant memory and a long purse; maw, a pregnant agility; pichet, a various invention; primero, a dextrous kinde of rashnesse, &c. *Horæ Vacivæ*, 1646, p. 150. Lord Worcester includes in his " Century of Inventions," 1663, two which may be thought to have been as well omitted. They refer to cheating tricks with cards and dice. " White silk," says his lordship, " knotted in the fingers of a pair of white gloves, and so contrived without suspicion, that playing at primero at cards, one may without clogging his memory keep reckoning of all sixes, sevens and aces, which he hath discarded." Again, the writer says: " A most dexterous dicing box, with holes transparent, after the usual fashion, with a device so dexterous, that with a knock of it against the table the four good dice are fastened, and it looseneth four false dice made fit for his purpose." Urquhart of Cromarty observes : " Verily, I think they make use of Kings, as we do of Card-Kings in playing at the Hundred; any one whereof, if there be appearance of a better game without him, (and that the exchange of him for another incoming card is like to conduce more for drawing of the stake), is by good gamesters without any ceremony discarded." *Discovery*, 1657, p. 237. Mr. W. H. Allnutt, of Oxford, found in a MS. diary of 1629 the following list: " Games at Chartes.—Ruffe, trumpe, slam'e, gleeke, Newcut, swigg, loadam, putt, primifisty, post and pair, bone-ace, anakin, seven cardes one and thirty, my sow has pig'd."

The earliest English example of an attempt to treat cards as an apologue appears to have been in the lost comedy of the *Play of Cards*, mentioned by Sir John Harington in his *Apologie of Poetrie*, accompanying his English *Ariosto*, 1591, in which, he tells us, is showed in Four Parasitical Knaves Four Principal Vocations of the Realme, videl. The vocation of soldiers, schollers, marchants, and husbandmen. The popular character of cards was the inducement to certain publishers to make them a vehicle of instruction in history and other topics; and we have from the time of James II. nearly to our own packs illustrated in a variety of ways, shewing historical episodes, leading points in geography, and even the outlines of grammar.

Card-tricks began at a very early date to be a deviation from the original and legitimate application of the objects, and Reginald Scot, in his *Discovery*, 1584, dedicates a section to the exposure of the frauds of sharpers of various types, among whom he tells us that there were some who affected, for the purpose of cosenage, to be drunk. In *A Notable Discovery of Cosenage*, 1592, *Dequoy, Mumchance, Catchdolt, or Irish One-and-Thirty, Non est possible, Dutch Noddy,* are quoted as the names of cheating games of cards then in vogue. In the margin of the text a note describes them as " the names of such games as Conycatchers vse."

Since Brand and Ellis wrote, several important works on this subject have appeared, particularly Singer's *Researches*, 1816, and Chatto's still more valuable work in 1848. See also P. Boiteau D'Ambly, *Cartes a Jouer et la Cartomancie*,1854, and the late Lady Charlotte Schreiber's monumental illustrated work. Copious notices of the different games will be found under their several heads and in the authorities there cited. In the 15th c. Italy had, besides chess, tables or backgammon, and triumphs or *tarocchi*, cards, running in suits like ours. These were usually *Cups, Swords, Coins, and Clubs.* Of these the *Tarrochi* were the most modern, and were composed of a series of 22 painted or engraved figures. The gambling tables were universally frequented, and reckless speculation on the part of both sexes prevailed. At Venice dice were introduced at a very remote date—perhaps the twelfth century—and chess was a favourite game among the higher classes. Hazlitt's *Venetian Republic*, 1900, i., 560, 758; ii., 456.

Care-Cloth. — Among the Anglo-Saxons the nuptial benediction was performed under a veil or square piece of cloth, held at each corner by a tall man, over the bridegroom and bride, to conceal her virgin blushes: but if the bride was a widow, the veil was esteemed useless. Strutt's *Manners and Customs*, i., 76. The most rational explanation of the meaning of *Care* here is that suggested in the last edition of Nares, 1859, making it equivalent to the Fr. *carré.* But I am afraid that Palsgrave, 1530, is wrong, as he and the author of the " Promptorium " (ed.

Way, in voce) intend an altogether different thing when they speak of Carde. See Scheller's Lex. art. Discerpiculum. According to the Sarum use, when there was a marriage before mass the parties kneeled together and had a fine linen cloth (called the care cloth) laid over their heads during the time of mass, till they received the benediction, and then were dismissed. In the Hereford Missal it is directed, that at a particular prayer the married couple shall prostrate themselves, while four clerks hold the pall, i.e., the care cloth over them. The rubric in the Sarum Missal is similar: "Prosternant se sponsus et sponsa in Oratione ad gradum Altaris: et tento pallio super eos, quod teneant quatuor Clerici in superpelliciis ad quatuor cornua." — *Missale ad Usum Sarum*, 1494. The York Manual differs here:—"Missa dein celebratur, illis genuflectentibus sub Pallio super eos extento, quod teneant duo Clerici in Superpelliceis." In the Appendix to Hearne's "Hist. and Antiq. of Glastonbury," p. 309, is preserved "Formula antiqua nuptias in iis partibus Angliæ (occidentalibus nimirum) quæ Ecclesiæ Herfordensis in ritibus Ecclesiasticis ordine sunt usi, celebrandi." The care-cloth seems to be described in the following passage: "Hæc Oratio 'S. propiciare Domini,' semper dicatur super Nubentes sub pallio prosternentes."

Careing Fair.—In the "Gentleman's Magazine" for 1785, p. 779, an advertisement, or printed paper, for the regulation of Newark Fair, is copied, which mentions that: "Careing Fair will be held on Friday before Careing Sunday"; and Mr. Nichols remarks on this passage, that he has heard an old Nottinghamshire couplet in the following words:

"Care Sunday, Care away,
   Palm Sunday, and Easter-day."

Carling, Carle or Care Sunday.—See *Passion Sunday.*

Carlings.—The vulgar, in the North of England, and also in the Midland Counties, give the following names to the Sundays of Lent, the first of which is anonymous:

"Tid, Mid, Misera,
   Carling, Palm, Paste Egg day."

This couplet is differently given by a writer in the "Gentleman's Magazine," for 1788, as follows:

"Tid, and Mid, and Misera,
   Carling, Palm, and Good-Pas-day."

The abbreviated form here found may present the commencing words of the Psalms: *Te Deum, Mi Deus,* and *Miserere mei.* In the "Festa Anglo-Romana," 1678, we are told that the first Sunday in Lent is called Quadragesima or *In-*

vocavit; the second, *Reminiscere;* the third, *Oculi;* the fourth *Lætare;* the fifth *Judica;* and the sixth *Dominica Magna. Oculi,* from the entrance of the 14th verse of the 25th Psalm. "Oculi mei semper ad Dominum," &c. *Reminiscere,* from the entrance of the 5th verse of Psalm 25, "Reminiscere Miserationum," &c., and so of the others. At Newcastle-upon-Tyne, and many other places in the North of England, and also in Lancashire and other counties, and in Scotland grey peas, after having been steeped a night in water, are fried with butter, given away, and eaten at a kind of entertainment on the Sunday preceding Palm Sunday, which was formerly called Care or Carle Sunday, as may be yet seen in some of our old almanacks. They are called carlings, probably, as we call the presents at fairs, fairings. In Yorkshire, as a clergyman of that county informed Brand, the rustics go to the public-house of the village on this day, and spend each his carling-groat, i.e., that sum in drink, for the carlings are provided for them gratis; and, he added, that a popular notion prevails there that those who do not do this will be unsuccessful in their pursuits for the following year. So in the popular old Scotish song, "Fy! let us all to the Briddel":

"Ther'll be all the lads and the lasses
   Set down in the midst of the ha,
With Sybows, and Risarts, and Carlings
   That are both sodden and ra."

Sybows are onions; and risarts radishes. The practice was a very ancient one; it is mentioned by Skelton in his *Colin Clout* (about 1520):

"Men call you therfor prophanes,
   Ye pycke no shrympes, nor pranes;
Salt-fyshe, stoc-fyshe, nor heryng,
   It is not for your werynge.
Nor, in holy Lenton season,
   Ye will netheyr benes ne peason.
But ye loke to be let lose,
   To a pygge or to a gose."

The above writer, in the "Gentleman's Magazine" for 1788, also gives a more particular account of the carlings or grey peas, and of the manner of dressing and eating them. See also "Gent. Mag." vol. lvi. p. 410, and Davis, *Suppl. Glossary,* 1881.

Carol (Christmas).—Dr. Furnivall thinks that the word Carol is derived from *Corolla* or *Chorolla.* Bishop Taylor observes that the "Gloria in Excelsis," the well-known hymn sung by the angels to the shepherds at our Lord's Nativity, was the earliest Christmas Carol. Bourne cites Durandus, to prove that in the earlier ages of the churches the bishops were accustomed on Christmas Day to sing carols among their clergy. This species of pious

song is undoubtedly of most ancient date.
Compare *Hagmena.* In 1521 was printed
a set of Christmas Carols. These, remarks
Warton, were festal chansons for enliven-
ing the merriments of the Christmas celebrity; and not such religious songs as are
current at this day with the common
people, under the same title, and which
were substituted by those enemies of innocent and youthful mirth, the Puritans,
The boar's head soused was anciently the
first dish on Christmas Day, and was carried up to the principal table in the hall
with great state and solemnity. For this
indispensable ceremony there was a carol.
"This carol," Warton adds, "yet with
many innovations, is retained at Queen's
College in Oxford," nor has it been discontinued since Warton's day. At present, it is usual for two atendants to bear
aloft into the hall on Christmas Day the
boar's head, on a large platter, preceded
by a fellow of the College in surplice: but
the head is fictitious, being merely a
painted counterfeit with a brawn enclosed.
Compare *Boar's Head.* William Cornish
received at Christmas, 1502, the sum of
13s. 4d. "for setting of a carralle upon
Christmas Day, in reward." In the "Para-
dyce of Daynty Devises," 1578, are hymns
by Jasper Heywood and Francis Kinwel-
mersh for Christmas Day, Whitsunday,
and Easter Day; and in the *Christmas
Prince,* 1607, occurs the carol sung by him
who brought into the hall the boar's head
at the celebration in St. John's College,
Oxford, in 1607. It is a species of burlesque. *The Christmas Prince,* ed. 1816,
p. 24. These older pious chansons were
sometimes borrowed from the early Christian poets, and the early Scotish writers
did not scruple to set their *guid and godly
ballates* to secular tunes. In the Churchwardens' accounts of St. Mary-at-Hill,
London, 1537, is the tantalizing entry:—
"To Sr. Mark for carolls for Christmas and
for 5 square Books. iijs. iiijd." Here is a
specimen from the first known impression
of the *Dundee Psalms,* 1578 :

"ANE SANG OF THE BIRTH OF CHRIST.

[*To be sung with the tune of Balulalow.*]
(*Angelus, ut opinor, loquitur.*)

"I come from heuin to tell
The best nowellis that euer befell ;
To yow the tythings trew I bring,
And I will of them say and sing.

This day to yow is borne ane Chylde
Of Mary meik and Virgin mylde ;
That blyssit bairne, bening and kynde,
Sall yow reioyce bath hart and mynde.

It is the Lord Christ, God and man,
He will do for yow what he can ;
Himself your Sauiour will be,
Fra sin and hell to mak yow fre.

He is your richt saluatioun,
From euerlasting dampnatioun,
That ye may ring in gloir and blis,
For euer mair in heuin with his.

Ye sall him find but mark or wying ,
Full sempill in ane cribe lying ;
Sa lyis he quhilk yow hes wrocht,
And all this warld maid of nocht.

Let us reioyce and be blyith,
And with the Hyrdis go full swyith,
And se quhat God of his grace hes done,
Throw Christ to bring vs to his throne.

My saull and lyfe, stand vp and se
Quha lys in ane cribe of tre,
Quhat Babe is that, so gude and fair?
It is Christ, Goddis Sone and air.
[.   .   .   .   .   .]

O God that maid all creature,
How art thow now becummin sa pure,
That on the hay and stray will ly
Amang the assis, oxin and ky?
[.   .   .   .   .   .]

O my deir hart, young Jesus sweit,
Prepair thy creddill in my spreit,
And I sall rocke the in my hart,
And neuer mair fra the depart.

But I sall praise the euer moir ,
With sangis sweit vnto thy gloir,
The kneis of my hart sall bow
And sing that richt Balulalow."
[.   .   .   .   .   .]

Lamb, in his Notes on the poem on the
"Battle of Flodden Field," 1774, tells us
that the Nurse's Lullaby Song, Balow (or
"He balelow"), is literally French, "He
bas! la le loup." "Hush! there's the
wolf."

At the end of Wither's "Fair Virtue,"
1622, is a "Christmas Carroll," in
which the customs of that season
are not overlooked. Among Herrick's
"Noble Numbers," is a "Christmas
Carol sung to the King in the presence at White Hall." The musical part composed by Mr. Henry Lawes.
Warmstrey, in his "Vindication of Christ's
Nativity, 1648, observes: "Christmasse
Kariles, if they be such as are fit for the
time, and of holy and sober composures,
and used with Christian sobriety and
piety, they are not unlawfull, and
may be profitable, if they be sung
with grace in the heart. New Yeares
Gifts, if performed without superstition, may be harmless provocations
to Christian love and mutuall testimonies thereof to good purpose, and
never the worse because the heathens have
them at the like times." In " Batt upon
Batt," a poem attributed to John Speed,
of St. John's College, Oxford, 1694, p. 4.

speaking of Batt's carving knives, &c., the author tells us:

"Without their help, who can good
　　Christmas keep?
Our teeth would chatter, and our eyes
　　would weep.
Batt is the cunning engineer, whose skill
Makes fools to carve the goose and shape
　　the quill :
Fancy and wit unto our meals supplies :
Carols, and not minc'd-meat, makes
　　Christmas pies.
'Tis mirth, not dishes, sets a table off ;
Brutes and phanaticks eat, and never
　　laugh."

In Goldsmith's time, as he tells us in his "Vicar of Wakefield," the rustics held the Christmas Carol in careful observance." "In the Scilly Islands they have a custom of singing carols on a Christmas Day at church, to which the congregation make contribution by dropping money into a hat carried about the church when the performance is over." Heath's *Account of the Scilly Islands,* p. 125.

A writer in the "Gentleman's Magazine" for May, 1811, says: "About six o'clock on Christmas Day, I was awakened by a sweet singing under my window; surprized at a visit so early and unexpected, I arose, and looking out of the window, I beheld six young women, and four men, welcoming with sweet music the blessed morn." In "Doctour Doubble Ale," a satire on the irregularities of the clergy in the time of Henry VIII., there is an anecdote of a parson who had a Christmas carol sung at a funeral. In a satirical tract, which was printed in 1642, the author, among other proposals made for the consideration of the Parliament, suggested that, "instead of carols, which farmers sonnes, and servants sing on Christ's Birth-day before they may eate or drink, you take order, that by some of your best City-Poets (who will write certainly to their capacity) there be some songs made of the great deeds that his Excelencie did at Worcester and Edgehill." *Antiq. Repert.,* 1807, iii., 32.

Several collections of old Christmas carols have been made since Mr. Brand's time. Among them may be mentioned the volume edited by Mr. Wright for the Percy Society, Mr. Sandys's book, and a little quarto volume edited by Dr. Rimbault, in which the carols are accompanied by the tunes. For a notice of all the early printed collections known to exist see my "Handbook of E. E. Lit." and *Bibl. Coll.* Art. Christmas. There are carols in many other books of usual occurrence, such as Tusser's "Points of

Husbandry," Aylet's "Wife not Ready Made but Bespoken," 1653, Herrick's "Hesperides," 1648, Furnivall's *Babees Book,* 1863, &c.

Carpet Knights, or Trencher Knights. — See Nares, *Glossary,* ed. 1859, in v. There is a scarce poetical volume, called *Pendragon, or the Carpet Knight, his Calendar,* 1698.

Carps (Ludus Carparum). — In a letter from Hearne to Dr. Richard Rawlinson, 1733, the former observes: "I am inquiring what sort of a game *Ludus Carparum* was. It is prohibited in some statutes, and is joined with cards, and reckoned as a kind of *alea.* . . . 'Twas, without doubt, call'd carps in English, and perhaps might be a sort of backgammon. The play was used in Oxford much; but being not mentioned in the New College statutes, I take it to have been brought up here since the foundation of that College." Nares and Halliwell render us no help here, nor Ducange.

Cartomancy. — The divination by cards, supposed to have been brought by the gypsies into Europe, and to have been familiar in the fifteenth century. See P. Boiteau D'Ambly, *Les Cartes à Jouer et la Cartomancie,* 1854.

Casting of Stones. — This is a Welsh custom, practised as they throw the blacksmith's stone in some parts of England. There is a similar game in the north of England called Long Bullets. The prize is to him that throws the ball furthest in the fewest throws. Compare *Quoits.*

Castor and Pollux. — Gregory observes: "Sailors have learned by experience that in great storms very frequently flames are seen upon the sails of ships, flashing hither and thither; these, if they appear double, portend the approach of a calm: if otherwise, sure and imminent shipwreck." He adds that through the superstition of ancient sailors the signs of Castor and Pollux were placed on the prows of ships. "Hoc certum satis, cum ejusmodi faculæ ardentes olim insidissent super capita Castoris & Pollucis ad Expeditionem Argonauticam, exinde Dioscuri in Deos indigites relati, et tanquam solida & sola Maris numina ab omnibus Navigantibus summa in veneratione habiti, cumque procellis suborientibus Tempestas immineat, astraque illa ab olim ominosa Antennis incubent, Castorem et Pollucem in auxilium adesse nemo dubitat." Pliny, in the second book of his *Natural History,* calls these appearances stars; and tells us that they settled not only upon the masts and other parts of ships, but also upon men's heads. Two of these lights forbode good weather and a prosperous voyage; and drive away the single one, which wears a threatening aspect. This the sailors call

Helen, but the two they call Castor and Pollux, and invoke them as gods. These lights do sometimes about the evening rest on men's heads. These appearances are called by the French and Spaniards inhabiting the coasts of the Mediterranean, St. Helmes or St. Telmes fires: by the Italians the fires of St. Peter and St. Nicholas, and are frequently taken notice of by the writers of voyages. Erasmus, in his dialogue entitled *Naufragium*, observes: " Nox erat sublustris et in summo malo stabat quidam e Nautis in Galea, circumspectans si quam terram videret: huic cœpit adsistere Spæra quædem ignea : id Nautis tristissimum ostentum est, si quando solitarius ignis est; felix, cum gemini. Hos Vetustas credidit Castorem et Pollucem. Mox globus igneus delapsus per funes devolvit sese usque ad Nauclerum : ubi paullisper commoratus, volvit se per margines totius Navis : inde per medios foros dilapsus evanuit. Fori sunt Tabulata Navis, ac veluti Tectum, sub meridiem cœpit magis ac magis incrudescere Tempestas." Cotgrave confirms what has already been said : " Feu d'-Helene, or Feu de S. Herme—St. Helens or S. Hermes fire ; a meteor that often appears at sea. *Dictionary*, 1650, vv. *Feu d'Heléne* and *Furote*. Among the apothegms at the end of Herbert's Remains, 1652, p. 194, is the following : " After a great fight there came to the camp of Gonsalvo the great Captain, a gentleman, proudly horsed and armed ; Diego de Mendoza asked the great captain, who's this ? who answered, 'Tis St. Ermyn that never appears but after a storm." Shaw tells us that in thick hazy weather he has observed those luminous appearances which at sea skip about the masts and yards of ships, and which the sailors call *corpusanse*, which is a corruption of the Spanish *Cuerpo Santo*. *Scotish Encyclopœdia*, v. *Lights*. Steevens quotes the subsequent passage from Hakluyt's Voyages, 1598 : " I do remember that in the great and boysterous storme of this foule weather, in the night there came upon the top of our maine yard and maine mast a certaine little light, much like unto the light of a little candle, which the Spaniards call the *Cuerpo Santo*. This light continued aboord our ship about three houres, flying from maste to maste, and from top to top ; and sometimes it would be in two or three places at once." *The British Apollo*, 1710, in reference to the vapor which by mariners is called a *corpo zanto*, usually accompanying a storm, informs us : " Whenever this meteor is seen, it is an argument that the tempest which it accompanied was caused by a sulphureous spirit, rarefying and violently moving the clouds. For the cause of the fire is a sulphurous and bituminous matter, driven downwards by the impetuous motion of the air and kindled by much agitation. Sometimes there are several of these seen in the same tempest, wandering about in various motions, as other ignes fatui do, tho' sometimes they appear to rest upon the sails or masts of the ship ; but for the most part they leap upwards or downwards without any intermission, making a flame like the faint burning of a candle. If five of them are seen near together, they are called by the Portugese *cora de nostra Senhora*, and are looked upon as a sure sign that the storm is almost over. Burton, in his " Anatomy," 1621, says that the " spirits or fire in form of fire-drakes and blazing-stars, sit on ship masts," &c. Hence the passage in the " Tempest " :

—" On the top masts,
The yards, and bowsprits, would I flame
distinctly."

Fryer, in his " Travels," quoted by Southey, observes. " I think I am not too positive in stating them to be a meteor-like substance, exhaled in the day, and at night (for except then they shew not themselves) kindled by the violent motion of the air, fixing themselves to those parts of the ship that are most attractive ; for I can witness they usually spent themselves at the spindles of the top-mast-heads or about the iron loops of the yard-arms, and if any went towards them they shifted always to some part of the like nature." So, in an account of " Fiery Impressions that appear mostly at Sea, called by mariners Castor and Pollux " : " When thin clammy vapours, arising from the salt water and ugly slime, hover over the sea, they, by the motion in the winds and hot blasts, are often fired ; these impressions will oftentimes cleave to the masts and ropes of ships by reason of their clamminess and glutinous substance and the mariners by experience find that when but one flame appears it is the forerunner of a storm ; but when two are seen near together, they betoken fair weather and good lucke in a voyage. The naturall cause why these may foretell fair or foul weather, is, that one flame alone may forewarn a tempest, forasmuch as the matter being joyn'd and not dissolved, so it is like that the matter of the tempest, which never wanteth, as winds and clouds, is still together, and not dissipate, so it is likely a storm is engendering ; but two flames appearing together, denote that the exhalation is divided, which is very thick, and so the thick matter of the tempest is dissolved and scattered abroad by the same cause that the flame is divided : therefore no violent storm can ensue, but rather a calme is promised." *History of Stormes*, 1704, p. 22.

Dickenson, in his *Greene in Conceipt*, 1598, p. 27, says :

"As when a wave-bruis'd barke, long
 tost by the windes in a tempest,
Straies on a forraine coast, in danger
 still to be swallow'd,
After a world of feares, with a winter of
 horrible objects—
The shipman's solace, faier Ledas
 twinnes at an instant
Signes of a calme are seen, and seene,
 are shrilly saluted."

Thomas Heyrick, a relative of the author of " Hesperides," writes :

"For lo ! a suddain storm did rend the
 air :
 The sullen Heaven, curling in frowns
  its brow,
 Did dire presaging omens show ;
 Ill-boding Helena alone was there."

Submarine Voyage, 1691, p. 2. The foregoing statements represent, for the most part, no scientific view of a subject, which was familiar to the ancients, even if they could not properly account for the phenomenon ; but is has long been reduced to an effect arising from natural causes ; and an excellent account of it may be found in the *Penny Magazine* for March, 1845. We should probably have never heard of this remarkable appearance, had our ancestors and preceding ages been acquainted with the laws of electricity and with metallic conductors.

Cat, or **Kit-Cat.**—In "The Captain," by Fletcher, written (and probably performed) before 1613, the cat-sticks, with which this game is played, are mentioned. Braithwaite, in his *Strappado for the Divell*, 1615, says :

"If mother Red-cap chance to haue an
 oxe
 Rosted all whole, O how you'le flye
  to it,
Like widgeons, or like wild geese in full
 flocks,
That for his pennie each may haue
 his bitte :

  * * * * *

Set out a pageant, whoo'l not thither
 runne?
As 'twere to whip the cat at Abington."

Lenton, in the "Young Gallants Whirligig," 1629, describes the young gallant (perhaps from personal experience), when he has reached the age for study, as preferring light literature to Littleton and Coke, and adds :

"———— instead of that
Perhaps hee's playing of a game at cat."

Poor Robin thus refers to it in his " Almanac " for 1709 :

"Thus harmless country lads and lasses
In mirth the time away so passes ;
Here men at foot-ball they do fall ;
There boys at cat and trap-ball.
Whilst Tom and Doll aside are slank,
Tumbling and kissing on a bank ;
Will pairs with Kate, Robin with Mary,
Andrew with Susan, Frank with Sarah.
In harmless mirth pass time away,
No wanton thoughts lead them astray,
But harmless are as birds in May."

Moor, in his *Suffolk Words*, describes it :—"A game played by boys. Three small holes are made in the ground triangularly, about twenty feet apart, to mark the positon of as many boys, who each holds a small stick, a little bigger than one's thumb, called cat, to be struck by those holding the sticks. On its being struck, the boys run from hole to hole, dipping the ends of their sticks in as they pass, and counting one, two, three, &c. as they do so, up to thirty-one, which is game. Or the greater number of holes gained in the innings may indicate the winners, as at cricket. If the cat be struck and caught, the striking party is out, and another of his sidesmen takes his place, if the set be strong enough to admit of it. If there be only six players, it may be previously agreed that three put-outs shall end the innings. Another mode of putting out is to throw the cat home, after being struck, and placing or pitching it into an unoccupied hole, while the in-party are running. A certain number of misses (not striking the cat) may be agreed on to be equivalent to a put-out. The game may be played by two, placed as at cricket, or four, or I believe more." The phrase " not big enough to whip a cat in" arose doubtless from this diversion, and not in reference to the animal so-called, although the contrary might be inferred perhaps from the well-known anecdote of Foote and his new house at Fulham.

Cat and Dog. — Jamieson tells us this is the name of an ancient sport used in Angus and Lothian. It is mentioned with other sports in the *Scotch Rogue*, 1722. "The following account," Jamieson adds, "is given of it." "Three play at this game, who are provided with clubs. They cut out two holes, each about a foot in diameter, and seven inches in depth. The distance between them is about twenty-six feet. One stands at each hole with a club. These clubs are called dogs. A piece of wood about four inches long, and one inch in diameter, called a cat, is thrown from the one hole towards the other by a third person. The object is, to prevent the cat from getting into the hole. Every time that it enters the hole, he who has the club at that hole, loses the club, and he who threw the cat gets possession both of the club and of the hole, while the former possessor is obliged to take charge of the cat. If the cat be struck, he who strikes it changes place with the person who holds the other club; and as often as these positions are changed, one is counted as won in the game, by the two who hold the clubs, and who are viewed as partners. "This is not unlike the stool-ball described by Strutt, but it more nearly resembles Club-ball, an ancient English game. It seems to be an early form of cricket."

Cat in Barrel.—"This is a sport which was common in the 18th century at Kelso on the Tweed. A large concourse of men, women, and children assembled in a field about half a mile from the town, and a cat having been put into a barrel stuffed full of soot, was suspended on a cross-beam between two high poles. A certain number of the whip-men, or husbandmen, who took part in this savage and unmanly amusement, then kept striking, as they rode to and fro on horseback, the barrel in which the unfortunate animal was confined, until at last, under the heavy blows of their clubs and mallets, it broke and allowed the cat to drop. The victim was then seized and tortured to death." *A Description of Kelso*, 1789. Steevens, on the passage in "Much Ado about Nothing":

"If I do, hang me in a bottle like a cat, and shoot at me";

observes that "in some counties in England, a cat was formerly closed up with a quantity of soot in a wooden bottle, (such as that in which shepherds carry their liquor), and was suspended on a line. He who beat out the bottom as he ran under it, and was nimble enough to escape its contents, was regarded as the hero of this inhuman diversion." He cites some passages that shew it was a custom formerly to shoot with arrows "at a catte in a basket." In a print entitled "Frost Fair," 1740, there is the following reference: "No. 6. Cat in the basket booth." Reed's quotations shew that a fictitious cat was sometimes used, and perhaps this booth was set apart for some sport not unlike cock-throwing (where a make-believe cock was oftener than not substituted for the real thing), or the modern Aunt Sally.

Cats.—Among omens, the movements of cats have always been regarded as important indications. The entrances and exits of strange cats are considered portentous by many even at the present time. When the cat washes its face, it was thought to be a sign of rain; so it was in Melton's time, and Herrick enumerates it among the current superstitions of his era, A modern writer maintains the same idea, and connects the practice with "the well-known disposition of that creature to the manifestation of electric phenomena." Couch of Polperro, *Illustrations of Instinct*, 1847, p. 13. But surely the cat washes its face after meals, as we do, or some of us, independently of the weather, and its neglect to perform this operation is usually ascribed to ill-health. Willsford remarks quaintly enough: "Cats coveting the fire more than ordinary, or licking their feet and trimming the hair of their heads and mustachios, presages rainy weather." This is explained elsewhere on scientific principles: "the moisture, which is in the air before the rain, insinuating itself into the fur of this animal, moves her to smooth the same and cover her body with it, so that she may less feel the inconvenience of winter, as, on the contrary she opens her fur in summer that she may the better receive the refreshing of the moist season."— *Athenian Oracle*, Suppl. 474. The poet-earl of Westmoreland had a cat with him in confinement, from which he used apparently to draw prognostications of the weather. The cat licking or scratching its ear was regarded in the light of an omen; and hence we get the well-worn proverb, "before the cat can lick her ear." The cat sneezing was considered as a lucky omen to a bride who was to be married the next day. Southey, when he was in Spain, found a belief current that the glossy appearance of the cat's skin portended fair weather. It was a vulgar notion, observes Mason, that cats, when hungry, would eat coals. In the "Woman's Prize, or Tamer Tamed," Tranio says to Moroso:

"I would learn to eat coals with an angry cat"—

and, in Fletcher's "Bonduca," the first daughter says:

"they are cowards,
Eat coals like compell'd cats—"

Trusler tells us, speaking of cats, that it has been judiciously observed that "the conceit of a cat's having nine lives hath cost at least nine lives in ten of the whole race of them. Scarce a boy in the street but has in this point outdone even Hercules himself, who was renowned for killing a monster that had but three lives," *Hogarth Moralized*, 134.

Brand seems to have thought that the prevailing antipathy to cats, which is incidental to many persons of the highest intelligence, was due to their supposed share in the sorceries of witches. The passage in Shakespear, where Lady Macbeth refers to the "poor cat in the adage," predisposes a dislike to wet, which has been generally ascribed to this animal. But the idea seems to be a popular fallacy. Even the tiger will wade some way into a river, and catch fish, General Robinson, an old Indian officer, once watched from a tree one engaged in this way, and continuing to catch and eat the fish till he was so surfeited that a buffalo, who had been tied to the tree as a bait, was left undisturbed, and the beast walked quietly off. In a *jeu-d'esprit* entitled " Les Chats," 8vo. Rotterdam, 1728, there are some very curious particulars relating to these animals, which are detailed with no common degree of learning. Compare *Witch's Cat.*

Catch-Fool. — This is named as a game, in the same sentence as Noddy, in Johnson's *Academy of Love,* 1641. It occurs under similar circumstances in a *Notable Discovery of Cosenage,* 1592; but it is there called *Catch-dolt.*

St. Catharine's or **St. Kattern's Day.** — (*November* 25). — Of St. Catherine of Alexandria, who is reputed to have suffered martyrdom on the wheel, whence we get the St. Catherine's wheel, there is an early metrical life printed in Halliwell's *Contributions to Early English Literature,* 1849. One of the ancient London Brotherhoods or Trading Gilds of Haberdashers was known as that of St. Catherine the Virgin. Hazlitt's Livery Companies, 1892, p. 115, 285. Camden says: " The very women and girls keep a fast every Wednesday and Saturday throughout the yeare, and some of them also on St. Catherine's Day; nor will they omit it though it happen on their birthday, or if they are ever so much out of order. The reason given by some for this is, that the girls may get good husbands, and the women better by the death or desertion of their present ones, or at least by an alteration in their manners." Woodes, in his *Conflict of Conscience,* 1581, tells us that we ought to pray to this Saint to cure " lawlessness of mind." St. Catharine is noticed in Naogeorgus as the favourer of learned men. The same writer adds :

" What should I tell what sophisters on Cathrins Day devise?
Or else the superstitious joyes that maisters exercise."

Miss Baker, in the appendix to her " Northamptonshire Glossary," 1854, says, in reference to the holiday on this day : " I have never been able to ascertain that it is observed at any place in this county, except at Peterborough, when, till the introduction of the new poor laws the female children belonging to the workhouse, attended by the master, went in procession round the city. They were all attired in white, and decorated with various coloured ribbons, principally scarlet; the tallest girl was selected to represent the queen, and was adorned with a crown and sceptre. The procession stopped at the houses of the principal inhabitants, and they sung the following rude ballad, begging for money at every house, as they passed along. (Here the ballad follows). St. Catharine being the patron of spinners, as well as of spinsters, and spinning being formerly the employment of the females in the workhouse, it naturally followed that they should be selected to commemorate the anniversary of this saint; and that this commemoration is of great antiquity appears from the early entries in the Dean and Chapter's accounts of payments, on St. Catherine's Day, for wheels and reels for the children of the workhouse." But a correspondent of " Notes and Queries," October 3rd, 1868, remarks that the usage, treated by the last writer as peculiar to Peterborough, is unquestionably of general observance in Northamptonshire, and is popularly supposed to be derived from one of the Queens Katherine in the time of Henry VIII.—probably Katherine Parr, who was a Northamptonshire woman. Mr. Plummer says, that this festival " is known to have been kept, for several generations, throughout the whole of the Northamptonshire lace-making districts, as well as those in Bedfordshire. By some it is called ' candle-day,' from its forming the commencement of the season for working at lace-making by candlelight. The popular tradition is that ' Queen Katherine was a great friend to the lacemakers.' " Another correspondent, in the same number, adds, that the wheelwrights also observe this as their holiday. Brome, in his " Travels," 1700, observes: " In Lothien, two miles from Edenburgh southward, is a spring called St. Katherines Well, flowing continually with a kind of black fatness, or oil, above the water, proceeding (as it is thought) from the parret coal, which is frequent in these parts; 'tis of a marvellous nature, for as the coal, whereof it proceeds, is very apt quickly to kindle into a flame, so is the oil of a sudden operation to heal all scabs and tumours that trouble the outward skin, and the head and hands are speedily healed by virtue of this oil, which retains a very sweet smell; and at Aberdeen is another well very efficacious to dissolve the stone, to expel sand from the reins and bladder, being good for the chollick and drunk in July and August, not inferior, they report, to the spaw in Germany." M. Le Roux de Lincy, in his " Livre des Proverbes Français," 1859, t. i. p. 119, notices two French proverbs relating to St. Catherine, but not the common one: " Coiffer Sainte-Catharine," i.e., to follow celibacy, or live and die an old maid. See " Notes and Queries," Oct. 31. 1868.

Cathern Bowl.—Mr. Halliwell, in his " Popular Rhymes and Nursery Tales," 1849, furnishes a set of verses sung by

Worcestershire children on this festival, "when they go round to the farmhouses, collecting apples and beer." "The Dean of Worcester," he adds, "informs me that the Chapter have a practice of preparing a rich bowl of wine and spices, called 'the Cathern Bowl,' for the inhabitants of the college precincts upon that day."

Catherning.—In the Churchwardens' accounts of Horley, Surrey, I find: "Mem. that reste in the hands of the wyffe of John Kelyoke and John Atye, 4 merkes, the yere of ower Lorde God 1521, of Sent Kateryn mony." "Mem. that rests in the hands of the wyff of John Atthy and the wyff of Rye Mansell, 3 pounds 2s. 9d. the yere of our Lorde God 1522, of Sent Kateryn mony." *Summa totalis S'cte Katerine* I[*irginis*] *Luminis*, remanet in manibus uxoris Johannis Peers et uxoris Wyl'i Celarer, an'o d'ni 1526, tres libras et undecim solidos. Summa totalis *S'cte Katerine Luminis*, remanet in manibus uxoris Wyl'i Cowper, & uxoris Thome Leakeford, an'o d'ni 1527, quatuor marcas. Summa totalis *Katerine Luminis*, remanet in manibus uxoris Thome Leakeforth, et uxoris Henrici Huett, an'o d'ni 1528, quatuor marcas. Item remanet in manibus uxoris Joh'is Bray, *de eodem Lumine*, anno supradicto 17s."—Ibid. Mr. Brand notes, that he bought the original MS. of Mr. Waight, bookseller in Holborn, Sept. 2, 1801, for 14s. According to La Motte, "St. Catherine is esteemed in the Church of Rome as the Saint and Patroness of the spinsters: and her holiday is observed, not in Popish countries only, but even in many places in this nation [France]: young women meeting on the 25th of November, and making merry together, which they call Catherning." "Essay on Poetry and Painting," 1730, p. 126.

Catoptromancy. — See *Glass (Looking)*.

Cattle Lore and Leechdom.— Reginald Scot tells us: Against witches "hang boughs (hallowed on Midsummer Day) at the stall door where the cattle stand." "Discovery of Witchcraft," 1584, ed. 1665, p. 144. He has "A special charm to preserve all cattel from witchcraft": At Easter, you must take certain drops that lie uppermost of the holy paschal candle, and make a little wax candle thereof: and upon some Sunday morning rathe, light it and hold it so as it may drop upon and between the horns and ears of the beast, saying, In nomine Patris et Filii, &c., and burn the beast a little between the horns on the ears with the same wax, and that which is left thereof, stick it cross-wise about the stable or stall, or upon the threshold, or over the door, where the cattle use to go in and out: and, for all that year your cattle shall never be bewitched." *Discovery*, p. 160. Browne, in his "Pastorals," 1613-14, alludes to what seems to have been a superstition in his time:

"Nor shall this helpe their sheep, whose stomacks failes,
By tying knots of wooll neere to their tailes:
But as the place next to the knot doth die,
So shall it all the bodie mortifie."

This is another form of the belief, which once actuated the farmers' wives in the Highlands, who used to tie a piece of red worsted thread round their cows' tails, to preserve them from evil influences. Coles tells us: "If asses chaunce to feed much upon hemlock, they will fall so fast asleep that they will seem to be dead: insomuch, that some thinking them to be dead indeed, have flayed off their skins, yet after the hemlock had done operating, they have stirred and wakened out of their sleep, to the griefe and amazement of the owners, and to the laughter of others. Wood nightshade, or bitter-sweet, being hung about the neck of cattell that have the staggers, helpeth them." *Introd.*, 1656, p. 69. Grose tells us that "a slunk or abortive calf, buried in the highway over which cattle frequently pass will greatly prevent that misfortune happening to cows. This is commonly practiced in Suffolk." A superstitious notion prevails in West Devonshire that, at twelve o'clock at night on Christmas Eve, the oxen in their stalls are always found on their knees, as in an attitude of devotion, and that (which is still more singular) since the alteration of the style they continue to do this only on the Eve of old Christmas Day. An honest countryman, living on the edge of St. Stephen's Down, near Launceston, Cornwall, informed Brand, October 28th, 1790, that he once, with some others, made a trial of the truth of the above, and watching several oxen in their stalls at the above time, at twelve o'clock at night, they observed the two oldest oxen only fall upon their knees, and, as he expressed it in the idiom of the country, make "a cruel moan like Christian creatures." Brand says: "I could not but with great difficulty keep my countenance: he saw, and seemed angry that I gave so little credit to his tale, and walking off in a pettish humour, seemed to marvel at my unbelief." There is an old print of the Nativity, in which the oxen in the stable, near the Virgin and Child, are represented upon their knees, as in a suppliant posture. This graphic representation has probably given rise to the above superstitious notion on this head."

"Charms," Pinkerton observes, "are the chief remedies applied for the diseases of animals. I have been myself acquainted with an Antiburgher clergyman in these parts, who pretended skill in these charms, two small pieces of wood, curiously wrought, to be kept in his father's cow-house, as a security for the health of his cows. It is common to bind into a cow's tail a small piece of mountain-ash-wood, as a charm against witchcraft. Few old women are now suspected of witchcraft: but many tales are told of the conventions of witches in the kirks in former times." *Heron's Journey through part of Scotland,* ii., 293. The minister of Logierait, Perthshire, writing in 1795, says: "Recourse is often had to charms, for the cure of diseases of horses and cows, no less than in the human species. In the case of various diseases, a pilgrimage is performed to a place called Strathfillan, forty miles distant from Logierait, where the patient bathes in a certain pool, and performs some other rites in a chapel which stands near. It is chiefly in the case of madness, however, that the pilgrimage to Strathfillan is believed to be salutary. The unfortunate person is first bathed in the pool, then left for a night bound in the chapel, and, if found loose in the morning, is expected to recover." *Stat. Acc.,* v. 84. "There is a disease," he adds, "called Glacach by the Highlanders, which, as it affects the chest and lungs, is evidently of a consumptive nature. It is called the Macdonalds' disease, 'because there are particular tribes of Macdonalds, who are believed to cure it with the charms of their touch, and the use of a certain set of words. There must be no fee given of any kind. Their faith in the touch of a Macdonald is very great.' " Similarly, the minister of Applecross, Co. Ross, describing the state of his parish about the same time, says: "There are none of the common calamities or distressful accidents incident to man or beast, but hath had its particular charm or incantation; they are generally made up of a group of unconnected words, and an irregular address to the Deity, or to some one of the saints. The desire of health, and the power of superstition reconciled many to the use of them; nor are they as yet, among the lower class, wholly fallen into disuse. Credulity and ignorance are congenial; every country hath had its vulgar errors; opinions early imbibed, and cherished for generations, are difficult to be eradicated."— *Stat. Acc. of Scotland,* iii., 379. Pennant tells us, in his "Tour in Scotland," "that the farmers carefully preserve their cattle

against witchcraft by placing boughs of mountain-ash and honey-suckle in their cow-houses on the second of May. They hope to preserve the milk of their cows, and their wives from miscarriage, by tying threads about them: they bleed the supposed witch to preserve themselves from her charms." Martin says: "It is a received opinion in these (the Western) Islands, as well as in the neighbouring part of the main land, that women, by a charm or some other secret way, are able to convey the increase of their neighbours cows' milk to their own use. and that the milk so charmed doth not produce the ordinary quantity of butter, and the curds made of that milk are so tough, that it cannot be made so firm as the other cheese, and also is much lighter in weight. The butter so taken away and joined to the charmer's butter is evidently discernible by a mark of separation, viz. the diversity of colours: that which is charmed being paler than the other. If butter, having these marks, be found on a suspected woman, she is presently said to be guilty. To recover this loss they take a little of the rennet from all the suspected persons, and put it into an eggshell full of milk : and when that from the charmer is mingled with it, it presently curdles, and not before. Some women make use of the root of groundsel as an amulet against such charms, by putting it among the cream. *Western Islands of Scotland,* p. 120.

Caul, or **Sely How.**—Cauls are little membranes found on some children, encompassing the head, when born, and which there may be some reason to ascribe to certain physical conditions between the man and the woman concerned, where unseasonable cohabitation has occurred. This is thought a good omen to the child itself, and the vulgar opinion is, that whoever obtains it by purchase will be fortunate, and escape dangers. An instance of great fortune in one born with this coif is given by Ælius Lampridius in his "History of Diadumenianus," who came afterwards to the sovereign dignity of the empire. This superstition was very prevalent in the primitive ages of the Church. St. Chrysostom inveighs against it in several of his homilies. He is particularly severe against one Prætus, a clergyman who, being desirous of being fortunate, bought such a coif of a midwife. Sir Thomas Browne thus attempts to account for this phenomenon: "To speak strictly," he says, "the effect is natural, and thus to be conceived: the infant hath three teguments or membranaceous filmes, which cover it in the womb, i.e. the corion, amnios, and allantois; the corion is the outward membrane, wherein are implanted the veins, arteries, and umbilical vessels, whereby its nourishment is conveyed; the allantois, a thin coat, seated under the corion, wherein are received the watery separations conveyed by the urachus, that the acrimony thereof should not offend the skin : the amnios is a general investment, containing the sudorous, or thin seriosity perspirable through the skin. Now about the time when the infant breaketh these coverings, it sometimes carrieth with it, about the head, a part of the amnios or neerest coat : which, saith Spigelius, either proceedeth from the toughness of the membrane or weaknesse of the infant that cannot get clear thereof and therefore herein significations are natural and concluding upon the infant, but not to be extended unto magical signalities, or any other person." Lemnius tells us, that if this caul be of a blackish colour it is an omen of ill fortune to the child; but if of a reddish one, it betokens every thing that is good. He observes "There is an old opinion, not only prevalent amongst the common and ignorant people, but also amongst men of great note, and physicians also, how that children born with a caul over their faces, are born with an omen, or sign of good or bad luck : when as they know not that this is common to all, and that the child in the womb was defended by three membranes." *Occult Miracles of Nature.* 1658, ii., 8. "In Scotland," says Ruddiman, "the women call a haly or sely How (i.e. holy or fortunate cap or hood), a film or membrane stretched over the heads of children new-born, which is nothing else but a part of that which covers the fœtus in the womb; and they give out that children so born will be very fortunate." *Glossary to Douglas's Virgil,* 1710. In the North of England, and in Scotland, a midwife is called a howdy or howdy wife. Grose says, that a person possessed of a caul may know the state of health of the party who was born with it : if alive and well, it is firm and crisp : if dead or sick, relaxed and flaccid. In Willis of Gloucester's "Mount Tabor," 1639, we are told that "There was one special remarkable thing concerning my self, who being my parents' first son, but their second child (they having a daughter before me), when I came into the world, my head, face, and foreparts of the body, were all covered over with a thin kell or skin, wrought like an artificiall veile; as also my eldest sonne, being likewise my second childe, was borne with the like extraordinary covering : our midwives and gossips holding such children as come so veiled into the world, to be very fortunate (as they call it), there being not one childe amongst many hundreds that are so borne; and this to fall out in the same

manner both to the father and the sonne being much more rare," &c. He goes on to make religious reflections thereupon, which are foreign to our present purpose. He entitles this chapter "Concerning an extraordinary veile which covered my body, at my comming into the world." Burton, in his "Anatomy," 1621, relates an odd story relevant to this part of the matter : "Guianerius speakes of a silly jealous fellowe, that seeing his child newborne included in a kell, thought sure a Franciscan that used to come to his house was the father of it, it was so like a friers cowle, and thereupon threatned the frier to kill him." A writer in the "Athenian Oracle" states that the virtues of the caul were transferred, in case it should be lost by the first owner, to the person who might find it.

This caul, thought medical in diseases, is also esteemed an infallible preservative against drowning, and, under that idea, is frequently advertised for sale in our public papers, and purchased by seamen. "To the gentlemen of the Navy, and others going long voyages to sea. To be disposed of, a child's caul. Enquire at the Bartlett Buildings Coffee House in Holborn. N.B. To avoid unnecessary trouble the price is Twenty Guineas."—*London Morning Post,* Aug. 21, 1779. I read also an advertisement, similar to the above, in the "Daily Advertiser," in July, 1790. In the "Times" for February 20, 1813, the following advertisement occurred : "A child's caul to be sold, in the highest perfection. Enquire at No. 2, Church Street, Minories. To prevent trouble, price £12." And, in the same newspaper for February 27, 1813, two advertisements of cauls together : Caul. A child's caul to be sold. Enquire at No. 2, Greystoke-Place, Fetter Lane."—"To persons going to sea. A child's caul, in a perfect state, to be sold cheap. Apply at 5, Duke Street, Manchester Square, where it may be seen." Advertisements of this nature still appear in the newspapers, and a very general belief continues to be entertained by the uneducated and more superstitious portion of the community in the virtue of child's cauls. Midwives used to sell this membrane to advocates, as an especial means of making them eloquent. They sold it also for magical use. Sir Thomas Browne says; " Thus we read in the Life of Antoninus by Spartianus, that children are sometimes born with this natural cap, which midwives were wont to sell to credulous lawyers, who held an opinion that it contributed to their promotion." Douce observes : "One is immediately struck with the affinity of the judges' coif to this practice of antiquity.

To strengthen this opinion it may be added that if ancient lawyers availed themselves of this popular superstition, or fell into it themselves, if they gave great sums to win these cauls, is it not very natural to suppose that they would feel themselves inclined to wear them?" Comp. Nares, *Glossary*, 1859, in v. "Etre né coiffé" is a proverb in the French language signifying birth under fortunate auspices, and the phenomenon occurs, when the child is born enveloped in the caul (a very rare event) so as to cover the head. In *Gil Blas* the robbers tell the hero of the story that he must have been *né coiffé* to fall into such good hands, since he had left Oviédo to seek his fortune. Livre 1, ch. iv. M. Le Roux de Lincy ("Proverbes Français," edit. 1859) has left a somewhat meagre account of this subject; but the present seemed to be hardly the proper place to supply his omissions. All the dictionaries tell us *what* a caul is; but none seems to say whence it arises, and the question may be worth putting whether it proceeds from physiological causes and from sexual relations at an advanced stage in the growth of the embryo. See *suprâ*. Its virtue is purely empirical.

Cent-Foot.—A game at cards, possibly the same as *foot-saunt* mentioned by Gosson in his *School of Abuse*, 1579. Roger, second Lord North of Kyrtling, who died in 1600, and who s ems to have been an ardent and unlucky gambler, mentions in his "Household Book" for 1575-6 having lost 15s. at Saint—probably this game of cent — on May 15, 1576. But 15s. was nothing to a man who frequently parted with £20 or £30 at one sitting. One cannot help suspecting that it was owing to his extravagance that the family estate fell shortly afterward into such hopeless decay. The game is referred to also by Braithwaite: "Playes at Cent-foot purposely to discover the pregnancy of her conceit." "Barnabæ Itinerarium," 1638, sign. H 2. and "Boulster Lecture," 1640, p. 163. Comp. Davies, *Suppl. Glossary*, 1881, p. 251.

Cerealia.—Shaw, in his account of Elgin and the Shire of Murray, tells us, "that in the middle of June, farmers go round their corn with burning torches, in memory of the Cerealia."

Chadwell, or St. Chad's Well.—Brand says: "I found on a visit to the source of the New River between Hertford and Ware, in August, 1793, an old stone inscribed 'Chadwell,' a corruption, no doubt, of St. Chad's Well. So copious a spring could not fail of attracting the notice of the inhabitants in the earliest times, who accordingly dedicated it to St. Chad, never once dreaming. perhaps, that in succeeding ages it should be converted to so beneficial a purpose as to supply more than half the capital of England with one of the most indispensable necessaries of human life."

Chameleon, The.—Ross asserts it to be true that this creature lives on air. (however Browne writes to the contrary), for the following reasons: "1. The testimonies both of ancient and modern writers, except a few, and the witnesses of some yet living, who have kept chameleons a long time, and never saw them feed but on air. 2. To what end hath Nature given it such large lungs beyond its proportion? Sure not for refrigeration; lesse lungs would serve for this use, seeing their heat is weak; it must be then for nutrition. 3. There is so little blood in it, that we may easily see it doth not feed on solid meat. 4. To what end should it continually gape more than other animals but that it stands more in need of air than they, for nutrition as well as generation? 5. He that kept the chameleon which I saw, never perceived it void excrements backwards: an argument it had no solid food."

Chancel. — Gilbert White says, in speaking of Selborne Church: "I have all along talked of the east and west end, as if the chancel stood exactly true to those points of the compass; but this is by no means the case, for the fabrick bears so much to the north of the east, that the four corners of the tower, and not the four sides, stand to the four cardinal points. The best method of accounting for this deviation seems to be, that the workmen, who probably were employed in the longest days, endeavoured to set the chancels to the rising of the sun." Hutton, speaking of St. Bartholomew's Chapel, Birmingham, observes : "The chancel hath this singular difference from others, that it veres toward the north. Whether the projector committed an error I leave to the critics. It was the general practice of the pagan church to fix their altar, upon which they sacrificed, in the east, towards the rising sun, the object of worship. The Christian Church, in the time of the Romans, immediately succeeded the Pagan, and scrupulously adopted the same method; which has been strictly adhered to." *History of Birmingham*, p. 113. It may not be generally known, that the presence of the monument of Shakespear in the chancel of Stratford Church was at all events partly due to his right to interment there as owner of the great tithes. Hazlitt, *Monograph on Shakespear*, 1903, pp. 46, 49.

Changeling. — It appears from Strype's Annals, under 1567, that then mid-wives took an oath, inter alia, not to "suffer any other bodies child to be set,

brought, or laid before any woman delivered of child in the place of her natural
child, so far forth as I can know and
understand. Also I will not use any kind
of sorcery or incantation in the time of
the travail of any woman." The word
changeling, in its modern acceptation,
implies one almost an idiot, evincing what
was once the popular creed on this subject, for as all the frail children were a
little backward of their tongue and seemingly idiots, therefore, stunted and idoti-
cal children were supposed changelings.

This superstition has not escaped the
learned Moresin : "Papatus credit alba-
tas Mulieres, et id genus Larvas, pueros
integros auferre, aliosque suggerere mons-
truosos, et debiles multis partibus ; aut ad
Baptisterium aliis commutare ; aut ad
Templi introitum." Papatus, p. 139.
It was thought that fairies could only
change their weakly and starveling
elves for the more robust offspring
of men before baptism, whence the
custom in the Highlands. One of the
methods of discovering whether a child
belongs to the fairies or not, is printed in
a book entitled "A Pleasant Treatise of
Witchcraft," 1673. In the highlands of
Scotland, as Pennant informs us, children
are watched till the christening is over,
lest they should be stolen or changed by
the fairies. This belief was entertained
by the ancients. Something like this obtained in England. Gregory mentions
' an ordinarie superstition of the old
wives, who dare not intrust a childe in a
cradle by itself alone without a candle."
This he attributes to their fear of night-
hags. In the "Gentle Shepherd," Bauldy
describing Mause as a witch, says of her :

"At midnight hours o'er the kirk-yard
    she raves,
And howks unchristen'd weans out of
    their graves."

To this notion Shakespear alludes when he
makes Henry IV., speaking of Hotspur,
in comparison with his own profligate son,
say as follows :

        "O that it could be prov'd
That some night-tripping fairy had ex-
    chang'd,
In cradle-cloaths our children where they
    lay,
And call'd mine Percy, his Plantaganet !
Then would I have his Harry, and he
    mine."

Spenser has the like thought in the first
book of the "Faery Queene" :
"From thence a fairy thee unweeting
    reft
There as thou slep'st in tender swad-
    ling band,

And her base Elfin brood there for thee
    left,
Such men do changelings call, so
    chang'd by fairy theft."

Willis relates a singular anecdote : —
' Vpon an extraordinary accident which
befel me in my swadling cloaths. When
we come to years, we are commonly told of
what befel us in our infancie, if the same
were more than ordinary. Such an accident (by relation of others) befel me within a few daies after my birth, whilst my
mother lay in of me being her second child,
when I was taken out of the bed by her
side, and by my suddain and fierce crying recovered again, being found sticking
between the beds head and the wall : and
if I had not cryed in that manner as I
did, our gossips had a conceit that I had
been quite carried away by the fairies
they know not whither, and some elfe or
changeling (as they call it) laid in my
room." He himself, however, discredit-
ing the gossips' account, attributes this
attempt to the devil. "Certainly, that
attempt of stealing me away as soone as
I was borne (whatever the midwives talk
of it) came from the malice of that archenemy of mankind, who is continually
going about seeking whom he may betray
and devoure." He concludes, "blessed
be the Lord our most gracious God, that
disappointed them then, and hath ever
since preserved and kept mee from his
manifold plots and stratagems of destruction : so as now in the seventieth yeare of
mine age, I yet live to praise and magni-
fie his wonderfull mercies towards me in
this behalfe." *Mount Tabor*, 1639, p. 92.
Gay, in his fable of the "Mother, Nurse,
and Fairy," laughs thus at the superstitious idea of changelings. A fairy's tongue
is the vehicle of his elegant ridicule :

"Whence sprung the vain conceited lye
That we the worid with fools supplye?
What ! give our sprightly race away
For the dull helpless sons of clay !
Besides, by partial fondness shown,
Like you, we doat upon our own.
Where ever yet was found a mother
Who'd give her booby for another?
And should we change with human
    breed,
Well might we pass for fools indeed."

Pennant, speaking of "the Fairy Oak,"
of which also he exhibits a portrait, relates (1796) this curious circumstance respecting it : "In this very century, a poor
cottager, who lived near the spot, had a
child who grew uncommonly peevish ; the
parents attributed this to the fairies, and
imagined that it was a changeling. They
took the child, put it in a cradle, and left
it all night beneath the tree, in hopes
that the *tylwydd têg* or fairy family, or
the fairy folk, would restore their own be-

fore morning. When morning came, they found the child perfectly quiet, so went away with it, quite confirmed in their belief." *Tour in Scotland*, 1796, p. 257.

Characts, or **Characters.** — Characts seem to have been charms in the form of inscriptions. "That he use ne hide ne charme, ne characte." Dugdale's *Orig. Jurid.*, p. 81. So Gower :

" With his carrecte would him en-
      chaunte."
" Through his carectes and figures."
" And his carecte as he was tawght
      He rad."

Confessio Amantis, Books i. and vi. In " Dives and Pauper," 1493, sign. C 2, we find censured : " Charmes in gadering of herbes, or hangynge of scrowes aboute man or woman or childe or beest for any seknesse with any scripture or figures and carectes, but if it be Pater Noster, Ave, or the Crede, or holy wordes of the Gospel, or of holy Wryt, for devocion nat for curiousite, and only with the tokene of the holy Crosse." In the " Burnynge of Paules Church," 1561, the author (Bishop Pilkington) writes : — " What wicked blindness is this than, to thinke that wearing prayers written in rolles about with theym, as S. Johns Gospell, the length of our Lord, the measure of our Ladye, or other like, thei shall die ne sodain death, nor be hanged, or yf he be hanged, he shall not die. There is to manye suche, though ye laugh, and beleve it not, and not hard to shewe them with a wet finger." Our author continues to observe that our devotion ought to " stande in depe sighes and gronings, wyth a full consideration of our miserable state and Goddes majestye, in the heart, and not in ynke or paper: not in hangyng written scrolles about the necke, but lamentinge unfeignedlye our synnes from the hart."

In the Earl of Northampton's " Defensative " we read : — " One of the Reysters which served under the Fernche Admirall, at the Siege of Poictiers, was found after he was dead, to have about his necke a purse of taffata, and within the same a piece of parchment full of characters in Hebrew ; beside many cycles, semicircles, tryangles, &c. with sundrie short cuttes and shreddings of the Psalmes. Deus misereatur nostri,' &c. ' Angelis suis mandavit de te,' &c. ' Super Aspidem et Basiliscum,' &c., as if the prophecies which properly belong to Christe, might be wrested to the safeguard and defence of every private man." *Defensative*, 1583, sign. O 4 verso, quoting *Histoire des Troubles*, livre viii. Lodge, speaking of curiosity, says : — " If you long to know this slave, you shall never take him without a book of characters in his

bosome. Promise to bring him to Treasure trove, and he will sell his land for it, but he will be couscened. Bring him but a table of led, with crosses, (and Adonai or Elohim written in it), he thinks it will heal the ague." *Wits Miserie*, 1596, sign. C 2. Ramesey says : " Neither doth fancie only cause, but also as easily cure diseases ; as I may justly refer all magical and jugling cures thereunto, performed, as is thought, by saints, images, relicts, holy-waters, shrines, avemarys, crucifixes, benedictions, charms, characters, sigils of the planets, and of the signs, inverted words, &c., and therefore all such cures are rather to be ascribed to the force of the imagination, than any virtue in them, or their rings, amulets, lamens," &c. *Elminthologia*, 1668, p. 289. Andrews tells us that " on all the old houses still existing in Edinburgh, there are remains of talismanic or cabalistical characters, which the superstition of earlier ages had caused to be engraven on their fronts. These were generally composed of some text of scripture, of the name of God, or, perhaps, of an emblematic representation of the Resurrection." *Continuation of Henry.* " To this kind," says Bingham, quoted by Bourne. " belong all ligatures and remedies, which the Schools of Physitians reject and condemn ; whether in inchantments or in certain marks, which they call characters, or in some other things which are to be hanged and bound about the body, and kept in a dancing posture. Such are ear-rings hanged upon the tip of each ear, and rings made of an ostriche's bones for the finger ; or, when you are told, in a fit of convulsions or shortness of breath, to hold your left thumb with your right hand." *Antiq. Vulg.* 1725, xxv. " It is recorded in divers authors (notes Mason) that in the image of Diana, which was worshipped at Ephesus, there were certaine obscure words or sentences, not agreeing together, nor depending one upon another: much like unto riddles written upon the feete, girdle and crowne of the said Diana : the which, if a man did use, having written them out, and carrying them about him, hee should have good lucke in all his businesses : and hereof sprung the proverbe *Ephesiæ Literæ*, where one useth anything which bringeth good successe." Our author also mentions the superstition of " Curing Diseases with certain wordes or characters." *Anotomie of Sorcerie*, 1612, 90. Compare Dr. Furnivall's *Political, Religious, and Love Poems*, 1866, p. 33, and *Love Charms*, infrâ.

Charms. — A charm has been defined to be " a form of word or letters, repeated or written, whereby strange things are pretended to be done, beyond the ordinary power of Nature." Mason derived the term from the Latin *carmen* (a verse or incantation). Lodge, speaking of lying, says: "He will tell you that a league from Poitiers, neere to Crontelles, there is a familie, that by a speciall grace from the father to the sonne, can heale the byting of mad dogs: and that there is another companie and sorte of people called sauveurs, that have Saint Catherines Wheele in the pallate of their mouthes, that can heale the stinging of serpents." *Wits Miserie*, 1596, pp. 12, 35. Felix, in his Anglo-Saxon Life of St. Guthlac (A.D. 749, or circâ), describes the cure of a man, whose flesh had festered through a prick from a thorn in the foot, by putting on the saint's garment. The biographer tells us in perfect good faith, that "no sooner was he (the patient) attired in the garment of so great a man, but the wound could not abide it: and lo! this same thorn, as an arrow speeds from the bow, so did it fly from the man, and go to a distance; and immediately at the same time all the swelling and all the wound departed from him, and he presently conversed with the holy man with blythe mood." Was this a physical or moral cure? For the sake of juxtaposition, the recovery of the Saxon boatman, "whose eyes had been for twelve months overspread with the white speck and dimness," by dropping on the afflicted organs some salt which the saint had consecrated, may be cited as a fair specimen of the credulity of former ages—a credulity after all, however, scarcely more gross than that we see at present around us. Gaule enquires "Whether pericepts, amulets, præfiscinals, phylacteries nioeteries ligatures, suspensions, charms, and spels, had ever been used, applyed, or carried about, but for magick and astrologie? Their supposed efficacy (in curing diseases and preventing of perils) being taught from their fabrication, configuration, and confection, under such and such sydereal aspects, conjunctions, constellations." His preceding observations upon alchymy are too pointed and sensible not to be retained: "Whether alchymie (that enticing yet nice harlot) had made so many fooles and beggars, had she not clothed or painted herself with such astrological phrases and magical practises? But I let this kitchen magick or chimney astrology passe. The sweltering drudges and smoky scullions (if they may not bring in new fuel to the fire) are soon taught (by their past observed folly) to ominate their own late repentance. But if they will obstinately persist, in hope to sell their smoak, let others beware how they buy it too dear." *Mag-astromancer posed*, p. 192.

Take the following passage: — "Others that they may colourably and cunningly hide their grosse ignorance, when they know not the cause of the disease, referre it unto charmes, witchcrafts, magnifical incantations, and sorcerie, vainely and with a brazen forehead affirming that there is no way to help them, but by characters, circles, figure-castings, exercismes, conjurations, and other impious and godlesse meanes. Others set to sale, at a great price, certaine amulets of gold and silver, stamped under an appropriate and selected constellation of the planets, with some magical character, shamelessly boasting that they will cure all diseases, and worke I know not what other wonders." The author concludes with the very sensible observation of "a great learned Clarke in our land, who in a daungerous sicknesse, being moved by some friends to use an unlettered Empericke, 'Nay, quoth he, I have lived all my life by the Booke, and I will now (God willing) likewise dye by the Booke."—*Beware of Pick-Purses*, 1605, p. 16 (a caveat against unskilful doctors). One of our early medical men, who turned author, favours us with some information under the present head, which may be worth preserving:—"If we cannot moderate these perturbations of the minde, by reason and perswasions, or by alluring their (the patients) mindes another way, we may politikely confirme them in their fantasies, that wee may the better fasten some cure upon them; as Constantinus Africanus (if it be his booke which is inserted among Galen's Works, de Incantatione, Adjuratione, &c.) affirmeth, and practised with good successe, upon one who was *impotens ad Venerem*, and thought himself bewitched therewith, by reading unto him a foolish medicine out of Cleopatra, made with a crowes gall and oyle: whereof the patient took so great conceit that, upon the use of it, he presently recovered his strength and abilitie againe. The like opinion is to bee helde of those superstitious remedies which have crept into our possession, of charmes, exorcismes, constellations, characters, pericepts, amulets, incense, holie-water, clouts crossed and folded superstitiously, repeating of a certaine number and forme of prayers or Ave Maries, offering to certaine saintes, * * * through the wedding ring, and a hundred such like toyes and gambols: which when they prevaile in the cure of diseases, it is not for any supernaturall vertue in them, either from God or the Divell, although perhaps the Divell may have a collaterall intent or worke therein, namely, to drawe us into superstition, but by reason of the confident perswasion which melancholike and passionate people may have in them;

according to the saying of Avicen, that the confidence of the patient in the meanes used is oftentimes more available to cure diseases then all other remedies whatsoever." Jorden's *Suffocation of the Mother*, 1603., p. 24. In Bell's MS. Discourse of Witchcraft I find the following : "28, Guard against devilish charms for men or beasts. There are many sorceries practised in our day, against which I would on this occasion bear my testimony, and do therefore seriously ask you, what is it you mean by your observation of times and seasons as lucky or unlucky? What mean you by your many spells, verses, words, so often repeated, said fasting, or going backward? How mean you to have success by carrying about with you certain herbs, plants, and branches of trees? Why is it, that fearing certain events, you do use such superstitious means to prevent them, by laying bits of timber at doors, carrying a Bible meerly for a charm without any farther use of it? What intend ye by opposing witchcraft to witchcraft, in such sort that when ye suppose one to be bewitched, ye endeavour his relief by burnings, bottles, horse-shoes and such-like magical ceremonies? How think ye to have secrets revealed unto you, your doubts resolved, and your minds informed, by turning a sieve or a key? or to discover by basons and glasses how you shall be related before you die? Or do you think to escape the guilt of sorcery, who let your Bible fall open on purpose to determine what the state of your souls is, by the first word ye light upon?"

Gay, in his "Pastorals," mentions the superstitious sowing of hempseed :

"At eve last Midsummer no sleep I
     sought,
But to the field a bag of hempseed
     brought;
—I scatter'd round the seed on every side,
And three times in a trembling accent
     cried,
'This hemp-seed with my virgin hand
     I sow ,
Who shall my true love be, the crop
     shall mow:
I straight look'd back, and, if my eyes
     speak truth,
With his keen scythe behind me came
     the youth.
'With my sharp heel I three times mark
     the ground,
And turn me thrice around, around,
     around.' "

Chaucer, in *Troilus and Cresseide*, writes :

"But canst thou playinraket to and fro,
Nettle in, docke out, now this, now that,
     Pandare— "

It appears from a communication to "Notes and Queries," that friction with a dock-leaf was then (as it is still) held in Northumberland to be a specific for the sting of a nettle. The charm to be repeated, while the rubbing process is proceeding, is :

"Nettle in, dock out,
Dock in, nettle out,
Nettle in, dock out,
Dock rub nettle out."

First Series, 111, 133. The remedy is mentioned by Fraunce in the Third Part of the Countess of Pembroke's Yvychurch, 1592. The subsequent charms were found by Mr. Brand in his Physical MS. of 1475:

"*A Charme to staunch Blood.*

Jesus that was in Bethleem born, and baptyzed was in the flumen Jordane, as stente the water at hys comyng, so stente the blood of thys Man N. thy servvaunt, thorw the vertu of thy holy Name — Jesu — and of thy Cosyn swete St. Jon. And sey thys charme fyve tymes with fyve Pater Nosters, in the worschep of the fyve woundys."

"*For Fever.*

Wryt thys wordys on a lorell lef ✠ Ysmael ✠ Ysmael ✠ adjuro vos per Angelum ut soporetur iste Homo N. and ley thys lef under hys head that he wete not therof, and let hym ete Letuse oft and drynk Ip'e seed smal grounden in a morter and temper yt with ale."

"*A Charme to draw out Yren de Quarell.*

Longius Miles Ebreus percussit latus Domini nostri Jesu Christi ; Sanguis exuit etiam latus ; ad se traxit lancea ✠ tetragramaton ✠ Messyas ✠ Sother Emanuel ✠ Saboath ✠ Adonay ✠ Unde sicut verba ista fuerunt verba Christi, sic exeat ferrum istud sive quarellum ab isto Christiano. Amen. And sey thys charme five tymes in the worschip of the fyve woundys of Christ.'

See also the Charms in Harl. MS. fol. 215 *verso*. Whitford, in his *Work for Householders*, 1530, observes : "The charmer is a good mà or a good womá & taketh here a pece of whyte breed / & sayth ouer that breed nothynge but onely ye Pat. nr. & maketh a crosse vpon ye breed / whiche thynges ben all good / than doth he nothynge els but lay ye pece of breed vnto ye tothe yt aketh or vnto ony other sore / turnynge ye crosse vnto ye sore or dysease / & so is ye persone healed." The writer calls this practice "euyll & dápnable." Ed. 1533, sign. C. 2 *verso*. In Bale's "Interlude concerning Nature, Moses, and Christ," 1538, idolatry is described with the following qualities :—

Mennes fortunes she can tell;
She can by sayenge her Ave Marye,
And by other charmes of sorcerye,
Ease men of the toth ake by and bye
  Yea, and fatche the Devyll from Hell.

And the same personage says:
With holy oyle and Water
I can so cloyne and clatter,
That I can at the latter
  Many sutelties contryve:

I can worke wyles in battell,
If I but ones do spattle
I can make corne and cattle
  That they shall never thryve.

   *   *   *   *   *

When ale is in the fat,
If the bruar please me nat
The cast shall fall down flat
  And never have any strength:

No man shall tonne nor bake
Nor meate in season make
If I agaynst him take
  But lose his labour at length.

   *   *   *   *   *

Theyr wells I can up drye,
Cause trees and herbes to dye
And slee all pulterye
  Whereas men doth me move:

I can make stoles to daunce
And earthen pottes to praunce,
That none shall them enhaunce,
  And I do but cast my glove.

I have charmes for the ploughe,
And also for the cowghe
She shall gyve mylke ynowghe
  So long as I am pleased:

Apace the myll shall go
So shall the credle do
And the musterde   querne also
  No man therwyth dyseased.

—Edit. 1562, sign. C 1-2. These specifics appear to partake, like others mentioned above under *Burlesque*, of a semi-serious character. Lord Northampton inquires: "What godly reason can any man alyve alledge why Mother Joane of Stowe, speaking these wordes, and neyther more nor lesse,

Our Lord was the first Man,
That ever thorne prick'd upon:
It never blysted nor it never belted,
And I pray God, nor this not may.

should cure either beasts, or men and women from diseases?" *Defensative*, 1583, sign. O04. Buttes, in his *Dyetts Dry Dinner*, 1599, asserts that "If one eate three small pomegranate flowers (they say) for an whole yeare he shall be safe from all maner of eye-sore." And that "It hath bene and yet is a thing which superstition hath beleeued, that the body anoynted with the iuyce of cichory is very availeable to obtaine the

fauour of great persons." King James enumerates 'Such kinde of charmes as commonly daft wives use for healing forspoken goods" (by goods he means here cattle) "for preserving them from evill eyes, by knitting roun trees, or sundrie kind of herbes, to the haire or tailes of the goodes, by curing the worme, by stemming of blood; by healing of horse crookes, by turning of the riddle; or by doing of such like innumerable things by words, without applying anything meete to the part offended, as mediciners doe: or else by staying married folkes to have naturally adoe with other, by knitting so many knots upon a point at the time of their marriage." *Demonology*, p. 100. Camden tells us that "to prevent kites from stealing their chicken, they hang up in the house the shells in which the chickens were hatched." Gough's edit. 1789, iii., 659. Lambarde, speaking of Kemsing, Kent, tells us that the farmers of that neighbourhood used to offer corn to the image of Edith, daughter of King Edgar, and Prioress of Wilton in Wiltshire, to protect their crops from mildew and other mishaps, and that the priest would take a handful of the quantity (keeping the rest himself, says Lambarde), sprinkle it with holy water, mumble a few words of conjuration over it, and then deliver it to the bringer to mingle with the whole harvest, to which it was supposed and pretended to communicate a sort of sanctity. *Perambulation of Kent*, 1570, ed. 1826, p. 457-8. Sir Thomas Browne mentions a rural charm against dodder, tetter, and strangling weeds, by placing a chalked tile at the four corners, and one in the middle of the fields, which though ridiculous in the intention, was rational in the contrivance, and a good way to diffuse the magic through all parts of the area *Quincunx Artificially Considered*, p. 111. I do not recollect to have seen the following mentioned among restoratives except in one of Webster's plays, Laodamia, in a mock-epistle to Protesilaus, says that when she faints,

"Under my nose they burn a feather,
And old shoes too with other leather,

—*Ovidius Exulans*, 1673, v. 51. The following rural charms are found in Herrick:
"This I'le tell ye by the way,
Maidens, when ye leavens lay,
Crosse your dow, and your dispatch
Will be better for your batch."

"In the morning when ye rise,
Wash your hands and cleanse your eyes.
Next be sure ye have a care
To disperse the water farre

For as farre as that doth light
So farre keeps the evil spright."

"If ye feare to be affrighted,
When ye are (by chance) benighted :
In your pocket, for a trust
Carrie nothing but a crust :
For that holie piece of bread
Charmes the danger and the dread."

Some other metrical charms noticed by Pepys in his *Diary*, under Dec. 31, 1664-5, may here be introduced :

"Unto the Virgin Mary our Saviour
was born,
And on his head he wore the crown of
thorn ;
If you believe this true and mind it
well,
This hurt will never fester, nor yet
swell."

The following one is for a scald or burn :

"There came three angels out of the
west,
One brought fire and two brought frost :
Out fire, and in frost,
In the name of Father, Son, and Holy
Ghost."

"Christ was of a virgin born,
And he was pricked by a thorn ;
And it did neither bell nor swell,
As I trust in Jesus this never will."

In "Trinum Magicum," p. 169, it is said : "Herbam Urticani tenens in manu cum millefolio, securus est ab omni metu, et ab omni phantasmate."

Shaw gives the following account, from personal observation, of some physical charms used in his time in Moray. In hectic and consumptive diseases they pared the nails of the fingers and toes of the patient, put these parings into a rag cut from his clothes, then waved their hand with the rag thrice round his head, crying *Deas soil*, after which they buried the rag in some unknown place. Pliny, in his "Natural History," mentions it as practised by the magicians or Druids of his time. When a contagious disease entered among the cattle, the fire was extinguished in some villages round ; then they forced fire with a wheel or by rubbing a piece of dry wood upon another, and therewith burned juniper in the stalls of the cattle, that the smoke might purify the air about them : they likewise boiled juniper in water, which they sprinkled upon the cattle ; this done, the fires in the houses were rekindled from the forced fire. It was, no doubt, a Druid custom. Hist. of Moray, p. 248. Coles says : "It is said that if a handfull of arsmart be put under the saddle, upon a tired horse's back, it will make him travaile fresh and lustily : If a footman take mugwort and put into his shoes in the morning, he may goe forty miles before noon and not be weary. The seed of fleabane (says he) strewed between the sheets causeth chastity. If one that hath eaten comin doe

but breathe on a painted face, the colour will vanish away straight. The seeds of docks tyed to the left arme of a woman do helpe barrenesse. All kinde of docks have this property, that what flesh, or meat, is sod therewith, though it be never so old, hard, or tough, it will become tender and meet to be eaten. Calamint will recover stinking meat, if it be laid amongst it whilst it is raw. The often smelling to basil breedeth a scorpion in the brain. That the root of male-piony dryed, tied to the neck, doth help the incubus, which we call the mare. That if maids will take wild tansey, and lay it to soake in buttermilke nine days, and wash their faces therewith, it will make them look very faire " (—a belief, which is also held in respect to May dew, as elsewhere stated). *Intro. to the Knowledge of Plants*, 1656, p 68. "Dew cakes with honey were given to those who entered Trophonius' Cave, to free them from any mischiefs from the phantoms which should appear. Loier's *Treatise of Spectres*, 1605, p. 136. Bulbianus says, that where Purslain is laid in the bed, those in it will not be disturbed by any vision that night. A diamond fastened to the left arm, so as to touch the skin, prevents all nocturnal fears To expel phantoms and rid people of folly, take the precious stone chrysolite, set it in gold, and let them weare it about em." Ostanes the magician prescribed the dipping of our feet in the morning in human urine as a preservative *against* charms. Warner, speaking of the old register of Christ Church, Hants, tells us that it contains some curious receipts of the seventeenth century in certain cases of indisposition, which his delicacy, however, forbad him to make public. *Hampshire*, 1795, 111, 131.

Mungo Park observes in his Travels in the interior of Africa that white chicken tied by the leg to a branch of a particular tree was thought by the people there to secure a prosperous issue to one's journey. Homer relates how Autolycus's sons staunched Ulysses's blood, flowing from a wound he received in hunting a wild boar, by a charm ; the same is observed by Pliny, who adds farther that 'sic Theophrastus ischidiacos sanari, Cato prodidit luxatis membris carmen auxiliari, Marcus Varro pod agris' : it was reported by Theophrastus, that the hip-gout was cured in the same manner ; by Cato, that a charm would relieve any member out of joint ; and by Marcus Varro, that it would cure the gout in the feet. Chiron in Pindar is said to use the same remedy in some distempers, but not in all."—Potter's *Greek Antiq.* i., 355. Grose observes that "Certain herbs, stones, and other substances ;

as also particular words written on parchment, as a charm, have the property of preserving men from wounds in the midst of a battle or engagement. This was so universally credited, that an oath was administered to persons going to fight a legal duel, 'that they had no charm, ne herb of virtue.' The power or rendering themselves invulnerable is still believed by the Germans: it is performed by divers charms and ceremonies: and so firm is their belief of its efficacy, that they will rather attribute any hurt they may receive, after its performance, to some omission in the performance, than defect in its virtue."

In the "Daily Telegraph" newspaper for December 11th, 1867, occurs this extraordinary piece of intelligence: "On the 9th inst., before the magistrates at Plymouth, a respectably dressed woman named Mary Catharine Murray, and who is about fifty years of age, was charged, under a warrant, with having 'unlawfully used certain subtle means and devices, to wit by a piece of parchment called a charm, and other subtle means to deceive and impose on one of her Majesty's subjects named Thomas Rendle.' The story told by Rendle, who is a poor farm labourer, living at Modbury is to the following effect: His wife, who is sixty-two years old, was taken ill about five months ago. He thought she was 'ill-wished,' and a nephew of his recommended him to go to the prisoner, as he was sure she, being wise, could cure the old woman. Rendle went to the prisoner's house in Plymouth on the 7th of August. She asked him what he was come for and he said, 'People tell me that my wife is ill-wished.' Prisoner asked him his age, and he told her 69. She opened a large book—her in two or three weeks, provided he him if he came for himself or any other person. He said he had come for his wife. She asked him his wife's age, and he said 62 next January. She said she could cure her in two or three weeks, provided she paid her one guinea to begin with. Prisoner said his wife had to go and see the planets, and would have to go into the churchyard and gather some herbs for twenty-one nights. She promised to send some medicine, and took down his address, and he then left. The following letter was sent to him about a week after: 'Sir and Madam—I find that it will be needful for you to have some powders to use, and a packet to wear. I have sent for the articles to make the powders. They will cost me 1s. each powder, and you will need to use two a day for three weeks. That will make 42 in the whole, and the packet, or the skin which makes the packet, will cost me 21s. That will last you as long as you live, if it should be 80 years longer.

The things I bought for you cost me 6s., and that will make £3 9s. You must have the things, and I should not send to you, but I am out of money, and the articles will be waiting at the station for me on Friday, so if you will remit me the money by the return of post, I will send it to you on Saturday, as you must put it on on Sunday, and also begin to use the powders on that day. Be sure you do not fail to send me an answer by return of post, and believe me to remain yours truly, M. C. MURRAY.' His wife had to take the medicine in a glass in the morning and evening. The packets of powder were to be burnt in the fire, one in the morning and the other in the evening. His wife took all the medicine, and she was at present worse. About two months afterwards the prisoner came to his house. She had a glass of water, and he saw some shadows in the water, and at her bidding his wife took up a poker and smashed the glass. The prisoner said she had seen a man and woman in the water, and the woman was the worst. She gave them a piece of parchment, on which were figures of the planets and extracts from foreign languages; this his wife was to wear. The prisoner then felt his wife's pulse. Altogether he paid the prisoner £4 10s. The prisoner acknowledged that what Rendle said was all true. He had thirty-one bottles of herbal mixture, at 3s. per bottle. She assured the magistrates that she believed in what they were pleased to call superstition. Rendle's niece said she had frequently seen the prisoner for the purpose of returning empty bottles, and also to get medicine. The prisoner had given her mother-in-law some powders to burn in her own room, which the prisoner said would do her good. The prisoner told her that her mother-in-law was ill-wished, and afterwards said she was bewitched. Her mother-in-law had had the parish doctor at Modbury attending her. The Mayor: Is the money paid to the prisoner the scrapings this old man has got together? Witness: Yes, sir; he has 10s. a week. The prisoner ordered the 91st Psalm to be read when the last powder packet was sent. The person that burnt the powder was to read the Psalm. The prisoner generally sent two packets at a time with the bottles. The prisoner denied saying anything about the Psalms, or about the woman being bewitched. The powders sent were for her to smell. She had cured Mr. Rendle's niece of paralysis. A Magistrate: Was there any charm in that case?—Prisoner: No, sir. After a short deliberation, the Mayor said, that as the prisoner had only just been apprehended, the Bench thought it right not to deal with the case then, and therefore would remand her until Thursday next.

Bail was refused." Such examples of ignorance in the latter half of the nineteenth century seem to shew that the time has come for initiating a general system of lay-education among the people. The subject of charms is one on which several volumes might be written. The nine series of "Notes and Queries" already completed contain a vast assemblage of material and illustration; and every week adds to the store. Fortunately, the excellent indexes supplied to that useful periodical render it worse than superfluous to transplant hither more than occasional passages. In the "Saxon Leech-

and Nursery Tales," 1849, and from Hazlitt's *Proverbs*, 1882.

Chase.—A point at the game of tennis beyond that struck by the adversary. Halliwell in v.

Chasing the Cheese.—At Birdlip, near Cheltenham, there is an ancient anniversary observance so termed. Its origin is not known, but it may be suggested that it has some consanguinity with an episode or traditional incident narrated in the *Gothamite Tales*, attributed to Andrew Borde, where the fourth story deals with a man of Gotham, who went to Nottingham to sell cheese, and, descending

CHESS-PLAYING.
(From an ancient MS.)

doms, and Wart Cunning, and Starcraft," edited by Mr. Cockayne, is a mass of matter on this subject. There are some curious charms in the "Mountebank's Masue," edited for the Shakespear Society, 1848, and in "Lancashire Folk-Lore," 1867. See several curious charms against thieves in Scot's Discovery of Witchcraft, b. ii. c. 17, and particularly St. Aldelbert's curse against them. That celebrated curse in Tristram Shandy, which is an original one, still remaining in Rochester Cathedral, is nothing to this, which is perhaps the most complete of its kind. Some additions to this section might easily have been introduced from Halliwell's "Popular Rhymes

the hill to Nottingham-bridge, one of his cheeses fell out of the cart, and rolled down the hill. Whereupon, seeing that they could run alone, he let loose all the others, charging them to meet him in the market place. But when he found they were not there, all having strayed or been taken, he took horse, and rode toward York, whither he conceived that they might have gone. Hazlitt's *Old English Jest Books*, 1864, iii., 6-7.

Chatelaine.—An article of use and ornament originating with the mediæval *chatelaine* or lady of the chateau. "An old marchant had hanging at his girdle, a pouch, a spectacle-case, a punniard, a pen and inckhorne, and a hand-kertcher, with many other trinkets besides: which a merry companion seeing, said, it was like a haberdashers shop of small wares."— Copley's *Wits, Fits, and Fancies*, 1595. In Erondel's "French Garden," 1605, in a dialogue describing a lady's dress, the mistress thus addresses her waiting woman: "Give me my girdle, and see that all the furniture be at it: looke if my cizers, the pincers, the pen-knife, the knife to close letters, with the bodkin, the ear-picker, and the seale be in the case: where is my purse to weare upon my gowne," &c. In Field's "A Woman's a Weather-cocke" act v. sc. 1, Bellafront is introduced with a knife hanging at her girdle, with which she threatens to stab herself if her father forces her to marry any other than Scudmore. This seems to have been a forerunner of the modern chatelaines, which some years ago were so favourite an article of ornament among our country-women, and were made receptacles for trinkets, keys, scissors, &c. Mr. Brand had an old print of a female foreigner entitled "Forma Pallii Mulieris Clevensis euntis ad forum," in which are delineated, as hanging from her girdle, her purse, her keys, and two sheathed knives.

Cheek.—Melton observes that " when the left cheek burnes, it is a signe somebody talks well of you; but if the right cheek burnes, it is a sign of ill." *Astrologaster*, 1620, p. 45. In a later writer we read: "That you shou'd think to deceive me! Why all the while I was last in your company, my heart beat all on that side you stood, and my cheek next you burnt and glow'd." Ravenscroft's *Canterbury Guests*, p. 20.

Cheesecake.—By the following passage in Ferne's "Glory of Generositie," p. 71, it should seem that cheesecakes composed a principal dainty at the feast of sheep-shearing. "Well vor your paines (if you come to our sheep-shearing veast) bum vaith yous taste of our cheese cake." This is put into the mouth of Columell the Ploughman.

Cherry Fair. — Cherry-fairs were often formerly, and may be still indeed, held in the cherry orchards; they were scenes of considerable licence. There are not many allusions to them in old writers or records; but in the story of "How the Wise Man Taught His Son," the transitory nature of man's life is not inelegantly likened to one of these scenes of temporary bustle and gaiety :

"And so, sone, thys worldys wele
Hyt fayrth but as a chery fayre."

And the same simile occurs in one of Hocclove's pieces. See Dyce's Skelton, ii., 85, and *Fairs*, infrâ.

Cherry Pit. — Cherry Pit is a play wherein they pitch cherry-stones into a little hole. It is noticed in Herrick's "Hesperides," 1648. But the earliest allusion to the sport is probably that found in the interlude of " The Worlde and the Chylde," 1522 :

"I can play at the chery pytte,
And I can wystell you a fytte,
Syres, in a whylowe ryne.'"

It is also mentioned by Skelton in " Speke Parot," written about the same time.

Chess.—This was a British or Welsh game, and is mentioned in the Triads. The board, on which it was played, was called the *tawlbwrd*, and one of these was held to be an essential feature in every gentleman's establishment. Chess-boards were made of wood, bone, or even ivory, the last being valued at three cows or sixty pence. Chess was also a favourite game in mediæval Italy and elsewhere abroad.

Chester.—King, speaking of the inhabitants of Chester, says, "touching their housekeeping, it is bountiful and comparable with any other shire in the realm: and that is to be seen at their weddings and burials, but chiefly at their wakes, which they yearly hold (although it be of late years well laid down)." *Vale Royal of England*, 20. In the same work there is an account that, at the City of Chester in the year 1533, " the offerings of ball and foot-balls were put down, and the silver bell offered to the Maior on Shrove Tuesday." *Vale Royal*, p. 94. King notes: " Anno 1575. This year Sir John Savage, maior, caused the Popish plays of Chester to be played the Sunday, Munday, Tuesday, and Wednesday after Mid-somer-Day, in contempt of an inhibition, and the Primat's Letters from York and from the Earl of Huntingdon." *Vale-Royal*, 1656, p. 88. "Anno 1563, upon the Sunday after Midsummer Day the History of Eneas and Queen Dido was play'd in the Roods Eye; and were set out by one William Croston, gent. and one Mr. Man, on which triumph there was made two forts and shipping on the water, besides many horsemen well armed and appointed." Collier's *Annals of the Stage*, 1831, i., 168, *et seqq.* We farther learn that Henry Hardware, Esq., mayor of Chester in 1599, " for his time, altered many antient customs, as the shooting for the sheriff's breakfast: the going of the giants at Midsommer, &c., and would not suffer any playes, bear-baits, or bull-bait." *Vale Royal*, 1656, p. 208. Pennant tells us of the place without the walls called the Rood Eye, where the lusty youth in former days exercised themselves in manly sports of the age; in archery, running, leaping, and wrestling; in mock fights and gallant and romantic triumphs. A standard was the prize of emulation, which was won in 1578 by Sheriff Montford on Shrove-Tuesday.

Childbirth.—In "A short Description of Antichrist," &c., 1554, is this passage: "I note all their Popishe traditions of confirmacion of yonge children wth oynting of oyle and creame, and with a ragge knitte aboute the necke of tho yonge babe," &c. This was the hallowed sheet. Bulwer remarks that "There is a tradition our midwives have concerning children borne open-handed, that such will prove of a bountiful disposition and frankhanded." The following occurs in the second part of Dekker's "Honest Whore," 1630: "I am the most wretched fellow: sure some left-handed priest christened me I am so unlucky." Coles says: "It hath been observed, that if a woman with childe eate quinces much, and coriander seed (the nature of both which is to represse and stay vapours that ascend to the braine) it will make the child ingenious: and, if the mother eate much onyons, or beanes, or such vapourous food, it endangereth the childe to become lunaticke, or of imperfect memory. Boemus relates, that in Darien in America the women eate an herb when they are great with childe, which makes them bring forth withoute paine." *Introduction to the Knowledge of Plants,* 69. Misson says: "The custom here is not to make great feasts at the birth of their children. They drink a glass of wine and eat a bit of a certain cake, which is seldom made but upon these occasions." *Travels,* translated by Ozell, p. 35. It was a belief in Angus that, if a child was put from the breast in the moon's wane, it would decay so long as the orb continued to decrease. These superstitions were generally diffused, and seem to have been entertained by the Scots in common with the Swedes, where the same ideas prevailed; nor can it be said that such notions are yet, or will for many a long day, be thoroughly rooted out. The following Scotish modern superstitions respecting new-born children are enumerated by Rosse in the *Fortunate Shepherdess,* 1778:

"Gryte was the care, and tut'ry that was ha'en,
Baith night and day about the bony Weeane,
The Jizzen-bed wi' rantry leaves was sain'd,
And sik like things as the auld Grannies kend,
Jeans paps wi' sa't and water washen clean,
Reed that her milk get wrang, fan it was green.

Neist the first hippen to the green was flung,
And thereat seeful words baith said and sung.
A clear brunt coal wi' the het tongs was ta'en
Frae out the Ingle-mids fu' clear and clean,
And throw the corsy-belly letten fa,
For fear the weeane should be ta'en awa;
Dowing and growing, was the daily pray'r,
And Nory was brought up wi' unco care."

Under "Natal or Natalitious Gifts," Blount observes that "among the Grecians, the fifth day after the child's birth, the neighbours sent in gifts, or small tokens; from which custom, that among Christians of the godfathers sending gifts to the baptized infant, is thought to have flowed: and that also of the neighbours sending gifts to the mother of it, as is still used in North Wales." It is very observable here, that there was a feast at Athens, kept by private families, called Amphidromia, on the fifth day after the birth of the child, when it was the custom for the gossips to run round the fire with the infant in their arms, and then, having delivered it to the nurse, they were entertained with feasting and dancing. Several French (or foreign) customs of child-birth are noticed in the "Traitè des Superstitions" of M. Thiers, vol. i. p. 320-34.

Childermass, or **Holy Innocents' Day.**—(December 26th.) This day is of most unlucky omen. None ever marries on a Childermas Day. It appears from the "Paston Letters," that the Coronation of Edward IV. was put off till the Monday, because the preceding Sunday was Childermass Day. Forby, in his "Vocabulary," 1830, says that the day on which this festival falls was reckoned unlucky for the commencement of any work or task. In the "Spectator," No. 7, we learn that the same notion of the weekly recurrence of this unlucky day was entertained at that time. The word itself is genuine Saxon, *childe masse dag.*

Childirmas-dai, in Wicklif's time. Childery-masse in Rob. Glouc. — "Gent. Mag." Jan. 1799. In the statutes of the Collegiate Church of St. Mary Ottery, founded in 1337. is a direction, that none of the singing boys shall be suffered to proceed beyond the boundaries of the parish on Innocents' Day. It is certainly curious that in 1278 Archbishop Peckham issued an injunction to restrain the performance of service by little girls (*parvulæ*) on this festival at Godstow nunnery. Processions of children on this day were forbidden by the proclamation of July 22nd, 1540. A curious Latin play or mystery on the Slaughter of the Innocents, and the flight into Egypt of Joseph and Mary, with the Infant Jesus, is termed Interfectio Puerorum, and strangely exhibits the primitive mediæval literalism in dealing with these subjects, in common with those English productions, with which readers are more familiar. Bourne tells us, chap. xviii. that "according to the monks it was very unlucky to begin any work on Childermas Day: and whatsoever day that falls on, whether on the Monday, Tuesday, or any other, nothing must be begun on that day through the year." Gregory observes that "It hath been a custom, and yet is elsewhere, to whip the children upon Innocents Day morning, that the memory of Herod's murder of the Innocents might stick the closer, and in a moderate proportion to act over the crueltie again in kinde." Gregorii *Posthuma*, 1649. See Cotgarve's "Dict." and the "Dictionn. de Furetiere."

Strype, under 1582, mentions a riot in Finsbury, about Christmas holidays, "by some loose young men of the Inns of Chancery, one of whom, named Light, was especially indicted for singing in the church, upon Childermas Day, Fallantida dilli, &c.—an idle loose song then used." In "Sir John Oldcastle," 1600, act ii. sc. 2, Murley objects to the rendezvous of the Wickliffites on a Friday:— "Friday, quoth'a, a dismal day; Childermas Day this year was Friday." Melton, in his "Astrologaster," 1620, p. 45, informs us it was formerly an article in the creed of popular superstition, that it was not lucky to put on a new suit, pare one's nails, or begin any thing on a Childermas Day.

Dufresne, in a note to Clement Marot's cxxxvth Epigram, observes, that on Innocents' Day there used to be a custom of slapping on the hinder parts any young folks who were surprised in bed on that morning, and occasionally it proceeded further. But this practice had even then fallen into disuse. The following is the passage in Dufresne:—"Innocentes. Allusion à un usage pratiqué lors en France, où les jeunes personnes qu'on pouvoit surprendre au lit le jour des Innocens, recevoient sur le derrière quelques claques, & quelque fois un peu plus, quand les sujet en valoient la peine. Cela ne se pratique plus aujourd'hui: nous sommes bien plus sages & plus reservés que nos pères." Douce cites a passage from *Le Voyageur à Paris*, to show that an odd species of burlesque was performed on this festival by some of the religious orders. Naogeorgus, in his Fourth Book, devotes

some space to this festival. See *Boy-Bishop*.

Children.—In John Bale's "Comedye concernynge thre Lawes of Nature, Moses, and Christ," 1538, Idolatry says:

"Yea, but now ych am a she
And a good mydwyfe perdé,
Yonge chyldren can I charme,
With whysperynges and whysshynges,
With crossynges and with kyssynges,
With blasynges and with blessynges,
That spretes do them no harme."

In Scotland (Edinburgh) a piece of silver, an egg, and some bread presented to a child on entering a house for the first time, are supposed to bring luck. Hutchinson tells us that children in Northumberland, when first sent abroad in the arms of the nurse to visit a neighbour, are presented with an egg, salt, and fine bread. *Northumberland*, ii., 4 and 13. He observes that "the egg was a sacred emblem, and seems a gift well adapted to infancy." Comp. *Cakes* and *Salt*. Herrick names a crust of holy bread laid under the head of a sleeping child as a charm against hags, and a knife placed near the child's heart with the point upward as a charm against peril in general. Among superstitions relating to children, the following is cited by Bourne from Bingham, on St. Austin:—"If when two friends are talking together, a stone, or a dog, or a child, happens to come between them, they tread the stone to pieces, as the divider of their friendship, and this is tolerable in comparison of beating an innocent child that comes between them. But it is more pleasant that sometimes the child's quarrel is revenged by the dogs: for many times they are so superstitious as to dare to beat the dog that comes between them, who turning again upon him that smites him, sends him from seeking a vain remedy, to seek a real physician indeed." *Antiq. Vulg.* ch. xii. Lupton says: "a piece of a child's navell string, born in a ring, is good against the falling sickness, the pains in the head, and the collick." *Notable Things*, ed. 1660, p. 92. There is a singular custom prevailing in the country of the Lesgins, one of the seventeen Tartarian nations. "Whenever the Usmei, or chief, has a son, he is carried round from village to village, and alternately suckled by every woman who has a child at her breast, till he is weaned. This custom by establishing a kind of brotherhood between the prince and his subjects, singularly endears them to each other." *European Magazine*, June, 1801, p. 408. See, for a singular notion about children's bread and butter, Petri Molinæi "Vates," p. 154. Compare *Bede's Well*, *Caul*, *Child-Birth*, and *Lying-In*.

Children's Games.—The essayist in the "Gentleman's Magazine" for February, 1738, says, that before the troubles, "cross-purposes was the game played at by children of all parties. Upon the death of Charles I. the ridicule of the times turned against monarchy; which during the Commonwealth was burlesqued by every child in Great Britain, who set himself up in mock majesty, and played at Questions and Commands; as for instance, King I am, says one boy; another answers, I am your man; then his Majesty demands, what service he will do him; to which the obsequious courtier replies, the best and worst, and all I can. During all Oliver's time, the chief diversion was, the Parson hath Lost his Fudling Cap: which needs no explanation. At the Restoration succeeded Love-Games, as I love my love with an A: a flower and a lady; and I am a lusty wooer—changed in the latter end of this reign, as well as all King James IId.'s, to 'I am come to torment you.' At the Revolution, when all people recovered their liberty, the children played promiscuously at what game they liked best—the most favourite one, however, was Puss in the Corner. Every body knows that in this play, four boys or girls post themselves at the four corners of a room, and a fifth in the middle, who keeps himself upon the watch to slip into one of the corner places, whilst the present possessors are endeavouring to supplant one another. This was intended to ridicule the scrambling for places — too much in fashion amongst the children of England, both spiritual and temporal."

Chin, The.—He was, says Forby, in his "Vocabulary of East Anglia, 1830," "a sort of imp which inhabits the chimneys of nurseries, and is sometimes called down to take away naughty children."

Chincough. — There is a belief in Cheshire that, if a toad is held for a moment within the mouth of the patient, it is apt to catch the disease, and so cure the person suffering from it. A correspondent of "Notes and Queries" speaks of a case, in which such a phenomenon actually occurred; but the experiment is one which would not be very willingly tried. Roasted mice were formerly held in Norfolk a sure remedy for this complaint; nor is it certain that the belief is extinct even now. A poor woman's son once found himself greatly relieved after eating three roast mice! A superstition still remains in Devonshire and Cornwall, that any person who rides on a pye-balled horse can cure the chin-cough.

Chiromancy.—Agrippa, speaking of chiromancy, says that, it "fancies seven mountains in the palm of a man's hand, according to the number of the seven planets; and by the lines which are there to be seen, judges of the complection, condition and fortune of the person; imagining the harmonious disposition of the lines to be, as it were, certain cælestial characters stamped upon us by God and Nature, and which, as Job saith, God imprinted or put in the hands of men, that so every one might know his works; though it be plain, that the divine author doth not there treat of vain chiromancy, but of the liberty of the will." He gives a great catalogue of names of such authors as have written on this science falsely so called, but observes that "none of them have been able to make any farther progress than conjecture and observation of experience. Now that there is no certainty in these conjectures and observations, is manifest from thence, upon the will; and about which the masters thereof of equal learning and authority do very much differ." *Vanity of Sciences*, p. 101. Ferrand tells us that "this art of chiromancy hath been so strangely infected with superstitions, deceit, cheating, and (if I durst say so) with magic also, that the canonists, and of late years Pope Sixtus Quintus, have been constrained utterly to condemn it. So that now no man professes publickly this cheating art, but theeves, rogues, and beggarly rascals; which are now every where knowne by the name of Bohemians, Egyptians, and Caramaras." *Erotomania*, 1640, p. 173. The lines in the palm of the hand, according to Indagine, are distinguished by formal names, such as the table line or line of fortune, the line of life or of the heart, the middle natural line, the line of the liver or stomach, &c., &c., &c., the triangle, the quadrangle. The thumb too, and fingers have their "Hills" given them, from the tops of which these manual diviners pretend that they had a prospect of futurity. The reader will smile at the name and not very delicate etymon of it, given in this work to the little finger. It is called the ear finger, because it is commonly used to make clean the ears. *Palmistry and Physiognomy*, trans. by F. Withers, 1656. Newton inquires whether the "governors of the commonwealth" "have suffered palmesters, fortune-tellers, stage-players, sawce-boxes, enterluders, puppit-players, loyterers, vagabonds, landleapers, and such like cozening makeshifts to practice their cogging tricks and rogish trades, within the circuite of their authoritie, and to deceive the simple people with their vile forgerie and palterie." *Tryall of a Man's Own Selfe*, 1602, p. 45. Mason ridicules the vanity and frivolity of palmistry, "where Men's fortunes are tolde by looking on the palmes of the hands." *Anatomie of Sorcerie*, 1612, p. 90. Gaule exposes the folly of palmistry which tells us, "that the lines spreading at the bottom joynt of the thumb, signe contentions; the line above the middle of the thumbe, if it meet round about, portends a hanging destiny; many lines transverse upon the last joynt of the fore-finger, note riches by heirdome; and right lines there, are a note of a jovial nature; lines in the points of the middle finger (like a gridiron) note a melancholy wit, and unhappy: if the signe on the little finger be conspicuous, they note a good witt and eloquent, but the contrary, if obscure. Equal lines upon the first joynt of the ring-finger, are marks of an happy wit." *Mag-Astromancer posed*, p. 188. "To strike another's palm," says Bulwer, in his Chirologia, 1644, pp 93, 105, "is the habit of expression of those who plight their troth, buy, sell, covenant, &c. He that would see the vigour of this gesture in puris naturalibus must repair to the horse-cirque or sheep-pens in Smithfield, where those crafty Olympique merchants will take you for no Chapman, unless you strike them with good lucke and smite them earnest in the palme."

Chrisome.—In Strype, it is said to be enjoined that, "to avoid contention, let the curate have the value of the chrisome, not under the value of 4d. and above as they can agree, and as the state of the parents may require." It is well known that "Chrisome (says Blount) signifies properly the white cloth, which is set by the minister of baptism upon the head of a child newly anointed with chrism (a kind of hallowed ointment used by Roman Catholics in the Sacrament of Baptism and for certain other unctions, composed of oyl and balm) after his baptism. Now it is vulgarly taken for the white cloth put about or upon a child newly christened, in token of his baptism; wherewith the women used to shroud the child, if dying within the month; otherwise it is usually brought to church at the day of purification." *Glossographia* in v. In Shipman's "Gossips," 1666, we read:

"Since friends are scarce, and neigh-
bours many,
Who will lend mouths, but not a penny,
I (if you grant not a supply)
Must e'en provide a chrisome pye."

In Henry V., ii., 3, Shakespear makes Falstaff go away, "an' it had been any Chrisom child."

Christ-Church, Oxford.—Every evening, at five minutes past nine, the great bell Tom rings 101 times in commemoration of the number of scholars, for which the foundation was at first erected.

Christ-Cross-row.—The alphabet, from the practice of writing it in the form of a cross on the horn-book or battledore.

Christening.—The following order for the christening of a prince or princess of England was established (or confirmed) in the reign of Henry VII.: "— ffor the cristynynge off the prince or a princese, the chirche or the chapelle dore where the cristynynge shalbe, the dore must be hangid roof and sides all wᵗ clothe of golde and carpets well vndyre the feet; then the font must be set on hight, yᵗ the pepill may see the cristenynge, and presse not to ny; and the font must be hangid withe a riche sele, and overlaid about wᵗ carpets on the greces (steps) and oyʳ places; and the font must be hangid all about wᵗ clothe of gold, and laid wᵗin withe small lyn clothe; and the chirche must be hangid all about the sides wᵗ arras; and the highe aucter muste be araid in the recheste wise, well carpetted afor the aucter; then in the side of the chirche be sides the font must be hangid a travers, and a feyre of coles well brynt or they come there, withe fumidory cast yʳin for the eyre, and a faire chauffure wᵗ water basyn of silver; Also yt muste be ordined that the gossepes be neghe loggid againste the Quenes delyverans; and when God sendithe tym that the prince be borne, then the gossapes to be redy to go wᵗ the childe to the chirche, and a duches to bere the cusyne afore it on her shulder on a kerchef of small reynes: and if it be a prince, an erle to bere his trayne; and it be a princes, a countesse to bere the trayne; and then yʳ must be born afore it to the chirche ij cc torches, xxiiij of them about the child, and the oyʳ dele borne wᵗ yomen afore it; and when yey com to the chirche, the torches to stand alle about the fonte, as ny the walles as they may: Then must the sargiant of the pantry be redy at the chirche dore wᵗ a towelle about his neke, wᵗ a faire salt sellere of gold in his hand, wᵗ salt yʳin; then the sergiant of the ewery to be there wᵗ basyn and ewere for the go-s sepes to wesche wᵗ; and the sergiant of the spicery and 2 butlers to be yʳ redy wᵗ spice and wine, that when the prince is cristenyde, the gossepes and oyʳ estats may take spice and wyne, and a bischope to crystyn the child: and when yᵉ childe is baptizede, all the torches to be lightide, and then to be born vp the highe auctere; and there to be confermyde; and then spice and wyne to be takyne, and the void to be hade; and there the yefts to be gevyne and the yefts takene, to erles, barrons, and baronetts [bannerets]; and they have to bere them afore the child to the Quenes chambre dore. . . . And if it be a Princese, then the wefts to be borne of ladys, and they to bere yem to the Quene." *Antiq. Repert*, 1807, i., 305. A curious representation of the procession at the christening of Prince Arthur, eldest son of Henry VII., here referred to, is given from a drawing in outline there. Grindal, writing from London to Henry Bullinger, Feb. 8, 1567, says: "Her (Mary's) eldest son was baptized in December last, after the popish manner by some mitred pseudo-bishop; but two only could be found out of the whole nobility of that kingdom, who thought proper to be present at the christening. The rest only accompanied the infant, both in going and returning, as far as the door of the chapel." *Zürich Letters*, Parker Soc. 1st Series, 182. It appears to have been anciently the custom at christening entertainments, for the guests not only to eat as much as they pleased, but also for the ladies, at least, to carry away as much as they liked in their pockets. In Strype's Stow accounts are given of two great christenings, in 1561 and 1562. After the first was "a splendid banquet at home"; and the other, we read, "was concluded with a great banquet, consisting of wafers and hypocras, French, Gascoign, and Rhenish wines, with great plenty, and all their servants had a banquet in the hall with divers dishes." Wafers and hippocras wine were the customary refreshment served up after the return from a christening, as appears from the case of Alderman White's child in 1559, when the Marquis of Winchester, Lord Treasurer, stood as one of the sponsors. The same entertainment was also very usual (with other dainties) at weddings about the same period. Compare *Wafers*. In Brathwaite's "Whimzies," 1631, speaking of a yealous (jealous) neighbour, the author says: "Store of bisket, wafers, and careawayes, hee bestowes at his childs christning, yet are his cares nothing lessned; he is perswaded that he may eate his part of this babe, and never breake his fast." At the christening entertainments of many of the poorer sort of people in the North of England (who are so unfortunate as to provide more mouths than they can with convenience find meat for) great collections are oftentimes made by the guests, such as will far more than defray the expenses of the feast of which they have been partaking. Moresin informs us of a remarkable custom, which he himself was an eye-witness of in Scotland. They take, says he, on their return from church, the newly-baptized infant, and vibrate it three or four times gently over a flame, saying, and repeating it thrice, "Let the flame consume thee now or never." *Papatus*, i., p. 72. Borlase writes: "The same lustration, by carrying of fire, is performed round about women after child-bearing, and round about children before they are christened, as an effectual means to preserve both the mother and the infant from the power of evil spirits." In the "Autobiography of Sir John Bramston," Sir John relates how after the death of King Edward VI., in

1553, Rose, a daughter of Sir William Lock, in the time of her first husband, Anthony Hickman, fled ultimately to Antwerp. from the persecution of Mary's government, they being Protestants. Mr. and Mrs. Hickman took two children abroad with them, and while they remained at Antwerp, she had a third, which she caused to be baptized in the house according to the rites of the Reformed Church. "The fashion was," writes the author of these memoirs," "to hange a peece of lawne out at the window where a child was to be baptised; and her house havinge two dores into two streetes, she hunge lawne out at each doore, soe the neighbours of each side, thinckinge the child was caried out at the other dore, inquired no farther." It is customary in the North also for the midwife, &c. to provide two slices, one of bread and the other of cheese, which are presented to the first person they meet in the procession to church at a christening. The person who receives this homely present must give the child in return three different things wishing it at the same time health and beauty. The gentleman who informed Brand of this, happening once to fall in the way of such a party, and to receive the above present, was at a loss how to make the triple return, till he bethought himself of laying upon the child which was held out to him, a shilling, a halfpenny, and a pinch of snuff. When they meet more than one person together, it is usual to single out the nearest to the woman that carries the child. The same sort of practice was in vogue in Durham and Northumberland in 1886; fruit-cake and cheese were the articles there and then presented. The cake was in fact a currant loaf. *Antiquary*, February, 1886, p. 84. In the "Statistical Account of Scotland," we read that the inhabitants "would consider it as an unhappy omen, were they by any means disappointed in getting themselves married, or their children baptized, on the very day which they had previously fixed in their mind for that purpose. Again, parish of Kilsinan, Argyleshire, we read: "There is one pernicious practice that prevails much in this parish, which took its rise from this source, which is, that of carrying their children out to baptism on the first or second day after birth. Many of them, although they had it in their option to have their children baptized in their own houses, by waiting one day, prefer carrying them seven or eight miles to church in the worst weather in December or January, by which folly they too often sacrifice the lives of their infants to the phantom of superstition." Again, the minister of the parishes of South Ronaldsay and Burray, Orkney, says: "Within these last seven years, (i.e.

circâ 1790), the minister has been twice interrupted in administering baptism to a female child before the male child, who was baptized immediately after. When the service was over, he was gravely told he had done very wrong, for as the female child was first baptized, she would, on her coming to the years of discretion, most certainly have a strong beard, and the boy would have none." Lastly, the minister of Logierait, Perthshire, says : " When a child was baptized privately, it was, not long since, customary to put the child upon a clean basket, having a cloth previously spread over it, with bread and cheese put into the cloth ; and thus to move the basket three times successively round the iron crook, which hangs over the fire, from the roof of the house, for the purpose of supporting the pots when water is boiled, or victuals are prepared. This might be anciently intended to counteract the malignant arts which witches and evil spirits were imagined to practice against new-born infants." Grose tells us there is a superstition that a child who does not cry when sprinkled in baptism will not live. He has added another idea equally well founded, that children prematurely wise are not long-lived, that is, rarely reach maturity ; a notion which we find quoted by Shakespear, and put into the mouth of Richard III. That an unbaptized infant cannot die, is a belief still entertaned in Lancashire ; but the authors of " Lancashire Folk-Lore, " 1867, do not appear to have been aware, that the superstiton is a very ancient and wide-spread one, and that this description of spirit was known as the Latewitch. There was formerly a custom of having sermons at christenings. I (says Mr. Brand) had the honour of presenting to the Earl of Leicester one preached at the baptism of Theophilus Earl of Huntingdon.

Christmas Box.—Hutchinson observes on these gifts to servants and mechanics, for their good services in the labouring part of the year, " The Paganalia of the Romans, instituted by Servius Tullius, were celebrated in the beginning of the year : an altar was erected in each village, where all persons gave money. This was a mode originally devised for gaining the number of inhabitants." *Hist. of Northumb.,* ii., 20. " Denique in nostris Ecclesiis nocte natali Parentes varia munuscula, Crepundia, Cistellas, Vestes Vehicula, Poma, Nuces, &c. liberis suis donant, quibus plerumque Virga additur, ut metu castigationis eo facilius regantur. Dantur hæc munuscula nomine S. Christi, quem per tegulas vel fenestras illabi, vel cum Angelis domos obire fingunt. Mos iste similiter a Saturnalibus Gentilium descendere videtur, in quibus Ethnicos sportulas sive varia Munera ultro citroque mi-

sisse, antiquissimus patrum Tertullianus meminit in lib. de Persecut. Hildebrandus, *De Diebus Festis,* 1735. See Du Cange's " Glossary," v. Natali. Drechler, in his Treatise " De Larvis," p. 30, quotes the 79th Canon of the General Council held at Constantiople in 690-1, for the apparent origin of this custom : " Quando aliqui post Diem Natalem Christi Dei nostri reperiuntur coquentes similam et se hanc mutuó donantes, prætextu scil. honoris secundinarum impollutæ Virginis Matris, statuimus ut deinceps nihil tale fiat a fidelibus." These cakes, Drechler imagines, were originally given as presents in remembrance of the Virgin, and other aritcles were, in course of time, added or substituted, the original object being kept in view. We are told that the Christmas Box money is derived hence. The Romish priests had masses said for almost every thing : if a ship went out to the Indies, the priests had a box in her, under the protection of some saint : and for masses, as their cant was, to be said for them to that saint, &c. the poor people must put something into the priest's box, which was not opened till the ship's return. The mass at that time was called Christmas : the box called Christmas Box, or money gathered against that time, that masses might be made by the priests to the saints to forgive the people the debaucheries of that time : and from this, servants had the liberty to get box money, that they too might be enabled to pay the priest for his masses, knowing well the truth of the proverb : " No Penny, No Pater Noster."— *Athenian Oracle,* by Dunton, i., 360. In the illustration of the cut to Blaxton's " English Usurer," 1634, the author, speaking of the usurer and swine, says : deficient in giving ; like the Christmas earthen boxes of apprentices, apt to take in money, but he restores none till hee be broken like a potters vessell into many shares." And in Mason's " Handful of Essaies," 1621, signat. c 2, we find a similar thought—" like a swine he never doth good till his death : as an apprentices box of earth, apt he is to take all, but to restore none till hee be broken." The box was evidently at one time of earthenware. Aubrey, in his " Natural History of Wiltshire," circa 1670, speaking of a pot in which some Roman Denarii were found, says : " it resembles in appearance an apprentices earthen Christmas box." " One asked a fellow, what Westminster Hall was like. Marry, quoth the other, it is like a butler's box at Christmas amongst gamesters : for whosoeuer loseth, the box will bee sure to be a winner."—Taylor's *Wit and Mirth,* 1629.

—— th'are some fair gamesters use
To pay the box well, especially at In and
In,

Innes of Court butlers would have but a Bad Christmas of it else."
—Cotgrave's *Treasury of Wit and Language*, 1655. Gay, in his "Trivia," mentions this:

"Some boys are rich by birth beyond all wants,
Belov'd by uncles, and kind, good, old aunts;
When time comes round, a Christmas box they bear,
And one day makes them rich for all the year."

In a catalogue of Presbyterian books, I find one, with the following title, "Christmas cordials fit for refreshing the souls and cheering the hearts; and more fit for Christmas-boxes than gold or silver."

"The Christmas box," (says the Connoisseur), "was formerly the bounty of well-disposed people, who were willing to contribute something towards rewarding the industrious, and supplying them with necessaries. But the gift is now almost demanded as a right, and our journeymen, apprentices, &c., are grown so polite, that instead of reserving their Christmas box for its original use, their ready cash serves them only for pocket-money; and instead of visiting their friends and relations, they commence the fine gentlemen of the week." The bestowing of Christmas boxes indeed, is one of those absurd customs of antiquity which, till within these few years had spread itself almost into a national grievance. The butcher and the baker sent their journeymen and apprentices to levy contributions on their customers, who were paid back again in fees to the servants of the different families. The tradesman had, in consequence, a pretence to lengthen out his bill, and the master and mistress to lower the wages on account of the vails. Presents were made by bakers to their customers at this time in old days: a baby of paste, or a cake with the figure of a lamb on it; but, although in the formation of cakes all sorts of fantastic shapes are still resorted to, and lambs in sugar and flour are still occasionally to be seen, the good ancient custom of giving such things away has died out. At Wrexham, in Denbighshire, the tradespeople unanimously resolved in 1867 to give no Christmas boxes and to present, instead, £35 to the local charities. Comp. Nares and Halliwell in v. Monsieur de Valois says that the Kings of France gave presents to their soldiers at this season.

Christmas Candle, the, at St. John's College, Oxford.—This candle, and the socket, which was still preserved in the Buttery, in 1813, used formerly to be burned at Christmas in an ancient stone socket, upon which was engraved a figure of the Holy Lamb. It was in use during the twelev days of Christmas, and stood on the public supper board. It was not, however, peculiar to St. John's. In the "Country Farmers' Catechism," 1703, occurs this passage: "She ne'er has no fits, nor uses no cold tea, as the 'Ladies Catechism' says, but keeps her body in health with working all the week, and goes to church on Sundays: my daughter don't look with sickly pale looks, like an unfit Christmas candle; they don't eat oatmeal, lime, or ashes, for pain at their stomachs; they don't ride on the fellows backs before they are twelve years old, nor lie on their own before they are fifteen, but look as fresh as new blown roses, with their daily exercise, and stay still they are fit for husbands before they have them."

Christmas Day.—This is observed without any real authority or probability of correctness on the 25th of December. Christmas Day, in the primitive Church, was always observed as the Sabbath Day, and, like that, preceded by an eve or vigil. Hence our present Christmas Eve. Bourne cites an oration of Gregory Nazianzen, which throws light upon the ancient rites of Christmas Day. "Let us not, says he, "celebrate the feast after an earthly, but an heavenly manner; let not our doors be crowned; let not dancing be encouraged; let not the cross-paths be adorned, the eyes fed, nor the ears delighted; let us not feast to excess, nor be drunk with wine." Certain coarse and obscene usages on Christmas Eve seem to be indicated by Barrington, where, speaking of the people, he says: "They were also, by the customs prevailing in particular districts, subject to services not only of the most servile, but the most ludicrous nature: 'Utpote die Nativitatis Domini coram eo saltare, buccas cum sonitu inflare et ventris crepitum edere." *Observ. on the Statutes,* p. 306. Upon Wednesday, December 22, 1647, the cryer of Canterbury, by the appointment of Master Mayor, openly proclaimed that Christmas Day, and all other superstitious festivals, should be put down, and that a market should be kept upon Christmas Day. See "Canterbury Christmas; or, a true Relation of the Insurrection in Canterbury on Christmas Day last," 1648. An order of Parliament, December 24, 1652, directed "that no observation shall be had of the five and twentieth day of December, commonly called Christmas Day; nor any solemnity used or exercised in churches upon that day in respect thereof." A credible person born and brought up in a village not far from Bury St. Edmunds, informed Mr. Brand that, when he was a boy, there was a rural custom there among the youths, of "hunting owls and squirrels on Christmas Day." Forby alludes to this now obsolete practice in his "Vocabulary of East Anglia," 1830. A correspondent of "Notes and Queries" for March 22 and June 21, 1862, points out that in some parts of the country (he was brought up in the West Riding of Yorkshire) a very curious superstition is connected with Christmas and New Year's mornings. It is that the first person who should enter the house on those two occasions ought, for luck, to have dark hair; and an old woman in his neighbourhood accounted for the belief by saying that Judas, the betrayer of the Saviour, had red hair, a circumstance which engendered a deep prejudice against that or any other light colour ever after. But it may be said here, as so often in relation to questions of the kind—*causa latet res ipsa notissima.* The writer observes: "All the ill-luck, that is, the untoward circumstances of the year, would be ascribed to the accident of a person of light hair having been the first to enter a dwelling on the mornings referred to. I have known instances, where such persons, innocently presenting themselves, have met with anything but a Christmas welcome. It was anciently believed that a child born on a Christmas-day, when that day fell on a Sunday, would be very fortunate. A MS. in the Bodleian has this passage:

"And what chyld on that day boorn be,
Of gret worscheyp schall he be."

Mr. Thomas Wright, in his "Essays," 1846, says: "It is still an article of popular faith in Scotland, that persons born at Christmas and on Good Friday, have more power of communicating with spirits and hobgoblins than other people," and quotes Scot's "Marmion" for an illustration so far at least as Christmas is concerned.

Christmas Eve.—It is customary on this night with young people in the North of England to dive for apples, or catch at them, when stuck upon one end of a kind of hanging beam, at the other extremity of which is fixed a lighted candle, and that with their mouths only, their hands being tied behind their backs. Nuts and apples chiefly compose the entertainment, and from the custom of flinging the former into the fire, or cracking them with their teeth, it has doubtless had its vulgar name of Nutcrack Night. Little troops of boys and girls still go about at Newcastle-upon-Tyne, and other places in the North of England (and in Yorkshire), some few nights before, on Christmas-eve night, and on that of the day itself. The Hagmena is still preserved among them, and they always conclude their begging song with wishing a merry Christmas and a happy New Year. Compare *Hagmena.* In Goldsmith's time, the country folks religiously observed this nutcracking festival, as he tells us in his "Vicar of Wake-

field." Stafford says, they (certain deluded men) "make me call to mind an old Christmas gambole, contrived with a thred which being fastened to some beame, hath at the nether end of it a sticke, at the one end of which is tied a candle, and at the other end an apple; so that when a man comes to bite at the apple, the candle burnes his nose. The application is as easy as the trick common." *Niobe,* 1611, p. 107. The catching at the apple and candle may be called playing at something like the ancient English game of the quintain, which is now almost totally forgotten. Hutchinson, somewhat fancifully perhaps, identified this Christian usage with the rites anciently observed in honour of Pomona. *Hist. of North.,* vol. ii. p. 18. Polwhele describes it in his "Old English Gentleman," p. 120:

"Or catch th' elusive apple with a
    bound,
As with its taper it flew whizzing
    round."

Luther, in his "Colloquia," i. 233, tells us that "upon the eve of Christmas Day the women run about and strike a swinish hour (pulsant horam suillam): if a great hog grunts, it denotes the future husband to be an old man, if a small one, a young man." Naogeorgus describes the midnight mass on Christmas Eve, the manner in which the priests used to pilfer the offerings laid on the altar, "least other should it have," and the wooden effigy of the Son of God, which used to be placed there likewise, that the children of both sexes might dance round it, the parents looking on, and applauding. Sir Herbert Croft informs us, that the inhabitants of Hamburg were obliged by custom to give their servants carp for supper on Christmas Eve. *Letter from Germany,* 1797, p. 82.

Christmas Holidays.—"If we compare," says Prynne, "our Bacchanalian Christmasses and New Years Tides with these Saturnalia and Feasts of Janus, we shall finde such near affinitye betweene them both in regard of time (they being both in the end of December and on the first of January) and in their manner of solemnizing (both of them being spent in revelling, epicurisme, wantonesse, idlenesse, dancing, drinking, stage-plaies, masques, and carnall pompe and jollity), that we must needes conclude the one to be but the very ape or issue of the other. Hence Polydor Virgil affirmes in expresse tearmes that our Christmas Lords of Misrule (which custom, saith he, is chiefly observed in England) together with dancing, masques, mummeries, stage-playes, and such other Christmas disorders now in use with Christians, were derived from these Roman Saturnalia and Bacchanalian festivals; which (concludes he) should cause all pious Christians eternally to abominate them." Selden was of opinion that from Christmas Day to Epiphany morning no one should fast save of his own option or at the bidding of the priest. *Analecton Anglo-Britannicum*, lib. ii., p. 208.

The Christmas of 1502 appears to have been kept with some splendour, for in the "Privy Purse Expenses of Elizabeth of York," there is a payment of twenty pounds to the grooms and pages of the Queen's chamber alone "against Cristmas." According to his biographer, Sir Thos. More "was, by his father's procurement, received into the house of the right reverend, wise, and learned prelate Cardinall Mourton, where (thoughe hee was yonge of yeares, yet) would he at Christmas tyd sodenly sometymes stepp in among the players, and never studinge for the matter, make a parte of his owne there presently amonge them, which made the lookers-on more sport than all the players besid. In whose witt and towardnesse the Cardinall much delightinge, would often say of him unto the nobles that divers tymes dyned with him : 'This child here wayting at the table, who soever shall live to see it, will prove a marveilous man.'" Andrews, in his "Hist. of Great Britain," vol. i. pt. 2, 4to. 1795, p. 329, mentions "the humorous Pageant of Christmas, personified by an old man hung round with savory dainties" which, he says, in common with "dancing round the Maypole and riding the hobby-horse," suffered a severe check at the Reformation. In the East of London, about Shoreditch and Mile-End, while the district was still open country, there were periodical celebrations of sports in holiday time. In 1577 we observe a licence to print the History of the High and Mighty William, Duke of Shoreditch, a personage named William Barlow, who had obtained the favour of Henry VIII. by his skill as a bowman, and on whom his Majesty had conferred this and other jocular titles. Nothing farther is known of such a publication, and of a later one in 1583 there is only a late print at the end of Wood's *Bowman's Glory*, 1682. In 1588 Queen Elizabeth attended a grand spectacle at Mile End, called *Arthur's Show*, q.v. Braithwaite, in his "Rules for the House of an Earle" (*circâ* 1640) laments the expenditure of money which would have been better laid out in the good old substantial fare, upon confectionery. He says : "I have known that the finest confectionary shoppe in Bearbinder Lane and the Blacke Fryers must be sought into for all kindes of conserved, preserved, and candied fruictes, and flowers, the chardge of a banquet arrising to as great a summe of monye as woulde have kept a good house all Christe-

mas, wherin should have been great dishes filled with great peeces of beefe, veale, swanne, venison, capons, and such like English meates." The same author, in his "Whimzies," 1631, describing a good and hospitable housekeeper, has left the following picture of Christmas festivities : "Suppose Christmas now approaching, the evergreen ivie trimming and adorning the portals and partcloses of so frequented a building ; the usual carolls, to observe antiquitie, cheerefully sounding ; and that which is the complement of his inferior comforts, his neighbours, whom he tenders as members of his owne family, joyne with him in this consort of mirth and melody." In the second part, he calls a piper " an ill wind that begins to blow upon Christmasse Eve, and so continues, very lowd and blustring, all the twelve dayes : or an airy meteor, composed of flatuous matter, that then appeares, and vanisheth, to the great peace of the whole family, the thirteenth day." Breton, also, in his "Fantasticks," 1626, has much that is highly interesting on this subject. Under November, he says : "The cooke and the comfitmaker make ready for Christmas, and the minstrels in the Countrey beat their boyes for false fingring." Of Christmas Day itself he observes : "It is now Christmas. and not a cup of drinke must passe without a carroll, the beasts, fowle, and fish, come to a general execution, and the corne is ground to dust for the bakehouse and the pantry : Cards and dice purge many a purse, and the youths shew their agility in shooing of the wild mare." The twelve days' rejoicing and merry-making at this season of the year are mentioned in "The Praise of Christmas," a ballad about 1630 :

"When Christmas-tide comes in like a bride,
　With holly and ivy clad,
Twelve days in the year, much mirth
　and good cheer
　In every household is had."

One of the most curious pictures in little of an old Christmas is that given (glimpselike) in Laurence Price's unique Christmas Book for 1657. He there describes the sea-faring man's Christmas dinner and the tradesman's, and admits us to the interior of an honest cobbler's house, where there was merry-making in an humble way, and music. One of the last pages is occupied with "The Cobbler's Song." In a tract of 1651, Old Christmas is introduced describing the former annual festivities of the season as follows : "After dinner we arose from the board and sate by the fire, where the harth was embrodered all over with roasted apples, piping hot, expecting a bole of ale for a cooler, which immediately was transformed into Lamb-wool. After which we discoursed merily, without either prophaness or obscenity; some went to cards; others sang carols and pleasant songs (suitable to the times); then the poor labouring hinds and maid-servants, with the plow-boys, went nimbly to dancing; the poor toyling wretches being glad of my company, because they had little or no sport at all till I came amongst them; and therefore they skipped and leaped for joy, singing a carol to the tune of Hey,

'Let's dance and sing, and make good cheer,
For Christmas comes but once a year.'

"Thus at active games and gambols of hot-cockles, shooing the wild mare, and the like harmless sports, some part of the tedious night was spent, and early in the morning I took my leave of them, promising they should have my presence again the next 25th of December." *Vindication of Christmas*, 4v. 1651. Stevenson, speaking of January, says, "For the recreations of this month, they are within doors, as it relates to Christmasse; it shares the chearfull carrols of the wassell cup. The Lord of Misrule is no meane man for his time; masking and mumming, and choosing king and queen." Under December are the following notices: "Now capons and hens, besides turkeys, geese, and ducks, with beef and mutton—must all die —for in twelve days a multitude of people will not be fed with a little. Now plumbes and spice, sugar and honey, square it among pies and broath. Now a journeyman cares not a rush for his master though he begs his plum-porridge all the twelve dayes. Now or never must the music be in tune, for the youth must dance and sing to get them a heat, while the aged set by the fire. The country maid leaves half her market, and must be sent againe if she forgets a pair of cards on Christmasse Even. Great is the contention of holly and ivy, whether master or dame weares the breeches. Dice and the cards benefit the butler: and, if the cook do not lack wit, he will sweetly lick his fingers."

"Christmase is come, make ready the good cheare:
Apollo will be frolicke once a yeare:
I speake not here of Englands twelve dayes madness,
But humble gratitude and hearty gladnesse.
These but observed, let instruments speak out,
We may be merry, and we ought, no doubt;
Christmas, 'tis the birth-day of Christ our King;
Are we disputing when the angels sing?"
—*Twelve Moneths*, 1661, p. 4. "Poor Robin" for 1677 notes the festive doings of Christmas as follows:

"Now grocer's trade
Is in request,
For plums and spices
Of the best.
Good cheer doth with
This month agree,
And dainty chaps
Must sweetned be.
Mirth and gladness
Doth abound,
And strong beer in
Each house is found.
Minc'd pies, roast beef
With other cheer
And feasting, doth
Conclude the year."

In 1682 appeared "The Christmas Ordinary, a private show; wherein is expressed the jovial Freedom of that Festival: as it was acted at a Gentleman's House among other Revels, by W. R. Master of Arts." Another account of the Christmas gambols occurs in Speed's "Batt upon Batt," 1694, p. 5:

"Our Batt can dance, play at high jinks with dice,
At any primitive, orthodoxal vice.
Shooing the wild mare, tumbling the young wenches,
Drinking all night, and sleeping on the benches.
Shew me a man can shuffle fair and cut,
Yet always have three trays in hand at Putt:
Shew me a man can turn up Noddy still,
And deal himself three fives too when he will:
Conclude with one and thirty, and a pair,
Never fail ten in stock, and yet play fair,
If Batt be not that wight, I lose my aim."

Misson says: "From Christmas Day till after Twelfth Day is a time of Christian rejoicing; a mixture of devotion and pleasure. They give treats, and make it their whole business to drive away melancholy. Whereas little presents from one another are made only on the first day of the year in France, they begin here at Christmas; and they are not so much presents from friend to friend, or from equal to equal (which is less practis'd in England now than formerly), as from superior to inferior. In the taverns the landlord gives part of what is eaten and drank in his house that and the next two days: for instance, they reckon you for the wine, and tell you there is nothing to pay for bread, nor for your slice of Westphalia," i.e., ham. He had observed, p. 29, "The English and most other Protestant nations are utterly unacquainted with those diversions of the carnival which are so famous at Venice, and known more or less in all other Roman Catholic countries. The great festival times here are from Christmas to Twelfth Day inclusive, at Easter, and at Whitsuntide." *Travels in England*, trans. by Ozell, p. 34. The Minister of Montrose tells us : " At Christmas and the New Year, the opulent burghers begin to feast with their friends, and go a round of visits, which takes up the space of many weeks. Upon such occasions, the gravest is expected to be merry, and to join in a cheerful song." *Stat. Acc. of Scotland*, v., 48. In the "World," No. 104, the following occurs : " Our ancestors considered Christmas in the double light of a holy commemoration and a chearful festival ; and accordingly distinguished it by devotion, by vacation from business, by merriment and hospitality. They seemed eagerly bent to make themselves and every body about them happy. With what punctual zeal did they wish one another a merry Christmas ? and what an omission would it have been thought, to have concluded a letter without the compliments of the season ? The great hall resounded with the tumultuous joys of servants and tenants, and the gambols they played served as amusement to the lord of the mansion and his family, who. by encouraging every art conducive to mirth and entertainment, endeavoured to soften the rigour of the season, and mitigate the influence of winter. What a fund of delight was the chusing King and Queen upon Twelfth Night ! and how greatly ought we to regret the neglect of minced pyes, which, besides the ideas of merrymaking inseparable from them, were always considered as the test of schismatics ! How zealously were they swallowed by the orthodox, to the utter confusion of all fanatical recusants ! If any country gentleman should be so unfortunate in this age as to lie under a suspicion of heresy, where will he find so easy a method of acquitting himself as by the ordeal of plumbporridge ? " " In Christmas holidays," says the author of " Round about our Coal Fire," (about 1730), " the tables were all spread from the first to the last ; the sirloins of beef, the minced pies, the plumb-porridge, the capons, turkeys, geese and plumb-puddings, were all brought upon the board : every one eat heartily, and was welcome, which gave rise to the proverb, 'Merry in the hall when beards wag all.' "

Sir Walter Scott, in a letter to Joanna Baillie, 1st January, 1819, says : " I wish you could have seen about a hundred children, being almost supported by their fathers' or brothers' labour, come down yesterday to dance to the pipes, and get a piece of cake and bannock, and pence apiece (no very deadly largess) in honour of Hagmanay. I declare to you, my dear

friend, that when I thought the poor fellows who kept these children so neat, and well taught, and well behaved, were slaving the whole day for eighteenpence or twentypence at the most, I was ashamed of their gratitude, and of their becks and bows." In another letter (Jan. 1, 1815), Scott says : " Yesterday being Hogmanay, there was a constant succession of *Guisards* i.e., boys dressed up in fantastic caps, with their shirts over their jackets, and with wooden swords in their hands. These players acted a sort of scene before us, of which the hero was one Goloskin."

In an amusing news-letter from John Pory to a friend, dated December 13th, 1632, the writer says :— " Sir William Curtis writes from Brussells, that the French there with the Queen Mother and monsieur made account to have kept a brave Christmas here in London, and for that purpose had trussed up their trinkets half-topmast high ; but it seemeth they reckoned before their host." An agreeable writer describes the busy and bright scene in the churches of Rome on this anniversary, when the people of all ranks flock thither, the peasantry in their holiday attire, and there are processions of priests everywhere. The ceremonial observances last during the whole night until the advent of Christmas Day itself. The Pope and College attend service at Santa Maria Maggiore. *Diary of an Invalid*, by H. Matthews, 1820.

Christmas Mummers.—A proclamation issued 8 Edward III., A.D. 1334, by the authorities of the City of London, concludes thus : " Also we do forbid, on the same pain of imprisonment, that any man shall go about at this feast of Christmas with companions disguised with false faces, or in any other manner, to the houses of the good folks of the City, for playing at dice there . . . . " Riley's *Memorials of London*, 1868, p. 192. At Tenby, among the Christmas mummings, was a dialogue between Father Christmas, St. George, Oliver Cromwell, and Beelzebub, where St. George is made to say :

" First, then, I fought in France ;
Second, I fought in Spain ;
Thirdly, I came to Tenby,
To fight the Turk again."

Where by *Turk* we are to understand the corsairs of Barbary, who at one time infested nearly every coast.

Christmas Pie.—Selden thought that the coffin of our Christmas pies, in shape long, is in imitation of the cratch, i.e., the manger wherein the infant Jesus was laid ; and they were long known as *coffin pasties*. The modern survival is the covered fruit tart in an oval dish. Scogin, in the edition of his " Jests," published in 1626, is made on his death-bed to say : " Masters, I tell you all that stand about mee, if I might live to eate a Christmasse pye, I care not if I dye by and by after : for Christmasse pyes be good meat.' In Robert Fletcher's poem styled "Christmas Day," we find the ingredients and shape of the Christmas pie :

" Christ-mass? give me my beads : the word implies
A plot, by its ingredients, beef and pyes.
The cloyster'd steaks with salt and pepper lye
Like nunnes with patches in a monastrie.
Prophaneness in a conclave? Nay, much more,
Idolatrie in crust ! Babylon's whore
Rak'd from the grave, and bak'd by hanches, then
Serv'd up in coffins to unholy men ;
Defil'd with superstition, like the Gentiles
Of old, that worship'd onions, roots, and lentiles ! "

Ex Otio Negotium, 1656, p. 114. Misson describes the composition of a Christmas pasty as follows : " In every family they make at Christmas a famous pie, which they call a Christmas pie. The making of this is a great science ; it is a learned medley of neats' tongue, the brawn of a chicken, eggs, sugar, currants, citron and orange-peel, various sorts of spice, &c." *Travels in England,* 322. In the " Gentleman's Magazine " for December, 1733, is an essay on " Christmas Pye," in which the author tells us : "That this dish is most in vogue at this time of the year, some think is owing to the barrenness of the season, and the scarcity of fruit and milk to make tarts, custards, and other desserts ; this being a compound that furnishes a dessert itself. But I rather think it bears a religious kind of relation to the festivity from whence it takes its name. Our tables are always set out with this dish just at the time and probably for the same reason that our windows are adorned with ivy. I am the more confirmed in this opinion from the zealous opposition it meets with from Quakers, who distinguish their feasts by an heretical sort of pudding known by their name, and inveigh against Christmas pye as an invention of the scarlet whore of Babylon, an hodgepodge of superstition, popery, the devil, and all his works. Lewis, speaking of the enthusiasts in the grand rebellion, tells us, that under the censure of lewd customs they include all sorts of public sports, exercises, and recreations, how innocent soever. Nay, the poor rosemary and bays, and Christmas Pye, is made an abomination. The famous Bickerstaffe rose up against such as would cut out the clergy from having any share in it. ' The

Christmas Pye,' says he ' is in its own nature a kind of consecrated cake, and a badge of distinction, and yet 'tis often forbidden to the Druid of the family. Strange ! that a sirloin of beef, whether boiled or roasted, when entire, is exposed to his utmost depredations and incisions : but if minced into small pieces, and tossed up with plums and sugar, changes its property, and forsooth is meat for his master.' Thus with a becoming zeal he defends the chaplains of noblemen in particular, and the clergy in general, who it seems were debarred, under pretence that a sweet tooth and a liqourish palate are inconsistent with the sanctity of their character."

" Come guard this night the Christmas-pie
That the thiefe, though ne'r so slie,
With his flesh hooks don't come nie
        To catch it ;
From him, who all alone sits there,
Having his eyes still in his eare,
And a deale of nightly feare
        To watch it."
                Herrick.

" Let Christmas boast her customary treat,
A mixture strange of suet, currants, meat,
Where various tastes combine, the greasy and the sweet."
        Oxford Sausage, p. FT.

In the North of England, a goose is always the chief ingredient in the composition of a Christmas pye. Ramsay, in his "Elegy on Lucky Wood," tells us, that among other baits by which the good ale-wife drew customers to her house, she never failed to tempt them at Christmas with a goose-pye.

" Than ay at Yule, whene'er we came,
        A bra' goose pye,
And was na that a good belly baum?
        None dare deny."

Christmas Prince.—In an audit book of Trinity College, Oxford, for 1559 Warton found a disbursement " Pro prandio Principis Natalicii." A Christmas Prince, or Lord of Misrule, he adds, corresponding to the Imperator at Cambridge, was a common temporary magistrate in the Colleges at Oxford. Wood, in his *Athenæ,* speaking of the " Christmas Prince of St. John's College, whom the juniors have annually for the most part elected from the first foundation of the College, says : " The custom was not only observed in that College, but in several other houses, particularly in Merton College, where, from the first foundation, the Fellows anually elected, about St. Edmund's Day, in November, a Christmas Lord or Lord of Misrule, styled in the registers Rex Fabarum and Rex Regni

Fabarum; which custom continued till the Reformation of Religion, and then, that producing Puritanism, and Puritanism Presbytery, the profession of it looked upon such laudable and ingenious customs as popish, diabolical and antichristian." It is to be collected from the pageant known as the *Christmas Prince*, that the students of St. John's College, Oxford, met on All-Hallow Eve, 1607, and a fire was lighted in the Hall, "accordinge to the custome and status of the same place, at wch time the whole companye, or most part of the students of the same house mette toogether to beginne their Christmas." On the next night, November 1, it seems, a second meeting was appointed, when it was proposed, for the preservation of order and peace, that a Christmas Lord or Prince of the Revels, should be chosen, We learn that no Christmas Lord had been created since 1577. In the present case, Thomas Tucker obtained a majority of suffrages, and being elected in his absence, was sought for, carried in triumph about the hall, and afterwards allowed to return to his own quarters, "to thinke of their loues and good will, and to consider of his owne charge and place." Is it worth while to inquire, if Thomas Tucker, Esq., had any conection with little Tom Tucker of the nursery rhyme?

Of this splendid and gay pageant there is the following contemporary description : — "On Christmas day in ye morning he (the Christmas lord or prince) was attended vnto prayers by ye whole company of the Bacchelours, and some others of his gentlemen vshers, bare before him. At diner beinge sett downe in ye Hall at ye high table in ye Vice Præsidents place (for ye Præsident himself was then allso psent) hee was serued wth 20 dishes to a messe, all wch were brought in by gentlemen of ye howse attired in his guards coats, vshered in by ye L^{rd} Comptroller, and other officers of ye Hall. The first mess was a boar's head, wch was carried by ye tallest and lustiest of all ye guard, before whom, (as attendants) wente first, one attired in a horsemans coate, wth a boars-speare in his hande, next to him an other huntsman in greene, wth a bloody falscion drawne; next to him 2 pages in tafatye sarcenet, each of y^{em} wth a mess of mustard next to whome came hee y^t carried ye boares-head, crost wth a greene silk scarfe, by wch hunge ye empty scabbard of ye faulchion, wch was carried before him." As the boar's head entered the hall, they sang a carol, and during the dinner the prince's musicians played. They had been sent for from Reading, because the town-music, it appears, had given His Highness "the slip," as they always did when any one wanted them particularly." After supper

there was an interlude, "contaynynge the order of ye Saturnalls, and shewinge the first cause of Christmas-candles, and in the ende there was an application made to the Day and Natiuitie of Christ." On the 26th, it had been intended to perform the tragical show of *Philomela*, but the carpenters were behindhand, and the show had to be postponed until the 29th. It seems that the person who represented Philomela on this occasion had so sweet a voice that the audience only regretted that it should be lost, and the coeval narrator quaintly says that they "could have found in their hartes that the story should have rather been falsified then so good a voyce lost." On New Year's Day the Prince sent to the President of St. John's, by the hands of Mr. Richard Swinnerton, one of the squires of his body, a pair of gloves, with these two verses :

"The prince and his councell in signe of their loves,
Present you their Præsident with these paire of gloves."

For further particulars of the quasi-dramatic exhibitions, and other merry-makings during the twelve days of Christmas, see the tract itself in *Miscellanea Antiqua Anglicana*, 1816.

Warton tells us that in an original draught of the statutes of Trinity College, Cambridge, founded in 1546, one of the Chapters is entitled, "De Præfecto Ludorum qui Imperator dicitur," under whose direction and authority Latin comedies and tragedies are to be exhibited in the Hall at Christmas ; as also six spectacula, or as many dialogues. With regard to the peculiar business and office of Imperator, it is ordered, that one of the masters of arts shall be placed over the juniors every Christmas, for the regulation of their games and diversions at that season of festivity. His sovereignty is to last during the twelve days of Christmas : and he is to exercise the same power on Candlemas Day. His fee is forty shillings. Fuller, in his "Good Thoughts in Worse Times," 1647, p. 139, tells us : "Some sixty yeares since, in the University of Cambridge, it was solemnly debated betwixt the heads to debarre young schollers of that liberty allowed them in Christmas, as inconsistent with the discipline of students. But some grave governors mentioned the good use thereof, because thereby, in twelve days, they more discover the dispositions of scholars than in twelve moneths before." The Lords of Misrule in colleges were preached against at Cambridge by the Puritans in the reign of James the First, as inconsistent with a place of religious education and as a relict of the Pagan ritual. An account of a splendid Christmas festival, in the Inner Temple is given by Gerard Leigh in his *Accidence of Armoury*, 1562,

The hero of the occasion was Dudley, Earl of Leicester, who assumed the designation of Palaphilos, Prince of Sophie. He was entertained by a chosen member of the Inn playing the part for the time of a sovereign prince, as at the Middle Temple, Lincoln's Inn, and Gray's Inn, and was attended by his Lord Chancellor, Privy Seal, Treasurer, Lord Chief Justice, Chief Baron of the Exchequer, besides many other dignitaries of the law, and upward of four-score guars. Dugdale, speaking of the Fooleries of the Lord of Misrule there on St. Stephen's Day, says : "Supper ended, the Constable-Marshall presented himself with drums afore him, mounted upon a scaffold born by four men, and goeth three times round about the harthe, crying out aloud, ' A Lord, a Lord,' &c. Then he descendeth, and goeth to dance, &c., and after he calleth his Court, every one by name, e.g. Sir Randle Rackabite, of Raskall-Hall, in the County of Rake-hell, &c. &c. This done, the Lord of Misrule addresseth himself to the banquet : which ended, with some minstralsye, mirth, and dancing, every man departeth to rest." A very magnificent pageant was exhibited at the Inner Temple in the Christmas which immediately succeeded the Restoration ; Charles II. and many of the nobility were present in person.

When the Societies of the Law performed these shows within their own respective refectories, at Christmas, or any other festival, a Christmas prince or revelmaster was constantly appointed. At a Christmas celebrated in the Hall of the Middle Temple in the year 1635, the jurisdiction, privileges, and parade of this mock-monarch are thus circumstantially described. He was attended by his lordkeeper, lord treasurer, with eight white staves, a captain of his band of pensioners, and of his guard ; and with two chaplains, who were so seriously impressed with an idea of his regal dignity, that when they preached before him on the preceding Sunday in the Temple Church, on ascending the pulpit they saluted him with three low bows. He dined both in the hall and in his privy chamber under a cloth of estate. The pole-axes for his gentlemen pensioners were borrowed of Lord Salisbury. Lord Holland, his temporary Justice in Eyre, supplied him with venison on demand, and the lord mayor and sheriffs of London. with wine. On twelfth-day, at going to church, he received many petitions, which he gave to his master of requests ; and, like other kings, he had a favourite, whom with others, gentlemen of high quality, he knighted at returning from church. His expences, all from his own purse, amounted to two thousand pounds. After he was deposed, the King

knighted him at Whitehall. In MS. Ashmole, 826, is a copy of the Writ of Privy Seal of the Christmas Prince of the Middle Temple, signed "Ri. Pr. de l'amour," directed "To our trusty and well-beloved servant, Mr. John Garrett," during his attendance at court, 26 Dec., 1635. Garrett was the person to whom Taylor the water-poet inscribed one of his facetious publications.

These events were not always restricted to Christmas itself, for a masque, composed at very short notice by Sir William Davenant, was exhibited in the Middle Temple Hall, 24 February, 1635, in honour of the Elector Palatine under the title of *The Triumphs of the Prince D'Amour*, with music and symphonies by Henry and William Lawes. In 1660 appeared a volume of miscellaneous poems entitled *Le Prince D'Amour*, and dedicated to the authorities of the Middle Temple. Dugdale, speaking of the Christmas festivities kept in Lincoln's Inn, cites an order dated 9th Hen. VIII., "that the King of Cockneys, on Childermas Day, should sit and have due service ; and that he and all his officers should use honest manner and good order, without any waste or destruction making in wine, brawn, chely, or other vitals : as also that he, and his marshal, butler, and constable marshal, should have their lawful and honest commandments by delivery of the officers of Christmas, and that the said King of Cockneys, ne none of his officers medyl neither in the buttery, nor in the stuard of Christmas his office, upon pain of 40s. for every such medling. And lastly, that Jack Straw, and all his adherents, should be thenceforth utterly banisht and no more to be used in this house, upon pain to forfeit, for every time, five pounds, to be levied on every Fellow hapning to offend against this rule." *Orig. Juridiciales*, 247. The King of Cockneys may be concluded to be the same character as Dugdale elsewhere describes, where he states that the Inn chose a king on Christmas Day. At Gray's Inn they had their Prince of Purpool or Portypool —the Manor in which the Inn lies—and in 1594 was performed here the *Gray's Inn Masque*, by Francis Davison, in the presence of Queen Elizabeth and her Court. It was ostensibly devised by his Highness's command. This performance remained in MS. till 1688. See Hazlitt's *Manual of Old Plays*, 1892, v. *Gesta Grayorum*. The Inn had distinguished itself so early as 1566 by presenting English dramatic versions of the *Jocasta* of Euripides (through an Italian version of Seneca's paraphrase), and the *Suppositi* of Ariosto. Dugdale, in his "Origines Juridiciales," p. 286, speaking of "Orders for Government— Gray's Inne," cites an order of 4 Car. I.

(Nov. 17) that "all playing at dice, cards, or otherwise, in the hall, buttry, or butler's chamber should be thenceforth barred and forbidden at all times of the year. the twenty days in Christmas onely excepted." An entertaining account of this annual buffoonery at the Inns of Court is given in "Noctes Templariæ," 1599. I must beg leave to refer the reader to this work, as the narrative is too long for transcription, and would scarcely bear curtailment. Manning's *Mem. of Sir B. Ruddyerd*, 1841. A Christmas Prince or King, however, acquired as early as Henry the Eighth's time a contemptuous signification, for in a letter of 1537 the Curate of St. Margaret's, Lothbury, writing to a correspondent at Plymouth, says, that the people made no more of God than if he had been "a Christmas King." And indeed, at Lincoln's Inn, according to what we have heard from Dugdale, he does not appear ever to have possessed so great a prestige or so exalted a jurisdiction as elsewhere. Churchyard, in the "Lamentacion of Freyndshypp," a ballad printed about 1565, says:

"Men are so used these dayes wyth wordes,
They take them but for jestes and boordes,
That Christmas Lordes were wonte to speke."

Guilpin, in his "Skialetheia," 1598, figures a man, who has been in the service of one of these characters, assuming on that account, lofty airs, and maintaining a disdainful silence—

"Thinks scorne to speake, especially now since
H' hath beene a player to a Christmas Prince."

Langley's Translation of Polydore Vergil, fol. 102 verso, mentions "The Christemass Lordes, that be commonly made at the nativitee of our Lorde, to whom all the householde and familie, with the Master himselfe, must be obedient, began of the equabilitie that the servauntes had with their masters in Saturnus Feastes that they were called Saturnalia: wherein the servauntes have like autoritie with their masters duryng the tyme of the sayd feastes."

Christmas Song.—"Poor Robin" for 1695, has the following:

"Now thrice welcome, Christmas,
Which brings us good cheer,
Minc'd pies and plumb-porridge,
Good ale and strong beer;
With pig, goose, and capon,
The best that may be,
So well doth the weather
And our stomachs agree.

Observe how the chimneys
Do smoak all about,
The cooks are providing
For dinner, no doubt;
But those on whose tables
No victuals appear,
O may they keep Lent
All the rest of the year!

With holly and ivy
So green and so gay;
We deck up our houses
As fresh as the day,
With bays and rosemary,
And lawrel compleat
And every one now
Is a king in conceit.
    *   *   *   *   *
But as for curmudgeons,
Who will not be free,
I wish they may die
On the three-legged tree."

Christmas Tree.—A very intelligent writer in Willis's "Current Notes" for February, 1854, observes: "The Christmas-tree has become a prevailing fashion in England at this season, and is by most persons supposed to be derived from Germany: such, however, is not the fact: the Christmas-tree is from Egypt, and its origin dates from a period long antecedent to the Christian era. The palm-tree is known to put forth a shoot every month, and a spray of this tree, with twelve shoots on it, was used in Egypt, at the time of the winter solstice, as a symbol of the year completed. Egyptian associations of a very early date still mingle with the tradition and custom of the Christmas-tree; there are as many pyramids, as trees used in Germany, in the celebration of Christmas by those whose means do not admit of their purchasing trees and the concomitant tapers. These pyramids consist of slight erections of slips of wood, arranged like a pyramidal epergne, covered with green paper, and decorated with festoons of paper-chain work, which flutters in the wind, and constitutes, a make-believe foliage. This latter, however, is an innovation of modern days." But the Christmas-tree, notwithstanding what has gone before, no doubt came to us from Germany directly, and is still a flourishing institution among us. It is usually an evergreen decorated with lights and also with presents for the guests, the latter depending, of course, on the means or generosity of the entertainer.

Christopher, St.—His history is in his name, Χριστοφορος being said to have carried our Saviour, when a child, over an arm of the sea. This legend is in Voragine, and in most of the works on the subject. By her will made in 1495, Cecily, Duchess of York, bequeathed to her daughter-in-law, the Queen of Edward IV., among other things, " a pix with the fleshe of Saint Christofer." Wills from Doctors' Commons, Camd. Soc. 1863, p. 2. A popular account of the saint occurs in " A helpe to Discourse." The noted incident described above is a very favourite and common subject in the early paintings on glass. See Ottley's " Hist. of Printing," ch ix. and Notes and Queries, Fourth Series, ii. 313, *et seqq.* This saint occurs on the coins of Würtemberg and other continental states and towns, doubtless from his association with the child Jesus.

Chudleigh Glen, Devonshire.
This is one of the places where the early practice of propitiation by leaving something in the nature of a clout or rag, or a handkerchief, is still said to prevail, especially among holiday-makers at Whitsuntide.

Church Ales.—Payments and receipts or accounts of these various church-ales are very frequent items in all the early Churchwardens' books. Attention may be particularly directed to Mr. Ouvry's Extracts from those of Wing, Co. Bucks, in the thirty-sixth volume of " Archæologia." The entries go back as far as 1527. We here meet with several credits given in the books under each year for the May ale, the Hock-tide ale, the Whitsun ale, and the Sepulchre ale. In 1537, the first-named, after all expenses paid, realised 34s. In 1550, the May ale produced £2 0s. 2d., but the amount of this and of the other ales was liable to much fluctuation both here and elsewhere. It depended on circumstances. In 1564, the May ale was worth £3 9s. 7d., and in later years the increase seems to have been steady ; but in some cases it is a little uncertain, whether the totals given are to be understood as gross or net. In 1562, at West Tarring, or Tarring Peverel, Sussex, the bill of fare included, *inter alia,* five calves, eight lambs, four sheep, five bushels of malt, two calves' heads, a leg of mutton, with pepper, saffron, and other spices. Lower's *Compendious History of Sussex,* 1870, ii. 198. In the Churchwardens' accounts of Minchin-hampton under 1580, among the receipts, occur " gathered the hoglyn money, which ys xs. iiijd. ; we made of oure Whiteson ale, iij. li. vs." " Archæol." vol. xxxv. p. 432. In 1588, the " clere gaine of the church ale " was £4 10s. and in 1589, £4 15s. Ibid. p. 435. It appears from Kethe's Sermon at Blandford, 1570, that it was the custom at that time for the church ales to be kept upon the sabbath day : which holy day, says our author, "the multitude call their revelyng day, which day is spent in bulbeatings, bearebeatings, bowlings, dicyng, cardyng, daunsynges, drunkennes and whoredome," "in so much as men could not keepe their servaunts

from lyinge out of theyr owne houses the same sabbath-day at night." Worsley, speaking of the parish of Whitwell, tells us, that there is a lease in the parish chest, dated 1574, " of a house called the church house, held by the inhabitants of Whitwell, parishioners of Gatcombe, of the lord of the manor, and demised by them to John Brode, in which is the following proviso : " Provided always, that, if the quarter shall need at any time to make a quarter-ale, or church-ale, for the maintenance of the chapel, that it shall be lawful for them to have the use of the said house, with all the rooms, both above and beneath, during their ale." Stubbes, in his " Anatomie of Abuses," 1585, p. 95, gives the following account of "The Maner of Church-Ales in England." : In certaine towns where dronken Bacchus beares swaie against Christmas and Easter, Whitson-daie, or some other tyme, the churchewardens of every parishe, with the consent of the whole parish, provide half a score or twenty quarters of mault, wherof some they buy of the churche stocke, and some is given them of the parishioners themselves, every one conferring somewhat, according to his abilitie ; which mault being made into very strong ale or beere, is sette to sale together in the church or some other place assigned to that purpose. Then when this is set abroche, well is he that can gette the soonest to it, and spend the most at it. In this kinde of practice they continue sixe weekes, a quarter of a yeare, yea, halfe a year together. That money, they say, is to repaire their churches and chappels with, to buy bookes for service, cuppes for the celebration of the Sacrament, surplesses for sir John, and such other necessaries. And they maintaine other extraordinarie charges in their parish besides.'
In his *Introduction to the Survey of North Wiltshire,* 1670, Aubrey remarks : "There were no rates for the poor in my grandfather's days ; but for Kington St. Michael (no small parish) the church ale at Whitsuntide did the business. In every parish is (or was) a church-house, to which belonged spits, crocks, &c., utensils for dressing provision. Here the housekeepers met, and were merry, and gave their charity." The following document was contributed, many years ago, to *Notes and Queries* : " An agreement of the inhabitants of the towns and parishes of Elvaston, Thurlaston, and Ambaston, of the one part, and the inhabitants of the town of Okebrook, within the said parish of Elvaston, in co. Derby, on the other part, by John Abbot of the Dale, Ralph Saucheverell, Esq., John Bradshaw, and Henry Tithel, gent. Witnesseth, that the inhabitants, as well of the said parish of Elvaston as of the said town of Okebrook, shall brew four ales, and every ale of one

quarter of malt—that at their own costs and charges, betwixt this and the feast of St. John Baptist next coming. And that every inhabitant of the town of Okebrook shall be at the several ales; and every husband and his wife shall pay two-pence, every cottager one penny; and all the inhabitants of Elvaston shall have and receive all the profits and advantages coming of the said ales to the use and behoof of the said church of Elvastòn, &c. And the inhabitants of Okebrook shall carry all manner of tymber being in the Dale wood now felled, that the said Prestchyrch of the said towns shall occupye to the use and profit of the said church."

Church Decorations at Christmas.—Bourne observes that this custom of adorning the windows at this season with bay and laurel is but seldom used in the North; but in the South, particularly at our Universities, it is very common to deck not only the common windows of the town, but also the chapels of the colleges, with branches of laurel, which was used by the ancient Romans as the emblem of peace, joy, and victory. In the Christian sense it may be applied to the victory gained over the Powers of Darkness by the coming of Christ. "Trimmyng of the temples," says Polydore Vergil, "with hangynges, floures, boughes, and garlondes, was taken of the heathen people, whiche decked their idols and houses with suche array." Bourne cites the Council of Bracara, Canon 73, as forbidding Christians to deck their houses with bay leaves and green boughs; but this extended only to their doing it at the same time with the Pagans. *Antiq. Vulg.* 173. "Non liceat iniquas observantias agere Kalendarum et ociis vacare Gentilibus, neque lauro, neque viriditate arborum cingere domos. Omnis enim hæc observatio Paganismi est."—Bracc Can. 73, Instell. Prynne, in his *Histrio-Mastix,* 1633, p. 581, cites nearly the same words from the 73d Canon of the Concilium Antisiodorense, in France, A.D. 614. In the same work, p. 21, he cites the Councils as forbidding the early Christians to "decke up their houses with lawrell, yvie, and greene boughes (as we used to doe in the Christian season)." Adding from Ovid *Fasti,* lib. iii.:

"Hedera est gratissima Baccho."

Compare also Tertull. de Idol. cap. 15. In the Roman Calendar, I find the following observation on Christmas Eve: Templa exornantur. Among the annual disbursements of St. Mary-at-Hill, London, there is the following entry: "Holme and ivy at Christmas Eve, iiijd." In the Churchwardens' accounts of St. Laurence's parish, Reading, 1505, quoted by Coates, we read: "It. payed to Makrell for the holy bush agayn Christmas, ijd." In the accounts of St. Martin Outwich, London, 1524, is: "Item for holy and ivy at Christmas, ijd. ob.—— 1525, Payd for holy and ivye at Chrystmas, ijd." In similar accounts for St. Margaret, Westminster, 1647, we read: "Item, paid for rosemarie and bayes that was stuck about the church at Christmas, 1s. 6d." Coles, in his "Art of Simpling," 1656, p. 64, tells us, "In some places setting up of holly, ivy, rosemary, bayes, yew, &c., in churches at Christmas is still in use." The use of box as well as yew, "to decke up houses in winter," is noticed in Parkinson's "Garden of Flowers," &c., 1629, p. 606.

Stow, in his "Survey," says that, "against the feast of Christmas, every man's house, as also their parish churches, were decked with holme, ivy, bayes, and whatsoever the season of the year afforded to be green. The conduits and standards in the streets were likewise garnished: among the which I read that in the year 1444, by tempest of thunder and lightning, towards the morning of Candlemas Day, at the Leadenhall. in Cornhill, a standard of tree, being set up in the midst of the pavement, fast in the ground, nailed full of holme and ivie, for disport of Christmas to the people, was torne up and caste down by the malignant spirit (as was thought), and the stones of the pavement all about were cast in the streets, and into divers houses so that the people were sore aghast at the great tempests." This illustrates the Spectator's observation, where he tells us that our forefathers looked into Nature with other eyes than we do now, and always ascribed common natural effects to supernatural causes. It should seem that this joy of the people at Christmas was death to their infernal enemy. Envying their festal pleasures, and owing them a grudge, he took this opportunity of spoiling their sport. In Herbert's "Country Parson," 1675, p. 56, the author tells us: "Our parson takes order that the church be swept and kept clean, without dust or cobwebs, and at great festivals strawed and stuck with boughs, and perfumed with incense."

"When rosemary and bays, the poet's crown,
Are brawl'd in frequent cries through all the town:
Then judge the festival of Christmas near,
Christmas, the joyous period of the year!
Now with bright holly all the temples strow
With lawrel green, and sacred mistletoe."

—Gay's *Trivia.* A writer in the "Gentleman's Magazine" for 1765, conjectures.

that the ancient custom of dressing churches and houses at Christmas with laurel, box, holly, or ivy. was in allusion to many figurative expressions in the prophets relative to Christ, the Branch of Righteousness, &c., or that it was in remembrance of the Oratory of wrythen Wands or Boughs, which was the first Christian Church erected in Britain. Before we can admit either of these hypotheses, the question must be determined whether or not this custom did not prevail at this season prior to the introduction of the Christian faith amongst us. The custom of decking churches at Christmas is still continued in Devonshire, as it was in Brand's day." Chandler tells us, in his "Travels in Greece," that it is related where Druidism prevailed the houses were decked with evergreens in December, that the sylvan spirits might repair to them, and remain unnipped with frost and cold winds, until a milder season had renewed the foliage of their darling abodes.

Churching of Women.—In a proclamation, dated 16th November, 30 Henry VIII., among many "laudable ceremonies and rytes" enjoined to be retained is the following: "Ceremonies used at purification of women delivered of chylde, and offerynge of theyr crysomes." In "A Part of a Register" (1593), in a list of "grosse poyntes of Poperie, evident to all men," is enumerated the following: "The churching of women with this psalme, that the sunne and moone shall not burn them": as is also, "The offeringe of the woman at hir churching." In the Chichester Articles of Inquiry, 1639, occurs the passage: "Doth the woman who is to be churched use the antient accustomed habit in such cases, with a white vail or kerchiefe upon her head?" It was anciently a custom for women in England to bear lights when they were churched, as appears from the following royal bon mot (for the historical truth of which there is no sufficient authority). William the Conqueror, by reason of sickness, kept his chamber a long time, whereat the French King, scoffing, said, "The King of England lyeth long in child-bed": which, when it was reported unto King William, he answered, "When I am churched, there shall be a thousand lights in France": "(alluding to the lights that women used to bear when they were churched): and after, wasting the French territories with that he performed within a few daies fire and sword." Compare *Carol* and *Yule*. In "The Burnynge of St. Paules Church in London, 1561," sign. I. 4 b. we read: "In Flaunders everye Saturdaye betwixt Christmas and Candlemas they eate flesh for joy. and have pardon for it, because our Ladye laye so long in childe-bedde, say they. We here may not

eat so; the Pope is not so good to us; yet surely it were as good reason that we should eat fleshe with them all that while that our Lady lay in child-bed, as that we shuld bear our candel at her churchinge at Candlemas with theym as they doe. It is seldome seene that men offer candels at womens churchinges, saving at our Ladies; but reason it is that she have some preferment if the Pope would be so good maister to us as to let us eat flesh with theym." Lupton says in his first book of "Notable Things": "If a man be the first that a woman meets after she comes out of the church, when she is newly churched, it signifies that her next child will be a boy; if she meet a woman, then a wench is likely to be her next child. This is credibly reported to me to be true." In the "Statistical Account of Scotland," it is said: "It was most unhappy for a woman, after bringing forth a child, to offer a visit, or for her neighbours to receive it, till she had been duly churched. How strongly did this enforce gratitude to the Supreme Being for a safe delivery! On the day when such a woman was churched, every family, favoured with a call, were bound to set meat and drink before her: and when they omitted to do so, they and theirs were to be loaded with her hunger. What was this, but an obligation on all who had it in their power to do the needful to prevent a feeble woman from fainting for want?" On a passage in his "History of Craven," where Master John Norton "gate leave of my old Lord to have half a stagg for his wife's churching." Whitaker observes in a note: "Hence it appears that thanksgivings after child-birth were anciently celebrated with feasting. He adds: "For this custom I have a still older authority: 'In iibur hosheveds vini albi empt' apud Ebor. erga purificationem Dominæ, tam post partum Mag'ri mei nuper de Clifford, quam post partum Mag'ri mei nunc de Clifford. . .lxvis. viijd.'" *Compotus Tho. Dom Clifford*, 15 *Henry VI.* Harrison, in his "Description of Britain," complains of the excessive feasting, as well at other festive meetings, as at "Purifications of women." It appears anciently to have been customary to give a large entertainment at the churching. In Deloney's "Thomas of Reading," 1632, signa. H iii. we read: "Sutton's Wife of Salisbury, which had lately bin delivered of a sonne, against her going to church prepared great cheare: at what time Simons wife of Southampton came thither, and so did divers others of the clothiers wives, onely to make merry at this churching-feast." In "The Batchellor's Banquet," 1603, attributed to Dekker, the lady (A 3) is introduced telling her husband: "You willed me (I was sent for) to go to Mistress M. Churching, and when I came thither I found great cheer and no small company of wives." And at c 2, the lady is asked : "If I had ever a new gown to be churched in." Among Shipman's Poems. is one dated 1667, and entitled, "The Churching Feast to Sr Clifford for a fat doe." Herrick, however, where he speaks of the churching ceremony omits reference to this entertainment. The ceremony of churching women in general sprang, no doubt, from the development of Candlemas into a festival of purification for the Virgin.

Church Steeples.—The custom of rustics in marking the outlines of their shoes on the tops of their church steeples, and engraving their names in the areas has been by Smart, in his "Hop-Garden," very sensibly referred to motives of vanity. As is the following, in the subsequent lines, to the pride of office :

> " With pride of heart the Churchwarden surveys
> High o'er the belfry, girt with birds and flow'rs,
> His story wrote in capitals : ' 'Twas I
> That bought the font ; and I repair'd the pews.' "

Churchyards.—It having been a current opinion in the times of heathenism, that places of burial were frequently haunted by spectres and apparitions, it is easy to imagine that the opinion has been transmitted from them, among the ignorant and unlearned, throughout all the ages of Christianity to this present day. The ancients believed that the ghosts of departed persons came out of their tombs and sepulchres, and wandered about the place where their remains lay buried. Thus Virgil tells us, that Mœris could call the ghosts out of their sepulchres and Ovid, that ghosts came out of their sepulchres and wandered about: and Clemens Alexandrinus upbraids them with the gods they worshipped; which, says he, are wont to appear at tombs and sepulchres, and which are nothing but fading spectres and airy forms. *Admonit. Ad. Gent*, p. 37. Mede observes from a passage of this same ancient father, that the heathens supposed the presence and power of Dæmons (for so the Greeks call the souls of men departed) at their coffins and sepulchres, as tho' there always remained some natural tie between the deceased and their relicts. Churchyards are certainly as little frequented by apparitions and ghosts as other places, and therefore it is a weakness to be afraid of passing through them. Superstition, however, will always attend ignorance ; and the night, as she continues to be the mother of dews, will also never fail of being the fruitful parent of chimerical fears. Even Shakespear says :

> " Now it is the time of night,
> That the graves all gaping wide,
> Ev'ry one lets forth his sprite
> In the church-way path to glide."

And Dryden :

> " When the sun sets, shadows that shew'd at noon
> But small, appear most long and terrible."

A more modern author follows on the same side :

> " Oft in the lone church yard at night I've seen
> By glimpse of moon-shine, checqu'ring thro' the trees,
> The school-boy, with his satchel in his hand,
> Whistling aloud to bear his courage up,
> And, lightly tripping o'er the long flat stones
> (With nettles skirted, and with moss o'ergrown),
> That tell in homely phrase who lie below.
> Sudden he starts ! and hears, or thinks he hears,
> The sound of something purring at his heels :
> Full fast he flies, and dares not look behind him,
> Till, out of breath, he overtakes his fellows ;
> Who gather round, and wonder at the tale
> Of horrid apparition, tall and ghastly,
> That walks at dead of night, or takes his stand,
> O'er some new open'd grave ; and (strange to tell !)
> Evanishes at crowing of the cock."

—*Blair's Grave.* We learn from Moresin, that churchyards were used for the purposes of interment in order to remove superstition.

Burial was in ancient times without the walls of cities and towns. Lycurgus, he tells us, first introduced grave stones within the walls, and as it were brought home the ghosts to the very doors. Thus we compel horses, that are apt to startle, to make the nearest approaches we can to the objects at which they have taken the alarm. "Christians," says Laurence, " distinguished their oratories into an atrium, a church yard ; a sanctum, a church ; a sanctum sanctorum, a chancell. They did conceive a greater degree of sanctitie in one of them, than in another, and on one place of them than another ; churchyards they thought profaned by sports ; the whole circuit both before and after Christ was privileged for refuge, none out of the communion of the kirke permitted to lie there, any consecrate ground preferred for interment before that which was not consecrat, and that in an higher esteem which was in an higher degree of consecration, and that in the highest which was neerest the altar." "Sermon preached before the King, &c.," p. 9, cited in "The Canterburian's Self-conviction, &c.," 1640, p. 83, note. Bailey tells us that, in ancient times amongst Christians, upon any extraordinary solemnity, particularly the anniversary dedication of a church, tradesmen used to bring and sell their wares even in the churchyards, especially upon the festival of the dedication; as at Westminster on St. Peter's Day; at London on St. Bartholomew's; at Durham on St. Cuthbert's Day, &c.; but riots and disturbances often happening, by reason of the numbers assembled together, privileges were by royal charter granted, for various causes, to particular places, towns, and places of strength, where magistrates presided to keep the people in order. In the Suffolk Articles of Enquiry, 1638, we read: "Have any playes, feasts, banquets, suppers, church ales, drinkings, temporal courts or leets, lay juries, musters, exercise of dauncing, stoole ball, foot ball, or the like, or any other prophane usage been suffered to be kept in your church, chappell, or church yard?" At Barnes, Surrey, among other ordinary benefactions, there was the Rose Acre, at present commuted for a sum in consols. The ground was left by a person so named, on condition that over his grave in the churchyard against the south wall of the church a rose-tree should be always kept growing and so it is unto this day. In "Magna Carta," 1556, I find the statute, "Ne Rector prosternet Arbores in Cemiterio."

Churn Supper.—There was a churn or kern supper (so they pronounce it vulgarly in Northumberland), and a shouting the church or kern. This, Aram informs us, was different from that of the Mell Supper: the former being always provided when all was shorn, the latter after all was got in. I should have thought that most certainly kern supper was no more than corn supper, had not Aram asserted that it was called the Churn Supper, because from immemorial times it was customary to produce in a churn a great quantity of cream, and to circulate it in cups to each of the rustic company, to be eaten with bread. This custom, in Aram's time, survived about Whitby and Scarborough, in the Eastern parts of Yorkshire, and round about Gisburne, &c., in the West. In other places cream has been commuted for ale, and the tankard politely preferred to the churn.

Cinque. — The famous Cornelius Scriblerus writes: "The play which the Italians call Cinque and the French Mourre is extremely antient. It was played by Hymen and Cupid at the marriage of Psyche, and was termed by the Latins *digitis micare*." The French game of Mourre is thus explained by Littrè: "un jeu qui consiste à montrer rapidement une partie des doigts leveé et l'autre fermée, afin de donner à deviner le nombre de ceux qui sont levès." Cornelius was apparently justified in dissuading Martin from bestowing his time on this recreation.

Cinque Ports.—Mr. Miall Green, of Streatham Hill, owner of the yachts Thalatta, Yolande, and Figaro, was on the 2nd December, 1901, elected deputy-mayor of Brightlingsea, an apanage of the Cinque Ports, in succession to Capt. Sycamore, of the Shamrock. The ceremony is a curious one, the council chamber being the tower of the parish church, while the vicar acts as recorder. Each elected freeman pays 11 pennies to the civic exchequer. Comp. *Brightlingsea*.

Clameur de Haro. — I presume that the Ara mentioned in Walford's *Fairs, Past and Present*, 1883, p. 9, is another form of Haro, being the cry when the settling time arrived at a certain stage in the operations. The following remarks appeared in the *Daily News* for June 1, 1882: "Several learned members of the French Académie des Sciences have come to the conclusion that the old fashioned 'Clameur de Haro' might be revived to advantage in civil procedure, as a means of enabling small landed proprietors and other humble owners of house property to fight their more wealthy opponents on better terms than they can under the existing laws. It is scarcely probable that the French Parliament will legislate in the sense suggested, but in the course of the discussion which has been going on, M. Glasson, who read a long essay on the subject, gave some very interesting information as to the origin of the word. According to M. Glasson the 'Clameur de Haro' is identical with the 'Legatro of the Bavarians and the Thuringians, and the first trace of it in France is to be found in the 'Grand Coutumier de Normandie.' The 'Clameur de Haro,' or cry for justice, only resorted to in criminal cases at first, is referred to under the name of 'Clamor Violentiæ' in the Saxon laws. It may be assumed, therefore, that when William the Conqueror came to England, he found the equivalent of the 'Clameur de Haro' in existence, and the changes which he made in the application of it tended to bring the English mode of procedure into closer conformity of detail with that which prevailed in Normandy. In course of time the 'Clameur de Haro' was made applicable to civil as well as to criminal affairs, and long after it had fallen into disuse for the latter—its utility becoming less and less as the organization of society grew more and more perfect—it was retained in use throughout the north-west provinces of France for cases of disputed possession, and was not actually repealed until the close of the 18th century. It still exists in the neighbouring Channel Islands, and the owners of property attach great value to it. A very striking instance of this was afforded in Jersey the other day, the owner of some property through which a railway was to be cut raising the 'Clameur de Haro.' He was so stout that he had great difficulty in fulfilling the indispensable formality of falling on his knees and getting up again with the cry in old French — 'Haro! Haro! A l'aide, mon Prince, on me fait tort.' It is not stated whether he gained his point; but there can be no doubt as to the attachment of the Channel Islanders to this survival of the Middle Ages." In the *Encyclopædia* of Chambers, 1874, v., 699 *back*, there is an implied suggestion, which is probably of no weight whatever, that *Haro* is a corruption or abbreviated form of Ha! Rollo! the appeal of the party having been originally to Duke Rollo.

Clavie.—Under the heading of "Relics of Fire-Worship in Scotland," the *Daily News* of January 4, 1878, has the following communication:—"On the last day of the year, old style, which falls on the 12th January, the festival of "The Clavie" takes place at Burghead, a fishing village near Forres. On a headland in that vilage still stands an old Roman altar, locally called the "Douro." On the evening of January 12 a large tar barrel is set on fire and carried by one of the fishermen round the town, while the assembled folks shout and holloa. If the man who carries the barrel falls, it is an evil omen. The man with the lighted barrel having gone with it round the town carries it up to the top of the hill, and places it on the Douro. More fuel is immediately added. The sparks as they fly upwards are supposed to be witches and evil spirits leaving the town; the people therefore shout at and curse them as they disappear in vacancy. When the burning tar barrel falls in pieces, the fisherwives rush in and endeavour to get a lighted bit of wood from its remains; with this light the fire on the cottage hearth is at once kindled, and it is considered lucky to keep in this flame all the rest of the year. The charcoal of the Clavie is collected and put in bits up the chimney, to prevent the witches and evil spirits coming into the house. The Duoro (i.e., the Roman altar) is covered with a thick layer of tar from the fires that are annually lighted upon it. Close to the Douro is a very ancient Roman well, and, close to the well, several rude but curious Roman sculptures can be seen let into a garden wall.

Clay-Daubing. — Brockett notices the Cumberland usage by which the friends of a newly-married couple met together, and erected them a cottage, before separating. This (he says) was called claydaubing.

Cleaver.—A school-boy's toy. See Halliwell in v.

Cleke.—See *Gleek.*

Clement's Day, St.—(November 23). Plot, describing a Clog Almanack, (which is now in the Bodleian library), says, "a pot is marked against the 23rd of November, for the Feast of St. Clement, from the ancient custom of going about that night to beg drink to make merry with." In the Privy Purse Expenses of the Princess Mary, under November, 1537, is this entry: "Itm. geuen to the bakers of the Prince house on saynt Clementes Even comyng wt theyr Bolle. . . .vs."; upon which the Editor (Sir F. Madden), referring to Hone's "Every Day Book," observes: "In more modern times, the blacksmiths seem to have usurped the privilege of the bakers." In a proclamation, July 22, 1540, it is ordered: "Neither that children should be decked, ne go about upon S. Nicholas, S. Katherine, S. Clement, the Holy Innocents, and such likes dayes." In some almanacks, this day is marked at Old Martinmass, because it is still here and there retained as one of the quarterly divisions of the year, on which payments fall due. At Tenby, on St. Clement's Day, the effigy of a carpenter was carried round the town, and subsequently cut to pieces. In Staffordshire, on this day, the children go about begging for apples, and singing these rude verses:

" Clemeny, Clemeny, God be wi' you,
  Christmas comes but once a ye-ar;
  When it comes, it will soon be gone,
  Give me an apple, and I'll be gone."

Closh.—A form of ninepins, noticed by Minsheu as forbidden by Statute 17 Edw. IV., cap. 3, and again in 18-20-23 Henry VIII. The ninepins were either of wood or of the shank-bones of a horse or ox. This sport was sometimes called closh-cayles. From a statement by Strutt it may be perhaps inferred that there were two varieties of closh or closh-cayles, that played with a ball, and that played with a club or stick, the latter resembling the French *jeu de quilles à baston.* The French word quille, however, —our cayles —was applied to the stick employed in other sports. Among our ancestors, as is still largely the case, all this family of recreations was popular rather than fashionable. Sir Thomas Elyot, in his *Governor*, 1531, classes *claishe pynnes* with bowls and quoits.

Coal.—Thomas Hill, in his *Natural and Artificial Conclusions*, 1581, describes "The vertue of a rare cole, that is to be found but one hour in the day, and one day in the yeare." "Divers authors," he adds, "affirm concerning the verity and vertue of this cole, viz., that it is onely to be found upon Midsummer Eve, just at noon, under every root of plantine and of mugwort; the effects whereof are wo derful: for whosoever weareth or beareth the same about with them, shall be freed from the plague, fever, ague, and sundry other diseases. And one author especially writeth, and constantly averreth, that he never knew any that used to carry of this marvellous cole about them, who ever were to his knowledge sick of the plague, or (indeed) complained of any other maladie." Lupton observes, "It is certainly and constantly affirmed that on Midsummer Eve there is found, under the root of mugwort, a coal which saves or keeps them safe from the plague, carbuncle, lightning, the quartan ague, and from burning, that bear the same about them: and Mizaldus, the writer hereof, saith, that he doth hear that it is to be found the same day under the root of plantane, which I know to be of truth, for I have found them the same day under the root of plantane, which is especially and chiefly to be found at noon." *Notable Things*, first printed in 1579, ed. 1660, book ii. p. 59. "The last summer," says Aubrey, "on the day of St. John Baptist, 1694, I accidentally was walking in the pasture behind Montague House, (Bloomsbury); it was 12 o'clock, I saw there about two or three and twenty young women, most of them well habited, on their knees, very busy, as if they had been weeding. A young man told me that they were looking for a coal under the root of a plantain, to put under their heads that night, and they should dream who would be their husbands. It was to be that day and hour."

Coat-Money.—See Davis, *Suppl. Glossary*, 1881, in v.

Cob or **Cobbing.**—A punishment used by seamen for petty offences or irregularities among themselves: it consists in bastanadoing the offender on the posteriors with a cobbing stick, or pipe staff; the number usually inflicted is a dozen. At the first stroke the executioner repeats the word watch, on which all persons present are to take off their hats, on pain of like punishment: the last stroke is always given as hard as possible, and is called the purse. Ashore, among soldiers, where this punishment is sometimes adopted, watch and the purse are not included in the number, but given over and above, or, in the vulgar phrase, free, gratis, for nothing. This piece of discipline is also inflicted in Ireland by the schoolboys on persons coming into the school without taking off their hats; it is there called school-butter."

Cob Loaf Stealing.—Compare *Aston*.

Cob-Nút.—A game which consists in pitching at a row of nuts piled up in heaps of four, three at the bottom and one at the top of each heap. Halliwell in v.

Cock.—A mode of evading the law against profane expressions, used both in conversation and literature in James I.'s time. It is common in the old plays. Compare Nares, 1859, in v. The modern equivalent is *Scott*. Our youths say *Great Scott* for *Great God*.

Cockal.—The game played with the huckle or pastern bone of the sheep, instead of dice, corresponding with the ancient *ludus talaris* or *astralagus*. Compare Nares, *Gloss.* 1859, in v. In Levinus Lemnius, we read: "The antients used to play at cokall or casting of huckle bones, which is done with smooth sheeps bones. The Dutch call them pickelen, wherewith our young maids that are not yet ripe use to play for a husband, and young married folks despise these as soon as they are married. But young men used to contend one with another with a kind of bone taken forth of oxe-feet. The Dutch call them Coten, and they play with these at a set time of the year. Moreover cockles which the Dutch call Teelings are different from dice, for they are square with four sides, and dice have six. Cockals are used by maids amongst us, and do no wayes waste any ones estate. For either they passe away the time with them, or if they have time to be idle, they play for some small matter, as for chesnuts, filberds, pins, buttons, and some such Juncats."— *Occult Miracles of Nature*, 1658, p. 768. In Kinder's translation from the same author of *A Sanctuarie of Salvation*, p. 144, these bones are called "Huckle-bones or coytes." In Polydore Vergil we have another description of this game: "There is a game also that is played with the posterne bone in the hynder foote of a sheepe, oxe, gote, fallowe or redde dere, whiche in Latin is called Talus. It hath foure chaunces, the ace point, that is named Canis, or Caniculas, was one of the sides; he that cast it leyed doune a peny or so muche as the gamers were agreed on; the other side was called Venus, that signifieth seven. He that cast the chaunce wan sixe and all that was layd doune for the castyng of Canis. The two other sides were called Chius and Senio. He that did throwe Chius wan three. And he that cast Senio gained foure. This game (as I take it) is used of children in Northfolke, and they call it the chaunce bone; they play with three or foure of those bones together; it is either the same or very lyke to it." Langley's Abridg., fol. 1. Herrick seems to speak of cockall as a children's sport, played with points and pins. For farther information relating to this game, as played by the ancients, the reader may consult Joannis Meursii Ludibunda, sivi de Ludis Græcorum, 1625, p. 7, πάσσαλος and Dan. Souterii "Palimedes," p. 81, but more particularly "I Tali ed altri Strumenti lusori degli antichi Romani discritti" da Fransecso de' Ficoroni, 1734. And for the Greek analogue St. John's *Manners and Customs of Ancient Greece*, 1842, i., 160-1.

Cockatrice or **Basilisk.** — Sir Thomas Browne informs us that the generation of a basilisk is supposed to proceed from a cock's egg hatched under a toad or serpent. A conceit which he observes is as monstrous as the brood itself. This writer endeavours to account for its killing at a distance. "It killeth at a distance — it poisoneth by the eye, and by priority of vision. Now that deleterious it may be at some distance, and destructive without corporal contaction, what uncertainty soever there be in the effect, there is no high improbability in the relation. For if plagues or pestilential atomes have been conveyed in the air from different regions: if men at a distance have infected each other: if the shadowes of some trees be noxious: if torpedoes deliver their opium at a distance, and stupifie beyond themselves: we cannot reasonably deny that there may proceed from subtiller seeds more agile emanations, which contemn those laws, and invade at distance unexpected. Thus it is not impossible what is affirmed of this animal; the visible rayes of their eyes carrying forth the subtilest portion of their poison which, received by the eye of man or beast, infecteth first the brain and is from thence communicated unto the heart." He adds: "Our basilisk is generally described with legs, wings, a serpentine and winding taile, and a crist or comb somewhat like a cock. But the basilisk of elder times was a proper kind of serpent, not above three palmes long, as some account, and differenced from other serpents by advancing his head and some white marks or coronary spots upon the crown, as all authentic writers have delivered." A cockatrice hatched from a cock's egg is described by a foreign author as one of the terrors of the superstitious man, and as an omen of the most pernicious sort. Werenfel's "Dissertation on Superstition," transl. into Engl. p. 7. This reminds us of Dryden's lines:

"Mischiefs are like the cockatrice's eye;
If they see first, they kill; if seen, they die."

Compare Nares, *Glossary*, 1859, in v.

Cockchafer.—I conclude that we must not allow the German children's invocation to the cockchafer or lady-bird

(lady-bug or lady-cow) to rank among modes of predestination; but it may be perhaps, in its present form, the relic of an older and more serious superstition:

"May-bug, May-bug, tell this to me,
How many years my life is to be?
One year, two years," &c.

Or, as the Swiss couplet runs (translated):
"O chafer, O chafer, fly off and awa',
For milk, and for bread, and a silver spoon bra'."

For which notices I am indebted to Mr. Atkinson. But there are variant versions. Comp. Halliwell's *Nursery Rhymes*, 6th ed. pp. 263, 272.

Cock-Crow.—The ancients, because the cock gives notice of the approach and break of day, have, with a propriety equal to any thing in their mythology, dedicated this bird to Apollo. They have also made him the emblem of watchfulness, from the circumstance of his summoning men to their business by his crowing, and have therefore dedicated him also to Mercury. With the lark he may be poetically styled the "Herald of the Morn." Philostratus, giving an account of the Apparition of Achilles' Shade to Apollonius Tyaneus, says, that it vanished with a little glimmer as soon as the cock crowed. "Vit. Apol." vol. iv. p. 16. Reed's "Shakespear," vol. iv. p. 16. Bourne very seriously examines the fact whether spirits roam about in the night, or are obliged to go away at cock-crow. The traditions of all ages appropriate the appearance of spirits to the night. The Jews had an opinion that hurtful spirits walked about in the night. The same opinion obtained among the ancient Christians, who divided the night into four watches called the evening, midnight, cock-crowing, and the morning. The opinion that spirits fly away at cock-crow is certainly very ancient, for we find it mentioned by the Christian poet Prudentius, who flourished in the beginning of the fourth century, as a tradition of common belief:

"They say the wandering powers, that love
The silent darkness of the night,
At cock-crowing give o'er to rove,
And all in fear do take their flight.
The approaching salutary morn,
Th' approach divine of hated day,
Makes darkness to its place return,
And drives the midnight ghosts away.
They know that this an emblem is,
Of what precedes our lasting bliss,
That morn when graves give up their dead
In certain hope to meet their God."

Bourne tells us he never met with any reasons assigned for the departure of spirits at the cock-crowing: "but," he adds, "there have been produced at that time of night, things of very memorable worth, which might perhaps raise the pious credulity of some men to imagine that there was something more in it than in other times. It was about the time of cock-crowing when our Saviour was born, and the angels sang the first Christmas carol to the poor shepherds in the fields of Bethlehem. Now it may be presumed, as the Saviour of the world was then born, and the heavenly Host had then descended to proclaim the news, that the Angel of Darkness would be terrified and confounded, and immediately fly away: and perhaps this consideration has partly been the foundation of this opinion." It was also about this time when our Saviour rose from the dead. "A third reason is, that passage in the Book of Genesis, where Jacob wrestled with the angel for a blessing, where the angels say unto him 'Let me go, for the day breaketh.'" Bourne, however, thinks this tradition seems more especially to have arisen from some particular circumstances attending the time of cockcrowing; and which, as Prudentius, before cited, seems to say, "are an emblem of the approach of the Day of Resurrection." "The circumstances, therefore, of the time of cock-crowing," he adds, "being so natural a figure and representation of the morning of the Resurrection; the night so shadowing out the night of the grave: the third watch, being, as some suppose, the time our Saviour will come to judgement at: the noise of the cock awakening sleepy man and telling him, as it were, the night is far spent, the day is at hand: representing so naturally the voice of the Arch-angel awakening the dead, and calling up the righteous to everlasting day: so naturally does the time of cock-crowing shadow out these things, that probably some good well-meaning men might have been brought to believe that the very devils themselves, when the cock crew and reminded them of them, did fear and tremble, and shun the light."

In the prose Life of St. Guthlac, Hermit of Crowland, by one Felix, *circâ* 749, there is the following passage: "It happened one night, when it was the time of cockcrowing, and the blessed man Guthlac fell to his morning prayers, he was suddenly entranced in light slumber—." I quote from Mr. Goodwin's translation of the Anglo-Saxon original. The following is from Chaucer's "Assemble of Foules," f. 235:

"The tame ruddocke and the coward kite,
The cocke, that horologe is of Thropes lite."

Spenser writes:
—— "The morning cocke crew loud;
And at the sound it shrunk in haste away,
And vanish'd from our sight."

Allot, in "England's Parnassus," 1600, printed the two following lines from Drayton's "Endimion and Phœbe, (1593)."
"And now the cocke, the morning's trumpeter,
Plaid hunts up for the day-starre to appeare."—

Where Gray has followed our poet:
"The cock's shrill clarion, or the echoing horn,
No more shall rouse them from their lowly bed."
"But soft, methinks I scent the morning air—
Brief let me be."

And again,
"The glow-worm shows the matin to be near."

In the "Merry Devil of Edmonton," 1608:
"More watchfull than the day-proclayming cocke."

It appears from a passage in "Romeo and Juliet," that Shakespear means that they were carousing till three o'clock:
"—— The second cock has crow'd,
The curfew-bell has toll'd; 'tis three o'clock."

Perhaps Tusser makes this point clear:
"Cocke croweth at midnight times few above six,
With pause to his neighbour to answer betwix:
At three aclocke thicker, and then as ye knowe,
Like all in to mattens neere day they doo crowe;
At midnight, at three, and an hour yer day,
They utter their language as well as they may."

By a passage in "Macbeth," "we were carousing till the second cock," it should seem to appear as if there were two separate times of cock-crowing. The commentators, however, say nothing of this. They explain the passage as follows: "Till the second cock:—Cock-crowing." So in "King Lear": "He begins at curfew, and walks till the first cock." Which is illustrated by a passage in the "Twelve Merry Jestes of the Widow Edith," 1525:
"The time they pas merely til ten of the clok,
Yea, and I shall not lye, till after the first cok."

"The cock crows and the morn grows on,
When 'tis decreed I must be gone."
—*Hudibras*, Canto i. p. iii.

In Blair's *Grave* is a passage which seems to form an exception from the general time of cock-crowing:

"Some say, that ever 'gainst that season comes,
Wherein our Saviour's birth is celebrated,
This bird of dawning singeth all night long.
And then, they say, no spirit dares stir abroad;
The nights are wholesome; then no planets strike,
No fairy takes, nor witch hath power to charm,
So hallow'd and so gracious is the time."

Bourne tells us, there is a tradition among the common people that at the time of cock-crowing the midnight spirits forsake these lower regions, and go to their proper places. Hence it is that in the country villages, where the way of life requires more early labour, the inhabitants always go cheerfully to work at that time: whereas if they are called abroad sooner, they are apt to imagine everything they see or hear to be a wandering ghost. Shakespear has given us an excellent account of this vulgar notion in his "Hamlet." The present writer suggested long since that the "early village cock" of Shakespear should be *early village clock*, as the word chanticleer has been given, and *cock* in the passage is a pleonasm. See my edition of W. Browne, 1868, i., 197. Peter Suavenius, who visited Scotland about 1535, relates in his MS. Diary that there is a place there, eight miles in circuit, where the cocks never crow.

Cock-Fighting.—Bailey tells us that the origin of this sport was derived from the Athenians on the following occasion: when Themistocles was marching his army against the Persians, he, by the way, espying two cocks fighting, caused his army to behold them, and addressed them as follows: "Behold, these do not fight for their household gods, for the monuments of their ancestors, nor for glory, nor for liberty, nor for the safety of their children, but only because the one will not give way unto the other." This so encouraged the Grecians that they fought strenuously and obtained the victory over the Persians; upon which cock-fighting was by a particular law ordained to be annually practised by the Athenians. Cock-fighting was an institution partly religious and partly political at Athens, and was continued there for the purpose of improving the seeds of valour in the minds of the Athenian youth. But it was afterwards abused and perverted, both there and in other parts of Greece, to a common pastime and amusement, without any moral, political, or religious intention,

and as it is now followed and practiced amongst us. Men have long availed themselves of the antipathy which one cock shows to another, and have encouraged that natural hatred with arts that may be said to disgrace human reason. Pegge has proved that though the ancient Greeks piqued themselves on their politeness, calling all other nations barbarous, yet they were the authors of this cruel and inhuman mode of diversion. The inhabitants of Delos were great lovers of this sport: and Tanagra, a city of Bœotia, the Isle of Rhodes, Chalcis in Eubœa and the country of Media, were famous for their generous and magnanimous race of chickens. It appears that the Greeks had some method of preparing the birds for battle. An account of the origin of this custom amongst the Athenians may be seen in Ælian," lib. ii. cap. xxviii. It may be worth noting that George Wilson, in his "Commendation of cocks and cock-fighting," 1607, endeavours to show that cock-fighting was before the coming of Christ. Lord Northampton says: "The Romaines tooke the crowing of a cocke for an abode of victory, though no philosopher be ignorant that this procedeth of a gallant lustinesse upon the first digestion." *Defensative*, 1583, sign. T. 2 *verso*. It is probable that cock-fighting was first introduced into this island by the Romans; the bird itself was here before Cæsar's arrival. *Bell-Gall.* v. sect. 12.

Fitzstephen is the first of our writers that mentions cock-fighting, describing it as the sport of school boys on Shrove-Tuesday. The cock-pit, it seems, was the school, and the master was the comptroller and director of the sport. Fitzstephen writes: " — that we may begin with the pastimes of the boys (as we have all been boys), annually on the day which is called Shrove-Tuesday, the boys of the respective schools bring to the masters each one his fighting-cock, and they are indulged all the morning with seeing their cocks fight in the school-room." Fd. 1772, p. 45. In the statutes of St. Paul's School, A.D. 1518, the following clause occurs: "I will they use no cock-fighting nor ridinge about of victorye, nor disputing at St. Bartilemewe, which is but foolish babling and losse of time." Knight's *Life of Dean Colet*, p. 362. From this time, at least, the diversion, however absurd and even impious, was continued among us. It was followed, though disapproved and prohibited in the 39 Edw. III.: also in the reign of Henry VIII. and in 1569. It has been called by some a royal diversion, and, as every one knows, the cock-pit at Whitehall was erected by Henry VIII. for the more magnificent celebration of the sport. It was prohibited, however, by an Act of March 31, 1654. Moresin informs us that

the Papists derived this custom of exhibiting cockfights on one day every year from
the Athenians, and from an institution of
Themistocles. "Cæl. Rhod." lib. ix.
variar lect. cap. xlvi. idem Pargami fiebat.
Alex. ab. Alex. lib. v. cap. 8., *Papatus*,
p. 66.

The Fathers of the Church inveigh
with great warmth against the spectacles of the arena, the wanton shed-
ding of human blood in sport; one
would have thought that with that
of the gladiators, cock-fighting would
also have been discarded under the
mild and human Genius of Christianity. But, as Pegge observes, it was reserved for this enlightened æra to practice
it with new and aggravated circumstances
of cruelty. In the *Privy Purse Expences
of Henry VII.*, under 1493, there is the
entry: "March 2. To Master Bray, for
rewardes to them that brought cokkes at
Shrovetide at Westmr., £1." In the
middle of the 16th century we find the
gentlemen of Yorkshire keenly interested
in this sport, and there is a letter from Sir
Henry Savile to William Plumpton, Esq.,
announcing "a meeting of cocks" at Sheffield, to which their common acquaintance
were expected to come, save from more or
less considerable distances. It was a match
between Lancashire, Derbyshire, and Hallamshire. *Plumpton Correspondence*, 1839,
pp. 250-1. Stubbes, in his "Anatomie of
Abuses," 1583, inveighs against cock-fighting, which in his day seems to have been
practiced on the Sabbath in England:

"*Cock Fightyng in Ailgna* [*Anglia*].

"Besides these exercises, they flock
thicke and threefolde to the cockfightes, an
exercise nothing inferiour to the rest,
where nothing is vsed, but swearing, for-
swearing, deceit, fraud, collusion, cosenage, skoldyng, railyng, conuitious talkyng,
fightyng, brawlyng, quarrelyng, drinkyng,
and whoryng, and whiche is worst of all,
robbing of one an other of their goodes,
and that not by direct, but indirecte
meanes and attempts. And yet to
blaunche and set out these mischeefs withall, (as though they were vertues), they
haue their appointed waies and set houres
when these deuilries must be exercised.
They haue houses erected to that purpose
flagges and ensignes hanged out, to giue
notice of it to others, and proclamation
goes out, to proclame the same, to the ende
that many maie come to the dedication of
this solemne feast of mischeefe." It is
odd enough, that the poverty of Roger Ascham, who was preceptor to Queen Elizabeth, and one of the most learned persons
of his time, was attributed by the no less
learned Camden to dicing and cock-fighting! It appears that James I. was remarkably fond of cock-fighting. Breton,

in his *Fantasticks*, 1626, says under Aug.:
"I had a touch at your recreations before,
and that your cock may not kick your
coyn out of your pocket, I shall give you
some marks to choose a good one by;
Know, then, that the best characters desirable in a fighting cock, are his shape,
colour, courage, and sharp heel; for his
shape, the middle size is ever accounted
best, because they be now most matchable
strong, nimble, and ready for your pleasure in his batel; and so the exceeding
little cock is as hard to match, and is commonly weak and tedious in his maner of
fighting; he would be of a proud and upright shape, with a small head, like a
spar-hawk, quick large eye, and a strong
back crooked, and big at the setting on,
and in colour suitable to the plume of his
feathers, as black, yellow, or reddish; the
beam of his legs would be very strong,
and according to his plume, blew, gray,
or yellow; his spurs long, rough and sharp,
and a little bending, and looking inward;
for his colour, the gray pyle, the yellow
pyle, or the red with the blanck breast, is
esteemed the best, the pyde is not so good,
and the white and dun are the worst; if
it be red about the head like scarlet, it is
a sign of lust, strength, and courage;
but if it be pale, it is a signe of sickness
and faintness; for his courage, you shall
observe it in his walk, by his treading,
and in the pride of his going, and in his
pen by his oft-crowing; for the sharpness
of his heel, it is only seen in his fighting;
for what cock is said to be sharp or narrow
heel'd, which every time he risketh, he hit-
teth and draws blood of his adversary,
gilding his spurs in blood, and threatening
at every blow an end of the battel. I wish
you such a Cock." I have quoted this interesting passage from Stevenson's *Twelve
Months*, 1661, but it is the same work as
Breton's under a different title.

Of this sport, as it was conducted in
London in 1669, an Italian resident has
left a graphic account. "The places
made for the cock-fights are a sort
of little theatre, where the spectators sit
all round on steps under cover. At the
bottom of these is a round table six *braccia*
in diameter, or thereabouts, and raised
about two *braccia* from the ground: it is
covered with matting all stained with the
blood of cocks. The days on which they
are going to have the contests are always
advertised by large printed bills, stuck
up at all the corners of the streets, and distributed through the city. When a large
crowd of people has been got together, two
cocks are brought out in sacks by two of
those men whose business it is to breed
them and look after them. One of these
men goes in at one side of the theatre, and
the other at the opposite entrance, and
having taken their cocks out of the bags,

they hold them in their hands, whilst the first betting is going on, which everyone does without any rule or regulation whatever, being solely actuated by his own judgment, which makes him fancy one cock more than another. The cocks have their wings cut and their crests removed. They are not generally finely-grown birds, but are very strong, and of extraordinary pluck. Half-way up their legs they are armed with a kind of spur of very sharp steel, with which, when they flutter up into the air, and come to close quarters with their beaks, they wound each other severely. As soon as they are set at liberty, the combatants glare at each other for a little while, and fix each other with their eyes. They then proceed to the contest with their necks stretched out, and all their feathers ruffled. At first they approach one another slowly, step by step; then all of a sudden they dart at one another, flapping their wings to raise themselves from the ground so as to attack each other in mid-air, and wound one another with their beaks with such fury that at the commencement you would think that a very keen contest was going to ensue. However, the truth is that they tire themselves by degrees, and the end becomes very tedious, simply reducing itself to this: that one sets to work to kill the other by the sheer fury of its pecking on the head and eyes of its enemy, which part of the scene will last over a quarter of an hour, and sometimes nearly half an hour. During the time that the contest lasts, you hear a perpetual buzz amongst those who are betting, who are doubling, trebling—nay, even quadrupling—their original bets; and there are those who make new ones, according as they see how the cocks are getting on. It often happens that when one of the birds appears to be conquered, and on the point of death, it will become restored to such wonderful vigour that it vanquishes the stronger and kills him, and when it happens, as in the last case, that the beaten cock seems roused up to courage again, then are the wildest bets made—twenty, thirty or a hundred to one. Sometimes it happens that both birds are left dead on the field of battle; sometimes when the first is dead, the other will drag itself on to the body of its enemy, and with the little breath that remains to it, will flap its wings and crow for victory. After this he will lay himself down to die. When one duel is finished, other cocks are brought on as long as there are people left to ask for them. You pay a shilling to enter, which goes into the purse of those who for this end breed the cocks. So that six or eight couples of cocks, which do not always die on the same day, are paid for with the sum of from forty to fifty crowns. This race of animal is not so plucky, when

once it is taken out of the island, it having been proved that in Normandy they do not do as well as in England. The hatred between them is natural, so that immediately they cease to be chickens they have to be fed separately, otherwise they would quickly kill one another." *Antiquary*, August 1884.

In the "Statistical Account of Scotland," vol. iii., p. 378, the minister of Applecross, co. Ross, speaking of the Schoolmaster's perquisites, says: "he has the cock-fight dues, which are equal to one quarter's payment for each scholar." In "Lluellin's Poems," 1646, is a song, in which the author seems ironically to satirize this cruel sport. In a copy of verses upon two cocks fighting, by Dr. R. Wild, the spirited qualities of the combatants are given in the following most brilliant couplet:

"They scorn the dunghill; 'tis their only prize
To dig for pearls within each other's eyes."

Our Poet makes his conquered or dying cock dictate a will, some of the quaint items of which follow:

"Imp. first of all, let never be forgot,
My body freely I bequeath to th' pot,
Decently to be boil'd, and for it's tomb,
Let me be buried in some hungry womb.
Item, executors I will have none
But he that on my side laid seven to one,
And like a gentleman that he may live,
To him and to his heirs my comb I give."

Misson, in his "Travels in England," about 1698, p. 39, says: "Cockfighting is one of the great English diversions. They build amphitheatres for this purpose, and persons of quality sometimes appear at them. Great wagers are laid; but I am told that a man may be damnably bubbled, if he is not very sharp." At p. 304 he tells us: "Cock fighting is a royal pleasure in England. The combats between bulls and dogs, bears and dogs, and sometimes bulls and bears, are not battels to death, as those of cocks." It appears that in 1763 there was no such diversion as public cock-fighting at Edinburgh. In 1783, there were many public cock-fighting matches, or mains, as they were technically termed; and a regular cock-pit was built for the accommodation of this school of gambling and cruelty, where every distinction of rank and character is levelled. In 1790, the cock-pit continued to be frequented." Gunning, in his "Reminiscences of Cambridge," under 1796, observes in a note: "Cock-fighting was much in fashion at this time, and as the races of the country towns approached, matches between the gentlemen of Cambridge and Suffolk were frequently announced." It seems that the defaulters at a cock-pit, like welchers at a horse-race, were roughly treated ; for Gunning, speaking of a noted hand at the game, adds : " The last account that reached the University was that he (the defaulter) was seen in the basket, at a cock-pit, the usual punishment for men who made bets which they were unable to pay—." In Brand's time cock-fighting still continued to be a favourite sport of the colliers in the North of England. The clamorous wants of their families solicited them to go to work in vain, when a match was heard of. Brand relates that in performing the service appropriated to the visitation of the sick with a collier, who died a few days afterwards, " to my great astonishment I was interrupted by the crowing of a game cock hung in a bag over his head. To this exultation an immediate answer was given by another cock concealed in a closet, to which the first replied, and instantly the last rejoined. I never remember to have met with an incident so truly of the tragi-comical cast as this, and could not proceed in the execution of that very solemn office, till one of the disputants was removed. It had been industriously hung beside him, it should seem for the sake of company. He had thus an opportunity of casting at an object he had dearly loved in the days of his health and strength, what Gray has well called " a long lingering look behind." The authors of " Lancashire Folk Lore," 1867, say : " About thirty years ago, cock-fighting formed a common pastime about Mellor and Blackburn. A blacksmith, named Miller, used to keep a large number of cocks for fighting purposes. He was said to have sold himself to the devil, in order to have money enough for betting, and it was remarked that he rarely won." They also notice that the Denton estates were held in 1780 under leases, the terms of which required the tenants to provide the landlord with a dog and a cock, or the equivalent in money. The late Mr. Thomas Miles, land-agent of Keyham, near Leicester, who probably knew more of the concerns of the families for miles round than any individual of his time, used to mention that Jones, the parson at Ashby, would have a cloth laid over the drawing-room carpet on Sundays between services, and have a couple of cocks in " to give them wind." This was about 1830. Cockfighting is much in vogue even now among the vulgar of all ranks in this country ; but it is no longer countenanced either legally or socially. " On Thursday, at the Birmingham Police-court, John Brown, a publican, was summoned to answer the complaint of the police for unlawfully keeping open his house, and acting in the management of a room, for the purpose of fighting of cocks, on the 27th of July last. A detective deposed to having obtained entrance to the defendant's house and to witnessing all the preparations for a cock-fight—the pit, birds, &c. In the evening he again went to the house and found traces of a fight having taken place, as well as cocks which had evidently been engaged in combat. For the defence it was alleged that there had neither been fighting nor intention to fight, and that the birds found trimmed as if for battle had merely been trimmed for the purpose of being painted on canvas The defendant was ordered to pay a fine of £5 and costs."—*Daily News* for Saturday, *Sept.* 26, 1868.

Carpentier's *Glossary* calls " Gallorum pugna " :—Ludi genus inter pueros scholares, non uno in loco usitati. Lit. remis. An. 1383, in Reg. 134. Chartoph. Reg. ch. 37. " En ce Karesme entrant. . . . à une feste ou dance que l'en faisoit lors d'Enfans pour la jouste des coqs, ainsi qu'il est accoustume (en Dauphiné)." In the same work under the words " Gallorum pugna," A.D. 1458, some differences are mentioned as subsisting between the Mayor and Aldermen of Abbeville, and the Dean and Chapter of the Church of St. Ulfra, which are made up on the following condition : " C'est assavoir que lesdiz Doyen et Cappitre, accordent que doresenavant ilz souffreront et consentiront, que cellui qui demourra Roy d' l'escolle la nuit des Quaresmiaulx apporte ou fache apporter devers le Maieur de laditte Ville ou Camp. S. George, le Cocq, qui demourra ledit jour ou autre jour victorieux, ou autre Cocq ; et que ledit Roy presente au dit Maieur *pour d'icellui faire le cholle en la maniere* accoutumée. Du Cange, in his " Glossary," tom. ii. col. 1679, says, that although this practice was confined to school-boys in several provinces of France, it was nevertheless forbidden in the Council of Copria (supposed to be Cognac) in the year 1260. The Decree recites " that although it was then become obsolete, as well in Grammar Schools as in other places, yet mischiefs had arisen, &c." Du Cange *in verbo*, and see Carpentier v. *Jasia*. In a MS. Book of Prayers, executed in the Netherlands at the end of the fifteenth century, one of the representations intended as ornamental designs for the volume, is a cock-fight.

Cock Lorel.—The name of a famous thief, said to have lived in the time of Henry VIII., and by one old writer described as a tinker by trade. The phrase seems to have become generic. Compare Nares, *Glossary*, 1859, in v., and Hazlitt's *Handbook*, 1867, p. 113. The true period of this celebrity is doubtful. Wynkyn de Worde printed a tract, entitled *Cock Lorels Bote*.

Cockney.—The term Cock applied to a man familiarly as a mark of affection is not known to be of any antiquity; but Cockney would otherwise seem to be a colloquial corruption of that monosyllable, and to signify an effeminate person, one who has been over-petted, or as we should say, a milk-sop. I am not so sanguine as Mr. Way ("Prompt. Parv." art. "Cockney,") that the word is to be traced to "Cockayne," an opinion which is apparently shared by Mr. Halliwell, "Archaic Dictionary," 1847, art. "Cockney," but rather think it is the other way. That, having originally signified a spoiled boy or man, it should have acquired the secondary meaning of a Londoner, is by no means strange, when it is considered that Londoners are even now, in the very extended sense of the phrase, looked upon by all the rest of the world as people good for very little beyond sedentary pursuits. In Nash's "Pierce Peniles," 1592, there is the following passage, leaving no doubt as to the writer's interpretation of the term at that period :—" A young heyre, or cockney, that is his mother's darling, if hee have playde the waste-good at the Innes of the Court, or about London, and that neither his students pension, nor his unthrifts credite, will serve to maintaine, &c.," and the citation from a MS. ascribed to the 14th century, in Pegge's *Anecdotes of the English Language*, 1844, p.v. exactly confirms this view: "Puer in deliciis matris nutritus, Anglice a cockney.'

Cock Penny. — The scholars at Clitheroe Free Grammar-School had to pay at Shrovetide what is called a cockpenny, which the authors of "Lancashire Folk-Lore," 1867, supposed to be a substitute for bringing the animal itself to school, which formerly was very common. This cock-penny used to be paid also at Burnley Grammar School, but has been long discontinued.

Cockpit. — This term was not only applied to a place where cock-fights were held, and to the theatres in Drury Lane and Whitehall originally devoted to the same purpose, but to the part of a vessel of war, where courts of inquiry were held. There is a tract in verse on this last acceptation by Charles Fletcher, M.D., 1787.

Cock's-Odin. — Cock's-Odin was, from its name, probably a traditionary game handed down from Danish times; for of the Danes there are many memorials scattered all over the Border. The play itself, however, throws no light upon any recognisable circumstance of their cruel invasions. It consisted merely of one boy sent forth to conceal himself within a certain range, and, after due law, the rest set out like so many hounds to discover and catch him if they could. What Odin could have to do with the fugitive I cannot conjecture; and whether the cock's victorious crow can be emblematical of triumph, is only a speculation worthy of a most inveterate Dryasdust.

Cock's-Spur. — Pliny mentions the spur, and calls it Telum, but the gafle is a mere modern invention, as likewise is the great, and, I suppose, necessary exactness in matching them. The Asiatics, however, use spurs that act on each side like a lancet, and which almost immediately decide the battle. Hence they are never permitted by the modern cock-fighters.

Cock-Throwing and **Thrashing.**—The writer of a pamphlet entitled "Clemency to Brutes, &c." 1761, has the following observation : " Whence it had its rise among us I could never yet learn to my satisfaction : but the common account of it is, that the crowing of a cock prevented our Saxon ancestors from massacring their conquerors, another part of our ancestors, the Danes, on the morning of a Shrove Tuesday, whilst asleep in their beds." " Battering with missive weapons a cock tied to a stake, is an annual diversion," says an essayist in the "Gentleman's Magazine," for Jan., 1737, "that for time immemorial has prevailed in this island." A cock has the misfortune to be called in Latin by the same word which signifies a Frenchman. "In our wars with France, in former ages, our ingenious forefathers," says he, "invented this emblematical way of expressing their derision of, and resentment towards that nation ; and poor Monsieur at the stake was pelted by men and boys in a very rough and hostile manner." He instances the same thought at Blenheim House, where over the portals is finely carved in stone the figure of a monstrous lion tearing to pieces a harmless cock, which may be justly called a pun in architecture. Among the games represented in the margin of the "Roman d'Alexandre," in the Bodleian, is a drawing of two boys carrying a third on a stick thrust between his legs, who holds a cock in his hands. They are followed by another boy, with a flag or standard emblazoned with a cudgel. Strutt has engraved the group in pl. xxxv. of his "Sports and Pastimes." He supposes, p. 293, that it represents a boyish triumph : the hero of the party having either won the cock, or his bird escaped unhurt from the dangers to which he had been exposed. The date of the illumination is 1343. Another early example of this custom may be adduced from the fifteenth century poem, "How the Goode Wif Thaught hir Daughter." It is where the good wife admonishes her child to avoid certain unbecoming pastimes; she says :

" Goe thou noght to wrastelynge ne she-
      tynge at the cokke,
As it were a strumpet or a gegelotte.''

Hence it appears that women and girls were fond of attending these diversions. In common with football, cockthrashing is mentioned, in 1409, as a sport then in vogue, on which certain persons used to levy money under pretence of applying it to the purposes of the players. In Smith's Life of the Fourth Lord Berkeley, who died in 1417, speaking of his recreations and delights, he tells the reader, "Hee also would to the threshing of the cocke, pucke with hens blindfolde and the like." Vol. ii. fol. 459. At Pinner, near Harrow, the cruel custom of throwing at cocks was formerly made a matter of public celebrity, as appears by an ancient account of receipts and expenditures. The money collected at this sport was applied in aid of the poor rates. "1682. Received for cocks at Shrovetide, 12s. 0d. 1628. Received for cocks in towne, 19s. 10d. Out of towne, 6d." This custom appears to have continued as late as the year 1680. Lysons' Environs, vol. ii. p. 588. Quarles, in his Preface to *Argalus and Parthenia*, 1629, allusively to the fate of that work, observes: "I have suffered him to live, that he might stand like a *Jack-a-Lent*, or a *Shroving Cake* for every one to spend a cudgel at." Grose tells us that, "To whip the cock is a piece of sport practised at wakes, horse-races, and fairs, in Leicestershire: a cock being tied or fastened into a hat or basket, half-a-dozen carters, blindfolded, and armed with their cart-whips, are placed round it, who, after being turned thrice about, begin to whip the cock, which if any one strikes so as to make it cry out, it becomes his property; the joke is that, instead of whipping the cock, they flog each other heartily." Hogarth has satirized this barbarity in the first of the prints called "The Four Stages of Cruelty." Trusler's description is as follows: "We have several groupes of boys at their different barbarous diversions; one is throwing at a cock, the universal Shrove-tide amusement, beating the harmless feathered animal to jelly." There is a passage in the "Newcastle Courant" for March, 15th, 1783. "Leeds, March 11th, 1783: Tuesday se'nnight, being Shrovetide, as a person was amusing himself along with several others, with the barbarous custom of throwing at a cock, at Howden Clough, near Birstal, the stick pitched upon the head of Jonathan Speight, a youth about thirteen years of age, and killed him on the spot. The man was committed to York Castle on Friday." In "Witt's Recreations," 1640, it is thus referred to:—

"Cock a-doodle-do, 'tis the bravest game,
Take a cock from his dame,
And bind him to a stake.

How he strutts, how he throwes,
How he swaggers, how he crowes,
As if the day newly brake.
How his mistris cackles ,
Thus to find him in shackles,
And ty'd to a pack-threed garter;
Oh the bears and the bulls
Are but corpulent gulls
To the valiant Shrove-tide martyr."

The custom of throwing at cocks at Shrove Tuesday was still retained in Mr. Brand's time (1794) at Heston in Middlesex, in a field near the church. Constables (says B.) have been often directed to attend on the occasion, in order to put a stop to so barbarous a custom, but hitherto they have attended in vain. I gathered the following particulars from a person who regretted that in his younger years he had often been a partaker of the sport. The owner of the cock trains his bird for some time before Shrove Tuesday, and throws a stick at him himself, in order to prepare him for the fatal day, by accustoming him to watch the threatened danger, and, by springing aside, avoid the fatal blow. He holds the poor victim on the spot marked out by a cord fixed to his leg, at the distance of nine or ten yards, so as to be out of the way of the stick himself. Another spot is marked, at the distance of twenty-two yards, for the person who throws to stand upon. He has three shys, or throws, for twopence, and wins the cock if he can knock him down and run up and catch him before the bird recovers his legs. The inhuman pastime does not end with the cock's life, for when killed it is put into a hat, and won a second time by the person who can strike it out. Broomsticks are generally used to shy with. The cock, if well trained, eludes the blows of his cruel persecutors for a long time, and thereby clears to his master a considerable sum of money. But I fear lest, by describing the mode of throwing at cocks, I should deserve the censure of Boerhaave on another occasion: "To teach the arts of cruelty is equivalent to committing them." This custom was retained in many schools in Scotland within the 18th century. The schoolmasters were said to preside at the battle, and claimed the run-away cocks, called fugees, as their perquisites. Akerman ("Wiltshire Glossary," 1842, *in voce*) notices this pastime under its local designation of "Cock-Sqwoilin." In "Newmarket: or an Esay on the Turf," 1771, vol. ii. p. 174, we read: "In the Northern part of England it is no unusual diversion to tie a rope across a street and let it swing about the distance of ten yards from the ground. To the middle of this a living cock is tied by the legs. As he swings in the air, a set of young people ride one after another, full speed, under the rope, and rising in their stirrups, catch at the animal's head, which is close clipped and well soaped in order to elude the grasp. Now he who is able to keepe his seat in the saddle and his hold of the bird's head, so as to carry it off in his hand, bears away the palm, and becomes the noble hero of the day." A print of this barbarous custom may be seen in the "Trionfi, &c. della Venetia"; see also Menestrier, "Traité des Tournois," p. 346. The Shrove-Tuesday's massacre of this useful and spirited creature is now virtually at an end, as are also those monstrous barbarities, the battle royal and Welsh main. Compare *Pancakes* and *Shrove-Tuesday.*

Cock Watt, mentioned by Decker in "Jests to make you Merrie," 1607, as "the walking Spirit of Newgate."

Cockle-Bread.—See *Hot Cockles.*

Cockle and Mussel Feast.— At the commencement of November, in accordance with a custom of very ancient origin, members of the Clitheroe Corporation assemble at the annual "cockle and mussel feast" for the purpose of choosing a Mayor for the ensuing year. Although this singular title is still retained, cockles and mussels form only an insignificant portion of the entertainment.

Coffee-Farthings. — See *Shrovetide.*

Coffin.—We have the very coffin of the present age described in Durandus. "Corpus lotum et sindone obvolutum, ac Luculo conditum, Veteres in cœnaculis, seu Tricliniis exponebant," *Rationale*, p. 225. Loculus is a box or chest. Thus in old registers I find coffins called kists, i.q. chests. Gough's *Sep. Mon.*, ii., *Introd.* In the *Squyr of Low Degrè*, the King's daughter encloses the hero, her lover, as she supposes, in a *maser tre*, i.e., a hollow trunk, with three locks. See *Embalming*, infrâ. "Uncovered coffins of wainscot," observes Mr. Atkinson, in the "Cleveland Glossary," 1868, "were common some years ago, with the initials and figures of the name and age studded on the lid in brass-headed nails; but coffins covered with black are now commonly seen. The coffin is almost never borne on the shoulders, but either suspended by means of towels passed under it, or on short staves provide for the purpose by the undertakers, and which were customarily, in past days, cast into the grave before beginning to fill it up. The author saw one of these bearing staves dug out when re-digging an old grave in August, 1863. Men are usually borne by men, women by women, and children by boys and girls according to sex. Women who have died in childbirth have white sheets thrown over their coffins." Compare *Funeral Customs.*

Colchester Trump.—See *Ruff.*

Coldharbour. — A name found in many parts of England, and under the local appellation elsewhere, and most reasonably explained to signify the shelters once existing in different parts of a country, where a disused residence, Roman or otherwise, had been fitted up for the accommodation of travellers content with temporary protection from the weather; and these places usually consisted of apartments with bare walls. The German equivalent is *Kalten-harberg.* Wright's *Domestic Manners and Sentiments*, 1862, p. 76.

Collop or **Shrove Monday.**— In the North of England, and elsewhere, the Monday preceding Shrove Tuesday or Pancake Tuesday, is called Collop Monday; eggs and collops composed an usual dish at dinner on this day, as pancakes do on the following, from which customs they have plainly derived their names. *Gentleman's Magazine*, 1790, p. 719. It should seem that on Collop Monday they took their leave of flesh in the papal times, which was anciently prepared to last during the winter by salting, drying, and being hung up. Slices of this kind of meat are to this day termed collops in the North, whereas they are called steaks when cut off from fresh or unsalted flesh; a kind of food which I am inclined to think our ancestors seldom tasted in the depth of winter. A collop is a slice of meat or cutlet from an animal, metaphorically a child, in which sense Shakespear and Lyly use it. The etymology is doubtful, unless it is from the old Latin *colponer*, to cut.

Colt-Pixy.—In Hampshire they give the name of colt-pixy to a supposed spirit or fairy, which, in the shape of a horse, wickers, i.e., neighs, and misleads horses into bogs, &c.

Columbaria. — Pigeon-houses, an inheritance, in common with so many others, from the ancient Hellenic farmyard, formerly maintained on a very large scale both in England and abroad. There was one at Hawthornden, the seat of Drummond the poet. These monastic and seigniorial adjuncts became very obnoxious by reason of the devastations of the pigeons among the crops and orchards, and their prolific increase. Occasionally the buildings were of an ornamental character; see Otto Jahn, *Die Wandgemälde des Columbariums in der Villa Pamfili*, München, 1857, with engravings.

Columbine.—Steevens, commenting on the mention of columbine in "Hamlet," says: "From Cutwode's 'Caltha Poetarum,' 1599, it should seem as if this flower was the emblem of cuckoldom:

'The blue cornuted columbine,
Like to the crooked horns of Acheloy.'"

"Columbine," says another of the commentators, S.W. "was an emblem of cuckoldom, on account of the horns of its nectaria which are remarkable in this plant." A third commentator, Holt White, says: "The columbine was emblematical of forsaken lovers:

'The columbine, in tawny often taken,
Is then ascrib'd to such as are forsaken.'"

Browne's *Britannia's Pastorals*, Book ii.

Combination-Room.—The apartment at Cambridge where the fellows retire after dinner for conversation and wine.

Comet.—(i.) In the Earl of Northampton's "Defensative," 1583, sign. v. 4, we read: "When dyvers, uppon greater scrupulosity than cause, went about to disswade her Majestye, lying then at Richmonde, from looking on the comet which appeared last; with a courage aunswerable to the greatnesse of her State, shee caused the windowe to be sette open, and cast out thys worde, *jacta est alea*, the dyce are throwne, affirming that her stedfast hope and confidence was too firmly planted in the Providence of God, to be blasted or affrighted with those beames, which either had a ground in Nature whereupon to rise, or at least no warrant out of Scripture to portend the mishappes of Princes." He adds: "I can affirm thus much, as a present witnesse, by mine owne experience." The writer is referring to the comet, or blazing star, which appeared on the 10th October, 1580, some months after the earthquake in April. The latter is supposed to be referred to in *Romeo and Juliet*. Francis Shakleton published an account of the comet of October. (ii.) A game at cards. See Davis, *Suppl. Glossary*, 1881, in v.

Commerce.—See *I am a Spanish Merchant*.

Communion Table.—See *Bowing*.

Communion Tokens.—Pieces of pewter formerly given to those who applied to receive the sacrament, after satisfying the minister that they were fit for such a ceremony.

Conduits.—Speaking of the different conduits in or about London, Strype, in his additions to Stow, says: "These conduits used to be in former times visited. And particularly, on the 18th of Sept., 1562, the Lord Mayor (Harper), Aldermen, and many Worshipful Persons, and divers of the Masters and Wardens of the Twelve Companies, rid to the conduit heads for to see them after the old custom; and afore dinner they hunted the hare, and killed her, and thence to dinner at the Head of the Conduit. There was a good number, entertained with good cheer by the Chamberlain. And after dinner they went to hunting the fox. There was a great cry for a mile; and at length the hounds killed him at the end of S. Giles's. Great hallowing at his death, and blowing of horns." *Survey*, 1720, i., 25.

Confarreation.—The following extract is from an old grant, cited in Du Cange, v. Confarreatio: "Miciacum concedimus et quicquid est Fisci nostri intra Fluminum alveos et *per sanctam Confarreationem et Annulum* inexceptionaliter tradimus." The ceremony used at the solemnnization of a marriage was called confarreation, in token of a most firm conjunction between the man and the wife, with a cake of wheat or barley. This, Blount tells us, is still retained in part with us by that which is called the bride-cake used at weddings. Moffet informs us that "the English, when the bride comes from church, are wont to cast wheat upon her head; and when the bride and bridegroom return home, one presents them with a pot of butter, as presaging plenty, and abundance of all good things." "Health's Improvement," p. 218. This ceremony of confarreation has not been omitted by Moresin ("Papatus," p. 165.) Nor has it been overlooked by Herrick ("Hesperides," p. 128). See also Langley's Polydore Vergil, fol. 9, verso. It was also a Hebrew custom. See Selden's "Uxor Hebraica" (Opera tom. iii. pp. 633, 668). Comp. *Bride-Cake* and *Wedding Cake*.

Conjuration.—There is a curious letter from the Abbot of Abingdon to Secretary Cromwell, about 1536, in which the writer gives an account of a priest who had been captured for practising conjuration. There is the following description of this person: "It shall please your Maistership to be advertised that my officers have taken here a Preyste, a suspecte person, and with hym certeyn bokes of conjuracions, in the whyche ys conteyned many conclusions of that worke; as fyndyng out of tresure hydde, consecratyng of ryngs with stones in theym, and consecratyng of a cristal stone wheryn a chylde shall looke, and se many thyngs. Ther ys also many fygors in hyt whiche haue dyvers thyngs in theym, and amongs all, one the whiche hath a swerde crossed ouer with a septor." King James, in his "Dæmonologie," says: "The art of sorcery consists in divers forms of circles and conjurations rightly joined together, few or more in number according to the number of persons conjurers (always passing the singular number), according to the qualitie of the circle and form of the apparition. Two principal things cannot well in that errand be wanted: holy water (whereby the Devil mocks the papists), and some present of a living thing unto him. There are likewise certain daies and houres that they observe in this purpose. These things being all ready and prepared, circles are made, triangular, quadrangular, round, double, or single, according to the form of the apparition they crave. But to speak of the diverse formes of the circles, of the innumerable characters and crosses that are within and without, and out-through the same; of the diverse forms of apparitions that the craftie spirit illudes them with, and of all such particulars in that action, I remit it over to many that have busied their heads in describing of the same. as being but curious and altogether unprofitable. And this farre only I touch, that, when the conjured spirit appeares, which will not be while after many circumstances long prayers, and much mutterings, and murmurings of the conjurers, like a papiste prieste dispatching a hunting mass—how soon, I say, he appears, if they have missed one jote of all their rites: or if any of their feete once slyd over the circle, through terror of this fearful apparition, he paies himself at that time, in his owne hand, of that due debt which they ought him and otherwise would have delaied longer to have paied him: I meane, he carries them with him, body and soul. If this be not now a just cause to make them weary of these formes of conjuration, I leave it to you to judge upon; considering the longsomeness of the labour, the precise keeping of daies and houres (as I have said), the terribleness of the apparition and the present peril that they stand in, in missing the least circumstance or freite that they ought to observe: and, on the other part, the devill is glad to moove them to a plaine and square dealing with them as I said before." "This," Grose observes, "is a pretty accurate description of this mode of conjuration, styled the circular method; but, with all due respect to his Majesty's learning, square and triangular circles are figures not to be found in Euclid or any of the common writers on geometry. But perhaps King James learnt his mathematics from the same system as Doctor Sacheverell, who, in one of his speeches or sermons, made use of the following simile: 'They concur like parallel lines, meeting in one common center.'"

Conjuror.—Scot tells us that with regard to conjurors, "The circles by which they defend themselves are commonly nine foot in breadth, but the Eastern magicians must give seven." *Discovery*, ed. 1665, 72. Melton, speaking of conjurors, says, "They always observe the time of the moone before they set their figure, and when they set their figure and spread their circle, first exorcise the wine and water, which they sprinkle on their circle, then mumble in an unknown language. Doe they not crosse and exorcise their surplus, their silver wand, gowne, cap, and every instrument they use about their blacke and damnable art? Nay, they crosse the place whereon they stand, because they think the Devill hath no power to come to it, when they have blest it." *Astrologaster*, 1620, p. 16. The following passage occurs in Dekker's "Strange Horse Race," 1613, sign. D 3, "He darting an eye upon them, able to counfound a thousand conjurors in their own circles (though with a wet finger they could fetch up a little devill)." Allusions to this character are not uncommon in our old plays. In "Albumazar," a comedy, 1615:

"He tels of lost plate, horses, and straye cattell
Directly, as he had stolne them all himselfe."

Again, in "Ram Alley," 1611:

— "Fortune-teller, a petty rogue
That never saw five shillings in a heape,
Will take upon him to divine Men's fate,.
Yet never knows himselfe shall dy a beggar,
Or be hanged up for pilfering tablecloaths,
Shirts, and smocks, hanged out to dry on hedges."

In Osborne's "Advice to his Son," 1656, p. 100, speaking of the soldiery, that author says, "they, like the spirits of conjurors, do oftentimes teare their masters and raisers in pieces, for want of other imployment." Butler says of his conjuror that he could

"Chase evil spirits away by dint
Of cickle, horse-shoes, hollow flint."

Addison, in his "Drummer, or the Haunted House," has introduced a rather apposite scene:
"Gardn. Prithee, John, what sort of a creature is a conjuror?
Butl. Why he's made much as other men are, if it was not for his long grey beard. His beard is at least half a yard long: he's dressed in a strange dark cloke, as black as a cole. He has a long white wand in his hand.
Coachm. I fancy 'tis made out of witchelm.
Gard. I warrant you if the ghost appears he'll whisk ye that wand before his eyes, and strike you the drum-stick out of his hand.
Butl. No; the wand, look ye, is to make a circle; and if he once gets the ghost in a circle, then he has him. A circle, you must know, is a conjuror's trap.

Coach. But what will he do with him, when he has him there?

Butl. Why then he'll overpower him with his learning.

Gard. If he can once compass him and get him in Lob's pound, he'll make nothing of him, but speak a few hard words to him, and perhaps bind him over to his good behaviour for a thousand years.

Coachm. Ay, ay he'll send him packing to his grave again with a flea in his ear, I warrant him.

Butl. But if the conjuror be but well paid, he'll take pains upon the ghost and lay him, look ye, in the Red Sea—and then he's laid for ever.

Gardn. Why, John, there must be a power of spirits in that same Red Sea. I warrant ye they are as plenty as fish. I wish the spirit may not carry off a corner of the house with him.

Butl. As for that, Peter, you may be sure that the steward has made his bargain with the cunning man before-hand, that he shall stand to all costs and damages."

Conquering. — This is a game in which schoolboys fit snail-shells together, point to point, and whichever succeeds in breaking the other, is said to be the conqueror. One shell is occasionally the hero, in this way, of a hundred battles, the strength of the shells being very unequal.

Consummation.—In the time of Montaigne, at least, it grew to be a belief in France that when any ill - will or jealousy existed against the husband, the latter might counteract the malignant influence by repeating a certain charm three times, tying at each turn a ribbon, with a medal attached to it, round his middle, the said medal or plate being inscribed with cabalistic characters. The plate was to be placed exactly upon the reins, and the third and last time was to be securely fastened, that it could not slip off, care being also taken to spread a gown on the bed, so as to cover both the man and the woman. We do not hear of any English analogue; yet it is a class of usage which might easily pass into desuetude and oblivion. The same writer has in his graphic and candid fashion adduced many other illustrations of nuptial practices in his country during the sixteenth century; but they fall outside our immediate range. *Essays*, by Hazlitt, 1902, i., 99. Compare *Amulets*, suprâ.

Coral. — The well - known toy, which is generally suspended from the necks of infants to assist them in cutting their teeth, is with the greatest probability supposed to have had its origin in an ancient superstition, which considered coral as an amulet or defensative against fascination: for this we have the authority of

Pliny. "Aruspices religiosum Coralli gestamen amoliendis periculis arbitrantur : et Surculi Lnfantiæ alligati tutelam habere creduntur." It was thought too to preserve and fasten the teeth in men. In Bartholomeus "de Proprietatibus Rerum," we read : "Wytches tell, that this stone (*coral*) withstondeth lyghtenynge.—It putteth of lyghtnyng, whirlwynde, tempeste and stormes fro shyppes and houses that it is in. The red coral helpeth ayenst the fendes gyle and scorne, and ayenst divers wonderous doyng and multiplieth fruite and spedeth begynnyng and ending of causes and of nedes." Coles, in his "Adam in Eden," speaking of coral, says : "It helpeth children to breed their teeth, their gums being rubbed therewith; and to that purpose they have it fastened at the ends of their mantles." And Plat, in his "Jewel-House of Art and Nature," 1594, says, "Coral is good to be hanged about children's necks, as well to rub their gums, as to preserve them from the falling sickness : it hath also some special sympathy with nature, for the best coral being worn about the neck, will turn pale and wan, if the party that wears it be sick, and comes to its former colour again, as they recover health." Scot, in his "Discovery of Witchcraft," 1584, says : "The coral preserveth such as bear it from fascination or bewitching, and in this respect they are hanged about children's necks. But from whence that superstition is derived, or who invented the lye I know not : but I see how ready the people are to give credit thereunto by the multitude of corrals that were employed." Steevens informs us that there appears to have been an old superstition that coral would change its colour and look pale when the wearer of it was sick. Reed's *Shakespear*, vii., 308. So in the play of "The Three Ladies of London," 1584 :

"You must say jet will take up a straw, amber will make one fat,
Coral will look pale when you be sick, and chrystal will stanch blood."

In Erondel's "French Garden," 1605, edit. 1621, signat. H 2, in a dialogue relative to the dress of a child, we have another proof of the long continuance of this custom: "You need not give him his corall with the small golden chayne, for I beleeve it is better to let him sleepe untill the afternoone."

Corby Pole Fair.—See *Fairs*.

Cork. — *Throwing the Dart by the Mayor of Cork,* an annual usage. See *Illustrated London News,* June 2, 1855.

Cornichon-va-devant.—A kind of game played in France in the sixteenth century, of which the precise nature is uncertain, and therefore whether there is or was any English analogue. Montaigne's *Essays*, by W. C. Hazlitt, 1902, iv., 275.

Corning.—Brand's servant, B. Jelks, informed him that there was a custom in Warwickshire for the poor on St. Thomas's Day, to go with a bag to beg corn of the farmers, which they called going a-corning.

Cornish Leechdoms.—Communicated by the late T. Q. Couch. There are numerous disjointed fragments of superstition which have been so sadly misshapen by time as to defy all attempts to classify them, and yet are worthy of being preserved against the period when the progress of education shall have rendered them obsolete. These are the superstitions connected with animals, plants, and things inanimate, and the medical or other virtues attributed to them. The domestic treatment of disease among our poor consists chiefly of charms and ceremonies, and even when recourse is had to material remedies, as much importance is attached to the rites which attend their employment as to the agents used. In many cases we may notice remnants of the old doctrine of signatures, and the idea of sympathies and antipathies between separate and dissimilar bodies. The brightest coloured decoctions, as saffron-water, are given to "throw out" exanthematous eruptions; whilst the nettle rash is treated by copious draughts of nettle tea. The fisherman, whose hand is wounded by a hook, is very careful to preserve the hook from rust during the healing of the wound.

The following instances will illustrate the household medicine of the poorer of our country people: If the infant is suffering from the thrush, it is taken, fasting, on three following mornings, to have its mouth blown into by a posthumous child. If afflicted with the hooping cough, it is fed with the bread and butter of a family, the heads of which bear respectively the names John and Joan. In the time of an epidemic, so numerous are the applications, that the poor couple have little reason to be grateful to their godfathers and godmothers for their gift of these particular names. Or, if a piebald horse is to be found in the neighbourhood, the child is taken to it, and passed thrice under the belly of the animal; the mere possession of such a beast confers the power of curing the disease. The owner of a piebald horse states that he has frequently been stopped on the road by anxious mothers, who inquired of him, in a casual way, what was good for the hooping cough? and the thing he mentioned, however inappropriate or absurd, was held to be a certain remedy in that particular case. The passing of children through holes in the earth, rocks, or trees,

was once an established rite, and the old Saxon penitentiaries record strict and protracted fasts against "the woman who useth any witchcraft to her child, or who draws it through the earth at the meeting of roads, because that is great heathenness." Remnants of this Pagan usage are still to be observed among the peasantry. Boils are said to be cured by creeping on the hands and knees beneath a bramble which has grown into the earth at both ends. Children afflicted with hernia are still passed through a slit made in an ash sapling, before sunrise, fasting, after which the slit portions are bound up, in the hope that, as they unite, the malady will be cured. The ash is a tree of many virtues: venomous reptiles are never known to rest under its shadow, and a single blow from an ash-stick is instant death to an adder; struck by any other wand, it is said to retain marks of life, till the sun goes down. The mountain ash, or care, has a still greater reputation in the curing of ills arising from supernatural as well as ordinary causes: it is the dread of evil spirits, and renders null the spells of the witch. The countryman will carry for years a small piece of it in his pocket, as a protection against the ill-wish, or as a remedy for the rheumatism. If his cow is out of health, and he suspects that she is overlooked, away he runs to the nearest wood and brings home branches of care, which he suspends over her stall, or wreathes round her horns, after which he considers her safe. The cure for warts are many and various. A piece of flesh is taken secretly, rubbed over the warts, and buried in the earth, and as the flesh decays the warts vanish. Or some mysterious vagrant desires to have them carefully counted, and, marking the number on the inside of his hat, leaves the neighbourhood, and takes the warts with him.

There are a few animals the subject of superstitious veneration, and a much greater number whose actions are supposed to convey intimations of the future. We are too little acquainted with the details of the practice of augury among the Druids, and the differences between it and its observance by our Saxon and Danish forefathers, to be able to mark the origin of each particular superstition; at all events the belief is too general to have been the result of local or individual observation, and has all the appearance of being a system once entire, but long since exploded. The desire to look into the future belongs to all times and all conditions; but the persistency and generality with which the faculty of foreshadowing coming events has been attached to particular animals is very remarkable. In some instances it would almost seem as if they were considered more in the light of causes than prognostics; yet as the doctrine of fatalism, in a restricted sense, runs through all our popular beliefs, we may consider, for instance, the conduct of the inhospitable housewife who drives off the cock that crows upon the door-step, warning her of the approach of strangers, as only a fresh illustration of a very old fallacy, which consists in the belief that when the prophet is silenced, his predictions are averted. Here are some of our superstitions connected with certain animals. The howling of dogs, the continued croaking of ravens over a house, and the ticking of the death-watch, portend death. The magpie is a bird of good or ill omen, according to the number seen at one time. A crowing hen is a bird of ill-luck. A country lad informed me that if, on first hearing the cuckoo, the sounds proceed from the right, it signifies "that you will go vore in the world"; if from the left, "that the ensuing year will be one of ill-fortune." Particular honour is paid to the robin and the wren. It is a very prevalent belief that a pillow stuffed with the feathers of wild birds delays the departure of the dying. Death is also thought to be prolonged until the ebb of the tide. The killing of the first adder seen for the season is a sign that the person is to triumph over his enemies. The slough of an adder hung to the rafters preserves the house against fire. The wonderful polity of bees could scarcely have escaped observation in the earliest ages, and they were accordingly supposed to be endued with a portion "divinæ mentis." Our forefathers appear to have been among those who considered bees as possessing something higher than ordinary instinct, for there is yet a degree of deference paid to them that would scarcely be offered to beings endowed with only the usual kind of animal intelligence. On the death of any relative, the husbandman takes care to acquaint the bees of it, by moving the hive, or putting it in mourning by attaching to it pieces of black cloth or crape; which neglected, they are said to leave the hive. The sale of bees is a very unlucky proceeding, so they are always given, and a bushel of wheat (the constant value of a swarm) is expected in return. In some house where death has occurred, the indoor plants are also hung with black, for if this be neglected they are said to droop and die. The cricket is a bringer of good luck, and its departure from a house is a sign of coming misfortune. Among the omens believed in, or existing in proverbs, we may further mention that the breaking of a looking-glass entails seven years' trouble, but no want. The dirgeful singing of children portends

a funeral. There is scarcely a sensation but has its meaning. If you shudder, it implies that some one is walking over the spot that is to be your grave. If the left palm itches, you will soon have to pay, if the right, to receive money. If the knee itches, you will kneel in a strange church. If the sole of the foot tingles, you will walk over strange ground. If the ear tingles, you will hear of "hastis" news. If the cheek burns, some one is talking scandal of you. I have frequently heard the following lines spoken:

"Right cheek! left cheek! why do you
    burn?
Cursed be she that doth me any harm.
If it be a maid, let her be staid:
If it be a widow; long let her mourn:
But if it be my own true love,
Burn, cheek, burn!"

Even the white patches at the roots of the nails, called *gifts*, are not without their significance.

Cornish Pixies, The.—The legends which follow are taken from a manuscript collection, all careful copies of oral traditions still extant; the first was communicated to the *Athenæum*, many years ago, by the late Jonathan Couch of Polperro; the remainder were furnished to the present writer by his son, the late Mr. Couch of Bodmin: A farmer, who formerly lived on an estate in this neighbourhood called Langreek, was returning one evening from a distant part of the farm, and in crossing a particular field, saw, to his surprise, sitting on a stone in the middle of it, a miserable looking creature, human in appearance, though dwarfish in size, and apparently starving with cold and hunger. Pitying its condition, and perhaps aware that it was of elfish origin, and that good luck would amply repay him for his kind treatment of it, he took it home, placed it by the warm hearth on a stool, fed it with milk, and shewed it great kindness. Though at first lumpish, and only half sensible, the poor bantling soon revived, and though it never spoke, became lively and playful. From the amusement it gave by its strange tricks, it soon became a general favourite in the family. After the lapse of three or four days, whilst it was at play, a shrill voice in the farm yard or "town place," was heard to call three times,—"Colman Grey!" at which the little fellow sprang up, and gaining voice, cried, "Ho! ho! ho! my daddy is come!" flew through the key-hole, and was never afterwards heard of. A field on the Langreek estate retains the name of "Colman Grey" to this day. The pixies seem to have delighted in mischief for its own sake. Old Robin Hicks, a fisherman of Polperro who, many years ago, lived in a house on the cliffs near the quay, has more than once, on stormy winter nights, been alarmed at his supper by a voice sharp and shrill, coming apparently through the key-hole—" Robin ! Robin ! your boat's adrift ! " He has risen and hastened down on the quay to find his boat riding safely at her moorings. The piskies would testify their joy at the success of their deceit by laughing and "tacking their hands." Another story is told by our fishermen but many of its particulars are forgotten. John Taprail, long since dead, had moored his boat in the evening beside a barge of much larger size belonging to John Rendle, who traded in her between this place and Plymouth. In the middle of the night he was awoke by a voice requesting him to get up and " shift his rope over Rendle." He accordingly rose, but found to his chagrin that he had been called unnecessarily, for both the boat and the barge were riding quietly at their ropes. On his way back again, when very near his home, he observed a number of the little people arranged in a circle under shelter of a boat that was lying high and dry on the beach. Each was holding his little cap in his hand, except one, who, sitting in the centre, was engaged in distributing a heap of money, throwing it into the caps after the manner in which cards are dealt. John Taprail crept slily towards them sheltered by the boat, and reaching round his own cap managed to introduce it into the circle. When it had received a good portion of the money, he slowly and cautiously withdrew it, and made off with the booty : the interloper, however, was discovered, and the whole circle joined in pursuing him. Having got a good start of the piskies, he managed to reach his house, and to close the door on his pursuers ; but his escape was a narrow one, for he had left the skirts of his sea coat in their hands. The next tradition well shows their caprice, and that they are easily offended by an offer of reward, however delicately tendered. A farmer, residing at a particular farmhouse in this neighbourhood, was surprised at the extraordinary quantity of corn which was threshed during the night, as well as puzzled to discover the mysterious agency by which it was effected. His curiosity led him to enquire closely into the matter. One moonlight night he crept stealthily to the barn-door, looked through a chink and, to his astonishment, saw a little fellow, clad in a ragged green suit, wielding the flail with great skill and rapidity. The farmer crept away unperceived, feeling very grateful to the pisky for his services. All night he lay awake, thinking in what way he could best show his gratitude. He settled, at length, that as the

little fellow's clothes were somewhat the worse for wear, the gift of a new suit would be the proper way to lessen the obligation ; so he had a suit of green made of what he judged to be the proper size, and this he carried early in the evening to the barn, and left there for the pisky's acceptance. At night he stole to the barn-door, to see how the gift was taken. He was just in time to see the elf put on the suit, with which he was very well pleased, for, looking down on himself, admiringly, he sang—

" Pisky fine, and pisky gay,
Now will pisky fly away."

From thenceforth the farmer received no assistance from the fairy flail. Another version of the pisky's song, equally common with the above, is—

" Pisky new coat, and pisky new hood,
Pisky now will do no more good."

It is said of another farmer that he discovered two piskies threshing lustily in his barn, now and then interrupting their work, and enquiring of each other, in the smallest falsetto voice, " I tweat ! you tweat ? " After a while the flails ceased, and they surveyed their work. " We've threshed enough," observed one. " Quite enough ! and thank ye ! " said the incautious farmer. The elves instantly vanished, and never more visited that barn. It will scarcely be necessary to remind the reader of the similarity of these tales and those which Milton speaks of as told by a country hearth. A farmer's boy, living at Portallow, was sent, one dark night, to procure some litle household necessaries from a shop at Polperro. He was trudging backwards, having executed his business at the grocer's, and had reached Talland-sand hill, when he heard some one say, " I'm for Portallow green ! " " As you are going my way," thought the lad, " I may as well have your company." Accordingly he listened for a repetition of the voice, intending to hail it. " I'm for Portallow green ! " was repeated after a short interval. " I'm for Portallow green !" shouted the boy. Quick as thought he found himself on the green, surrounded by a throng of little laughing pixies. They were, however, scarcely settled before the cry was heard from several tiny voices, " I'm for Seaton beach !" (a fine expanse of sand on the coast between Looe and Plymouth, and about seven miles distant from Portallow). Whether he was charmed by this brief taste of pisky society, or was taken with their pleasant mode of travelling, is not stated, but he immediately rejoined, " I'm for Seaton beach !" Off he was whisked, and in a moment found himself on Seaton beach, engaged in a dance of the most lively and fantastic kind, for the nimble manner in which his feet were flung about, in measure with the fairy tune which was played by one of the elves, was a perfect wonder to himself. After they had for a while danced "their ringlets to the whistling wind," the cry was changed to " I'm for the King of France's cellar !" Strange to say, he offered no objection even to so long a journey. " I'm for the King of France's cellar !" shouted the adventurous youth, as he threw his parcel on the edge of the beach, near the tide. Immediately he found himself in a spacious cellar engaged with his mysterious companions in tasting the richest of wines, after which they passed through grand rooms, fitted up with a splendour which quite dazzled him. The tables were covered with fine plate and rich viands, as if in expectation of a feast. Thinking it would be as well to take away with him some small memorial of his travels, he pocketed a rich silver goblet. After a short stay, the piskies said, "I'm for Seaton beach," which was repeated by the boy, and he was taken back as quickly as he went, reaching the beach in time to recover his parcel from the flowing tide. Their next destination was Portallow Green, where they left our wondering traveller, who soon reached his home, delivered his message, and received a compliment from the good wife for his dispatch. "You'd say so, if you only know'd where I've been," said he. " I've been with the piskies to Seaton beach, and I've been to the King of France's cellar, and all in five minutes." "The boy is mazed," said the farmer. "I thought you'd say I was mazed, if I didn't bring something with me to show vor't," he replied, at the same time producing the goblet. The farmer and his family examined it, wondered at it, and finished by giving a full belief to the boy's strange story. The goblet is unfortunately not now to be produced in proof to those who may still doubt, but we are told that it remained the property of the boy's family for generations after. Our legend of the pisky midwife is so well related by Mrs. Bray, in her book on the "Tamar and Tavy," that it need not be again told, the only material difference being, that it was the accidental application to her right eye of the soap with which she was washing the baby that opened to her the secrets of fairy-land. I have been unable to discover any traces of a belief in water spirits. An old man, just deceased, was accustomed to relate that he saw on a stormy day a woman, her face buried in her long dank locks, sitting on the rocks at Talland sand, and weeping. On his approach, she slid into the sea, and disappeared. The story is easily accounted for by supposing that he saw a seal (an animal that has been noticed in that locality on more than one occasion), the long hair being an allowable embellishment. Our fishermen talk of "môrmaids," and the egg-cases of the rays and sharks are popularly called " môrmaids' purses." It is extremely doubtful whether they formed a part of the old mythology.

Besides the piskies, but of a widely different character and origin, are the spectre huntsman and his pack, known as the "Devil and his dandy dogs." The genius of this tradition is essentially Scandinavian, and reminds us of the " Wirtend heer," and the grim sights and terrible sounds which affright the peasant at night in the forests of the north. Though at first the frightful spectres were the ghosts of slain warriors speeding from Valhalla, and pursuing their prey through the murky air, the tradition has become variously altered in different countries, but in all retaining enough of the terrible to mark its derivation. The " Devil and his dandy dogs" frequent our bleak and dismal moors on tempestuous nights, and are also occasionally heard in the more cultivated districts by the coasts, where they are less frightful in their character. They are most commonly seen by those who are out at nights on wicked errands, and woe betide the poor wretch who crosses their path. An interesting legend will illustrate the little we have heard of this superstition in its wilder forms. A poor herdsman was journeying homeward across the moors one windy night, when he heard, at a distance among the tors, the baying of hounds which, time and circumstances considered, he immediately recognised as the dismal chorus of the dandy dogs. Very much alarmed, he hurried onwards as fast as the treacherous nature of the soil and the uncertainty of the path would allow; but the melancholy yelping of the hounds, and the holloa of the huntsman as it sounded across the waste, became every moment nearer and nearer. After a considerable run, they had so gained upon him, that on looking back he could distinctly see hunter and dogs. The former was terrible to look at, and had the usual complement of "saucer" eyes, horns, and tail, accorded by the common consent of story-tellers to the legendary devil. He was, of course, black, and carried a long hunting-pole. The dogs, too, were black, many in number, each of them snorting fire, and uttering a yelp of peculiarly frightful character. With no cottage, rock, or tree to give him shelter, in despair he was about to abandon himself to their fury, when at once a happy thought suggested a resource. Just as they were about to rush upon him he fell on his knees in prayer, earnest no doubt. Immediately, as if resistance had been offered, the whole pack stood at bay, howling loudly and dismally. The hunter shouted "bo shrove!" "which," says my informant, "means in the old language, 'the boy prays!'" and at the words they all drew off and disappeared. The dandy dogs are not unfrequently seen on the sea-coast, and the stories told are so well attested, that there is reason to conclude the narrators have really seen a pack of weasels, of which it is well known that they hunt gregariously at night, and when so engaged do not scruple to attack man.

It is certainly surprising to find those stories which we have been taught to associate with a particular house or family told of persons and places very remote. There is, however, only space here to point to certain instances of this community of fable. There is a great similarity, for instance, between the story of Colman Grey, and that of Gilpin Homer, as given in the notes to the "Lay of the Last Minstrel," and we are reminded of the same story when reading of the "Killcrops," in Luther's "Colloquia Mensalia." Our story of the pisky thresher has its counterpart in the fairy lore of almost all the countries in Europe, and so close is the resemblance, that the pisky song would seem almost a verbatim translation from one language to another. In England, at Hilton Hall, the fairy sang—

"Here's a cloak, and here's a hood !
The cauld lad of Hilton will do no more good."

The brownie of Scotland is offended in like manner at a present of clothes, and cries :

"A new mantle and a new hood !
Poor Brownie ! ye'll ne'er do mair gude."

The tale of the midwife is also of very wide distribution, and may be found, with slight variation, in Gervase of Tilbury. The legend of "I'm for Portallow green" resembles, in many points, that told of Lord Duffus, in the "Minstrelsy of the Scottish Border"; and that related of a butler in the noble house of Monteith. The reader will also be reminded of the story of the "Haunted Cellar," by Crofton Croker. These curious superstitions have received many modifications in the course of ages. The promulgators of later creeds appear to have despaired at the task of rooting out old and stubborn prejudices, and to have preferred grafting their new doctrines on the old. As instances of these modifications may be mentioned, the widely spread belief that piskies are the souls of unbaptized children ; the modern name of the spectre huntsman and his hounds ; and the efficacy of prayer in driving off the latter. From the little I know of the fairy superstitions of Cornwall (which little has been gleaned entirely from oral tradition), it would not be easy to classify the beings of the popular creed : still there are characteristics which, when more is known of them, may serve to distribute them into classes resembling those of the continental nations, whose mythology has kept its distinctions more definitely than our own. Our domestic spirit, who rewards the thrifty servant, and punishes the slattern, and who, in the old manor house at Killigarth, when the family was at church, was wont to watch the joint as it roasted on the spit, and to admonish the servant to remove it when sufficiently drest, agrees with the gobelin of Normandy, the kobold of Germany, the nisse of Norway, the Tomte gubbe of Sweden, and the brownie of Scotland, and may be found distinct from our little pastoral fairy, whose chief amusement is music and dancing, laughter and mischief, and who makes those rings in our meadows "of which the ewe not bites."

In Cornwall we might expect to find the "swart fairy of the mine" occupying a prominent place in our mythology. It would therefore be interesting to know whether this is the case from those who are acquainted with the "folk lore" of our mining districts, especially as it has been a disputed point whether the Duegars or dwarf tribe dwelling in hills and caverns, and distinguished for their skill in metallurgy really formed a portion of the old belief, or were, as Sir Walter Scott thought them, the diminutive natives of the Lappish and Finnish nations, driven to the mountains by their invaders. The general belief seems to be "that they are personifications of the subterranean powers of nature" : for. as Keightley observes, "all parts of every ancient mythology are but personified powers, attributes, and moral qualities."

There is "An account of Anne Jefferies, now living in the county of Cornwall, who was fed for six months by a small sort of airy people called fairies ; and of the strange and wonderful cures she performed, with salves and medicines she received from them, for which she never took one penny of her patients : In a letter from Moses Pitt to the right reverend Father in God, Dr. Edward Fowler, Lord Bishop of Gloucester : 1696." This tract states that Anne Jefferies (for that was her maiden name) was born in the parish of St. Teath in the county of Cornwall, in December, 1626, and is still living, 1696, aged 70. She is married to one William

Warren, formerly hind to the late eminent physician Dr. Richard Lower, deceased, and now to Sʳ. Andrew Slanning of Devon, Bart.—That A.D. 1645, as she was one day sitting knitting in an arbour in the garden there came over the hedge of a sudden, six persons of a small stature all clothed in green, which frighted her so much as to throw her into a great sickness. They continued their appearance to her, never less than two at a time, nor never more than eight, always in even numbers, 2, 4, 6, 8. "She forsook eating our victuals" (continues the narrator in whose family she lived as a servant) "and was fed by these fairies from the harvest time to the next Christmas Day; upon which day she came to our table and said, because it was that day she would eat some roast beef with us, which she did, I myself being then at table. One day," he adds, "she gave me a piece of her fairy bread, which I did eat, and think it was the most delicious bread that ever I did eat, either before or since. One day," the credulous narrator goes on, "these fairies gave my sister Mary a silver cup which held about a quart, bidding her give it my mother; but my mother would not accept it. I presume this was the time my sister owns she saw the fairies. I confess to your lordship I never did see them. I have seen Anne in the orchard dancing among the trees; and she told me she was then dancing with the fairies." Morgan's "Phœnix Britannicus," p. 545. Morgan tells us that the copy from which he reprinted it had at the bottom of its title-page this N.B in MS.: "Recommended by the Right Rev. to his friend Mrs. Eliz. Rye." He means, no doubt, the above Bishop of Gloucester, who it should seem had tacked to his creed this article of belief in fairies. It is with great diffidence that I shall venture to consider Anne's case *en Medicin;* yet I presume some very obvious physical reasons might be given why a wench of nineteen should fall into sickness and see objects that were green without the smallest necessity of calling in the aid of the marvellous. It appears that Anne was afterwards thrown into gaol, as an impostor, nor does even the friendly narrator of her singular story, Moses Pitt, give us any plausible account why the fairies, like false earthly friends, forsook her in the time of her distress.

Cornlaiters.—Hutchinson, speaking of the parish of Whitbeck, says: "Newly married peasants beg corn to sow their first crop with, and are called cornlaiters." *Cumberland,* i., 553.

Corporal Oath is supposed to have been derived—"not from the touching of the New Testament, or the bodily act of kissing it, but from the ancient use of touching the *Corporale,* or cloth which covered the consecrated elements."

Corpus Christi Day. — Corpus Christi Day, a moveable feast, is in all Roman Catholic countries celebrated with music, lights, flowers strewed all along the streets, their richest tapestries hung out upon the walls, &c. In the Municipal Records of York, there are vestiges of the performance of the Corpus Christi Play in that city as far back as 1388, and from a fragment of the Chamberlain's Account for 1397, which is extant, we learn that in the latter year the King was present at the spectacle; but from the general tenor of later entries among the archives, there can be no question, that the practice was of far higher antiquity than the reign of Richard II. Mr. Davies, who enters into long details on this subject, says: "The Corporation took great pains to render the exhibition acceptable to their royal visitor. Barriers were erected for the King's accommodation; the pageant was repaired and newly painted; four new scenes and a new banner were provided; the players and the city minstrels were paid additional rewards; and the minstrels of the king and his suite, which probably took part in the performances, received a liberal gratuity." In the Extracts, 18 Edward IV., are two entries relative to the performance of the Corpus Christi play at York in that year: "And paid for a banner of Thomas Gaunt, for the Corpus Christi play, at the inn of Henry Watson, 4d. And paid Margaret the sempstress for the repair of the banners of the Corpus Christi play, 3d." Mr. Davies observes: "We possess no authentic information of the time, when the observance of the festival was first introduced into England."

The Chronicle of Sprott, which notices its institution by Pope Urban IV., whose pontificate commenced in 1261, records 'the confirmation of the festival of Corpus Christi' in the year 1318; and perhaps, during this interval, it was transplanted from Italy into other parts of the Christian world. . . In the year 1313, Philip the Fair gave in Paris one of the most sumptuous fêtes that had been seen for a long time in France. The King of England, Edward II., was invited expressly, and crossed the sea with his Queen Isabella, and a splendid train of nobility. . . In the reign of Edward II. was written the miracle play of the 'Harrowing of Hell,' the earliest dramatic composition hitherto discovered in the English language. It seems therefore not improbable that the celebration of the Corpus Christi festival on its first introduction into this country was accompanied by the exhibition of pageant plays produced by the several companies, into which the tradesmen and artizans of cities and towns were then incorporated." Extracts from the Records of York, 1843, "Appendix," p. 228-9; York Plays, edited by Miss Toulmin Smith, 1885, Introduction.

The following is an account of the expenses incurred on the occasion: "And in expenses incurred this year by the Mayor, aldermen, and many others of the Council of the Chamber at the Feast of Corpus Christi, seeing and directing the play in the house of Nicholas Bewick, according to custom, together with 40s. 4d. paid for red and white wine, given and sent to knights, ladies, gentlemen, and nobles then being within the city; and also 9s. paid for the rent of the chamber, and 3s. 4d. paid to one preaching and delivering a sermon on the morrow of the said feast, in the Cathedral Church of St. Peter of York, after the celebration of the procession, according to the like custom. . . . £4 18s. 11d." In the churchwardens' and chamberlain's accounts at Kingston occur these entries: "21 Hen. VII. Mem. That we, Adam Backhous and Harry Nycol, amountyd of a Play. . . . £4 0s. 0d. 27 Hen. VII. Paid for pack-thred on Corpus Christi day, 1d." "This," Lysons observes, "was probably used for hanging the pageants, containing the History of our Saviour, which were exhibited on this day, and explained by the Mendicant Friars." In the same accounts for St. Mary at Hill, London, 17 and 19 Edw. IV., the following entry occurs: "Garlands on Corpus Christi Day. xd." I find also among the Church disbursements: "For four (six, or eight) men bearing torches about the parish" on this day, payments of 1d. each. Among the same accounts, for the 19 and 20 Edward IV., we have: "For flaggs and garlondis, and pak-thredde for the torches, upon Corpus Christi Day, and for six men to bere the said torches, iiijs. vijd." And in 1845, "For the hire of the garments for pageants, is. viijd." In the Wax-Chandlers' account, 1512, a charge of 2s. 8d. is made for garnishing eight torches on Corpus Christi Day. Rose-garlands on Corpus Christi Day are also mentioned under 1524 and 1525, in the accounts of St. Martin Outwich. In "John Bon and Mast Person" (1548), by Luke Shepherd, the parson commends John for leaving his work early in order to attend the celebration of Corpus Christi, for, says he:—

"— Surely some ther be wyl go to
   ploughe an carte,
And set not by thys holy Corpus Christi
   even.
   John. They are more to blame, I
   swere by saynt Steuen,

But tell me, mast person, one thing,
   and you can;
What Saynt is Copsi Curtsy, a man or a
   woman?"

At the celebration of the Feast of Corpus Christi, at Aix in Provence, there is a procession of saints, among whom St. Simeon is represented with a mitre and cap, carrying in his left hand a basket of eggs. *Hist. de la Fête Dieu*, p. 100. Douce. Naogeorgus ("Popish Kingd." transl. by Googe, 1570, fol. 53 verso) describes at some length the customs prevalent in his day in Germany on Corpus Christi Day.

Corpus Christi Eve.—In North Wales, at Llanasaph, there is a custom of strewing green herbs and flowers at the doors of houses on Corpus Christi Eve.— *Pennant.*

Corvina Stone.—A sort of amulet named in the work of John Florio, 1625, as having been given by Ferdinando, Grand Duke of Tuscany, to Anne of Denmark, and as having passed into the possession of the testator who bequeathed it to William Earl of Pembroke. Florio describes it in his *Italian Dictionary*, 1611, as a stone of many virtues, which they say is found in a raven's nest, fetcht thither by the raven, if in her absence a man have sodden bad eggs, and laid them in the nest again, to make them new again. *Corvina* readily suggests the etymology *corvo*.

Coscinomantia.—Of *coscinomantia* it is said, that this method of divination is assisted by spirits, and that it was considered a surer one than any other by the people on the continent. The process was accomplished by two persons holding the sieve with a forceps or pair of pincers by their middle fingers, and repeating six unintelligible words over it; whereupon, the names of all those who are suspected of the theft, act of violence, or whatever it may be that they seek to discover, being called, at the mention of the culprit the utensil moves, trembles, or turns round under the influence of the presiding (though invisible) spirit, and the divination is completed. Delrio's account is similar, *Disguis. Magicæ*, 245; and it has been merely translated (as it were) by Grose. Holiday, an English author, who repeats the same description, adds, that the ceremony was also employed for the purpose of ascertaining whom such an one was to have in marriage. *Marriage of the Arts*, 1618, ed. 1630, 92. The charm is not overlooked by Mason and Melton. *Anotomie of Sorcerie*, 1612, 9; *Astrologaster*, 1620, 45. Lodge seems to intimate that it was sometimes performed by a sieve and key, *Wits Miserie*, 1596, p. 12, which was no doubt the case, as this other form of the operation is explained in a later work thus: "A Bible having a key fastened in the middle, and being held between the two forefingers of two persons, will turn round after some words said; as, if one desires to find out a thief, a certain verse taken out of a Psalm is to be repeated, and those who are suspected nominated, and if they are guilty, the book and key will turn, else not." *Athenian Oracle*, i., 425. Scot tells us that "Popish Priests, as the Chaldeans used the divination by sive and sheers for the detection of theft, do practice with a Psalter and key fastened upon the forty-ninth (fiftieth) Psalm to discover a thief; and when the names of the suspected persons are orderly put into the pipe of the key at the reading of these words of the Psalm 'If thou sawest a thief thou did'st consent unto him,' the Book will wagg, and fall out of the fingers of them that hold it, and he whose name remaineth in the key must be the thief." *Discovery*, ed. 1665, p. 286. This is called in the *Athenian Oracle* (ii., 309) "The trick of the sieve and Scizzars, the coskiniomancy of the Antients, as old as Theocritus:"

"To Agrio too I made the same demand,
A cunning woman she, I cross'd her hand:
She turn'd the sieve and sheers, and told me true,
That I should love, but not be lov'd by you."

The original words are:—

Εἶπε καὶ Ἀγροιὼ ταλαθέα, κοσκινόμαντις,
Ἁ πρὰν ποιωλογεῦσα, παραιβάτις, οὕνεκ' ἐγὼ μεν
Τὶν ὅλος ἔγκειμαι· τὺ δὲ μεῦ λόγον οὐδένα ποιῇ.

Agrippa devotes the 21st chapter of his *Occult Philosophy* to this subject, and furnishes a representation from an iron plate of the mode of performing this species of divination. He says: "Huc enim Coscinomantia scribenda venit, quæ Dæmone urgente, per Cribrum Divinationem suscitari docet, quis rei patratæ author sit, quis hoc commiserit furtum, quis hoc dederit vulnus, aut quicquid tale fuerit. Cribrum enim inter duorum astantium medios digitos, per forcipem suspendunt, ac dejuratione facta per sex Verba, nec sibi ipsis, nec aliis intellecta, quæ sunt: *Dies Mies Jeschet Bendoftet, Dovvina Enitemaus*, Dæmonem in hoc compellunt ut reo nominato (nam omnes suspectos nominare oportet) confestim circum agatur sed per obliquum instrumentum è forcipe pendens, ut reum prodat: Iconem hic ponimus. Annis abactis plus minus triginta, ter hujus divinationis genere sum ipse usus—ubi semper pro voto aleam cecidisse comperi. Hanc Divinationem cæteris arbitrabantur veri-

orem, sicut etiam Erasmus scribit in proverbio, 'Cribro divinare.'"
Butler mentions this:—

"Th' oracle of sieve and shears,
That turns as certain as the spheres."

Hudibras, Part 2, iii., 559. But, after all, it may remain a matter of legitimate doubt, whether this superstition was ever widely prevalent in England. Scot is the earliest writer of our nation who refers to it, and his testimony does not seem to disturb an impression that all the English accounts (which implicitly follow each other) are borrowed from the continental writers, and do not establish the existence of this mode of detection as a genuine English practice or belief, except as a marriage charm.

Cotswold Games.—These were athletic sports annually held in those parts, especially about Willersley and Chipping-Campden. They seem to have been established by Robert Dover, an attorney of Barton on the Heath, in Warwickshire, son of John Dover, a Norfolk man; and James I. allowed him to appropriate for the temporary purpose a certain open space, while Endimion Porter, a gentleman whose name is agreeably associated with those of many of the literary celebrities of the time, procured him some of the King's wardrobe, including a hat and feather, and ruff. Dover entered with great spirit into this entertainment, which seems to have spread over two days; a large concourse of people assembled to witness the proceedings; and in 1636 an account of the custom, with encomiastic verses by poets of the day, appeared, embellished with a frontispiece illustrative of some of the features of the programme. The usage was interrupted by the Civil War, but subsequently revived and still remained in vogue in the time of Rudder the Gloucestershire historian. The anniversary was then celebrated at a point called Dover's Hill, on Thursday in Whitsun week. *Poetical Works of William Basse* (1602-53), 1893, pp. 105-6.

Coxcomb.—Originally the fool's cap, from the comb with which it was decorated. Comp. Nares, 1859, in v. In a secondary and now more usual sense the word now denotes a vain, conceited, meddling fellow. *Reed's Shakespear*, 1803, vol. xvii. p. 358. In "The First Part of Antonio and Mellida," 1602, we read: "Good faith, Ile accept of the cockescombe so you will not refuse the bable."

Crack-Nut Sunday.—The Sunday next before Michaelmas Eve. The practice was carried on in Church by all ages, so as to disturb the service. See Brayley and Britton's *Surrey*, iii., 41, referring particularly to Kingston.

Cramp.—In "Ovid Travestie," 1673, Epistle of Hero to Leander, the following charms are facetiously mentioned as specifics against cramp:

"——Wear bone ring on thumb, or tye Strong pack-thread below your thigh."

In the North of England, the children run round the tree, repeating these verses:

"Cramp, be thou painless,
As our Lady was sinless,
When she bare Jesus."

Mr. Brand remembered that is was a custom in the North of England for boys that swam, to wear an eel skin about their naked leg to prevent the cramp. Rings made from coffin-hinges are supposed to do so. See Grose's "Dictionary of the Vulgar Tongue," v. Scower.

Cramp-Rings.—Borde, in his "Introduction to Knowledge," 1542, speaking of England, says: "The Kynges of Englande doth halowe every yere crampe rynges, y⁰ which rynges worne on ones fynger doth helpe them whych hath the crampe." The same author, in his "Breviary of Health," 1557, fol. 166, speaking of the cramp, adopts the following superstition among the remedies thereof: "The Kynges Majestie hath a great helpe in this matter in halowyng crampe ringes, and so geven without money or petition." The ceremonies of blessing cramp rings on Good Friday will be found in Waldron's "Literary Museum," 1789.—*Douce.* In Cartwright's *Ordinary.* apparently written in 1634, Moth the Antiquary betrothes the widow Potluck with "his biggest cramp-ring." In the *Life of Benvenuto Cellini*, by himself, (1500-71), it is stated that these rings were imported from England into Italy in the sixteenth century, and cost tenpence. They were then known as *anelli del granchio;* but they now term them *anelli di salute.* Note in the Engl. transl. by J. A. Symonds, 3rd ed. p. 301.

Creeling.—In the "Statistical Account of Scotland," 1792, the minister of Galston, in Ayreshire, informs us of a singular custom there: "When a young man wishes to pay his addresses to his sweetheart, instead of going to her father's and professing his passion, he goes to a publichouse; and having let the landlady into the secret of his attachment, the object of his wishes is immediately sent for, who never almost refuses to come. She is entertained with ale and whiskey, or brandy; and the marriage is concluded on. The second day after the marriage a creeling, as it is called, takes place. The young wedding pair, with their friends, assemble in a convenient spot. A small creel or basket is prepared for the occasion, into which they put some stones: the young men carry it alternately, and allow themselves to be caught by the maidens, who have a kiss when they succeed. After a great deal of innocent mirth and pleasantry, the creel falls at length to the young husband's share, who is obliged to carry it generally for a long time, none of the young women having compassion upon him. At last, his fair mate kindly relieves him from his burden; and her complaisance in this particular is considered as a proof of her satisfaction with the choice she has made. The creel goes round again; more merriment succeeds; and all the company dine together and talk over the feats of the field." Ramsay, in his "Poems," 1721, refers to the creeling usage, and adds in a note: "'Tis a custom for the friends to endeavour the next day after the wedding to make the new-married man as drunk as possible." Perhaps the French phrase, 'Adieu, panniers, vendages sont faites,' may allude to a similar custom."

Creeping to the Cross.—The Catholic ceremony of "creeping to the cross" on Good Friday is given, from an ancient book of the "Ceremonial of the Kings of England," in the Notes to the Northumberland Household Book. The Usher was to lay a carpet for the Kinge to "creepe to the Crosse upon." The Queen and her ladies were also to "creepe to the Crosse." In a proclamation, dated 26th February, 30 Henry VIII., we read: "On Good Friday it shall be declared howe creepyng to the Crosse signifyeth an humblynge of ourselfe to Christe before the Crosse, and the kyssynge of it a memorie of our redemption made upon the Crosse." This usage was retained for some time after the restoration of the Protestant religion under Elizabeth. In a letter written about 1566 by the Bishop of London to Sir W. Cecil, the Bishop speaks of some who, "att Dunbarre, on Good Frydaye sawe certeyn persons goo barefooted and barelegged to the churche, to creepe to the crosse." See also Bonner's "Injunctions," A.D. 1555, signat. A. 2. In "A short Description of Antichrist," &c. the author notes the Popish custom of "creepinge to the Crosse with egges and apples."

Cremation. — The ancient Christians, to testify the abhorrence of heathen rites, rejected the Pagan custom of burning the dead, depositing the inanimate body entire in the ground. Thus I found at Rutchester, one of the stations upon the Roman Wall in Northumberland, a sepulchre hewn out of the living rock, wherein Leland says Paulinus who converted the Northumbrians to Christianity was interred. The whole subject of cremation is ably taken up and treated in the thirty-seventh volume of the Archæologia by William Michael Wylie, Esq. Mr. Wylie shews that the burning of the dead was commonly put in practice in this country in early times; and he observes: "The recent researches of Mr. Akerman, in a Keltic cemetery at Brighthampton in Oxfordshire, disclosed a great number of examples of cremation, unmixed with inhumation.

It may not be generally known that there is an Earth-to-Earth Society, established to resist and discountenance this method of dissolution. Its published reasons against cremation are mainly legal or clerical. Perhaps this matter ought not to be dismissed without a passing reference to the rather revolting practice of destroying the remains of executed convicts by means of quick lime, partly no doubt in consequence of the law, which directs that such persons shall be buried within the precincts of the gaol at which the execution occurred. It is well-known that the body of Ritson the antiquary, by his own express desire, underwent this barbarous form of combustion, which all the ingenuity of the author of "Urn-Burial" could not reconcile with Christian ideas.

Cresset.—See Nares and Halliwell in v., and Hazlitt's *Livery Companies*, 1892, p. 310.

Cricket.—This sport, now so common and popular, has only of recent years attracted archæological notice, and been found in some form or other to go back to the fourteenth, if not thirteenth, century. By some it is supposed to be an evolution from club-ball, and it is cognate with rounders and hockey. A Bodleian MS. of 1344 represents a female figure bowling to a man, who holds in his hand a bat prepared to strike; and in 1350 John Parish. of Guildford, enclosed a plot of ground there for the purpose of playing at cricket. Whether the allusion in 1305, cited in the *Antiquary*, intends cricket under the designation of *creag*, seems uncertain. During the seventeenth century references to the game are not numerous, which may possibly arise from its familiarity at that time. as it is one of the pastimes enumerated in a news-letter of May 6. 1670, from the chaplain of the ship Assistance, lying off Antioch. when he speaks of the sailors occupying their leisure in this sort of way. the curious feature being that they should have found the means of doing so in such a locality without having taken the implements with them. The fact appears to be that what we at present recognise as cricket was simply club or bat-and-ball at the outset. and that wicket. wicket-keeper, scouts and other accessories came afterward—long afterward.

In the ancient romance of *Merlin*, where the King's messengers are in search for a particular object of a child born without a mortal father, they meet with a party of children, who are said in the popular summary by Dunlop to be playing at cricket, Merlin being the number. Of course this is no authority for the game; but the occupation of the miraculous boy and his comrades may very well have been club-ball— a pastime of the highest antiquity. In Chamberlain's *Angliæ Notitia*, 1694, the game is thus explicitly named :—"The natives will endure long and hard labour; inasmuch that after 12 hours' hard work, they will go in the evening to football, stool ball, cricket, prison-base, wrestling, cudgel-playing, or some such like vehement exercise for their recreation." It is said, in the *World Bewitch'd*, 1699, p. 22, that, on the approach of summer, "Quoits, cricket, nine-pins, and trap-ball will be very much in fashion, and more tradesmen may be seen playing in the fields than working in their shops." But Lillywhite does not seem to trace back farther than 1746. at all events for any events of importance. *Cricket Scores and Biographies of Celebrated Cricketers*, 1862-3. The print published by Bowles and Carver in 1784 of this game, as it was then played by the Gentlemen's Club, White Conduit House, exhibits the usual accessories of wickets, stumps, fielders, batsman, and bowler. The party wears knee-breeches, shoes or high-lows, and all, except two, who are seated on the ground, and may be umpires, are in shirt-sleeves. The seated figures, and one or two of the others have pigtails, and the former cloaks and sombrero hats. The length of the course in the engraving seems less than would suit modern experts. The wicket is in the form of two forked stumps; the bat resembles a club. A few years earlier (1779), a match was played at Sevenoaks in Kent, between the Countess of Derby and other noble ladies, all represented in a contemporary print as attired in ordinary outdoor dress and elaborate head-gear. The bowler is stooping to serve the ball, and the wicket has only two stumps. The cricket grounds at Darnall, near Sheffield, appear to have been celebrated in the earlier part of the last century (1820), and there is a coloured engraving by Robert Cruikshank, shewing the North East view of the place. It is not many years since this sport was played by men and boys wearing their tall hats, nor indeed is the practice yet entirely discontinued. A friend has seen a print of the boys at Tonbridge School in the earlier part of the century in which they are so represented.

As far back as 1800, in the Court Rolls of the Manor of Wimbledon, complaints were registered of the annoyance and danger arising from cricket balls to passengers and vehicles near the gate leading from Windsor-street to Barnes on Lower Putney Common. The Wimbledon Cricket Club has periodically printed for the use of its members an account of the matches and scores since the establishment of the institution in 1871. Lord's Cricket Ground, still so celebrated, owed its name to Thos. Lord, one of the attendants at the White Conduit Club at the end of the 18th century. Lord subsequently established the Marylebone Club, now Lord's.

Smith, in his *Book for a Rainy Day,* 1861, tells us that in 1803 the Duke of Dorset, Lord Winchelsea, Lord Talbot, and others, played at this game in an open field near White Conduit House. The Marylebone Club appears to have been one of the more prominent institutions of this character in old days. In 1823 Henry Bentley printed "A correct Account of all the Cricket Matches which have been played by the Mary-le-Bone Club and all the other principal Matches from 1786 to 1822," and in 1825 appeared at Basingstoke a small duodecimo volume entitled "Laws of the game of Cricket as revised by the Cricket Club at St. Marylebone." The encouragement of the game in Kent was largely due to Sir Horace Mann, the correspondent of Horace Walpole. Mann, with the Duke of Dorset and Lord Tankerville, presidents of the Surrey and Hants Elevens, Sir William Draper and others, formed a committee, which met at the Star and Garter, in Pall Mall, and drew up rules for the game, about 1770. In the *Kentish Gazette* for April, 1794, is an advertisement of a game of cricket to be played under the auspices of Sir Horace Mann at Harrietsham on ponies. Some incidental particulars about the game and those who were distinguished as players under George II. and George III., may be gathered from the Notes by Scriblerus Maximus to an heroic poem entitled *Cricket,* published without date, and dedicated to John Earl of Sandwich (1729-92). The Kentish men appear at this time to have held high rank as cricketers. But the game had evidently been long ere this well established. The men of Wareham in Sussex, also acquired in the eighteenth century a great name for their proficiency in the sport. Lower's *Compend. Hist. of Sussex,* 1870, ii., 231. Dr. Furnivall informs me that he met, in a 17th century book, with the term yorker in the use of a ball, which is so pitched by the bowler as to strike the ground between the batsman's feet, and make it impossible for him to hit it. Comp. *Cat and Dog,* &c., and see Halliwell in v.

Cricket, The.—Pliny mentions the cricket as much esteemed by the ancient magicians: there is no doubt that our superstitions concerning these little domestics have been transmitted to us from his times. *Nat. Hist.*, book xxix. It is a lucky sign to have crickets in the house :

> "*Ad Grillum.*
> O qui meæ culinæ,
> Argutulus choraules,
> Et hospes es canorus
> *Quacunque commoreris*
> *Felicitatis Omen.*"

—Bourne's *Poematia,* edit. 1764, p. 133. Grose says it is held extremely unlucky to kill a cricket, perhaps from the idea of its being a breach of hospitality, this insect taking refuge in houses. Several old writers mention this superstition as strong and general. Melton, in his *Astrologaster,* 1620, p. 45, tells us that the abandonment of a chimney by crickets is a fatal sign, and Gay in his *Pastoral Dirge,* and an early dramatist seem to say that the shrieking of the insect in the oven or chimney was to be viewed in the same unfavourable light. Dodsley's *Old Plays,* 1780, vi. 357. In the Spectator's day the voice of the cricket was held to be potent for good or evil. In Dryden and Lee's "Œdipus," it is even ranked with the owl and the raven, birds of the worst omen. To come to a more modern and intelligent writer, White of Selborne observes to us : "they" (crickets) "are the housewife's barometer, foretelling her when it will rain, and are prognostic sometimes, she thinks, of ill or good luck, of the death of a near relation, or the approach of an absent lover. By being the constant companions of her solitary hours, they naturally become the objects of her superstition. Tender insects, that live abroad, either enjoy only the short period of one summer, or else doze away the cold, uncomfortable months in profound slumbers; but these residing, as it were, in a torrid zone, are always alert and merry; a good Christmas fire is to them like the heats of the dog-days. Though they are frequently heard by day, yet it is their natural time of motion in the night."

Croquet. — A game probably of French origin, as it is depicted in an engraving, dated 1624, by Callot, representing the players at Nancy in Lorraine at that time. It is said in some verses accompanying the series of prints, of which this forms one, to be a diversion of the spring of the year. A Wimbledon correspondent of *Notes and Queries* (Jan. 4, 1873), thus describes the illustration :— "The scene of the pastime is a broad, straight walk, running between parterres, and apparently 100 feet in length. At either end is erected a single hoop, of width and height seemingly 2¼ feet. Several balls are grouped close to one of these hoops, round which stand some players, mallet in hand; while, a few feet in front of the other hoop, another player is about to deliver a stroke, and is evidently aiming to send his ball up among its companions near the goal opposite him. Mallets, balls, hoops, and players, though on a minute scale, are all so distinctly drawn, that no mistake can occur in perceiving at a glance the action of performers and the instruments of performance. All the players are males; and in this respect most certainly the croquet which was going on before Callot's eyes at Nancy, in the Year of Grace, 1624, is sadly at a disadvantage, when compared with the modern reproduction.

Cross.—Hall, in his "Characters," 1608, speaking of the superstitious man, says: "Some wayes he will not go, and some he dares not; either there are bugs, or he faineth them. Every lanterne is a ghost, and every noise is of chaines. He knows not why, but his custom is to go a little about, and to leave the Cross still on the right hand." In Articles to be enquired of within the Archdeaconry of Yorke, 1640, I find the following:— "Whether at the death of any there be praying for the dead at crosses, or places where crosses have been, in the way to the church." In "The Canterburian's Self-Conviction," 1640, chap. 6. is this passage: "They avow that signing with the signe of the Crosse at rysing or lying downe, at going out or ccming in, at lighting of candles, closing of windowes, or any such action, is not only a pious and profitable ceremonie, but a very apostolick tradition." The following very curious "Old Wives' Prayer" is found in Herrick's "Hesperides," p. 205:

"Holy-rood, come forth and shield
Us ith' citie, and the field:
Safely guard us, now and aye,
From the blast that burns by day;
And those sounds that us affright
In the dead of dampish night.
Drive all hurtful Feinds us fro,
By the time the cocks first crow."

Pennant, in his "Tours in Wales," says: "At the delivery of the bread and wine at the Sacrament, several, before they receive the bread or cup, though held out to them, will flourish a little with their thumb, something like making the figure of the Cross. They do it (the women mostly) when they say their prayers on their first coming to church." In Boswell's "Life of Johnson," it is observed: "In days of superstition they thought that holding the poker before the fire would drive away the witch, who hindered the fire from burning, as it made the sign of the Cross."

Cross and Pile.—See *Heads and Tails.*

Cross Days.—These are the Monday, Tuesday, and Wednesday preceding Holy Thursday in Rogation Week. They are referred to under this name in the *Plumpton Correspondence*, under date of May 18, 1501. It appears that in North Wales, among the slate quarrymen of Penrhyn, there is a superstition still prevalent that, if any work is done on Ascension Day, some accidents will follow, and the *Daily News* of June 10, 1878, reports that "during last week thousands of men employed at the Welsh slate quarries here refused to work on Ascension Thursday." It adds: "A few years ago the agents persuaded the men to break through the superstitious observance, and there were accidents each year, a not unlikely occurrence, seeing the extent of the works carried on and the dangerous occupation of the men. This year, however, the men one and all refused to work."

Cross in Writing.—I have no doubt but that this is a remain of Popery. Thus persons, who cannot write, are directed to make their marks, instead of signing their names, which is generally done in the form of a cross. From the form of a cross at the beginning of a horn-book, the alphabet is called the Christ-Cross row. The cross used in shop books Butler seems to derive from the same origin:

"And some against all idolizing
The cross in shop-books or baptizing."

Hudibras, p. 3, c. 2, l. 313. The round O of a milk-score is, if I mistake not, also marked with a cross for a shilling, though unnoted by Lluellin in a passage where he speaks of the barmaid writing—

"For a tester half a moone,
And a great round O for a shilling."

A not unusual superscription to early letters was a cross with or without the word Jesus. Dalrymple, in his "Travels in Spain," says, that there "not a woman gets into a coach to go a hundred yards, nor a postillion on his horse, without crossing themselves. Even the tops of tavern-bills and the directions of letters are marked with crosses."

Cross-Legged. — Sir Thomas Browne cites Pliny for the opinion of the ancients that to sit cross-legged was unlucky and improper, and Athenæus for the fact, that it was regarded as a practice which had power to hinder childbirth. Park, on the contrary, noted in his copy of Bourne and Brand: "To sit cross-legged, I have always understood, was intended to produce good or fortunate consequences. Hence it was employed as a charm at school by one boy who wished well for another, in order to deprecate some punishment which both might tremble to have incurred the expectation of. At a card-table, I have also caught some superstitious players sitting cross-legged with a view of bringing good luck." It was a point of belief that a witch, by sitting cross-legged, could prevent a woman's delivery, and Heywood, in his " Silver Age," 1613, has bestowed on Juno this power, where the goddess hinders the labour of Alcmena. The dramatist followed the classical legend to a certain extent, while he made it conform to the superstitious creed of his own country. Flecknoe, speaking of "your fanatick reformers," says: "Had they their will, a bird should not fly in the air with its wings across, a ship with its cross-yard sail upon the sea, nor prophane taylor sit cross-legged on his shop-board, or have cross-bottoms to winde his thread upon." This whimsical detestation of the cross-form, no doubt, took its rise from the odium at that time against everything derived from Popery.

Cross Monday.—In Bridges " History of Northamptonshire " are recorded various instances of having processions on Cross Monday.

Cross Point.—See *Horse-Trick*.

Cross-Questions.—Said to be a game by Nares, *Glossary*, in v. Perhaps allied to *Questions and Commands*, and to *Cross-Questions and Cross-Answers*. Compare Hazlitt's *Handbook* and *Bibl. Coll.* v. Breton, and *Children's Games* suprâ.

Cross Ruff.—This is a species of ruff, a game at cards. There was ruff (q.v.), double-ruff, and cross-ruff. In *A Notable Discovery of Cosenage*, 1591, the preface states, among other matters, how the author, going into the West of England, found at a country ale-house half-a-dozen farmers playing at cross-ruff, and hoped to win all their money, when he found to his disappointment that they had read Greene's exposure of *conycatchers*, and were on their guard. This, with others, is quoted in " Poor Robin's Almanac" for 1693 :

" Christmas to hungry stomachs gives relief,
With mutton, pork, pies, pasties, and roast beef :
And men at cards spend many idle hours,
At loadum, whisk, cross-ruff, put, and all-fours."

Crowdie.—In Scotland, Eden says, they used to eat crowdie on Shrove Tuesday, as in England they did pancakes. He adds : " On this day there is always put into the bason or porringer, out of which the unmarried folks are to eat, a ring, the finding of which, by fair means, is supposed to be ominous of the finder's being first married." Crowdie is made by pouring boiling water over oat-meal and stirring it a little. It is eaten with milk or butter. The more modern manner of preparing is described in the *Musæ Anglicanæ*, 1689, ii., 86.

Crow-Keeper.—See Nares, *Glossary*, in v., and Hazlitt's *Proverbs*, 1882, p. 181.

Cry.—See *Auctions*, where the employment of the *Preco* or *Crier* is recorded. But the cry was used on a multifarious diversity of occasions : 1, for the announcement of the issue of new money ; 2, for the publication of the decrees of Councils ; 3, for the advertisement of plays to be performed ; 4, for the recovery of lost property ; 5, for proclaiming the approach of royal or high personages to their seats ; 6, for the notification of any local event, not only prior to typography and journalism, but down to the present time in some rural districts. In ancient times the crier or usher carried, not a bell, but a trumpet. Lacroix, *Mœurs et Usages*, 1872, p. 337 ; Hazlitt's *Venetian Republic*, 1900, ii., 355, 457 ; Hazlitt's Monograph on Shakespear, 1902, p. 103. The heraldic *Oyez* and the legal *Oyer and Terminer* are evolutions from the ancient use of the cry in manifold cases ; and *Oyentia* is a feudal term for the public indication of the time for paying a periodical tribute. Maigne D'Arnis *Lexicon Mediæ et Infimæ Latinitatis*, 1856, in v.

Cry Coke.—To cry *Coke* is in vulgar language synonymous with crying Peccavi. Coke, says Ruddiman, in his Glossary to Douglas's "Virgil," is the sound which Cocks utter, especially when they are beaten, from which Skinner is of opinion they have the name of Cock.

Crying the Mare.—There is a harvest sport in Hertfordshire, called " Crying the Mare " (it is the same in Shropshire), when the reapers tie together the tops of the last blades of corn, which is Mare, and standing at some distance, throw their sickles at it, and he who cuts the knot, has the prize, with acclamations and good cheer. I was informed of the following custom on this occasion at Hitchin in the same county where each farmer drives furiously home with the last load of his corn, while the people run after him with bowls full of water in order to throw on it : this is also accompanied with great shouting. Blount tells us farther that " after the knot is cut, then they cry with a loud voice three times, ' I have her.' Others answer, as many times, ' What have you ? ' — ' A mare, a mare, a mare.'

—'Whose is she?' thrice also.— J. B. (naming the owner three times).— 'Whither will you send her?'—'To J. à Nicks,' (naming some neighbour who has not all his corn reaped); then they all shout three times, and so the ceremony ends with good cheer. "In Yorkshire upon the like occasion they have a Harvest Dame, in Bedfordshire a Jack and a Gill."

Crying the Nack.—A harvest custom in Dorsetshire and Devonshire. A correspondent of *Notes and Queries* writes:—"I was present last year at a farm in North Devon where the curious old custom of "calling the nack" was observed. The reapers were gathered round a pond, where they sang three times, first in low tones, gradually increasing in loudness, the words:—

"Arnack, arnack, arnack,
We haven, we haven, we haven,
God send the nack."

After which they all laughed and shouted. They then retired to the house—not to supper, for the ceremony was not yet over. One of the party had the "nack" secreted on his person. A member of the farmer's family tried to discover the possessor, before he entered the kitchen in order to drench him, or, as they said, "wet the nack," with a bucket of water. Failing to do this, the farmer was obliged to supply a larger quantity of beer than would otherwise have been given to each individual after supper. The "nack" is preserved in the farmer's kitchen for the year."

Cucking, or Goging Stool.—Called also a tumbrel, tribuch, and trebuchet; also a thewe. In the "Promptorium Parvulorum," "Esyn, or Cukkyn," is interpreted by *stercoriso*: and in the "Domesday Survey," in the account of the City of Chester," we read: "Vir sive mulier falsam mensuram in civitate faciens deprehensus, iiii. solid. emendab'. Similiter malam servisiam faciens, aut in Cathedrâ, ponebatur Stercoris, aut iiii. solid. dab' prepositis." See Cowel in v. ex Carta Joh. regis, dat. 11 Jun. anno regni 1. It is called *thewe* in Lambarde's "Eirenarcha," lib. i. c. 12. The following extract from Cowel, in v. Thew, (with the extract just quoted from Lysons) seems to prove this : "Georgius Grey Comes Cantii clamat in maner. de Bushton & Ayton punire delinquentes contra Assisam Panis et Corvisiæ, per tres vices per amerciamenta, & quarta vice Pistores per Pilloriam, Braciatores per Tumbrellam, & Rixatrices per Thewe, hoc est, ponere eas super scabellum vocat. a Cucking Stool. Pl. in Itin. apud Cestr. 14 Hen. VII." But comp. *Stool of Repentance*, infrâ. The cucking-stool was an engine invented for the punishment of scolds and unquiet women, by ducking them in the water, after having placed them in a stool or chair fixed at the end of a long pole, by which they were immerged in some muddy or stinking pond. Blount tells us that some think it a corruption from ducking stool, but that others derive it from Choaking Stool. Though of the most remote antiquity, it is now, it should seem, totally disused. An essayist in the "Gentleman's Magazine," for May, 1732, observes that "The stools of infamy are the ducking stool, and the stool of repentance. The first was invented for taming female shrews. Lysons gives us a curious extract from the churchwardens' and chamberlain's accounts at Kingston-upon-Thames in 1572, which contains a bill of expenses for making one of these cucking stools, which, he says, must have been much in use formerly, as there are frequent entries of money paid for its repair. *Environs*, i., 233. Blakeway, in his *History of Shrewsbury*, 1779, p. 172, furnishes the subjoined entries:—"1572. The making of the cucking stool, 8s.; iron work for the same, 3s.; timber for the same, 7s. 6d.; 3 brasses for the same and three wheels, 4s. 10d." There is an order of the Corporation of Shrewsbury, 1669, that "A ducking stool be erected, for the punishment of all scolds." Borlase tells us that: "Among the punishments inflicted in Cornwall, of old time, was that of the cocking-stool, a seat of infamy where strumpets and scolds, with bare foot and head, were condemned to abide the derision of those that passed by, for such time as the bailiffs of manors, which had the privilege of such jurisdiction, did appoint. *Nat. Hist. of Cornwall*, p. 303. A certificate of the punishment of an incorrigible scold by ducking, dated 1673, and addressed by the churchwardens of Waddington, co. York, to Thomas Parker, Esq., of Browsholme, hereditary bowbearer of Bolland Forest under the Duke of Buccleuch, is to be seen in "Current Notes" for December, 1855.

In Skene's "Regiam Majestatem," ch. 69, this punishment occurs as having been used anciently in Scotland: speaking of Browsters, i.e. "Wemen quha brewes aill to be sauld" it is said, "gif she makes gude ail, that is sufficient. Bot gif she makes evill ail, contrair to the use and consuetude of the burgh, and is convict thereof, she sall pay ane unlaw of aucht shillings, or sal suffer the justice of the burgh, that is, she sall be put upon the cock-stule, and the aill sall be distributed to the pure folke." Braithwaite, speaking of a Xantippean, says: "He (her husband) vowes therefore to bring her in all disgrace to the cucking-stoole : and shee vowes againe to bring him with all contempt, to the stoole of repent-ance." *Whimzies*, 1631, p. 182. In one of the jest-books, there is the following anecdote : "Some gentlemen travelling, and coming near to a town, saw an old woman spinning near the ducking stool : one, to make the company merry, asked the good woman what that chair was made for? Said she, you know what it is. In-deed, said he, not I, unless it be the chair you use to spin in. No, no, said she, you know it to be otherwise : have you not heard that it is the cradle your good mother hath often layn in?" *New Help to Discourse*, 1684, p. 216. These stools seem to have been in common use when Misson, the French traveller, visited this country, and when Gay wrote his Pasto-rals : they are thus described by the latter :

"I'll speed me to the pond, where the high stool
On the long plank hangs o'er the muddy pool,
That stool, the dread of every scolding queen," &c.

Misson says : "La maniere de punir les femmes querelleuses et debauchées est assez plaisante en Angleterre. On attache une chaise à bras à l'extremité de deux Especes de Solives, longues de douze ou quinze pieds et dans un eloignement paral-lele, en sorte que ces deux pieces de bois embrassent par leur deux bouts voisins la chaise qui est entre deux, & qui y est at-tachée par la côte comme avec un essieu, de telle maniere, qu'elle a du Jeu, et qu'elle demeure toujours dans l'etat na-turel & horisontal auquel une Chaise doit être afin qu'on puisse s'asseoir dessus, soit qu'on l'éleve, soit qu'on l'abaisse. On dresse un pôteau sur le bord d'un Etang ou d'une Riviere, & sur ce poteau on pose presque en equilibre, la double piece de bois à une des extremitez de laquelle la Chaise se trouve au dessus de l'eau. On met la Femme dans cette Chaise et on la plonge ainsi autant de fois qu'il a été ordonné, pour raffraichir un peu sa chaleur immoderée." See Ozell's Translation, p. 65. In "Miscellaneous Poems," &c., by Benjamin West, of Wee-don-Beck, Northamptonshire, 8vo. 1780, is preserved a copy of verses, said to have been written near sixty years ago, entitled "The Ducking Stool." A note informs us, "To the honour of the fair sex in the neighbourhood of R***y. this machine has been taken down (as useless) several years." The stool is represented in a cut annexed to the "Dumps," designed and engraved by Louis du Guernier, and also in the frontispiece of "The old Woman of Ratcliff Highway." A specimen was to be seen within a few years on the banks of the Stour at Fordwich in Kent. Some ad-ditional particulars, illustrating this obso-lete usage, but to the same purport, were printed in Willis's "Current Notes" for February and April, 1854. See Wright and Fairholt's *Archæological Album*, 1845, p. 49-54, and Halliwell's *Dict.*, 1860, in v. Morant, speaking of Canuden, in the hun-dred of Rochford, mentions "Cuckingstole Croft, as given for the maintenance of a light in this church, as appears by inquisi-tion, 10 Eliz." *Essex*, i., 317.

CUCKING STOOL.

Cuckold.—I know not how this word, which is generally derived from cuculus, a cuckoo, has happened to be given to the injured husband, for it seems more pro-perly to belong to the adulterer, the cuckoo being well known to be a bird that deposits its eggs in other bird's nests. The Romans seemed to have used this cu-culus in its proper sense as the adulterer, calling with equal propriety the cuckold himself Carruca or hedge - sparrow, which bird is well known to adopt the other's spurious offspring. Richardson and Worcester, in their Dictionaries, en-dorse Tooke's etymology of cuckold, which seems, after all, to be the correct one, namely, cucol, from the Italian cucolo, a cuckoo; the word should be cucol, as in some of our old writers, and not cucold (or cuckold), and we get the word from the past participle of the English verb formed from the Italian substantive : cucolo, cucol, cucol'd. Douce says : "That the word cuculus was a term of reproach amongst the antients there is not the least doubt, and that it was used in the sense of our cuckold is equally clear. Plautus has so

introduced it on more than one occasion.
In his *Asinaria* he makes a woman thus
speak of her husband :

" Ac etiam cubat Cuculus, surge, Ama-
    tor, i domum" :

and again :

" Cano capite te Cuculum Uxor domum
    ex lustris rapit."

And yet in another place, where Pseudolus
says to Callidorus " Quid fles, Cucule?"
the above sense is out of the question, and
it is to be taken merely as a term of reproach. Horace certainly uses the word
as it is explained by Pliny in the passage
already given, and the conclusion there
drawn appears to be that which best re-
conciles the more modern sense of the
term, being likewise supported by a note
in the Variorum Horace, from "Historia
Mirabilium," by Carystius. The application of the above passage to our use of the
word cuckold, as connected with the cuckoo, is that the husband, timid, and in-
capable of protecting his honour, like that
bird, is called by its name, and thus converted into an object of contempt and
derision. In the "Athenian Oracle" it is
remarked of cuckoldry: "The Romans
were honourable, and yet Pompey, Cæsar,
Augustus, Lucullus, Cato and others had
this fate, but not its infamy and scandal."
In "Paradoxical Assertions," by Robert
Heath, 1664, it is said : "Since Plautus
wittily, and with more reason calls the
adulterer, and not him whose wife is adul-
terated, Cuculum, the cuckold, because he
begets children on others wives, which the
credulous father believes his own : why
should not he then that corrupts another
man's wife be rather called the Cuckow,
for he sits and sings merrily whilst his eggs
are hatched by his neighbour's hens?"
Chaucer, in his "Prosopopeia of Jealousie," brings her in with a garland of gold
yellow, and a cuckoo sitting on her fist.
Two items in *A. C. Mery Talys*, 1526, turn
on this somewhat unconventional topic :
the story of the wife whose pigs died in
farrowing, and who being told that she
should get a cuckold's hat, and farrow
them therein, applied to a female neighbour, whereupon the latter angrily re-
torted that her husband was no cuckold,
and so had no hat, and the woman, after
inquiring all round, declared that if she
lived another year, she would get one of
her own ; the second, the account of the
miller's rejoinder to the merchant, who observed that he had heard say every true
miller had a golden thumb. " Truth it
is," quoth he, " that my thumb is gilt,
how be it ye have no power to see it, for
there is a property incident thereto,
that he that is a cuckold shall never have
power to see it." Comp. Hazlitt's *Pro-

verbs, 1882, p. 56, where the converse is
suggested, in which case we should conclude that the reason was because his jaun-
diced eye would take the thumb to be yellow or golden.

There is a song in Ritson's collection in
which a jealous wife is represented as
putting on her yellow hose.

    " Here is Maryone Marchauntes at All-
        gate,
    Her husbòde dwells at yᵉ signe of yᵉ
        Cokoldes Pate."

—*Cock Lorels Bote*. In the *Boke of Mayd
Emlyn* (about 1540), it is stated that the
lady had five husbands, all cuckolds, and
that she *made their beards*, whether they
liked or not, and gave them a pretty hood-
ful of bells to wear. Hazlitt's *Popular
Poetry*, iv., 83. Dickenson, in " Greene in
Conceipt," 1598, uses this expression of a
cornute : " but certainely, beleeved, that
Giraldo his master was as soundly armde
for the heade, as either Capricorne, or the
stoutest horned signe in the Zodiacke."
" It is said,—Many a man knows no end
of his goods : right : many a man has good
horns, and knows no end of them. Well,
that is the dowry of his wife ; 'tis none of
his own getting. Horns? Even so :—
Poor men alone?—No, no ; the noblest
deer hath them as huge as the rascal."—
As You Like It, act iii., sc. 3. Among the
witticisms on cuckolds that occur in our
old plays, must not be omitted the following in " Ram Alley," 1611 :

" Why, my good father, what should
    you do with a wife?
Would you be crested? Will you needs
    thrust your head
In one of Vulcan's helmets? Will you
    perforce
Weare a city cap and a Court feather?"

The following passage is in "Plaine
Percevall, the peacemaker of England " : — You say true, Sal sapit
omnia ; and service without salt, by
the rite of England, is a cuckold's fee if
he claim it."

" On Dr. Cuckold.
" Who so famous was of late,
He was with finger pointed at :
What cannot learning do, and single
    state?
" Being married, he so famous grew,
As he was pointed at with two :
What cannot learning and a wife now
    do? "

Flecknoe's *Diarium*, 1656. Butler, in his
" Hudibras," informs us for what a singular purpose carvers used formerly to invoke the names of cuckolds. This allusion
arose, according to a passage in the 59th
No. of the " British Apollo," from the dexterity of one Thomas Web, carver to the
Lord Mayor in Charles the First's time,

and his fame in a less favourable respect, whence came the proverb, "Think of a cuckold," addressed to one who cannot carve the joint before him. In Hazlitt's *Early Popular Poetry,* 1864 - 6, vol. i., will be found the curious Arthurian piece, called the Cuckold's *Dance,* with a body of notices illustrative at the present subject, including the dance of *Cuckolds all a-row.* The latter became at the Restoration a favourite dance-tune. Compare the same writer's *Proverbs,* 1882. In the background of Hogarth's signboard of " The Man Loaded with Mischief," is an inn called "The Cuckold's fortune." Cuckold's Point, below Rotherhithe or Redriff, was anciently known as Cuckold's Haven. In " Tarlton's Jests," first publshed probably about 1590, we are told, " How Tarlton landed at Cuckold's Hauen," " whereupon one gaue him this theame next day :

' Tarlton, tell mee, for fayne would I know,
If thou wert landed at Cuckold's hauen, or no?
Tarlton answered thus :
' Yes, sir, I take 't in no scorne,
For many land there, yet misse of the horne.' "

The following is an extract from Hentzner's " Travels in England," 1598 : "Upon taking the air down the river (from London), on the left hand lies Ratcliffe, a considerable suburb. On the opposite shore is fixed a long pole, with ram's horns upon it, the intention of which was vulgarly said to be a reflection upon wilful and contented cuckolds." Pennant, in his " Zoology," 1776, speaking of the cuckoo, says : " His note is so uniform, that his name in all languages seems to have been derived from it, and in all other countries it is used in the same reproachful sense. The reproach seems to arise from this bird making use of the bed or nest of another to deposit its eggs in ; leaving the care of its young to a wrong parent ; but Juvenal, in his 6th Satire, with more justice, gives the infamy to the bird in whose nest the supposititious eggs were layed,

' Tu tibi tunc Curruca places—' "

A case lately occurred in which a cuckoo was found to have deposited its eggs in the nest of a wagtail, which was sitting upon them. *Daily News,* Sept. 4, 1879. Johnson, in his Dictionary, says : " The cuckow is said to suck the eggs of other birds, and lay her own to be hatched in their place ; from which practice it was usual to alarm a husband at the approach of an adulterer by calling ' cuckoo,' which by mistake was in time applied to the husband." He was vulgarly supposed to suck other birds' eggs to make his voice clear as in the old rhyme :

" He sucks little birds' eggs,
To make his voice clear ;
And when he sings cuckoo,
The summer is near."

The following item is from the *Morning Post of* May 17, 1821 : " A singular custom prevails in Shropshire at this period of the year, which is peculiar to that county. As soon as the first cuckoo has been heard, all the labouring classes leave work, if in the middle of the day, and the time is devoted to mirth and jollity over what is called the cuckoo ale." The annexed communication was made by a writer, signing himself G., to the *Daily News* of Sept. 5, 1879 : " In July last, at a small road-side crossing on the London and South Western Railway on the banks of the Axe, in Dorsetshire, and at a place well known to anglers, called Tytherleigh-bridge, I had in my hands a full-fledged young cuckoo which had just dropped from the nest of a small finch that haunts the river side and goes by some local name I am not at this moment prepared to spell. The man at the station, who rejoices equally in the name of Joe, a wooden leg, and an unblemished reputation, is in his way a bit of a naturalist, and took almost as much interest in the young cuckoo as in the flowers which cover and surround his cottage. He had watched the bird for some time, and seemed from other instances to have no doubt as to the truth of the tradition. The young cuckoo, when once removed from the nest and before it can use its wings, will not remain there, but scrambles down and gets into the hedges at the roadside. In that case it generally dies ; but the foster parents, which in this instance we saw in a painful state of agitation on the telegraph wires and neighbouring trees, will in the meantime follow it and feed it. The young cuckoo just fledged was certainly larger than a fullgrown thrush or black-bird, and was as savage as a young eagle. From the size of the nest it must have very much inconvenienced the foster parents. One can easily understand that the old hen cuckoo before depositing its own egg would clear out the eggs of the finch, as tradition relates."

In the March number of the "Gentleman's Magazine" for 1895, among the general articles, G. W. Murdoch has one ridiculing the popular myth that the cuckoo arrives in March. It is, he says, a fiction of the imagination, and he only admits one probable authentication of so early an arrival of the cuckoo in half-a-century—all personal testimonies to the contrary notwithstanding. He also goes as far as to say that the myth of the March cuckoo can be disproved beyond the shadow of a scientific doubt, and, pursuing the scientific branch of the subject, goes on to say that for reasons which branch off and take root in several departments of human cult in relation to the phenomena of pyschological and pure animistic evolution, the cuckoo holds quite an unique position in avi-fauna life. It holds, too, no inconsiderable place in the dim, and now almost intangible, relics of Totemistic worship, and fills a very large space in the traditional records and literature of folk-lore. In ornithic science it has been the subject of the most profound study, has stimulated the liveliest controversies—not settled yet—and inspired many delightful prose treatises and imperishable poems. Even at the present day the cuckoo is regarded as a sacred bird by the peasantry of some parts of Ireland, and in Connaught and Connemara it is believed to be unlucky to kill it, even by accidentally mistaking it for the sparrow-hawk, with which it is habitually confounded by superficial observers. In that respect the cuckoo holds a position analogous to the robin, and the universality of the superstition among primitive folks is an established canon of the literature of Totemistic cult. But the article is not all scientific argument. Mr. Murdoch has some stories to tell.

At Hefful or Heathfield Fair in Sussex, on April 14, the first cuckoo is said to be let out of a basket by an old woman, or, in other words, the note of the bird is popularly supposed to be first heard on that occasion. The following is a childish game (if it may be so described) :

"Cuckoo in cherry tree,
Come down and tell me
How many years I have to live."

The cuckoo has been long considered as a bird of omen. Gay, in his "Shepherd's Week," in the fourth Pastoral, describes the popular dread of hearing the first song of the cuckoo in the spring, and the usage of taking off the shoe of the left foot. Greene, in "A quip for an upstart Courtier," 1592, calls a cuckoo the cuckold's quirister : "It was just at that time when the cuckolds quirrister began to bewray Aprill gentlemen, with his never chaunged notes." In the play of "Timon," edited by Mr. Dyce, act i. sc. 2, Eutrapelus says to Abyssus : "Di'st euer heare a cuckowe of a note more inauspicious?" In the same drama, act ii. sc. 5, Timon himself is made to say, in allusion to horns :

"A common badge to men of eache degree,
How many hange their heades downe,
leaste they splitte
The signe posts with their hornes—"

Guilpin, in his "Skialetheia," 1598, says :

"For let Severus heare
A cuckow sing in June, he sweats for feare--"

Why the writer chooses June, I do not know ; the proverbial lines run :

"In April,
The cuckoo shews his bill ;
In May,
He sings all day ;
In June,
He alters his tune ;
In July,
Away he'll fly ;
Come August,
Away he must."

In Clarke's "Polimanteia," 1595, we read : "the nightingall and the cuckow both grow hoarse at the rising of Syrius, the dogge-starre."

In the introduction to a reprint of the *Gothamite Tales*, 1630, inserted in *Old English Jest Books*, 1864, the present writer drew attention to the familiar myth of the Wise Men of Gotham hedging in the cuckoo ; and on the title of the old edition is a woodcut representing this profitable occupation. I am not at present in a positon to say whether the emblem of the Belgian lion-rampant enclosed in a hedge, and grasping in one claw a staff surmounted by the Stadtholder's bonnet, which occurs on some of the copper money of the Netherlands in the early part of the seventeenth century, is connected with the same tradition. The type of *Le lion à la haie* occurs on a piece of William IV., Count of Hainault (1404-17), struck at Valenciennes, and on money of Jacqueline of Bavaria, Countess of Hainault, from 1427 to 1433.

Among the many human and animistic transformation - records to be found in the Slavonic folk tales translated by Mr. A. H. Wratislaw, M.A., is a charming one of a young damsel who fell in love with a snake and bore it two children, one of whom was turned into a nightingale, and the other into a cuckoo. Among the Danes and Norwegians the early note of the bird is welcomed in divers but very human ways. Young girls, on hearing it, kiss their hands "in the direction from which the music comes. and cry out. 'When shall I be married?' while the aged ask, 'When shall I be relieved from pain and affliction?'" *Globe*, March 2, 1895.

Cuckoo-Spit.—The larvæ of the cicada.

Cuerpo Santo. — See *Castor and Pollux.*

Curcuddoch, Curcuddie.—"To dance Curcuddie or Curcuddoch," (says Jamieson, in his Dictionary) "is a phrase used in Scotland to denote a play among children in which they sit on their houghs, and hop round in a circular form. Many of these old terms," Dr. Jamieson adds, "which now are almost entirely confined to the mouths of children, may be overlooked as nonsensical or merely arbitrary. But the most of them, we are persuaded, are as regularly formed as any other in the language. The first syllable of this word is undoubtedly the verb *curr*, to sit on the houghs or hams. The second may be from Teut. *kudde*, a flock; *kudd-en*, coire, convenire, congregari, aggregari; *kudde-wijs*, gregatim, catervatim, q. 'to curr together.' The same game is called Harry Hurcheon in the north of Scotland, either from the resemblance of one in this position to a hurcheon or hedge-hog, squatting under a bush; or from the Belg. *hurken*, to squat, to hurkle." This seems to be a form of *Cockle-Bread* or *Hot Cockles*.

Curfew.—Peshall says: "The custom of ringing the Curfew Bell at Carfax every night at eight o'clock was by order of King Alfred, the restorer of our University, who ordained that all the inhabitants of Oxford should, at the ringing of that bell, cover up their fires and go to bed, which custom is observed to this day, and the bell as constantly rings at eight as Great Tom tolls at nine. It is also a custom, added to the former, after the ringing and tolling this bell, to let the inhabitants know the day of the month by so many tolls." *History of Oxford*, p. 177. A similar practice prevailed in parts of North Wales till very recently. The curfew is commonly believed to have been of Norman origin. A law was made by William the Conqueror that all people should put out their fires and lights at the eight o'clock bell, and go to bed. *Stow's Survey*, 1754, v. i., c. 15. The practice of this custom, we are told, to its full extent, was observed during that and the following reign only. Thomson has inimitably described its tyranny. In the second mayoralty of Sir Henry Colet, Knt. (father of Dean Colet), A.D. 1495, and under his direction, the solemn charge was given to the quest of wardmote in every ward, as it stands printed in the Custumary of London: "Also yf ther be anye paryshe clerke that ryngeth curfewe after the curfewe be ronge at Bowe Chyrche, or Saint Brydes Churche, or Saint Gyles without Cripplegat, all suche to be presented." From "A C. Mery Talys," 1526, we see that, in the time of Henry VIII. it was the duty of the sexton to ring the curfew-bell. In the Faversham Articles, 22 Hen. VIII., we read: "Imprimis, the sexton, or his sufficient deputy, shall lye in the church-steeple; and at eight o'clock every night shall ring the curfewe by the space of a

quarter of an hour, with such bell as of old time hath been accustomed." I find, however, in "The Merry Devil of Edmonton," 1608, the sexton says:

"Well, 'tis nine a'clocke, 'tis time to ring curfew."

Shakespear, in "King Lear," act iii. sc. 4, writes:

Edgar: "This is the foul fiend Flibbertigibbet: He begins at curfew, and walks to the first cock." The following is an extract from the Churchwardens' and Chamberlain's Accounts of Kingston-upon Thames: "1651. For ringing the curfew bell for one year, £1 10s. 0d." Bridges, speaking of Byfield Church, tells us: "A bell is rung here at four in the morning, and at eight in the evening, for which the clerk hath 20s. yearly, paid him by the Rector." *Northamptonshire*, i., 110. Hutchins, speaking of Mappouder Church, mentions land given "to find a man to ring the morning and Curfeu Bell throughout the year." Also, under Ibberton, is mentioned one acre given for ringing the eight o'clock bell, and £4 for ringing the morning bell. *Dorsetshire*, ii., 267. Macaulay says: "The custom of ringing Curfew, which is still kept up at Claybrook, has probably obtained without intermission since the days of the Norman Conqueror." *Hist. of Claybrook*, 1791, p. 128. In 1848 the curfew was still rung at Hastings from Michaelmas till Lady-day, and the same was the case at Wrexham in North Wales, and elsewhere, till even a later date. Barrington, *Observations on the Statutes*, p. 153, tells us that "Curfew is written Curphour in a Scotish poem written before 1568. It is observed in the annotations on these poems, that by Act 144, Parl. 13, Jam. I., this bell was to be rung in boroughs at nine in the evening: and that the hour was afterwards changed to ten, at the solicitation of the wife of James Stewart, the favourite of James the sixth. There was a narrow street in Perth in the last century still called Couvre-Feu-Row, leading west to the Black Friars, where the Couvre Feu Bell gave warning to the inhabitants to cover their fires and go to rest when the clock struck ten. We find the Couvre feu mentioned as a common and approved regulation on the Continent. It was used in most of the monasteries and towns of the North of Europe, the intent being merely to prevent the accidents of fires. All the common houses consisted at this time of timber. Moscow, therefore, being built with this material, generally suffered once in 20 years, and it was much the same at Stockholm, where in comparatively recent days persons were not allowed to smoke in the streets, and it was obligatory on all to co-operate at call in extinguishing fires. In mediæval Venice there was an analogous regulation, from which only the Barber's Quarter was exempt, because the members of that Gild probably united the surgical faculty, as with us, and their aid might be required during the night..

Curling.—See "Curling, an Ancient Scottish Game." By James Taylor, M.A., with illustrations by C. A. Doyle, 8vo., 1884.

Cushion-Dance.—A riotous sort of dance, formerly usual at weddings. It is thus mentioned in the "Apothegms of King James," 1658, p. 60. A wedding entertainment is spoken of. "At last when the masque was ended, and time had brought in the supper, the cushion led the dance out of the parlour into the hall," &c. In "The Dancing Master," 1698, p. 7, is an account of "Joan Sanderson, or the Cushion Dance, an old Round Dance. This dance is begun by a single person (either man or woman), who taking a cushion in his hand, dances about the room, and at the end of the tune he stops and sings, ' This dance it will no further go.' The musician answers, 'I pray you good Sir, why say you so?' Man. ' Because Joan Sanderson will not come to.' Musick. ' She must come to, and she shall come to, and she must come whether she will or no.' Then he lays down the cushion before a woman, on which she kneels and he kisses her, singing, ' Welcom, Joan Sanderson, welcom, welcom.' Then she rises, takes up the cushion, and both dance, singing, ' Prinkum-prank'um is a fine dance, and shall we go dance it once again, and once again, and shall we go dance it once again?' Then making a stop, the woman sings as before, ' This dance it will no farther go.' Musick. ' I pray you. Madam, why say you so?' Woman. 'Because John Sanderson will not come to.' Musick. 'He must come to,' &c., (as before). And so she lays down the cushion before a man who, kneeling upon it, salutes her, she singing, ' Welcome John Sanderson,' &c. Then he taking up the cushion, they take both hands and dance round, singing as before, and thus they do till the whole company are taken into the ring. Then the cushion is laid before the first man, the woman singing, ' This dance,' &c. (as before), only instead of ' Come to,' they sing ' Go fro,' and instead of ' Welcome,' John Sanderson,' &c., they sing ' Farewell John Sanderson, farewell, farewell,' and so they go out, one by one. as they came in. Note, the woman is kiss'd by all the men in the ring, at her coming in, and going out, and likewise the man by the women." A correspondent of *Notes and Queries* thus de-

scribes the cushion-dance, as it was performed in Derbyshire, about sixty years since :—" The company were seated round presently, one carrying a large square cushion, the other an ordinary drinking-horn, china bowl, or silver tankard, according to the possessions of the family. The one carrying the cushion locked the door, putting the key in his pocket. Both gentlemen then went to the fiddler's corner, and after the cushion-bearer had put a coin in the vessel carried by the other, the fiddler struck up a lively tune, to which the young men began to dance round the room, singing or reciting to the music :—

> " Frinkum, frankum is a fine song,
> An' we will dance it all along;
> All along and round about,
> Till we find the pretty maid out."

After making the circuit of the room, they halted on reaching the fiddler's corner, and the cushion-bearer, still to the music of the fiddle, sang or recited :

> " Our song it will no further go ! "

The fiddler :—

> " Pray, kind sir, why say you so—"

The cushion-bearer :—

> " Because Jane Sanders won't come to."

The fiddler :—

> " She must come to, she shall come to,
> An' I'll make her whether she will or no ! "

The cushion-bearer and vessel-holder then proceeded with the dance, going as before round the room, singing " Frinkum, frankum," &c., till the cushion-bearer came to the lady of his choice, before whom he paused, placed the cushion on the floor at her feet, and knelt upon it. The vessel-bearer then offered the cup to the lady, who put money in it and knelt on the cushion in front of the kneeling gentleman. The pair kissed, arose, and the gentleman, first giving the cushion to the lady with a bow, placed herself behind her, taking hold of some portion of her dress. The cup-bearer fell in also, and they danced on to the fiddler's corner, and the ceremony was again gone through as at first with the substitution of the name of " John " for " Jane," thus :—

The lady :—

> " Our song it will no further go ! "

The fiddler :—

> " Pray, kind miss, why say you so? "

The lady :—

> " Because John Sandars won't come to."

The fiddler :—

" He must come to, he shall come to,
 An' I'll make him whether he will or
   no."

The dancing then proceeded, and the lady, on reaching her choice (a gentleman, of necessity), placed the cushion at his feet. He put money in the horn and knelt. They kissed and rose, he taking the cushion and his place in front of the lady, heading the next dance round, the lady taking him by the coat-tails, the first gentleman behind the lady, with the horn-bearer in the rear. In this way the dance went on till all present, alternately a lady and gentleman, had taken part in the ceremony. The dance concluded with a romp in file round the room to the quickening music of the fiddler, who at the close received the whole of the money collected by the horn-bearer." Compare, for farther particulars Nares, *Glossary*, 1859, in v., and Halliwell's *Dict.*, 1860, in v.

Cuthbert, St., Bishop of Durham.—The anniversary of the death of this holy and eminent personage, March 20, 687, in voluntary retirement, is one of the festivals of the church. An unusually long and complete account of his life and work may be seen in Chambers's *Encyclopædia.* Comp. *Bromfield* and *Luck of Eden Hall.* In Kensington Church, Middlesex, there is a painted window, in which St. Cuthbert is said to be represented playing at golf. He was by birth, one understands, an Irishman, but by original employment a North-country shepherd.

Cutting Off the Fiddler's Head.—See *Manx.*

Cuzship. — They had formerly in printing offices an usage called *cuzship*, which is described by Gent, the York printer of the last century, in his *Autobiography*, where he speaks of his attachment to the staff of Mr. Mears, the stationer and printer. He tells us that, in addition to *Beer-money*, he was obliged to submit to the immemorial custom of being sworn a cuz, the origin of which he could not learn. He proceeds :—"It commenced by walking round the chapel (printing rooms being called such, because first begun to be practised in Westminster Abbey) singing an alphabetical anthem, tuned literally to the vowels ; striking me, kneeling, with a broadsword, and pouring ale upon my head ; my title was exhibited, and to this effect : ' Thomas Gent, Baron of College Green, Earl of Fingall, with power to the limits of Dublin bar, captain-general of the Teagues, near the Lake of Allen, and lord high admiral over all the bogs in Ireland.' " He adds that they even gave

him godfathers, which his Presbyterian training had not previously accorded.

Cymmortha, or Cymmorth Gwan.—Pughe remarks : " The wearing of the leek on St. David's Day probably originated from the custom of *Cymhortha*, or the neighbourly aid practised among farmers, which is of various kinds. In some districts of South Wales, all the neighbours of a small farmer without means appoint a day when they all attend to plough his land, and the like ; and at such a time it is a custom for each individual to bring his portion of leeks, to be used in making pottage for the whole company : and they bring nothing else but the leeks in particular for the occasion." Anciently it was a custom in Wales, to institute associations among neighbours and friends for the performance of any work or undertaking, and this usage, which appears to have had its rise in motives of industrial expediency, was gradually turned both to political and social account. These Cymmortha formed the pretext, as early as the reign of Henry IV. for insurrectionary gatherings, and by 4 Hen. iv. c. 27, it was ordained, " that no westrye, rhymer, minstrel, nor vagabond be in any wise sustained in the land of Wales to make Cymmorthas or gatherings upon the common people there." Sir H. Ellis, to whom I am indebted for this information, (" Orig. Letters," 2nd Series, 1827), adds, that " Wood, speaking of Bala, says, ' It is a small town at the bottom of the lake of that name, and is celebrated for its vast trade in woollen stockings, in the knitting of which men, women, and children are incessantly employed. They assemble in the winter at each other's houses, listening to some ancient song, or provincial tale, and this meeting is called *Cymmorth Gwan*, or Knitting Assembly.' " The Cymmortha (or Comortha) was, in fact, a sort of Primitive Trades' Union, and part of the system was the relief of those members of it, who, by some unavoidable cause, happened to fall into distress. That such was the case is pretty evident from a letter addressed to Lord Burghley by Richard Price of Brecknock, January 31, 1575-6. The Cymmortha was more than once forbidden by statute : but the Bishop of Coventry and Lichfield, in a letter to Thomas Cromwell, describes an odd privilege granted by the King to a gentleman in pecuniary straits, one George Mathew, Esquire, in the twenty-seventh year of his reign ; it was the right of holding a Commortha for his personal benefit, " any statute, ordinaunce, or other thing to the contrary hereof notwithstanding." The Bishop estimates the value of the Royal license to Mathew at not less than 1,000 marks. Owen's *Welsh Dictionary*, v.v. *Cawa*, and

Cymborth, may be consulted; but there is nothing of importance which is not noticed above.

Cypress.—It is doubtful whether the cypress was meant by the ancients to be an emblem of an immortal state, or of annihilation after death; since the properties of the tree apply, happily enough, to each. The cypress was used on funeral occasions, say the commentators on Virgil, "vel quia cariem non sentit, ad gloriæ immortalitatem significandam; vel quia semel excisa, non renascitur, ad mortem exprimendam"; Servius' Com. on Œneid. iii., p. 64, and the Delphin edit.; but, instead of that, the ancient Christians used the things before mentioned, and deposited them under the corpse in the grave to signify that they who die in Christ, do not cease to live; for though, as to the body, they die to the world, yet, as to their souls, they live and revive to God. And as the carrying of these evergreens is an emblem of the soul's immortality, so it is also of the resurrection of the body: for as these herbs are not entirely plucked up, but only cut down, and will, at the returning season, revive and spring up again; so the body, like them, is but cut down for a while, and will rise and shoot up again at the resurrection. For, in the language of the evangelical prophet, our bones shall flourish like an herb. The reader conversant with the classics will call to mind here the beautiful thought in the Idyllium on Bion by Moschus: though the fine spirit of it will evaporate when we apply it to the Christian doctrine of the resurrection. The antithesis will be destroyed. Moschi *Idyll*, iii., l. 100.

The cypress, however, appears to have been retained to later times. Coles says: "Cypresse garlands are of great account at funeralls amongst the gentiler sort, but rosemary and bayes are used by the commons both at funeralls and weddings. They are all plants which fade not a good while after they are gathered, and used (as I conceive) to intimate unto us that the remembrance of the present solemnity might not dye presently, but be kept in minde for many yeares." *Introduction to the Knowledge of Plants*, 64. The line,

"And cypress which doth biers adorn,"

is cited in Poole's "English Parnassus," 1657. Spenser mentions

"The aspin, good for staves, the cypress funerall."

Dekker, in his "Wonderfull Yeare," 1603, signat. c 3 verso, describes a charnell-house pavement, "instead of greene rushes, strewde with blasted rosemary, wither'd hyacinthes, fatalle cypresse, and ewe, thickly mingled with heapes of dead men's bones." He says, signat. D 2 verso, "Rosemary, which had wont to be sold for twelve pence an armefull, went now" (on account of the Plague), "at six shillings a handfull." In "The Exequies," by Stanley, we read:

> "Yet strew
> Upon my dismall grave,
> Such offerings as you have,
> Bind with cypresse and sad ewe,
> For kinder flowers can take no birth
> Or growth from such unhappy earth."

Poems, 1651, p. 54. In "The Marrow of Complements," &c., 1655, is "A Mayden's Song for her dead Lover," in which cypress and yew are particularly mentioned as funeral plants:

> "Come you whose loves are dead,
> And, whilst I sing,
> Weepe and wring
> Every hand, and every head
> Bind with cypresse and sad ewe,
> Ribbands black, and candles blue;
> For him that was of men most true.
> "Come with heavy moaning,
> And on his grave
> Let him have
> Sacrifice of sighes and groaning,
> Let him have faire flowers enough,
> White, and purple, green, and yellow,
> For him that was of men most true."

In "Round about our Coal Fire," circâ 1730, I find the following passage on this subject:—"The rooms were embowered with holly, ivy, cyprus, bays, laurel, and Miseltoe, and a bouncing Christmas log in the chimney." In this acount the cypress is quite a new article. Indeed, I should as soon have expected to have seen the yew as the cyprus used on this joyful occasion.

Dab.—Pegge, in the "Gentleman's Magazine" for September, 1767, derives the word *Dab*, in the phrase of "a dab at such or such a thing," as a vulgar corruption of the Latin *adeptus*.

Daffodil.—Herrick describes a

> "*Divination by a Daffodil.*
> When a Daffadil I see,
> Hanging down her head t'wards me;
> Guesse I may, what I must be:
> First, I shall decline my head;
> Secondly, I shall be dead,
> Lastly, safely buried."

Hesperides, 1648, p. 40.

Dagger-Money.—See *Newcastle-on-Tyne.*

Dancing at Weddings.—Among the Anglo-Saxons, after the nuptial feast, "the remaining part of the day was spent by the youth of both sexes in mirth and dancing, while the graver sort sat down to their drinking bout, in which they highly delighted." Among the higher ranks there was, in later times, a wedding sermon, an epithalamium, and at night a masque. It was a general custom between the wedding dinner and supper to have dancing. In "The Christian State of Matrimony," 1543, fol. 49, we read : " After the bancket and feast, there begynnethe a vayne, madde, and unmanerlye fashion, for the bryde must be brought into an open dauncynge place. Then is there such a rennynge, leapynge, and flyngyng amonge them, then is there suche a lyftynge up and discoverynge of the damselles clothes and other womennes apparell, that a man might thynke they were sworne to the Devels Daunce. Then muste the poore bryde kepe foote with al dauncers and refuse none, how scabbed, foule, droncken, rude, and shameles soever he be. Then must she oft tymes heare and se much wyckednesse and many an uncomely word ; and that noyse and romblyng endureth even tyll supper." So, in the " Summe of the Holy Scripture," 1547, signat. H 3 verso : " Suffer not your children to go to weddings or banckettes ; for nowe a daies one can learne nothing there but ribaudry and foule wordes." In Selden's " Table Talk," first printed in 1689, under the head " Excommunication," is an allusion to the custom of dancing at weddings : " Like the wench that was to be married : she asked her mother, when 'twas done, if she should go to bed presently ? No, says her mother, you must dine first. And then to bed, mother ? No, you must dance after dinner. And then to bed, mother ? No, you must go to supper," &c. " Quas epulas omnes Tripudia atque Saltationes comitantur. Postremo Sponsa adrepta ex Saltatione subito atque Sponsus in Thalamum deducuntur." " Antiq. Convivial.," fol. 68. This requisite has not been omitted in the " Collier's Wedding." :

" The pipers wind and take their post,
And go before to clear the coast."

I do not know to what particular revel-day Browne refers in the second song of his First Book, where he speaks of the shepherd, who wears the trophies of his manly skill or strength :

" Piping he sate, as merry as his looke,
And by him lay his bottle and his hooke.
His buskins (edg'd with siluer) were of silke,
Which held a legge more white then mornings milk.
Those buskins he had got and brought away
For dancing best vpon the reuell day."

Works, by Hazlitt, 1868, i., 68. In Heywood's " Fayre Mayd of the Exchange," 1607, Bernard enters with news of a wedding in Gracechurch Street, where dancing is going on : —

" Bernard. By Jesu ! the rarest dancing in Christendom.
Bowdler. Sweet rascal, where ? Oh, do not kill my soul
With such delays. . . .
Ber. At a wedding in Gracious Street.
Bowd. Come, come away ; I long to see the man
In dancing art that does more than I can.
Ber. Than you, sir ? he lives not.
Bowd. Why, I did understand thee so.
Ber. You only excepted, the world besides
Cannot afford more exquisite dancers
Than are now cap'ring at that brideale house."

The following passage is curious, from its enumeration of several old dances, which were usual at weddings :

" J. Slime. I come to dance, not to quarrel. Come, what shall it be ? Rogero ?
Jem. Rogero ! no ! we will dance the beginning of the world.
Sisly. I love no dance so well as John come kiss me now.
Nich. I that have ere now deserv'd a cushion, call for the cushion-dance.
R. Brick. For my part, I like nothing so well as Tom Tyler.
Jem. No ; we'll have the Hunting of the Fox.
J. Slime. The hay ; the hay ! there's nothing like the hay—
Nich. I have said, do say, and will say again—
Jem. Every man agree to have it as Nick says.
All. Content.
Nich. It hath been, it now is, and it shall be—
Sisly. What, Master Nicholas ? What ?
Nich. Put on your smock o' Monday.
Jem. So the dance will come cleanly off. Come, for God's sake agree of something : if you like not that, put it to the musicians, or let me speak for all, and we'll have Sellengers round."

Elsewhere we read : " The custom of dancing in the church-yard at their feasts and revels is universal in Radnorshire, and very common in other parts of the Principality. Indeed this solemn abode is rendered a kind of circus for every sport and exercise. The young men play at fives and tennis against the wall of the church. It is not, however, to be understood that they literally dance over the graves of their progenitors. This amusement takes place on the north side of the Church-yard, where it is the custom not to bury. It is rather singular, however, that the association of the place, surrounded by memorials of mortality, should not deaden the impulses of joy in minds, in other respects not insensible to the suggestions of vulgar superstition." Malkin's *S. Wales*, 1804, p. 261. Again, under Aberedwy, "In this church yard are two uncommonly large yew trees, evidently of great age, but in unimpaired luxuriance and preservation, under the shade of which an intelligent clergyman of the neighbourhood informed me that he had frequently seen sixty couple dancing at Aberedwy Feast on the 14th of June. The boughs of the two trees intertwine, and afford ample space for the evolutions of so numerous a company within their ample covering." Every Englishman has heard of the "Dance round our coal fire," ridiculed by the Duke of Buckingham in the *Rehearsal*; which receives illustration from the probably ancient practice of dancing round the fires in our Inns of Court (and perhaps other halls in great men's houses). This practice was still in 1733 observed at an entertainment at the Inner Temple Hall, on Lord Chancellor Talbot taking leave of the house, when the Master of the Revels took the Chancellor by the hand, and he, Mr. Page; who, with the judges, serjeants, and benchers, danced round the coal fire, according to the old ceremony, three times, and all the times the antient song, with music, was sung by a man in a Bar gown."

Dandies.—See *Cockal*.

Dark Lantern.—Barrington, speaking of the Curfew, observes "that there is a general vulgar error, that it is not lawful to go about with a dark lantern. All popular errors," he adds, "have some foundation : and the regulation of the curfew may possibly have been the occasion of this." But he derives this notion from Guy Fawkes' dark lantern. *Observations on the Statutes*, 154 *note*.

Darvel Gathern, Worship of. — 5th April. — It appears that one of the objects of pilgrimage in the Principality of Wales before the Reformation, was the Image of Darvell Gathern in the diocese of St. Asaph; who or what Darvell Gathern was, does not appear; but the superstition is mentioned by Hall the Chronicler and others. In a letter from Ellis Price to Secretary Cromwell, dated 6th April, 1538, there is the following account of it :— "There ys an Image of Darvellgadarn, within the said diocese, in whome the people have so greate confidence, hope, and truste, that they cumme dayly a pillgramage unto hym, somme withe kyne, other with oxen or horsis, and the reste withe money : in so muche that there was fyve or syxe hundrethe pilgrimes to a mans estimacion, that offered to the saide image the fifte daie of this presente monethe of Aprill. The innocente people hath ben

sore aluryd and entised to worship the saide image, in so muche that there is a commyn sayinge as yet amongst them that who so ever will offer anie thinge to the saide Image of Darvellgadern, he hathe power to fatche hym or them that so offers oute of Hell when they be dampned." Besides this "commyn sayinge," there appears from Hall to have been a prophecy current "that the image should set a whole forest on fire " ; and this was supposed to be fulfilled, when the idol was burnt in Smithfield with a friar so named, in May, 1538. For a few farther particulars, the reader may turn to Ellis's "Original Letters," First Series, pages 83-4 of the second volume. There is a second letter from Ellis Price to Cromwell, at a somewhat later date; but we do not get any nearer to a solution of the mystery as to Darvel Gadern, beyond the patent fact that he was held in great veneration by the Welsh. Sir H. Ellis in a note indeed quotes the following passage from Michael Woodde's "Dialogue between two Neighbours," 1554 : "If the Welshman would have a purse, he praied to Darvel Gatherne." Pennant calls him St. Derfel Gatherne.

Date-Stone.—The following legend, intended to honour the Virgin Mother, was considered by Brand worth inserting, and I have retained it : "Eating some dates with an old man, but a credulous Christian, he said : that the letter O remained upon the stone of a date for a remembrance that our blessed Lady, the Virgin, with her divine Babe in her arms, resting herself at the foot of a palm-tree (which inclined her branches and offered a cluster of dates to her Creator), our lady plucked some of the dates, and eating, satisfied with the taste and flavour, cryed out in amazement, 'O how sweet they are !' This exclamation engraved the letter O, the first word of her speech, upon the date stone, which being very hard, better preserved it.'"

Daubing.—See *Bride-Wain*.

David's Day (March 1).—St. David, Archbishop of Menevy, now from him called St. David's, in Pembrokeshire, flourished, according to Pits, in the fifth and sixth centuries of the Christian era, and died at the age of a hundred and forty years. In the "Episcopal Almanack for 1677," he is described as uncle to King Arthur. There is a Welsh pedigree which shows him to have been the son of Caradog, Lord of Cardiganshire, by Non, daughter of Ynyr, of Caer Gawch. "The Britons on this day constantly wear a leek, in memory of a famous and notable victory obtained by them over the Saxons, they, during the battle, having leeks in their hats for their military colours and distinction of themselves, by the persuasion of the said prelate, St. David." Another account adds, that they were fighting, under their king Cadwallo, near a field that was replenished with that vegetable. But the battle is recorded by Jeffrey of Monmouth in the 8th and 9th chapters of his twelfth book. In the "Chronicles of Englonde," edit. 1500, signat. C 3, we have, in allusion to the Welsh :

"They haue gruell to potage,
And lekes kynde to companage—"

And again—

"Atte mete and after eke,
Her solace is salte and leke."

The "Salisbury Primer" contains the following :

"Davyd of Wales loveth well lekes.
That wyll make Gregory lene chekes ;
Yf Edwarde do eate some with them,
Mary sende hym to Bedlem."

Sir John Harington, in his "Brief View of the State of the Church," 1653, speaks of an indulgence of Pope Calixtus II., by which one pilgrimage to St. David's was made equivalent to two to Rome, whence came the distich :

"Roma semel quantum,
Bis dat Menevia tantum."

Henry VII., having Welsh blood in his veins, was supposed to be under rather peculiar obligations, possibly, as regarded the observance of St. David's festival ; on the anniversary of 1494-5, under the date of March 6, we find in that prince's "Privy Purse Expenses" ; "To the Walshemen towards ther feste, £2,"—meaning the Welshmen who happened to be about the *Dance*, with a body of notices illustrative of the present subject, including Court. The feast given to the Welshmen on this festival remained in force during the reign of Henry VIII. On two or three occasions, the yeomen of the guard presented the Princess Mary with a leek, for which they received 15s. in reward.

Dr. Owen Pughe says : "In consequence of the romances of the middle ages which created the Seven Champions of Christendom, St. David has been dignified with the title of patron Saint of Wales : but this rank, however, is hardly known among the people of the Principality, being a title diffused among them from England in modern times. The writer of this account never heard of such a patron saint, nor of the leek as his symbol, until he became acquainted therewith in London." *Cambrian Biography*, 1803, p. 86. The following lines occur in Harl. MS., 1977, fol. 9 :

"I like the leeke above all herbes and flowers.
When first we wore the same the feild was ours.
The leeke is white and green, whereby is ment
That Britaines are both stout and eminent ;
Next to the lion and the unicorn,
The leeke the fairest emblyn that is worne."

In Shakespear's "Henry the Fifth," act v. sc. i., Gower asks Fluellen, "But why wear your leek to-day? Saint Davy's Day is past." From Fluellen's reply we gather that he wore his leek in consequence of an affront he had received but the day before from Pistol whom he afterwards compels to eat the leek, skin and all, in revenge for the insult, quaintly observing to him "When you take occasions to see leeks hereafter, I pray you, mock at them, that is all." Gower too upbraids Pistol for mocking "at an ancient tradition—begun upon an honourable respect, and worn as a memorable trophy of pre-deceased valour." In "The Bishop's last Goodnight," 1642, the 14th stanza runs thus :

"Landaff, provide for St. David's Day,
Lest the leeke and red-herring run away :
Are you resolved to go or stay?
You are called for, Landaff :
Come in, Landaff."

There is a poetical broadside in double columns, entitled : "The Welsh-mens Glory, or the famous Victories of the Ancient Britons obtained upon St. David's Day." It begins :

"The honor, glory, and the grace,
Of valiant Brute's tryumphant race,
Shewing the reasons wherefore they
Wear leeks upon St. David's Day.

Ursula is introduced in "The Vow-breaker, or, the fayre Maid of Clifton," 1636, act i. sc. i. as telling Anne—"Thou marry Gorman ! His head's like a Welchman's crest on St. Davy's Day ! He looks like a hoary frost in December ! Now, Venus blesse me ! I'd rather ly by a statue." From a notice in the "Flying Post" for 1699, it appears that it was then usual for the Court to wear a leek on this day :—"Yesterday, being St. David's Day, the King, according to custom, wore a leek in honour of the ancient Britons, the same being presented to him by the Serjeant-porter, whose place it is, and for which he claims the cloaths which his Majesty wore that day. The courtiers, in imitation of his Majesty, wore leeks likewise." Misson, in his "Travels in England," translated by Ozell, p. 334, says, speaking of the Welsh custom of wearing leeks, "The King himself is so complaisant as to bear them company." Coles, in his "Adam in Eden" says, concerning leeks, "The gentlemen in Wales have them in great regard, both for their feeding, and to wear in their hats upon St. David's Day." To a querist in "The British Apollo," the following answer is given : "The ceremony is observed on the first of March, in commemoration of a signal victory obtained by the Britons, under the command of a famous general, known vulgarly by the name of St. David. The Britons wore a leek in their hats to distinguish their friends from their enemies in the heat of the battle." There is the following proverb on this day :

"Upon St. David's Day, put oats and
   barley in the clay."

It is a custom still kept up on this festival, for each of the scholars at Westminster, being Welshmen, to receive a guinea from some ancient endowment made for the purpose. About twenty received it in 1879. See *Eton School.*

Dawzin.—The faculty of divination is believed in the west to be confined to certain favoured persons, and is termed Dawzin.

Days.—See *Lucky and Unlucky,* and *Perilous Days,* infrà.

Dead Body, Seizure of a, for Debt.—The earliest instance on record occurs, perhaps, in the Romance of Sir Amadace. The security was retained till the claim was satisfied. It is difficult, Daines Barrington observes, to account for many of the prevailing vulgar errors with regard to what is supposed to be law. Such are that the body of a debtor may be taken in execution after his death : which, however, was practised in Prussia before Frederic II. abolished it by the Code Frederique. A singular case occurred at Venice in 1763, where the attempt was made to seize the remains of a Doge on this account. See Hazlitt's *Venetian Republic,* 1900, ii., 308 and *Errors,* infra. In Massinger's "Fatall Dowry," 1632, act ii. sc. 1, are some curious thoughts on this subject, spoken at the funeral of a marshal in the army, who died in debt, on account of which the corpse was arrested :

"What ! weepe ye, souldiers? . . .
The jaylors and the creditors do
   weepe ; . . . .
Be these thy bodies balme : these and
   thy vertue
Keepe thy fame ever odoriferous—
Whilst the great, proud, rich, undeserving man. . . .
Shall quickly, both in bone and name
   consume,
Though wrapt in lead, spice, seare-cloth,
   and perfume.

—This is a sacrifice : our Showre shall
   crowne
His sepulcher with olive, myrrh, and
   bayes,
The plants of peace, of sorrow, victorie."

Death-Howl.—Howling at funerals appears to have been of general use in the Papal times from the following passage in Veron, in his *Hunting of Purgatory,* 1561, where, speaking of St. Chrysostom, he says : "No mention at al doth he make of that manner of singinge or rather unsemely howling that your Papists use for the salvation of theyr dead, therby, under a pretence of godlinesse, picking the purses of the pore simple and ignorant people." Stafford observes : "It is a wonder to see the childish whining we nowadayes use at the funeralls of our friends. If we could houl them back againe, our lamentations were to some purpose ; but as they are, they are vaine, and in vain." *Meditations and Resolutions,* 1612, p. 16. The minister of Nig, co. Kincardine, reported in 1793, of the people thereabout : "On the sudden death of their relations, or fear of it, by the sea turning dangerous, the fisher people, especially the females, express their sorrow by exclamation of voice and gesture of body, like the Eastern nations, and those in an early state of civilization." Mungo Park, in his "Travels," relates that among the Moors, a child died in one of the tents, "and the mother and the relations immediately began the death-howl. They were joined by a number of female visitors, who came on purpose to assist at this melancholy concert. I had no opportunity of seeing the burial, which is generally performed secretly in the dusk of the evening, and frequently at only a few yards distance from the tent. Over the grave they plant one particular shrub ; and no stranger is allowed to pluck a leaf, or even to touch it." Speaking elsewhere of the negroes, he says : "When a person of consequence dies, the relations and neighbours meet together and manifest their sorrow by loud howlings." Compare *Ireland.*

Death-Omens. — Nearly all the death-omens then credited are set forth by Deloney in his romance of "Thomas of Reading," probably published anterior to 1600. Lupton, in his *Third Book,* says : "If the forehead of the sick wax red, and his brows fall down, and his nose wax sharp and cold, and his left eye becomes little, and the corner of his eye run, if he turn to the wall, if his ears be cold, or if he may suffer no brightness, and if his womb fall, if he pulls straws or the cloaths of his bed, or if he pick often his nostrils with his fingers, and if he wake much, these are almost certain tokens of death." The sharpness of the nose and the pulling of the bed-clothes were adopted by Shakespear in the deathbed scene of Falstaff in Henry V. By the flying and crying of ravens over their houses, especially in the dusk evening, and where one is sick, they conclude death: the same they conclude by the much crying of owles in the night, neer their houses at such a time," according to the author of *Demonology*, 1597. Werenfels says, p. 7, " The superstitious person could wish indeed that his estate might go to his next and best friends after his death, but he had rather leave it to any body than make his will, for fear lest he should presently die after it." The subsequent lines, from Dryden and Lee's *Œdipus*,iv., 1, need no apology for their introduction :

" For when we think Fate hovers o'er
    our heads,
Our apprehensions shoot beyond all
    bounds,
Owls, ravens, crickets seem the Watch
    of Death ;
Nature's worst vermin scare her godlike
    sons ;
Echoes, the very leavings of a voice,
Grow babling ghosts and call us to our
    graves :
Each mole-hill thought swells to a huge
    Olympus,
While we, fantastic dreamers, heave and
    puff,
And sweat with an imagination's
    weight ;
As if, like Atlas, with these mortal
    shoulders
We could sustain the burden of the
    world."

Hear Molinæus :—" Si visitans Ægrum, lapidem inventum per viam attollat et sub lapide inveniatur Vermis se movens, aut formica vivens, faustum Omen est, et indicium fore ut æger convalescat ; si nihil inveniatur, res est conclamata, et certa mors, ut docet Burchardus, Decretorum, lib. xix." " Vates," p. 154. Lupton, in his third book of *Notable Things*, says : " If a firr tree be touched, withered, or burned with lightening, it signifies that the master or mistresse thereof shall shortly die." Comp. *Bay-Tree*. In Heylin's " Life of Laud," it is stated, that " the Bishop, going into his study, which nobody could get into but himself, found his own picture lying all along on its face, which extremely perplexed him, he looking upon it as ominous." Grose tells us that, besides general notices of death, many families have particular warnings or notices ; some of the appearance of a bird, and others by the figure of a tall woman dressed all in white, who goes shrieking about the house. This apparition is common in Ireland, where it is called Benshea and the Shrieking

Woman. Pennant says, that many of the great families in Scotland had their dæmon or genius, who gave them monitions of future events. Thus the family of Rothmurchas had the bodack au dun, or the ghost of the hill : Kinchardines the spectre of the bloody hand. Gartinbeg House was haunted by Bodach Gartin, and Tulloch Germs by Maug Monlack or the girl with the hairy left hand. The Synod gave frequent orders that inquiry should be made into the truth of this apparition ; and one or two declared that they had seen one that answered the description.

Camerarius writes : '' There bee some Princes of Germanie that have particular and apparent presages and tokens, full of noise, before or about the day of their death, as extraordinairie roaring of lions and barking of dogs, fearful noises and bustlings by night in castles, striking of clocks, and tolling of bels at undue times and howres, and other warnings whereof none could give any reason." *Living Librarie*, 1621, p. 284. Delrio adds, that in Bohemia a female spectre in mourning is accustomed to appear in a certain castle of an illustrious family, before one of the wives of its seigneurs dies. *Disquisitiones Magicæ*, p. 592. Compare *Luck of Eden Hall*, infrâ, and Hazlitt's *Proverbs*, 1882, p. 763.

Death-Rattle.—The dead or death rattle, a particular kind of noise made in respiring by a person in the extremity of sickness, is still considered in the North, as well as in other parts, of England, as an omen of death. Levinus Lemnius, in his " Occult Miracles of Nature," lib. ii. ch. 15, is very learned concerning it : " In Belgica regione, totoque Septentrionalis plagæ tractu, morituri certa argumenta proferunt emigrandi, edito sonitu murmuloso, nec est, qui absque hujusmodi indicio vitam non finiat. Siquidem imminente morte sonum edunt, tanquam aquæ labentis per salebras, locaque anfractuosa atque incurva, murmur, aut qualem Siphunculi ac Fistulæ in aquæ ductibus sonitum excitant. Cùm enim vocalem arteriam occludi contingat, spiritus qui confertim erumpere gestit, nactus angustum meatum, collapsamque fistulam, gargarismo quodam prodit, ac raucum per lævia murmur efficit, scatebrisque arentes deserit artus. Conglomeratus itaque spiritus, spumaque turgida commixtus, sonitum excitat, reciprocanti maris æstui assimilem. Quod ipsum in nonnullis etiam fit ob panniculos ac membranas in rugas contractas, sic ut spiritus obliquè ac sinuoso volumine decurrat. Hi, autem, qui valido sunt vastoque corpore, et qui violenta morte periunt, gravius resonant, diutiusque cum morte luctantur, ob humoris copiam ac densos crassosque spiritus. Iis vero qui extenuato sunt corpore, ac lenta morte con-

tabescunt, minus impetuose lenique sonitu
fertur Spiritus, ac sensim placideque
extinguuntur, ac quodammodo obdormis-
cunt."

Death - Watch. — "How many
people have I seen, says Defoe, "in the
most terrible palpitations for months together, expecting every hour the approach
of some calamity, only by a little worm,
which breeds in old wainscot, and, endeavouring to eat its way out, makes a
noise like the movement of a watch." *Duncan Campbell*, 1732, p. 61. Wallis gives
the following account of the insect so
called, whose ticking has been thought by
ancient superstition to forbode death in a
family. "The small scarab called the
Death-Watch (Scarabæus galeatus pulsa-
tor) is frequent among dust and in decayed
rotten wood, lonely and retired. It is one
of the smallest of the Vagipennia, of a
dark brown, with irregular light brown
spots, the belly plicated, and the wings
under the cases pellucid; like other beetles,
the helmet turned up, as is supposed for
hearing; the upper lip hard and shining.
By its regular pulsations, like the ticking
of a watch, it sometimes surprises those
that are strangers to its nature and properties, who fancy its beating portends a
family change, and the shortening of the
thread of life. Put into a box, it may
be heard and seen in the act of pulsation,
with a small proboscis against the side of
it, for food more probably than for hyme-
næal pleasure as some have fancied."
History of Northumberland, i., 367.
Baxter observes that "There are
many things that ignorance causeth
multitudes to take for prodigies. I
have had many discreet friends that
have been affrighted with the noise
called a death-watch, whereas I have since,
near three years ago, oft found by trial,
that it is a noise made upon paper, by a
little, nimble, running worm, just like a
louse, but whiter, and quicker; and it is
most usually behind a paper pasted to a
wall, especially to wainscot: and it is
rarely, if ever heard, but in the heat of
summer." Then immediately after he
adds : "But he who can deny it to be a
prodigy, which is recorded by Melchior
Adamus, of a great and good man, who
had a clock-watch that had layen in a
chest many years unused; and when he lay
dying, at eleven o'clock, of itself, in that
chest, it struck eleven in the hearing of
many." *World of Spirits*, 1691, 203.

Deaths.—The custom, formerly only
too much diffused, of removing the pillow
from the head of a dying person in order
to accelerate the end, is sometimes ascribed to the superstitious notion, that
the presence of a pigeon's feather among
the rest prevents the fatal catastrophe.

But there was also a belief that this practice afforded relief to the individual *articulo mortis*.

Dedication of Churches.—As
in the times of Paganism annual festivals
were celebrated in honour and memory of
their gods, goddesses, and heroes, when the
people resorted together at their temples
and tombs; and as the Jews constantly
kept their anniversary feast of Dedication
in remembrance of Judas Maccabæus their
deliverer; so it hath been an ancient custom among the Christians of this island to
keep a feast every year upon a certain
week or day, in remembrance of the finishing of the building of their parish church,
and of the first solemn dedicating of it to
the service of God, and committing it to
the protection of some guardian saint or
angel. At the conversion of the Saxons,
says Bourne, by Austin the monk, the
heathen Paganalia were continued among
the converts, with some regulations, by
an order of Gregory I., to Melitus the Abbot, who accompanied Austin in his mis-
sion to this island. His words are to this
effect : On the day of dedication, or the
birth-day of Holy Martyrs, whose relics
are there placed, let the people make to
themselves booths of the boughs of trees,
round about those very churches which
had been the temples of idols, and in a religious way to observe a feast : that beasts
may no longer be slaughtered by way of
sacrifice to the devil but for their own
eating and the glory of God : and that
when they are satisfied they may return
thanks to him who is the giver of all good
things. Silas Taylor says, that "in the
days of yore, when a Church was to be
built, they watched and prayed on the
Vigil of the Dedication, and took that
point of the horizon where the sun arose
for the east, which makes that variation,
so that few stand true except those built
between the two equinoxes. I have experimented some churches, and have found
the line to point to that part of
the horizon where the sun rises,
on the day of that Saint to whom the
church is dedicated." But it being observed that the number of holidays was
excessively increased, to the detriment of
civil government and secular affairs,
and also that the great irregularities and
licentiousness which had crept into these
festivities by degrees, especially in the
churches, chapels, and churchyards, were
found highly injurious to piety, virtue,
and good manners, statutes and canons
were made to regulate them : and by an
Act of Convocation passed by Henry the
Eighth in 1536, their number was in some
measure lessened. The Feast of the Dedication of every Church was ordered to be
kept upon one and the same day everywhere; that is, on the first Sunday in Octo-

ber: and the saint's day to which the church was dedicated entirely laid aside. This act is now disregarded; but probably it arose thence that the Feast of Wakes was first put off till the Sunday following the proper day, that the people might not have too many avocations from their necessary and domestic business. "Ut die Dedicationis, vel Natalitiis Sanctorum Martyrum, quorum illic Reliquiæ ponuntur, tabernacula sibi circa easdem Ecclesias, quæ ex fanis commutatæ sunt de ramis arborum faciant," &c.—*Bed.* lib. . . . cap. 30. Borlase says, the Parish Feasts instituted in commemoration of the dedication of parochial churches were highly esteemed among the primitive Christians, and originally kept on the saint's day to whose memory the church was dedicated. The generosity of the founder and endower thereof was at the same time celebrated, and a service composed suitable to the occasion. This is still done in the colleges of Oxford, to the memory of the respective founders. On the eve of this day prayers were said and hymns were sung all night in the church; and from these watchings the festivals were styled Wakes; which name still continues in many parts of England, though the vigils have been long abolished. Dugdale's *Warwickshire*, p. 575; and compare *May - Day.* The following entries occur in the accounts of St. - Mary - at - Hill, 1495: "For bred and wyn and ale to Bowear (a singer) and his co., and to the Quere on Dedication Even, and on the morrow, i.s. vjd." 1555. "Of the Sumcyon of our Ladys Day, which is our church holyday, for drinkyng over-night at Mr. Haywards, at the King's Head, with certen of the parish and certen of the chapel and other singing men, in wyne, pears, and sugar, and other chargis, viiis. jd. For a dynner for our Ladys Day, for all the syngyng men and syngyng children, il. For a pounde and halfe of sugar at dinner, is. vijd. ob. 1557. For garlands for our Ladys Day & for strawenge yerbes, ijs. ijd. For bryngyng down the images to Rome Land and other things to be burnt." In these accounts, "To singing men and children from the King's Chapel, and elsewhere," on some of the grand festivals, particularly the parish feast (our Lady's Assumption), a reward in money and a feast are charged in several years. Carew, who wrote about 1585, tells us that "The Saints Feast is kept upon the Dedication Day by every householder of the parish, within his own dores, each entertaining such forrayne acquaintance, as will not fayle ,when their like turne cometh about, to requite them with the like kindness." *Survey of Cornwall*, 1602, p. 69. But Borlase informs us that, in his time, it being very inconvenient, especially in harvest

time, to observe the parish feast on the saint's day, they were by the bishop's special authority transferred to the following Sunday. Charles I. in his "Book of Sports," 1633, removed the prohibition which had been exercised against these dedication-feasts. This tract is little more than a re-issue of James the First's Book, 1618. In Aubrey's "Natural History of Wiltshire," first printed in 1847, we read: "The night before the Day of Dedication of the Church, certain officers were chosen for gathering the money for charitable uses. Old John Wastfield of Langley was Peter man at St. Peter's Chapel there," and from the same source it appears that it was customary to spend the eve of the Dedication-day in fasting and prayer. In the southern parts of this nation, says Bourne, most country villages are wont to observe some Sunday in a more particular manner than the rest, i.e., the Sunday after the day of dedication, or day of the saint to whom the church was dedicated. Then the inhabitants deck themselves in their gaudiest clothes, and have open doors and splendid entertainments for the reception and treating of their relations and friends, who visit them on that occasion from each neighbouring town. The morning is spent for the most part at church, though not as that morning was wont to be spent, in commemorating the saint or martyr, or in gratefully remembering the builder and endower. The remaining part of the day is spent in eating and drinking. Thus they also spend a day or two afterwards in all sorts of rural pastimes and exercises: such as dancing on the green, wrestling, cudgelling &c. *Antiq. Vulg.*, ch. 30. "In the Northern Counties," says Hutchinson, "these holy feasts are not yet abolished; and in the county of Durham many are yet celebrated. They were originally feasts of dedication in commemoration of the consecration of the church, in imitation of Solomon's great convocation at the consecrating the Temple of Jerusalem. The religious tenor is totally forgotten, and the Sabbath is made a day of every dissipation and vice which it is possible to conceive could crowd upon a villager's manners and rural life. The manner of holding these festivals in former times was under tents and booths erected in the church-yard, where all kinds of diversions were introduced. Interludes were there performed, being a species of theatrical performance consisting of a rehearsal of some passages in Holy Writ personated by actors. This kind of exhibition is spoken of by travellers, who have visited Jerusalem, where the religious even presume to exhibit the Crucifixion and Ascension with all their tremendous circumstances. On these celebrations in this country, great feasts were displayed, and vast abundance of meat and drink." *History of Northumberland*, ii., 26. In Bridges' "Northamptonshire" are very many instances recorded of the wake being still kept on or near to the day of the saint to whom the church was dedicated. In the "Spectator," No. 161, for Sept. 4, 1711, the writer, speaking of this anniversary, tells us, that "the squire of the parish treats the whole company every year with a hogshead of ale; and proposes a beaver hat as a recompense to him who gives most falls." In this country an element of licentiousness undoubtedly crept into this description of festival, and we find a clergyman, one Rosewell, in a sermon which he published in 1711, earnestly opposed to the continuance of the wake on the eve before the dedication. But when an order had been made in 1627 and in 1631, at Exeter and in Somersetshire, for the suppression of the wakes, both the ministers and the people desired their continuance, not only for preserving the memorial of the dedication of their several churches, but for civilizing their parishioners, composing differences by the mediation and meeting of friends, increasing of love and unity by these feasts of charity, and for the relief and comfort of the poor.

Kirchmaier, or Naogeorgus, in his *Popish Kingdom*, translated by Googe, 1570, draws a curious and edifying picture of the enthusiasm and licentiousness attendant by degrees in this festival abroad:

"The dedication of the Church is yerely had in minde,
With worship passing Catholicke, and in a wondrous kinde:
From out the steeple hie is hangde a crosse and banner fayre,
The pavement of the temple strowde with hearbes of pleasant ayre,
The pulpits and the aulters all that in the Church are seene,
And every pewe and piller great, are deckt with boughes of greene:
The tabernacles opened are, and images are drest,
But chiefly he that patron is, doth shine above the rest:
A borde there standes, whereon their bulles and pardons thick they lay,
That given are to every one that keepes this holyday:
The Idoll of the Patron eke, without the doore doth stande,
And beggeth fast of every man, with pardons in his hande:
Who for bicause he lackes his tongue, and hath not yet the skill
In common peoples languages when they speak well or ill:

He hath his own interpretor, that alwayes standeth by,
And vnto every man that commeth in or out doth cry:
Desiring them the Patrone there, with giftes to have in minde,
And Popishe pardons for to buie, release of sinnes to finde.

*   *   *   *   *

On every side the neighbours come, and such as dwell not nere,
Come of their owne good willes, and some required to be there.
And every man his weapon hath, their swords and launces long,
Their axes, curriars, pystolets, with pikes and darts among.
The yong men in their best array, and trimmest maydes appeare,
Both jeasters, roges, and minstrels with their instruments are heare.
The pedlar doth his pack untrusse, the host his pots doth fill,
And on the table breade and drinke doth set for all that will:
Nor eyther of them their heape deceyves, for of the others all,
To them th' advauntage of this feaste, and gaine, doth chiefly fall.
The service done, they eyther to the taverne fast doe flie,
Or to their neighbours house, whereas they feede unreasonablie:
For sixe or seven courses they vnto the table bring,
And for their suppers may compare with any heathen king.
The table taken up, they rise, and all the youth apace,
The minstrell with them called go to some convenient place:
Where when with bagpipe hoarce, he hath begon his musicke fine,
And vnto such as are preparde to daunce hath given signe,
Comes thither streight both boys and girls, and men that aged bee,
And maryed folkes of middle age, there also comes to see,
Old wrinckled hagges, and youthfull dames, that minde to daunce aloft,
Then sundrie pastimes do begin, and filthie daunces oft:
When drunkards they do lead the daunce with fray and bloody fight,
That handes, and eares, and head, and face, are torne in wofull plight.
The streames of bloud run downe the armes, and oftentimes is seene.
The carkasse of some ruffian slaine, is left upon the greene.
Here many, for their lovers sweete, some daintie thing do buie,
And many to the taverne goe, and drink for companie,
Whereas they foolish songs do sing, and noyses great do make:

Some in the meane while play at cardes,
    and some the dice do shake.
Their custome also is, the priest into the
    house to pull :
Whom when they have, they thinke their
    game accomplished at full :
He farre in noise exceedes them all, and
    eke in drinking drie
The cuppes, a prince he is, and holdes
    their heades that speewing lie."

Compare *Wake.*

Demoniac.—The very curious and
extraordinary "Saxon Leechdoms," edited
by Mr. Cockayne, contain a receipt for
" a fiend-sick man, or *demoniac.*" It was
" a spew-drink, or emetic : lupin, bishopwort, henbane, cropleek ; pound these together, add ale for a liquid, let it stand
for a night, add fifty libcorns, or cathartic
grains, and holy water. A drink for a
fiend-sick man, to be drunk out of a church
bell : githrife, cynoglossum, yarrow, &c.,
work up the drink off clear ale, sing seven
masses over the worts, add garlic and holy
water, and drip the drink into every
drink which he will subsequently drink,
and let him sing the psalms, Beati Immaculati, and Exsurgat, and Salvum me fac,
deus, and then let him drink out of a
church bell, and let the mass priest after
the drink sing this over him, Domine,
sancte pater omnipotens." Following
these two specifics for fiend-sick men, is a
third, equally repugnant to modern ideas
of common sense, for a lunatic.

Denier à Dieu.—See *God's Penny.*

Denier de Foi.—Douce, in a paper
read before the Society of Antiquaries in
January, 1810, observes : " The small piece
of silver, that accompanies this paper is
inscribed *Denier de Foy* or *pour Epouser,*
having on one side a heart between two
hands, and on the other two fleurs de lis.
It is not in reality a current piece of
money, but only a local or a particular
token or symbol of property. It is, as the
inscription imports, a French betrothing
penny, given before the marriage ceremony." I do not think that Douce proves
more than the delivery of a token in earnest of dower, and of his betrothing penny
there are, to the best of my knowledge, no
Anglo-Saxon or English examples in existence. There is another sort inscribed
Denier Tournois pour Epouser. These
pieces occur both in gold and silver ; see
supplement to Hazlitt's *Coins of Europe,*
1897, p. 33. But, after all, the token exhibited by Douce appears to have been
nothing more than an example of the festing-penny, familiar enough in the northern counties of England, and no doubt properly identified with the Danish custom of
hiring or binding apprentices with some
such token. Festing is, of course, a form
of fasting or fastening. The fœsteninge-

ring was similarly the betrothing-ring or,
as it is now called, the engaged-ring. To
fest, in the North of England, is to bind
as an apprentice. Mr. Atkinson, in his
Cleveland Glossary, 1868, after observing
that the festing-penny of the North of
England is analogous to the Scandinavian
betrothing penny (shown by Douce to have
been also known in France), adds : " if a
servant who has been duly hired and received her hiring or festing-penny, wishes
to cancel her bargain. . . she always sends
back the festing penny. . . Two instances
of this kind have occurred in this (Danby)
parish in the course of the spring hiring-
time of the present year, 1865."

Dequoy or **Decoy.**—See *Cards.*

Dessil.—Martin says : " In this Island
of Lewis there was an antient custom to
make a fiery circle about the houses, corn,
cattle, &c., belonging to each particular
family. A man carried fire in his right
hand, and went round, and it was called
Dessil, from the right hand, which, in the
antient language, is called Dess. There is
another way of the dessil, or carrying fire
round about women before they are
churched, and about children until they
be christened, both of which are performed
in the morning and at night. They told
me this fire round was an effectual means
to preserve both the mother and the infant from the power of evil spirits, who
are ready at such times to do mischief,
and sometimes carry away the infants, and
return them poor meagre skeletons, and
these infants are said to have voracious
appetites, constantly craving for meat.
In this case it was usual for those who believed that their children were thus taken
away, to dig a grave in the fields upon
Quarter Day, and there to lay the fairy
skeleton till next morning : at which time
the parents went to the place, where they
doubted not to find their own child instead
of the skeleton." *Hist. of W. Islands,* p.
116. He elsewhere observes, " Loch-siant
Well in Skie is much frequented by strangers as well as by the inhabitants of the
Isle, who generally believe it to be a specifick for several diseases ; such as stitches,
headaches, stone, consumption, megrim.
Several of the common people oblige themselves by a vow to come to this well and
make the ordinary tour about it, called
Dessil, which is performed thus : They
move thrice round the well, proceeding
sun-ways, from east to west, and so on.
This is done after drinking of the water ;
and when one goes away from the well, it
is a never-failing custom to leave some
small offering on the stone which covers
the well. There is a small coppice near it,
of which none of the natives dare venture
to cut the least branch, for fear of some
signal judgement to follow upon it." *Description of W. Islands of Scotland,* 140.

He also speak of a well of similar quality, at which, after drinking, they make a tour and then leave an offering of some small token, such as a pin, needle, farthing, or the like, on the stone cover which is above the well.

Deuce.—Deuce may be said to be another popular name for the Devil. Few, perhaps, who make use of the expression "Deuce take you," particularly those of the softer sex, who accompanying it with the gentle pat of a fan, cannot be supposed to mean any ill by it, are aware that it is synonymous with "sending you to the Devil." Dusius was the ancient popular name for a kind of demon or devil among the Gauls, so that this saying, the meaning of which so few understand, has at least its antiquity to recommend it. It is mentioned by St. Augustine (*De Civitate Dei*, c. 23) as a libidinous demon, who used to violate the chastity of women, and, with the incubus of old, was charged with doing a great deal of mischief of so subtle a nature, that, as none saw it, it did not seem possible to be prevented. Later times have done both these devils justice, candidly supposing them to have been much traduced by a certain set of delinquents, who used to father upon invisible and imaginary agents the crimes of real men.

Devil.—In some of the early Mysteries Satan is introduced as *Saint Mahown*. The Glossary to Burns mentions Hornie as one of his Majesty's names. And another is *Old Boots*, whence the saying, "It rains like Old Boots."

There is a story in one of the Chronicles, under the year 1165, that the Devil was seen riding like a great black horse, before a storm which happened in Yorkshire in that year, and that the marks of his feet were visible in several places, particularly on the cliff at Scarborough, where he sprang into the sea. Not many years ago, an extraordinary sensation was produced in the South of England, by the discovery of marks in various parts of the country, which could not be identified with the prints of any known beast or bird, unless it was that there was some similitude to a donkey's shoe. The people in those parts did not like to say it was the Devil, perhaps; but it is not unlikely that some of them thought so. At the same time, no explanation of the mystery has, I believe, been offered to this day. Perhaps this extraordinary presence may have been nothing more than the cloven hoof which, in the deep snows of winter, is said to haunt the Dewerstone, a rocky elevation on the borders of Dartmoor. But this latter phenomenon is reported to be accompanied by a naked human foot, of which a case occurred in Devonshire, and created a wide and long

sensation, many years since. Several instances of mysterious footprints are collected in "Lancashire Folk - Lore," 1867. There is no vulgar story of the Devil having appeared anywhere without a cloven foot. It is observable also that this infernal enemy, in graphic representations of him, is seldom or never pictured without one. Othello says:

"I look down towards his feet; but that's a fable;
If that thou be'st a devil, I cannot kill thee";

which Johnson explains : "I look towards his feet, to see, if, according to the common opinion, his feet be cloven." Grose says :—"Although the devil can partly transform himself into a variety of shapes, he cannot change his cloven foot, which will always mark him under every appearance." Scott has the following curious passage on this subject : "In our childhood, our mother's maids have so terrified us with an ugly devil, having horns on his head, fire in his mouth, and a tail in his breech, eyes like a basin, fangs like a dog, claws like a bear, a skin like a Niger, and a voyce roaring like a lyon, whereby we start and are afraid when we hear one cry Bough!" He adds: "and they have so frayed us with bul-beggars, spirits, witches, urchens, elves, hags, fairies, satyrs, pans, faunes, sylens, Kit with the canstick, Tritons, centaures, dwarfes, gyants, imps, calcars, conjurers, nymphes, changelings, incubus, Robin Good-fellow, the spoorn, the mare, the man in the oak, the Hell-wain, the fire-drake, the puckle, Tom-thombe, hob-goblin, Tom-tumbler. Boneless, and such other bugs, that we are afraid of our own shadowes; insomuch that some never feare the devil but in a darke night, &c. *Discovery*, ed. 1665. p. 65. Philip Stubbes, in his "Two wonderful and rare examples" (1581), describes a remarkable case which happened to Mistress Bowcer, at Donnington, in Leicestershire : "And nowe," says Stubbs, I will proceede to shewe one other as straunge a judgement happening in Leicestershire, in a towne called Donnington, where dwelled a poore man named Iohn Twell, who deceased, owing unto one Oswald Bowcer the summe of fiue shilling, which the sayde Oswalde did forgiue the sayde man before named, as he lay vpon his death bedde; but the sayde Oswaldes wife, called Ioane, would in no way forgive the said Twell, as long (she sayde) as she had to liue. Whereupon, not long after, the Deuill appeared vnto her in the form of the sayd Twell deceased, expressing all the lyneamentes of the body of the dead man : which might well be, for we reade in the Bible, in the like order did Satan counterfeit the body of Samuell. But to proceede to the matter: this euill spirit uttered vnto her these speeches, and said he had brought her money from Iohn Twell deceased, and willed her incontinent to disburse the sayd money vnto her husband for his paines. Which she, with as covetous a desire, receyved, saying, God thanke you. She had no sooner named God, but the money consumed away from betweene her handes, as it were a vapour of smoake, tyll it was all consumed: wherewith the Deuill, giving her a most fearfull and sore stroke, vanished out of her sight. Wherewith her whole body became as blacke as pitche, replenished all over with a moste filthy scurfe and other things."

The Rev. George Gordon, who drew up the old statistical account of Sorn, co. Ayr, in 1798, observes: "There is a tradition well authenticated that King James the fifth honoured his treasurer Sir William Hamilton with a visit at Sorn Castle, on occasion of the marriage of his daughter to Lord Seton. The King's visit at Sorn Castle took place in winter; and being heartily tired of his journey through so long a track of moor, moss, and miry clay, where there was neither road nor bridge, he is reported to have said with that good-humoured pleasantry which was a characteristic of so many of his family, that 'were he to play the Deil a trick, he would send him from Glascow to Sorn in winter.'" "The trick now-a-days," continues the writer, "would not prove a very serious one; for Satan, old as he is, might travel very comfortably one half of the way in a mail-coach, and the other half in a post-chaise. Neither would he be forced, like King James, for want of better accommodation, to sit down about mid-way, by the side of a well (hence called King's Well), and there take a cold refreshment in a cold day. At the very same place he might now find a tolerable inn and a warm dinner." *S.A.*, xx. 170. An early writer, speaking of a man who desired an interview with the Prince of Darkness, says that he was recommended to go in quest of him to wild Scotland, his favourite sojourn, but that when the traveller proceeded to act on this advice, he failed to discover his majesty, and merely met with an old woman, who pretended to have some knowledge of him. Michel, *Les Ecossais en France*, 1862, p. 2. At this time, no doubt, the farther extremities of the country, at least, were practically a *terra incognita*, about which any legends might be set afloat. Winslow, in his *Good News from New England*, 1624, speaking of the sacrifices of the Indians to the Devil, says: "They have told me I should see the Devil at those times come to the vestry; but I assured myself and them of the con-

trary: which so proved. Yea, themselves have confessed, they never saw him, when any of us were present." In a tract in the Huth library, printed about 1645, among other "Signs and Wonders from Heaven," is an account how the Evil One came to a farmer's house at Swaffham in West Norfolk under the form of a gentlewoman on horseback. In Massinger's "Virgin Martyr," 1622, act iii. sc. 1, Harpax, an evil spirit, following Theophilus in the shape of a secretary, speaks thus of the superstitious Christian's description of his infernal master:

" I'll tell you what now of the Devil:
He's no such horrid creature; cloven-
    footed,
Black, saucer-ey'd, his nostrils breath-
    ing fire,
As these lying Christians make him."

In a contemporary description of the appearance of the Devil at St. Alban's, Herts, in 1648, it is said that he then assumed the likeness of a ram, and that a butcher cut his throat, sold a portion of the flesh, and cooked the remainder for himself and a select party of friends, all of which was "attested by divers letters of persons of very good credit," and the tract itself purported to have been published "for confutation of those that believe there are no such things as spirits or devils." Hone's *Ancient Mysteries*, 1823, p. 89. This infernal visitant appears in no instance to have been treated with more *sang froid* on his appearing, or rather perhaps his imagined appearance, than by one Mr. White of Dorchester, assessor to the Westminster Assembly at Lambeth, as recorded by Mr. Samuel Clarke: "The Devil, in a light night, stood by his bedside: he looked awhile whether he would say or do anything, and then said, 'If thou hast nothing else to do, I have': and so turned himself to sleep." Baxter's *Certainty of the World of Spirits*, 1691, p. 63. He adds, that "Many say it from Mr. White himself." One has only to wonder, on this occasion, that a person who could so effectually lay the Devil, could have been induced to think, or rather dream, of raising him. Sir Thomas Browne is full on this subject of popular superstition in his "Vulgar Errors": "The ground of this opinion at first," says he, "might be his frequent appearing in the shape of a goat," (this accounts also for his horns and tail), "which answers the description. This was the opinion of the antient Christians, concerning the Apparition of Panites, Fauns, and Satyrs; and of this form we read of one that appeared to Anthony in the Wilderness. The same is also confirmed from expositions of Holy Scripture. For whereas it is said, Thou shalt not offer unto Devils: the original word is Seghuirim, that is, rough and hairy goats, because in that shape the Devil most often appeared, as is expounded by the Rabins, as Tremellius hath also explained, and as the word Ashimah, the God of Emath, is by some conceived." He observes, also, that the goat was the emblem of the sin-offering, and is the emblem of sinful men at the Day of Judgment. It is observed in the "Connoisseur," No. 109, that "the famous Sir Thomas Browne refuted the generally-received opinion, that the Devil is black, has horns upon his head, wears a long curling tail and a cloven stump: nay has even denied that, wheresoever he goes, he always leaves a smell of brimstone behind him." Baxter tells us that "Devils have a greater game to play invisibly than by apparitions. O happy world, if they did not do a hundred thousand times more hurt by the baits of pleasure, lust, and honour, and by pride, and love of money, and sensuality, than they do by witches." *World of Spirits*, 1691, p. 223. In "Sphinx and Œdipus," (part of "A Helpe to Discourse," 1627), I read that "the Devil never appears in the shape of a dove, or a lamb, but in those of goats, dogs, and cats, or such like: and that to the Witch of Edmonton he appeared in the shape of a dog, and called his name Dom." An essayist in the "Gentleman's Magazine" for October, 1732, observes that, "As for the great Evil Spirit, 'tis for his interest to be masked and invisible. Amongst his sworn vassals and subjects he may allow himself to appear in disguise at a public paw-wawing, (which is attested by a cloud of travellers), but there is no instance of his appearing among us, except that produced by Mr. Echard, to a man in so close confederacy with him, that 'twas reasonable to suppose they should now and then contrive a personal meeting."

The old ceremonies used in raising the devil, such as making a circle with chalk, setting an old hat in the centre of it, repeating the Lord's Prayer backward, and so forth, even when Brand wrote about 1795, had become, he says, "altogether obsolete, and seem to be forgotten even amongst our boys." Obsession of the devil is distinguished from possession in this. In possession the evil one was said to enter into the body of the man. In obsession, without entering into the body of the person, he was thought to besiege and torment him without. To be lifted up into the air, and afterwards to be thrown down violently, without receiving any hurt; to speak strange languages that the person had never learned; not to be able to come near holy things or the sacraments, but to have an aversion to them; to know and foretell secret things; to perform things that exceed the person's strength; to say or do things that the person would not or durst not say, if he were not externally moved to it, were the ancient marks and criterions of possessions. Jorden observes: "I doe not deny but there may be both possessions, and obsessions, and witchcraft, &c., and dispossession also through the prayers and supplications of God's servants, which is the only means left unto us for our reliefe in that case. But such examples being verye rare now-a-dayes, I would in the feare of God advise men to be very circumspect in pronouncing of a possession: both because the impostures be many, and the effects of naturall diseases be strange to such as have not looked thoroughly into them." *Suffocation of the Mother*, 1603, Dedic. The semi-mythical legend of Faustus, of which the most authentic version, so to speak, is in the Editor's *National Tales and Legends*, 1892, introduces us to a plurality of demons, having Lucifer as their chief and Mephistopheles as an agent on earth; and there is a scene in the story where a parliament of devils assembles, under the eyes of Faustus. In the *History of Friar Rush*, a romance of the 16th century, the Evil One is represented as holding occasional receptions, or levees of his emissaries, and listening to their reports of the most recent achievements performed by them in his behalf. One of them was Rush himself. Another bore the unusual name of Norpell. The more atrocious their exploits, the warmer of course was his Satanic majesty's commendation. There was an early metrical tract under the title of the *Parliament of Devils*, two or three times printed about 1520, and possibly responsible for the suggestion of the *Rush* piece just mentioned. Cassian, mentioning a host of devils who had been abroad in the night, says, that as soon as the morn approached, they all vanished and fled away: which farther evinces that this was the current opinion of the time. Vallancey *Coll.* viii., c. 16.

Devil on Two Sticks.—A correspondent of *Notes and Queries* (about 1880) writes as follows:—"I possess the means of playing the game, but not the art. Sometimes, when I see the stick and hour-glass shaped 'devil,' I wish I could handle them, for I have seen an old friend display great skill with the sticks in his garden, sending the 'devil' humming on high, and catching it with great accuracy. My old uncles used to talk of it: they knew and played the game early in this century. It may be of interest to know that such games have been found very useful *faute de mieux*. I remember one day, more than thirty years ago, paying a visit to one of the dearest old ladies I ever knew, named

Lady Scovell, the wife of Sir George Sco-vell, whom she had accompanied in his Peninsular campaigns when he was one of the most useful and most trusted of the Duke's staff. I found her disentangling a number of cups and balls, the strings of which had been all mixed by a carpet-crawling urchin, who had upset the basket containing them. I was surprised at the variety of shapes and sizes. The balls had to be caught on common average cups, cups flattened almost to a table, cups cut away on both sides till only a crescent was left, and, of course, the usual spike. On my asking her how she came by such a col-lection she told me that during the war she came home one winter to see her friends whilst the army was in quarters, and whilst at home she got a letter from Sir Rowland (Lord) Hill, saying the weather was so bad they very often could not get out, and he begged her to bring with her on her return any indoor games for himself and staff. Lady Scovell said she at once got these varieties of cups and balls and devils on two sticks made, and (having taken them to Spain) she added that they answered the purpose admir-ably, but it was rather funny to see the general and staff in the afternoon, when the day's work was finished, moving about the rooms hard at work at these games, and one backing himself against another." And this was seventy years ago.

Devil's Bit.—Coles tells us that "there is one herb, flat at the bottome, and seemeth as if the nether part of its root were bit off, and is called Devil's-bit, whereof it is reported that the devill, knowing that that part of the root would cure all diseases, out of his inveterate malice to mankind, bites it off." *Know-ledge of Plants*, 1656, p. 37.

Devil-Worship.—Dr Paul Carus, in his *History of the Devil*, makes the Spirit of Evil the primary object of pro-pitiatory homage on the part of archaic communities more disposed to dread the apparent source of what they suffered than that of what they enjoyed. On the principal of Dualism, in a more enlight-ened age, it still remains in a way a salu-tary inducement to rectitude to suppose the existence of a Power not merely able, but anxious, to punish the evil-doer. The modern popular theories of the Devil are the converse of that of universal original subjection to such a creation as the Thibe-tan All-Devourer, and depict man as originally pure and sinless, and the Evil One as a rebellious and degraded minister of God.

Dew.—Willsford tells us: "Mettals in general, against much wet or rainy weather, will seem to have a dew hang upon them, and be much apter to sully or foul any thing that is rubbed with the metal; as you may see in pewter dishes against rain, as if they did sweat, leaving a smutch upon the table cloaths: with this Pliny concludes as a signe of tempests ap-proaching. . . . . Stones against rain will have a dew hang upon them; but the sweating of stones is from several causes, and sometimes is a sign of much drought. Glasses of all sorts will have a dew upon them in moist weather: Glasse windows will also shew a frost, by turning the air that touches them into water, and then congealing of it." *Nature's Secrets*, p. 138. This depends, of course, on the dif-ference between the internal and external temperature. At Hertford Assizes, 4 Car. I., the following testimony, which of course, merely reflects the popular view of the subject, was taken by Sir John May-nard, Serjeant at Law, from the deposi-tion of the minister of the parish where a murder was committed: "That the body being taken out of the grave thirty days after the party's death, and lying on the grass, and the four defendants (suspected of murdering her) being required, each of them touched the dead body, whereupon the brow of the dead, which before was of a livid and carrion colour, began to have a dew, or gentle sweat, arise on it, which encreased by degrees, till the sweat ran down in drops on the face, the brow turned to a fresh and lively colour; and the de-ceased opened one of her eyes, and shut it again three several times: she likewise thrust out the ring or marriage finger three times, and pulled it in again, and the finger dropt blood on the grass." The minister of the next parish, who also was present, being sworn, gave evidence ex-actly as above. *Gentleman's Magazine*, 1731. Compare *May-Day.*

Dice.—In the Municipal Records of the City of London we first become aware of the employment of dice by reason of abuses in connection with the introduction of them under 1311 for the purpose of cheating. Unsuspecting persons were even then enticed into taverns by well-dressed sharpers, and robbed in this way. Other notices, where false dice occur, may be found under 1334 and 1376, where tables or backgammon is mentioned as a second amusement and medium of deceit. Riley's *Memorials*, 1868, pp. 86, 193, 395. In the account of the entertainment given to Richard, son of the Black Prince, in 1337, the mummers shewed by a pair of dice their desire to play with the young Prince. Hazlitt's *Warton*, 1871, iii., 161. Sir T. Elyot, in his "Governor," 1531, has some remarks on this subject, which, as illustrating the state of feeling in Henry VIII.'s time, may be worth a place here: "I suppose there is not a more playne figure of idlenesse, then playing at dice. For besides, that therin is no maner of exercise of the body or minde, they which play thereat, must seeme to haue no portion of witte or cunnyng, if they will be called fayre players, or in some company auoyde the stabbe of a dagger, if they bee taken with any craftie conueyance." In "The Common Cries of London," an early Elizabethan ballad by W. Turner, there is a curious passage seeming to shew that the street-hawkers used sometimes to carry dice in their pockets either for amusement, or for the purpose of practising on some inexperienced customer :

"Ripe, cherry ripe !
    The costermonger cries ;
Pippins fine or pears !
    Another after hies,
With a basket on his head,
    His living to advance,
And in his purse a pair of dice,
    For to play at mumchance."

Comp. *London*. Dr. Wilde left a sum of money by will, the interest of which was to be invested in the purchase of Bibles, which were to be tossed for every year at the Communion-table at the parish church at St. Ives, in Huntingdonshire, by six boys and six girls, being parishioners. The operation now takes place in the vestry. Jonson seems to have informed Drummond of Hawthornden in 1619. that at Christmas Eve, when Queen Elizabeth would play at dice, there were special ones provided for her, so that her highness might always win. *Masson's Drummond*, 1873, p. 94. Compare *Cards*.

Dick o' Tuesday.—See *Will o' the Wisp*.

Diet or **Debates (The).**—A social game at cards, played with a pack of 24. Twelve of the cards have costume figures. The inscriptions are in French, German, and English. The set before me appears to belong to 1830 or thereabouts.

Dish Fair.—Drake tells us that " A Fair is always kept in Mickle Gate (York) on St. Luke's Day, for all sorts of small wares. It is commonly called Dish Fair, from the great quantity of wooden dishes, ladles, &c., brought to it. There is an old custom used at this fair of bearing a wooden ladle in a sling on two stangs about it, carried by four sturdy labourers, and each labourer was formerly supported by another. This, without doubt, is a ridicule on the meanness of the wares brought to this fair, small benefit accruing to the labourers at it. Held by Charter Jan. 25, an. Reg. Regis, Hen. vii. 17." *Eboracum*, p. 219.

Distaff's (St.) or **Rock Day.**— (January 7). So this day is jocularly termed by Herrick in his *Hesperides*,

1648, and by Henry Bold, in his *Wit a Sporting*, 1657, in some lines copied from the earlier writer.

Divinations. — Divinations differ from omens in this, that the omen is an indication of something that is to come to pass, which happens to a person, as it were by accident, without his seeking for it : whereas divination is the obtaining of the knowledge of something future by some endeavour of his own, or means which he himself designedly makes use of for that end. There were among the ancients divinations by water, fire, earth, air ; by the flight of birds, by lots, by dreams, by the wind, &c. Gaule enumerates as follows the several species of divination : "Stareomancy, or divining by the elements ; äeromancy, or divining by the ayr ; pyromancy, by fire ; hydromancy, by water ; geomancy, by earth ; theomancy, pretending to divine by the revelation of the spirit, and by the Scriptures or word of God ; dæmonomancy, by the suggestions of evill dæmons, or devils ; idolomancy, by idolls, images, figures ; psychomancy, by men's souls, affections, wills, religious or morall dispositions ; antinopomancy, by the entrails of men, women, and children ; theriomancy, by beasts ; ornithomancy, by birds ; ichtyomancy, by fishes ; botanomancy, by herbs ; lithomancy, by stones ; cleromancy, by lotts ; orniromancy, by dreams ; onomatomancy, by names ; arithmancy, by numbers ; logarithmancy, by logarithmes ; sternomancy, from the breast to the belly ; gastromancy, by the sound of or signs upon the belly ; omphalomancy, by the navel ; chiromancy, by the hands ; pedomancy, by the feet ; onychomancy, by the nayles ; cephalonomancy, by brayling of an asses head ; tuphramancy, by ashes ; capnomancy, by smoak ; livanomancy, by burning of frankincence ; carromancy, by melting of wax ; lecanomancy, by a basin of water ; catoxtromancy, by looking glasses ; chartomancy, by writing in papers" (this is retained in chusing valentines, &c.). ; "macharomancy, by knives or swords ; christallomancy, by glasses ; dactylomancy, by rings ; coseinomancy, by sieves ; axinomancy, by sawes ; cattabomancy, by vessels of brasse or other metall ; roadomancy, by starres ; spatalomancy, by skins, bones, excrements ; sciomancy, by shadows ; astragalomancy, by dice ; oinomancy, by wine ; sycomancy, by figgs ; typomancy, by the coagulation of cheese ; alphitomancy, by meal, flower, or branne ; critomancy, by grain or corn ; alectomancy, by cocks or pullen ; gyromancy, by rounds or circles ; lampadomancy, by candles and lamps ; and in one word for all, nagomancy or necromancy, by inspecting, consulting, and divining by, with or from the dead.

Borlase says that the Druids "besides the ominous appearance of the entrails, had several ways of divining. They divined by augury, that is, from the observations they made on the voices, flying, eating, mirth or sadness, health or sickness of birds." *Antiq. of Cornwall*, p. 133. A later writer tells us that Boadicea or Bonduca is said to have taken an omen with a hare, and that on that account this animal was eschewed as an article of food—a fact mentioned by Cæsar in his *Commentaries*. But he proceeds to mention that the hare was not eaten by the Cymry in the tenth century. and was regarded as worthless, insomuch, that in the laws of Hoel Dda it was not protected as the goose was, by any fine; and there was a notion indeed that it changed its sex from year to year, becoming alternately a male and a female. *Notes on Ancient Britain*, by W. Barnes, 1858, p. 5. In Caxton's "Description of England," we read: "It semeth of these men a grete wonder that in a boon of a wethers ryght sholder whan the fleshe is soden awaye and not rosted, they knowe what have be done, is done, and shall be done, as it were by spyryte of prophecye and a wonderful crafte. They telle what is done in ferre countres, tokenes of peas or of warre, the state of the royame, sleynge of men, and spousebreche, such thynges theye declare certayne of tokenes and sygnes that is in suche a sholder bone." Drayton mentions:

"A diuination strange the Dutch-made-
    English haue
Appropriate to that place (as though
    some power it gaue)
By th' shoulder of a ram from off the
    right side par'd
Which vsuallie they boile, the spade-
    boane being bar'd,
Which when the wizard takes, and
    gazes there-vpon,
Things long to come fore showes, as
    things done long agon."

He alludes to a colony of Flemings in Pembrokeshire. *Polyolbion*, Song v., p. 81, 84-5. We are referred to Giraldus Cambrensis, i., cap. 11. Selden writes hereupon: "Under Hen. II., one William Mangunel, a gentleman of those parts, finding, by his skill of prediction, that his wife had played false with him, and conceiued by his own nephew, formally dresses the shoulder-bone of one of his own rammes; and, sitting at dinner, (pretending it to be taken out of his neighbours' flocke), requests his wife (equalling him in these divinations) to giue her judgment: she curiously observes, and at last with great laughter casts it from her; the gentleman importun-

ing her reason of so vehement an affection, receiues answer of her, that his wife, out of whose flocke that ram was taken, had by incestuous copulation with her husband's nephew fraughted herself with a yong one. Lay all together, and iuge, gentlewomen, the sequele of this cross accident. But why she could not as well diuine of whose flocke it was, as the other secret, when I haue more skill in osteomantie, I will tell you." Pennant gives an account of this sort of divination as used in Scotland and there called sleinanachd, or reading the speal bone, or the blade-bone of a shoulder of mutton, well scraped (Mr. Shaw says picked; no iron must touch it). When Lord Loudon, he says, was obliged to retreat before the rebels to the Isle of Skie, a common soldier, on the very moment the battle of Culloden was decided, proclaimed the victory at that distance, pretending to have discovered the event by looking through the bone. "Tour in Scotland," 1769, p. 155. See also his "Tour to the Hebrides," p. 282, for another instance of the use of the speal bone. The word speal is evidently derived from the French *espaule*, humerus.

Hanway gives us to understand, that in Persia, too, they have a kind of divination by the bone of a sheep. *Travels*, i., 177. Owen, in his "Welch Dictionary," voce Cyniver, mentions "A play in which the youth of both sexes seek for an even-leaved sprig of the ash: and the first of either sex that finds one, calls out Cyniver, and is answered by the first of the other that succeeds; and these two, if the omen fails not, are to be joined in wedlock." Divination by arrows is ancient, according to Gibbon, and famous in the East. *D. and F.*, 4°, ed. x., 345. Brooke, in his "Ghost of Richard the Third," 1614, figures the king in his youth endeavouring by one of the ancient forms of divination to ascertain his destiny. The poem is, in imitation of the "Mirror for Magistrates," written in the first person:

"——Then at the slaughter-house, with
    hungry sight,
Vpon slaine beasts my sensuall part did
    feede;
And (that which gentler natures might
    affright)
I search'd their entrayles, as in them to
    reade
(Like th' ancient bards) what fate
    should thence betide."

Lilly the astrologer made, it should seem by the desire of Charles I. an experiment, to know in what quarter of the nation the King might be most safe, after he should have effected his escape, and not be discovered until he himself pleased. Madame Whorewood was deputed to receive Lilly's judgment. He seems to have had high fees, for he owns he got on this occasion twenty pieces of gold. It seems to have been believed that there was some divination, or other supernatural medium, by which the robbers of orchards might be detected, for in "Cataplus, a Mock Poem," 1672, the writer says of the Sibyl:

"Thou canst in orchard lay a charm
To catch base felon by the arm."

Randolph, in his "Amyntas," 1638, makes fairies declare a partiality for apples stolen from orchards in the night:

"*Jocastus.* What divine noise fraught with immortal harmony
Salutes my ears?
Bromius. Why this immortal harmony
Rather salutes your orchard: these young rascals,
These pescod shellers do so cheat my master,
We cannot have an apple in the orchard,
But straight some fairy longs for 't."

Of course, however, in this particular case, the fairies are counterfeit, like those in the "Merry Wives of Windsor"; while in the story in *A C. Mery Talys*, 1526, folio v. the depredators are mistaken for evil spirits. Charms or spells for divining purposes are, or not very long ago at least were, made by our peasantry in various districts from the blades of the oat, wheat, and even, according to Miss Baker, of the reed. Clare describes the special uses of these in his *Shepherd's Calendar*. It is still a common amusement with girls to ascertain, as they pretend, whom they are going to marry, to take some description of grass, and to count the spiral fronds, saying:

Tinker,
Tailor,
Soldier,
Sailor,
Rich man,
Poor man,
Beggar man,
Thief,

till they come to the end of them, and it is supposed to be the last frond, which decides it.

"Tu ne quæsieris scire nefas quem mihi, quem tibi
Finem Di dederint, Leuconoë: nec Babylonios
Tentaris numeros."
Hor. *Carm.* lib. i. Od. ii.

Diviner.—John of Salisbury enumerates no fewer than thirteen different kinds of diviners or fortune tellers, who (in his time) pretended to foretell future events, some by one means and some by another. *De Nugis Curialium*, lib. i., c. 12. Henry tells us that, "after the Anglo-Saxons and Danes embraced the Christian religion, the clergy were commanded by the canons to preach very frequently against diviners, sorcerers, auguries, omens, charms, incantations, and all the filth of the wicked and dotages of the Gentiles." *Hist. of Gr. Britain*, ii., 550, 4°, ed. He cites Johnson's *Eccl. Canons*, A.D. 747, c. 3.

Divining Rod.—Not only the Chaldeans used rods for divination, but almost every nation, which has pretended to that science, has practised the same method. Herodotus mentions it as a custom of the Scythians, Ammianus Marcellinus, of a tribe of that nation, the Alani, and Tacitus of the old Germans. *Bartholinus*, p. 676. Divination by the rod or wand is mentioned in the prophecy of Ezekiel. Hosea, too, reproaches the Jews as being infected with the like superstition: "My people ask counsel at their stocks, and their staff declareth unto them." We read in the *Gentleman's Magazine* for November, 1751: "So early as Agricola the divining rod was in much request, and has obtained great credit for its discovering where to dig for metals and springs of water; for some years past its reputation has been on the decline, but lately it has been revived with great success by an ingenious gentleman who from numerous experiments hath good reason to believe its effects to be more than imagination. He says that hazel and willow rods, he has by experience found, will actually answer with all persons in a good state of health, if they are used with moderation and at some distance of time, and after meals, when the operator is in good spirits. The hazel, willow, and elm are all attracted by springs of water: some persons have the virtue intermittently; the rod in their hands will attract one half hour, and repel the next. The rod is attracted by all metals, coals, amber, and lime stone, but with different degrees of strength. The best rods are those from the hazel or nut tree, as they are pliant and tough, and cut in the winter months. A shoot that terminates equally forked is to be preferred, about two feet and a half long; but as such a forked rod is rarely to be met with, two single ones, of a length and size, may be tied together with thread, and will answer as well as the other." It has been alleged that "the experiment of a hazel's tendency to a vein of lead ore is limited to St. John Baptist's Eve, and that with an hazel of that same year's growth." *Athenian Oracle*, Suppl., 234. Gay describes some other rustic methods of divination with hazel nuts, and he mentions two other kinds by the lady-fly and by apple-parings. Pennant mentions that this was still employed and credited within his memory, and was supposed, by having a sympathy with the hidden ore, to supersede the necessity for ordinary methods of searching. The instrument used by a foreign adventurer in the writer's neighbourhood is described by him as being no more than a rod forked at one end, which had been cut in a planetary hour, on Saturn's day and hour, because Saturn was the significator of lead. Jupiter, Venus, Sol, and Mercury, also participated in the operation according to their reputed several attributes and powers. *Tours in Wales*, 1810, i., 75.

"*Virgula divina.*"

Some sorcerers do boast they have a rod,
 Gather'd with vows and sacrifice,
And (borne about) will strangely nod
  To hidden treasure where it lies;
Mankind is (sure) that rod divine,
For to the wealthiest (ever) they incline."

Sheppard's *Epigr.* 1651, p. 141. I find the following account from Theophylact on the subject of *rabdomanteia* or rod divination : " They set up two staffs; and having whispered some verses and incantations, the staffs fell by the operation of dæmons. Then they considered which way each of them fell, forward, backward, to the right or left hand, and agreeably gave responses, having made use of the fall of their staffs for their signs." *Bell's MS. Discourse on Witchcraft*, 1705, p. 41. In Camerarius we read : " No man can tell why forked sticks of hazill (rather than sticks of other trees growing upon the very same places) are fit to shew the places where the veines of gold and silver are, the sticke bending itselfe in the places, at the bottome, where the same veines are." *Living Librarie*, 1621, p. 283. In the " Gentleman's Magazine" for February, 1752, it is observed : "M. Linnæus, when he was upon his voyage to Scania, hearing his secretary highly extol the virtues of his divining wand, and willing to convince him of its insufficiency, and for that purpose concealed a purse of one hundred ducats under a ranunculus, which grew by itself in a meadow, and bid the Secretary find it if he could. The wand discovered nothing, and M. Linnæus' mark was soon trampled down by the company who were present; so that when M. Linnæus went to finish the experiment by fetching the gold himself, he was utterly at a loss where to seek it. The man with the wand assisted him, and he pronounced that it could not lie the way they were going, but quite the contrary : so pursued the direction of his wand, and actually dug out the gold. M. Linnæus adds, that such another experiment would be sufficient to make a proselyte of him." The notion, still prevalent in the North and other mining districts of England, of the

hazel's tendency to a vein of lead ore, seam or stratum of coal, &c., seems to be a vestige of this rod divination. The *virgula divina*, or *baculus divinatorius*, is a forked branch in the form of a Y, cut off an hazel or apple-stick of twelve months' growth by means whereof people have pretended to discover mines or springs, &c., under ground. The method of using it is this : the person who bears it, walking very slowly over the places where he suspects mines or spring may be, the effluvia exhaling from the metals, or vapour from the water impregnating the wood, makes it dip or incline, which is the sign of a discovery. The manner was, to hold the rod with both hands horizontally, and to go along the tract of land where the lode was supposed to lie, until the rod bent of itself, which at once indicated the presence of the desired metal. Such an experiment is known to have been made, in perfect good faith, not many years since. Mr. Baring-Gould stated in 1866 that it was still employed in Wiltshire (and on the Continent) for this purpose. See Vallemont " Physique Occulte, ou Traité de la Baguette Divinatoire; et de son utilité pour la decouverte des sources de l'eau de rivières, de Trésors cachez, &c." 1693. Also Lilly's " History of his Life and Times," p. 32, for a curious experiment (which he confesses however to have failed in) to discover hidden treasure by the hazel rod. As regards the discovery of springs underground by this process, the belief in it is said still to have survived in Normandy in 1874. *Vaux de Vire*, of Jean le Houx, by Muirhead, 1875, p. xvi.

With the divining rod seems connected a *lusus naturæ* of ash tree bough, resembling the *litui* of the Roman augurs and the Christian pastoral staff, which still obtains a place, if not on this account I know not why, in the catalogue of popular superstitions. In the last century Brand himself saw one of these, which he thought extremely beautiful and curious, in the house of an old woman at Beer Alston, in Devonshire, of whom he would most gladly have purchased it; but she declined parting with it on any account, thinking it would be unlucky to do so. Gostling has some observations on this subject. He thinks the *lituus* or staff with the crook at one end, which the augurs of old carried as badges of their profession and instruments in the superstitious exercise of it, was not made of metal, but of the substance above mentioned. Whether, says he, to call it a work of art or nature may be doubted : some were probably of the former kind : others Hogarth, in his "Analysis of Beauty," calls *lusus naturæ*, found in plants of different sorts, and in one of the plates to that work gives a specimen of a very elegant one, a branch of ash. I should rather, continues he, style it a distemper or distortion of nature ; for it seems the effect of a wound by some insect which, piercing to the heart of the plant with its proboscis, poisons that, while the bark remains uninjured, and proceeds in its growth, but formed into various stripes, flatness and curves, for want of the support which Nature designed it. The beauty some of these arrive at might well consecrate them to the mysterious fopperies of heathenism, and their rarity occasion imitation of them by art. The pastoral staff of the Church of Rome seems to have been formed from the vegetable litui, though the general idea is, I know, that it is an imitation of the shepherd's crook. The engravings given in the "Antiquarian Repertory" are of carved branches of the ash. *Antiq. Repert.*, 1807, ii., 164. Moresin, in his "Papatus," v. 126, says : "Pedum Episcopale est Litui Augurum, de quo Livius, i."

Divisions of Time.—The day, civil and political, has been divided into thirteen parts. The after-midnight and the dead of the night are the most solemn of them all, and have therefore, it should seem, been appropriated by ancient superstition to the walking of spirits. 1. After midnight. 2. Cock-crow. 3. The space between the first cock-crow and break of day. 4. The dawn of the morning. 5. Morning. 6. Noon. 7. Afternoon. 8. Sunset. 9. Twilight. 10. Evening. 11. Candle-time. 12. Bed-time. 13. The dead of the night. The Church of Rome, according to Durandus *De Nocturnis*, made four nocturnal vigils : the conticinium, gallicinium or cock-crow, intempestum, and antelucinum. There is a curious discourse on this subject in Peck's "Desiderata Curiosa," vol. i. p. 223, *et seq.* The distribution of the day into two equal terms of twelve hours *ante* and *post meridiem* was in early times only partially observed. Hazlitt's *Venetian Republic*, 1900, ii., 607.

Dog.—An opinion prevails that the howling of a dog by night in a neighbourhood is a presage of death to any that are sick in it. Keuchenii Crepundia, 113. Dogs have been known to stand and howl over the bodies of their masters, when they have been murdered, or died an accidental or sudden death : taking such note of what is past, is an instance of great sensibility in this faithful animal, without supposing that it has in the smallest degree any prescience of the future. Keuchenius adds, that when dogs rolled themselves in the dust, it was a sign of wind ; which is also mentioned by Gaule and Willsford in their often-quoted works. The latter observes : "Dogs tumbling and wal-

lowing themselves much and often upon the earth, if their guts rumble and stink very much, are signs of rain or wind for certain." Shakespear, in Henry VI., part iii., act v. sc. 6, ranks this among omens :

"The owl shriek'd at thy birth—an evil
      sign !
The night-crow cry'd, aboding luckless
      time ;
Dogs howl'd, and hideous tempest shook
      down trees."

Home speaks of this portent as a sign of death ; which, adds Alexander Ross, is "plaine by historie and experience." *Demonologie*, 1650, p. 60. Grose substantiates this view, and indeed the superstition is still a common one among all classes of people. The following passage is cited in Poole's *English Parnassus*, 1657, v. *Omens* :

"The air that night was fill'd with dismal groans,
And people oft awaked with the howls
Of wolves and fatal dogs."

"Julius Obsequens sheweth" (says Alexander Ross) that there was an "extraordinary howling of dogs before the sedition in Rome, about the dictatorship of Pompey : he sheweth also, (c. 127) that before the civil wars between Augustus and Antonius, among many other prodigies, there was great howling of dogs near the house of Lepidus the Pontifice. Camerarius tells us that some German princes have certain tokens and peculiar presages of their deaths, amongst others are the howling of dogs. Capitolinus tells us that the dogs by their howling presaged the death of Maximinus. Pausanias (in Messe) relates that before the destruction of the Messenians, the dogs brake out into a more fierce howling than ordinary ; and we read in Fincelius that in the year 1553, some weeks before the overthrow of the Saxons, the dogs in Mysina flocked together, and used strange howlings in the woods and fields. The like howling is observed by Virgil, presaging the Roman calamities in the Pharsalick War. So Statius and Lucan to the same purpose." Defoe clearly leant to this belief, "unaccountable as it might seem," in cases, of course, where the howling was spontaneous. *Mem. of Duncan Campbel*, 1732, p. 76. Homer, in the "Odyssey," makes the dogs of Eumæus recognize Minerva, while the goddess remains invisible to Telemachus. I scarcely know if Douce thought that this was an evidence that the ancients credited the animal with the faculty of seeing ghosts : but the heathen divinities were endowed with the power of manifesting themselves to any particular person in a company, without being seen by the others. In the

Treasury of St. Denis they are said to preserve the silver keys of the saint, which by being laid on the face of the patient, cure the bite of a mad dog. *Les Raretez qui se voyent dans l'Eglise Royale de S. Denis*, 1749, p. 4.

Dog-Whipper. — See *St. Luke's Day.*

Dole.—The giving of a dole, and the inviting of the poor on this occasion, are synonymous terms. There are some strong figurative expressions on this subject in St. Ambrose's Funeral Oration on Satyrus, cited by Durandus. Speaking of those who mourned on the occasion, he says :— " The poor also shed their tears ; precious and fruitful tears, that washed away the sins of the deceased. They let fall floods of redeeming tears." From such passages as the above in the first Christian writers, literally understood, the Romanists may have derived their superstitious doctrine of praying for the dead. " Preterea con-vocabantur et invitabantur necdum Sacer-dotes et Religiosi, sed et egeni pauperes." *Durandus.* Had Pope an eye to this in ordering by will poor men to support his pall? Doles were used at funerals, as we learn from St. Chrysostom, to procure rest to the soul of the deceased, that he might find his judge propitious. *Homilia in Matthei* cap. 9.

In "Dives and Pauper," 1493, we read : " *Dives.* What seyst thou of them that wole no solemnyté have in their buryinge, but be putt in erthe anon, and that that shulde be spent aboute the buriyng they bydde that it shulde be yoven to the pore folke blynde and lame?—*Pauper.* Comonly in such prive buriynges bene ful smalle doles and lytel almes yoven, and in solemne buriynges been grete doles and moche almesse yoven, for moche pore people come thanne to seke almesse. But whanne it is done prively, fewe wytte therof, and fewe come to axe almesse ! for they wote nat whanne ne where, ne whom they shulde axe it. And therefore I leve sikerly that summe fals executoures that wolde kepe all to themself biganne firste this errour and this foyle, that wolden make themself riche with ded mennys godes, and nat dele to the pore after dedes wylle, as nowe all false executoures use by custome." By the will of William de Montacute, Earl of Salisbury (1397), he directs " that twenty-five shillings should be daily distributed among three hundred poor people from the time of his death to the arrival of his body at the Conventual Church of Bustle-ham [Bustleton] in which it was to be deposited." Warner's *Hampshire*, 11, 73. Strutt tells us that Sir Robert Knolles, in the eighth year of Henry IV. died at his Manor in Norfolk, and his dead body was brought in a litter to London with great pomp, and much

torch-light, and it was buried in the White Friars Church, " where was done for him a solemn obsequie, with a great feaste and lyberal dole to the poore." This custom, says Strutt, of giving a funeral feast to the chief mourners, was universally practised all over the kingdom, as well as giving alms to the poor, in proportion to the quality and finances of the deceased. *Manners and Customs*, ii., 109. Nichols, speaking of Stathern in Framland Hun-dred, says : " In 1790, there were 432 in-habitants ; the number taken by the last person who carried about bread, which was given for dole at a funeral ; a custom formerly common throughout this part of England, though now fallen much into disuse. The practice was some-times to bequeath it by will ; but, whether so specified or not, the cere-mony was seldom omitted. On such occasions a small loaf was sent to every person, without any distinction of age or circumstances, and not to receive it was a mark of particular disrespect." *Leicestershire*, vol. ii., part i., p. 357. Ly-sons's *Env.*, iii., 341. Pennant says :— " Offerings at funerals are kept up here (Whiteford), and I believe, in all the Welsh Churches." *Hist. of Whiteford*, p. 99. The same writer observes : " In North Wales, pence and half-pence (in lieu of little rolls of bread) which were hereto-fore, and by some still are, given on these occasions, are now distributed to the poor, who flock in great numbers to the house of the dead before the corpse is brought out. When the corpse is brought out of the house, layd upon the bier and covered, be-fore it be taken up, the next of kin to the deceased, widow, mother, daughter, or cousin (never done by a man), gives over the corps to one of the poorest neighbours three 2d. or four 3d. white loaves of bread, or a cheese with a piece of money stuck in it, and then a new wooden cup of drink, which some will require the poor person who receives it immediately to drink a little of. When this is done, the minister, if present, says the Lord's Prayer, and then they set forward for church. The things mentioned above as given to a poor body, are brought upon a large dish, over the corpse, and the poor body returns thanks for them, and blesses God for the happiness of his friend and neighbour de-ceased." Compare *Sin-Eater* and Ditch-field, chap.18. In the 18th century, it ap-pears that at Glasgow large donations at funerals were made to the poor, " which are never less than £5, and never exceeded ten guineas, in which case the bells of the city are tolled." *Stat. Acc. of Scotland*, v. 523. It was formerly customary for a sum of money to be given to certain per-sons or institutions, with whom or which the deceased had been connected. This usage is illustrated by a document inserted among the "Egerton Papers," being the memoranda relating to the will of one of the Rokeby family, who died in 1600. Among the items are gifts of sums of money to the principals of Lincoln's Inn, Furnival's Inn, and Thavis' Inn, for drink to be supplied to the members of those societies in honour of the occasion. This custom of funeral libations is still not uncommon in the country. By his will made in 1639, Francis Pynner, of Bury St. Edmunds, directed that out of certain rents and revenues accruing from his property, from and after the Michaelmas following his decease, forty poor parishioners of St. Mary's, Bury, should, on coming to the church, be entitled to a twopenny wheaten loaf on the last Friday in every month throughout the year, for ever. See a curious account of doles in Ducarel's *Tour through Normandy.*

Dolemoors.—Collinson says: "In the parishes of Congresbury and Puxton, are two large pieces of common land called East and West Dolemoors, (from the Saxon dal, which signifies a share or portion), which are divided into single acres, each bearing a peculiar and different mark cut in the turf, such as a horn, four oxen and a mare, two oxen and a mare, a pole-axe, cross, dung-fork, oven, duck's-nest, hand-reel, and hare's-tail. On the Saturday before Old-Midsummer, several proprietors of estates in the parishes of Congresbury, Puxton, and Week St. Lawrence, or their tenants, assemble on the commons. A number of apples are previously prepared, marked in the same manner with the before-mentioned acres, which are distributed by a young lad to each of the commoners from a bag or hat. At the close of the distribution each person repairs to his allotment, as his apple directs him, and takes possession for the ensuing year. An adjournment then takes place to the house of the overseer of Dolemoors (an officer annually elected from the tenants) where four acres, reserved for the purposes of paying expenses, are let by inch of candle, and the remainder of the day is spent in that sociability and hearty mirth so congenial to the soul of a Somersetshire yeoman." *Somersetshire,* iii., 586.

Door-Drink.—See *Bridling Cast and Stirrup Cup.*

Dore, Mary.—Warner, mentioning Mary Dore, the "parochial witch of Beaulieu," who died about 1750, says, "her spells were chiefly used for purposes of self-extrication in situations of danger; and I have conversed with a rustic whose father had seen the old lady convert herself more than once into the form of a hare or cat, when likely to be apprehended in wood-stealing, to which she was somewhat addicted. *Hampshire,* 1793, ii., 241.

Doree.—Pennant informs us that "Superstition hath made the Doree rival to the Hadock for the honour of having been the fish out of whose mouth St. Peter took the tribute-money, leaving on its sides those incontestible proofs of the identity of the fish, the marks of his finger and thumb." *Zoology,* 1776, iii., 221. It is rather difficult at this time to determine on which part to decide the dispute; for the doree likewise asserts an origin of its spots of a similar nature, but of a much earlier date than the former. St. Christopher, in wading through an arm of the sea, having caught a fish of this kind *en passant,* as an eternal memorial of the fact, left the impression on its sides to be transmitted to all posterity.

Dorrish.—The story of the Squire of Dorrish, an ancient Devonshire family, is related as follows: "Returning home late on a winter night after a considerable consumption of brandy punch at the house of a neighbouring squire, he fell from his horse where a brook, running at the foot of a hill on which stands the house of Dorrish, is crossed by a narrow bridge, and was killed. This was early in the 18th century. From that time to this his spirit has been gradually advancing up the hill toward the house, at the rate of a "cockstride" in every moon. A bridge as narrow and as sharp as the edge of a sword is provided for the unfortunate squire. Whenever he falls off (and it is supposed that this must occasionally happen), he is obliged to return to the stream where his life was ended, and to begin again. His present position is therefore quite uncertain, but there is no doubt that he will one day reach his own front door, and what may then happen no one can possibly foresee. The sharp sword here unquestionably represents the "brig of dread" of the northern Lykewake:—

'This ae night, this ae night,
  Everie night and alle
To brig of dread thou comes at last—
  And Christ receive thy sawle.' "

Double Hand.—Taylor the Water-poet, in his "Great Eater of Kent," 1630, says: "I have known a great man very expert on the Jewe-harpe, a rich merchants wife a quicke gamester at Irish (especially when she came to bearing of men) that she wolde seldome misse entring. Monsieur le Ferr, a Frenchman, was the first inventor of the admirable game of double-hand, hot-cockles; and Gregorie Dawson, an Englishman, devised the unmatchable mystery of blindman buffe."

Doublets or **Dublets.**—See *Tick-Tack.*

Dough.—*Dough* or *Dow* is vulgarly used in the North for a little cake, though it properly signifies a mass of flour tempered with water, salt and yeast, and kneaded fit for baking. It is derived, as Junius tells us, from the Dutch *Deeg*, which comes from the Theostican *thihen*, to grow bigger, or rise, as the bakers term it. The sailors call pudding dough, but pronounce it duff. Du Cange says : "Panis Natalitius, cujusmodi fieri solet in die Natalis Domini, et præberi Dominis a prædiorum conductoribus, in quibusdam Provinciis, qui ex farina delicatiori, ovis et lacti confici solent : *Cuignets* appellant Picardi, quod in cuneorum varias species efformentur." Gloss. v. *Panis Natalitius.* See also Ihre *Gloss. Suio-Goth*, i., 1009.

Dough-Nut Day.—A name formerly given to Shrove-Tuesday by the children at Baldock, Herts, from small cakes fried in brass skillets over the fire with hog's lard.

Douro.—See *Clavie.*

Dove.—A correspondent of "Notes and Queries" sent the following account in 1857 to that miscellany. "A month or two back, a family, on leaving one of the Channel Islands, presented to a gardener (it is uncertain whether an inhabitant of the island or no) some pet doves, the conveyance of them to England being likely to prove troublesome. A few days afterwards the man brought them back, stating that he was engaged to be married, and the possession of the birds might be (as he had been informed) an obstacle to the course of true love running smooth." This was put in the shape of a query, but no answer appeared. 2nd S., iv., 25. Doves were formerly threshed in some places at Shrove-tide.

Dovercourt, Rood of.—"In the same year of our Lord, 1532, there was an Idoll named the Roode of Dovercourt, whereunto was much and great resort of people. For at that time there was a great rumour blown abroad amongst the ignorant sort, that the power of the *Idoll of Dovercourt* was so great that no man had power to shut the church doore where he stood, and therefore they let the church dore, both night and day, continually stand open, for the more credit unto the blinde rumour." Fox's *Book of Martyrs*, ii. 302. He adds that four men, determining to destroy it, travelled ten miles from Dedham, where they resided, took away the rood, and burnt it, for which act three of them afterwards suffered death. In *Grim the Collier of Croydon* (Hazlitt's Dodsley, viii., 398) Miles Forest says :

"Have you not heard, my lords, the wondrous feats
Of Holy Dunstan, Abbot of Canterbury?
What miracles he hath achieved of late ;
And how the rood of Dovercourt did speak,
Confirming his opinion to be true?—"

Dovercourt was the mother-church of Harwich.

Dover's Games.—Sports held from time immemorial on the hill in the Cotswolds, still known as Dover's Hill. Robert Dover, called Captain Dover, promoted their revival, when they had grown more or less obsolete, about 1596. In 1636, a collection of poems by various writers appeared with a frontispiece representing Dover in a suit, which had been given to him by James I. Among the writers is Randolph, who contributes *An Eclogue on the noble Assemblies revived on Cotswold Hills by Master Robert Dover.*

Down Plat.—See *St. Luke's Day.*

Draco Volans.—See *Aërolites.*

Dragon.—In the old romances the dragons are frequently denominated worms, a phrase employed by our forefathers with considerable latitude, as I think will be allowed when I mention that, in the "Towneley Mysteries," the plague of locusts in Egypt is described as a visitation of "wyld wormes." The modern Greeks seem to have classed what we now are sufficiently familiar with under the denomination of the water-spout among dragons. Mr. Wright, in his "Essays," 1846, quotes a curious extract from the chronicle of John of Bromton in confirmation of this theory. The spout is described by the chronicler as a great black dragon descending from the clouds, and hiding its head in the water, while its tail reached to the sky ; and he tells us that any ships which were passing at the time, he swallowed up with all their contents. The theatre of this reputed monster's depredations was the Gulf of Satalia. It was supposed that a serpent, to become a dragon, must eat a serpent. This partly realizes the ophiophagous genus of serpents, which does not thereby suffer such a metamorphosis. I found the following note in "The Muses' Threnodie," by Henry Adamson, 1638, repr. 1774 : "We read of a cave called 'The Dragon Hole,' in a steep rock on the face of Kinnoul Hill, of very difficult and dangerous access. On the first day of May, during the era of Popery, a great concourse of people assembled at that place to celebrate superstitious games, now," adds the writer, "unknown to us, which the Reformers prohibited under heavy censures and severe penalties, of which we are informed from the ancient records of the Kirk Session of Perth." It may, perhaps, be mentioned that the Chinese to this day believe in the existence of dragons, and attribute natural phenomena, such as eclipses, to their malignant agency. They shout at the dragon when there is an eclipse, and as soon as the solar or lunar orb has recovered its usual splendour, it is the dragon which has been discomfited and put to flight.

Dragon's Blood.—A resinous compound, which is still employed by young girls, chiefly in the rural districts, as a charm for restoring to the person, who burns it, and repeats over the flame certain cabalistic words, the object of affection. But it is also employed by married women who have become estranged from their husbands, and desire reconciliation. *Antiquary*, June and July, 1891.

Draw Gloves.—There was a sport entitled "Draw Gloves," of which, however, I find no description. The following *jeu d'esprit* is found in Herrick:

Draw Gloves.

"At Draw-gloves we'l play,
And prethee let's lay
   A wager, and let it be this;
Who first to the summe
Of twenty shall come,
   Shall have for his winning a kisse."

And in another poem by him, "To the Maides to Walk Abroad" there is the following:

"Come sit we under yonder tree,
Where merry as the maids we'l be,
And as on primroses we sit,
We'l venter (if we can) at wit:
If not, at draw-gloves we will play :
So spend some minutes of the day;
Or else spin out the threed of sands,
Playing at questions and commands."
See Davis, *Suppl. Glossary*, 1881, p. 202.

Draw Straws, To.—In the *Vaux de Vire* of Jean le Houx, Muirhead's translation, 1875, p. 103, we find:

"If after mirth our wine
Run short, in pleasant way
We draw straws, to divine
   Who for some more shall pay."

I have not met with any English parallel of this, no doubt, at one time common Norman usage.

Dreams.—Dreams, as the sacred writings inform us, have on certain occasions, been used as the divine mediums of revelation. As connected with our present design, they may either come under the head of omens or that of divination. Homer has told us that dreams come from Jupiter, and in all ages and every kingdom the idea that some knowledge of the future is to be derived from them, has always composed a very striking article in the creed of popular superstitions. Bartholinus, *De Causis contemptæ a Danis Mortis*, p. 678. Henry tells us: "We find Peter of Blois, who was one of the most learned men of the age in which he flourished, writing an account of his dreams to his friend the Bishop of Bath, and telling him how anxious he had been about the interpretation of them; and that he

had employed for that purpose divination by the Psalter. The English, it seems probable, had still more superstitious curiosity, and paid greater attention to dreams and omens than the Normans; for when William Rufus was dissuaded from going abroad on the morning of that day on which he was killed, because the Abbot of Gloucester had dreamed something which portended danger, he is said to have made this reply : 'Do you imagine that I am an Englishman, to be frighted by a dream, or the sneezing of an old woman?" *Hist. of Gr. Britain*, 111, 572. Cornelius Agrippa, speaking of "Interpretation of Dreams," says: "To this delusion not a few great philosophers have given not a little credit, especially Democritus, Aristotle, and his follower Themistius, Sinesius also the Platonick, so far building upon examples of dreams, which some accident hath made to be true; and thence they endeavour to persuade men that there are no dreams but what are real. But as to the causes of dreams, both external and internal, they do not all agree in one judgment. For the Platonicks reckon them among the specifick and concrete notions of the soul. Avicen makes the cause of dreams to be an ultimate intelligence moving the moon in the middle of that light with which the fancies of men are illuminate while they sleep. Aristotle refers the cause thereof to common sense, but placed in the fancy. Averroes places the cause in the imagination. Democritus ascribes it to little images or representatives separated from the things themselves. Albertus, to the superior influences which continually flow from the skie through many specifick mediums. The physicians impute the cause thereof to vapours and humours : others to the affections and cares predominant in persons when awake. Others joyn the powers of the soul, celestial influences and images together, all making but one cause. Artemidorus and Daldianus have written of the interpretation of dreams : and certain books go about under Abraham's name, whom Philo, in his Book of the Gyants and of Civil Life, asserts to have been the first practiser thereof. Other treatises there are falsified under the names of David and Solomon, wherein are to be read nothing but meer dreams concerning dreams. But Marcus Cicero, in his Book of Divination, hath given sufficient reasons against the vanity and folly of those that give credit to dreams, which I purposely here omit." *Vanity of Sciences*, p. 105. Every dream, according to Wolfius, takes its rise from some sensation, and is continued by the succession of phantasms in the mind. His reasons are that when we dream we imagine something, or the mind produces phantasms;

but no phantasms can arise in the mind without a previous sensation. Hence neither can a dream arise without some previous sensation. Here it may be stated, says Douce, that if our author meant a previous sensation of the thing dreamt of, it is certainly not so.

> "Dreams are but the rais'd
> Impressions of premeditated things,
> Our serious apprehension left upon
> Our minds, or else th' imaginary shapes
> Of objects proper to the complexion,
> Or disposition of our bodies."

Cotgrave's *English Treasury of Wit and Language*, 1655. Physicians seem to be the only persons at present who interpret dreams. Frightful dreams are perhaps always indications of some violent oppression of Nature, especially of dyspepsia. Hippocrates has many curious observations on dreams. Ennius made that very sensible remark, that what men studied and pondered in the day-time the same they dreamed on at night. Scot informs us of "The art and order to be used in digging for money, revealed by dreams." "There must be made," says he, "upon a hazel wand three crosses, and certain words must be said over it, and hereunto must be added certain characters and barbarous names. And whilst the treasure is a digging, there must be read the Psalms De Profundis, &c., and then a certain prayer: and if the time of digging be neglected, the Devil will carry all the treasure away." *Discovery*, ed. 1665, 102. Some verses on this occasion are preserved by Aubrey. *Miscellanies*, 1696, ed. 1857, 132. A writer in the "Gentleman's Magazine" for September, 1751, wittily observes that "Dreams have for many ages been esteemed as the noblest resources at a dead lift: the dreams of Homer were held in such esteem that they were styled golden dreams: and among the Grecians we find a whole country using no other way for information, but going to sleep. The Oropians, and all the votaries of Amphiaraus are proofs of this assertion, as may be seen in Pausan. Attic." In the "Gentleman's Magazine" for January, 1799, are some curious rhymes on the subject of dreams, from Harl. MS. 541, fol. 228 verso:

> "Vpon my ryght syde y maie leye, blesid lady to the y Ᵽ y
> For the teres that ye lete vpon your swete sonnys feete,
> Sende me grace for to slepe, & good dremys for to mete
> Slepyng wakyng til morowe daye bee.
> Owr lorde is the frevte, oure lady is the tree
> Blessid be the blossom that sprange lady of the.
> In nôie patris & filii & sp's sā amen."

In "Mery Tales and Quicke Answeres" (circâ 1540) is a not very delicate story "of him that dreamed he founde gold." See "Old English Jest-Books," i. In "A C. Mery Talys," 1525, is the story of Sir Richard Whittington's Dream (ibid.) In the "Opticke Glasse of Hvmors," by T. W. 1607, there is a curious section on this subject (ed. 1639, p. 141). In Lyly's "Sapho and Phao," 1584, are some pleasant observations on dreams, act iv. sc. 3: "And can there be no trueth in dreams? Yea, dreams have their trueth.—Dreames are but dotings, which come either by things we see in the day, or meates that we eate, and so the common sense preferring it to be the imaginative. 'I dreamed,' says Ismena, 'mine eye tooth was loose, and that I thrust it out with my tongue.' 'It fortelleth,' replies Mileta, 'the losse of a friend: and I ever thought thee so ful of prattle, that thou wouldest thrust out the best friend with the tatling.'" In Overbury's "Character of a Milkmaid" is the passage: "Her dreams are so chaste that shee dare tell them: only a Fridaies dream is all her superstition: that she conceales for feare of Anger." There is a nursery adage:

> "Friday night's dream
> On the Saturday told,
> Is sure to come true,
> Be it never so old."

Various are the popular superstitions, or at least the faint traces of them that still are made use of to procure dreams of divination: such as fasting St. Agnes' Fast; laying a piece of the first cut of the groaning cheese under the pillow, to cause young persons to dream of their lovers, and putting a Bible in the like situation, with a sixpence clapped in the Book of Ruth, and so on. Strutt says: "Writing their name on a paper at twelve o'clock, burning the same, then carefully gathering up the ashes, and laying them close wrapp'd in a paper upon a looking-glass. marked with a cross, under their pillows: this should make them dream of their loves." *Manners and Customs*, 111, 180. Mr. Brand observed that in his day, except amongst the most ignorant and vulgar, the whole imaginary structure had fallen to the ground; but surely this assertion was a little premature, looking at the still extensive belief, even among intelligent people, in this class of revelation, one that will never, perhaps, wholly be extinguished under any circumstances.

Dreams, Interpretation of.— The following may in some measure supply what Agrippa thought proper to omit in a passage above-cited: "Cicero, among others, relates this. A certain man dreamed that there was an egg hid under his bed; the soothsayer to whom he applied himself for the interpretation of the dream told him that in the same place where he imagined to see the egg there was treasure hid; whereupon he caused the place to be digged up, and there accordingly he found silver, and in the midst of it a good quantity of gold, and, to give the interpreter some testimony of his acknowledgment he brought him some pieces of the silver which he had found; but the soothsayer, hoping also to have some of the gold, said: "And will you not give me some of the yolk too?'" Amyraldus, translated by Lowde, 1676. Bacon observes that the interpretation of natural dreams has been much laboured, but mixed with numerous extravagancies, and adds, that at present it stands not upon its best foundation. Shylock, in the "Merchant of Venice," says:

"There is some ill a brewing towards my rest,
For I did dream of money-bags to-night."

Hall, in his "Characters of Vertues and Vices," 1608, speaking of the superstitious man, observes: "But, if his troubled fancie shall second his thoughts with the dreame of a fair garden, or greene rushes, or the salutation of a dead friend, he takes leave of the world, and sayes he cannot live."—"There is no dream of his without an interpretation, without a prediction, and if the event answer not his exposition, he expounds it according to the event." Melton says: "That if a man dreame of egs or fire, he shall heare of anger." "That to dreame of the Devil is good lucke." "That to dreame of gold good lucke, but of silver ill." *Astrologaster*, 1620, No. 13. In another old work, it is said: "To dreame of eagles flying over our heads, to dreame of marriages, dancing and banquetting, foretells some of our kinsfolkes are departed: to dream of silver, if thou hast it given to thyselfe, sorrow: of gold, good fortune: to lose an axle toth or an eye, the death of some friend: to dream of bloody teeth, the death of the dreamer: to weepe in sleepe, joy: to see one's face in the water, or to see the dead, long life: to handle lead, to see a hare, death: to dream of chickens and birds, ill-luck," &c. *Help to Discourse*, 1633, p. 330. In a "Strange Metamorphosis of Man," &c., 1634, it is observed: "Nor is he (the bay-tree) altogether free from superstition; for he wil make you beleeve that if you put his leaves under your pillow, you shall be sure to have true dreames." In Sampson's "Vôw-Breaker," 1636, act iii. sc. 1, Ursula speaks: "I have heard you say that dreames and visions were fabulous; and, yet one time I dreamt fowle water ran through the floore, and the next day the house was on fire. You us'd to say hobgoblins, fairies and the like, were nothing

but our owne affrightments, and yet o' my troth, cuz, I once dream'd of a young batchelour, and was ridd with a night-mare." "He that dreams he hath lost a tooth, shall lose a friend, (he has lost one), and he that dreams that a rib is taken out of his side, shall ere long see the death of his wife." See Lowde's Amyraldus, p. 22, and the passage from Lyly already cited. Gaule gives us "the snorting in sleep," the dreaming of gold, silver, eggs, gardens, weddings, dead men, dung," &c. *Mag-Astromancer posed*, p. 181. Some extracts from *A Treatise of the Interpretation of Sundry Dreames*, 1601 (licensed for the press in 1566) may not be unacceptable:

"1. First, to see the ayre faire and cleere, promiseth good vnto all persons: especially vnto such, which seeke after things lost, and would iourney into strange places: for all things be made apparent to a cleare ayre. 2. To see the ayre darkned, mysty, or cloudy, doth then portend the hinderance of actions, or heauinesse. 3. To see rayne fall without a tempest or with wind, signifieth good (in a manner) vnto all persons. 4. To see showres, haile, thick cloude, and tempests, doe pronounce troubles, harmes, and perills vnto all persons, except to seruants and such in present troubles. 5. To see fire in the ayre, cleere, pure, and little, doth foreshow threatnings of some noble estates: but vnto many, this dreame portendeth the incursion of enemies, pouerty and hunger. 6. To see lightning passe neere by him, without a tempest, and not to touch the body, doth after threaten banishment out of the place, in which he dwelleth. 7. To think himselfe striken with lightning, promise vnto him which lacketh a wife, to marry one, whether hee bee poore or rich. And married, the separation of his wife from him: and the like to be vnderstood of brethren, friends, kinsfolke and acquaintance, to become enemies vnto him. 8. A certaine person dreamed that hee saw the outward pillar or bed-post smitten and burnt with lightning, and not long after dyed his wife. 9. To thinke thy selfe drawne by force of a dead person knowne to thee, vnto a place vnknowne, doth after signifie, that he shall be taken with a grieuous sicknes, of which he shall dye: but if hee escape, it shall be very hardly. 10. Hee which thinketh hee seeth a dead person sleeping, such a person shall dye quietly. 11. To see either father or mother that be dead, is lesser euill, then to see any other dead person. 12. He which seeth a dead person, looking sad, deformed and in torne clothes, doth after signifie a misfortune to ensue vnto the dreamer. 13. The sick person to dreame that he maried a maiden, signifieth death to ensue. But good it is vnto him which beginneth a new businesse, for that it shall come into a good purpose. 14. To marie a widow, signifieth the compassng of old matters or businesses, but contrarie in the new. 15. To see the sun rising out of the east, cleere and fair, and setting the like in the west, signifieth good vnto all persons. 16. And a sicke person to see the sun rising out of the west, signifieth amendment vnto health. 17. And the sonne seeming darke or bloody, or for the great heat making a noyse, is dangerous & euill vnto all persons, for that it declareth vnto some, the hindrance of actions, and vnto others sicknesse, and perill vnto their children, or disease and paine of their eyes. 18. Hee which seeth his image in the moone, not hauing children, doth foreshew the birth of a sonne to ensue; but to the woman like dreaming, to haue a daughter. 19. To see the starres fall from heauen, doth signifie vnto the rich much pouerty and care to ensue. 20. He which seeth a great starre fall from heauen on his head doth after promise great good luck to ensue. 21. To see thy house faire swept with a broome, signifieth the consumption of thy money. 22. To see another man's faire swept, signifieth that the dreamer shall possesse the money of that house. 23. To seeme to open a new doore, shall after mary a wife profitable vnto him. 24. To dreame, to cut downe a tree, or plucke it vp by the rootes, doth after signifie that hee shall slay a man or a beast. 25. To dreame to see a hoy or crayer, or other small vessel to enter into a house & after to go out againe: signifieth that the principall of the same house shal after die, and the rather, if water appeareth there, for that the same signifieth teares, and the vessel the coffin, in which dead bodies be caried. 26. And beeing in a ship, whosoeuer dreameth to see fire in any part of the ship, from that side or part of the ship shal the wind arise the next morrow. 27. Whatsoeuer seemeth to happen to the ship, whiles thou thinkest thy selfe in her, the same shall hapen vnto thy wife: or being a widower, vnto thy children. 28. Whosoeuer dreameth to see any lanterne light in a ship or other barke, it doth after signifie a great calme, or quietnesse of the wind to ensue. 29. Whosoeuer beeing on the sea, dreameth to see sea-gulles, sea-pies, or any other like sea-birds, it doth signifie vnto saylers or mariners to bee after in very great perill, but no losse altogether. 30. He that dreameth to haue a mill, & doth grind in the same, promiseth good vnto the dreamer, and a prosperous life. 31. He that thinketh to eate fresh fish, shall talke euilly of men. 32. To eat salt fish, signifieth the losse of his money, either by fraud, or by a wile. 33. To dreame to ride on a blacke horse, signifieth losse & sorrow to ensue. 34. To see red oxen in the dream declares the mightier & sharper sicknesses. 35. To see oxen lying or sleeping, declareth euill or harme to happen vnto the dreamer.''

"Somniandi modus Franciscanorum hinc duxit originem. Antiqui moris fuit Oracula et futurorum præscientiam quibusdam adhibitis sacris per insomnia dari: qui mos talis erat, ut Victimas cæderent, mox Sacrificio peracto sub pellibus cæsarum Ovium incubantes, somnia, captarent, eaque lymphatica insomnia verissimos exitus sortiri. Alex. ab Alex. lib. iii. c. 26. Et Monachi super storea cubant in qua alius Frater ecstaticus fuerat somniatus. sacrificat missam, preces et jejunia adhibet, inde ut communiter fit de amoribus per somnia consulit. redditque responsa pro occurrentibus spectris," &c. Moresini *Papatus*, 1594, p. 162. Compare *Dumb-cake*.

Drinking, A.—In the "Statistical Account of Scotland" the minister of Kirmichael tells us: "In extraordinary cases of distress, we have a custom which deserves to be taken notice of; and that is, when any of the lower people happen to be reduced by sicknesses, losses or misfortunes of any kind, a friend is sent to as many of their neighbours as they think needful, to invite them to what they call a drinking. This drinking consists in a little small beer, with a bit of bread and cheese, and sometimes a small glass of brandy or whiskey, previously provided by the needy persons or their friends. The guests convene at the time appointed, and after collecting a shilling a-piece, and sometimes more, they divert themselves for about a couple of hours with music and dancing, and then go home. Such as cannot attend themselves, usually send their charitable contribution by any neighbour that chooses to go. These meetings sometimes produce five, six and seven pounds to the needy person or family." *Stat. Acc.*, i., 59. In the same work, it is said, under the parish of Gargunnock, co. Stirling: "There is one prevailing custom among our country people, which is sometimes productive of much evil. Everything is bought and sold over a bottle. The people who go to the fair in the full possession of their faculties, do not always transact their business, or return to their homes, in the same state." *Stat. Acc.*, xviii., 123. This, however, was in the eighteenth century.

Drinking Usages. — In Nash's "Pierce Pennilesse," 1592, occurs: "Nowe he is nobody that cannot drinke Supernagulum, carouse the hunters hoope, quaffe upse freze crosse, with healths, gloves, mumpes, polockes, and a thousand such domineering inventions." In Young's "England's Bane," 1617, are some curious passages (partly taken direct from other authors) concerning the then customs of drinking: "I myselfe have seen and (to my grief of conscience) may now say have in presence, yea, and amongst others been an actor in the businesse, when upon our knees, after healthes to many private punkes, a health have been drunke to all the whoores in the world." Again: "He is a man of no fashion that cannot drinkee supernaculum, carouse the hunters hoop, quaffe upseyfreese crosse, bowse in Permoysant, in Pimlico, in crambo, with healthes, gloves, numpes, frolicks, and a thousand such domineering inventions, as by the bell, by the cards, by the dye, by the dozen, by the yard, and so by measure we drink out of measure. There are in London drinking schooles: so that drunkennesse is professed with us a liberal arte and science." Again: "I have seene a company among the very woods and forests," (he speaks of the New Forest and Windsor Forest), "drinking for a muggle. Sixe determined to try their strengths who could drink most glasses for the muggle. The first drinkes a glasse of a pint, the second two, the next three, and so on every one multiplieth till the last taketh sixe. Then the first beginneth againe and taketh seven, and in this manner they drink thrice a peece round, every man taking a glasse more then his fellow, so that hee that dranke least, which was the first, drank one and twentie pints, and the sixth man thirty-six." Our author observes: "Before we were acquainted with the lingering wars of the Low Countries, drunkennes was held in the highest degree of hatred that might be amongst us." "Ebrius experiens, or the Drunkard's Humor," signat. M 3. Some remarkable anecdotes of this class are given also by Ward of Ipswich, in his "Woe to Drunkards," 1622. The term *Upsey freeze*, so often employed by the writers of the times of James I. and Charles I., is a corrupt form of *op zyn Vriesch*, in the Friesland fashion, and was introduced when the English became better acquainted with the Low Countries under Elizabeth. Robert Harris speaks, in the dedication to his *Drunkard's Cup*, of drinking as a sort of profession at this time: "There is (they say) an art of drinking now, and in the world it is become a great profession. There are degrees and titles, given under the names of roaring boyes, damned crew, &c. There are lawes and ceremonies to be observed both by the firsts and seconds, &c. There is a drinking by the foot, by the yard, &c., a drinking by the douzens, by the scoures, &c., for the wager, for the victory, man against man, house against house, town against town, and how not? There are also terms of art, fetched from Hell, (for the better distinguishing of the practitioners); one is coloured, another is

foxt, a third is gone to the dogs, a fourth is well to live," &c. In the body of the sermon, he mentions "the strange saucinesse of base vermine, in tossing the name of his most excellent Majesty in their foaming mouthes, and in dareing to make that a shooing horne to draw on drink, by drinking healths to him." He adds elsewhere explanatorily: "I doe not speak of those beasts that must be answered and have right done them in the same measure, gesture, course, &c., but of such onely as leave you to your measure (You will keepe a turne and your time in pledging); is it any hurt to pledge such? How pledge them? You mistake if you think that we speak against any true civility If thou lust to pledge the lords prophets in woes, pledge good fellowes in their measures and challenges: if not so, learne still to shape a peremptory answer to an unreasonable demand. Say —I will pray for the King's health, and drinke for mine owne." He uses "somewhat whitled," and "buckt with drink" as terms expressing the different degrees of drunkenness. In another (well-known) work, I find a singular passage. which I confess I do not thoroughly understand, concerning the then modes of drinking. The writer is describing a drinking bout of female gossips: "Dispatching a lusty rummer of Rhenish to little Periwig, who passed it instantly to Steephen Malten, and she conveigh'd with much agility to Daplusee, who made bold to stretch the Countesses gowne into a pledge, and cover and come, which was the only plausible mode of drinking they delighted in: This was precisely observ'd by the other three, that their moistned braines gave leave for their glibb'd tongues to chat liberally." Gayton's *Notes on Don Quixote*, 1654, p. 234. In Shakespear's "Timon of Athens," act i. sc. 5, is the following passage:

> "If I
> Were a huge man, I should fear to
>   drink at meals,
> Lest they should spy my wind pipe's
>   dangerous notes;
> Great men should drink with harness on
>   their throats":

Upon which Strutt observes: "The old manner of pledging each other when they drank, was thus: the person who was going to drink, asked any one of the company who sat next him, whether he would pledge him, on which he answering that he would, held up his knife or sword, to guard him whilst he drank; for while a man is drinking he necessarily is in an unguarded posture, exposed to the treacherous stroke of some hidden or secret enemy." Strutt's authority was William of Malmesbury, and he observes from the delineation he gives us (and it must be noted that his plates, being copies of ancient illuminated manuscripts, are of unquestionable authority), that it seems perfectly well to agree with the reported custom; the middle figure is addressing himself to his companion, who seems to tell him that he pledges him, holding up his knife in token of his readiness to assist and protect him. After all, I cannot help hazarding an opinion that the expression meant no more than that if you took your cup or glass I pledged myself to you that I would follow your example. The common ellipsis, "to" is wanting. Thus we say, "I'll give you," instead of "I'll give to you"; "I'll pledge you," and "I'll pledge to you." But I offer this with great deference to the established opinions on the subject. But the custom is said to have first taken its rise from the death of Edward the Martyr, who was by the contrivance of Elfrida, his stepmother, treacherously stabbed in the back as he was drinking. Daines Barrington illustrates the former danger to which life was subject: He says, "The *Speculum Regale* advises the courtier, when he is in the King's presence, to pull off his cloak; and one of the reasons given is, that he shews by this means that he hath no concealed weapons to make an attempt upon the King's life." *Observ. on the Statutes*, 1775, p. 206. In 1553, during Wyatt's rebellion the seven serjeants and other lawyers in Westminster Hall pleaded in harness. Compare *Healths, Supernaculum, &c.*

Drinking Vessels. — Heywood says: "Of drinking cups divers and sundry sorts we have; some of elme, some of box, some of maple, some of holly, &c. Mazers, broad-mouth'd dishes, noggins, whiskins, piggins, crinzes, ale-bowls, wassell-bowls, court-dishes, tankards, kannes, from a pottle to a pint, from a pint to a gill. Other bottles we have of leather, but they are most used among the shepheards and harvest people of the countrey: small jacks wee have in many ale-houses of the Citie and suburbs, tip't with silver, besides the great black jacks and bombards at Court, which when the Frenchmen first saw, they reported, at their returne into their countrey, that the Englishmen used to drink out of their bootes: we have, besides, cups made of hornes of beasts, of cocker-nuts, of goords, of the eggs of estriches, others made of the shells of divers fishes brought from the Indies and other places. and shining like mother of pearl. Come to plate, every taverne can afford you flat bowles, French bowles, prounet cups, beare bowles, beakers: and private householders in the Citie, when they make a feast to entertain their friends, can furnish their cupbords with flagons, tankards, beere-cups, wine-bowles, some white, some percell guilt, some guilt all over, some with covers, others without,

of sundry shapes and qualities. . . There is now profest an eighth liberal art or science, call'd *Ars Bibendi*, i.e., the art of drinking. The students or professors thereof call a greene garland, or painted hcope hang'd out, a colledge: a signe where there is a lodging, mansmeate, and horse-meate, an inne of court, an hall, or an hostle: where nothing is sold but ale and tobacco, a grammar schoole: a red or blew lattice, that they terme a free schoole for all commers. . . . The bookes which they study, and whose leaves they so often turne over, are, for the most part, three of the old translations and three of the new. Those of the old translation: 1. The Tankard. 2. The black Jack. 3. The quart-pot rib'd, or thorondell. Those of the new be these: 1. The jugge. 2. The beaker. 3. The double or single can, or black pot." Among the proper phrases belonging to the library occur, "to drink upse-phreese, supernaculum, to swallow a flap-dragon, or a rawe egge—to see that no lesse than three at once be bare to a health. . . Many of our nation have used the Lowe-countrey-warres so long, that though they have left their money and clothes behind, yet they have brought home their habit of drinking." At p. 60, he gives the following phrases then in use for being drunk. "He is foxt, hee is flawed, he is flustered, hee is suttle, cupshot, cut in the leg or backe, hee hath seene the French king, he hath swallowed an haire or a taverne-token. hee hath whipt the cat, he hath been at the scriveners and learn'd to make indentures, hee hath bit his grannam, or is bit by a barne-weesell, with an hundred such-like adages and sentences." *Philocothonista*, 1635, p. 45.

Drive Knaves out of Town.— See *Troule-in-Madame*.

Drowned Bodies.—Several correspondents of *Notes and Queries* writing from Peterborough and elsewhere, refer to the notion, a very foolish one, that, where a person has been drowned, a button from his waistcoat, mounted on a piece of wood, will indicate the spot, where the body lies, by ceasing to float on its arrival thither. The annexed extract is from the *Echo*, 1874: "Students of folk-lore will bear us out in the assertion that the recovery of drowned bodies was formerly made the occasion of a variety of superstitious practice, ranging from the horrible to the grotesque. Had any enthusiastic collector of such waifs from the ebbing flood of past folly been standing on the bridge of Namur a few days since, he might have witnessed a spectacle, doubtless common enough in the middle ages, but extremely rare in our own. Four individuals, sitting on a trough, drifted down the Sambre between the bridge and the lock. Three of them held boat-hooks, the fourth read aloud some formula out of a book, and a lighted candle, stuck in a washerwoman's tub, floated by the side of the trough. These persons were looking for a drowned man; the reader was evoking the deceased by means of sacred words, while the candle was expected to stop and go out as soon as it stood over the spot where the corpse lay. The party did not, indeed, trust wholly to their mediæval recipe, but supplemented it by sounding the bed of the river with their poles, yet there was, it must be owned, enough in their conduct to suggest to the *Organ de Namur* the indignant query, 'Is it possible that in the year of grace, 1874, adult and vaccinated citizens know no better than this?'"

Druid's Eggs, or Ova Anguina. —The ancient Britons, says Pennant, *Zoology*, iii. 31, had a strange superstition in respect of the viper, and of which there still remained in his time (if it is even yet extinct) in Wales a strong tradition. The account Pliny (*Nat. Hist.* lib. xxix., c. 12) gives of it we find thus translated by Mason in his "Caractacus." The person speaking is a Druid:

" —— The potent adder stone
Gender'd 'fore th' autumnal moon:
When in undulating twine
The foaming snakes prolific join;
When they hiss, and when they bear
Their wondrous egg aloof in air;
Thence, before to earth it fall
The Druid, in his hallow'd pall.
    Receives the prize,
    And instant flies,
Follow'd by th' envenom'd brood
Till he cross the crystal flood."

This wondrous egg seems to be nothing more than a bead of glass, used by the Druids as a charm to impose on the vulgar, whom they taught to believe that the possessor would be fortunate in all his attempts, and that it would give him the favour of the great. Our modern Druidesses, he adds, give much the same account of the ovum Anguinum, *Glain Neidr*, as the Welsh call it, or the adder gem, as the Roman philosopher does, but seem not to have so exalted an opinion of its powers, using it only to assist children in cutting their teeth, or to cure the Chin-cough, or to drive away an ague. He gives a plate of these bands, made of glass of a very rich blue colour: some of which are plain and others streaked.

"Near Aberfraw," in the Isle of Anglesey," says Gough, "are frequently found the Glain Naidr or Druid glass rings. Of these the vulgar opinion in Cornwall and most part of Wales is, that they are produced through all Cornwall by snakes joining their heads together and hissing, which forms a kind of bubble like a ring about the head of one of them, which the rest by continual hissing blow on till it comes off at the tail, when it immediately hardens and resembles a glass ring. Whoever found it was to prosper in all his undertakings. These rings are called Glain Nadroedh, or Gemmæ Anguinæ. Glûne in Irish signifies glass. In Monmouthshire they are called Maen magl, and corruptly Glaim for Glain. They are small glass annulets, commonly about half as wide as our finger rings, but much thicker, usually of a green colour, though some are blue, and others curiously waved with blue, red, and white. Mr. Lluyd had seen two or three earthen rings of this kind, but glazed with blue, and adorned with transverse strokes or furrows on the outside. The smallest of them might be supposed to have been glass beads worn for ornaments by the Romans, because some quantities of them, with several amber beads, had been lately discovered in a stone pit near Garford in Berkshire, where they also dug up Roman coins, skeletons, and pieces of arms and armour. But it may be objected, that a battle being fought there between the Romans and Britons, as appears by the bones and arms, these glass beads might as probaly belong to the latter. And indeed it seems very likely that these snake stones, as we call them, were used as charms or amulets among our Druids of Britain on the same occasion as the snake-eggs among the Gaulish Druids. Thus, continues Mr. Lluyd, we find it very evident that the opinion of the vulgar concerning the generation of these adder-beads, or snake-stones, is no other than a relic of the superstition or perhaps imposture of the Druids; but whether what we call snake stones be the very same amulets that the British Druids made use of, or whether this fabulous origin was ascribed formerly to the same thing, and in aftertimes applied to these glass beads, I shall not undertake to determine. As for Pliny's Ovum Anguinum it can be no other than a shell (marine or fossil) of the kind we call *Echinus marinus*. whereof one sort, though not the same he describes, is found at this day in most parts of Wales. Dr. Borlase, who had penetrated more deeply into the Druidical monuments in this Kingdom than any writer before or since. observes that instead of the natural anguinum which must have been very rare, artificial rings of stone, glass, and sometimes baked clay, were substituted as of equal validity." The Doctor adds, from Mr. Lluyd's Letter, March 10th, 1701, that "the Cornish retain variety of charms, and have still, towards the Land's End, the amulets of Maen Magal and Glainneider, which latter they call a Melprev (or Milprev, i.e., a thousand worms), and have a charm for the snake to make it, when they have found one asleep, and stuck a hazel wand in the centre of her spiræ." Gough's *Camden*, 1789, ii., 571; Rowlands, *Mona Antiqua*, 342. "The opinion of the Cornish," Borlase continues, "is somewhat differently given by Carew. The country-people have a persuasion that the snakes here breathing upon a hazel wand, produce a stone ring of blue colour, in which there appears the yellow figure of a snake, and that beasts bit and envenom'd being given some water to drink, wherein this stone has been infus'd, will perfectly recover of the poison." *Antiq. of Cornwall,* p. 137. These beads are not unfrequently found in barrows, or occasionally with skeletons whose nation and age are not ascertained. Stukeley's *Abury*, p. 44. Bishop Gibson engraved three: one of earth enamelled blue, found near Dolgelly, in Merionethshire; a second of green glass, found at Aberfraw; and a third, found near Maes y Pandy, co. Merioneth.

Subjoined is the original passage from Pliny:— "Præterea est ovorum genus in magna Galliarum fama, omissum Græcis. Angues innumeri æstate convoluti, salivis faucium corporumque spumis artifici complexu glomerantur anguinum appellatur. Druidæ sibilis id dicunt in sublime jactari, sagoque oportere intercipi, ne tellurem attingat. Profugere raptorem equo: serpentes enim insequi, donec arceantur amnis alicujus interventu. Experimentum ejus esse, si contra aquas fluitet vel auro vinctum. Atque, ut est Magorum solertia occultandis fraudibus sagax, certa Luna capiendum censent, tanquam, congruere operationem eam serpentium, humani sit arbitrii. Vidi equidem id ovum mali orbiculati modici magnitudine, crusta cartilaginis, velut acetabulis brachiorum polypi crebris, insigne Druidis. Ad victorias litium, ac regum aditus, mire laudatur: tantæ vanitatis, ut habentem id in lite in sinu equitem Romanum e Vocontiis, a Divo Claudio Principe interemptum non ob aliud sciam."—*Plinii Hist. Nat.*, *edit. Harduin*, lib. xxix. 12.

Drumming-Well. — Baxter gives the following anecdote of himself: "When I was a school-boy at Oundle, in Northamptonshire, about the Scots coming into England, I heard a well, in one Dob's Yard, drum like any drum beating a march. I heard it at a distance: then I went and put my head into the mouth of the well, and heard it distinctly, and nobody in the well. It lasted several days and nights so as all the country people came to hear it. And so it drummed on several changes of times. When King Charles the Second died, I went to the Church carrier at the Ram Inn in Smithfield, who told me their well had drumm'd, and many people came to hear it, and I heard it drumm'd once since." *World of Spirits,* 1691, 157. Dodsley refers to the same phenomenon: "In Northamptonshire I observed, as in most other places, the superstition of the country people with regard to their local wonders. The well at Oundle is said to drum against any important event; yet nobody in the place could give me a rational account of their having heard it, though almost every one believes the truth of the tradition." Dodsley's *Travels of Tom Thumb*, 17.

Drunkard's Cloak. — According to Gardiner's *England's Grievance*, 1656, in the time of the Commonwealth, the magistrates of Newcastle punished scolds with the branks, and drunkards by making them carry a tub, with holes in the sides for the arms to pass through, called the drunkard's cloak, through the streets of that town.

Drunken Groat.—It appears from Allan Ramsay, that in Scotland, of those "wha had been fow yestreen," i.e., drunk the night before, "payment of the drunken groat is very peremptorily demanded by the common people, next morning: but if they frankly confess the debt due, they are passed for two-pence."

Drunkenness.—That it is good to be drunk once a month, says the author of the "Vulgar Errors," is a common flattery of sensuality, supporting itself upon physic and the healthful effects of inebriation. It is a striking instance of "the doing ill," as we say, "that good may come out of it." It may happen that inebriation, by causing vomiting, may cleanse the stomach, &c., but it seems a very dangerous kind of dose, and of which the "repetatur haustus," too quickly repeated, will prove that men may pervert that which Nature intended for a cordial into the most baneful of all poisons. It has been vulgarly called "giving a fillip to Nature." But it is at the present time a not uncommon maxim among physicians that occasional indulgence is rather beneficial to the system than the reverse.

Duck and Drake.—A game played by throwing shells or stones along the surface of the water. See Halliwell in v. It appears from the *Nomenclator* of Junius, 1585, quoted by Nares, that the full original name was *A duck and a drake and a halfpenny cake*. It was an amusement known to the Greeks. St. John's *Manners and Customs of Ancient Greece*, 1842, i., 153. Butler makes it one of the important qualifications of his conjurer to tell:

"What figur'd slates are best to make,
On watry surface duck or drake."
Hudibras, part 2, c. iii.

Duckstone.—A game played by trying to knock a small stone off a larger one which supports it. Halliwell in v.

Duke Humphrey.—The common expression "to dine with Duke Humphrey" was applied to persons who, being unable to procure a dinner, walked about and loitered during the dinner time in the open spaces about St. Paul's, to which, in the earlier part of the day, many persons used to resort for exercise, to hear news, &c. One of the aisles was called Duke Humphreys Walk, not that there ever was in reality a cenotaph there to the Duke's memory who, every one knows, was buried at St. Albans, but because, says Stowe, ignorant people mistook the monument of Sir John Beauchamp, who died in 1358, for that of Humphrey Duke of Gloucester. Stow's *Survey*, 1720, iii., 165. The error is also pointed out by Fuller. See Hazlitt's *Proverbs*, 1882, p. 428. On this mistake the following dialogue is founded :

"What ancient monument is this?
It is, as some say, of Duke Humphrie of
    Gloucester,
Who is buried here.
They say that he hath commonly his
    Lieftenant
Here in Paules, to know if there be
Any newes from Fraunce or other
    strange Countries.
'Tis true my friend, and also he hath
His steward, who inviteth the bring-
    ers of
These newes to take the paines to dine
    with His Grace."

Elyot's *Fruits for the French*, 1593, part 2, 165. Now, it appears from one of Anthony Munday's Additions to Stow, that it was the fashion in the time of James I. for certain persons, under the false impression that the monument of Sir John Beauchamp was that of the Duke to make annually "a solemn meeting at his tomb, on St. Andrew's Day, in the morning, (before Christmas), and to conclude on a breakfast or dinner——." It therefore seems, that there was a good foundation for the phrase in absolute fact and the probability is, that the ridicule attached (even in Stow's time) to the practice of paying homage to the wrong man, or to the right man in the wrong place, led eventually to the adoption of the idea and saying in derision of such unfortunates as paced the open spaces about St. Paul's during the dinner hour for want of something better to do, "in idle and frivolous opinion of whom," farther observes Munday, "some men, of late times, have assured themselves to be servants, and to hold diversity of offices under the good Duke Humphrey." Munday notices a curious ceremony performed by the tankard bearers, watermen, and others, on May-day, also in honour of the Duke, "by strewing herbs, and sprinkling fair water" on the tomb. An abundance of passages in the works of our old writers tend to confirm this explanation. Thus in "A Health to the gentlemanly profession of servingmen," 1598, the writer says : "I meete a gentleman that may dispende yeerely by his reuenues, 2000 pounds of good and lawfull English money, with onely one boy at his heeles, walking up Ludgate hill, and by that tyme I come to Paules middle walke, I shall see Dauie Debet, with vi. or viii. tall fellowes attending him, whetting their kniues readie to dine with Duke Humfrie." Harvey, in his "Fovre Letters and Certaine Sonnets," &c., 1592, speaks of a poverty-stricken person who has left home "to seek his dinner in Poules with Duke Humfrey ——." In "The Return of the Knight of the Post from Hell," 1606, we have : "In the end comming into Poules to behold the old Duke and his guests." In Nash's satirical "Prognostication" for 1591, we read : "Sundry fellows in their silkes shall be appointed to keepe Duke Humfrye company in Poules, because they know not where to get their dinners abroad."

"'Tis Ruffio: trow'st thou where he
    din'd to day?
In sooth I saw him sit with Duke Hum-
    fràÿ :
Many good welcoms and much gratis
    cheere
Keepes hee for everie stragling cava-
    liere :
An open house, haunted with great re-
    sort."

Hall's *Virgidemiæ*, 1597. "To the ninth of this month, it will be as good dining well in a matted chamber, as dialoguing with Duke Humphrey in Paules." *Vox Graculi*, 1623. p. 54. Speaking of the monument in St. Paul's of Owen the Epigrammatist, Gayton says :

"He was set up with such a peaking
    face,
As if to the Humphreyans h'had been
    saying grace."

The same writer elsewhere inquires :

"Wherefore we do amand Duke Hum-
    phrey's guest,
For their provision truly is o'th'least :
A dog doth fare much better with his
    bones,
Than those whose table, meat, and drink
    are stones."

—*Art of Longevity*, 1659, p. 1. Compare Nares. *Glossary*, 1859 in v.

Dulce Domum.—At St. Mary's College. Winton, the Dulce Domum is sung on the evening preceding the Whitsun holidays; the masters, scholars, and choristers, attended by a band of music, walk in procession round the courts of the college, singing it. It is, no doubt, of very remote antiquity, and its origin must be traced not to any ridiculous tradition, but to the tenderest feelings of human nature :

"Concinamus, O Sodales !
Eja ! quid silemus?
Nobile canticum !
Dulce melos, domum !
Dulce domum resonemus !

Chorus.—Domum, domum, dulce domum !
Domum, domum, dulce domum !
Dulce, dulce, dulce domum !
Dulce domum resonemus," &c.

But the Dulce Domum is one of those usages which are fast wearing out; it was not confined to Winchester School, but was general. In my time, it was regularly sung every Christmas, before the breaking up, at Merchant Taylors' School, and I remember that the whole school, in the presence of the masters, suddenly, as if by previous concert, burst into a full chorus.

Dumb Borsholder of Chart.— There was, till of late years, says Hasted, a singular, though a very ancient custom, kept up, of electing a deputy to the Dumb Borsholder of Chart, near Wateringbury, in Kent, claiming liberty over fifteen houses in the precinct of the hamlet of Sizein - Well, every householder of which was formerly obliged to pay the keeper of this borsholder one penny yearly. The Dumb Borsholder was always first called at the Court-Leet holden for the hundred of Twyford, when its keeper, who was yearly appointed by that Court, held it up to his call, with a neckcloth or handkerchief put through the iron ring fixed at the top, and answered for it. The Borsholder and the Court Leet have been discontinued for about fifty years : and the Borsholder, who is put in by the Quarter Sessions for Wateringbury, claims over the whole parish. This Dumb Borsholder is made of wood, about three feet and a half an inch long, with an iron ring at the top, and four more by the sides, near the bottom, where it has a square iron spike fixed, four inches and a half long, to fix it in the ground, or, on occasion, to break open doors, &c. which used to be done, without a warrant of any Justice, on suspicion of goods having been unlawfully come by and concealed in any of these fifteen houses. It is not easy, at this distance of time, to ascertain the origin of this dumb officer. Perhaps it might have been made use of as a badge or ensign by the office of the market here. The last person who acted as deputy to it was one Thomas Clampard, a blacksmith, who died in 1748, whose heirs have it now in their possession. *History of Kent*, folio ed., ii., 284.

Dumb-Cake.—The dumb-cake is a species of dreaming bread, prepared by unmarried females, with ingredients traditionally suggested in witching doggerel. When baked, it is cut into three divisions : a part of each to be eaten, and the remainder to be put under the pillow. When the clock strikes twelve, each votary must go to bed backwards, and keep a profound silence, whatever may appear. Indeed, should a word be uttered, either during the process or before falling asleep, the spell is broken, and some direful calamity may be dreaded. Those who are to be married, or are full of hope, fancy they see visions of their future partners hurrying after them ; while they who are to live and die old maids are not very sanguine of obtaining their errand, seeing nothing at all.

Dun's in the Mire.—We find this game noticed at least as early as Chaucer's time, in the "Manciples Prologue" :

"Then gan our hoste to jape and to play
And sayd : sires, what? Dun is in the mire."

In Rowlands' "Humors Ordinarie," 1600, I see it enumerated among other pastimes :

"At shoue-groat, venter-poynt, or crosse and pile. . . .
At leaping ore a Midsommer bone-fier,
Or at the drawing dunne out of the myer."

But in Drue's "Dutchess of Suffolke," 1631, signat. E 3, the expression is used in a different way:

"Well done, my masters, lend 's your hands,
Draw dun out of the ditch,
Draw, pull, helpe all, so, so, well done."
"They pull him out."

They had shoved Bishop Bonner into a well and were pulling him out. "Dun is in the mire," says Gifford, "is a Christmas gambol, at which I have often played. A log of wood is brought into the midst of the room : this is Dun (the cart-horse), and a cry is raised that he is stuck in the mire. Two of the company advance either with or without ropes, to draw him out. After repeated attempts, they find themselves unable to do it, and call for more assistance. The game continues, till all the company take part in it, when Dun is extricated of course ; and the merriment arises from the awkward and affected efforts of the rustics to lift the log, and from sundry arch contrivances to let the ends of it fall on one another's toes." Dun's in the mire hence, no doubt, became a proverbial expression. Dyce's *Beaumont and Fletcher*, vol. i. p. 71, note; Hazlitt's *Proverbs*, 1882, p. 123.

Dunmow Flitch.—A custom formerly prevailed. and is still observed, at Dunmow, in Essex, of giving a flitch of bacon to any married man or woman, who would swear that neither of them, in a year and a day, either sleeping or waking, repented of their marriage. Blount attributes the origin of this ceremony to an institution of the Lord Fitzwalter, in the reign of Henry III. who ordered that "whatever married man did not repent of his marriage, or quarrel with his wife in a year and a day after it, should go to his Priory, and demand the bacon, on his swearing to the truth, kneeling on two stones in the church-yard." The form and ceremony of the claim, as made in 1701 by William Parsley, of Much Easton, in the County of Essex, butcher, and Jane his wife, are detailed in the same work. Dugdale, "Mon. Angl." vol. ii. p. 79; Morant's "Essex," vol. ii., p. 429; and "Antiq Repert." edit. 1807, vol. iii., p. 341-4. The author of "Piers Ploughman" (1362) and Chaucer in his "Wife of Bath's Prologue," refer to the Dunmow flitch :—

"I sette hem so on werke, by my fay,
   That many a night they songen wey-
       laway.
The bacoun was nought set for hem, I
     trowe,
That som men fecche in Essex at Don-
     mowe."

We also find a reference to the usage in a MS. which is supposed to have been written not much more than half a century after the death of Chaucer :

"I can fynd no man now that wille
     enquere,
The parfyte wais unto Dunmowe ;
For they repent hem within a yere,
And many within a weke, and sonner,
     men trow ;
That cawsith the weis to be rowgh and
     over grow,
That no man may find path or gap,
The world is turnyd to another shap."

The usage is mentioned in the Chartulary of Dunmow Priory, under 1445, 1467, and 1510. It is to be collected from a MS. in the College of Arms, written by Sir Richard St. George, Garter, about 1640, that this notable usage originated either in Robert Fitzwater, a favourite of Henry II., or in one of his successors in the lordship of Dunmow and its Priory. It is said of this Fitzwater, by the writer of the MS., that "he betooke himself in his latter dayes to prayers and deeds of charity. . . and reedified the decayed priorie of Dunmow. . . . in which priorie arose a custome begune and instituted either by him or some other of his successors . . . .

I have enquired of the manner of yt, and can learne no more but that yt continued untill the Dissolution, of that house as also the Abbey." St. George proceeds to say, that in his time two hard-pointed stones were to be seen in the churchyard, on which the claimant was required to take the oath kneeling humbly in the presence of the prior, convent, and people ; which process, together with the length and elaborate character of the declaration exacted, "with solemn singing" into the bargain, seems to have brought St. George to the conclusion that the "partie or pilgrim for bacon," as he terms him, had rather a "painful pilgrimage." We are to infer, from Garter's account, that it was at that time considered sufficient for the husband to attend ; and he acquaints us that, after the endurance of the solemn ordeal, he was, if his claim were admitted, carried in triumph through the town, with his flitch before him. The quantity given does not seem to have been strictly uniform, for Garter says, "I find that some had a gammon and others a fleeke, or a flitch." The earliest record of the presentation of the flitch appears to be in 7 Edw. IV., when Stephen Samuel, of Ayrton, in Essex, claimed and obtained his gammon, on satisfying the usual conditions. In 23 Hen. VI., Richard Wright, of Badborough, near Norwich, was similarly awarded the palm of conjugal harmony ; but in his case it was only a flitch. Again, in 1510, 2 Hen. VIII., Thomas Lefuller, of Cogshall, Essex, was allowed the full gammon. But on what grouud this variation was made, we do not learn. The singular oath administered to them ran thus, according to Dugdale :

"You shall swear by the Custom of our
     Confession,
That you never made any nuptial trans-
     gression,
Since you were married to your wife,
By household brawles, or contentious
     strife ;
Or otherwise, in bed or board
Offended each other in deed or word ;
Or since the Parish Clerk said Amen,
Wished yourselves unmarried agen.
Or in a twelvemonth and a day
Repented not in thought any way.
But continued true and in desire,
As when you joined hands in the Holy
     Quire.
If to these conditions without all feare
Of your own accord you will freely
     swear,
A Gammon of Bacon you shall receive,
And beare it hence with love and good
     leave ;
For this is our custom in Dunmow well
     known,
Though the sport be ours, the Bacon's
     your own."

It is scarcely necessary to observe, that the preceding lines have every mark of being a modern local version of the more ancient formula, now apparently not preserved. Dugdale, however, thought them worth printing in his " Monasticon." In Playford's *Catch that Catch Can,* 1685, is a copy of the oath set to music. See a letter from Horace Walpole to Lady Aylesbury, August 23rd, 1760. The parties were to take this oath before the prior and convent and the whole town, humbly kneeling in the churchyard upon the two hard pointed stones, as has just been noticed. They were afterwards taken upon men's shoulders, and carried, first, about the priory churchyard, and after through the town, with all the friars and brethren, and all the townsfolk, young and old, followed them with shouts and acclamations, with their bacon before them. Brand describes a large print, entitled " An exact perspective view of Dunmow, late the Priory in the County of Essex, with a representation of the ceremony and procession in that Mannor, on Thursday the 20th of June, 1751, when Thomas Shapeshaft of the parish of Weathersfield in the county aforesaid, weaver, and Anne his wife, came to demand, and did actually receive a gammon of bacon, having first kneeled down upon two bare stones within the church doore and taken the oath, &c. N.B. Before the dissolution of monasteries it does not appear, by searching the most antient records, to have been demanded above three times, and, including this, just as often since. Taken on the spot and engraved by David Ogborne." The *Gentleman's Magazine,* xxi., 282, calls the individual John Shakeshanks, woolcomber.

It seems that no religious distinctions were observed, but that the flitch was open to all comers, who had lived in a state of absolute content and felicity a year and a day from the date of their union. It was also stipulated that it was to hang up in the hall of the Manor-house, " redy arrayde all times of the yere, bott in Lent." Instead of one claimant, namely, the husband, it became customary, it appears, at a later date, for both the man and the woman to attend, and a large oak chair was preserved in Dunmow Church in the present century, in which the fortunate couple were installed, so soon as the decision in their favour was made known. It is probably still to be seen; at any rate an engraved view of it is given in the " Antiquarian Repertory." It is there described as " undoubtedly of great antiquity, probably the official chair of the prior, or that of the lord of the manor." In 1902 fourteen couples entered for the prize, but were reduced to two, Mr. and Mrs. Wallis of Derby, and Mr. and Mrs. Brook of Bromley, Kent. Both parties were successful before the judge in the case, Mr. J. V. Mackenzie, in establishing their claims, and duly received their flitches. The claimants had their own counsel, and the donors of the bacon theirs; and a composite jury of six maidens and six bachelors had been, as usual, empanelled to consider the evidence. It is said that down to 1772 only eight claims were preferred or allowed, and that the custom was falling into disuse, until it revived about 1850 under the auspices of Mr. Harrison Ainsworth.

According to the " Contes d'Eutrapel," cited by Tyrwhitt, it was a Breton usage, prevailing at St. Helaine, near Rennes. But Dr. Bell, in his researches into Shakespear's " Puck " has shown that the usage has also a German counterpart; and I am inclined certainly to acquiesce in the line of argument, which seems to secure for the idea in its origin a Teutonic source. Comp. *Whichenovre.*

Dwarf.—It appears that the Saxons treated the malady which is now well known under the name of convulsions, as the visitation of a dwarf. It was a belief which they brought with them from the north of Europe, and which was common to the whole Gothic family. The Saxon Leechdoms furnish a receipt for this disease or affliction, which was said to be " doing away a dwarf." Unlike the night-mare, which was exclusively a nocturnal visitor, the dwarf came to his victim, as may be supposed from the character of the complaint which the superstition thus personifies, at any time during the four-and-twenty hours. Mr. Cockayne has some remarks on this matter in his preface.

Dyzemas Day. — In Northamptonshire, or some parts of it, Titheday is known as Dyzemas Day. Miss Baker observes: " A sexagenarian, on the southern side of the county, to whom I was indebted for the name, informed me that within his remembrance this day was kept as sacred as the sabbath, and it was considered very unlucky to commence any undertaking, or even to wash on the same day of the week throughout the year, on which the anniversary of this day last fell." *Northamptonshire Glossary,* 1854, in v. But the latter notion is not peculiar to the county in question. It is also current in the North of England and elsewhere. According to some authorities, the day is also called Dyzeman's Day in the North.

Earnest.—See *God's Penny.*

Ear-Omens. — Itching in the ear, or on the lobes of it, is still received as a symptom that one is being talked of behind one's back; but we may perhaps collect from one of John Heywood's Epigrams, 1562, that in his day it bore another signification, and portended that the party, whose ear itched, had been guilty of an untruth; and the same sense is evidently from the context to be given to a passage in the interlude of *Jack Juggler* (about 1550):—

"But I promise you, I do curstlie feare,
For I feel a vengeable burning in my left ere"—

The speaker has been inventing a falsehood. Browne, in his "Vulgar Errors," adds: "He (Pliny) supposes it to have proceeded from the notion of a signifying genius, or universal Mercury, that conducted sounds to their distant subjects, and taught to hear by touch." Delrio and Keuchenius seem to have been of opinion that a tingling in the right ear portended good, and in the left the reverse, in which they are supported by the old Scotish saying, cited by Douce in his MSS. notes on Brand: "Right lug, left lug, whilk lug lows. If the left ear, they talk harm; if the right, good." Delrio, "Disquis. Magic." p. 473; Keuchenius "Crepundia," 1662, p. 113. In "Much Ado About Nothing," 1600, act iii. sc. 2, Beatrice says: "What fire is in mine ears?" which Warburton explains as alluding to a proverbial saying of the common people, that their ears burn when others are talking of them. On which Reed observes that the opinion is mentioned by Pliny. Moreover is not this an opinion generally received, that when our ears do glow and tingle, some there be that in our absence doe talke of us?"—Holland's "Translation," b. xxviii. p. 297. Pliny's own words are: "Absentes tinnitu Aurium præsentire sermones de se receptum est." Gaule has not omitted in his list of "Vain Observations and Superstitious Ominations thereupon," the tingling of the ear, the itching of the eye, &c." *Mag-Astromancer posed*, 181, and Home tells us: "If their ears tingle, they say it is a signe they have some enemies abroad, that doe or are about to speake evill of them: so, if their right eye itcheth, then it betokens joyfull laughter: and so, from the itching of the nose, and elbow, and severall affectings of severall parts, they make severall predictions too silly to be mentioned, though regarded by them." *Demonology*, 1650, p. 61.

Herrick refers to this belief:

"*On himselfe.*

"One eare tingles; some there be,
That are snarling now at me;
Be they those that Homer bit,
I will give them thanks for it."

Easter. — Turner, in his "History of the Anglo-Saxons," derives Easter from the Saxon Goddess Eostre, and probably this etymology is the true one. In Lysons' "Environs," vol. i. p. 230, among his curious extracts from the Churchwardens' and Chamberlain's Books at Kingston-upon-Thames, are the following entries concerning some of the ancient doings on Easter Day:—"5 Hen. VIII. For thred for the Resurrection, 1d.; for three yerds of dornek for a pleyers cote, and the makyng, 1s. 3d. 12 Hen. VIII. Paid for a skin of parchment and gunpowder, for the play on Easter Day, 8d. For brede and ale for them that made the stage and other things belonging to the play, 1s. 2d." By the subsequent entry these pageantries should seem to have been continued during the reign of Queen Elizabeth, 1565. "Rec^d of the players of the stage at Easter, £1 2s. 1½d." Among the ancient annual disbursements of the Church of St. Mary-at-Hill, I find the following entry against Easter: "Three great garlands for the crosses, of roses and lavender: three dozen other garlands for the quire: 3s." The same also occurs in the Churchwardens' Accounts, ibid. 1512. Also among the Church disbursements, ibid. in the Waxchandler's Accompt, "for making the Pascal at Ester, 2s. 8d." Ibid. 1486. "At Ester, for the howllyn people for the pascal, 11s. 5d." In the Churchwardens' Accompts of St. Martin Outwich, London, under the year 1525, is the following item: "Paid for brome ageynst Ester, 1^d." It seems from the "Privy Purse Expenses of Elizabeth of York," 1502, that it was then customary to present gratuities to the officers of the kitchen, saucery, and scullery, and to the gateporters; and in the "Northumberland Household Book," 1512, there is a long enumeration of the bounty which the Earl and his family were accustomed to distribute on this festival. A pair of gloves was a present at Easter, as well as at Christmas. Whitelocke's *Liber Famelicus*, 1858, under 1615. "To houl over the paschal," is mentioned among the customs of the Roman Catholics censured by John Bale in his "Declaration of Bonner's Articles," 1554. There is a proverb:

"If Easter falls in Lady Day's lap,
Beware, Old England, of a clap."

Easter, Pasch, or **Paste Eggs.**—Gebelin informs us that this custom of giving eggs at Easter is to be traced up to the theology and philosophy of the Egyptians, Persians, Gauls, Greeks, Romans, &c., among all of whom an egg was an emblem of the universe, the work of the supreme Divinity; and Hutchinson indeed remarks that "Eggs were held by the Egyptians as a sacred emblem of the renovation of mankind after the Deluge. The Jews adopted it to suit the circumstances of their history, as a type of their departure from the land of Egypt; and it was used in the feast of the Passover as part of the furniture of the table, with the paschal lamb. The Christians have certainly used it on this day, as retaining the elements of future life, for an emblem of the Resurrection. It seems as if the egg was thus decorated for a religious trophy after the days of mortification and abstinence were over, and festivity had taken their place; and as an emblem of the resurrection of life, certified to us by the Resurrection, from the regions of death and the grave." The ancient Egyptians, if the resurrection of the body had been a tenet of their faith, would perhaps have thought an egg no improper hieroglyphical representation of it. The extraction of a living creature by incubation, after the vital principle has lain a long while dormant, or seemingly extinct, is a process so truly marvellous, that, if it could be disbelieved, would be thought by some as a thing incredible to the full, as that the Author of Life should be able to reanimate the dead. Easter, says Gebelin, and the New Year, have been marked by similar distinctions: among the Persians, the New Year is looked upon as the renewal of all things, and is noted for the triumph of the Sun of Nature, as Easter is with Christians for that of the Sun of Justice, the Saviour of the World, over death by his Resurrection. The Feast of the New Year, he adds, was celebrated at the Vernal Equinox, that is, at a time when the Christians removing their New Year to the Winter Solstice, kept only the Festival of Easter. Hence, with the latter, the feast of eggs has been attached to Easter, so that eggs are no longer made presents of at the New Year. Bryant says, "An egg, containing in it the elements of life, was thought no improper emblem of the ark, in which were preserved the rudiments of the future world: hence in the Dionusiaca and in other mysteries, one part of the nocturnal ceremony consisted in the consecration of an egg. By this, as we are informed by Porphyry, was signified the world. It seems to have been a favourite

symbol, and very antient, and we find it adopted among many nations. It was said by the Persians of Orosmasdes, that he formed mankind and inclosed them in an egg. A writer in the "Gentleman's Magazine," for July, 1783, supposes the egg at Easter "an emblem of the rising up out of the grave, in the same manner as the chick entombed, as it were, in the egg, is in due time brought to life." He takes the flowers which are used to decorate the churches at this time to bear the same import. A correspondent of "Notes and Queries," traces to pagan times and to the Mahometan feast of nooroose, or the waters, an anniversary celebration of the Creation and Deluge, the Christian practice of offering eggs at Easter. He cites Sir R. Ker Porter's "Travels in Georgia, Persia, &c.," 1821, in confirmation of this theory. Le Brun, in his "Voyages," tells us that the Persians, on the 20th of March, 1704, kept the festival of the Solar New Year, which he says lasted several days, when they mutually presented each other, among other things, with coloured eggs. They were sometimes tinted yellow, sometimes red, sometimes sky-blue. In Italy, Spain, and in Provence, says Father Carmeli, where almost every ancient superstition is retained, there are in the public places certain sports with eggs. This custom he derives from the Jews or the Pagans, for he observes it is common to both. This custom still prevails in the Greek Church. Chandler, in his "Travels in Asia Minor," gives the following account of the manner of celebrating Easter among the modern Greeks: "The Greeks now celebrated Easter. A small bier, prettily deckt with orange and citron buds, jasmine, flowers, and boughs, was placed in the church, with a Christ crucified, rudely painted on board, for the body. We saw it in the evening, and, before day-break, were suddenly awakened by the blaze and crackling of a large bonfire, with singing and shouting in honour of the Resurrection. They made us presents of coloured eggs and cakes of Easter bread." "They (the Russians) have an order at Easter, which they alwaies observe, and that is this: every yeere, against Easter, to die or colour red, with Brazzel (Brazil wood), a great number of egges, of which every man and woman giveth one unto the priest of the parish upon Easter Day in the morning. And, moreover, the common people use to carrie in their hands one of these red egges, not only upon Easter Day, but also three or foure days after, and gentlemen and gentlewomen have egges gilded, which they carry in like maner. They use it, as they say, for a great love, and in token of the Resurrection, whereof they rejoice. For when two friends meete during the Easter holydayes they come and take one another by the hand, the one of them saith, ' The Lord, or Christ, is risen ' ; the other answereth, ' It is so, of a trueth ' ; and they then kiss, and exchange their egges, both men and women, continuing in kissing four dayes together." Our ancient voyage-writer means no more here, it should seem, than that the ceremony was kept up for four days. Le Brun, in his "Travels," 1702, noticed the same custom, when he visited Russia, and, after him, the Abbé d'Auteroche describes in his journey to Siberia, this ceremonial as still kept up with unabated enthusiasm. Le Brun says that it lasted fifteen days, and among people of all ranks. The author of "Le Voyageur à Paris," tom. ii. p. 112, "supposes that the practice of painting and decorating eggs at Easter, amongst the Catholics, arose from the joy which was occasioned by their returning to this favourite food after so long an abstinence from it during Lent. 'Dans plusieurs villes,' he adds, ' les clercs des Eglises, les etudians des Ecoles et les autres jeunes Gens, s'assemblaient sur une place au bruit des Sonnettes et des Tambours, portant des etandarts burlesques pour se rendre a l'Eglise principale, ou ils chantoient laudes avant de commencer leur quête d'œufs.' " — Douce. Ihre, in his "Glossarium Suio-gothicum," 1769, v. egg, explains a Paskegg to mean one that at Easter time is sent by persons to each other, variously ornamented and coloured, and in token of rejoicing at the termination of the Lenten fast. Among the Russians it was not thought too great a freedom, he says, according to travellers, to offer such eggs to the Emperor.

Hyde, in his "Oriental Sports," tells us of one with eggs among the Christians of Mesopotamia on Easter Day and forty days afterwards, during which time their children buy themselves as many eggs as they can, and stain them with a red colour in memory of the blood of Christ shed as at that time of his Crucifixion. Some tinge them with green and yellow. Stained eggs are sold all the while in the market. The sport consists in striking their eggs one against another, and the egg that first breaks is won by the owner of the egg that struck it. Immediately another egg is pitted against the winning egg, and so they go on, till the last remaining egg wins all the others, which their respective owners shall before have won. This sport, he observes, is not retained in the Midland parts of England, but seems to be alluded to in the old proverb, "An egg at Easter," because the

liberty to eat eggs begins again at that festival, and thence must have arisen this festive egg-game. For neither the Romanists nor those of the Eastern Church begin to eat eggs till Easter.

That the Church of Rome has considered eggs as emblematical of the Resurrection, may be gathered from the subsequent prayer which the reader will find in an extract from the Ritual of Pope Paul the Fifth, for the use of England, Ireland, and Scotland. It contains various other forms of benediction. "Bless, O Lord ! we beseech thee, this thy creature of eggs, that it may become a wholesome sustenance to thy faithful servants, eating it in thankfulness to thee, on account of the Resurrection of our Lord," &c. In the Roman Calendar I find the following : " Ova annunciatæ, ut aiunt, reponuntur." Le Brun plausibly suggests that these eggs were kept for luck (as we say) from Good Friday to Good Friday, like our cross-buns. In Bale's "Yet a Course at the Romishe Foxe," 1542, signat. D 4, the author enumerates some "auncyent rytes and lawdable ceremonyes of holy churche" then it should seem laid aside, in the following censure of the Bishop : "Than ought my Lorde also to suffre the same selfe ponnyshment for not rostyng egges in the Palme ashes fyre," &c. In the Beehive of the Romish Church, 1579, they are termed Holy Pace Eggs. Coles, in his "Latin Dictionary," renders the Pasch, or Easter egg, by "Ovum Paschale croceum, seu luteum." In the Household of Edward the First, in his eighteenth year (" Archæol." 1805) is the following item in the Accounts of Easter Sunday :—"For four hundred and a half of eggs, eighteen pence." The original item runs thus : "Pro iiij°. di' ov' xviij^{d}." In the North of England, observes Hyde, in Cumberland and Westmoreland, boys beg, on Easter Eve, eggs to play with, and beggars ask for them to eat. These eggs are hardened by boiling, and tinged with the juice of herbs, broom-flowers, &c. The eggs being thus prepared, the boys go out and play with them in the fields : rolling them up and down, like bowls, upon the ground, or throwing them up, like balls, into the air. Eggs, stained with various colours in boiling, and sometimes covered with leaf-gold, are at Easter presented to children, at Newcastle-upon-Tyne, and other places in the North, where these young gentry ask for their "paste eggs," as for a fairing, at this season. In the neighbourhood of Newcastle, they are tinged yellow with the blossoms of furze, called there whin-bloom. The title of a tract, printed in 1644, "To Sion's Lovers, being a golden Egge, to

avoid Infection, &c." undoubtedly refers
to this superstition. "On y fit aussi des
deffences de vendre des œufs de couleur
apres Pasques, parce que les enfans s'en
joüoyent auparavant, qui estoit de mau-
vais exemple."—*Satyre Menippée de la
Vertu du Catholicon d'Espagne*, 8vo.,
1595, fol. 94. The English version of this
work renders *œufs de couleur* speckled
eggs.

Easter Eve.—Various superstitions
crept in by degrees among the rites of
this day : such as putting out all the fires
in churches and kindling them anew from
flint, blessing the Easter wax, &c. According to Naogeorgus, the ceremony of
extinguishing the fires in order to re-
kindle them, was common on the Continent among the Catholics. The paschal
taper, which Naogeorgus describes as ty-
pical of "Christ that conquered hell,"
and which on the Continent and
among us used to be hallowed, and
perfumed with frankincense, was an
important item in the ceremonies and also
in the expenses of this feast. It appears
that, in 1557, the taper used in the Abbey
Church at Westminster was of 300 lbs.
weight. In the ancient annual Church
Disbursements of St. Mary-at-Hill, in
the City of London, I find the following
article : "For a quarter of coles for the
hallowed fire on Easter Eve, 6d." Also
the subsequent : "To the Clerk and Sexton (for two men) for watching the Sepulchre from Good Friday to Easter Eve,
and for their meate and drink, 14d." I
find also in the Churchwardens' Accounts,
ibid. 5th Hen. VI. the following entries :
"For the Sepulchre, for divers naylis and
wyres and glu, 9d. ob. Also payd to
Thomas Joynor for makyng of the same
Sepulchre, 4s. Also payd for bokeram for
penons, and for the makynge, 22d." In
Coates's "Hist. of Reading," p. 130,
under Churchwardens' Accounts for the
year 1558, &c., there are several quotations of money laid out for this purpose.
Part of the cost consisted in hiring men,
who should watch the sepulchre in imitation of the soldiers, who actually performed the duty. It appears too, that
with true parochial instinct the materials
were sold when the time was up, and the
next year took care of itself. Two of the
entries are : "Paide to Roger Brock for
watching of the Sepulchre, 8d." "Paide
more to the saide Roger for fyres and
colles, 8d." In "A Short Description of
Antichrist, &c.," the author censures,
among other popish customs, "the halowyng of fiere." They had a custom in Dorsetshire formerly of forming a procession
of boys on Easter Eve, with torches and a
small black flag. The procession chanted
these lines :

"We fasted in the light,
For this is the night."

Easter Eve is, in some places, known as
Holy Saturday. It is a great day among
the Irish Catholics, who hold high festival
at midnight for a few hours, and then
retire till sunrise, when they get up to
see that luminary dance in honour of the
Resurrection. Nor is this usage confined
to the lower classes.

Easter Holidays.—Easter has
ever been considered by the Church as a
season of great festivity. By the law
concerning holidays, made in the time of
King Alfred the Great, it was appointed
that the week after Easter should be kept
holy. It seems from Fitzstephen, cited
by Stowe, that the water-quintain was a
popular diversion at this season. Beli-
thus, a ritualist of ancient times, tells us
that it was customary in some churches
for the bishops and archbishops themselves to play with the inferior clergy at
hand-ball, and this, as Durandus asserts,
even on Easter-day itself. Why they
should play at hand-ball at this time,
rather than any other game, Bourne tells
us he has not been able to discover; certain it is, however, that the present custom of playing at that game on Easter
holidays for a tanzy-cake has been derived
from thence. Erasmus, speaking of the
proverb, "Mea est pila," that is "I've
got the ball," tells us, that it signifies
"I have obtained the victory. I am
master of my wishes." The Romanists
certainly erected a standard on Easter-
day in token of our Lord's victory; but
it would perhaps be indulging fancy too
far to suppose that the Bishops and governors of churches, who used to play at
hand-ball at this season, did it in a mystical way, and with reference to the trium-
phal joy of the season. Certain it is,
however, that many of their customs and
superstitions are founded on still more
trivial circumstances, even according to
their own explanations of them, than this
imaginary analogy. In the Privy Purse
Expenses of Henry VII. Mr. Brand found
the following article : "From 16 to 18
Nov. 9 Hen. VII. Item, to Walter Alwyn
for the revells at Estermess xiijli. vjs.
viijd." Durandus tells us, that on Easter
Tuesday, wives used to beat their husbands, on the day following the husbands
their wives. The custom is still retained at
the City of Durham in the Easter holidays.
On Easter Sunday, in Yorkshire, the
young men in the villages of that county
had a custom of taking off the young girls'
buckles. On Easter Monday, the young
men's shoes and buckles were taken off by
the young women. On the Wednesday they
were redeemed by little pecuniary forfeits,
out of which an entertainment, called a

tansey-cake, was made, with dancing.
Naogeorgus writes:

" At midnight then with carefull minde,
　　they up to mattens ries,
The Clarke doth come, and, after him,
　　the priest with staring eies."
" At midnight strait, not tarying till
　　the daylight doe appeere,
Some getes in flesh and glutton lyke,
　　they feede upon their cheere.
They rost their flesh, and custardes
　　great, and egges and radish store,
And trifles, clouted creame, and cheese,
　　and whatsoeuer more
At first they list to eate, they bring into
　　the Temple straight,
That so the Priest may halow them with
　　wordes of wond'rous waight.
The Friers besides, and pelting Priestes
　　from house to house do roame,
Receyving gaine of every man that this
　　will have at home.
Some raddish rootes this day doe take
　　before all other meate,
Against the quartan ague, and such
　　other sicknesse great."
" Straight after this, into the fieldes
　　they walke to take the viewe,
And to their woonted life they fall, and
　　bid the reast adewe."

In *Wit and Drollery*, 1682, there is a
graphic account of the sort of company,
which flocked to Westminster Abbey at
this time:—" You must suppose it to be
Easter Holy Days: at what time Sisly
and Dol, Kate and Peggy, Moll and Nan
are marching to Westminster, with a
Leash of Prentices before 'em; who go
rowing themselves along with their right
arms to make more hast, and now and
then with a greasy hanckercher wipe away
the dripping that bathes their forehead.
At the Door they meet crow'd of Wapping
Seamen, Southwark Broom-men, the Inhabitants of the Bank-Side, with a Butcher or two prick't in among them. There
awhile they stand gaping for the Master
of the Show, staring upon the suburbs of
their dearest delight, just as they stand
gaping upon the painted Cloath before
they go into the Puppet Play. By and
by they hear the Bunch of Keys which re-
joyces their hearts like the sound of the
Pancake-Bell. For now the Man of Comfort peeps over the spikes, and beholding
such a learned Auditory, opens the Gate
of Paradise, and by that time they are
half got into the first Chappel, for time is
very pretious, he lifts up his Voice among
the Toombs, and begins his Lurrey in
manner and form following." Then we
get a metrical rehearsal of the inmates of
the several monuments, which at this
time of day we regard with qualified credulity.

It is related in Aubanus's description of ancient rites in Germany,
that there were at this season foot-courses
in the meadows, in which the victors carried off each a cake, given to be run for,
as we say, by some better sort of person
in the neighbourhood. Sometimes two
cakes were proposed, one for the young
men, another for the girls; and there was
a great concourse of people on the occasion. This is a custom by no means unlike the playing at hand-ball for a tanzy-
cake, the winning of which depends chiefly
upon swiftness of foot. It is a trial too
of fleetness and speed, as well as the foot-
race.

Easter King.—Charles the Fifth,
whilst he was in possession of his regal
dignity, thought so slightingly of it, that
when, one day, in passing through a village in Spain, he met a peasant who was
dressed with a tin crown upon his head,
and a spit in his hand for a truncheon, as
the Easter King (according to the custom
of that great festival in Spain), who told
the Emperor that he should take off his
hat to him: " My good friend," replied
the Prince, " I wish you joy of your new
office: you will find it a very troublesome
one, I can assure you."

Easter Monday.—They have an
ancient custom at Coleshill, in the county
of Warwick, that if the young men
of the town can catch a hare, and bring
it to the parson of the parish before ten
o'clock on Easter Monday, the parson is
bound to give them a calf's head and a
hundred of eggs for their breakfast, and a
groat in money. Hazlitt's Blount, 1874,
p. 78.

Easter Offering.—Originally a
halfpenny, then a penny, later on raised
to half a silver groat or twopence, payable
by each parishioner waiting on the incumbent of the parish, who was expected
to return it in entertainment. Subsequently the charge became a groat, and
the minister offered no equivalent. These
payments continue customary; but it is
believed that there is no obligation beyond
fourpence a head, to be collected by the
clergyman or his sufficient deputy. In
Doctor Double Ale, a poem written about
1550 (Hazlitt's *P. P.*, iii., 311) we are
told:

" This man, to sum mens thinking,
Doth stay hym much vpon the Kyng,
As in the due demaunding,
Of that he calleth an head peny,
And of the paskall halfpenny."

Comp. Machyn's *Diary*, Camd. Soc., p.
62.

Easter Sunday or **Easter Day.**
—Eggs and green sauce, the latter composed of herbs, were a very usual repast
on the Continent and here on Easter Day.
It is mentioned in the " Doctrine of

the Masse Book" as an authorised dish for this occasion. At Gray's Inn, and perhaps at the other Inns of Court, there is the testimony of Dugdale that the commons used to consist on this day of the same sort of viands (so to speak), and until the 23 Eliz. the charge of providing the repast for the students devolved on the chief cook; after that, it was defrayed by the Society. A superstitious practice appears to have prevailed upon the Continent, of abstaining from flesh on Easter Sunday, to escape a fever for the whole year. I know not whether it ever reached this Island. It was condemned by the Provisional Council of Rheims in 1583, and by that of Toulouse in 1590. See "Traite des Superstitions," vol. i., p. 319, 320. The first dish that was brought up to the table on Easter Day, was a red herring riding away on horseback; i.e., a herring ordered by the cook something after the likeness of a man on horseback, set in a corn-salad. The custom of eating a gammon of bacon at Easter, which is still kept up in many parts of England was founded on this, viz., "to shew their abhorrence to Judaism at that solemn commemoration of our Lord's Resurrection." Aubrey (1679). It was the practice in Germany (during the sixteenth century at least) for the preachers to intermix their sermons with facetious stories on Easter Day. This may be gathered from the "Convivialium Sermonum Liber." Bas. 1542, sig. K8. Douce's *MSS. Notes.* It is still a common usage, of which the origin is assuredly not held in remembrance by many of those who observe it, of wearing something new on Easter Sunday. Poor Robin says:

"At Easter let your clothes be new,
Or else be sure you will it rue."

Lamb is very usually eaten for the first time on this festival. An old - established usage at Northmore, near Witney, in Oxfordshire, was for the men and women, after evening service, to throw apples in the churchyard, those that had been married within the year throwing thrice as many as the rest; and all subsequently adjourned to the minister's house, where they were entertained on bread and cheese. Hearne's *Diary,* Jan. 19, 1725, and Note. Comp. *Sun.*

Eating.—If, says Grose, in eating, you miss your mouth, and the victuals fall, it is very unlucky, and denotes approaching sickness.

Eden Hall.—See *Luck of Eden Hall.*

Edgeware.—Sir William Blackstone says, that it was usual for the lord of this manor to provide a minstrel or piper for the diversion of the tenants, while they were employed in his service. He refers to the manor-rolls which are among the Archives of All-Souls' College.—Lysons' *Environs,* 1st ed., ii., p. 244. Lysons searched the rolls without success, but accepts the statement on Blackstone's authority; and he adds that a piece of ground in the parish still (1795) goes by the name of Piper's Green.

At a Court of the manor of Edgeware, anno 1552, the inhabitants were presented for not having a tumbrel and cucking-stool. This looks as if the punishments were different. Lysons' *Environs,* ii., 244. At a court of the same Manor, in 1555, "it was presented that the butts at Edgeware were very ruinous, and that the inhabitants ought to repair them; which was ordered to be done before the ensuing Whitsontide."

Edgewell Tree.—Allan Ramsay, speaking of Edge-well Tree, describes it to be "an oak tree which grows on the side of a fine spring, nigh the Castle of Dalhousie, very much observed by the country people, who gave out, that before any of the family died, a branch fell from the Edge-well Tree. The old tree some few years ago fell altogether, but another sprung from the same root, which is now tall and flourishing, and lang be't sae."

Egg and Spoon.—An amusement which consists in a certain number running a race, each carrying an egg on a flat spoon, and the one, who arrives at the goal without disaster, wins. We seem here to have an evolution from the Venetian egg-game, described in Zompini's *Cries of Venice,* 1785.

Egg Feast.—The Egg Feast, mentioned in the Oxford Almanack, and formerly held there on Egg Saturday, that immediately preceding Shrove Tuesday, was held when the scholars took leave of that kind of food. Comp. Halliwell, v. *Egg-Feast.* Novelties in Easter eggs are constantly introduced from year to year in the English market. For 1903 they advertised natural eggs, chocolate eggs, plover's eggs, wooden eggs with snakes, globes, skipping ropes, and other toys inside.

Egg Saturday.—The Saturday before Shrove Tuesday. See *Easter Eggs.*

Egg Service.—One, where eggs are contributed for some special purpose, as when at Biggar, Lanarkshire, eighty dozen were quite recently collected, and sent to the children's hospitals in Glasgow and Edinburgh.

Egg Shell.—To break the egg-shell after the meat is out, is a relic of superstition mentioned in Pliny. Sir Thomas Browne tells us that the intent of this was to prevent witchcraft; for lest witches should draw or prick their names therein, and veneficiously mischief their persons, they broke the shell, as Delecampius has observed. Delrio, in his "Disquisitiones

Magicæ," has a passage on this subject. Scot says: "Men are preserved from witchcraft by sprinkling of Holy Water, receiving consecrated salt; by candles hallowed on Candlemas Day, and by green leaves consecrated on Palm Sunday." Coles tells us that "Matthiolus saith that Herba paris takes away evill done by witchcraft, and affirms that he knew it to be true by experience." In Fletcher's *Women Pleased* occurs:

"The Devil should think of purchasing
     that egg-shell
To victual out a witch for the Bur-
     moothes."

Eggs.—Stocker, on the line in Persius, Sat. v., 1, 185:

"Tunc nigri Lemures *ovoque pericula rupto*,"

observes: "If an egg broke when put on the fire, it portended jeopardy to the person or property of the individual." The Rev. James Layton informed Mr. Roach Smith that the East Anglian rustics had a general custom when an egg was eaten, of thrusting the spoon through the bottom of the shell, so that the witches might not sail in it. But the Romans, according to Pliny, observed a similar usage.   C. R. Smith's *Richborough*, 1850, p. 206.

Elder. — Gerarde, "Herball," ed. 1633, p. 1428, says: "The Arbor Judæ is thought to be that whereon Judas hanged himself, and not upon the elder tree as it is vulgarly said." I am clear (says Brand) that the mushrooms or excrescences of the elder tree, called Auricula Judæ in Latin, and commonly rendered "Jews' Eares," ought to be translated "Judas' Eares" from the popular superstition above-mentioned. Coles says: "It" (Jewes' Eares) "is called in Latine Fungus Sambucinus and Auricula Judæ: some having supposed the elder tree to be that whereon Judas hanged himself, and that, ever since, these mushrooms, like unto eares, have grown thereon, which I will not persuade you to believe." There was an early Italian belief that the tree was the carob or St. John's Bread-tree, which is mentioned in St. Luke, chap. xv. v. 16, and by Pulci in his *Morgante Maggiore*. The late Mr. Dyce was acquainted with a gentleman, a great travellor, who had seen the tree, whether the ordinary elder or the *Arbor Judæ*, is not clear. Mitford's *Notes on Beaumont and Fletcher* and *Shakespeare*, 1856, p. 41.

Lupton, in his fifth book of "Notable Things," edit. 1660, p. 132, says: "Make powder of the flowers of elder, gathered on Midsummer Day, being before well dried, and use a spoonfull thereof in a good draught of borage-water, morning and evening, first and last, for the space of a month: and it will make you seem young a great while." Blagrave writes: "It is reported that if you gently strike a horse that cannot stale, with a stick of this elder, and bind some of the leaves to his belly, it will make him stale presently. It is also said, and some persons of good credit have told me, (but I never made any experiment of it), that if one ride with two little sticks of elder in his pockets, he shall not fret nor gaul, let the horse go never so hard." Supplement to Culpeper's *English Physician*, 1674, p. 62. The first of these superstitions is again mentioned in Coles's "Adam in Eden." In the "Athenian Oracle" is the following relation: "A friend of mine being lately upon the road a horseback, was extremely incommoded by loss of leather; which coming to the knowledge of one of his fellow travellers, he over-persuaded him to put two elder sticks in his pocket, which not only eased him of his pain, but secured the remaining portion of his posteriours, not yet excoriated, throughout the rest of his journey," 111, 545. Coles says: "It hath beene credibly reported to me from severall hands, that if a man take an elder stick, and cut it on both sides so that he preserve the joynt, and put in his pocket when he rides a journey, he shall never gall." *Introduction to the Knowledge of Plants*, 1656, p. 63. Flecknoe also mentions, in his *Diarium*, 1656, p. 65:—

"How alder-stick in pocket carried,
By horseman who on high-way feared
His breech should nere be gall'd or
          wearied,
Although he rid on trotting horse,
Or cow, or cowl-staff which was worse,
It had, he said, such vertuous force,
Where Vertue oft, from Judas came
(Who hang'd himself upon the same,
For which, in sooth, he was to blame.)
Or't had some other magick force,
To harden breech, or soften horse,
I leave't to th' learned to discourse."

In the *Anatomy of the Elder*, 1653, are some particulars in connexion with this part of the subject. "The common people keep as a great secret in curing wounds, the leaves of the elder which they have gathered the last day of April; which, to disappoint the charms of witches, they had affixed to their dores and windows." There is mentioned an amulet against the erysipelas, "made of the elder on which the sunn never shined. If the piece betwixt the two knots be hung about the patient's neck, it is much commended. Some cut it in little pieces, and sew it in a knot in a piece of a man's shirt, which seems superstitious." Two instances of its success are recorded. "There is likewise set down," against the epilepsia, "a singular amulet made of the elder growing on a sallow. If in the month of October, a little before the full moon, you pluck a twig of the elder, and cut the cane that is betwixt two of its knees, or knots, in nine pieces, and these pieces being bound in a piece of linnen, be in a thread, so hung about the neck, that they touch the spoon of the heart, or the sword-formed cartilage; and that they may stay more firmly in that place they are to be bound thereon with a linnen or silken roller wrapt about the body, till the thred break of itself. The thred being broken and the roller removed, the amulet is not at all to be touched with bare hands, but it ought to be taken hold on by some instrument and buried in a place that nobody may touch it." We are told, "Some hang a cross, made of the elder and sallow, mutually inwrapping one another about the children's neck," pp. 54, 207, 211. Among other rustic charms may be mentioned : Curing a lame pig by boring a little hole in his ear, and putting a small peg of elder into it. In the epilogue to Lyly's "Campaspe," 1584, a passage is found which implies that elder was given at that time as a token of disgrace : "Laurell for a garland and ealder for a disgrace." So again, in "An Hue and Cric after Cromwell," 1649, p. 4, we read :

"Cooke, the Recorder, have an elder tree,
And steel a slip to reward treacherie."

There is a vulgar prejudice that "if boys be beaten with an elder-stick, it hinders their growth."

Elephants. — There is a belief founded on observation, that this quadruped will not only start at the grunt of the wild pig, but at a lizard or other small object, from which he may feel a difficulty in protecting himself. This is constantly noticed in respect to the specimens which are brought to Europe, and are disconcerted by a mouse in the den among the straw. Charles Gibbon, in his *Order of Equality*, 1604, merely mentions that elephants are terrified by the grunting of pigs. He should have explained that the pig in question was the tenant of Indian jungles.

Elf. — The elf was also called urchin or goblin. The "Urchins' Daunce" is preserved in one of Ravenscroft's musical volumes, and has been republished in Dr. Rimbault's book of "Songs and Ballads," 1851.

Elf-Disease. There appear to have been two kinds of elf-disease, land-elf disease, and water-elf disease. The symptoms and treatment were different. The nostrums which were prescribed by our Saxon doctors in each case are described at length in Mr. Cockayne's "Saxon Leechdoms." Mr. Cockayne includes a "salve against the elfin race and nocturnal goblin visitors, and for the women with whom the devil hath carnal commerce." The specific is as follows : "Take the ewe hop plant, wormwood, bishopwort, lupin, ashthroat, harewort, vipers bugloss, heathberry plants, cropleek, garlic, grains of hedgerise, githrise, fennel; put these worts into a vessel, set them under the altar, sing over them nine masses, boil them in butter and sheep's grease, add much holy salt, strain through a cloth, throw the worts into running water." If any one was troubled by night elves, his forehead was to be smeared with this salve, and also his eyes, and any sore parts of his body, and he was to be "censed with incense," and signed frequently with the cross, and then his condition would soon be better. A disease, consisting of a hardness of the side, was called in the dark ages of superstition the elf-cake. In the seventh book of Lupton's "Thousand Notable Things," No. 55, is the following prescription which, it is said, will help the hardness of the side called the elf-cake. "Take the root of gladen, and make powder thereof, and give the diseased party half a spoon-ful thereof to drink in white wine, and let him eat thereof so much in his pottage at one time, and it will help him within a while." A cure for the above disorder is in Harl. MS. 2378, f. 47 and 57 : "For the elf-cake." This is of the time of Henry VI., and the same as that from Lupton. Camden says : "When any one in Ireland happens to fall, he springs up again, and turning round three times to the right, digs the earth with a sword or knife, and takes up a turf, because they say the earth reflects his shadow to him : (quod illi terram umbram reddere dicunt : they imagine there is a spirit in the earth) : and if he falls sick within two or three days after, a woman skilled in those matters is sent to the spot, and there says, 'I call thee P. from the east, west, south, and north, from the groves, woods, rivers, marshes, fairies white, red, black, &c.' and, after uttering certain short prayers, she returns home to the sick person, to see whether it be the distemper which they call esane, which they suppose inflicted by the fairies, and whispering in his ear another short prayer, with the Pater-noster, puts some burning coals into a cup of clear water, and forms a better judgment of the disorder than most physicians." *Britannia*, 1789, iii., 668.

Elf-Fire or the *ignis fatuus.*—"Wredeld vocatur Ignis qui ex attritu duorum

Lignorum elicitur, & quia superstitiosis varie usurpari dicitur." Ihre, "Glossar. Suio-Goth." 1769. Comp. *Will o' the Wisp.*

Elf-Locks.—A matted lock of hair in the neck. See the glossary to Kennet's "Parochial Antiquities," v. Lokys. "His haires are curl'd and full of elves-locks, and nitty for want of kembing." He is speaking of a "Ruffian, a swash buckler, and a braggart." Lodge's "Wits Miserie," 1596, p. 62. So Shakespear, in "Romeo and Juliet," 1597:

———"This is that very Mab,
That plats the manes of horses in the night,
And brakes the elf-locks in foul sluttish hairs,
Which once untangled, much misfortune bodes."

Warburton thought this superstition had its origin in the "Plica Polonica." Again, in "King Lear," Edgar says, "Elf all my hair in knots." Drayton, in his "Poems," 1637, says:

"O, that I were but a witch but for her sake!
Yfaith her Queenship little rest should take;
Id scratch that face, that may not feel the aire,
And knit whole ropes of witch-knots in her haire."

Mr. Halliwell, who cites the above passage in illustration of the word witch-knot, in his "Archaic Dictionary," 1847, adds, under Elf: "To Elf—To entangle in knots." In Holland's "Don Zara del Fogo, a mock romance," 1656, "My guts, quoth Soto, are contorted like a dragons tayle, in elf-knots, as if some tripe-wife had tack't them together for chitterlings."

Elf-Shot. — Fairies were sometimes thought to be mischievously inclined by shooting at cattle with arrows headed with flint-stones. These were often found, and called elf-shots. They were simply the stone arrow-heads used by the aboriginal Irish and by the early Scots. They are still occasionally found in different parts of the world, having been in universal use, before weapons were made of metal. It was thought that if the part of the animal affected by the elf-shot was rubbed with the arrow-head, and was then put into the water which it drank, there was no danger of fever or other ill-effect. Plot, speaking of elf-arrows, says: "These they find in Scotland in much greater plenty, especially in the præfectuary of Aberdeen, which, as the learned Sir Robert Sibbald informs us, they there called elf-arrows, lamiarum sagittas, imagining they drop from the clouds, not being to be found upon a dili-

gent search, but now and then by chance in the high beaten roads. The animal affected was, in order to a cure, to be touched with one of these, or made to drink the water in which one of them had been dipped." *Staffordshire,* p. 369. Allan Ramsay, in his "Poems," 1721, p. 224, explains elf-shot thus: "Bewitch'd, shot by fairies. Country people tell odd tales of this distemper amongst cows. When elf-shot, the cow falls down suddenly dead; no part of the skin is pierced, but often a little triangular flat stone is found near the beast, as they report, which is called the elf's arrow." In an authoritative Scotish publication of the 18th century, we are told that stone or flint arrow heads, called elf, or fairy-stones, used not uncommonly to be found in various districts, as at Lauder, at Wick (Caithness), and Fordice (co. Banff). About 1793, the minister of Wick reported: "Some small stones have been found which seem to be a species of flint, about an inch long and half an inch broad, of a triangular shape, and barbed on each side. The common people confidently assert that they are fairies' arrows, which they shoot at cattle, when they instantly fall down dead, though the hide of the animal remains quite entire. Some of these arrows have been found buried a foot under ground, and are supposed to have been in ancient times fixed in shafts, and shot from bows." Again: "Elves, by their arrows, destroyed, and not seldom unmercifully, cows and oxen." But now, it is added: "the elf has withdrawn his arrow." *Stat. Acc. of Scotland,* i., 78, x. 15; xxi., 148. The subsequent lines are found in Collins:

"There ev'ry herd by sad experience knows
How, wing'd with fate, their elf-shot arrows fly,
When the sick ewe her summer food foregoes,
Or stretch'd on earth the heart-smit heifers lie."

Odes, p. 10. The author of the "Whitby Glossary," quoted by Atkinson, tells us that, "to cure an awf- (or elf-) shotten animal it must be touched with one of the shots, and the water administered in which one of them has been dipped." Mr. Atkinson adds: "In one district of Jutland it is believed that cattle, when elf-shot, become stiff, and surely die, unless speedy help is at hand. The quickest and surest remedy consists in driving the beast up out of the moss, and firing a shot over it; only care must be taken to fire from the head in the direction of the tail." *Cleveland Glossary,* 1868, v. *Elf.* The naturalists of the dark ages owed many obligations to our fairies, for whatever they found wonderful and could not account for, they easily got rid of by charging to their account.

Eligius, St., Eloy, or Loy.— (December 1). This saint was Bishop of Noyon, and flourished in the sixth century. The late Mr. Robert Bell, in a note to Chaucer's "Freres Tale," observes: "The 'Book of Homilies,' in enumerating the different forms of invoking the Saints, gives as an example, 'to the horse, God and Saint Loy save thee.'" In Chaucer it is a carter is addressing his horse:

"'Hayt now,' quod he, 'ther Jhesu Crist yow blesse,
And al his hondwerk, bothe more and lesse !
That was wel twight, myn oughne lyard boy,
I pray God save thy body and Saint Loy.'"

Chaucer makes his Prioress swear by St. Eloy :

"Hire gretest othe was but by seint Eloy."

Lyndsay, in his "Monarke," 1554, says :
"Sum makis offrande to sanct Eloye,
That he thare hors may weill conuoye."

And again Woodes, in the *Conflict of Conscience*, 1581, says :
"Sent Loy saue your horse, Sent Anthony your swyne."

Taylor the Water-poet has an anecdote of a countryman who was saying his devotions before an old image of the saint, when it fell down, and hurt him severely. It is in "Wit and Mirth," 1629. In the "Booke in Meeter of Robin Conscience" (circa 1585), one of the interlocutors swears by St. Loy. We read in the account of Tottenham High Cross in "The Ambulator," 1790 : "In a brick field, on the west side of the great road, belonging to Mr. Charles Saunders, is St. Loy's Well, which is said to be always full, and never to run over : and in a field, opposite the Vicarage House, rises a spring called 'Bishop's Well,' of which the common people report many strange cures."

Eligius in his lifetime was moneyer to Dagobert I. and II., Kings of Paris, and became after death and canonization patron of the Goldsmiths and Farriers. See Hazlitt's supplement to his *Coins of Europe*, 1897, v. *Paris*, and Idem, *Remains of the Early Popular Poetry of England*, 1864-6, iii., 236.

Elizabeth's Day, St.—This was the 19th November, and had no original reference to English customs, but to the natal day of Elizabeth, daughter of Alexander, King of Hungary, who was canonized, and of whom there is a life in English. See Hazlitt's *Bibl. Coll.*, i., 285. The anniversary was subsequently adopted as a festival in honour of the accession of Elizabeth of England on the 17th of the month.

Elizabeth's, Queen, Accession.—(*St. Hugh's Day*, Nov. 17). From a variety of notices scattered in different publications, the anniversary of Queen Elizabeth's Accession appears to have been constantly observed even within the 18th century ; and in many of the almanacks was noted, certainly as late as 1684, and probably considerably later. In "The Pleasant Conceits of Old Hobson," 1607, inserted in "Old English Jest-Books," there is the following reference to St. Hugh's Day and its observances : "Vpon Saint Hewes day being the seventeenth of November, upon which day the tryumph was holden for Queene Elizabeths happy government, as bonefiers, ringing of bells, and such like ; but in the parish where Maister Hobson dwelled, he being Churchwarden, was no ringing at all, by reason the steeple was a-mending and the bells downe." It appears from the "Status Scholæ Etonensis," 1560, that the scholars at Eton elected their Boy on this day, as the members of the college were accustomed to do on the feast of St. Nicholas. The author of "A Protestant Memorial for the Seventeenth of November, being the Inauguration Day of Queen Elizabeth," 1713, mentions this as still in observance, and adds : "I say we have now a new motive to this zeal, the preservation of our most gracious queen Anne being to be added to the vindication of the most gracious queen Elizabeth."

Elmo's, St., Fire.—See *Castor and Pollux*. We hear of the phenomenon occurring to Helen of Troy and to Servius Tullius, when the future King of Rome was a boy in the household of Tarquinius Priscus. Donaldson's *Miscellanea Virgiliana*, 1825, pp. 176-7, where other examples or allusions are cited from Virgil and Horace.

Elvish-Marked.—Shakespear has the expression elvish-marked, on which Steevens observes: "The common people in Scotland (as I learn from Kelly's 'Proverbs') have still an aversion to those who have any natural defect or redundancy, as thinking them marked out for mischief." In Ady's *Candle in the Dark*, 1659, p. 120, we read : "There be also often found in women with childe, and in women that do nurse children with their breasts," and on other occasions, "certain spots, black and blue, as if they were pinched or beaten, which some common ignorant people call fairy-nips, which, notwithstanding do come from the causes aforesaid : and yet for these have many ignorant searchers given evidence against poor innocent people (that is, accused them of being witches)."

Embalming.—This was a very common practice in this country in Catholic times, and remains so abroad to this day. In one of the most interesting of our early romances, "The Squyr of Low Degre," there is a description of the manner in which the daughter of the King of Hungary buried and embalmed the body (as she supposed) of her lover the squire, but in reality that of the false steward :

"Into the chamber she dyd him bere ;
His bowels soone she dyd out drawe,
And buryed them in goddes lawe.
She sered that body with specery,
With wyrgin waxe and commendry ;
And closed hym in a maser tre,
And set on hym lockes thre.
She put him in a marble stone,
With quaynt gynnes many one,
And set hym at hir beddeshead,
And euery day she kyst that dead."

Hazlitt's *Popular Poetry*, ii., 49. Some embalmed remains were discovered at Bury St. Edmunds in 1772, which, on examination, were found to be in as perfectly sound a condition as an Egyptian mummy. Even the brain, the colour of the eyes and hair, the shape of the features, every thing, had remained through hundreds of years inaccessible to decomposing influences. *Antiq. Repertory*, 1808, iii., 331-2. The remains of Napoleon I., embalmed in 1821, were found to be in perfect state in 1840, when the tomb was opened preparatory to their removal to France. The Egyptians embalmed even their cats, and vast numbers of these mummies have been in modern times converted to common use.

Ember or **Imber Days.** — The "Festyvall," speaking of the Quatuor Tempora, or Ymbre Days, now called Ember Days, fol. 41, b., says they were so called, "bycause that our elder fathers wolde on these dayes ete no brede but cakes made under ashes." But in Tarlton's "Newes out of Purgatorie," 1590, the anonymous author perhaps semi-seriously ascribes the term to a different cause, "one pope," says he, "sat with a smocke about his necke, and that was he that made the imbering weekes, in honor of his faire and beautifull curtizan, Imbra."

Englewood, or **Inglewood, Cumberland.**—"At Hesket (in Cumberland) yearly on St. Barnabas's Day, by the highway-side, under a thorn tree, (according to the very ancient manner of holding assemblies in the open air), is kept the court for the whole Forest of Englewood"—the "Englyssh-wood" of the ballad of *Adam Bel*.

Ensham, Oxfordshire. — See *Whitsuntide*.

Ephialtes.—The ephialtes, or nightmare, is called by the common people witch-riding, and Wytche is the old English name for the complaint. This is, in fact an old Gothic or Scandinavian superstition. The term Ephialtes may be accounted scarcely correct, as it is merely the traditional name of one of the giants, who made war against the gods, and was slain by Apollo. Marca, whence our nightmare is derived, was in the Runic theology a spectre of the night, which seized men in their sleep, and suddenly deprived them of speech and motion. A great deal of curious learning upon the night-mare, or nacht-mare, as it is called in German, may be seen in Keysler and in Ihre. *Antiquitates Selectæ Septentrionales*, p. 497, *et seqq; Glossarium Suio-Gothicum*, ii., 135. According to Pliny's "Natural History," the antients believed that a nail drawn out of a sepulchre, and placed on the threshold of the bedchamber-door, would drive away phantoms and visions which terrified people in the night. The night-mare is, of course, now almost universally referred to its true origin, dyspepsia or indigestion, but even now it is easy to account for the prevalence of the superstition among a credulous and uneducated people, when the frightfully painful nature of the struggle during its continuance, and the astonishingly vivid phantoms conjured up before us, are considered. In Scot there is the following spell against this incubus :

"S. George, S. George, our Ladies Knight,
He walkt by day, so did he by night,
Until such time as he her found :
He her beat, and he her bound,
Until her troth she to him plight,
He would not come to her that night."

Dyce's *Beaumont and Fletcher*, vii., 388, *Note*.

"*Black Jesting Pawn.* So make him my white jennet, while I prance it. After the Black Knight's litter.

White Pawn. And you'd look then Just like the Devil striding o'er a nightmare,
Made of a miller's daughter."

A Game at Chesse, by Thomas Middleton, 1624 ("Works," 1840, vol. iv. p. 368). Comp. Halliwell v. *Night-Mare*.

There is an account of Johannes Cuntius of Pertsch, in Silesia, inserted in the "Antiquarian Repertory," from Henry More's Philosophical Writings. This person was suspected of having sold one of his sons, and of having made a contract with the Devil; he died suddenly under painful circumstances: and the narrative informs us (ii. 321), "He had not been dead a day or two, but several rumours were spread in the town, of a spiritus incubus or ephialtes, in the shape of Cuntius, that would have forced a woman. But this ephialtes seems to be different from our conception of the night-mare.

Epiphany.—See *Twelfth Day.*

Epping Forest Stag-Hunt.—The "Chelmsford Chronicle" of April 15, 1805, contained a notice to the following effect: "On Monday last Epping Forest was enlivened, according to ancient custom, with the celebrated stag hunt. The road from Whitechapel to the 'Bald-faced Stag,' on the Forest, was covered with Cockney sportsmen, chiefly dressed in the costume of the chace, viz. scarlet frock, black jockey cap, new boots, and buckskin breeches. By ten o'clock the assemblage of civic hunters, mounted on all sorts and shapes, could not fall short of 1,200. There were numberless Dianas also of the chace, from Rotherhithe, the Minories, &c., some in riding habits, mounted on titups, and others by the sides of their mothers, in gigs, tax-carts, and other vehicles appropriate to the sports of the field. The Saffron Walden stag-hounds made their joyful appearance about half after ten, but without any of the Mellishes or Bosanquets, who were more knowing sportsmen than to risque either themselves, or their horses, in so desperate a burst! The huntsman having capped their half-crowns, the horn blew just before twelve, as a signal for the old fat one-eyed stag (kept for the day) being enlarged from the cart. He made a bound of several yards, over the heads of some pedestrians, at first starting—when such a clatter commenced, as the days of Nimrod never knew. Some of the scarlet jackets were sprawling in the high road a few minutes after starting—so that a lamentable return of maimed! missing! thrown! and thrown-out! may naturally be supposed." In the *Standard* newspaper of April 24, 1870, occurs the subjoined paragraph: "Lieut. Colonel Palmer, the verderer of the Forest and judge of the Forest Courts, attended the King's Oak, High Beach, to receive any of the Royal Princes, the Lord Mayor and aldermen of London, and such of the citizens of London and others from the vicinity who might see fit to attend for the sake of exercising their ancient privilege of hunting a stag in Epping Forest on Easter Monday. The Hon. Frederick Petre lent his pack of stag hounds for the purpose, and a fine deer was turned out about three o'clock in the afternoon, in the presence of a very large

assemblage of sporting and peaceable holiday folks of all ranks, trades, and ages. The stag showed much sport, and after a run of 45 minutes was taken upon the border of Sir Thomas Fowell Buxton's Park, at Warlies. A strong body of the Metropolitan Police were upon the ground at the request of some of the parties who have made illegal inclosures of portions of the Forest, in the expectation that the fences would be thrown down; but nothing of the kind was attempted, or ever intended, as such encroachments as have been made in this forest, and which it may be necessary to throw out, will be removed in a strictly legal manner by the forest officers, when the freeholders of the County of Essex and her Majesty's ministers fulfil the engagements they recently entered into by the desire of the majority of the House of Commons, and which have received the sanction and cordial approbation of her Most Gracious Majesty the Queen." And it is also noticed in the journals for 1875. But in 1883, an announcement appeared that it was to be at last discontinued.

Erasmus, St.—There were two saints of this name. St. Eline, one of the martyrs of the fourth century, was also called St. Erasmus: his day is Nov. 25. The life of the bishop and martyr, whose day is June 2, was printed by Julian Notary in 1520. He was supposed to exercise a beneficial influence in certain diseases, especially the colic. There is a letter from Henry Lord Stafford to Cromwell, then Lord Privy Seal, about 1539, in which the writer speaks of the destruction of an image of St. Erasmus. He describes it as "an idoll, callid of ignorant persons Sainct Erasmus."

Eringo.—See a notice of its supposed aphrodysiac qualities in Nares *Glossary*, 1859, in v.

Erra Pater.—See a good account in Nares, *Glossary*, 1859, in v.

Errors, Vulgar or **Popular.**—The *Schola Salernitana* records some curious fallacies: that rue sprinkled in a house kills all the fleas; that, when the young swallows are blind, the mother, by applying the plant celendine, can make them see: that watercresses taken as a beverage, or as an ointment, are specifics against baldness and the itch; that willow-juice poured into the corn-ear will kill the blight; and that the rind of the tree boiled in vinegar will remove warts; and the present catalogue of absurdities might be enlarged with great ease. Vaughan informs us, "That the mole hath no eyes, nor the elephant knees, are two well known vulgar errors: both which notwithstanding, by daily and manifest experience are found to be untrue." *Brief Natural History*, p. 89, Comp. Hazlitt's *Proverbs*, 1882, p. 228, where deafness is falsely ascribed to the adder in a popular saying. There is a vulgar error that the hare is one year a male and the other a female. That a wolf if he see a man first, suddenly strikes him dumb. To the relators this Scaliger wishes as many blows as at different times he has seen wolves without losing his voice. That there is a nation of pigmies, not above two or three feet high, and that they solemnly set themselves in battle array to fight against the cranes. Strabo thought this a fiction; but in our age geographical research has made us acquainted with nations of warlike dwarfs. A writer in the "Gentleman's Magazine" for June, 1771, refutes the following errors: asserting "that the Scorpion does not sting itself when surrounded by fire, and that its sting is not even venomous." "That the tarantula is not poisonous, and that music has no particular effects on persons bitten by it, more than on those stung by a wasp." "That the lizard is not friendly to man in particular, much less does it awaken him on the approach of a serpent." "That the stroke of the cramp fish is not occasioned by a muscle." "That the bite of the spider is not venomous, that it is found in Ireland too plentifully, that it has no dislike to fixing its web on Irish oak, and that it has no antipathy to the toad." "That the porcupine does not shoot out its quills for annoying his enemy; he only sheds them annually, as other feathered animals do." "That the jackall, commonly called the lion's provider, has no connection at all with the lion," &c. Barrington says, it is supposed to be penal to open a coal mine, or to kill a crow, within five miles of London: as also to shoot with a wind-gun: as to the wind-gun, he takes that to arise from a statute of Henry VII. prohibiting the use of a cross-bow without a licence; but this, I apprehend, refers to statute 6 Hen. VIII. It is also a vulgar error to suppose that there is a statute which obliges the owners of asses to crop their ears, lest the length of them should frighten the horses which they meet on the road.

In the "Gentleman's Magazine" for September, 1734, we have the following from Bayle: "There is nothing strange in errors becoming universal, considering how little men consult their reason. What multitudes believe, one after another, that a man weighs more fasting than full; that a sheepskin drum bursts at the beat of a wolfskin drum; that young vipers destroy the old females when they come to the birth, (of which

Scaliger from his own experience asserted the falsehood) and strike the male dead at the instant of their conception, with many other truths of equal validity?" To these vulgar errors, adds Barrington, *Observations on the Statutes*, p. 474, may be added perhaps the notion, that a woman's marrying a man under the gallows, will save him from the execution. This probably arose from a wife having brought an appeal against the murderer of her husband; who afterwards, repenting the prosecution of her lover, not only forgave the offence, but was willing to marry the appellee. In the case of Margaret Clark, executed for firing her master's house in Southwark, 1680, it is said, at her execution, "there was a fellow who designed to marry her under the gallows (according to the antient laudable custome) but she being in hopes of a reprieve, seemed unwilling, but when the rope was about her neck, she cryed she was willing, and then the fellow's friends dissuaded him from marrying her; and so she lost her husband and her life together." But among some savage tribes a woman may save a person of the other sex, who has been taken prisoner, from a cruel death by demanding him in marriage. Captain Marryat has introduced this incident into one of his novels.

I may likewise add to these that any one may be put into the Crown office for no cause whatsoever, or the most trifling injury. It is a legal fiction rather than an error to describe those born or drowned at sea as parishioners of Stepney. Other vulgar errors are, that the old statutes have prohibited the planting of vineyards or the use of sawing mills, relating to which I cannot find any statute: they are however established in Scotland, to the very great advantage both of the proprietor and the country. One of Mr. Brand's correspondents sent him a notice of two other vulgar errors, viz.: When a man designs to marry a woman who is in debt, if he take her from the hands of the priest, clothed only in her shift, it is supposed that he will not be liable to her engagements. The second is that there was no land tax before the reign of William the Third. Barrington supposes that an exemption granted to surgeons from serving on juries is the foundation of the vulgar error that a surgeon or butcher (from the barbarity of their business) may be challenged as jurors. *Observations on the Statutes*, 475. This is still a prevailing notion; and it may perhaps hardly be out of place to add that it is no vulgar error, but a matter of established and recognised usage, that no butcher, attorney, or (I think) brewer shall be placed on the commission of the peace.

The Lord Chancellor sends a notice to this effect to any new borough, which has to forward for his approval the list of candidates.

Ethelberg, St., or Alburg's Day.—(October 11). Fosbrooke mentions, amidst the annual store of provision at Barking Nunnery, "wheat and milk for Frimitè upon St. Alburg's Day."

Ethelreda, St., otherwise *St. Audrey*, or *Auldrey*, whence it is alleged that we get the word tawdry, because at the Saint's Fair held at various places, Ely included, on the 17th October, a great deal of cheap finery was offered for sale. This holy lady is said to have died from a swelling in her throat occasioned by the divine anger at her vanity, when young, in wearing fine necklaces; but the story also goes, that she was on religious grounds peculiarly abstemious in her use of water for washing purposes.

Eton School. — At Eton College, in place of a boy-bishop and his crozier, they introduced a captain and an ensign, replacing the religious by a sort of military element, and the chieftain of the band conducted his followers to a scene of action in the open air, where no consecrated walls were in danger of being profaned, and where the gay striplings could at least exhibit their wonted pleasantries with more propriety of character. The exacting of money from the spectators and passengers, for the use of the principal, remained much the same, but, it seems, no evidence has been transmitted whether the deacons then, as the salt-bearers did afterwards, made an offer of a little salt in return when they demanded the annual subsidy. I have been so fortunate, however, as to discover, in some degree, a similar use of salt, that is, an emblematical one; among the scholars of a foreign university, at the well-known ceremony of Deposition, in a publication dated at Strasburg in Alsace, so late as A.D. 1666. The consideration of every other emblem used on the above occasion, and explained in that work, being foreign to my purpose, I shall confine myself to that of the salt alone, which one of the heads of the college explains thus to the young academicians: "With regard to the ceremony of salt," says the writer of the account of the Strasburg "Depositio," "the sentiments and opinions both of divines and philosophers concur in making salt the emblem of wisdom or learning; and that, not only on account of what it is composed of, but also with respect to the several uses to which it is applied. As to its component parts, as it consists of the purest matter, so ought

wisdom to be pure, sound, immaculate, and incorruptible: and similar to the effects which salt produces upon bodies, ought to be those of wisdom and learning upon the mind." There are twenty plates illustrating the several stages of ·the Depositio. The last represents the giving of the salt, which a person is holding on a plate in his left hand, and with his right hand about to put a pinch of it upon the tongue of each Beanus or Freshman. A glass holding wine (I suppose), is standing near him. Underneath is the following couplet, which is much to our purpose; for even the use of wine was not altogether unknown in our Montem procession at Eton:

"Sal Sophiæ gustate, bibatis vinaque læta,
Augeat immensus vos in utrisque Deus!"

In another part of the oration he tells them, "This rite of salt is a pledge or earnest which you give that you will most strenuously apply yourselves to the study of good arts, and as earnestly devote yourselves to the several duties of your vocation." How obvious is it then to make the same application of the use of salt in the old ceremony at Eton! Here, too, is said to have been formerly one of the pleasantries of the salt-bearers to fill any boorish looking countryman's mouth with it, if, after he has given them a trifle, he asked for anything in return, to the no small entertainment of the spectators.

I should conjecture that Salt Hill was the central place where anciently all the festivities used on this occasion were annually displayed, and here only, it should seem, the salt was originally distributed, from which circumstance it has undoubtedly had its name. See the "Status Scholæ Etonensis," 1560, Mense Januarii. I have heard it asserted, but find no foundation of the fact, that in the papal times there was an exclusive grant to Eton College, from the Pope, to sell consecrated salt for making holy water. In a letter from John Byrom to John Aubrey, 1693, the writer informs his correspondent that he had heard of the college holding certain lands by the custom of salting. He thought that the practice was to be traced to the Scriptural quotation: "Ye are the salt of the earth," and to the idea of purification. Aubrey's Letters, &c., 1813, ii., 168. The custom of having a procession of the scholars can be clearly proved as far back as the reign of Elizabeth, who, when she visited this College, desired to see an account of all the antient ceremonies observed there from its foundation to that period, in the number of which it appears that an annual procession of the scholars was one, and that at such times verses were repeated, and sums of money were gathered from the public for a dinner, &c. to which fund was added the small pittances extorted from the boys who were recently admitted, by those of a longer standing." Mr. Cambridge, an old Etonian, informed Mr. Brand, August 9th, 1794, that, in his time, the salt-bearers and scouts carried, each of them, salt in a handkerchief, and made every person take a pinch out of it before they gave their contributions.

In Huggett's MSS. Collections for the History of Windsor and Eton College is the following account of "Ad Montem": "The present manner is widely different from the simplicity of its first institution. Now the Sales Epigrammatum are changed into the Sal purum; and it is a play-day without exercise. Here is a procession of the school quite in the military way. The scholars of the superior classes dress in the proper regimentals of captain, lieutenant, &c., which they borrow or hire from London on the occasion. The procession is likewise in the military order, with drums, trumpets, &c. They then march three times round the school-yard, and from thence to Salt Hill, on which one of the scholars, dress'd in black and with a band, as chaplain, reads certain prayers: after which a dinner dressed in the College kitchen is provided by the captain for his guests at the inn there; the rest getting a dinner for themselves at the other houses for entertainment. But long before the procession begins, two of the scholars called salt-bearers, dressed in white, with a handkerchief of salt in their hands, and attended each with some sturdy young fellow hired for the occasion, go round the College, and through the town, and from thence up into the high road, and offering salt to all, but scarce leaving it to their choice whether they will give or not: for money they will have, if possible, and that even from servants. The fifth and sixth forms dine with the captain. The noblemen usually do, and many other scholars whose friends are willing to be at the expence. The price of the dinner to each is 10s. 6d. and 2s. 6d. more for salt-money. Every scholar gives a shilling for salt, the noblemen more. At this time also they gather the recent money, which is . . . . from every scholar that has been entered within the year. Dinner being over, they march back in the order as before into the school yard, and with the third round the ceremony is concluded. The motto on the ensign

colours is, "Pro More et Monte." Every scholar, who is no officer, marches with a long pole, focii or two and two. At the same time and place the head-master of the school makes a dinner at his own expence for his acquaintance, assistants, &c. Of late years the captain has cleared, after all expences are paid, upwards of £100. The Montem day used to be fixed for the first Tuesday in Hilary Term, which begins January 23rd. In the year 1759, the day was altered to Tuesday in the Whitsun week (which was then June 5th); the Whitsun holidays having a few years before been altered from five weeks holiday at election. This procession to Montem is every third year, and sometimes oftener." In one of the "Public Advertisers," in 1778, is the oldest printed account of the ceremony I have been able to find. It was then biennial: On Tuesday, being Whit Tuesday, the gentlemen of Eton School went, as usual, in military procession to Salt Hill. This custom of walking to the Hill returns every second year, and generally collects together a great deal of company of all ranks. The King and Queen, in their phæton, met the procession at Arbor-hill, in Slough-road. When they halted, the flag was flourished by the ensign. The boys went, according to custom, round the mill, &c. The parson and clark were then called, and there these temporary ecclesiasticks went through the usual Latin service, which was not interrupted, though delayed for some time by the laughter that was excited by the antiquated appearance of the clerk, who had dressed himself according to the ton of 1745, and acted his part with as minute a consistency as he had dressed the character. The procession began at half-past twelve from Eton. The collection was an extraordinary good one, as their Majesties gave, each of them, fifty guineas." Warton has preserved the form of the acquittance given by a Boy-bishop to the receiver of his subsidy, then amounting to the considerable sum of £3 15s. 1d. ob. The sum collected at the Montem on Whit-Tuesday, 1790, was full £500. This sum went to the captain, who was the senior of the collegers at the time of the ceremony. The motto for that year was "Pro More et Monte." Their majesties presented each a purse of fifty guineas. The fancy dresses of the salt bearers and their deputies, who were called scouts, were usually of different coloured silks, and very expensive. Formerly the dresses used in this procession were obtained from the theatres. In the "Gentleman's Magazine" for June, 1793, is the following account of the Montem procession for that year:—"On Whit-

Tuesday, according to triennial custom, the procession of the young gentlemen educated at Eton-School to Salt Hill took place. About eleven, the gentlemen assembled in the school-yard, and were soon after properly arranged in the procession, according to their rank in the school. Their Majesties, with the Prince of Wales, Princesses Royal, Augusta, Elizabeth, and Amelia, the Duchess of York, and Prince William of Gloucester, arrived at the College about twelve, and took their station in the stable-yard. The young gentlemen marched twice round the school yard, and then went, in true military parade, with music playing, drums beating, and colours flying, into the stable yard, where they passed the royal family, the ensign having first flourished the flag, by way of salute to their Majesties. The procession then moved on, through the playing fields, to Salt Hill, where they were again received by the royal family; when, after again marching by, and saluting them, the young gentlemen paraded to dinner. To the honour of Eton, the number of gentlemen who marched in the procession amounted to 500. The collection for the benefit of the captain far exceeded all former ones; the sum spoken of amounts to near £1,000. The motto on the flag, and on the tickets distributed on the occasion, was "Mos pro Lege." Their Majesties, the Prince of Wales, Princesses and Duchess of York, made their donations to the salt-bearers. In the evening the gentlemen returned, in proper military uniform, to Eton; and afterwards the salt-bearers and scouts appeared on the terrace in their dresses, and were particularly noticed by their Majesties."

> "When boys at Eton, once a year
> In military pomp appear;
> He who just trembled at the rod,
> Treads it a hero, talks a god,
> And in an instant can create
> A dozen officers of state.
> His little legion all assail,
> Arrest without release or bail;
> Each passing traveller must halt,
> Must pay the tax, and eat the salt.
> You don't love salt, you say; and storm—
> Look o' these staves, sir—and conform."

—*The Tunbridge Miscellany,* 1712. A long article on the Montem at Eton will be found in "Notes and Queries" for November 9, 1867. The custom was abolished in 1876. It appears from the "Status Scholæ Etonensis," 1560, that the Eton Scholars used to act plays in the Christmas holidays. St. Nicholas Day continued in Mr. Brand's time to be a gaudy-day in Eton College; and

though the Montem was then generally kept on Whit Tuesday, yet it is certain that it was formerly kept in the winter time, a little before the Christmas holidays, as a person of high rank, who had been a scholar there, told Brand; or, as others informed him, in February. Dr. Davies, one of the provosts, remembered when they used to cut a passage through the snow from Eton to the hill called Salt Hill, upon which, after the procession had arrived there, the chaplain with his clerk used to read prayers; upon the conclusion of which it was customary for the chaplain to kick his clerk down the hill. It is said that the first time Queen Charlotte was present at this ceremony, she thought this sort of sport so very irreligious, and expressed her royal dissatisfaction at it so much, that the kicking part of the service was very properly laid aside. It is observable that in Latin verses in the "Musæ Etonenses," 1755, pp. 62 and 113, to both of which "Pro More et Monte" is the motto, the season is described to be winter.

It is also a practice at Eton School which, unlike the Montem, is still kept up, to present each new head master by the hand of the captain, upon his entry into office, that is, at the first eleven o'clock school, over which he presides, with a birch tied up with blue ribbons. On this occasion the captain makes a short address, and the master is expected to reply, deprecating the necessity of chastisement, and hoping the present state of mutual confidence may remain unaltered. The Barring-out ceremony, already described at length under *Bromfield*, was long used here. The boys used on the day of the Circumcision, in former times, to play for little New Year's gifts before and after supper: and they had a custom that day, for good luck's sake, of making verses, and sending them to the Provost, Masters, &c., as also of presenting them to each other. "Status Scholæ Etonensis," A.D. 1560, MS. Brit. Mus. Donat. 4843, fol. 423. It was the custom on Shrove Monday for the scholars to write verses either in praise or dispraise of Father Bacchus: poets being considered as immediately under his protection. He was therefore sung on this occasion in all kinds of metres, and the verses of the boys of the seventh and sixth and some of the fifth forms, were affixed to the inner doors of the College. Verses are still written and put up on this day; but I believe the young poets are no longer confined to the subject of writing eulogiums on the god of wine. It still however retains the name of the *Bacchus.* "Status Scholæ Etonensis," fol. 423. On Shrove Tuesday the boys were allowed to play from eight o'clock for the whole day; and mention occurs in the work so often cited of the cook coming and fastening a pancake to a crow, which the young crows are calling upon, near it, at the school-door. The crows generally have hatched their young at this season.

In 1560, on Ash Wednesday, it was the custom of the scholars to choose themselves confessors out of the masters or chaplains, to whom they were to confess their sins. *Status Scholæ Etonensis*, fol. 425. It is stated that, on the day of St. Philip and St. James, if it be fair weather, and the Master grants leave, those boys who choose it may rise at four o'clock to gather May branches, if they can do it without wetting their feet: and that on that day they adorn the windows of the bed-chamber with green leaves, and the houses are perfumed with fragrant herbs. The boys of the School had anciently their bonfires on the east side of the Church, on St. Peter's Day, and at midsummer on St. John's Day. After morning prayers, also, they used to sing three antiphones in the church, and their beds they decorated with prints and verses descriptive of events in the life of the saint and his predecessors. *Status Scholæ Etonensis*, 1560. It seems from the same authority that in September, "on a certain day," most probably the fourteenth, the boys were to have a play-day, in order to go out and gather nuts, with a portion of which, when they returned, they were to make presents to the different masters. It is ordered, however, that before this leave be granted them, they should write verses on the fruitfulness of autumn, the deadly colds, &c., of advancing winter. There is on St. David's Day (March 1) an annual procession of boats. This year (1903) the day falling on a Sunday, the ceremony was observed on the 28th February. There were nine 8-oars and one 10-oars, and each had its own colours.

"It was an ancient custom," says Huggett, "for the butcher of the College to give on the election Saturday a ram to be hunted by the scholars; but by reason (as I have heard) of the ram crossing the Thames, and running through Windsor market-place with the scholars after it, where some mischief was done, as also by long courses in that hot season, the health of some of the scholars being thereby thought endangered, about thirty years ago the ram was ham-strung, and, after the speech, was with clubs knocked on the head in the stable-yard. But, this carrying a show of barbarity in it, the custom was entirely left off in the election of 1747; but the ram, as usual, is served

up in pasties at the high table. "Browne Willis would derive this custom from what is (or was) used in the manor of East Wrotham, Norfolk (the rectory and, I believe, the manor of which belongs to this College) where the lord of the manor after the harvest gave half an acre of barley and a ram to the tenants thereof. The which ram, if they caught it, was their own, if not, it was for the lord again." Hazlitt's *Blount*, 1874, p. 382. In the "Gentleman's Magazine" for August, 1731, is the following: "Monday, August 2, was the election at Eton College, when the scholars, according to custom, hunted a ram, by which the Provost and Fellows hold a manor." Even in Beckwith's time, however, this usage had been given up. Edit. of *Blount*, 1815, p. 495; Carlisle's *Endowed Grammar Schools*, 1818.

Even or Odd? i.q., *Odd or Even?* a game of chance mentioned in the dedication by the anonymous writer to Mr. William Lilly, of "Pantagruel's Prognostication," about 1645. He classed it with Handy-dandy. It was played by the boys in ancient Greece.

Evil Eye.—The following passage is cited from one of Bacon's works. It seems some have been so curious as to note that the times when the stroke, or percussion of an envious eye does most hurt, are particularly when the party envied is beheld in glory and triumph." *Minor Morals*, i., 124. Lupton says: "The eyes be not only instruments of enchantment, but also the voice and evil tongues of certain persons; for there are found in Africk, as Gellius saith, families of men, that, if they chance exceedingly to praise fair trees, pure seeds, goodly children, excellent horses, fair and well-liking cattle, soon after they will wither and pine away, and so dye. No cause or hurt known of their withering or death. Thereupon the custome came, that, when any do praise any thing, that we should say, God blesse it or keepe it. Arist. in Prob. by the report of Mizaldus." *Notable Things*, ed. 1660, p. 201. In the 18th century, if not now, the evil eye was an article of general faith in Scotland. In 1795, however, the minister of Monzie, co. Perth, reported: "The power of an evil eye is still believed, although the faith of the people in witchcraft is much enfeebled." It appears that the people of Stirlingshire then still clang to some of their old prejudices. A writer says: "The dregs of superstition are still to be found. The less informed suspect something like witchcraft about poor old women, and are afraid of their evil eye among the cattle. If a cow is suddenly taken ill, it is ascribed to some extraordinary cause. If a person when called to see one does not say 'I wish her luck,' there would be a suspicion he had some bad design." *Stat. Acc. of Scotland*, xiv., 526. Pinkerton acquaints us that "Cattle are subject to be injured by what is called an evil eye, for some persons are supposed to have naturally a blasting power in their eyes with which they injure whatever offends, or is hopelessly desired by them. Witches and warlocks are also much disposed to wreak their malignity on cattle." *Heron's Journey*, ii., 223. Martin says: — "All these (Western) Islanders, and several thousands of the neighbouring Continent, are of opinion that some particular persons have an evil eye, which affects children and cattle. This, they say, occasions frequent mischances, and sometimes death." *Description of the Western Islands of Scotland.* p. 123. The same author, speaking in the last century of the Isle of Harris, says: "There is a variety of nuts, called molluska beans, some of which are used as amulets against witchcraft or an evil eye, particularly the white one : and upon this account they are wore about children's necks, and if any evil is intended to them. they say the nut changes into a black colour. That they did change colour I found true by my own observation. but cannot be positive as to the cause of it. Malcolm Campbell, steward of Harris, told me that some weeks before my arrival there, all his cows gave blood instead of milk for several days together : one of the neighbours told his wife that this must be witchcraft, and it would be easy to remove it, if she would but take the white nut, called the Virgin Mary's nut, and lay it in the pail into which she was to milk the cows. This advice she presently followed, and having milked one cow into the pail with the nut in it, the milk was all blood, and the nut changed its colour into dark brown. She used the nut again, and all the cows gave pure good milk, which they ascribe to the virtue of the nut. This very nut Mr. Campbell presented me with, and I still keep it by me." In going once to visit the remains of Brinkburne Abbey in Northumberland, Brand himself found a reputed witch in a lonely cottage by the side of a wood, where the parish had placed her to save expenses, and keep her out of the way. On enquiry at a neighbouring farm house, he was told, though he was a long while before he could elicit anything from the inhabitants in it concerning her, that every body was afraid of her cat, and that she herself was thought to have an evil eye, and that it was accounted dangerous to meet her in a morning "black-fasting." Volney, in his "Travels in Egypt and Syria," vol. i. p. 246, says : "The ignorant mothers of many of the modern Egyptians, whose hollow eyes, pale faces, swoln bellies, and meagre extremities make them seem as if they had not long to live, believe this to be the effect of the evil eye of some envious person, who has bewitched them ; and this ancient prejudice is still general in Turkey." "Nothing," says Mr. Dallaway, in his "Account of Constantinople," 1797, p. 391, "can exceed the superstition of the Turks respecting the evil eye of an enemy or infidel. Passages from the Koran are painted on the outside of the houses, globes of glass are suspended from the ceilings, and a part of the superfluous caparison of their horses is designed to attract attention, and divert a sinister influence." That this superstition was known to the Romans we have the authority of Virgil :

"Nescio quis teneros oculus mihi fascinat agnos."

Ecl. iii. Comp. *Spitting.*

Evil May Day.—What is known as Evil May-day was an insurrection of the apprentices of London in 1517. It is described sufficiently at large in the chronicles. Johnson, in his "Crowne-Garland of Goulden Roses," 1659, has the "Story of Ill May-day in the time of King Henry VIII., and why it was so called, and how Queen Katherine begged the lives of two thousand London 'prentices. To the tune of ' Essex's Last Good night.' " But the Queen does not seem to have been present on the occasion, and it was Wolsey, who interceded, not for 2,000, but for 400, apprentices brought before the King barefoot, with halters round their necks. A sedition of a very similar character occurred in 1586, and is referred to in a letter from Fleetwood, Recorder of London, to the Lord Treasurer Burleigh. But in one from the Venetian Resident in London, Sebastian Giustinian, to his Government, dated from Westminster, Sept. 26, 1517, it appears that a second conspiracy had been arranged for Michaelmas Eve, to murder all strangers, and sack their houses, while the King and Wolsey were out of town. Three of the ringleaders were arrested, and 3,000 householders and public functionaries were under arms for the protection of life and property. Nothing farther seems to have occurred.—*Four Years at the Court of Henry VIII.*, edited by R. Brown, ii., 130. These movements indicate the growth of the foreign or alien element in the commercial life of London.

Exequies.—See *Funeral Customs.*

Exhibition.—A term now limited to academical instruction and to men studying at the Universities. But it was formerly understood of fees payable for the education of children at home or otherwise. In a letter, 26th November, 1501, to Sir Robert Plumpton, the writer states in reference to a payment made by her: "What parte, or how much thereof, my sayd nevue, Germayne, hath sent to your mastership, I am ignorant, saving that he shewed me that he sendeth you but xli. towards the exhibicions of my nese, his wyfe." The latter, though described as married, was probably betrothed only, and resident under the paternal roof. *Plumpton Correspondence*, 1839, p. 163.

Exorcism. — The following spell is from Herrick:

"Holy Water come and bring;
Cast in salt, for seasoning;
Set the brush for sprinkling:

Sacred spittle bring ye hither;
Meale and it now mix together;
And a little oyle to either:

Give the tapers here their light;
Ring the saints-bell to affright
Far from hence the evill sprite."

Adamson, in his "Muses' Threnodie," 1638, (repr. 1774, p. 213) observes: "Many are the instances, even to this day, of charms practised among the vulgar, especially in the Highlands, attended with forms of prayer. In the Miscellaneous MS., written by Baillie Dundee, among several medicinal receipts, I find an exorcism against all kinds of worms in the body, in the name of the Father, Son, and Holy Ghost, to be repeated three mornings, as a certain remedy. The poor women who were prosecuted for witchcraft, administered herbs and exorcized their patients." Upon the subject of exorcising, the following books may be consulted with advantage: "Fustis Dæmonum, cui adjicitur Flagellum Dæmonum," 1608, (a prohibited book among the Roman Catholics); and Polidorus "Practica Exorcistarum ad Dæmones expellendum," 1606. From this last Bourne's form has been taken. Comp. *Charms and Sorcery*.

Eye. — In the third idyll of Theocritus, paraphrased by Thomas Bradshawe under the title of the "Shepherd's Starre," 1591, Corydon says: "But my right eye watreth, 'tis a signe of somewhat, do I see her yet?" In Creech's later version the same passage runs:

"My right eye itches, and shall I see
My love?"

The watering or itching was sometimes treated as a lucky omen, sometimes the reverse. Compare *Ear Omens*.

Eye, Black's your. — There is a vulgar saying in the North, and probably in many other parts of England, "No one can say black is your eye." In Wanley's "Vox Dei," 1658, p. 85, the author, speaking of St. Paul having said that he was teaching the righteousness which is in the law blameless, observes upon it, "No man could say (as the proverb hath it) black was his eye"; meaning that nobody can justly speak ill of you. In his "Discovery," 1584, says Reginald Scot: "Many writers agree with Virgil and Theocritus in the effect of bewitching eyes, affirming that in Scythia there are women called Bithiæ, having two balls, or rather blacks, in the apples of their eyes. These, forsooth, with their angry looks do bewitch and hurt, not only young lambs, but young children." The phrase occurs, however, in Parrot's "Mastive or Young Whelpe of the old Dog," 1615. One of the epigrams is as follows:

"Doll, in disdaine, doth from her
heeles defie:
The best that breathes shall tell her
black's her eye:
And that it's true she speaks, who can
say nay?
When none that lookes on't but will
sweare 'tis gray."

Fabulous Creatures of the Middle Ages. — In the *Archæological Album*, 1845, pp. 174-86, will be found a valuable description of many of these fanciful objects of dread to our ancestors, some doubtless realities under written descriptions or pictorial forms, which do not enable us to identify them. Such was the attercop, a poisonous spider, perhaps a sort of tarantula, concerning which is an anecdote of the fourteenth century, connected with Shrewsbury and the magical properties of St. Winifred's Well, and which collaterally illustrates the evolution from reptiles into birds, as the accompanying cut from a Saxon herbal may shew; the white bird, called *caladrius*,

ATTERCOP.

which haunted the halls of kings and princes, and if any sick person was going to die, averted its head from him, but if he was about to recover, looked him in the face; the *serra* or *serre*, with the head of a lion and the tail of a fish, with wings, which could stay a ship, so long as it could remain in the air; and the mediæval syren, which followed the type of the ancient myth. Some of these early superstitions have been extinguished by the progress of scientific knowledge, even the belief in the disastrous consequences attendant on the slaughter of the albatross, which forms the plot of Coleridge's crude *Rime of the Ancient Mariner.* Comp. *Remora* and *Unicorn.*

Face - Cloth. — The face - cloth is of great antiquity. Strutt tells us that "after the closing of the eyes, &c., a linen cloth was put over the face of the deceased. Thus we are told that Henry the Fourth, in his last illness, seeming to be dead, his Chamberlain covered his face with a linen cloth." Stafford says: "I am so great an enemie to ceremonies, as that I would onelie wish to have that one ceremonie at my buriall, which I had at my birth; I mean, swadling: and yet I am indifferent for that too."

Facer. — Allan Ramsay mentions a set of drinkers called Facers, who, he says, "were a club of fair drinkers who inclined rather to spend a shilling on ale than twopence for meat. They had their name from a rule they observed of obliging themselves to throw all they left in the cup in their own faces: Wherefore, to save their face and their cloaths, they prudently sucked the liquor clean out."

Fain Play.—See *St. Nicholas's Day* and *Touch.*

Fairies.—In the "British Apollo," 1708, No. I. supernumerary for April, we are told : "The opinion of fairies has been asserted by Pliny and several historians, and Aristotle himself gave some countenance to it, whose words are these : Εστι δε ὁ τοπος &c., i.e. Hic Locus est quem incolunt Pygmei, non est Fabula, sed pusillum Genus ut aiunt: wherein Aristotle plays the sophist. For though by 'non est Fabula' he seems at first to confirm it, yet coming in at last with his 'ut aiunt,' he shakes the belief he had before put upon it. Our Society, therefore, are of opinion, that Homer was the first author of this conceit, who often used similies, as well to delight the ear as to illustrate his matter: and in his third Iliad compares the Trojane to manes, when they descend against fairies. So that, that which was only a pleasant fiction in the fountain, became a solemn story in the stream, and current still among us." Bishop Percy tells us that, on the assurance of a learned friend in Wales, the existence of fairies is alluded to by the most ancient British bards, among whom their commonest name was that of the spirits of the mountains. *Reliques*, iii., 207. "It will afford entertainment," says he, "to a contemplative mind to trace these whimsical opinions up to their origin. Whoever con-

siders how early, how extensively, and how uniformly they have prevailed in these nations, will not readily assent to the hypothesis of those who fetch them from the East so late as the time of the Croisades. Whereas it is well known that our Saxon ancestors, long before they left their German forests, believed the existence of a kind of diminutive Demons, or middle species between men and spirits, whom they called Duergar or dwarfs, and to whom they attributed many wonderful performances far exceeding human art." "I made strict inquiries" (Brand says) "after the fairies in the uncultivated wilds of Northumberland, but even there I could only meet with a man who said that he had seen one that had seen fairies. Truth is hard to come at in most cases. None, I believe, ever came nearer to it in this than I have done." Chaucer is very facetious concerning them in his "Canterbury Tales," where he puts his creed of fairy mythology into the mouth of the Wife of Bath :

"In olde dayes of the kyng Arthour
Of which that Britouns speken gret
    honour,
All was this lond fulfilled of fayrie;
The elf-queen with hir joly compaignie,
Daunced ful oft in many a grene mede,
This was the old oppynyoun as I rede.
I speke of many hundrid yeres ago,
But now can no man see noon elves mo.
For now the grete charite and prayeres
Of lymytours and other holy freres,
That sechen every lond and every
    streme,
As thick as motis in the sonne-beme.

*   *   *   *   *   *   *

That makith that ther ben no fayeries
For ther as wont was to walken an elf,
Ther walkith noon but the lymytour
    himself,
As he goth in his lymytatioun,
Wommen may now go safely up and
    doun,
In every bussch, and under every tre,

There is none other incubus but he," &c. The genius of Shakespear converting whatever it handled into gold, has been singularly happy in its display of the fairy mythology. I know not whether anything can be imagined to go beyond the flights of his imagination on the subject; and it seems to realize all that has been fabled of magic, when he exerts his creative fancy in giving to

    "These airy nothings,
    A local habitation and a name."

That accomplished antiquary, the Rev. Joseph Hunter, long since drew attention to the work of Leo Allatius on certain Greek superstitions of modern times, printed in 1645, as illustrating the fairy mythology of *A Midsummer Night's Dream*, and he remarks that at that date at all events the Greeks were as familiar as ourselves with all these legends and fancies, and that Robin Goodfellow or Puck was invested with the same attributes as he is held to possess here. *New Illustrations of Shakespear*, 1845, i., 286. An amusing scene is introduced into the "Merry Wives of Windsor," 1602, where Falstaff is pinched black and blue by the pretended fairies, Mistress Quickly and her confederates. Selden observes that there was never a merry world since the fairies left dancing and the parson left conjuring. The opinion of the latter kept thieves in awe, and did as much good in a country as a Justice of Peace. In the superstitions and customs concerning children, I have before noticed their practice of stealing unbaptized infants and leaving their own progeny in their stead. Puttenham mentions this as an opinion of the nurses. *Arte of English Poesie*, 1589, p. 144. It is also noticed in the "Irish Hudibras," 1689 : —

"Drink dairies dry, and stroke the Cattle :
Steal sucklings, and through key-holes fling,
Topeing and dancing in a ring."

—P. 122. It was an article in the popular creed concerning fairies, that they were a kind of intermediate beings, partaking of the nature both of men and spirits : that they had material bodies and yet the power of making themselves invisible and of passing them through any sort of enclosures. They were thought to be remarkably small in stature, with fair complexions, from which last circumstance they have derived their English name. The habits of both sexes of fairies are represented to have been generally green. With all the passions and wants of human beings, they are represented as great lovers and patrons of cleanliness and propriety, for the observance of which they were said frequently to reward good servants by dropping money into their shoes in the night ; and on the other hand they were reported to punish most severely the sluts and slovens by pinching them black and blue. This tradition is illustrated by "Robin Good-Fellow, his Mad Prankes and Merry Jests," 1628, where the tricks of the fairies are related. But Jonson, in his song, "The Pranks of Puck," has deviated from the old prose narrative, which, though not now known in any impression earlier than in 1628, was clearly in existence before Jonson began to write, and also from the metrical tale founded on it, entitled "The Merry

Puck." Jonson attributes to Robin, on what appears to be insufficient authority what the "Mad Prankes" and the poem give to the fairies Pinch and Pach. Hazlitt's *Fairy Tales*, &c., 1875. Thus Lluellin :

— "We nere pity girles, that doe
 Find no treasure in their shoe,
But are nip't by the tyrannous fairy.
 List the noice of the chaires,
 Wakes the wench to her pray'rs
Queen Mab comes worse than a witch in,
 Back and sides she entailes
 To the print of her nailes,
She'l teach her to snort in the kitchin."

And in Browne's "Pastorals," 1614 :

 "Where oft the Fairy Queen
At twy-light sate and did command her Elues
To pinch those maids that had not swept their shelues :
And further, if by maidens ouer-sight
Within doores water were not brought at night :
Or if they spread no table, set no bread,
They shall haue nips from toe vnto the head :
And for the maid that had perform'd each thing
She in the water-paile bade leaue a ring."

Roxb. Lib., ed. i., 66. Lilly, in his "Life and Times," tells us that fairies love neatness and cleanness of apparel, a strict diet, and upright life : "fervent prayers unto God," he adds, "conduce much to the assistance of those who are curious these ways." He means, it should seem, those who wish to cultivate an acquaintance with them. Concerning fairies, King James has the following passages : "That there was a king and queene of Phairie, that they had a jolly court and traine—they had a teynd and dutie, as it were of all goods—they naturally rode and went, eate and dranke, and did all other actions like natural men and women. Witches have been transported with the phairie to a hill, which opening, they went in and there saw a faire Queen, who being now lighter, gave them a stone that had sundrie vertues." *Demonology*, p. 132. In Poole's "Parnassus," 1657, are given the names of the fairy court : "Oberon the Emperor, Mab the Empress. Perriwiggin, Perriwinckle, Puck, Hob-goblin, Tomalin, Tom Thumb, Courtiers. Hop, Mop, Drop, Pip, Trip, Skip, Tub, Tib, Tick, Pink, Pin, Quick, Gill, Im, Tit, Wap, Win, Nit, the maids of honour. Nymphidia, the mother of the Maids." An old writer undertakes to explain why Englishmen creep to the chimney in winter and summer also : — "Doth not the warm zeal of an Englishman's devotion (who was ever observed to contend most stifly pro aris et focis) make them maintain and defend the sacred hearth, as the sanctuary and chief place of residence of the tutelary lares and household gods, and the only court where the lady fairies convene to dance and revel?" *Paradoxical Assertions* by R. H., 1664, part 2, p. 14. Randolph, in his "Amyntas," 1638, describes the Queen's palace: "A curious park paled round about with pick-teeth—a house made all with mother of pearle—an ivory tennis court—a nutmeg parlour—a saphyre dairy room—a ginger hall—chambers of agate—kitchens all of crystal—the jacks are gold—the spits are all of Spanish needles." "Grant that the sweet fairies may nightly put money in your shoes, and sweepe your house cleane," occurs as one of the good wishes introduced by Holiday in his "Marriage of the Arts," 1618, signat. E verso.

Gertrude. Good lord, that there are no fairies nowadays, Syn.

Syndefy. Why, Madam?

Gertrude. To do miracles, and bring ladies money."—*Eastward Hoe*, 1605, v. 1. "My grandmother," says the author of "Round about our Coal Fire," (circa 1730), "has often told me of fairies dancing upon our greene, and that they were little little creatures clothed in green." The author has these farther particulars of the popular notions concerning them. "The moment anyone saw them and took notice of them, they were struck blind of an eye. They lived under ground, and generally came out of a molehill." The same writer has the subsequent passage: "When the master and mistress were laid on their pillows, the men and maids, if they had a game at romps and blundered up stairs, or jumbled a chair, the next morning every one would swear 'twas the fairies, and that they heard them stamping up and down stairs all night, crying Water's lock'd, Water's lock'd, when there was not water in every pail in the kitchen." P. 42. I know not why, but they are reported to have been particularly fond of making cakes, and to have been very noisy during the operation. It was a common superstition that, if the gifts or favours of a fairy were revealed by the recipient, they vanished or were discontinued. Of this we have an example in the injunction given by the fairy to Sir Launfal, and elsewhere. Field, in "A Woman's a Weathercock," 1612, makes Nevill say to Scudamore:

"I see you labour with some serious thing,
And think (like fairy's treasure) to reveal it
Will cause it vanish."

A charm against fairies was turning the coat. Thus Bishop Corbet in his "Iter Boreale":

—"William found
A meanes for our deliv'rance; turn your cloakes,
Quoth hee, for Pucke is busy in these oakes:
If ever we at Bosworth will be found
Then turne your cloakes, for this is fairy ground."

From another passage, it should seem that there was a popular belief that if you struck a fairy or walking spirit, that it would dissolve into air. Our prelate was just mentioning the turning of the cloak above:

"But, ere the witchcraft was perform'd, we meete
A very man, who had not cloven feete,
Tho' William, still of little faith, doth doubt,
'Tis Robin or some spirit walkes about.

Strike him, quoth he, and it will turne to aire,
Crosse yourselves thrice, and strike him—strike him that dare
Thought I, for sure this massie Forester
In blows will prove the better conjurer."

The Bishop was right, for it proved to be the keeper of the forest, who showed them their way which they had lost. The following on the same subject is from the ode by Collins on *The Superstitions of the Highlands*, 1788 :

—' Still 'tis said, the Fairy people meet
Beneath each birken shade on mead or hill.
There each trim lass, that skims the milky store,
To the swart tribes their creamy bowls allots;
By night they sip it round the cottage door,
While airy minstrels warble jocund notes."

I have printed in my *Fairy Mythology of Shakespear*, 1875, some "Conjurations for Fairies," from two MSS. In the three old madrigals from Ravenscroft and Weelkes, inserted in the same volume, there seems to be no sufficient distinction made between two things very broadly distinct, I apprehend — the fairies or nymphs of Grecian mythology and the fairies or elves or modern European folk-lore.

Compare *Knockers*. The historian Wace informs us, in "Le Roman de Rou," that he went expressly to the forest of Brecheliant, in Bretagne, on a report which had reached him that there fairies were to be veritably seen; but he hunted every corner of the forest, and returned from his sleeveless errand, not a little vexed at his disappointment. "A fool," says he, "I went, and a fool I returned." Alfred Maury, *Les Forêts de la Gaule*, 1867, p. 331.

Fairies in Scotland.—It appears that in Scotland formerly "Fairies held from time immemorial certain fields which could not be taken away without gratifying those merry sprites by a piece of money": but that at a later period (the 18th century) "Fairies, without requiring compensation, have renounced their possessions." From the same source we derive the following details respecting a remarkably romantic linn formed by the water of the Crichup, co. Dumfries, inaccessible in a great measure to real beings. *Stat. Acc. of Scotland*, xxi., 148. "This linn was considered as the habitation of imaginary ones; and at the entrance into it there was a curious cell or cave, called the Elf's Kirk, where, according to the superstition of the times, the imaginary inhabitants of the Linn were supposed to hold their meetings. This cave, proving a good free stone quarry, has lately (1794) been demolished for the purpose of building houses, and from being the abodes of elves, has been converted into habitations for men." Ibid., xiii., 245. "The Queen of Fairie, mentioned in Jean Weir's Indictment, is probably the same Sovereign with the Queen of Elf-land, who makes a figure in the case of Alison Pearson, 15th May, 1588; which I believe is the first of the kind in the Record." *Additions and Notes to Maclaurin's Arguments and Decisions in remarkable Cases.* Law Courts, Scotland, 1774, p. 726. In 1795, the statistical report on Stronsay and Eday, two parishes in Orkney, supplied the annexed items of information: "The common people of this district remain to this day so credulous, as to think that fairies do exist; that an inferior species of witchcraft is still practiced, and that houses have been haunted, not only in former ages, but that they are haunted, at least noises are heard which cannot be accounted for on rational principles, even in our days. An instance of the latter happened only three years ago, in the house of John Spence, boat-carpenter." xv., 430. Under another head (Parish of Kirkmichael) the report states: "Not more firmly established in this country is the belief in ghosts than that in fairies. The legendary records of fancy, transmitted from age to age, have assigned their mansions to that class of genii, in detached hillocks covered with verdure, situated on the banks of purling brooks, or surrounded by thickets of wood.

These hillocks are called sioth-dhunan, abbreviated sioth-anan, from sioth, peace, and dun, a mound. They derive this name from the practice of the Druids, who were wont occasionally to retire to green eminences to administer justice, establish peace, and compose differences between contending parties. As that venerable order taught a Saoghl hal, or World beyond the present, their followers, when they were no more, fondly imagined, that seats where they exercised a virtue so beneficial to mankind, were still inhabited by them in their disembodied state. In the autumnal season, when the moon shines from a serene sky, often is the wayfaring traveller arrested by the musick of the hills, more melodious than the strains of Orpheus. Often struck with a more solemn scene, he beholds the visionary hunters engaged in the chace, and pursuing the deer of the clouds, while the hollow rocks, in long-sounding echoes, reverberate their cries. "There are several now living, who assert that they have seen and heard this aërial hunting, and that they have been suddenly surrounded by visionary forms, and assailed by a multitude of voices. About fifty years ago (this was written about 1793), a clergyman in the neighbourhood, whose faith was more regulated by the scepticism of philosophy than the credulity of superstition, could not be prevailed upon to yield his assent to the opinion of the times. At length, however, he felt from experience that he doubted what he ought to have believed. One night as he was returning home, at a late hour, from a presbytery, he was seized by the fairies, and carried aloft into the air. Through fields of æther and fleecy-clouds he journied many a mile, descrying, like Sancho Panza on his Claviléno, the earth far distant below him, and no bigger than a nut-shell. Being thus sufficiently convinced of the reality of their existence, they let him down at the door of his own house, where he afterward often recited to the wondering circle the marvellous tale of his adventure." xii., 461. A note adds: "Notwithstanding the progressive increase of knowledge and proportional decay of superstition in the Highlands, these genii are still supposed by many of the people to exist in the woods and sequestered valleys of the mountains, where they frequently appear to the lonely traveller, clothed in green, with dishevelled hair floating over their shoulders, and with faces more blooming than the vermil blush of a summer morning. At night in particular, when fancy assimilates to its own preconceived ideas every appearance and every sound, the wandering enthusiast is frequently entertained by their musick, more melodious than he ever before heard. It is curious to observe, how much this agreeable delusion corresponds with the superstitious opinion of the Romans, concerning the same class of genii, represented under different names. The Epicurean Lucretius describes the credulity in the following beautiful verses :

"Hæc loca capripedes satyros, nymphasque tenere
Finitimi pingunt, et faunos esse loquuntur;
Quorum noctivago strepitu, ludoque jocanti
Adfirmant volgo taciturna silentia rumpi
Chordarumque sonos fieri, dulcesque querelas
Tibia quas fundit digitas pulsata cantentum" :

A farther note by Brand himself in reference to the above incident says :
"In plain English, I should suspect that spirits of a different sort from fairies had taken the honest clergyman by the head, and though he has omitted the circumstance in his marvellous narration, I have no doubt but that the good man saw double on the occasion, and that his own mare, not fairies, landed him safe at his own door."

In a statistical report of the condition of Strachur and Stralachlan, co. Argyle, in the 18th century, occurs the subjoined passage: "About eight miles to the eastward of Cailleachvear, a small conical hill rises considerably above the neighbouring hills. It is seen from Inverary, and from many parts at a great distance. It is called Sien-Sluia, the fairy habitation of a multitude": adding in a note, "A belief in fairies prevailed very much in the Highlands of old : nor at this day is it quite obliterated. A small conical hill, called Sien, was assigned them for a dwelling, from which melodious music was frequently heard, and gleams of light seen in dark nights." *Stat. Acc.*, iv., 560. Pinkerton, writing in 1799, informs us that "The fairies are little beings of doubtful character, sometimes benevolent, sometimes mischievous. On Hallowe'en and on some other evenings, they and the Gyar-Carlins are sure to be abroad and to stap those they meet and are displeased with, full of butter and heare-awns. In winter nights they are heard curling on every sheet of ice. Having a septennial sacrifice of a human being to make to the Devil, they sometimes carry away children, leaving little vixens of their own in the cradle. The diseases of cattle are very commonly attributed to their mischievous operation. Cows are often elf-shot." *Heron's Journey*, ii., 227. A writer describing the superstitions current in the vicinity of

St. Andrew's, Scotland, says : "In private breweries, to prevent the interference of the fairies, a live coal is thrown into the vat. A cow's milk no fairy can take away, if a burning coal is conducted across her back and under her belly immediately after her delivery. The same mischievous elves cannot enter into a house at night if, before bedtime, the lower end of the crook or iron chain, by which a vessel is suspended over the fire, be raised up a few links." *Letter from Professor Playfair to Mr. Brand*, January 26, 1804.

Fairy Butter.—A species of gelatine. See Forby's *Vocabulary of East Anglia*, 1830, p. 108.

Fairy Poetry.—In the "Maydes Metamorphosis," 1601, occurs the following fairy song:—

"Round about, round about, in a fine ring-a :
Thus we dance, thus we dance, and thus we sing-a :
Trip and go, to and fro, over this green-a,
All about, in and out, for our brave queen-a.

Round about, round about, in a fine ring-a :
Thus we dance, thus we dance, and thus we sing-a :
Trip and go, to and fro, over this green-a,
All about, in and out, for our brave queen-a.

We've danc'd round about in a fine ring-a :
We have danc'd lustily, and thus we sing-a :
All about, in and out, over this green-a,
To and fro, trip and go, to our brave queen-a."

So, again, Drayton :
"*Doron.* Come, frolick youth, and follow me,
My frantique boy, and I'le show thee
The countrey of the fayries."

—*Muses Elizium*, 1630, p. 24. Randolph describes fairy hunting :
"*Dor.* I hope King Oberon and his royal Mab are well?
Joe. They are. I never saw their Graces eat such a meal before.
Joe. They are rid a hunting.
Dor. Hare, or deer, my lord?
Joe. Neither: a brace of snails of the first head."

I find the following in Herrick's "Hesperides :

"*The Fairies.*"
If ye will with Mab finde grace,
Set each platter in its place;
Rake the fier up and get
Water in ere sun be set:

Wash your pailes and clense your
    dairies,
Sluts are loathsome to the fairies:
Sweep your house, who doth not so,
Mab will pinch her by the toe."

There are some allusions in Corbet's
ballad entitled "The Fairies Farewell."

" Farewell rewards and fairies,
  Good house wives now may say;
For now fowle sluts in dairies
  Do fare as well as they :
And, though they sweepe their hearths
    no lesse
Then maides were wont to doe,
Yet who of late for cleanlinesse
  Findes six pence in her shooe?

Lament, lament, old Abbies,
  The fairies lost command,
They did but change priest's babies,
  And now grown puritanes,
Who live as changelings ever since
  For love of your demaines.

At morning and at evening both
  You merry were and glad,
So little care of sleepe and sloath
  These pretty ladies had :
When Tom came home from labour,
  Or Cisse to milking rose,
Then merrily went their tabor,
  And nimbly went their toes.

Witnesse those rings and roundelayes
  Of theirs which yet remaine,
Were footed in Queene Maries dayes
  On many a grassy plaine.

A tell-tale in their company
  They never could endure,
And who so kept not secretly
  Their mirth was punisht sure.
It was a iust and Christian deed
  To pinch such black and blew :
O how the Common-wealth doth need
  Such Iustices as you !"

The following is in Poole's *Parnassus*,
1657, p. 333 :

" There is Mab, the mistress fairy,
That doth nightly rob the dairy,
And can help or hurt the churning
As she please, without discerning.
She that pinches country wenches
If they rub not clean their benches :
And with sharper nails remembers,
When they rake not up the embers.
But if so they chance to feast her,
In their shooe she drops a tester.
This is she that empties cradles,
Takes out children, puts in ladles.
Trains forth midwives in their slum-
    ber
With a sive, the holes to number ;
And then leads them from their
    boroughs
Thorough ponds and water-furrows."

Here is Dr. King's description of "Orpheus' Fairy Entertainment " :—

" A roasted ant that's nicely done
By one small atom of the sun ;
These are flies eggs in moon - shine
    poach'd ;
This is a flea's thigh in collops scotch'd,
'Twas hunted yesterday i' th' Park,
And like t' have scap'd us in the dark.
This is a dish entirely new,
Butterflies brains dissolv'd in dew ;
These lovers' vows, these courtiers'
    hopes.
Things to be eat by microscopes :
These sucking mites, a glow-worm's
    heart,
This is a delicious rainbow-tart."

King's Works, 1776, 111, 112. And Pope
says :

" Of airy elves by moon-light shadows
    seen,
The silver token and the circled green."
—*Rape of the Lock.*

Fairs. — A fair is a greater kind of
market, granted to any town by privilege,
for the more speedy and commodious providing of such things as the place stands
in need of. Fairs are generally kept once
or twice in a year. Proclamation is to be
made how long they are to continue, and
no person is allowed to sell any goods after
the time of the fair is ended, on forfeiture
of double their value. The term appears
to be derived from Latin *foris*, outside the
town, whence the French *foire*, because
fairs, as distinguished from markets, were
held beyond the urban precincts. Warton tells us, that before flourishing towns
were established, and the necessaries of
life, from the convenience of communication and the increase of provincial civility,
could be procured in various places, goods
and commodities of every kind were
chiefly sold at fairs ; to these, as to one
universal mart, the people resorted periodically, and supplied most of their wants
for the ensuing year. The display of
merchandise and the conflux of customers,
at these principal and almost only em-
poria of domestic commerce, were prodigious : and they were often held on open
and extensive plains on that account as
well as to prevent infection. Robert of
Brunne, in 1303, notices that fairs disappeared in a night. He likens to their
short existence ill-gotten wealth :

" Here mayst thou se, euyl wunne
    thyng,
With eyre shal neuer make gode endyng ;
Namly with thyng of holy cherche
Shalt thou neuer spede wel to werche,
That mayst thou se by parsones eyres :
Hyt fareth wyth hem as doth with these
    feyres ;

Now ys the feyre byggede weyl,
And on the morne ys ther neuer a deyl.
Ryche tresoure now furthe men leye,
And on the touther day hyt ys all
aweye."

Handlyng Synne, i. ed. Furnivall, p.
292. A constant incidence of the grant
of manors in ancient times was the leave
to establish local fairs and markets, to
the tolls of which the lord might be entitled, and which would gradually tend to
develope his property. Of attendance at fairs on the Sabbath, Humphrey
Roberts of King's Langley speaks in his
"Complaint for Reformation," 1572:
"Leaue therefore," he says, "your carefull toyle and labours vpon the Saboth
day : as cartyng, carying of sackes and
packes, byinge and sellyng : yea keping
of faiers and markets—." Sometimes,
when the day fell on the Sabbath, the fair
was held on the Monday, as Hearne says
of Wantage Fair in 1723, where among
other sports introduced were backsword or
cudgel-play between the hill-country and
the vale-country, Berkshire being celebrated for this amusement. Wantage at
this time enjoyed three fairs, one on July
7 (Translation of St. Thomas á Becket), a
second on October 6 (St. Faith's Day),
and a third, of recent origin, called
the Constable's Fair, granted by the high
constable after being chosen for Wantage.
Hearne's *Diary*, July 10, 1723. In 1872
the fairs at Charlton, near Woolwich, and
Blackheath, were held for the last time.
The former was known as Horn Fair, and
from the disorderly character of the proceedings arose the proverb, "All is fair
at Horn Fair." Hazlitt's *Proverbs*, 1882,
p. 49. Greenwich Fair was still kept within
living memory, one of the attractions being
that of rolling down the hill. There
is a small broadside account in doggerel verse of the humours of Bow Fair.
Among the attendants at fairs in the
olden time, the sharpers and pickpockets
mustered pretty strongly. In the ballad
of "Ragged and Torn and True," it is
said :

"The pick-pockets in a throng,
    At a market or a faire,
Will try whose purse is strong,
    That they may the money share."

In the *Life and Adventures of
Bamfylde Moore Carew*, 1745, we read
how at Bridgewater Fair the deaf,
blind, dumb, lame, and other sham-
mers were present in great force,
and how on one occasion the mayor
having let it be known that he intended
to cure them of their complaints, caused
them to be taken to the Darkhouse, where
a medical man examined them, but (per-

haps intentionally) leaving the door unlocked, they all decamped.

There are two old English proverbs that
relate to fairs : "Men speak of the fair
as things went with them there" ; as also,
"To come a day after the fair." The
first seems intended to rhyme. The second
is still perfectly common.

Mr. Cornelius Walford has collected
in his volume on the subject, 1883,
a large body of information on Fairs
in England, their origin, antiquity,
development, and disappearance. Some
of those still held date from Anglo-
Saxon times, and were established by virtue of royal grants ; they necessarily occasioned a body of statutory enactments
peculiarly bearing on their incidence, of
which not the least remarkable and
troublesome was the complication arising
from the strong alien element in these
institutions. C. Walford, *Fairs, Past
and Present*, 1883, p. 19, et seqq. ; Wheatley, *Round about Piccadilly and Pall
Mall*, 1870, pp. 200-02. In his valuable
paper on the *King's Peace*, Mr. Hubert
Hall has explained the meaning and
origin of the "Peace of the Fair," or in
other words the official regulations for the
maintenance of order and justice in view
of the large body of foreigners whom these
institutions gradually attracted. *Antiquary*, November 1888, p. 189.

At the Lammas Fair at Exeter
and at Barnstaple the opening of
the proceedings was denoted by the
hoisting of a large glove on a pole,
and at the latter place, in more
recent times, the pole was dressed
with dahlias. By the Statute of 2 Edw.
III. c. 13, it was ordered that "A cry
shalbe made at the begynnyng of euery
feyre how longe it shall indure & that
none shall sell after vpon payne to be gre-
uously punyshed agaynst the Kynge."
The authority of the proprietor or lord
of the fair was only co-existent in duration with the fair itself ; merchants continuing to trade after the legal conclusion
of the fair were amerced in double the
value of the goods so sold ; nothing but
the necessaries of life were to be on sale
on feast-days and Sundays; except only
"fore sonday in the heruyst" ; the Londoners were permitted to attend all fairs
under pain of ten pounds' fine to the hin-
derer or hinderers. The articles are
"Wine, wax, beiffes, muttons, wheite, &
malt." This proves that fairs still continued to be the principal marts for purchasing necessaries in large quantities,
which now are supplied by frequent trading towns : and the mention of beiffes and
muttons (which are salted oxen or sheep)
shews that at so late a period they knew
little of breeding cattle. It may seem
surprising that their own neighbourhood,

including the cities of Oxford and Coventry, could not supply them with commodities neither rare nor costly : which they thus fetched at a considerable expense of carriage. It is a rubric in some of the monastic rules, " De Euntibus ad Nundinas " ; i.e., concerning those who go to fairs. Warton's *H. E. P.* by Hazlitt, ii., 260.

Prior to 1406, at Oswestry in Shropshire, the Welsh tenants of the lord were accustomed to keep watch and ward for three days and nights at the four gates of the town during the fairs of St. Andrew and St. Oswald ; but owing to the irregularities committed by their men the service was commuted for a payment, which went to hire Englishmen to perform the same duty. Pennant's *Tours in Wales,* 1810, i., 345-6. Minstrels and ballad-singers, it seems, attended fairs in the time of Elizabeth, and we hear of two men, Outroaring Dick and Wat Wimbers, gaining twenty shillings a day at Braintree fair in Essex. They were noted trebles. Hazlitt's Warton, 1871, iv., 428. Great complaint was made in the reign of Henry VI. of the irregularities and disorderly proceedings at our English fairs, especially on festivals, such as Sunday, Good Friday, Ascension Day, and so forth, and in 23 Hen. VI. we find a petition submitted to that monarch for the suppression of fairs throughout the country on holy days set apart for the service of the Church, including the Sabbath itself. The petitioners required the fulfilment of their prayer from after the next Michaelmas then ensuing in perpetuity ; but the king declined, in his response, to make more than a partial and temporary concession. *Antiq. Repert.,* 1807, iii., 444-5. It appears from the " Northumberland Household Book," 1512, that the stores of his lordship's house at Wresill, for the whole year, were laid in from fairs. From the ancient fabliau of the " Merchant turned Monk," and from other sources, we gather that the same was the case in France, if not in other continental countries, at this early period. Braithwaite, in describing what ought to be the qualifications of the chief officers of an earl, writes : "They must be able to iudge, not onely of the prices, but of the goodnes of all kindes of corne, cattell, and other household provisions ; and the better to enable themselves therto, are oftentimes to ride to fayres and great markets, and ther to have conference with graziers and purveiors, being men of witt and experience—" Some Rules and Orders for the government of the house of an Earle. (circâ 1640), *apud Miscell. Antiq. Angl.,* 1821. Hearne furnishes an interesting account of St. Frideswide's Fair at Oxford, originally granted by

Henry I. to be held for twelve days together within the precincts of the priory, beginning with the feast of St. Benedict, but removed by Henry III. to St. Frideswide's Day, October 19. It was kept in St. Frideswide's meadow, and during its continuance the prior exercised supreme jurisdiction over the village of Oxford, and subsequently over the city, of which the keys were delivered to him for the time being. Abuses, however, gradually led to the discontinuance of this custom in the reign of Richard II., when the Chancellor of the University interdicted the farther visits of the traders, and so abolished the fair. Hearne's *Diary,* June 8, 1730. In *Canidia, or the Witches,* by R. D., 1683, is furnished a not very flattering account of the proceedings at Sturbridge Fair, vulgarly called Stirbitch Fair. It is curious to find, however, that in 1686 the library of James Chamberlaine was sold there.

The ceremonial of proclaiming Bridge Fair was duly observed at Peterborough in 1898. At noon on the 4th of October the Mayor and Corporation walked in procession to the bridge spanning the river, where the Town Crier declared the fair open, to be held as well in Northamptonshire as in Huntingdonshire. The original charter dates back to the time of Henry VIII. According to custom, the Mayor afterwards entertained the members of the Corporation to a sausage and champagne luncheon at an hotel adjacent to the fair field. In the Churchwardens' Accounts of St. Laurence Parish, Reading, A.D. 1499, is the following article : — " Receypt. It. Rec. at the Fayer for a stonding in the Church porch, iiijd." Coates' *History of Reading,* p. 214. By " Advertisements partly for due order in the publique administration of Common Prayers," &c., 25 Jan. 7 Eliz., it was enjoined, " that in all faires and common markets, falling uppon the Sunday, there be no shewing of any wares before the service be done." Machyn in his Diary mentions that on St. Peter's Day (June 29), 1557, a small fair, for the sale of wool and other like commodities, was held in the churchyard of St. Margaret's, in the City of London.

A conspicuous feature in the management of these institutions was the system of tolls exacted from the frequenters, especially in the case of foreigners. It used to be said that in some of the principal French fairs the dues absorbed half the profits of alien vendors. At the same time, it seems to have been often customary to allow goods imported from other countries to enter, and the unsold portion to leave, ports on a reduced scale of harbour and

excise dues. But at Corby, co. of Northampton, between Kettering and King's
Cliff, they still hold, once in twenty years,
under a charter of Elizabeth, confirmed
by Charles II., what is termed Pole Fair
on May 19. By the said charter the men
and tenants of the ancient demesne of
Corby, once belonging to the St. Johns,
subsequently to the Willoughby D'Eres-
bys and Latimers, and now to Lady Cardigan, were freed from town and bridge
tolls throughout the kingdom, and from
serving on juries and in the Militia. The
charter is read at four o'clock in the morning at each entrance to the village; the
stocks are brought out; bars or poles are
laid across all the approaches; and all,
who do not pay the toll, are carried—the
men on poles, and the women on chairs,
round the streets, and placed in durance,
till the demand is met. In 1902 the fair
was very numerously attended, and on the
21st May the President of the National
Record Association visited the village, and
was pleased to find that the ancient usage
had not been relinquished. The president
was himself chaired, and borne through
the streets, preceded by a band, placed in
the stocks with the oldest inhabitant, and
duly released on compliance with the re-
quisition.

At Barnet Fair, they at all events,
when we were last there, sold a varied
assortment of gilt gingerbread, representing soldiers, animals, and other
figures. The four Cambridge fairs were:
Reach Fair, held in Rogation Week:
Barnwell or Midsummer Fair; the Nuns'
or Garlic Fair; and Stourbridge Fair. The
best account of the last is in Gunning's
Reminiscences (1789 - 1854). Compare
Sturbridge Fair, infrâ. A picture of
Harlow Bush Fair, Essex, was formerly
on the wall of the first-floor room at the
old Elephant Tavern in Fenchurch Street,
and was attributed to Hogarth. Timbs,
Clubs and Club-Life, 1872, p. 401. It was
at the Fair of Abingdon in Berkshire,
that the servants of the house were absent when Amy Robsart was murdered at
Cumnor. A fair is usually held at Reading on Candlemas Day for cattle and
horses; but of late the day for holding it
has not always been rigidly observed. Mr.
Brand gathered from a newspaper that
an annual fair was then held in the Broad
Gate at Lincoln on the 14th September,
called Fool's Fair, for the sale of cattle,
so called, on that authority, as follows:
"King William and his Queen having
visited Lincoln, while on their tour
through the Kingdom, made the citizens
an offer to serve them in any manner
they liked best. They asked for a fair,
though it was harvest, when few people
can attend it, and though the town had

no trade nor any manufacture. The King
smiled, and granted their request; observing, that it was a humble one indeed."
In the eighteenth century Thomas Day,
author of *Sandford and Merton*, 1786, instituted what was known as Fairlop Fair,
which used to be opened in Epping Forest
by drawing a ship made of one fir tree
on a trunk with six horses round a certain area in the Forest three times.

Among the Hardwicke Papers, recently sold to the British Museum,
were grants by the Crown of fairs
to Hawarden, co. Flint, Woburn, co.
Bedford (on the 1st of January yearly,
&c., from 1762), and to Westcot, near
Dorking (1726). In the last century, Lysons, speaking of the numerous fairs at
Okehampton, Devon, says that the holiday fair held on the Saturday after Christmas was called the Giglet. *Magna Britannia, Devonshire*, p. 370. At Faversham,
in Kent, two fairs were formerly allowed,
each lasting ten days. One, called St.
Valentine's Fair, commenced on February 14, the other on August 1st. In the
18th century, in the parish of Wamphray,
in Scotland, it seems that hiring fairs
used to be much frequented. "Those,"
it is said "who are to hire, wear a green
sprig in their hat: and it is very seldom
that servants will hire in any other
place." *Stat. Acc.*, xxi., 457. Whit-
stable Fair was held on Good Friday. In
two poetical writings of the earlier half
of the 18th century are descriptions of the
old-fashioned fair worth reproducing:

"Now pedlars' stalls with glitt'ring
　toys are laid,
The various fairings of the country
　maid;
Long silken laces hang upon the twine,
And rows of pins and amber bracelets
　shine.
Here the tight lass, knives, combs and
　scissars spies,
And looks on thimbles with desiring
　eyes.
The mountebank now treads the stage,
　and sells
His pills, his balsams, and his ague-
　spells;
Now o'er and o'er the nimble tumbler
　springs,
And on the rope the ventrous maiden
　swings;
Jack Pudding in his party-colour'd
　jacket
Tosses the gloves, and jokes at every
　packet;
Here raree-shows are seen, and Punch's
　feats,
And pockets pick'd in crouds, and vari-
　ous cheats."
　—*Gay's Sixth Pastoral.*

" Next morn, I ween, the village char-
  ter'd fair,
A day that's ne'er forgot throughout
  the year :
Soon as the lark expands her auburn
  fan,
Foretelling day, before the day began,
Then ' Jehu Ball ' re-echoes down the
  lane,
Crack goes the whip, and rattling
  sounds the chain.
With tinkling bells the stately beast
  grown proud.
Champs on the bit, and neighing roars
  aloud.
The bridles dotted o'er with many a
  flow'r,
The six-team'd waggon forms a leafy
  bow'r.
Young Damon whistled to Dorinda's
  song,
The fiddle tuneful play'd the time along.
At length arriv'd, the statute fills the
  fair,
Dorcas and Lydia, Bella too was there :
Favours and gauzes, variegated gay,
Punch loudly squeaks, the drum pro-
  claims the play.
The pole high rear'd, the dance, the
  gambol shew'd
Mirth and diversion to the gaping
  crowd :
Sam with broad smile, and Poll with
  dimpled face,
Revers'd the apron, shews she wants a
  place.
The race in sacks, the quoit, the cir-
  cling reel,
While Prue more thoughtful buys a
  spinning wheel.
The grinning Andrew perch'd on Folly's
  stool,
Proves th' artificial, not the natural
  fool :
For Hodge declares he thinks, devoid of
  art,
He must be wise, who acts so well his
  part !"
—H. Rowe's *Poems*, 1796.

One of the constant attractions in fairs
both in London and in the provinces was
the theatrical show, usually in a booth,
and limited to a brief representation, to
suit a succession of spectators. Favourite subjects were the *Creation, Noah's
Flood*, the *Nine Worthies*, and *Punchinello*, or *Punch and Judy*.   Hazlitt's
Manual of Old Plays, 1892, pp. 34, 167,
187. The Towneley series of Mysteries is
described as having been periodically exhibited at Woodkirk Fair, as well
as at Wakefield, and it is sometimes referred to as the Woodkirk series.

We are told that in the 18th century a
practice still continued at Dundonald, in
Ayrshire, " of kindling a large fire, or
tawnle as it is usually termed, of wood,

upon some eminence, and making merry
around it, upon the eve of the Wednesday
of Marymass Fair in Irvine (which begins
on the third Monday of August and continues the whole week). As most fair
days in the country were formerly popish
holidays, and their eves were usually
spent in religious ceremonies and in diversions, it has been supposed that tawnles
were first lighted up by our Catholic
fathers, though some derive their origin
from the Druidical Times."   From the
same source we learn that Christ's Kirk
May Fair, Kenethmont, Aberdeenshire,
" was kept on the Green, and in the
night ; hence it was by the people called
Sleepy - market. About a century ago,
the proprietor changed it from night
to day ; but so strong was the pre-
possession of the people in favour of the
old custom, that, rather than comply with
the alteration, they chose to neglect it
altogether."   The same account, speaking of Marykirk, co. Kincardine, says :
" On the outside of the church, strongly
fixed to the wall, are the Joggs. These
were made use of, where the weekly market and annual fair stood, to confine and
punish those who had broken the peace,
or used too much freedom with the property of others. The stocks were used for
the feet, and the joggs for the neck of the
offender, in which he was confined, at
least, during the time of the fair."
Though the worthy minister who drew up
this account has omitted the etymology of
joggs, I should think it a very obvious
one—from *Jugum*, a yoke. *Stat. Account
of Scotland*, vii., 622 ; xiii., 77 : xviii, 612.

In Mr. G. L. Gomme's *Presidential Address* to the Folk-Lore Society, 1894, occurs an account of an early usage at a
place in Lanarkshire, about the time of
St. Luke's Fair, and the President points
out that the Kourds have a precisely similar cult. The narrative is rather long ;
but it is too curious to omit or abridge,
and so I crave leave to reproduce it :—

" An ancient custom, for the observance
of which Rutherglen has long been famous, is the baking of sour cakes. Some
peculiar circumstances attending the operation render an account of the manner
in which it is done not altogether unnecessary. About eight or ten days before St.
Luke's Fair (for they are baked at no
other time of the year), a certain quantity
of oatmeal is made into dough with warm
water, and laid up in a vessel to ferment.
Being brought to a proper degree of fer-
mentation and consistency, it is rolled up
into balls, proportionable to the intended
largeness of the cakes. With the dough
is commonly mixed a small quantity of
sugar, and a little aniseed or cinnamon.
The baking is executed by women only,

and they seldom begin their work till after sunset, and a night or two before the fair. A large space of the house, chosen for the purpose, is marked out by a line drawn upon it. The area within is considered as consecrated ground, and is not, by any of the bystanders, to be touched with impunity. A transgression incurs a small fine, which is always laid out on drinks for the use of the company. This hallowed spot is occupied by six or eight women, all of whom, except the toaster, seat themselves on the ground in a circular figure, having their feet turned towards the fire. Each of them is provided with a bake-board about two feet square, which they hold on their knees. The woman who toasts the cakes, which is done on a girdle suspended over the fire, is called the queen or bride, and the rest are called her maidens. These are distinguished from one another by names given them for the occasion. She who sits next the fire towards the east is called the Todler; her companion on the left hand is called the Hodler, and the rest have arbitrary names given them by the bride —as Mrs. Baker, best and worst maids, etc. The operation is begun by the Todler, who takes a ball of the dough, forms it into a small cake, and then casts it on the bake-board of the Hodler, who beats it out a little thinner. This being done, she in her turn throws it on the board of her neighbour, and thus it goes round from east to west in the direction of the course of the sun, until it comes to the toaster, by which time it is as thin and smooth as a sheet of paper. The first cake that is cast on the girdle is usually named as a gift to some well-known cuckold, from a superstitious opinion that thereby the rest will be preserved from mischance. Sometimes the cake is too thin as to be carried by the current of air up into the chimney. As the baking is wholly performed by the hand, a great deal of noise is the consequence. The beats, however, are not irregular, nor destitute of an agreeable harmony, especially when they are accompanied with vocal music, which is frequently the case. Great dexterity is necessary, not only to beat out the cakes with no other instrument than the hand, so that no part of them shall be thicker than another, but especially to cast them from one board to another without ruffling or breaking them. The toasting requires considerable skill, for which reason the most experienced person in the company is chosen for that part of the work. One cake is sent round in quick succession to another, so that none of the company is suffered to be idle. The whole is a scene of activity, mirth, and diversion, and might afford an excellent subject for a picture. As there is no account, even by

tradition itself, concerning the origin of this custom, it must be very ancient. The bread thus baked was, doubtless, never intended for common use. It is not easy to conceive why mankind, especially in a rude age, would strictly observe so many ceremonies, and be at so great pains in making a cake which, when folded together, makes but a scanty mouthful. Besides, it is always given away in presents to strangers who frequent the Fair. The custom seems to have been originally derived from paganism, and to contain not a few of the sacred rites peculiar to that impure religion—as the leavened dough, and the mixing it with sugar and spices, the consecrated ground, etc., etc. But the particular deity for whose honour these cakes were at first made is not, perhaps, easy to determine."

In his *Jolly Beggars*, Burns makes the girl, who is enamoured of "Soldier laddie," meet him at Cunningham Fair, dressed out in all his military finery.

Fosbrooke tells us, "Much quarrelling and fighting sometimes attended the monastic fairs, held in the churchyard; and Henry observes from Muratori, that, "When a fair was held in Italy within the precincts of a cathedral or monastery, it was not uncommon to oblige every man to take an oath at the gate, before he was admitted, that he would neither lie, nor steal, nor cheat, while he continued in the fair." *British Monachism*, ii., 217. According to Olaus Magnus, the ancient Northern nations held annual ice fairs. Frost fairs and blanket fairs have been known on the Thames. The last great frost fair among us was in 1814. See "Old Ballads illustrating the Great Frost of 1683-4" (Percy Soc.); and Handbook of Early English Lit. Art. Frosts. Down to our own time, the great fair at Nijni Novgorod in Russia formed the source of supply and exchange on a scale of unparalleled magnitude and variety. C. Walford's *Fairs Past and Present*, 1883. Compare *Ascension Day, Cherry Fairs, Cuckoo, Greenwich Fair, Bartholomew Fair, Honey Fair, Horn Fair, Sturbridge Fair*, &c.

Fairing.—It was customary at all fairs to present fairings, which are gifts, bought at these annual markets. The custom prevailed in the days of Chaucer, as appears by the subsequent passage in the "Wife of Bathes Prologue," where she boasts of having managed her several husbands so well:

"I governed hem so well after my lawe
  That eche of hem ful blisful was, and
    fawe
To bringe me gay thinges fro the faire
They were ful glad," &c.

And in "Rusticæ Nundinæ," 1730:

"Ad sua quisque redit; festivis Daphnen Amyntas
Exonerat Xeniis, dandoque astringit Amores."

When these institutions were more general and more important, considerable sums were laid out by wealthier persons in this way. The first Earl of Bristol, in his *Diary*, 1735-6-8, notes sums of £6 15s. 0d., £3 12s. 0d., and £7 7s. 0d., bestowed on members of his family for the purchase of fairings at Bury St. Edmunds. But of course, the more usual, and at least equally interesting and characteristic, home-bringings were of a humbler description, like that mentioned in the old song:—

"O dear! what can the matter be?
Johnny's so long at the fair:
He promis'd to buy me a bunch of blue ribbons
To tie up my bonnie brown hair."

Fairy Rings.—The haunts of fairies were thought to have been groves, mountains, the southern sides of hills, and verdant meadows, where their diversion was dancing hand in hand in a circle, as alluded to by Shakespear in his "Midsummer Night's Dream." The traces of their tiny feet are supposed to remain visible on the grass long afterward, and are called fairy-rings or circles. Shakespear's words are:

"To dance on ringlets to the whistling wind."

"Ringlets of Grass," Dr. Grey observes, "are very common in meadows, which are higher, sowrer, and of a deeper green than the grass that grows round them: and by the common people are usually called fairy circles." Again, in "The Tempest," act v. sc. 1, Prospero says:

"Ye elves ———you demy puppets, that
By moon-shine do the green-sour ringlets make,
Whereof the ewe not bites."

So again,

"To dew her orbs upon the green."

And Drayton:

"They in their courses make that round,
In meadows and in marshes found,
Of them so call'd the fairy ground."

They are again alluded to in Randolph's "Amyntas":

"They do request you now
To give them leave to dance a fairy ring."

Browne, the Devonshire poet, describes:

—"a pleasant mead
Where fairies often did their measures tread,
Which in the meadows made such circles greene,
As if with garlands it had crowned beene.
Within one of these rounds was to be seene
A hillocke rise, where oft the fairy queene
At twy-light sate."

—*Pastorals* (Roxb. Lib. ed. i., 66). "They had fine musicke always among themselves," says an author already cited, "and danced in a moon-shiny night, around, or in a ring, as one may see at this day upon every common in England where mushroomes grow." *Round about our Coal Fire*, p. 41. The author of "Mons Catherinæ" has not forgotten to notice these ringlets in his poem:

"Sive illic Lemurum populus sub nocte choreas
Plauserit exiguas, viridesque attriverit herbas."

They are also mentioned in George Smith's "Pastorals," 1770, p. 24.

Olaus Magnus, "De Gentibus Septentrionalibus," writes: "Similes illis spectris, quæ in multis locis, præsertim nocturno tempore, suum saltatorium Orbem cum omnium Musarum concentu versare solent." It appears from the same author (ibid. p. 410) that these dancers always parched up the grass, and therefore it is properly made the office of Puck to refresh it. See Steevens's Note on Reed's edit. of Shakespear, 1803, vol. iv. p. 343. The most clear and satisfactory remarks by earlier writers on the origin of fairy rings are probably those of Dr. Wollaston, made during a few years' residence in the country. The cause of their appearance he ascribes to the growth of certain species of agaric, which so entirely absorb all nutriment from the soil beneath that the herbage is for a while destroyed. Mr. Herbert Spencer, following in the same track, shews that fairy rings are nothing more than the seeds shed by a particular kind of fungus, which, as Wollaston had previously observed, impoverishes the ground in which it grows to such an extent as to prevent the procreation of a new root in the second year. Thus the old fungus sheds its seed in a circular form, and perishes, leaving only the ring formed round it. But the same sort of process is observable of other species of vegetation, and in particular of the iris, which exhausts the soil in which it immediately grows, and throws out new roots beyond in search of fresh nourishment. A learned German, Baron von Reichenbach, reducing this superstition to that level of scientific commonplace which has already degraded the nightmare into indigestion, and the dwarf into convulsions, is inclined to recognise in these fancied fairy-rings or dances nothing more than "the operation of the phenomenon termed 'the odylic light' emitted from magnetic substances." But it seems proper to mention that in the "British Apollo," 1710, a physical cause was suspected, the rings being there assigned to the direct agency of lightning. In support of this hypothesis the reader may consult Priestley's "Present State of Electricity." See also No. cxvii. p. 391, of the "Philosophical Transactions," where it is stated that Mr. Walker, walking abroad after a storm of thunder and lightning, observed a round circle of about four or five yards diameter, whose rim was about a foot broad, newly burnt bare, as appeared from the colour and brittleness of the grass roots. See "Gent. Mag." for Dec. 1790. But in fact, Brand himself says : Some ascribe the phænomenon of the circle or ring, supposed by the vulgar to be traced by the fairies in their dances, to the effects of lightning, as being frequently produced after storms of that kind, and by the colour and brittleness of the grass-roots when first observed. The "Athenian Oracle," mentions a popular belief that "if a house be built upon the ground where fairy rings are, whoever shall inhabit therein does wonderfully prosper."

Fairy Sparks, &c.—Certain luminous appearances, often seen on clothes in the night, are called in Kent fairy sparks or shell-fire, as Ray informs us in his "East and South Country Words." I was (says Brand) told by Mr. Pennant, that there is a substance found at great depths in crevices of lime-stone rocks, in sinking for lead ore, near Holywell, in Flintshire, which is called Menyn Tylna Teg, or fairies' butter. So also in Northumberland the common people call a certain fungous excrescence, sometimes found about the roots of old trees, fairy butter. After great rains, and in a certain degree of putrefaction, it is reduced to a consistency which, together with its colour, makes it not unlike butter, and hence the name.

Faith's, St., Day.—(October 6). See *Love Charms.*

Falling Stars.—See *Aërolites.*

Falstaff, Shakespear's.—See *Death-Omens.*

Faring.—This is mentioned as a popular game at cards, or dice, or both,

in the "English Courtier and the Countrey Gentleman," 1586.

Faro.—Sometimes called *Pharaoh.* See Davis, *Suppl. Glossary,* 1881, p. 488.

Fast and Loose.—This game, played with a skewer and a leathern belt or girdle placed in folds edgewise on a table, is also known as Pricking at the Belt. A description of it by Sir John Hawkins occurs in a note to Davenport's *City Night-Cap* in Hazlitt's edition of Dodsley. It was a game at which vagrants (so-called gypsies) cheated common people out of their money. Comp. Nares, 1859, in v.

Fast-E'en Tuesday.—See *Shrove Tuesday.*

Faustus or **Faust.** — See my *National Tales and Legends,* 1892, for the earliest attempt to place this story on its true footing.

Favours. — In the "Defence of Conny-Catching," 1592, Signat, C 3, verso, is the following passage : "Is there not heere resident about London, a crew of terryble hacksters in the habite of gentlemen wel appareled, and yet some weare bootes for want of stockings, with a locke worne at theyr lefte eare for their mistrisse favour." The subsequent is taken from Lodge's "Wit's Miserie," 1596, p. 47 : "When he rides, you shall know him by his fan : and, if he walke abroad, and misse his mistres favour about his neck, arme, or thigh, he hangs the head like the soldier in the field that is disarmed." In Marston's "Dutch Courtezan," a pair of lovers are introduced plighting their troth as follows :

"*Enter Freeville.* Pages with torches. Enter Beatrice above." After some very impassioned conversation, Beatrice says : "I give you faith ; and prethee, since, poore soule ! I am so easie to beleeve thee, make it much more pitty to deceive me. Weare this slight favour in my remembrance" (throweth down a ring to him).

"*Freev.* Which, when I part from, Hope, the best of life, ever part from me !
——Graceful mistresse, our nuptiall day holds.
"*Beatrice.* With happy Constancye a wished day."

Of gentlemen's presents on similar occasions, a lady, in Beaumont and Fletcher's "Cupid's Revenge," 1615, Dyce's B. and F., 11, 390, says :

"Given earings we will wear ;
Bracelets of our lovers' hair,
Which they on our arms shall twist
With their names carv'd, on our wrist."

In England these knots of ribbons were

distributed in great abundance formerly, even at the marriages of persons of the first distinction. They were worn at the hat, (the gentlemens', I suppose), and consisted of ribbons of various colours. If I mistake not, white ribbons are the only ones used at present.

> "What posies for our wedding-rings,
> What gloves we'll give, and ribbanings."
> —*Herrick.*

Bride favours appear to have been worn by the peasantry of France on similar occasions on the arm. Favours are still assumed on a variety of occasions.

Faw.—See *Gypsies.*

Fawkes, Guy.—(Nov. 5). The ignorant processions of boys, who carry about the effigy of the unfortunate Yorkshire gentleman, sing the following verses, which are, perhaps, scarcely worth insertion on any other ground than the gradual evanescence of all our old vulgar usages :

> Remember, remember
> The fifth of November,
>   Gunpowder treason and plot :
> I see no reason,
> Why gunpowder treason
>   Should ever be forgot.
> Guy Fawkes Guy,
> Hit him in the eye, etc.

The late Mr. Robert Davies, the scholarly Town Clerk of York, devoted a pamphlet to the family history of the Fawkes's of York, small 8vo., 1850. Good and sensible Bishop Sanderson exclaims : "God grant that we nor ours ever live to see November the fifth forgotten or the solemnity of it silenced." The figures of the Pope and the Devil were formerly burnt on this occasion. There is an account of the remarkable cavalcade on the evening of this day in the year 1679, at the time the Exclusion Bill was in agitation. The Pope, it should seem, was carried in a pageant representing a chair of state covered with scarlet, richly embroidered and fringed; and at his back, not an effigy, but a person representing the Devil, acting as his holiness's privy-councillor; and "frequently caressing, hugging, and whispering him, and oftentimes instructing him aloud." The procession was set forth at Moorgate, and passed first to Aldgate, thence through Leadenhall Street, by the Royal Exchange and Cheapside to Temple Bar. The statue of the Queen on the inner or eastern side of Temple Bar having been conspicuously ornamented, the figure of the Pope was brought before it, when, after a song, partly alluding to the protection afforded by Elizabeth to Protestants, and partly to the existing circumstances of the times, a vast bonfire having been prepared "over against the Inner Temple Gate, his holiness, after some compliments and reluctances, was decently toppled from all his grandeur into the impartial flames; the crafty Devil leaving his infallibilityship in the lurch, and laughing as heartily at his deserved ignominious end as subtle Jesuits do at the ruin of bigoted lay Catholics, whom themselves have drawn in." This enlightened demonstration was found so attractive, that, in 1680 it was repeated with additions. In 1715, the effigy of the old Pretender was burnt by the people, as well as those of the Pope and the Devil, on this anniversary, and the additional feature in the demonstration does not seem to have been given up, even when the Jacobite cause was finally abandoned.

This is one of the grand days with the Societies of the Temple, when an extra bottle of wine is allowed to each mess in hall; it used to be observed as a holiday at some of the public schools and offices. Before the custom declined in popularity everywhere, it was the practice of the boys to dress up an image of Guy Fawkes, holding in one hand a dark lanthorn, and in the other a bundle of matches, and to carry it about the streets begging money in these words, "Pray remember Guy Fawkes!" In the evening there are bonfires, and these frightful figures are burnt in the midst of them. In "Poor Robin" for 1677 are the following observations :

> "Now boys with
>   Squibs and crackers play,
> And bonfires' blaze
>   Turns night to day."

This old usage finds no favour with the High Church party at present so paramount, or with the community at large, and is in fact happily dying out.

Feathers. — There is a well-known article of popular belief in some districts, particularly in the eastern counties, that the presence of game-feathers in a feather bed will prolong the agonies of death. There is a curious paper on this subject by Mr. Albert Way, in the fourth volume of "Notes and Queries." 1st series. The same idea is entertained in some parts of Yorkshire with regard to pigeon's feathers, and in Cumberland respecting those of the turkey. The objection to game feathers is widely prevalent, occurring in Derbyshire and in several parts of Wales; and I hardly think that the superstition can be explained on the utilitarian theory propounded by the writer in the "Athenæum," "that none of these feathers are fit for use, being too hard and sharp in the barrel." It is impossible, according to Grose, for a person to die, while resting on a pillow stuffed with the feathers of a dove; but he will struggle with death in the most exquisite torture. The pillows of dying persons are therefore taken away, says he, when they appear in great agonies, lest they may have pigeons' feathers in them. A more ridiculous or degrading superstition can scarcely be imagined, and as to the removal of the pillow from under the head of a dying person, it is almost always followed by suffocation. Nurses, when they are not carefully watched, will snatch this support away suddenly, to accelerate the result, and save trouble. The "British Apollo" very properly characterizes this as an "old woman's story," and adds: "But the scent of pigeon's feathers is so strong, that they are not fit to make beds with, insomuch that the offence of their smell may be said (like other strong smells) to revive any body dying, and if troubled with hysteric fits. But as common practice, by reason of the nauseousness of the smell, has introduced a disuse of pigeons' feathers to make beds, so no experience doth or hath ever given us any example of the reality of the fact."

Fernseed. — The ancients, who often paid more attention to received opinions than to the evidence of their senses, believed that fern bore no seed (Pliny's "Nat. Hist.," by Holland, lib. xxvii. ch. 9). Our ancestors imagined that this plant produced seed which was invisible. Hence, from an extraordinary mode of reasoning, founded on the fantastic doctrine of signatures, they concluded that they who possessed the secret of wearing this seed about them would become invisible. This superstition Shakespear's good sense taught him to ridicule. It was also supposed to seed in a single night, and is called in Browne's Pastorals, 1614:

"The wond'rous one-night seeding ferne."

Johnson the Botanist, in his edition of Gerarde, 1633, says: "Fern is one of those plants which have their seed on the back of the leaf, so small as to escape the sight. Those who perceived that fern was propagated by semination, and yet could never see the seed, were much at a loss for a solution of the difficulty; and, as wonder always endeavours to augment itself, they ascribed to fernseed many strange properties, some of which the rustick virgins have not yet forgotten or exploded." In a MS. of the time of Queen Elizabeth there is the following receipt: "Gather fearne-seed on Midsomer Eve betweene 11 and 12 noone and weare it about thee continually." It is said to be also gatherable at night. Fernseed, according to a passage quoted by Grose, was looked upon as having great magical powers, and must be gathered on

Midsummer Eve. A person who once went to gather it reported that the spirits whisked by his ears, and sometimes struck his hat and other parts of his body, and at length, when he thought he had got a good quantity of it, and secured it in papers and a box, when he came home, he found both empty. A respectable countryman at Heston, in Middlesex, informed Brand in June, 1793, that when he was a young man, he was often present at the ceremony of catching the fern-seed at midnight, on the eve of St. John Baptist. The attempt, he said, was often unsuccessful, for the seed was to fall into the plate of its own accord, and that too without shaking the plant. Dr. Rowe, of Launceston, apprised him, October 17th, 1790, of some rites with fern-seed which were still performed at that place. Mr. Couch of Bodmin observes: "Midsummer-day, the feast of the Summer Solstice, is marked only (among the Cornish tinners) by the elevation of a bush or a tall pole, on the highest eminence of the stream work."

Torreblanca, in his "Demonologia," suspects those persons of witchcraft who gather fern-seed on this night. Lemnius tells us: "They prepare fern gathered in a tempestuous night, rue, trifoly, vervain, against magical impostures." In "The Pylgremage of Pure Devotyon, newly translatyd into Englishe," is this passage: "Peraventure they ymagyne the symylytude of a tode to be there, evyn as we suppose when we cutte the fearne-stalke there to be an egel, and evyn as chyldren (whiche they se nat indede) in the clowdes, thynke they see dragones spyttynge fyre, and hylles flammynge with fyre, and armyd men encounterynge." Of course this notion about fernseed is perfectly fanciful and equally groundless. Shakespear justly ridicules it in *Henry IV.*, i., 2:

"*Gadshill.* We steal as in a castle, cocksure; we have the receipt of fern-seed, we walk invisible."

Chamberlain. Nay, I think rather you are more beholden to the night than to the fern-seed, for your walking invisible."

Steevens remarks : "This circumstance [its gift of invisibility] relative to the fern-seed is alluded to in Beaumont and Fletcher's 'Fair Maid of the Inn':—

'Had you Gyges' ring?
Or the herb that gives invisibility?'

"Again, in Ben Jonson's 'New Inn':
'I had
No medicine, Sir, to go invisible,
No fern-seed in my pocket.'"

In "Flaine Percevall the Peace-maker of England," sign. C 3, the author remarks : "I thinke the mad slave hath tasted on a

fern-stalke, that he walkes so invisible."
Butler alludes to this superstitious
notion :

"That spring like fern, that infect weed
Equivocally, without seed."

Addison laughs at a doctor who was arrived at the knowledge of the green and
red dragon, and had discovered the female
fern-seed.—*Tatler*, No. 240.

Festing Penny.—See *Denier de
Foi.*

Fetch or **Fetich.**—There are, says
Grose, the exact figures and resemblances
of persons then living, often seen not only
by their friends at a distance, but many
times by themselves : of which there are
several instances in Aubrey's "Miscellanies." These apparitions are called
fetches, and in Cumberland swarths : they
most commonly appear to distant friends
and relations, at the very instant preceding the death of the person whose figure
they put on. Sometimes there is a
greater interval between the appearance
and death. For a particular relation of
the appearance of a fetch-light or dead-
man's candle, to a gentleman in Carmarthenshire, see the "Athenian Oracle,"
vol. i. pp. 76, 77, and ibid., vol. iii. p. 150 ;
also, Aubrey's "Miscellanies," p. 176 ;
and Baxter's "World of Spirits," 1691,
pp. 131-137.

Field-Ale or **Filkdale.**—Refreshment furnished in the field or open air to
bailiffs of hundreds, and supplied from
funds contributed by the inhabitants of
the particular hundred. It has long fallen into disuse. Tomlins, *Law Dict.*,
1835, in v.

Field Mice.—The following illustration of the barbarous practice of enclosing field-mice was received by Mr. Brand
in a letter, dated May 9, 1806, from Robt.
Studley Vidal, Esq., of Cornborough near
Bideford, a gentleman to whom he was
much indebted for incidental information
on the local customs of Devonshire :

"An usage of the superstitious kind
has just come under my notice, and which,
as the pen is in my hand, I will shortly
describe, though I rather think it is not
peculiar to these parts. A neighbour of
mine, on examining his sheep the other
day, found that one of them had entirely
lost the use of its hinder parts. On seeing it I expressed an opinion that the
animal must have received a blow across
the back or some other sort of violence
which had injured the spinal marrow, and
thus rendered it paralytic : but I was
soon given to understand that my remarks
only served to prove how little I knew of
country affairs, for that the affection of
the sheep was nothing uncommon, and
that the cause of it was well known,

namely a mouse having crept over its
back. I could not but smile at the idea ;
which my instructor considering as a mark
of incredulity, he proceeded very gravely
to inform me that I should be convinced
of the truth of what he said by the means
which he would use to restore the animal ;
and which were never known to fail. He
accordingly dispatched his people here
and there in quest of a field mouse ; and
having procured one, he told me that he
should carry it to a particular tree at
some distance and, inclosing it within a
hollow in the trunk, leave it there to
perish. He further informed me that he
should bring back some of the branches of
the tree with him for the purpose of their
being drawn now and then across the
sheep's back, and concluded by assuring
me, with a very scientific look, that I
should soon be convinced of the efficacy of
this process, for that, as soon as the poor
devoted mouse had yielded up his life a
prey to famine, the sheep would be restored to its former strength and vigour.
I can, however, state with certainty, that
the sheep was not at all benefited by this
mysterious sacrifice of the mouse. The
tree, I find, is of the sort called witchelm or witch-hazel." It is more properly
described as the wych elm or hazel.

Fifollets or **Feux Follets.**—See
Will o' the Wisp.

Fifteen or **Eleven.**—Some old
trick (? at cards). See Thynne's *Debate between Pride and Lowliness* (1570),
p. 51 of repr.

Fifth of November. — See
Fawkes (Guy) and *St. Hugh's Day.*

Fig Sunday.—A popular name for
the Sunday before Easter, in allusion to
Jesus Christ's alleged desire to eat that
fruit on his way from Bethany. Brand
says that it is known under this name in
Northamptonshire and Hertfordshire.
Miss Baker, writing in 1854, says : "It is
the universal custom with both rich and
poor to eat figs on this day. On the Saturday preceding this day, the market at
Northampton is abundantly supplied with
figs, and there are more purchased at this
time than throughout the rest of the year :
even the charity children in some places
are regaled with them. . ." *Northampt.
Gloss.*, 1854. A correspondent of Hone,
in the "Year Book," col. 1593, remarks :
"At Kempton in Hertfordshire, five miles
from Hertford, it hath long been, and, for
aught the writer knoweth, still is a custom for the inhabitants, 'rich and poor,
great and small,' to eat figs on the Sunday
before Easter, there termed 'Fig Sunday.'
A dealer in 'groceries,' resident at
Kempton, affirmed to me from his own
lengthy observations, that more figs are
sold in the village the few days previous

than in all the year beside." This was written in 1832.

Figging Craft.—A term applied in a tract elsewhere mentioned (See *Mumchance*) to cheaters at dice.

Figgy Pudding.—Plum pudding, so called in some parts. The Editor's father always used this form.

Finding or Losing Things.—Melton says : "That if a man, walking in the fields, finde any foure-leaved grasse, he shall in a small while after find some good thing. That it is nought for a man or woman to lose their hose garter. That it is a sign of ill lucke to find money." *Astrologaster*, 1620, p. 46. Greene in "The Groundworke of Conny-catching," 1592, (an alteration of Harman's "Caveat," 1567), sign. B, tells us, "'Tis ill lucke to keepe found money. Therefore it must be spent." Mason mentions as an omen of good luck, "If drinke be spilled upon a man ; or if he find old iron." Hence it is accounted a lucky omen to find a horse shoe. *Anatomie of Sorcerie*, 1612, 90, and *Horseshoe*, infrâ. Homes remarks : "How frequent is it with people (especially of the more ignorant sort, which makes the things more suspected), to think and say, (as Master Perkins relates), if they finde some pieces of iron, it is a prediction of good luck to the finders. If they find a piece of silver, it is a foretoken of ill luck to them. *Demonologie*, 1650, p. 60. Even the learned Boyle admits that he once stooped to pick up a horse-shoe, but it was only, he tells us, "to make merry with this fond conceit of the superstitious vulgar." *Occasional Reflections*, 1665, p. 217. It was considered unlucky to let a pin lie on the floor. So the common nursery rhyme instructs us :

> "See a pin and pick it up,
> All the day you'll have good luck ;
> See a pin and let it lay,
> Bad luck you'll have all the day."

Fire.—There is some curious matter bearing on this prolific subject in Mr. Wright's "Essays on the Superstitions of the Middle Ages," 1846, in the chapter devoted to mythology. One of the magical devices, against which there is a general protest in a Saxon homily, quoted by this learned writer, was directed against any one "who places his child on the roof, or in a furnace, for the recovery of his health. . . ." That a belief in the power of resuscitation by fire had at one time some hold on the popular mind in our country, we have evidence in the strange production called "The Treatyse of the Smyth whych that forged hym a new dame," printed about the middle of the sixteenth century, but a great deal older than the date of publication in its structure and doctrine. The piece may be seen in Hazlitt's *Popular Poetry*, 1864-6.

Fire-Balls.—See *Aërolites*.

Fire-Drake.—(*Draco volans*). White calls the fiery dragon "a weaker kind of lightning. Its livid colour, and its falling without noise and slowly, demonstrate a great mixture of watry exhalation in it. 'Tis sufficient for its shape that it has some resemblance of a dragon, not the expresse figure." *Institutions*, 1656, p. 156. By the subsequent description, copied by Blount from Bullokar's "Expositor," 1616, the fire-drake should seem to be a distinct appearance from the ignis fatuus : "There is a fire sometimes seen flying in the night, like a dragon : it is called a fire-drake. Common people think it a spirit that keeps some treasure hid ; but philosophers affirm it to be a great unequal exhalation inflamed between two clouds, the one hot, the other cold (which is the reason that it also smokes), the middle part whereof, according to the proportion of the hot cloud, being greater than the rest, makes it seem like a belly, and both ends like a head and tail." I suppose our author, when he says the above is like a dragon, refers to the common graphic description of that imaginary creature. The name is used in 1663 as characteristic of a ruffianly knight-adventurer. Hazlitt's *Handbook*, 1867, p. 198. In the "Life of Anthony a Wood," under date of May 16, 1668, is the following : "Between 9 and 10 of the clock at night, there was seen by them, Matthew Hutton and Anthony Wood and those of the family of Borstall near Brill, in Bucks, a draco volans fall from the sky. It made the place so light for a time, that a man might see to read. It seemed to A. W. to be as long as All Saints' steeple in Oxon, being long and narrow ; and when it came to the lower region, it vanished into sparkles, and as some say, gave a report. Great raines and inundations followed, &c." *Lives of Leland, Hearne and Wood*, 1772, ii., 212.

"A Fire-Drake," says Steevens, "is both a serpent, antiently called a brenning-drake or dipsas, and a name formerly given to a Will o' the Wisp, or ignus fatuus. So in Drayton's 'Nymphidia' ;

> 'By the hissing of the snake,
> The rustling of the fire-drake.' "

Again, in the anonymous play of "Cæsar and Pompey," 1607 :

> "So have I seene a fire-drake glide along
> Before a dying man, to point his grave,
> And in it stick and hide."

Aubanus, p. 270, speaking of his German experiences or observations, tells us: " Ignis fit, cui Orbiculi quidam lignei perforati imponuntur, qui quum inflammantur, flexilibus virgis præfixi, arte et vi in aërem supra Moganum amnem excutiuntur : Draconem igneum volare putant, qui prius non viderunt."

Plot, in his " Oxfordshire," fol. 203, mentions " that, about the year 750, a battle was fought near Burford, perhaps on the place still called Battle-Edge, west of the town towards Upton, between Cuthred or Cuthbert, a tributary king of the West Saxons, and Ethelbald king of Mercia, whose insupportable exactions the former king not being able to endure, he came into the field against Ethelbald, met, and overthrew him there, winning his banner, whereon was depicted a golden dragon; but this was an ordinary device or cognizance, and not an artificial *draco volans*, like that of Aubanus. Comp. *Excerpta Historica*, 1833, p. 404.

Fire Omens.—Willsford tells us: " When our common fires do burn with a pale flame, they presage foul weather. If the fire do make a huzzing noise, it is a sign of tempests near at hand. When the fire sparkleth very much, it is a sign of rain. If the ashes on the herth do clodder together of themselves, it is a sign of rain. When pots are newly taken off the fire, if they sparkle (the soot upon them being incensed), it presages rain. When the fire scorcheth, and burneth more vehemently than it useth to do, it is a sign of frosty weather; but if the living coals do shine brighter than commonly at other times, expect then rain. If wood or any other fuel do crackle and break forth wind more than ordinary, it is an evident sign of some tempestuous weather neer at hand; the much and suddain falling of soot presages rain." *Nature's Secrets*, 1658, p. 120. Defoe seems to say that in his time superstitious persons imagined every variety of shape in the fire: swords, and other weapons, buildings of all kinds, wedding-rings, bags of money, and, in fact, whatever they wished. *Mem. of Duncan Campbel*, 1732, p. 61. In the " Vicar of Wakefield," among the omens of the Doctor's daughters, are " Purses bounded from the fire." In the North of England, the cinders that bound from the fire are carefully examined by old women and children, and according to their respective forms are called either coffins or purses, and consequently thought to be the presages of death or wealth. A coal, says Grose, in the shape of a coffin, flying out of the fire to any particular person, betokens their death not far off. But, on the other hand, according to Moulin,

the flame suddenly bursting from the ashes was a good sign. *Vates*, p. 219.

" So when a child, as playful children use,
Has burnt to tinder a stale last year's News,
The flame extinct, he views the roving fire—
There goes my lady, and there goes the squire,
There goes the parson, oh ! illustrious spark,
And there, scarce less illustrious, goes the clerk !"

—Cowper's *Poems*, 1798, vol. i., p. 272. A flake of soot hanging at the bars of the grate, says Grose, also denotes the visit of a stranger. Some clap their hands when they see the latter, and by the number of times they do this, they judge the number of days that will elapse before the person comes. Many fantastic shapes are discerned in the fire, in the candle, and in the tea-cup by some people. I have had the figure of a dog carrying a parcel shown to me in the last-mentioned; but I hardly know whether this was supposed to be indicative of good or the reverse. I do not know whether this has anything to do with Cowper's idea, in his " Winter Evening," that the fungus in the candle " implies the arrival of a parcel."

Fires.—That fires were very frequent in London, Fitzstephen proves. The Saxon Chronicle also makes frequent mention of towns being burned, which might be expected for the same reason, the Saxon term for building being ꞅeꞇꞵmbꞟꞹꝥan. " Solæ pestes Londoniæ sunt Stultorum immodica potatio, et frequens Incendium."

Firing at the Apple Trees.—In Devonshire, on Twelfth Day Eve, the farmers used to rally out with guns and blunderbusses, and fire with powder only at the apple-trees in the orchards, pronouncing an invocation in doggerel, praying for a bountiful harvest of fruit. A representation of this ceremony was given in the *Illustrated London News* of January 11, 1851, and is reproduced on a smaller scale in the *Antiquary* for March, 1895, where the verses are given, with an account by a correspondent at Exeter. The origin of this custom is said to be unknown; the harmless fusillade may have been intended either as a salute to the good genius of the orchard or as a conjuration against evil spirits. The ancients attributed to their sylvan deities the prosperity of their fruit-seasons or otherwise.

First Foot or **Qual-tagh.** — In the North of England the first person who enters the house on Christmas or New Year's Eve is called, says Brockett, the First Foot.

Fives.—See *Tennis.*

Flapdragon.—See Halliwell in v.

Fleas.—I find the following in Hill's "Natural and Artificial Conclusions," 1581 : " A very easie and merry conceit to keep off fleas from your beds or chambers. Plinie reporteth that if, when you first hear the cuckow, you mark well where your right foot standeth, and take up of that earth, the fleas will by no means breed either in your house or chamber, where any of the same earth is thrown or scattered." So M. Thiers, "La première fois qu'on entend le Coucou, cerner la terre qui est sous le pied droit de celuy qui l'entend, & la répandre dans les maisons afin d'enchasser les puces." Among the jests of Scogin is "How Scogin sold Powder to Kill Fleas." He broke up some wood from a rotten post, and went about among the old wives, pretending that it was a famous receipt. Comp. *Old English Jest Books,* 1864, ii., 84.

Flibbertigibbet. — See Nares, *Gloss.,* 1859, in v.

Flies.—Willsford says : "Flies in the spring or summer season, if they grow busier or blinder than at other times, or that they are observed to shroud themselves in warm places, expect then quickly for to follow, either hail, cold storms of rain, or very much wet weather ; and if those little creatures are noted early in autumn to repare unto their winter quarters, it presages frosty mornings, cold storms, with the approach of hoary winter. Atomes or flies, swarming together and sporting themselves in the sunbeams, is a good omen of fair weather." *Nature's Secrets,* 1658, p. 135. " Amongst our deep sea fishermen at Greenock there is a most comical idea, that if a fly falls into the glass from which any one has been drinking, or is about to drink, it is considered a sure and true omen of good luck to the drinker, and is always noticed as such by the company."—*Notes and Queries,* Dec. 22, 1855. An anecdote in an early jest book possibly alludes to this idea. A traveller being at a banquet, where a fly chanced to fall into his glass, he took it out before he drank, but afterwards put it in again. Being asked his reason, he answered, that for his own part he did not like flies, but others might.

Flouncing.—The custom of flouncing is said to be peculiar to Guernsey. It is an entertainment given by the parents of a young couple, when they are engaged, and the match has received approval. The girl is introduced to her husband's family and friends by her future father-in-law, and the man similarly by hers : after this, they must keep aloof from all flirtation, however lengthy the courtship may prove. The belief is, that if either party break faith, the other side can lay claim to a moiety of his or her effects.

Flowers, Herbs, &c., on Days of Humiliation and Thanksgiving.—In the Parish Accounts of St. Margaret, Westminster, under 1650-1, are the following items, the interest of two of which is more than archæological :

"Item, paid for herbs that were strewed in the windows of the church, and about the same, att two severall daies of Humiliation, 3s. 10d. Item, paid for herbs that were strewed in the church upon a daie of thanksgiving, 2s. 6d. Item, paid for herbs that were strewed in the church on the 24th day of May, 1651, being a day of humiliation, 3s. Item, paid to the ringers, for ringing on the 24th of October, being a day of thanksgiving for the victorie over the Scotts at Worcester, 7s. Item, paid for hearbes and lawrell that were strewed in the church the same day, 8s." Mrs. Joyce Jeffries, of Hereford and other places, in the time of Charles I. used, as her account-books shew, to have her pew in All Saints' Church, Hereford, dressed with flowers at Christmas by the clerk's wife. It is still the universal practice to deck churches and private dwellings with holly at Christmas, and the evergreen is usually left to the end of February, or till Good Friday. In towns the custom is rather a mechanical habit, it is to be feared, than any genuine homage to a time-honoured observance. *Archæologia,* xxxvii., 200

Flowers, &c., at Marriages. —There was anciently a custom at marriages of strewing herbs and flowers, as also rushes, from the house or houses where persons betrothed resided, to the church. Herrick and Braithwaite refer to this usage. The former writes :

" All haile to Hymen and his marriage day,
Strew rushes and quickly come away ;
Strew Rushes, maides, and ever as you strew,
Think one day, maydes, like will be done for you."

Hesp., 1648, p. 129. *Strappado for the Divell,* 1615, p. 74. Browne, who wrote his Pastorals before 1614, evidently in the following lines describes some village wedding in his native Devon :

" As I haue seene vpon a Bridall day
Full many maids clad in their best array,
In honour of the Bride come with their flaskets
Fill'd full with flowers: others in wicker baskets

Bring from the marish rushes, to o'er-
    spread
The ground, whereon to church the
    louers tread :
Whilst that the quaintest youth of all
    the plaine
Vshers their way with many a piping
    straine."

Every one will call to mind the passage
in Shakespear to this purpose:

" Our bridal flowers serve for a buried
    corse."

Armin's "History of the Two Maids of
Moreclacke," 1609, opens thus, preparatory to a wedding : " Enter a maid strewing flowers, and a serving-man perfuming
the door. The maid says ' strew, strew,'
—the man, ' the muscadine stays for the
bride at Church.' " So in Brooke's "Epithalamium " :—

" Now busie maydens strew sweet
    flowres."

Engl. Hel., ed. 1614, R 1 v°. The strewing herbs and flowers on this occasion, as
mentioned in a note upon Barrey's play
of "Ram Alley," 1611, to have been practised formerly, is still kept up in Kent
and many other parts of England. Dodsley's *O. P.*, by Hazlitt, x., 366. In the
drama just cited, we read : " Enter Adri-
ana, and another strawing hearbes."

"*Adr.* Come straw apace. Lord ! shall
    I never live,
To walke to church on flowers? O, 'tis
    fine,
To see a bride trip it to church so
    lightly,
As if her new choppines would scorne
    to bruze
A silly flower !"

In "Oxford Drollery," 1671, p. 118, is a
poem styled " A Supposition," in which
the custom of strewing herbs is thus alluded to :

" Suppose the way with fragrant herbs
    were strowing,
All things were ready, we to church
    were going :
And now suppose the priest had joyn'd
    our hands," &c.

Flowers, &c., on Graves.—
Gough says : " The Greeks used the ama-
ranth and the polianthus, one species of
which resembles the hyacinth, parsley,
myrtle. The Romans added fillets or
bandeaux of wool. The primitive Christians reprobated these as impertinent
practices : but in Prudentius's time they
had adopted them, and they obtain in a
degree in some parts of our own country,
as the garland hung up in some village
churches in Cambridgeshire, and other

counties, after the funeral of a young
woman, and the inclosure of roses round
graves in the Welsh church yards, testify." He adds : " Aubrey takes notice
of a custom of planting rose trees on the
graves of lovers by the survivors, at Oak-
ley, Surrey, which may be a remain of
Roman manners among us : it being in
practice among them and the Greeks to
have roses yearly strewed on their graves,
as Bishop Gibson remarks from two inscriptions at Ravenna and Milan. The
practice in Propertius of burying the
dead in roses is common among our country people ; and to it Anacreon seems to
allude, in his 53rd Ode. *Sep. Mon. Introd.*
ii., xvii. and cciv. Bishop Gibson is also
cited as an authority for this practice by
Strutt. "Mann. and Customs, Anglo-
Saxon Era," vol. i. p. 69. See also Bray's
"Surrey," vol. ii. p. 165. I do not find
that the custom is at present retained.—
Ellis.

Moresin observes, at p. 61: "Flores
et Serta, educto Cadavere, certatim
injiciebant Athenienses." Sir Thomas
Browne, in his " Urneburiall," tells us
that among the antients " the funerall
pyre consisted of sweet fuell, cypresse,
firre, larix, yewe, and trees perpetually
verdant." And he observes, " Whether
the planting of yewe in church yards
holds its original from antient funerall
rites, or as an embleme of Resurrection
from its perpetual verdure, may also admit conjecture." Virgil, in Dryden's
version, describing Anchises grieving for
Marcellus, makes him say :

" Full canisters of fragrant lilies bring,
  Mix'd with the purple roses of the
    spring :
Let me with fun'ral flow'rs his body
    strow,
This gift which parents to their chil-
    dren owe,
This unavailing gift, at least I may
    bestow."

The custom of strewing flowers upon the
graves of departed friends, which has
been already incidentally noticed, is also
derived from a custom of the ancient
Church. St. Ambrose has these words :
" I will not sprinkle his grave with flowers, but pour on his spirit the odour of
Christ. Let others scatter baskets of
flowers : Christ is our Lily, and with this
I will consecrate his relicks." And St.
Jerome tells us : " Whilst other husbands
strewed violets, roses, lilies, and purple
flowers upon the graves of their wives,
and comforted themselves with such like
offices, Pammachius bedewed her ashes
and venerable bones with the balm of
alms." *Epistola ad Pammachium de
obitu Uxoris.* Durandus tells us that the

ancient Christians, after the funeral, used to scatter flowers on the tomb. P. 237. There is a great deal of learning in Moresin upon this subject. *Papatus,* 157. It appears from Pliny's "Natural History," from Cicero in his "Oration on Lucius Plancus," and from Virgil's sixth Æneid, that this was a funeral rite among the Romans. They used also to scatter them on the unburied corpse. Gough has the following passage: "The ancients used to crown the deceased with flowers, in token of the shortness of life, and the practice is still retained in some places in regard to young women and children. The Romish Ritual recommends it in regard of those who die soon after baptism, in token of purity and virginity. It still obtains in Holland and parts of Germany. The primitive Christians buried young women with flowers, and martyrs with the instruments of their martyrdom. I have seen fresh flowers put into the coffins of children and young girls." "Sep. Mon." vol. ii. introd. p. 5. "Cum igitur infans vel Puer baptizatus defunctus fuerit ante usum Rationis, induitur juxta ætatem, et imponitur ei Corona de floribus, seu de herbis aromaticis et odoriferis, in signum integritatis Carnis et Virginitatis." "Ordo Baptizandi, &c., pro Anglia, Hibernia, et Scotia," 1626, p. 97.

Bourne further remarks that, as the form of procession is an emblem of our dying shortly after our friend, so the carrying in our hands of ivy, sprigs of laurel, rosemary, or other evergreens, is an emblem of the soul's immortality. In the account of the funeral expenses of Sir John Rudstone, Mayor of London, 1531, I find the following article: "For yerbys at the bewryal, £0 1s. 0d." So, in a song in "Wit's Interpreter," 1655, we read:

"Shrouded she is from top to toe
With lillies which all o'er her grow,
   Instead of bays and rosemary."

In a book by Dr. Case, the author says: "I wil end with death, the end of all mortality, which though it be the dissolution of Nature and parting of the soul from the body, terrible in itself to flesh and blood, and amplified with a number of displeasant and uncomfortable accidents, as the shaving of the head, howling, mourning apparel, funeral boughs of yeu, box, cipresse, and the like, yet we shall find by resorting to antiquities, that musick hath had a share amongst them, as being unseasonable at no time." *Praise of Musicke,* 1586, F 8 v°. Friar Laurence in "Romeo and Juliet" says:

"Dry up your tears, and stick your Rosemary
On this fair corse."

Of Paris, the intended husband of Juliet, who, to all appearance, died on their wedding day, it is said, in the language of Shakespear,

"He came with flowers to strew his ladies grave,"

when he provoked and met his fate by the hand of Romeo. Overbury, in his "Characters," describing the "faire and happy milkmaid," says: "Thus lives she, and all her care is that she may die in the Spring time, to have store of flowers stucke upon her winding-sheet;" which has a complete parallel in the Breton usage commemorated in the traditional ballad or song, *The Flowers of May* (Bleuniou Mae), of which the concluding lines are:

"Heureuses les jeunes personnes, qui meurent au printemps!
Heureuses les jeunes personnes que l'on couvre de fleurs nouvelles."

Chants Populaires de la Bretagne, par Villemarqué, 1846, ii., 265. Gay describes thus the strewing of flowers upon the graves:

"Upon her grave the rosemary they threw,
The daisy, butter'd-flow'r, and endive blue."

He adds the custom is still used in the South of England, of fencing the graves with osiers, &c.; and glances at clerical economy, for which there is oftentimes too much occasion, in the last two lines:

"With wicker rods we fenced her tomb around,
To ward from man and beast the hallow'd ground.
Lest her new grave the parson's cattle raze,
For both his horse and cow the church yard graze."

Gough says: "It is the custom at this day all over Wales to strew the graves both within and without the church, with green herbs, branches of box, flowers, rushes and flags, for one year; after which, such as can afford it lay down a stone. *Sep. Mon.* ii., Introd. 294. The common Welsh graves are curiously matted round with single or double matting, and stuck with flowers, box, or laurel, which are frequently renewed." Pepys in his *Diary,* April 26, 1662, mentions a churchyard near Southampton, where the graves were "accustomed to be all sowed with sage." In Lancashire, it is still usual in some districts for each mourner to carry with him to the place of interment a sprig of box prepared for the purpose, and cast it, before leaving, into the grave of the departed. *Notes and Queries,* Dec. 26, 1868.

Flowers, &c., on Graves in South Wales.

Mr. Brand borrowed some notes from Malkin's *South Wales*, which, though perhaps of no great authority, I scarcely like to disturb: "The bed on which the corpse lies is always strewed with flowers, and the same custom is observed after it is laid in the coffin. They bury much earlier than we do in England; seldom later than the third day, and very frequently on the second. The habit of filling the bed, the coffin, and the room, with sweet-scented flowers, though originating probably in delicacy as well as affection, must of course have a strong tendency to expedite the progress of decay. It is an invariable practice, both by day and night, to watch a corpse; and so firm a hold has this supposed duty gained on their imaginations, that probably there is no instance upon record of a family so unfeeling and abandoned as to leave a dead body in the room by itself, for a single minute, in the interval between the death and burial. Such a violation of decency would be remembered for generations. The hospitality of the country is not less remarkable on melancholy than on joyful occasions. The invitations to a funeral are very general and extensive, and the refreshments are not light and taken standing, but substantial and prolonged. Any deficiency in the supply of ale would be as severely censured on this occasion as at a festival. The grave of the deceased is constantly overspread with plucked flowers for a week or two after the funeral. The planting of graves with flowers is confined to the villages and the poorer people. It is perhaps a prettier custom. It is very common to dress the graves on Whitsunday and other festivals, when flowers are to be procured: and the frequency of this observance is a good deal affected by the respect in which the deceased was held. My father-in-law's grave in Cowbridge Church has been strewed by his surviving servants every Sunday morning for these twenty years. It is usual for a family not to appear at church till what is called the month's end, when they go in a body, and then are considered as having returned to the common offices of life. It is a very antient and general practice in Glamorgan to plant flowers on the grave; so that many church yards have something like the splendour of a rich and various parterre. Besides this, it is usual to strew the graves with flowers and evergreens, within the church as well as out of it, thrice at least every year, on the same principle of delicate respect as the stones are whitened. No flowers or evergreens are permitted to be planted on graves but such as are sweet-scented: the pink and polyanthus, sweet Williams, gilliflowers, and carnations, mignonette, thyme, hyssop, camomile, and rosemary, make up the pious decoration of this consecrated garden. Turnsoles, pionies, the African marigold, the anemone, and many others I could mention, though beautiful, are never planted on graves, because they are not sweet-scented. It is to be observed, however, that this tender custom is sometimes converted into an instrument of satire; so that where persons have been distinguished for their pride, vanity, or any other unpopular quality, the neighbours whom they may have offended plant these also by stealth upon their graves. In the Easter week most generally the graves are newly dressed, and manured with fresh earth, when such flowers or ever-greens as may be wanted or wished for are planted. In the Whitsuntide holidays, or rather the preceding week, the graves are again looked after, weeded, and otherwise dressed, or if necessary, planted again. It is a very common saying of such persons as employ themselves in thus planting and dressing the graves of their friends, that they are cultivating their own freeholds. This work the nearest relations of the deceased always do with their own hands, and never by servants or hired persons. Should a neighbour assist, he or she never takes, never expects, and indeed is never insulted by the offer of any reward, by those who are acquainted with the ancient customs.

The vulgar practice and illiberal prejudice against old maids and old bachelors subsists among the Welsh in a very disgraceful degree, so that their graves have not unfrequently been planted by some satirical neighbours, not only with rue, but with thistles, nettles, henbane, and other noxious weeds. When a young unmarried person dies, his or her ways to the grave are also strewed with sweet flowers and ever-greens; and on such occasions it is the usual phrase, that those persons are going to their nuptial beds, not to their graves. There seems to be a remarkable coincidence between these people and the ancient Greeks, with respect to the avoiding of ill-omened words. None ever molest the flowers that grow on graves; for it is deemed a kind of sacrilege to do so. A relation or friend will occasionally take a pink, if it can be spared, or a sprig of thyme, from the grave of a beloved or respected person, to wear it in remembrance; but they never take much, lest they should deface the growth on the grave. This custom prevails principally in the most retired villages; and I have been assured, that in such villages where the right of grazing the church yard has been enforced, the practice has alienated the affections of very great numbers from the clergymen and their churches; so that many have become Dissenters for the singularly uncommon reason that they may bury their friends in Dissenting burying-grounds, plant their graves with flowers, and keep them clean and neat, without any danger of their being cropt. The white rose is always planted on a virgin's tomb. The red rose is appropriated to the grave of any person distinguished for goodness, and especially benevolence of character. The natives of the principality pride themselves much on these antient ornaments (the yews) of their church yards; and it is nearly as general a custom in Brecknockshire to decorate the graves of the deceased with slips either of bay or yew, stuck in the green turf, for an emblem of pious remembrance, as it is in Glamorganshire to pay a tribute of similar import, in the cultivation of sweet-scented flowers on the same spot. The graves of Glamorganshire, decorated with flowers and herbs, at once gratify the relations of the departed and please the observer."

Flying Coaches.—The older name of the merry-go-round at fairs. They are mentioned in *Poor Robin* for 1733. See the passage quoted in Nares, *Gloss.*, *in v.*

Flying Machine.—The name bestowed on the mail-coaches, which left London to convey passengers along all the great roads in the eighteenth century. It is found described in *Coaching Days and Coaching Ways*, 1903.

Font.—The font was usually covered, and the cover was made fast with a lock, in order to guard against malignant influences. There was more reason in the practice which formerly prevailed of securing the poor-boxes in the churches with locks and keys, and even iron plates, not *propter sortilegia*, but to guard the donations of the charitable against common-place depredators. "Archæologia," vol. x. p. 207-8, where "Gent. Mag." vol. xliv. p. 500 and vol. xlv. p. 13 are cited. The passage requiring this protection to fonts is curious :" Fontes baptismales sub sera clausi teneantur propter sortilegia."

Fool (Christmas).—In representations of the Fool, who took part in dramatic performances and in sports at festivals, he appears with all the badges of his office; the bauble in his hand, and a coxcomb hood, with asses' ears, on his head. The top of the hood rises into the form of a cock's neck and head, with a bell at the latter : and "Minshew's Dictionary," 1617, under the word *Coxcomb*, observes, that "natural idiots and fools have accustomed and still do accustome themselves to weare in their capes cockes feathers, or a hat with the necke

and head of a cock on the top, and a bell thereon." His hood is blue, guarded or edged with yellow at its scalloped bottom, his doublet is red, striped across, or rayed with a deeper red, and edged with yellow, his girdle yellow, his left-side hose yellow, with a red shoe, and his right-side hose blue, soled with red leather. In Gibson's "Memoranda," 1510-11, a charge of a halfpenny is made for "a turnyd ladyll spent for the foole," in connection with the Court Revel of the 15th November in that year. It seems from the prologue to "Henry the Eighth," that Shakespear's Fools should be dressed "in a long motley coat, guarded with yellow," which is illustrated by a passage in Rowlands:

"My sleeves are like some Morris-dauncing fellow,
My stockings, ideot-like, red, greene, and yeallow :—"

Comp. Nares, *Glossary*, 1859, in v., for an excellent note on this subject.

Fool (Court). — In the " Privy Purse Expenses of Henry VII." numerous entries occur of money given to fools " in reward." Under date of Jan. 12, 1492-3, there is, "To Peche the fole in reward, 6s. 8d." Two other fools present themselves in this record : the *Duke of Lancas-*

A COURT FOOL (15*th* Cent.).

ter and Diego the Spanish fool. Steevens notices that the calf-skin coats, worn formerly by the professional fools in great houses, were designed to mark their calling, and to protect them from chastisement by those indisposed to tolerate their extravagances; and this custom, in his time, was still retained in Ireland, in the Christmas mummings. He observes of the later jesters : "Sometimes these gentlemen over-passed the appointed limits, and they were therefore corrected or discharged. The latter misfortune happened to Archibald Armstrong, jester to King Charles the First." Rushworth says: "It so happened that, on the 11th of the said March (1637-8), that Archibald, the King's Fool, said to his Grace the Archbishop of Canterbury, as he was going to the Council-table, 'Whea's feule now? doth not your Grace hear the news from Striveling about the Liturgy?' with other words of reflection: this was presently complained of to the Council, which produced the order for his expulsion from Court." There is in Olaus Magnus a delineation of a fool, or jester, with several bells upon his habit, with a bauble in his hand, and he has on his head a hood with asses' ears, a feather, and the resemblance of the comb of a cock. The Lord Mayor of London had his fool.

Fool (Domestic).—The following passage occurs in Lodge's "Wit's Miserie," 1596, p. 73 : "He is like Captain Cloux, Foole of Lyons, that would needs die of the sullens, because his master would entertaine a new foole besides himself." Comp. *Newcastle*. A character of this kind was the unfortunate person, who might in the good old days be "begged" for a fool, if he was heir to an estate, and had no friends. These abuses were once frequent. See Thoms' *Anecdotes and Traditions*, 1839, p. 7, and Lyly's *Midas* (Works, 1858, ii., 74).

Fool Plough.—In the North of England there is a custom used at or about Shrovetide which, as will be seen, was anciently observed also in the beginning of Lent. The Fool Plough goes about, a pageant that consists of a number of sword dancers dragging a plough, with music, and one, sometimes two, in very strange attire ; the Bessy, in the grotesque habit of an old woman, and the fool, almost covered with skins, a hairy cap on, and the tail of some animal hanging from his back. The office of one of these characters. in which he is very assiduous, is to go about rattling a box amongst the spectators of the dance, in which he receives their little donations. It is also called the fond plough, aliter the white plough, so denominated because the gallant young men that compose it appear to be dressed in their shirts (without coat or waistcoat) upon which great numbers of ribbands folded into roses are loosely stitched on. It appears to be a very airy habit at this cold season, but they have on warm waistcoats under it. Hutchinson, speaking of the dress of the sword-dancers at Christmas, adds : "Others, in the same kind of gay attire, draw about a plough, called the Stot Plough, and, when they receive the gift, make the exclamation *Largess!*

but if not requited at any house for their appearance, they draw the plough through the pavement, and raise the ground of the front in furrows. I have seen twenty men in the yoke of one plough." He concludes thus : "The stot-plough has been conceived by some to have no other derivation than a mere rural triumph, the plough having ceased from its labour." *History of Northumberland*, ii., 18. The Fool Plough upon the Continent appears to have been used after the solemn service of Ash Wednesday was over. Hospinian gives a very particular account of it from Naogeorgus, and explains the origin of its name.

Fools (Feast of).—See Du Cange, v. Kalendæ, and Du Tilliott, "Memoires pour servir à l'Histoire de la Fête des Foux," 1751 (as well as the present work under April Fools' Day). Du Cange, v. Cervula, Carpentier Supplem. ad Du Cange, ibid. and under *Abbas Lætitiæ*, and Delrio "Disquisit. Magis.", L. iii. P. ii. Quœst. 4. Sect. 5, p. 477. See also Hospinian "de Orig. Fest. Christ." fol. 32 b. where the practice is mentioned nearly in the same words.

Foot-Ale.—Grose says, "There is a kind of beverage called 'Foot-Ale' required from one entering on a new occupation." A person in this position is even now, in many businesses, expected to pay his footing, as it is called, in kind. Auctioneers, when they hold their first sale, are sometimes expected to treat the company all round.

Football or **Camp.**—The sport named by Fitzstephen was almost certainly hand-ball. But football was one of the most popular games in the city in the middle ages, and regulations relating to it are found at intervals in the Corporation archives. It was prohibited in the fields near the City as early as 1314. But in 1409 a proclamation of Henry IV. forbad anyone to levy money on pretence of it being for the games of football or cockfighting. Riley's *Memorials*, 1868, p. 571. In the early part of the fifteenth century there was a gild of the Football Players, and they held their meetings at Brewers' Hall. Mr. Stahlschmidt found it recorded in an old MS. book belonging to the Brewers' Company. It is alluded to in a deed of 30 Henry VI. The ballad of *Sir Hugh, or, The Jew's Daughter*, opens with a scene in which Sir Hugh is playing at the game on Hallowday, when school boys are let out to engage in their amusements :—

"Yesterday was brave Hallowday,
And, above all days in the year,
The schoolboys all got leave to play,
And little Sir Hugh was there.

" He kicked the ball with his foot,
And kepped it with his knee,
And even in at the Jew's window
He gart the bonnie ba' flee— "

As to its antiquity two passages in the *Sussex Archæological Collections*, cited in *Notes and Queries*, may be acceptable here :—" In the proof of age of William Selwyne (baptized in 1403), a witness, John Hendyman, aged fifty-four, deposed that he knew the date, because after the baptism, he played football and broke his leg. post mort., 3 Henry VI., No. 51, cit. xv. S.A.C., 213). Again, as to the age of Robert Tank (baptized 1404), John Coumbes remembers it because he was playing football afterwards and broke his leg (Inq. p. m., 4 Hen. VI., No. 42, cit. xii. S.A.C., 43). Hence it is inferable that the game was not unusually played after christenings. Sir T. Elyot, in his *Governor*, 1531, decries the sport : "Some men wolde say that in the mediocritie, which I have soo moche praysed in shoot-ynge, why shuld not bouling, claishe pynnes, and koytynge, be as moche commended? Veryly as for the two laste, they be to be vtterly abiected of all noble men, in lyke wyse foote balle, wherein is nothynge but beastely fury, and extreme violence, where-of procedeth hurte, and consequently rancour and malice do remayn with them that be wounded, wherefore it is to be put in perpetual sylence." King Lear having chastised Goneril's steward, the latter replies, " I'll not be struck, my Lord,"— " Nor tripped neither, you base football player," replied the Earl of Kent, tripping up his heels. (I. iv.). Ray says that in his time it prevailed most in Norfolk, Suffolk, and Essex. To Sir Thomas Browne, who came among us from another kingdom of the Octarchy, it was new ; and he puts the word camp (or as he spells it, kamp) into his small collection of Norfolk words." The following description is from Forby's " Vocabulary," 1830. The writer says, that in his time two kinds of camp were recognised : rough-play and civil-play. " In the latter there is no boxing. But the following is a general description of it as it was of old, and in some places still continues. Two goals are pitched at the distance of 120 yards from each other. In a line with each are ranged the combatants : for such they truly are. The number on each side is equal ; not always the same, but very commonly twelve. They ought to be uniformly dressed in light flannel jackets, distinguished by colours. The ball is deposited exactly in the mid-way. The sign or word is given by an umpire. The two sides, as they are called, rush forward. The sturdiest and most active of each encounter those of the other. The contest for the ball begins, and never ends without black eyes and bloody noses, broken heads or shins, and some serious mischiefs. If the ball can be carried, kicked, or thrown to one of the goals, in spite of all the resistance of the other party, it is reckoned for one towards the game ; which has sometimes been known to last two or three hours. But the exertion and fatigue of this is excessive . . . The prizes are commonly hats, gloves, shoes, or small sums of money."

I shall transcribe hither what I find in a quarter where it might scarcely be looked for : "This rough and, it must be confessed, somewhat dangerous sport, originally in all probability introduced into this country by the Romans, may still on Shrove Tuesday be witnessed in certain towns of South Wales. The balls consist of bulls' bladders protected by a thick covering of leather, and blown tight. Six or eight are made ready for the occasion. Every window in the town is shut by break of day, at which time all the youths of the neighbourhood assemble in the streets. The ball is then thrown up in front of the town-hall ; and the multitude, dividing into two parts, strive with incredible eagerness and enthusiasm to kick the football to the other extremity of the town. In the struggle several kicks and wounds are given, and many fierce battles take place. The ball sometimes ascends thirty or forty feet above the tops of the highest houses, and falls far beyond, or goes right over into the gardens, whither it is immediately followed by a crowd of young men. The sport is kept up all day, the hungry combatants recruiting their strength from time to time by copious horns of ale and an abundant supply of the nice pancakes which the women sell in baskets at the corner of every street. To view this sport thousand of persons assemble from all the country round, so that to the secluded population of those districts it is in some sort what the battle in the Platanistas was to the Spartans, or even what the Isthmian and Nemean games were to the whole of Greece." St. John's *Manners and Customs of Ancient Greece*, 1842, i., 157. The same thing is still kept up at Dorking, Epsom, and Kingston, in Surrey ; but there has been a movement so far unsuccessful (1903) at Dorking for its discontinuance. "At the Surrey Quarter Sessions at Kingston yesterday the ancient custom of playing football in the principal streets of Dorking on Shrove Tuesday was referred to in the report of the Standing Joint Committee to the Justices. The committee stated that a petition signed by upwards of one hundred inhabitants of Dorking had been received, urging the committee to adopt necessary measures to put a stop to the practice. The reasons given were that it caused a complete cessation of business on the afternoon of that day; that it caused great danger to vehicular and pedestrian traffic; that the ancient custom has now entirely lost its significance in consequence of the totally different conditions now prevailing; and that it had become an intolerable nuisance. The petitioners stated that they had decided to discontinue closing their shops and barricading against an unlawful proceeding.—The Committee reported that they were making exhaustive inquiries on the subject with a view to the suppression of the custom, and would shortly make some definite announcement."—*Daily Graphic*, 1897. A very curious practice prevails at Sedgwick in Durham, where a match is periodically played between the tradespeople and the country-folk at Chester-le-Street, and probably elsewhere, and the ball on each occasion becomes public property, and returns to its custodian, the town-clerk, by the latter putting it thrice through the bull-ring prior to proceedings and at the close. *Antiquary* for April, 1896. In the volume for 1898, there is a very animated description of the Shrovetide celebration there in that year. At Pocklington, in the East Riding of Yorkshire, there is a narrow strip of ground, where, after the races, they play at football, and it sometimes happens that one of the players throws the ball to a man attending on horseback, who rides off with it, and unless he is overtaken by one belonging to the opposite side, carries it into his own parish, where he is secure. This is also the case in Morbihan, Brittany, as described in Mr. Weld's interesting work, 1856, but the sport seems to have been there carried to almost brutal extremities. Mr. Brand was informed that, at Alnwick Castle, in Northumberland, the waits belonging to the town come playing to the castle every year on Shrove-Tuesday, at two o'clock p.m., when a football was thrown over the castle walls to the populace. He saw this done Feb. 5th, 1788.

Football in Scotland.—In Sinclair's "Statistical Account of Scotland," the minister of Kirkmichael, in Perthshire, speaking of the manners and customs of the inhabitants, says, "Foot-ball is a common amusement with the schoolboys, who also preserve the custom of cock-fighting on Shrove Tuesday." On Shrove-Tuesday at Inverness there is a standing match at football between married and unmarried women, in which the former are always victors. Every year on Shrove-Tuesday the bachelors and married men drew themselves up at the Cross of Scone, on opposite sides. A ball was then thrown up, and they played from two o'clock till sun-set. The game was this. He who at any time got the ball into his hands, ran with it till overtaken by one of the opposite party, and then, if he could shake himself loose from those on the opposite side who seized him, he ran on: if not, he threw the ball from him, unless it was wrested from him by the other party; but no person was allowed to kick it. The object of the married men was to hang it; i.e., to put it three times into a small hole in the moor, the dool or limit on the one hand: that of the bachelors was to drown it: i.e., to dip it three times into a deep place in the river, the limit on the other. The party who could effect either of these objects won the game. But, if neither party won, the ball was cut into equal parts at sunset. In the course of the play one might always see some scene of violence between the parties; but, as the proverb of this part of the country expresses, 'All was fair at the Ball of Scone.' *Stat. Acc. of Scotland*, xviii., 82. "This custom is supposed to have had its origin in the days of chivalry. An Italian (it is said) came into this part of the country, challenging all the parishes, under a certain penalty in case of declining his challenge. All the parishes declined the challenge except Scone, which beat the foreigner, and in commemoration of this gallant action the game was instituted. Whilst the custom continued, every man in the parish, the gentry not excepted, was obliged to turn out and support the side to which he belonged; and the person who neglected to do his part on that occasion was fined: but the custom being attended with certain inconveniences, was abolished a few years ago."

The allusions to the game in early writings are very numerous. Tusser says:

"In meadow or pasture (to grow the
    more fine)
Let campers be camping in any of
    thine;
Which if ye do suffer when low is the
    spring,
You gain to yourself a commodious
    thing."

Chamberlain, in a letter to Carleton, March 5, 1600-1, says: "You may do well, if you have any idle time, to play the good fellow and come and see our matches at football, for that and bowling wilbe our best entertainment." Henry Spelman, in his *Relation of Virginia*, 1609, says: "They vse beside football play, wch women and young boyes doe much play at, the men neuer. They make ther gooles as ours, only they neuer fight nor pull one another doone. The men play wth a litell balle lettinge it falle out of ther hand and striketh wth the tope of his foot, and he that can strike the balle farthest, winnes that they play for." This is the earliest American reference to the game which I remember to have seen. I quote from a modern edition of the original MS., possibly not a very accurate text. But the sense is sufficiently clear, except that the writer seems to say in one place that the men in Virginia did not play, only the women and boys, and presently he alludes to the way in which his own sex did play.

"Football with us may be with them balloon :
As they at tilt, so we at quintain, run."

Randolph, *Eclogue on the Cotswold Games* (Works, 1875, 621-3). Day in the *Blind Beggar of Bednal Green*, 1659, makes Tom Strowd say : " I'll play a gole at Campball or wrassell a fall of the hip or the hin turn with ere a Courtnoll of ye all for 20 quarters of malt, and match me height for height." Strowd's was probably the rough play, like the modern Rugby. Under date of January, 1664-5, Pepys notes : "The street full of footballs, it being a great frost." Misson, writing about 1690, says : " In winter foot-ball is a useful and charming exercise. It is a leather ball about as big as one's head, fill'd with wind. This is kick'd about from one to t'other in the streets, by him that can get at it, and that is all the art of it." There is a proverb : " All fellows at football," which means that it is a case where every man must take his chance. It is a game which levels artificial distinctions. " We are hale fellows, well met, not onely at foot-ball, but at every thing else." *Ludus Ludi Literarius*, 1672, p. 73. Comp. *Liber Albus*, Rolls ed., p. 440 ; Halliwell's *Dictionary* in v. ; and Antiquary, xxxii., 99-100. It appears that this sport was known to the Mexicans prior to the Spanish conquest.

Football Money.—In the North of England, among the colliers, &c., it is customary for a party to watch the bridegroom's coming out of church after the ceremony, in order to demand money for a football, a claim that admits of no refusal. Thiers refers to an analogous abuse in France, and describes such practices as " insolences proscrites." " Traité des Superstitions," 1794, tom. iii., p. 477.

Foot-Saunt.—See *Cent-Foot.*

Forespoken Water.—See *Orkneys.*

Forester of the Fee.—A person who had for some service to the crown a perpetual right of hunting in a forest on payment of a certain rent. Halliwell in v. From Forester as an employment we get the proper names, *Forrester, Forester, Forster,* and *Foster.*

Forfeits in a Barber's Shop. —In " Measure for Measure," the author has written :—

—" the strong Statutes
Stand like the forfeits in a barber's shop,
As much in mock as mark ;"

On which Warburton observes, " Barbers' shops were, at all times, the resort of idle people :

'Tronstrina erat quædam : hic solebamus ferè
Plerumque eam opperiri.'——

Donatus calls it *apta sedes otiosis.* Formerly with us the better sort of people went to the barber's shop to be trimmed ; who then practised the under parts of surgery ; so that he had occasion for numerous instruments which lay there ready for use ; and the idle people, with whom his shop was generally crouded, would be perpetually handling and misusing them. To remedy which, I suppose, there was placed up against the wall a table of forfeitures, adapted to every offence of this kind ; which it was not likely would long preserve its authority." Dr. Henley adds : " I perfectly remember to have seen them " (the list of forfeits) "in Devonshire, printed like King Charles's Rules. See Nares, 1859, in v.

Fortune-Telling.—The following passage is from Lodge's *Wit's Miserie*, 1596, p. 17 : " There are many in London now adaies that are besotted with this sinne, one of whom I saw on a white horse in Fleet Street, a tanner knave I never lookt on, who with one figure (cast out of a schollers studie for a necessary servant at Bocordo) promised to find any man's oxen were they lost, restore any man's goods if they were stolne, and win any man love, where or howsoever he settled it, but his jugling knacks were quickly discovered." Baxter speaks of those men that tell men of things stolen and lost, and that show men the face of a thief in a glass, and cause the goods to be brought back, who are commonly called white witches. " When I lived," he says, " at Dudley, Hodges at Sedgley two miles off, was long and commonly counted such a one. And when I lived at Kedderminster one of my neighbours affirmed, that having his yarn stolen, he went to Hodges (ten miles off) and he told him that at such an hour he should have it brought home again, and put in at the window, and so it was ; and as I remember he shewed him the person's face in a glass.

Yet I do not think that Hodges made any known contract with the Devil, but thought it an effect of art." *World of Spirits*, 1691, p. 184. Comp. *Witches.*

In the *Daily Telegraph* newspaper for December 11, 1867, appeared the annexed paragraph : "At Leamington yesterday, a woman named Hannah Maria Moore was charged with fortune-telling. The defendant resided at a lonely cottage in the cutskirts of Leamington, and has long been celebrated for her knowledge of the occult arts, and her skill in divining the future. If report be true, the rich were as credulous as the poor, and even carriages might be seen waiting after night-fall in the vicinity of her dwelling. At last, so notorious did the scandal become, that the police took steps to obtain a conviction. Accordingly, on Monday night, the wives of two of the constables paid her a visit. If her powers of divination are to be judged by what she revealed to them, they certainly were not great, for she not only failed to discover the true object of their visit, but showed great consideration for them, and, out of compassion for their indigence, only charged threepence for all her glowing promises of sweethearts, weddings, and a long line of descendants. It would appear, however, from a letter found in her possession when apprehended, that she occasionally engaged to exercise her arts so as to send sweethearts to young women, as in the communication alluded to her correspondent upbraided her for not having fulfilled her promises, and exhorted her to redouble her efforts. The bench committed her to gaol for a month with hard labour."

Fox and Geese.—On the 4th March, 1587-8, John Wolfe the printer entered at Stationers' Hall the Gynnye game, Cheste game, and Foxe and Geese."

Fox in the Hole.—A boys' game as far back as the reign of Elizabeth. See Halliwell in v. It is mentioned by Herrick in his "New Yeares Gift sent Sir Simeon Steward," preserved among the Hesperides," 1648.

Foy.—A bad husband is described at the end of *England's Jests*, 1687, as "a passionate lover of morning-draughts, which he generally continues till dinner-time ; a rigid exacter of Num-Groats, and Collector General of Foys and Biberidge. He admires the produce of that apothegm, Lets drink first: and would rather sell 20 per cent. to loss than make a dry-bargain." Eden, in his "State of the Poor," 1797, vol. i., p. 560, gives us the following passage from Fergusson's "Farmer's Ingle":

"On some feast day, the wee-things busk it braw,
Shall heeze her heart up wi' a silent joy,
Fu' cadgie that her head was up, and saw
Her ain spun cleething on a darling Oy,
Careless tho' death should make the feast her foy."

After explaining Oy in a note to signify grand-child, from the Gaelic *Ogha*, he tells us "A Foy is the feast a person, who is about to leave a place, gives to his friends before his departure."

Freemen of Highgate.—See *Horns.*

Free Warren.—As far back as the reign of Henry II., the citizens of London had the right of free warren in Middlesex, Hertfordshire, the Chiltern country, and in Kent, as far as the Cray. This right was probably renewed in 1226, in which year Stow erroneously places its original concession. A limitation on the primitive liberty of hunting, fowling, &c., seems to have been made in the reign of Henry VI., when the parks, from which the venison was to be taken, were specified by the lords of the Council. In the time of Elizabeth, the right had been formally commuted for a yearly warrant from the government upon the keepers of certain parks within the county of Middlesex, for the delivery of bucks to the mayor and aldermen. Comp. Hazlitt's *Bibl. Coll.*, 2nd Series, 118 v. *Charter Warren.*

St. Frethmund, Fredysmund, or **Fremund.**—Son of Offa, King of Mercia, and his queen Botilda, murdered by a servant of the king his father, and canonised about 790 A.D. A long account of him from various early authorities is printed in the *Antiquary* for May, 1893, where it is stated that he is supposed to have been buried at Cropedy Church, Lincolnshire. In 1488, St. Frethmund had a chapel in the cathedral at Lincoln, as we learn from the will of Richard Danvers of Prescott, co. Oxford, made in that year, where he leaves 20s. to the chaplain to pray for his soul, and a shrine in Cropedy Church, to the repairs of which a similar amount is dedicated by the testator. It may be added that Nicolas, in his *Chronology of History*, calls him hermit and martyr, and states that his anniversary was May 11. The son of this Danvers, Sir John Danvers, died in 1514, and also left benefactions to Cropedy Church and St. Fremund's Church ; and above his tomb in Dauntsey Church, Wilts, was formerly a window stained with glass, illustrating the legend.

Friar Rush, mentioned in Harsnet's *Declaration of Popish Impostures*, 1603, as a Christmas game; but its nature is not explained.

Friar Tuck.—Tollett describes this character upon his window as in the full clerical tonsure, with a chaplet of white and red beads in his right hand: and, expressive of his professed humility, his eyes are cast upon the ground. His corded girdle and his russet habit denote him to be of the Franciscan Order, or one of the Grey Friars (the only one exempt from episcopal jurisdiction, as Tollett himself pointed out). His stockings are red, his red girdle is ornamented with a golden twist, and with a golden tassel. At his girdle hangs a wallet for the reception of provision, the only revenue of the mendicant orders of religion, who were named Walleteers or budget-bearers. Steevens supposes this Morris Friar designed for Friar Tuck, of Fountain's Dale, chaplain to Robin Hood, as King of May. The Friar's coat, as appears from some of the extracts of Churchwardens' and Chamberlain's Accounts of Kingston, was generally of russet. The original character was one of the heroes of the Robin Hood epic. Hazlitt's *National Tales and Legends*, 1892, p. 273.

Friday (Good).—See *Good Friday.*

Friday in Lide.—The first Friday in March is so called from Llyd, Anglo-Saxon for *tumult* or *loud.* "This day," says Mr. Couch, "is marked by a serio-comic custom of sending a young lad on the highest bound or hillock of the work, and allowing him to sleep there as long as he can; the length of his siesta being the measure of the afternoon nap for the tinners throughout the ensuing twelvemonth. The weather which commonly characterizes Friday in Lide is, it need scarcely be said, scarcely conducive to prolong sleep. In Saxon times the labourers were usually allowed their mid-day sleep; and I have observed that it is even now permitted to husbandmen in some parts of East Cornwall, during a stated portion of the year. Tusser speaks of it in his 'Five Hundred Points of Good Husbandry':

' From May to mid August an hour or two,
Let Patch sleep a snatch, howsoeuer ye do:
Though sleeping one hour refresheth his song,
Yet trust not Hob Grouthead for sleeping too long.' "

Browne, in the third eclogue of the "Shepheard's Pipe," 1614, clearly alludes to this usage, where he makes Thomalin say:

" Where is euery piping lad
That the fields are not yclad
With their milk-white sheep?
Tell me: Is it Holy-day,
Or if in the month of May
Use they long to sleepe? "

The same author has the practice in view, where he says in the third song of his first Book of *Pastorals*, in reference to the song-birds in the woodland:

" Whose pleasing noates the tyred swaine have made
To steale a nap at noone-tide in the shade."

Frindsbury, Kent.—Ireland, in his "Views of the Medway," speaks of a singular custom which used to be annually observed on May Day by the boys of Frindsbury and the neighbouring town of Stroud. "They met on Rochester Bridge, where a skirmish ensued between them. This combat probably derived its origin from a drubbing received by the monks of Rochester in the reign of Edward I. These monks, on occasion of a long drought, set out on a procession for Frindsbury to pray for rain; but the day proving windy, they apprehended the lights would be blown out, the banners tossed about, and their order much discomposed. They, therefore, requested of the Master of Stroud Hospital leave to pass through the orchard of his house, which he granted without the permission of his brethren; who, when they had heard what the master had done, instantly hired a company of ribalds, armed with clubs and bats, who way-laid the poor monks in the orchard, and gave them a severe beating. The monks desisted from proceeding that way, but soon after found out a pious mode of revenge, by obliging the men of Frindsbury, with due humility, to come yearly on Whit Monday, with their clubs in procession to Rochester, as a penance for their sins. Hence probably came the by-word of Frindsbury clubs."

Fritters or **Frutters Thursday.**—In Leeds and the neighbourhood, they eat a sort of pancake on the Thursday, which in that part they call frutters (fritters) Thursday. The Leeds fritter, it is said in the "Dialect of Leeds," 1862, p. 307, is "about one-fourth the size of a pancake, thicker, and has an abundance of currants in it."

Frog in the Middle.—A game played by both sexes, and consisting of a party of four or more, of whom one sat in the middle (the frog), and was playfully buffeted by the others, till he or she could catch one of them, who had then to take the place. A representation of the mode of playing this game occurs in Wright's

Domestic Manners, 1862, p. 233. *Frog in the Middle* seems to date back to an early period.

Fullam.—Compare a note in Nares, *Gloss.* in v. where there is a cross-reference to *Gourds*, and *High-Men* ibid., and see *Huth Cat*, p. 1005.

Funeral Customs.—"All funerals," says Adam, in his "Roman Antiquities," p. 476, "used antiently to be solemnized in the night time with torches, that they might not fall in the way of magistrates and priests, who were supposed to be violated by seeing a corpse, so that they could not perform sacred rites, till they were purified by an expiatory sacrifice. Serv. in Virg. xi. 143; Donat. Ter. And. i. I, 81. And hence we get the term itself, as the primitive lights were formed of small ropes or cords (funes) dipped in wax or tallow. But in after ages public funerals (funera indictiva) were celebrated in the daytime, at an early hour in the forenoon, as it is thought from Plutarch, in Syll. with torches also. Serv. in Virg. Æn. vi. 224. Tacit. Ann. iii. 4. Private or ordinary funerals (tacita) were always at night. *Fest. in Vespilones.* Sir Thomas Browne, speaking of the ancients, observes, that "they poured oyle upon the pyre, while the intention rested in facilitating the accension: but to place good omens in the quick and speedy burning, to sacrifice unto the windes for a dispatch in this office, was a low form of superstition." *Hydriotaphia*, p. 59. But when the remains were calcined, wine was poured over them, and when they were intended for preservation, they were then collected in a vase or urn, the which in the Homeric age was finally deposited with honours in the ground or in a barrow. Such or similar rites are described as attendant on the sepulture of Beowulf.

The Greek, Roman, and Anglo-Saxon methods of interment appear to have presented close analogies, and even domestic utensils, weapons and jewelry were favourite accompaniments of the departed; and instances are recorded, where, for some unknown reason, but probably because the persons had died abroad, the barrow was a cenotaph, containing only the complimentary accessories or the affectionate homage—in one case (at Bourne Park, Kent), a shield, a horse's bit, and other similar articles at home, perhaps by a soldier on foreign service or a crusader. "Their last valediction thrice uttered by the attendants was also very solemn; 'Vale, Vale, Vale, nos te ordine quo Natura permittet sequemur': and somewhat answered by Christians, who thought it too little, if they threw not the earth

thrice upon the enterred body." Gough says: "The women of Picardy have a custom of calling the deceased by his name, as he is carried to the grave. So do the Indians, and expostulate with him for dying, which reminds us of the Irish: "Och! why did ye die?" Χαιρε was among the Greeks a common parting exclamation.

Bourne tells us, that they followed the corpse to the grave, because it presented to them what would shortly follow, how they themselves should be so carried out. *Antiq. Vulg.* ch. iii. In Langley's abridgement of Polydore Vergil, 1546, we read: "In burials the old rite was that the ded corps was borne afore, and the people folowed after, as one should saie we shall dye and folowe after hym, as their laste woordes to the coarse did pretende. For thei used to say, when it was buried, on this wise, farewell, wee come after thee, and of the folowyng of the multitude thei were called exequies." It appears that among the primitive Christians the corpse was sometimes kept four days. Pelagia, in Gregory of Tours, requests of her son, that he would not bury her before the fourth day. In the will of John Hales, of Eton, "the ever-memorable," proved in March, 1666, there is a passage, in which he says that he desires to be buried "the next evening-song after he shall die," in a plain simple manner, "without sermon or ringing of bells, commensations, compotations, or such like solemnities."

Misson, speaking of funerals, says: "They let the body lie three or four days, as well to give the dead person an opportunity of coming to life again, if his soul has not quite left his body, as to prepare mourning and the ceremonies of the funeral. They send the beadle with a list of such friends and relations as they have a mind to invite; and sometimes they have printed tickets which they leave at their houses. A little before the company is together for the march," he continues, "they lay the body into the coffin upon two stools, in a room, where all that please may go and see it; then they take off the top of the coffin, and remove from off the face a little square piece of flannel, made on purpose to cover it, and not fastened to any thing. Being ready to move, one or more beadles march first, each carrying a long staff, at the end of which is a great apple, or knob of silver. The body comes just after the minister or ministers attended by the Clerk. The relations in close mourning, and all the guests, two and two, make up the rest of the procession." *Travels in England*, transl. by Ozell, 90.

It was customary, in the Christian burials of the Anglo-Saxons, to leave the head and shoulders of the corpse uncovered till the time of the burial, that relations, &c., might take a last view of their deceased friend. To this day we yet retain (in our way) this old custom, leaving the coffin of the deceased unscrewed till the time of the burial. They were wont, says Bourne, to sit by the corpse from the time of death till its exportation to the grave, either in the house it died in, or in the church itself. To prove this he cites St. Austin, concerning the watching the dead body of his mother Monica; and Gregory of Tours, concerning that of St. Ambrose, whose body was carried into the church the same hour he died. In the monumental effigy of Berengaria, queen of Richard Cœur de Lion, at Le Mans, the figure holds a book, on the covers of which is embossed a representation of the departed, lying on a bier, with waxen torches burning in candlesticks by her side. Fairholt's *Costume in England*, 1860, p. 82. This practice was general, and is still in vogue among the Romanists. Pope refers to the practice of setting candles upon the bier during the wake or watching time:

" Ah hopeless lasting flames ! like those that burn
To light the dead, and warm th' unfruitful urn."
—*Eloïsa to Abelard.*

Some of the earliest notices of funeral observances in England, dating back to Anglo-Norman times, are connected with the Gilds of the City of London, and particularly with that of the Saddlers. A convention made between the latter and the monastery of St. Martin's-le-Grand, immediately contiguous to their ancient quarters, in 1154, shews that the brethren of the Company enjoyed the privileges of sepulture in the burial ground of the holy fraternity on payment for the ringing of the bell and the reception of the body, the sum of eightpence. Many of the London gilds still preserve the rich palls, which used to be thrown over the coffin on its passage to the place of interment within the civic precincts. Hazlitt's *Livery Companies of London*, 1892, pp. 602, 608, *et passim*. A reference to the same authority will shew the former universality of lights maintained in churches and chapels for the souls of the departed, out of funds bequeathed by testators and others. Misson mentions, under the head of funerals, " the washing the body thoroughly clean, and shaving it, if it be a man, and his beard be grown during his sickness." Pennant, in his "Tours in Wales," informs us that, " at these words 'we commit the body

to the ground,' the minister holds the spade and throws in the first spadeful of earth." He adds : " At Skiv-'og from the Park to the Church I have seen the bier carried by the next of kin, husband, brothers, and father in law. All along from the house to the church yard at every cross-way, the bier is laid down, and the Lord's Prayer rehearsed, and so when they first come into the church yard, before any of the verses appointed in the service be said. There is a custom of ringing a little bell before the corps, from the house to the church yard (Dymerchion.) Some particular places are called resting-places." " Skyvi'og. When a corpse is carried to church from any part of the town, the bearers take care to carry it so that the corps may be on their right hand, though the way be nearer and it be less trouble to go on the other side; nor will they bring the corps through any other way than the south gate. If it should happen to rain while the corps is carried to church, it is reckoned to bode well to the deceased, whose bier is wet with the dew of Heaven. At church the evening service is read, with the Office of Burial. The minister goes to the altar, and there says the Lord's Prayer, with one of the prayers appointed to be read at the grave: after which the congregation offer upon the altar, or on a little board for that purpose fixed to the rails of the altar, their benevolence to the officiating minister. A friend of the deceased is appointed to stand at the altar, observing who gives, and how much. When all have given, he counts the money with the minister, and signifies the sum to the congregation, thanking them all for their good will." The same writer informs us that the Scotish and Irish practice of howling or shrieking at burials was equally prevalent in Wales. *Tours in Wales*, 1810, ii., 175. Not improbably it was a Celtic usage. We learn from the inscription in a copy of the *Bowman's Glory*, 1682, by W. Wood, that he was buried at Clerkenwell, attended by the Company of Archers, who shouted three times over his grave. *Gent. Mag. Lib.*, (*Bibl. Coll.*, 222). In Thomas Hill's Book on Dreams, signat. M i., is the following passage: " To a sicke person to have or weare on white garments doothe promyse death, for that dead bodyes bee caryed foorth in white clothes. And to weare on a blacke garmente, it doothe promyse, for the more parte, healthe to a sicke person, for that not dead personnes, but suche as mourne for the deade, do use to be clothed in blacke." At the funerals of unmarried persons of both sexes, as well as infants, the scarves, hatbands, and gloves given as mourning are white. Pepys saw in Westminster Hall Mistress Lane and the rest of the maids, who had been at the funeral service over a young bookseller in the Hall, and who all wore their white scarves. This was in January, 1659-60. Laying out the corpse is an office always performed by women, who claim the linen, &c., about the person of the deceased at the time of performing the ceremony. It would be thought very unlucky to the friends of the person departed, were they to keep back any portion of what is thus found. These women give this away in their turn by small divisions; and they who can obtain any part of it, think it an omen or presage of future good fortune to them or theirs.

The following is an extract from the old Register-book of Christ Church, Hants: — "April 14, 1604. Christian Steevens, the wife of Thomas Steevens, was buried in child-birth, and buried by women, for she was a Papishe." *Warner*, ii., 130. Pennant states: "The people kneel, and say the Lord's Prayer on the graves of their dead friends for some Sundays after their interment: and this is done generally upon their first coming to Church, and, after that, they dress the grave with flowers. Llanvechan." Gough adds that in Flintshire they say the prayer as the body leaves the house. *Sep. Mon.*, ii., cciv. In the time of Durandus coals, holy water, and frankincense were, in some places, put into the grave. The holy water was to drive away the devils; the frankincense to counteract the ill smells of the body." *Rationale*, vii., 35, 38. Sir Thomas Browne, in his "Urne-burial" observes, that "the custom of carrying the corpse as it were out of the world with its feet forward, is not inconsonant to reason, as contrary to the native posture of man, and his production first into it." Macaulay observes: "At the funeral of a yeoman, or farmer, the clergyman generally leads the van in the procession, in his canonical habiliments; and the relations follow the corpse, two and two, of each sex, in the order of proximity, linked in each other's arms. At the funeral of a young man it is customary to have six young women, clad in white, as pall-bearers; and the same number of young men, with white gloves and hatbands, at the funeral of a young woman. But these usages are not so universally prevalent as they were in the days of our fathers." *Hist. of Claybrook*, 1791, 131.

Judging from an illustration in an early Breviary in the British Museum, the body was at first consigned to the ground in the funeral cerements, but without any coffin, and the latter was not introduced down to a comparatively late period. *Archæol. Album*, 1845, p. 90. A similar practice is followed by the Mohammedans, and ap-

pears to have prevailed on the European continent, which doubtless derived it from the East, as England may have done from her immediate neighbours across the Channel. There is a story laid in Picardy, in fact, where a woman taken to be dead, but only in a lethargy, was followed to the grave, wrapped in a sheet, and the bearers, going too near a hedge, the thorns penetrated the covering, and restored vitality. Hazlitt's Studies in Jocular Literature, 1890, p. 120. It is this tale, to which Tallemant des Reaux seems to refer; but he gives it a various reading. *Historiettes*, ed. 1854,

BURIAL WITHOUT A COFFIN.

i., 437. Speaking of the peculiarities in the conduct of a Cleveland funeral, Mr. Atkinson says (1868): "Till lately, when the corpse of an unmarried female was carried to the churchyard, the bearers were all single, and usually young women dressed in a kind of uniform, in some places all in white, in other in black dresses with white shawls and white straw bonnets trimmed with white. The servers (the young women who wait at the arval-supper) also always preceded the coffin, as it approached the churchyard, sometimes in white, more usually in black with a broad white ribbon worn scarf-wise over one shoulder, and crossing over the black shawl; or else with knots or rosettes of white on the breast." In Cornwall, the manner among the lower orders is to bear the coffin almost level with the ground, slung on trestle boards, the members of the procession taking turns; and the dead body occupies the centre of the group. There is no hearse or vehicle of any kind (1875). In the Cotswolds there appears to be a pretty and appropriate custom at the burials of little children, by which the coffin is borne in the case of a boy by four children of that sex in black dresses and white hats, and in that of a girl by as many young females of the village similarly attired. This probably ancient usage will doubtless grow obsolete, as the neighbourhood becomes more conventional. *Graphic*, Oct. 25, 1902. At the recent interment of a bailiff, belonging to a farmhouse among the hills on the borders of Devonshire and West Dorsetshire, the body was borne to the churchyard in a waggon decorated with heather, the coffin being hidden under bunches of oats. Three cart-horses, whose manes were embellished with black rosettes, drew the vehicle; the lord of the manor headed the procession on a black hunter, and a hundred labourers from the farm and the neighbourhood followed the remains. *Daily Mail*, Sept. 5, 1903.

In the heart of London, in the neighbourhood of the Seven Dials, among the costermongers who are of superior standing and means, the last tribute to the defunct often costs a considerable sum, and involves a good deal of ceremony. The body is duly prepared, and laid upon a truck—the one used by the departed—with a pall over it, and the friends having assembled, a procession threads all the adjoining thoroughfares, preparatory to the departure for the place of interment. Where the deceased person was popular, as many as 400 or 500 will attend the committal to the earth, and the funeral cortège will consist of a dozen well-appointed carriages. It yet (1903) remains a characteristic trait of the English poorer class to expend a disproportionate amount on burials.

Grose says:— "If you meet a funeral procession, or one passes by you, always take off your hat: this keeps all evil spirits attending the body in good humour, but this, though very usual abroad, is very rarely practised here, at least in large towns."

In relation to the stage of the burial service where the minister says, *Earth to Earth*, and casts a handful over the coffin after deposition, there is the passage in Herrick's *Hesperides*, 1648, where, in speaking of his youthful years, the poet says, that he shall never again visit Westminster or Cheapside:

> "Where the earth
> Of Julian Herrick gave to me my birth."

It is observed that in sandy, wet soils twenty years suffice to obliterate every vestige of a coffin and its contents except perhaps the brass plate and a few nails, where no artificial precautions have been taken. This point may be collated with a familiar passage in *Hamlet*.

In some excavations undertaken in 1576, according to Stow, in Spitalfields, certain Roman cinerary urns were brought to light, which in company with the ashes, contained a small coin of the contemporary emperor, and in the tomb of Canute, opened at Winchester in modern times, one of the hands held a silver penny of that ruler. The precise object of this practice has not been determined, although it has been suggested that it might have been a tradition from later Hellenic folklore and the ferryman Charon who, however, only accepted fares in the shape of persons canonically buried. A different class of association between coins and the dead was the deposit of money in tombs commemorative of the reign of a sovereign, as in the case of Napoleon at St. Helena in 1821.

Funerals, Ceremonial Usages at. — When the tomb of King John in Worcester Cathedral was opened in 1797, the remains were found to have been deposited in the earth, habited in the same manner as the monumental effigy outside. The King wore a supertunic of crimson embroidered with gold, with red hose and black shoes; his gilt spurs were fastened to his feet by straps of light blue, striped with green and yellow. The beard was closely trimmed. But the most remarkable variation was that on the head was a monk's cowl, corroborating the statement of the chroniclers, that John had assumed that article of dress in his last moments as a protection from the Devil. Fairholt's *Costume in England*, 1860, p. 83-4. The identical notion recurs elsewhere, as the subjoined extract shews:— "On the 13th May, 1220, (4 Hen. iii.) died Robert the second Lord Berkelye, ætis. 55 or thereabouts, and was buried in the North Isle of the Church of the Monastery of St. Augustines (Bristol) over against the high altar, in a monck's cowle, an usual fashion for great peeres in those tymes, esteemed as an amulet or defensative to the soule, and as a Scala Cœli, a ladder of life eternal." Smyth's *Berkeley MSS.*, i., 117. This was Robert de Berkeley, second baron by tenure under a charter of Queen Eleanor. In Ceremonies and Services at Court in the reign of Henry VII. there is a reference to the manner in which the body of Henry V. was brought over to England from France in 1422: "In conveynge over of King Henry V[th]. out of France into Englond," the narrative informs us, "his coursers were trappid w[t] trappers of party coloures: one sid was blewe velvet embrodured w[t] antilopes drawenge iij. iuillis; the toy[r] sid was grene velvet embrowdered withe antelopes sittinge on stires w[t] long flours springinge betwene the hornes; the trappers aftur, by the conandment of kinge Henry the VIth, were sent to the Vestry of Westminst[r]; and of every coloure was mad a cope, a chesabille, and ij tenacles; and the gefereys of one coloure was of the clothe of oy[r] coloure." Many other curious and important particulars relative to funeral ceremonies may be gathered from the same paper ("Antiq. Repert." ed. 1807, vol. i. p. 311.). Somewhat later we find a high authority deprecating unbecoming expenditure on these occasions. Archbishop Warham in his will, 1530, says:— "Non convenit enim eum quem humiliter vivere decet, pomposé sepeliri, nisi velit, et id frustrâ, cadaveri mortuo majores honores deberi quam corpori vivo." Extravagant outlay on burials was forbidden by the ancient Greek law, which does not appear to have been uniformly respected any more than such enactments in modern times.

In the first funeral which he seems to have witnessed after the accession of Queen Elizabeth, and the return to Protestantism, Machyn is rather minute in his description. He says: "Ther was a gret compene of pepull, ij and ij together, and nodur (neither) prest nor clarke, the nuw (new) prychers in ther gowne lyke leymen, nodur nor sayhyng tyll they cam to the grave, and a-for she was put into the grayff a collect in Englys, and then put in-to the grayff, and after took some heythe (earth) and caste yt on the corse, and red a thynge . . . for the same, and contenent (incontinently) cast the heth in-to the grave, and contenent red the pystyll of sant Poll to the Stesselonians (Thessalonians) the . . chapter, and after that they song paternoster in Englys, boyth prychers and odur, and (. . .) of a nuw fassyon, and after on of them whent in-to the pulpytt and mad a sermon." This narrative, in spite of its uncouth phraseology and orthography, seemed worth transcribing, as being the earliest account we have of a funeral rite subsequently to the re-establishment of the reformed faith. At the funeral of Lady Cicily

Mansfield, in 1558, Lady Petre was chief mourner.

During two centuries and a half the Dyotts of Lichfield buried their dead in the family vault in the north aisle of St. Mary's-in-the-Market by torchlight; and the usage survived down to recent times. In the *Antiquary* for 1891, there is an account of the disorderly scenes on two of these occasions; and in his monograph, *The Curiosities of the Church*, Mr. Andrews, without citing this case, has a section on torchlight burial, which, as I have noted, was habitual among the ancients. An interesting paper on Traditions and Customs Relating to Death and Burial in Lincolnshire, from the pen of Miss Florence Peacock of Bottesford Manor, appeared in the *Antiquary* for November, 1895. Monsieur Jorevin, in his *Travels in England*, 1672, describing a lord's burial near Shrewbury, tells us: "The relations and friends being assembled in the house of the defunct, the minister advanced into the middle of the chamber, where, before the company, he made a funeral oration, representing the great actions of the deceased, his virtues, his qualities, his titles of nobility, and those of the whole family, &c. It is to be remarked that during his oration, there stood upon the coffin a large pot of wine, out of which every one drank to the health of the deceased. This being finished, six men took up the corps, and carried it on their shoulders to the church." "The coffin," he adds, "was covered with a large cloth, which the four nearest relations held each by a corner with one hand, and in the other carried a bough"; (this must have been a branch of rosemary:) "the other relations and friends had in one hand a flambeau, and in the other a bough, marching thus through the street, without singing or saying any prayer, till they came to the church." After the burial service, he adds, the clergyman, "having his bough in his hand like the rest of the congregation, threw it on the dead body when it was put into the grave, as did all the relations, extinguishing their flambeaux in the earth with which the corps was to be covered. This finished, every one retired to his home without farther ceremony." *Antiq. Repert.* iv., 549, 585. Braithwaite mentions that it was the function of the gentleman of the horse to lead the earl's charger caparisoned in black velvet after the body, and that these trappings remained the official's perquisites. *Rules for the Government of the House of an Earle*, (about 1640), apud *Miscellanea Antiq. Anglicana*, 1821, p. 16. The infant son of Sir Simonds D'Ewes, who died in

March, 1629-30, was carried to the burial-place in his father's private carriage.

Funeral Customs in Scotland.—In the Minute Book of the Society of Antiquaries of London, July 21, 1725, we read : " Mr. Anderson gave the Society an account of the manner of a Highland lord's funeral. The body is put into a litter between two horses, and, attended by the whole clan, is brought to the place of burial in the churchyard. The nearest relations dig the grave, the neighbours having set out the ground, so that it may not encroach on the graves of others. While this is performing, some hired women, for that purpose, lament the dead, setting forth his genealogy and noble exploits. After the body is interred, a hundred black cattle, and two or three hundred sheep, are killed for the entertainment of the company." The minister of Borrowstones, Linlithgow, reported in 1796 : " At the burials of the poor people, a custom, almost obsolete in other parts of Scotland, is continued here. The beadle perambulates the streets with a bell, and intimates the death of the individual in the following language : ' All brethren and sisters, I let ye to wit, there is a brother (or sister) departed at the pleasure of the Almighty, (here he lifts his hat), called —— All those that come to the burial, come at —— of clock. The corpse is at ——.' He also walks before the corpse to the church-yard, ringing his bell." Pennant, in his " Tour in Scotland," tells us, that on the death of a highlander, the corpse being stretched on a board, and covered with a coarse linen wrapper, the friends lay on the breast of the deceased a wooden platter, containing a small quantity of salt and earth, separate and unmixed. The earth an emblem of the corruptible body ; the salt an emblem of the immortal spirit. All fire is extinguished where a corpse is kept : and it is reckoned so ominous for a dog or cat to pass over it, that the poor animal is killed without mercy. A common funeral at Avoch, in Rosshire, in the 18th century, is thus described : " The corpse is preceded by the parish officer tolling a hand-bell. The pall or mort cloth is of plain black velvet, without any decoration, except a fringe. An immense crowd of both sexes attend ; and the lamentations of the women, in some cases, on seeing a beloved relative put into the grave, would almost pierce a heart of stone." *Stat. Acc. of Scotland*, xv., 636. The Scots used to believe that " It disturbed the ghost of the dead, and was fatal to the living, if a tear was allowed to fall on a winding sheet. What was the intention of this, but to prevent the effects of a wild or frantic sorrow ? If a cat was permitted to leap over a corpse, it portended misfortune.

The meaning of this was to prevent that carnivorous animal from coming near the body of the deceased, lest, when the watchers were asleep, it should endeavour to prey upon it" &c. These notions appear to have been called in Scotland "frets." *Stat. Acc.*, xxi., 147. " In Scotland," observes the Rev. John Black, " it is the custom of the relations of the deceased themselves to let down the corpse into the grave, by mourning cords, fastened to the handles of the coffin : the chief mourner standing at the head, and the rest of the relations arranged according to their propinquity. When the coffin is let down and adjusted in the grave, the mourners first, and then all the surrounding multitude, uncover their heads : there is no funeral service read : no oration delivered : but that solemn pause, for about the space of ten minutes, when every one is supposed to be meditating on death and immortality, always struck my heart in the most awful manner : never more than on the occasion here alluded to. The sound of the cord, when it fell on the coffin, still seems to vibrate on my ear." *Poems*, 1799, p. 10. Speaking of Scotish manners in the 18th century, it is said : The desire of what is called a decent funeral, i.e., one to which all the inhabitants of the district are invited, and at which every part of the usual entertainment is given, is one of the strongest in the poor. The expence of it amounts to nearly two pounds. This sum, therefore, every person in mean circumstances is anxious to lay up, and he will not spare it, unless reduced to the greatest extremity." Again : " Complaints occur against the expensive mode of conducting burials in the parish of Dunlop, in Ayrshire. It is pointed out as an object of taxation." In the same publication, parish of Lochbroom, co. Ross, " At their burials and marriages," we are told, the inhabitants " too much adhere to the folly of their ancestors. On these occasions they have a custom of feasting a great number of their friends and neighbours, and this often at an expence which proves greatly to the prejudice of poor orphans and young people : although these feasts are seldom productive of any quarrels or irregularities among them." And, under parish of Campsie, co. Stirling, we read : " It was customary, till within these few years, when any head of a family died, to invite the whole parish : they were served on boards in the barn, where a prayer was pronounced before and after the service, which duty was most religiously observed. The entertainment consisted of the following parts : first, there was a drink of ale, then a dram, then a piece of short-bread, then another dram of some other species of liquor, then a piece of currant-bread, and a third dram, either of spirits or wine, which was followed by loaves and cheese, pipes and tobacco. This was the old funeral entertainment in the parish of Campsie, and was stiled their service: and sometimes this was repeated, and was then stiled a double service; and it was sure of being repeated at the Dredgy. A funeral cost, at least, a hundred pounds Scots, to any family who followed the old course. The most active young man was pointed out to the office of server; and, in those days, while the manners were simple, and at the same time serious, it was no small honour to be a server at a burial. However distant any part of the parish was from the place of the interment, it was customary for the attendants to carry the corpse on hand spokes. The mode of invitation to the entertainment was, by some special messenger; which was stiled bidding to the burial, the form being nearly in the following words:— 'You are desired to come to such-a-one's burial to-morrow, against ten hours.' No person was invited by letter; and, though invited against ten of the clock, the corpse never was interred till the evening: time not being so much valued in those days." The minister of Gargunnock, co. Stirling, reported, (1796): "The manner of conducting funerals in the country needs much amendment. From the death to the interment, the house is thronged by night and day, and the conversation is often very unsuitable to the occasion. The whole parish is invited at ten o'clock in the forenoon of the day of the burial, but it is soon enough to attend at 3 o'clock in the afternoon. Everyone is entertained with a variety of meats and drinks. Not a few return to the dirge, and sometimes forget what they have been doing, and where they are. Attempts have been lately made to provide a remedy for this evil; but old customs are not easily abolished." The minister of Carmunnock, co. Lanark, tells us: "We must mention a custom, which still prevails, and which certainly ought to be abolished. It is usual, in this parish, as in many other parts of Scotland, when a death has taken place, to invite on such occasions the greater part of the country round, and though called to attend at an early hour in the forenoon, yet it is generally towards evening, before they think of carrying forth the corpse to the churchyard for interment. While, on these occasions, the good folks are assembled, though they never run into excess, yet no small expense is incurred by the family: who often vie with those around them, in giving, as they call it, an honourable burial to their deceased friend. Such a custom is attended with many evils, and frequently involves in

debt, or reduces to poverty many families otherwise frugal and industrious, by this piece of useless parade and ill-judged expence." *Stat. Acc.*, vi., 487; ix., 543; xv., 372; xxiii., 123, 174.

In 1612, appended to the *Abridgement of the Scots Chronicles*, in "The Description of the Isles of Scotland," by J. Monipenny, under the Island of Rona, is the following passage: "There is in this island a chapel dedicated to St. Ronan: wherein (as aged men report) there is alwayes a spade wherewith when as any is dead, they find the place of his grave marked." See Gough's *Topography*. In Sutherlandshire, in the 18th century, a contemporary says: "The friends of the deceased, and neighbors of the village, who came to witness the interment, are drawn up in rank and file, by an old sergeant, or some veteran who has been in the Army, and who attends to maintain order, and give as they term it here, the word of relief. Upon his crying Relief! the four under the bier prepare to leave their stations, and make room for other four, that instantly succeed. This progression is observed at the interval of every five minutes, till the whole attendants come in regularly, and, if the distance requires it, there is a second, a third, or a fourth round of such evolutions gone through. When the persons present are not inflamed with liquor, there is a profound silence generally observed, from the time the corpse has been taken up till the interment is over." In another part of the same description we read: "Country burials are not well regulated. The company are invited at 11 o'clock forenoon, but they are probably not all arrived at 2. Till of late a pipe and tobacco was provided for every one of the company; but this custom is entirely laid aside. *Stat. Acct. of Scotland*, iii., 525; vii., 622. The minister of Kilsinichen and Kilviceven, co. Argyll, writing in the 18th century, says: The inhabitants "are by no means superstitious, yet they still retain some opinions handed down by their ancestors, perhaps from the time of the Druids. It is believed by them that the spirit of the last person that was buried watches round the churchyard till another is buried, to whom he delivers his charge." *Stat. Acc. of Scotland*, iv., 210. In the same work, it is said, "in one division of this county, where it was believed that the ghost of the person last buried kept the gate of the church yard till relieved by the next victim of death, a singular scene occurred, when two burials were to take place in one church yard on the same day. Both parties staggered forward as fast as possible to consign their respective friend in the first place to the dust. If they met at the gate, the dead were thrown down till the living decided by blows whose ghost should be condemned to porter it. *Stat. Acc.*, xxi., 144.

Funeral Customs in Ireland.
—See *Irish Funeral Customs, Wakes,* and two papers in the *Penny Magazine* for July, 1844.

Funeral Customs Abroad.—
In foreign countries, no less than among ourselves, it was a peremptory regulation and usage to bury instantaneously all victims to epidemics; and it is to the lasting honour of the Venetians that in 1576, Titian dying of the plague, his remains were specially allowed to lie in state. In some places abroad, it is customary to set out the departed person's toilette, and go through many of the same forms which he or she observed in life. In the Island of Madeira, they are in the habit of closing the chamber of death during a twelve-month after the event. Armstrong says: "I have seen an old woman placed on a bier, dressed like a Franciscan monk, and so conducted by the good brothers of that order, with singing and the tinckling of the hand-bell, to their church." *History of Minorca*, p. 212. This superstition, which, as I have just noticed, was not wholly unknown in England, was observed by Milton; for when describing the Paradise of Fools, he does not forget to mention those—

'—— Who to be sure of Paradise,
Dying, put on the weeds of Dominick,
Or in Franciscan think to pass dis-
       guis'd.'"
—*Paradise Lost*, p. 111.

The accompanying elaborate account of the funeral ceremony at the obsequies of Alfonso XII., of Spain, is taken from the *Daily News* of November 30, 1885: "The funeral of the late King took place to-day. Early in the morning the Royal Family heard mass near the body. Then, after leaving flowers, they retired. The Queen, looking heartbroken, was the last to leave the hall. At 10 o'clock the coffin was carried downstairs by the grandees. A procession was formed of the Royal household, the equerries, the King's Body Guard, the Halberdiers, and priests. The roads were lined with troops. The crowd was extremely dense. All heads were uncovered as the coffin passed. The Ministers and the Bishop of Madrid received the body at the station, the bands playing the Royal March. The train left amidst the firing of cannon and the tolling of bells. The ceremony at the Escurial was imposing. The procession from the station slowly wound up the hill to the Monastery. When the funeral car reached the principal door

it was closed. The Lord Chamberlain knocked for admittance. A voice inside asked, 'Who wishes to enter?' The answer given was 'Alfonso XII.' The doors were then thrown open. The Prior of the Monastery appeared. The body was carried into the church and placed on a raised bier before the grand altar. The coffin was then covered with the four cloaks of the noble orders. A thousand tapers were lighted, and the church assumed a magnificent appearance. Black hangings embossed with the arms of Spain covered the stone walls. A mass was said and the Miserere sung. The coffin was raised once more and carried to the entrance of the stairs leading down to the vaults. No one descended there except the Prior, the Minister of Grace and Justice, and the Lord Chamberlain. The coffin was placed on a table in a magnificent black marble vault, in which the Kings of Spain lie in huge marble tombs all around. Now came the most thrilling part of the ceremony. The Lord Chamberlain unlocked the coffin, which was covered with cloth of gold, raised the glass covering from the King's face, then after requesting perfect silence, knelt down and shouted three times in the dead monarch's ear, 'Señor, Señor, Señor.' Those waiting in the church upstairs heard the call, which was like a cry of despair, for it came from the lips of the Duke of Sexto, the King's favourite companion. The Duke then rose, saying, according to the ritual, 'His Majesty does not answer. Then it is true the King is dead.' He locked the coffin, handed the keys to the Prior, and taking up his wand of office, broke it in his hand, and flung the pieces at the foot of the table. Then every one left the monastery, as the bells tolled, and the guns announced to the people that Alfonso XII. had been laid with his ancestors in the gloomy pile of Philip II." This was on the Sunday at the Escurial.

The *Times* of December 3, 1889, describes the last tribute to Luis I. of Portugal: "A singular traditional usage was carried out at Lisbon some days after the funeral of the late King. At three principal places in the city platforms were erected covered with black cloth. A procession passed from one place to the other. The chief municipal officers of the city and the chief personages of the late Royal household, all clad in deep mourning, formed the procession, which was preceded and followed by cavalry in mourning, the colours draped with black. Military bands accompanied the march, playing sad strains. Four shields, on which were painted the Royal arms, were borne aloft on long staves. A multitude of people, all suitably dressed, were present, several walking with the procession. Arrived at the platform all the principal persons took up their places upon it, and one of the shield-bearers, advancing to the front, cried out in a chanting tone, ' Weep, O Portuguese, for your King Dom Luis I. is dead.' He then dashed the shield to the ground with such violence that it was shattered. This ceremony was repeated at the other platforms. Then the procession moved to the church of Santo Antonio da Sé, where a solemn requiem service was held. During the whole ceremony all the bells of the city tolled."

Funeral Psalmody.—Various are the proofs of the ancient custom of carrying out the dead with psalmody in the primitive church: in imitation of which it is still customary in many parts of this nation, to carry out the dead with singing of psalms and hymns of triumph; to show that they have ended their spiritual warfare, that they have finished their course with joy, and are become conquerors. This exultation, as it were, for the conquest of their deceased friend over hell, sin, and death, was the great ceremony used in all funeral processions among the ancient Christians. Bourne cites Socrates Scholasticus telling us "that when the body of Babylas the Martyr was removed by the order of Julian the Apostate, the Christians, with their women and children, rejoiced and sung psalms all the way as they bore the corpse from Daphne to Antioch. Thus was Paula buried at Bethlehem, and thus did St. Anthony bury Paul the Hermite." The following passage is curious on the subject of singing psalms before the corpse: "Cantilena feralis per Antiphonas in pompa funebri et Fano debacchata hinc est. Inter Græcos demortui cadavere deposito in inferiori domus aula ad portam, et peractis cæteris Ceremoniis, Cantores funerales accedunt et threnon canunt, quibus per intervalla respondebant domesticæ servæ, cum assistentium corona, neque solum domi, sed usque ad Sepulchrum præcedebant feretrum ita canentes." Guichard. lib. ii. cap. 2. "Funeral," apud Moresini "Papatus," &c., p. 32. Durandus cites one of the ancient councils, in which it is observed the psalms were wont to be sung, not only when the corpse was conducted to church, but that the ancients watched on the night before the burial, and spent the vigil in singing psalms. Gough tells us that music and singing made a part of the funerals. Macrobius assigns as a reason that it implied the soul's return to the origin of harmony or heaven. Hyginus understands it to mean a signal of a decent disposal

of the dead, and that they came fairly by their death, as the tolling bell among Christians." *Sep. Mon.*, ii., introd. vii. Stopford says : " The heathens sang their dead to their graves or places of burial." *Pagano-papismus*, p. 282, citing Alex. ab Alexandro, " Gen. Dier." lib. iii., cap. 7, And Macrobius, *In Somnium Scipionis*, ii., 37, affirms,. that this custom was according to the institutions of several nations, and grounded upon this reason, because they believed that souls after death returned to the original of musical sweetness, that is Heaven : and therefore in this life every soul is taken with musicall sounds, &c." Other reasons are assigned by Kirkman, and several authorities urged for this custom. *De Funeribus Romanorum*, ii., 4. In "The Burnynge of Paules Church," 1561, we read : " In burials we do not assemble a number of priestes to swepe purgatorye, or bye forgivenes of synnes, of them whiche have no authoritye to sell, but accordinge to Saint Jeroms example we followe. At the death of Fabiola, sais he, the people of Ro. were gathered to the solemnite of the buriall. Psalmes were songe, and Alleluia sounding oute on height, did shake the gildet celinges of the Temple. Here was one companye of yonge menne and there another which did singe the prayses and worthy dedes of the woman. And no mervaile if men rejoyce of her salvation, of whose conversion th' angells in heaven be glad. Thus Jerom used burialls." Ed. 1563, sign. G 6 vᵒ. I find the following passage in Dickenson's "Greene in Conceipt," 1598, p. 43 : " It is a custome still in use with Christians, to attend the funerall of their deceased friendes, with whole chantries of choyce quire-men, singing solemnly before them : but behinde follows a troope all clad in blacke, which argues mourning : much have I marveled at this ceremony, deeming it some hidden paradox, confounding thus in one things so opposite as these signes of joy and sorrowe."

Aubrey has preserved for our advantage a song, which he had from Mr. Meautis, and which could be traced back to 1626. It is connected with a Yorkshire superstition that the souls of the departed went over Whinny Moor. Some portions of the production seem to bespeak a far greater antiquity. Thoms has printed the verses entire, and very pertinently points out that Sir Walter Scott, in quoting them in the *Minstrelsy*, omits to give a portion of one line in a stanza, where the approach to purgatory is described. The missing words are here given in italics; they occur in Aubrey's MS. in the margin, but clearly belong to the text :—

" From Brig o' Dread, *na brader than
   a thread*,
   Every night and awle,
To Purgatory fire thou comest at last,
   And Christ receive thy sawle."

The bridge no broader than a thread is a
fine imaginative touch, and is such an object as many of us have encountered in
nightmares. The song used in Aubrey's
time to be sung at funerals in Yorkshire,
and is substantially identical with Scott's
Lykewake Dirge. Atkinson, in his
Cleveland Glossary, 1868, furnishes a different version and other similar composi-
tions; and Pennant tells us that in his
day (about 1775) a custom prevailed in
North Wales of singing psalms all the way
to the church.

Funeral Rings.—The practice of
offering rings at funerals is introduced in
the early romance of *Sir Amadas.* Anne of
Cleves, who survived Henry VIII. several
years, left by her will very numerous bequests, and among them we meet with
several mourning-rings of various value
to be distributed among her friends and
dependents. By the will of Lady Anne
Drury, of Hardwicke, Suffolk, who died
in 1621, in the possession of considerable
property, rings were to be given to all her
brother's wives, to her brothers themselves, to her two brothers-in-law, and to
such of her friends as the executors
thought fit. This lady was the sister of
Sir Edmund Bacon, Knt., of the Suffolk
family of that name. Mr. Wright, in
" Miscellanea Graphica," 1857, describes
a gold enamelled mourning ring, "formed
of two skeletons, who support a small sar-
cophagus. The skeletons are covered with
white enamel, and the lid of the sarco-
phagus is also enamelled, and has a Mal-
tese cross in red on a black ground studded
with gilt hearts, and when removed displays another skeleton. Under his
will in 1616 Shakespear bequeathed
26s. 8d. apiece to five of his friends to buy
them memorial rings. Halliwell-Phillipps,
Outlines, 6th ed. ii., 170-1.

Funeral Sermons.—Funeral sermons are of great antiquity. Durandus,
Rationale, 236. This custom used to be
very general in England. But the earliest funeral sermon in English, at all
events in print, seems to be that preached
by Bishop Fisher for the Countess
of Richmond and Derby, 1509. Mr.
Brand says: " I know no where that it is
retained at present, except upon Portland
Island, Dorsetshire, where the minister
has half-a-guinea for every sermon he
preaches, by which he raises annually a
very considerable sum. This species of
luxury in grief is very common there, and
indeed, as it conveys the idea of posthumous honour, all are desirous of procuring
it even for the youngest of their children
as well as their deceased friends. The fee
is nearly the same as that mentioned by
Gay in his dirge :

" Twenty good shillings in a rag I laid,
Be ten the parson for his sermon
   paid."

Gough says : " From funeral orations over
Christian martyrs have followed funeral
sermons for eminent Christians of all denominations, whether founded in esteem or
sanctioned by fashion, or secured by reward. Our ancestors, before the Reformation, took especial care to secure the repose and well-being of their souls, by
masses and other deeds of piety and charity. After that event was supposed to
have dispelled the gloom of superstition,
and done away the painful doctrine of
Purgatory, they became more solicitous to
have their memories embalmed, and the
example of their good works held forth to
posterity. Texts were left to be preached
from, and sometimes money to pay for
such preaching. Gratitude founded commemorative sermons as well as commemorative dinners for benefactors." *Sepulchral Monuments,* ii., Introd. xi. In the
Genevan "Forme of prayers," 1561, occurs
" the maner of buriall," in which there is
the following direction : " The corps is
reverentlie brought to the grave, accompanied with the congregation, without
any further ceremonies: which being
buried, the Minister, if he be present, and
required, goeth to the Church, if it be not
farr off, and maketh some comfortable exhortation to the people, touching death
and resurrection." Even the " comfortable exhortation " is struck out in the
Middleborough Book, 1587. In " The
Burnynge of Paules Church," 1561, we
read : " Gregory Nazanzene hais his funerall sermons and orations in the commen-
dacion of the party departed ; so hais Ambrose for Theodosius and Valentinian the
Emperours, for his brother Statirus," &c.

In the Public Library at Cambridge, Dd. xii., 19, is the funeral
oration pronounced at Leiden by John
Dinley over Sir Albert Morton. Misson says: "The common practice is
to carry the corpse into the body
of the church, where they set it down
upon two tressels, while either a funeral
sermon is preached, containing an eulogi-
um upon the deceased, or certain prayers
said, adapted to the occasion. If the body
is not buried in the church, they carry it
to the church yard, where it is interred,
(after the minister has performed the service which may be seen in the book of common prayer), in the presence of the guests,
who are round the grave, and do not leave

it till the earth is thrown in upon it. Then they return home in the same order that they came." *Travels in England*, p. 93. It was till lately a custom for the Ordinary of Newgate to preach a funeral sermon before each execution. In Cotgrave's "Treasury of Wit and Language," p. 35, we read :

"In all this sermon I have heard little commendations
Of our dear brother departed : rich men doe not go
To the Pit-hole without complement of Christian buriall."

Granger quotes Fuller (*Appeal of Injured Innocence*, iii., 75) for this : "When one was to preach the funeral sermon of a most vicious and generally hated person. all wondered what he would say in his praise ; the preacher's friends fearing, his foes hoping, that, for his fee, he would force his conscience to flattery. For one thing, said the minister, this man is to be spoken well of by all ; and, for another, he is to be spoken ill of by none. The first is, because God made him ; the second, because he is dead." Even such an infamous character as Madame Cresswell had her funeral sermon. She desired by will to have a sermon preached at her funeral, for which the preacher was to have ten pounds ; but upon this express condition, that he was to say nothing but what was well of her. A preacher was, with some difficulty, found, who undertook the task. He, after a sermon preached on the general subject of mortality, and the good uses to be made of it, concluded with saying, " By the will of the deceased it is expected that I should mention her, and say nothing but what was well of her. All that I shall say of her, therefore, is this : she was born well, she lived well and she died well ; for she was born with the name of Cresswell, she lived in Clerkenwell, and she died in Bridewell."

Bishop White Kennet, under *Orationes Funerales*, acquaints us that : "At the burial of the dead it was a custom for the surviving friends to offer liberally at the altar for the pious use of the priest, and the good estate of the soul of the deceased. This pious custom does still obtain in North Wales, where at the rails which decently defend the Communion Table, I have seen a small tablet or flat-board, conveniently fixt, to receive the money, which at every funeral is offered by the surviving friends, according to their own ability, and the quality of the party deceased. Which seems a providential augmentation to some of those poor churches." *Par. Antiq. Gloss.* in v.

Funeral Suppers.—The ancients had several kinds of suppers made in honour of the deceased. First, that which was laid upon the funeral pile, such as we find in the 23rd Book of Homer and the 6th Æneis of Virgil, in Catullus (Ep. lv.) and Ovid (Fasti ii.) Secondly, the supper given to the friends and relations at their return from the funeral ; as in the 24th Book of Homer's Ilias, in honour of Hector. This kind of supper is mentioned in Lucian's Treatise of Grief, and Cicero's third Book of Laws. Thirdly, the Silicernium, a supper laid at the sepulchre, called Ἑκάτης δειπνον. Others will have it to be a meeting of the very old relations, who went in a very solemn manner after the funeral, and took their leaves one of the other, as if they were never to meet again. The fourth was called Epulum Novendiale. Juvenal, in his fifth Satire, mentions the *cœna feralis*, which was intended to appease the ghosts of the dead, and consisted of milk, honey, water, wine, olives, and strewed flowers. The modern arvals, however, are intended to appease the appetites of the living, who have upon these occasions superseded the manes of the dead. Gough says : " An entertainment or supper, which the Greeks called Περιδειπον, and Cicero *Circompotatio*, made a part of a funeral, whence our practice of giving wine and cake among the rich, and ale among the poor." *Sep. Mon.*, ii., Introd. vi. Among Smith's Extracts from the Berkeley MSS. (printed in 1821), the following occurs : " From the time of the death of Maurice the fourth Lord Berkeley, which happened June 8, 1368, untill his interment, the reeve of his Manor of Hinton spent three quarters and seaven bushells of beanes in fatting one hundred geese towards his funerall, and divers other reeves of other Manors the like, in geese, duckes, and other pultry." In Strype's edition of Stow we read : " Margaret Atkinson, widow, by her will, October 18, 1544, orders that the next Sunday after her burial there be provided two dozen of bread, a kilderken of ale, two gammons of bacon, three shoulders of mutton, and two couple of rabbits. Desiring all the parish, as well rich as poor, to take part thereof ; and a table to be set in the midst of the church, with every thing necessary thereto." Ed. 1720, i., 259. At the funeral of Sir John Gresham, Knight, Mercer (1556), the church and streets were all hung with black and arms great store. A sermon was preached by the Archdeacon of Canterbury, " and after, all the company came home to as great a dinner as had been seen for a fish day, for all that came. For nothing was lacking." Again : At the funeral of Thomas Percy, 1561, late skinner to Queen Mary, he was "attended to his burial in Saint Mary Aldermary Church with twenty black gowns and coats, twenty clerks singing, &c. The floor strewed with rushes for the chief mourners. Mr. Crowley preached. Afterwards was a great dole of money; and then all went home to a dinner. The company of Skinners, to their Hall, to dine together. At this funeral, all the mourners offered: and so did the said company." A.D. 1562, at the funeral of Sir Humphrey Brown, Knight, Lord Chief Justice, Dec. 15, Mr. Reneger made the sermon, "and after, they went home to a great dinner. The church was hung with black and arms. The helmet and crest were offered (on the altar), and after that his target; after that his sword; then his coat-armour; then his standard was offered, and his penon: and after all, the mourners, and judges, and serjeants of the law, and servants offered." In connection with the subject of "funeral baked meats," Henry Machyn notes in his Diary, under 1552-3, March 22: "The same day, wyche was the xxij day of Marche, was bered master John Heth, dwellynge in Fanchyrche Strett, and ther whent a-ffor hym a C. Childeryn of Grey freres, boys and gyrlles, ij and iij together, and he gayff (left) them shurts and smokes, and gyrdulls, and moketors, and after they had wyne and fygs and good alle, and ther wher a grett dener; and ther wher the cumpene of Panters, and the Clarkes, and ys cumpony had xxs. to make mere with-alle at the tavarne." Machyn relates that after the interment of Sir John Rainford, Kt. on the 20th September, 1559, there was a grand dinner proposed for the mourners, at which the widow, however, did not show herself. When the party had left, her ladyship came down, and had her dinner—four eggs and a dish of butter. At the obsequies of Francis, Earl of Shrewsbury, in 1560, the funeral banquet consisted of 320 messes, each mess containing eight dishes.

Misson, under the head of funerals, says: "Before they set out, and after they return, it is usual to present the guests with some thing to drink, either red or white wine, boiled with sugar and cinnamon, or some other such liquor. Every one drinks two or three cups." Butler, the keeper of a tavern, (the Crown and Sceptre in St. Martin's Street), told Mr. Brand that there was a tun of red port wine drunk at his wife's burial, besides mull'd white wine. Note, no men ever go to womens burials, nor the women to mens, so that there were none but women at the drinking of Butler's wine.

The expressions "Forth bringing" and "bringing home" are very interesting memorials of old notions in connection with the last act of our humanity. A correspondent of *Notes and Queries* has collected examples from a variety of sources extending over 120 years (1523-1645):—

1523. Will of Isabel Chetham, of Manchester: "The residue of all my goods not beqwethed, after my furth bryngyng made," &c.

1543. Will of Hugh Habergam, of Bradlegh in Hapton, co. Lanc., husbandman: "To be bestowed on a drynkyng at my forth bryngyng, a noble," &c.

1556. Will of John Davenport, of Henbury, co. Chester, Esq.: "Also I will that Kateryn my wife shall have, after my forthe bryngyng, my funeral expencys discharged, the rest and residue of all my hole goodes, &c.

1571. Will of John Booth, of Barton-upon-Irwell, co. Lanc., Esq.: "Shall after my death bestowe upon my funeralls and bringinge furthe," &c.

1572. Will of Philip Mainwaring, of Peover, co. Chester, Esq.: "I will that my debts, funeralls,, and bringing home shall be discharged," &c.

1584. Will of Richard Hall, Fellow of the College of Manchester: "And after my forth bringinge, the rest of my goodes to be divided," &c.

1597. Will of Alice Garsyde, of Oldham: "The charge of my forth bringing being taken out of the whole of my goods," &c.

1630. Will of Andrew Gartside, of Denshaw, in the parish of Saddleworth: "I will that my forthbringinge, funerall expenses," &c., be paid.

1633. Will of Richard Buckley, of Grottonhead, in the parish of Saddleworth: "My will is that my forthbringinge, funerall expenses be discharged," &c.

1645. Will of Thomas Leadbeater, of Cranage, co. Chester: "My desire is ..... that my children shall bring me home with bread and cheese and drink."

A writer in the "Gentleman's Magazine" for March, 1780, says: "Our ancient funerals, as well as some modern ones, were closed with merry makings, at least equal to the preceding sorrow, most of the testators directing, among other things, victuals and drink to be distributed at their exequies; one in particular, I remember, orders a sum of money for a drinking for his soul." Another writer, apparently describing the manners of Yorkshire, in the volume for July, 1798, says: "At funerals, on which occasions a large party is generally invited, the attendant who serves the company with ale or wine has upon the handle of the tankard a piece of lemon-peel, and also upon her left arm a clean white napkin. I believe these customs are invariably observed. From what cause they originated, some ingenious correspondent may be able to inform me." Hutchinson, speaking of Eskdale chapelry, says: "Wakes and doles are customary; and weddings, christenings, and funerals are always attended by the neighbours, sometimes to the amount of a hundred people. The popular diversions are hunting and cock-fighting." *Cumberland*, i., 579. "At the funerals of the rich in former days," says the compiler of the "Whitby Glossary," (quoted by Atkinson, in his "Cleveland Glossary," 1868), "it was here a custom to hand burnt wine to the company in a silver flagon, out of which every one drank. This cordial seems to have been a heated preparation of port wine with spices and sugar. And if any remained, it was sent round in the flagon to the houses of friends for distribution."

An allusion to these entertainments occurs in the Romance of Sir Degore (about 1500):

"A great feaste would he holde
Upon his quenes mornynge day,
That was buryed in an abay."

So Dickenson, in "Greene in Conceipt," 1598: "His corpes was with funerall pompe conveyed to the church and there solemnly entered, nothing omitted which necessitie or custom could claime: a sermon, a banquet, and like observations." We are all familiar with the passage in *Hamlet*, 1603-4, where, speaking of his mother's marriage, Hamlet says:

"The funeral bak'd meats
Did coldly furnish forth the marriage-tables."

Upon which Steevens noted: "It was anciently the general custom to give a cold entertainment to mourners at a funeral. In distant counties this practice is continued among the yeomanry." In Lord North's "Forest of Varieties," 1645, is the following: "Nor are all banquets (no more than musick) ordained for merry humors, some being used even at funeralls." In his "Whimsies," 1631, p. 89, speaking of a launderer, Braithwaite says: "So much she hath reserv'd out of all the labours of her life, as will buy some small portion of diet bread, comfits, and burnt claret, to welcome in her neighbours now at her departing, of whose cost they never so freely tasted while she was living." Again, in describing a jealous neighbour, he concludes with observing: "Meate for his funerall pye is shred, some few ceremonial teares on his funerall pile are shed; but the

worms are scarce entered his shroud, his corpse flowers not fully dead, till this jealous earth-worme is forgot, and another more amorous, but lesse jealous mounted his bed." Flecknoe, speaking of a "curious glutton," observes: "In fine, he thinks of nothing else, as long as he lives, and when he dyes, onely regrets that funeral feasts are quite left off, else he should have the pleasure of one feast more, (in imagination at least), even after death; which he can't endure to hear of, onely because they say there is no eating nor drinking in the other world." *Characters*, 1658, ed. 1665, p. 14.

"In Northern customs duty was exprest
To friends departed by their fun'ral feast.
Tho' I've consulted Hollingshead and Stow,
I find it very difficult to know
Who to refresh th' attendants to the grave,
Burnt claret first, or Naples-bisket gave."

King's Art of Cookery, p. 65. The writer of "Pleasant Remarks on the Humours of Mankind" observes: "How like epicurists do some persons drink at a funeral, as if they were met there to be merry, and make it a matter of rejoycing that they have got rid of ther friends and relations."

Funerals, References in the Poets to.—A writer in the "Gorgious Gallery of Gallant Inventions," 1578, describing the death of Pyramus and Thisbe, says:

"And mulberries in signe of woe, from white to blacke turnde were."

So in "Romeo and Juliet," 1597:

"All things, that we ordained festival,
Turn from their office to black funeral;
Our instruments, to melancholy bells;
Our wedding cheer, to a sad burial feast;
Our solemn hymns to sullen dirges change;
Our bridal flowers serve for a buried corse,
And all things change them to their contraries."

In "Cymbeline," act iv. sc. 2, Arviragus, speaking of the apparently dead body of Imogen, disguised in men's clothes, says:

"And let us, Polydore, sing him to the ground,
As once our mother; use like note and words,
Save that Euriphile must be Fidele."

"Let my bier
Be borne by virgins, that shall sing by
  course
The truth of maids and perjuries of
  men."

—Beaum. and Fl. *Maids Tragedy*, 1619.
Compare *Arval, Bidding, Burial, Death, Dole, Flowers, Graves, Lichway,* &c.

Furmety.—Furmety is made of what is called, in a certain town in Yorkshire, "kneed wheat," or whole grains first boiled plump and soft, and then put into and boiled in milk sweetened and spiced." In Ray's "North Country Words," "to cree wheat or barley, is to boil it soft." Gower tells us: "I cannot avoid reminding you upon the present occasion that furmenty makes the principal entertainment of all our country wakes: our common people call it 'Firmitry.' It is an agreeable composition of boiled wheat, milk, spice, and sugar." *Sketch of the Materials for a History of Cheshire.* Beckwith, in the "Gentleman's Magazine" for February, 1784, tells us that, in the country about Rotherham, in Yorkshire, furmety used, in his remembrance, to be always the breakfast and supper on Christmas Eve. In his epistle before Greene's *Arcadia*, 1589, Thomas Nash takes occasion to observe that "a tale of Ioane of Brainfords will, and the vnlucky frumenty, will be as soone entertained into their Libraries as the best Poëme that euer Tasso eternis'ht." He refers to a fugitive piece of verse by G. Kyttes, called *The Vnlucky firmentie*, of which there seems to be a MS. copy under the title of *Panche* in Bishop Percy's Folio MS.

Furmety Sunday.—See *Mothering*.

Furry Day.—A writer in a periodical for 1790 says: "At Helstone, a genteel and populous borough town in Cornwall, it is customary to dedicate the eighth of May to revelry (festive mirth, not loose jollity). It is called the Furry Day, supposed Flora's Day; not, I imagine, as many have thought, in remembrance of some festival instituted in honour of that goddess, but rather from the garlands commonly worn on that day. In the morning, very early, some troublesome rogues go round the streets with drums, or rather noisy instruments, disturbing their sober neighbours, and singing parts of a song, the whole of which nobody now recollects, and of which I know no more than that there is mention in it of 'the grey goose quill,' and of going to the green wood to bring home 'the Summer and the May-o.' And, accordingly, hawthorn flowering branches are worn in hats. The commonalty make it a general holiday; and if they find any person at work, make him ride on a pole, carried on men's shoulders, to the river, over which he is to leap in a wide place, if he can; if he cannot, he must leap in, for leap he must, or pay money. About 9 o'clock they appear before the school, and demand holiday for the Latin boys, which is invariably granted; after which they collect money from house to house. About the middle of the day they collect together, to dance hand-in-hand round the streets, to the sound of the fiddle, playing a particular tune, which they continue to do till it is dark. This they call a 'Faddy.' In the afternoon, the gentility go to some farmhouse in the neighbourhood, to drink tea, syllabub, etc., and return in a Morrice dance to the town, where they form a faddy, and dance through the streets till it is dark, claiming a right of going through any person's house, in at one door, and out at the other. And here it formerly used to end, and the company of all kinds to disperse quietly to their several habitations; but latterly corruptions have in this as in other matters crept in by degrees. The ladies — all elegantly dressed in white muslins, are now conducted by their partners to the ball-room, where they continue their dance till supper time; after which they all faddy it out of the house, breaking off by degrees to their respective houses. The mobility imitate their superiors, and also adjourn to the several public houses, where they continue their dance till midnight. It is, upon the whole, a very festive, jovial, and withall sober, and I believe singular custom." The song, which follows from another source, seems to betray a faint reminiscence of the Spanish Armada:

THE FURRY-DAY SONG.
"Robin Hood and Little John,
  They both are gone to the fair,
And we'll go to the merry green wood,
  And see what they do there.
For we were up as soon as any day
  For to fetch the summer home,
The summer and the May, O,
  For the summer now has come!
Where are those Spaniards
  That make so great a boast?
They shall eat the grey goose feather,
  And we will eat the roast.
As for the brave St. George,
  St. George he was a knight;
Of all the knights in Christendom.
  St. Georgy is the right.
God bless Aunt Mary Moses,
  And all her powers and might,
And send us peace in merry England,
  Both day and night!"
The Furry Day was duly observed in 1903.

Fye.—In Scotland a ghost seems to have been known as a fye. Witness the following anecdote : " Some observing to an old woman, when in the 99th year of her age, that in the course of Nature she could not long survive—'Ay,' said the good old woman, with pointed indignation, 'what fye-token do you see about me?'" *Stat. Acc.*, xxi., 148; *Parish of Menghittes.*

Gabriel, the Archangel. — (March 26 and April 13).—The Salutation of the Virgin by this personage was supposed to be commemorated by the chapel of Our Lady at Nazareth, on the model of which that at Walsingham is reported to have been built by a lady named Richold, A.D. 1061. See *Foundation of the Chapel of Walsingham*, printed about 1495, in Hazlitt's *Fugitive Tracts*, 1875, 1st Series. In the *Vertue of the Masse* (circâ 1500), by Lydgate, St. Gabriel is named as the patron of " good rydynge "; but the whole passage seems worth copying, especially as it mentions one or two points not generally known :

" Herynge of masse dooth passynge grete auayle,
At nede at myschefe folke it doth releue,
Causeth saynt Nicholas to gyue good counsayle,
And saynt Iulyan good hostel at eue ;
To beholde saynt Crystofer none enemy shall hym greue,
And saynt Loy your Iourney shall preserue,
Horse ne caryage that daye shall not myscheue,
Masse herde before who dooth these sayntes serue.
Partynge fro masse begynnynge your Iourney,
Call saynt Myghell you to fortefye,
For sodayne haste and good prosperyte,
And for good rydynge saynt Gabryell shall you gye."

Gabriel-Rachet, The. — This, says Mr. Atkinson, in his "Cleveland Glossary," 1868, is a name for a yelping sound heard at night, more or less resembling the cry of hounds or yelping of dogs, probably due to flocks of wild geese (*anser segetum*) which chance to be flying by night, and is taken as an omen or warning of approaching death to the hearer or some one connected with him or her." Mr. Atkinson speaks of a Cleveland tradition about the local origin of the Gabriel-rachet ; but probably very slight credit is due to the legend narrated by him. It seems to be nothing more or less than a form of the belief current all over the world from the remotest times in spectral apparitions and sounds seen or heard in the deadness of night. Compare Lucas, *Studies in Nidderdale*, pp. 156-7.

Gambling.—A very curious sketch of the early passion for speculation, even of the wildest character, in playing at games both of skill and chance, is given by Mr. Wright. *Domestic Manners and Sentiments in England during the Middle Ages*, 1862, ch. x. Comp. *Games* below.

Game.—"Formerly," says Mr. Tanswell, "Lambeth was celebrated for game of all sorts, but principally in the neighbourhood of Brixton. In the 5th of Elizabeth a licence was granted to Andrew Perne, D.D., Dean of Ely (who resided at Stockwell), 'to appoint one of his servants, by special name, to shoot with any cross-bow, hand-gonne, hacquebut, or demy-hack, at all manner of deadmarks, at all manner of crows, rooks, cormorants, kytes, puttocks, and suchlike, bustards, wyld swans, barnacles, and all manner of sea-fowls, and fen-fowls, wild doves, small birds, teals, coots, ducks, and all manner of deare, red, fallow, and roo.' In the reign of James I., Alexander Glover received, as 'Keeper of the game about Lambeth and Clapham, 12d. per diem, and 26s. 8d. per annum for his livery': in all £36 10s." *History of Lambeth*, 1858, p. 15. And at the same period Putney Park was a royal demesne with deer and a keeper under the Crown. The site is still remembered in Putney Park Lane.

Game at the Hole.—So named in an entry at Stationers' Hall in 1587. The full title is : " The game at the hole, otherwise, if you be not pleased, you shall be eased."

Games.—Dr. Arbuthnot used to say, that notwithstanding all the boasts of the safe conveyance of tradition, it was no where preserved pure and uncorrupt but amongst school-boys, whose games and plays are delivered down invariably the same from one generation to another.

Benedictus Abbas has preserved a very curious edict, which shews the state of gaming in the Christian army commanded by Richard the First King of England, and Philip of France, during the Crusade in the year 1190. No person in the army is permitted to play at any sort of game for money, except knights and clergymen ; who in one whole day and night shall not, each, lose more than twenty shillings, on pain of losing one hundred shillings to the archbishops of the army. The two Kings may play for what they please, but their attendants not for more than twenty shillings. Otherwise, they are to be whipped naked through the army for three days. The monarchs probably played at *Quatuor Reges* or chess, and their followers at dice. Many of the early romances comprise notices of amusements enjoyed by the characters introduced; but it is sometimes, of course, difficult to judge how much is exaggeration; and in the *Books of Hours* we often meet with interesting illustrations of this class, intended as ornamental accessories. In the 13th. c. fabliau of *Blonde of Oxford and Jean de Dammartin*, the hero and heroine play at chess, tables, and dice; and in a MS. of the romance of *Meliadus de Lyonnois*, of the fourteenth century, there are representations of parties engaged in games at chess and cards—the latter perhaps the earliest graphic view of that amusement, and apparently prior to anything known to Chatto. *Archæol. Album*, 1845, p. 75. In a fine MS. in the Bodleian, cited by Strutt, and after him by Brand, there is a series of representations of the more popular games then (1343) in favour. It is remarkable that among them are to be found many of the amusements still in fashion among the old or young, such as top-spinning, cock-fighting, chess, bowls, dice, &c., while others have completely disappeared. In a volume of Homilies of the 14th century, there is a strong illustration of the ungovernable propensity among our countrymen and countrywomen for enjoying themselves in ways, which were not in all cases highly proper. The Homily says: "*p*er is an o*p*er lepre of yonge folk: *p*at *p*ei ben moche smyttid with now a daies/ and *p*is is veyn laughtre, and idul wordis, and many o*p*er vayn iapis; *p*at seelden or neuer *p*ei kunnen stynte from hem/ *p*ei taken noon heede of goddis word. *p*ei rennen to enterludes with gret delijt; yhe, *p*at is more reu*p*e, to strumpetis daunce / *p*e preest for hem mai stonde alone in *p*e chirche, but *p*e harlot in *p*e clepyng shal be hirid for good money: to tellen hem fablis of losengerie/ but to such maner folk : christ sei*p* ful sharplei *p*ese wordis./ wo to you *p*at now lawen : for ye shuln wepe ful fore her-aftir/" This notice concurs with what a later writer observes respecting the desertion of the churches and the devotion of the people to frivolous and wicked sports. Harl. MS. 2276, fol. 37. I am indebted to my friend Mr. F. J. Furnivall for this extract.

Du Cange informs us, that the Council of Salzburg, in 1274, prohibited certain *ludi noxii* on account of the licence used at them. Wright supplies from one of the Royal MSS. in the British Museum a short list of fourteenth century games, of which the exact character is not known. *Domestic Manners*, 1862, p. 210. A farther list occurs at p. 229, and is liable to the same objection.

Some of these forgotten pastimes are of French or foreign origin; but since at the period, to which they appertain, relations between France at all events and ourselves were so constant and intimate, it may be useful to annex the names, by which they were once currently known :

Propre confusion.	Tessera.
Qui perd, se sauve.	Calculus.
Qui est large, est sage.	Urio vel Dardana pugna.
Meschief fait homme penser.	Tricolus.
La chasse de ferce (queen) et de chevalier.	Senio. Monarchus. Orbiculi. Taliorhicus.
Dames et demoiselles.	Vulpes.
La Bataille de rokes.	Tabula.

Some of these are recognizable as still surviving institutions, while others are obsolete variations of the game of chess. The subjoined literary notices are interesting :

"Herlotes walkes thurghe many tounes Wyth speckede mantels and bordouns; And ate ilke mannes house ga *p*ai inne, *p*are *p*ai hope oght for to wynne. Bote 'herlotes' mene calles comonlye Alle *p*at hauntes herlottrye : Herlotes falles to stande on *p*e flore, And play some tyme ate *p*e spore, Atte *p*e beyne, and ate *p*e cate,— A foule play holde I *p*ate,— And *p*are agayne may *p*ai noght be Whene mene byddes *p*aim for *p*aire fe, ffor *p*e rewele of *p*aire relygyoune Es swylke, thurgh *p*aire professyoune ; *p*is es a poynte of *p*aire reule ilke tyme, To lykene mene *p*are *p*ai come, in ryme. zhyte haunte *p*ai oft other Iapes; Some ledes beres, and some ledes apes *p*at mus sautes and solace *p*at sees : All *p*ise are bote foly and nycetees."

William of Nassyngton, *Myrrour of Lyfe* (14th century).

"Also use not to pley at the dice ne at the tablis, Ne none maner gamys uppon the holidais ; Use no tavernys where be jestis and fablis, Syngyng of lewde balettes, rondelettes, or virolais ; Nor erly in mornyng to fecche home fresch mais, For yt makyth maydins to stomble and falle in the breirs, And afterward they telle her councele to the freirs."

MS. Laud 416, (circâ 1460) apud *Rel. Antiq.* vol. ii., p. 27. By the Statute 6 Hen. iv. c 4, labourers and servants playing at unlawful games were made liable to imprisonment for six days, and any magistrate or other officer neglecting to take cognizance of such offences was subject to a penalty. By the statute 17 Edw. IV. c. 3, this earlier enactment was confirmed as follows: "Laborers and seruauntys that vse dyse and other sych games shall haue imprisonment of .vi. dayes," and it was also provided, that "noo gouerner of howse, tenement or gardeyn suffer wyllyngly any person to occupy to playe at the classe keyles [ninepins,] halfe bowle, handyn handout or quekbourd vpon payn or inprisonment by .iii. yerys," &c. By 11 Hen. VII. c. 2, and 19 Hen. VII. c. 12, it was laid down that "no apprentyce nor seruant of husbandry, laborer, nor seruant artificer play at the tablys, tenyse, dyse, cardys, bowlys, nor at none other vnlawfull game owt of the tyme of Crystmas but for mete and drynke, and in crystmas to playe onely in the dwellyng howse of his mayster or in the presence of hys mayster."

In an account of the visit of Louis of Bruges and his suite to England in 1472 there are references to the amusements of the Court at Windsor. The Queen and her ladies played at the *morteaulx*, a game supposed to be allied to bowls, and others at *closkeys*, or ninepins, which are described as being of ivory, but were more probably of bone. *England as seen by Foreigners*, by W. B. Rye, 1865, p. xli. In the contemporary narrative of the marriage of Catherine of Arragon to Prince Arthur of England, in 1501, mention occurs of galleries and other buildings fitted up in the royal gardens:—"In the lougher ende of this gardeyn both pleasaunt gallerys, and housis of pleasure to disporte inn, at chesse, tables, dise, cardes, bylys; bowling aleys, butts for archers, and goodly tenes play." *Antiq. Repert.*, ii., 316. The statutes of Wadham College, Oxford, drawn up in 1613, prescribe that gaming with cards or dice was not permissible except on All Saints' Day, Christmas Day, and the Purification of the Blessed Virgin, when cards might be used, provided the stakes were small, and suitable hours were observed. "Thei hauke, thei hunt, they card, thei dice, they pastyme in theyr prelacies with gallaunte gentlemen, with theyr daunsinge minyons, and with theyr freshe companions, so that ploughinge is set a syde."—Latimer's *Sermon of the Plough*, 1548. Humphrey Roberts, in his "Complaint for Reformation," 1572, represents that his countrymen "vpon the Saboath Day resorte rather to bearebayting, bulbayting, daunsing, fenceplaying and suche lyke vayn exercises then to the Church."

Roberts adds: "— in London, other cyties, and in the countrey townes also, there are many other places of concourse of people: As dycing houses, bowling aleys, fencyng scooles, yea tauerns and ale-houses: wherin are such a nomber of ruffians and cutters (as they call them): that those places are become yonge helles, suche is their wickednesse. So that the tender yonglyngs, beynge come of good houses: and all others (once vsynge suche places), are, as it were, translated, or chaunged, into monsters." The resort to amusements on Sundays was evidently not unusual. In *A Devonshire Yeoman's Diary*, under 1602, we find the following entry: "August 22. I went to Trusham Church. After evening prayers went to bowles." *Antiquary*, 1892, p. 259. In the dedication to "Mihil Mumchance, his discoverie of the Art of Cheating in false Dice play," 1597, we read, "making the divel to daunce in the bottome of your purses, and to turne your angels out of their houses like bad tenants." In the same tract, "Novum, Hassard, and Swift-foot-passage" occur as games. Some of the undermentioned games, quoted here from Rowlands' "Letting of Hvmors Blood," &c., 1611, are overlooked not only by Brand, but by Strutt and Hone:

> "Man, I dare challenge thee to throw the sledge,
> To iumpe, or leape ouer ditch or hedge;
> To wrastle, play at stoole-ball, or to runne;
> To pich the bar, or to shoote off a gunne:
> To play at loggets, nine holes, or tenpinnes;
> To try it out at foot-ball by the shinnes,
> At ticktacke, Irish, noddy, maw, and ruffe:
> At hot-cockles, leap-frog, or blindmanbuffe:
> To drinke halfe pots, or deale at the whole can:
> To play at base, or pen and Inck-horne sir Ihan:
> To daunce the Mirris, play at barlybreake:
> At all exployts a man may thinke or speake,
> At shoue-groat, venter-poynt, or crosse & pile,
> At beshrow him thats last at yonder stile:
> At leaping ore a Midsommer bone-fier:
> Or at the drawing dunne out of the myer."

In Erondel's "French Garden," 1605, the titles of the following games occur:—"Trompe — Dice — Tables — Lurch—Draughts — Perforce — Pleasant—Blowing—Queen's Game—Chesse." There is added: "The maydens did play at Purposes—at Sales—To Thinke—at Wonders—at Stakes—at Vertues—at Answers, so that we could come no sooner," &c. A list of games, to which the keys seem to have been lost, is printed in *Notes and Queries*, being transcribed from three sources as under:

"We went to a sport called selling a horse for a dish of eggs and herrings."—Pepys, *Diary*, Feb. 2, 1659-60.

"The merry game of The parson has lost his cloak."—*Spectator*, N. 268.

"'What say you, Harry; have you any play to show them?'" 'Yes, sir,' said Harry, 'I have a many of them; there's first leap-frog and thrush-a-thrush."—H. Brooke, *Fool of Quality*, i. 25 (ed. 1859).

"One fault brought me into another after it, like *Water my chickens come clock.*"—Ib., i. 272.

"Can you play at draughts, polish, or chess?"—Ib., i. 267.

"Some reminded him of his having beaten them at boxing, others at wrestling and all of his having played with them at prison-bars, leap-frog, shut the gate, and so forth."—Ib., ii. 168.

Several games of the middle of the 17th century are enumerated in "Wit Restor'd," 1658:

"Here's children's bawbles and mens too,
  To play with for delight.
Here's round-heads when turn'd every way
  At length will stand upright.
Here's dice, and boxes if you please
  To play at in and inn,
Here is a sett of kettle pinns
  With bowle at them to rowle:
And if you like such trundling sport
  Here is my ladyes hole.
Here's shaddow ribbon'd of all sorts,
  As various as your mind,
And here's a windmill like your selfe
  Will turne with every wind.
And heer's a church of the same stuff
  Cutt out in the new fashion."

In Cotgrave's *Wit's Interpreter*, third edition, 1671, we meet with directions for playing the courtly games of L'Ombre, Piquit, Gleek, and Cribbage; and in Cotton's *Compleat Gamester*, 1674 he adduces the usual and most gentile games on cards, dice, billiards, trucks, bowls, or chess. In a later impression, 1709, the amusements enumerated are more varied: Piquet, gleek, l'ombre, a Spanish game, cribbage, all-fours, English ruff, and honours *alias* slam, whist, French ruff, five cards, a game called costly colours, boneale, put, the high game, wit and reason, the art of memory, plain dealing, Queen Nazareene, lanterloo, penneech, bankafalet, beast or la béte, and basset.

Edward Chamberlayne, in his "Angliæ Notitia," 1676, enumerates what were at that time the principal recreations and exercises both of the upper and lower classes of society in this country:

"For variety of divertisements, sports, and recreations, no nation doth excel the English. The King hath abroad, his forests, chases, and parks, full of variety of game; for hunting red and fallow deer, foxes, otters; hawking, his paddock courses, horse-races, &c., and at home, tennis, pelmel, billiard, enterludes, balls, ballets, masks, &c. The Nobility and gentry have their parks, warrens, decoys, paddock-courses, horse-races, huntings, coursing, fishing, fowling, hawking, setting dogs, tumblers, lurchers, duck-hunting, cock-fighting, guns for birding, lowbells, bat-fowling; angling, nets, tennis, bowling, billiard tables, chess, draughts, cards, dice, catches, questions, purposes, stage-plays, masks, balls, dancing, singing, all sorts of musical instruments, &c. The citizens and peasants have hand-ball, foot-ball, skittles or nine-pins, shovelboard, stow-ball, goffe, trol-madame, cudgels, bear-baiting, bull-baiting, bow and arrow, throwing at cocks, shuttlecock, bowling, quoits, leaping, wrestling, pitching the bar, and ringing of bells, a recreation used in no other countrey of the world. Amongst these, cock-fighting seems to all foreigners too childish and unsuitable for the gentry, and for the common people; bull-baiting and bearbaiting seem too cruel; and for the citizens, foot-ball and throwing at cocks, very uncivil, rude, and barbarous within the City." In the "Life of the Scotch Rogue," 1722, p. 7, the following sports occur: "I was but a sorry proficient in learning: being readier at cat and dog, cappy hole, riding the hurley hacket, playing at kyles and dams, spang-bodle, wrestling, and foot-ball, and (such other sports as we use in our country), than at my book."

"Julius Pollux," (observes Cornelius Scriblerus) "describes the Omilla or chuck-farthing; tho' some will have our modern chuck-farthing to be nearer the aphetinda of the ancients. He also mentions the basilinda or King I am; and myinda, or hoopers-hide. But the chytindra described by the same author is certainly not our hot-cockle; for that was by pinching, and not by striking; tho' there are good authors who affirm the rathapygismus to be yet nearer the modern hot cockles. My son Martin may use either of them indifferently, they being equally antique. Building of houses and riding upon sticks, have been used by children in all ages; *Ædificare casas, equitare in arundine longa.* Yet I much doubt whether the riding upon sticks did not come into use after the age of the Centaurs. There is one play which shews the gravity of ancient education, called the Acinetinda, in which children contended who could longest stand still. This we have suffered to perish entirely; and if I might be allowed to guess, it was certainly first lost among the French. I will permit my son to play at Apodidascinda, which can be no other than our Puss in a corner. Julius Pollux, in his ninth Book, speaks of the melolonthe, or the kite; but I question whether the kite of antiquity was the same with ours, and though the Ορτυτοποπία, or **quail-fight**ing, is what is most taken notice of, they had doubtless cock-matches also, as is evident from certain antient gems and relievos. In a word, let my son Martin disport himself at any game truly antique, except one which was invented by a people among the Thracians, who hung up one of their companions in a rope, and gave him a knife to cut himself down; which if he failed in, he was suffered to hang till he was dead; and this was only reckoned a sort of joke. I am utterly against this as barbarous and cruel." Misson says: "Besides the sports and diversions common to most other European nations, as tennis, billiards, chess, tick-tack, dancing, plays, &c., the English have some which are particular to them, or at least which they love and use more than any other people." *Travels in England*, p. 304. See a little volume entitled: "Games most in use in England, France, and Spain, viz., Basset, Piquet, Primero, L'Ombre, Chess, Billiards, Grand-tricktrack, Verquere, &c., some of which were never before printed in any language. All regulated by the most experienced Masters." Published by J. Morphew about 1710. The editions of Charles Cotton's *Compleat Gamester*, and the earlier issues of Hoyle's *Games* may also be consulted. Hollar published in 1607 "Paidopœgnion, sive puerorum ludentium schemata varia, pictorum usui aptata."

The Gantelupe or **Gauntlet, To Run.**—See *Penny Magazine* for 1837, p. 339, where it is described as a military and naval punishment; but it was not confined to this country or to civilized nations. It occurs in accounts of travels among savage communities, and in works of fiction founded on them.

Garden-House.—The older *summer-house.* See Nares, *Glossary*, 1859, in v.

Garlands.—Nuptial garlands are of the most remote antiquity. They appear to have been equally used by the Jews and the Greeks and Romans. Selden's *Uxor*

Hebraica in *Opera*, iii., 655. "Among the Romans, when the marriage-day was come, the bride was bound to have a chaplet of flowers or hearbes upon her head, and to weare a girdle of sheeps wool about her middle, fastned with a true-loves-knot, the which her husband must loose. Hence rose the proverb: He hath undone her virgin's girdle: that is, of a mayde he hath made her a woman." Vaughan's *Golden Grove*, 1600, ed. 1608, sign O 2. In Ihre's "Glossarium," 1769, v. Krona, we read: "Sponsarum ornatus erat coronæ gestamen, qui mos hodieque pleno usu apud Ruricolas viget."

Among the Anglo-Saxons, after the benediction in the church, both the bride and bridegroom were crowned with crowns of flowers, kept in the church for that purpose. In the Eastern Church the chaplets used on these occasions appear to have been blessed. Selden, *ubi suprâ*, p. 661. "Coronas tenent a tergo paranymphi, quæ Capitibus Sponsorum iterum a Sacerdote non sine benedictione solenni aptantur." The form is given, p. 667. "Benedic, Domine, Annulum istum et Coronam istam, ut sicut Annulus circumdat digitum hominis et Corona Caput, ita Gratia Spiritus Sancti circumdet Sponsum et Sponsam, ut videant Filius et Filias usque ad tertiam aut quartam Generationem, &c." We ought not to overlook the miraculous garland given by the father in the Wright's Chast Wife in the tale of that name from the "Gesta Romanorum." He says to the wright, on presenting it as the only gift it is in his power to make:

"Haue here thys garlonde of roses ryche,
In alle thys lond ys none yt lyche,
    For ytt wylle euer be newe.
Wete thou wele withowtyn fable,
Alle the whyle thy wyfe ys stable,
    The chaplett wolle hold hewe."

In "Dives and Pauper, 1493, "The fixte Precepte," chap. 2, is the following curious passage: "Thre ornamentys longe pryncypaly to a wyfe. A rynge on hir fynger, a broch on hir brest, and a garlond on hir hede. The ringe betokenethe true love, as I have seyd, the broch betokennethe clennesse in herte and chastitye that she oweth to have, the garlande bytokeneth gladnesse and the dignitye of the sacrament of wedlok." At the marriage of Blonde of Oxford to Jean de Dammartin, in the 13th century, the bride is made to wear a gold chaplet. Compare *Nuptial Usages, infrâ.* In dressing out Grisild for her marriage in the "Clerk of Oxenford's Tale" in Chaucer, the chaplet is noted: "A corune on

hire hed they han ydressed." The nuptial garlands were sometimes made of
myrtle. In England, in the time of
Henry VIII., the bride wore a garland of
corn ears, sometimes one of flowers. Wax
appears to have been used in the formation of these garlands from the subsequent passage in Hyll's book on Dreams:
" A garlande of waxe (to dream of) signifyeth evill to all personnes, but especiallye to the sicke, for as much as it is
commonlye occupyed aboute burialls."
Gosson, in his " Ephemerides of Phialo,"
1579, remarks: " In som countries the
bride is crowned by the matrons with a
garland of prickles, and so delivered unto
her husband that hee might know he
hath tied himself to a thorny plesure."
Among the wares on sale or supply by
Newbery in his *Dives Pragmaticus,* 1563
(Hazlitt's *Fugitive Tracts,* 1875, vol. i.),
figure:

" Fyne gay and straunge garlands, for
    Bryde & Brydegrome."

In the Churchwardens' Accounts of St.
Margaret's, Westminster, under 1540, is
the following item: " Paid to Alice
Lewis, a goldsmith's wife of London;
for a serclett to marry maydens in, the
26th day of September, £3 10s." The
following occurs in Marston's " Dutch
Courtezan":

" I was afraid, I'faith, that I should
    ha seene a garland on this beauties
    herse."

In Field's " Amends for Ladies," 1618,
scene the last, when the marriages are
agreed upon, there is a stage direction
to set garlands upon the heads of the
maid and widow that are to be married.
These garlands are thus described by
Gay:

" To her sweet mem'ry flow'ry garlands
    strung,
On her now empty seat aloft were
    hung."

These emblems were apparently hung up
in churches, and where they were composed of fresh flowers withered. Newton, under Breaches of the second
Commandment, censures " the adorning
with garlands, or presenting unto any
image of any Saint, whom thou hast made
speciall choise of to be thy patron and
advocate, the firstlings of thy increase, as
Corne and Graine, and other oblations."
Tryall of a Man's Own Selfe, 1586, 54.
Coles, probably speaking of the metropolis only, says: " It is not very long
since the custome of setting up garlands
in churches hath been left off with us."
Intro. to the Knowledge of Plants, 64,
But in the Ely Articles of Enquiry, 1662,

p. 7, I read as follows: " Are any garlands and other ordinary funeral ensigns
suffred to hang where they hinder the
prospect, or until they grow foul and
dusty, withered and rotten?" Aubanus,
in his Description of the Rites at Marriages in his country and time, has not
omitted garlands. Dallaway tells us that
" Marriage is by them (of the Greek
Church) called the Matrimonial Coronation, from the crowns or garlands with
which the parties are decorated, and
which they solemnly dissolve on the eighth
day following." Brand likewise refers
to a French work, where it is mentioned
that, at the weddings of the poorer sort,
a chaplet or wreath of roses was customary in France; but these illustrations,
even when they are very apt, which is
not often, it must be owned, the case, are
only interesting parallel examples.

The Masters and Wardens of some of the
Gilds of London formerly used Election
Garlands, which were often made of
sumptuous materials. See particularly
the fine large illustrations in Black's
History of the Leathersellers, 1871,
where the examples date from 1539.

Garrett.—For a notice of this place,
otherwise known as Garvett, and its mock
mayor, &c., see Additions to Hazlitt's
Blount, 1874, in *Antiquary* for September, 1885. Its evolution from a single
house to a hamlet has had many ana-
logues, such as Vauxhall, and Schaffhau-
sen, Mühlhausen, &c., abroad. During
a considerable number of years, Sir Jeffrey Dunstan, a dealer in wigs, and Sir
Henry Dimsdale, a muffin-seller, subsequently a hardware man, were successively returned as mayors of Garrett. The
former was nicknamed *Old Wigs,* and the
latter *Honeyjuice* or *Sir Harry.*

Garters at Weddings.—There
was formerly a custom in the North of
England, which will be thought to have
bordered very closely upon indecency,
and strongly marks the grossness of manners that prevailed among our ancestors:
it was for the young men present at a
wedding to strive immediately after the
ceremony, who could first pluck off the
bride's garters from her legs. This was
done before the very altar. The bride
was generally gartered with ribbons for
the occasion. Whoever were so fortunate
as to be victors in this singular species of
contest, during which the bride was often
obliged to scream out, and was very frequently thrown down, bore them about
the church in triumph. Brand says: "A
clergyman in Yorkshire told me, that to
prevent this very indecent assault, it is
usual for the bride to give garters out of
her bosom. I have sometimes thought
this a fragment of the ancient ceremony

of loosening the virgin zone, or girdle, a custom that needs no explanation." From passages in different works, it should seem that the striving for garters was originally after the bride had been put to bed. Among the lots in the lottery presented in 1601, there occurs:

"*A Payre of Garters.*

"Though you have fortunes garters, you must be
More staid and constant in your steps than she."

Sir Abraham Ninny, in Field's "A Woman's a Weather-Cocke," 1612, act i. sc. 1, declares:

"Well, since I am disdain'd; off garters blew;
Which signifies Sir Abram's love was true.
Off cypresse blacke, for thou befits not me;
Thou art not cypresse of the cypresse tree,
Befitting Lovers: out green shoe-strings, out,
Wither in pocket, since my Luce doth pout."

In Brooke's "Epithalamium," 1614, we read:

"Youths; take his poynts; your wonted right:
And maydens, take your due, her garters."

In Aylet's Poems, 1654, is a copy of verses "on a sight of a most honorable Lady's Wedding Garter." A note to George Stuart's "Discourse between a Northumberland Gentleman and his Tenant," 1686, p. 24, tells us: "The piper at a wedding has always a piece of the bride's garter ty'd about his pipes." These garters, it should seem, were anciently worn as trophies in the hats. Misson says: "When bed-time is come, the bride-men pull of the bride's garters, which she had before unty'd, that they might hang down and so prevent a curious hand from coming too near her knee. This done, and the garters being fasten'd to the hats of the gallants, the bride maids carry the bride into the bride-chamber, where they undress her and lay her in bed." I am of opinion that the origin of the *Order of the Garter* is to be traced to this nuptial custom, anciently common to both court and country. It is the custom in Normandy for the bride to bestow her garter on some young man as a favour, or sometimes it is taken from her.

Gate Penny.—A customary tribute from tenants to their landlords. See Halliwell in v.

Gawby Day.—(December 28). This day at Wrexham is called Gawby Day, perhaps from *Gauby*, a Northern term for a countryman or a bumpkin; and the town is filled with servants, both men and women. Formerly and originally they came up from the country to be hired; but now it has become a mere holiday. See Atkinson's *Cleveland Glossary*, 1868, in v.

George's Day, St.—(April 23rd). Among the ordinances made by Henry V. for his army abroad, printed in "Excerpta Historica," 1833, is one "For theim that bere not a bande of Seinte George"; and it appears that all the English soldiers were bound, under severe penalties, to carry this distinguishing badge. Compare *Amulet*. It is curious that the same Ordinances, which were promulgated by Henry V. in 1415, served the same purpose in 1513, when Henry VIII. made his expedition to Boulogne, *mutatis mutandis*. In Coates's "History of Reading," p. 221, under Churchwardens' Accounts in the year 1536, are the following entries:

"Charg' of Saynt George.
"Ffirst payd for iii caffes-skynes, and ii horse-skynnes, iii^s. vi^d.
Payd for makeyng the loft that Saynt George standeth upon, vi^d.
Payd for ii plonks for the same loft, viij^d.
Payd for iiij pesses of clowt lether, ij^s ij^d.
Payd for makeyng the yron that the hors resteth vpon, vj^d.
Payd for makeyng of Saynt George's cote, viij^d.
Payd to John Paynter for his labour, xlv^s.
Payd for roses, bells, gyrdle, sword, and dager, iij^s. iiij^d.
Payd for settyng on the bells and roses, iij^d.
Payd for naylls necessarye thereto, x^d. ob."

In the hamlet of Y Faerdref, in the commote of Isdulas, in Denbighshire, is a small village called St. George, on the churchyard-wall of which it was formerly believed that the print of the shoes of St. George's horse could be seen. The neighbouring woods were supposed to be haunted by fairies and other spirits. *Denbigh and its Lordship*, by John Williams, 1860, pp. 217-18. Machyn the Diarist notes that, on St. George's Day, 1559, the Knights of the Garter went about the Hall singing in procession in the morning, and in the afternoon was the election of new knights. Machyn appears, in one place, to insinuate, a sort of dissatisfaction at the occasional departure from the old usage of holding the chapter of the order of the garter at Westminster instead of Windsor, as was the case once or twice in the early part of Elizabeth's reign. Comp. Evelyn's *Diary*, April 23, 1667.

It seems to be the case that at ceremonial observances in St. George's Chapel at Windsor in the case of installations or otherwise the choristers demanded as a fee the King's spurs, which were redeemed by a pecuniary payment. In the Privy Purse Expenses of Henry VII., under 1495, we find : " To the children for the King's spoures, 4s.," and there are similar entries in the Expenses of Henry VIII. under 1530.

It appears that blue coats were formerly worn by people of fashion on St. George's Day. Hazlitt's *Dodsley*, x., 349. Among the Fins, whoever makes a riot on St. George's Day is in danger of suffering from storms and tempests.

Germanus, St., Bishop of Auxerre.—Pennant remarks that the Church of Llanarmon in Denbighshire is dedicated to this personage, who with St. Lupus, says he, " contributed to gain the famous *Victoria Alleluiatica* over the Picts and Saxons near Mold." *Tours in Wales*, 1810, ii., 17. Owing to this circumstance it doubtless was that Bishop Germanus was a favourite in Wales, and had many churches dedicated to him. There were apparently two or three sainted persons of this name, nor is it clear to which Woodes refers where in his *Conflict of Conscience*, 1581, he makes one of the characters say :

" Sent Iob heale the pore, the agew Sent Germayne."

Ghosts.—" A ghost," according to Grose, " is supposed to be the spirit of a person deceased, who is either commissioned to return for some especial errand, such as the discovery of a murder, to procure restitution of land or money unjustly withheld from an orphan or widow, or, having committed some injustice whilst living, cannot rest, till that is redressed. Sometimes the occasion of spirits revisiting this world is to inform their heir in what secret place, or private drawer in an old trunk, they had hidden the title deeds of the estate ; or where, in troublesome times, they buried their money or plate. Some ghosts of murdered persons, whose bodies have been secretly buried, cannot be at ease till their bones have been taken up, and deposited in consecrated ground, with all the rites of Christian burial. This idea is the remain of a very old piece of heathen superstition : the ancients believed that Charon was not permitted to ferry over the ghosts of unburied persons, but that they wandered up and down

the banks of the river Styx for a hundred years, after which they were admitted to a passage. This is mentioned by Virgil :

' Hæc omnis quam cernis, inops inhumataque turba est :
Portitor ille, Charon ; hi quos vehit un da, sepulti.
Nec ripas datur horrendas, et rauca, fluenta,
Transportare prius quam sedibus ossa quierunt.
Centum errant annos, volitantque hæc littora circum :
Tum, demum admissi, stagna exoptata revisunt.'

Sometimes ghosts appear in consequence of an agreement made, whilst living, with some particular friend, that he who first died should appear to the survivor. Glanvil tells us of a ghost of a person who had lived but a disorderly kind of life, for which it was condemned to wander up and down the earth, in the company of evil spirits, till the Day of Judgment. In most of the relations of ghosts they are supposed to be mere aërial beings, without substance, and that they can pass through walls and other solid bodies at pleasure. A particular instance of this is given in Relation the 27th in Glanvil's Collection, where one David Hunter, neat-herd to the Bishop of Down and Connor, was for a long time haunted by the apparition of an old woman, whom he was by a secret impulse obliged to follow whenever she appeared, which he says he did for a considerable time, even if in bed with his wife ; and because his wife could not hold him in his bed, she would go too, and walk after him till day, though she saw nothing ; but his little dog was so well acquainted with the apparition, that he would follow it as well as his master. If a tree stood in her walk, he observed her always to go through it. Notwithstanding this seeming immateriality, this very ghost was not without some substance : for, having performed her errand, she desired Hunter to lift her from the ground, in the doing of which, he says, she felt just like a bag of feathers. We sometimes also read of ghosts striking violent blows ; and that, if not made way for, they overturn all impediments, like a furious whirlwind. Glanvil mentions an instance of this, in Relation 17th of a Dutch lieutenant, who had the faculty of seeing ghosts ; and who, being prevented making way for one which he mentioned to some friends as coming towards them, was, with his companions, violently thrown down, and sorely bruised. We further learn, by Relation 16th, that the hand of a ghost is ' as cold as a clod.'

"The usual time at which ghosts make their appearance is midnight, and seldom before it is dark; though some audacious spirits have been said to appear even by day-light: but of this there are few instances, and those mostly ghosts who have been laid, perhaps in the Red Sea (of which more hereafter), and whose times of confinement were expired: these, like felons confined to the lighters, are said to return more troublesome and daring than before. No Ghosts can appear on Christmas Eve: this Shakespear has put into the mouth of one of his characters in Hamlet." "Ghosts," Grose adds, "commonly appear in the same dress they usually wore whilst living; though they are sometimes cloathed all in white; but that is chiefly the churchyard ghosts, who have no particular business, but seem to appear *pro bono publico*, or to scare drunken rustics from tumbling over their graves. I cannot learn that ghosts carry tapers in their hands, as they are sometimes depicted, though the room in which they appear, if without fire or candle, is frequently said to be as light as day. Dragging chains is not the fashion of English ghosts; chains and black vestments being chiefly the accoutrements of foreign spectres, seen in arbitrary governments; dead or alive, English spirits are free. If, during the time of an apparition, there is a lighted candle in the room, it will burn extremely blue: this is so universally acknowledged, that many eminent philosophers have busied themselves in accounting for it, without once doubting the truth of the fact. Dogs too have the faculty of seeing spirits, as is instanced in David Hunter's relation, above quoted; but in that case they usually shew signs of terror, by whining and creeping to their master for protection: and it is generally supposed that they often see things of this nature when their owner cannot; there being some persons, particularly those born on a Christmas Eve, who cannot see spirits. The coming of a spirit is announced some time before its appearance, by a variety of loud and dreadful noises; sometimes rattling in the old hall like a coach and six, and rumbling up and down the staircase like the trundling of bowls or cannon balls. At length the door flies open, and the spectre stalks slowly up to the bed's foot, and opening the curtains, looks steadfastly at the person in bed by whom it is seen; a ghost being very rarely visible to more than one person, although there are several in company. It is here necessary to observe that it has been universally found by experience, as well as affirmed by divers apparitions themselves, that a

ghost has not the power to speak till it has been first spoken to; so, that, notwithstanding the urgency of the business on which it may come, every thing must stand still till the person visited can find sufficient courage to speak to it; an event that sometimes does not take place for many years. It has not been found that female ghosts are more loquacious than those of the male sex, both being equally restrained by this law.

The mode of addressing a ghost is, by commanding it, in the name of the three persons of the Trinity, to tell you who it is, and what is its business; this it may be necessary to repeat three times; after which it will, in a low and hollow voice, declare its satisfaction at being spoken to, and desire the party addressing it not to be afraid, for it will do him no harm. This being premised, it commonly enters into its narrative, which being completed, and its request or commands given, with injunctions that they be immediately executed, it vanishes away, frequently in a flash of light; in which case some ghosts have been so considerate as to desire the party to whom they appear to shut their eyes: sometimes its departure is attended with delightful music. During the narration of its business, a ghost must by no means be interrupted by questions of any kind; so doing is extremely dangerous; if any doubts arise, they must be stated after the spirit has done its tale. Questions respecting its state, or the state of any of their former acquaintance, are offensive, and not often answered, spirits, perhaps, being restrained from divulging the secrets of their prison-house. Occasionally spirits will even condescend to talk on common occurrences, as is instanced by Glanvil in the apparition of Major George Sydenham to Captain William Dyke, Relation 10th. Wherein the Major reproved the Captain for suffering a sword he had given him to grow rusty, saying, 'Captain, Captain, this sword did not used to be kept after this manner when it was mine.' This attention to the state of the weapon was a remnant of the Major's professional duty when living.

It is somewhat remarkable that ghosts do not go about their business like the persons of this world. In cases of murder, a ghost, instead of going to the next Justice of the Peace, and laying its information, or to the nearest relation of the person murdered, appears to some poor labourer who knows none of the parties, draws the curtains of some decrepit nurse or almswoman, or hovers about the place where his body is deposited. The same circuitous mode is pursued with respect to redressing injured orphans or widows: when it seems as if the shortest and most certain way would be, to go to the person guilty of the injustice, and haunt him continually till he be terrified into a restitution. Nor are the pointing out lost writings generally managed in a more summary way, the ghost commonly applying to a third person, ignorant of the whole affair, and a stranger to all concerned. But it is presumptuous to scrutinize too far into these matters: Ghosts have undoubtedly forms and customs peculiar to themselves. If, after the first appearance, the persons employed neglect, or are prevented from, performing the message or business committed to their management, the ghost appears continually to them, at first with a discontented, next an angry, and at length with a furious countenance, threatening to tear them in pieces if the matter is not forthwith executed: sometimes terrifying them, as in Glanvil's Relation 26th, by appearing in many formidable shapes, and sometimes even striking them a violent blow. Of blows given by ghosts there are many instances, and some wherein they have been followed by an incurable lameness. It should have been observed that ghosts, in delivering their commissions, in order to ensure belief, communicate to the persons employed some secret, known only to the parties concerned and themselves, the relation of which always produces the effect intended. The business being completed, ghosts appear with a cheerful countenance, saying they shall now be at rest, and will never more disturb any one; and, thanking their agents, by way of reward communicate to them something relative to themselves, which they will never reveal. Sometimes ghosts appear, and disturb a house, without deigning to give any reason for so doing: with these the shortest and only way is to exorcise and eject them, or, as the vulgar term is, lay them. For this purpose there must be two or three clergymen, and the ceremony must be performed in Latin; a language that strikes the most audacious ghost with terror. A ghost may be laid for any term less than a hundred years, and in any place or body, full or empty; as, a solid oak—the pommel of a sword—a barrel of beer, if a yeoman or simple gentleman, or a pipe of wine, if an esquire or justice. But of all places the most common, and what a ghost least likes, is the Red Sea; it being related in many instances, that ghosts have most earnestly besought the exorcists not to confine them in that place. It is nevertheless considered as an indisputable fact,

that there are an infinite number laid there, perhaps from it being a safer prison than any other nearer at hand; though neither history nor tradition gives us any instance of ghosts escaping or returning from this kind of transportation before their time."

It is to be suspected that the ancient ideas of a ghost were as indefinite and loose as those now prevalent among us. *St. John's Manners and Customs of Ancient Greece*, 1842, i., 364, *et seqq.* The vulgar superstition, that ghosts walk about in white sheets or clothes seems to have had existence at an early date: for in the story of the Miller and the Tailor in "A C. Mery Talys," 1526, the sexton mistakes the miller in his white coat for the dead farmer's troubled spirit risen from the grave. But in the "Awntyrs of Arthur at the Ternewathelyn" there is a description of an apparition, which proceeds on a somewhat more intelligent theory, so to speak:

"Bare was hir body, and blak to
    the bane,
  Vnbeclosut in a cloude, in clethyng
    evyl clad;
Hit zaulut, hit zamurt, lyke a woman,
  Nauthyr of hyde, nyf of heue, no hyl-
    lyng hit had.
  . . . .

Alle gloet as the gledes, the gost qwere
    hit glidus,
  Was vnbyclosut in a cloude, in cle-
    thing vn-clere,
Was sette aure with serpentes, that
    sate to the sydus;
  To telle the todus ther opon with
    tung were to tere."

Shakespear's ghosts excel all others. The terrible indeed is his forte. How awful is that description of the dead time of night, the season of their perambulation!

"'Tis now the very witching time of
    night,
When churchyards yawn, and hell itself
    breathes out
Contagion to this world."

I append two other early notices:

"I know thee well, I heare the watch-
    full dogs,
With hollow howling tell of thy ap-
    proach,
The lights burne dim, affrighted with
    thy presence:
And this distemper'd and tempestuous
    night
Tells me the ayre is troubled with some
    devill."

    Merry Devil of Edmonton, 1608.

"Ghosts never walk till after midnight,
If I may believe my Grannam."
Beaumont and Fletcher, *Lovers Progress*,
act iv.

"Various ways," says a writer in the *Gentleman's Magazine*, 1732, "have been proposed by the learned for laying of ghosts. Those of the artificial sort are easily quieted. Thus when a fryer, personating an apparition, haunted the chambers of the late Emperor Josephus, the present King Augustus, then at the Imperial Court, flung him out of the window, and laid him effectually. The late Dr. Fowler, Bishop of Gloucester, and the late Mr. Justice Powell, had frequent altercations upon this subject. The Bishop was a zealous defender of ghosts; the Justice somewhat sceptical, and distrustful of their being. In a visit the Bishop one day made his friend, the Justice told him, that since their last disputation he had had ocular demonstration to convince him of the existence of ghosts. How, says the Bishop, what! ocular demonstration? I am glad, Mr. Justice, you are become a convert; I beseech you let me know the whole story at large. 'My Lord,' answers the Justice, 'as I lay one night in my bed, about the hour of twelve, I was wak'd by an uncommon noise, and heard something coming upstairs, and stalking directly towards my room. I drew the curtain, and saw a faint glimmering of light enter my chamber.'—'Of a blue colour, no doubt,' (says the Bishop),—'Of a pale blue' (answers the Justice): the light was follow'd by a tall, meagre, and stern personage, who seemed about 70, in a long dangling rugg gown, bound round with a broad leathern girdle; his beard thick and grizly; a large furr-cap on his head, and a long staff in his hand; his face wrinkled and of a dark sable hue. I was struck with the appearance, and felt some unusual shocks; for you know the old saying I made use of in Court, when part of the lanthorn upon Westminster Hall fell down in the midst of our proceedings, to the no small terror of one or two of my brethren,

Si fractus illabatur Orbis,
Impavidum ferient Ruinæ.

But, to go on: it drew near and stared me full in the face.' 'And did you not speak to it?' (interrupted the Bishop); there was money hid or murder committed, to be sure.' 'My Lord, I did speak to it'—'And what answer, Mr. Justice?' 'My Lord, the answer was, (not without a thump of the staff and a shake of the lanthorn), that he was the watchman of the night, and came to give me notice that he had found the streetdoor open; and that unless I rose and shut it, I might chance to be robbed before break of day.' The Judge had no sooner ended, but the Bishop disappear'd." The same author adds: "The cheat is begun by nurses with stories of bug-bears, &c. from whence we are gradually led to the traditionary accounts of local ghosts, which, like the genii of the ancients, have been reported to haunt certain family seats and cities, famous for their antiquities and decays. Of this sort are the apparitions at Verulam, Silchester, Reculver, and Rochester: the Dæmon of Tidworth, the Black Dog of Winchester, and the Bar-guest of York. The story of Madam Veal has been of singular use to the editors of Drelincourt on Death." And he afterward ironically observes: "When we read of the ghost of Sir George Villiers, of the Piper of Hamelm, the Dæmon of Moscow, or the German Colonel mentioned by Ponti, and see the names of Clarendon, Boyle, &c. to these accounts, we find reason for our credulity; till, at last, we are convinc'd by a whole conclave of ghosts met in the works of Glanvil and Moreton." The Madame Veal above-mentioned was the same as the person of whom Defoe wrote. Mr. Locke assures us we have as clear an idea of spirit as of body."

In the "Antiquarian Repertory" is a singular narrative of a man named Richard Clarke, a farming-labourer at Hamington, in Northamptonshire, who was haunted by the ghost of another man, name apparently unknown, who declared to Clarke once, through a large hole in the wall of one of the rooms of his (Clarke's) house, that he had been murdered near his own house 267 years, 9 months, and 2 days ago, (this was in 1675), and buried in the orchard. He added that his wife and children, who had lived in Southwark, never knew what became of him; that he had some treasures and paper buried in the cellar of a house near London, and that Clarke must seek for it, and that he (the ghost) would meet him in the cellar, to assist him in the search. Clarke asked time to consider; but the ghost was peremptory. He told him that, as soon as the money and the writings were found, and duly delivered to certain relatives of his in Southwark at such an address, removed from him in the fourth generation, he (the ghost) would cease to visit him, and would leave him in peace; at present he said "that he rece'd much hurt in his cattele by him, yᵗ he shooke the house when his first wife lay in, and frighted her so, she dyed of it." Hereupon Clarke went to town, and on London Bridge the ghost passed him, and conducted him to the house, where his wife had lived four generations before. Clarke found everything answerable to the account which the ghost had given him; the money and the documents were discovered, the writ-

ings on vellum found, but those on paper
decayed. Clarke divided the money, and
acted exactly as the ghost of the murdered
man directed him to do, and the latter
"lookt chearfully upon him, and gave
him thankes, and said now he should be
at rest, and spoke to those other persons
which were of his generation, relations,
but they had not courage to answer; but
Clarke talked for them." Morgan, the
writer of the letter, in which this story
appears, quite believed in the account,
and he says, alluding to the money: "It
must be coyne of Hen. 4 time and will
come amongst the goldsmiths one time or
other, if care be taken in it; methinks it
should make some noise in Southwarke,
and might be found out there. He (Clarke)
hath several brothers in London whom he
was w^th; perhaps some discovery may be
made from them of the place. I
had this story from Mr. Clarke himself."
Original letter from Fr. Morgan at
Kingsthorpe near Northton (Northampton) to a correspondent at Garraway's
Coffee-house, printed in A. R. ed. 1808,
vol. iv. p. 635-7. "Tout est prodige
pour l'ignorance, qui, dans le cercle étroit
de ses habitudes, voit le cercle ou se meut
l'univers. Pour le philosophe, il n'y a
pas de prodiges: une naissance monstru-
euse, l'eboulement subit de la roche la plus
dure, resultent, il le sait, de causes aussi
naturelles, aussi necessaires, que le retour
alternatif du jour et de la nuit."—Salverte, *Des Sciences Occultes*, p. 7.

Gifts.—See *Nails.*

Giles's, St., Day.—(September 1.)
An account of this Saint and of the origin
of the consecration of the 1st of September to his memory in our calendar, may
be found in the "Book of Days." Many
churches bear his name. There is the following description in Machyn's "Diary,"
of the procession in the city of London in
1556, round the parish of St. Giles,
Cripplegate: "The furst day of September was Sant Gylles day, and ther was a
goodly processyon abowt the parryche
with the whettes (waits), and the canepe
borne, and the sacrament, and ther was
a goodly masse songe as has bene hard;
and master Thomas Greuelle, waxchandler, mad a grett dener for master Garter
(lord mayor) and my lade, and master
Machylle the shreyffe and ys wyff, and
boyth the chamburlayns, and mony wor-
shefull men and women at dener, and the
whettes playng and dyver odur mynstrelles, for ther was a grett dener."
Brand has observed silence respecting St. Giles's Bowl, the flagon or jug of
ale, which was in the old times presented
to the condemned convict at St. Giles's
Hospital, on the road to Tyburn. It
appears to be established with tolerable

certainty, that the gallows stood on the
site of a portion of Connaught Square;
but I am not aware that the precise spot
has been settled beyond dispute. . A correspondent of "Current Notes" for
August 1856, quotes Burton the Leicestershire historian's account of this ceremony. "At the Hospital of St. Giles in
the Fields, without the bar of the old
Temple, London, and the *Domus Conver-
sorum* (now the Rolls), the prisoners conveyed from the City of London towards
Teybourne, there to be executed for trea-
sons, felonies, or other trespasses, were
presented with a great bowle of ale thereof to drinke at their pleasure, as to be
their last refreshing in this life." The
writer goes on to say that Parton, in his
account of St. Giles's Hospital and Parish, 1822, refers to this as a peculiar custom; but he points out that "the custom
was not so peculiar, but appears to have
been an observance of Popish times." He
seems rather to mean Catholic countries, for the period, of which he had
been before speaking, was antecedent, of
course, to the Reformation, and he just
afterwards cites some examples of a similar usage among the French in the XVth
century. Churchyard also refers to it in
his "Mirror and Manners of Men," 1594:

"Trusting in friendship makes some be
    trust up,
Or ride in a cart to kis Saint Giles his
    cup."

There is a Yorkshire proverb: "He will
be hanged for leaving his liquor, like the
saddler of Bawtrey," which refers to a
similar usage. A saddler from Bawtrey,
on his way to execution declined the
proffered bowl of ale, and was consequently turned off, just before a reprieve
arrived.

In Lyndsay's time, and long before,
the inhabitants of Edinburgh used
to carry about the town, on St. Giles's
Day, what the poet calls "an auld stock
image," and likens to the image of Bel,
which they bore in procession at Babylon.
The passage is in the "Monarke," first
printed about 1554:

"On thare feist day, all creature may
    se:
Thay beir an auld stock image throuch
    ye toun,
With talbrone, trompet, schalme, and
    clarioun,
Quhilk hes bene vsit mony one zeir
    bigone;
With priestis and freris, in to proces-
    sioun,
Siclyke as bell wes borne throuch Babi-
    lone.' '

"The arm-bone of St. Giles," observes
Mr. D. Laing, "was regarded as a relique

of inestimable value, when brought to this country by William Prestoun of Gourtoun, who bequeathed it to ' our mother kirk of Sant Gele of Edynburgh,' 11th of January, 1454-5." Notes to reprint of "Dundee Psalms," 1868, p. 257. Mr. Laing refers us to the "Charters of the Collegiate Church of St. Giles." Bann. Club, 1859.

Giles's, St., Fair. — One of the chief fairs was that of St. Giles's Hill or Down, near Winchester: the Conqueror instituted it and gave it as a kind of revenue to the Bishop of Winchester. It was at first for three days, but afterwards, by Henry III., prolonged to sixteen days. Its jurisdiction extended seven miles round, and comprehended even Southampton, then a capital and trading town. Merchants who sold wares at that time within that circuit forfeited them to the bishop. Officers were placed at a considerable distance, at bridges and other avenues of access to the fair, to exact toll of all merchandize passing that way. In the meantime, all shops in the city of Winchester were shut. A court, called the Pavilion, composed of the bishop's justiciaries and other officers, had power to try causes of various sorts for seven miles round. The bishop had a toll of every load or parcel of goods passing through the gates of the city. On St. Giles's Eve the Mayor, bailiffs, and citizens of Winchester delivered the keys of the four gates to the bishop's officers. Many and extraordinary were the privileges granted to the bishop on this occasion, all tending to obstruct trade and to oppress the people. Numerous foreign merchants frequented this fair; and several streets were formed in it, assigned to the sale of different commodities. The surrounding monasteries had shops or houses in these streets, used only at the fair; which they held under the bishop, and often let by lease for a term of years. Different counties had their different stations. In the Revenue Roll of William of Waynflete, An. 1471, this fair appears to have greatly decayed; in which, among other proofs, a district of the fair is mentioned as being unoccupied : "Ubi Homines Cornubiæ stare solebant."

Gilligate, Durham. — The septennial Capital Court of the Marquess of Londonderry for the borough and manor of "Gilligate" — the ancient name for that part of Durham city now called Gilesgate—was held May 8, 1902. After the officials had been chosen, and local differences righted, the steward and his suite, with a crowd of the inhabitants, proceeded to perambulate the boundaries, in the course of which many curious gifts have to be provided by his lordship's retainers. Sports and a dinner wound up the day's proceedings.

Gimmal Ring. — See *Rings* and compare Nares, *Glossary*, 1859, in v.

Ginger.—See *Nuptial Usages.*

Girdle.—See *Lying-In.*

Gisborough, co. York.—In an old account of the Lordship of Gisborough, Yorkshire, and the adjoining coast, speaking of the fishermen, it is stated, that "upon St. Peters Daye they invite their friends and kinsfolk to a festyvall kept after their fashion with a free hearte and noe shew of nigardnesse : that daye their boates are dressed curiously for the shewe, their mastes are painted, and certain rytes observed amongste them, with sprinkling their prowes with good liquor, sold with them at a groate the quarte, which custome or superstition suckt from their auncestors, even contynueth down unto this present time." *Antiq. Repertory*, iii., 304.

Glass, Looking.—Potter says: "When divination by water was performed with a looking-glass, it was called catoptromancy : sometimes they (the Greeks) dipped a looking glass into the water, when they desired to know what would become of a sick person : for as he looked well or ill in the glass, accordingly they presumed of his future condition. Sometimes, also, glasses were used and the images of what should happen, without water. *Greek Antiquities*, i., 350. Douce's MSS. notes add that "washing hands in the same water is said to forbode a quarrel." "Some magicians," writes an old author, " being curious to find out by help of a looking-glass, or a glasse-viall full of water, a thiefe that lies hidden, make choyce of young maides, or boyes unpolluted, to discerne therein those images or sights which a person defiled cannot see. Bodin, in the third book of his " Dæmonomachia," chap. 3, reporteth that in his time there was at Thoulouse a certain Portugais, who shewed within a boyes naile things that were hidden. And he added that God hath expressly forbidden that none should worship the Stone of Imagination. His opinion is that this Imagination or Adoration (for so expoundeth he the first verse of the 26th chapter of Leviticus, where he speaketh of the idoll, the graven image, and the painted stone) was smooth and cleare as a looking-glasse, wherein they saw certaine images or sights of which they enquired after the things hidden. In our time conjurers use christall, calling the divination chrystallomantia, or onychomantia, in which, after they have rubbed one of the nayles of their fingers, or a piece of chrystall, they utter I know not what words, and they call a boy that is pure and no way corrupted, to see therein that which they require, as the same Bodin doth also make mention." Molle's *Living Librarie*, 1621, p. 2.

In the "Marriage of the Arts," by Barten Holiday, 1618, is this: "I have often heard them say, 'tis ill luck to see one's face in a glass by candle-light." Among unlucky portents must also be noticed the strong objection which persons even of enlightened views and good position in society still have to allow a young baby to see itself in the glass. The reason is not particularly obvious; but in such a case perhaps a lady's reason ought to be accounted sufficient. When a looking glass is broken, it is an omen that the party to whom it belongs will lose his best friend. See the Greek Scholia on the *Nubes* of Aristophanes, p. 169. Grose tells us that "Breaking a looking glass betokens a mortality in the family, commonly the master."

Glastonbury Thorn.—Collinson, speaking of Glastonbury, says: "Southwest from the town is Wearyall Hill, an eminence so-called (if we will believe the monkish writers) from St. Joseph and his companions sitting down here, all weary with their journey. Here St. Joseph struck his stick into the earth, which, although a dry hawthorn stick, thenceforth grew, and constantly budded on Christmas-Day. It had two trunks or bodies till the time of Queen Elizabeth, when a Puritan exterminated one, and left the other, which was the size of a common man, to be viewed in wonder by strangers; and the blossoms thereof were esteemed such curiosities by people of all nations, that the Bristol merchants made a traffick of them, and exported them into foreign parts. In the Great Rebellion, during the time of King Charles I., the remaining trunk of this tree was also cut down: but other trees from its branches are still growing in many gardens of Glastonbury and in the different nurseries of this kingdom. It is probable that the monks of Glastonbury procured this tree from Palestine, where abundance of the same sort grew, and flower about the same time. Where this thorn grew is said to have been a nunnery dedicated to St. Peter, without the Pale of Weriel Park, belonging to the Abbey. It is strange to say how much this tree was sought after by the credulous: and though a common thorn, Queen Anne, King James, and many of the nobility of the realm, even when the times of monkish superstition had ceased, gave large sums of money for small cuttings from the original." *Somersetshire*, ii., 265.

I have no doubt but that the early blossoming of the Glastonbury Thorn was owing to a natural cause. It is mentioned by Gerard and Parkinson in their herbals. Camden also notices it. Ashmole tells us that he had often heard it spoken of, "and by some who have seen it whilst it flourished at Glastonbury." He adds: "Upon St. Stephen's Day, Anno 1672, Mr. Stainsby (an ingenious enquirer after things worthy memorial) brought me a branch of hawthorne having green leaves, faire buds, and full flowers, all thick and very beautifull, and (which is more notable) many of the hawes and berries upon it red and plump, some of which branch is yet preserved in the plant booke of my collection. This he had from a hawthorne tree now growing at Sir Lancelote Lake's house, near Edgworth (Edgeware) in Middlesex, concerning which, falling after into the company of the said knight, 7 July, 1673, he told me that the tree, whence this branch was plucked, grew from a slip taken from the Glastonbury Thorn about sixty years since, which is now a bigg tree, and flowers every winter about Christmas." Appendix to Hearne's *Antiquities of Glastonbury*, p. 303. Sir Thomas Browne remarks: "Certainly many precocious trees, and such as spring in the winter, may be found in England. Most trees sprout in the fall of the leaf or autumn, and if not kept back by cold and outward causes, would leaf about the solstice. Now if it happen that any be so strongly constituted as to make this good against the power of winter, they may produce their leaves or blossoms at that season, and perform that in some singles which is observable in whole kinds: as in ivy, which blossoms and bears at least twice a year, and once in the winter: as also in Furze, which flowereth in that season." "This tree," says Worlidge, "flourished many years in Wilton Garden, near Salisbury, and, I suppose, is there yet; but is not altogether so exact to a day as its original from whence it came was reported to be; it's probable the faith of our ancestors might contribute much towards its certainty of time. For imagination doth operate on inanimate things, as some have observed." *Systema Horticulturæ*, 1677, p. 88.

In the metrical life of Joseph of Arimathea, probably written in the reign of Henry VII., three hawthorns are mentioned:

"Thre hawthornes also that groweth in werall
Do burge and bere grene leaves at Christmas
As fresshe as other in May whan ye nightyngale

Wrestes out her notes musicall as pure
as glas
Of al wodes and forestes she is ye chefe
chauntres
In wynter to synge yf it were her
nature
In werall she might haue a playne place
On those hawthornes to shewe her notes
clere."

Lyfe of Joseph of Arimathea, 1520, sig.
B 2. Dr. Leighton, writing to Cromwell
about 1537, says : " Pleesith it your worship to understand that yester night we
came from Glastonbury to Bristow? I here
send you for relicks two flowers wrapped
up in black sarcenet, that on Christmas
even will spring and burgen, and bear
flowers." Manningham, in his *Diary*,
May 2, 1602, records, apparently as something of which he had heard, that " At
Glastenbury there are certaine bushes
which beare May flowers at Christmas and
in January."

A writer in the "World" has
the following irony on the alteration
of the stile in 1752 : " It is well known
that the correction of the Calendar was
enacted by Pope Gregory the thirteenth,
and that the Reformed Churches have,
with a proper spirit of opposition, adhered to the old calculation of the Emperor Julius Cæsar, who was by no means
a Papist. Nearly two years ago the
Popish Calendar was brought in (I hope
by persons well affected). Certain it is
that the Glastonbury Thorn has preserved
its inflexibility, and observed its old anniversary. Many thousand spectators
visited it on the parliamentary Christmas
Day—not a bud was to be seen !—on the
true nativity it was covered with blos-
some. One must be an infidel indeed to
spurn at such authority." *Paper of
March 8*, 1753. The following account
was communicated to the "Gentleman's
Magazine" for January, 1753, by a correspondent at Quainton, in Buckinghamshire : " Above two thousand people came
here this night with lanthorns and
candles, to view a black thorn which
grows in this neighbourhood, and which
was remembered (this year only) to be a
slip from the famous Glastonbury Thorn,
that always budded on the 24th, was full
blown the next day, and went all off at
night; but the people finding no appearance of a bud, 'twas agreed by all, that
Dec. 25th, N.S. could not be the right
Christmas Day, and accordingly refused
going to church, and treating their friends
on that day as usual : at length the affair
became so serious, that the ministers
of the neighbouring villages, in order to
appease the people, thought it prudent
to give notice, that the old Christmas
Day should be kept holy as before. A

vast concourse of people attended the
noted thorns at Glastonbury on Christmas
Eve, new style; but to their great disappointment, there was no appearance of
its blowing, which made them watch it
narrowly the 5th of January, the Christmas Day old style, when it blowed as
usual."

Gleek.—A game at cards, played by
three persons with 44 cards. See Halliwell in v. The game of *cleke*, for which
in the *Privy Purse Expenses of Henry
VII.*, under September 15, 1503, one Weston receives £2 on the King's account,
was apparently our gleek. In Gayton's
"Notes on Don Quixote," 1654, is the
following : " A lady once requesting a
gentleman to play at gleeke, was refused,
but civilly, and upon three reasons : the
first whereof, madam, said the gentleman,
is I have no money. Her ladyship knew
that was so materiall and sufficient, that
she desired him to keep the other two
reasons to himself." Under date of Jan.
13, 1661-2, Pepys wrote : " My aunt
Wright and my wife and I to cards, she
teaching us to play at Gleeke, which is a
pretty game; but I love not my aunt so
far as to be troubled with it." However,
on the 17th of the following month the
Diarist was sufficiently composed to play
at it, and won 9s. 6d. clear—" the most
that ever I won in my life. I pray God
it may not tempt me to play again."
There is no farther reference to it. We
are told that the Lord Keeper Guildford was fond of this and other similar
amusements. The best account of this
amusement is in Cotgrave's *Wits Interpreter*, 1655.

Gloves.—Felix, in his Anglo-Saxon
Life of St. Guthlac, Hermit of Crowland, circâ A.D. 749, mentions the use of
gloves as a covering for the hand in chap.
xi., and it is related of the consort of
Domenigo Selvo, Doge of Venice (1071-84)
that she always wore gloves. Hazlitt's
Venetian Republic, 1900, ii., 767-8. Gloves
were in use in France in the beginning
of the ninth century. Johannes de Garlandia in his *Dictionary*, (13th century),
speaks of the glovers of Paris as cheating
the scholars by selling them gloves of inferior material. He describes them as of
lambskin, fox-fur, and rabbit's-skin ; and
he refers to leathern mittens. Wright's
Vocabularies, 1857, p. 124 ; see also Fairholt's *Costume in England*, 1860, p. 460-
463 ; and Hazlitt's *Livery Companies*,1892,
pp. 520-3. In the "Year Book of Edw.
I." 1302, it is laid down that, in cases of
acquittal of a charge of manslaughter, the
prisoner was obliged to pay a fee to the
justices' clerk in the form of a pair of
gloves, besides the fees to the marshal. A
good deal of interesting and authentic in-

formation under this head may be found in Pegge's "Curialia," 1818, to which, the work being so accessible, it would be useless to do more than refer the reader. A custom still prevails at maiden assizes, i.e., when no prisoner is capitally convicted, to present the judges, &c., with white gloves. It should seem, by the dedication of Clavell's "Recantation of an ill-led life," 1628, to some of the judges, that anciently this present was made by such prisoners as received pardon after condemnation. Fuller says: "It passeth for a general report of what was customary in former times, that the sheriff of the county used to present the judge with a pair of white gloves, at those which we call mayden-assizes, viz., when no malefactor is put to death therein." Among the lots in "A Lottery presented before the late Queenes Maiesty at the Lord Chancellor's (Keeper's) house, 1601," is A Pair of Gloues with a posy. Davison's "Poetical Rapsodie," 1611, p. 44. Also at p. 44, of ed. 1621, and in Nicolas's, ed. vol. i. p. 7. This lottery is given rather differently in "Early Poetical Miscellanies" (Percy Soc.) The Lord Keeper was Sir T. Egerton. There is some pleasantry in the very common notion, and not exclusively vulgar one, as Brand alleged, that if a woman surprizes a man sleeping, and can steal a kiss without waking him, she has a right to demand a pair of gloves. Thus Gay in his Sixth Pastoral:

"Cic'ly, brisk maid, steps forth before
          the rout,
And kiss'd with smacking lip the sno-
          ring lout :
For custom says, whoe'er this venture
          proves,
For such a kiss demands a pair of
          gloves."

It was customary in Tusser's day to give the reapers gloves when the wheat was thistly, and Hilman, the author of "Tusser Redivivus," 1710, observes that the largess, which seems to have been usual in the old writer's time, was still a matter of course, of which the reapers did not require to be reminded. Can the custom of dropping or sending the glove, as the signal of a challenge, have been derived from the circumstance of it being the cover of the hand, and therefore put for the hand itself? The giving of the hand is well known to intimate that the person who does so will not deceive, but stand to his agreement. To "shake hands upon it" would not, it should seem, be very delicate in an agreement to fight, and therefore gloves may possibly have been deputed as substitutes. We may, perhaps, trace the same idea in wedding gloves.

But there was equally a custom in former times to wear a glove in the hat as a signal of challenge as well as in token of the favour of a mistress or of the loss of a friend. Fairholt's *Costume in England,* 1860, p. 461. But Edgar, in *Lear,* is made to say that he wore them in his cap, when he was a serving-man. A pair of gloves used to be both a Shrovetide and a Christmas gift. See Whitelocke's *Liber Famelicus,* 1858, p. 49, under date of 1615.

Gloves at Funerals. — Gloves were not less common at funerals than at weddings. In some cases, where the family was rich, or at least in good circumstances, as many as an hundred pairs were given away. In our time, the undertaker provides gloves for the mourners, and the friends of the departed usually get kid gloves, the servants worsted. But only those who are present, or are unavoidably absent, receive any. At the funeral of John Wilson, a Sussex gentleman, in 1640, there were one hundred and fifty pairs of gloves. *Sussex Arch. Coll.,* xi., 147. I may call attention to a very serviceable paper by Mr. Henry John Feasey on Bishops' gloves in the *Antiquary* for 1898, with general remarks on the subject and an engraving of a mediæval pontifical glove.

Gloves at Weddings.—It appears from Selden, that the Belgic custom at marriages was for the priest to ask of the bridegroom the ring, and, if they could be had, a pair of red gloves, with three pieces of silver money in them (arrhæ loco)—then putting the gloves into the bridegroom's right hand, and joining it with that of the bride, the gloves were left, on loosing their right hands, in that of the bride. "Uxor Hebraica," Opera, tom. iii. p. 673: "De More Veterum mittendi Chirothecam in rei fidem cum Nuntio, quem quopiam ablegabant alibi agetur vocabatur id genus Symbolum Jertekn." Ihre's "Glossarium," v. Handske. Du Cange says: "Chirothecam in signum Consensus dare." "Etiam Rex in signum sui Consensus, suam ad hoc mittere debet Chirothecam." In Arnold's Chronicle, 1502, among "the artycles upon whiche is to inquyre in the visitacyons of ordynaryes of churches," we read: "Item, whether the curat refuse to do the solemnysacyon of lawfull matrymonye before he have gyftes of money, hoses, or gloves." Mr. Halliwell prints a posy supposed to accompany the present of a pair of gloves from a gentleman to his mistress, and notices the incident in "Much Ado About Nothing," where the Count sends Hero a pair of perfumed gloves. The posy runs as follows:

"Love, to thee I send these gloves;
    If you love me,
    Leave out the G,
And make a pair of loves."

Popular Rhymes and Nursery Tales, 1849, p. 250. The custom occurs in "The Miseries of inforced Marriage" (by George Wilkins the Elder, 1607), and in Herrick. White gloves still continue to be presented to the guests on this occasion. Sir Dudley Carleton, describing to Winwood, in a letter of January, 1604-5, the marriage between Sir Philip Herbert and the Lady Susan, says: "No ceremony was omitted of bride-cakes, points, garters, and gloves." In Jonson's "Silent Woman," Lady Haughty observes to Morose: "We see no ensigns of a wedding here, no character of a bridale; where be our scarves and our gloves?" The bride's gloves are noticed by Stephens: "She hath no rarity worth observance, if her gloves be not miraculous and singular: those be the trophy of some forlorne sutor who contents himself with a large offering, or this glorious sentence, that she should have been his bed-fellow." *Essays and Characters,* 1615. At Wrexham in Flintshire," says Dr. Lort, in his copy of Bourne and Brand, 1777, "on occasion of the marriage of the surgeon and apothecary of the place, August 1785, I saw at the doors of his own and neighbours' houses, throughout the street where he lived, large boughs and posts of trees, that had been cut down and fixed there, filled with white paper, cut in the shape of women's gloves, and of white ribbons."

Goat.—There is a popular superstition relative to goats: they are supposed never to be seen for twenty-four hours together; and that, once in that space, they pay a visit to the Devil in order to have their beards combed. This is common both in England and Scotland. The Rev. Donald McQueen, in the "Gentleman's Magazine" for February, 1795, speaking of the Isle of Skye, says: "In this hyperborean country, in every district, there is to be met with a rude stone consecrated to Gruagach or Apollo. The first who is done with his reaping, sends a man or a maiden with a bundle of corn to his next neighbour, who hath not yet reaped down his harvest, who when he has finished, dispatches to his own next neighbour, who is behind in his work, and so on, until the whole corns are cut down. This sheaf is called the Cripple Goat, an Gaobbir Bhacagh, and is at present meant as a brag or affront to the farmer, for being more remiss, or later than others in reaping the harvest, for which reason the bearer of it must make as good a pair of heels, for fear of being ill-used for his indiscretion, as he can. Whether the appelation of cripple goat may have any the least reference to the Apollonian Altar of Goats' Horns, I shall not pretend to determine."

Godfathers and Godmothers.—This was probably an ancient secular custom and form of suretyship spiritualized by the Church in the same way as the rite of marriage itself. Ralph Sadler, in a letter to Cromwell, without date, but about 1532-3, asking him to stand sponsor for his newly-born child, says: "I wold also be right glad to have Mr. Richards wyf, or my lady Weston to be the godmother. Ther is a certen superstycious opynyon and vsage amongst women, which is, that in case a woman go with childe she may chrysten no other mannes childe as long as she is in that case: and therfore not knowing whether Mr. Richards wyf be with childe or not, I do name my lady Weston." Queen Elizabeth stood sponsor in person or by proxy for a great number of the children of her courtiers and favourites, and some of her predecessors had done the same to a certain extent. In the Privy Purse Expenses of our early kings are many entries, shewing that where they did not honour the ceremony with their presence, they sent a suitable person to represent them, and a gift. Strype, in his "Annals," A.D. 1559, informs us that "on the 27th of October of that year, the Prince of Sweden, the Lord Robert and the Lady Marchioness of Northampton, stood sureties at the christening of Sir Thomas Chamberlaynes son, who was baptized at St. Benet's Church, at Paul's Wharf. The church was hung with cloth of arras; and, after the christening, were brought wafers, comfits, and divers banquetting dishes, and hypocras and Muscadine wine, to entertain the guests." On the 17th of December, 1566, James, the son of Mary, Queen of Scots, was baptized according to the rites of the Popish Church, at Edinburgh. Queen Elizabeth had been asked to become one of the sponsors, and sent the Earl of Bedford with a gold font as a present. The prince was held up by the Countess of Argyll in the behalf of the English queen; after the baptism had been solemnized, the names and the titles of the royal infant were proclaimed to the sound of trumpets. In Stow's "Chronicle" by Howes, 1631, speaking of the life and reign of King James, he observes: "At this time, and for many yeares before, it was not the use and custome (as now it is) for godfathers and godmothers generally to give plate at the baptisme of children (as spoones, cupps, and such like), but onely to give christening shirts, with little bands and cuffs, wrought either with silke or blew threed, the best of them, for chiefe persons weare, edged with a small lace of blacke silke and gold, the highest price of which for great men's children was seldom above a noble, and the common sort, two, three, or foure, and five shillings a piece." At the christening of Prince Charles, afterwards Charles I., in 1630, the Duchess of Richmond, who stood proxy for the queen-mother of France, presented a jewel valued at £7000 or £8000, and gave the melch, or wet-nurse, a chain of rubies of the estimated worth of £200. Cowell says : " It was a good old custom for godfathers and godmothers, every time their god-children asked them blessing, to give them a cake, which was a gods-kichell ; it is still a proverbial saying in some countries, ' Ask me a blessing, and I will give you some plum-cake." *Law Dictionary, v. Kichell.* In a tract of the 18th century it is said : " The godmother, hearing when the child's to be coated, brings it a gilt coral, a silver spoon, and porringer, and a brave new tankard of the same metal. The godfather comes too, the one with a whole piece of flower'd silk, the other with a set of gilt spoons, the gifts of Lord Mayors at several times." *Fifteen Comforts of Wooing,* p. 162. At ordinary christenings, at least, it appears to have been the custom in Pepys's day (*Diary,* August 25th, 1667), for the godfather to give the name in the case of a boy, and the godmother otherwise. At the baptism of Bamfylde Moore Carew in 1693, his godfathers being the Hon. Hugh Bamfylde and Major Moore, these two gentlemen tossed up whose name should stand first, and Bamfylde won the precedence. *Life and Adventures of B. M. Carew,* 1745, p. 2.

God's Penny.—In the story of the *Heir of Linne,* John o' the Scales exclaims, when the hero has engaged to sell his patrimony : " I draw you to record, lords, and a God's penny, lo ! I cast to the Heir of Linne." Hazlitt's *Tales and Legends,* 1892, p. 381. Percy notes : " Godspennie, i.e., earnest-money ; from the French ' Denier á Dieu.' " The bishop adds : " At this day, (1794) when application is made to the Dean and Chapter of Carlisle to accept an exchange of the tenant under one of their leases, a piece of silver is presented by the new tenant, which is still called a God's Penny." Mr. Atkinson, " Cleveland Glossary," 1868, p. 225, says : " God's penny. Earnest money, given to a servant on concluding the hiring compact : customarily half-a-crown." It is still customary in the West of England, when the conditions of a bargain are agreed upon, for the parties to ratify it by joining their hands, and at

the same time for the purchaser to give an earnest.

Gog and Magog.—Bishop Hall, in his " Satires," 1597-8, speaks of the old figures as then in their places in Guildhall. Stow mentions the older figures as representations of a Briton and a Saxon. In Smith's " De Urbis Londini Incendio," 1667, the carrying about of pageants once a year is confirmed ; and in Marston's " Dutch Courtezan," we read : " Yet all will scarce make me so high as one of the giant's stilts that stalks before my Lord Maiors Pageants." Sir H. Ellis refers to Hatton's " New View of London," 1708, as an authority for believing that Gog and Magog were restored in 1707. Bragg says, " I was hemmed in like a wrestler in Moorfields ; the cits begged the colours taken at Ramilies, to put up in Guildhall. When I entered the Hall, I protest, Master, I never saw so much joy in the countenances of the people in my life, as in the cits on this occasion ; nay, the very giants stared at the colours with all the eyes they had, and smiled as well as they could." In Grosley's Tour to London, translated by Nugent, 1772, vol. ii. p. 88, we find the following passage :

" The English have, in general, a rambling taste for the several objects of the polite arts, which does not even exclude the Gothic : it still prevails, not only in ornaments of fancy, but even in some modern buildings. To this taste they are indebted for the preservation of the two giants in Guildhall. These giants, in comparison of which the Jacquemard of St. Paul's at Paris is a bauble, seem placed there for no other end but to frighten children : the better to answer this purpose, care has frequently been taken to renew the daubing on their faces and arms. There might be some reason for retaining those monstrous figures, if they were of great antiquity, or if, like the stone which served as the first throne to the Kings of Scotland, and is carefully preserved at Westminster, the people looked upon them as the palladium of the nation ; but they have nothing to recommend them, and they only raise, at first view, a surprise in foreigners, who must consider them as a production, in which both Danish and Saxon barbarism are happily combined." Hone devotes the 11th section of his " Ancient Mysteries Described," 1823, to this subject, and gives representations of the giants. He refers us to a small tract entitled The *Gigantick History of the two famous Giants in Guildhall,* 1741, and points out the error of Noorthouck in his account of London, 1773, in stating the figures to be formed of pasteboard, like the giant at Salisbury.

The latter is still preserved in the Museum there.

Goitre.—A correspondent of "Notes and Queries" for May 24, 1851, furnishes two remedies then in use at Withyam, Sussex, for goitre, which is common to all regions, where the water is unduly charged with lime : "A common snake, held by its head and tail, is slowly drawn by someone standing by nine times across the front part of the neck of the person affected, the reptile being allowed, after every third time, to crawl about for a while. Afterwards the snake is put alive into a bottle, which is corked tightly, and then buried in the ground. The tradition is, that as the snake decays, the swelling vanishes. The second mode of treatment is just the same as the above, with the exception of the snake's doom. In this case it is killed, and its skin, sewn in a piece of silk, is worn round the diseased neck. By degrees the swelling in this case also disappears." But Dr. Bell has shown that the belief in the efficacy of sacrifice as a charm was not confined to Sussex or to reptiles. *Shakespear's Puck*, i., 117-19.

Golf, Goff, or **Gouf.** (*Dutch Kolef* or *Kolf*.)—Strutt considers this as one of the most ancient games played with the ball that require the assistance of a club or bat. A ball, let us bear in mind, is the basis of some of our own, and other nations' and ages,' most permanent and favourite pastimes. Ball, pure and simple, foot-ball, club-ball, golf, hockey, rounders, cricket, fives, tennis, hurling, and croquet. "In the reign of Edward the third, the Latin name *Cambuca* was applied to this pastime, and it derived the denomination, no doubt, from the crooked club or bat with which it was played ; that bat was also called a bandy from it being bent, and hence the game itself is frequently written in English bandy-ball. Jamieson derives golf from the Dutch kolf a club. Wachter derives it from klopp-en to strike, from Keltic goll, the hand, which, curiously enough, degenerated in the course of time into a mere vulgarism, like our modern phrase paw.

I find the following description of this sport in an ancient church writer, which evinces its high antiquity : "Pueros videmus certatim gestientes, testarum in mare jaculationibus ludere. Is lusus est, testam teretem, jactatione Fluctuum lævigatam, legere de litore : eam testem plano situ digitis comprehensam, inclinem ipsum atque humilem, quantum potest, super undas irrotare : ut illud jaculum vel dorsum maris raderet, vel enataret, dum leni impetu labitur : vel summis fluctibus tonsis emicaret, emergeret, dum assiduo saltu sublevatur. Is se in pueris victorem ferebat, cujus testa et procurreret longius, et frequentius exsiliret." *Minucius Felix*, 1712, p. 28. St. Cuthbert, Bishop of Durham, a North-country man, who died in 687, is said to have been acquainted with the game. Why not? The idea is simple and obvious enough. Golf and foot-ball appear to have been prohibited in Scotland by James II. in 1457 ; and again in 1491 by James IV. The ball used at this game was stuffed very hard with feathers. Northbrooke, a native of Devonshire, speaks of it as a favourite amusement in that county in the reign of Elizabeth. His treatise against dicing and other profanities appeared in 1577. Strutt says that this game is much practiced in the north of England ; and Jamieson, that it is a common game in Scotland. In the *North American Review* for July, 1899, Mr. Andrew Lang has an interesting paper, entitled : "Golf from a St. Andrew's point of view," where it is suggested that the game probably came to Scotland from Holland, as the terms are Dutch, and where the writer enumerates the eminent personages, from Mary Stuart downward, who have taken pleasure in this sport. The patronage of golf by the Stuarts was not continued in England after their fall by their successors ; but it has now been introduced again with full honours, having always survived in North Britain, and having had many distinguished historical characters of the eighteenth century among its votaries. There is proof that the ancient Dutch method of playing the game was not dissimilar from ours. There are Dutch prints of the 17th century, displaying the method then used, and an etching by Rembrandt, where the amusement is called *Kolef*. But in an account of the voyage of the Hollanders in 1596-7, which was signalized by the discovery of Spitzbergen, the crew of one of the vessels made a staff to play at Colfe, thereby to stretch their joints. Prince Henry, eldest son of James I., who died in 1612, is said by Sir Simonds D'Ewes to have been "rather addicted to martial studies and exercises than to pale-maille, whilst his schoolmaster stood talking with another and marked not his highness warning him to stand further off, the prince thinking he had gone aside, lifted up his goff-club to strike the ball; mean tyme one standing by said to him, Beware that you hit not master Newton, wherewith he, drawing back his hand, said, Had I done so, I had but paid my debts.'"

There was in the 18th century a Society of Golfers at Blackheath, and we have a large portrait of a member by Abbott, 1792, accompanied by his servant, carrying his sticks. Of this painting there is a print.

At the end of Ferrier's *Guide to North Berwick*, 1881, are "Rules for the game of golf, as it is played on the Links" there. A writer in the "Book of Days" ascribes to this sport, of which he gives a very good account, the origin of the common phrase, getting into a scrape.

This etymology may be correct; the expression itself was used at least as far back as the time of George III. in its present sense. M. Berjeau, who refers to two curious works on the game, both published in the last century, seems to consider that golf resembled "the present fashionable game of croquet." *Bookworm*, iii., 173-4. The fact is, that the game was susceptible of modifications, according to circumstances, or the opportunity of those playing at it. In the French rules printed at Paris in 1717, it is said that the club and ball were both to be made of the root of the box-tree. The caddie, who follows the players with the sticks and reserve balls, is the same as the Edinburgh *cadie* or running stationer of the eighteenth century.

Good Friday.—"The Festival," 1511, fol. 36, says: "This day is called, in many places, Goddes Sondaye: ye knowe well that it is the maner at this daye to do the fyre out of the hall, and the blacke wynter brondes, and all thynges that is foule with fume and smoke shall be done awaye, and there the fyre was shall be gayly arayed with fayre floures, and strewed with grene rysshes all aboute." It may have been termed Good Friday to distinguish it from the other Fridays of the year, as it was considered an unlucky day. It was customary in the popish times to erect on Good Friday a small building to represent the Sepulchre of our Saviour. In this was placed the host, and a person set to watch it both that night and the next; and the following morning very early, the host being taken out, Christ was said to have arisen. Hospinian tells us that the Kings of England had a custom of hallowing rings with much ceremony on Good Friday, the wearers of which will not be afflicted with the falling sickness. He adds, that the custom took its rise from a ring, which had

been long preserved with great veneration in Westminster Abbey, and was supposed to have great efficacy against the cramp and falling sickness, when touched by those who were afflicted with either of those disorders. This ring is reported to have been brought to King Edward by some persons coming from Jerusalem, and which he himself had long before given privately to a poor person who had asked alms of him for the love he bare to St. John the Evangelist. In his "Curialia Miscellanea," 1818, Appendix 3, Pegge has printed the formulary at length. It was usual, at this season, to eschew ordinary butter, and to substitute almond butter, which formed an element in English cookery from a very remote date. In a collection of culinary recipes, attributed to the reign of Richard II., there is one for making this article of diet. It is mentioned in the printed Wardrobe Accounts of Edward IV., 1480, and elsewhere. In the List of Church Plate, Vestments, &c., in the Churchwardens' Accounts of St. Mary at Hill, 10 Hen. VI., occurs also: "an olde Vestment of red silke lyned with yelow for Good Friday." On Good Friday the Roman Catholics offered unto Christ Eggs and Bacon to be in his favour till Easter Day was past; from which we may at least gather with certainty that eggs and bacon composed a usual dish on that day.—Keth's *Sermon*, 1570, p. 18. In Braithwaite's "Whimzies," 1631, p. 196, we have this trait of "a zealous brother": "he is an antipos to all Church-government: when she feasts he fasts; when she fasts he feasts: Good Friday is his Shrove Tuesday: he commends this notable carnall caveat to his family — eate flesh upon dayes prohibited, it is good against Popery." "To holde forth the crosse for egges on Good Friday" occurs among the Roman Catholic customs censured by John Bale, in his "Declaration of Bonner's Articles," 1554, Signat. D 3, as is ibid D 4, verso, "to creape to the Crosse on Good Friday featly." Compare *Creeping to the Cross.*

Among Good Friday customs still observed, may be enumerated that of laying one-and-twenty sixpences on the spot in the churchyard of St. Bartholomew the Great, Smithfield, in London, supposed to be the resting-place of a lady who left the fund for as many aged widows, on condition that each recipient should be able to stoop, and pick up the coin without help. A small sum is also payable from the same source for a sermon on this day. At All Hallows, Lombard Street, after the service, sixty of the younger scholars from Christ's Hospital were presented by the incumbent, under the will of Peter Symonds (1687), with a new penny and a packet of raisins. In Langbourne Ward, such of the school-children as assisted in the choir received hot-cross buns and trifling gratuities in money. At Tenby there was the old custom of walking to church barefoot on this day, and the people about the same time collected long reeds from the river to make Christ's bed."

It was an ancient belief in Flanders, that children born on Good Friday possessed the power of curing themselves, without aid, of fevers and other ailments. It used to be thought that eggs laid on this day were capable of extinguishing fires, and that three loaves baked then, and buried in corn, were safe from the depredation of all vermin. There is a curious usage still in vogue among the Spanish and Portuguese sailors who happen to be in the English Docks at this time, of flogging an effigy, which they called Judas Iscariot (in commemoration of Judas's share in Christ's death). The author of the "Popish Kingdom" describes the worship of the Cross on Good Friday, and the absurd burlesque on the burial of the Saviour. The opening lines are too ludicrous to be omitted:

"Two priestes, the next day following,
　vpon their shoulders beare
The image of the Crucifixe, about the
　altar neare,
Being clad in coape of crimozen die,
　and dolefully they sing:
At length, before the steps, his coate
　pluckt off, they straight him bring:
And vpon Turkey carpettes lay him
　down full tenderly !"

The *Globe* newspaper of April 24, 1897, published the following account: "Yesterday was the Greek Good Friday, and in view of the particular circumstances of the occasion the celebration was marked by much emotion on the part of the inhabitants. Unusually large crowds assembled in the streets in the evening to witness the customary processions, and Constitution-square, where all the processions meet about 10 o'clock, was densely packed with thousands of people, all holding lighted candles. Viewed from the balconies and windows overlooking the square, the spectacle was an extremely striking one. The procession to the Cathedral, where the King and Queen attended Mass, included the whole of the officials of the capital, and was headed by the Metropolitan wearing his gold embroidered robes and a glittering tiara on his head. As the procession passed, choirs chanted the prayers for the day, set to melodious and extremely impressive music. In the middle of the square the procession stopped, while the Metropolitan, in a loud, clear voice, offered prayers invoking the protection of God for the soldiers who had gone to defend the national honour and to fight for the glory of the Cross. At this moment the emotion of the people reached its height, the silence of the multitude, standing bareheaded in the light of the flickering candles, being only broken by the occasional sound of uncontrollable sobs. The different processions afterwards returned to their respective churches."

Good Friday Bun.—Hutchinson, in his "History of Northumberland," following Mr. Bryant's "Analysis," derives the Good Friday Bun from the sacred cakes which were offered at the Arkite Temples, styled boun, and presented every seventh day. Bryant has the following passage on this subject: "The offerings which people in ancient times used to present to the gods, were generally purchased at the entrance of the Temple; especially every species of consecrated bread, which was denominated accordingly. One species of sacred bread which used to be offered to the gods was of great antiquity, and called boun. The Greeks who changed the *nu* final into a *sigma*, expressed it in the nominative, but in the accusative more truly, Boun. Hesychius speaks of the boun, and describes it a kind of cake with a representation of two horns. Julius Pollux mentions it after the same manner, a sort of cake with horns. Diogenes Laertius, speaking of the same offering being made by Empedocles, describes the chief ingredients of which it was composed: "He offered one of the sacred Liba, called a bouse, which was made of fine flour and honey." It is said of Cecrops that he first offered up this sort of sweet bread. Hence we may judge of the antiquity of the custom, from the times to which Cecrops is referred. The prophet Jeremiah takes notice of this kind of offering, when he is speaking of the Jewish women at Pathros, in Egypt, and of their base idolatry; in all which their husbands had encouraged them. The women, in their expostulation upon his rebuke, tell him: "Did we make her cakes to worship her?" Jerem. xilv. 18, 19; vii. 18. Hutchinson concludes: "We only retain the name and form of the boun; the sacred uses are no more."

A writer in *Once a Week* observes: "Do our Ritualists eat hot cross-buns on Good Friday? Perhaps they do not, but consider the consumption of such cakes to be a weak concession to the childish appetites of those who would not duly observe their Lenten fastings; and who, had they lived in the days of George III., would have been among the crowds who clustered beneath the wooden porticoes of the two royal and rival bun-houses at Chelsea. But there is the cross-mark on the surface of the bun to commend it to the minds which are favourably disposed to symbolism; and there is the history of the cross-bun itself, which goes back to the time of Cecrops, and to the *liba* offered to Astarte, and to the Jewish passover cakes, and to the eucharistic bread, or cross-marked wafers, mentioned in St. Chrysostom's Liturgy, and thence adopted by the early Christians. So that the Good Friday bun has antiquity and tradition to recommend it; and indeed its very name of bun is but the oblique *boun*, from *bous*, the sacred ox, the semblance of whose horns was stamped upon the cake. There, too, they also did duty for the horns of Astarte, in which word some philologists would affect to trace a connection with Easter. The substitution by Greeks of the cross-mark in place of the horn-mark would seem to have chiefly been for the easier division of the round bun into four equal parts. Such cross-marked buns were found at Herculaneum."

Hazlitt, in his *Livery Companies*, 1892, p. 104, quotes Maitland's *Account of London*, 1739, for the origin of this usage: "The bakers, probably perceiving that great profits arose to the clergy by the use of the symbols of the cross, *Agnus Deis*, and name of Jesus, to oblige their customers (for their own interest) began to imprint upon their bread the like representations." This practice seems to have been interdicted by a royal mandate of 1252, but it has been more or less continued ever since. The people in the North of England and elsewhere make with a knife many little cross-marks on their cakes before they put them into the oven. It is still a common belief that one cross-bun should be kept for luck's sake from Good Friday to Good Friday. It seems that, in Dorsetshire, a loaf baked on the day, and hung over the chimney-piece, will have the effect, in the popular estimation, of preventing the bread baked in the house during the year from going reamy or stringy. The small loaf of bread, not unusually baked on Good Friday morning by many country folks, is carefully preserved as a medicine for diarrhœa. It is considered that a little of the Good-Friday loaf, grated into a proper proportion of water, is an infallible remedy for this complaint. A relative of the present writer had a loaf of this description, baked on the Good Friday after her marriage in 1856; and it was long kept with this view. The lower classes of society do not monopolize these superstitions.

Good Man's Croft.—Andrews tells us, on the authority of Arnot, that "In 1594, the Elders of the Scotish Church exerted their utmost influence to abolish an irrational custom among the husbandmen, which with some reason gave great offence. The farmers were apt to leave a portion of their land untilled and uncropt year after year. This spot was supposed to be dedicated to Satan, and was styled 'the Good Man's Croft,' viz. the Landlord's Acre. It seems probable that some Pagan ceremony had given rise to so strange a superstition": no doubt as a charm or peace-offering, that the rest might be fertile. Cont. of *Henry's History of Great Britain*, p. 502 Note.

Gooding on St. Thomas's Day.—I find some faint traces of a custom of going a gooding (as it is called) on St. Thomas's Day, which seems to have been done by women only, who, in return for the alms they received, appear to have presented their benefactors with sprigs of evergreens, probably to deck their houses with at the ensuing festival. Perhaps this is only another name for the Northern custom to be presently noticed, of going about and crying Hagmena. In the "Gentleman's Magazine" for April, 1794, where the writer is speaking of the preceding mild winter, he says: "The women who went a gooding (as they call it in these parts) on St. Thomas's Day, might, in return for alms, have presented their benefactors with sprigs of palm and bunches of primroses." Ellis was informed that this practice was still kept up in 1813 in Kent, in the neighbourhood of Maidstone. Miss Baker, in the "Northamptonshire Glossary," 1854, says: "In some villages in the county, I am informed, they formerly went about with a two-handled pad or gossiping-pot, begging furmety, or wheat, for making it. My good old grandfather always, on this day, gave a bowl of wheat to any of the poor in the village who chose to come for it. . . Going a gooding is, I understand, still continued at Peterborough, and in some few villages, but it is going fast into desuetude." In some places they speak of these days as "goodish days." The subjoined is from "Notes and Queries" for December 19, 1857: "In the Staffordshire parish, from which I write, St. Thomas's Day is observed thus: not only do the old women and widows, but representatives also from each poorer family in the parish, come round for alms. The clergyman is expected to give one shilling to each person. . . Some of the parishioners give alms in money, others in kind. Thus some of the farmers give corn, which the miller grinds gratis. The day's custom is termed 'Gooding.' In neighbouring parishes no corn is given, the farmers giving money instead; and in some places the money collected is placed in the hands of the clergyman and churchwardens, who, on the Sunday nearest to St. Thomas's Day, distribute it at the vestry. The fund is called St. Thomas's Dole, and the day itself is termed Doleing Day." The custom which children have of going about before Christmas, to collect fruit, or anything which people choose to bestow on them, has always been common to this country, and to its continental neighbours. Comp. *Corning*.

It is thus described by Naogeorgus:

"Three weekes before the day whereon
    was borne the Lorde of Grace,
And on the Thursdaye boyes and girls
    do runne in every place,
And bounce and beate at every doore,
    with blowes and lustie snaps,
And crie, the Advent of the Lord not
    borne as yet perhaps.
And wishing to the neighbours all, that
    in the houses dwell,
A happie yeare, and every thing to
    spring and prosper well:
Here have they peares, and plumbs, and
    pence, ech man gives willinglie,
For these three nights are alwayes
    thought vnfortunate to bee:
Wherein they are afrayde of sprites and
    cankred witches spight,
And dreadfull devils blacke and grim,
    that then have chiefest might."

Goose.—An early author, speaking of the goose, says: "She is no witch, or astrologer, to divine by the starres, but yet hath a shrewd guesse of rainie weather, being as good as an almanack to some that beleeve in her." *Strange Metamorphosis of Man*, 1634. There is a proverbial phrase in Skelton's *Garland of Laurel*, 1523:

"When the rain raineth, and the goose
    winketh,
Little wots the gosling, what the goose
    thinketh."

A German writer cited by Mr. Atkinson in his "Cleveland Glossary," 1868, says: "From the breast-bone of a goose eaten at Martinmas Eve (old style), it is possible to ascertain what the winter is likely to be. When picked, it must be held up to the light, and the white marks then discernible betoken snow, the darker ones, frost and cold weather. It should also be remarked, that the front part of the bone foretells the weather before Christmas, the hinder part the weather after Christmas."

Goose.—A game mentioned in the Stationers' Register under 1597, and described as "new and most pleasant." It does not seem to be otherwise known, but that it was popular, and long continued in vogue seems to be shown by an advertisement as late as 1670, at the end of Robert Pricke's translation of Le Muet's Architecture, of this pastime as a publication then in print.

Goose-Grass.—See *Whittlegait*.

Goose Intentos.—Corrupted into *goose in ten toes*, the goose popularly regarded by the husbandmen in Lancashire as due to them for a dinner on the sixteenth Sunday after Pentecost, when the old prayer for the day concluded with *præstet esse intentos*. Blount and Halliwell in v.

Goose, Winchester.—The venereal disease, from the stews at Southwark, formerly under the jurisdiction of the see of Winchester. It is one of the species of *goose* enumerated and described by Taylor the Water-poet, in his cognominal tract, 1621. In a tract printed under Edward VI.'s reign, called the *Upchering of the Mass*, it is referred to as the "Winchester gosling."

Goose Riding.—A goose, whose neck is greased, being suspended by the legs to a cord tied to two trees or high posts, a number of men on horseback riding at full-speed attempt to pull off the head, which if they accomplish they win the goose. This has been practised in Derbyshire within the memory of persons lately living. Douce says, his worthy friend Mr. Lumisden informed him that when young he remembered the sport of "riding the goose" at Edinburgh. A bar was placed across the road, to which a goose, whose neck had been previously greased, was tied. At this the candidates, as before mentioned, plucked.

Gooseberry Fair.—See *Running for the Smock*. In Paulinus "de Candore," p. 264, we read: "In Dania, tempore quadragesimali Belgæ rustici in Insula Amack, Anserem (candidum ego vidi), fune alligatum, inque sublimi pendentem, habent, ad quem citatis Equis certatim properant, quique caput ei prius abruperit, victor evasit." Concerning the practice of swarming up a pole after a goose placed at top, see Sauval, "Antiquités de Paris," tom. ii. p. 696.

At the present day a leg of mutton or a pig is frequently scrambled for in the same manner at fairs and regattas.

Gospel Oak.—The place called Gospel Oak, near Kentish Town, doubtless derived its name from the same custom as the Gospel Trees mentioned elsewhere. Comp. *Parochial Perambulations*.

Gossiping-Pot.—See *Gooding*.

Gossip's Cake.—In his *Twelve Months*, 1661, Stevenson, speaking of the month of August, observes: "The new wheat make the Gossips Cake, and the Bride-Cup is carryed above the heads of the whole parish."

Govor's, St., Well.—St. Govor's Well, in Kensington Gardens, London, is still visited by persons who have faith in the virtues of the water. It is, I believe, an artesian spring. The name of this saint, who does not belong to the English series, and is consequently unnoticed by Butler, has been corrupted into Go'or, whence Kensington Gore, in the immediate vicinity, seems to have been derived.

Graal, or **Grail.**—A dish supposed to have held the paschal lamb at the Last Supper, and which, after being brought (as it was said) to England by Joseph of Arimathea, was lost, and formed the object of quest for knights-errant. See a rather long note in Nares, *Glossary* in v. In the common translation of "Don Quixote," the holy Graal is called Saint Graal, a very unauthorized accession to the Romish Calendar; and an eminent historian of our own day has discovered a new saint in the Holy Vial, of which he speaks as Saint Ampoule.

Grace-Cup.—Milner, on an ancient cup ("Archæologia," vol. xi. p. 240), informs us that the introduction of Christianity amongst our ancestors did not at all contribute to the abolition of the practice of wassailing. On the contrary, it began to assume a kind of religious aspect; and the wassail bowl itself, which in the great monasteries was placed on the Abbot's table, at the upper end of the refectory or eating hall, to be circulated among the community at his discretion, received the honourable appellation of 'Poculum Charitatis.' This in our Universities is called the Grace-cup."

Grail. — An abbreviated form of *Graduale*, one of the ancient musical service books of the Church in Romish times. There is one for the use of Salisbury.

Graves. — Graves were anciently called pyttes, and in large towns and cities in and after the middle ages a common pit for the dead was provided in some retired spot. See Strutt's "Manners and Customs," vol. iii., p. 172. But the converse was and remains true; for in Lincolnshire the potato-mounds raised above the ground and covered with earth are known as graves, although they are not dug. I find in Durandus, lib. vii. De Officio Mortuorum, cap. 35-39, the following: "Debet autem quis sic sepeliri, ut capite ad occidentem posito, pedes dirigat ad Orientem, in quâ quasi ipsa positione orat : et innuit quod promptus est, ut de occasu festinet ad ortum: de Mundo ad Seculum." Cullum says: "There is a great partiality here, to burying on the south and east sides of the church yard. About twenty years ago, when I first became rector, and observed how those sides (particularly the south), were crowded with graves, I prevailed upon a few persons to bury their friends on the north, which was entirely vacant; but the example was not followed as I hoped it would: and they continue to bury on the south, where a corpse is rarely interred without disturbing the bones of its ancestors. This partiality may perhaps at first have partly arisen from the antient custom of praying for the dead; for as the usual approach to this and most country churches is by the south, it was natural for burials to be on that side, that those who were going to divine service might, in their way, by the sight of the graves of their friends, be put in mind to offer up a prayer for the welfare of their souls; and even now, since the custom of praying for the dead is abolished, the same obvious situation of graves may excite some tender recollection in those who view them, and silently implore 'the passing tribute of a sigh.' That this motive has its influence, may be concluded from the graves that appear on the north side of the church yard, when the approach to the church happens to be that way; of this there are some few instances in this neighbourhood." *Hist. and Antiq. of Hawsted, Suffolk.* 1784, apud *Bibl. Top. Brit.*, xxiii. "As to the position in the grave, though we decline," says Browne in his "Urne-burial," "the religious consideration, yet in cœmeterial and narrower burying-places, to avoid confusion and cross-position, a certain posture were to be admitted. The Persians lay north and south; the Megarians and Phœnicians placed their heads to the east: the Athenians, some think, towards the west, which Christians still retain: and Bede will have it to be the posture of our Saviour. That Christians bury their dead on their backs, or in a supine position, seems agreeable to profound sleep and the common posture of dying; contrary also to the most natural way of birth; not unlike our pendulous posture in the doubtful state of the womb. Diogenes was singular, who preferred a prone position in the grave; and some Christians like neither, (Russians, &c.) who decline the figure of rest, and make choice of an erect posture." In the Ely Articles of Enquiry, (with some directions intermingled), 1662, it is asked, "When graves are digged, are they made six foot deep, (at the least), and east and west?" In the position of the graves the common and honourable direction is from east to west, the dishonourable one from north to south. Hearne had such correct notions on this head, that he left orders for his grave to be made straight by a compass, due east and west: in consequence of which his monument, which I have often seen, is placed in a direction not parallel with any of the other graves. Its being placed seemingly awry, gives it a very remarkable appearance.

In the Cambrian Register is the following very apposite passage respecting church-yards in Wales. "In country church yards the relations of the deceased crowd them into that part which is south of the church; the north side, in their opinion, being unhallowed ground, fit only to be the dormitory of stillborn infants and suicides. For an example to his neighbours, and as well to escape the barbarities of the sexton, the writer of the above account ordered himself to be buried on the north side of the church yard. But as he was accounted an infidel when alive, his neighbours could not think it creditable to associate with him when dead. His dust, therefore, is likely to pass a solitary retirement, and for ages to remain undisturbed by the hands of men." 1796, p. 374, *Notes*. In "Cymbeline," act iv. sc. 2, Guiderius, speaking of the disguised and (supposed) dead Imogen, says: "Nay, Cadwal, we must lay his head to the east; my father has a reason for't." And in *Guy Mannering* we similarly have: "Na, na! Not that way: the feet to the east." Moresin says that in Popish burying grounds, those who were reputed good Christians lay towards the south and east; others, who had suffered capital punishment, laid violent hands on themselves, or the like, were buried towards the north: a custom that had formerly been of frequent use in Scotland. In "Martins Months Mind," 1589, we read: "He died excommunicate, and they might not therefore burie him in Christian buriall, and his will was not to come there in any wise. His bodie should not be buried in any church, (especiallye cathedrall, whichever he detested), chappell, nor church yard; for they have been profaned with superstition. He would not be laid east and west, (for he ever went against the haire), but north and south: I think because 'Ab Aquilone omne malum,' and the south wind ever brings corruption with it." In tho trial of Robert Fitzgerald Esq., and others, for the murder of Patrick Randal M'Donnel, Esq. (in Ireland in 1786), we read: "The body of Mr. Fitzgerald, immediately after execution, was carried to the ruins of Turlagh House, and was waked in a stable adjoining, with a few candles placed about it. On the next day it was carried to the church yard of Turlagh, where he was buried on what is generally termed the wrong side of the church, in his cloaths, without a coffin." Craven Ord, Esq. informed Brand that "at the east end of the chancel, in the church yard, of Fornham All Saints, near Bury, Suffolk, is the coffin-shaped monument of Henrietta Maria Cornwallis, who died in 1707. It stands north and south, and the parish tradition says that she ordered that position of it as a mark of penitence and humiliation." Pennant, in allusion to Whiteford Church, says: "I step into the churchyard and sigh over the number of departed which fill the inevitable retreat. In no distant time the north side, like those of all other Welsh Churches, was through some superstition to be occupied only by persons executed, or by suicides. It is now nearly as much crowded as the other parts." He adds, that, in North Wales none but excommunicated or very poor and friendless people, are buried on the north side of the church yard. *Hist. of Whiteford*, p. 102. Gilbert White, speaking of Selborne church yard, observes: "Considering the size of the church, and the extent of the parish, the church yard is very scanty; and especially as all wish to be buried in the south side, which is become such a mass of mortality, that no person can be there interred without disturbing or displacing the bones of his ancestors. There is reason to suppose that it once was larger, and extended to what is now the Vicarage Court and garden. At the east end are a few graves; yet none, till very lately, on the north side; but as two or three families of best repute have begun to bury in that quarter, prejudice may wear out by degrees, and their example be followed by the rest of the neighbourhood." In "Paradoxical Assertions," &c., by R. H., 1664, we read:

"Cœlo tegitur, qui non habet urnam." "Doubtless that man's bones in the north church yard rest in more quiet than his that lies entomb'd in the chancel." Benjamin Rhodes, steward to one of the earls of Elgin, requested, it seems, "to be interred in the open church yard, on the north side (to crosse the received superstition, as he thought, of the constant choice of the south side), near the new chapel." Rhodes was interred in Malden Church in Bedfordshire. "Life and Death of Mr. Benjamin Rhodes," &c., by P. Samwaies, his lordship's chaplain, 1657, p. 27. One of Mr. Brand's lady correspondents seems to have thought that if she died an old maid, she would have to lie in her grave with her face downwards.

In the poet Mason's time, it appears to have been usual to whiten the head and footstones of graves at Christmas, Easter, and Whitsuntide; but of course the custom was one which would vary exceedingly. I do not exactly know the origin of the phrase, to mark with a white stone, employed in allusion to a lucky or auspicious day in one of Hazlitt's Essays.

Gray's-Inn.—See *Antients, Pension,* and *Lord of Misrule.*

Greengoose or **Goose Fair.**— A fair formerly held at Stratford-le-Bow on Thursday in Whitsun week, when green geese were the chief features in the entertainment. See Nares, *Glossary* in v. The fair seems to have flourished in 1694, when a popular tract made its appearance with the title of *The Three Merry Wives of Greengoose Fair,* including a story similar to that of the *Crucified Priest,* in La Fontaine. Hazlitt's *Bibl. Coll.,* i., 455.

Green Men or **Wild Men.**—See Halliwell in v., and Hazlitt's *Livery Companies,* 1892, p. 311.

Greenock Fair.—A correspondent of "Notes and Queries" describes the pompous ceremonial which attended the opening of this fair. A Greenock correspondent informs the Editor that it is still kept up on the first Thursday in July and the fourth Tuesday in November, and with more than questionable advantage to the locality and neighbourhood. Formerly at least the offices and other places of business were closed for the day, and he recollects going as a lad, like all the rest, to see the show. *Letter from Allan Park Paton,* April 30, 1897.

Greenwich Fair.—The rolling of young couples down Greenwich-hill, at Easter and Whitsuntide, while the fair was held there, appears by the following extract from R. Fletcher's "Ex Otio Negotium," 1656, p. 210, in a poem called "May Day," to be the vestige of a May game :

" The game at best, the girls now rould
    must bee,
Where Coryden and Mopsa, he and
    shee,
Each happy pair make one Hermophro-
    dite,
And tumbling, bounce together, black
    and white."

This custom, which many still among us must remember, has died with the abolition of Greenwich Fair.

Gregory's, St., Day. — Gregory mentions a singular superstition : " Some are so superstitiously given, as upon the

night of St. Gregory's Day, to have their children ask the question in their sleep, whether they have anie minde to book or no; and if they saie yes, they count it a very good presage : but if the children answer nothing, or nothing to that purpose, they put them over to the plough." *Posthuma,* 1649, 113. In Hazlitts' *Handbook,* 1867, p. 244, there is a notice of an unique life of this saint's mother in verse, published about 1540.

Grimp.—St. Evremond, in a letter to Henry Jermyn, Earl of St. Albans, speaks of playing at *ombre* and *grimpe* as an agreeable way of passing a man's last moments. It was probably a game of cards, perhaps only a French game.

Groaning Chair.—An essayist in the " Gentleman's Magazine ' 'for May, 1732, observes : " Among the women there is the groaning chair, in which the matron sits to receive visits of congratulation. This is a kind of female ovation due to every good woman who goes through such eminent perils in the service of her country."

" For a nurse, the child to dandle
Sugar, sope, spic'd pots, and candle,
A groaning chair, and eke a cradle.—
Blanckets of a several scantling
Therein for to wrap the bantling :
Sweetmeats from comfit-maker's
    trade
When the child's a Christian made—
Pincushions and other such knacks
A child-bed woman always lacks,
Caudles, grewels, costly jellies, &c."
—*Poor Robin* for 1676.

Groaning Cheese.—Against the time of the good wife's delivery, it used to be everywhere the custom for the husband to provide a large cheese and a cake. These, from time immemorial, have been the objects of ancient superstition. It is customary at Oxford to cut the cheese (called in the North of England, in allusion to the mother's complaints at her delivery, the Groaning Cheese) in the middle when the child is born, and so by degrees form it into a large kind of ring, through which the child must be passed on the day of the christening. It was not unusual to preserve for many years, I know not for what superstitious intent, pieces of the groaning cake. Thus I read in Gayton : " And hath a piece of the groaning cake (as they call it) which she kept religiously with her Good Friday bun, full forty years un-mouldy and un-mouse-eaten." *Festivous Notes on Don Quixote,* 1654, p. 17. In other places the first cut of the sick wife's cheese (so also they call the groaning cheese) is to be divided into little pieces and tossed in the midwife's smock, to cause young women to dream of their lovers. Slices of the first cut of the groaning cheese are in the North of England laid under the pillows of young persons for the above purpose. In "The Vow-Breaker," by W. Sampson, 1636, in a scene where is discovered "a bed covered with white; enter Prattle, Magpy, Long-tongue, Barren with a childe, Anne in bed" : Boote says, "Neece, bring the groaning cheece, and all requisites, I must supply the father's place, and bid god-fathers."

Guinea Game.—A sport or amusement, so-called, is mentioned in the Stationers' Register under 1587-8.

Gule of August, or Lammas Day.—Pettingal derives "Gule" from the Celtic or British "Wyl," or "Gwyl," signifying a festival or holyday, and explains "Gule of August" to mean no more than the holyday of St. Peter ad Vincula in August, when the people of England under popery paid their Peter pence. This is confirmed by Blount, who tells us that Lammas Day, the first of August, otherwise called the Gule or Yule of August, may be a corruption of the British word "Gwyl Awst, signifying the feast of August." Vallancey says that *Cul* and *Gul* in the Irish implies a complete wheel, a belt, a whul, an anniversary. It may be synonymous with *Yule.* Spelman, in his Glossary, under the Gules of August, observes : "It often occurs in ancient parchments (especially legal ones) for the Feast of St. Peter ad Vincula, which is celebrated on the same calends of August. Durandus, in his Rationale, suggests, as a reason for this among others that, the Tribune Quirinus having a daughter whose throat was diseased, the girl was ordered by the Pope to kiss the chains wherewith St. Peter had been shackled, which wrought her complete cure, and led to the institution of the festival, as well as the erection of a memorial church." Vallancey cites Cormac, Archbishop of Cashel in the tenth century, in his Irish Glossary, as telling us that, "in his time, four great fires were lighted up on the four great festivals of the Druids; viz., in February, May, August, and November." Vallancey also tells us that "this day was dedicated to the sacrifice of the fruits of the soil. La-ith-mas was the day of oblation of grain. It is pronounced La-ee-mas, a word readily corrupted to Lammas. *Ith* is all kinds of grain, particularly wheat and mas, fruit of all kinds, especially the acorn, whence mast." Mr. Way, in a note to the word Lammas, in his edition of the "Promptorium Parvulorum," 1865, observes : "On the calends, or first of August, the festival of St. Peter *ad vincula*, it was customary in Anglo-Saxon times to make a votive offering of the first fruits of the harvest, and thence the feast was termed hlaf mæsse, Lammas, from hlaf, panis, and mæsse, missa, festum." Lammas day is called in the "Red Book of Derby hlaꝼ mæꝛꝛe ꝺæᵹ." But in the "Saxon Chronicle" it is hlam mæꝛꝛe. Mass was a word for festival ; hence our way of naming the festivals of Christmass, Candlemass, Martinmass, &c ∴ The remark in the Calendar of the Romish Church, under the first of August, is :

　　"Chains are worshipped," &c.

　　"Catenæ coluntur ad Aram in Exquiliis Ad Vicum Cyprium juxta Titi thermas."

Comp. *Lammas.*

Gwindy or **Wine-House.**—A curious institution in Wales in former days, where friends, neighbours, &c., assembled, *ymgampio*, or to perform feats of strength and activity, as archery, wrestling, throwing the sledge, and afterward the company called for wine, which the master supplied at a profit. This practice became an abuse, as criminals were sheltered at these places. Pennant's *Tours in Wales,* 1810, ii., 129-30. This gwindy was different from the summerhouse surmounting a cellar which the same writer notes as having at his own residence, and to which the gentlemen of a party withdrew after dinner to take their wine and converse more freely. *Hist. of Whiteford and Holywell,* 1796, p. 28.

Gypsies. — The history and migration of the gipsies, says Professor Sayce, have been traced step by step by means of an examination of their lexicon. The grammar and dictionary of the Romany prove that they started from their kindred, the Játs, on the north-western coast of India, near the mouths of the Indus, not earlier than the tenth century of the Christian era ; that they slowly made their way through Persia, Armenia and Greece, until, after a sojourn in Hungary, they finally spread themselves through western Europe into Spain on the one side and England on the other. The views of the old writers on this subject, cited below, are rather uncritical.

Ralph Volaterranus affirms that they first proceeded, or strolled, from among the Uxi, a people of Persia. Sir Thomas Browne cites Polydore Vergil as accounting them originally Syrians : Philip Bergoinas as deriving them from Chaldea ; Æneas Sylvius as from some part of Tartary ; Bellonius, as from Wallachia and Bulgaria ; and Aventinus as fetching them from the confines of Hungary. He adds that "they have been banished by most Christian Princes. The great Turk at least tolerates them near the Imperial City: he is said to employ them as spies: they were banished as such by the Emperor Charles the fifth." Sir Thomas Browne gives this general account of the gipsies: "They are a kind of counterfeit Moors, to be found in many parts of Europe, Asia, and Africa. They are commonly supposed to have come from Egypt, whence they derive themselves. Munster discovered in the Letters and Pass, which they obtained from Sigismund the Emperor, that they first came out of Lesser Egypt, that having turned apostates from Christianity and relapsed into Pagan rites, some of every family were enjoined this penance, to wander about the world. Aventinus tells us, that they pretend, for this vagabond course, a judgment of God upon their forefathers who refused to entertain the Virgin Mary and Jesus, when she fled into their country." *Vulgar Errors*, p. 280. He adds: "Their first appearance was in Germany since the year 1400. Nor were they observed before in other parts of Europe, as is deducible from Munster, Genebrard, Crantsius, and Ortelius." *Ibid.* p. 287. Yet Bellonius, who met great droves of gipsies in Egypt, in villages on the banks of the Nile, where they were accounted strangers and wanderers from foreign parts, as with us, affirms that they are no Egyptians. *Observat.* lib. ii. Blackstone, in his "Commentaries," has the following account of them: "They are a strange kind of commonwealth among themselves of wandering impostors and juglers, who first made their appearance in Germany about the beginning of the sixteenth century. Munster, it is true, who is followed and relied upon by Spelman, fixes the time of their first appearance to the year 1417: but as he owns that the first he ever saw were in 1529, it was probably an error of the press for 1517, especially as other historians inform us, that when Sultan Selim conquered Egypt in 1517 several of the natives refused to submit to the Turkish yoke, and revolted under one Zinganeus, whence the Turks call them Zinganees; but being at length surrounded and banished, they agreed to disperse in small parties all over the world, where their supposed skill in the black art gave them an universal reception in that age of superstition and credulity. In the compass of a very few years they gained such a number of idle proselytes, (who imitated their language and complexion, and betook themselves to the same arts of chiromancy, begging, and pilfering), that they became troublesome and even formidable to most of the States of Europe.

Hence they were expelled from France in the year 1560, and from Spain 1591, and the Government of England took the alarm much earlier, for in 1530 they are described, Stat. 22 Hen. VIII. c. x., as an 'outlandish people calling themselves Egyptians, using no craft, nor feat of merchandize, who have come into this realm and gone from shire to shire, and place to place, in great company, and used great, subtle, and crafty means to deceive the people, and also have committed many heinous felonies and robberies.' Wherefore they are directed to avoid the realm, and not to return under pain of imprisonment and forfeiture of their goods and chattells; and upon their trials for any felony which they may have committed, they shall not be intitled to a jury *de medietate linguæ*. And afterwards it was enacted by Statutes 1 and 2 Ph. and Mary, c. iv., and 5 Eliz. c. xx., that if any such persons shall be imported into the kingdom, the importers shall forfeit forty pounds. And if the Egyptians themselves remain one month in the kingdom, or if any person, being fourteen years old, whether natural-born subject or stranger, which hath been seen or found in the fellowship of such Egyptians, or which hath disguised him or herself like them, shall remain in the same one month at one or several times, it is felony without benefit of clergy. And Sir Matthew Hale informs us that at one Suffolk Assize no less than thirteen persons were executed upon these Statutes a few years before the Restoration. But to the honour of our national humanity, there are no instances more modern than this of carrying these laws into practice."

The subsequent passage, from the "British Critic," exhibits a proof of the same tendency. "In a late meeting of the Royal Society of Gottingen, Professor Blumenbach laid before the members a second Decad of the crania of persons of different nations contrasted with each other, in the same manner as in the first, and ranged according to the order observed by him in his other works. In the first variety was the cranium of a real gipsey, who died in prison at Clausenburg, communicated by Dr. Patacki of that place. The resemblance between this and that of the Egyptian mummy in the first dead was very striking. Both differed essentially from the sixty-four crania of other persons belonging to foreign nations, in the possession of the author: a circumstance which, among others, tends to confirm the opinion of Profess. Meiners, that the Hindoos, from whom Grielman derives the gipsies, came themselves originally from Egypt." The gipsies, as it should thus seem, came originally from Hindostan, where they are supposed to have been of the lowest class of Indians, namely Parias, or, as they are called in Hindostan, Suders. They are thought to have migrated about A.D. 1408 or 1409,when Timur Beg ravaged India for the purpose of spreading the Mahometan religion. On this occasion so many thousands were made slaves and put to death, that an universal panic took place, and a very great number of terrified inhabitants endeavoured to save themselves by flight. As every part towards the north and east was beset by the enemy, it is most probable that the country below Multan, to the mouth of the Indus, was the first asylum and rendezvous of the fugitive Suders. This is called the country of Zinganen. Here they were safe, and remained so till Timur returned from his victories on the Ganges. Then it was that they first entirely quitted the country, and probably with them a considerable number of the natives, which will explain the meaning of their original name. By what track they came to us cannot be ascertained. If they went straight through the southern Persian deserts of Sigistan, Makran, and Kirman, along the Persian Gulf to the mouth of the Euphrates, from thence they might get, by Bassora, into the great deserts of Arabia, afterwards into Arabia Petræa and so arrive in Egypt by the Isthmus of Suez. They must certainly have been in Egypt before they reached us, otherwise it is incomprehensible how the report arose that they were Egyptians. Pasquier, in his "Recherches de la France," has the following: "On August 17, 1427, came to Paris twelve Penitents (penanciers) as they call themselves, viz., a duke, an earl, and ten men, all on horseback, and calling themselves good Christians. They were of lower Egypt, and gave out that not long before the Christians had subdued their country, and obliged them to embrace Christianity, or put them to death. Those who were baptized were great lords in their own country, and had a King and Queen there. Some time after their conversion, the Saracens overran their country and obliged them to renounce Christianity. When the Emperor of Germany, the King of Poland, and other Christian Princes heard this, they fell upon them and obliged them all, both great and small, to quit their country, and go to the Pope at Rome, who enjoined them seven years penance to wander over the world without lying in a bed; every bishop and abbot to give them once 10 livres tournois; and he gave them letters to this purpose, and his blessing. They had been wandering five years when they

came to Paris. They were lodged by the police out of the City, at Chapel St. Denis. Almost all had their ears bored, and one or two silver rings in each, which they said was esteemed an ornament in their country. The men were very black, their hair curled; the women remarkably ugly and black, all their faces scarred (deplayez), their hair black, like a horse's tail, their only habit was an old shaggy garment (flossoye) tied over their shoulders with a cloth or cord-sash, and under it a poor petticoat or shift. In short they were the poorest wretches that had ever been seen in France; and, notwithstanding their poverty, there were among them women who, by looking into people's hands, told their fortunes *et meirent contens en plusieurs mariages;* for they said, thy wife has played thee false (Ta femme t'a fait coup) and what was worse, they picked people's pockets of their money and got it into their own by telling these things by art, magic, or the intervention of the Devil or by a certain knack." It is added that they were expelled from France in 1561.

At a comparatively early date the terms *Œgyptian* and *Bohemian* were rather wrongly applied to them. For in Grielman's *Dissertation on the Gypsies,* translated by Raper, 1787, we read that, in 1418, the gipsies first arrived in Switzerland near Zürich and other places, to the number, men, women, and children, of fourteen thousand. In a provincial council, held at Tarragona in 1591 there was the subjoined decree promulgated against them: "Curandum etiam est ut publici Magistratus eos coerceant qui se Ægyptiacos vel Bohemianos vocant, quos vix constat esse Christianos, nisi ex eorum relatione; cum tamen sint mendaces, fures, et deceptores, et aliis sceleribus multi eorum assueti." "Ægyptiaci," says Ducange, "vagi homines, harioli ac fatidici, qui hac & illac errantes ex manus inspectione futura præsagire se fingunt, ut de marsupiis incautorum nummos corrogent."

In Grielman a very copious catalogue is given of gipsy and Hindostan words collated, by which it appears that every third gipsy word is likewise an Hindostan one, or still more, that out of every thirty gipsy words eleven or twelve are common to Hindostan. This agreement will appear uncommonly great if we recollect that the above words have only been learned from the gipsies within these very few years, consequently after a separation of near four complete centuries from Hindostan, their supposed native country, among people who talked languages totally different, and in which the gipsies themselves conversed; for under the constant and so long continued influx of these languages, their own must necessarily have suffered great alteration. In this learned work there is also a comparison of the gipsies with the above cast of Suders: but I lay the greatest stress upon those proofs which are deduced from the similarity of the languages. In the supplement it is mentioned that Marsden had obtained as many words as he could get, and that by a correspondence from Constantinople he procured a collection of words used by the Cingaris thereabouts; and these, together with the words given by Ludolph in his "Historia Æthiopica," compared with Hindostan vulgar language, show it to be the same that is spoken by the gipsies and in Hindostan.

Harrison, in his "Description of England," describing the various sorts of cheats practised by the voluntary poor, after enumerating those who maim or disfigure their bodies by sores, or counterfeit the guise of labourers or serving men, or mariners seeking for ships which they have not lost, to extort charity, adds: "It is not yet full threescore years since this trade began: but how it hath prospered since that time it is easie to judge, for they are now supposed of one sex and another to amount vnto aboue 10,000 persons, as I haue heard reported. Moreouer. in counterfeiting the Egyptian roges, they haue deuised a language among themselues which they name Canting, but others Pedlers French, a speach compact thirtie yeares since of English and a great number of od words of their owne deuising, without all order or reason: and yet such is it as none but themselues are able to vnderstand. The first deuiser thereof was hanged by the necke, a iust reward no doubt for his deceits and a common end to all of that profession." *Holinshed*, 1587, p. 183. In Rid's *Art of Jugling*, 1612, sign.B b, is the following account:— "These kind of people about an hundred years agoe, about the twentieth yeare of King Henry the eight, began to gather an head, at the first heere about the Southerne parts, and this (as I am informed) and as I can gather, was their beginning. Certaine Egiptians, banished their cuntry, (belike not for their good conditions), arrived heere in England, who being excellent in quaint tricks and devises, not known heere at that time among us, were esteemed and had in great admiration, for what with strangeness of their attire and garments, together with their sleights and legerdemaines, they were spoke of farre and neere, insomuch that many of our English loyterers joyned with them, and in time learned their crafte and cosening. The speach which they used was

the right Egyptian language, with whome our Englishmen conversing with, at least learned their language. These people continuing about the country in this fashion, practicing their cosening art of fast and loose legerdemaine, purchased themselves great credit among the cuntry people, and got much by palmistry and telling of fortunes, insomuch they pitifully cosened the poore contry girles, both of money, silver spones, and the best of their apparrell, or any good thing they could make, onely to hear their fortunes." "This Giles Hather (for so was his name) together with his whore, Kit Calot, in short space had following them a pretty traine, he terming himself the King of the Egiptians, and she the quene, ryding about the cuntry at their pleasure uncontrolld." He then mentions the statute against them of the 1st and 2d of Philip and Mary, on which he observes— "But what a number were executed presently upon this statute, you would wonder: yet, notwithstanding, all would not prevaile: but still they wandred, as before, up and downe, and meeting once in a yeare at a place appointed: sometime at the Devil's A—— in Peake in Darbishire, and otherwhiles at Ketbrooke by Blackheath. or elsewhere, as they agreed still at their meeting." Speaking of his own time, he adds: "These fellowes seeing that no profit comes by wandring, but hazard of their lives, do daily decrease and breake off their wonted society, and betake themselves, many of them, some to be pedlers, some tinkers, some juglers, and some to one kinde of life or other." William Bullein, in his Treatise "of Simples and Surgery," accompanying his *Bulwarke of Defence*, 1562, in which the author speaks of dog-leeches and Egyptians, and Jews: all pretending to the telling of fortunes and curing by charms. "They" (dog-leeches) "buy some gross stuff, with a box of salve and cases of tools to set forth their slender market withal, &c. Then fall they to palmistry and telling of fortunes, daily deceiving the simple. Like unto the swarms of vagabonds, Egyptians, and some that call themselves Jews: whose eyes were so sharp as lynx. For they see all the people with their knacks, pricks, domifying, and figuring, with such like fantasies. Faining that they have familiers and glasses, whereby they may find things that be lost. And, besides them, are infinite of old doltish witches with blessings for the fair and conjuring of cattel." Strype's *Annals*, ii., 611. In Dekker's *Lanthorne and Candlelight*, 1608, Sign. G 2, the gipsies are called Moone-men, and a section is devoted to an account of "a strange wild people, very dangerous to townes and country villages," as they are called; and Dekker draws a picture of them, which closely corresponds with our experience of their modern descendants or representatives. I am sorry that his account is too long for transfer hither. "In "Witt's Recreations," a long piece called "The gipsies" occurs, which is curious, as it contains a good deal of phraseology evidently supposed by the writer to be peculiar to the class, but then, as now, common to all the mendicant fraternity. In Harman's time (1566) many of the terms were current among thieves and beggars, which are familiar to modern ears. Spelman's portrait of the gipsy fraternity in his time, which seems to have been taken *ad vivum*, is as follows: "Egyptiani. Errorum Impostorumque genus nequissimum: in Continente ortum, sed ad Britannias nostras et Europam reliquam pervolans:—nigredine deformes, excocti sole, immundi veste, et usu rerum omnium fœdi.—Fœminæ cum stratis et parvulis, jumento invehuntur. Literas circumferunt Principum, ut innoxius illis permittatur transitus.—Oriuntur quippe et in nostra et in omni Regione, spurci hujusmodi nebulones, qui sui similes in Gymnasium sceleris adsciscentes; vultum, cultum, moresque supradictos sibi inducunt. Linguam (ut exotici magis videantur) fictitiam blaterant, provinciasque vicatim pervagantes, auguriis et furtis, imposturis & technarum millibus plebeculam rodunt et illudunt, linguam, hanc Germani Rotwelch, quasi rubrum Wallicum, id est Barbarismum; Angli Canting nuncupant." In "The Character of a Quack Astrologer," 1673, sign. A 3 verso, our wise man, "a gypsey of the upper form," is called "a three-penny prophet that undertakes the telling of other folks fortunes, meerly to supply the pinching necessities of his own." At sign. B 3 our cunning man is said to "begin with theft, and to help people to what they have lost, picks their pockets afresh; not a ring or spoon is nim'd away, but pays him twelvepence toll, and the ale-drapers' often-straying tankard yields him a constant revenue: for that purpose he maintains as strict a correspondence with gilts and lifters, as a mountebank with applauding midwives and recommending nurses: and if at any time, to keep up his credit with the rabble, he discovers anything, 'tis done by the same occult Hermetic learning, heretofore profest by the renowned Mall-Cut-Purse." These used still, in Brand's time, to be called "Wise Men" in the villages of Durham and Northumberland. Gay, in his "Pastorals," speaking of a girl who is slighted by her lover, thus describes the gipsies:

"Last Friday's eve, when as the sun
    was set,
I, near yon stile, three sallow gipsies
    met;
Upon my hand they cast a poring look,
Bid me beware, and thrice their heads
    they shook:
They said that many crosses I must
    prove,
Some in my worldly gain, but most in
    love.
Next morn I miss'd three hens and our
    old cock,
And, off the hedge, two pinners and a
    smock."

In the North of England and Scotland they seem to have enjoyed some share of indulgence. Before the middle of the sixteenth century we meet with "'Letters of Defence and Concurrence to John Fall, Lord and Earl of Little Egypt, for assisting him in the execution of Justice upon his Company, conform to the Laws of Egypt, February 15th, 1540-1.' These are supposed to have been a gang of gypsies associated together in defiance of the State under Fall, as their head or king, and these the articles of association for their internal government, mutual defence and security, the embroil'd and infirm state of the Scotish nation at that time not permitting them to repress or restrain a combination of vagrants, who had got above the laws, and erected themselves into a separate community as a set of banditti." There is a curious letter of the justices of Durham to the Earl of Shrewsbury, Lord President of the North, dated at Durham, Jan. 19, 1549-50, concerning the gipsies and Faws. A writ of Privy Seal, dated 1549, supports John Faw, Lord and Earl of Little Egypt, in the execution of justice on his company and folk, conform to the laws of Egypt, and in punishing certain persons there named, who rebelled against him, left him, robbed him, and refused to return home with him. James's subjects are commanded to assist in apprehending them, and in assisting Faw and his adherents to return home. There is a like writ in his favour from Mary Queen of Scots, 1553; and in 1554 he obtained a pardon for the murder of Nunan Small. So that it appears he had staid long in Scotland, and perhaps some time in England, and from him this kind of strolling people might receive the name of Faw Gang, which they still retain. "Privy Seal Book of Edinburgh," no. xiv. fol. 59, quoted in "Gent. Mag." for Oct. 1785. This document is noticed by Ellis in his first series of "Original Letters," 1825. Lodge's "Illust. of British History," vol. i. p. 135. Mr. Hampton has pointed out, in his most interesting "Origines Patriciæ," 1846, that Johnny Faw, the familiar name for the old gipsy chiefs, was corrupted from Fowde or Faad, the Danish name for a governor, and the same writer mentions that, in the Acts of James VI. of Scotland, 1581, the term is used in the sense of bailiff.

In Scotland, in the eighteenth century, the gipsies appear to have been tolerably abundant. A person writing from Eaglesham, Co. Renfrew, about 1795, says: "There is no magistrate nearer than within four miles; and the place is oppressed with gangs of gipsies, commonly called tinkers or randy-beggars, because there is nobody to take the smallest account of them." *Stat. Acc.* ii., 124. There is a well-known Scotish song entitled "Johnny Faa, the Gypsie Laddie." An advertisement in the "Newcastle Courant," July 27, 1754, offers a reward for the apprehending of John Fall and Margaret his wife, William Fall and Jane, otherwise Ann his wife, &c. "commonly called or known by the name of Fawe," &c. Gipsies still continue to be called "Faws" in the North of England. Since the repeal of the Act against this people in 1788 they are said to have declined in numbers. In May, 1797, their settlement at Norwood was broken up, and they were treated as vagrants. The number of genuine gipsies in England is not large; but there are thousands of women fortune-tellers, who pretend to be gipsies, and affect to understand palmistry and divination. The gipsies are universally considered in the same light, i.e., of cheats and pilferers. Witness the definition of them in Ducange and the curious etchings of them by Callot. The engraver does not represent them in a more favourable light than the lexicographer, for, besides his inimitable delineations of their dissolute manner of living, he has accompanied his plates with verses, which are very far from celebrating their honesty. It appears from many preceding allusions that the modern artifices in practice among this class of persons date somewhat far back. We find in the old ballad of "The brave English Gipsey," that the still familiar trick of dyeing the face with walnut-juice was in vogue in the time of Charles I. :

"Our dye is not in vaine;
For we do dye in graine:
The walnut-tree supplies our lacke;
What was made faire, we can make blacke."

The whole piece is curious, and worthy of perusal, as it shews that the gipsy has always led a pretty similar kind of existence in this country, employing the same shifts, and known by the same characteristics. The ballad was an imitation of one written on the same plan under the title of "The Spanish Gipsy."

The late Dr. Diamond, of Twickenham, told me that when he was a boy, a gipsy chief died in his neighbourhood, and over the place of interment his followers laid a black coffin-shaped stone of peculiar appearance; and it was their practice every year to come and sit in a circle round the stone, as a mark of homage to the departed. So lately as September, 1894, in the Chapelry of Withernsea, in the East Riding of Yorkshire, after the death of "Fiddler Jack," his clothes and effects were burnt, to prevent any dispute among his relatives, who had to begin again, and buy their own belongings; and a second motive was that the widow might not be wooed for the sake of her property. *Antiquary*, November, 1894.

The subjoined paragraph in a newspaper of the 19th Nov. 1903, seems barely credible:—The effects of the Queen of the Boswell tribe of Gipsies, who died and was buried in Falkirk last week, have been destroyed at the gipsy encampment in accordance with a native custom of the tribe, which is invariably followed. The goods destroyed were of the value of £150, including five bags full of valuable costumes, a solid silver George III. tea set, antique china, silver teaspoons and forks. The caravan of the deceased, which cost £130, is also to be destroyed by fire.

In the present editor's boyhood there was a song in common use, of which he remembers one stanza :

"Hark, hark, the dogs do bark;
The gipsies are coming to town;
Some in rags, and some in jags,
And some in velvet gown."

Twiss, in his "Travels," gives the following account of them in Spain : "They are very numerous about and in Murcia, Cordova, Cadiz, and Ronda. The race of these vagabonds is found in every part of Europe; the French call them Bohemiens, the Italians Zingari, the Germans Zigeunen, the Dutch Heydenen (Pagans), the Portuguese Siganos, and the Spaniards Gitanos, in Latin Cingari. Their language, which is peculiar to themselves, is everywhere so similar, that they undoubtedly are all derived from the same source. They began to appear in Europe in the 15th century, and are probably a mixture of Egyptians and Ethiopians. The men are all thieves, and the women libertines. They follow no certain trade, and have no fixed religion. They do not enter into the order of society, wherein they are only tolerated. It is supposed there are upwards of 40,000 of them in Spain, great numbers of whom are inn-keepers in the villages and small towns, and are everywhere fortune-tellers. In Spain they are not allowed to possess any lands, or even to serve as soldiers. They marry among themselves, stroll in troops about the country, and bury their dead under water. They are contented if they can procure food by showing feats of dexterity, and only pilfer to supply themselves with the trifles they want; so that they never render themselves liable to any severer chastisement than whipping for having stolen chickens, linen, &c. Most of the men have a smattering of physic and surgery, and are skilled in tricks performed by sleight of hand. The foregoing account is partly extracted from le Voyageur François, vol. xvi. but the assertion that they are all so abandoned as that author says, is too general." In the " Pall Mall Gazette," 1869, it was stated that the Pope went out of Rome to bless some Bohemians, encamped on the outskirts of the city, and inspected their quarters.

See upon the subject Pasquier, " Recherches de la France," p. 392; " Dictionnaire des Origines, v. Bohemiens"; De Pauw, " Recherches sur les Egyptiens," tom. i. p. 169; Camerarius, " Horæ Subsecivæ": " Gent. Mag.", vol. liii. p. 1009; ibid. vol. lvii. p. 897. " Antiquarian Repertory," ed. 1807, vol. iii. p. 375-9; Borrow's " Bible in Spain " and " Gipsies in Spain," &c.

Hab-Nab.—The exposition offered by Isaac Reed seems most consonant with truth. It occurs in a note upon that passage in " Twelfth Night," where a character speaking of a duellist says, " His incensement at this moment is so implacable that satisfaction can be none but by pangs of death, and sepulchre; hob, nob, is his word; give't or take't." In Anglo-Saxon, habban is to have, and næbban to want. May it not therefore be explained in this sense, as signifying, " Do you chuse a glass of wine, or would you rather let it alone?" An even earlier author has the following passage:

" Where wooers hoppe in and out, long
    time may bryng
Him that hoppeth best, at last to have
    the ryng.
I hoppyng without for a ringe of a rush,
And while I at length debate and beate
    the bushe,
There shall steppe in other men, and
    catch the burdes,
And by long time lost in many vaine
    wurdes.
Betwene these two wives, make slouth
    speede confounde
While betweene two stooles my tayle
    goe to the ground.

By this, sens we see slouth must breede
    a scab,
Best sticke to the tone out of hand, hab
    or nab."

The phrase occurs in Ben Jonson's 'Tale of a Tub':

' I put it
Even to your Worship's bitterment hab
    nab
I shall have a chance o' the dice for't,
    I hope.' "

And Malone adds a passage from Holinshed: " The citizens in their rage shot habbe or nabbe, at random." In Harington's " Epigrams," book iv., ep. 91, we read:

" Not of Jack Straw, with his rebellious
    crew,
    That set King, realme, and lawes at
      hab or nab,
Whom London's worthy Maior so
    bravely slew
    With dudgeon dagger's honourable
      stab."

In " The New Courtier," a ballad, preserved in " Le Prince 'Amour," 1660, we find hab nab thus introduced:

" I write not of religion
For (to tell you truly) we have none.
If any me to question call,
With pen or sword, hab nab's the word,
Have at all."

It is said of the quack astrologer: " He writes of the weather hab nab, and as the toy takes him, chequers the year with foul and fair." So we perceive that the true sense of the expression was gradually forgotten. On the other hand, in *Appius and Virginia*, 1575 (Hazlitt's Dodsley, iv., 127), we have:

" There is no more ways, but *hap or
    hap not* "—

Hackin. — Hackin, a large sort of sausage, being a portion of the cheer provided for Christmas festivities, from to hack or chop, hackstock being still a chopping-block in the Scotish dialect." Nares *Gloss.*, 1859, in v. In " Round about our Coal-Fire " (circâ 1730) I find the following account of the usual diet and drink of this season, with other curious particulars: " An English gentleman at the opening of the great day, i.e., on Christmas Day in the morning, had all his tenants and neighbours enter his hall by day-break. The strong beer was broached, and the black-jacks went plentifully about with toast, sugar, nutmegg, and good Cheshire cheese. The Hackin (the great sausage) must be boiled by day-break, or else two young men must take the maiden (i.e., the cook), by the arms, and run her

round the market-place till she is ashamed
or her laziness."

Haddock.—Pennant tells us that,
"On each side beyond the gills of a haddock is a large black spot. Superstition
assigns this mark to the impression St.
Peter left with his finger and thumb,
when he took the tribute out of the mouth
of a fish of this species, which has been
continued to the whole race of haddocks
ever since that miracle." "Zoology,"
vol. iii., p. 182, edit. 1776.

> "But superstitious haddock, which
> appear
> With marks of Rome, St. Peter's finger
> here."

Haddock has spots on either side, which
are said to be marks of St. Peter's fingers,
when he catched that fish for the tribute."
—"Metellus his dialogues," &c., 1693, p.
57:

> "O superstitious dainty, Peter's fish,
> How com'st thou here to make so godly
> dish?"

Ibid.

**Haddon or Hardwicke, Co.
Derby, Headless Steeds of.**—
The superstitious notion that a coach
drawn by headless steeds, and driven by a
headless coachman, haunted this locality,
appears to have been common to Parsloes
in Essex, and several other places. The
late Mr. Thoms, under the *nom de plume*
of Ambrose Merton, wrote a letter to the
Athenæum about 1857 on the subject. A
correspondent of the same paper, replying
to Thoms, enquired whether the neighbourhood of Haddon or of Hardwicke was
still visited by the phantom coach. Comp.
Allies' *Antiquities of Worcestershire*,
1856, p. 462.

Haggs.—There is sometimes an appearance of phosphorus upon the manes
of horses or men's hair *(flammæ lam-
bentes)*, called "Haggs." Blount says,
"Hags are said to be made of sweat or
other some vapour issuing out of the
head: a not unusual sight among us when
we ride by night in summer time. They
are extinguished like flames by shaking
the horses' manes; but I believe rather it
is only a vapour reflecting light, but fat
and sturdy, compacted about the manes
of horses, or men's hair." Hyll, in his
Contemplation of Mysteries (1568), sign.
E 2, speaking of "the fire cleaving and
hanging on the parts of men and beasts,"
observes: "This impression for troth is
prodigious without any phisicke cause expressing the same when as the flame or
fire compasseth about anye persons heade.
And this straunge wonder and sight doth
signifie the royal assaultes of mightie
monarchies, and kinges, the governments
at the Emperie, and other matters wor-

thie memory, of which the Phisicke Causes
sufficient cannot be demonstrated. Seeing
then such fyers or lightes are, as they wer,
counterfets or figures of matters to come,
it sufficiently appeareth, that those not
rashely do appeare or showe but by Gods
holy will and pleasure sent, that they
maye signifie some rare matter to men.
This light doth Virgill write of in the
seconde Booke of Æneados of Ascanius,
which had a like flame burning without
harme on his heade. Also Livius in his
first Book, and Valerius Maximus reporte
of Servius Tullius, a childe who, sleeping
on bedde, such a flame appeared on his
heade and burned rounde about the heade
without harme, to the wonder of the beholders: which sight pronounced after his
ripe age the comming unto royall Estate."
He devotes another section to the consideration of the question: "What is to be
thought of the flame of fyre, which cleav-
eth to the heares of the heade and to the
heares of beastes?" He says here: "Experience witnesseth, that the fyre do
cleave manye times to the heades and eares
of beastes, and often times also to the
heades and shoulders of men ryding and
going on foote. For the exhalations dis-
pearsed by the ayre, cleave to the heares of
horses, and garments of men: which of the
lightnesse doe so ascend, and by the heate
kindled. Also this is often caused when
men and other beastes by a vehement and
swift motion wax very hote, that the
sweate, fattie and clammye, is sent forth,
which kindled yeldeth this forme. And
the like maner in all places, (as afore
uttered), as eyther in moyst and clammie
places, and marishes, in churchyards, cloy-
sters, kitchins, under galosses, valleys,
and other places, where many deade bodies
are laide, doe such burning lightes often
appeare. The reason is that, in these places
the earth continually breatheth forth
fatte fumes, grosse and clammy, which
come forth of dead bodyes: and when the
fume doth continually issue forth, then is
the same kindled by the labouring heate,
or by the smiting togither: even as out
of two flint stones smitten togither fyre is
gotten. To conclude, it appeareth that
such fyres are seene in moyst kitchins,
sinckes, or guttours, and where the orfall
of beastes killed are thrown: or in such
places most commonly are woont to be
seene. Such fires cleaving, doe marvey-
lously amase the fearfull. Yet not all
fires which are seene in the night are per-
fite fiers in that many have a kinde without a substaunce and heate, as those
which are the delusions of the devill, well
knowne to be the Prince of the World, and
flyeth about in the ayre." In a work
already cited, occurs an account "of
flames that appear upon the hairs of men
and beasts, their cause. These are some-

times clammy exhalations scattered in the air in small parts, which, in the night, by the resistance of the cold, are kindled, by cleaving to horse's ears and men's heades and shoulders, riding or walking; and that they cleave to hair or garments, it is by the same reason the dew cleaves to them, they being dry and attractive, and so more proper to receive them. Another kind of these flames are when the bodies of men and beasts are chafed and heated, they send forth a fat clammy sweat, which in like manner kindles, as is seen by sparkles of fire that fly about when a black horse is very hard curryed in the dark, or as the blue fire on the shells of oysters, caused by the nitrous salt. Livy also tells us of one Marius, a knight of Rome who, as he was making an oration to his soldiers in Spain with such vehemency as heated him, his head appeared to them all in a flame, though himself was not aware of it." *Account of Storms,* 1704, p. 79.

Hagmena.—The word "Hagmena" is by some supposed of an antiquity prior to the introduction of the Christian Faith. On the Norman *Hoquinanno* Douce observes: "This comes nearer to our word, which was probably imported with the Normans. It was also by the French called Haguillennes and Haguimento, and I have likewise found it corrupted into Haguirenleux," (and he refers to Carpentier, Menage, and other authorities). He says also: "I am further informed that the words used upon this occasion are 'Hagmena, Hagmena, gives us cakes and cheese, and let us go away.' Cheese and oaten-cakes, which are called farls, are distributed on this occasion among the cryers." Subjoined is all that appears to have survived of the Yorkshire Hagmena Song:

"To-night it is the New Year's night,
    to-morrow is the day,
And we are come for our right and for
    our ray,
As we used to do in old King Henry's
    Day:
Sing fellows, sing, hag-man, ha!
If you go to the bacon-flick cut me a
    good bit;
Cut, cut and low, beware of your maw.
Cut, cut, and round, beware of your
    thumb,
That me and my merry men may have
    some:
Sing, fellows, sing, hag-man, ha!
If you go to the black ark, bring me
    ten mark;
Ten mark ten pound, throw it down
    upon the ground,
That me and my merry men may have
    some;
Sing, fellows, sing, hag-man, ha!"

For the following lines, which the common people repeat upon this occasion, on New Year's Day, in some parts of France, I am indebted to M. Olivier:

"Aguilaneuf de céans
  On le voit a sa fenêtre,
  Avec son petit bonnet blanc,
  Il dit qu'il sera le Maître,
  Mettera le Pot au feu;
  Donnez nous, ma bonne dame,
  Donnez nous Aguilaneuf."

A writer in the "Gentleman's Magazine" for July, 1790, tells us: "In Scotland, till very lately (if not in the present time), there was a custom of distributing sweet cakes and a particular kind of sugared bread, for several days before and after the New Year; and on the last night of the old year (peculiarly called Hagmenai), the visitors and company made a point of not separating till after the clock struck twelve, when they rose, and, mutually kissing, wished each other a happy New Year. Children and others, for several nights, went about from house to house as guisarts, that is, disguised, or in masquerade dresses, singing:

"'Rise up, good wife, and be no swier
To deal your bread as long's your here,
The time will come when you'll be dead,
And neither want nor meal nor bread.'

"Some of those masquerades had a fiddle, and, when admitted into a house, entertained the company with a dramatic dialogue, partly extempore."

We read in the "Scotch Presbyterian Eloquence Displayed" that "it is ordinary among some plebians in the South of Scotland, to go about from door to door upon New Year's Eve, crying Hagmena, a corrupted word from the Greek for *holy month.* John Dixon, holding forth against this custom once, in a sermon at Kelso, says: 'Sirs, do you know what Hagmane signifies? It is, the Devil be in the house! that's the meaning of its Hebrew original.'" Page 102. Comp. *Tappy Tousie.*

Hair (i.) Customs.—The Countess of Dorset, Pembroke, and Montgomery, in her *Day-Book,* 1676, notes the visits of one Richard Goodgeon to Brougham Castle to cut her ladyship's hair. The custom of wearing the hair down the back loose, and a coif between the crown and the head, seems to have been preserved for a long time, and to have been in vogue on the Continent. The Princess Catherine of Aragon is described as wearing her hair so arranged in the contemporary narrative of her journey to England, previously to her espousal to Prince Arthur, son of Henry VII., and her ladies-in-waiting appear to have followed the same fashion. *Antiq. Repert.*, 1807, ii., p. 278. At the coronation of Elizabeth of York, in November, 1487, the Queen is described as wearing her fair yellow hair plain behind her back, with a caul of pipes over it, somewhat, perhaps, in the later Roman style, as we see it on coins. Compare *Marriage*, infrâ. This habit was not confined, however, to women, for the younger portraits of Henry VII. on his coins represent him with long unkempt hair, somewhat like that worn by Lorenzo dé Medici in the paintings or prints of him, by members of the Della Rovera, Visconti, Este, and other families on coins of nearly the same period, and by Louis XII. of France on his Franco-Italian money, as well as in fact the fashion followed in the 15th and 16th centuries by all male personages of rank on the Continent. On the title of an edition of Donatus the Grammarian, printed by Wynkyn de Worde about 1496, are four figures with their hair similarly left to fall over the neck and shoulders, and numerous illustrations of the fashion occur in Fairholt and Planché. The mode may be taken to have been borrowed from Italy.

Hair (ii.) Superstitions.—There is a vulgar notion that men's hair will sometimes turn grey upon a sudden and violent fright, to which Shakespear alludes in a speech of Falstaff to Prince Henry: "Thy father's beard is turned white with the news." Grey remarks: "This whimsical opinion was humorously bantered by a wag in a coffee-house; who, upon hearing a young gentleman giving the same reason for the change of his hair from black to grey, observed that there was no great matter in it, and told the company that he had a friend, who wore a coal-black wig, which was turned grey by a fright in an instant." Of late years the large sums offered by the trade for hair of a particular hue and length have overcome in many instances the old repugnance to part with this ornament, not only on the ground of pride or vanity, but on that of superstitious fear; for it was anciently a current vulgar belief, that if any portion of hair was left about, the birds would steal it to build their nests with, a fatal consequence to the owner, especially if the bird was a pie. Going still farther back, we arrive at the barbarous idea, of which Scott has availed himself in the "Pirate," that hair thrown into the sea had the power of kindling a storm, or (as Scott has it) of appeasing the waters. The hair from a calf's tail, inserted in the cow's ear, is supposed, or was formerly, to be efficacious in making the mother forget the loss of its young one; and the hair of a dog, which has bitten you, is held to be an antidote against any evil consequences, if given by the owner to the person bitten. But compare Hazlitt's *Proverbs*, 1882, p. 19.

Halcyon or **Kingfisher.**—See, as to the superstition about this bird, Nares, *Glossary*, 1859, in v., *Halcyon*.

Hallow Eve at Oxford. — See *Christmas Prince.*

Hallow E'en.—In North Wales, according to Pennant, there was a custom upon all Saints' Eve of making a great fire called Coel Coeth, when every family about an hour in the night makes a great bonfire in the most conspicuous place near the house, and when the fire is almost extinguished, every one throws a white stone into the ashes, having first marked it; then having said their prayers turning round the fire, they go to bed. In the morning, as soon as they are up, they come to search out the stones, and if any one of them is found wanting they have a notion that the person who threw it in, will die before he sees another All Saints' Eve. They have a custom also of distributing Soul Cakes on All Souls' Day, at the receiving of which poor people pray to God to bless the next crop of wheat. But many of these customs, even in Pennant's time, had fallen into disuse. In Owen's account of the Bards we read: "The autumnal fire is still kindled in North Wales, being on the eve of the first day of November, and is attended by many ceremonies; such as running through the fire and smoke, each casting a stone into the fire, and all running off at the conclusion to escape from the black short-tailed sow: then supping upon parsneps, nuts, and apples: catching at an apple suspended by a string with the mouth alone, and the same by an apple in a tub of water: each throwing a nut into the fire; and those that burn bright, betoken prosperity to the owners through the following year, but those that burn black and crackle, denote misfortune. On the following morning the stones are searched for in the fire, and if any be missing, they betide ill to those who threw them in." Owen prefaced these curious particulars by the following observations: "Amongst the first aberrations may be traced that of the knowledge of the great Huon, or the Supreme Being, which was obscured by the hieroglyphics or emblems of his different attributes, so that the grovelling minds of the multitude often sought not beyond those representations for the objects of worship and adoration. This opened an inlet for numerous errors more minute; and many superstitions became attached to their periodical solemnities, and more particularly to their rejoicing fires, on the appearance of vegetation in spring, and on the completion of harvest in autumn."

Hallow E'en in Scotland.—

Shaw, in his *Account of Moray*, seems to consider the festivity of this night as a kind of harvest home rejoicing: "A solemnity was kept," says he, "on the eve of the first of November as a thanksgiving for the safe in-gathering of the produce of the fields. This I am told, but have not seen it, is observed in Buchan and other counties, by having Hallow Eve fire kindled on some rising ground." Martin tells us that the inhabitants of St. Kilda, on the festival of All Saints, baked "a large cake, in the form of a triangle, furrowed round, and which was to be all eaten that night." "The passion of prying into futurity," says Burns, in the notes to his poem, "makes a striking part of the history of human nature, in its rude state, in all ages and nations; and it may be some entertainment to a philosophic mind to see the remains of it among the more unenlightened in our own." He gives therefore the principal charms and spells of this night, so big with prophecy to the peasantry in the West of Scotland. One of these by young women is by pulling stalks of corn: another by the blue clue: a third by eating the apple at the glass. Burns goes on to enumerate several other very observable customs of divination on this even of Allhallows. The first is "Sowing Hemp seed." The second is: "To winn three wechts o'naethings." Others are: "to fathom the stack three times," "to dip your left shirt sleeve in a burn where three Lairds' lands meet"; and the last is a singular species of divination "with three luggies or dishes." The minister of Logierait, in Perthshire, says: "On the evening of the 31st of October, O.S. among many others, one remarkable ceremony is observed. Heath, broom, and dressings of flax are tied upon a pole. This faggot is then kindled. One takes it upon his shoulders, and, running, bears it round the village. A crowd attend. When the first faggot is burnt out, a second is bound to the pole, and kindled in the same manner as before. Numbers of these blazing faggots are often carried about together, and when the night happens to be dark they form a splendid illumination." The minister of Callander says: "On All Saints' Even they set up bonfires in every village. When the bonfire is consumed, the ashes are carefully collected into the form of a circle. There is a stone put in near the circumference, for every person of the several families interested in the bonfire: and whatever stone is moved out of its place, or injured next morning, the person represented by that stone is de-

voted or fey, and is supposed not to live twelve months from that day. The people received the consecrated fire from the Druid priests next morning, the virtues of which were supposed to continue for a year." The minister of Kirkmichael, in Perthshire, says: "The practice of lighting bonfires on the first night of winter, accompanied with various ceremonies, still prevails in this and the neighbouring highland parishes. Formerly the Hallow Even fire, a relic of Druidism, was kindled in Buchan. Various magic ceremonies were then celebrated to counteract the influence of witches and demons, and to prognosticate to the young their success or disappointment in the matrimonial lottery. These being devoutly finished, the hallow fire was kindled, and guarded by the male part of the family. Societies were formed, either by pique or humour, to scatter certain fires, and the attack and defence were often conducted with art and fury."—"But now the hallow fire, when kindled, is attended by children only: and the country girl, renouncing the rites of magic, endeavours to enchant her swain by the charms of dress and of industry." Pennant tells us, in his "Tour in Scotland," that the young women there determine the figure and size of their husbands by drawing cabbages blind-fold on Allhallow Even. "The first ceremony of Hallow-e'en is pulling each a stock or plant of kail. They must go out, hand-in-hand, with eyes shut, and pull the first they meet with. Its being big or little, straight or crooked, is prophetic of the size and shape of the grand object of all their spells—the husband or wife. If any yird or earth stick to the root, that is tocher or fortune; and the taste of the custoc, that is the heart of the stem, is indicative of the natural temper and disposition. Lastly, the stems, or to give them their ordinary appellation, the runts, are placed somewhere above the head of the door; and the christian names of the people whom chance brings into the house, are, according to the priority of placing the runts, the names in question."

Of the scanty particulars known to us of the great Watt one is that his grandfather, Thomas Watt, was a baillie at Greenock, till his death in 1734, and in this capacity fined evil-doers on Hallow E'en night. The *Dundee Advertiser*, reporting the celebration of the old Scotish festival of "Hallowe'en" at Balmoral Castle in 1871, says:—"The demonstration has come to be known in Balmoral and throughout the district as 'The Queen's Hallowe'en;' and in accordance with the royal desire, and following the custom of past years, most of the people, both on the Balmoral and Abergeldie estates, turned out on Tuesday night, and formed a torchlight procession, which had a picturesque and imposing appearance. There were altogether from 180 to 200 torch-bearers; and her Majesty, with several members of the Royal family, viewed the scene with evident pleasure and satisfaction. Her Majesty remained for fully an hour an interested spectator of the proceedings. After the torch-bearers had promenaded for some time, the torches were heaped in a pile on the roadway a litle to the west, and in full view from the windows of the Castle. Empty boxes and other materials were soon added, and in a short time a splendid bonfire blazed famously, a gentle breeze helping to fan the flames. Her Majesty, the Prince and Princess Louise, the Princess Beatrice, and the ladies and gentlemen of the suite, then retired indoors, and took up positions at the windows to see the rest of the merry-making. Dancing was begun with great vigour round the bonfire. The demonstration culminated in a vehicle containing a well got-up effigy of the Hallowe'en witch being drawn to the fire by a band of sturdy Highlanders. The witch had a number of boys for a guard of honour, headed by the piper, and in the rear came Mr. Cowley, her Majesty's yager, whose workmanship the effigy was. The fire was kept up for a long time with fresh fuel, and when all had danced till they could almost dance no longer, the health of her Majesty was proposed by Mr. Cowley, and responded to with the utmost enthusiasm, accompanied by three times three rounds of vociferous cheering. Later in the evening the servants and others about the Castle enjoyed a dance in the ghillie hall. The ball broke up at an early hour on Wednesday morning." In a newspaper of 1877, this custom is described as still existing in Perthshire.

Hallowmass. — In the "Festyvall," 1511, is the following passage: "We rede in olde tyme good people wolde on All halowen daye bake brade and dele it for all crysten soules." On Allhallows' Day, or Hallowmass, it was an ancient English custom for poor persons and beggars to go a-souling, which signified to go round asking for money, to fast for the souls of the donors of alms or their kinsfolk. In the "Two Gentlemen of Verona," Shakespear makes Speed speak of some one puling, "like a beggar at Hallowmass." But the usage is referred to by Scot in his "Discovery of Witchcraft," 1584. In Shropshire (and perhaps elsewhere) the children still go souling, as they did in Aubrey's day, on Hallowmass, and they sing the following verses, for which I am indebted to a correspondent of "Notes and Queries":

"Soul! soul! for a soul-cake;
Pray, good mistress, for a soul-cake.
One for Peter, two for Paul,
Three for them that made us all.
Soul! soul! for an apple or two;
If you've got no apples, pears will do.
Up with your kettle, and down with your pan :
Give me a good big one, and I'll be gone.
                Soul! soul! &c.
An apple or pear, a plum or a cherry,
Is a very good thing to make us merry.
                Soul! soul! &c.

Some of the richer sorts of persons in Lancashire and Herefordshire (among the papists there) used to give cakes of oaten bread to the poor on this day: and they, in retribution of their charity, hold themselves obliged to say this old couplet:

—"God have your Saul,
Beens and all."

In the Cleveland country these loaves are called similarly Sau'mas Loaves. In the Whitby Glossary, they are described as "sets of square farthing cakes with currants in the centre, commonly given by bakers to their customers; and it was usual to keep them in the house for good luck." In this last respect they resembled the Good Friday bread and cross-buns. Mr. Brand's servant, who was a native of Warwickshire, told him that seedcakes at Allhallows were also usual in that country. Harvey, the Dublin conjurer, states that, on this Eve, which he characterizes as an "anile, chimerical solemnity," his servants demanded apples, ale, and nuts, and left him alone, while they went to enjoy themselves.

In the Churchwardens' Accounts of Heybridge, Essex, under 1517, are the following items: "Payed to Andrew Elyott, of Maldon, for newe mendynge of the bell knappelle agenste Hallowmasse, £0 1s. 8d. Item, payed to John Gidney, of Maldon, for a new bell-rope agenste Hallowmasse, £0 0s. 8d." In the time of Henry VIII. "the Vigil and ringing of bells all the night long upon Allhallow day at night," was abolished. In the appendix also to Strype's "Annals," the following injunction, made early in the reign of Elizabeth, occurs: "that the superfluous ringing of bels, and the superstitious ringing of bels at Alhallown tide, and at All Souls' Day with the two nights next before and after, be prohibited." It is stated in Kethe's Sermon preached at Blandford, 1570, that "there was a custom, in the papal times, to ring bells at Allhallow-tide for all Christian souls." No. 130 of "Mery Tales and Quicke Answers," 1567, however, is "Of the gentilman that checked his seruant for talke of ryngyng." "A Gentilman, brought vp at London in an In of court, was maryed, and kepte an house in the countrey : and as he sate at supper with his neyghbours aboute hym, vpon an alhalow daie at night, amonge other communication, he talked of the solemne ringyng of the belles (as was the vsage than)." The feast of Allhallows is said to drive the Finns almost out of their wits.

Hallowmass in Scotland.—

Martin, speaking of the Isle of Lewis, says that it was long before the minister there could persuade the people to relinquish a ridiculous custom they had of going by night on Hallow-tide to the Church of St. Mulvay, whence one of their number went into the sea up to his waist, with a cup of ale brewed for the occasion with malt contributed by the inhabitants (each family giving a peck), and pouring the liquid into the water, addressed a propitiatory allocution to a sea-god called Shony, who was supposed to have an influence over the crops. They then returned to church, observed a moment's dead silence, then extinguished at a given signal the candle on the altar, and proceeded to the fields, where the rest of the night was spent in revelry.

Hand, The.—

It is probable that if an exhaustive research into the subject were undertaken, the folk-lore of the Hand would occupy a considerable space, and develop many curious particulars.

The practice of holding up the right hand as a mark of submission or assent is extremely ancient and very widely spread. A small silver coin of Udalric, Duke of Bohemia (1012-37), bears on one side an open hand, which might have stood as a symbol of the Deity, or as a signification of allegiance to his suzerain ; and the same type occurs in pennies of Edward the Elder, (901-57) and Ethelred II. of England, who began to reign in 979. In a coin of the former the third and fourth fingers are closed in token of the bestowal of the Latin benediction. Barrington says that it was anciently the custom for a person swearing fealty "to hold his hands joined together between those of his lord ; the reason for which seems to have been that some Lord had been assassinated under pretence of paying homage ; but, while the tenant's hands continued in this attitude, it was impossible for him to make such an attempt." *Observations on the Statutes*, 1775, p. 206. In the *Squire of Low Degree*, where the King of Hungary takes the hero out of prison, and makes him swear to keep his counsel, it is said :

"The squyer there helde vp his hande,
His byddyng neuer he should withstande."

In the old story of *Adam Bel*, printed before 1536, and reproducing far earlier notions, we find the hand introduced where the outlaws come into the presence of the king:

"And when they came before our kyng,
As it was the lawe of the lande,
They kneled down without lettynge,
And eche held vp his hande."

Cetewayo held up his hand to our Queen, but he stood erect.

It may be suggested that the custom of elevating the right hand—the hand which usually held the weapon—may have been designed, on the same principle as that indicated by Barrington, at the outset as a guarantee of good faith and an assurance of security. In some Popish countries, and in our Canadian possessions, which include the old Colony of New France, the usage of holding up the right hand in making oath is supplemented by the obligation of doing so before a crucifix, which is suspended in the Court for that purpose. Where there is a search for weapons, the person concerned usually raises both his arms. Bingham has a quotation from St. Austin on superstitious observations, among which, he says, "You are told in a fit of convulsion or shortness of breath, to hold your left thumb with your right hand." Cited by Bourne, *Antiq. Vulg.*, c. 18. There is a superstition that the forefinger of the right hand is venomous, and is therefore not fit to touch any wound or sore. "That a yellow death-mould may never appear upon your hand, or any part of your body," occurs among the omens introduced in Holiday's "Marriage of the Arts," 1618. It is still usual in parts of the country to tap the back of the hand or the forearm thrice to avert a bad omen (*absit omen!*)when a person has been speaking of his or her good health or good fortune. This I saw done at Bowdon, near Manchester, in 1870, by the late Mrs. Alexander Ireland. Gaule ridicules the popular belief that "a great thick hand denotes one not only strong but stout : a little slender one a person weak but timorous : a long hand and long fingers betoken a man not only apt for mechanical artifice, but liberally ingenious ; but those short, on the contrary, note a foole and fit for nothing : an hard brawny hand signes dull and rude ; a soft hand, witty but effeminate ; an hairy hand, luxurious ; longe joynts signe generous, yet if they be thick withal, not so ingenious ; the often clapping and folding of the hands note covetous ; and their much moving in speech, loquacious; an ambidexter is noted for ireful, crafty, injurious; short and fat fingers mark a man out for intemperate and silly; but long and leane, for witty; if his fingers crook upward, that shewes long nailes and crooked, signe one brutish, ravenous, unchaste; very short nails, pale, and sharp, shew him false, subtile, beguiling; and so round nails, libidinous; but nails broad, plain, white, thin and reddish, are the token of a very good wit." *Mag-Astromancer posed*, 187. It is not unusual in a family to see some of the children follow the father in possessing long slender hands and fingers, and others the mother in having short and thick, or *vice versâ*. A moist hand is vulgarly accounted a sign of an amorous constitution. The Chief Justice, in "Henry IV., Part IV." enumerates a dry hand among the characteristics of age and debility.

The Cagots, a persecuted race in the Pyrenees, have been said to possess the power of making an apple decay by holding it within the hand, their hands being remarkable for moist heat. Hence I heard a lady from Penrith say gravely that her mother was thought to have Cagot blood in her, because her hand was unusually hot and moist.

According to Grose, the Hand of Glory at one time formed a staple article of belief among housebreakers in many parts of France, Germany, and Spain. From *Les Secrets du petit Albert*, 1751, he translates the following passage: "I acknowledge that I never tried the Secret of the Hand of Glory, but I have thrice assisted at the definitive judgement of certain criminals, who under the torture confessed having used it. Being asked what it was, how they procured it, and what were its uses and properties? they answered, first, that the use of the Hand of Glory was to stupefy those to whom it was presented, and to render them motionless insomuch that they could not stir any more than if they were dead; secondly that it was the hand of a hanged man; and thirdly, that it must be prepared in the manner following:—Take the hand, right or left, of a person hanged and exposed on the highway; wrap it up in a piece of a shroud or winding-sheet, in which let it be well squeezed, to get out any small quantity of blood that may have remain'd in it: then put it into an earthen vessel, with zimat, salt-petre, salt, and long pepper, the whole well powdered; leave it fifteen days in that vessel; afterwards take it out, and expose it to the noon-tide sun in the dog-days, till it is thoroughly dry; and if the sun is not sufficient, put it into an oven heated with fern and vervain: then compose a kind of candle with the fat of a hanged man, vir-

gin wax, and sisame of Lapland. The Hand of Glory is used as a candlestick to hold this candle, when lighted. Its properties are that wheresoever any one goes with this dreadful instrument, the persons to whom it is presented will be deprived of all power of motion. On being asked if there was no remedy or antidote to counteract this charm, they said the Hand of Glory would cease to take effect, and thieves could not make use of it, if the threshold of the door of the house, and other places by which they might enter, were anointed with an unguent composed of the gall of a black cat, the fat of a white hen, and the blood of a screech-owl; which mixture must necessarily be prepared during the dog-days." Grose adds that the mode of preparation appears to have been given by a judge. In the latter there is a striking resemblance to the charm in Macbeth. Grose says that "a dead man's hand is supposed to have the quality of dispelling tumours, such as wens, or swelled glands, by striking with it nine times the place affected. It seems as if the hand of a person dying a violent death was deemed particularly efficacious, as it very frequently happens that nurses bring children to be stroked with the hands of executed criminals, even whilst they are hanging on the gallows." He adds: "Moss growing on a human skull, if dried, powdered, and taken as snuff, will cure the head-ach." "The chips or cuttings of a gibbet or gallows, on which one or more persons have been executed or exposed, if worn next the skin, or round the neck in a bag, will cure the ague, or prevent it." Brand relates that he saw about 1790 some saw-dust, in which blood was absorbed, taken for the purpose of charming away some disease or other from off the scaffold on the beheading of one of the rebel lords in 1746. In a newspaper, 1777, it is said: "After he (Doctor Dodd) had hung about ten minutes, a very decently dressed young woman went up to the gallows in order to have a wen in her face stroked by the Doctor's hand, it being a received opinion among the vulgar that it is a certain cure for such a disorder. The executioner, having untied the doctor's hand, stroked the part affected several times therewith." But at the execution of Crowley the murderer at Warwick in 1845 a similar scene is described in the newspapers: "At least five thousand persons were mustered on this occasion to witness the dying moments of the unhappy culprit. . . . As is usual in such cases, a number of females were present, and scarcely had the soul of the deceased taken its farewell flight from its earthly tabernacle, than the scaffold was crowded by members of the 'gentler sex' afflicted with wens in the neck, with white swellings in the knees, &c., upon whose afflictions the cold clammy hand of the sufferer was passed to and fro for the benefit of his executioner."

I have somewhere read, that the custom of kissing the hand by way of salutation is derived from the manner in which the ancient Persians worshipped the sun : which was by first laying their hands upon their mouths, and then lifting them up by way of adoration. A practice which receives illustration from a passage in the Book of Job, a work replete with allusions to ancient manners—" If I beheld the sun, when it shined, or the moon walking in brightness ; and my heart hath been secretly enticed, or my mouth hath kissed my hand." *Archæologia*, xxxi., 26-7. In a paper in the *Antiquary* for 1891, on Handprints and Footprints on Stones, Margaret Stokes instances cases of hand-markings or impressions of hands or fingers associated in the popular mind abroad or in the East with miraculous properties.

Handball or **Jeu de Paume.**— One of the most ancient games, perhaps, in the world, which was known to the Greeks under the name of Sphairisis, and to the Romans as Pila. It is introduced on some of the coins of Larissa in Thessaly (Head's *Historia Numorum*, 1887, p. 254). It was originally, even among the modern nations, played with the hand, which was protected by a thick glove ; hence came the French jeu de paume ; and the racket was a comparatively recent improvement. Fitzstephen seems to allude to this sport, where he says : " After dinner, all the youths go into the fields, to play at the ball. The scholars of every school have their ball, or bastion, in their hands. The antient and wealthy men of the city come forth on horseback, to see the sport of the young men, and to take part of the pleasure, in beholding their agility. See Halliwell in v., where Stowe's *Survey*, 1720, is cited for the custom of playing at this on Easter-day for a tansy cake. The following beautiful description in the " Mons Catharinæ " may almost equally be applied to hand-ball :

" His datur orbiculum
Præcipiti—levem per gramina mittere
    lapsu :
Ast aliis, quorum pedibus fiducia
    major
Sectari, et jam jam salienti insistere
    prædæ ;
Aut volitantem altè longéque per aëra
    pulsum
Suspiciunt, pronosque inhiant, captan-
    que volatus,

Sortiti fortunam oculis ; manibusque
    paratis
Expectant propriorem, intercipiuntque
    caducum."—p. 6.
Compare what has been said under *Golf*.

Hand-Fasting.—There was a remarkable kind of marriage-contract among the ancient Danes called Hand-festing. It is mentioned in Ray's " Glossarium Northanhymbricum" in his collection of local words. " Hand-fæstning, promissio, quæ sit stipulata manu, sive cives fidem suam principi spondeant, sive mutuum inter se matrimonium inituri, a phrasi *fæsta* hand, quæ notat dextram dextræ jungere." Ihre " Glossar, Suio-Gothicum," in v. ; Ibid. in v. Bröllop. Brudkaup. In " The Christian State of Matrimony," 1543, p. 43 verso, we read : " Yet in thys thynge also must I warne everye reasonable and honest parson, to beware that in contractyng of maryage they dyssemble not, ner set forthe any lye. Every man lykewyse must esteme the parson to whom he is handfasted, none otherwyse than for his owne spouse, though as yet it be not done in the church ner in the streate.—After the handfastynge and makyng of the contracte yᵉ churchgoyng and weddyng shuld not be differed to longe, lest the wickedde sowe hys ungracious sede in the meane season. Into this dysh hath the Dyvell put his foote and mengled it wythe many wycked uses and coustumes. For in some places ther is such a maner, wel worthy to be rebuked, that at the handefasting ther is made a greate feaste and superfluous banc-ket, and even the same night are the two handfasted personnes brought and layed together, yea, certan wekes afore they go to the chyrch."

In 1794, the Minister of Eskdalemuir, Dumfries, mentioning an annual fair held time out of mind at the meeting of the Black and White Esks, now entirely laid aside, reported : " At that fair it was the custom for the unmarried persons of both sexes to choose a companion according to their liking, with whom they were to live till that time next year. This was called hand-fasting, or hand in fist. If they were pleased with each other at that time, then they continued together for life : if not they separated, and were free to make another choice as at the first. The fruit of the connection (if there were any) was always attached to the disaffected person. In later times, when this part of the country belonged to the Abbacy of Melrose, a priest, to whom they gave the name of Book i'bosom (either because he carried in his bosom a Bible, or perhaps a register of the marriages), came from time to time to confirm the marriages. This place is only a small distance from the Roman encampment of Castle-o'er. May not the fair have been first instituted when the Romans resided there? And may not the 'hand-fasting' have taken its rise from their manner of celebrating marriage, ex usu, by which, if a woman, with the consent of her parents or guardians, lived with a man for a year, without being absent three nights, she became his wife? Perhaps, when Christianity was introduced the form of marriage may have been looked upon as imperfect, without confirmation by a priest, and therefore, one may have been sent from time to time for this purpose." Compare *Betrothal, Trothplight,* &c., and Hazlitt's Monograph on Shakespear, 2nd edit. 1903, p. 9, where the case of the poet and his wife is treated.

Handicap.—Under September 18, 1660, Pepys notes, that some of his party, at the Mitre in Wood Street, "fell to handicap, a sport that I never knew before, which was very good"; but unfortunately he has furnished no particulars. Was it an early anticipation of a table game of race-horses?

Hand in and Hand Out.—Halliwell thus describes this amusement: "A company of young people are drawn up in a circle, when one of them, pitched upon by lot, walks round the band, and, if a boy, hits a girl, or if a girl, she strikes a boy whom she chooses, on which the party striking and the party struck run in pursuit of each other, till the latter is caught, whose lot it then becomes to perform the same part." It seems equally impossible to determine whether this was identical with the hand-out mentioned by Sir John Harington or with the Hand-in-Hand-out prohibited by 17 Edw. IV. c. 2. If the latter were the case, some licentious outgrowth from the original game has to be supposed, and it seems more logical to infer that the Edward statute had a different pastime in view, though Harington's Hand-out may very well have been the one objected to by the law, and still more or less pursued.

Handkerchief.—We gather from Howes's Additions to Stow's Chronicle that, in the reign of Queen Elizabeth, "it was the custome for maydes and gentilwomen to give their favorites, as tokens of their love, little handkerchiefs of about three or four inches square, wrought round about, and with a button or a tassel at each corner, and a little one in the middle, with silk and threed: the best edged with a small gold lace or twist, which being foulded up in foure crosse foldes, so as the middle might be seene,

gentlemen and others did usually weare them in their hatts, as favours of their loves and mistresses. Some cost six pence apiece, some twelve pence, and the richest sixteene pence." It appears, from a passage in Heywood's "Fayre Mayde of the Exchange," 1607, that it was not unusual to furnish these handkerchiefs with amorous devices worked in the corners. It is where Phillis brings the handkerchief to the Cripple of Fanchurch to be so embroidered. She says:

"Only this handkercher, a young gentlewoman
Wish'd me to acquaint you with her mind herein:
In one corner of the same, place wanton Love,
Drawing his bow, shooting an amorous dart—
Opposite against him an arrow in an heart:
In a third corner picture forth Disdain,
A cruel fate unto a loving vein;
In the fourth draw a springing laurel-tree,
Circled about with a ring of poesy."

In Sampson's play of "The Vow-Breaker," 1636, act i. sc. 1, Miles, a miller, is introduced telling his sweetheart, on going away to the wars: "Mistress Ursula, 'tis not unknowne that I have lov'd you; if I die, it shall be for your sake, and it shall be valiantly: I leave an hand-kercher with you: 'tis wrought with blew Coventry: let me not, at my returne, fall to my old song, she had a clowte of mine sowde with blew Coventry, and so hang myself at your infidelity." In an account of Dunton Church, in Barnstable Hundred, Essex, is the following remark: "Here has been a custom, time out of mind at the churching of a woman, for her to give a white Cambrick Handkerchief to the minister as an offering. Morant's *Essex*, i., 219. This is observed by Mr. Lewis in his 'History of the Isle of Thanet,' where the same custom is kept up."

Handsel.—The first money taken at a market or fair. It is still usual, both here and abroad, to spit on it, and in Italy and Portugal, in the case of an ordinary gift to the poor, the recipient will spit on it, press it to his forehead, and cross himself with the benefaction. Lemon's *Dictionary*, 1783, explains "Handsell," "the first money received at market, which many superstitious people will spit on, either to render it tenacious that it may remain with them, and not vanish away like a fairy gift, or else to render it propitious and lucky, that it may draw more money to it." It is quoted in the "Pedlar's Lamentation," an old ballad (circâ 1640):

> "Come, pretty fair maids, then make
>   no delay,
> But give me your handsel, and pack
>   me away."

Handsel Monday and Tuesday.—"The minister of Moulin, in Perthshire, informs us, that 'beside the stated fees, the master (of the parochial school there) receives some small gratuity, generally two-pence or three-pence, from each scholar, on Handsel-Monday or Shrove-Tuesday. It is worth mentioning that one William Hunter, a collier, was cured in the year 1758 of an inveterate rheumatism or gout, by drinking freely of new ale, full of barm or yest. The poor man had been confined to his bed for a year and a half, having almost entirely lost the use of his limbs. On the evening of Handsel Monday, as it is called, (i.e., the first Monday of the New Year, O.S.) some of his neighbours came to make merry with him. Though he could not rise, yet he always took his share of the ale, as it passed round the company, and, in the end, became much intoxicated. The consequence was, that he had the use of his limbs the next morning, and was able to walk about. He lived more than twenty years after this, and never had the smallest return of his old complaint."

Handy-Dandy.—By far the most copious and satisfactory account of this ancient English game is to be found in Mr. Halliwell's "Popular Rhymes and Nursery Tales," 1849, to which I must beg to refer the reader. The earliest allusion to it yet discovered is the passage in "Piers Ploughman," cited by Mr. Halliwell. Browne, in the fifth song of "Britannia's Pastorals," 1614, describes it as a boy's game:

> "Who so hath seene young lads (to
>   sport themselues),
> Run in a low ebbe to the sandy shelues:
> Where seriously they worke in digging
>   wels,
> Or building childish forts of cockle-
>   shels;
> Or liquid water each to other bandy;
> Or with the pibbles play at handy-
>   dandy—"

This game is mentioned in the dedication to Mr. William Lilly, by Democritus Pseudomantis, of Pantagruel's Prognostication, about 1645. But Halliwell (*Archaic Dictionary*, in v.) cites the Nomenclator of Adrianus Junius for some description of handy-dandy different from the ordinary game, "the play called handie dandie or the casting or pitching of the barre." Perhaps this was some foreign variety.

Cornelius Scriblerus, in forbidding certain sports to his son Martin till he is better informed of their antiquity, says: "Neither cross and pile, nor ducks and drakes, are quite so ancient as handy-dandy, tho' Macrobius and St. Augustine take notice of the first, and Minutius Foelix describes the latter; but handy-dandy is mentioned by Aristotle, Plato, and Aristophanes."

Hanging out the Besom.—The appearance of a besom on the top of a ship's mast is certainly not always an indication of the vessel being for sale, as it is also usual to place it there, when the craft is in port being cleaned or under repair. To hang out a besom from a house is in some places received as a sign that the master is from home. Comp. *Broom.*

Hangman's Wages.—In a letter to Edward King, Esq., President of the Society of Antiquaries, Dr. Pegge has entered with some minuteness and care into this question, and into the origin of the old, but now obsolete, practice of presenting the public executioner with thirteen pence halfpenny (the Scotish merk, minus two placks), as his wages for performing the unenviable task. Pegge's paper ought to be read as it stands without curtailment. But it is certainly strange that Brand and his editor should, both of them, have overlooked this point, which was worth at least a reference to the place, where it is discussed. It is generally known, that the hangman is ex-officio the sheriff's deputy, and that, in default of a person to execute the office, the sheriff himself would even now be obliged to act. It is observable, as regards the wages of the executioner, that by Halifax Law no man could be punished capitally for a theft not exceeding thirteenpence halfpenny: the coincidence is curious; but it may be nothing more than a coincidence. The earliest example of the grant of a prisoner's clothes to anyone is not to the executioner, but to the person whom the authorities chose to dig the grave. Thus in *Adam Bel*, 1536:—

> The Justice called to hym a ladde,
> Cloudesles clothes sholde he haue,
> To take the mesure of that yeman,
> And therafter to make hys graue.

It reads as if the Justice himself performed the office in this particular case; yet the sheriff was present.

Happy Foot.—In a statistical account of the parish of Forglen, co. Banff, drawn up about 1795, it is said: "There are happy and unhappy feet. Thus they wish bridegrooms and brides a happy foot, and to prevent any bad effect, they salute those they meet on the road with a kiss. It is hard, however, if any misfortune happens when you are passing, that you should be blamed, when neither you nor your feet ever thought of the matter." *Stat. Acc.* xiv., 541.

Hare.—The ancient Romans made use of hares for the purposes of divination. They were never killed for the table. Borlase tells us of "a remarkable way of divining related of Bonduca or Boadicea Queen of the Iceni—when she had harangued her soldiers to spirit them up against the Romans, she opened her bosom and let go a hare, which she had there concealed, that the augurs might thence proceed to divine. The frighted animal made such turnings and windings in her course, as, according to the then rules of judging, prognosticated happy success. The joyful multitude made loud huzzas, Boadicea seized the opportunity, approved their ardour, led them straight to their enemies, and gained the victory." *Antiq. of Cornwall*, p. 135. 'Tis perhaps hence that they have been accounted ominous by the vulgar. *Cæsar's Comment,.* p. 89. An opinion was formerly entertained both in England and abroad, that a hare crossing the path of any one was a portent of misfortune, and a warning to return, or retrace one's steps; and of this almost universal superstition our own early writers, and those of the Continent, abound in confirmations. Sir Thomas Browne tells us, "if an hare cross the highway, there are a few above three score years that are not perplexed thereat, which, notwithstanding, is but an augurial terror, according to that received expression Inauspicatum dat iter oblatus lepus. And the ground of the conceit was probably no greater than this, that a fearful animal, passing by us, portended unto us something to be feared : as, upon the like consideration, the meeting of a fox presaged some future imposture. These good or bad signs sometimes succeeding according to fears or desires, have left impressions and timorous expectations in credulous minds for ever." Home adds: ". . . In so much as some in company with a woman great with childe have upon the crossing of such creatures, cut or torn some of the clothes off that woman with childe, to prevent (as they imagined) the ill luck that might befall her. I know I tell you most true; and I hope in such a subject as this, touching these superstitions, I shall not offend in acquainting you with these particulars." *Demonologie*, 1650, p. 50. Among the Forfarshire fishermen, the portent of the hare crossing the path, which in many other places is regarded as unlucky, has sufficient influence to deter any one from going out. See Machin's "Dumb Knight," 1608, Hazlitt's Dodsley, x; Hall's "Characters of Vertues and Vices,"

1608; Melton's "Astrologaster," 1620, p. 45; Burton's "Anatomy of Melancholy," 1621, p. 214; Ellison's "Trip to Benwel," p. lx.; Mason's "Anatomie of Sorcery," 1612, p. 85; Gaule's "Mag-Astromancer Posed," etc., p. 181; Ramsey's "Elminthologia," 1668, p. 271. Alexander ab Alexandro, "Geniales Dies," vol. v. p. 13; Bebelius, "Facetiæ," 1516, sign. E 3; Townson's "Travels in Hungary." Pepys seems to have believed in the virtues of a hare's foot as a preservative against the colic; but he did not at first apply it properly; for in the *Diary*, January 20, 1664-5, there is this odd entry : "Homeward, in my way buying a hare, and taking it home, which arose upon my discourse to-day with Mr. Batten, in Westminster Hall, who showed me my mistake, that my hare's foot hath not the joynt to it, and assures me he never had his cholique since he carried it about with him; and it is a strange thing how fancy works for I no sooner handled his foot, but I became very well, and so continue."

Hare and Hounds.—An out-door sport, where a youth (the hare) starts in advance, and traverses a line of country, dropping, as he proceeds, something to indicate his route, and is followed by the others—the hounds, who have to get up to him, and capture him. All are dressed in jerseys, and the amusement seems to have nothing to recommend it, as the exercise is too violent to suit many boys or young men. Saturday afternoons during all seasons of the year are occupied in this way by seekers of active recreation.

Harper. — Puttenham speaks of "blind harpers or such like tauerne minstrels that give a fit of mirth for a groat, and their matters being for the most part stories of old time, as the Tale of Sir Topas, the Reportes of Bevis of Southampton, Guy of Warwicke, Adam Bell, and Clymme of the Clough, and such other old romances, or historicall rimes, made purposely for recreation of the common people at Christmasse diners and Brideales, and in tauernes and ale-houses, and such other places of base resort." There is the tract by Martin Parker, 1641, entitled *The Poet's Blind Man's Bough; or, Have among You, my Blind Harpers.* Possibly the blindness, real or supposed, was found remunerative.

Harvest.—Macrobius tells us that, among the ancients, the masters of families, when they had got in their harvest, were wont to feast with their servants, who had laboured for them in tilling the ground. In exact conformity to this, it is common among us, when the fruits of the earth are gathered in and laid in their proper repositories, to provide a plentiful supper for the harvest men and the servants of the family. At this entertainment all are in the modern revolutionary idea of the word perfectly equal. Here is no distinction of persons; but master and servant sit at the same table, converse freely together, and spend the remainder of the night in dancing, singing, &c., in the most easy familiarity. *Saturn. Conviv.* cap. 10. Durandus mentions that it was formerly usual among the Gentiles for the servants, both male and female, to take their masters' or employers' places after the gathering-in of the harvest, and usurp their authority for a time. *Rationale.* vi., 86. Bourne thinks the original of both these customs is Jewish, and cites Hospinian, who tells us that the heathens copied this custom of the Jews, and at the end of their harvest, offered up their first fruits to the gods. For the Jews rejoiced and feasted at the getting in of the harvest. This festivity is undoubtedly of the most remote antiquity. In the "Roman Calendar" I find the following observation on the eleventh of June: (the harvests in Italy are much earlier than with us). "The season of reapers, and their custom with rustic pomp." Theophylact mentions "Scenopegia, quod celebrant in gratiarum actionem propter convectas Fruges in Mense Septembri. Tunc enim gratias agebant Deo, convectis omnibus fructibus, &c."— Theoph. in 7 cap. Joan. Vacuna, so called, as it is said, *à vacando,* among the ancients, was the name of the goddess to whom rustics sacrificed at the conclusion of harvest.

That men in all nations where agriculture flourished should have expressed their joy on this occasion by some outward ceremonies, has its foundation in the nature of things. Sowing is hope; reaping, fruition of the expected good. To the husbandman, whom the fear of wet, blights, &c., had harrassed with great anxiety, the completion of his wishes could not fail of imparting an enviable feeling of delight. Festivity is but the reflex of inward joy, and it could hardly fail of being produced on this occasion, which is a temporary suspension of every care. The respect shown to servants at this season seems to have sprung from a grateful sense of their good services. Every thing depends at this juncture on their labour and dispatch. In Carew's "Survey of Cornwall," p. 20, verso, "an ill kerned or saved harvest" occurs. We do not recognise among more modern European societies any analogue to the Roman *Fornacalia* or rites to the goddess Fornax for the happy taking of the corn, which concluded, with the harvest itself and other early local institutions, with a period of licence, known as *Stultorum Feriæ.* The *Fornacalia,* traditionally established by Numa, was held on the 18th of February.

Harvest in Scotland. Moresin tells us that Popery, in imitation of this, brings home her chaplets of corn, which she suspends on poles, that offerings are made on the altars of her tutelar gods, while thanks are returned for the collected stores, and prayers are made for future ease and rest. Images too of straw or stubble, he adds, are wont to be carried about on this occasion; and that in England he himself saw the rustics bringing home in a cart a figure made of corn, round which men and women were singing promiscuously, preceded by a drum or piper. *Papatus,* p. 173, v. *Vacona.* Johnson tells us, in his "Tour to the Hebrides," that he saw the harvest of a small field in one of the Western Islands. The strokes of the sickle were timed by the modulation of the harvest song, in which all their voices were united. They accompany, in the Highlands, every action which can be done in equal time with an appropriate strain, which has, they say, not much meaning, but its effects are regularity and cheerfulness. The ancient proceleusmatic song, by which the rowers of gallies were animated, may be supposed to have been of this kind. There is now an oar song used by Hebridians. In the "Statistical Account of Scotland," it is said, "There is one family on the Cupar-Grange Estate, which has been there a century. The former tenant in that family kept a piper to play to his shearers all the time of harvest, and gave him his harvest-fee. The slowest shearer had always the drone behind him. In Henry IV.'s time, the French peasants were accustomed to regale after the getting in of the harvest, on what was called a harvest Gosling. Armstrong says: "Their harvests are generally gathered by the middle of June: and, as the corn ripens, a number of boys and girls station themselves at the edges of the fields, and on the tops of the fence walls, to fright away the small birds with their shouts and cries. This puts one in mind of Virgil's precept in the first book of his Georgicks,

'Et sonitu terrebis aves'——

and was a custom, I doubt not, among the Roman farmers, from whom the ancient Minorquins learned it. They also use, for the same purpose, a split reed: which makes a horrid rattling, as they shake it with their hands. *Hist. of Minorca,* 177. A personal friend of the writer saw a farmer near Edinburgh, about ten years ago, personally superintending the inning process, assisted by his daughter; and he was a man of large fortune.

Harvest Doll.—An old woman,

who in a case of this nature is respectable authority, at a village in Northumberland, informed Mr. Brand, that in the first half of the 18th century, they used every where to dress up something similar to the figure above described, at the end of harvest, which was caled a Harvest Doll or Kern Baby. This northern word is plainly a corruption of corn baby or image, as is the Kern Supper or Corn Supper. Comp. *Harvest.*

Harvest Home. — In Tusser's "Husbandry," 1580, under August, are the following lines alluding to this festivity :

"In harvest time, harvest folke, servants and all,
Should make, alltogither, good cheere in the hall,
And fill out the black bol of bleith to their song,
And let them be merie al harvest time long.
Once ended thy harvest, let none be begilde,
Please such as did please thee, man, woman, and child.
Thus doing, with alway suche helpe as they can,
Thou winnist the praise of the labouring man."

On which is this note in Hilman : "This, the poor labourer thinks, crowns all, a good supper must be provided, and every one that did any thing towards the inning must now have some reward, as ribbons, laces, rows of pins to boys and girls, if never so small, for their encouragement; and, to be sure, plumb-pudding. The men must now have some better than best drink, which, with a little tobacco and their screaming for their largesses, their business will soon be done." *Tusser Redivivus*, 1710, ed. 1749, 104. In another part of Tusser's work under "The Ploughman's Feast Days," are these lines :

"For all this good feasting, yet art thou not loose,
Til ploughman thou givest his harvest home goose ;
Though goose go in stubble, I passe not for that,
Let goose have a goose, be she lean, be she fat."

On which Hilman remarks: "The goose is forfeited, if they overthrow during harvest." In his "Travels," in England and elsewhere, temp. Elizabeth, speaking of Windsor, Hentzner says, "As we were returning to our inn we happened to meet some country people celebrating their harvest home ; their last load of corn they crown with flowers, having besides an image richly dressed, by which perhaps they

would signify Ceres: this they keep moving about, while men and women, men and maid-servants, riding through the streets in the cart, shout as loud as they can till they arrive at the barn." In Cornwall, it should seem, they have "Harvest Dinners" ; and these, too, not given immediately at the end of the harvest. "The harvest dinners," says Carew, "are held by every wealthy man, or, as we term it, every good liver, between Michaelmas and Candlemas, whereto he inviteth his next neighbours and kindred. And, though it beare only the name of a dinner, yet the ghests take their supper also with them, and consume a great part of the night after in Christmas rule. Neither doth the good cheere wholly expire (though it somewhat decrease) but with the end of the weeke." *Survey*, 1602, 68. Stevenson thus glances at the customs of harvest home. "The furmenty pot welcomes home the harvest cart, and the garland of flowers crowns the captain of the reapers; the battle of the field is now stoutly fought. The pipe and the tabor are now busily set a-work, and the lad and the lass will have no lead on their heels. O, 'tis the merry time wherein honest neighbours make good cheer and God is glorified in his blessings on the earth." *Twelve Moneths*, 1661, p. 37 (August).

"Hoacky is brought
Home with hallowin,
Boys with Plumb-cake,
The cart following.

Poor Robin for 1676. A newspaper for 1773 says : "A few days ago a melancholy accident happened near Worcester at a harvest home. As near thirty persons were coming from the field in a waggon, it overturned, whereby great part of the company had one or other of their limbs broken, or were dangerously bruised, and one young wcman was killed on the spot." Thomson, in his "Seasons," (Autumn), has left us a beautiful description of this annual festivity of harvest home. Other terms for it are the *Mell, Kern,* or *Chern Supper,* and the *Ingathering* or *Inning.* Cuthbert Bede, in *Notes and Queries*, October 12, 1875, gives the following account of a Rutland custom :— "On Wednesday evening, Sep. 18, 1875, I was at a farm-house in the county of Rutland, and saw "the last load" brought in. As marking the conclusion of harvest, and, as they termed it, "harvest home," the load (of beans) was decorated with green boughs; and on the top of the load were several children, who were lustily cheering as the waggon came lumbering along the road. It was eight o'clock, and a resplendent harvest-moon was just rising over the trees that girdled the old church hard by the farmer's stackyard. A company of us stood at his gate to watch the scene. Near to us, but concealed by the hedge, were the female and other servants, ready prepared with buckets of water and pitchers, and also with baskets of apples. As the last load passed us, with its drivers and occupants shouting "Harvest home!" and cheering, the liers-in-wait behind the hedge suddenly rose up to view and pelted the waggon-load with a shower of apples, and also dashed pitchers full of water over men, horses, children and beans. This had to be done quickly, while the waggon was moving by; so they who ran the gauntlet were not much damaged, and the children on top of the load got more apples than water, and were proportionately thankful and applausive. But the waggon had to go to the bean-stack in the well-filled stack-yard, whither it was followed by those who had already received it with the salute of apples and water, and where also all the labourers on the farm were waiting for it. A liberal supply of buckets of water was there at hand for the reception of the last load and its attendants; and we followed to see the fun. As the waggon drew up at the appointed spot, and the ladder was reared against its side to assist the children from the top of the load, the signal was given for a species of free fight with buckets and pails of water. The children evidently did not relish their douche bath, and were helped down from the top of the bean-load, sobbing bitterly, and bewailing their soaked condition. Friend and foe seemed to be treated with equal impartiality, and the water was scooped out of the buckets and dashed indiscriminately over male and female. A reverend gentleman, who was making off round the stack, was not recognized (let us hope!) in the semi-darkness, and, falling between two fires, received a ducking. I had just left him, in order to follow the sobbing children and administer to them pecuniary comfort; so I escaped with dry clothes, being, I think, the only one on the spot who did so."

Harvest Home Song.—Formerly, it should seem, there was a harvest home song. Kennett tells us : " Homines de Hedyngton ad curiam Domini singulis annis inter festum S. Michaelis et festum S. Martini venient cum toto et pleno Dyteno, sicut hactenus consueverunt." This, he adds, is singing harvest home. *Gloss. to Paroch. Antiq. v. Dytenum.* Mr. Brand notes : " I have often observed at Newcastle-upon-Tyne (and I suppose it is the same in other sea-port towns) that the sailors, in heaving their anchors, made use of a similar kind of song. In ploughing with oxen in Devonshire, I observed a song of the same kind."

Harvest Lord and Lady.—The two principal reapers are known in the eastern counties as the Harvest Lord and Lady. The former, says Forby, used to be addressed as " My Lord." He directs the operations of his companions. There is no other dignity attached to the rank, unless it be the first and second place respectively at the harvest home. In the *Penny Magazine* for November, 1835, is a representation of the Hop Queen, who appears to be the same as the harvest lady above mentioned. Possibly she, with a male associate, *Lord* or *King*, presided over the festivities at the conclusion of the work. Comp. *Harvest Queen* below.

Harvest Queen. — Hutchinson, speaking of the parish of Easington, in Durham, observes, " In this part of the country are retained some ancient customs evidently derived from the Romans, particularly that of dressing up a figure of Ceres, during harvest, which is placed in the field while the reapers are labouring, and brought home on the last evening of reaping, with musick and great acclamation. After this a feast is made, called the mell-supper, from the ancient sacrifice of mingling the new meal." *Hist. of Durham*, ii., 583. " I have seen," he elsewhere says, " in some places an image apparelled in great finery, crowned with flowers, a sheaf of corn placed under her arm, and a scycle in her hand, carried out of the village in the morning of the conclusive reaping day, with musick and much clamour of the reapers, into the field, where it stands fixed on a pole all day, and when the reaping is done, is brought home in like manner. This they call the Harvest Queen, and it represents the Roman Ceres." *Hist. of North.*, ii., 17. Clarke in his "Travels," incidentally observes : " At the Hawkie (at Cambridge), as it is called, I have seen a clown dressed in woman's clothes, having his face painted, his head decorated with ears of corn, and bearing about him other symbols of Ceres, carried in a waggon, with great pomp and loud shouts, through the streets, the horses being covered with white sheets; and when I enquired the meaning of the ceremony, was answered by the people that they were drawing the Harvest Queen."

Hawkie.—The name of a place at Cambridge, formerly dedicated to the holding of the fair, and apparently a corruption of the Breton *Hourquie*, Latin *Furcia*. See Hazlitt's *Coins of Europe*, 1893, p. 134 ; and see above.

Head.—Gaule mentions as a notion current in his day (in which he by no means concurred :"That a great head is an omen, or a sign of a sluggish fool "—this reminds one of the old saying, " Great head and little wit")—" A little head of a subtile knave. A middle head, of a liberal head. A round head, of a senselesse irrational fellow. A sharp head, of an impudent sot," &c. Our author's remarks, or rather citation of the remarks, upon round heads above, seem not to have been over-well timed, for this book was printed in 1652, and is dedicated to Cromwell. *Mag-Astromancer posed*, p. 183.

Head-Ache.—John London, writing to Cromwell, about 1536, mentions a recipe for the head-ache, which was supposed at that time to have great virtue. He writes: "In the body of the Churche at Tellisford Cross (or Crutched) Friars, Somersetshire, wasse an image at an awters end callid Mayden Cutbrogh, and vnder her feete wasse a trowgh of wodde descending vnder the awter wich wasse hollow. Thyder resortyd such as wer trobely with the hedde ache, or hadde any slottiche wydowes lockes, viz. here growen to gether in a tufte. Ther must they putt in to the trowgh a pecke of oots, and when they wer oons slydyd vndre the awter, the Crosse Fryers schuld behynd the awter pryvily stele them owt, and the sykk person must geve to the Fryer a peny for a pynte of these Mayden Cutbrogh owts, and then ther heds schuld ak no more till the next tyme."

Head-Penny.—A payment in former times to a parson for burying a poor parishioner or otherwise; but it was the old silver coin. The money was also applicable to the purchase of bread and wine. Comp. *Easter Offering.*

Heads and Points.—A child's game, played with pins. It seems to have been popular in Scotland in 1724. Chambers, *Dom. Annals*, iii., 491.

Heads or Tails.—This is the modern game of toss, and corresponds to the *Capita aut Navia* of the Romans. It was known, it appears, in Edward II.'s time, and formed a favourite diversion of that prince, who won and lost money at it, as is to be collected from entries among his privy purse expenses: "Item paid to the King himself to play at Cross and Pile by the hands of Richard de Mereworth, the receiver of the Treasury, 12 pence. Item paid there to Henry, the King's barber, for money which he lent to the King to play at cross and pile. . . 5s. Item paid there to Peres Barnard Usher of the King's Chamber money which he lent to the King, and which he lost at cross and pile to monsieur Robert Wattewylle. . . eightpence." In the preface to *Plantagruel's Prognostication* (about 1645) it is called Cross *or* Pile.

Healths.—The Greeks and Romans used at their meals to make libations, pour out, and even drink wine, in honour of the gods. The classical writings abound with proofs of this. The Greeks had the practice of toasting the nine Muses as Three times Three, of which the origin and antiquity may not be generally known, and which is yet followed both in England and abroad.

The Greek and Roman writers have also transmitted to us accounts of the graceful custom of drinking to the health of our benefactors and of our acquaintances:

> " Pro te, fortissime, vota
> Publica suscipimus: Bacchi tibi sumimus haustus."

It appears that the men of gallantry among the Romans used to take off as many glasses to their respective mistresses as there were letters in the name of each. Thus Martial:

> " Six cups to Nævia's health go quickly round,
> And be with seven the fair Justina's crown'd."

How exceedingly similar to our modern custom of saying to each of the company in turn ,"Give us a lady to toast," is the following:

> " Da puere ab summo, age tu interibi ab infimo da suavium."

Plauti *Asinaria*, v. 2. In the "Maner of the tryumphes at Caleys & Bullen," 1532, Henry VIII. and the French king are described as drinking to each other: "And than they dyd lyght of theyr horses & dranke eche to other/the frenshe kyng dranke fyrst to our kynge/ & whan they had dronke/ they embraced eche other agayn with great loue/" Francis I. drank before his guest in this case, perhaps, in order to prove that there was no foul play. Pasquier, in his "Recherches," p. 501, mentions that Mary, Queen of Scots, previously to her execution, drank to all her attendants, desiring them to pledge her. See what the same author has said in p. 785 of his work concerning this custom. In Decker's *Lanthorne and Candle-light*, 1608, sign. H 2, we have: "The third man squires her to a play, which being ended, and the wine offered and taken (for she's no Recusant, to refuse anything) him she leanes too ; and being set vpon by a fourth, him she answers at his own weapon, sups with him, and drincks Vpsie Freeze. . . ." In the second part of Dekker's " Honest Whore," 1630, signat. 1 verso, is the following: "Will you fall on your maribones and pledge this health, 'tis to my mistris?" So in Marmion's " Antiquary," act ii. :

" Drank to your health whole nights in
　Hippocrase,
Upon my knees, with more religion
Than e'er I said my prayers, which
　Heaven forgive me."
Pledging is again mentioned in act iv.:
" To our noble Duke's health, I can drink
no lesse, not a drop lesse; and you his
servants will pledge me, I am sure."
Braithwaite says: " These cups proceed
either in order or out of order.　In order,
when no person transgresseth or drinkes
out of course, but the cup goes round according to their manner of sitting: and
this we call an health cup, because in our
wishing or confirming of any one's health,
bare-headed and standing, it is performed
by all the company.　It is drunke without
order, when the course or method of order
is not observed, and that the cup passeth
on whomsoever we shall appoint."Again :
" Some joyne two cups one upon another
and drinke them together."　*Laws of
Drinking*, 1617, p. 9.　It seems to have
been formerly usual for a man in company,
not contented with taking what he chooses,
to bind another to drink the same quantity that he does.　In the following passage one proposes a health which another
pledges to honour by drinking to it an
equal quantity with him that proposed
it :
" Oh, how they'll wind men in, do what
　they can,
By drinking healths, first unto such a
　man,
Then unto such a woman.　Then they'll
　send
An health to each man's mistresse or his
　friend ;
Then to their kindreds or their parents
　deare,
They needs must have the other jug of
　beere.
Then to their captains and commanders
　stout,
Who for to pledge they think none shall
　stand out,
Last to the King and Queen, they'll
　have a cruse,
Whom for to pledge they think none
　dare refuse."

Ward of Ipswich, in his *Woe to Drunkards*, 1622, strenuously, but vainly exhorted his countrymen to abandon " that
foolish and vicious custome, as Ambrose
and Basil call it, of drinking healths, and
making that a sacrifice to God for the
health of others, which is rather a sacrifice to the Devill, and a bane of their
owne."　It appears from the same writer,
that it was a custom to drink healths at
that time upon their bare knees.　The
author is speaking of pot-wits and spirits
of the buttery, " who never bared their
knees to drink healthes, nor ever needed

to whet thir wits with wine, or arme their
courage with pot-harnesse." In Braithwaite's " Times Curtaine drawne," 1621,
is the subsequent passage :
" I was conjured by my kissing friend
To pledge him but an health, and then
　depart,
Which if I did I'de ever have his heart.
I gave assent ; the health five senses
　were,
(Though 'scarce one sense did 'twixt us
　both appeare)
Which as he drunk I pledg'd ; both
　pledg'd and drunk,
Seeing him now full charg'd, behinde I
　shrunke," &c.
In Marmion's " Antiquary," 1641, act iv.,
is the following passage : " Why they are
as jovial as twenty beggars, drink their
whole cups, sixe glasses at a health."
Douce's MSS. Notes say : " It was the
custom in Beaumont and Fletcher's time,
for the young gallants to stab themselves
in the arms or elsewhere, in order to drink
the healths of their mistresses, or to write
their names in their own blood." So, in
a song to a Scotish tune, the following
lines occur :
" I stab'd mine arm to drink her health,
　The more the fool I, the more the fool
　　I," &c.
And
" I will no more her servant be
　The wiser I, the wiser I,
　Nor pledge her health upon my
　　knee," &c.
At Christmas, 1623, the gentlemen of the
Middle Temple, according to one of the
Harleian MSS., quoted in the " Life of
Sir Simonds D'Ewes," drank a health to
Princess Elizabeth who, with her husband
the King of Bohemia, was then in great
straits, and stood up, one after the other,
their cup in one hand, and their sword in
the other, and pledged her, swearing to
die in her service, which is said to have
greatly offended James I. Herrick writes :
" Remember us in cups full crown'd,
And let our Citie-health go round,
Quite through the young maids and the
　men,
To the ninth number, if not tenne ;
Untill the fired chestnuts leape
For Joy to see the Fruits ye reape.
From the plumpe Challice and the Cup
That tempts till it be tossed up."
Hesperides, 1648, pp. 146, 87.　The fol-
lowing is a curious epigram of Owen on
this subject :
" Quo tibi potarum plus est in ventre
　　Salutum,
　Hoc minus epotis, hisce Salutis habes.
Una salus sanis, nullam potare Salutem,
　Non est in potâ vera Salute salus."
Part I. lib. ii. Ep. 42.

561. HEALTH.

" Even from my heart much health I
　wish,
No health I'll wash with drink,
Health wish'd, not wash'd, in words,
　not wine,
To be the best I think."

Witts Recreat., 1667. Evelyn, speaking
of taverns, says, " Your L. will not believe me that the ladies of greatest quality
suffer themselves to be treated in one of
these taverns, but you will be more as-
tonisht when I assure you that they
drink their crowned cups roundly, strain
healths through their smocks, daunce after
the fiddle, kiss freely, and term it an honourable treat. There is a sort of perfect
debauchees, who stile themselves Hectors,
that in their mad and unheard of revels,
pierce their veins to quaff their own blood,
which some of them have drank to that
excess, that they died of intemperance. . .
I don't remember, my Lord, ever to have
known (or very rarely), a health drank in
France, no, not the King's; and if we
say *a vôtre Santé, Monsieur,* it neither
expects pledge or ceremony. 'Tis here so
the custome to drink to every one at the
table, that by the time a gentleman has
done his duty to the whole company, he
is ready to fall asleep, whereas with us,
we salute the whole table with a single
glass onely. *Character of England,*
1659, pp. 34-6-7. In his *Diary*, June 19,
1663, Pepys observes: " To the Rhenish
wine-house, where Mr. Moore showed us
the French manner, when a health is
drunk, to bow to him that drunk to you,
and then apply yourself to him, whose
lady's health is drunk, and then to the
person that you drink to, which I never
knew before; but it seems it is now the
fashion." In 1666, at the Bear Garden,
on a thanks-giving day, the Diarist drank
Mercer's health with his hat off. But in
1668, at Sir George Carteret's at Cran-
bourne, the party drank to the Duke of
York's health on their knees in turn, the
King included. *Pepys*, 23rd Sept. 1668.
M. Jorevin, who was here in Charles
II.'s time, speaking of Worcester and the
Stag Inn there, observes: "According to
the custom of the country, the landladies
sup with strangers and passengers, and if
they have daughters, they are also of the
company, to entertain the guests at table
with pleasant conceits, where they drink
as much as the men. But what is to me
the most disgusting in all this is, that
when one drinks the health of any person
in company, the custom of the country
does not permit you to drink more than
half the cup, which is filled up, and presented to him or her whose health you
have drank." *Antiq. Repert*, 1808, iv.,

563. In " Folly in Print," 1667, in a
catch made before the King's coming to
Worcester with the Scotish army, is something to the purpose:

" Each man upon his back
Shall swallow his sack,
　This health will endure no shrink-
　　ing;
The rest shall dance round
Him that lyes on the ground;
　Fore me this is excellent drinking."

Misson has some curious remarks on the
manner of drinking healths in England
in his time. An author who wrote at
about the same period, alludes to a custom at the Old Crown Inn, at Ware, by
which every one coming to see the great
bed there preserved, was expected to
drink " a small can of beer," and to repeat some health, but the gentleman unluckily forgot what this was. *A Journey
from London to Scarborough*, 1734, p. 4.

Healths in Scotland.—Ramsay
mentions as in use among the Scots, " Hy
jinks," " a drunken game, or new project
to drink and be rich; thus, the quaff or
cup is filled to the brim, then one of the
company takes a pair of dice, and after
crying Hy-jinks, he throws them out:
the number he casts up points out the
person must drink, he who threw, beginning at himself number one, and so round
till the number of the persons agree with
that of the dice, (which may fall upon himself if the number be within twelve); then
he sets the dice to him, or bids him take
them: he on whom they fall is obliged to
drink, or pay a small forfeiture in money;
then throws, and so on: but if he forgets
to cry Hy-jinks he pays a forfeiture into
the bank. Now he on whom it falls to
drink, if there be anything in bank worth
drawing, gets it all if he drinks. Then,
with a great deal of caution he empties
his cup, sweeps up the money, and orders
the cup to be filled again, and then
throws; for, if he err in the articles, he
loses the privilege of drawing the money.
The articles are (1) drink. (2) draw. (3)
fill. (4) cry Hy-jinks. (5) Count just.
(6) Chuse your doublet man, viz. when two
equal numbers of the dice are thrown, the
person whom you chuse must pay a double
of the common forfeiture, and so must you
when the dice is in his hand. A rare project this," adds honest Allan, " and no
bubble, I can assure you; for a covetous
fellow may save money, and get himself
as drunk as he can desire in less than an
hour's time." The following passage is
curious: " Now to drink all out every
man: (Drinking and Carrowsing) which
is a fashion as little in use amongst us, as
yᵉ terme itselfe is barbarous and strange:
I meane, Ick bring you, is sure a foule

thing of itselfe, and in our countrie so coldly accepted yet, that we must not go about to bring it in for a fashion. If a man doe quaffe or carrouse unto you, you may honestly say nay to pledge him, and geveing him thankes, confesse your weaknesse, that you are not able to beare it: or else to doe him a pleasure, you may for curtesie sake taste it: and then set downe the cup to them that will, and charge yourselfe no further. And although this, Ick bring you, as I have heard many learned men say, hath beene an auncient custome in Greece: and that the Grecians doe much commend a good man of that time, Socrates by name, for that hee sat out one whole night long, drinking a *Vie* with another good man, Aristophanes: and yet the next morning, in the breake of the daye, without any rest uppon his drinking, made such a cunning geometrical instrument, that there was no maner of faulte to be found in the same: bycause the drinking of wine after this sorte in a *Vie*, in such excesse and waste, is a shrewde assault to trie the strength of him that quaffes so lustily." Della Casa's *Galateo*, 1576, transl. by Peterson, sign. Q 2.

"Healths and Toasts," says Lord Cockburn, in his *Memorials*, were special torments—oppressions which cannot now be conceived. Every glass during dinner required to be dedicated to the health of some one. It was thought sottish and rude to take wine without this, as if forsooth there was nobody present worth drinking with. I was present about 1803, when the late Duke of Buccleuch took a glass of sherry by himself at the table of Charles Hope, then Lord Advocate, and this was noticed afterwards as a piece of direct contempt." Cockburn refers to the period, when he and Sir Walter Scott were young men; and he proceeds to describe the ceremonious manner in which the healths were proposed and drunk. The master or the landlord, as the case might be, was privileged to include several persons in the same health. Among the modern Germans offence is apt to be taken if a stranger, invited to drink wine with them, declines the compliment. It is a method of qualifying the person for companionship, a sort of credentials.

Heam.—Waller, in his *Advice to a Painter*, 1681, has the following passage:

" barking bear-ward—
Whom pray'e dont forget to paint with's Staff,
Just at this green bear's tail,——
Watching (as carefull neat-herds do their kine)
Lest he should eat her nauseous secundine.

Then draw a haw-thorn bush, and let him place
The Heam upon't, with faith, that the next race
May females prove "—

with this explanation at p. 13:—"This alludes to a little piece of superstition which the country people use, carefully attending their calving cows, lest they should eat their after-burthen, which they commonly throw upon a hawthorn bush, with steadfast belief they shall have a cow-calf the next year after." Heam is explained to mean "the same in beasts as the secundine or skin that the young is wrapped in." It is apparently akin to *halm*, *heaulme*, and *helm*.

Heaving.—"The counties of Shropshire, Cheshire, and Lancashire, boast a custom which they call heaving, and perform with the following ceremonies, on the Monday and Tuesday in the Easter week. On the first day, a party of men go with a chair into every house to which they can get admission, force every female to be seated in their vehicle, and lift them up three times, with loud huzzas. For this they claim the reward of a chaste salute, which those who are too coy to submit to may get exempted from by a fine of one shilling, and receive a written testimony, which secures them from a repetition of the ceremony of that day. On the Tuesday the women claim the same privilege, and pursue their business in the same manner, with this addition—that they guard every avenue to the town, and stop every passenger, pedestrian, equestrian, or vehicular."—*Public Advertiser*, April 13, 1787. See also on this subject "Gent. Mag." for 1783, p. 378; the same for 1798, p. 325; and comp. *Hoke-Tide* and *Lifting*.

Hedgehog. — Philip de Thaun, in his Anglo-Norman Bestiary, circâ 1120, has this odd fallacy: "Hear," says he, " of the hedgehog, what we understand by it. Physiologus says of it in his writings, ' It is made like a little pig, prickles in its skin—in the time of wine-harvest it mounts the tree, when the cluster of grapes is; it knows which is the ripest, and knocks down the grapes: it is a very bad neighbour to it (the tree): then it descends from the tree, spreads itself out upon the grapes, then folds itself up upon them, round like a ball; when it is well charged, and has stuck its prickles into the grapes, thus by kind it carries its food to its children." *Wright's Popular Treatises on Science*, 1841, p. 103.

Helen's, St., or Eline's Day.— (May 2). "The 2nd of May, St. Helen's Day," says Mr. Atkinson, 1868, "is Rowan-tree (mountain-ash) day, or

Rowan-tree Witch-day, and on that day, even yet with some, the method of proceeding is for some member of the household or family to go the first thing in the morning, with no thought of any particular rowan-tree. From this tree a sufficient supply of branches is taken and (a different path home having been taken, by the strict observers, from that by which they went) on reaching home twigs are stuck over every door of every house in the homestead, and scrupulously left there, till they fall out of themselves. A piece is also always borne about by many in their pockets or purses, as a prophylactie against witching. Not so very long since, either, the farmers used to have whipstocks of rowan-tree wood—rowan-tree gads they were called—and it was held that, thus supplied, they were safe against having their draught fixed, or their horses made restive by a witch." In the "Plumpton Correspondence," under the date of 1489-90 circiter, is a letter from Edward Plumpton, in which he says that he has made an appointment to meet a person at Knaresborough "the Wednesday next after Saynt Eline Day." This was also called the Invention of the Holy Cross, in commemoration of the discovery of that sacred relic by the Empress Helena. A sufficiently ample account of this legend is given in "The Book of Days." And the Holy Cross or Holy Rood Day will be noticed elsewhere, the Emperor Heraclius having also been the fortunate finder of a portion of the cross, and the founder of a festival in honour of the incident on the 14th September. "Two pieces off the holye crosse," occur in an inventory of Reading Abbey in 1537, and probably there was not a religious house in the kingdom without a similar curiosity in its possession; so that to assume all these relics genuine, we must also assume the cross itself to have been of considerable dimensions. In the *Northumberland Household Book* mention occurs of Saint Elyn Day as a day when certain servants were to receive their yearly allowance for horse-meat; but the editor supposes (I do not know why) that the reference is to dies Helenæ regis, viz., May 21; and I see that Nicolas, in the *Chronology of History*, makes only one saint of this name fall in May, namely, Queen Helena, on the 21st. See *Castor and Pollux.*

Hen and Chickens.—This is a Devonshire legend. I cannot resist the temptation of transcribing the account of it I find in "Notes and Queries": "The vicar of a certain Devonshire parish was a distinguished student of the black art, and possessed a large collection of mysterious books and MSS. During his absence

at church one of his servants entered his study, and, finding a large volume open on the desk, imprudently began to read it aloud. He had scarcely read half a page, when the sky became dark and a great wind shook the house violently; still he read on, and in the midst of the storm the doors flew open, and a black hen and chickens came into the room. They were of the ordinary size, when they first appeared, but gradually became larger and larger, until the hen was of the bigness of a good-sized ox. At this point the Vicar (in the church) suddenly closed his discourse, and dismissed his congregation, saying he was wanted at home, and hoped he might arrive there in time. When he entered the chamber, the hen was already touching the ceiling. But he threw down a bag of rice, which stood ready in the corner; and whilst the hen and chickens were busily picking up the grains, the vicar had time to reverse the spell." The same writer adds: "I believe a hen and chickens is sometimes found on the bosses of early church roofs: a sow and pigs certainly are. A black sow and pigs haunt many cross-roads in Devonshire."

Hens.—
"At Shroftide to shroving, go thresh the fat hen,
If blindfold can kill her, then give it thy men."

These lines from Tusser, in "Tusser Redivivus" (by Daniel Hilman), 1710, p. 80, are explained in a note: "The hen is hung at a fellow's back, who has also some horse-bells about him, the rest of the fellows are blinded, and have boughs in their hands, with which they chase this fellow and his hen about some large court or small enclosure. The fellow with his hen and bells shifting as well as he can, they follow the sound, and sometimes hit him and his hen; other times, if he can get behind one of them, they thresh one another well favouredly; but the jest is, the maids are to blind the fellows, which they do with their aprons, and the cunning baggages will endear their sweethearts with a peeping-hole, while the others look out as sharp to hinder it. After this the hen is boiled with bacon, and store of pancakes and fritters are made. In Baron's "Cyprian Academy," 1648, p. 53, a clown is speaking. "By the maskins I would give the best cow in my yard to find out this raskall. And I would thrash him as I did the henne last Shrove Tuesday." Mr. Jones informed Mr. Brand that, in Wales, such hens as did not lay eggs before Shrove Tuesday were, when he was a boy, destined to be threshed on that day by a man with a flail, as being no longer good for anything. If the man hit the hen, and consequently killed her, he got her for his pains.

Herne the Hunter.—Of this legendary character, mentioned in the *Merry Wives of Windsor*, and introduced into Ainsworth's *Windsor Castle*, there appear to be no authentic memorials. We merely hear in a vague manner that he was at some remote period a keeper in the Forest. The story may be a graft from one of the numerous Teutonic myths of the same class.

Hiccius Doctius.—"A common term among our modern sleight of hand men. The origin of this is probably to be found among the old Roman Catholics. When the good people of this Island were under their thraldom, their priests were looked up to with the greatest veneration, and their presence announced in the assemblies with the terms hic est doctus! hic est doctus! and this probably is the origin of the modern corruption Hiccius doctius. M.F." Note in ed. of Brand, 1813.

Hide Fox and All After.—Supposed to be an old form and name of the modern children's sport of *Hide and seek*, *Whoop and hide*, &c. The idea of the fox may correspond with the present amusement among young lads of fox and hounds. Comp. *All-Hid*.

High Wycombe.—The old ceremony of weighing the Mayor and Corporation on November 9 is still observed here. The origin of the custom has not been ascertained. It is not mentioned by Lysons.

Hob.—Mr. Atkinson, in his "Cleveland Glossary, 1868," observes: "Probably, like the nisses of popular faith in Denmark, there were many hobs, each with a 'local' habitation and a 'local' name. Thus there is a Hob Hole at Runswick, a Hob Hole near Kempswithen, a Hob's Cave at Mulgrave, Hobt'rush Rook on the Farndale Moors, and so on."

Hobby-Horse.—The sport which Plot describes as having been performed within his memory at Abbot's or Paget's Bromley, under the name of the Hobby-horse dance, is nothing more than the common rustic diversion, not disused till of late years, in which a man, carrying the image of a horse between his legs, and in his hands holding a bow and arrow, plays the horse. "The latter," says Douce, "passing through a hole in the bow, and stopping on a shoulder, made a snapping noise when drawn to and fro, keeping time with music. With this man danced six others, carrying on their shoulders as many reindeer heads, with the arms of the chief families to whom the revenues of the town

belonged. They danced the heys and other country dance. To the above hobby-horse dance there belonged a pot, which was kept by turns by the reeves of the town, who provided cakes and ale to put into this pot; all people who had any kindness for the good intent of the institution of the sport giving pence a-piece for themselves and families. Foreigners also that came to see it contributed; and the money, after defraying the expense of the cakes and ale, went to repair the church and support the poor : which charges, adds Plot, are not now perhaps so cheerfully borne." Tollett is induced to think the famous hobby horse to be the King of the May, thogh he now appear as a juggler and a buffoon, from the crimson foot-cloth fretted with gold, the golden bit, the purple bridle, with a golden tassel, and studded with gold, the man's purple mantle with a golden border, which is latticed with purple, his golden crown, purple cap, with a red feather and with a golden knop. The foot-cloth, however, was used by the Fool. In Braithwaite's "Strappado for the Divell," 1615, p. 30, we read :

"Erect our aged fortunes make them
  shine
(Not like the Foole in's foot-cloath but)
  like Time
Adorn'd with true experiments," &c.

"Our hobby," Tollett adds, "is a spirited horse of pasteboard, in which the master dances and displays tricks of legerdemain, such as the threading of the needle, the mimicking of the whigh-hie, and the daggers in the nose, &c., as Ben Jonson acquaints us, and thereby explains the swords in the man's cheeks. What is stuck in the horse's mouth I apprehend to be a ladle, ornamented with a ribbon. Its use was to receive the spectator's pecuniary donations." "The colour of the hobby horse is a reddish white, like the beautiful blossom of the peach-tree. The man's coat or doublet is the only one upon the window that has buttons upon it, and the right side of it is yellow, and the left red." In a tract of 1601, speaking of Weston the Jesuit, the writer says : "He lifted up his countenance, as if a new spirit had been put into him, and tooke upon him to controll, and finde fault with this and that : (as the comming into the hall of the hobby-horse in Christmas :) affirming that he would no longer tolerate these and those so grosse abuses, but would have them reformed." There is a passage in Kemp's "Nine Daies Wonder," 1600 : "On Munday morning, very early, I rid the 3 myles that I daunst the Satterday before ; where alighting, my taberer struck up, and lightly I tript forward, but I had the heauiest way that euer mad Morrice-dancer trod ; yet

With hey and ho, through thicke and
thin,
The Hobby-horse quite forgotten,
I followed, as I did begin,
Although the way were rotten."

See Mr. Hunter's "New Illustrations of
Shakespear," vol. ii. p. 248. Shakespear,
in "Hamlet," acted in 1602, makes his
Anglo-Danish hero complain of the oblivion into which the hobby-horse had then
fallen. And in the ballad introduced into
Weelkes's "Ayres," 1608, there is the
same allusion :—

"Since Robin Hood, Maid Marian,
And Little John are gone—a ;
The hobby-horse was quite forgot,
When Kempe did daunce alone a."

This character is introduced into several
of the old comedies. In "Patient Grissil," 1603, there is the following :

"*Urc.* No more of these jadish tricks :
here comes the hobby-horse.
Far. Oh, he would dance a morrice
rarely, if he were hung with bells.
Urc. He would jangle villainously."

And again :

"*Gelas.*—Dost thou know where
Are any wodden horses to be sould,
That neede noe spurre nor haye? Ile
aske this stranger.
Pœd. H'st, master, what say to a hobby
horse?—"

Timon, a Play, i. 4. In "The Vow-
Breaker," 1636, by William Sampson, is
the following dialogue between Miles, the
Miller of Ruddington, and Ball, which
throws great light upon this now obsolete
character :

"*Ball.* But who shall play the hobby
horse? Master Major?
"*Miles.* I hope I looke as like a hobby
horse as Master Major. I have not liv'd
to these yeares, but a man woo'd thinke
I should be old enough and wise enough to
play the hobby horse as well as ever a
Major on 'em all. Let the Major play the
hobby horse among his brethren, and he
will ; I hope our towne ladds cannot want
a hobby horse. Have I practic'd my
reines, my carree'res, my pranckers, my
ambles, my false trotts, my smooth ambles,
and Canterbury paces, and shall Master
Major put me besides the hobby horse?
Have I borrow'd the fore horse-bells, his
plumes, and braveries, nay, had his mane
new shorne and frizl'd and shall the Major
put me besides the hobby-horse? Let him
hobby-horse at home, and he will. Am I
not going to buy ribbons and toyes of
sweet Ursula for the Marian, and shall I
not play the hobby horse?
"*Ball.* What shall Joshua doe?
"*Miles.* Not know of it, by any meanes ;
hee'l keepe more stir with the hobby horse

then he did with the pipers at Tedbury
Bull-running : provide thou for the
Dragon, and leave me for a hobby horse.
"*Ball.* Feare not, I'le be a fiery Dra-
gon."
And afterwards, when Boote askes him :
"Miles, the Miller of Ruddington,
gentleman and souldier, what make you
here?
"*Miles.* Alas, Sir, to borrow a few rib-
bandes, bracelets, eare-rings, wyertyers,
and silke girdles and hand-kerchers for a
Morice, and a show before the Queene.
"*Boote.* Miles, you came to steale my
Neece.
"*Miles.* Oh Lord ! Sir, I came to furnish the hobby horse.
"*Boote.* Get into your hobby horse,
gallop, and be gon then, or I'le Moris-
dance you—Mistris, waite you on me.
Exit.
"*Ursula.* Farewell, good hobby horse.
—*Weehee. Exit.*"
We perhaps owe to the hobby horse not
only the familiar expression, "to ride a
hobby," that is to say, to indulge a crot-
chet, but "to ride the great horse," which
is mentioned in a paper inserted by Gutch
in his "Collectanea Curiosa," 1781, in
apparent reference to Sir Balthazar Gerbier's project for a Royal Academy or
College of Honour, conceived by him in
the reign of James I. This great horse
was, so far as one can collect, the new
system or curriculum, which Gerbier was
then endeavouring to institute. In the
later literature of the seventeenth century, if not in that of Shakespear's own
day, hobby-horse evidently stands very
often for a children's horse, the toy which
has been elaborated by modern art into
a rocking-horse. Thus, in "Musarum Deliciæ," 1656 :

"Another sware, that I no more did
ride,
Then children, that a hobby-horse be-
stride."

But Bayes's Troop in the Duke of Buckingham's *Rehearsal* is said by Douce to
afford a fair idea of the hobby horse in the
Morris. Comp. *Irish Hobby.*

Hobgoblin.—As to this term, I find
it difficult to concur with Wedgwood (*Dict.*
in v.) ; I think a more rational solution of
the word to be a clownish spirit, or supernatural Hob, who might be supposed to
partake of the awkwardness of the mortal
rustic.

Hock-Cart or **Hockey-Cart.**—
That which brings the last corn and the
children rejoicing with boughs in their
hands, with which the horses also are attired. Herrick addressed to the poet-earl
of Westmoreland, author of "Otia Sacra,"
1648, a copy of verses, in which he pleasantly describes the usages of the harvest

home. He alludes to the crowning of the hock-cart, and the other ceremonies observed after the gathering-in of the crop. Lord Westmoreland himself tells us :

" How the hock-cart with all its gear Should be trick'd up, and what good chear."

Hockey.—This is a game played with a ball and sticks. Several persons may partake in the recreation, and the sport consists in driving the ball in different directions, each player being provided with a stick, with which, by the exercise of a good deal of agility and quickness of eye, he may succeed in outstripping his competitors, and bringing the ball to the appointed goal. Hockey has, of late years, rather increased in popularity ; like other diversions, the interest fluctuates from period to period.

Hockey Cake.—That distributed to the people at *Harvest-home.*

Hocus-pocus or **Hoax.**—Vallancey, speaking of hocus pocus, derives it from the Irish " *Coic* an omen, a mystery ; and *bais*, the palm of the hand : whence is formed *Coiche-bais*, legerdemain ; Persicé *choko-baz* : whence the vulgar English hocus pocus." He is noticing the communication in former days between Ireland and the East. *Collect.* xiii., 93. Ady, speaking of common jugglers, that go up and down to play their tricks in fairs and markets, says : " I will speak of one man more excelling in that craft than others, that went about in King James his time, and long since, who called himself the Kings Majesties most excellent Hocus Pocus, and so was he called, because that at the playing of every trick, he used to say ' Hocus pocus, tontus, talontus, vade celeriter jubeo,' a dark composure of words, to blinde the eyes of the beholders." *Candle in the Dark*, 1659, p. 29. Archbishop Tillotson tells us that " in all probability those common jugling words of hocus pocus are nothing else but a corruption of *hoc est Corpus*, by way of ridiculous imitation of the priests of the Church of Rome in their trick of Transubstantiation," &c. *Discourse on Transubstantiation.* With due submission to his Grace, this appears rather a fanciful etymology. In 1634 was published a tract entitled *Hocus Pocus Junior, the Anatomy of Legerdemain*, which passed through about ten impressions, and is illustrated with wood-cuts of the various tricks. Butler has these lines :

" With a slight Convey men's interest, and right, From Stiles's pocket into Nokes's As easily as hocus pocus."

Hodening.—Busby, in his " Concert-Room Anecdotes," gives an account of this usage, which is merely another form of the " Mari Llwyd " hereafter described.

Hognell or **Hogling Money.**—See *Hoke-Tide.*

Hoisting.—A process to which soldiers were subjected on returning to barracks for the first time after being married.

Hoke-Tide or **Hoc-Tide.**—This festival was celebrated, according to ancient writers, on the Quindena Paschæ, by which, Mr. Denne informs us, the second Sunday after Easter cannot be meant, but some day in the ensuing week : and Matthew Paris and other writers have expressly named Tuesday. There are strong evidences remaining to shew that more days were kept than one. As it is observed in the " Glossary " of Nares, Hoke Day cannot be the anniversary of any fixed event, as it is a movable feast, varying with Easter-tide. Matthew Paris (who is the oldest authority for the word), has the following passages concerning Hoctide. " Post diem Martis quæ vulgariter Hokedaie appellatur, factum est Parliamentum Londini," p. 963. " Die videlicet Lunæ quæ ipsum diem præcedit proximò quem Hokedaie vulgariter appellamus," p. 834. " In quindena Paschæ quæ vulgariter Hokedaie appellatur," p. 908. On these passages Watts, in his Glossary, observes, " adhuc in ea die solent mulieres jocose vias Oppidorum funibus impedire, et transeuntes ad se attrahere, ut ab eis munusculum aliquod extorqueant, in pios usus aliquos erogandum " ; and then refers to Spelman. But there can be no doubt that the term is derived from hoch-zeit, the high tide, a festival, which in modern German signifies marriage. I find that Easter is called " Hye-tyde " in Robert of Gloucester, vol. i. p. 156. Colonel Vallancey communicated to Mr. Brand a curious paper in his own hand-writing, to the following effect : " Hoc-Tide. In Erse and Irish oach or oac is rent, tribute. The time of paying rents was twice in the year, at La Samham, the day of Saman (2nd Nov.) and La Oac, the day of Hock (April). See La Saman, ' Collectanea,' No. 12. " Hoguera (Spanish) el fuego que se haze con hacina de lennos que levanta llama ; y assi se enciende siempre en lugar descubierto. Hazian hogueras los antiguos para quemar los cuerpos de los difuntos, y en ciertas fiestas que llamavam lustros ; y en tiempo de peste se han usado para purificar el aire. Por regoziio se hazen hogueras en la fiesta de san Juan Baptista, y otros Santos, y en las alegrias por nacimientos de principes, y por otras causas. El saltar por encima de las hogueras se haze agora con simplicidad ; pero antiguamente tenia cierto genero de superstition; y tuvo origen de los Caldeos, segun escriven autores graves. Llevadme cavallera, y sea a la hoguera. Esto dixo una hechizera, llevandola a quemar. Acostumbran en muchas partes llevar a losque han de justiciar por su pie : y pienso que la costumbre de llevarlos en Castilla cavalleros es pia y llegada a razon; porque el que va a padecer va debilitado, temblando con todo su cuerpo: y con esta fatiga puede ser, que no vaya tan atento, ni los religiosos que le van confortando. Vltra desto, como va levantado en alto, venle todos, para exemplo, y para comiseracion."—Tesoro de la Lingua Castellana por Don Seb. de Cobarruvias Orosco, fol. Madr. 1611.

Blount, in his edition of Cowell's Glossary, says, that Hoc Tuesday money was a duty given to the landlord, that his tenants and bondsmen might solemnize that day on which the English mastered the Danes, being the second Tuesday after Easter week. Neither Alfred of Beverley, Hardyng, nor the anonymous writer of the Chronicle usually called Caxton's, mentions the massacre. Higden says it happened on St. Brice's night, fol. 244 b. Fabyan says it happened on St. Brice's day, and began at Welwyn in Hertfordshire, p. 259. Grafton follows him in the same words. Holinshed makes it to have taken place on St. Brice's day in the year 1012; and adds, that the place where it began is uncertain, some saying at Welwyn, and others at Howahil, in Staffordshire, 1st edit. fol. 242. Matthew of Westminster gives more particulars of the massacre than any other historian, and makes it to have happened in 1012, but says nothing of Hoctide in that place. Stowe very briefly mentions the fact as having happened on St. Brice's day, 1002. Mr. Brand himself observed, that the strongest testimony against the hypothesis that the festival was instituted to commemorate the destruction of the Danes by Ethelred in 1002, is that of Henry, Archdeacon of Huntingdon, who expressly says that the massacre of the Danes happened on the feast of St. Brice, which is well known to be on the thirteenth of November. Other ancient authorities for the mention of Hoctide are, 1. "Monast. Anglic." vol. i., p. 104, "A die quæ dicitur Hokedai usque ad festum S. Michaelis." 2. An instrument in Kennett's "Paroch. Antiq." dated 1363, which speaks of a period between Hoke Day and St. Martin's Day. 3. A Chartulary at Caen, cited by Du Cange, p. 1150, in which a period between "Hocedei usque ad Augustum" is mentioned. 4. An Inspeximus in Madox's "Formulare," p. 225, dated 42 Ed. III. in which mention is made of "die Martis proximo post Quin-

denam Paschæ qui vocatur Hokeday." In "an indenture constituting John att Hyde steward of the Priory of Poghley," among many other things granted him, are two oxen for the larder on Hoke-day. "Item ii. Boves pro lardario apud Hoccoday." It is dated on the feast of the Annunciation, in the 49th of Edward the Third.

By a proclamation of Henry IV. in 1409, this sport was to be permitted as for that year on Hock-Monday and Tuesday in the City of London and suburbs, without hinderance or exception, within doors and without. Riley's *Memorials*, 1868, p. 571. There is preserved in the fifth volume of Leland's "Collectanea," 1770, p. 298, a curious inhibition of John, Bishop of Worcester, against the abuses of the "Hoc-days," dated 6th April, 1450. The expression Hock, or Hoketyde, comprizes both days. Hoke-Monday was for the women, and Hock Tuesday for the men. On both days the men and women, alternately, with great merriment intercepted the public roads with ropes, and pulled passengers to them, from whom they exacted money to be laid out in pious uses. So that Hoketyde began on the Monday immediately following the second Sunday after Easter, in the same manner as several feasts of the dedications of churches, and other holidays, commenced on the day or the vigil before, and was a sort of preparation for, or introduction to, the principal feast. In Coates's Extracts from the Accounts of St. Laurence's parish, Reading, under 1499, 14 Hen. VII. are the following entries: "It. rec. of Hok money gaderyd of women, xxs." "It. rec. of Hok money gadyeryd of men iiijs.'"— *History of Reading*, p. 214. Among the "Privy Purse Expenses of Henry VII." many of which shew that prince's kindness of heart and generosity of character, is one to this point: "To Lendesay for the wyffs at Greneviche upon Hockmonday, 3s. 4d.'" The date is March 9, 1505-6. It appears clearly, from these and other extracts, that the women made their collection on the Monday : and it is likewise shown that the women always collected more than the men. Plot expressly mentions that in his time they had two Hocdays, viz., "The Monday for the women," which, says he, "is the more solemn, and the Tuesday for the men, which is very inconsiderable." Blount, in his own "Law Dictionary," v. Hokeday, says he has seen a lease, without date, reserving so much rent payable "ad duos anni terminos, scil. ad le Hokeday, et ad festum S. Mich." He adds, that in the accounts of Magdalen College, in Oxford, there is yearly an allowance pro mulieribus hocantibus, in some manors of theirs in Hampshire, where the men hoc the women on the Monday, and contra on Tuesday. In some Churchwardens' Accounts, appertaining to the parochial affairs of Bletchingley, in Surrey, printed in the "Loseley MSS.," 1836, occurs an item called Hognell money —presumably connected with this occasion. In the Churchwardens' Accounts of Cheddar, co. Somerset, under 1612 and 1631, are two entries of amounts received as hogling money, namely, £9 13s. 4d. and £9 3s. 4d. I conclude this to be connected with Hoc or Hoke Tide; yet the amounts collected are far in excess of what seems to have been usual. *Notes and Queries,* 3rd Ser., iii., 423. The custom of men and women heaving each other alternately on Easter Monday and Easter Tuesday in North Wales (mentioned by Pennant) must have been derived from this hocking each other on Hok-days, after the keeping of the original days had been set aside. I find this, amongst other sports, exhibited at Kenilworth Castle by the Earl of Leicester, for the entertainment of Queen Elizabeth, A.D. 1575, under the superintendence of Captain Cox. "And that there might be nothing wanting that these parts could afford, hither came the Coventre men, and acted the ancient play, long since used in that city, called Hocks-Tuesday, setting forth the destruction of the Danes in King Ethelred's time, with which the Queen was so pleas'd, that she gave them a brace of bucks, and five marks in money, to bear the charges of a feast." The play was an annual event here.

Plot says that one of the uses of the money collected at Hoketyde was the reparation of the several parish churches where it was gathered. This is confirmed by extracts from the Lambeth Book:

"1556—1557. Item, of Godman Rundells wife, Godman Jacksons wife, and Godwife Tegg, for Hoxce money by them received to the use of the Church, xijs."

"1518—1519. Item, of William Elyot and John Chamberlayne, for Hoke money gyderid in the pareys, iijs. ixd."

"Item of the gaderyng of the Churchwardens wyffes on Hoke Monday, viijs. iijd."

In "Peshall's History of the City of Oxford," under St. Mary's parish, are the following curious extracts from old records:

P. 67. "1510, sub tit. Recepts. Recd. atte Hoctyde of the wyves gaderynge, xvs. ijd. From 1522 to 3, sub tit. Rec. for the wyfes gatheryng at Hoctyde de claro, xvis. xd."

P. 83. Parish of St. Peter in the East. "1662. About that time it was customary for a parish that wanted to raise money to do any repairs towards the church to keep a Hocktyde, the benefit of which was often very great: as, for instance, this parish of St. Peter in the

East gained by the Hocktide and Whitsuntide, anno 1664, the sum of £14.

"1663. Hocktide brought in this year £6.

"1667. £4 10s. gained by Hocktide." *Archæologia,* vii., 252. In the Churchwardens' Accounts of St. Mary at Hill, London, under the year 1496, is the following article: "Spent on the wyves that gaderyd money on Hob Monday, 10d." Ibid. 1518, there is an order for several sums of money gathered on Hob Monday, &c. to go towards the organs, but crossed out with a pen afterwards. Ibid. 1497. "Gatherd by the women on Hob Monday, 13s. 3d. By the men on the Tuesday, 5s." There are many other entries to the same effect. See Nichols' "Illust." 1797. In Lysons' extracts from the Churchwardens' and Chamberlain's Books at Kingston-upon-Thames are the following concerning Hocktide:

"1 Hen. VIII. Recd. for the gaderyng at Hocktyde, 14s.

2 Hen. VIII. Payd for mete and drink at Hoc-tyde, 12d."

The last time that the celebration of Hocktyde appears is in 1578:

"Recd. of the women upon Hoc Monday, 5s. 2d."

Ibid. vol. ii. p. 145. Parish of Chelsea. "Of the women that went a hocking, 13 April, 1607, 45s." There is a passage in Wither's "Abuses stript and whipt," 1613, which seems to imply that Hock-tide was then still generally observed. It declined soon after the Restoration, yet as late as 1667 there is a trace of it in Parish Books.

Holed or **Pierced Stones.**— See *Stones.*

Holling.—The Eve of the Epiphany is so called at Brough in Westmoreland, where there is an annual procession of an ash-tree, lighted on the tops of its branches, to which combustible matter has been tied. This custom is in commemoration of the star of the Wise Men of the East. Halliwell's *Dict.,* 1860, in v.

Holly.—"Mary," says Gascoigne, in the *Pleasures at Kenilworth,* 1576, "there are two kinds of holly, that is to say, he holly and she holly. Nowe some will say that the she holly hath no prickes, but thereof I entermeddle not." Poems by Hazlitt, ii., 139. From a carol in praise of the holly, temp. Hen. VI. in Harl. MS. 5396, it should seem that holly was used only to deck the inside of houses at Christmas: while ivy was used not only as a vintner's sign, but also among the evergreens at funerals.

Holly-Boy and Ivy-Girl. — A sport formerly practised in East Kent. A writer in the *Gentleman's Magazine* for 1779 says: "Mr. Urban being on a visit on

Tuesday last in a little obscure village in this county, I found an odd kind of sport going forward : the girls, from eighteen to five or six years old, were assembled in a crowd, and burning an uncouth effigy, which they called an Holly-Boy, and which it seems they had stolen from the boys, who, in another part of the village were assembled together, and burning what they called an Ivy-Girl, which they had stolen from the girls : all this ceremony was accompanied with loud huzzas, noise, and acclamations. What it all means I cannot tell, although I inquired of several of the oldest people in the place, who could only answer that it had always been a sport at this season of the year." A correspondent of Mr. Brand described the Ivy Girl to him somewhat differently, namely, as a figure composed of some of the best corn the field produces, and made, as well as they can, into a human shape ; this is afterwards curiously dressed by the women, and adorned with paper trimmings, cut to resemble a cap, ruffles, handkerchief, &c. of the finest lace. It is brought home with the last load of corn from the field upon the waggon, and they suppose entitles them to a supper at the expense of their employers. Naogeorgus or Kirchemair seems to allude to a similar practice in his *Popish Kingdom*, translated by Googe, 1570 :

" Now when at length the pleasant time
    of Shrove-tide comes in place,
And cruell fasting dayes at hand ap-
    proch with solemne grace :
Then olde and yong are both as mad, as
    ghestes of Bacchus feast,
And foure dayes long they tipple square,
    and feede and never reast.
Downe goes the hogges in every place,
    and puddings every wheare
Do swarme : the dice are shakte and
    tost, and cardes apace they teare :
In every house are showtes and cryes,
    and mirth, and revell route.
And daintie tables spred, and all be set
    with ghestes about :
With sundrie playes and Christmas
    games, and feare and shame away,
The tongue is set at libertie, and hath
    no kinde of stay.
All thinges are lawfull then and done,
    no pleasure passed by,
That in their mindes they can deuise, as
    if they then should die."

Purchas, speaking of the Peruvian superstitions, mentions an usage rather analogous to the English one : " In the sixt moneth they offered a hundred sheepe of all colours, and then made a feast, bringing mayz from the fields into the house, which they yet vse. This feast is made, comming from the farme to the house, saying certaine songs, and praying that the mayz may long continue. They put a quantitie of the mayz (the best that groweth in their farmes) in a thing which they call Pirua, with certaine ceremonies watching three nights. Then doe they put it in the richest garment they haue, and, being thus wrapped and dressed, they worship this Pirua, holding it in great veneration, and saying, It is the mother of the mayz of their inheritances, and that by this meanes the mayz augments and is preserued. In this moneth they make a particular sacrifice, and the witches demand of this Pirua if it hath strength enough to continue vntill the next yeere. And if it answeres no, then they carrie this maiz to the farme whence it was taken, to burne and make another Pirua as before : and this foolish vanitie still continueth." " Pilgrimes," vol. v., lib. ix., c. 12. He cites Acosta, lib. vi. c. 3.

Holly Bussing.—The " Newcastle Express," quoted by "Notes and Queries," May 2, 1857, thus describes the local practice of holly bussing. " On Easter Tuesday, the lads and lasses of the village and vicinity (of Netherwitton, Northumberland) meet, and accompanied by our worthy parish clerk, who plays an excellent fiddle, . . . proceed to the wood to get holly, with which some decorate a stone cross that stands in the village, while others are ' bobbing around ' to ' Speed the Plough ' or ' Birnie Bouzle.' Accordingly, on Tuesday last, a merry party assembled, and after going through the usual routine, dancing was kept up on the green till the shades of evening were closing on them."

Holydays.—Philip de Thaun, in his " Livre des Creatures," circâ A.D. 1121, says, respecting the Latin term *Feriæ:*

" Mais ço truvum lisant en cel compot
    Gerlant.
Que li bers Sainz Silvestre, qui de Rume
    fud mestre,
Feries les apelat, e lur nuns tresturnat,
Pur ço que cristiens ne cresisant paiens
De fole entenciun ne de male raisun."

Wright's *Popular Treatises on Science*, 1841, p. 28.

There is an order from the Bishop of Worcester, given in April, 1450, to the Almoner of Worcester Cathedral and others, that all persons within the jurisdiction of the diocese should cease woodcutting and dishonest sports on the days vulgarly called holy-days, under pain of excommunication. Hooker says : "Holy-days were set apart to be the landmarks to distinguish times." In " Barten Holiday to the Puritan in his Technogamia," in " Witts Recreations," 1640, the writer says:

" 'Tis not my person, nor my play,
 But my sirname, Holiday,
 That does offend thee, thy complaints
 Are not against me, but the Saints."

Holy Dust.—Among the Britons and early Saxons the idea of sanctity was not limited to those who had received canonization or to gods. Bede apprises us that the dust of Oswald, King of Northumbria, was preserved as a cure for sickness, and narrates an anecdote of a countryman who had travelled far to collect this precious medicine, which he carried home, wrapped up in a linen cloth. Barnes, *Notes on Ancient Britain*, 1858, p. 22.

Holy Hand.—A communication to *Notes and Queries* (August 31, 1872), intimates the survival of the belief at Lancaster and the vicinity that the touch of Father Arrowsmith's right hand was efficacious in curing various complaints. It will be better to append the account itself :—" At last week's meeting of the Wigan Board of Guardians, a case was brought forward relating to an extraordinary superstition in Lancaster. The assistant-overseer of Ashton-in-Makerfield had sent to the Wigan workhouse a woman who gave the name of Catherine Collins, and who had been sitting all day on a doorstep, and was wholly destitute. She stated that she had come out of Salford Workhouse, on leave, to have the holy hand applied to her paralysed side. Mr. Clarke, one of the Guardians for Ashton, stated to the Board that hundreds of persons visited the township for similar purposes. The holy hand is kept by the Roman Catholic priest at Garswood, in Ashton township, and is preserved with great care in a white silk bag. Many wonderful cures were said to have been wrought by this saintly relic, which is alleged to be the hand of Father Arrowsmith, a priest who was put to death for his religion at Lancaster. When about to suffer he desired his spiritual attendant to cut off his right hand, which should then have the power to work miraculous cures on those who had faith to believe in its efficacy."

Holy Name of Jesus.—(August 7.) In the " Plumpton Correspondence " occurs a letter to Sir Richard Plumpton from John Pullen, under the supposed date of 1499, in which the writer says : " Sir, as hartylie as I can, I commaund me unto you ; and within a box to my lady . . . is the fest of Nomen Jesu with Utas.". . . The Editor conjectures, and doubtless properly, that what Pullen sent to Lady Plumpton was the book or MS. containing the service used on this particular day, with the octave or Utas. Of this, however, Pynson printed at least two editions, and one of these may have been the book above mentioned. Hone, in his *Every-Day Book*, gives an account of the anniversary.

Holy-Rood Day.—(Sept. 14.) This festival, called also Holy Cross Day, was instituted on account of the recovery of a large piece of the Cross by the Emperor Heraclius, after it had been taken away, on the plundering of Jerusalem by Chosroes, King of Persia, about 615. Churchwardens' Accounts, previous to the Reformation, are usually full of entries relating to the Rood-loft. In the accounts of St. Mary at Hill, 5 Hen. VI. we have : " Also for makynge of a peire endentors betwene William Serle, carpenter, and us, for the Rode lofte and the under clerks chambre, ijs. viijd. Also refs. of certeyn men for the Rod loft ; fyrst of Ric. Goslyn, £10 ; also of Thomas Raynwall, £10 ; also of Rook 26s. 7d." ; and eighteen others. " Summa totalis £95 11s. 9d." Sir H. Ellis remarks that the carpenters on this occasion appear to have had what in modern language is called " their drinks " allowed them over and above their wages. " Also the day after St. Dunstan, the 19 day of May, two carpenters with her nonsiens (nuncheons or luncheons)." Other entries respecting the Rood-loft occur in the above-cited accounts :

" Also payd for a rolle and 2 gojons of iron and a rope, xiiijd.

Also payd to 3 carpenters removing the stallis of the quer, xxd.

Also payd for 6 peny nail and 5 peny nail, xjd.

Also for crochats, and 3 iron pynnes and a staple, xiijd.

Also for 5 yardis and a halfe of grene Bokeram, iijs. iijd. ob.

Also for lengthyng of 2 cheynes and 6 zerdes of gret wyer, xiiijd.

Also payd for eleven dozen pavyng tyles, iijs. iijd."

Ellis points out that, in Howes' edition of Stow, 2 Edw. VI. 1547, we read : "The 17 of Nov. was begun to be pulled down the Roode in Paules Church, with Mary and John, and all other images in the church, and then the like was done in all the Churches in London, and so throughout England, and texts of Scripture were written upon the walls of those churches against images, &c." He adds : "Many of our Rood-lofts, however, were not taken down till late in the reign of Queen Elizabeth."

It appears to have been the custom to go a nutting upon this day, from the following passage in " Grim the Collier of Croydon," 1662 :

"This day, they say, is called Holy-
   rood Day,
And all the youth are now a nutting
   gone."
Hazlitt's *Dodsley*, vii., 443.

Holy Saturday.—See *Easter Eve*.

Holy Thursday.—Various rites
appear to have been performed on Holy
Thursday at wells, in different parts of
the kingdom: such as decorating them
with boughs of trees, garlands of tulips,
and other flowers, placed in various fancied devices. In some places indeed it
was the custom, after prayers for the day
at the church, for the clergyman and singers even to pray and sing psalms at the
wells. At the village of Tissington, in the
county of Derby, a place remarkable for
fine springs of water, it has been the custom from time immemorial. *Gents. Mag.*,
Feb., 1794. This usage is still in force,
and was observed in 1903. I subjoin the
acount of it in the *Daily Mail* of May 22:
"After service in the parish church the
clergy led a procession round the wells,
which were attractively decorated with
flowers. The designs included representations of a lighthouse, castles, and St.
George's encounter with the dragon. At
one the hymn, "Rock of Ages," was flor-
ally illustrated. Over each well was an
appropriate inscription. It is said that
the custom originated in 1615 as a form of
thanksgiving for a bounteous supply of
water during a season of exceptional
drought." A writer in the "Gentleman's
Magazine" for March, 1794, says: "The
same custom was observed of late years, if
not at the present time, at Brewood and
Bilbrook, two places in the county of
Stafford." Plot tells us: "They have a
custom in this county, which I observed
on Holy Thursday at Brewood and Bilbrook, of adorning their wells with boughs
and flowers. This, it seems, they doe too
at all gospell-places, whether wells, trees,
or hills: which being now observed only
for decency and custom sake, is innocent
enough. Heretofore, too, it was usual to
pay this respect to such wells as were eminent for cureing distempers, on the Saint's
Day whose name the well bore, diverting
themselves with cakes and ale, and a little
musicke and dancing; which, whilst within these bounds, was also an innocent recreation. But whenever they began to
place sanctity in them, to bring alms and
offerings, or make vows at them, as the
antient Germans and Britons did, and the
Saxons and English were too much inclined to, for which St. Edmund's Well,
without Saint Clements near Oxford, and
St. Laurence's at Peterborough, were famous heretofore: I doe not find but they
were forbid in those times, as well as now,
this superstitious devotion being called

Wilþeopþunga, which Somner rightly translates Well-worship, and was strictly
prohibited by our Anglican Councils as
long agoe as King Edgar; and in the reign
of Canutus; not long after again in a
Council at London under S. Anselm, Archbishop of Canterbury, A.D. 1102, as it was
also particularly at these two wells near
Oxford and Peterborough, by Oliver Sutton, Bishop of Lincoln." *Staffordshire*,
p. 318.

A writer in *Notes and Queries* (Mr.
A. P. Allsopp) says:—"The belief
that rain-water, caught on Holy Thursday and put into a bottle and corked
will keep good for any length of time is
not confined to Surrey, but is also prevalent in some parts of Worcestershire, e.g.,
in the parishes of Martley and Hindlip,
especially among the old women. The
daughter of one of our servants was
troubled with sore eyes whilst she was living at Harrow some years ago, but by the
application of some rain-water, which
had been caught on Holy Thursday and
carefully preserved in a bottle by an old
friend in Buckinghamshire, the sore eyes
were cured. The water was quite fresh,
and as clear as crystal, although many
years had elapsed since it was first caught.
Aubrey, who wrote about 1670, says in
his "Remains of Gentilism and Judaism": "The fellows of New College have,
time out of mind, every Holy Thursday,
betwixt the hours of eight and nine, gonne
to the hospitall called Bart'lemews neer
Oxford, when they retire into the chapell,
and certaine prayers are read, and an an-
theme sung: from thence they goe to the
upper end of the grove adjoyning to the
chapell (the way being beforehand strewed
with flowers by the poor people of the
hospitall), they place themselves round
about the well there, where they warble
forth melodiously a song of three, four,
or five parts; which being performed, they
refresh themselves with a morning's
draught there, and retire to Oxford before
sermon." Hearne notes in his *Diary*,
Jan. 19, 1725: "They have a custom in
St. Aldgate's parish, Oxford, for people of
the parish to eat sugar sopps out of the
font in the church every holy Thursday,
and this is done in the morning." Mr.
Brand's servant B. Jelkes, who lived several years at Evesham in Worcestershire,
informed him of an ancient custom in that
place for the master-gardeners to give
their workpeople a treat of baked peas,
both white and grey (and pork) every year
on Holy Thursday. Compare *Rogation
Week*.

Holy Water.—The ancient Greeks
were perfectly acquainted with the
use and supposed virtue of holy water.
St. John's *Manners and Customs of*

Ancient Greece, 1842, i., 367. All the Romish service books contain the *Benedictio Salis et Aquæ*. But the sanctification of water for medical and sanitary purposes was carried on to some considerable extent. The " Durham Ritual " contains a benedictio for cases of sore eyes, bodily infirmity, &c. There seems to have been scarcely an article of use or consumption, which was not brought within the operation of holy water. Pennant communicated to Brand a MS. account of customs in North Wales, in which occurred the following passage : " If there be a Fynnon Vair, Well of our Lady or other Saint in the parish, the water that is used for baptism in the font is fetched thence. Old women are very fond of washing their eyes with the water after baptism. It is still a common article of popular belief in North Wales, even among educated people that the holy water used in baptism should never be thrown away afterwards, but should be employed to moisten some tree or shrub, to whose growth it is held to be propitious. The nurses and gossips in the same part of the country also maintain that a child should cry at the baptismal font, or it is a sign that it will not live. They will even pinch it, rather than the lucky omen should be wanting. Rose, in a note to his translation of " Amadis of Gaul, 1803, mentions that in the romance of " Petit Jean de Saintres," the king's chamber is " sprinkled at night with holy water as a protection against evil spirits." In the " Life of Henrietta Maria," 1669, p. 3, we read : " On the 25th of June, 1610, she was carried with her brother to perform the Ceremony of casting Holy-water on the corps of her dead father (Henry the Fourth of France), who was buried the 28th following." Comp. *Orkneys*.

Mungo Park, in his " Travels," tells us, " At Baniseribe—a Slatee having seated himself upon a mat by the threshold of his door, a young woman (his intended bride) brought a little water in a calabash, and kneeling down before him, desired him to wash his hands : when he had done this, the girl, with a tear of joy sparkling in her eye, drank the water ; this being considered as the greatest proof of her fidelity and love."

Holy Wells and Fountains.— The custom of giving names to wells and fountains is of the most remote antiquity. In giving particular names to inanimate things it is obviously the principal intention to secure or distinguish the property of them. A well was a most valuable treasure in those dry and parched countries which composed the scene of the Patriarchal History, and therefore we find in one of the earliest of human writings, the Book of Genesis, that it was a frequent subject of contention (*Genesis*, xxi., 31, also xxvi.), and so it continued to be down to modern days, and even in Western Europe as frequently the sole source of water supply to a village or district. The association of a holy name with such spots was actuated, no doubt, by a desire to protect them from injury and pollution. At Rome Fontinalia was a religious feast, celebrated on the 13th of October, in honour of the nymphs of wells and fountains. The ceremony consisted in throwing nosegays into the fountains, and putting crowns of flowers upon the wells. We judge that the ancients discerned some supernatural influence behind these gifts of Nature. " Horace, in one of his odes, made a solemn promise that he would make a present of a very fine kid, some sweet wine, and flowers, to a noble fountain in his own Sabine villa. See Ovid's " Fasti," lib. iii., 300 :

" —Fonti rex Numa mactat ovem."

Comp. *Holy Thursday*. In the Papal times there was a custom in this country, if a well had an awful situation, if its waters were bright and clear, or if it was considered as having a medicinal quality, to dedicate it to some saint, by honouring it with his name. We find that the superstitious adoration of fountains is forbidden so early as in the 16th of the canons made in the reign of Edgar, A.D. 960 : as also in the canons of St. Anselm made in 1102. There are interdictions of this superstition in the laws of Canute, also preserved in Wheloc's edition of Lambarde's " Archaionomia," 1644.

Fitzstephen, in his account of London in the time of Henry II., writes : " There are also about London, on the north of the suburbs, choice fountains of water, sweet, wholesome and clear, streaming forth among the glistering pebble-stones : in this number, Holy-well, Clerken-well, and Saint Clement's-well, are of most note, and frequented above the rest, when scholars and the youths of the city take the air abroad in the summer evenings." Our British topography abounds with accounts of holy wells, or such as had assigned them, by ancient superstition, most extraordinary properties. These ideas, so far from being worn out in a more enlightened age, were long retained by the vulgar, not only in the distant provinces, but also close to the metropolis itself. The custom of affixing ladles of iron, &c. by a chain to wells, is of great antiquity. Strutt, in his " Anglo-Saxon Æra," tells us, that Edwine caused ladles or cups of brass to be fastened to the clear springs and wells, for the refreshment of the passengers. Venerable Bede is his authority, Eccles. Hist. ii. 16. The passage is as follows : " Tantum quoque rex idem utilitati suæ gentis consuluit, ut plerisque in locis ubi fontes lucidos juxta publicos viarum transitus conspexit, ibi ob refrigerium viantium erectis stipitibus et æneos caucos suspendi juberet, neque hos quisquam nisi ad usum necessarium contingere præ magnitudine vel timoris ejus auderet, vel amoris vellet."

The present class of superstition appears to have been very prevalent in this island till the age before the Reformation, and is not even yet entirely extinguished among the Roman Catholics and the common people. In the parish of Ilam, Staffordshire, there used to be the tomb, well, and ash of St. Bertram, who was a worker of miracles in the county. The ash grew over the spring, and was regarded as inviolable. *England's Gazetteer*, 1751, v. *Ilam*.

Borlase observes: "A very singular manner of curing madness, mentioned by Carew in the parish of Altarnun—was to place the disordered in mind on the brink of a square pool, filled with water from St. Nun's Well. The patient, having no intimation of what was intended, was, by a sudden blow on the breast, tumbled into the pool, where he was tossed up and down by some persons of superior strength, till, being quite debilitated, his fury forsook him; he was then carried to Church, and certain masses sung over him. The Cornish call this immersion Boossenning, from beuzi or bidhyzi in the Cornu-British and Armoric, signifying to dip or drown." *Antiq. of Cornwall*, 138. *Nat. Hist. of Cornwall*, 302; Carew's *Survey*, 1602, p. 123.

"In thys estate rode lamentabillye,
Tyll he approched, certes, sodenlye,
The fontayn and well of Thursty Gladnesse
(As said is, it came of the fayrie)."

Romance of Partenay (or Melusine), circâ 1500, ed. Skeat, 18.

"For to that holy wood is consecrate
A virtuous well, about whose flowery banks
The nimble-footed fairies dance their rounds
By the pale moonshine, dipping oftentimes
Their stolen children, so to make them free
From dying flesh and dull mortality—"

Fletcher's *Faithful Shepherdess* (1610). I find the following recipe for making a holy well: "Let them finde out some strange water, some unheard of spring. It is an easie matter to discolour or alter the taste of it in some measure (it makes no matter how little). Report strange cures that it hath done. Beget a superstitious opinion of it. Good fellowship shall uphold it, and the neighbouring townes shall all sweare for it." Powell's *Tom of all Trades*, 1631, p. 31. Compare *Bromfield*.

Holy Wells and Fountains in Scotland.

—Shaw, in his "History of the Province of Moray," tells us "that true rational Christian knowledge, which was almost quite lost under Popery, made very slow progress after the Reformation. That the prevailing ignorance was attended with much superstition and credulity: heathenish and Romish customs were much practised: Pilgrimages to wells and chapels were frequent." Henry Adamson says, in the "Muses Threnodie," St. Conil's Well, in Scotland. "This well, dedicated to St. Conwall, whose anniversary was celebrated on the 18th of May, is near to Ruthven Castle or Hunting Tower. It is sufficient to serve the town of Perth with pure, wholesome water, if it were brought down by pipes. In the days of superstition this well was much resorted to." *Repr. of Ed.* 1638, 175. We find that in the last century there was at Balmanno "a fine spring-well, called St. John's Well, which in antient times was held in great estimation. Numbers, who thought its waters of a sanative quality, brought their rickety children to be washed in its stream. Its water was likewise thought a sovereign remedy for sore eyes, which, by frequent washing, was supposed to cure them. To shew their gratitude to the Saint, and that he might be propitious to continue the virtues of the waters, they put into the well presents, not indeed of any great value, or such as would have been of the least service to him, if he had stood in need of money, but such as they conceived the good and merciful apostle, who did not delight in costly oblations, could not fail to accept. The presents generally given were pins, needles, and rags taken from their cloaths. This may point out the superstition of those times. "Stat. Acc. of Scotl." vol. xviii., p. 630, Parish of Mary-kirk, co. Kincardine. Comp. *Blessing of Clouts*.

It appears, that in the last century, it was usual at Nigg, co. Kincardine, in the month of May, for many of the lower ranks from around the adjacent city (Aberdeen) to come to drink of a well in the Bay of Nigg, called Downey Well; and, proceeding a little farther, to go over a narrow pass, the Brigge of ae Hair, to Downy-Hill, a green island in the sea, where young people cut their favourites' names in the sward. It seems to have been the remains of some superstitious respect to the fountain and retreat of a reputed saint gone into an innocent amusement. *Stat. Acc. of Scotland*, vii., 213. The minister of Kirkmichael, Banffshire, about the same time, made these general remarks on the subject: "The same credulity that gives hair-formed inhabitants to green hillocks and solitary groves, has given their portion of genii to rivers and fountains. The presiding spirit of that element, in Celtic mythology, was called Neithe. The primitive of this word signifies to wash or purify with water. To this day fountains are regarded with particular veneration over every part of the Highlands. The sick, who resort to them for health, address their vows to the presiding powers, and offer presents to conciliate their favour. These presents generally consist of a small piece of money, or a few fragrant flowers. The vulgar in many parts of the Highlands, even at present, not only pay a sacred regard to particular fountains, but are firmly persuaded that certain lakes are inhabited by spirits. In Strathspey there is a lake called Lochnan Spioradan, the Lake of Spirits. Two frequently make their appearance — the Horse, and the Bull of the Water. The Mermaid is another. Before the rivers are swelled by heavy rains, she is frequently seen, and is always considered as a sure prognostication of drowning. In Celtic mythology to the above-named is a fourth spirit added. When the waters are agitated by a violent current of wind, and streams are swept from their surface and driven before the blast, or whirled in circling eddies aloft in the air, the vulgar, to this day, consider this phenomenon as the effect of the angry spirit operating upon that element. They call it by a very expressive name, the Mariach shine, or the Rider of the Storm." It is added: "Near the kirk of this parish there is (1794) a fountain, once highly celebrated, and antiently dedicated to St. Michael. Many a patient have its waters restored to health, and many more have attested the efficacy of its virtues. But, as the presiding power is sometimes capricious, and apt to desert his charge, it now lies neglected, choked with weeds, unhonoured and unfrequented. In better days it was not so; for the winged guardian, under the semblance of a fly, was never absent from his duty. If the sober matron wished to know the issue of her husband's ailment, or the love-sick nymph that of her languishing swain, they visited the Well of St. Michael. Every movement of the sympathetic fly was regarded in silent awe; and as he appeared cheerful or dejected, the anxious votaries drew their presages; their breasts vibrated with correspondent emotions. Like the Delai Lama of Thibet, or the King of Great Britain, whom a fiction of the English law supposes never to die, the Guardian Fly of the Well of St. Michael was believed to be exempted from the laws of mortality.

To the eye of ignorance he might sometimes appear dead, but agreeably to the Druidic system, it was only a transmigration into a similar form, which made little alteration on the real identity." "Not later than a fortnight ago," (it is added) "the writer of this account was much entertained to hear an old man lamenting with regret the degeneracy of the times; particularly the contempt in which objects of former veneration were held by the unthinking crowd. If the infirmities of years and the distance of his residence did not prevent him, he would still pay his devotional visits to the Well of St. Michael. He would clear the bed of its ouze, open a passage for the streamlet, plant the borders with fragrant flowers, and once more, as in the days of youth, enjoy the pleasure of seeing the Guardian Fly skim in sportive circles over the bubbling wave, and with its little proboscis imbibe the panacean dews." Ordiquhill, Banffshire. The Mineral Well, "dedicated to the Virgin Mary, was formerly, at certain seasons, much resorted to by the superstitious as well as the sick." "There are in Perthshire several wells and springs dedicated to St. Fillan, which are still places of pilgrimage and offerings, even among the Protestants. They are held powerful in cases of madness, and in cases of very late occurrence lunatics have been left all night bound to the holy stone, in confidence that the saint would cure and unloose them before morning." *Stat. Acc.*, xvii., 377. Again: Parish of Little Dunkeld, Perthshire. "Here there are a fountain and the ruins of a chapel, both dedicated by antient superstition to St. Laurence"; and again: "Near Tarbat, (Synod of Ross), there is a plentiful spring of water, which continues to bear the name of Tobair Mhuir, or Mary's Well." Glenorchay and Inishail, Argyleshire. "Near the parish school, is the well of St. Connon," the tutelar saint of the county, "memorable for the lightness and salubrity of its water." Trinity Gask, Perthshire. "The most noted well in the parish is at Trinity Gask. It is remarkable for the purity and lightness of its water; the spring is copious and perennial. Superstitions, aided by the interested artifices of Popish priests, raised, in times of ignorance and bigotry, this well to no small degree of celebrity. It was affirmed that every person who was baptized with the water would never be seized with the plague. The extraordinary virtue of Trinity Gask Well has perished with the downfall of superstition." *Stat. Acc. of Scotl.*, vi., 384, 431; viii., 351; xii., 464; xvi., xviii, 487.

Martin observes, "Loch-siant Well in Skie is much frequented by strangers as well as by the inhabitants of the Isle, who generally believe it to be a specifick for several diseases; such as stitches, headaches, stone, consumptions, megrim. Several of the common people oblige themselves by a vow to come to this Well and make the ordinary tour about it, called dessil, which is performed thus: They move thrice round the well, proceeding sun-ways, from east to west, and so on. This is done after drinking of the water; and when one goes away from the well, it's a never failing custom to leave some small offering on the stone which covers the well. There is a small coppice near it, of which none of the natives dare venture to cut the least branch, for fear of some signal judgement to follow upon it." He also speaks of a well of similar quality, at which, after drinking, they make a tour and then leave an offering of some small token, such as a pin, needle, farthing, or the like, on the stone cover which is above the well.

In the *Antiquary* for 1890, Mr. Hope printed a long series of notices of wells and fountains of reputed sanctity in different parts of the kingdom. It has been shown (ibid. 1884) that the practice of well-dressing, or decking the wells with garlands and flowers, inherited from the Roman *Fontinalia*, yet lingered in some parts of the country down to about 1830. It is to be regarded as one of the numberless vestiges and survivals of Paganism. See *St. Andrew's Well, Bede's Well, Stones*, and *Waking the Well.*

Camerarius gives us a minute account of presaging fountains: "I have heard a Prince say, that there is in his territories a fountaine that yeelds a current of water which runs continually; and ever when it decreaseth, it presageth dearnesse of victuals: but when it groweth drie, it signifieth a dearth. There is a fountaine in Glomutz, a citie of Misnia, a league from the river Elbis, which of itself making a pond, produceth oftentimes certaine strange effects, as the inhabitants of the country say, and many that have seene the same witnesse. When there was like to be a good and fruitful peace in all the places about, this fountaine would appeare covered with wheat, oats, and akornes, to the great joy of the country people that flock thether from all parts to see the same. If any cruell war doe threaten the countrey, the water is all thick with blood and with ashes, a certaine presage of miserie and ruine to come. In old times the Vandals Sorabes came everie yeare in great troupes to this wonderfull fountaine, where they sacrificed to their idols and enquired after the fruitfulnesse of the yeare following. And myselfe know some gentlemen that confesse, if a certaine fountaine (being otherwise very cleane and cleare), be suddenly troubled by meanes of a worme unknowne, that the same is a personall summons for some of them to depart out of the world." Dallaway, speaking of the Bosphorus, tells us "Frequent fountains are seen on the shore, of the purest water, to which is attached one of the strongest and most antient superstitions of the Greek Church. They are called 'ayasmà,' and to repeat certain prayers at stated seasons, and to drink deeply of them, is held to be a most salutary act of their religion. *Constantinople*, 1797, 144. Commander Cameron, in his well-known *Narrative of a Journey across Africa*, mentions several instances of the idolatrous veneration of the natives for springs, which they imagine to be the abiding-places of spirits, and into which they cast a bead or so for the purpose of propitiation.

Honey Fair.—At Wrexham, in North Wales, this used, before the introduction of railways, to be held four times a year, and March Honey Fair lasted a fortnight. There were squares of shops, where the produce from various parts was on sale: The Birmingham Square, the Yorkshire Square, &c. All the shopkeepers in North Wales, as well as private persons, attended to make purchases. Honey was almost exclusively the article offered; but Irish lace and Belfast linen were other specialities. At present the trade in honey is chiefly conducted on the two last Thursdays in September in the General Market as part of the business; the old Squares have been pulled down or converted to other purposes. *Mr. John Bury of Wrexham's Letter to the Editor*, 20 Feb., 1897.

Honeymoon.—The honeymoon does not seem to have been observed of old, and no stated time was understood to elapse between the nuptials and the reception of friends at home by the married couple. Thomas Copley, Esq., of Gatton, county Surrey, in a letter to Sir Thomas Cawarden, July 18th, 1558, says that he was going to be married on the Sunday following, and that on the Wednesday he should be happy to see Sir Thomas at Gatton, "at wᶜʰ daie I thynke we shall come home." In the "Wright's Chast Wife," a poem supposed by Mr. Furnivall to have been written about 1462, it is said of the Wright and his magical rose garland:

"Of thys chaplett hym was fulle fayne,
And of hys wyfe, was nott to layne;
He weddyd her fulle sone,
And ladde her home wyth solempnite,
And hyld her brydlle dayes thre,
Whan they home come."

This poem is laid in a humble sphere of life; and even now it is not usual for working folks to remain more than a few days away after the marriage.

The French have the equivalent, which they know as *Lune de Miel*.

Hoodman-Blind or **Hooper's Hide.** — Variant names for blindman's buff. Nares, *Gloss.* in v. cites a passage, where the second name is figuratively applied.

Hoop.—A boy's game from very ancient days. See St. John's *Manners and Customs of Ancient Greece*, 1842, i., 147-8. It probably evolved from the improved wheel, as that may have done from the mathematical circle. Hoop occurs among the puerile sports delineated in the Missal seen by Strutt in the possesion of Mr. Ives. It is also noticed by Charlotte Smith in her "Rural Walks":

"Sweet age of blest delusion! blooming boys,
Ah! revel long in childhood's thought-less joys;
With light and pliant spirits, that can stoop
To follow sportively the rolling hoop;
To watch the sleeping top with gay delight,
Or mark with raptur'd gaze the sailing kite:
Or eagerly pursuing pleasure's call,
Can find it centred in the bounding ball!"

and Gray recalls in his verses his youthful experiences in this direction at Eton. Some of the Latin poets allude to *plectrum*, or hoop-stick. Both hoop and conductor were originally of wood.

Hopping is derived from the A.-S. *hoppan*, to leap, or dance. Dancings in the North of England, and I believe (colloquially) in other parts, are called Hops. The word in its original meaning is preserved in grass-hopper. The word "hoppe" occurs in Chaucer, in the beginning of the "Cokes Tale." In many villages in the North of England these meetings are still kept up, under the name of Hoppings. We shall hope that the rejoicings on them are still restrained in general within the bounds of innocent festivity; though it is to be feared they sometimes prove fatal to the morals of our swains, and corrupt the innocence of our rustic maids. In "A Joco-serious Discourse between a Northumberland Gentleman and his Tenant" (by George Stuart), 1686, p. 32, we read:

"To horse-race, fair, or hoppin go,
There play our casts among the whip-sters,
Throw for the hammer, lowp for flippers,
And see the maids dance for the ring,
Or any other pleasant thing;
——for the Pigg, lye for the Whet-stone,
Or chuse what side to lay our betts on."

Hop Queen.—See *Harvest Lord and Lady*.

Hopscotch.—A common children's game. See Halliwell in v.

Horn. — It is well known that the word horn in the sacred writings denotes fortitude and vigour of mind; and that in the classics personal courage (metaphorically from the pushing of horned animals) is intimated by horns. Horn is used vulgarly to signify the virile symbol: "His horn shall be exalted"; "The horn of my salvation," &c. Comp. *Horns*.

Horn, Tenure by the.—Compare Hazlitt's ed. of Blount's *Tenures*, 1874, pp. 248, 346. It may be added that at Queen's College, Oxford, there is a drinking horn, presented by the foundress, Philippa, queen of Edward III., holding two quarts Winchester measure, and securing the ownership of a manor in Dorsetshire.

Horn-Book or **Battledore.**—See Halliwell in v., and the late Mr. A. W. Tuer's monograph.

Horn Dance.—An amusement pursued at Abbot's Bromley, a village on the borders of Needwood Forest, in Staffordshire, since ancient times, and described and illustrated in the *Strand Magazine* for November, 1896.

Horn Fair.—Grose mentions a fair called Horn-Fair, held at Charlton, in Kent, on St. Luke's Day, the 18th October. It consisted of a riotous mob, who, after a printed summons dispersed through the adjacent towns, met at Cuckold's Point, near Deptford, and marched from thence in procession through that town and Greenwich to Charlton, with horns of different kinds upon their heads; and at the fair there were sold rams' horns and every sort of toy made of horn; even the ginger-bread figures had horns. A sermon used to be preached at Charlton Church on the fair day. Tradition attributes the origin of this licentious fair to King John, who being detected in an adulterous amour, compounded for his crime by granting to the injured husband all the land from Charlton to Cuckold's Point, and established the fair as a tenure. It appears that it was the fashion in William Fuller's time to go to Horn Fair dressed in women's clothes. "I remember being there upon Horn Fair day, I was dressed in my land-lady's best gown, and other women's attire, and to Horn Fair we went, and as we were coming back by water, all the cloaths were spoiled with dirty water, &c., that was flung on us in an inundation, for which I was obliged to present her with two guineas, to make atonement for the damage sustained." &c. *Life of W. Fuller*, 1703, p. 122. In an extract from an old newspaper, I find it was formerly a custom for a procession to go from some of the inns in Bishopsgate Street, in which were a king. a queen, a miller, a councillor, &c., and a great number of others, with horns in their hats, to Charlton, where they went round the church three times, &c. So many indecencies were committed upon this occasion on Blackheath (as the whipping of females with furze, &c.), that it gave rise to the proverb of " all is fair at Horn Fair." This account is perhaps connected with that given in a tract of 1711, which is a letter announcing a meeting of the most Ancient Company of Fumblers at the annual festival at Horn Fair, October 14th, when it appears that they wore horns on their head and carried pickaxes, shovels. &c., in their hands. Lysons in his " Environs," says, the burlesque procession has been discontinued since the year 1768.

Horning.—A Scotish method of proclaiming an offender. There is a warrant under the date 1680 for imprisoning and putting to the horn one Roderick Mackenzie. Under the old Scotish law a witness might be debarred from deposing or giving his evidence, and tendering his oath, by horning, and in the same way he was bound to compear and respond on a future occasion at the horn under pain of contumacy. Spotiswood's *Form of Process,* 1711, p. 78.

Hornpipe.—Henry Spelman, in his *Relation of Virginia,* 1609., says, under the head of *Pastimes,* " When they meet at feasts or otherwise, they vse sports much like to ours heare in England, as ther daunsinge, wch is like our darbysher Hornepipe, a man first and then a woman, and so through them all, hanging all in a round ; ther is one wch stands in the midest wth a pipe and a rattell, wth wh. when he begins to make a noyse all the rest gigetts about, wriinge ther neckes and scrapings on ye ground." Humphrey King, in his *Halfe-Pennyworth of Wit,* 1613, refers to " a harsh Lancashire Horn-pipe."

Horns (i.).—Hearne, in his Preface to " Robert of Gloucester," p. xviii., speaking of the old custom of drinking out of horns, observes : "'Tis no wonder, therefore, that, upon the Jollities on the first of May formerly, the custom of blowing with, and drinking in, horns so much prevailed, which, though it be now generally disus'd, yet the custom of blowing them prevails at this season, even to this day, at Oxford, to remind people of the pleasantness of that part of the year, which ought to create mirth and gayety, such as is sketch'd out in some old books of Offices, such as the ' Prymer of Salisbury,' printed at Rouen, 1551, 8vo." That the twofold use of the horn for drinking and blowing purposes is very ancient seems to be shown

by the poem entitled " The Cokwolds Daunce " ("Remains of E. P. Poetry of Eng." i.). Aubrey, in his " Remains of Gentilisme and Judaisme," MS. Lansd. 226, fol. 5 b. says : " Memorandum, at Oxford the boys do blow cow horns and hollow canes all night ; and on May Day the young maids of every parish carry about garlands of flowers, which afterwards they hang up in their churches."

Horns (ii.).—There used to be a vulgar saying that " a husband wears horns," or is a Cornute, when his wife proves false to him ; as also that of the meaning of the word cuckold, which has for many ages been the popular indication of the same kind of infamy. The following is extracted from the " Gentleman's Magazine " for December, 1786 : " I know not how far back the idea of giving his head this ornament may be traced, but it may be met with in Artemidorus (Lib. ii.) and I believe we must have recourse to a Greek epigram for an illustration :

Οστις εσω πυροος καταλαμβανει ουκ αγοραζων,

Κεινον Αμαλθειας ἡ γυνη εστι κερg.

" ————— Namque in malos asperrimus Parata tollo Cornua."—Horat. *Epod.*
" Jam feror in pugnas & nondum Cornua sumpsi."

Ovid *De Ebrietate.* It is said to have been a custom of the Emperor Andronicus to hang up in a frolic, in the porticoes of the Forum, the stag's horns he had taken in hunting, intending, as he says, by this new kind of insignia, to denote at once the manners of the city, the lasciviousness of the wives he had debauched, and the size of the animals he had made his prey, and that from hence the sarcasm spread abroad that the husband of an adulterous wife bare horns. The twofold application of the horn is suggested in a passage in the *Boke of Mayd Emlyn* (about 1540) :

" She wude byte and whyne
Whan she saw her tyme,
And with a prety gynne
Gyue her husbande an horne,
To blow with on the morne :
Beshrewe her whyte skynne."

Hazlitt's *Popular Poetry,* iv., 84. There is a singular passage upon this subject, which I shall give, and leave, too, without comment, as I find it. The historians are speaking of the monument of Thomas the first Lord Wharton, in the church of Kirby Stephen in Westmoreland, the crest of whose arms was a bull's head : " The consideration of horns, generally used upon the crest, seemeth to account for what hath hitherto by no author or other person ever been accounted for ; namely the connexion betwixt horns and cuckolds. The notion of cuckolds wearing horns prevails through all the modern European languages, and is of four or five hundred years standing. The particular estimation of badges and distinction of arms began in the time of the Crusades, being then more especially necessary to distinguish the several nations of which the armies were composed. Horns upon the crest, according to that of Silius Italicus,

' Casside cornigera dependens Insula ' were erected in terrorem; and after the husband had been absent three or four years, and came home in his regimental accoutrements, it might be no impossible supposition that the man who wore the horns was a cuckold. And this accounts, also, why no author at that time, when the droll notion was started, hath ventured to explain the connexion: for, woe be to the man in those days that should have made a joke of the Holy War; which indeed, in consideration of the expence of blood and treasure attending it, was a very serious affair." Nicolson and Burn's "History of Westmoreland and Cumberland," vol. i., p. 540. Bulwer, in his *Chironomia*, says: "To present the index and eare-finger (i.e. the fore and little finger) wagging, with the thumb applied unto the temples is their expression who would scornfully reprove any. The same gesture, if you take away the motion, is used, in our nimble-fingered times, to call one cuckold, and to present the Badge of Cuckoldry, that mentall and imaginary horn; seeming to cry, ' O man of happy note, whom Fortune meaning highly to promote, hath stucke on thy forehead the earnest penny of succeeding good lucke."

In Greene's *Disputation between a He Conycatcher and a She Conycatcher*, 1592, is the following witticism on this head: "Hee that was hit with the horne was pincht at the heart." Again: "Let him dub her husband Knight of the forked Order." In "Titus Andronicus," 1594, act ii., sc. 3, the following occurs:

"Under your patience, gentle Emperess,
'Tis thought you have a goodly gift in horning.
Jove shield your husband from his hounds to day!
'Tis pity, they should take him for a stag."

Shakespear and Ben Jonson seem both to have considered the horns in this light: "Well, he may sleep in security, for he hath the horn of abundance, and the lightness of his wife shines through it: and yet he cannot see, though he has his own lanthorn to light him."

"What! never sigh,
Be of good cheer, man, for thou art a cuckold.
'Tis done, 'tis done! nay, when such flowing store,
Plenty itself, falls in my wife's lap,
The Cornu Copiæ will be mine, I know."

So in *Othello*, 1622:

"O curse of marriage!
—'Tis Destiny, unshunnable like Death.
Even then this forked plague is fated to us,
When we do quicken."—Act iii., sc. 3.

There is the following curious epigram in "Witts Recreations," 1640:

"*To Festus.*
"Festus th' art old, and yet wouldst maryed be:
Ere thou do so, this counsel take of me:
Look into Lillies Grammar, there thou'lt find,
Cornu a horn, a word still undeclin'd."

The following passage occurs in "The Horne exalted," 1661: "Horns are signified by the throwing out the little and fore-finger when we point at such whom we tacitly call cuckolds." In "The English Fortune Teller," by Philips, 1703, the author, speaking of a wanton's husband, says: "He is the wanton wenches game amongst themselves, and Wagges sport to poynt at with two fingers."

Armstrong says, the inhabitants of Minorca bear hatred to the sight and name of a horn: "for they never mention it but in anger, and then they curse with it, saying *Guerno*, as they would *Diablo*." *Hist. of Minorca*, 2nd ed., 1756, p. 170. In Spain it is a crime as much punishable by the laws to put up horns against a neighbour's house, as to have written a libel against him. It was an offence also in the eye of the law among the Venetians, and a doge's son was severely punished on this account in the fourteenth century. Hazlitt's *Venice*, 1900, ii., 742. We are told that even among the Indians it was the highest indignity that could be offered them even to point at a horn. Comp. *Cuckoldom and Skimmington.*

Horns at Highgate, to Swear on the.— A sufficient account of this usage may be found in Hone and other readily accessible authorities. The Green Dragon at Highgate, demolished in 1899, was one of the houses where the burlesque oath was administered in the coaching days. The Old Red Lion was another. See Hazlitt's *Proverbs*, 1882, p. 167.

Hornage.—A quantity of corn formerly given yearly to the lord of the manor for every ox worked in the plough on lands within his jurisdiction. *Halliwell.*

Horoscopes.—Sheridan says: "To give some little notion of the ancients concerning horoscopes. The Ascendant was understood by them, to be that part of Heaven which arises in the East the moment of the child's birth. This, containing thirty degrees, was called the first house. In this point the astrologers observed the position of the celestial constellations, the planets, and the fixed stars, placing the planets and the signs of the zodiac in a figure, which they divided into twelve houses, representing the whole circumference of Heaven. The first was Angulus Orientis, (by some called the Horoscope), shewing the form and complexion of the child then born: and likewise the rest had their several significations, too tedious to be inserted here, because of no use in the least. The heathen astrologers, in casting nativities, held that every man's genius was the companion of his horoscope, and that the horoscope was tempered by it: hence proceeded that union of minds and friendship which was observed among some. This appears from Plutarch in his Life of Anthony, concerning the Genii of Anthony and C. Octavius. Those who have the curiosity of being farther informed in these astrological traditions, let them consult Ptolemy, Alcabitius, Albo Hali, Guido Bonat, &c." *Notes on Persius,* p. 79, ed. 1739.

Horse.—Brand says:—"Perhaps it will be thought no uninteresting article in this little Code of Vulgar Antiquities to mention a well-known interjection used by the country people to their horses, when yoked to a cart, &c. Heit or Heck! I find this used in the days of Chaucer:

'Thay seigh a cart, that chargid was with hay,
Which that a carter drop forth in his way,
Deep was the way, for which the carte stood:
This carter smoot and cryde as he wer wood,
'Hayt, brok; hayt, scot;' what, spare ye for the stoones!'

The name of Brok is still in common use amongst farmers' draught oxen. A learned friend says, "the exclamation 'Geho, Geho,' which carmen use to their horses is not peculiar to this country, as I have heard it used in France." In the "Mactatio Abel," one of the Towneley series of Mysteries, there are some curious interjectional forms of this class. But in "John Bon and Mast Person," 1548, we get the form 'ree who' instead of 'gee

wo.' Hobs the tanner, in Heywood's Edward IV. 1600, says of his mare, "Why, man, Brock my mare knows ha and ree, and will stand when I cry ho." As to the meaning of the term brock, see Halliwell's "Archaic Dictionary," 1847, *ad vocem.* Forby, in his "Vocabulary," says that ge-ho means go-stop, and ge-wo go-go. In fact, when a driver wishes his horse to stop, he should say ho! and when he desires him to proceed, wo! The two words are at present confused. Ge—go seems to present itself in a reduplicated form in ge-ge, the nursery name for a horse. In "The Cold Yeare, 1614. A Deepe Snow, &c." printed in 1615, we find: "After the collier they (the team) ran, who cryed, hey, and hoe, and ree, and gee; but none of his carterly rethoricke was able to stay them." "In olde time," (it is said in the *Man in the Moon,* telling fortunes to Englishmen, 1609, sign. G 3), "such as solde horses were wont to put flowers or boughes upon their heads, to reveale that they were vendible." But the following passage from Flecknoe's Epigrams shews that ribbons were, as at present, also usual:

"As horse-coursers their horses set to sale,
With ribonds on their foreheads and their tail;
So all our poets' gallantry now-a-days
Is in the prologues and epilogues of their plays."

In the *Character of a Quack Astrologer,* 1673, speaking of "Itch of picture in the Front," the author says: "This sets off the pamphlet in a country fair, as the horse sells the better for the ribbon, wherewith a jockey tyes up his tail."

As regards the names of horses, one of the earliest English Lists seems to be that of certain horses destined to accompany the forces engaged in the French war at the time of the battle of Agincourt in 1415, where a very interesting entry presents itself in the mention of Thomas Chaucer, Butler of England, and of a horse, probably his, described as Bayard Chaucer. Other equine designations are Lyard, Grey, Morell, and Sorell. See Hunter's *Agincourt,* 1850, pp. 43, 54. Morel, Moriel, or Morrell became a favourite designation for a horse. In the *fabliau* of Eustace the Monk that daring adventurer makes off with Moriel, the horse of the Count of Boulogne, an animal of matchless swiftness. Among the Plumpton Correspondence, under 1466, there is a mention of "good morrel and his felow." *Pl. Corr.,* p. 17. In *John Bon and Mast Person* (1548) the concluding lines seem to point to contemporary terms for horses employed at the plough:

" Ha ! browne done ! forth, that horson crabbe ! . . .
haight, blake hab !
Have agayne, bald before, hayght, ree who !—"

—Hazlitt's *Popular Poetry*, 1864-6, iv., 16. In the Diary of the first Earl of Bristol (1665-1751) a series of equine appellations will be found. The list has been recently (1904) communicated by the present writer to the *Connoisseur*. Morel continued to be a common term for a dark-coloured horse in the time of Elizabeth, and occurs in the familiar story of the *Wife lapped in Morel's Skin*. In *Twelfth Night*, iii., 4, Sir Andrew Aguecheek is made to propose the gift of his horse Grey Capilet to the man, whose anger he is desirous of averting.

The horse ridden by Charles VIII. of France at the battle of Fornovo in 1495 was called Savoy, and was remarkable for his swiftness. Hazlitt's *Venetian Republic*, 1900, ii., 137. Presents of horses were frequently made to Henry VIII. by foreign potentates with a view to propitiating him. Ibid., ii, 408.

In Homeric times the Greeks prided themselves on their breeds of horses ; but some of the most celebrated came from the East. As it was with the Romans they employed the swiftest and most enduring, not in the way that the modern nations do, but in their chariot races. St. John's *Manners and Customs of Ancient Greece*, 1842, ii., 280-2. The tradition of the winged steed Pegasus was of course founded on his speed ; the Hellenic thorough-breds were said to have the velocity of birds. The horse of Alexander, called *Bucephalus*, suggests an animal with a short, thick neck, and in the mediæval MSS., where horses are portrayed, this type is conspicuous. Equine nomenclature, as we know, dates very far back into antiquity. Aristotle mentions a mare named *Dicæa*. Amongst the better classes at Rome and in the Roman colonies the names of horses were placed over the stall which each animal occupied, and these memorials have in some cases been preserved in the remains of buildings. Comp. *May-Day and Omens* infrâ, and Hazlitt's *Proverbs*, 1882, pp. 37, 108.

Horse and Hattock.—Aubrey, in his " Miscellanies," gives us the following most important piece of information respecting fairies : " When fairies remove from place to place they are said to use the words Horse and Hattock."

Horse-block.—A familiar object outside doors in country-houses and inns, to enable persons, especially ladies, to mount. They were in use at Pompeii,

and go back to an era, when riders had no stirrups. Fosbrooke's *Encyclopædia*, 1843, p. 314.

Horse, Dr. Story's Wooden, of Troy.—The executioner's cart. See Halliwell's *Books of Characters*, 22. Dr. Story was hanged in 1571. See Hazlitt's *Bibl. Coll.*, General Index in v.

Horse-Races.—The earliest appear to have been instituted in England in Hyde Park about 1637, when Shirley's *Hyde Park* was published. Before 1646 Charles I. established the races at Newmarket, and we have the name of a horse which won the cup there in Shirley's *Poems*, 1646.—Bay Tarrall. The resort to Epsom Downs does not seem to have been anterior to the closing years of the reign of Anne ; but under Charles II. there were races at Leith under the control of the Lord Provost of Edinburgh, as we learn from the Rules or Articles drawn up for their management, and printed as a folio broadside. Compare Haydn's *Dict. v. Races* for a very fair outline of the subject, and Hazlitt's *Manual of Old Plays*, 1892, v. *Hyde Park*. In 1654 and 1658 proclamations appeared forbidding for a certain term the usual horse-races throughout England and Wales. But Scotland and Ireland are not indicated.

Horse-Shoe.—Nailing of horse-shoes seems to have been practised as well to keep witches in, as to keep them out. Douce's notes say : " The practice of nailing horse-shoes to thresholds resembles that of driving nails into the walls of cottages among the Romans, which they believed to be an antidote against the plague : for this purpose L. Manlius, A. U. C. 390, was named Dictator, to drive the nail." " That the horse-shoe may never be pul'd from your threshold," occurs among the good wishes introduced by Holiday in " The Marriage of the Arts," 1618. Aubrey tells us that " it is a thing very common to nail horse-shoes on the thresholds of doors : which is to hinder the power of witches that enter into the house. Most houses of the West end of London have the horse-shoe on the threshold. It should be a horse-shoe that one finds." But the horse-shoe, as it has been elsewhere explained, was used for other purposes. " In the Bermudas they use to put an iron into the fire when a witch comes in. Mars is enemy to Saturn." Aubrey adds : " under the porch of Staninfield Church in Suffolk, I saw a tile with a horse-shoe upon it, placed there for this purpose, though one would imagine that holy water would alone have been sufficient. I am told there are many other similar instances." *Miscellanies*, p. 148. In Gay's fable of "The Old Woman and her Cats," the supposed witch complains as follows:

—"Crouds of boys
Worry me with eternal noise;
Straws laid across my pace retard,
The horse-shoe's nailed, (each thresh-
 old's guard),
The stunted broom the wenches hide,
For fear that I should up and ride;
They stick with pins my bleeding seat,
And bid me show my secret teat."

Misson, speaking on the subject of the horse-shoe nailed on the door, tells us: "Ayant souvent remarqué un fer de Cheval cloüe au Seuils des portes (chez les Gens de petite etoffe) j'ai demandé a plusieurs ce que cela vouloit dire? On m'a repondu diverses choses differentes; mais la plus generale Reponse a eté, que ces fers se mettoient pour empêcher, les Sorciers d'entrer. Ils rient en disant cela, mais ils ne le disent pourtant pas tout-a-fait en riant; car ils croyent qu'il y a là dedans, ou du moins qu'il peut y avoir quelque vertu secrete: et s'ils n'av-oient pas cette opinion, ils ne s'amuse-roient pas a clouer ce fer à leur porte." *Travels in England*, p. 192. In Mon-mouth-street, says Brand, "many horse-shoes nailed to the thresholds are still to be seen (1797). There used to be one at the corner of Little Queen-street, Hol-born. Sir H. Ellis, on the 26th of April, 1813, counted no fewer than seventeen horse-shoes in Monmouth-street nailed against the steps of doors. There was one in 1869 over the door of a private dwelling in Fulham, near the Bishop's Palace. There is a saying: "When a fool finds a horse-shoe, he thinks aye the like to do." The Editor was driv-ing with the late Mr. Henry Stopes, an East Anglian, in a hansom cab in the Borough in 1887, when the horse slipped its shoe, and Mr. Stopes at once leapt out of the cab and secured it, to place it over the door of his office. It is a piece of Scotish folk-lore, that a horse-shoe nailed to the mast of a fishing-smack will pro-tect it against the weather.

The bawds of Amsterdam believed (in 1687) that a horse-shoe which had either been found or stolen, placed on the chim-ney-hearth, would bring good luck to their houses. They also believed that horse's dung dropped before the house, and put fresh behind the door, would produce the same effect. *Putanisme d'Amsterdam*, pp. 56-7.

Horse-Trick.—A nuptial scene is introduced into Heywood's "Woman Kilde with Kindnesse," 1607. Among the steps in dancing mentioned there, I observe the horse-trick and the cross-point. These two terpsichorean accomplishments

are unnoticed by Strutt, Halliwell, Nares, and others.

Hot Cockles or **Hautes Co-quilles.**—Aubrey says that at funerals in parts of Yorkshire one of the pastimes was Hot Cockles, and what follows illus-trates this observation to a certain ex-tent, although Aubrey does not notice the connection. "Young wenches," says he, "have a wanton sport, which they call moulding of cockle-bread, viz., they gett upon a table-board, and then gather up their knees and their coates with their hands as high as they can, and then they wabble to and fro and say these words, viz.:

My dame is sick and gonne to bed,
And I'll go mowld my cockle-bread.

In Oxfordshire the maids, when they have put themselves into the fit posture, say thus:

My granny is sick, and now is dead,
 And wee'l goe mould some cockle-
 bread.
Up wth my heels and down with my
 head,
And this is the way to mould cockle-
 bread.

I did imagine nothing to have been in this but mere wantonness of youth. (Here he misquotes Juvenal, vi., 129.) But I find in Burchardus, in his *Methodus Con-fitendi*, on the VII. Commandment, one of ye Articles of interrogating a young woman is, if she did ever *subigere panem clunibus*, and then bake it, and give it to one that she loved to eate, *ut in majo-rem modum exardesceret amor?* So here I find it to be a relique of Naturall Mag-ick, an unlawfull philtrum." The full question put to the woman was, accord-ing to Grimm's citation of Burchardus, "Fecisti quod quædam mulieres facere solent, prosternunt se in faciem, et disco-opertis natibus jubent, ut supra nudas nates conficiatur panis, et eo decocto tradunt maritis suis ad comedendum. Hoc ideo faciunt ut plus exardescant in amo-rem illarum." Cockle seems to be, in fact, a corruption of the French coquille, which Le Roux (*Dictionnaire Comique*, 1786, v. *Coquille*) says, "Dans le sens libre signifie á mots couverts la nature d'une femme," for which he quotes a passage from the *History of Francion*. Hot Cockles is therefore Hautes Coquilles; and the custom is very likely to have been introduced hither from France. We know that cockle-bread was the term applied to bread of a coarse brand, made partly of cockle, and it seems very likely that in England the two phrases were confused, and at an early period the distinction lost between the thing supposed to be made and the part, on which it was to be kneaded, our cockle and the French co-quille being so near in sound. The quotation from Burchardus is important, because it demonstrates that the practice was not confined to the young, but was a general usage among females. The late Mr. Coote had heard part of the rhyme given above employed in his time by a nurse to a baby, as she tossed it in her lap:

Up with your heels, and down with your head,
That is the way to make cockle-bread,

which is a singular instance not only of survival, but of distortion. Taking this usage of cockle-bread and its sundry outgrowths as a whole, it has merely to be predicated of it, I think, that we owe our knowledge of such practices to the casual removal of the veil, and by men working on totally different lines, like Aubrey and Burchardt, from the darker phases of the human character and the hidden impurities of life. That libidinous impulses are capable of these and similar excesses, no one required to be told; but the Apostles of Folk-lore, Aubrey, and Burchardt, the publisher of real or supposed scenes in the Confessional, have, each from his own point of view, disclosed here a touch of the less divine part of their own physiology and ours. They have given a few paragraphs where they might have given volumes. After all, I entertain a conviction that, with respect to these hot cockles and likewise to leap-candle, we are merely on the threshold of the inquiry; there is more than Aubrey says, or than appears on the surface, pretty clearly; and the question stands at present much as if one had picked up by accident the husk of some lost substance. Speaking conjecturally, but with certain sidelights to encourage me, this seems a case of the insensible degradation of rite into custom.

Wright furnishes an account of this sport, as practised both here and abroad, tending to shew that its character was modified, and possibly its original incidence forgotten, at a later period, unless there were different types. For the description and accompanying illustrations seem to go no farther than to portray a variety of blindman's buff or hoodman blind, while the one above given represents something infinitely less innocent, and is not even suggested by Mr. Wright. In the following passage from Stevenson's *Twelve Moneths*, 1661, under October, (which work, let us recollect, was originally a reissue of a 1626 book), a different recreation seems to be intended: — "It is now not amisse

to play at hot-cockles hot, unlesse coals be the cheaper." Possibly it is the same as is described in the *Vindication of Christmas*, 1651, as "a harmless sport." Compare Nares, *Gloss.*, 1859, in v. We have here probably the transition successively from a rite to what Nares makes of it, and to a meaningless nursery rhyme. But, again, Mr. Ditchfield (*Old English Customs*), 1896, p. 64, informs us independently that at Norwich on Shrove Tuesday they sell at the bakers' and confectioners' shops a small currant-loaf called a *coquille*, and that in the shop-windows a notice is set up, that "hot coquilles" are to be had at eight in the morning and four in the afternoon. This is survival with a difference, and another type of coquille, and the form is curious in connection with the Lowestoft *largie*.

House, Haunted.—Pliny tells us that houses were anciently hallowed against evil spirits with brimstone! Gay gives us a fine description of a haunted house:

" Now there spreaden a rumour that everich night
The rooms ihaunted been by many a sprite,
The miller avoucheth, and all thereabout,
That they full oft hearen the hellish rout;
Some saine they hear the gingling of chains,
And some hath heard the Psautries straines,
At midnight some the headless horse imeet,
And some espien a corse in a white sheet,
And oother things, faye, elfin, and elfe,
And shapes that fear createn to itself."

Bourne has preserved the form of exorcising a haunted house, a truly tedious process for the expulsion of demons, who, it should seem, have not been easily ferreted out of their quarters, if one may judge of their unwillingness to depart by the prolixity of this removal-warrant. *Antiq. Vulg.*, 1725, ch. ii.

House-Warming.—This is to the present day a well-understood expression for the entertainment which it is usual to give on removal to a new house, or establishment of a household. The phrase occurs in a letter from Fleetwood, Recorder of London, to Lord Burleigh, July 30, 1577: " Upon Tuesday we had little or no business, saving that the Shoemakers of London [the Cordwainers' Gild], having builded a faire and a newe Hall, made a royalle feast for theire friends, which they call their house-warming." It would not be difficult to accumulate instances of the use of the term in later correspondence; but I do not happen to have met with any earlier example. Pepys, in his *Diary*, Nov. 1, 1666, notes having received a noble cake as a gift, and going the same day with his wife and others, and the addition of some wine, to house-warm Betty Michell. The ceremony has long been exclusively performed at the cost of the householder himself.

Houseleek.—It was thought formerly (and the idea is not perhaps entirely extinct) "that if the herb houseleek, or syngreen, do grow on the house-top, the same house is never stricken with lightning or thunder." It is still common in many parts of England, to plant the herb house-leek upon the tops of cottage houses.

Hove-Dance. — The Court-dance. *Halliwell.*

Huers.—Persons employed to watch on the Cornish coasts, and to give the alarm through a long trumpet, which they carry, of the approach of the shoals of pilchards.

Hugh's St., Day.—The best popular account of St. Hugh, Bishop of Lincoln, may be read in Hone's "Every-Day Book," under Nov. 17. This was also the Shoemakers' feast, St. Hugh being the patron of the "gentle craft," and from a notice in "The Christmas Prince," 1607, the fraternity are to be suspected of having sometimes overstepped the bounds of strict decorum and sobriety on the great professional holiday :

"Bouzer I am not, but mild, sober Tuesday,
As catt in cap case, if I light not on St. Hewsday."

Compare *Queen Elizabeth's Accession.*

Hunt the Slipper.—This game is noticed by Rogers in the "Pleasures of Memory," l. 35:

"Twas here we chas'd the slipper by its sound."

It is a holiday game which was till lately in vogue, and is played by children of various growths, sitting on the carpet in a circle.

Hunting of the Ram.—See *Eton School.*

Hunting the Fox.—An early boy's game. See Halliwell in v.

Huntingdon. — The whole of the freemen of the borough assemble in the market-place on the morning of September 15th. The skull of an ox, borne on two poles, is placed at the head of a procession composed of the freemen and their sons, a certain number of them bearing spades and sticks. Three cheers having been given, the procession moves out of the town, and proceeds to the nearest point of the borough boundary, where the skull is lowered. The procession then moves along the boundary line of the borough, the skull being dragged along the line as if it were a plough. The boundary-holes are dug afresh, and a boy thrown into the hole and struck with a spade. At a particular point called Blackstone Leys refreshments are provided, and the boys compete for prizes. The skull is then raised aloft, and the procession returns to the market-place, and then disperses after three more cheers have been given. *Antiquary,* 1892.

Hunt's Up.—A tune played on the horn to awaken the huntsmen on the morning of the chase. See Halliwell in v.

Hurling.—A game at ball, played with two sides, and a favourite pastime in Cornwall, where at present it is exclusively pursued. A description of it may be found in the *Antiquary,* January, 1888. The rocks called the Hurlers, near Liskeard, are traditionally said to have owed their origin to the conversion into stone of certain players at this game on a Sunday. As early as 1654 a hurling match was played in Hyde Park before the Protector and his council between fifty Cornishmen wearing red caps and fifty others wearing white.

Hurly-Hacket.—An early school boy's diversion in Scotland, which appears to have consisted in sliding down a sharp incline. It is mentioned by Sir David Lyndsay as common to adults in a passage quoted in Southey's *Commonplace Book,* 2nd Series, p. 310.

Hyde Park Fair.—A cant expression for Tyburn. See Hazlitt's *Handbook,* 1867, under *T. R.*

Hydromancy.—Very anciently a species of hydromancy appears to have been practised at wells. "The Druids," says Borlase, "(as we have great reason to think) pretended to predict future events, not only from holy wells and running streams, but from the rain and snow water, which, when settled, and afterwards stirr'd either by oak-leaf, or branch or magic wand, might exhibit appearances of great information to the quick-sighted Druid, or seem so to do to the credulous enquirer, when the priest was at full liberty to represent the appearances as he thought most for his purpose." *Antiq. of Cornwall,* 137. To the divination by water also must be referred the following passage in a list of superstitious practices preserved in the "Life of Harvey the

Conjuror," 1728, p. 58. "Immersion of wooden bowls in water, sinking incharmed and inchanted amulets under water, or burying them under a stone in a grave in a churchyard." I suppose the following species of divination must be considered as a vestige of the ancient hydromancy. An essayist introduces "a person surprising a lady and her company in close cabal over their coffee; the rest very intent upon one, who by her dress and intelligence he guessed was a tire-woman; to which she added the secret of divining by coffee-grounds: she was then in full inspiration, and with much solemnity observing the atoms round the cup: on one hand sat a widow, on the other a maiden lady, both attentive to the predictions to be given of their future fate. The lady (his acquaintance), tho' marryed, was no less earnest in contemplating her cup than the other two. They assured him that every cast of the cup is a picture of all one's life to come: and every transaction and circumstance is delineated with the exactest certainty." *Gents. Mag.*, March, 1731. The same practice is noticed in the "Connoisseur," No. 56, where a girl is represented divining to find out of what rank her husband shall be : "I have seen him several times in coffee grounds with a sword by his side; and he was once at the bottom of a tea cup in a coach and six with two footmen behind."

Hynny-Pynny. — A game played with marbles in Devon and Somerset. See Halliwell in v.

I.

I am a Spanish Merchant.—A writer in the *Gentleman's Magazine* for 1738 says: "Queen Elizabeth herself is believed to have invented the play 'I am a Spanish Merchant'; and Burleigh's children were the first who played at it. In this play, if any one offers to sale what he hath not his hand upon or touches, he forfeits—meant as an instruction to traders not to give credit to the Spaniards. The Play of Commerce succeeded, and was in fashion during all her reign."

Ider.—A form of oath by St. Iderius formerly usual in Applecross, co. Ross.—*Stat. Acc. of Scotland*, iii., 380.

Ignis Fatuus. — See *Will o' the Wisp*.

I Love my Love with an A, etc.—Pepys, under March 4,1668-9, notes being at Whitehall, "And there," says he, "I did find the Duke of York and Duchess, with all the great ladies, sitting upon a carpet on the ground, there being no chairs, playing at 'I love my love with an A, because of this and that'; and some of them, but particularly the Duchess herself, and my Lady Castlemaine, were very witty."

Images, etc.—In the Churchwardens' Accounts of Minchinhampton, under 1576, there is an entry of an allowance of 6s. 8d. to John Mayowe and John Lyth for "pullynge downe, dystroyenge, and throwynge out of the churche sundrye superstycyous thinges tendinge to the maynetenaunce of idolatrye." *Archæologia*, xxxv., 430.

A very curious case, illustrative of this branch of our subject, occurred in Scotland in the earlier part of the reign of James VI. The parties to an intended murder first tested their probable success by shooting with arrows of flint at images of their proposed victims, made of butter. *Dom. Annals of Scotland*, i., 232.

Immaculate Conception.—See *Mary of Nazareth*.

Imperator at Cambridge.—See *Christmas Prince*.

In and In.—"In-and-in," says the "Compleat Gamester," 1680, (quoted by Mr. Dyce in a note), "is a game very much used at an ordinary, and may be play'd by two or three, each having a box in his hand. It is play'd with four dice." This game is referred to in Fletcher's play of the "Chances," written prior to 1625. There Don Frederick says:

> " 'Tis strange
> I cannot meet him; sure, he has encounter'd
> Some light o' love or other, and there means
> To play at in-and-in for this night—"

Of course the allusion here is playful or facetious. Perhaps these double meanings were in some favour. In Nevile's "Newes from the New Exchange," 1650, the author, speaking of Lady Sands, says: "She out drinkes a Dutch-man, outvies a courtesan, and is good at all games, but loves none like In and In." In-and-in also occurs as a popular recreation in Lenton's "Young Gallants Whirligig," 1629. Comp. Halliwell and Nares in v.

Indulgences, Papal. — See Hazlitt's *Bibl. Collections and Notes*, 1903, p. 194, for a notice of two issues of a printed document, granting under certain specified conditions, 32,755 years of pardon to the person, whose name is filled in, these forms being generally issued with a blank or blanks left for the ecclesiastic concerned to complete. At the end of a sort of metrical allegory, called *Piers of Fulham* (14th century), in Hazlitt's *Popular Poetry*, 1864, ii., occurs the moral, with this apparently facetious or satirical notification: "Iff any man and woman that hath a deuocyon to heire hit, they shall

haue peraventure for theire meede not
past C dayes of pardon"; so that
these absurdities and impostures were
even then discredited and ridiculed. At
a later period, John Heywood, in
his interlude of the *Pardoner and
the Friar*, written in or before 1521,
makes the former rehearse all the
benefits which accrue from the purchase of the relics, which he carries with
him, or from a subscription to his calls.
Five, ten, and even twelve, thousand years
of pardon are mentioned, but not 32,755.
Contributors to crusades against the infidels were, during the 15th and 16th centuries, shareholders in these *paullo-post-
futuro* securities.

Inner Temple.—See *Christmas
Prince* and *Inns of Court.*

Inning Goose.—In some parts of
Yorkshire, as a clergyman of that county
informed Brand, there is given at the end
of shearing or reaping the corn a prize
sheaf to be run for, and when all the
corn is got home into the stack-yard, an
entertainment is given, called the Inning
Goose.

Innocents' Day.—See *Childermas.*

Inns of Court.—See *Christmas, Inner Temple, Lord of Misrule,* &c. An extraordinary pageant or masque, in which
all the four principal Inns co-operated,
was the *Triumph of Peace*, by James Shirley, 1633, which is of course in Dyce's edition of the dramatist. It was performed
in the banquetting House at Whitehall.
Martin Parker wrote a ballad called *The
Honour of the Inns of Court Gentlemen,
or a briefe recitall of the Magnificent and
Matchlesse Show, that passed from Hatton and Ely house in Holborne to Whitehall, on Monday night, being the third
of February, and the next day after
Candlemas, to the Tune of our Noble King
in his Progresse.*

Inns of Court.—Christmas Sports.
See Leigh's *Accidence of Armoury*, 1562.

Irish.—This was a species of tables or
backgammon, which was a very old game
in this country. Fletcher, in the "Scornful Lady," 1616, makes the lady say:

"I would have vex'd you
More than a tir'd post horse, and been
    longer bearing,
Than ever after-game at Irish was—"

Upon which Mr. Dyce observes: "See the
'Compleat Gamester,' where we are informed that it requires a great deal of
skill to play it (Irish) well, especially the
after-game; bearing, a term of the game,
was frequently, as in the present passage,
used with a quibble—." Shirley mentions Irish in his play of "St. Patrick for
Ireland," 1640, and Hall, in his "Horæ

Vacivæ," 1646, observes: "The inconstancy of Irish fitly represents the change-
ablenesse of humane occurrences, since it
ever stands so fickle that one malignant
throw can quite ruine a never so well-built
game. Art hath here a great sway, by
reason if one cannot well stand the first
assault, hee may safely retire back to an
after game." From a passage in the
"Honest Man's Fortune" (1613), it may
be inferred that in Beaumont and Fletcher's day there were two kinds of Irish,
for there we hear of "two hand Irish."

Irish Baal or **Sun Worship.**—
In Ireland, says Piers, in his *Description
of Westmeath*, 1682, "on the Eves of
St. John Baptist and St. Peter, they always have in every town a bonfire late in
the evenings, and carry about bundles of
reeds fast tied and fired; these being dry,
will last long, and flame better than a
torch, and be a pleasing divertive prospect to the distant beholder; a stranger
would go near to imagine the whole country was on fire. On Midsummer's Eve
every eminence, near which is a habitation, blazes with bonfires; and round these
they carry numerous torches, shouting and
dancing, which affords a beautiful sight,
and at the same time confirms the observation of Scaliger." *Survey of the South
of Ireland*, p. 232. "I have however
heard it lamented that the alteration of
the style had spoiled these exhibitions;
for the Roman Catholics light their fires
by the new style, as the correction originated from a pope; and for that very same
reason the Protestants adhere to the old."
"The sun," says the writer, "was pro-
pitiated here by sacrifices of fire: one was
on the first of May, for a blessing on the
seed sown. The first of May is called, in
the Irish language, La Beal-tein, that
is, the day of Beal's fire. Vossius says it
is well known that Apollo was called Beli-
nus, and for this he quotes Herodian, and
an inscription at Aquileia, Apollini Belino.
The gods of Tyre were Baal, Ashtaroth,
and all the Host of Heaven, as we learn
from the frequent rebukes given to the
backsliding Jews for following after Sido-
nian idols: and the Phenician Baal or
Baalam, like the Irish Beal or Bealin,
denotes the sun, as Asturoth does the
moon." The writer in the "Gent. Magazine" for Feb. 1795, attributes the Irish
worship of the sun and fire to the Roman
Catholics, who have artfully yielded to the
superstitions of the natives, in order to
gain and keep up an establishment, grafting Christianity on Pagan rites. The
chief festival in honour of the sun and
fire is upon the 21st of June, when the
sun arrives at the summer solstice, or
rather begins its retrograde motion. Correspondents of "Notes and Queries" es-

tablish the existence of this custom, not many years ago, in Ireland. In the course of ages, its ancient ceremonial and symbolic import has, no doubt, grown a little indistinct in the minds of those who still practise it; but it is curious that, at so remote a date, the old Baal-worship should survive among us even in any form. The Irish in Liverpool still burned very recently the midsummer fires on St. John's Eve. Yet Vallancey seems to say that in Ireland itself, even in his time, candles had been substituted for fires.

Irish Christmas Usages.—Sir Richard Cox, in his "History of Ireland," mentions some very ridiculous Christmas customs, which continued in the year 1565. In Ireland "On Twelve-Eve in Christmas, they use to set up as high as they can a sieve of oats, and in it a dozen of candles set round, and in the centre one larger, all lighted. This in memory of our Saviour and his Apostles, lights of the world." Sir Henry Piers' *Description of the County of Westmeath*, 1682, in Vallancey, vol. i. No. 1, p. 124.

Irish Drinking Customs. — Barnaby Rich, describing the mode of drinking healths in his time, tells us: "He that beginneth the health, hath his prescribed orders: first uncovering his head, hee takes a full cup in his hand, and setling his countenance with a grave aspect, hee craves for audience: silence being once obtained, hee begins to breathe out the name, peradventure of some honourable personage, that is worthy of a better regard, than to have his name polluted amongst a company of drunkards: but his health is drunke to, and hee that pledgeth must likewise off with his cap, kisse his fingers, and bowing himselfe in signe of a reverent acceptance. When the leader sees his follower thus prepared: he soups up his broath, turnes the bottom of the cup upward, and in ostentation of his dexteritie, gives the cup a phillip, to make it cry Twango. And thus the first scene is acted. The cup being newly replenished to the breadth of an haire, he that is the pledger, must now beginne his part, and thus it goes round throughout the whole company, provided alwaies by a cannon set downe by the founder, there must be three at the least still uncovered, till the health hath had the full passage: which is no sooner ended, but another begins againe." *Irish Hubbub*, 1617, ed. 1619, p. 24. Brown, Bishop of Cork, being a violent Tory, wrote a book to prove that drinking memories was a species of idolatry, in order to abolish a custom then prevalent among the Whigs of Ireland of drinking the glorious memory of King William the Third. But, instead of cooling, he only inflamed the rage for the toast, to which they afterwards tacked the following rider, "And a f*** for the Bishop of Cork." "Survey of the South of Ireland," p. 421. The Bishop's work was entitled "Of drinking in remembrance of the Dead"; 8vo. Lond. 1715, where, in p. 54, he asserts that "an Health is no other than a liquid sacrifice in the constant sense and practice of the heathen." And at page 97, he tells us of a curious "Return given by the great Lord Bacon to such as pressed him to drink the King's Health"; namely, that "he would drink for his own health, and pray for the King's." In Ireland, "on the Patron Day, in most parishes, as also on the feasts of Easter and Whitsuntide, the more ordinary sort of people meet near the alehouse in the afternoon, on some convenient spot of ground, and dance for the cake: here to be sure the piper fails not of diligent attendance. The cake to be danced for is provided at the charge of the ale-wife, and is advanced on a board on the top of a pike, about ten feet high; this board is round, and from it riseth a kind of garland, beset and tied round with meadow flowers, if it be early in the summer: if later, the garland has the addition of apples, set round on pegs, fastened unto it. The whole number of dancers begin all at once in a large ring, a man and a woman, and dance round about the bush (so is this garland called), and the piper, as long as they are able to hold out. They that hold out longest at the exercise, win the cake and apples, and then the ale-wife's trade goes on." Piers, *Description of Westmeath*, 1682, ap. Vallancey i., 123.

Irish Election Custom.—There was an old ceremony in Ireland of electing a person to any office by throwing an old shoe over his head, according to the author of the *Idol of the Clowns*, 1654, p. 19.

Irish Fairy Lore.—The late Mr. T. Crofton Croker classes the Irish fairies under the heads of shefro, cluricaune, banshee, phooka, merrow, dullahan and the fir darrig. The name shefro literally signifies a fairy-house or mansion, and is adopted as a generic name for the elves who are supposed to live in troops or communities, and were popularly supposed to have castles or mansions of their own. The cluricaune was distinguished by his solitary habits. The banshee, an attendant fairy or spirit, especially observed to mourn on the death of any member of a family to which it attached itself. The phooka appears to be a modification of Robin Goodfellow or Puck. The merrow is a mermaid. The dullahan is a malicious, sullen spirit, or goblin, and the fir darrig a little merry red man, not unlike in its disposition and movements to Puck." Brand's *P. A.*, ed. 1848. "Sith-bhreog, the same as Sigh-brog, a fairy; hence bean-sighe, plural mna-sighe, women fairies; credulously supposed by the common people to be so affected to certain families, that they are heard to sing mournful lamentations about their houses by night, whenever any of the family labours under a sickness, which is to end by death: but no families, which are not of an ancient and noble stock (of Oriental extraction he should have said), are believed to be honoured with this fairy privilege." O'Brien's *Dict. Hib.*, cited by Vallancey, Collect. iii. 461.

Dr. Moore, a Wicklow schoolmaster, in the time of Charles II., had, it seems, "been often told by his mother and several others of his relations, of spirits which they called fairies, who used frequently to carry him away, and continue him with them for some time, without doing him the least prejudice: but his mother being very much frighted and concerned thereat, did, as often as he was missing, send to a certain old woman, her neighbour in the country, who by repeating some spells or exorcisms, would suddenly cause his return." His friend very naturally disbelieved the facts, "while the doctor did positively affirm the truth thereof." But the most strange and wonderful part of the story is, that during the dispute the doctor was carried off suddenly by some of those invisible gentry, though forcibly held by two persons; nor did he return to the company till six o'clock the next morning, both hungry and thirsty, having, as he asserted "been hurried from place to place all that night." At the end of this marvellous narration is the following advertisement: "For the satisfaction of the licenser, I certifie this following" (it ought to have been preceding) "Relation was sent to me from Dublin by a person whom I credit, and recommended in a letter bearing date the 23rd of November last as true news much spoken of there. John Cother." This sort of certificate usually accompanies all the old narratives of marvels, as if the narrators entertained a secret misgiving as to the extent of popular credulity on the subject. Here was a man assuring the government official that everything was perfectly correct! "Strange and Wonderful News from the County of Wicklow," &c., 1678.

In the "Survey of the South of Ireland," p. 280, I read as follows: "The fairy mythology is swallowed with the wide throat of credulity. Every parish has its green and thorn, where these little people are believed to hold their merry meetings, and dance their frolic **rounds. I have seen one of those elf-**stones, like a thin triangular flint, not half an inch in diameter, with which they suppose the fairies destroy their cows. And when these animals are seized with a certain disorder, to which they are very incident, they say they are elf-shot." Vallancey, in his "Collectanea de Rebus Hibernicis," No. xiii., description of Plate 11, tells us, that "what the peasants in Ireland call an elf-arrow is frequently set in silver, and worn about the neck as an amulet against being elf-shot." "In Ireland," says Grose, "they (the fairies) frequently lay bannocks, a kind of oaten cakes, in the way of travellers over the mountains; and if they do not accept of the intended favour, they seldom escape a hearty beating or something worse." Comp. *Elf-Shot*.

Irish Funeral Customs.—In the "Irish Hudibras," 1689, is given the following description of the burial of an Irish piper:

> "They mounted him upon a bier,
> Through which the whattles did appear,
> Like ribs on either side made fast,
> With a white velvet (i.e. blanket) over cast:
> So poor Macshane, God rest his shoul,
> Was after put him in a hole;
> In which, with many sighs and scrieches,
> They throw his trouses and his breeches;
> The tatter'd brogue was after throw,
> With a new heel-piece on the toe;
> And stockins fine as friez to feel,
> Worn out with praying at the heel;
> And in his mouth, 'gainst he took wherry,
> Dropt a white groat to pay the ferry.
> Thus did they make this last hard shift,
> To furnish him for a dead lift."

The following is copied from the "Argus," Aug. 5, 1790. "Dublin, July 31: Sunday being St. James's Day, the votaries of St. James's Church Yard attended in considerable crowds at the Shrines of their departed friends, and paid the usual tributary honours of paper gloves and garlands of flowers on their graves." Compare *Irish Wakes*.

Irish Hobby.—The hobby-harness mentioned in the Wardrobe Accounts of Edward IV., 1480, was intended, not for a hobby-horse, but for an Irish hobby, or small horse imported into this country from Ireland at an early date.

Irish Marriage Rites. In Piers' *Description of Westmeath*, 1682, it is stated, that "in their marriages, especially in those countries where cattle abound, the parents and friends on each side meet on the side of a hill, or, if the weather be cold, in some place of shelter about mid-way between both dwellings. If agreement ensue, they drink the Agreement-Bottle, as they call it, which is a bottle of good Usquebaugh," (i.e. whisky, the Irish *aqua vitæ*, and not what is now understood by Usquebaugh), " and this goes merrily round. For payment of the portion, which generally is a determinate number of cows, little care is taken. Only the father, or next of kin to the bride, sends to his neighbours and friends *sub mutuæ vicissitudinis obtentu*, and every one gives his cow or heifer, which is all one in the case, and thus the portion is quickly paid ; nevertheless, caution is taken from the bridegroom, on the day of delivery, for restitution of the cattle, in case the bride died childless within a certain day limited by agreement, and in this case every man's own beast is restored. Thus care is taken that no man shall grow rich by often marriages. On the day of bringing home, the bridegroom and his friends ride out, and meet the bride and her friends at the place of treaty. Being come near each other, the custom was of old to cast short darts at the company that attended the bride, but at such a distance that seldom any hurt ensued : yet it is not out of the memory of man that Lord Hoath on such an occasion lost an eye : this custom of casting darts is now obsolete." Camden says, that "they (the Irish) are observed to present their lovers with bracelets of women's hair, whether in reference to Venus' Cestus or not, I know not." Gough's ed. 1789, iii., 658. The following is from the "Gentleman's Magazine" for March, 1767 : " The antient custom of seizing wives by force, and carrying them off, is still practised in Ireland. A remarkable instance of which happened lately in the county of Kilkenny, where a farmer's son, being refused a neighbour's daughter of only twelve years of age, took an opportunity of running away with her ; but being pursued and recovered by the girl's parents, she was brought back and married by her father to a lad of fourteen. But her former lover, determining to maintain his priority, procured a party of armed men, besieged the house of his rival : and in the contest the father-in-law was shot dead, and several of the besiegers were mortally wounded, and forced to retire without their prize."

Irish May-day Customs.—Piers

says (*Description of Westmeath*, 1682), " On May Eve, every family sets up before their door a green bush, strewed over with yellow flowers, which the meadows yield plentifully. In countries where timber is plentiful, they erect tall slender trees, which stand high, and they continue almost the whole year ; so as a stranger would go nigh to imagine that they were all signs of ale-sellers, and that all houses

were ale-houses." He also tells us that the Irish " have a custom every May-day, which they count their first day of summer, to have to their meal one formal dish, whatever else they have, which some call stir-about, or hasty-pudding, that is flour and milk boiled thick ; and this is holden as an argument of the good wife's good huswifery, that made her corn hold out so well as to have such a dish to begin summer fare with ; for if they can hold out so long with bread, they count they can do well enough for what remains of the year till harvest ; for then milk becomes plenty, and butter, new cheese and curds and shamrocks, are the food of the meaner sort all this season. Nevertheless, in this mess, on this day, they are so formal, that even in the plentifullest and greatest houses, where bread is in abundance all the year long, they will not fail of this dish, nor yet they that for a month before wanted bread." Camden says : "They fancy a green bough of a tree, fastened on May Day against the house, will produce plenty of milk that summer." Vallancey, speaking of the first of May, says : "On that day the Druids drove all the cattle through the fires, to preserve them from disorders the ensuing year. This pagan custom is still observed in Munster and Connaught, where the meanest cottager worth a cow and a wisp of straw practises the same on the first day of May, and with the same superstitious ideas."

Irish Michaelmas Custom.—

" In Ireland a sheep was killed in every family that could afford one, at Michaelmas ; and it was ordained by law that a part of it should be given to the poor. This, as we gather from Keating, and a great deal more, was done in that kingdom, to perpetuate the memory of a miracle wrought there by St. Patrick through the assistance of the Archangel. In commemoration of this, Michaelmas was instituted a festal day of joy, plenty, and universal benevolence."

Irish Superstitions. — Giraldus

Cambrensis, who visited Ireland about the end of the twelfth century, speaks thus of some relics of superstition :—" Hoc etiam non praetereundum puto, quod campanas bajulas, baculosque sanctorum in superiore parte recurvos, auro et argento vel ære confectos, tam Hiberniæ et Scotiæ quam et Walliæ populus et clerus in magna reverentia habere solent : ita ut sacramenta supra hæc, longe magis quam super Evangelia, et præstare vereantur et pejerare. Ex vi enim quadam occulta, et his quasi divinitus insita, nec non et vindicta (cujus praecipue sancti illi appetibiles esse videntur) plerumque puniuntur contemptores." "Topog. Hiber." l. iii. c. 33, and l. ii. c. 23, edit. 1867.

"On the Oidche Shamhna (Ee Owna) or Vigil of Saman," Vallancey says, "The peasants in Ireland assemble with sticks and clubs (the emblems of laceration) going from house to house, collecting money, bread-cake, butter, cheese, eggs, &c., &c., for the feast, repeating verses in honour of the solemnity, demanding preparations for the festival in the name of St. Colomb Kill, desiring them to lay aside the fatted calf, and to bring forth the black sheep. The good women are employed in making the griddle cake and candles; these last are sent from house to house in the vicinity, and are lighted up on the (Saman) next day, before which they pray, or are supposed to pray, for the departed soul of the donor. Every house abounds in the best viands they can afford: apples and nuts are devoured in abundance; the nut-shells are burnt, and from the ashes many strange things are foretold: cabbages are torn up by the root: hemp seed is sown by the maidens, and they believe that if they look back, they will see the apparition of the man intended for their future spouse: they hang a smock before the fire, on the close of the feast, and sit up all night, concealed in a corner of the room, convinced that his apparition will come down the chimney and turn the smock: they throw a ball of yarn out of the window, and wind it on the reel within, convinced that if they repeat the Pater Noster backwards, and look at the ball of yarn without, they will then also see his sith or apparition: they dip for apples in a tub of water, and endeavour to bring one up in the mouth: they suspend a cord with a cross stick, with apples at one point, and candles lighted at the other, and endeavour to catch the apple, while it is in circular motion, in the mouth. These, and many other superstitious ceremonies, the remains of Druidism, are observed on this holiday, which will never be eradicated while the name of Saman is permitted to remain." I do not know whether Saman has an affinity to the Turanian Shaman.

In Ireland, "On the first Sunday in harvest, viz., in August, they will be sure to drive their cattle into some pool or river and therein swim them: this they observe as inviolable as if it were a point of religion, for they think no beast will live the whole year thro' unless they be thus drenched. I deny not but that swimming cattle, and chiefly in this season of the year, is healthful unto them, as the poet hath observed:

'Balantemque gregem fluvio mersare salubri.'—*Virg.*
In th' healthful flood to plunge the bleating flock.

but precisely to do this on the first Sunday in harvest, I look on as not only superstitious but profane." Piers, *Descr. of Westmeath*, 1682, ap. Vallancey, i., 121. In "The Irish Hudibras," 1689, we have the following allusion to the Irish visits to holy wells on the patron's day:

" Have you beheld, when people pray
At St. John's Well on Patron-Day,
By charm of priest and miracle,
To cure diseases at this well;
The valleys fill'd with blind and lame,
And go as limping as they came."

This refers to a well in the North of Ireland. Camden says: " If they never give fire out of their houses to their neighbours, they fancy their horses will live the longer and be more healthy. If the owners of horses eat eggs, they must take care to eat an even number, otherwise some mischief will betide the horses. Grooms are not allowed eggs, and the riders are obliged to wash their hands after eating them. When a horse dies, his feet and legs are hung up in the house, and even the hoofs are accounted sacred. It is by no means allowable to praise a horse or any other animal, unless you say God save him, or spit upon him. If any mischance befalls the horse, in three days after they find out the person who commended him, that he may whisper the Lord's Prayer in his right ear. They believe some men's eyes have a power of bewitching horses; and then they send for certain old women who, by muttering short prayers, restore them to health. Their horses' feet are subject to a worm, which gradually creeping upwards produces others of its own species, and corrupts the body. Against this worm they call in a witch, who must come to the horse two Mondays and one Thursday, and breathe upon the place where the worm lodges, and after repeating a charm the horse recovers. This charm they will, for a sum of money, teach to many people, after first swearing them never to disclose it." Gough's *Camden*, 1789, iii., 668: Jorden's *Suffocation of the Mother*, 1603, p. 24. The former adds: "They think women have charms divided and distributed among them; and to them persons apply according to their several disorders, and they constantly begin and end the charm with Pater Noster and Ave Maria." And again, "They look through the hare blade-bone of a sheep, and if they see any spot in it darker than ordinary, foretell that somebody will be buried out of the house." Ed. 1789, iii., 659, 668. " If a cow becomes dry, a witch is applied to, who, inspiring herself with a fondness for some other calf, makes her yield her milk." He also tells us: " The women who are turned off (by their husbands) have recourse to witches, who are supposed to inflict barrenness, impotence, or the most dangerous diseases, on the former husband or his new wife." Also, they account every woman who fetches fire on May-day a witch, nor will they give it to any but sick persons, and that with an imprecation, believing she will steal all the butter next summer. On May-day they kill all hares they find among their cattle, supposing them the old women who have designs on the butter. They imagine the butter so stolen may be recovered if they take some of the thatch hanging over the door and burn it." *Britannia*, 1789, iii., 659.

According to a writer of the Georgian era, the Irish were partial to philtres. He observes: "The spark that's resolved to sacrifice his youth and vigour on a damsel, whose coyness will not accept of his love-oblations, he threads a needle with the hair of her head, and then running it thro' the most fleshy part of a dead man, as the brawn of the arms, thigh, or the calf of the leg, the charm has that virtue in it, as to make her run mad for him whom she so lately slighted." *Comical Pilgrim's Voyage into Ireland.* We read, in *Memorable Things noted in the Description of the World*, pp. 111-13, "About children's necks the wild Irish hung the beginning of St. John's Gospel, a crooked nail of an horse-shoe, or a piece of wolves-skin, and both the sucking child and nurse were girt with girdles finely plated with woman's hair: so far they wandered into the ways of errour, in making these arms the strength of their healths." . . . "Of the same people Solinus affirmeth, that they are so given to war, that the mother, at the birth of a man child, feedeth the first meat into her infant's mouth upon the point of her husband's sword, and with heathenish imprecations wishes that it may dye no otherwise then in war, or by sword." Giraldus Cambrensis saith, "At the baptizing of the infants of the wild Irish, their manner was not to dip their right arms into the water, that so as they thought they might give a more deep and incurable blow." Here is a proof that the whole body of the child was anciently commonly immersed in the baptismal font. Camden relates that, "if a child is at any time out of order, they sprinkle it with the stalest urine they can get."

Scot, in his *Discovery*, 1584, writes: "The Irishmen affirm that not only their children, but their cattle are (as they call it) Eyebitten, when they fall suddenly sick." This statement is repeated by Ady (*Candle in the Dark*, 1659, p. 104). Among the Irish, when a woman milks her cow, she dips her finger into the milk, with which she crosses the beast, and

piously ejaculates a prayer, saying, "Mary and our Lord preserve thee, until I come to thee again." "The Irish, when they put out a candle, say, 'May the Lord renew, or send us the light of Heaven,'" Defoe's *Memoirs of Duncan Campbel*, 1734, p. 202. The subsequent passage is in Osborne's "Advice to his Son," 1656, p. 79, "The Irish or Welch, during eclipses, run about beating kettles and pans, thinking their clamour and vexations available to the assistance of the higher orbes." A foreign editor of English, or rather Irish, antiquities, informs us, that the inhabitants of the sister-island were accustomed, when they first beheld the new moon, to fall down on their knees, repeat the Lord's prayer, and then cry aloud, addressing the planet, "Leave us all well as thou hast found us." Du Chesne's *History of England*, p. 18. Vallancey also says: "The vulgar Irish at this day retain an adoration to the new moon, crossing themselves and saying, 'May thou leave us as safe as thou has found us.'" *Collectanea*, xiii., 91. Camden, speaking of Ireland, says: "In the town when any enter upon a public office, women in the streets, and girls from the windows, sprinkle them and their attendants with wheat and salt. And before the seed is put into the ground the mistress of the family sends salt into the field." Gough's Camden, iii., 659. See *Jack-Stones.*

Irish Wakes.—The *Conclamatio* among the Romans coincides with the Irish cry. The "Mulieres præficæ" exactly corresponds with the women who lead the Irish band, and who make an outcry too outrageous for real grief.

"Ut qui conducti plorant in funere,
    dicunt
Et faciunt prope plura dolentibus ex
    animo."

That this custom was Phœnician we may learn from Virgil, who was very correct in the costume of his characters. The conclamatio over the Phœnician Dido, as described by him, is similar to the Irish cry:

"Lamentis gemituque et fœmineo ulu-
    latu
Tecta fremunt."

The very word "ululatus," or "hulluloo," and the Greek word of the same import, have all a strong affinity to each other. Campbell mentions that the custom obtained here of placing a plate of salt over the heart. It should seem as if he had seen Moresin's remark, by his supposing that they consider the salt as the emblem of the incorruptible part. "The body itself," says he, "being the type of corruption." *Survey of the South of Ireland*, 1777, p. 210. Some have said that instead of salt the relatives place snuff, of which the mourners and visitors partake. Rich, in his "Irish Hubbub," 1616, writes: "Stanyhurst, in his History of Ireland, 1584, maketh this report of his countreymen: they follow the dead corps to the ground, with howling and barbarous outcries, pitifull in appearance, whereof (as he supposeth) grew this proverb, 'to weep Irish.' Myselfe am partly of his opinion, that (indeede) to weepe Irish, is to weep at pleasure, without either cause or greefe, when it is an usuall matter amongst them, upon the buriall of their dead, to hire a company of women, that for some small recompence given them, they will follow the corpse, and furnish out the cry with such howling and barbarous outcries, that hee that should but heare them, and did not know the ceremony, would rather thinke they did sing than weep. And yet in Dublin itselfe, there is not a corps carried to the buriall, which is not followed with this kind of mourners, which you shall heare by their howling and their hollowing, but never see them to shed any tears. Suche a kinde of lamentation," he adds, it is "as in the judgement of any man that should but heare, and did not know their custome, would think it to bee some prodigious presagement, prognosticating some unlucky or ill successe, as they use to attribute to the howling of doggs, to the croaking of ravens, and the shrieking of owles, fitter for infidels and barbarians, than to bee in use and custome among Christians."

Piers, in his *Description of Westmeath*, 1682, observes: "In Ireland at funerals they have their wakes, which as now they celebrate, were more befitting heathens than christians. They sit up commonly in a barn or large room, and are entertained with beer and tobacco. The lights are set up on a table over the dead; they spend most of the night in obscene stories and bawdye songs, untill the hour comes for the exercise of their devotions; then the priest calls on them to fall to their prayers for the soul of the dead, which they perform by repetition of aves and paters on their beads, and close the whole with a 'De Profundis,' and then immediately to the story or song again, till another hour of prayer comes. Thus is the whole night spent till day. When the time of burial comes, all the women run out like mad, and now the scene is altered, nothing heard but wretched exclamations, howling and clapping of hands, enough to destroy their own and others' sense of hearing: and this was of old the heathenish custom as Virgil hath observed in Dryden's translation:

'The gaping croud around the body stand,
All weep . . . . . his fate,
And hasten to perform the fun'ral state.'

"This they fail not to do, especially if the deceased were of good parentage, or of wealth and repute, or a landlord, &c. and think it a great honour to the dead to keep all this coyl, and some have been so vain as to hire these kind of mourners to attend their dead; and yet they do not by all this attain the end they seem to aim at, which is to be thought to mourn for the dead; for the Poet hath well observed:

'Fortiter ille dolet, qui sine teste dolet.'

"At some stages, where commonly they meet with great heaps of stones in the way, the corpse is laid down and the priest or priests and all the learned fall again to their aves and paters, &c. During this office all is quiet and hushed. But this done, the corpse is raised, and with it the out-cry again. But that done, and while the corpse is laying down and the earth throwing on, is the last and most vehement scene of this formal grief; and all this perhaps but to earn a groat, and from this Egyptian custom they are to be weaned. In some parts of Connaught, if the party deceased were of good note, they will send to the wake hogsheads of excellent stale beer and wine from all parts, with other provisions, as beef, &c., to help the expence at the funeral, and oftentimes more is sent in than can well be spent." *Vallancey*, i., 124. The same writer (Sir H. Piers) adds: "After the day of interment of a great personage, they count four weeks; and that day four weeks all priests and friars, and all gentry, far and near, are invited to a great feast (usually termed the Month's Mind); the preparation to this feast are masses, said in all parts of the house at once, for the soul of the departed; if the room be large, you shall have three or four priests together celebrating in the several corners thereof; the masses done, they proceed to their feastings; and after all, every priest and friar is discharged with his largess." *Vallancey*, i., 126. The author of "The Comical Pilgrim's Pilgrimage into Ireland," 1723, says: "When a virgin dies, a garland made of all sorts of flowers and sweet herbs, is carried by a young woman on her head, before the coffin, from which hang down two black ribbons, signifying our mortal state, and two white, as an emblem of purity and innocence. The ends thereof are held by four young maids, before whom a basket full of herbs and flowers is supported by two other maids, who strew them along the streets to the place of burial : then, after the deceased, follow all her relations and acquaintance." In "The Irish Hudibras," 1689, is an exaggerated description of what is called in the margin " An Irish Wake." In the early part of the 18th century, this fashion and taste for howling at Irish funerals still prevailed. "The Comical Pilgrim's Pilgrimage into Ireland," 1723, p. 92. The following is from a paper by the third Lord Chesterfield : — " When the lower sort of Irish, in the most uncivilized parts of Ireland, attend the funeral of a deceased friend or neighbour, before they give the last parting howl, they expostulate with the dead body, and reproach him with having died, notwithstanding that he had an excellent wife, a milch cow, seven fine children, and a competency of potatoes." *The World*, No. 24. In the " Gentleman's Magazine " for August, 1771, it is said of a girl who was killed by lightning in Ireland, that " she could not be waked within doors, an expression which is explained as alluding to a custom among the Irish of dressing their dead in their best cloaths, to receive as many visitors as please to see them; and this is called keeping their wake. The corpse of this girl, it seems, was so offensive, that this ceremony could not be performed within doors." The author of the " Philosophical Survey of the South of Ireland," says, p. 207: " It was formerly usual to have a bard to write the elegy of the deceased, which contained an enumeration of his good qualities, his genealogy, his riches, &c., the burden being, ' O why did he die?' " A modern writer on Ireland tells us : " It is the custom of this country to conduct their dead to the grave in all the parade they can display; and as they pass through any town, or meet any remarkable person, they set up their howl. "Survey of the South of Ireland," pp. 206, 209-10. A good account of the Wake is to be found, as Sir H. Ellis pointed out, in the Glossary to Miss Edgeworth's " Castle Rackrent."

Ivo or **Ives, St.**—The patron saint of lawyers, on whose feast day, May 19, in Normandy, at least, the members of the profession in towns used to assemble, and partake of good cheer. *The Vaux-de-Vire* of Jean le Houx, by Muirhead, 1875, p. li.

Ivy.—In " Witts Recreations," 1640, occurs an epigram on " Christmasse Ivy":

" At Christmasse men do alwayes ivy get,
And in each corner of the house it set.
But why do they, then, use that Bacchus weed?
Because they mean then Bacchus-like to feed."

In the piece called "Hankins Heigh-ho," printed in Musarum Deliciæ, 1656, we have :

" Thrice had all new-yeares guests their yewl guts fill'd
With embalm'd veal, buried in Christmas past :
Thrice had they ivy herby wreath well pill'd ;——"

Aubrey says that, in his time (1678) it was customary in several parts of Oxfordshire " for the maidservant to ask the man for ivy to dress the house, and if the man denies, or neglects to fetch in ivy, the maid steals away a pair of his breeches, and nails them up to the gate in the yard or highway."

Ivy-Bush.—Comp. *Bush*, and see Nares, 1859, v. *Ivy-Bush.*

Ivy-Girl.—See *Holly-Boy.*

Ivy-Leaf.—Lupton, in his " Tenth Book of Notable things," No. 87, says: "Lay a green ivie-leaf in a dish, or other vessel of fair water, either for yourselfe or for any other, on New Year's Even at night, and cover the water in the said vessel, and set it in a sure or safe place, until twelfe even nexte after, (which will be the 5th day of January), and then take the said ivie-leafe out of the said water, and mark well if the said leafe be fair and green as it was before, for then you, or the party for whome you lay it into the water, will be whole and sound, and safe from any sickness all the next year following. But if you find any black spots thereon, then you or the parties for whome you laid it into the water, will be sicke the same year following. And if the spots be on the upper part of the leafe toward the stalke, then the sicknesse or paine will be in the head, or in the neck, or thereabout. And if it be spotted nigh the midst of the leaf, then the sicknesse will be about the stomach or heart. And likewise judge, that the disease or grief will be in that part of the body, according as you see the black spots under the same in the leafe, accounting the spots in the nether or sharp end of the leafe to signify the paines or diseases in the feet. And if the leafe bee spotted all over, then it signifies that you, or the partie, shall dye that yeare following. You may prove this for many or few, at one time, by putting them in water, for everie one a leaf of green ivie (so that every leafe be dated or marked to whom it doth belong). This was credibly told me to be very certain." Edit. 1660, p. 300.

Jack in the Green. — See *May Games.*

Jack o' or **w' a Lanthorn.**—See *Will o' the Wisp.*

Jack o' Lent.—A Jack o' Lent was

a puppet, formerly thrown at, in our own country, in Lent, like Shrove-cocks. So in "The Weakest goes to the Wall," 1600, we have, "A mere anatomy, a Jack of Lent." Again, in the "Four Prentices of London," 1615: "Now you old Jack of Lent, six weeks and upwards." Again, in "Green's Tu quoque," 1614, "For if a boy, that is throwing at his Jack o' Lent, chance to hit me on the shins," &c. Taylor the Water-poet, in a tract printed in 1620, personifies under this form the observances of the season, with the mad pranks of Jack's gentleman-usher Shrove-Tuesday, and his footman Hunger. Jonathan Couch of Polperro, in his account of that Cornish fishing village, 1871, observes: "An old custom, now quite defunct, was observed here not long since in the beginning of Lent. A figure, made up of straw and cast-off clothes, was carried round the town, amid much noise and merriment, after which it was either burnt, shot at, or brought to some other ignominious end. This image was called 'Jack o' Lent,' and was doubtless intended to represent Judas Iscariot. A dirty slovenly fellow is often termed a 'Jack o' Lent.'"

"Then Jake a Lent comes justlinge in
　　With the hedpeece of a herynge,
And saythe, repent yowe of yower syn,
　　For shame, syrs, leve yower swerynge;
And to Palme Sunday dcethe he ryde,
And sprots and herryngs by hys syde,
And makes an ende of Lenton tyde!"
Elderton's *Ballad of Lenten Stuffe*, 1570,

Jack Pudding. — See *Merry Andrew.*

Jack Stones or Gobstones. — Divination at marriages was practised in times of the remotest antiquity. Vallancey tells us that in the "Memoirs of the Etruscan Academy of Cortona" is the drawing of a picture found in Herculaneum, representing a marriage. In the front is a sorceress casting the five stones. The writer of the memoir justly thinks she is divining. The figure exactly corresponds with the first and principal cast of the Irish purin: all five are cast up, and the first catch is on the back of the hand. He has copied the drawing: On the back of the hand stands one, and the remaining four on the ground. Opposite the sorceress is the matron, attentive to the success of the cast. No marriage ceremony was performed without consulting the Druidess and her purin. Juvenal tells us: "Auspices solebant nuptias interesse." Vallancey adds: "This is now played as a game by the youths of both sexes in Ireland. The Irish Seic Seona (Shec Shona) was readily turned into Jack Stones, by an English ear, by which name

this game is now known by the English in Ireland. It has another name among the vulgar, viz., Gobstones."

James's Day, St. — (July 25). The blessing of new apples upon this day is preserved in the "Manuale ad Usum Sarum":

　　"Benedictio Pomorum in Die Sancti Jacobi."

"Te deprecamur omnipotens Deus ut benedicas hunc fructum novorum pomorum: ut qui esu arboris letalis et pomo in primo parente justa funeris sententia mulctati sumus; per illustrationem unici filii tui Redemptoris Dei ac Domini nostri Jesu Christi & Spiritus Sancti benedictionem sanctificata sint omnia atque benedicta: depulsisque primi facinoris intentatoris insidiis, salubriter ex hujus diei anniversaria solennitate diversis terris edenda germina sumamus per eundem Dominum in unitate ejusdem. Deinde sacerdos aspergat ea aquâ benedictâ." Edit. Rothomagi, 1555, fol. 64-5. In Wiltshire and Somersetshire the apples are said to be christened on St. James's Day. Hasted tells us that "the rector of Cliff, in Shamel hundred, by old custom, distributes at his parsonage house on St. James's Day, annually, a mutton pye and a loaf, to as many persons as chuse to demand it, the expence of which amounts to about £15 per annum." "Hist. of Kent," vol. i. p. 537, folio ed. The hay crop is in a sufficiently forward state by this time to enable the growers to judge of the prospects of a good or bad harvest, and there is a proverbial expression bearing on this:

"Till St. James's Day be come and gone,
There may be hops, or there may be none."

The "Book of Days" says that this is a Herefordshire adage; but it is current in all the hop-districts. On St. James Day, old style, oysters come in in London; and there is a popular superstition still in force, like that relating to goose on Michaelmas Day, that whoever eats oysters on that day will never want money for the rest of the year.

James's, St., Fair. — St. James's Fair, held at Westminster on the 25th July, was, in the year 1560, so largely attended, that a pig was not to be had there, we are told by Machyn the diarist, "for mony." And he adds that the ale-wives could get nothing to eat or drink till three in the afternoon, and "the chese went very well away for 1d. p. the pounde." On Thursday, the 17th of July, 1651, the Parliament passed a resolution, "That the fair usually held and kept yearly at St. James's, within the Liberty of the City of Westminster, on or about the 25th of July, be forborn this year; and that no fair be kept or held there by any person or persons whatsoever, until the Parliament shall take further order." Comp. *May-Fair*.

James's, St., Fair, Bristol.— A fair was formerly held at Bristol on St. James's Day, and it is related by the author of Tarlton's "Jests," 1611, that that celebrated comedian and his fellow-players went down to perform there on one occasion while the theatres were closed in London. Probably it was at the same time that they visited Gloucester and other places mentioned in the "Jests." The player seems also to have been engaged at private houses in the country to give entertainments. This must have been prior to 1588, when Tarlton died.

Jericho.— A bye-name for Blackmore Priory, Essex, after the Dissolution, when the house was adopted by Henry VIII. as an occasional resort. Here was born the King's natural son by Elizabeth Tachboro, afterward created Duke of Richmond. Blackmore belonged to the manor of Fringreth.

Jericho, Rose of.—See *Rose*.

Jews.— The modern Jews, on the first day of the first month Tisri, have a splendid entertainment, and wish each other a happy New Year. Vallancey says that "there is a passage in Ruth, chap. iv. v. 7, which gives room to think that the marriage ring was used by the Jews as a covenant." He adds, that the Vulgate has translated Narthick (which ought to be a ring) a shoe. "An Irish Nuirt is an amulet worn on the finger, or arm, a ring." Sphæra solis est Narthick, says Buxtorf in his Chaldee Lexicon. *Collect.* xiii., 98. The Jews have a custom at this day, when a couple are married, to break the glass in which the bride and bridegroom have drunk, to admonish them of mortality. This custom of nuptial drinking appears to have prevailed in the Greek Church. Leo Modena, speaking of the Jews' contracts and manner of marrying, says that before the writing of the bride's dowry is produced, and read, "the bridegroom putteth a ring upon her finger, in the presence of two witnesses, which commonly used to be the rabbines, saying withal unto her: 'Behold, thou art my espoused wife, according to the custome of Moses and of Israel.'" *Hist. of the Rites of the Jews*, translated by Chilmead, 1650, 176. Something like the care-cloth is used by the modern Jews: from whom it has probably been derived into the Christian Church. Leo Modena says: "There is a square vestment called Taleth, with pendants about it, put over the head of the bridegroom and the bride together," and Levi

seems to show that this "square vestment," or canopy, was of velvet. White, in his "History of Selborne," remarks: "Deborah, Rebekah's nurse, (Gen. xxxv. 8) was buried under an oak; the most honourable place of interment, probably, next to the Cave of Macphelah (Gen. xxiii. 9), which seems to have been appropriated to the remains of the patriarchal family alone. We read that when any of the sick among the Jews have departed, the corpse is taken and laid on the ground, and a pillow put under its head; and the hands and feet are laid out even, and the body is covered over with a black cloth, and a light is set at its head." Levi's "Account of the Rites and Ceremonies of the Modern Jews," p. 163. Levi says, that among the modern Jews, "the corpse is carried forward to the grave and interred by some of the Society; and as they go forth from the burying-ground, they pluck some grass and say, 'They shall spring forth from the city, as the grass of the earth'; meaning at the Day of Resurrection." *Rites and Ceremonies of the Jews*, 169. Bourne cites Gregory as observing, that it was customary among the ancient Jews, as they returned from the grave, to pluck up the grass two or three times, and then throw it behind them, saying these words of the Psalmist, "They shall flourish out of the city, like grass upon the earth," which they did to shew that the body, though dead, should spring up again as the grass. Gregory, *Posthuma*, 1649, c. 26. The Jews, in celebrating their Passover, placed on the table two unleavened cakes, and two pieces of the Lamb: to this they added some small fishes, because of the Leviathan: a hard egg, because of the bird Ziz: some meal, because of the Behemoth: these three animals being, according to their Rabbinical doctrines, appointed for the feast of the elect in the other life. The Jewish wives, at this Feast, upon a table prepared for that purpose, place hard eggs, the symbols of Ziz, concerning which the Rabbins have a thousand fabulous accounts. Mr. Brand saw at the window of a baker's shop in London, on Easter Eve, 1805, a Passover Cake, with four eggs, bound in with slips of paste, crossways, in it. He went into the shop, and enquired of the baker what it meant: he assured him it was a Passover Cake for the Jews.

To strike one with a shoe, or cast a shoe at one, was regarded by the ancient Jews as a mark of indignity and contempt, as in the passage of the Psalms: "Moab is my washpot; over Edom will I cast out my shoe"—if, indeed, it did not imply a resolve to reduce to subjection, where the leader of a besieging force threw a shoe into the city he was about to beleaguer. The Arabs, too, seem to have treated this act in a similar light; a person removing his shoe, and throwing it towards another, signified thereby his readiness to do him homage and be at his bidding. Bynæus *On the Shoes of the Hebrews*, lib. ii. Leo Modena, speaking of the modern Jews, tells us that "Some of them observe, in dressing themselves in the morning, to put on the right stocking and right shoe first, without tying it; then afterward to put on the left, and so return to the right; that so they may begin and end with the right side, which they acount to be most fortunate."

Jodhian-morian, or **Breastplate of Judgment.**—A Druidical ornament worn upon the breast of the chief priest, and supposed to possess the power of strangling the deliverer of a false decision or sentence. A specimen, from the original in the museum of the Royal Irish Academy, is engraved in Fairholt's *Costume*, 1860, p. 16.

Joggs.—See *Fairs in Scotland*.

John, St., the Baptist's Day. —June 30th). Sir John Smythe, in his "Instructions, Observations, and Orders Militarie," 1595, says:— "An ensigne-bearer in the field, carrieing his ensigne displayed ought to carry the same upright, and never, neither in towne nor field, nor in sport, nor earnest, to fetche flourishes about his head with his ensigne-staffe, and taffata of his ensigne, as the ensigne-bearers of London do upon Midsommer Night." Among the domestic regulations in the household of Robert Wynn, Esq., of Bodscallan, North Wales, 17th century, was one that no liquor but black stock, seven years old, 4 bushels to a hogshead, refined with some roast wheat thrown into it, should be drunk on this anniversary.

The Rev. William Jones, in his "Life of Bishop Horne," says: "A letter of July the 25th, 1755, informed me that Mr. Horne, according to an established custom at Magdalen College in Oxford, had begun to preach before the University, on the day of St. John the Baptist. For the preaching of this annual sermon, a permanent pulpit of stone is inserted into a corner of the first quadrangle; and so long as the stone pulpit was in use (of which I have been a witness), the quadrangle was furnished round the sides with a large fence of green boughs, that the preaching might more nearly resemble that of John the Baptist in the Wilderness; and a pleasant sight it was: but for many years the custom has been discontinued, and the assembly have thought it safe to take shelter under the room of the chapel. In the Treasury of St. Denis, according to an account printed in 1749, one of the holy relics is a shoulder-bone of the Baptist, sent by the Emperor Heraclius to Dagobert in the 7th century.

John, St., the Baptist's Vigil or **Eve.**—The Pagan rites of this festival at the summer solstice, may be considered as a counterpart of those used at the winter solstice at Yule-tide. There is one thing that seems to prove this beyond the possibility of a doubt. In the old Runic Fasti, as will be shown elsewhere, a wheel was used to denote the Festival of Christmas. This wheel is common to both festivities. Thus Durandus, speaking of the rites of the Feast of St. John Baptist, informs us of this curious circumstance, that in some places they roll a wheel about to signify that the sun, then occupying the highest place in the zodiac, is beginning to descend. "Rotam quoque hoc die in quibusdam locis volvunt, ad significandum quod Sol altissimum tunc locum in Cœlo occupet, et descendere incipiat in Zodiaco." Harl. MSS. 2345 (on vellum), Art. 100, is an Account of the rites of St. John Baptists's Eve, in which the wheel is also mentioned. In the amplified account of these ceremonies given by Naogeorgus, we read that this wheel was taken up to the top of a mountain and rolled down thence: and that, as it had previously been covered with straw, twisted about it and set on fire, it appeared at a distance as if the sun had been falling from the sky. And he further observes, that the people imagine that all their ill-luck rolls away from them together with this wheel. At Norwich, says a writer in *Current Notes* for March, 1854, the rites of St. John the Baptist were anciently observed, "When it was the custom to turn or roll a wheel about, in signification of the sun's annual course, or the sun, then occupying the highest place in the zodiac, was about descending." There is a very plausible suggestion to be drawn from a passage in Durandus; it is that these fires had to some extent their origin in the necessity for an annual fumigation of the atmosphere, wells, springs, &c. The popular belief was that at this season noxious serpents infected the air and water. In Polydore Vergil, we read: "Oure Midsomer bonefyers may seme to have comme of the sacrifices of Ceres Goddesse of Corne, that men did solemnise with fyres, trusting thereby to have more plenty and aboundance of corne. Moresin appears to have been of opinion that the custom of leaping over these fires is a vestige of the ordeal where to be able to pass through fires with safety was held to be an indication of innocence. To strengthen the probability of this conjecture, we may observe that not only the young and vigorous, but even those of grave character used to leap over them, and there was an interdiction of ecclesiastical authority to deter clergymen from this superstitious instance of agility. From the Roman Calendar it seems that spices were given on St. John's Eve, and that the festivities included carol-singing, processions with garlands, for the purpose of collecting money (when recusants were freely anathematized by the itinerant petitioners), and that fern was gathered for the sake of the virtue supposed to reside in its seed. The reader will join me in thinking the following extract from the Homily " De Festo Sancti Johannis Baptistæ," a pleasant piece of absurdity :

" In worshyp of Saint Johan the people waked at home, and made three maner of fyres : one was clene bones, and noo woode, and that is called a bone fyre ; another is clene woode, and no bones, and that is called a wode fyre, for people to sit and wake therby ; the thirde is made of wode and bones, and it is callyd Saynt Johannys fyre. The first fyre, as a great clerke Johan Belleth telleth he was in a certayne countrey, so in the countrey there was soo greate hete the which causid the dragons to go togyther in tokenynge that Johan dyed in brennynge love and charyte to God and man, and they that dye in charyte shall have parte of all good prayers, and they that do not, shall never be saved. Then as these dragons flewe in th' ayre they shed down to that water froth of ther kynde, and so enven͏ymed the waters, and caused moche people for to take theyr deth therby, and many dyverse sykenesse. Wyse clerkes knoweth well that dragons hate nothyng more than the stenche of brennynge bones, and therefore they gaderyd as many as they mighte fynde, and brent them ; and so with the stenche therof they drove away the dragons, and so they were brought out of greete dysease. The second fyre was made of woode, for that wyl brenne lyght, and wyll be seen farre. For it is the chefe of fyre to be seen farre, and betokennynge that Saynt Johan was a lanterne of lyght to the people. Also the people made blases of fyre for that they shulde be seene farre, and specyally in the nyght, in token of St. Johans having been seen from far in the spirit by Jeremiah. The third fyre of bones betokenneth Johans martyrdome, for hys bones were brente, and how ye shall here." The homilist accounts for this by telling us that after John's disciples had buried his body, it lay till Julian, the apostate Emperor, came that way, and caused them to be taken up and burnt, "and to caste the ashes in the wynde, hopynge that he shuld never ryse again to lyfe."

Cleland, in his "Institution of a

Young Nobleman," 1607, very aptly calls these observances "follies al forged by the infernal Cyclops and Plutoes seruants." Hutchinson says it was usual to raise fires on the tops of high hills, and in the villages, and sport and dance around them ; and the same writer, speaking of the parish of Cumwhitton in Cumberland, says : "They hold the wake on the Eve of St. John, with lighting fires, dancing, &c. The old Bel-teing." Bonfires were lately, or still continue to be, made on Midsummer Eve, in the villages of Gloucestershire. Brand was so informed in passing from Bath to Oxford, May 21, 1786. They still prevailed also, on the same occasion, in Brand's time, in the northern parts of England. Pennant informs us that small bonefires were made on the Eve of St. John Baptist at Daro-wen, in Wales. On Whiteborough (a large tumulus with a foss round it), on St. Stephen's down, near Launceston, in Cornwall, as Mr. Brand learnt at that place in October, 1790, there was formerly a great bonefire on Midsummer Eve : a large summer pole was fixed in the centre, round which the fuel was heaped up. It had a large bush on the top of it. Round this were parties of wrestlers contending for small prizes. An honest countryman informed him, who had often been present at these merriments, that at one of them an evil spirit had appeared in the shape of a black dog, since which none could wrestle, even in jest, without receiving hurt : in consequence of which the wrestling was, in a great measure, laid aside. The rustics hereabout believe that giants are buried in these tumuli, and nothing would tempt them to be so sacrilegious as to disturb their bones. The boundary of each tin mine in Cornwall is marked by a long pole, with a bush at the top of it. These on St. John's Day are crowned with flowers. It is usual at Penzance to light fires on this occasion, and dance and sing round them. In a Collection of Ancient Traditional Songs, edited by Mr. Dixon for the Percy Society, is inserted one, which, according to Mr. Sandys, has been sung for a long series of years in that locality on St. John's Day. A clergyman of Devonshire informed Brand that, in that county the custom of making bonefires on Midsummer Eve, and of leaping over them, still continued. This was about 1790. At Barnwell, in Cambridgeshire, St. John's Eve used to be celebrated in a somewhat similar manner. Comp. *Barnwell Fair.* In "Lancashire Folklore," 1867, it is said, "In parts of Lancashire, especially in the Fylde, these traces (the fires) of a heathen custom still linger." In "Perth Assembly," 1619, the writer speaks of the-midsummer fires, and cites Bellarmine and Scaliger for them. The former says: "Fire is accustomed to be kindled for the signifying of joy, even in profane things," and Scaliger has this remark, that "the candles and torches lighted on Midsummer Eve are the footsteps of antient gentilism."

"I was so fortunate," (says a Skye correspondent of the "Gent. Mag." for February, 1795), "in the summer of 1782 as to have my curiosity gratified by a sight of this ceremony to a very great extent of country. At the house where I was entertained, it was told me that we should see at midnight the most singular sight in Ireland, which was the lighting of fires in honour of the sun. Accordingly, exactly at midnight, the fires began to appear, and taking the advantage of going up to the leads of the house, which had a widely extended view, I saw on a radius of thirty miles, all around, the fires burning on every eminence which the country afforded. I had a farther satisfaction in learning, from undoubted authority, that the people danced round the fires, and at the close went through these fires, and made their sons and daughters, together with their cattle, pass through the fire; and the whole was conducted with religious solemnity." In the "Statistical Account of Scotland," parish of Mongahitter, it is said: "The Midsummer Even fire, a relic of Druidism, was kindled in some parts of this county." The late Mr. Samuel Laing, the highly distinguished writer, who was born in 1810, relates that, when he was young, these fires were lighted on the highest hills of Orkney and Shetland. "As a boy," he writes, "I have rushed with my playmates through the smoke of those bonfires without a suspicion that we were repeating the homage paid to Baal in the Valley of Hinnom." *Human Origins*, 1897, p. 161. Among the Privy Purse Expenses of Henry VII. we have, under date of June 23, 1493: "To the makyng of the bonefuyr on Middesomer Eve, 10s." In the Privy Purse Expenses of Elizabeth of York, 1502, there is the following entry: "Itm., the xxviijth day of Juyn, to the gromes and pages of the halle for making bonefyres upon the evyns of Saint John Baptist and Saint Peter, 5s."

In the Churchwardens' Accounts of St. Martin Outwich we have: "1524. Payde for byrche and bromes at Mydsom^r, ijd." "1525. Payde for byrch and bromes at Mydsom^r. iijd." In Dekker's "Seaven deadly Sinnes of London," speaking of "Candell-light, or the Nocturnall Triumph," he says: "What expectation was there of his coming? setting aside the bon-

fiers, there is not more triumphing on Midsommer Night." In the same writer's "Wonderful Yeare," 1603, signat. B. we read: "Olive-trees (which grow no where but in the Garden of Peace) stood (as common as beech does at Midsomer) at every mans doore." In Brown's "Shepheards Pipe," 1614, occur the following lines:

"Neddy, that was wont to make
Such great feasting at the wake,
And the blessing-fire—"

with a marginal note upon blessing fire (by the author) informing us that "the Midsummer fires are tearmed so in the west parts of England." Stow tells us that the rites of St. John Baptist's Eve were also used on the Eve of St. Peter and St. Paul. Piers, *Description of Westmeath*, 1682, apud Vallancey, makes the same remark touching Ireland or at least that part of it: and Moresin informs us that in Scotland the people used, on this latter night, to run about on the mountains and higher grounds with lighted torches, like the Sicilian women of old in search of Proserpine. Moresin thinks this a vestige of the ancient Cerealia. Compare *St. Peter's Day*. In Niccols' "London Artillery," 1616, p. 97, is preserved a long description of the great doings anciently used in the streets of London on the vigils of St. Peter and St. John the Baptist: "when," says our author, "that famous marching-watch, consisting of two thousand, beside the standing watches, were maintained in this citie. It continued from temp. Henrie III. to the 31st of Henry VIII. when it was laid down by licence from the King, and revived (for that year only) by Sir Thomas Gresham, Lord Mayor, 2 Edw. VI."

Mr. Brand saw in the possession of Douce a French print, entitled "L'esté le Feu de la St. Jean," from the hand of Mariette. In the centre was the fire made of wood piled up very regularly, and having a tree stuck up in the midst of it. Young men and women were represented dancing round it hand in hand. Herbs were stuck in their hats and caps, and garlands of the same surrounded their waists, or were slung across their shoulders. A boy was represented carrying a large bough of a tree. Several spectators were looking on. The following lines were at the bottom:—

"Que de Feux brulans dans les airs!
Qu'ils font une douce harmonie!
Redoublons cette melodie
Par nos dances, par nos concerts!"

In the "Traité des Superstitions" we read: "Whoever desires to know the colour of his future wife's hair has only to walk three times round the fire of St.

John, and when the fire is half-extinguished he must take a brand, let it go out, and then put it under his pillow, and the next morning he will find encircling it threads of hair of the desired colour. But this must be done with the eyes shut." Tom. iii. p. 455. We are further told that where there is a widow or a marriageable girl in a house, it is necessary to be very careful not to remove the brands, as this drives away lovers. Midsummer Eve festivities are still kept up in Spain. "At Alcala, in Andalusia," says Dalrymple, in his "Travels through Spain and Portugal," "at twelve o'clock at night, we were much alarmed with a violent knocking at the door. 'Quiens es?' says the landlord; 'Isabel de San Juan,' replied a voice: he got up, lighted the lamp, and opened the door, when five or six sturdy fellows, armed with fusils, and as many women, came in. After eating a little bread, and drinking some brandy, they took their leave; and we found that, it being the Eve of St. John, they were a set of merry girls with their lovers, going round the village to congratulate their friends on the approaching festival." A gentleman who had resided long in Spain informed me that in the villages they light up fires on St. John's Eve, as in England. Lemnius, in his "Treatise de Occultis Naturæ Miraculis," lib. iii. cap. 8, remarks upon the enthusiasm with which the ceremonies peculiar to St. John's Day were observed, not only by the Jews and Christians, but by the Moors and other peoples not professing Christianity. The same writer remarks, that the Low Dutch have a proverb, that "when men have passed a troublesome night's rest, and could not sleep at all, they say, We have passed St. John Baptist's Night; that is, we have not taken any sleep, but watched all night; and not only so, but we have been in great troubles, noyses, clamours, and stirs, that have held us waking." "Some," he previously observes, "by a superstition of the Gentiles, fall down before his image, and hope to be thus freed from the epileps; and they are further persuaded, that if they can but gently go unto this Saint's shrine, and not cry out disorderly, or hollow like madmen when they go, then they shall be a whole year free from this disease; but if they attempt to bite with their teeth the Saint's head they go to kisse, and to revile him, then they shall be troubled with this disease every month, which commonly comes with the course of the moon, yet extream juglings and frauds are wont to be concealed under this matter."

Pecock, in his "Repressor of over much Blaming of the Clergy," refers to the custom which held in London on the Eve of St. John the Baptist, of decorating the houses with flowers. "Certis," says he, "thouz Crist and his Apostlis weren now lyvyng at Londoun, and wolde bringe so as is now seid braunchis fro Bischopis wode and flouris fro the feeld into Loundoun, and wolden delyvere to men that thei make there with her housis gay, into remembraunce of Seint Johan Baptist," &c. Stow, in his "Survey," tells us, "that, on the vigil of St. John Baptist, every man's door being shadowed with green birch, long fennel, St. John's wort, orpin, white lilies, and such like, garnished upon with garlands of beautiful flowers, had also lamps of glass with oil burning in them all the night. Some," he adds, "hung out branches of iron, curiously wrought, containing hundreds of lamps lighted at once." Coles, in his "Adam in Eden," speaking of the birch-tree, says: "I remember once, as I rid through Little Brickhill, in Buckinghamshire, which is a town standing upon the London-road, between Dunstable and Stony-Stratford, every signe-post in the towne almost was bedecked with green birch." This had been done, no doubt, on account of Midsummer Eve. Pennant informs us that, in Wales "they have the custom of sticking St. John's wort over the doors on the eve of St. John Baptist." It was formerly believed that if anyone fell asleep in the church porch on Midsummer Eve, he would die the same year.—Spence's *Anecdotes*, 1858, 371, note. Bourne cites from the Trullan Council a singular species of divination on St. John Baptist's Eve: "On the 23rd of June, which is the eve of St. John Baptist, men and women were accustomed to gather together in the evening by the sea-side, or in some certain houses, and there adorn a girl, who was her parents' first-begotten child, after the manner of a bride. Then they feasted and leaped after the manner of Bacchanals, and danced and shouted as they were wont to do on their holidays: after this they poured into a narrow-neck'd vessel some of the sea-water, and put into it certain things belonging to each of them. Then, as if the Devil gifted the girl with the faculty of telling future things, they would enquire with a loud voice about the good or evil fortune that should attend them: upon this the girl would take out of the vessel the first thing that came to hand, and shew it, and give it to the owner, who, upon receiving it, was so foolish as to imagine himself wiser, as to the good or evil fortune that should attend him." The following occurs in "The Practice" of Paul Barbette: "For the falling sickness some ascribe much to coals pulled out (on St. John Baptist's Eve) from under the roots of mugwort: but those authors are deceived, for they are not coals, but old acid roots, consisting of much volatile salt, and are almost always to be found under mugwort: so that it is only a certain superstition that those old dead roots ought to be pulled up on the eve of St. John Baptist, about twelve at night." Bishop Hall says that, St. John is implored for a benediction wine upon his day." In *Current Notes*, April, 1853, it is mentioned, on the authority of Aubrey, that near Bisley Church, in Surrey, there is a well dedicated to St. John the Baptist, which is cold in summer and warm in winter. This was usually, not always, the Merchant Taylors' feast-day. St. John the Baptist is said in the Scriptural narrative to have fed, during his sojourn in the wilderness, on locusts and wild honey. The locust or carob-tree is still common in the Levant, and yields a pulp, contained in a pod. It is vulgarly known to this day as St. John's Bread. Comp. *Bonfires, Coal, Midsummer.*

John, St., the Evangelist.—(December 27). The custom of giving wine on the Day of St. John the Evangelist is noticed under St. Stephen's Day. It appears that the common people in the Moray parish of Duffus, used to "celebrate (perhaps without ever thinking of the origin of the practice) St. John's Day, St. Stephen's Day, Christmas Day, &c. by assembling in large companies to play at football, and to dance and make merry. That horror at the name of holidays which was once a characteristic of the Puritans and true blue Presbyterians, never took possession of them." "Stat. Account of Scotland," vol. viii., p. 399; parish of Duffus, county of Moray. I append what Naogeorgus says:—

"Nexte John the sonne of Zebedee hath his appoynted day,
Who once by cruell tyraunts will, constrayned was they say
Strong poyson up to drinke, therefore the Papistes doe beleeve
That whoso puts their trust in him, no poyson them can greeve.
The wine beside that halowed is, in worship of his name,
The Priestes doe give the people that bring money for the same.
And after with the selfe same wine are little manchets made
Agaynst the boystrous winter stormes, and sundrie such like trade.
The men upon this solemne day, do take this holy wine
To make them strong, so do the maydes to make them faire and fine."

The Popish Kingdome, translated by Googe, 1570, fol. 45.

Johnny Cake.—A cake made of Indian flour without yeast, and baked on a pewter plate before the fire. It was a standing dish at the afternoon meal in New England about 1785. It is yet remembered, if not so usual. W. C. Hazlitt's *Four Generations of a Literary Family,* 1897, i., 38.

Judas Candles.—In the Churchwardens' Accompts of St. Martin Outwich, London, under the year 1510, is the following article: "Paid to Randolf Merchaunt, wex-chandiler for the Pascall, the tapers affore the Rode, the Cross candelles and Judas Candelles, ixˢ. iiijᵈ."

Juego de Cañas.—This, as a note in the Diary of Henry Machyn informs us, was an amusement introduced by the Spaniards, who were very numerous in London in the reign of Mary. Machyn mentions the pastime as one of the entertainments prepared at the marriage of Lord Strange to the Earl of Cumberland's daughter in February, 1554-5. But the fact is, that the sport is as ancient as the twelfth century, and was known in Italy, at least, as early as the reign of our Richard I. Strutt prints an anecdote illustrative of this from Hoveden. In the particular instance recorded by Machyn, the cane play was not introduced till after supper, and was then carried on by torchlight. The editor of Machyn has illustrated his entry respecting the game by an interesting note. It is possible, however, that the sport was not much used in England till the reign of Henry VIII., and there may be no specific record of it ever having been practised before 1518; but that it was known in this country at a much earlier date seems, at all events, open to argument. Francis Yoxley, writing to Sir W. Cecil from the Court, 12th Oct. 1554, says: "Uppon Thursday next, there shalbe in Smithfield Guioco di Canne: where the King and Quene wolbe.—" Ellis's *Orig. Letters,* 3rd S. iii., 313. In Lawrence Twyne's *Patterne of Painfull Adventures,* first published about 1576, it is mentioned under the name of *ioco di can* among the sports at the wedding of Appollonius and Lucina. Hazlitt's *Shakespear's Library,* 1875, iv., 279. James Howell must refer to some other unknown sport, where, in a letter to Sir Thomas Lake, July 3, 1629, he says: "I have shewed Sir Kenelm Digby both our translations of Martials 'Vitam quæ faciunt beatoriem,' &c., and to tell you true, he adjudged yours the better; so I shall pay the wager in the place appointed and try whether I can recover myself at Gioco d'amore, which the Italian saith is a play to cozen the Devil."

Jugglers.—Like his contemporary Shakespear, Bacon did not scruple or disdain to avail himself of all possible vehicles for illustration or comparison. When he wrote in his admirable *Sylva Sylvarum* the passage copied below, he had in his remembrance a scene at which he had been present; it is a curious bit—a fragment of the popular street-life of London, which one would have rather expected to encounter in the pages of Strutt or Brand:

"What a little moisture will doe in vegetables, even though they be dead, and severed from the earth, appeareth wel in the Experiment of Iuglers. They take the beard of an oate; which, (if you mark it well), is wreathed at the bottome, and one smooth entire straw at the top. They take onely the part that is wreathed, and cut off the other, leaving the beard halfe the breadth of a finger in length. Then they make a little crosse of a quill, longwayes of that part of the quill, which hath the pith: and crosse-wayes of that peece of the quill without pith; the whole crosse being the breadth of a finger high. Then they pricke the bottome where the pith is, and thereinto they put the oaten-beard, leaving halfe of it sticking forth of the quill: Then they take a little white box of wood, to deceive men, as if somewhat in the box did work the feat: in which, with a pinne, they make a little hole, enough to take the beard, but not to let the crosse sink downe, but to stick. Then likewise by way of imposture, they make a question; as, who is the fairest woman in the company? or, Who hath a glove or card? and cause another to name divers persons: And upon every naming they stick the crosse into the box, having first put it towards their mouth, as if they charmed it: and the crosse stirreth not; but when they come to the person that they would take; as they hold the cross to their mouth, they touch the beard with the tip of their tongue, and wet it; and so stick the crosse in the box; and then you shall see it turne finely and softly, three or foure turnes; which is caused by the untwining of the beard by the moisture. You may see it more evidently, if you sticke the crosse betweene your fingers in stead of the box; and therefore you may see, that this motion, which is effected by so little wet, is stronger than the closing or bending of the head of a marigold." The Essay of Hazlitt on a Performance of Indian Jugglers was partly with a view to vindicate the pretensions of physical or mechanical ingenuity.

Julian, St.—"There were three or four saints of this name; but the best known was the saint, who is the supposed patron and protector of pilgrims and travellers. The history of this St. Julian is in the "Gesta Romanorum" and elsewhere. He was a knight, who found, on returning to his house one day, two persons asleep in his bed. He thought that his wife had been unfaithful to him, and immediately slew the supposed guilty pair, who turned out to be his father and mother, who had travelled from a distant land to see him. He thereupon founded a hospital for travellers: hence he acquired the name of Hospitator, or the gude herberjour. "Simon the Leper," it is noted by Warton, "at whose house our Saviour lodged in Bethany, is called in the legends Julian the good herborow, and Bishop of Bethpaze. In the Tale of Beryn, St. Julian is invoked to revenge a traveller, who had been traitorously used in his lodgings." He is mentioned in the "Kyng and the Hermyt":

"I have herd pore men call at morrow,
Seynt Julyan send yem god harborow,
    When that they had nede.
Seynt Julian as I am trew knyzt,
Send me grace this iche nyght
    Of god harborow to sped—"

And again in the same:—

"Then seyd the Kyng that tyde,
Now, seynt Julian, a boune ventyll,
As pylgrymes know full wele"—

Hazlitt's *Popular Poetry,* 1864, i. 16-17. In the "Ancren Riwle" (13th century) we have: "Surely they (the pilgrims) find St. Julian's inn, which way faring men diligently seek." Chaucer had the familiar attribute of St. Julian before him, when he described his Frankeleyn, or country gentleman:

"An housholder, and that a grete, was he:
Seint Julian he was in his contré."

Justina of Padua, St.—(October 7). See Hazlitt's *Venetian Republic,* 1900, ii., 380. The Battle of Lepanto was gained on her name-day, 1571, and two types of coins in silver, the *giustina maggiore* and *minore,* were struck to commemorate the victory. They remained in circulation and use long after the occurrence.

Kate Kennedy's Day in St. Andrews.—In the *Daily News* of February 21, 1874, occurs:—"The annual demonstration by the fourth year students of St. Andrew's University, in commemoration of Kate Kennedy, supposed to have been a daughter of Bishop Kennedy, the founder of the College, was observed this afternoon with more than the usual pomp and brilliancy of display. Attempts have frequently been made by several of the professors to stamp the demonstration out, but their interference has only had the effect of imparting to it a vigour and importance it never before possessed. To-day's celebration was fully equal to that of any former year. About noon "Kate," equipped in riding habit, appeared, followed by a retinue, gorgeously attired. The College and Professors' houses were duly honoured with a call. During their progress throughout the city the processionists busied themselves vending their "annual" and the *carte*. Principal and Professors are represented as an assembly of immortals on Mount Olympus considering the Lady Students question. Kneeling before the presiding deity is a lady student, while in the background is seen the shade of John Stuart Mill, bearing in his hand the gift of £5,000. The demonstration passed off with the usual *éclat*.

Kayles.—From the French *quilles*. The original nine-pins. In France, during the middle ages, if not among us, there was a variety known as *jeu de quilles à baston*, where the player aimed with a stick at the pins, instead of with a bowl. This form was known in England, at all events at an early date, as *club-kayles*. Wright's *Domestic Manners*, 1862, p. 236, where an illustration of club-kayles may be seen.

Kelpie.—In the "Statistical Account of Scotland," under Parish of St. Vigeans, co. Caithness, we are told : "A tradition had long prevailed here, that the Water-Kelpy (called in Home's 'Douglas' the angry Spirit of the Water), carried the stones for building the church, under the fabrick of which there was a lake of great depth." Mr. Campbell, in *Popular Tales of the West Highlands*, 1860, ii 193-4, says very little about this spectre, and what he does say, I confess that I do not perfectly follow. But in Mr. George Macdonald's *Ronald Bannerman's Boyhood*, 1871, there is a curious and rather thrilling account, which seems worth copying hither. It occurs in one of the tales which Kirsty, the female farm-servant, used to relate to the children—not, one hopes towards bedtime, if they partook of the same character as this. The kelpie is described as an awful aquatic creature, emerging from its native element only to pursue human prey. One afternoon it appears that a shepherd's daughter, remarkable for her beauty, went to the glen to meet her lover, and after staying with him till it was dark, returned home, passing on the way the kelpie's lair. He had seen her, and because she was so fair, he desired to eat her. She heard a great whish of water behind her. That was the water tumbling off the beasts's back as he came up from the bottom. If she ran before, she flew now. And the worst of it was that she could not hear him behind her,

so as to tell whereabouts he was. He might be just opening his mouth to take her every moment. At last she reached the door, which her father, who had gone out to look for her, had set wide open that she might run in at once; but all the breath was out of her body, and she fell down flat just as she got inside. "Here Allister jumped up from his seat, clapping his hands, and crying 'Then the kelpie didn't eat her !—Kirsty ! Kirsty !' 'No, but as she fell, one foot was left outside the threshold, so that the rowan branch (which the shepherd kept over the door to prevent the kelpie from ever entering) would not take care of it. And the beast laid hold of the foot with his great mouth, to drag her out of the cottage and eat her at his leisure.' Here Allister's face was a picture to behold ! His hair was almost standing on end, his mouth was open, and his face as white as my paper. 'Make haste, Kirsty,' said Turkey, 'or Allister will go in a fit.' 'But her shoe came off in his mouth, and she drew in her foot, and was safe.'" But the more natural solution of the difficulty may be that the kelpie was a creature supposed or alleged to lurk among the kelp or sea-weed, which in some coasts not only grows to an incredible height and size, but disposes itself in all sorts of fantastic and weird forms. The kelp manufacture used in the eighteenth century to be a staple industry in the Orkneys and Hebrides, and during the Peninsular War became for a time enormously lucrative. Superstition made the Scotish spirit one-eyed, as an imperfectly authorized tradition makes Polyphemus and his countrymen, or rather Polyphemus, for of the rest no description is given in the Odyssey. Mr. Campbell says the Cyclops was a water-spirit, as well as the kelpie, for no better reason apparently than because he was sometimes fabled to be the son of Neptune. There is surely no hint of such an idea in Homer. There is a good deal of uncertainty and confusion about the Cyclopes, which it might be both practicable and profitable to remove. But the connection between them and the kelpie is not manifest, since Polyphemus at least was one-eyed, and nowhere appears as a marine monster. Kelpie is supposed to owe itself to *kelp*, its lurking-place, although the word is also traced to the German *chalp* or *kalb*, from the roar which the monster utters ; and the kelpie is elsewhere described as a horse-fiend which lures riders by its attractive aspect, and then bears them off, where it may devour them at its leisure. Allies' *Antiquities of Worcestershire*, 2nd ed. 1856, p. 468. The more probable etymology, however, seems to be that first suggested. The legend is easily explained by the constant howling of the ocean on a wild shore and the fantastic forms assumed by the sea-weed, especially if seen after dusk.

Kenan, St., of Ireland.—See Mr. Hart's *Lectionarium*, printed from an unique MS., 1869. This saint's day was November 24th.

Kenelm's, St., Salop.—At the wake held at the small village of St. Kenelm's, co. Salop, called Kenelm's Wake, or Crab Wake, the inhabitants have a singular custom of pelting each other with crabs: and even the clergyman seldom escapes as he goes to, or comes from, the chapel. *Gent. Mag.*, Sept. 1797.

Kern or **Corn Baby.**—See *Harvest Doll.*

Kern Supper.—See *Harvest.*

Keyna or **Keyne, St., the Virgin.**—(October 8). Mr. Pengelly, in his *Antiquity of Man in the South West of England*, 1887, p. 13, speaks of a pilgrimage, which this saint paid to St. Michael's Mount in A.D. 490, on the authority of Borlase. *Antiquities of Cornwall*, 1769, p. 385. Her well is among the traditionary stories of the county. Carew, in his "Survey," written long before it was printed in 1602, refers to it. Subjoined is the well-known ballad on the subject:

" ' Now art thou a bachelor, stranger?'
    quoth he,
' For an if thou hast a wife,
The happiest draught thou hast drunk
    this day
    That ever thou didst in thy life.
Or has thy good woman, if one thou
    hast,
    Ever here in Cornwall been?
For an if she have, I'll venture my life
    She has drunk of the well of St.
    Keyne.'
' I have left a good woman who never
    was here,'
    The stranger he made reply,
' But that my draught should be better
    for that,
    I pray you answer me why?'
' St. Keyne,' quoth the Cornishman,
    'many a time
    Drank of this crystal well,
And before the angel summon'd her,
    She laid on the water a spell:—
If the husband of this gifted well
    Shall drink before his wife,
A happy man henceforth is he,
    For he shall be master for life.
But if the wife should drink of it first,—
    Oh, pity the husband then!'
The stranger stoop'd to the well of St.
    Keyne,
    And drank of the water again.

' You drank of the well I warrant be-
    times?'
He to the Cornishman said:—
But the Cornishman smiled as the stran-
    ger spake,
    And sheepishly shook his head."

Kidderminster. — At Kidderminster is a singular custom. On the election of a bailiff, the inhabitants assemble in the principal streets to throw cabbage stalks at each other. The townhouse bell gives signal for the affray. This is called lawless hour. This done (for it lasts an hour), the bailiff elect and corporation, in their robes, preceded by drums and fifes (for they have no waits), visit the old and new bailiff, constables, &c., &c., attended by the mob. In the meantime, the most respectable families in the neighbourhood are invited to meet and fling apples at them on their entrance. I have known forty pots of apples expended at one house.

Kilken.—"In the Parish of Kilken, on the side of the turnpike-road, not far from Kilken Hall, is the noted Ffynnon Leinw, or the flowing well: a large oblong well with a double wall round it. This is taken notice of by Camden for its flux and reflux, but the singularity has ceased since his time, according to the best information I can receive." Pennant's "Tours in Wales," ed. 1810, vol. ii. p. 59-60.

King by Your Leave.—This occurs without any explanation, as a phrase in the mouth of the clown, toward the end of the play of *Mucedorus*, 1598. Humphrey King says: "Methinks a King by birth, as I am, should not debase himselfe to intreate so much. And yet I remember an old school-boyes game of *King by your leare* (ever since I was a boy my selfe), and so I am afraid you will cry, 'King by your leave, we are to haue a bout with you, beare it off with the head and shoulders how you can.'" *Halfepennyworth of Wit*, 1613, Dedic.

One of the company assumes the right of occupying a certain spot, generally elevated, and if a mound of earth, so much the better, and drives his companions off with

" I am the King of the Castle :
" Get out, you dirty rascal ! "
till one of the rascals succeeds in dethroning the monarch, and usurps his place. It is far from impossible that this game may really be of some antiquity, and may have originated in some political source. The hidden moral does not strike us as far below the surface.

King-Game or **Kingham.** — The pageant of the three Kings of Cologne. See *Three Kings of Cologne*, infrâ, and Nares, *Glossary*, 1859, in v. Under the parish of St. Laurence, Reading, we read: "A.D. 1499. It. payd for horse mete to the horses for the kyngs of Colen on May-day, vjd." A note adds: "This was a part of the pageant called the King-play, or King-game, which was a representation of the Wise Men's Offering, who are supposed by the Romish Church to have been kings, and to have been interred at Cologne." Then follows: "It. payd to mynstrells the same day, xijd." Lysons, in his Extracts from the Churchwardens' and Chamberlain's Accounts at Kingston-upon-Thames ("Environs of London," vol. i. p. 225), affords us some curious particulars of the King-game, and in another quotation from the same accounts, 24 Hen. VII. the "cost of the Kyngham and Robyn-Hode" appears in one entry, viz.:

	£	s.	d.
A kylderkin of 3 halfpennye bere and a kilderkin of singgyl bere	0	2	4
7 bushels of whete	0	6	3
2 bushels and ½ of rye	0	1	8
3 shepe	0	5	0
A lamb	0	1	4
2 calvys	0	5	4
6 pygges	0	2	0
3 bushels of colys	0	0	3
The coks for their labour	0	1	11½

The clear profits, 15 Henry VIII. (the last time Lysons found it mentioned) amounted to £9 10s. 6d., a very considerable sum. Was the child's game called "King I am" a derivative from this? Comp. *Children's Games.*

King of Cockneys (At Lincoln's Inn).—See *Christmas Prince.*

King of the Castle.—See *King by your leave.*

King's Evil.—Scot says: "To heal the King or Queen's Evil, or any other soreness in the throat, first touch the place with the hand of one that died an untimely death: otherwise let a virgin fasting lay her hand on the sore and say: Apollo denyeth that the heat of the plague can increase where a naked virgin quencheth it: and spet three times upon it." *Discovery,* ed. 1665, 137. The seventh son of a seventh son is accounted an infallible doctor. Lupton says: "It is manifest, by experience, that the seventh male child, by just order, (never a girle or wench being born between) doth heal only with touching (through a natural gift) the King's Evil: which is a speciall gift of God, given to kings and queens, as daily experience doth witnesse." There was, in the 18th century, in the parish of Kilfynichen, a man named Tunis who touched for the evil. He was a seventh son, and was firmly credited with the faculty of a ring. An official report of the day says: "He

touches or rubs over the sore with his hand, two Thursdays and two Sundays successively, in the name of the Trinity, and says, 'It is God that cures.' He asks nothing for his trouble. It is believed if he did, there would be no cure. He is often sent for out of the country; and, though he asks nothing, yet the patients or their friends make him presents. He is perfectly illiterate, and says he does not know how the cure is effected, but that God is pleased to work it in consequence of his touch." Stat. Acc., xiv., 210. The author of the old account of Gisborough, in Yorkshire, describes this knowledge as a species of intuition, and states that the mere touch would suffice. *Antiq. Repert.,* 1807, iii., 304. Lupton says: "Three nails made in the vigil of the nativity of St. John Baptist, called Midsommer Eve, and driven in so deep that they cannot be seen, in the place where the party doth fall that hath the falling sicknesse, and naming the said parties name while it is doing, doth drive away the disease quite." He says in the same page, "The root of vervin hanged at the neck of such as have the king's evil, it brings a marvellous and unhoped help." *Notable Things,* ed. 1660, p. 40. "Squire Morley, of Essex," according to the Rev. George Ashby, "used to say a prayer which he hoped would do no harm, when he hung a bit of vervain root from a scrophulous person's neck. My aunt Freeman had a very high opinion of a baked toad in a silk bag, hung round the neck." *Note in his copy of Brand and Bourne.* The virtue of the seventh son of a seventh son is a belief also current on the continent. Thiers, *Traité des Superstitions,* i., 436-7, Delrio. *Disq. Magicæ,* i., 3. Delrio adds that fasting was considered a necessary preparation on the part of the intending healer; but the writer is candid enough to add that he had no personal faith in the efficacy of the charm, and was acquainted with instances proving directly to the contrary.

The earliest of our monarchs, who performed this ceremony, is said to have been Edward the Confessor (1042-66). In the Privy Purse Expenses of Henry VII., under 1491, we find: "For healing of a seke body this day, 6s. 8d."; and numerous entries of a similar kind occur in those of Henry VIII. In the "Gentleman's Magazine" for 1751, we read: "The solemn words, 'I touch, but God healeth,' were those our former kings always pronounced, when they touched for the evil; but this was never done but in the presence of a bishop or priest, who introduced the patient to the royal presence for that salutary intention. Then also a form of prayer for the divine blessing was used, and the king hung a small piece of silver about the person's neck, which he was required to wear during his life." The piece in question was known as a *touch-piece*, and usually had a ship on one side, and the Archangel Michael and the dragon on the other. It was more frequently in gold, but in either case was known, it seems, as the Angel. The ceremonies and service used on this occasion were repeatedly printed in broadside or book form. Part of it runs: "As often as the King putteth the Angel about their necks, repeat these words: 'That Light was the true Light which lighteth every man into the world.' After this the Lord's Prayer is said, and another prayer on the behalf of the diseased, that they, receiving health, may give thanks to God, &c." Borde, in his "Breviary of Health" (1547), among the remedies of the king's evil has the following: "For this matter, let every man make frendes to the Kynges Majestie, for it doth perteyne to a kynge to helpe this infirmitie by the grace of God, the which is geven to a king anoynted. But for as much as some men doth judge divers times a fystle or a French pocke to be the king's evyll, in such matters it behoveth not a kynge to medle withall." We now, without the smallest danger of incurring the suspicion of disloyalty, can safely pronounce that the royal touch for the king's evil is to be referred to the head of physical charms, evincing that no order of men escaped the ancient contagion of superstition. It appears that King Henry the Eighth was accustomed to make a gratuity of 7s. 6d. to all persons whom he touched, and this circumstance, which is borne out by entries in his "Privy Purse Expenses," for 1529-32, may induce a suspicion that patients occasionally shammed, in order to get what, to a poor person, was at that time by no means a contemptible sum of money. Dr. Cox in *Notes and Queries* observes: "James I. was not supposed to possess this royal virtue when king of Scotland; but the power is said to have come to him immediately after his accession to the English throne." A proclamation of March 25, 1616, forbad patients to approach the king during the summer.

Dr. Nicholson is mistaken in thinking that the exercise of this superstition was in abeyance for any time prior to James I., as Elizabeth repeatedly went through the ceremony. In common no doubt with other searchers, in old parish registers, I have frequently come across instances of certificates granted by their parish priest to those seeking to be royally healed. The latest instance that I have noted in this county is in the Measham registers, under March, 1687. A folio prayer book of 1706, now before me, has the office "At the healing" on a leaf between the Form of Prayer for the Accession and the Articles. With respect to this may I ask another question? What is the earliest and latest edition of the Prayer Book containing this office, and is the form used by Queen Anne, the same as that of other post-reformation monarchs? Bulwer observes: "This miraculous imposition of the hand in curing the disease called the struma, which, from the constant effect of that sovereigne salve, is called the king's evil, his sacred majestie that now is hath practiced with as good success as any of his royal progenitours." *Chirologia,* 1644, p. 149. But a case is reported as having occurred at Deptford in Kent in 1649, where a girl was cured of blindness by a handkerchief, which had been dipped in the king's blood! *A Miracle of Miracles,* 1649. In one of the papers inserted from MSS. in Peck's "Desiderata Curiosa," 1779, is another similar story: "A young gentlewoman of about sixteen years of age, Elizabeth Stevens, of Winchester, came (7 October, 1648) into the presence-chamber to be touched for the evill, which she was supposed to have; and therewith one of her eyes (that namely on the left side) was so much indisposed, that by her owne and her mother's testimony (who was then also present), she had not seene with that eye of above a month before. After prayers, read by Dr. Sanderson, the maide kneeled downe among others, likewise to be touched. And his majestie touched her, and put a ribbon, with a piece of money at it, in usuall manner, about her neck. Which done, his majestie turned to the lords (viz. the duke of Richmond, the earl of Southampton, and the earl of Lindsey) to discourse with them. And the said young gentlewoman of her own accord said openly: 'Now, God be praised! I can see of this sore eye.' And afterwards declared she did see more and more by it, & could, by degrees, endure the light of the candle. All which his majestie, in the presence of the said lords & many others, examined himself, & found it to be true. And it hath since been discovered that, some months agone, the said young gentlewoman professed that, as soon as she was come of age sufficient, she would convey over to the king's use all her land; which to the valew of about £130 per annum, her father deceased had left her sole heyre unto." Sixty or seventy years ago Ashburnham Church, Sussex, was a resort of scrofulous persons, who believed that by touching a shirt and pair of drawers, which were there deposited, and which had fallen from the possession of Charles I. to that of one of his attendants, John Ashburnham, they might be cured of their disease. Camden's *Remains*, ed. 1870, p. 5, *Note*. Dr. Johnson, when he was about two and a half years old, was taken up to London by his mother to be touched by Queen Anne, who gave him a touch-piece, and whose appearance on this occasion Boswell tells us that his friend faintly recalled. Barrington tells us of an old man who was witness in a cause, and averred that when Queen Anne was at Oxford, she touched him whilst a child for the evil. Barrington, when he had finished his evidence, " asked him whether he was really cured? upon which he answered with a significant smile, that he believed himself never to have had a complaint that deserved to be considered as the evil, but that his parents were poor, and had no objection to the bit of gold." This accounts well for the great resort of patients and supposed miraculous cures on this occasion. *Observations on the Statutes*, p. 107. It seems rather doubtful whether the perforation in these pieces of touch-money which almost invariably occurs, was for the purpose of suspension or for good luck, or both. For a proclamation concerning the cure of the king's evil, see Rushworth's " Collections," part ii., vol. i., p. 49. Dr. Pegge, in his " Curialia Miscellanea," 1818, has devoted a section to this subject. The obsolete usage is described in " Macbeth," iv., 3:

" —— strangely visited people,
All swoln and ulcerous, pitiful to the eye,
The mere despair of surgery, he cures :
Hanging a golden stamp about their necks,
Put on with holy prayers—"

Osborne, advising his son, says : " Be not therefore hasty to register all you understand not in the black Calendar of Hell, as some have done the weapon salve, passing by the cure of the king's evill altogether, as improbable to sense. Neither rashly condemn all you meet with that condemns the common received opinion, lest you remain a fool upon record." *Works*, ed. 1682-92.

Kings of Cologne, Three.—See *Kingham* and *Virgins of Cologne*. In the 16th c. the Festival of the Three Kings was kept with great solemnity and merriment throughout Northern Germany. Gostwick and Harrison, *Outlines of German Literature*, 1873, p. 111.

Kissing Usages.—From the following passage in the " Towneley Mysteries" it may be perhaps deduced that it was formerly usual for the commoner sort of people, before a carouse, to kiss each other, as a mark of good fellowship :

" *Secundus Pastor.* Yit a botelle here is.
Tercius Pastor. That is well spoken ;
    By my thryft we must kys—
Secundus Pastor. That had I forgotten."

By a note in Reed's Shakespear we learn that in dancing, " a kiss was anciently the establish'd fee of a lady's partner." So in Lovel's " Dialogue between Custom and Veritie," 1581 :

" But some reply, what foole would daunce,
    If that when daunce is doone,
He may not have at ladyes lips
    That which in daunce he woon."

This custom is still prevalent among the country people in many, perhaps all, parts of the kingdom. Shakespear makes his dancers on the sea shore take hands, curtsey and kiss.

Kiss, Nuptial, in the Church.—This nuptial kiss in the church, which was originally an act of religious symbolism, is enjoined both by the York Missal and the Sarum Manual. " Accipiat Sponsus pacem (the Pax) a Sacerdote, et ferat Sponsæ, osculans eam, et neminem alium, nec ipse nec ipsa." 1553, Rubrick, fol. 69. " Surgant ambo, Sponsus et sponsa, et accipiat sponsus pacem a Sacerdote, et ferat Sponsæ, osculans eam, et neminem alium, nec ipse nec ipsa." This liturgical precept appears to have developed or degenerated into the priest himself kissing the bride and into the more modern practice of the husband, and even relatives, saluting her at the conclusion of the ceremony. The subsequent particulars are from Randolph's " Letters," where he is speaking of the marriage of Mary Queen of Scots to Lord Darnley : " She had on her back the great mourning gown of black, with the great wide mourning hood, &c. The rings, which were three, the middle a rich diamond, were put on her finger. They kneel together, and many prayers were said over them ; she tarrieth out the mass, and he taketh a kiss, and leaveth her there, and went to her chamber, whither, within a space, she followeth and being required, (according to the solemnity) to cast off her cares, and leave aside these sorrowful garments, and give herself to a more pleasant life, after some pretty refusal (more, I believe, for manner sake than grief of heart), she suffereth them that stood by, every man that could approach, to take out a pin, and so, being committed to her ladies, changed her garments, but went not to bed : to signifie to the world that it was not lust that moved them to marry, but only the necessity of her country, not, if God will, to leave it without an heir." It is expressly mentioned in the following line from Marston's " Insatiate Countess " :

"The kisse thou gav'st me in the church
here take."

Vaughan, in his "Golden Groue,"
1600, says: "Among the Romans the
future couple sent certain pledges one
to another, which most commonly they
themselves afterwards being present would
confirme with a religious kisse." Aubrey, writing about 1670, relates that
when he was a boy, it was usual for the
bride and bridegroom to kiss over the
cakes at the table. He adds that the cakes
were laid at the end of the dinner, one
on another, like the shew-bread in the
old Bible-prints. The bridegroom was expected to wait at table on this occasion.
In "The Collier's Wedding," the bride is
introduced as being waylaid, after the
ceremony, at the church stile, for this purpose. It was once customary among persons of middling rank, as well as
the vulgar, in most parts of England for the young men present at
the marriage ceremony to salute the
bride, one by one, the moment it
was concluded. This, after officiating in
the ceremony himself, Mr. Brand saw frequently done. But it is now usual only
among the common people. It seems from
the account left us by Guthrie, that in the
18th century the nuptial kiss described by
Theocritus in his fifth idyll as usual among
his countrymen, that is to say, the form,
where the man takes the woman by the
ears to kiss her, was still preserved among
the Russians.

Kitchen Fires.—In Yorkshire there
is, or was, a house where a niece of
Charles Richardson, the lexicographer,
visited, and where they would think it a
bad omen if the kitchen fire went out;
and I understand from this lady that it
had been kept up incessantly where she
lived for some years. The custom used
to be observed in many other districts.

Kitchen Furniture.—Gough, in
his edition of Camden, 1789, says: "At
Therfield, as at Braughing, was till lately
a set of kitchen furniture lent to the poor
at weddings."

Kitch-Witch, The.—In Norfolk,
and perhaps elsewhere, a female attired
in some grotesque and frightful manner
is called a kitch-witch, of which the etymology is not clear. Formerly the streets
of Yarmouth were occasionally infested
by troops of these creatures, who made a
sort of house to house visitation, and
levied toll on some ground or other. They
wore men's shirts over their own dresses,
and had their faces smeared with blood.
It is supposed, probably enough, that
Kittywitch Row owes its appellation to
this happily obsolete usage.

Kites.—These may be the same as the
paper windmills seen in the hands of the
younger sort of children in Mr. Ives's
Missal.

Kit-Kat.—A boy's game. See Halliwell in v. and under *Stand Holes.*

Kit-Kat-Cannio.—This is described
by Moor: "A sedentary game, played by
two with slate pencil or pencil and paper
like kit-cat, easier learned than described.
It is won by the party who can first get
three marks (o's or x's) in a line; the
marks being made alternately by the players o or x in one of the nine spots equidis-
tant in three rows, when complete. He
who begins has the advantage, as he can
contrive to get his mark in the middle."

Knack.—At Werington in Devonshire the clergyman of the parish informed
Mr. Brand, about 1795, that when a farmer finishes his reaping, a small quantity
of the ears of the last corn are twisted or
tied together into a curious kind of figure,
which is brought home with great acclamations, hung up over the table, and kept
till the next year. The owner would think
it extremely unlucky to part with this,
which is called "a knack." The reapers
whoop and hollow "A Knack! a knack!
well cut! well bound! well shocked!" and,
in some places, in a sort of mockery, it
is added, "Well scattered on the ground."
A countryman gave him a somewhat different account as follows: "When they
have cut the corn, the reapers assemble to
gether: a knack is made, which one placed
in the middle of the company holds up,
crying thrice 'a Knack,' which all the
rest repeat: the person in the middle says

'Well cut! well bound!
Well shock'd! well saved from the
ground.'

he afterwards cries 'Whoop' and his
companions hollow as loud as they can.
He applied for one of them. No farmer
would part with that which hung over his
table; but one was made on purpose for
him." I should suppose that Moresin alludes to something like this when he says:
"Et spiceas papatus (habet) coronas, quas
videre est in domibus, &c." *Papatus*, p.
163, v. Spicæ. See the last ed. of Nares'
Gloss. art. Knack, and *Harvest Doll*,
suprâ.

Knight of the Common Hall.
—Skelton uses the term in relation to a
person in a certain predicament. He is
speaking of "la belle Isolde," the wife
of King Mark:

"Some say she was lyght,
And made her husband knyghte
Of the common hal
What cuckoldes men cal—"

In "Tarltons Newes out of Purgatory,"
1590, we have "The Tale of Three Cuckolds, of their impresses and mottoes."

Knives, &c.—It is unlucky, says Grose, to lay one's knife and fork crosswise. Crosses and misfortunes are likely to follow. Melton observes, "that it is naught for any man to give a pair of knives to his sweetheart, for feare it cuts away all love that is betweene them." *Astrologaster*, 1620, p. 45. Thus Gay in his second Pastoral:

"But woe is me! such presents luckless prove,
For knives, they tell me, always sever love."

It is, says Grose, unlucky to present a knife, scissors, razor, or any sharp or cutting instrument to one's mistress or friend, as they are apt to cut love and friendship. To avoid the ill-effects of this, a pin, a farthing, or some trifling recompense must be taken. To find a knife or a razor denotes ill luck and disappointment to the party." Compare, however, *Bride-Knives*.

Knockers.—Subterranean spirits, supposed in Wales in former times to have by their sounds denoted the whereabouts of minerals. Miss Costello's *North Wales*, 1845, pp. 124-6. Grose quotes Lewis, in his correspondence with Baxter, describing them as little statured, and about half a yard long; and adding that at this very instant there are miners on a discovery of a vein of metal on his own lands, and that two of them are ready to make oath they have heard these knockers in the day time. The Germans believed in two species of fairies of the mines, one fierce and malevolent, the other a gentle race, appearing like little old men dressed like miners, and not much above two feet high.

Knocking Down at Lincoln's Inn.—It was formerly usual, when the dinner in term-time had been placed on the tables, for the butler to strike thrice with a wooden mallet on the sideboard, probably by way of commanding silence, in order that the chaplain might say grace. The same observance was followed preparatory to the grace after dinner. This was known as *Knocking Down*. *Penny Magazine* for February, 1836.

Kyneburg, St., of Gloucester.—See Mr. Hart's privately printed *Lectionarium*, 1869, from an unique MS. St. Kyneburg's Day was March 6.

Lady in the Straw.—An expression, which carries us back to very primitive times, when some kind of rude arrangement preceded the institution of the palliasse both in England and abroad. From the nursery rhyme of "See-Saw, Margery Daw," it is inferrible that the mattress had then grown into use, and that the archaic straw lair was accounted derogatory. In old Bedlam the inmates lay on straw in chains. Comp. *Childbirth* and *Lying-in*.

Lady of the Lamb.—"At Kidlington, or Kidington, in Oxfordshire," observes Blount, "the custom is that, on Monday after Whitsun week, there is a fat live lamb provided; and the maids of the town, having their thumbs tied behind them, run after it, and she that with her mouth takes and holds the lamb, is declared Lady of the Lamb, which being dressed, with the skin hanging on, is carried on a long pole before the lady and her companions to the green, attended with music, and a Morisco dance of men, and another of women, where the rest of the day is spent in dancing, mirth, and merry glee. The next day the lamb is part baked, boiled, and roast, for the Lady's Feast, where she sits majestically at the upper end of the table, and her companions with her, with music and other attendants, which end the solemnity." Hazlitt's edit. of Blount, 1874, p. 181. Hearne, however, thought that the true place was Kirtleton, but was the latter a local pronounciation of Kidlington? Hearne's *Diary*, under 1723.

Lady of the Wake.—See *Wakes*.

Lady's Thistle. — The purple-flowered Lady's Thistle, the leaves of which are beautifully diversified with numerous white spots, like drops of milk, is vulgarly thought to have been originally marked by the falling of some drops of the Virgin Mary's milk on it, whence, no doubt, its name Lady's, i.e., Our Lady's Thistle. An ingenious little invention of the dark ages, and which, no doubt, has been of service to the cause of superstition.

Lake-Wake.—See *Lych Wake*.

Lambs, Looking at.—The late Mr. Robert Roberts of Boston, Lincolnshire, writes: "In these parts it is commonly believed that the first lamb you see ought to have its head turned towards you. I believe the superstition is pretty general. We also say that you ought to have money in your pocket on these occasions, silver at least, but gold is better still, and that it is very unlucky to be without it."

Lamb's Wool.—A Nottinghamshire correspondent of the "Gentleman's Magazine" for 1784, states, "that when he was a boy at school the practice on Christmas Eve was to roast apples on a string till they dropt into a large bowl of spiced ale, which is the whole composition of Lamb's Wool." It is probable that from the softness of this popular beverage it has gotten the above name. See Shakespear's "Midsummer Night's Dream."

——"Sometimes lurk I in a gossip's bowl,
In very likeness of a roasted crab;

And when she drinks, against her lips
  I bob,
And on her wither'd dew-lap pour the
  ale."

The writer in the "Gentleman's Magazine" for May, 1784, says, he has "often met with lambs' wool in Ireland, where it is a constant ingredient at a merry-making on Holy Eve, or the evening before All Saints' Day; and it is made there by bruising roasted apples and mixing them with ale, or sometimes with milk. Formerly, when the superior ranks were not too refined for these periodical meetings of jollity, white wine was frequently substituted for ale. To lambs' wool, apples and nuts are added as a necessary part of the entertainment, and the young folks amuse themselves with burning nuts in pairs on the bar of the grate, or among the warm embers, to which they gave their name and that of their lovers, or those of their friends who are supposed to have like attachments, and from the manner of their burning and direction of the flame, draw such inferences respecting the constancy or strength of their passions as usually promote mirth and good humour." For Vallancey's Etymology of lambs' wool, see "Collectanea," vol. iii., p. 444.

Lammas Lands.—Property anciently appropriated to the celebration of Lammas. In the *West London Advertiser* for April 28, 1877, the annexed report appeared of a vestry meeting at Fulham on the 24th:—"The business was to take into consideration a recommendation from the Lammas Rights' Committee. Mr. Mugford moved: 'That the Lammas Rights' Committee be requested to hold a meeting and be empowered to call and receive evidence respecting existing Lammas Rights of this parish, in order, if necessary, to assert the rights of parishioners.' He considered the proper time had arrived when the vestry should be in possession of a map setting forth the limits of Lammas Rights. He was very much astonished to find that they had not a single trace of any document showing the Lammas Rights. This would strengthen the hands of their legal advisers. If they found that the Lammas Rights were in the hands of other people, they could call on them to prove their title. Mr. Lammin said there were eight or ten old inhabitants who were able to give evidence on this question. He had no doubt the rights of copyholders existed over the parish, but fences had been allowed to grow up and the rights had apparently lapsed. At present they could only proceed with such parts as those near the river, and, perhaps, in the Fulham Fields. Mr. Schofield said there

had been a road down to the river for centuries. There were cottages down there to which there was a right of way, and they were placed under sanitary regulations. The Lammas Rights in respect to those cottages, had slipped away. It was high time they had a fresh 'school' to look after the rights of the parish. Mr. Rawkins seconded the motion. To talk of Lammas Rights near the Thames was nonsense. That part of their rights was hardly worth fighting for. The Fulham market gardens were laid out on Lammas lands. They belonged to Fulham charities, and they had been allowed to lapse." A recent Act of Parliament has extinguished the Lammas rights at Petersham in Surrey in favour of the Earl of Dysart, who surrendered in exchange a valuable riparian area which his lordship might otherwise have let to the builder.

Lampas Ardens.—At a very remote period an impost was levied, if voluntary benevolences were not forthcoming for the supply of artificial light outside certain religious buildings in continental cities, as a means of security for passengers and as a clue to the locality. These lights were usually dedicated to a saint. They were in Italy known as cesendele, a term borrowed from the fire-flies, which early travellers describe as swarming after sunset in some parts of Lombardy. The Greeks took their word for a glow-worm λαμπουρις from that for a torch. In England these lights were more commonly employed inside churches and other ecclesiastical establishments, and were frequently supported by funds secured on land or other property, whence came the term *candle-meadow*. See White Kennett's *Parochial Antiquities*, 1695, ed. 1818, *Glossary*, v. *Luminare*.

Langemark Day.—In the "Statistical Account of Scotland," vol. xv., p. 45, Parish of Lanark, we read of "the riding of the marches, which is done annually upon the day after Whitsunday Fair by the magistrates and burgesses, called here the Landsmark or Langemark Day, from the Saxon *langemark*. It is evidently of Saxon origin, and probably established here in the reign of, or sometime posterior to Malcolm I."

Langholm, Co. Dumfries.—There is still an annual custom of "Riding the Marshes" here on July 27. In 1901 it is said that a drum and fife band paraded the town at 5.30 a.m., and that at a later hour a hound race or trail took place over a six-mile course. There was subsequently a procession through the place of hundreds of boys and girls bearing heather besoms. A large thistle, a barley bannock, and a salt herring were carried aloft. *Antiquary*, xxxvii., 281.

Lanterloo.—See Chatto's *Playing Cards*, 1848, p. 166.

Lanthorn Fly.—Merian has given us an account of the famous Indian lanthorn fly, published among her *Insects*, at Surinam. "It has a hood or bladder on its head, which gives a light like a lanthorn in the night, but by daylight is clear and transparent, curiously adorned with stripes of red or green colour. Writing of tolerable large character may be read by the light of it at night. It is said that the creature can either dilate or contract the hood or bladder over its head at pleasure, and that when taken it hides all its light, which only when at liberty it affords plentifully."

Largesse.—To the festivities of harvest home must be referred the popular custom among the hop-pickers in Kent, described by Smart, and of which he gives an engraved representation in the title-page to his "Poems." He is describing their competitions:

"Who first may fill
The bellying bin, and cleanest cull the hops.
Nor ought retards, unless invited out
By Sol's declining, and the evening's calm,
Leander leads Lætitia to the scene
Of shade and fragrance—Then th' exulting band
Of pickers, male and female, seize the fair
Reluctant, and with boisterous force and brute,
By cries unmov'd, they bury her in the bin.
Nor does the youth escape — him too they seize,
And in such posture place as best may serve
To hide his charmer's blushes. Then with shouts
They rend the echoing air, and from them both
(So custom has ordain'd) a Largess claim."

"Hop-Garden," lib. 2, l. 177 ("Poems," 1752). In Northamptonshire, according to the testimony of Miss Baker, there is after the harvest what is termed a largesse, a phrase in general use, but in a different and less special sense. It is in fact nothing more than a voluntary contribution made by the inhabitants of a village towards the harvest supper, which was usually held in a barn, and kept up tolerably late with singing, drinking, and other jollity. The term largesse, among the gamins at Lowestoft, in Suffolk, was corrupted into *largie*. They would run after you, crying "Largie, largie."

Lattice, Green or Red. — As Douce long ago pointed out, ale-house lattices were at times occasionally blue, or perhaps a bluish green, and by no means invariably red. The literary allusions are, however, almost invariably to the latter. George Steevens traced to this source the later *checquers*. In Shakespear's "Henry IV.," part ii., Falstaff's page speaking of Bardolph, says, "He called me even now, my lord, through a red lattice, and I could see no part of his face from the window." In Marston's "Antonio and Mellida," we read: "as well knowen by my wit, as an ale-house by a red lattice." In the last will and Testament of Lawrence Lucifer, the old Batchiler of Limbo, at the end of the "Blacke Booke," 1604, is the following passage: "Watched sometimes ten houres together in an ale-house, ever and anon peeping forth, and sampling thy nose with the red lattice." Again, in "The Miseries of inforc'd Marriage," 1607:

—"'tis treason to the red lattice, enemy to the sign-post."

So in Marmion's "Fine Companion," "A Waterman's Widow at the sign of the Red Lattice in Southwark." But in Arden of Faversham, 1592, the colour is not defined:

—"his sign pulled down, and his lattice born away."

This designation of an ale-house is not altogether lost, though the original meaning of the word is, the sign being converted into a green lettuce; of which an instance occurs in Brownlow-street, Holborn. Apart from its use in this connection a lattice in front of windows was a common mode of securing privacy in dwellings; and at the coronation of Elizabeth of York in 1487, Henry VII. is said to have witnessed the ceremony behind a lattice.

Laugh and Lay Down.—A juvenile game at cards. The expression was common in 1605, and seems to have gained an under-meaning. See Halliwell in v., Hazlitt's *Bibl. Coll.*, i., 415, and his ed. of Herrick, 1890, i., 122.

Laundress.—The term employed at the Inns of Court from very early times for the woman who attends to the lawyers' chambers. More than one of our professional men, who eventually acquired celebrity, married his laundress. It has been conjectured that the word *meretrix* found in many ancient documents in the sense of a camp-follower ought to be interpreted in this way, and not in a less favourable one. See Hazlitt's ed. of Blount's *Tenures*, 1874, pp. 119, 433. The same female personage is styled by Braithwaite a *launderer*, as we perceive from a passage in his

Whimzies, 1631, quoted under *Funeral Feasts.*

Lavender.—From the subsequent passage in Greene's "Quip," 1592, it should seem that lavender was somehow or other vulgarly considered as emblematical of cuckoldom : "There was loyal lavender, but that was full of cuckow-spittes, to show that women's light thoughts make their husbands heavy heads."

Lawrence Lazy, Sir, or **Lazy Lawrence.**—A metonym for a sluggard. There is a chapman's story-book, entitled "The Infamous History of Sir Lawrence Lazy," of which the earliest impressions have disappeared. Mr. Durrant Cooper, in his "Sussex Vocabulary," 1853, seems to think that this Lawrence is rather "A kind of imaginary saint or fairy, whose influence produces indolence," and quotes the well-known saying, "I've got a touch of old Lawrence to-day." But it seems preferable to derive the expression from some real or fabulous human personage so named, proverbial for such qualities, and not seek any divine or supernatural solution of the mystery. In 1594, a ballad called "Lusty Lawrence" was licensed for the press by the Stationers' Company ; it reads like a parody or imitation of "Lazy Lawrence" (unless the converse was the case), but what its precise character was, there are no means of ascertaining, to my knowledge. See Fletcher's play of the *Captain*, iv., 3.

Lawrence, St.—Deacon and Martyr, whose day is August 10, is associated with the uncomfortable tradition of the gridiron, on which he is said to have been roasted alive. He was adopted by one or two places on the continent as their patron saint, and appears on the coins of Wismar, on the Baltic, and elsewhere, holding the instrument of martyrdom before him. It is an evident error to identify the name with the Lazy and Lusty Lawrence of popular literature and belief. Near Bodmin in Cornwall is the small village of St. Lawrence, where an annual fair is held, and a mayor elected for the occasion.

Leabharfein.—A form of asseveration by the Bible, or rather by *the great Sabbath*, formerly usual in the Western Isles of Scotland. *Stat. Acc.,* 1792, Applecross, co. Ross, vol. iii., 380. Supposed to correspond to the Danish *Inhoire*, customary at that period in the Isle of Lewis. Comp. *Bible.*

Leap-Candle.—"The young girls in and about Oxford (notes Aubrey) have a sport called Leap-candle, for which they set a candle in the middle of the room in a candlestick, and then draw up their coats in the form of breeches, and dance over the candle back and forth, with these words :

'The taylor of Bisiter he has but one eye,
He cannot cut a pair of green Galligaskins, if he were to die.' "

"Remains of Gentilism and Judaism," Folk-Lore Soc. ed. p. 44-5. This sport in other parts is called dancing the candle-rush.

Leaping the Well on St. Mark's Day.—Brockett, in his "Glossary of North-Country Words," 1825, describes this as "going through a deep and noisome pool on Alnwick Moor, called the Freeman's Well— a sine quâ non to the freedom of the borough." Brockett has the following account of the ceremony : "On St. Mark's Day, the aspirants proceed in great state, and in equal spirits, from the town to the moor, where they draw up in a body, at some distance from the water, and, on a signal being given, they scramble through the mud with great labour and difficulty. They may be said to come out in a condition not much better than the heroes of the 'Dunciad' after diving in Fleet Ditch. There is a current tradition, that this strange and ridiculous custom—rendered more ludicrous by being performed in white clothing—was imposed by that capricious tyrant, King John, who, it is said, was bogged in this very pool. I witnessed the ceremony a few years ago, and I can assure my friend, Mr. Surtees, that there is no foundation for his supposition, that they contrive to keep the pond dry."

Leechdom.—A considerable degree of attention has been recently paid to the subject of ancient leechdom, perhaps not much more, relatively perhaps not at all more, empirical than that of our own time. Supernatural influence and agencies entered, however, more largely into it. A very curious remedy for disease in general was the cincture of a patient with a fillet or girdle, which had been previously secured round the shrine or reliquary of a saint, supplemented by the application of a bent silver penny to the affected part ; and this process could be accomplished either on the spot or at a distance, when the sufferer could not travel, and lived in another district. The penny afterwards lapsed to the Church. In one of the Lays of Marie de France there is a singular account of a weasel restoring one of its dead fellows to life by fetching a flower, and placing it in the mouth of the defunct creature. The same remedy was subsequently applied to one of the heroines of the tale with equal success. Ellis's *Early English Metrical Romances*, 1848, p. 73. So late as 1903, a mother at Heywood in Lancashire placed a necklace of beads strung together with white thread on the neck of her child, who suffered from a fat or swollen neck.

Lee Fair.—The anonymous author of the "Dialect of Leeds," 1862, notices the great fair which was anciently held at Lee-Fair, a village in the parish of Woodkirk, (a cell of Black canons to Nostal Priory), and which terminated on St. Bartholomew's Day. This fair was not only for purposes of buying and selling, barter and exchange, but scholastic exercises and disputations were held there. It is supposed that it was a chartered institution allowed to Nostal as a privilege and source of revenue.

Lee Penny or **Lee Stone.**—The Lee-penny, or Lee-stone, is a curious piece of antiquity belonging to the family of Lee in Scotland, on which Scott's tale of "The Talisman" is founded. But the idea is probably, or rather almost certainly, much older, even than the Scotish tradition. It is a cornelian of a triangular shape, and its size about half an inch on each side. It is set in a groat of Edward III. It has been, by tradition, in the Lee family since the year 1320, that is, a little after the death of King Robert Bruce, who having ordered his heart to be carried to the Holy Land, there to be buried, one of the noble family of Douglas was sent with it, and it is said got the crowned heart in his arms from that circumstance; but the person who carried the heart was Simon Locard of Lee, who just about this time borrowed a large sum of money from Sir William de Lindsay, a prior of Ayr, for which he granted a bond of annuity of ten pounds of silver, during the life of the said Sir William de Lindsay, out of his lands of Lee and Cartland. The original bond, dated 1323, and witnessed by the principal nobility of the country, is still remaining among the family papers. As this was a great sum in those days, it is thought it was borrowed for that expedition; and from his being the person who carried the royal heart, he changed his name to Lockheart, as it is sometimes spelt, or Lockhart, and got a heart within a lock for part of his arms, with the motto *Corda serata pando.* This Simon Lockhart having taken prisoner a Saracen prince or chief, his wife came to ransom him, and on counting out the money or jewels, this stone fell out of her purse, which she hastily snatched up; which Simon Lockhart observing, insisted to have it, else he would not give up his prisoner. Upon this the lady gave it him, and told him its many virtues, viz., that it cured all diseases in cattle, and the bite of a mad dog both in man and beast. It is used by dipping the stone in water, which is given to the diseased cattle to drink; and the person who has been bit, and the wound or part infected, is washed with the water. There are no words used in the dipping of the stone, nor any money taken by the servants, without incurring the owner's displeasure. Many are the cures said to be performed by it; and people come from all parts of Scotland, and even as far up in England as Yorkshire, to get the water in which the stone is dipped, to give their cattle, when ill of the murrain especially, and black leg. A great many years ago, a complaint was made to the ecclesiastical courts, against the Laird of Lee, then Sir James Lockhart, for using witchcraft. It is said, when the plague was last at Newcastle, the inhabtiants sent for the Lee-penny, and gave a bond for a large sum in trust for the loan; and that they thought it did so much good, that they offered to pay the money, and keep the Lee-penny; but the gentleman would not part with it. A copy of this bond is very well attested to have been among the family papers, but supposed to have been spoiled along with many more valuable ones, about fifty years ago, by rain getting into the charter-room during a long minority, and no family residing at Lee. "The most remarkable cure performed upon any person, was that of Lady Baird, of Sauchton Hall, near Edinburgh; who having been bit by a mad dog, was come the length of hydrophobia; upon which, having sent to beg the Lee-penny might be sent to her house, she used it for some weeks, drinking and bathing in the water it was dipped in, and was quite recovered. This happened about eighty years ago; but it is very well attested, having been told by the lady of the then Laird of Lee, and who died within these thirty years. She also told, that her husband, Mr. Lockhart, and she were entertained at Sauchton Hall, by Sir Robert Baird and his lady, for several days, in the most sumptuous manner, on account of the lady's recovery, and in gratitude for the loan of the Lee-penny so long, as it was never allowed to be carried from the house of Lee. It was tried by a lapidary, and found to be a stone; but of what kind he could not tell."

It seems to be rather a curious coincidence that much about the same time Sir Richard-at-Lee borrowed money of St. Mary's Abbey at York, and mortgaged his lands to it, as we see in the Robin Hood epic. Hazlitt's *Tales and Legends*, 1892, 258-60, 294.

Leg, Foot, &c. Charms.—When Coleridge was at Christ's Hospital in the 18th century, there were the following metrical charms, he tells us, and he concludes that they might have been in use there long before his time:—

"The devil is tying a knot in my leg!
Mark, Luke, and John, unloose it, I beg:
Crosses three we make to ease us:
Two for the thieves, and one for Christ Jesus!"

And the form for a numbed foot was:—

"Foot, foot is fast asleep!
Thumb, thumb, thumb, in spittle we steep:
Crosses three, &c.—"

The remedy was held to apply to a stitch in the side.

Lent.—So-called from the lengthening of the day, varied with Easter, when it occurs. What was called clean Lent is mentioned in the "Plumpton Correspondence," under 1502-3, as occurring on the 5th of March, or Quadragesima Sunday. Camd. Soc. ed. 173. In Fosbrooke's "British Monachism," is the following: "At Barking Nunnery the annual store of provision consisted, inter alia, of green peas for Lent; green peas against midsummer"; with a note copied from the "Order and Government of a Nobleman's House" in the XIIIth volume of the "Archæologia," p. 373, that "if one will have pease soone in the year following, such pease are to be sowenne in the waine of the moone, at St. Andro's tide before Christmas." In Smith's "Lives of the Lords of Berkeley," we read that on the anniversary of the founder of St. Augustine's, Bristol, i.e., Sir Robert Fitzharding, on the 5th of February, "At that Monastery there shall be one hundred poore men refreshed, in a dole made unto them in this forme: every man of them hath a chanons loafe of bread, called a myche, and three hearings thearewith. There shalbe doaled also amongst them two bushells of Pesys."—"And in the anniversary daye of Dame Eve, (Lady Eve, wife of the above Lord, Sir Robert Fitzharding), our Foundresse, i.e., 12 Marcii, a dole shalbe doled in this forme: that daye shalbe doled to fifty poore men fifty loafes called miches, and to each three hearings, and, amongst them all, one bushell of pease." Lord Robert Fitzharding died Feb. 5th, 1170 [-1] 17 Hen. II., aged about 75 years. Dame Eve, who herself founded and became prioress of the house called the Magdalens, by Bristol, died prioress thereof March 12th, 1173 [-4].

In the Churchwardens' Account of St. Mary-at-Hill, in the City of London, A.D. 1492, is the following article:

"For dyssplying Roddys, ij^d."

And again, Ibid. 1501. "For paintynge the Cross Staffe for Lent, iiij^d." Herrick

in his "Noble Numbers," 1647, in his poem "To keep a True Lent," writes:

"—'Tis a fast to dole
Thy sheaf of wheat,
And meat,
Unto the hungry soule.

"It is to fast from strife,
From old debate,
And hate;
To circumcise thy life.

"To show a heart grief-rent
To starve thy sin,
Not bin;
And that's to keep thy Lent."

At Dijon, in Burgundy, it is the custom upon the first Sunday in Lent to make large fires in the streets, whence it is called Firebrand Sunday. This practice originated in the processions formerly made on that day by the peasants with lighted torches of straw, to drive away, as they called it, the bad air from the earth.

Letiche.—See *Whiteness.*

Letter.—Defoe says: "I have seen people who, after writing a letter, have prognosticated to themselves the ill success of it, if by any accident it happened to fall to the ground; others have seemed as impatient, and exclaiming against their want of thought, if, thro' haste or forgetfulness, they have chanced to hold it before the fire to dry; but the mistake of a word in it is a sure omen, that whatever request it carries shall be refused." *Mem. of Duncan Campbel,* 1732, 202.

Level Coil.—This is the name of a game mentioned by our old play-writers, and by Gifford is supposed to have been something like the modern child's sport called catch-corner (or puss-in-the-corner), "in which each of the parties strives to supplant and win the place of the other. In Coles's Dictionary it is derived from the Italian *levar il culo,* which is supported by Minsheu, and is no doubt correct. Whatever may be thought of this etymology, the diversion appears to have been a rather riotous one, and the phrase hence obtained a figurative sense, which still survives in the colloquial phrase coil." In the last edition of the "Glossary of Nares" (1859), a more particular description of level-coil occurs, so that it seemed unnecessary to enter into farther detail here. But I must add, that, unless I derive a very wrong inference from a perusal of the article in Nares, there were two games (as indeed Gifford seems to have partly suspected), one called level-coil, the other, level-sice, which were quite distinct.

Lich-Gate, or **Gate of the Dead.**—The gate at or near the entrance to a church, where the funeral service was in former times often conducted.

Lich-Wake or **Lake-Wake.**—It is otherwise known as the Lych-wake, Like-wake, and Late-wake. Atkinson's *Cleveland Gloss.*, 1868, p. 327-8. These appear to be variant forms of pronunciation, The word is plainly derived from the Anglo-Saxon lic or lice, a corpse, and wæcce, a wake, vigil, or watching. It is used in this sense by Chaucer in his "Knight's Tale":

> "Shall not be told by me
> How that Arcite is brent to ashen cold,
> Ne how that there the Liche-Wake was
> yhold
> All that night long."

St. Gregory, in the Epistle treating of the death of his sister Macrina, says: "Cum igitur nocturna Pervigilatio, ut in Martyrum celebritate canendis Psalmis perfecta esset, et Crepusculum advenisset," &c. That watching with the corpse was an ancient custom everywhere practised, numerous passages from ecclesiastical writers might be cited to prove, could there be any doubt of the antiquity of a custom, which, owing its origin to the tenderest affections of human nature, has perhaps on that account been used from the infancy of time. Ruddiman observes: "Proper Like Wakes (Scotish) are the meetings of the friends of the deceased, a night or nights before the burial." *Glossary to Douglas's Æneid*, v. *Walkin*. Jamieson says: "This antient custom most probably originated from a silly superstition with respect to the danger of a corpse being carried off by some of the agents of the invisible world, or exposed to the ominous liberties of brute animals. But, in itself, it is certainly a decent and proper one; because of the possibility of the person, considered as dead, being only in a swoon. Whatever was the original design, the lik-wake seems to have very early degenerated into a scene of festivity extremely incongruous to the melancholy occasion." *Etym. Dict.* v. *Lyk-Wake*. Hutchinson, speaking of the parish of Whitbeck in Cumberland, says: "People always keep wake with the dead," and we learn from another source "that the Late Wake was in the last century a practice common in many parts of Scotland, and not yet exploded in Aberdeenshire, of people sitting up all night with the dead corps, in the chamber of the deceased." Again, we read: "It was customary for the folks at Campsie, co. Stirling, to have at least two lyke-wakes (the corpse being kept two nights before the interment) where the young neighbours watched the corpse, being merry or sorrowful, according to the situation or rank of the de-

ceased." *Cumberland*, i., 553; *Stat. Acc. of Scotland*, v., 435, xv., 372.

"In North Wales," says Pennant (speaking of the manners of the 18th century), "the night before a dead body is to be interred, the friends and neighbours of the deceased resort to the house the corpse is in, each bringing with him some small present of bread, meat, drink, (if the family be something poor); but more especially candles, whatever the family be: and this night is called *wyl nôs*, whereby the country people seem to mean a watching night. Their going to such a house, they say, is *i wilior corph*, i.e. to watch the corpse; but wylo signifies to weep and lament, and so wyl nôs may be a night of lamentation: while they stay together on that night, they are either singing psalms, or reading some part of the Holy Scriptures. "Whenever any body comes into the room where a dead body lyes, especially the wyl nôs and the day of its interment, the first thing he does, he falls on his knees by the corpse, and says the Lord's Prayer."

The abuse of this vigil is of pretty old standing. The 10th Canon at the provincial Synod held in London temp. Edw. III. "endeavours to prevent the disorders committed at people's watching a corpse before burial. Here the Synod takes notice that the design of people's meeting together upon such occasions, was to join their prayers for the benefit of the dead person; that this antient and serviceable usage was overgrown with superstition and turned into a convenience for theft and debauchery: therefore, for a remedy against this disorder, 'tis decreed that, upon the death of any person, none should be allowed to watch before the corpse in a private house, excepting near relations and friends of the deceased, and such as offered to repeat a set number of psalms for the benefit of his soul." The penalty annexed is excommunication. This is also mentioned in Becon's "Reliques of Rome," 1563, and comprized in the catalogue of crimes that were anciently cursed with bell, book and candle

Bourne complains of the sport, drinking, and lewdness used at these Lake Wakes in his time. Even in Brand's day, they still continued to resemble too much the ancient Bacchanalian orgies. Pennant, in describing Highland ceremonies, says: "The lake wake is a ceremony used at funerals. The evening after the death of any person, the relations or friends of the deceased meet at the house attended by a bagpipe or fiddle: the nearest of kin, be it wife, son, or daughter, opens a melancholy ball, dancing and greeting, i.e. crying violently at the same time; and this continues till day-light, but with such gambols and frolicks among the younger part of the company, that the loss which occasioned them is often more than supplied by the consequences of that night. If the corpse remain unburied for two nights, the same rites are renewed. Thus, Scythian-like they rejoice at the deliverance of their friends out of this life of misery." He tells us in the same place that "the Coranich or singing at funerals is still in use in some places. The songs are generally in praise of the deceased, or a recital of the valiant deeds of their ancestors." *Tour in Scotland,* 1769, 112.

In Jamieson's time the Lych-Wake was retained in Sweden, where it was called Wakstuga, from wak-a, to watch, and perhaps stuga, a room, an apartment, or cottage. Ihre observes, that "although these wakes should be dedicated to the contemplation of our mortality, they have been generally passed in plays and compotations, whence they were prohibited in public edicts." *Etym. Dict.* v. *Lyk-Waik; Gloss. Suio-Goth.* v. *Wake.*

Lich-Way.—A way most direct for a funeral procession on foot from the house to the place of burial, and where a precedent had been set, it was thought that a right was created for others to use the route even across private property. This belongs to the rather long roll of popular errors. The lich-way is cognate to the better-known lichgate and to the locality originally called Lichfield or the Field of the Dead.

Lidford Law.—See Hazlitt's *Proverbs,* 1882, p. 141, and Lysons' *Magna Britannia,* Devonshire, 512, where it is stated that the lords of the manor of Tiverton had formerly the power of capital punishment. In Browne's Poems, by Hazlitt, 1869, p. 352, a passage in the verses headed *Lidford Journey* suggests that offences against the laws of the Stannaries were punished by confinement in the gaol here; for the writer thus concludes:

"At sixe a clock I came away
And prayde for those that were to stay
Within a place so Arrant:
Wild and ope to winds that rore,
By Gods grace Ile come there no more,
Vnlesse by some Tin Warrant."

Lifting Monday.—In the "Household Expences, 18 Edw. I." is this curious account: "Domine de camera Regine. XV. die Maii, vii dominabus et domicellis regine, quia ceperunt dominum regem in lecto suo, in crastino Pasche et ipsum fecerunt finire versus eas pro pace regis, quam fecit de dono suo per manus Hugonis de Cerru, Scutiferi domine de Weston.

xiiijli." *Archæologia* for 1805. The taking Edward Longshanks in his bed by the above party of ladies of the bedchamber and maids of honour, on Easter Monday, was very probably for the purpose of heaving or lifting the king, on the authority of a custom which then doubtless prevailed among all ranks throughout the kingdom, and which is yet not entirely laid aside in some of our distant provinces; a custom, by which, however strange it may appear, they intended no less than to represent our Saviour's Resurrection. At Warrington, Bolton, and Manchester, and in many other places, as Liverpool, Shrewsbury, and in North Wales, on Easter Monday, the women, forming parties of six or eight each, still continue to surround such of the opposite sex as they meet, and, either with or without their consent, lift them thrice above their heads into the air, with loud shouts at each elevation. On Easter Tuesday, the men, in parties as aforesaid, do the same to the women. By both parties it is converted into a pretence for fining or extorting a small sum, which they always insist on having paid them by the persons whom they have thus elevated. In the "Gentleman's Magazine" for February, 1784, p. 96, a gentleman from Manchester says, that "Lifting was originally designed to represent our Saviour's Resurrection. The men lift the women on Easter Monday, and the women the men on Tuesday. One or more take hold of each leg, and one or more of each arm, near the body, and lift the person up, in a horizontal position, three times. It is a rude, indecent, and dangerous diversion, practised chiefly by the lower class people. Our magistrates constantly prohibit it by the bellman, but it subsists at the end of the town; and the women have of late years converted it into a money job. I believe it is chiefly confined to these Northern counties." See *Hoke-Tide,* suprà, Monthly Magazine for April, 1798, p. 273; and Halliwell's *Dict.* in v.

Lights in Churches (Mediæval). —See *Antiquary* for January, 1892, for a paper on this subject.

Limiter or **Limitour.**—A friar licensed to beg within a certain radius.

Lincoln Green.—See Nares, *Gloss.* in v. and a passage in Hazlitt's *Tales and Legends,* 1892, p. 295-6, where mention occurs of scarlet cloth as well as green. In 1515 Henry VIII. and his companions celebrated May-Day, clad in liveries of Lincoln Green in imitation of Robin Hood and his men.

Lincoln's Inn.—See *Christmas, Lord of Misrule,* &c. In 1662-3, the Prince de la Grange, Lord-Lieutenant of Lincoln's-Inn, entertained Charles II. with a pageant called *Universal Motion.*

Linen Armourer.—The original vocation of the Merchant-Tailor, who quilted the armour worn in the middle ages; the process is shown to some extent by the old arms of the Gild engraved in Hazlitt's work, 1892.

Lin-Shords.—A Lent custom at Ilfracombe. See Halliwell in v.

Liquoring of the Clouts.—The drinking bout formerly usual, when a lying-in was in prospect at a house, and the lady's linen was being aired in readiness for the occasion. On October 1, 1721, the Earl of Rochester's house at Petersham was burnt down, and his fine library destroyed, by the inmates going up to bed intoxicated, and leaving the clothes at the fire.

Little John (otherwise *Micklejohn*), the renowned comrade of Robin Hood, and also a *dramatis persona* in the May games. Among the extracts given by Lysons from the Churchwardens' and Chamberlain's Accounts at Kingston, there is an entry "for Little Johns cote." Both forms of the name are still current.

Liturgical Uses.—These are of Salisbury, York, Salisbury and York jointly or in common, Hereford, Bangor, and England in general. In many leading respects they differed little from the rituals printed for circulation abroad, and a considerable proportion of them were from the presses of Paris and Rouen. These service-books consisted of Missals, Horæ, Primers in Latin and English or in English alone, Officia, Manualia or Breviaries, Portifolia, Benedictiones, Antiphonalia, Gradualia or Grails, and Processionalia. They are for the most part of signal rarity, except a few of the later Primers, missals and manuals. Some have the reputation of being unique. All are difficult to find in good state. The sole text of the Durham Benedictional is defective; it is in Latin with an interlinear Anglo-Saxon gloss, and is probably the most ancient of the series, to which it belongs; the nearest to it may be the Salisbury use, founded on Bishop Osmund's eleventh century prototype. There is a very early Antiphonal belonging to the church of Bangor, co. Down, Ireland, and the Huth Library possesses a *Missal* ascribed to Bangor use, presented to the high altar of Oswestry parish church in 1554 (? 1454) by Sir Morris Griffith, priest. Mr. Maskell, to whom the volume formerly belonged, judged it to be for the Welsh Bangor; but there were constant relations between the Welsh borders and Ireland in remote times, and the attribution is at any rate dubious. The oldest processional in type appears to be that of 1508, reprinted with variations in 1517, 1523, and later. There is a fine Sarum Graduale of 1532. In regard to the mixed uses, MSS. *Horæ* occur, in which many English prayers and even saints are found, although the service is nowhere expressly said to be in English in the exordium, and there are only occasional offices stated to be *ad usum Sarum*. This is the case, but far more rarely, with the York use, which was also widely diffused. There are monographs by Dickinson and others relating to them, and bibliographical descriptions in my *Collections and Notes*.

Livery Cloth.—The *Times* of Dec. 4, 1889, says: "Yesterday a very ancient custom—a relic of the days when the freemen and apprentices of the various companies used to wear the livery of their respective guilds—was observed at Guildhall by the inspection and selection by the Court of Aldermen of the gifts of what is called "livery cloth," which are made, at this season to the great officers of state and other personages. The Lord Chancellor, the Lord Chief Justice, the Master of the Rolls, the Lord Chamberlain, the Vice-Chamberlain, the Lord Steward, the Treasurer and Controller of the Household, the Home Secretary, the Foreign Secretary, the Attorney-General, the Solicitor-General, the Recorder, and the Common Serjeant each receive annually four and a half yards of the best black cloth; the Town Clerk receives six yards of black and six of green cloth, and the principal clerk in the Town Clerk's offices receives four yards of black and four yards of green cloth."

Llandegla, Denbighshire.—Pennant, speaking of the Church dedicated to St. Tecla, Virgin and Martyr, at Llandegla, says: "About two hundred yards from the church, in a quillet called Gwern Degla, rises a small spring. The water is under the tutelage of the saint, and to this day held to be extremely beneficial in the falling sickness. The patient washes his limbs in the well; makes an offering into it of four-pence; walks round it three times; and thrice repeats the Lord's Prayer. These ceremonies are never begun until after sunset, in order to inspire the votaries with greater awe. If the afflicted be of the male sex, like Socrates, he makes an offering of a cock to his Æsculapius, or rather to Tecla Hygeia; if of the fair sex, a hen. The fowl is carried in a basket, first round the well; after that into the church-yard; when the same orisons and the same circum-ambulations are performed round the church. The votary then enters the church; gets under the Communion Table; lies down with the Bible under his or her head, is covered with the carpet or cloth, and rests there till break of day; departing after offering sixpence, and leaving the fowl in the church. If the bird dies, the cure is supposed to have been effected, and the disease transferred to the devoted victim." *Tours in Wales*, 1810, ii., 15.

Loaves.—While walking by the river at King's Cliffe, two young men found the body of the lad who was drowned in the flooded stream a fortnight ago. Many attempts had been made to find the body, the most curious being to float down the river loaves of bread containing mercury, in the belief that bread so "charmed" will never go past a corpse. Strange to say, the body has been found in the stretch of water where the bread "stopped short." The superstitious have their beliefs in the potency of mercurised bread considerably strengthened. *Daily Mail*, Nov. 16, 1903.

Lodam.—An old game at cards. See Nares, *Glossary*, 1859, in v., and the authorities there cited.

Loggats.—Steevens says, "This is a game played in several parts of England even at this time. A stake is fixed into the ground; those who play, throw loggats at it, and he that is nearest the stakes wins. I have seen it played in different counties at their sheep-shearing feasts, where the winner was entitled to a black fleece, which he afterwards presented to the farmer's maid to spin for the purpose of making a petticoat, and on condition that she knelt down on the fleece to be kissed by all the rustics present." Malone says, "Loggeting in the fields is mentioned for the first time among other new and crafty games and plays, in the statute of 33 Hen. VIII. c. 9. Not being mentioned in former acts against unlawful games, it was probably not practised long before the statute of Henry the eighth was made." "A loggat-ground," says Blount, "like a skittle-ground, is strewed with ashes, but is more extensive. A bowl much larger than the jack of the game of bowls is thrown first. The pins, which I believe are called loggats, are much thinner, and lighter at one extremity than at the other. The bowl being first thrown the players take the pins up by the thinner and lighter end, and fling them towards the bowl, and in such a manner that the pins may once turn round in the air, and slide with the thinner extremity towards the bowl. The pins are about one or two-and-twenty inches long."

Long Bullets.—A game played by casting stones. See Davis, *Suppl. Glossary*, 1881, p. 384.

Long Hundred, The.—We learn from Hickes's "Thesaurus," that the Norwegians and Islandic people used a method of numbering peculiar to themselves, by the addition of the words, Tolfræðr, or Tolfrœd, or Tolfræt (whence our word twelve), which made ten signify twelve; a hundred, a hundred and twenty; a thousand, a thousand two hundred; &c. The reason of this was, that the nations above-named had two decads or tens: a lesser, which they used in common with other nations, consisting of ten units; and a greater, containing twelve (tolf) units. Hence, by the addition of the word Tolfræðr, or Tolfræd, the hundred contained not ten times ten, but ten times twelve, that is a hundred and twenty. The Doctor observes that this Tolfrædic mode of computation by the greater decads, or tens, which contain twelve units, is still retained amongst us in reckoning certain things by the number twelve, which the Swedes call dusin, the French douzain, and we dozen. And I am informed, he adds, by merchants, &c., that in the number, weight, and measure of many things the hundred among us still consists of that greater tolfrædic hundred which is composed of ten times twelve. Hence then without doubt is derived to us the present mode of reckoning many things by six score to the hundred. By the statute, 25 Hen. VIII., c. 13, no person shall have above two thousand sheep on his land; and the twelfth section (after reciting that the hundred in every county be not alike, some reckoning by the great hundred, or six score, and others by five score), declares that the number two thousand shall be accounted ten hundred for every thousand, after the number of the great hundred, and not after the less hundred, so that every thousand shall contain twelve hundred after the less number of the hundred. Percy observes, upon the Northumberland Household Book, "It will be necessary to premise here, that the antient modes of computation are retained in this book: according to which it is only in money that the hundred consists of five score: in all other articles the enumerations are made by the old Teutonic hundred of six score, or a hundred and twenty." In the 18th century, a man died at Parton in Scotland, aged above ninety, who, about eight months before his death, got a complete set of new teeth, which he employed till near his last breath to excellent purpose. He was four times married, had children by all his wives, and, at the baptism of his last child, which happened not a year before his death, with an air of complacency expressed his thankfulness to his Maker for having "at last sent him the cled score," i.e. twenty-one. See Hazlitt's *Proverbs*, 1882, p. 142.

Long Rope Day.—At Brighton, Good Friday goes under the name of "Long Rope Day." The children of all growths bring up the ropes from the beach, and skip about the streets. This was done as lately as 1863.

Lord, have Mercy upon Us!—
The inscription on houses infected with
the plague. See Nares, *Gloss.* in v., and
Hazlitt's *Handbook*, 1867, and *Bibl. Coll.*,
iii., 36.

Lord of Misrule.—"In the feast
of Christmas," says Stow in his "Survey,"
"there was in the King's House, wheresoever he lodged, a Lord of Misrule, or
Master of merry disports, and the like had
ye in the house of every nobleman of honour or good worship, were he spiritual or
temporal. The Mayor of London and
either of the sheriffs had their several lords
of misrule, ever contending, without quarrel or offence, who should make the rarest
pastime to delight the beholders. These
lords, beginning their rule at Allhallond
Eve, continued the same till the morrow
after the feast of the Purification, commonly called Candlemas Day: in which
space there were fine and subtle disguisings, masks, and mummeries, with playing
at cards for counters, nayels, and points
in every house, more for pastimes than for
gaine." Ellis prints a letter from the
Council of the Princess Mary's household
to Cardinal Wolsey, supposed to have been
written in 1525, several years before the
date of the "Privy Purse Expenses" published by Madden; in this document we
get a glimpse of unusually splendid and
costly prepartions for the then approaching Chrismas holidays. The letter is
dated Tewkesbury, November 27, without
any note of the year. The following passage may be worth extracting : "We humbly beseche the same (your grace) to let
us knowe youre gracious pleasure concernyng aswell a ship of silver for the almes
dishe requysite for her high estate, and
spice plats, as also for trumpetts and a
rebek to be sent, and whyther we shall ap-
poynte any Lord of Mysrule for the said
honorable householde, or provide for en-
terluds, disgysyngs, or pleyes in the said
fest, or for banket on twelf nyght."
Among the Loseley Papers, printed by
Kempe in 1836, are several relating to
George Ferrers, of St. Albans, Herts, who
was Lord of Misrule to Edward VI. Ferrers, in this official capacity, composed a
variety of masques and interludes, which
are no longer known to exist, and he is
also the author of one or two of the legends in the "Mirror for Magistrates," of
which Mr. Kempe, by an oversight, describes him as the principal writer. Ferrers received his appointment at Christmas, 1551, and although his literary performances as lord of misrule seem to have
perished, a good deal of valuable correspondence illustrative of his functions and
proceedings is inserted in Mr. Kempe's
volume from the originals at Loseley.
There is one singularly interesting letter

in this series, in which Ferrers narrates
the manner of his entry into London in
1551, and the proposed devices for the
same ceremony in the following year. "As
towching my Introduction," he writes to
Sir Thomas Cawarden, "whereas the last
yeare my devise was to cum of oute of the
mone, this yeare I imagine to cum oute
of a place called vastum vacuum, the
great waste, as moche to saie as a place
voide or emptie w^{th}out the worlde, where
is neither fier, ayre, nor earth; and that
I have bene remayning there sins the last
yeare." He desired to be attired in blue
velvet, and he wished, if possible, to be
with the King on St. Stephen's Day before
dinner. He had provided a man to play
on a kettle-drum, with his boy, and another drummer with a fife, who were to be
dressed like Turks; and so forth. Comp.
my *Prefaces, Dedications, and Epistles*,
1874, p. 69. There cannot, perhaps,
be a more remarkable proof of the
importance which was attached to
these mummeries at Christmas than the
form, in which the warrants were
drawn up for any arrangements connected
with them; even the order for a fool's coat
is signed by six of the Privy Council.
Henry Percy, fifth Earl of Northumberland, it seems from his Household-book for
1512, was accustomed, when he was at
home at Christmas, to engage a lord of
misrule, who had 30s. in reward.

Henry Machyn notes in his "Diary"
under January 4, 1551-2 : "The iiij. day
of Januarii was mad a grett skaffold in
chepe hard by the crosse, agaynst the
kynges lord of myssrule cummyng from
Grenwyche; and he landed at Towre warff,
and with hym yonge knyghts and gentyll-
men a gret nombur on hosse bake sum in
gownes and cotes and chaynes abowt ther
nekes, and on the Towre hyll ther they
went in order, furst a standard of yelow
and grene sylke with Saint George, and
then gonnes and skuybes (squibs) and
trompets and bagpipes, and drous-
selars and flutes, and then a gret
compeny all in yelow and gren, and doc-
turs declaryng my lord grett, and then
the mores danse dansyng with a tabret,"
&c. In the Christmas of 1553, it is recorded that Sheriff Maynard "had a lord
of misrule, and the mores dansse, with a
good compeny." This lord, we learn from
Stow's *Chronicle*, 1631, p. 608, was Serjeant Vawce or Vaux. The pastime seems
to have engaged the attention of the Diarist, for he inserts several entries under
the same head in various years. The
Sheriff's lord met the King's lord on the
present occasion, and on others, and the
two joined in procession through a portion
of the City, till the King's lord took leave
of his brother-mome at Tower wharf by

Sheriff Maynard's procession with his torch-light. Machyn's description of lord of misrule, in 1553, is too curious and picturesque to be omitted. "The xvij day of March cam thrug London, from Algatt, Master Maynard, the sheryff of London, wyth a standard and dromes, and after gyants boyth great and smalle, and theur hobe-horsses, and after them the g . . ., and affter grett horsses and men in cotes of velvet, with chains of gold a-bowt ther nekes, and men in harnes; and then the mores dansse, and then mony mynsterells; and after came the sergantes and yomen on horsse-bake with rebyns of green and whyte abowtt ther nekes, and then la. . . . . late beyng lord of myssrulle, rod gorgyusly in cloth of gold, and with cheynes of gold abowt hys neke, with hand fulle of rynges of gret waluw, the which serjants rod in cotes of velvet with cheynes of gold; and then com the dullo, and a sawden, and then a priest shreyffyng Jack-of-lent on horss-bake, and a doctor ys fezyssyoun, and then Jack-of-lents wyff browght him ye fessyssyouns and bad save ys lyff, and he shuld give him a thowsand li. for ys labur; and then cam the carte with the wyrth hangyd with cloth of gold, and fulle of banners and mynsterels plahyng and syng-yng." Sheriff Maynard, Machyn else-where tells us, kept a large establishment. He was buried on the 12th November, 1557.

These costly proceedings appear to have been disapproved by the citizens: for by an Act of Common Council, 1 and 2 Phil. and Mary, for retrenching expenses among other things, it was ordered, "that from henceforth there shall be no wyth fetcht home at the Maiors or Sheriffs Houses. Neither shall they keep any lord of misrule in any of their houses." Strype's Stow, Book i. p. 246. Machyn describes a gorgeous lord of misrule who rode through London in 1561, followed by an hundred gentlemen on horseback, with gold chains; and Machyn says that my lord himself was "in clene complett har-nes, gylt."

Stubbes affords the following account of the Lord of Misrule: "Firste, all the wilde heades of the Parishe, con-uentyng together, chuse them a graund Capitaine (of mischeef) whom they innoble with the title of my Lorde of Misserule, and hym they crown with great solemni-tie, and adopt for their kyng. This kyng anoynted, chuseth for the twentie, fortie, three-score, or a hundred lustie guttes like to hymselfe, to waite vppon his Lordely maiestie, and to guarde his noble persone. Then euery one of these his menne he in-uesteth with his liueries, of greene, yel-

lowe, or some other light wanton colour. And as though that were not (baudie) gaudy enough I should saie, they bedecke themselues with scarffes, ribons, and laces, hanged all ouer with golde rynges, preci-ous stones, and other jewelles: this doen, they tye about either legge twentie or fourtie belles with rich hande-kercheefes in their handes, and somtymes laied a crosse ouer their shoulders and neckes, borrowed for the moste parte of their pretie Mopsies and loouyng Bessies for bussyng them in the darcke. Thus all thinges sette in order, haue they their hobbie horses, dragos, and other antiques, together with their baudie pipers, and thunderyng drommers, to strike vp the Deuilles Daunce withall, then marche these heathen companie towardes the churche and churche-yarde, their pipers pipyng, their drommers thonderyng, their stumppes dauncyng, their belles iynglyng, their handkerchefes swyngyng about their heades like madmen, their hobbie horses, and other monsters skirmishyng amongest the throng: and in this sorte they goe to the churche, (though the minister bee at praier or preachyng) dauncyng and swingyng their handkercheefes ouer their heades, in the church, like Deuilles incar-nate, with suche a confused noise, that no man can heare his owne voice. Then the foolishe people, they looke, they stare, they laugh, they fleere, and mount vpon formes and pewes, to see these goodly pageauntes, solemnized in this sort. Then after this, about the churche they goe againe and againe, and so forthe into the churche yarde, where they have commonly their Sommer haules, their bowers, ar-bours, and banquettyng houses set vp, wherein they feaste, banquet, and daunce all that daie, and (peraduenture) all that night too. And thus these terrestrial furies spend their Sabbaoth daie. Then for the further innoblyng of this honorable Lur-dane (Lorde I shoulds aye) they have also certaine papers, wherein is paynted some babblerie or other, of imagerie worke, and these thei call my Lord of Misrules badges. these thei geue to euery one, that will geue money for thé to maintaine them in this their heathenrie, diuelrie, whoredome, dronkennesse, pride, and what not. And who will not shewe himselfe buxome to them, and geue the money for these the deuilles cognizaunces, they shall be mocked, and shouted at shamefully. And so assotted are some that they not onely giue them money, to maintain their ab-homination withall, but also weare their badges and cognizances in their hattes, or cappes openly. An other sorte of fan-tasticall fooles, bring to these helhoundes (the lorde of Misrule and his complices) some bread: some good ale, some newé chese, some olde cheese, some custardes, some cakes, some flaunes, some tartes, some creame, some meate, some one thing, some an other : but if they knewe that as often as they bring any to the maintenance of these execrable pastymes, they offer sacrifice to the Deuill and Sathanas, they would repent, and withdrawe their hands, whiche God graunt they maie."

In the "Lincoln Articles," 1585, one is :—"Whether your Minister or Churchwardens have suffered any lord of Misrule, or Sommer lords, or ladies or any disguised person in Christmas, or at Maigames, or morris dancers or at any other time, to come unreverently into the churchyard, and there to daunce or play any unsemely part with scoffs, iestes, wanton gestures, or ribald talk, namely in the time of common praier?" I find the following in the York Articles (any year till 1640) :— "Whether hath your church or churchyard beene abused and prophaned by any fighting, chiding, brawling, or quarrelling, and playes, Lords of Misrule, summer lords, morris-dancers, pedlers, bowlers, bearewards, butchers feastes, schooles, temporal courts, or leets, lay-juries, musters, or other prophane usage in your church or church-yard."

Lodge, in his "Wits Miserie," 1596, p. 84, speaking of a jeaster, says : "This fellow in person is comely, in apparel courtly, but in behaviour a very ape, and no man ; his studye is to coine bitter jeastes, or to show antique motions, or to sing baudie sonnets and ballads : give him a little wine in his head, he is continually flearing and making of mouths ; he laughs intemperately at every little occasion, and dances about the houses, leaps over tables, outskips men's heads, trips up his companions' heeles, burns sacke with a candle, and hath all the feates of a Lord of Missrule in the countrie. It is a special marke of him at table, he sits and makes faces." Hinde, in his "Life of Bruen," p. 86, censures those gentlemen "who had much rather spend much of their estate in maintaining idle and base persons to serve their owne lustes and satisfie the humour of a rude and profane people as many do their hors-riders, faulkeners, huntsmen, lords of misrule, pipers, and minstrels, rather to lead them and their followers (both in their publick assemblies and private families) a dance about the calfe, than such a dance as David danced before the Arke, with spiritual rejoicing in God's mercies,' &c." Urquhart, in "The Discovery of a most exquisite Jewel, &c." 1651, p. 238, says : "They may be said to use their King as about Christmas we used to do the King of Misrule, whom we invest with that title to no other end, but to countenance the Bacchanalian riots and preposterous disorders of the family where he is installed." Christmas, says Selden, in his "Table Talk," succeeds the Saturnalia, the same time, the same number of holy days : then the Master waited upon the servant like the lord of misrule. The name only of the Lord of Misrule is now remembered. In Scotland he was known as the *Abbot of Misrule*, or of *Bon Accord*.

In a similar way, Peter the Great of Russia had his prince-pope, who was head of a College of Fools. One of Peter's last acts was to hold an election to supply the place of Buturlin ; and an account of the ceremony has been given in a Transatlantic magazine, Scribner's *Monthly*, xxii., 886. This Abbot of Misrule, or Unreason, appears to have borne much resemblance to the *Abbas Stultorum*, who presided over the Feast of Fools in France. At Rodez, the capital of the Province of Rovergue in France, they had an Abbé de la Malgouverné, who corresponds exactly with our Abbot of Misrule. See Warton's "Obs. on the F. Q." vol. ii., p. 211. See also Fuller's "Church History," 1655. "Hist. of Cambridge," p. 159. Life of Dr. Dee in Joan. Glastoniensis Chronica, ed. 1726, append. p. 502, Dugd. "Orig. Jurid." ed. 1671, pp. 154, 156, 247, 285. In a *Calendar Historical*, printed at Geneva, 1569, the only holy-day marked is February 18 : "The holie-day of foles and misrules was kept at Rome." This entry seems to refer to the ecclesiastical *Feast of Fools*, a survival in an altered form of the Roman *Saturnalia*. Wright's *Archæological Album*, 1845, pp. 161-4, where a very interesting account may be found of this continental and Catholic festival and orgy.

Lordship or **Seigniorialty.**—The germinal or primary notion and principle resident in rule of any kind by a man over his fellow-men were the engagement to provide them with the means of sustenance ; and the first idea of conquest is to be similarly sought in the need on the part of growing communities of additional sources of food. Hampton's *Origines Patriciæ*, 1846, chapters iii. and iv. Selden puts the matter differently, goes down less to the root, where he writes : "A king is a thing men have used for their own sakes, for quietness' sake. Just as in a family one man is appointed to buy the meat. . . ." *Table Talk*, 1689, ed. 1860, p. 172. The development and evolution of royalty have overlaid the foundation of it, and in the modern kingship and kingly prerogative and majesty we lose the commencement of the system. The term lady equally owes itself to the idea of food, signifying Loaf-Giver.

Love.—To play at a game of chance

for love is to play for nothing. At the game of ping-pong the two parties engaged are said to be so many to love, that is, so many to nothing.

Love Charms, Philtres, &c.—Theocritus and Virgil have both introduced women into their pastorals, using charms and incantations to recover the affections of their sweethearts. In Bradshaw's "Shepherd's Starre," 1591, sig. B, which is a paraphrase of the third of the Canticles of Theocritus, Dialoguewise. Amaryllis. Corydon. Tityrus, Corydon says: "There is a custome amongest us swaynes in Crotona, (an auncient towne in Italy, on that side where Sicilia bordereth), to elect by our divination Lordes and Ladies, with the leaf of the flower telephilon, which being laide before the fier leapeth unto them whom it loveth, and skippeth from them whom it hateth. Tityrus and I, in experience of our lott, whose happe it should be to injoye your love, instead of Telephilon we burned mistletoe and boxe for our divination, and unto me Amaryllis you fled, and chose rather to turne to an unworthy shepherd, then to burne like an unworthy lover." Again, at sig. G 2, occurs :— "Lately, I asked counsell of Agræo, a prophetesse, how to know Amaryllis should ever love mee, shee taught mee to take telephilon, a kinde of leafe that pepper beareth, so called of Δηλιφιλον, because it foreseweth love, and to clap the leaves in the palme of my hand. If they yeelded a great sound, then surely shee should love me greatly ; if a little sound, then little love. But either I was deafe, being fenceles through love, or else no sound at all was heard, and so Agræo the Divinatrix tolde me a true rule. Now I preferre my garlande made in sorrowfull hast, of which the flowers, some signifying death, and som mourning, but none belonging to marriage, do manifest that Amaryllis hath no respect of meane men." He had before said : "I will go gather a coronet, and will weave and infolde it with the knottes of truest love, with greene lawrell Apollos scepter, which shall betoken her wisedome, and with the myrtle faire Venus poesie, which shall shewe her beautie. And with Amaranthus Dianas Herbe, whereby bloud is stenched, so may shee imitate the herbe, and have remorce." Newton enquires, under breaches of the seventh commandment, "Whether, by any secret sleight or cunning, as drinkes, drugges, medicines, charmed potions, amatorious philters, figures, characters, or any such like paltering instruments, devises, or practises, thou hast gone about to procure others to doate for love of thee." *Tryall of a man's own Selfe,* 1586, p. 116. Ferrand adds : "It is most certain that Botanomancy,

which is done by the noise or crackling that Kneeholme, box, or bay-leaves make when they are crushed betwixt one's hands, or cast into the fire, was of old in use among the Pagans, who were wont to bruise poppy flowers betwixt their hands, by this meanes thinking to know their loves : and for this cause Theocritus cals this hearb Τηλιφιλον, quasi Δηλιφιλον, as if we should say Tel-love." The same author, speaking of the ancient love charms, characters, amulets, or such like periapses, says, they are "such as no Christian Physitian ought to use : notwithstanding that the common people doe to this day too superstitiously believe and put in practice many of these paganish devices." *Erotomania,* 1640, pp. 176, 310. It is said elsewhere of the quack astrologer that "He trapans a young heiress to run away with a footman, by perswading a young girl 'tis her destiny : and sells the old and ugly philtres and love-powder to procure them sweethearts." *Character of a Q. A.,* 1675, sign. C 2. Lyly, in "Euphues and his England," 1580, makes one of his characters say : "I haue hearde often-tymes that in loue there are three things for to bee vsed : if time serue, violence, if wealth be great, gold, if necessitie compel, sorcerie. But of these three but one can stande me in-steede, the last, but not the least, which is able to worke the mindes of all the woemen like wax, when the others can scarce wind them like a with." He proceeds to enumerate various spells and charms, which seem to be intended satirically by the author. Lovers, indeed, have always been fond of enchantment. Shakespear has represented Othello as accused of winning his Desdemona "by conjuration and mighty magic." Brabantio, for instance, says to Othello, referring to Desdemona :

——"Thou hast practis'd on her with
    foul charms;
Abus'd her delicate youth with drugs
    or minerals
That weaken motion : "—
Again, the same person exclaims :
"She is abus'd, stol'n from me, and
    corrupted
By spells and medicines bought of
    mountebanks."
——"I therefore vouch again
That with some mixtures powerful o'er
    the blood,
Or with some dram conjur'd to this
    effect
He wrought upon her."
Act i., sc. 2-3.

"*Gelas.* Doe you thinck,
Is't possible to obteyne a maydens loue
By pouders or by philtres?
Pseud. Art thou Venus vassall?

Gelas. I am a man compact of flesh
  and blood;
I feel a stirring heate.
  Pseud. Vpon the mountaines of Thes-
    salia
I doe remember that I sawe an oake,
That brought forth goulden akornes of
  greate price:
If any young man had but one of theis,
The maides would almost dye for loue of
  him."

Timon, a Play, i., 4. In the "Letting of
Humours Blood in the Head-Vaine," 1600,
by S. Rowlands, the author speaks of an
odd kind of charm or philtre for procuring love:

———"(sayes he) take me a turtle-doue,
And in an ouen let her lie and bake
So dry, that you may powder of her
  make:
Which being put into a cup of wine,
The wench that drinkes it, will to loue
  incline."

Browne, the Devonshire poet, instructs
us that there was formerly a kind of love-
charm performed with the leaves of the
alder:

"Then comes another, and her hand
  bereaues
The soone slipt alder of two clammy
  leaues,
And clapping them together, bids him
  see
And learne of loue the hidden mystery.
Braue Flood (quoth she) that hold'st vs
  in suspence,
And shew'st a God-like powre in abstin-
  ence,
At this thy coldnesse we doe nothing
  wonder,
These leaues did so, when once they grew
  asunder;
But since the one did taste the others
  blisse,
And felt his partners kinde, partake
  with his,
Behold how close they ioyne."

He refers to another, which also does not
seem to be elsewhere on record:

"Those, seen of one who every herbe
  would try,
And what the blood of elephants im-
  parts
To coole his flame, yet would he (forced)
  cry,
Love! why to wounde her had I not thy
  darts?"

Loudon describes the Scabiosa as a kind of
medicinal weed, used in cutaneous complaints, and the elephant is a variety of
this. The subsequent passage from Swet-
nam's "Arraignment of Women," 1615,
points out some of the vagaries of lovers

of that age: "Some thinke, that if a
woman smile on them she is presentlie
over head and eares in love. One must
weare her glove, another her garter, another her colours of delight." Heath, in his
"House of Correction," 1619, has an epigram "In Pigmæum," which shrewdly
animadverts upon this folly of the age.
Herrick has—

"*A Charme, or an Allay, for Love.*"
  If so be a toad be laid
  In a sheep-skin newly flaid,
  And that ty'd to man, 'twil sever
  Him and his affections ever."

Aubrey has the following direction for
anybody who wishes to know whom he
shall marry: "You must lie in another
county, and knit the left garter about the
right-legged stocking (let the other garter
and stocking alone), and, as you rehearse
these following, at every comma, knit a
knot:

'This knot I knit,
To know the thing I know not yet,
That I may see,
The man (woman) that shall my hus-
  band (wife) be,
How he goes, and what he wears,
And what he does, all days, and years.'"

Miscellanies, ed. 1857, chapter on *Magic*.

"In the True Fortune Teller," an early
chap-book, there is a recipe "To know
whether a woman will have the man she
wishes":—"Get two lemon-peels, wear
them all day, one in each pocket; at night
rub the four posts of the bedstead with
them; if she is to succeed, the person will
appear in her sleep, and present her with
a couple of lemons; if not, there is no
hope!" Girls made trial also of the fidelity of their swains by sticking an apple-
kernel on each cheek; or, according to a
writer in the "Connoisseur," two on the
forehead. That which fell first indicated
that the love of him whose name it bore
was unsound. Something of this kind
occurs in the eighth chapter of Beroaldus's
"Life of Claudius Cæsar." If a person
desires to be revenged on a false lover,
take a bird's heart, and at midnight stick
it full of pins: a likeness of the person,
whom you have thus published, will immediately appear to you in great agony.
Among the poorer classes, some dragon's
blood, carefully wrapped in paper, and
thrown on to the fire, while the person
using the charm repeats—

"May he no pleasure or profit see,
Till he comes back again to me—"

was supposed to have efficacy in conjuring
back a neglectful or perfidious lover. This
practice is of kin to the Turkish creed,
that the hyæna (probably in a state of
solution, but how taken does not appear

anywhere) was of service in love-philtres as a means contributing to the recovery of estranged affections. It appears to have been considered formerly an efficacious method of causing a man to dream of his mistress, or a woman of her lover, to "Hide some dazy-roots under your pillow, and hang your shoes out of the window." Scott's *Mock Marriage*, 1696, Sign. G. The young girls in Northamptonshire pull out the threads from the blossom of the knapweed, and deposit them in their bosoms, and if they name their lover, and guess right, the bud within an hour will flower again. The young women of Craven, observes Carr, "have a custom of using kale by way of a charm, when they are desirous of knowing whom they shall afterwards marry. The rules observed by the person who practices it are these: At bedtime she stands on something on which she never stood before, and repeats the following lines, holding in her hand a pot of cold kale:

"Hot kale, or cold kale, I drink thee,
If ever I marry a man, or a man marry me,
I wish this night I may him see, to-morrow may him ken
In church, fair, or market above all other men.'

"She then drinks nine times, goes to bed backwards, and during the night she expects to see, in a dream, her future husband." *Dialect of Craven*, 1828, in v. Kale. They have another love-charm in the North, peculiar to St. Faith's Day, the 6th of October. A flour-cake is made (the ingredients being flour, spring-water, salt and sugar) by three maidens or three widows, each taking an equal part. It is baked before the fire in an oven, no one speaking during the process, and each must turn it three times. It is divided, when ready, into three equal parts; each cuts her share into nine small slices, and passes each slice three times through a wedding-ring, the property of some woman who has been married not less than seven years. Then they undress, and during the time they are so occupied, they must eat the slices, repeating these lines:

"O, good St. Faith, be kind to night,
And bring to me my heart's delight:
Let me my future husband view,
And be my visions chaste and true."

They all sleep in one bed, and the ring must be placed at the head of it; and then they are sure to obtain the desired object. Compare *Charms*.

Love-Feast.—An annual feast celebrated in some parishes on the Thursday next before Easter. Halliwell in v.

Love Powder or **Potion.**—In the "Connoisseur," No. 56, was publicly advertised a most efficacious love powder, by which a despairing lover might create affection in the bosom of the most cruel mistress. We have in Gay's "Shepherd's Week":

"Strait to the 'Pothecary's shop I went,
And in love powder all my money spent,
Behap what will, next Sunday after prayers,
When to the ale-house Lubberkin repairs,
These golden flies into this mug I'll throw,
And soon the swain with fervent love shall glow."

Werenfels says: "Whenever the superstitious person is in love, he will complain that tempting powder has been given him." Miss Blandy, who was executed for poisoning her father, persisted to the last in affirming that she thought the powder which her villainous lover, Cranston, sent her to administer to him was a love powder, which was to conciliate her father's affection to the villain. She met her death with this asseveration, and I presume that those who have considered the wonderful power of superstition, added to the fascination of love, will be half persuaded to believe that she did not go out of the world with a lie in her mouth. Her dying request, too, to be buried close to her father, appears to me a corroborating proof that she was not, in the blackest sense of the word, his wilful murderess.

Loving Cup.—The cup, one with two handles, and generally of silver, used at the public banquets of municipal bodies, in particular the Corporation of London and City Companies. The ceremony is too familiar to require description.

Low or **White Sunday.**—(First Sunday after Easter). Sometimes called Quasimodo Sunday, or the *Little Sunday after Easter*. It is spelled Loe Sunday in a printed copy of the sermon delivered by the King's Chaplain, before James I., his family, and council, on that anniversary in the year 1606. The word *Whit* may be derived from the Dutch *Uit*; in that Liturgy the festival is so termed. Fry's *Bibliogr., Memoranda.*, 1816, p. 42. This day appears to have received its designation of Low from the circumstance that it is the lowest, i.e. latest day for discharging the Easter Dues or offerings, and of white, because on that day the neophytes discontinued the white garments assumed by them on Easter Eve, or Holy Saturday. Blount, in his *Jocular Tenures* (Hazlitt's ed., 1874, p. 206-7), speaks of a custom, which once prevailed on Low Sunday at Lostwithiel, in Cornwall: "On Low Sunday, the freeholders of the town and manor assembled in an adjoining field, and from amongst them one was chosen, whom they dressed in the most sumptuous manner, with a crown on his head, a sceptre in his hand, and, being mounted on a fine horse, a sword of state was carried before him, while all the freeholders walked in procession through the principal street to the church. When he arrived at the great gate, the curate, dressed in his best robes, received him, and conducted him to a princely seat in the church to hear mass. This being over, he repaired, in the same pompous manner, to a house provided for that purpose, where a feast was made for all his attendants, he sitting at the head of the table, and being served by the principal townsmen, kneeling, together with all other marks of respect usually shown to regal dignity."

Lubin, The.—I do not find that there has ever been any traditional belief in a creature of this sort in England. It appears to have been credited in France, or at least in some parts of that country, that a spirit, in the likeness of a wolf, haunted the vicinity of cemeteries and churchyards, in the endeavour to prey on the bodies of the dead, like the ghoul of Arabian fiction.

Lubrican.—I find Lubrican as the name of a spirit in the second part of Dekker's "Honest Whore," 1630, signat. E 3:

—"As for your Irish Lubrican, that
   spirit
Whom by preposterous charmes thy lust
   hath raised
In a wrong circle, him Ile damne more
   blacke
Then any tyrants soule."

A jealous husband is threatening an Irish servant, with whom he suspects his wife to have played false.

Luck-Money. — A payment still made, but not in the same general way as formerly, by the salesman to the buyer at fairs and markets: 2s. per score on sheep and 1s. a head on bullocks, an essential feature in the transaction being that the recipient should spit on the coin or coins. This is a practice and belief borrowed from the ancient Egyptians by the inhabitants of modern Egypt, and derived through the former and the Greeks and Romans by ourselves. It is common to most parts of the European continent, and is distinct from the *Handsel* or *Handgeld*.

Luck of Eden Hall.—Hutchinson, speaking of Eden-Hall, says : "In this house are some good old-fashioned apartments. An old painted drinking glass, called the Luck of Eden Hall, is preserved with great care. In the garden near to the house, is a well of excellent

spring water, called St. Cuthbert's Well, (the church is dedicated to that saint); this glass is supposed to have been a sacred chalice ; but the legendary tale is, that the butler going to draw water, surprised a company of fairies, who were amusing themselves upon the green, near the well : he seized the glass, which was standing upon its margin ; they tried to recover it ; but after an ineffectual struggle, flew away, saying,

  'If that glass either break or fall,
    Farewell the luck of Eden Hall.'"

This cup is celebrated in the Duke of Wharton's ballad upon the remarkable drinking match held at Sir Christopher Musgrave's. Another reading of the lines said to have been left with it, is

  "Whene'er this cup shall break or fall,
    Farewell the luck of Eden Hall."
Cumberland, i., 269.

Lucky or **Unlucky Days.** — Bourne observes, "that among these (the ancients) were lucky and unlucky days: some were *dies atri*, and some *dies albi*. The atri were pointed out in their calendar with a black character, the albi with a white. The former, to denote it a day of bad success, the latter a day of good. Thus have the monks, in the dark unlearned ages of Popery, copy'd after the heathens, and dream'd themselves into the like superstitions, esteeming one day more successful than another." He tells us, also that St. Austin, upon the passage of St. Paul to the Galatians against observing days, and months, and times, and years, explains it to have this meaning: "The persons the Apostle blames, are those who say, I will not set forward on my journey because it is the next day after such a time, or because the moon is so; or I'll set forward, that I may have luck, because such is just now the position of the stars. I will not traffick this month, because such a star presides, or I will because it does. I shall plant no vines this year, because it is leap year," &c. *Antiq. Vulg.* ch. 18. I find an observation on the 13th of December in the "Romish Calendar," that on this day prognostications of the months were drawn for the whole year. As also, that on the day of St. Barnabas, and on that of St. Simon and St. Jude, a tempest often arises. In the "Schola Curiositatis," ii., 236, we read: "Multi nolunt opus inchoare die Martis tanquam infausto die." In the Calendar prefixed to Grafton's "Abridgment," 1565, the unlucky days, according to the opinion of the astronomers, are noted, which I have extracted as follows: "January 1, 2, 4, 5, 10, 15, 17, 29, very unlucky. February 26, 27, 28, unlucky; 8, 10, 17, very unlucky. March 16, 17, 20, very unlucky.

April 7, 8, 10, 20, unlucky; 16, 21, very unlucky. May, 3, 6, unlucky; 7, 15, 20, very unlucky. June, 10, 22, unlucky; 4, 8, very unlucky. July, 15, 21, very unlucky. August, 1, 29, 30, unlucky; 19, 20, very unlucky. September 2, 4, 21, 23, unlucky; 6, 7, very unlucky. October 4, 16, 24, unlucky; 6, very unlucky. November 5, 6, 29, 30, unlucky; 15, 20, very unlucky. December 15, 22, unlucky; 6, 7, 9, very unlucky." In "Erra Pater," 1565, the unlucky days vary from these of Grafton.

At the end of an old MS. mentioned in the Duke de la Valliere's Catalogue, i. 44 (Add.), there is part of a Calendar in which the following unlucky days are noticed: "Januar. iiii. Non. (10th) dies ater et nefastus. viii. Id. (25th) dies ater et nefastus. Mar. vi. Non. (10th) non est bonum nugere (q. nubere?) Jan. iiii. Kal. (2nd) dies ater." Some days, however, are commonly deemed unlucky: among others, Friday labours under that opprobrium; and it is pretty generally held that no new work of enterprise should commence on that day. Likewise, respecting the weather there is this proverb:

———"Friday's moon,
Come when it will, it comes too soon."

It is yet accounted unlucky to be married on a Friday or on the 13th of the month, the latter having the same sinister significance as the presence of thirteen at table.

A respectable merchant of the city of London informed Mr. Brand about 1790 that no person there will begin any business on a Friday, and this is yet a common superstition. Sailors do not like starting on a voyage on that day. Moryson, in his "Itinerary," 1617, speaking of the King of Poland at the port of Dantzic in 1593, says: "The next day the king had a good wind, but before this (as those of the Romish religion are very superstitious), the king and the queen (being of the house of Austria), while sometimes they thought Monday, sometimes Friday, to be unlucky days, had lost many fair winds." The Spaniards hold Friday to be a very unlucky day, and never undertake anything of consequence upon it. "Voyage en Espagne par le Marquis de Langle," tom. ii. p. 36. Brockett, in his "North Country Glossary," 184, has noticed that Buchanan in the 6th volume of the "Asiatic Researches," points out that the Burmese held this superstition respecting the inauspicious character of Friday as well as ourselves. Among the Finns whoever undertakes any business on a Monday or Friday must expect very little success. Tooke's "Russia," vol. i., p. 47. And yet from

the following extract, it should seem to appear that Friday is elsewhere considered in a different light: "On Friday the 28th of Zkand, his Majesty (Aurengzebe) performed his morning devotions in company with his attendants: after which, as was frequently his custom, he exclaimed, 'O that my death may happen on a Friday, for blessed is he who dieth on that day.'"

It was considered improper to partake of goose, to be let blood, or to take any medicinal draught, on three particular Mondays in the year, if the days in question fell on a Monday, viz., March 22, August 20, and the last Monday in December. The "Schola Salernitana" adds, that the first of May, and the last of April and September were also considered unsuitable for phlebotomy, and for the use of goose as a diet. The "Schola" does not support the opinion. In some verses in a manuscript at Cambridge it is said that if the anniversary of Christ's birth falls on a Sunday, there will be a good winter, and heavy winds; the summer dry and fair, with plenty of sheep and bees, but scarcity of other victual. There will be peace in the land, but

"Who so stelyth oght schalbe takyn sone,
And what chyld on that day boorn be,
Off gret worschyp schall he be."

—Hazlitt's *Popular Poetry*, ii., 2. Lord Burghley, in his *Precepts*, 1636, p. 36, expresses himself thus: "Though I think no day amisse to undertake any good enterprize or businesse in hande, yet have I observed some, and no meane clerkes, very cautionarie to forbeare these three Mundayes in the yeare, which I leave to thine owne consideration, either to use or refuse, viz. 1. The first Munday in April, which day Caine was born, and his brother Abel slain. 2. The second Munday in August, which day Sodome and Gomorrah were destroyed. 3. The last Munday in December, which day Judas was born, that betrayed our Saviour Christ." Grose tells us that many persons have certain days of the week and month on which they are particularly fortunate, and others in which they are as generally unlucky. These days are different to different persons. Aubrey has given several instances of both in divers persons. Thursday was noted as a fatal day to King Henry VIII. and his posterity. Stow's *Annals*, 1631, p. 812. September 3 was more than once an auspicious day to the Protector Cromwell, and on that day, too, he died. Newton enquires under "sinnes externall and outward" against the first commandment, "whether, for the procuring of anything good or bad, thou hast used any unlawfull meanes, or superstitious and damnable helps. Of which sort bee the observation and choise of dayes, of planetarie houres, of motions and courses of starres, mumbling of prophane praiers, consisting of words both strange and senselesse, adjurations, sacrifices, consecrations, and hallowings of divers thinges, rytes and ceremonies unknowne to the Church of God, toyish characters and figures, demanding of questions and aunsweares of the dead, dealing with damned spirits, or with any instrument of phanaticall divination, as basons, rings, cristalls, glasses, roddes, prickes, numbers, dreames, lots, fortune tellings, oracles, soothsayings, horoscoping, or marking the houres of nativites, witchcraftes, enchauntments, and all such superstitious trumperie :—the enclosing or binding of spirits to certain instruments, and such like devises of Sathan the Devill." Under the same head he asks,' "Whether the apothecarie have superstitiously observed or fondly stayed for choise dayes or houres, or any other ceremonious rites in gathering his herbs and other simples for the making of drougs and receipts." *Tryall of a Man's own Self*, 1586, p. 44.

The following passage on this subject is taken from Melton's "Astrologaster," 1620 : "Those observers of time are to be laught at that will not goe out of their house before they have had counsell of their almanacke, and will rather have the house fall on their heads than stirre if they note some natural effect about the motion of the aire, which they suppose will varie the lucky blasts of the starres, that will not marry, nor traffique, or doe the like, but under some constellation. These, sure, are no Christians : because faithfull men ought not to doubt that the Divine Providence from any part of the world, or from any time whatsoever, is absent. Therefore we should not impute any secular businesse to the power of the starres, but to know that all things are disposed by the arbitrement of the King of Kings. The Christian faith is violated when, so like a pagan and apostate, any man doth observe those days which are called Ægyptiaci, or the calends of Januarie, or any moneth, or day, or time, or yeere, eyther to travell, marry, or to doe any thing in." Mason enumerates among the superstitious of his age "Regarders of times, as they are which will have one time more lucky then another : to be borne at one hower more unfortunate then at another : to take a journey or any other enterprize in hand, to be more dangerous or prosperous at one time then at another : as likewise if such a festival day

fall upon such a day of the weeke, or such like, we shall have such a yeare following : and many other such like vaine speculations, set downe by our astrologians, having neither footing in God's word, nor yet natural reason to support them ; but being grounded onely upon the superstitious imagination of man's braine." *Anatomie of Sorcerie*, 1612, p. 25. Lodge, in his "Wits Miserie," 1596, p. 12, glances as follows at the superstitious observer of lucky and unlucky times : "He will not eat his dinner before he hath lookt in his almanacke." Hall, in his "Characters," 1608, speaking of the superstitious man, observes : "If his journey began unawares on the dismal day, he feares a mischiefe." This individual would only go to sea on a Sunday. A good deal of additional information on this subject is to be found in John Gibbon's *Day Fatality*, 1678 and 1686, and in Aubrey's *Miscellanies*, 1696, 1721, 1857.

Lucky and Unlucky Days in Scotland.—The Minister of Logierait, in Perthshire, says: "In this parish, and in the neighbourhood, a variety of superstitious practices still (1793) prevail among the vulgar, which may be in part the remains of ancient idolatory, or of the corrupted Christianity of the Romish Church, and partly, perhaps, the result of the natural hopes and fears of the human mind in a state of simplicity and ignorance. Lucky and unlucky days are by many anxiously observed. That day of the week upon which the 14th of May happens to fall, for instance, is esteemed unlucky through all the remainder of the year ; none marry or begin any business upon it. None chuse to marry in January or May ; or to have their banns proclaimed in the end of one quarter of the year, and to marry in the beginning of the next. Some things are to be done before the full moon ; other after. In fevers the illness is expected to be more severe on Sunday than on the other days of the week ; if easier on Sunday, a relapse is feared," v. 80. The minister of Kirkwall and St. Ola, Orkney, remarks : "In many days of the year they will neither go to sea in search of fish, nor perform any sort of work at home," vii., 560. Again, we are told : "There are few superstitious usages among them. No gentleman, however, of the name of Sinclair, either in Canisbay, or throughout Caithness, will put on green apparel, or think of crossing the Ord upon a Monday. They were dressed in green, and they crossed the Ord upon a Monday, in their way to the Battle of Flodden, where they fought and fell in the service of their country, almost without leaving a representative of their name behind them. The day and the dress are accordingly regarded as inauspicious. If the Ord must be got beyond on Monday, the journey is performed by sea," viii., 156, xv., 541. "There are happy and unhappy days for beginning any undertaking. Thus few would choose to be married here on Friday, though it is the ordinary day in other quarters of the Church." Ibid. vol. xv. p. 258. Parish of Monzie, Perth: "The inhabitants are stated to be not entirely free from superstition. Lucky and unlucky days are still attended to, especially about the end and beginning of the year. No person will be proclaimed for marriage in the end of one year, or even quarter of the year, and be married in the beginning of the next." Ibid. vol. xxi. p. 148. "Lucky and unlucky days, dreams, and omens, are still too much observed by the country people." Barnabe Googe thus translates the remarks of Naogeorgus on this subject:

"And first, betwixt the dayes they make
    no little difference,
For all be not of vertue like, nor like
    preheminence.
But some of them Egyptian are, and
    full of jeopardee,
And some againe, beside the rest, both
    good and luckie bee.
Like diffrence of the nights they make,
    as if the Almightie King,
That made them all, not gracious were
    to them in every thing."
—*Popish Kingdom*, 1570, p. 42.

"Sed et circa dies injecta est animis religio. Inde dies nefasti, qui Ἀπόφραδες Græcis, quibus iter aut aliquid alicujus momenti indipisci, periculosum existimatur."—"De quibus diebus faustis aut infaustis, multa, Hésiodus Ἡμέραις et Virgilius primo Georgicon. Quam scrupulosam superstitioném, sese illigantem delira formidine, damnat Apostolus ad Galatas, 4:—'Observatis dies, et menses, et tempora, et annos: metuo ne incassum circa vos me fatigaverim.'" Pet. Molinæi Vates, p. 155. The modern Greeks view Tuesday in an inauspicious light. See on this subject, Selden "De Jure Nat. Gen." lib. iii. cap. 17, et Alexand. ab Alexandro "Genial. Dier." lib. iv. c. 20. Comp. *Perilous Days.*

Lucy, St.—See Nares, 1859, in v.

Lug and a Bite.—A boy's game played with apples. See Halliwell in v.

Luke's Day, St.—In Chapman's *Monsieur D'Olive*, 1606, sign. F 4, verso, D'Olive says: "As St. Valentine's Day is fortunate to choose louers, St. Luke's to choose husbands, so shall this day be to the choosing of Lordes." The author of the *Mastive or Young Whelpe of the Olde Dogge*, 1615,

in his preface, observes:—"I'll not defile my hands by giuing such the least of chastisement, but leave them peremptorily for the lashing of the dogge-whipper for those curres provided." Drake tells us, that St. Luke's Day is known in York by the name of Whip-Dog Day, from a strange custom that school-boys use here of whipping all the dogs that are seen in the streets that day. Whence this uncommon persecution took its rise is uncertain: yet, though it is certainly very old, I am not of opinion, with some, that it is as ancient as the Romans. The tradition that I have heard of its origin seems very probable, that in times of popery, a priest celebrating mass at this festival in some church in York, unfortunately dropped the Pax after consecration: which was snatched up suddenly and swallowed by a dog that lay under the altar table. The profanation of this high mystery occasioned the death of the dog, and a persecution began, and has since continued, on this day, to be severely carried on against his whole tribe in our city." Eboracum, p. 219. Mr. Atkinson gives a somewhat different account:—"Dog-whipper. A parish official whose duties consisted in expelling any dog or dogs which might intrude into the church during the performance of any service. The office was usually joined with that of sexton and pew-opener. The short, stout dog-whip was a regular part of the dog-whipper's equipment... In Derby Church the office has existed down to the year 1861, and has become almost hereditary in one family..." But, as is so often the case, the usage was not confined to this country, and I remember to have seen an engraving in Lacroix of a scene in an old French church, where a man is engaged in whipping a dog out of the building. *Cleveland Glossary*, 1868, p. 145. It appears that in King Charles II.'s time, it was customary at Hull to carry home what they called the Down-Plat on St. Luke's Night with great formality and show. *Poems*, by W. C., 1684, p. 48. St. Luke is the patron saint of the Worshipful Company of Painters from his legendary association with that art.

Luke's Fair, St.—See *Fairs.*

Lullaby. — Dr. Rimbault, in "A Little Book of Songs and Ballads," 1851, has printed from a collection of music with the words, published about 1530, an ancient lullaby song, which commences with this stanza:

"By by, lullaby,
Rockyd I my chyld:
In a dream late as I lay,
Methought I heard a mayden say
And spak these wordys mylde:

My lityl sone with the I play,
And ever she song by lullaby,
Thus rockyd she hyr chyld.
By by, lullaby,
Rockid I my child, by by."

But there is an earlier production of the same class in a MS. on paper before me of the first half of the fifteenth century which contains a second harmonized :

Lullay Lullay thow lytil child slep & be wel style
The kynge of blys thy fader is as it was his wille
Thys other nyzt y say a syght a mayde a cradel kepe
Lullay scho songe & seyde amonge ly stille my childe & slepe.
How schold y slepe y ma not for wepe so sor y am by gone
Slepe y wolde y may not for colde & clothys han y none
ffor adams gult man kinde is spilde & that me rewyth sore
ffor adam & eve y schal leve herᵹ thryt-ty wintᵹ & more.

Lurch.—A reference to this may be found under *Ticktack*.

Lych-Gate}
Lych-Way } See *Lich-Gate* and *Way*.

Lying-In. — Henry tells us, that "amongst the antient Britons, when a birth was attended with any difficulty, they put certain girdles made for that purpose, about the woman in labour, which they imagined gave immediate and effectual relief. Such girdles were kept with care, till very lately in many families in the Highlands of Scotland. They were impressed with several mystical figures; and the ceremony of binding them about the woman's waist was accompanied with words and gestures which shewed the custom to have been of great antiquity, and to have come originally from the Druids." *Hist. of Britain*, i., 459. Under December, 1502, in the Privy Purse Expenses of Elizabeth of York, there is this entry : " — to a monke that brought our Lady gyrdelle to the Quene in rewarde . . . vjs. viijd."—upon which the editor notes : "Probably one of the numerous relicks, with which the monasteries and abbeys then abounded, and which might have been brought to the Queen for her to put on when in labour, as it was a common practice for women in this situation to wear blessed girdles." Comp. *Relics*. It appears that lying-in women were also accustomed sometimes to wrap round them under similar circumstances a long scroll, containing the Magnificat written upon it. In a letter to Lord Cromwell from Dr. Leighton, about 1537, ocurs this passage : "I send you also Our Ladys Girdle

of Bruton red silke, a solemn relike, sent to women in travail." The phrase *enceinte* applied to a woman with child doubtless came from this source. The unusual tenderness for women in childbed is pleasantly illustrated by an ordinance of Henry V., published for the information of his army abroad, to the effect that any Engglish soldier found robbing a woman so situated should forfeit all his goods and hold his life at the King's mercy. From a MS. once in the possession of Peter Le Neve, Norroy, containing an account of Ceremonies and Services at the Court of Henry VII., the following directions to be observed at the lying-in of the queen appear :—

"Item, as for the delyverance of the Quene, it must be knowene in what chambre she shalbe delyvered by the grace of God : And that chambre must be hangid, so that she may haue light, wᵗʰ riche arras, rooffe, sides, and windowes and all, except one windowe whereby she may haue light, when it plessithe hir : wᵗ a rialle bedde there in : The flore must be laid wᵗ carpets over and over ; and there must be ordined a faire pailet wᵗ all the stuf longinge yʳto, wᵗ a riche sparvere hanging ouer ; and there muste be set a cupbord faire coueryd wᵗ sute of the same that the chambre is hangid wᵗ. And when it plessithe the Quene to take hir chambre, she shalbe brought thedur wᵗ lords and ladys of estat, and to be brought vnto the chapelle or the chirche, and there to ressaue hir Godde ; and then to com into the gret chambre, and there to take spice & wyne vnder the clothe of estat ; and that done, ij of the gretest estats to led hir into hyr chambre, where she shall be delyuerid, and they to take there leve of the Quene ; then all the ladys & gentille women to go in wᵗ hir, and no man after to come in to the chambre saue women ; and women to be incid ; al maner of officers, butlers, panters, sewers, and all maner officers shall bring yᵐ al maner things that them shall nede to the gret chambre dore, and the women officers to ressaue it." *Antiq. Repertory*, 1807, i., 304-5. It is stated that when the queen of King Henry VII. tok her chamber in order to her delivery, "the Erles of Shrewsbury and of Kente hyld the towelles, whan the Quene toke her rightes ; and the torches were holden by knights. When she was comen into hir great chambre, she stode undre hir clothe of estate : then there was ordeyned a voide of espices and swet wyne : that doone, my Lorde, the Quenes Chamberlain, in very goode wordes desired in the Quenes name, the pepul there present to pray God to sende hir the goode oure : and so she departed to her inner chambre." The naming of the term Rights is elucidated by the following passage in the "Examination of the Masse," (circâ 1550), signat. B 8: "Yf the Masse and Supper of yᵉ Lord be al one thyng, the Rightes, the Housell, the Sacramente of Christes bodye and bloude, and the Supper of the Lord are all one thyng." From a MS. formerly in the collection of Herbert, dated 1475, I transcribe the following charm, or more properly charect, to be bound to the thigh of a lying-in woman: "For woman that travelyth of chylde, bynd thys wryt to her thye: In nomine Patris ✠ et Filii ✠ et Spiritus Sancti ✠ Amen. ✠ Per virtutem Domini sint medicina mei pia crux et passio Christi. ✠. Vulnera quinque Domini sint medicina mei. ✠ Sancta Maria peperit Christum. ✠ Sanct Anna peperit Mariam. ✠. Sancta Elizabet peperit Johannem. ✠. Sancta Cecilia peperit Remigium. ✠. Sator Arepo tenet opera rotas. ✠. Christus vincit. ✠. Christus regnat. ✠. Christus dixit Lazare veni foras. ✠. Christus imperat. ✠. Christus te vocat. ✠ Mundus te gaudet. ✠. Lex te desiderat. ✠ Deus ultionum Dominus. ✠. Deus preliorum Dominus libera famulam tuam N. ✠ Dextra Domini fecit virtutem. a. g. l. a. ✠ Alpha ✠ et Ω. ✠. Anna peperit Mariam, ✠ Elizabet precursorem, ✠ Maria Dominum nostrum Jesum Christum, sine dolore et tristicia. O infans sive vivus sive mortuus exi foras ✠ Christus te vocat ad lucem. ✠. Agyos ✠. Agyos. ✠ Agyos. ✠ Christus vincit. ✠ Christus imperat. ✠ Christus regnat. ✠ Sanctus ✠ Sanctus ✠ Sanctus ✠ Dominus Deus. ✠ Christus qui es, qui eras, ✠ et qui venturus es. ✠ Amen. bhurnon ✠ blictaono ✠ Christus Nazarenus ✠ Rex Judeorum fili Dei ✠ miserere mei ✠ Amen."

In Bale's *Comedy of Three Laws*, 1538, Hypocrisy is introduced mentioning the following charms against barrenness:

"In Parys we have the mantell of Saynt Lewes,
Which women seke moch, for helpe of their barrenness:
For be it ones layed upon a wommanys bellye,
She go thens with chylde, the myracles are seene there daylye.
And as for Lyons, there is the length of our Lorde
In a great pyller. She that will with a coorde
Be fast bound to it, and take soche chaunce as fall,
Shall sure have chylde, for within it is hollowe all."

Thomas Thacker, in a letter to Thomas Cromwell, written about 1538, refers to "the image of Seint Moodwyn of Burton

upon Trent, with hir red kowe and hir staff, which wymen laboryng of child in those parties were very desirous to have with them to leane upon, and to walke with yt." It is a traditional belief among the Cornish fishwomen, that the use of the ray-fish, which is common on the north coast, is conducive to parturition. In Bonner's Injunctions at his Visitation from September 3rd, 1554, to October 8th, 1555, we read: "A mydwyfe (of the diocese and jurisdiction of London) shal not use or exercise any witchecrafte, charmes, sorcerye, invocations or praiers other than suche as be allowable and may stand with the lawes and ordinances of the Catholike Church." In Articles to be enquired in the Visitacyon, 1 Eliz. 1559, the following occurs: "Item, whether you knowe anye that doe use charmes, sorcery, enchauntmentes, invocations, circles, witchecraftes, south-sayinge, or any like craftes or imaginacions invented by the Devyl, and specially in the tyme of womens travayle."

It should seem that the expression of "the lady in the straw," meant to signify the lady who is brought to bed. is derived from the circumstance that all beds were anciently stuffed with straw, so that it is synonymous with saying "the lady in bed," or that is confined to her bed. It appears that even so late as King Henry the VIII.'s time there were directions for certain persons to examine every night the straw of the King's bed, that no daggers might be concealed therein. In "Plaine Percevall, the Peace-maker of England," 1589, we find an expression which strongly marks the general use of straw in beds during that reign: "These high-flying sparks will light on the heads of us all, and kindle in our bed-straw." In an old book of receipts we read "How and wherewith, the child-bed woman's bed ought to be furnished. A large boulster, made of linnen cloth, must be stuffed with straw, and be spread on the ground, that her upper part may lye higher than her lower; on this the woman may lye, so that she may seem to lean and bow, rather than to lye drawing up her feet unto her that she receive no hurt." *A Rich Closet of Physical Secrets*, p. 9. In the old Herbals we find descriptions of a herb entitled "The Ladies Bed-Straw." Pecock, in his "Repressor of Over-much Blaming of the Clergy," observes: "Sum other vntrewe opinioun of men is . . . . that iij sistris (whiche ben spirits) comen to the cradilis of infantis, for to sette to the babe what schal bifalle to him." These are, of course, the Three Weird Sisters, or Parcæ.

It is related that when Mary, Queen of Scots was lying in, the Countess of Athole, who was supposed to have magical powers, was at the same place in a similar situation; and it is stated by someone who was at Edinburgh Castle at the time that Lady Athole cast the pains of her own childbirth on the lady who was attending on the Queen. Chambers remarks: "It was a prevalent belief of that age, that the pains of parturition could be transferred by supernatural art; and not merely to another woman, but to a man or to one of the lowest animals. Amongst the charges against an enchantress of the upper ranks called Eupham McCalyean, twenty-five years after this time, is one to the effect that, for relief of her pain at the time of the birth of her own sons, she had had a bored stone laid under her pillow, and enchanted powder rolled up in her hair, likewise "your guidman's sark taen aff him, and laid whomplit under your bed-feet: the whilk being practisit, your sickness was casten aff you unnaturally upon ane dog, whilk ran away, and was never seen again." *Dom. Annals*, i., 39.

It was stated (1877) in the *Daily News*, that the practice was known at Berne in Switzerland, of the husband lying down in the wife's stead; and it is also still believed that a pregnant woman may be exempt from suffering or pain, if her husband bears it by proxy. This same strange illusion is said to prevail among the Chinese.

Pennant informs us that the Highland midwives gave new-born babes a small spoonful of earth and whisky, as the first food they take. Gough's *Camden*, iii., 658, It is considered lucky for the mother before she goes downstairs after her confinement, to ascend one step, and back; and I believe that it is considered sufficient by the learned, if the lady lifts her foot, and lays it for a moment on a stool or any other similar object. In "Seven Dialogues" (from Erasmus), by W. Burton, 1606, in that of the woman in child-bed occurs the following passage: "Eut. By chaunce I (passing by these houses) sawe the crowe, or the ring of the dore bound about with a white linnen cloth, and I marvelled what the reason of it should be. Fab. Are you such a stranger in this countrey that you doe not know the reason of that? doe you not knowe that it is a signe that there is a woman lying in where that is?" So, in *A Voyage to Holland by an English Gentleman*, 1691: "Where the woman lies in the ringle of the door does pennance, and is lapped about with linnen, either to shew you that loud knocking may wake the child, or else that for a month the ring is not to be run at: but if the child be dead there is thrust out a nosegay tied to a stick's end; perhaps for an emblem of the life of man, which may wither as soon as born; or else let you know, that though these fade upon their gathering, yet from the same stock the

next year a new shoot may spring." Bartholinus informs us that the Danish women, before they put the new-born infant into the cradle, place there or over the door as amulets, to prevent the evil spirit from hurting the child, garlick, salt, bread, and steel, or some cutting instrument made of that metal. *Century of Rare Anatomical Histories*, p. 19. Compare *Children*.

Mab, Queen.—Shakespear's portrait of Queen Mab must not be omitted here. He puts it into the mouth of Mercutio, in "Romeo and Juliet," 1597:

"She is the fairies' midwife; and she comes
In shape no bigger than an agate-stone
On the fore-finger of an alderman,
Drawn with a team of little atomies
Athwart men's noses as they lie asleep:
Her waggon-spokes made of long spinners' legs;
The cover, of the wings of grasshoppers;
Her traces, of the smallest spider's web;
Her collars, of the moonshine's wat'ry beams;
Her whip, of cricket's bone; the lash, of film:
Her waggoner, a small grey-coated gnat,
Not half so big as a round little worm
Prick'd from the lazy finger of a maid:
Her chariot is an empty hazelnut,
Made by the joiner squirrel, or old grub,
Time out of mind the Fairies' coach-makers.
And in this state she gallops night by night
Through lovers' brains, and then they dream of love:
On courtiers' knees, that dream on court'sies straight:
O'er lawyers' fingers, who straight dream on fees:
O'er ladies' lips, who straight on kisses dream;
Which oft the angry Mab with blisters plagues,
Because their breaths with sweet-meats tainted are.
Sometimes she gallops o'er a courtier's nose,
And then dreams he of smelling out a suit:
And sometimes comes she with a tithe-pig's tail,
Tickling a parson's nose as 'a lies asleep,
Then dreams he of another benefice:
Sometimes she driveth o'er a soldier's neck,
And then he dreams of cutting foreign throats,
Of breaches, ambuscadoes, Spanish blades,
Of healths five fathoms deep; and then anon

Drums in his ear; at which he starts,
and wakes;
And, being thus frighted, swears a
prayer or two,
And sleeps again."

Mace Monday. — (July 26). A feast of bacon and beans is held on this day in Newbury in Berks, and elsewhere. It is mentioned in the "Devonshire Dialogue," 1839. A cabbage stuck on a pole serves as a substitute for a mace, and all the other emblems of civic grandeur are similarly parodied.

Macham.—An Irish game of cards.

Madron or **Madern, St., Well of, Cornwall.**—This well is reputed to possess medicinal properties of a very high order, and its fame is of considerable antiquity. The most celebrated cure recorded in connection with it is, doubtless, that of the cripple, John Trelille, which is narrated by Bishop Hall in his treatise "On the Invisible World," and again (from a contemporary writer) in the "Cornish Magazine" for 1828. The latter account the late Mr. Couch, of Bodmin, sent to the "Journal of the Royal Institution of Cornwall" in 1864, where it is printed : "I will relate one miracle more done in our own country, to the great wonder of the inhabitants, but a few years ago, viz. : about the year 1640. The process of the business was told the King when at Oxford, which he caused to be further examined. It was this :—A certain boy, of twelve years of age, called John Trelille, on the coast of Cornwall, not far from the Land's End, as they were playing at foot-ball, snatching up the ball, ran away with it ; whereupon a girl, in anger, struck him with a thick stick on the backbone, and so bruised or broke it that for sixteen years after he was forced to go creeping on the ground. In this conditon he arrived to the twenty-eighth year of his age, when he dreamed that if he did but bathe in St. Madern's Well, or in the stream running from it, he should recover his former strength and health. This is a place in Cornwall frequented at this time by many on the Thursday in May ; near to which Well is a chapel dedicated to St. Madern, where is yet an altar, and right against it a grassy hillock, (made every year anew by the country people), which they call St. Madern's Bed. The chapel roof is quite decayed ; but a kind of thorn, of itself shooting forth out of the old walls, so extends its boughs that it covers the whole chapel, and supplies, as it were, a roof. On Thursday in May, assisted by one Perriman, his neighbour, entertaining great hopes from his dream, thither he went, and, laying before the altar, and praying very fervently that he

might regain his health and the strength of his limbs, he washed his whole body in the stream that flowed from the well, and ran through the chapel. After which, having slept about one hour and a half in St. Madern's Bed, through the extremity of pain he felt in his nerves and arteries, he began to cry out, and, his companions helping and lifting him up, he perceived his limbs and joints somewhat expanded, and himself become stronger, insomuch that, partly with his feet, partly with his hands, he went more erect than before. Before the following Thursday he got two crutches, resting on which he would make a shift to walk, which before he could not do ; and, coming to the chapel as before, after having bathed himself, he slept on the same bed, and awaking, found himself much stronger and more upright ; and so, leaving one crutch in the chapel, he went home with the other. The third Thursday, he returned to the chapel, and bathed as before, slept, and when he awoke rose up quite cured ; yea, grew so strong that he wrought day-labour among other hired servants ; and, four years after, enlisted himself a soldier in the King's army, where he behaved himself with much stoutness both of mind and body ; at length in 1644 he was slain at Lyme in Dorsetshire." *R. P. Francisci Convent : Paralip. Philos.*, iv., 48. A letter dated Penzance, May 17, 1819, was communicated to "Current Notes" for February, 1856 ; it contains some information on this subject, which appeared to be worth quoting. "In Cornwall," says the writer, "there are several wells, which bear the name of some patron saint, who appears to have had a chapel consecrated to him, or her, on the spot. These chapels probably were simply oratories, but in the parish of Maddern (now called Madron) is a well called 'Maddern Well,' inclosed in a complete Baptistery : the walls, seats, doorway, and altar of which still remain. . . . I was surprised at being informed that the superstitious of the neighbourhood attend on the first Thursday in May to consult this oracle by dropping pins, &c. Why on the Thursday? May not this be some vestige of the day on which the baptisteries were opened after being kept closed and sealed during Lent, which was Maundy Thursday? My informant told me that Thursday was the particular day of the week, though some came on the second and third Thursday. May was the first month after Easter, when the waters had been especially blessed : for then was the great time of baptism."

Magdalen College, Oxford.— On St. John's Day, in the quadrangle, where the Yeoman's open-air pulpit is found, rushes, grass, and green boughs, are spread about, and a sermon delivered to the audience assembled, the accessories mentioned being supposed (oddly enough) to be significant of the Baptist's sojourn in the Wilderness. In 1501, Henry VII. having given the advowsons of Slimbridge, co. Gloucester. and Fyndon, co. Sussex, to this College, with an acre of land in each parish, a service was annually performed on Trinity Sunday in honour of the royal benefactor, and after the King's death a service or requiem. At present the choristers and other members of the College and their friends assemble at or about half-past four on May-Day morning at the top of Magdalen Tower, erected in 1492, and, seated with their faces toward the East, the choir sings, on the stroke of five, a Latin hymn in honour of the Trinity. A considerable crowd usually gathers on the bridge adjacent, and the voices on the tower may, it is said, be sometimes heard at two miles' distance. At the conclusion of this part of the ceremony, all heads are covered again, and the belfry rings out a peal in celebration of the anniversary, while the boys blow on tin horns. The hymn has been attributed to Benjamin Rogers in the time of Charles II., and appears formerly to have been used at Magdalen daily as an after-grace. The rents arising from the property above-mentioned were originally divided among the fellows; but the money is now applied to the provision of an entertainment for the choir. The present writer attended the observance in 1901, and was sensible of the oscillation of the great tower.

Magic.—Moresin affirms that the ancients, who believed in spells and other magical influences, were surpassed far by the Roman Catholics, who held that God himself was to be reached by incantations and exorcisms, so that it was impossible that anything, the most secret thoughts of the human heart, could be kept from discovery. *Papatus*, 1594, p. 7. Avicenna, to prove that there are charms, affirms that all material substances are subject to the human soul; but another writer more judiciously observes that when the minds of men are haunted with dreams of charms and enchantments, they are apt to fancy that the most common occurrences in nature are the effects of magical art. Some very interesting information on this subject will be found in the learned Preface by Mr. Richard Price to Warton's "History of Poetry," 1871; it seemed to be scarcely worth while, or even desirable to transplant it hither.

In the City of London Records under 1382 there is a case of a cobbler, who pretended to have the power of discovery in charges of theft, where a certain Paris kerchief had been stolen from a married woman, named Alice Trigg. This fellow, William Norhampton, also foretold that Alice would within a month be drowned, and so terrified her that she was on the point of death, for he happened to be in possession of certain particulars of her private concerns, and thus made her credit his supernatural insight. It was acknowledged by him, on being charged with the matter, that he knew nothing about it, or about magical arts, and had acted deceitfully, and he was sentenced to the pillory. Riley's *Memorials*, 1868, p. 475-6. In the same year a similar offence was committed by one Robert Berewold, who undertook by certain means to reveal the person, who had purloined a cup from Matilda de Eye. He thereupon took a loaf, and fixed in the top of it a round peg of wood, and four knives at the four sides, cruciformly, and then pronounced magical incantation over it. Which, when he had finished, he declared Johanna Wolsy the culprit. The accusation being proved false, the said Berewold was condemned to stand in the pillory with the loaf, and the peg and knives, hung round his neck. Ibid. 472-3. In the Life of Montaigne, by Bayle St. John, 1858, we hear of a magician, who proposed to render the dresses and under-garments of the ladies about the Court transparent for the benefit of Francis I. and his friends; but we do not know whether the scheme was adopted or proved successful. In any case the account suggests an anticipation of the system of rays, by which science now penetrates all sorts of interiors from a man's stomach to his portmanteau. Comp. *Sorcery, Witchcraft*, &c.

Magpie.—Magot-pie is the original name of the bird; magot being the familiar appellation given to pies, as we say Robin to a red-breast, Tom to a titmouse, Philip to a sparrow, &c. The modern mag is the abbreviation of the ancient magot, a word which we had from the French. But it has also been supposed that mag is a short form of Margaret or Margery, as we speak of Jack-Daw. "Skata, Pica. Quum illius plurimum in Auguriis usus fuerit, v. Plinii 'Hist. Nat.' lib. x. 18, interque aves sinisterioris Ominis semper locum invenerit, unde etiam videmus, veteris Superstitionis tenacem plebem nostram volucrem hanc Stabulorum portis expansis alis suspendere, ut, quod ait Apuleius, suo corpore luat illud Infortunium quod aliis portendit: hinc arbitror a *scada* nocere, A.S. scathian nomen illi inditum fuisse. Vocatur alias Skjura, forté a garritu, ut etiam Latinà Garrulus nuncupabatur."—Ihre. Such is the opinion of the common people in

Sweden. Shakespear says in *Macbeth*, iii., 4 :—

"Augurs, and understood relations, have
By magot-pies and choughs and rooks brought forth
The secret'st man of blood."

on which Steevens observes :—"In Cotgrave's Dictionary a magpie is called Magatapie. In the "Night Raven," by S. Rowlands, 1620, we have :

'I neither tattle with Jack Daw
Or maggot-pye on thach'd house straw."

The form magatipie is still found in the West of England. Scot says that to prognosticate that guests approach to your house, upon the chattering of pies or haggisters, (haggister in Kent signifies a magpie) is altogether vanity and superstition. *Discovery*, ed. 1665, p. 95. Gaule almost repeats this observation. Home, in his "Dæmonologie," 1650, speaking of popular superstitions, page 59, tells us : "By the chattering of magpies, they know they shall have strangers."

Ross tells us that, in the time of Charles VIII. of France, the battle fought between the French and Bretons, in which the latter were overthrown, was foreshewed by a skirmish between magpies and Jack Daws. *App. to Arcana Microcosmi*, p. 219. The chattering of a magpie is ranked by Bourne among omens. *Antiq. Vulg.*, p. 71. It is very observable that, according to Lambarde, Editha persuaded her husband to build a monastery at Oseney near Oxford, upon such a prognostication. *Topographical Dictionary*, p. 260. It is unlucky, says Grose, to see first one magpie, and then more, but to see two, denotes marriage or merriment; three, a successful journey; four, an unexpected piece of good news; five, you will shortly be in a great company. The bad omen is thought to be averted by turning thrice round or by spitting three times. In 1865, a gentleman on horseback saw a magpie, and took no notice. Presently after he was thrown. He said he would never forget again to spit at a magpie. In Lancashire it is accounted very unlucky to see two magpies (called there pynots; in Northumberland, pyanots) together; thus Tim Bobbin says: "I saigh two rott'n Pynots (hongum) that wur a sign o bad fashin: for I heard my Gronny say hoode os leef o seen two owd Harries (devils) os two pynots." *Lancashire Dialect*, 1775, p. 31. In Lincolnshire the superstition as to number also prevails. See Hazlitt's *Proverbs*, 1882, p. 321.

Maiden Feast.—In the "Statistical Account of Scotland," we read, "It was in the last century, the custom to give what was called a Maiden Feast, upon the finishing of the harvest : and to prepare for which, the last handful of corn reaped in the field was called the Corn Lady or Maiden. This was generally contrived to fall into the hands of one of the finest girls in the field, and was dressed up with ribbands, and brought home in triumph with the music of fiddles or bagpipes. A good dinner was given to the whole band, and the evening spent in joviality and dancing, while the fortunate lass who took the Maiden was the Queen of the Feast; after which this handful of corn was dressed out generally in the form of a cross, and hung up with the date of the year in some conspicuous part of the house. This custom is now entirely done away, and in its room each shearer is given 6d. and a loaf of bread. However, some farmers, when all their corns are brought in, give their servants a dinner and a jovial evening, by way of harvest-home." xix., 550, par. of Lansforgan, co. Perth.

Maid Marian.—Tollett thus describes Maid Marian, who, as Queen of May, has a golden crown on her head, and in her left hand a red pink, as emblem of Summer. Her vesture was once fashionable in the highest degree. Margaret, the eldest daughter of Henry the Seventh, was married to James King of Scotland with the crown upon her head and her hair hanging down. Betwixt the crown and the hair was a very rich coif, hanging down behind the whole length of the body. This simple example sufficiently explains the dress of Marian's head. Her coif is purple, her surcoat blue, her cuffs white, the skirts of her robe yellow, the sleeves of a carnation colour, and her stomacher red, with a yellow lace in cross-bars. In Shakespear's "Henry the Eighth," Anne Boleyn, at her coronation, is in her hair, or as Hollingshed put it, her hair hanged down, but on her head she had a coif, with a circlet about it full of rich stones. In the Marriage of Joseph and the Virgin, a painting formerly at Strawberry Hill, and now in the possession of his Grace the Duke of Buccleuch, Mary is represented with her hair hanging down exactly in the same manner, and with a coronet on her head, the latter feature common to the early Bavarian and other coins, where the Virgin appears as part of the type. This costume may help to fix the date of the picture, which Walpole erroneously supposed to represent the nuptials of Henry VI.—*Anecd. of Painting*, ed. 1862, p. 34. Maid Marian, "the Lord Fitzwater's Daughter" of the Poets, is mentioned in a subjoined extract from a MS. of the 15th century:

" At Ewle we wonten gambole, daunse,
    to carol, and to sing,
To have gud spiced sewe, and roste, and
At Easter Eve, pampuffes; gangtide-
    plum pie for a king;
    gates did holie masses bring;
At Paske begun oure Morris, and ere
    Pentecoste oure May.
Thro' Roben Hood, litell John, Frier
    Tuck and Mariam deftly play,
And lord and ladie gang 'till kirk with
    lads and lasses gay ;
Fra masse and een songe sa gud cheere
    and glee on every green.
As save oure wakes 'twixt Eames and
    Sibbes, like gam was never seene.
At Baptis-day, with ale and cakes, bout
    bonfires neighbours stood :
At Martlemas wa turn'd a crabbe, thilk
    told of Roben Hood,
Till after long time myrke, when blest
    were windowes, dores, and lightes,
And pailes were fild, and harthes were
    swept, gainst fairie elves and
    sprites :
Rock and Plow Monday gams sal gang
    with saint feasts and kirk sightes."

In Coates' " History of Reading," p. 220,
in the Churchwardens' Accounts of St.
Lawrence Parish, is the following entry :
" 1531. It. for ffyve ells of canvas for a
cote for Made Maryon, at iii. ob. the ell.
xvijᵈ. ob." In the old play of " Robin
Hood." and many other dramatic performances where she happened to be introduced, Maid Marian was usually imper-
sonated by some pretty boy of feminine
appearance. In the " Downfal of Robert
Earl of Huntingdon," 1601, Skelton the
chorus exclaims: " What, our Maid
Marian, leaping like a lad !" After the
morris degenerated into a piece of coarse
buffoonery, and Maid Marian was personated by a clown, this once elegant Queen
of May obtained the name of Malkin. To
this Fletcher alludes in " Monsieur
Thomas" :

" Put on the shape of order and human-
    ity,
Or you must marry Malkyn, the May-
    lady."

It appears by one of the extracts given in
Lysons' " Environs," that in the reign
of Henry VIII. at Kingston-upon-Thames,
the character was performed by a woman
who received a shilling each year for her
trouble. Comp. *Midsummer Ale* and
Robin Hood.

Maid's Money.—At the town-hall,
Guildford, on January 23, 1902, two
domestic servants threw dice to decide
which should be the recipient of " the
maid's money," left in 1674 by John How
for the servant who had been upwards of
two years in the same situation in the

borough, and who threw the highest number with two dice in competition with another qualified servant. Clara Howard,
who had been in one service over eight
years, scored the highest number, and received a cheque for twelve guineas.

Making and Marring. — See
White and Black.

Mallard.—At All Souls' College, Oxford, on the 14th January, they used to
have a supper, and sit up all night drinking and singing, which was known as "All
Souls' College Mallard." The song was
called *The Mallard,* and originally the fellows rambled about the College precincts
with sticks and poles in search of the mallard. The meaning of the custom seems to
be unknown. Hearne's *Diary,* Jan. 18,
1722-3.

Manciple.—A person employed in
former times as a purveyor in great
houses, in the Inns of Court, and in the
Universities. The term is nearly forgotten. But the functionary so called is introduced by Chaucer as the narrator of
one of his series of Tales. He tells the
story of the Crow, when the party had
reached Bob-up-and-Down or Harble-
down. Comp. Nares, *Gloss.* in v.

Man in the Moon.—This is one of
the most ancient as well as one of the
most popular superstitions. It is supposed to have originated in the account
given in the Book of Numbers, of a man
punished with death for gathering sticks
on the Sabbath-day. In one of the drawings representing this extraordinary and
familiar character, he appears as a man
with a staff over his shoulder, on which
he carries his fatal bundle of sticks, followed by a dog. It was formerly, as it
still remains, a common tavern-sign, and
two or three differing portraitures of the
renowned sabbath-breaker have been
handed down. " History of Sign-boards,"
1867, plates 8 and 17. The vulgar
parody on the old legend, apparent in the
former of these engravings, may have
something to do with the saying, which
was so popular and well understood, "The
Man in the Moon drinks claret." Peacock,
in his " Repressor," enumerates among
" vntrewe opiniouns," the one that " a
man which stale sumtyme a birthan of
thornis was sette into the moone, there for
to abide for evere." In the old play of
" Timon," act iv. sc. 3, Stilpo says : " The
man in the moone is not in the moone
superficially, although he bee in the
moone (as the Greeks will haue it), cata-
podially, specificatiuely, and quiddita-
tiuely." In the " Midsummer Night's
dream," Quince the carpenter, in arrang-
ing his dramatis personæ for the play
before the Duke, directs that " One must
come in with a bush of thorns and a lan-

tern, and say, he comes to disfigure, or to present, the person of moonshine," which we afterwards find done. "All that I have to say," concludes Moon, in act v. sc. i., "is, to tell you that the lantern is the moon; I, the man in the moon; this thorn bush, my thorn bush; and this dog, my dog." And such a character appears to have been familiar to the old English stage. See also the *Tempest*, ii., 2. The man in the moon is thus alluded to in the second act of Dekker's "Honest Whore," 1630, signat. D 2: "Thou art more than the moone, for thou hast neither changing quarters, nor a man standing in thy circle with a bush of thornes." Mr Baring Gould notices a representation of the man in the moon in Gyffin church, near Conway. It is in the roof of the chancel, where are symbols of the sun, moon, and stars, &c.; and in the disk of the lunar orb is the man, with his bundle of sticks, but not his dog. The same writer draws attention to a deed 9 Edw. III. which bears a seal, with the man in the moon as a device, and this legend:

" Te, Waltere, docebo
cur spinas phebo
gero."

It is necessary to explain that the document is a deed of conveyance from Walter de Grendesse of Kingston-upon-Thames, to his mother.

Man, Isle of.—See *Manx*.

Mandrake.—The earliest references to the Mandragoria or Mandrake and its extraordinary properties is, so far as I know, in Genesis, respecting which Cruden has a note, in the course of which he says: "It is reported that in the province of Pekin there is a kind of mandrake so valuable, that a pound of that root is worth thrice its weight in silver, for they say it so wonderfully restores the sinking spirits of dying persons that there is often time for the use of other means, and thereby recovering them to life and health. Those mandrakes which Reuben brought home to his mother, are by some called violets, by others lilies or jessamins, by others citrons. Some reckon them to be such agreeable flowers of the field wherewith children were pleased, Reuben that gathered them being only about five or six years of age."

In his Anglo-Norman "Bestiary," written in the first half of the twelfth century, Philip de Thaun writes: "He (Isidore) says of the mandragore, that it has two roots, which have the make of man and woman; the female root resembles woman and girl; the female is leaved like a leaf of lettuce; the male

remains leaved as the heart is (i.e. has the leaves peculiar to the plant). It is gathered by a stratagem. . . . The man who is to gather it must fly round about it; must take great care that he does not touch it; then let him take a dog bound—let it be tied to it—which has been close tied up, and has fasted three days—and let it be shown bread, and call from afar; the dog will draw it to him; the root will break; it will send forth a cry; the dog will fall down dead at the cry which he will hear—such virtue this herb has, that no one can hear of it, but he must always die; and if the man heard it, he would directly die—therefore he must stop his ears, and take care that he hear not the cry, lest he die, as the dog will do, which shall hear the cry. When one has this root, it is of great value for medicine, for it cures of every infirmity — except only death." Wright's *Popular Treatises on Science*, 1841, 101-2, where a cut of a female

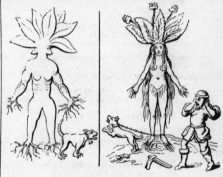

MANDRAKE.

mandrake is given. In the Anglo-Norman *Bestiary* cited just above, it is said that the elephant is of so cold a nature that the male does not seek the company of a female till wandering in the direction of Paradise, he find the mandrake, which has aphrodisiac virtues. Wright's *Archæological Album*, 1845, 177-8. This idea tallies with the story of Rachel in the Bible. But the belief in the semi-human character and physiology of the mandrake appears to have been shaken at a very early date in our country, for in the "Grete Herball," 1526, the idea of a herb endowed with human faculties and sensibilities is expressly declared to be inadmissible. A cut of a female mandrake is here given, very similar to one copied by Berjeau's *Bookworm*, iii., 106-7, from an old Dutch Herbal. It is in both cases the figure of a naked woman with the plant shooting into leaf and flower from her head. But even in some of the early lists the mandrake is mentioned without any reference to its miraculous properties or double gender; and Gerarde in his Herbal, 1597, derides the whole notion.

The superstitious belief in mandrakes not unnaturally led to a trade in imitations formed of briony and other plants, which lent themselves to such a purpose. Lupton, in his "Thousand Notable Things," 1579, refers to this imposture, and he is followed by Sir Thomas Browne in his *Vulgar Errors*, and others.

Even when the faith in its miraculous nature no longer existed, however, the mandragoria or mandrake was still regarded as a strong narcotic, a property which may perhaps explain the medicinal virtue just imputed to it. Massinger, in the "Unnatural Combat," makes the usher say :

"Here's music
In this bag shall wake her, though she
    had drunk opium,
Or eaten mandrakes—"

Shakespear himself makes Iago say of Othello :

"—— Not poppy, nor mandragora,
Nor all the drowsy syrups of the world,
Shall ever medicine thee to that sweet
    sleep
Which thou ow'dst yesterday."

The mandrake is mentioned in the "Flying betwixt Montgomery and Polwart," 1629 :

"The Weird Sisters wandring, as they
    were wont then,
Saw reavens rugand at that ratton, be
    a Ron ruit,
They mused at the mandrake, vnmade
    lik a man ;
A beast bund with a bonerand, in ane
    old buit."

This is what Dekker refers to in his "Newes from Hell," 1606. Randolph, in the "Jealous Lovers," 1632, makes Dipsos say to Chremylas :

"The ravens, screech-owls, and the
    mandrakes voice
Shall be thy constant musick."

Nabbes, in his play of "Totenham Court," 1638, has this passage ; it is Worthgood, who speaks :

"—— The dismal shrieks
Of fatall owles, and groanes of dying
    mandrakes,
Whilst her soft palme warm'd mine,
    were musicke to me."

"The fleshy mandrake, where it doth
    grow
In noonshade of the mistletow,
And where the phœnix airyes."—
Drayton's *Muses Elizium*, 1630, p. 24.

The value of the mandrake or mandragoria as a narcotic has been noted above in the sketch of the subject in its more popular aspect. But it will have been perceived that even some of our own early writers disbelieved the properties ascribed to it by folklore or vulgar superstition. It was in fact familiar to the ancients and throughout the middle ages as a powder which, dissolved in wine or otherwise, assuaged pain, and produced temporary insensibility during surgical operations. Edouard Fournier, *Le Vieux-Neuf*, 1877, i, 86-7.

Manna.—Peacham tells us, "There are many that believe and affirm the manna which is sold in the shoppes of our apothecaries, to be of the same which fell from Heaven, and wherewith the Israelites were fedde." He then proceeds to give reasons why this cannot be. *Truth of our Times*, 1638, p. 174. Not unlike what is popularly known as manna is the sweet gum, which is yielded by the damson and other trees in this country, and which accumulates on the bark. We all remember the line in Virgil, where he feigns that when the golden age should return under the auspices of Asinius Gallus, among other prodigies,

"—— duræ quercus sudabunt roscida
    mella—"

This is, of course, our mel-dew or honeydew : it drops, to a modified extent, from the full-leaved lime ; but in New Zealand, the manuka-tree exudes a resin, which readily clots into a hard substance, very agreeable to the palate, and much liked. See W. Browne's Works by Hazlitt, ii., Notes v. *Mel-Dew*.

Manx Christenings.—Waldron, speaking of the Manx christenings, says : "The whole country round are invited to them ; and, after having baptized the child, which they always do in the church, let them live ever so distant from it, they return to the house, and spend the whole day, and good part of the night, feasting." *Works*, p. 170.

Manx Customs.—In a statistical account of Campbelton, Argyleshire, in 1794, it is said : "We read of a King of the Isle of Mann sending his shoes to his Majesty of Dublin, requiring him to carry them before his people on a high festival, or expect his vengeance." This good Dublinian King discovers a spirit of humanity and wisdom rarely found in better times. His subjects urged him not to submit to the indignity of bearing the Manksman's shoes. "I had rather," said he, "not only bear but eat them, than that one province of Ireland should bear the desolation of war." A communication to *Notes and Queries*, about 1875, says: "In a lately published tale, entitled 'Green Hills by the Sea,' the scene of which is laid in the Isle of Man, a strange Manx custom is described. It appears that up to the year 1845, and perhaps still, in a capital trial the bishop and archdeacon were required to appear upon the bench. The question put to the jury was not, as in England, "Guilty" or "Not Guilty," but "May the man of the chancel continue to sit?" The answer was a plain "Yes" or "No." In the latter case the departure of the clergy was followed by a sentence of death. An excellent account, almost too long for the immediate purpose, of the usages and beliefs of the island may be found in Glover's *Illustrated Guide*, 1866. Many of these local practices are analogous to those observed elsewhere at Easter, May-day, Midsummer, and Christmas. Particular attention may be directed to the *Caa'l Breeshey*, or festival in honour of St. Bridget, on the 1st of February, and to the custom of blowing horns on the mountains on *lao Baaldyn, or May-Day*. I suppose that the proverbial expression current in the Isle of Man :

"On Shrove Tuesday night, though the supper be fat,
Before Easter day thou mayst fast for that"—

arose from the improvident expenditure customary at this season of almost universal jubilee. In the Isle of Man, according to Waldron, the month of May is every year ushered in with the following ceremony :— "In almost all the great parishes, they chuse from among the daughters of the most wealthy farmers a young maid for the Queen of May. She is drest in the gayest and best manner they can, and is attended by about twenty others, who are called maids of honour; she has also a young man, who is her captain, and has under his command a good number of inferior officers. In opposition to her is the Queen of Winter, who is a man dressed in woman's clothes, with woollen hoods, furr tippets, and loaded with the warmest and heaviest habits one upon another : in the same manner are those who represent her attendants drest, nor is she without a captain and a troop for her defence. Both being equipt as proper emblems, of the beauty of the Spring, and the deformity of the Winter, they set forth from their respective quarters; the one preceded by

violins and flutes, the other with the rough musick of the tongs and cleavers. Both companies march till they meet on a common, and then their trains engage in a mock battle. If the Queen of Winter's forces get the better so far as to take the Queen of May prisoner, she is ransomed for so much as pays the expences of the day. After this ceremony, Winter and her company retire, and divert themselves in a barn, and the others remain on the green, where, having danced a considerable time, they conclude the evening with a feast : the Queen at one table with her maids, the Captain with his troop at another. There are seldom less than fifty or sixty persons at each board, but not more than three knives."

Manx Folk-Lore.—Waldron tells us : "On the 24th of December, towards evening, all the servants in general have a holiday; they go not to bed all night, but ramble about till the bells ring in all the churches, which is at twelve o'clock : prayers being over, they go to hunt the wren; and, after having found one of these poor birds, they kill her, and lay her on a bier with the utmost solemnity, bringing her to the parish church, and burying her with a whimsical kind of solemnity, singing dirges over her in the Manx language, which they call her knell; after which, Christmas begins."

Train, in his "Historical and Statistical Account of the Isle of Man," 1845, goes somewhat at large into this ancient custom : "Hunting the wren has been a pastime in the Isle of Man from time immemorial. In Waldron's time it was observed on the 24th December, which I have adopted, though for a century past it has been observed on St. Stephen's Day. This singular ceremony was founded on a tradition, that in former times a fairy of uncommon beauty exerted such undue influence over the male population, that she, at various times, induced by her sweet voice numbers to follow her footsteps, till by degrees she led them into the sea, where they perished. This barbarous exercise of power had continued for a great length of time, till it was apprehended that the island would be exhausted of its defenders, when a knight-errant sprang up, who discovered some means of countervailing the charms used by this syren, and even laid a plot for her destruction, which she only escaped at the moment of extreme hazard, by taking the form of a wren. But, though she evaded instant annihilation, a spell was cast upon her by which she was condemned on every succeeding New Year's Day to reanimate the same form with the definitive sentence, that she must ultimately perish by human hand. In consequence of this well-authenticated legend, on the specific anniversary, every man and boy in the island (except those who have thrown off the trammels of superstition) devote the hours between sunrise and sunset to the hope of extirpating the fairy, and woe be to the individual birds of this species who show themselves on this fatal day to the active enemies of the race; they are pursued, pelted, fired at, and destroyed without mercy, and their feathers preserved with religious care, it being an article of belief, that every one of the relics gathered in this laudable pursuit is an effectual preservative from shipwreck for one year, and that fishermen would be considered as extremely foolhardy, who should enter upon his occupation without such a safeguard. When the chase ceases, one of the little victims is affixed to the top of a long pole, with its wings extended, and carried in front of the hunters, who march in procession to every house, chanting the following rhyme :

'We hunted the wren for Robbin the Bobbin,
We hunted the wren for Jack of the Can,
We hunted the wren for Robbin the Bobbin,
We hunted the wren for every one.'

"After making the usual circuit and collecting all the money they could obtain, they laid the wren on a bier, and carried it in procession, to the parish churchyard, where, with a whimsical kind of solemnity, they made a grave, buried it, and sung dirges over it in the Manks language, which they called her knell. After the obsequies were performed, the company outside the churchyard wall formed a circle, and danced to music which they had provided for the occasion. At present there is no particular day for pursuing the wren : it is captured by boys alone, who follow the old custom, principally for amusement. On St. Stephen's Day, a group of boys go from door to door with a wren suspended by the legs, in the centre of two hoops, crossing each other at right angles, decorated with evergreens and ribands, singing lines called Hunt the Wren. If, at the close of this rhyme, they be fortunate enough to obtain a small coin, they gave in return a feather of the wren ; and before the close of the day, the little bird may sometimes be seen hanging almost featherless. The ceremony of the interment of this bird in the churchyard, at the close of St. Stephen's Day, has long since been abandoned ; and the sea-shore or some waste ground was substituted in its

place." A longer version of the song given above may be seen in Halliwell's *Archaic Dictionary*, 1860. Mr. Ditchfield remarks : "Fanciful interpreters have seen in the stoning of the wren a connection with the stoning of St. Stephen, whose martyrdom occurred on the day of the observance of this barbarous custom. Another legend is that one of St. Stephen's guards was awakened by a bird just as his prisoner was about to escape. *Old English Customs*, 1896, p. 33. Waldron adds : "There is not a barn unoccupied the whole twelve days of Christmas, every parish hiring fiddlers at the publick charge. On Twelfth Day the fiddler lays his head in some one of the wenches' laps, and a third person asks, who such a maid, or such a maid shall marry, naming the girls then present one after another ; to which he answers according to his own whim, or agreeable to the intimacies he has taken notice of during the time of merriment. But whatever he says is as absolutely depended on as an oracle ; and if he happens to couple two people who have an aversion to each other, tears and vexation succeed the mirth. This they call cutting off the fiddler's head ; for, after this, he is dead for the whole year."

"The old story of infants being changed in their cradles, is here in such credit, that mothers are in continual terror at the thoughts of it. I was prevailed upon myself to go and see a child, who, they told me, was one of these changelings, and indeed must own was not a little surprized as well as shocked at the sight. Nothing under Heaven could have a more beautiful face : but tho' between five and six years old, and seemingly healthy, he was so far from being able to walk or stand that he could not so much as move any one joint : his limbs were vastly long for his age, but smaller than an infant's of six months : his complexion was perfectly delicate, and he had the finest hair in the world : he never spoke nor cryed, ate scarce anything, and was very seldom seen to smile ; but if anyone called him a fairy-elf he would frown, and fix his eyes so earnestly on those who said it, as if he would look them through. His mother, or at least his supposed mother, being very poor, frequently went out a charing, and left him a whole day together : the neighbours, out of curiosity have often looked in at the window to see how he behaved when alone, which, whenever they did, they were sure to find him laughing, and in the utmost delight. This made them judge that he was not without company more pleasing to him than any mortal's could be ; and what made this conjecture seem the more reasonable, was, that if he were left ever so dirty, the woman, at her return, saw him with a clean face, and his hair combed with the utmost exactness and nicety." Waldron also mentions "Another woman, who, being great with child, and expecting every moment the good hour, as she lay awake one night in her bed, she saw seven or eight little women come into her chamber, one of whom had an infant in her arms. They were followed by a man of the same size, in the habit of a minister." A mock christening ensued, and "they baptized the infant by the name of Joan, which made her known she was pregnant of a girl, as it proved a few days after, when she was delivered."

Waldron tells us that there is in the Isle of Man, "The Fairies Saddle, a stone termed so, as I suppose, from the similitude it has of a saddle. It seems to lie loose on the edge of a small rock, and the wise natives of Man tell you, it is every night made use of by the fairies, but what kind of horses they are, on whose backs this is put, I could never find any of them who pretended to resolve me." He also tells us that "the Manks confidently assert that the first inhabitants of their islands were fairies, and that these little people have still their residence among them. They call them the good people, and say they live in wilds and forests, and on mountains, and shun great cities because of the wickedness acted therein. All the houses are blessed where they visit, for they fly vice. A person would be thought imprudently prophane, who should suffer his family to go to bed without having first set a tub, or pail full of clean water, for these guests to bathe themselves in, which the natives aver they constantly do, as soon as the eyes of the family are closed, wherever they vouchsafe to come. If anything happen to be mislaid, and found again, they presently tell you a fairy took it and returned it. If you chance to get a fall and hurt yourself, a fairy laid something in your way to throw you down, as a punishment for some sin you have committed." Again, we are told the fairies are supposed to be fond of hunting. "There is no persuading the inhabitants but that these huntings are frequent in the island, and that these little gentry, being too proud to ride on Manks horses, which they might find in the field, make use of the English and Irish ones, which are brought over and kept by gentlemen. They say that nothing is more common than to find these poor beasts in a morning all over sweat and foam, and tired almost to death, when their owners believe they have never been out of the stable. A gentleman of Balla-fletcher assured me he had three or four of his best horses killed with these

nocturnal journeys." *Descr. of the Isle of Man*, Works, p. 136.

"The natives tell you, that, before any person dies, the procession of the funeral is acted by a sort of beings, which for that end render themselves visible. I know several that have offered to make oath, that, as they have been passing the road, one of these funerals has come behind them, and even laid the bier on their shoulders, as tho' to assist the bearers. One person, who assured me he had been served so, told me that the flesh of his shoulder had been very much bruised, and was black for many weeks after. There are few or none of them who pretend not to have seen or heard these imaginary obsequies, (for I must not omit that they sing psalms in the same manner as those do who accompany the corpse of a dead friend), which so little differ from real ones, that they are not to be known till both coffin and mourners are seen to vanish at the church doors. These they take to be a sort of friendly demons; and their business, they say, is to warn people of what is to befall them: accordingly, they give notice of any stranger's approach, by the trampling of horses at the gate of the house where they are to arrive." "As to circles in the grass, and the impression of small feet among the snow, I cannot deny but I have seen them frequently, and once I thought I heard a whistle as tho' in my ear, when nobody that could make it was near me."

Higden, in the "Polychronicon," tells us that the witches in the Isle of Man anciently sold winds to mariners, and delivered them in knots tied upon a thread exactly as the Laplanders did. Stories of mermaids, water-bulls, and other marine phenomena, are current among the inhabitants. Waldron mentions a charact, a copy of an inscription, found under a cross (which was carefully preserved and carried to the vicar, who wrote copies of it and dispersed them over the Island). "They tell you," says he, "that they are of such wonderful virtue to such as wear them, that on whatever business they go, they are certain of success. They also defend from witchcraft, evil tongues, and all efforts of the devil or his agents; and that a woman wearing one of them in her bosom, while she is pregnant, shall by no accident whatever lose the fruit of her womb. I have frequently rode by the stone under which they say the original paper was found, but it would now be looked upon as the worst sacrilege to make any attempt to move it from the place." He gives also the tenor of the inscription: "Fear God, obey the Priesthood, and do by your neighbour as you would have him to do to you." *Descr. of the Isle of Man,* Works, 174.

Waldron says: "No person will go out on any material affair without taking some salt in their pockets, much less remove from one house to another, marry, put out a child, or take one to nurse, without salt being mutually interchanged; nay, tho' a poor creature be almost famished in the streets, he will not accept any food you will give him, unless you join salt to the rest of your benevolence." The reason assigned by the natives for this is too ridiculous to be transcribed, i.e., "the account given by a pilgrim of the dissolution of an inchanted Palace on the Island, occasioned by salt spilt on the grond."

The belief in second sight is illustrated by a second passage: "As difficult as I found it to bring myself to give any faith to this, I have frequently been very much surprised, when, on visiting a friend, I have found the table ready spread, and everything in order to receive me, and had been told by the person to whom I went, that he had knowledge of my coming, or some other guest, by these good-natured intelligencers. Nay, when obliged to be absent some time from home, my own servants have assured me, they were informed by these means of my return, and expected me the very hour I came, though perhaps it was some days before I hoped it myself at my going abroad. That this is fact, I am positively convinced by many proofs. Waldron's *Description of the Isle of Man,* Works, 130, 187.

Speaking of a crypt **or** souterrain chapel near Peel Castle, he says, "within it are thirteen pillars, on which the whole chapel is supported. They have a superstition that whatsoever stranger goes to see this cavern out of curiosity, and omits to count the pillars, shall do something to occasion being confined there." *Ibid.,* 104. See some valuable papers on this branch of the subject in the *Antiquary* for 1886 and 1895.

Manx Funeral Customs.—In the Isle of Man, observes Train, "When a person dies, the corpse is laid on what is called a straightening-board ; a trencher, with salt in it, and a lighted candle, are placed on the breast, and the bed, on which the straightening-board bearing the corpse rests, is generally strewed with strong-scented flowers." Waldron says that "When a person dies, several of his acquaintance come to sit up with him, which they call the wake. The Clerk of the parish is obliged to sing a psalm, in which all the company join ; and after that they begin some pastime to divert themselves, having strong beer and tobacco allowed them in great plenty. This is a

custom borrowed from the Irish, as indeed are many others much in fashion with them. They give no invitation, but every body that had any acquaintance with the deceased comes, either on foot or horseback. I have seen sometimes, at a Manks Burial, upwards of a hundred horsemen and twice the number on foot : all these are entertained at long tables, spread with all sorts of cold provisions, and rum and brandy flies about at a lavish rate." "The procession of carrying the corpse to the grave is in this manner: when they come within a quarter of a mile of the church, they are met by the parson, who walks before them singing a psalm, all the company joining with him. In every church yard there is a cross round which they go three times before they enter the church." A weird and amusing story of the Manx *bogane* is told by the Rev. R. C. Cowell in the *Antiquary* for December, 1886.

Manx Superstitions.—*See Manx Folklore,* suprâ.

Manx Weddings.—Waldron says: "Notice is given to all the friends and relations on both sides, tho' they live ever so far distant. Not one of these, unless detained by sickness, fails coming and bringing something towards the feast : the nearest of kin, if they are able, commonly contribute the most, so that they have vast quantities of fowls of all sorts : I have seen a dozen of capons in one platter and six or eight fat geese in another ; sheep and hogs roasted whole, and oxen divided but into quarters. They are preceded to church by musick, who play all the while before them the tune, The Black and the Grey, and no other is ever used at weddings." He adds, "that when they arrive at the church-yard, they walk three times round the church before they enter it." "They have bridemen and brides-maids, who lead the young couple as in England, only with this difference, that the former have ozier wands in their hands, as an emblem of superiority." *Descr. of the Isle of Man,* Works, 169. For the Statutes of the Island see *Train,* ii., 167.

Marbles.—Marbles had no doubt their origin in bowls, and received their name from the substance of which the bowls were formerly made. Taw is another name of this play, but the taw was and is, strictly speaking, a marble of larger size used to aim at the others. Rogers notices marbles in his "Pleasures of Memory," l. 137.:

"On yon gray stone that fronts the chancel-door
Worn smooth by busy feet, now seen no more,
Each eve we shot the marble through the ring."

Notwithstanding Dr. Cornelius Scriblerus's Injunctions concerning playthings of "primitive and simple antiquity," we are told "he yet condescended to allow Martinus the use of some few modern playthings; such as might prove of any benefit to his mind, by instilling an early notion of the Sciences. For example, he found that marbles taught him percussion and the laws of motion; nutcrackers the use of the lever, swinging on the ends of a board the balance; bottlescrews the vice; whirligigs the axis and peritrochia; bird-cages the pulley; and tops the centrifugal motion." Bob cherry was thought useful and instructive, as it taught, "at once, two noble virtues, patience and constancy; the first in adhering to the pursuit of one end, the latter in bearing disappointment." In a Coventry penny token of 1801 the boys are represented playing at marbles in the free school.

Mare, to Cry the.—A harvest custom in Herefordshire. See Halliwell in *v.*, and *Crying* suprâ.

Margaret's, St., Day.—(July 20). Butler, in his "Lives of the Saints," dates the commencement of this saint's celebrity in our country from the Crusades. In the third volume of the "Shakespear Society's Papers," Collier notices several entries in the registers of St. Saviour's, Southwark, relating to dramas and other festive celebrations on this day in the olden time. Among these is a record belonging to 30 Hen. VI., as follows : "Fyrste, ayd to the pleyers vpon Seynt Margrets Day, vijˢ." Again, in the Churchwardens' Accounts of Basingbourne, Cambridgeshire, appears this memorandum : "Received at the play held on St. Margaret's Day, A.D. MDXI., in Basingborn, of the holy martyr St. George . . . : Received of the Township of Royston, xijˢ., Tharfield, viˢ. viijᵈ, Melton, vˢ. iiijᵈ."; and so on, and at the end occur these two curious items: "Item, received of the Town of Basingborn on the Monday and Friday after the play, together with other comers on the Monday, xivˢ. vᵈ. Item, received on the Wednesday after the play, with a pot of ale at Kneesworth, all costs deducted, iˢ. vijᵈ. It may be noted that Queen's College, Cambridge, was founded in 1446 by Margaret of Anjou, consort of Henry VI., and called "The College of St. Margaret and St. Bernard," to whom it was jointly dedicated. A separate life of this Saint was printed more than once in the 16th century.

Mari Lhwyd.—It has been satisfactorily shown that the *Mari Lhwyd*, or horse's skull decked with ribbons, which used to be carried about at Christmas in Wales, was not exclusively a Welsh custom, but was known and practised in the Border-counties. It was undoubtedly a form of an old English hobby-horse, one universally prevalent as a popular sport, and conducted, as the readers of Strutt, Douce, and others are already well aware, with all kinds of grotesque and whimsical mummery. The etymology of the term is doubtful. Instinct prompts one to suggest an association with a practice intended to commemorate Maid Marian.

Maritagium or **Amabyr.**—The fine payable to the King or Crown on the marriage of an heir or heiress. The Cinque Ports claimed within their liberties an exemption. See Morris's Chaucer (*Life of Chaucer*, 19-20), where it is stated that on the 28th December, 1375, the King granted Chaucer the custody of five solidates of rent in Solys in Kent, which were in the royal hands in consequence of the minority of the heir of John Solys, deceased, together with the marriage of the said heir. In the Year-book of xxx. Edward I. a case at law is described, in the course of which it was elicited that, in Cornwall, it was then a manorial custom where a bondwoman married out of the manor where she was *reseant*, that she should find surety to the lord of the said manor to return to it after the death of her husband, if he pre-deceased her. It was also laid down at the same time, that where a bondwoman, or neyfe married a freeman, the act of marriage merely enfranchised her during the lifetime of her husband; but when she married the lord of the manor, she was thereby enfranchised for ever. *Gobyr-merch* is explained to be the Welsh term for the maiden's fee or fine payable on marriage. It might be in the form of money or kind. In some places it was redeemed or commuted for a sum payable to the lord, as in the Honour of Clun, appertaining to the Earl of Arundel, who granted for £60 in the time of Elizabeth perpetual exemption from this tax.

Mark.—Some years ago, a gentleman, writing in the "Athenæum," observed : "I can tell you of a fancy that some people have in the wilder parts of Craven, that if the mark of a dead person (the body, however, not being cold) be put to a will, it is valid in law. A few years ago, a case of this nature occurred. A farmer had omitted to make his will; he died, and before the body was cold, a will was prepared by some relative (of course in his own favour), and a mark, purporting to be that of the deceased, was made by putting the pen into the hand of the dead man, and so making his mark to the will. The body of the man was not then cold. The will was contested by some parties, and, I believe, proceeded to trial at law:

when the circumstances of the belief of the parties came out in evidence."

Market-Penny.—Money for the purchase of liquor at market. The reference is of course to the old silver coin.

Markets.—The distinction between the fair and the market has been already pointed out (*Fairs*). The latter outlived the former, because it was less liable to objection, as building and population increased; but both are gradually disappearing under the pressure of social and political changes, and the universality of the shop and store. In and around the metropolis the markets were at a period well within living recollection numerous enough. Those at Covent Garden, Leadenhall, Smithfield and Billingsgate are still flourishing. But we long had others scattered in various directions, and successively suppressed or abandoned as inconsistent with modern conditions and requirements. I may specify:—

Stocks Market on the site of the Mansion House. Hence the Poultry and Coney-hope Lane; The Hay Market in St. James's; Newgate Market; Farringdon Market; Clare Market; Bloomsbury Market; Newport Market; Shepherd's Market; Chelsea Market; Knightsbridge Market; Oxford Market; Carnaby Market; Cumberland Market (formerly St. James's Market).

The Hay-Market or St. James's Market had ceased almost before the time of men now living to be what its name implies, and what it was in the old days in its particular way as much as Covent Garden or Leadenhall. Suckling alludes to it in the Ballad of a Wedding:

" At Charing Cross, hard by the way,
　Where thou and I, Dick, sell our hay,
　— There is a house with stairs—"

In comparatively recent times Lady Burdett-Coutts endeavoured to establish Columbia Market.

Mark's St., Day or **Eve.** (April 25th). — Strype, in his "Annals of the Reformation," under 1559, informs us: "The 25th April, St. Mark's Day (that year), was a procession in divers parishes of London, and the citizens went with their banners abroad in their respective parishes, singing in Latin the Kyrie Eleeson, after the old fashion." "Althoughe Ambrose saye that the churche knewe no fastinge day betwix Easter and Whitsonday, yet beside manye fastes in the Rogation weeke, our wise popes of late yeares have devysed a monstrous fast on Saint Markes Daye. All other fastinge daies are on the holy day even, only Saint Marke must have his day fasted. Tell us

a reason why, so that will not be laughen at. We knowe wel ynough your reason of Tho. Beket, and thinke you are ashamed of it: tell us where it was decreed, by the Churche or Generall Counsell. Tell us also, if ye can, why the one side of the strete in Cheapeside fastes that daye, being in London diocesse, and the other side, beinge of Canterbury diocesse, fastes not? and soe in other townes moe. Could not Bekets holynes reache over the strete, or would he not? If he coulde not, he is not so mighty a Saint as ye make hym; if he would not, he was maliciouse, that woulde not doe soe muche for the citye wherein he was borne."—*The Burnynge of Paules Churche* (1561), 1563, by Bp. Pilkington. There is a superstitious notion in the North of England that if any of the family die within the year, the mark of the shoe will be impressed on the ashes in the hearth, which it is usual to sift on this eve. It is customary in Yorkshire, as a clergyman of that county informed me, for the common people to sit and watch in the church porch on St. Mark's Eve, from eleven o'clock at night till one in the morning. The third year (for this must be done thrice), they are supposed to see the ghosts of all those who are to die the next year, pass by into the church. When any one sickens that is thought to have been seen in this manner, it is presently whispered about that he will not recover, for that such, or such an one, who has watched St. Mark's Eve, says so. This superstition is in such force, that if the patients themselves hear of it, they almost despair of recovery. Many are said to have actually died by their imaginary fears on the occasion; a truly lamentable, but by no means incredible, instance of human folly. Brockett, in his "North Country Glossary," 1846, notices a similar custom of watching for the ghosts of those who were to die the next year, and who were alleged to pass in procession before the watchers in their ordinary dress. It was an usage which became very troublesome, because the persons, who kept the vigil, real or pretended, paid any grudge by giving out, that they had seen the ghost of such an one.

There is still some vestige preserved of an old superstitious practice, followed by our ancestors on this Eve, of riddling chaff as a method of divining the death of persons connected with the family or the operators themselves. Mr. Atkinson, in the "Cleveland Glossary," 1868, describes this absurd species of augury thus: "The riddle is filled with chaff, the scene of operations being the barn-floor with both barn-doors set wide open; the hour is midnight or just before, and each person of the party takes the riddle in succession, and riddles the contents. Should no appearance present itself during the action, death is not imminent to the person operating, or to his friends. But, on the other hand, the appearance of a funeral procession, or even of persons simply bearing a coffin, is a certain augury of death, either to the then riddler himself, or to some one near to him." Sir William Vaughan of Merioneth says, in his *Golden Grove*, 1600, " In the yeare of our Lord, 1589, I being as then but a boy, do remember that an ale wife, making no exception of dayes, would needes brue upon Saint Markes days ; but loe, the marvailous worke of God ! whiles she was thus laboring, the top of the chimney took fire : and, before it could be quenched, her house was quite burnt. Surely, a gentle warning to them that violate and prophane forbidden daies." Bishop Hall says : " On St. Mark's day, blessings upon the corn are implored." Pennant says, that in North Wales no farmer dare hold his team on St. Mark's Day, because, as they believe, one man's team was marked that did work that day with the loss of an ox. The Church of Rome observes St. Mark's Day as a day of abstinence, in imitation of St. Mark's disciples, the first Christians of Alexandria, who, under this Saint's conduct, were eminent for their great prayer, abstinence, and sobriety.

Marlow Fair.—This annual affair, held on the last three days of October, was originally a concession in 1324 by Edward II. to Hugh Marlow, lord of the manor of Chipping Marlow. The fair has been lately (1903) abolished as a nuisance, and General Owen Williams, the present lord of the manor, received £200, raised by public subscription, to indemnify him for the loss of the attendant profit.

Marriage Lines.—The familiar name among the poorer classes for the marriage certificate, which costs under the Act of William IV. half a crown, but which the officiating minister not unfrequently presents to the bride in the case of persons of humble means—of course transcribing from the register in the vestry.

Martinmas.— (November 11). In the Roman Calendar I find the subsequent observations on the 11th of November :— " Wines are tasted and drawn from the lees. The Vinalia, a feast of the ancients, removed to this day. Bacchus in the figure of Martin." Stukeley, speaking of Martinsall-hill, observes : " I take the name of this hill to come from the merriments among the Northern people, call'd Martinalia, or drinking healths to the memory of St. Martin, practis'd by our Saxon and Danish ancestors. I doubt not but upon St. Martin's Day, or Martinmas,

all the young people in the neighbourhood assembled here, as they do now upon the adjacent St. Ann's hill, upon St. Ann's Day." In the Churchwardens' Accounts of St. Martin Outwich, London, are the following articles :—A.D. 1517. " Payd on Seynt Martens Day for bred and drynke for the syngers, vd." A.D. 1524. " It'm for mendyng of the hovell on Sent Marten, vjd." It'm for rose garlands, brede, wyne, and ale, on ij Sent Martens Days, xvd. ob." A.D. 1525. " Payd for brede, ale, and wyne, and garlonds, on Seynt Martyns Day, y° translacyon, xvjd." In the " Debate and Stryfe betwene Somer and Wynter " (a translation from the French circâ 1520), Winter says :

" Somer, men make great joy what tyme
    I com in
For companyes gadereth togyther on
    the eue of seynt martyn :
Ther is nother greate nor small but than
    they will drinke wyne,
If they sholde lay theyr cote to gage to
    drynke it or it fine."

This little glimpse is probably alike applicable to our continental neighbours and ourselves. Hazlitt's *Popular Poetry*, iii., 38. Douce says, that on St. Martin's night boys expose vessels of water, which they suppose will be converted into wine. The parents deceive them by substituting wine. Does this artifice throw any sidelight on the miracle at the marriage at Cana of Galilee? And are we entitled to put a similar interpretation on a harmless stratagem of an analogous kind noticed under St. Nicholas's Day? This, in some districts, is corruptly called Martlemas. In the Glossary to Kennett's " Parochial Antiquities," Salt-Silver is explained to be, " One penny paid at the Feast of Saint Martin by the servile tenants to their lord, as a commutation for the service of carrying their lord's salt from market to his larder." This was for the purpose of curing stock for winter use, including Martlemas beef. Formerly a custom prevailed everywhere amongst us, though generally confined at present to country villages, of killing cows, oxen, swine, &c., at this season, which were cured for the winter, when fresh provisions were seldom or never to be had. In Tusser's " Husbandry," under June, are the following lines :

" When Easter comes who knows not
    than
That veale and bacon is the man?
And Martilmas Beefe doth beare good
    tacke,
When countrey folke do dainties lacke."

With this note in " Tusser Redivivus," 1744, p. 78. " Martlemas beef is beef dried in the chimney, as bacon, and is so called, because it was usual to kill the beef for this provision about the feast of St. Martin, Nov. 11th. Hall, in his "Satires," 1597, mentions

—" dried flitches of some smoked beeve, Hang'd on a writhen wythe since Martins Eve."

"A piece of beef hung up since Martlemas" is also mentioned in the play of the "Pinder of Wakefield," 1599. About a hundred years ago, between Hallowmas and Christmas, when the people of Forfar laid in their winter provisions, about twenty-four beeves were killed in a week; the best not exceeding sixteen or twenty stone. A man who had bought a shilling's worth of beef, or an ounce of tea, would have concealed it from his neighbours like murder. At Martilmas, the inhabitants of Kircudbright killed an old ewe or two, as their winter provision, and used the smoked sheep (braxy) that had died on the moors, in the latter end of autumn. A practice common to the North of England down to modern days, as we learn from Lucas' *Studies in Nidderdale*, and other sources. Almost no beef, and very little mutton, was formerly used by the common people in Wigton, generally no more than a sheep or two, which were killed about Martinmas, and salted up for the provision of the family during the year. The weather on Martinmas Eve is anxiously watched by the farmers in the Midland counties, as it is supposed to be an index to the barometer for about two or three months forward. That this belief is wholly unfounded, is almost a superfluous remark. The fine weather often experienced about this season is known as "St. Martin's little summer."

The feast of St. Martin is a day of debauch among Christians on the Continent: the new wines are then first tasted, and the saint's day is celebrated with carousing. Aubanus tells us, at p. 372, that in Franconia there was a great deal of eating and drinking at this season; no one was so poor and niggardly that on the feast of St. Martin had not his dish of the entrails either of oxen, swine, or calves. They drank, too, as he also informs us, very liberally of wine on the occasion. See also Dupré's "Conformity," p.97. Aubanus tells us, that in Germany there was in his time a kind of entertainment called the "Feast of Sausages or Gut-puddings," which was wont to be celebrated with great joy and festivity. *Antiq. Conviv.* p. 62. From Frolich's "Viatorium," p. 254, I find that St. Martin's Day is celebrated in Germany with geese, but it is not said in what manner. See "Sylva jucund. Serm." p. 18, Stanley says: "St. Martin's Day,

in the Norway clogs, is marked with a goose; for on that day they always feasted on a roasted goose; they say, St. Martin being elected to a bishoprick, hid himself, (noluit episcopari) but was discovered by that animal. We have transferred the ceremony to Michaelmas."

Martin's, St., Rings.—In "Plaine Percevall the Peace-maker of England," 1589, we read: "I doubt whether all be gold that glistereth, sith St. Martins Rings be but copper within, though they be gilt without, sayes the goldsmith." In "The Compters Commonwealth," by W. Fennor, 1617, p. 28, is the following passage: "This kindnesse is but like alchimy or Saint Martins rings, that are faire to the eye, and have a rich outside, but if a man should break them assunder and looke into them, they are nothing but brasse and copper."

Martlemas.—Corrupted from Martinmas, q.v. See Nares, *Glossary*, 1859, in v.

Mary Magdalen's Day, St.—(July 22). In Collinson's "Somersetshire," vol. i. Abdick and Bulston Hundred, p. 64, speaking of Stocklinch, St. Magdalen Parish, the author says: "A revel is held here on St. Mary Magdalen's Day." The Paganalia or country feasts of the ancients were of the same stamp with this of the wake. Spelman says: "Hæc eadem sunt quæ apud Ethnicos Paganalia dicebantur," &c.

Mary of Nazareth.—Of this personage, the daughter of Anne, and wife of Joseph the house-builder, to whom she bore several children, among the rest one named Jesus, a fair account is to be found in the *Dictionary of the Bible*, 1863. We hear of her immaculate conception as an afterthought on the part of the Romanists, of her purification, and of her assumption; but of the broad facts of her career we know little, especially of her early life. Nearly the whole narrative touching her is evidently fabulous, and the three cardinal points, the immaculate conception by her mother, her own purification, and her transit or assumption, are absurdities, which seem scarcely deserving of serious debate. In some of the admirable books of the late Mr. S. Laing farther particulars will be found, and the present writer has entered into the subject more at large in his *Ourselves in Relation to a Deity and a Church*, 3rd ed. 1904.

Masse Blanche.—The collective names given to the 300 martyrs who were cast into a cauldron of live coals at Utica (August 18).

Matachin.—A dance with swords, of Spanish origin, in which three persons took part. See Nares, *Glos.*, 1859. in v.,

Matthew's, St. Day.—(September 21). Philip de Thaun, in his "Livre des

Creatures," written about 1121, says: "And now we see the reason, why we ought to keep the feast of St. Matthew, of which many men say, that they do not know how to keep it, or which day to celebrate. When the bissextile falls on the following day, according to the understanding of mankind, I tell you briefly, pay close attention, on the day which comes nearest that keepest its vigil, it is not to be doubted, a day must not be interposed between that holy day and the vigil day: but therein the feast shall be kept and celebrated." Wright's Translation of the Anglo-Norman original ("Popular Treatises on Science," 1841, p. 51).

The following is from the *Daily News* of September 22, 1868; the usage to which the description refers, has been overlooked by Hone and the Editor of the "Book of Days.": "Yesterday being St. Matthew's Day, in accordance with a time and well-honoured custom, the senior scholars of Christ's Hospital, or what is more familiarly known as the Blue Coat School, delivered orations in the presence of the Lord Mayor and Sheriffs of the City of London. Early in the forenoon, the City dignitaries and boys of the school attended divine service at Christ's Church. Service being over, the scholars repaired to the great hall of the school, where a very large audience, principally composed of ladies, was assembled to hear the delivery of the speeches. Following the example of previous years, those Grecians who are about to proceed to the Cambridge University delivered addresses on the benefits resulting from those metropolitan hospitals which are called royal. Robert William Le Mesurier, fifth Grecian, chose the Greek language in which to convey his opinion of the great blessings resulting from these charities, while Charles Albert Stokes, first Grecian, Thompson, mathematical medallist and Montefiore prizeman, 1868, spoke in English; Alf. George Arthur Robarts, fourth Grecian, spoke in Latin; and Frederick J. Biden, second Grecian and French prizeman, 1868, spoke in French. Each of these scholars was allowed to treat the subject in his own way, though, for the most part, there was little difference in them, the same cardinal points being touched upon in each. Allusion was made to the establishment, now three centuries ago, of the royal hospitals by the pious and youthful Edward VI. These hospitals were founded in a time of peace, and shortly after the Reformation, and as an emblem of it, and they have lasted through the dangerous and anarchical times of the reign of Queen Mary and of the Commonwealth. Christ's Hospital and St. Bartholomew's are in close proximity, the one keeping its door constantly open to receive the sick, while the other maintains and educates more than a thousand children, and it was only the other day that her Majesty the Queen laid the foundation of a new building in which the good work of St. Thomas's Hospital will in future be carried on. Referring more particularly to Christ's Hospital, Charles Albert Stokes, in his English oration, said this foundation instructed its children for every branch of useful and honourable life, and everywhere on the face of the globe where there are Englishmen, are her scholars to be found. Some proceed to the Universities, some to either branch of the navy, very many are engaged in the business of commerce, of whom it has been said that they are generally characterised for their intelligence, activity, and integrity, a greater honour than which could not be desired either for them or for the school. The various points of the addresses, whether delivered in the English or other tongues, were taken up by the boys and loudly cheered. After the delivery of the addresses on the subject of the royal hospitals, several other scholars proceeded to give miscellaneous orations in Latin and Greek, these embracing a translation from 'Henry VI.' into Greek iambics, by Reginald Heber Hoe; a translation into Latin Elegiacs of the 'Battle of Linden,' by Arthur Lionel Smith; a translation into Greek Hexameters of Kirke White's 'Time,' by Alfred Joshua Butler: and a translation into Latin Sapphics of the 'Burial of the Minnisink,' by Samuel Wood. Orations were also given, one in Latin by Edward Maclaine Field, and the other in Greek by Frank Henry Carter."

Matthias, St., the Apostle.— (February 24). Before the alteration of the style, according to Nicolas (*Chronology of History*, p. 162), this anniversary was observed in leap years on the 25th of February: but according to a tract entitled *The True Time of Keeping St. Matthias's Day*, 1711, the change was made by Archbishop Sancroft.

Maund.—A basket, a word formerly in common use. In a letter from Mrs. Hazlitt, wife of the essayist, to her son, dated July 10, 1831, she says: "Your letter, which I received by the maund last night. . . . ." But it appears to have been completely forgotten in this sense.

Maundy or **Shere Thursday**— Cowell describes Maundy Thursday as the day preceding Good Friday, when they commemorate and practice the commands of the Saviour, in washing the feet of the poor, &c., as our Kings of England have long practised the good old custom on that day of washing the feet of poor men in number equal to the years of their reign, and giving them shoes, stockings, and money. Some derive the word from *mandatum*, command, but others, and I think much more probably, from maund, a kind of great basket or hamper, containing eight bales, or two fats. In the Privy Purse Expenses of Henry VII., under 1494, we have : "To thirty eight poer men in almes, £6 0s. 4d. For thirty-eight smale purses, 1s. 8d."—*Excerpta Historica*, 1833, p. 97. King Henry VIII., after the dissolution of his marriage with Katherine of Arragon in 1533, refused to allow her to keep her maundy as Queen, but permitted her to do so, if she thought proper, as Princess-Dowager, in much the same manner that the mother of Henry VII. had in former years. Ellis prints a letter on this subject from the Treasurer of Henry VIII's Household to Thomas Cromwell.

The following is from the "Gentleman's Magazine" for April 1731 : "Thursday, April 15, being Maunday Thursday, there was distributed at the Banquetting House, Whitehall, to forty-eight poor men and forty-eight poor women (the king's age forty-eight) boiled beef and shoulders of mutton, and small bowls of ale, which is called dinner after that, large wooden platters of fish and loaves, viz. undressed, one large old ling, and one large dried cod ; twelve red herrings and twelve white herrings, and four half quarter loaves. Each person had one platter of this provision ; after which was distributed to them shoes, stockings, linen, and woollen cloth, and leathern bags with one penny, two penny, three penny, and four penny pieces of silver, and shillings ; to each about four pounds in value. His grace the Lord Archbishop of York, Lord High Almoner, performed the annual ceremony of washing the feet of a certain number of poor in the Royal Chapel, Whitehall, which was formerly done by the kings themselves, in imitation of our Saviour's pattern of humility, &c. James the Second was the last King who performed this in person." The ceremony of keeping a maundy is now entirely disused. King William III. deputed his almoner to perform the pious office, which his predecessors had executed themselves.

Among the receipts and disbursements of the Canons of the Priory of St. Mary in Huntingdon, we have : "Item, gyven to 12 pore men upon Shere Thorsday, 2s." In an account of Barking Abbey, we read, *inter alia*, in transcripts from the Cottonian Manuscripts and the "Monasticon." "Deliveryd to the Co'vent coke, for rushefals for Palme Sundaye, xxi. pounder fygges. Item, delyveryd to the seyd coke on Sher Thursday viii pounde ryse. Item, delyveryd to the said coke for Shere Thursday xviii pounde almans." Nichols' "Illustrations of the Manners and Expences of Ancient Times in England," p. 294. That it was formerly customary on this day to give, not only money, but pairs of shoes, appears by an entry in the "Privy Purse Expenses of Elizabeth of York," 1502 : "Itm, for xxxvij payre shoes for xxxvijti poore women at the Queenes Maundy at vd. the payre, xvs. vd." Among the ancient annual church disbursements of St. Mary at Hill, in the City of London, I find the following entry : "Water on Maundy Thursday and Easter Eve, 1d."

A writer in the "Gentleman's Magazine" states that "it is a general practice of people of all ranks in the Roman Catholic Church countries to dress in their very best cloaths on Maundy Thursday. The churches are unusually adorned, and everybody performs what is called the Stations ; which is, to visit several churches, saying a short prayer in each, and giving alms to the numerous beggars who attend upon the occasion." According to another correspondent, the inhabitants of Paris and Naples made formerly this day the occasion for much religious display.

Maw or **Mack.**—In the Household Book of Roger, second Lord North, under 1575, occurs this entry : "Aug 6. Lost at Maw w^h the Queen, xxviij*li*." The next item is, "Lost at Primerow" (apparently also with Queen Elizabeth), "xxxij*li*." On November 2 following his lordship lost to her majesty "at play," £32, and on the 22nd February, 1575-6, £70. He was with Elizabeth at Kenilworth, and there she won £50 more of him. It seems that in the later years of Elizabeth's reign, Maw, from having been a vulgar country game, grew into favour and fashion at Court, for in a tract printed in 1580, it is said : "Master Rich. Drake, a gentleman well bearing himselfe alwayes, . . . advised M. Hall as his friende. . . specially for the giving signes of hys game at Mawe, a play at cardes growne out of the country, from the meanest, into credite at the courte with the greatest." What follows presently is curious : "In truth, quoth Hall, yesternight he trode on my foote, I being at mawe at Mistresse Arundels, the old and honorable ordinary table, as I may terme it, of England ; but what he ment thereby I know not, I thnke no evil." *A Letter sent by F. A. touching a quarell between Arthur Hall and Melchisedech Mallerie.*

to his very friend L. B. &c. (1580, repr. in "Miscellanea Antiqua Anglicana," 1816. In the "True Tragedie of Richard the Third," 1594, a citizen, speaking of Lord Hastings, says: "He is as good as the ase of hearts at maw." But the Four has been thought to have been the best card. See Hazlitt's Dodsley, x, 539. Randolph thus alludes to it in his (posthumous) poems, 1638:

> "Histrio may
> At maw, or gleek, or at primero play,
> Still Madam goes to stake—"

In the comedy of "Patient Grissil," 1603, a stage direction says: "A drunken feast: they quarrel and grow drunk, and pocket up the meat: the dealing of cans, like a set at mawe." Among the Huth broadsides, is one in prose, *sine ullâ notâ*, entitled, "The Groome-porters Lawes at Mawe, to be observed for fulfilling the due order of the game." These laws are sixteen in number. The duties of the groom-porter are defined at large in the "Antiquarian Repertory," ed. 1807, vol. ii. p. 201. See also Dyce's Middleton, 1840, ii., 197, and the authority there quoted, Pepys's *Diary*, Jan. 1, 1667-8, and Nares, *Glossary*, 1859, p. 389. Taylor the Waterpoet facetiously says of his hero, Nicholas Wood, of Harrietsham, the Great Eater of Kent (1630): "Hee is no gamester, neither at dice, or cards, yet there is not a man within forty miles of his head, that can play with him at maw."

May.—May is generally held to be derived from *Maia*, the mother of Mercury, to whom the Romans offered sacrifices on this day. But perhaps there is an intermixture in the ceremonies observed at this season of the ancient homage paid to Maia and to Flora, the latter the goddess of vernal productiveness. Our British forefathers appear to have lighted fires on the Crugall or Druid's mound on May-day, perhaps on the same principle that such a practice was afterwards celebrated on St. John the Baptist's Eve; and they are, moreover, said to have been accustomed to draw or hale each other over or through these fires as a pastime, which may have led to the tradition of human sacrifices. These fire-games are noticed in a Welsh triad, and probably involved occasional disasters. Barnes, *Notes on Ancient Britain*, 1858, p. 18. A wet and cold May seems generally to have been regarded as a good portent. In our own language we get the proverb, "A hot May makes a fat church-hay," and M. Michel, in his "Pays Basque," 1857, notices a similar superstition as prevalent in that region.

May-Babies.—It seems that in some parts of Devonshire they have a custom of dressing up dolls, which they call May-babies, in commemoration of Charles II. and his concealment in the oak. The women and children carry these about, enclosed in a box, and covered with a loose cloth. The precise origin of the usage has not been hitherto traced. In the same neighbourhood the people make an effigy of straw, which they dress up in royal attire, even to the Blue Ribbon and Garter, and carry in procession. This also belongs to Oak-apple Day, and is more clearly indicative, primâ facie, of a desire to perpetuate the memory of the Restoration.

May-Cats. — A correspondent of "Notes and Queries" states, that in Wiltshire and Devonshire cats born in May are not valued, because it is believed they will catch no mice or rats, and will, on the contrary, "bring in snakes and slow-worms."

May-Day.—

> "To Islington and Hogsdon runnes the streame
> Of giddie people, to eate cakes and creame.

Tollet, in the description of his painted window (first inserted in Steevens's Shakespear, 1778), says: "Better judges may decide that the institution of this festival originated from the Roman Floralia, or from the Celtic La Beltine (Bal-tein), while I conceive it derived to us from our Gothic ancestors." Olaus Magnus says: "That after their long winter, from the beginning of October to the end of April, the Northern nations have a custom to welcome the returning splendour of the sun with dancing, and mutually to feast each other, rejoicing that a better season for fishing and hunting was approached." In honour of May Day the Goths and Southern Swedes had a mock battle between summer and winter, which ceremony is retained in the Isle of Man, where the Danes and Norwegians had been for a long time masters. Borlase, in his account of Cornwall, has this observation: "This usage is nothing more than a gratulation of the spring"; and every house exhibited a proper signal of its approach, "to testify their universal joy at the revival of vegetation. An ancient custom still retained by the Cornish is that of decking their doors and porches on the first day of May with green boughs of sycamore and hawthorn, and of planting trees, or rather stumps of trees, before their houses." In the Roman Calendar I find the following observation on the 30th of April:

> "The boys go out Maying."

There was a time when this custom was observed by noble and royal personages, as well as the vulgar. Thus we read, in Chaucer's "Court of Love," that, early on May Day, "fourth goth al the Court, both most and lest, to fetche the flouris fresh, and braunch, and blome." Stow tells us : "Of these Mayings we reade, in the raigne of Henry the Sixt, that the aldermen and sheriffes of London being, on May Day, at the Bishop of London's wood, in the parish of Stebunheath (Stepney), and having there a worshipfull dinner for themselves and other commers, Lydgate the Poet, that was a monke of Bery, sent to them by a pursuant a joyfull commendation of that season, containing sixteen staves in meter roiall, beginning thus :

'Mightie Flora, Goddesse of fresh flowers,
Which clothed hath the soyle in lustie greene,
Made buds spring, with her swete showers,
By influence of the sunne-shine.
To doe pleasance of intent full cleane,
Vnto the States which now sit here,
Hath Vere downe sent her owne daughter deare."

In a Royal Household Account, communicated by Craven Ord, Esq., of the Exchequer, I find the following article :— "July 7, 7 Hen. VII. Item, to the Maydens of Lambeth for a May, 10sh." So, among "Receipts and Disbursements of the Canons of the Priory of St. Mary, in Huntingdon," in Mr. Nichols's "Illustrations of the Manners and Expences of Ancient Times in England," 1797, p. 294, we have: "Item, gyven to the Wyves of Herford to the makyng of there May, 12d." Of the celebration of May-day by Henry VIII. and Queen Catherine in 1515 the Venetian ambassador, Sebastian Giustinian, who was present, has left us by far the best account :—"On the first day of May his Majesty sent two English lords to the Ambassadors, who were taken by them to a place called Greenwich, five miles hence, where the King was for the purpose of celebrating May Day. On the ambassadors arriving there, they mounted on horseback, with many of the chief nobles of the kingdom, and accompanied the most Serene Queen into the country to meet the King." The writer, whose letter to his government is dated May 3, adds that her majesty proceeded with her retinue two miles out of Greenwich, into a wood, "where they found the King with his guard, all clad in a livery of green, with bows in their hands, and about a hundred noblemen on horseback, all gorgeously arrayed." Henry indulged more than once in the earlier part of his reign in this diversion. At that time the Robin Hood tradition was three centuries younger than it is now.

It may be necessary to observe that the May-game was not confined to the month, from which it has de-

rived its name, and to which it had been, doubtless, originally limited: for, on the 3rd June, 1555, there was, according to Machyn, "a goodly May-gam at Westmynster as has ben synes." There were, he adds, "gyantes, morespykes, gunes, and drumes, and duwylles (devils), and iij mores-dansses, and bag-pypes and wyolles, and mony dysgyssyd, and the lord and lade of May rod gorgyously, with mynsterelles dyvers playng." In a May-game which took place on the 30th of May, 1557, in Fenchurch Street, Henry Machyn's " Diary " informs us that the "Nine Worthies" were also represented. They also took part in the one which was celebrated on the 24th June, 1559. On May Day, 1559, a company of people gathered at Westminster, in boats opposite the palace, and began throwing eggs and oranges at each other, and some set fire to squibs, one of which fell upon a barrel of gunpowder, and nearly caused the death of several persons, but by good fortune only one was drowned.

In parts of Huntingdonshire, the poor people go " sticking," or gathering sticks for fuel in Warboys Wood on May Day.

There is an engraving of the 18th century where a fiddler and two women described as milkmaids are dancing, one of the dancers having on her head a silver plate, which was borrowed for the occasion. Bourne tells us that, in his time, in the villages in the North of England, the juvenile part of both sexes were wont to rise a little after midnight on the morning of that day, and walk to some neighbouring wood, accompanied with music and the blowing of horns, where they broke down branches from the trees and adorned them with nosegays and crowns of flowers. This done, they returned homewards with their booty, about the time of sunrise, and made their doors and windows triumph in the flowery spoil. See *Magdalen College, Oxford.*

Shakespear says, it was impossible to make the people sleep on May morning, and that they rose early to observe the rites of May. Stubbes, in his " Anatomy of Abuses," 1583, shews the darker side of the picture: "Against Maie—every parishe, towne, and village, assemble themselves together, bothe men, women, and children, olde and yong, even all indifferently : and either goyng all together, or deuidyng themselves into companies, they goe some to the woodes and groves, some to the hilles and mountaines, some to one place, some to another, where they spende all the night in pastymes, and in the mornyng they returne, bringing with them birch, bowes, and braunches of trees, to deck their assemblies withall." — " I have heard it credibly reported," he adds, " (and that *viva voce*) by men of great gravitie, credite, and reputation, that of fourtie, three score, or a hundred maides goying to the woode ouer night, there have scarcely the thirde parte of them returned home againe undefiled." In Braithwaite's "Whimzies," 1631, p. 132, speaking of a Ruffian, the author says: "His soveraignty is showne highest at May-games, wakes, summerings, and rush-bearings." In "The Laws of the Market," 1677, under "The Statutes of the Streets of this City against Noysances," 29, (reprinted from Stowe's *Survey*, 1633), I find the following: "No man shall go in the streets by night or by day with bow bent, or arrows under his girdle, nor with sword unscabbar'd under pain of imprisonment; or with hand-gun, having therewith powder and match, except it be in a usual May-game or sight." The Court of James I. and the populace long preserved the observance of the day, as Spelman remarked. "May is the merry moneth—on the first day, betimes in the morning, shall young fellowes and mayds be so enveloped with a mist of wandring out of their wayes, that they shall fall into ditches one upon another. In the afternoone, if the skie cleare up, shall be a stinking stirre at Pickehatch, with the solemne revels of morice-dancing, and the hobbie-horse so neatly presented, as if one of the masters of the parish had playd it himselfe. Against this high-day, likewise, shall be such preparations for merry meetings, that divers durty sluts shall bestow more in stuffe, lace, and making up of a gowne and a peticote, then their two yeares wages come to, besides the benefits of candles' ends and kitchen stuffe."— *Vox Graculi*, 1623. A few other literary allusions may be interesting:

——"If thou lov'st me then,
Steal forth thy father's house to-morrow night;
And in the wood, a league without the town,
Where I did meet thee once with Helena,
To do observance to a morn of May,
There will I stay for thee."
Mids. N. Dream, act i. sc. 1.

"And though our May-lord at the feast,
Seemed very trimly clad,
In cloth by his owne mother drest,
Yet comes not neere this lad."
Browne's *Shepherd's Pipe*, 1614.

"*On May Morning.*
"Now on the bright morning star, day's harbinger,
Comes dancing from the East, and leads with her

The flow'ry May, who from her green lap throws
The yellow cowslip and the pale primrose.
Hail! bounteous May! that dost inspire
Mirth and youth and warm desire:
Woods and groves are of thy dressing,
Hill and dale doth boast thy blessing.
Thus we salute thee with our early song,
And welcome thee, and wish thee long."
—*Milton*. In Herrick's "Hesperides" are several allusions to customs on May Day.

In the "Life of Mrs. Pilkington" the writer says, "They took places in the waggon, and quitted London early on May morning; and it being the custom in this month for the passengers to give the waggoner at every inn a ribbon to adorn his team, she soon discovered the origin of the proverb, 'as fine as a horse'; for, before they got to the end of their journey, the poor beasts were almost blinded by the tawdry party-coloured flowing honours of their heads." The *Sheffield Daily Telegraph* of May 2, 1889, says: "Yesterday the annual parade of dray horses owned by the Midland Railway Company took place. Of the 113 animals forming the Sheffield stud no less than a hundred put in an appearance at the Wicker Goods Station. The horses were, without exception, in splendid condition, and the decorations showed that the draymen had taken great pains in polishing the harness and general equipment. A dray horse at work is not expected to be a thing of beauty; but yesterday the horses attending the annual parade looked as gay as circumstances would permit, with bright ribbons attached to their manes and tails, and with the brasswork of the harness polished to brilliancy. In order to encourage the men to groom the horses well and to keep the harness in condition, a number of prizes are annually given for the best-groomed horses.

On New May Day the cart, waggon, and brewers' horses are usually decorated with ribbons and rosettes, and in many cases now new reins and whips are provided. This happened in 1903. In 1892, May-Day falling on a Sunday, the observance took place on the day previous.

Martin, speaking of the Isle of Lewis, says that "the natives in the village Barvas retain an antient custom of sending a man very early to cross Barvas river every first day of May, to prevent any females crossing it first; for that, they say, would hinder the salmon from coming into the river all the year round. They pretend to have learn'd this from a foreign sailor, who was ship-wreck'd upon that coast a long time ago. This observation they

maintain to be true, from experience."
For an account of the May-day celebrations in France before the Revolution of 1789, see Douce's " Illust. of Shakespear," vol. ii., pp. 463, 468, 471. Compare *Evil May Day*, *Irish May Customs*, and *Morris Dance*.

May-Day, Old.—May 11. In the *Tears of Old May Day*, ascribed to Lovibond, are some stanzas in allusion to the alteration in the style.

May-Dew.—It was long an article of popular faith in Eastern and Western Europe, that a maiden, washing herself with dew from the hawthorn on the first day of May at daybreak, would preserve her beauty for ever, the operation being of course annually repeated. In 1515 we find Catherine of Arragon, accompanied by twenty-five of her ladies, sallying out on May-Day to gather the dew for the purpose of preserving her complexion, and in 1623 the Spanish Infanta Maria is described by Howell in one of his *Familiar Letters* as doing the same thing in the country, where she was staying at a *casa de campo* belonging to her royal father near Madrid, while Prince Charles was paying his addresses to her. In the *Morning Post*, Monday, May 2nd, 1791, it was mentioned, " that yesterday, being the first of May, according to annual and superstitious custom, a number of persons went into the fields and bathed their faces with the dew on the grass, under the idea that it would render them beautiful." At a village in Sussex, about 1810, the lasses used to repair to the woods early on May morning, and gather the dew, which they sprinkled over their faces as a preservative against freckles, and to secure their good looks until the next anniversary.

Pepys notes in his " Diary," under May 28, 1667 : " My wife away down with Jane and W. Hewer to Woolwich, in order to a little ayre and to lie there to-morrow, and so to gather May-dew tomorrow morning, which Mrs. Turner hath taught her is the only thing in the world to wash her face with ; and I am contented with it." On the 9th of May, 1669, Mrs. Pepys " went with her coach abroad " for the same purpose. Lord Braybrooke refers to Hone's " Every Day Book," where the case of belief in this dissolvent (as Aubrey calls it) in 1791, is noticed. See Aubrey's *Miscellanies*, 1696, ed. 1857, p. 127.

At Venice, as early as 1081, mention occurs of a Dogaressa, who, when she rose, bathed her cheeks with dew ; but this was a daily process, undertaken from a similar motive. She was by birth a Greek. Hazlitt's *Venetian Republic*, 1900, ii., 752.

May Fair.—St. James's Fair (q. v.) was removed to Brookfield, Westminster, adjoining to Piccadilly, in 1688, and was held annually on May-Day and for about a fortnight after. It proved as great a nuisance in its new place of settlement as it had in its original one. In 1709 a pamphlet appeared, giving reasons for the suppression of this fair. " Multitudes of the booths erected in this Fair," we are told, " are not for trade and merchandise, but for musicke, shows, drinking, raffling, lotteries, stage-plays, and drolls. It is a very unhappy circumstance of this Fair, that it begins with the prime beauty of the year, in which many innocent persons incline to walk into the fields and outparts of the city to divert themselves, as they very lawfully may." A farther account of May Fair may be found in Mr. Wheatley's *Piccadilly*, 1870, pp. 200-208.

May Garlands.—In Martin Parker's ballad of " The Milkmaid's Life," there is a passage to the immediate purpose :—

" Upon the first of May,
With garlands fresh and gay,
With mirth and music sweet,
For such a season meet,
They passe their time away—"

These garlands are described by Robert Fletcher in his " Poems," 1656 :—

"Heark, how Amyntas in melodious loud
Shrill raptures tunes his horn-pipe !
　　whiles a crowd
Of snow-white milk-maids, crowned with
　　garland gay,
Trip it to the soft measures of his lay ;
And fields with curds and cream like
　　green-cheese lye ;
This now or never is the Gallaxie.
If the facetious gods ere taken were
With mortal beauties and disguis'd, 'tis
　　here.
See how they mix societies, and tosse
The tumbling ball into a willing losse,
That th' twining Ladyes on their necks
　　might take
The doubled kisses which they first did
　　stake."

In the dedication to " Col. Marten's Familiar Epistles to his Lady of Delight," by E. Gayton, 1663, we have the following allusion to this custom : " What's a May-day milking-pail without a garland and a fiddle ? " " An antient poor woman " (an old writer relates) " went from Wapping to London to buy flowers, about the 6th or 7th of May, 1660, to make garlands for the day of the King's proclamation (that is, May 8th), to gather the youths together to dance for the garland ; and when she had bought the flowers, and was going homewards, a cart went over part of her body, and bruised her for it, just before the doors of such as she might vex thereby. But since, she remains in a great deal of misery by the bruise she had gotten, and cryed out, the devil! saying the devil had owed her a shame, and now thus he had paid her. It's judged at the writing hereof that she will never overgrow it." Henri Misson, who was in England in the time of Charles II., says: "On the first of May, and the five or six days following, all the pretty young country girls that serve the town with milk, dress themselves up very neatly, and borrow abundance of silver plate, whereof they make a pyramid, which they adorn with ribbands and flowers, and carry upon their heads, instead of their common milk-pails. In this equipage, accompanied by some of their fellow milk-maids and a bag-pipe or fiddle, they go from door to door, dancing before the houses of their custo-mers, in the midst of boys and girls that follow them in troops, and every body gives them something." The children at Islip, in Oxfordshire, used to carry about their May garlands, singing:

"Good morning, Missis and Master,
I wish you a happy day;
Please to smell my garland,
Because it is the first of May."

A writer in the *Morning Post*, May 2, 1791, says: "I remember that in walking that same morning between Hounslow and Brentford, I was met by two distinct par-ties of girls with garlands of flowers, who begged money of me, saying 'Pray, Sir, remember the garland.'"

May Gosling.—In the North of England, they appear to have had a May gosling, equivalent to the April Fool. A correspondent of the "Gent. Mag." for April, 1791, says:—"A May gosling, on the first of May, is made with as much eagerness, in the North of England, as an April Noddy or Fool, on the first of April."

May Hirings.—At those, which were held in Lincolnshire in 1902, not one girl in twenty, engaged for the farmhouse, would undertake the duties of milking, which was once a *sine quâ non* of almost every such domestic. The majority of ser-vants now stipulate for a weekly holiday, and in most cases at least one evening or one afternoon "off" per week has to be conceded. The wages demanded, too, show a substantial increase over those which obtained a few years ago. Girls of 14 and 15 years of age going into general service asked as many pounds per year, and boys for the farm were equally pre-cocious."—*Daily Telegraph*, May, 22, 1902.

May, Lord and Lady or **Queen of.**—In "The Knight of the Burning

Pestle," 1613, Rafe, one of the characters, appears as Lord of the May:

"And, by the common-councell of my
fellows in the Strand,
With gilded staff, and crossed skarfe,
the May-Lord here I stand."

He adds:

"The Morrice rings while hobby horse
doth foot it featously;"

and, addressing the group of citizens as-sembled around him, "from the top of Conduit-head," says:

"And lift aloft your velvet heads, and
slipping of your gowne,
With bells on legs, and napkins cleane
unto your shoulders ti'de,
With scarfs and garters as you please,
and Hey for our town cry'd:
March out and shew your willing minds,
by twenty and by twenty,
To Hogsdon or to Newington, where
ale and cakes are plenty.
And let it nere be said for shame, that
we, the youths of London,
Lay thrumming of our caps at home,
and left our custome undone.
Up then, I say, both young and old,
both man and maid, a Maying,
With drums and guns that bounce
aloud, and merry taber playing."

"It appears," says Douce, "that the Lady of the May was sometimes carried in procession on men's shoulders; for Ste-phen Batman, speaking of the Pope and his ceremonies, states that he is carried on the backs of four deacons, 'after the maner of carying whytepot queenes in Western May games. There can be no doubt that the Queen of May is the legiti-mate representative of the Goddess Flora in the Roman Festival." Browne thus describes the Queen or Lady:

"As I haue seene the Lady of the May
Set in an arbour (on a Holy-day)
Built by the May-pole, where the iocund
swaines
Dance with the maidens to the bagpipes
straines,
When enuious night commands them to
be gone,
Call for the merry youngsters one by one,
And for their well performance soone
disposes,
To this a garland interwoue with roses;
To that, a carued hooke or well-wrought
scrip;
Gracing another with her cherry lip:
To one her garter, to another then
A hand-kerchiefe cast o're and o're
agen:
And none returneth emptie that hath
spent
His paines to fill their rurall meri-
ment—"

In the "Gent. Mag." for October, 1793, there is a curious anecdote of Dr. Geddes, the well-known translator of the Bible, who, it should seem, was fond of innocent festivities. He was seen in the summer of that year, "mounted on the poles behind the Queen of the May at Marsden Fair, Co. Oxon." At Cambridge they beg money for "the poor May Lady," a figure dressed grotesquely by the children.

"The bush of hawthorn," observes a writer, "or, as it is called, May, placed at the doors on this day, may point out the first fruits of the Spring, as this is one of the earliest trees which blossoms." Ihre, in his "Suio-Gothic Glossary," makes mention of the King or Lord of May upon the Continent (tom. ii. p. 118, sub. v.). The designation of "Lady of May" conferred by the anonymous author of the "Justes of the Moneths of May and June," 1507, on the Princess Mary, as patroness of the Lists, has, of course, no connection with the old English custom here illustrated. But it shews that the title was sufficiently popular at that time to tempt the author of the "Justes" to employ it for his own purposes. Hazlitt's *Popular Poetry*, ii, 109 *et seqq*. Much the same is to be predicated of the pretty pageant, which takes place annually at Whitelands College, under the initiative of the late Mr. Ruskin.

Maypole.—Bourne, speaking of the first of May, tells us: "The after-part of the day is chiefly spent in dancing round a tall poll, which is called a May poll; which being placed in a convenient part of the village, stands there, as it were consecrated to the Goddess of Flowers, without the least violation offered to it, in the whole circle of the year." The author of "The Way to Things by Words," &c., very properly points out, that May-pole is a pleonasm, for the French call the same thing the *Mai*. We are told by the same writer that the column of May (whence our May-pole) was the great standard of justice in the Ey-Commons or Fields of May. Here it was that the people, if they saw cause, deposed or punished their governors, their barons, and their kings. The judge's bough or wand (at this time discontinued and only faintly represented by a trifling nosegay), and the staff or rod of authority in the civil and in the military (for it was the mace of civil power and the truncheon of the field officers), are both derived hence. Keysler, says Borlase, thinks that the custom of the Maypole took its rise from the earnest desire of the people to see their king, who seldom appearing at other times, made his procession at this time of year to the great assembly of the States held in the open air. In the "British

Apollo," (it is said): "It was a custom among the ancient Britons, before converted to Christianity, to erect these Maypoles, adorned with flowers, in honour of the Goddess Flora; and the dancing of the milk-maids may be only a corruption of that custom in complyance with the town." Tollett tells us, that the May Pole in his window "is painted yellow and black, in spiral lines." Spelman's "Glossary" mentions the custom of erecting a tall May Pole, painted with various colours, and Shakespear, in "A Midsummer Night's Dream," act iii. sc. 2, speaks of a painted May Pole. Upon our pole (adds Mr. Tollett) are displayed St. George's red cross or the banner of England, and a white penon or streamer, emblazoned with a red cross, terminating like the blade of a sword; but the delineation thereof is much faded. Stukeley, in his "Itinerarium," 1724, p. 29, says: "There is a May Pole near Horn Castle, Lincolnshire, where probably stood an Hermes in Roman times. The boys annually keep up the festival of the Floralia on May Day, making a procession to this hill with May gads (as they call them) in their hands. This is a white willow wand, the bark peel'd off, ty'd round with cowslips, a thyrsus of the Bacchanals. At night they have a bonefire, and other merriment, which is really a sacrifice, or religious festival." Borlase, speaking of the manners of the Cornish people, says:—"From towns they make excursions on May Eve into the country, cut down a tall elm, bring it into the town with rejoicings, and having fitted a straight taper pole to the end of it, and painted it, erect it in the most public part, and, upon holidays and festivals, dress it with garlands of flowers, or ensigns and streamers." Owen, in his "Welsh Dictionary," voce "Bedwin," a birch-tree, explains it also by "a May-pole, because it was always," he says, "made of birch. —It was customary to have games of various sorts round the Bedwen; but the chief aim, and on which the fame of the village depended, was, to preserve it from being stolen away, as parties from other places were continually on the watch for an opportunity; who, if successful, had their feats recorded in songs on the occasion."

It appears from a stage direction in the "Mountebanks' Masque"—"Paradox his Disciples, and the May-pole, all daunce" —that the latter was much like the modern "Jack in the Green," and formed, like it, the central figure in the dance. In an account of Parish Expences in Coates's "Hist. of Reading," p. 216, A.D. 1504, we have: "It. payed for felling and bryngy'g home of the bow (bough) set in the M'cat-place, for settyng up of the same, mete and drink, viii^d." In the Chapel Warden's

Accounts of Brentford, under the year 1623, is the following article : "Received for the May-pole, £1 4s." In Northbrooke's "Treatise against Dicing," &c., 1577, is the following passage : "What adoe make our yong men at the time of May? Do they not vse nightwatchings to rob and steal yong trees out of other mens grounde, and bring them home into their parishe with minstrels playing before : and, when they haue set it vp, they will decke it with floures and garlandes, and daunce round, (men and women togither, moste vnseemly and intolerable, as I haue proued before), about the tree, like vnto the children of Israell that daunced about the golden calfe that they had set vp," &c. Stubbes, in his "Anatomie of Abuses," 1583, says : "But their cheefest jewell they bring home from thence (the woods) is their Maie poole, whiche they bring home with greate veneration, as thus. They have twentie or fourtie yoke of oxen, every oxe havyng a sweete nosegaie of flowers tyed on the tippe of his hornes, and these oxen drawe home this Maie poole, (this stinckyng idoll rather), which is covered all over with flowers and hearbes, bounde rounde aboute with stringes, from the top to the bottome, and sometyme painted with variable colours, with two or three hundred men, women, and children followyng it, with greate devotion. And thus beyng reared up, with handkercheifes and flagges streamyng on the toppe, they strawe the ground aboute, binde greene boughes about it, sett up Sommer haules, bowers, and arbours hard by it. And then fall they to banquet and feast, to leaps and daunce aboute it, as the heathen people did at the dedication of their idolles, whereof this is a perfect patterne, or rather the thyng itself." Lodge, in his "Wits Miserie," 1596, p. 27, describing usury, says : "His spectacles hang beating . . . like the flag in the top of a May pole." James I. published his ordinance in respect to lawful sports, among which this is included, in 1618, and by Charles I.'s warrant, dated Oct. 18. 1633, it had been similarly enacted, that, "for his good peoples lawfull recreation, after the end of Divine Service, his good people be not disturbed, letted, or discouraged from any lawfull recreation : such as dancing, either men or women; archery for men, leaping, vaulting, or any other such harmless recreations; nor from having of May games, Whitson Ales, and Morris dances, and the setting up of May poles, and other sports therewith used; so as the same be had in due and convenient time, without impediment or neglect of Divine Service. And that women shall have leave to carry rushes to the church, for the decorating of it, according to their old custom. But

with all his Majesty doth hereby account still as prohibited, all unlawful games to be used on Sundays only, as bear and bull-baitings, interludes, and, at all times in the meaner sort of people by law prohibited, bowling."—Harris's *Life of Charles I.*, p. 48, note. It was against this royal manifesto that Henry Burton directed his *Judgments upon Sabbath-Breakers*, 1641—an evidence of the increasing power of the Puritans. Here we of course find many particulars about May-games and the May-pole :—

"At Dartmouth, 1634, upon the coming forth and publishing of the 'Book of Sports,' a company of yonkers, on May-day morning, before day, went into the country to fetch home a May-pole with drumme and trumpet, whereat the neighbouring inhabitants were affrighted, supposing some enemies had landed to sack them. The pole being thus brought home, and set up, they began to drink healths about it, till they could not stand so steady as the pole did : whereupon the mayor and justice bound the ringleaders over to the sessions; whereupon, these complaining to the Archbishop's Vicar-generall, then in his visitation, he prohibited the justices to proceed against them in regard of the King's Book. But the justices acquainted him they did it for their disorder in transgressing the bounds of the book. Hereupon, these libertines scorning at authority, one of them fell suddenly into a consumption, whereof he shortly after died. Now, although this revelling was not on the Lord's Day, yet being upon any other day, and especially May-day, the May-pole set up thereon giving occasion to the prophanation of the Lord's Day the whole year after, it was sufficient to provoke God to send plagues and judgments among them." The greater part of the examples are levelled at summer-poles. By an ordinance of the Long Parliament, in April 1644, among other references, all May poles were taken down, and removed by the constables, church-wardens, &c. The ordinance states :—

"And because the prophanation of the Lords Day hath been heretofore greatly occasioned by May-poles (a heathenish vanity, generally abused to superstition and wickedness), the Lords and Commons do further order and ordain, that all and singular Maypoles, that are, or shall be erected, shall be taken down and removed by the Constables, Borsholders, Tything men, petty Constables, and Church Wardens of the parishes and places where the same be; and that no May pole shall be hereafter set up, erected, or suffered to be within this Kingdome of England or Dominion of Wales."—Die Sabbathi, 6 April, 1644. The officers were to be fined five shillings weekly, till the poles were removed. Husband's "Collection," 1646, p. 479. During a long succession of years, however, notwithstanding the Puritan antipathy to them, May-poles continued to flourish, and to be a favourite feature in the May sports. William Fennor, in his *Pasquil's Palinodia*, 1619, has left us a curious description of this object and usage :

"Fairely we marched on, till our approach
  Within the spacious passage of the Strand,
Objected to our sight a summer-broach,
  Ycleap'd a May Pole, which, in all our land,
No city, towne, nor streete can parallel,
  Nor can the lofty spire of Clarken-well,
Although we have the advantage of a rocke,
Pearch up more high his turning weather-cock.
"Stay, quoth my Muse, and here behold a signe
Of harmlesse mirth and honest neighbourhood,
Where all the parish did in one combine
  To mount the rod of peace, and none withstood :
When no capritious constables disturb them,
Nor justice of the peace did seek to curb them,
Nor peevish puritan, in rayling sort,
Nor over-wise church-warden, spoyl'd the sport.
"Happy the age, and harmlesse were the dayes,
  (For then true love and amity was found),
When every village did a Maypole raise,
  And Whitson-ales and May-games did abound :
And all the lusty yonkers, in a rout,
With merry lasses daunc'd the rod about,
Then Friendship to their banquets bid the guests,
And poore men far'd the better for their feasts.

"The lords of castles, mannors, townes, and towers,
  Rejoic'd when they beheld the farmers flourish,
And would come downe unto the summer bowers
To see the country gallants dance the Morrice.
      *   *   *   *   *   *
"But since the Summer poles were overthrown,
  An all good sports and merriments decay'd,
How times and men are chang'd, so well is knowne,

It were but labour lost if more were said.
      *   *   *   *   *   *
" Alas, poore May Poles; what should be the cause
  That you were almost banish'd from the earth?
Who never were rebellious to the lawes ;
  Your greatest crime was harmlesse, honest mirth :
What fell malignant spirit was there found,
To cast your tall Pyramides to ground
To be some envious nature it appeares,
That men might fall together by the eares.

" Some fiery, zealous brother, full of spleene,
  That all the worlde in his deepe wisdom scornes,
Could not endure the May-pole should be seene
  To weare a coxe-combe higher than his hornes :
He took it for an idoll, and the feast
For sacrifice unto that painted beast ;
Or for the wooden Trojan asse of sinne,
By which the wicked merry Greeks came in.

" But I doe hope once more the day will come,
  That you shall mount and pearch your cocks as high
As ere you did, and that the pipe and drum
  Shall bid defiance to your enemy ;
And that all fidlers, which in corners lurke,
And have been almost starv'd for want of work,
Shall draw their crowds, and, at your exaltation,
Play many a fit of merry recreation.

" And you, my native town, which was, of old,
  (When as thy bonfires burn'd and May-poles stood,
And when thy wassall-cups were uncontrol'd),
  The summer bower of peace and neighbourhood.
Although, since these went down, thou lyst forlorn,
By factious schismes and humours overborne,
Some able hand I hope thy rod will raise,
That thou mayst see once more thy happy daies."

In "The Honestie of this Age," by Barnabe Rych, 4to. Lond. 1615, p. 5, is the following passage : "the country swaine, that will sweare more on Sundaies, dancing about a May pole, then he will doe all the week after at his work, will have a cast at me." "This day shall be erected long wooden idols, called May-poles; whereat many greasie churles shall murmure, that will not bestow so much as a faggot sticke towards the warming of the poore: an humour that, while it seemes to smell of conscience, favours indeed of nothing but covetousnesse."—*Vox Graculi*, 1623. It is to be suspected, nevertheless, that, as Cromwell's personal ascendancy asserted itself, greater tolerance prevailed. There are in a volume printed in 1657, called "Wit a-Sporting," by Henry Bold, some verses, which were not improbably conveyed from an earlier writer (much of his matter was stolen from Herrick):

"The May Pole.
"The May Pole is up,
  Now give me the cup,
I'll drink to the garlands around it,
  But first unto those
  Whose hands did compose
The glory of flowers that crown'd it."

After the Restoration, May poles were permitted to return. Hall, however, protested against this revival in his "Funebria Floræ, the Downfall of May Games," 1660. At the end is a copy of verses (in which he makes the May-pole recapitulate *propriâ personâ*) the evils with which its introduction was fraught to the cause of religion and morality. Another copy of the verses is to be found in Harl. MS., 1221, and is there entitled: "A May Pooles Speech to a Traveller." Possibly the lines were merely appropriated by Hall. The May-Pole is made to say:

"I have a mighty retinue,
The scum of all the raskall crew
Of fidlers, pedlers, jayle-scap't slaves,
Of tinkers, turn-coats, tospot knaves,
Of theeves and scape-thrifts many a one,
With bouncing Besse, and jolly Jone,
With idle boyes, and journey-men,
And vagrants that their country run:
Yea, hobby-horse doth hither prance,
Maid-Marrian and the Morrice-dance.
My summons fetcheth, far and near,
All that can swagger, roar, and swear,
All that can dance, and drab and drink,
They run to mee as to a sink.
These mee for their commander take,
And I do them my blackguard make.
The honour of the Sabbath-day
My dancing-greens have ta'en away,
Let preachers prate till they grow wood,
Where I am they can do no good."

At page 10, Hall says: "The most of these May-poles are stollen, yet they give out that the poles are given them."—"There were two May-poles set up in my parish (King's-Norton); the one was stollen, and the other was given by a profest

papist. That which was stollen was said to be given, when 'twas proved to their faces that 'twas stollen, and they were made to acknowledge their offence. This pole that was stollen was rated at five shillings: if all the poles one with another were so rated, which were stollen this May, what a considerable sum would it amount to! Fightings and bloodshed are usual at such meetings, insomuch that 'tis a common saying, that 'tis no festival unless there bee some fighting." "If Moses were angry," he says in another page, "when he saw the people dance about a golden calf, well may we be angry to see people dancing the morrice about a post in honour of a whore, as you shall see anon." "Had this rudeness," he adds, "been acted only in some ignorant and obscure parts of the land, I had been silent; but when I perceived that the complaints were general from all parts of the land, and that even in Cheapside itself the rude rabble had set up this ensign of prophaneness, and had put the lord-mayor to the trouble of seeing it pulled down, I could not, out of my dearest respects and tender compassion to the land of my nativity, and for the prevention of the like disorders (if possible) for the future, but put pen to paper, and discover the sinful rise and vile prophaneness that attend such misrule." In "The Lord's Loud Call to England," published by H. Jessey, 1660, there is given part of a letter from one of the Puritan party in the North, dated "Newcastle, 7th of May, 1660": "Sir, the countrey, as well as the town, abounds with vanities; now the reins of liberty and licentiousness are let loose: May-poles, and players, and juglers, and all things else, now pass current. Sin now appears with a brazen face," &c. But the resistance and exposure were vain. The May-pole was never again suppressed, till modern feeling operated against it. Pepys notes the erection of the Strand May-pole under date of June 1, 1663. The Rural Dance about the May-pole, and the tune to which the first figure is danced at Mr. Young's ball, May, 1671, is described in "Westminster Drollery," 1671:

"Come lasses and lads, take leave of your dads,
  And away to the May-pole hie;
For every he has got him a she,
  And the minstrel's standing by.
For Willy has gotten his Jill, and Johnny has got his Joan.
To jig it, jig it, jig it, jig up and down.

"Strike up, says Wat. Agreed, says Kate,
  And, I prithee, fidler, play:
Content, says Hodge, and so says Madge,

For this is a holiday!
Then every man did put his hat off to
　　his lass,
And every girl did curchy, curchy,
　　curchy on the grass.

"Begin, says Hall.　Aye, aye, says
　　Mall,
We'll lead up Packington's Pound:
No, no, says Noll.　And so, says Doll,
We'll first have Sellenger's Round.
Then every man began to foot it round
　　about,
And every girl did jet it, jet it, jet
　　it, in and out.

"You're out, says Dick.　'Tis a lie, says
　　Nick;
The fiddler played it false:
'Tis true, says Hugh; and so says Sue,
And so says nimble Alce.
The fiddler then began to play the tune
　　again,
And every girl did trip it, trip it, trip
　　it to the men."

A shorter version of this is given by
Rimbault, in his *Book of Songs and Bal-
lads*, 1851.　Shakespear makes dancers
kiss:
"Come unto these yellow sands,
　　And then join hands.
Curtsied when you have, and kist,
　　The wild waves wist!——"

In "Polwart on the Green," we have at
the very commencement (I quote from
"Orpheus Caledonius," 1733):
"At Polwart on the Green,
　　If you'll meet me the morn,
Where lasses do convene,
　　To dance about the thorn;
A kindly welcome you shall meet
　　Frae her who likes to view
A lover and a lad complete,
　　The lad and lover you."

"The Mayings," says Strutt, "are in
some sort yet kept up by the milk-maids
at London, who go about the streets with
their garlands and music, dancing; but
this tracing is a very imperfect shadow of
the original sports; for May-poles are set
up in the streets, with various martial
shows, Morris dancing and other devices,
with which, and revelling, and good chear,
the day was passed away.　At night they
rejoiced, and lighted up their bonfires."
"Manners and Customs," vol. ii. p. 99.
The young chimney-sweepers, some of
whom are fantastically dressed in girls'
clothes, with a great profusion of brick-
dust by way of paint, gilt paper, &c.,
making a noise with their shovels and
brushes, were long the most striking objects in the celebration of May Day in the
streets of London.　But the May-pole, and
the May customs generally, are now almost

quite neglected in London and other great
centres.
　　Consult Vossius "De Orig. & Prog.
Idolatriæ," lib. ii. Spelman's *Glossary*,
1687, v. "Maiuma," Ducange, v. "Maiuma," and Carpentier's "Glossary," v.
"Maium."

Meadow Verse.—To the Harvest
festivities must be referred the Meadow
Verse.　In Herrick's "Hesperides," 1648,
p. 161, we have:
"*The meadow Verse, or Anniversary,
　　to Mistris Bridget Lowman.*

"Come with the Spring-time forth, fair
　　Maid, and be
This year again the Meadows Deity.
Yet ere ye enter, give us leave to set
Upon your head this flowry coronet;
To make this neat distinction from the
　　rest,
You are the Prime, and Princesse of
　　the feast:
To which with silver feet lead you the
　　way,
While sweet-breath nimphs attend you
　　on this day.
This is your houre; and best you may
　　command,
Since you are Lady of this fairie land.
Full mirth wait on you, and such mirth
　　as shall
Cherrish the cheek, but make none
　　blush at all.

*The Parting Verse, the Feast there
　　ended.*

Loth to depart, but yet at last, each one
Back now must go to's habitation:
Not knowing thus much, when we once
　　do sever,
Whether or no, that we shall meet here
　　ever."
　　　　　　　　　　　　"If fates do give
Me longer date, and more fresh springs
　　to live,
Oft as your field shall her old age renew,
Herrick shall make the meddow-verse
　　for you."

Medard, St.—"I had always imagined that St. Médard was the rainy saint
of France, and St. Godelièvc the St.
Swithin of Flanders.　In France the popular saying is:
"S'il pleut le jour de la Saint Médard
Il pleut quarante jours plus tard."
St. Médard, however, unlike St. Swithin,
has not absolute control over the weather
at this season, his decision being subject
to that of St. Barnabé, whose fête day
falls three days later, the 11th of June;
and even should these two saints combine
to bring terror to the heart of the agricul-
turist, there is a forlorn hope left, for SS.
Gervais and Protais, whose fête day is on
the 19th of the month, may yet ordain,
that the weather shall be fine.　The *Jour-*

nal de Roubaix of the 11th of June quotes the following lines anent this superstition :

> 'Quand il pleut à la Saint Médard,
> Prends ton manteau sans nul retard :
> Mais s'il fait beau pour Barnabé,
> Qui va lui couper l'herbe sous le pied,
> Ton manteau chez toi peut rester.
> Enfin, s'il pleut ces deux jours,
> Si Médard et Barnabé, comme toujours,
> S'entendaient pour te jouer des tours,
> Tu auras encore Saint Gervais,
> Accompagné de Saint Protais,
> Que le beau temps va ramener.'

The legend runs that St. Médard was one day crossing a plain when a drenching shower fell. Every one was wetted to the skin except the saint, over whom an eagle spread its wings as a shelter." *G. Perratt* in *Notes and Queries.*

Mell-Sheaf.—The last leaf of the harvest was called the Mell-Sheaf, and says Mr. Atkinson, "used to be formed, on finishing the reaping, with much observance, and care." He adds, that it "was frequently made of such dimensions as to be a heavy load for a man, and within a few years comparatively was proposed as the prize to be won in a race of old women. In other cases, it was carefully preserved, and set up in some conspicuous place in the farm-house." *Cleveland Glossary,* 1868.

Mell-Supper.—The Mell-Supper, the entertainment usual after harvest, is derived from *Mehl*, farina or meal, as is proposed by Dr. Pegge in a letter to Mr. Brand of Aug. 12, 1786. Nares, *Glossary,* ed. 1859, v. Mell-Supper. In the "Life of Eugene Aram," 1759, there is an Essay on "The Mell-Supper, and shouting the Churn," by that extraordinary man. Bread, or cakes, he says, composed part of the Hebrew offering, as appears by Leviticus, xxiii. 13; and we gather from Homer in the first Book of his "Iliad," that a cake thrown upon the head of the victim was also part of the Greek offering to Apollo. Apollo, continues Aram, losing his divinity on the progress of Christianity, what had been anciently offered to the god, the reapers as prudently eat up themselves. At last the use of the meal of new corn was neglected, and the supper, so far as the meal was concerned, was made indifferently of old or new corn, as was most agreeable to the founder. He adds, as .the harvest was last concluded with several preparations of meal, or brought to be ready for the mell, this term became, in a translated signification, to mean the last of other things : as when a horse came last in the race, they often say in the North, he has got the mell."

Mensa Paschæ.—"The month or quinzaine of Easter, i.e. the eight days preceding and the eight days following Easter Day." *Plumpton Correspondence* under 1476, p. 37, Note. Robinet Plumpton, writing to Sir William Plumpton, 1 April, 1476, says : "And for the Day of Appearance of Ailmer wyfe, is *mense Paske*; so that she be here the morrow after *Mense Paske.*"

Mercheta Mulierum.—"Merchet," says Tomline in his *Law Dictionary,* 1835, " was a fine or composition paid by inferior tenants to the lord, for liberty to dispose of their daughters in marriage. No baron or military tenant could marry his sole daughter and heir, without such leave purchased from the king, *pro maritandâ filiâ*; and many of our servile tenants could neither send their sons to school nor give their daughters in marriage, without express licence from their superior lord." Freemen were not, it seems, liable to this mercheta, at least in all cases. "Mercheta," observes Whitaker, " is certainly British. This term, which has given rise to that fiction of folly in the best histories of Scotland, that the lord had a privilege to sleep with the bride of his vassal on her wedding night. . . is apparently nothing more than the merched of Howel-Dhu, the daughterhood or the fine for the marriage of a daughter." This view is supported by the passage quoted by Brand himself from one of the Cottonian MSS. "Rentale de Tynemuth, factum A.D. 1378.—Omnes Tenentes de Tynemouth cum contigerit, solvent Layrewite filiabus vel Ancillis suis et etiam Merchet pro filiabus suis maritandis." Vitellius, E. 5. Buchanan testifies to the prevalence of this usage in Scotland under a law of King Eugenius (perhaps Eugenius III.) in its original form, and tells us that a later prince in the eleventh century, yielding to the prayers of his consort, first sanctioned a pecuniary commutation in the shape of half a mark of silver; but whether this was a coin or a measure of weight, seems uncertain. *Rerum Scoticarum Historia,* 1582. The present Editor has the impression that this mercheta was at the outset both here and elsewhere an incidence of serfdom, that it was subsequently commuted by a fine, but that, as I have shown in my Blount, a freeman could plead exemption even from the latter. But I believe that in Scotland, Wales, and Ireland, the practice, like every other relic of antiquity, lingered much longer, and that the commutation was not so great, or the line of distinction so clearly defined : and the laxity in this respect, when the laws of property began to assert themselves, may have had something to do with the discredit cast on the first issue of a marriage among the lower class, and the tendency to favour the second son in testamentary dispositions. It has been said that there was a similar usage in Germany, whence indeed the English may have derived it. There is a publication, which the writer has not seen, entitled: "Les Nuits d'Epreuve des Villageoises Allemandes avant le mariage," small 8°, Bruxelles, 1877, probably one of those meretricious and silly books, which are worse than useless. Compare *Maritagium* suprâ and Hazlitt's Blount, 1874, p. 433.

Meretrix. — See *Whores, Punishment of*.

Meritot, Shuggy-Shaw or **Swing.**—Speght, in his "Glossary to Chaucer," says : "Meritot, in Chaucer, a sport used by children by swinging themselves in bell-ropes, or such-like, till they are giddy. In Latin it is called Oscillum, and is thus described by an old writer : "Oscillum est genus ludi, scilicet cum funis dependitur be trabe, in quo pueri & puellæ sedentes impelluntur huc et illuc." This sport is described as follows by Gay :

"On two near elms, the slacken'd cord I hung,
Now high, now low, my Blouzalinda swung."

So Rogers :

"Soar'd in the swing, half-pleas'd and half afraid,
Thro' sister elms that wav'd their summer shade."

See Halliwell in v.

Merry Andrew.—Pennant, in his "Zoology," tells us : "It is very singular that most nations give the name of their favourite dish to the facetious attendant on every mountebank : thus the Dutch call him Pickle Herring, the Italians Macaroni, the French Jean Potage, the German Hans Wurst, i.e., Jack Sausage; and we dignify him with the title of Jack Pudding." It has been conjectured (with no particular probability) that Andrew Borde, the facetious physician of Henry the Eighth's time, was the original Merry Andrew.

Merry-trotter.—Corrupted from *meritot*, a swing. See above.

Michaelmas. — Michaelmas, says Bailey, is a festival appointed by the Church to be observed in honour of St. Michael the Arch-angel, who is supposed to be the chief of the Host of Heaven, as Lucifer is of the infernal [one], and as he was supposed to be the protector of the Jewish, so is he now esteemed the guardian and defender of the Christian Church. In the "Observations on Days in the Romish Calendar," I find on St. Michael's Day the following :

"Arx tonat in gratiam tutelaris Numinis,"

which I translate :

"Cannon is fired from the citadel in honour of the tutelar saint."

It has long been and still continues the custom at this time of the year, or thereabouts, to elect the governors of towns and cities, the civil guardians of the peace of men, perhaps, as Bourne supposes, because the feast of angels naturally enough brings to our minds the old opinion of tutelar spirits, who have, or are thought to have, the particular charge of certain bodies of men, or districts of country, as also that every man has his guardian angel, who attends him from the cradle to the grave, from the moment of his coming in to his going out of life. His appearance in Cornwall on the Mount which bears his name in the fifth, or according to others in the eighth, century is a matter of local tradition. Pengelly, *Antiquity of Man in the South West of England*, 1887, p. 13.

A red velvet buckler was formerly preserved in a castle in Normandy, which the Arch-angel made use of, when he combated the Dragon. At Mont St. Michel in Brittany Michaelmas Day is of course the grand anniversary, when the Bishop of the diocese comes over, and thousands of persons visit the spot. But on the Saint's Vigil there is an interesting and impressive ceremony in the evening, the priests and choristers forming in procession in the town below, and winding up the ascent to the church with lighted candles, singing hymns. A service succeeds.

Michaelmas Goose.—There is an old custom still in use among us, of having a roast goose to dinner on Michaelmas Day. Beckwith says : "Probably no other reason can be given for this custom but that Michaelmas Day was a great festival, and geese at that time most plentiful. In Denmark, where the harvest is later, every family has a roasted goose for supper on St. Martin's Eve."

Moresin refers the great doings on this occasion, which, he says, were common to almost all Europe in his time, to an ancient Athenian festival observed in honour of Bacchus, upon the eleventh, twelfth, and thirteenth days of the month Anthesterion, corresponding with our November. Aubanus seems to confirm this conjecture, though there is no mention of the slaughter of any animal in the description of the rites of the Grecian festival. It is observable that the fatted goose, so common in England at Michaelmas, is, by the above foreign authors and others, marked as one of the delicacies in common use at every table on the continent at Martinmas. Walpole, in "The World," No. 10, tells us : "When the reformation of the Calendar was in agitation, to the great disgust of many worthy persons who urged how great the harmony was in the old establishment between the holidays and their attributes (if I may call them so), and what confusion would follow if Michaelmas Day, for instance, was not to be celebrated when stubble-geese are in their highest perfection ; it was replied, that such a propriety was merely imaginary, and would be lost of itself, even without alteration of the calendar by authority : for if the errors in it were suffered to go on, they would in a certain number of years produce such a variation, that we should be mourning for good King Charles on a false thirtieth of January, at a time of year when our ancestors used to be tumbling over head and heels in Greenwich Park in honour of Whitsuntide : and at length be choosing king and queen for Twelfth Night, when we ought to be admiring the London Prentice at Bartholomew Fair."

Among other services John de la Hay was bound (10 Edw. IV.) to render to William Barnaby, Lord of Lastres, in the county of Hereford, for a parcel of the demesne lands, one goose fit for the lord's dinner on the Feast of St. Michael the Archangel. Blount's *Tenures*, ed. 1874, p. 188. In Deering's "Nottingham," p. 107, mention occurs of "hot roasted geese" having formerly been given on Michaelmas Day there by the old Mayor, in the morning, at his house, previous to the election of the new one. Queen Elizabeth is said to have been dining on this dish, no doubt in her time perfectly usual as it is with us, when she received tidings of the destruction of the Armada. I append a group of literary notices or allusions. In Gascoigne's Poems is the following passage :

"And when the tenauntes come to paie their quarters rent,
They bring some fowle at Midsummer, a dish of fish in Lent,
At Christmasse a capon, at Michaelmas a goose ;
And somewhat else at New-yeres tide, for feare their lease flie loose."

In "A Health to the Gentlemanly Profession of Serving-men," by J. M., 1598, signat. I 2, is the following passage : "He knoweth where to haue a man . . . . that will stande him in lesse charge. . . . his neighbours sonne, who will not onely maynteine him selfe with all necessaries, but also his father will gratifie his maisters kindnes at Christmas with a New-yeeres gyft, and at other festiuall times

with pigge, goose, capon, or other such like householde prouision." It appears by the context that the father of the serving-man does this to keep his son from going to serve abroad as a soldier. Buttes, in his "Dyets dry Dinner," 1599, says that "a goose is the emblem of meere modestie."

"Geese now in their prime season are,
Which, if well roasted, are good fare :
Yet, however, friends, take heed
How too much on them you feed,
Lest, when as your tongues run loose,
Your discourse do smell of goose."

Poor Robin for 1695. According to the "British Apollo," 1708 :

"The custom came up from the tenants presenting
Their landlords with geese, to incline their relenting
On following payments."

In King's "Art of Cookery," p. 63, we read :

"So stubble geese at Michaelmas are seen
Upon the spit; next May produces green."
"September, when by custom (right divine)
Geese are ordain'd to bleed at Michael's shrine."

—*Churchill*. It is a popular saying, "If you eat goose on Michaelmas Day you will never want money all the year round." The practice of eating goose at Michaelmas does not appear to prevail in any part of France. Upon St. Martin's Day they eat turkeys at Paris. They likewise eat geese upon St. Martin's Day, Twelfth Day, and Shrove Tuesday, there. Green geese form a common summer dish at the Inns of Court and elsewhere. Comp. *Harvest-Home*.

Michael's, St., Cake or **Bannock.**—Martin, speaking of the Protestant inhabitants of Skie, says : "They observe the festivals of Christmas, Easter, Good Friday, and that of St. Michael's. Upon the latter they have a cavalcade in each parish, and several families bake the cake called St. Michael's Bannock." *Western Islands of Scotland*, p. 213. Speaking of Kilbar Village, he observes : "They have likewise a general cavalcade on St. Michael's Day in Kilbar Village, and do then also take a turn round their church. Every family, as soon as the solemnity is ended, is accustomed to bake St. Michael's Cake, and all strangers, together with those of the family, must eat the bread that night." *Ibid.* 100. Macaulay, in his *History of St. Kilda*, p. 82, says : "It was, till of late, an universal custom among the Islanders, on Michaelmas Day, to prepare in every family a loaf or cake of bread, enormously large, and compounded of different ingredients. This cake belonged to the Arch-Angel, and had its name from him. Every one in each family, whether strangers or domestics, had his portion of this kind of shew-bread, and had, of course, some title to the friendship and protection of Michael."

Middle Temple.—See *Lord of Misrule.*

Mid-Lent Sunday.—The fourth Sunday in Lent, says Wheatley "on the Common Prayer," (8vo. Lond. 1741, p. 227) is generally called Mid-Lent, "though Bishop Sparrow, and some others, term it Dominica Refectionis, the Sunday of Refreshment: the reason of which, I suppose, is the gospel for the day, which treats of our Saviour's miraculously feeding five thousand; or else, perhaps from the first lesson in the morning, which gives us the story of Joseph's entertaining his brethren." He is of opinion that "the appointment of these scriptures upon this day might probably give the first rise to a custom still retained in many parts of England, and well known by the name of Mid-lenting or Mothering." I find in Kelham's "Dictionary of the Norman or old French language," Mid-Lent Sunday, Dominica Refectionis, is called "Pasques Charnieulx." In the Household Roll of 18 Edward I., is the following item on Mid-lent Sunday:

"*Pro pisis* j*d.*"

The question is, whether these peas were substitutes for furmenty, or Carlings which are eaten at present in the North of England on the following Sunday, commonly called Passion Sunday, but by the vulgar in those parts Carling Sunday.

Aubanus speaks of a practice in Franconia of eating milk peas and dried pears on this day, but it was, according to him, only partial. It is also called Passion Sunday and Care or Carling Sunday in some old Almanacks.

Midsummer Ale.—In Marmion's "Antiquary," 1641, act 4, is the following passage: "A merry world the while, my boy and I, next Midsommer Ale, I may serve for a fool, and he for Maid Marian."

Midsummer Day. — Hutchinson mentions a custom used on this day; it is, "to dress out stools with a cushion of flowers. A layer of clay is placed on the stool, and therein is stuck with great regularity an arrangement of all kinds of flowers, so close as to form a beautiful cushion. These are exhibited at the doors of houses in the villages, and at the ends of streets and cross-lanes of larger towns," (this custom is very prevalent in the city

of Durham), "where the attendants beg money from passengers, to enable them to have an evening feast and dancing." He adds: "This custom is evidently derived from the Ludi Compitalii of the Romans; this appellation was taken from the Compita or cross lanes, where they were instituted and celebrated by the multitude assembled before the building of Rome. Servius Tullius revived this festival after it had been neglected for many years. It was the Feast of the Lares or Household Gods, who presided as well over houses as streets. This mode of adorning the seat or couch of the Lares was beautiful, and the idea of reposing them on aromatic flowers, and beds of roses, was excellent.—We are not told there was any custom among the Romans of strangers or passengers offering gifts. Our modern usage of all these old customs terminates in seeking to gain money for a merry night."

Midsummer Eve.—Aubrey, who is followed by Grose almost word for word, tells us, "that any person fasting on Midsummer Eve, and sitting in the church porch will, at midnight, see the spirits of the persons of that parish who will die that year, come and knock at the church door, in the order and succession in which they will die. One of these watchers, there being several in company, fell into a sound sleep, so that he could not be waked. Whilst in this state, his ghost or spirit was seen by the rest of his companions knocking at the church door." Grose says: "Any unmarried woman fasting on Midsummer Eve, and at midnight laying a clean cloth, with bread, cheese, and ale, and sitting down as if going to eat, the street door being left open, the person whom she is afterwards to marry will come into the room and drink to her by bowing; and after filling the glass will leave it on the table, and, making another bow, retires. The *Connoisseur,* No. 56, fixes the time for watching in the church porch on Midsummer Eve: "I am sure my own sister Hetty, who died just before Christmas, stood in the church porch last Midsummer Eve. to see all that were to die that year in the parish; and she saw her own apparition." This superstition was more generally practiced, and, I believe, is still retained in many parts, on the Eve of St. Mark.

Midsummer Fires.—Sometimes the ceremony was postponed by reason of the inclement weather; but it seems that at Whalton in Northumberland it has been customary to carry out the observance on July 4. Ths was done in 1903. *Antiquary,* January, 1904. See *St. John's Eve.*

Midsummer Men.—See *Orpine.*

Midsummer Pageants.—Puttenham speaks of "Midsommer Pageants in London, where, to make the people wonder, are set forth great and uglie gyants marching as if they were alive, and armed at all points, but within they are stuffed full of browne paper and tow, which the shrewd boyes, underpeering do guilefully discover and turne to a greate derision." *Arte of English Poesie*, 1589, p. 128. Compare *Gog and Magog.*

Midsummer Watch. — Niccols at p. 97 of his *London's Artillery*, 1616, observes: "King Henrie VIII., approving this marching watch, as an auncient commendable custome of this cittie, lest it should decay thro' neglect or covetousnesse, in the first yeare of his reign, came privately disguised in one of his guards coates into Cheape, on Midsummer Even, and seeing the same at that time performed to his content, to countenance it, and make it more glorious by the presence of his person, came after on St. Peter's Even, with Queen Katherine, attended by a noble traine, riding in royall state to the Kings-heade in Cheape, there to behold the same; and after, anno 15 of his reigne, Christerne, King of Denmark, with his Queene, being then in England, was conducted through the cittie to the King's-heade, in Cheape, there to see the same." We read, in one of the Breviat Chronicles, printed by John Byddell, under the year 1527: "This yere was the sweatinge sicknesse, for the which cause there was no watche at Mydsommer." See also Grafton's "Chronicle," p. 1290, in ann. 1547, when the watch appears to have been kept both on St. John Baptist's Eve and on that of St. Peter. The Midsummer Watch was perhaps organised in connection with the festive or religious observances of the time. The charge on the City grew so heavy, that the usage was gradually discontinued.

Miller.—There is a kind of large white moth, popularly known in Somersetshire as the miller, which the children persecute in expiation of the supposed delinquencies of his namesake. They usually sing the following rhyme over the doomed insect, before they dispatch him:

"Millery! Millery! Dousty-poll! How many sacks hast thou stole?"

—*Notes and Queries*, 1st Series, iii., 133. Compare *Strickler.*

Miller's Eye, putting out the.—This expression is held to apply to the over-wetting of meal for bread or paste. See Hazlitt's *Proverbs*, 1882, p. 444. Miss Baker observes, that the phrase has no reference to the eye of a miller, but probably refers to that part of the machinery of a mill termed the mill-eye. *Northamptonshire Glossary*, 1854, ii., 21. To drown the miller is a well-understood expression at present for weakening unduly any spirituous beverage.

Miller's Golden Thumb.—In Chaucer, the Miller is thus described:

"Well couth he steale corne and told it thrise,
And yet he had a thombe of gold pardè.
A white coate and a blew hode weared he"—&c.

In "A C. Mery Talys," 1526, Number 10, is the story "Of the mylner with the golden thombe." It runs as follows:—"A Merchant that thought to deride a myllner seyd vnto y⁰ myllner syttyng among company. Sir, I haue hard say that euery trew mylner that tollyth trewlye hathe a gyldeyn thombe. The mylner answerd and sayd it was trewth. Then quod the merchaunt: I pray the let me see thy thombe; & when the mylner shewyd hys thomb the merchaunt sayd: I can not perceyue yᵗ thy thombe is gylt: but it is as all other mennys thombis be. To whom the mylner answeryd & seyd: Syr, trewthe yt ys that my thomb is gylt; how be it ye haue no power to se it: for ther is a properte euer incydét therto, he yᵗ ys a cokecold shall neuer haue power to se yt." Ed. 1887, sign. B ii. This passage does not seem to support Tyrwhitt's view at all. In Somersetshire the saying is:—"An honest miller hath a golden thumb: but none but a cuckold can see it." The sense appears to me to be facetious, and as tantamount to saying that there is no such thing as an honest miller. In "The Common Cries of London," an early ballad, by W. Turner, it is said:

"The miller and his golden thumb,
And his dirty neck,
If he grind but two bushels,
He must needs steal a peck."

In "The Vow-Breaker," by William Sampson, 1636, signat. D., Miles, a miller, is introduced saying: "Fellow Bateman farwell, commend me to my old Wind-Mill at Rudington, Oh the Mooter Dish, the Millers thumbe, and the maide behinde the hopper?" The mooter dish is the same as the toll-dish. I suspect "The Miller's Thumb" to have been the name of the Stickle used in measuring corn, the instrument with which corn is made level and struck off in measuring: in Latin called "Radius," which Ainsworth renders "a stricklace or strike, which they use in measuring of corn." Compare *Strickler.* See several sayings about millers in my "Collection of Proverbs," 1882, (index in v.)

Miller's Thumb.—In Ainsworth's Dictionary, "A Miller's Thumb" is rendered "Capito, cephalus fluvialis." Capito is explained, ibid. "Qui magno est capite, unde et piscis ita dictus. 1. A Jolthead; 2, also a kind of cod fish, a pollard." In Cotgrave's "Dictionary," "A Miller's Thumb" is rendered, "Cabot, Teste d'Asne, Musnier."

Mince-pie.—In Sheppard's "Epigrams," 1651, Mince, Minch, or Minced Pies are called Shrid-pies.

Epig. 19.
"*Christmas Day.*

"No matter for plomb-porridge, or Shrid-pies,
Or a whole oxe offered in sacrifice
To Comus, not to Christ," &c.

In Dekker's "Warres, Warres, Warres," 1628, sign. C. 4, these pies are called "Minched Pies." Minced pies are thus mentioned in "The Religion of the Hypocritical Presbyterians in meeter," 1661:

"Three Christmas or minc'd pies, all very fair,
Methought they had this motto, 'Though they slir
And preach us down, *sub pondere crescit virtus.*'"

Jonson in his "Masque of Christmas," printed in his "Works," 1616, has introduced "Minced-Pye" and "Babie-cake," who act their parts in the drama. We have never been witnesses, says Dr. Johnson in his "Life of Butler," of animosities excited by the use of minced pies and plumb-porridge, nor seen with what abhorrence those who could eat them at all other times of the year, would shrink from them in December.

Minning Day.—The first anniversary or year's mind of a death. "Article 7. All the day and night after the buriall they vse to have excessive ringinge for yᵉ dead, as also at the twel-monthes day after, which they call a minninge day. All which time of Ringinge, theire vse is to have theire privat devotions at home for the soule of the dead. But while the partie liethe sicke, they will never require to have the Belle knowled, no, not at the pointe of deathe; whereby the people showld be sturred vp to prayer in due time; neither will any allmost at that time desire to have the minister to come to him for comfort and instruction."—Ab. 1590, 'The Manifolde Enormities of the Ecclesiastical State in the most partes of the Countie of Lancaster,' &c. *Mr. Earwaker's Information printed in Chetham Miscellanies,* vol. v.

Mirrors.—See *Beryl.*

Mistle-child.—Sir Hugh Platt says:—"By sitting vppon a hill late in an evening, neare a wood, in a few nights a firedrake will appeare; marke where it lighteth, and there you shall find an oake with Mistletoe therein, at the roots wherof there is a mistel child, wherof many strange things are conceived. Beati qui non crediderunt. *Flora's Paradise,* 1608, p. 80.

Mistletoe.—This sacred epidendron is described by Virgil in the 6th Æneid :—

"Quale solet silvis brumali frigore Viscum
Fronde virere nova, quod non sua seminat Arbos,
Et croceo fœtu teretes circumdare truncos:
Talis erat species," &c.

Christie observes hereupon: "We find by the allusion of Virgil, who compared the golden bough in Infernis to the mistletoe, that the use of this plant was not unknown in the religious ceremonies of the antients, particularly the Greeks, of whose poets he was the acknowledged imitator." *Inquiry,* 1801, p. 131. A writer in Willis's "Current Notes" for August, 1852, says:—"The Gaelic name for this plant forms a singular link and clue to its real meaning; it is uile-ice, the mistletoe, the all-heal—'lus sior uaine a tharuingeas a bhith o phlannt eile, an ever-green tree that draws its existence from another plant.' It evidently refers us to the Saxon Se Hælend, the Healer, the Saviour of Mankind. The Saxon mis-el-tu is a compound of three Sancrit words, viz. Mas, vishnu (the Messiah): tal, a pit (metaph. the womb): and tu, motion to or from. . . . The ivy and mistletoe being evergreens, denote the everlasting life through faith in the promised Messiah. Kissing under the mistletoe has now lost its import: its primary meaning is obvious. I believe the . . . branch, Ezekiel viii. 17, refers to the mistletoe, the viscum in Virgil's "Æneid," vi. 205: but the Hebrew signifies a branch not torn off, nor broken off, but cut from the tree."

Mr. G. Williams tells us, that "Guidhel, Misletoe, a magical shrub, appears to be the forbiddon tree in the middle of the trees of Eden; for in the Edda, the mistletoe is said to be Balder's death, who yet perished through blindness and a woman." *Gents. Mag.,* Feb. 1791. Selden, in Notes on the 9th Song of the "Polyolbion," tells us "that on this Druidical custome (of going out to cut the mistletoe) some haue grounded that vnto this day vsed in France; where the younger country fellowes, about New-yearstide, in euery village giue the wish of good fortune at the inhabitants dores, with this acclamation, 'Au guy l'an neuf,' (i.e. to the mistletoe this New year) ; which, as I remember, in Rabelais is read all one word, for the same purpose." He cites here "Jo. Goropius Gallic. 5, et alii." "Aguilanleu, par corruption, pour An gui l'an neuf : ad Viscum, Annus novus." —Menage. See also Cotgrave in verbo "Au-guy-l'an neuf." The Celtic name for the oak was gue or guy. Vallancey, in his "Grammar of the Irish Language," observes : "The mistletoe was sacred to the Druids, because not only its berries, but its leaves also, grow in clusters of three united to one stock. The Christian Irish hold the Seamroy, or Shamrock, sacred in like manner, because it has three leaves united to one stalk." Borlase says : "When the end of the year approached, the old Druids marched with great solemnity to gather the mistletoe of the oak, in order to present it to Jupiter, inviting all the world to assist at this ceremony with these words : 'The New year is at hand, gather the Mistletoe.' " He cites Keysler to prove that "the footsteps of this custom still remain in some parts of France." *Antiq. of Cornwall,* 91-2.

Stukeley mentions the introduction of mistletoe into York Cathedral on Christmas Eve as a remain of Druidism. Speaking of the Winter Solstice, our Christmas, he says : "This was the most respectable festival of our Druids, called Yule-tide ; when mistletoe, which they called Allheal, was carried in their hands, and laid on their altars, as an emblem of the salutiferous advent of Messiah. This mistletoe they cut off the trees with their upright hatchets of brass, called Celts, put upon the ends of their staffs, which they carried in their hands. Innumerable are these instruments found all over the British Isles. *Medallic History of Carausius.* ii., 163-4. "The custom is still preserved in the North, and was lately at York : on the Eve of Christmas-Day they carry mistletoe to the high altar of the Cathedral, and proclaim a public and universal liberty, pardon, and freedom to all sorts of inferior and even wicked people at the gates of the city, towards the four quarters of Heaven." But Brand was of opinion, although Gay mentions the mistletoe among those evergreens that were put up in churches, that it never entered those sacred edifices but by mistake, or ignorance of the sextons ; for it was the heathenish and prophane plant, as having been of such distinction in the pagan rites of Druidism, and it therefore had its place assigned it in kitchens, where it was hung up in great state with its white berries, and whatever female chanced to stand under it, the young man present had a right or claimed one of saluting her, and of plucking off a berry at each kiss. I have made many diligent inquiries after the truth of this. I learnt at Bath that it never came into the churches there.

An old sexton at Teddington in Middlesex informed Brand that some mistletoe was once put up in the church there, but was by the clergyman immediately ordered to be taken away. Coles, speaking of mistletoe, says : "It is carryed many miles to set up in houses about Christmas time, when it is adorned with a white glistening berry." Sir John Colbatch, in his dissertation concerning mistletoe, 1720, which he strongly recommends as a medicine very likely to subdue not only the epilepsy, but all other convulsive disorders, observes that this beautiful plant must have been designed by the Almighty "for further and more noble purposes than barely to feed thrushes, or to be hung up superstitiously in houses, to drive away evil spirits." He tells us also, that "the high veneration in which the Druids were anciently held by people of all ranks, proceeded in a great measure from the wonderful cures they wrought by means of the mistletoe of the oak : this tree being sacred to them, but none so that had not the mistletoe upon them." The mistletoe of the oak, which is very rare, was vulgarly said to be a cure for wind-ruptures in children. Colbatch asserts that the kind that is found upon the apple is good for fits. But Sir John endeavours to evince that that of the crab, the lime, the pear, or any other tree, is of equal virtue. In the "Statis. Acc. of Scot." vol. xiii. p. 520, parish of Kiltarlity, Inverness, it is said, "In Lovat's Garden are a great number of standard trees. On two standard apple trees here misletoe grows, which is a very rare plant in this country." For a curious story about the mistletoe, see Willis's Current Notes for May, 1853.

Christie speaks of the respect the Northern nations entertained for the mistletoe, and of the Celts and Goths being distinct in the instance of their equally venerating the mistletoe about the time of the year when the sun approached the winter solstice. *Inquiry,* 1801, 2nd Dissert., p. 129.

Mitcham Fair.—On the 12th of August, 1871, Mitcham pleasure-fair was proclaimed open for three days by gong and kettle-drum.

Mock-beggar's-hall.—The popular bye-name for a large house ill kept up. See Nares, *Glossary,* in v.

Moles.—In the *Husbandman's Prac-*

tice, ed. 1658, p. 153, some of the ideas formerly entertained on this subject are given with much simplicity and freedom, as for example : " If the man shall have a mole on the place right against the heart, doth denote him undoubtedly to be wicked. If a mole shall be seen either on the man's or woman's belly, doth demonstrate that he or she to be a great feeder, glutton. If a mole in either the man or woman shall appear on the place right against the spleen, doth signify that he or she shall be much passionated and oftentimes sick." The following tokens are enumerated by Lupton : " A mole on the feet and hands shews there are others on the testes, and denotes many children. Moles on the arm and shoulder, denote great wisdom ; on the left, debate and contention. Moles near the the armhole riches and honour. A mole on the neck commonly denotes one near the stomach, which denotes strength. A mole on the neck and throat, denotes riches and health. A mole on the chin, another near the heart, signifies riches. A mole on the lip, another on the testes, signifies good stomacks and great talkers. A mole on the right side of the forehead, is a sign of great riches both to men and women ; and on the other side the quite contrary. Moles on the right ear of men or women, denote riches and honour ; and on the left, the quite contrary. A mole between the eye-brow and edge of the eye-lid, there will be another between the navel and the secrets. A red mole on the nose of a man or woman, there will be another on the most secret parts, and sometimes on the ribs, and denotes great lechery. Moles on the ankles or feet, signify modesty in men, and courage in women. A mole or moles on the belly, denote great eaters. A mole on or about the knees, signifies riches and virtue ; if on a woman's left knee, many children. A mole on the left side of the heart, denotes very ill qualities. A mole on the breast, denotes poverty. A mole on the thighs denotes great poverty and infelicity." *Notable Things*, ed. 1660, xii. It must remain an astounding monument of the gross indelicacy of former times that among the sights at Bartholomew Fair in the reign of James II., (and both earlier and later, perhaps), was a girl of fifteen with strange moles on a particular part of her person. James Percy the trunkmaker who, in 1680, claimed the Earldom of Northumberland, tried to throw discredit on his rival William Percy because the latter had not the well known mark of the family, whereas he had it very distinctly (a mole like a half moon.) It is almost superfluous to observe that the Parliament paid no regard

to this divine signature, as James called it, for he did not succeed to the Earldom of Northumberland. *Claim*, 1680, sign. D. The following additional information on this belief, which, absurd as it is, is so far worth commemorating and illustrating that it is fast passing away, is from a chap-book called " The Greenwich Fortune-Teller " :

" A mole against the heart undoubtedly denotes wickedness. A mole on the belly signifies a glutton. A mole on the bottom of the belly signifies weakness. A mole on the knee signifies obtaining a comely, wealthy wife. If a woman have a mole on her right knee, she will be honest and virtuous ; if on the left, she will have many children. If a man hath a mole athwart his nose he will be a traveller. A mole on a woman's nose, signifies she will travel on foot through divers countries. A mole on a man's throat shows that he will become rich. If a woman have a mole on the lower jaw, it signifies she shall lead her life in sorrow and pain of body. A mole in the midst of the forehead, near the hair, denotes a discourteous, cruel mind, and of unpleasant discourse ; if it is of honey colour, will be beloved ; if red, sullen and furious ; if black, inexpert and wavering, if raised more like a wart, very fortunate ! But if a woman, shows her to be a slut ; and if in her forehead black, treacherous, consents to evil and murder. A mole on the right side, about the middle of the forehead, declares a man to abound in benefits by friendship of great men ; will be loaded with command, esteemed and honoured ; the paler the colour the greater the honour ; if red, he is loved by the clergy ; if black, let him beware of the resentment of great men ; if warty, it increaseth good fortune. A woman having this shall be fortunate in all her actions ; but if black, beware of her tongue. A mole on the left side of the forehead, near the hair, predicts misery and abundance of tribulations to a man, by means of his own misconduct ; if honey-coloured or red, his sorrows are lessened ; but if black, unfortunate in every undertaking. A mole on the left side of the forehead, about midway, threatens a man with persecutions from his superiors ; if of a honey colour, he prodigally wastes his estate ; if red, will become poor ; if black, let him beware of the wrath or malice of great men ; if a woman, it threatens sorrow by the perfidy of some men ! if black, let him beware of the wrath or of misery. A mole on the left side of the forehead, a litle above the temple, if it appear red, he has excellent wit and understanding ; if black, in danger of being branded for his falsehoods ; if he has a wart, his fate is mitigated. To a woman it shows justification of innocence, though not deserved; if black, malignity, and it represents every evil. A mole on any part of the lip, signifies a great eater or a glutton, much beloved and very amorous. A mole on the chin signifies riches. A mole on the ear signifies riches and respect. A mole on the neck promises riches. A mole on the right breast threatens poverty. A mole near the bottom of the nostrils is lucky. A mole on the left side of the belly denotes affliction. A mole on the right foot denotes wisdom. A mole on the left foot denotes dangerous rash actions. A mole on the eyebrow means speedy marriage and a good husband. A mole on the wrist, or between that and the fingers' ends, shows an ingenious mind. If many moles happen between the elbow and the wrist, they foretell many crosses towards the middle of life, which will end in prosperity and comfort. A mole near the side of the chin shows an amiable disposition, industrious, and successful in all your transactions."

Monacella, St. (January 31).—St. Monacella is not even mentioned by Hone, Brand, Nicolas, and Chambers. She is the Welsh Melange, however, whose day was January 31. "The Legend of St. Monacella," says a correspondent of "Current Notes" for March, 1857, "relates that she was the daughter of an Irish monarch, who had determined to marry her to a nobleman of his court. She had, however, vowed celibacy, fled from her father's dominions, and took refuge in Wales, where she lived fifteen years without seeing the face of a man. At length, Brochwel Yscythrog, Prince of Powis, one day hare-hunting, pursued his game till he came to a great thicket, where he was amazed to find a virgin of surprising beauty, engaged in deep devotion, with (under her robe) the hare he had been pursuing, boldly facing the dogs, who retired howling to a distance, notwithstanding all the efforts of the prince's followers to make them seize their prey. Even when the huntsman attempted to blow his horn, it stuck to his lips. The prince heard her story, and gave to God and her a parcel of land, to be a sanctuary to all that fled there. . . ." St. Monacella died lady superior of the abbey she founded in consequence, at an advanced age, and was buried in the adjoining church, called from her Pennant-Melangell. Pennant the historian records a visit paid by him to this spot in 1784. *Tours in Wales*, 1810, iii., 173-4.

Monday, Saint.—This does not belong to the calendar, but is merely introduced here to notice, that it is so jocularly christened by those mechanics and others, who make Monday a *dies non* in a working sense, not to say Tuesday. In fact, if we reckon in the new Saturday half-holiday (which is, however, rather, a revival slightly altered) certain classes of our operatives only keep strictly to their work from Tuesday to Saturday at noon. In some parts of Yorkshire, any day devoted to idleness is called Cobbler's Monday, from the fact that members of that vocation seldom ply their trade till the Tuesday; this is not confined to Yorkshire, but is general, and applies to a few other crafts. Benjamin Franklin, in his autobiography, expressly states that he gained the good will of his master in early days by never making a Saint Monday. C. Knight's *Shadows of the Old Booksellers*, 1865, p. 87.

Monitor Lizard.—This inhabitant of the Nile district and of the Transvaal is popularly supposed to utter a sort of warning in the shape of a hissing sound at the approach of a crocodile. See one, recently added to the Regent's Park collection, delineated in the *Daily Graphic*, March 16, 1897.

Monks.—Gaule says: "Meeting of monks is commonly accounted as an ill omen, and so much the rather if it be early in the morning: because these kind of men live for the most part by the suddain death of men; as vultures do by slaughters."

Month's Mind, The.—Bede speaks of this as *Commemorationis Dies*—Minding Days. It was also an anniversary observance. "Minnyng Days," says Blount, "from the Saxon Lemynde, days which our ancestors called their Monthes mind, their Years Mind, and the like, being the days whereon their souls, (after their deaths), were had in special remembrance, and some office or obsequies said for them: as Obits, Dirges, &c. This word is still retained in Lancashire; but elsewhere they are more commonly called anniversary days. The common expression of 'having a Month's Mind,' implying a longing desire, is probably derived hence." The following is in Peck: "By saying they have a month's mind to it, they antiently must undoubtedly mean, that, if they had what they so much longed for, it would (hyperbolically speaking) do them as much good (they thought) as they believed a month's mind, or service said once a month, (could they afford to have it), would benefit their souls after their decease." *Desiderata Curiosa*, i., 230. But this expression, which was originally special and strict, being applied to the masses or other funeral services performed in remembrance of the departed, acquired the general meaning of a commemoration, as in the case of Robert Tofte's "Alba, or the Month's Mind of a Melancholy Lover," 1598.

We read in " Fabian's Chronicle " that "in 1439 died Sir Roberde Chicheley, Grocer, twice Mayor of London, the which wylled in his Testament that upon his Mynde Day a good and competent dyner should be ordayned to xxiiii. C. pore men, and that of housholders of the Citee, yf they myght be founde. And over that was xx pounde distributed among them, which was to every man two pence." Fabyan the historian himself also, in his will, gives directions for his month's mind: " At whiche tyme of burying, and also the Monethis Mynde, I will that myne Executrice doo cause to be carried from London .xii. newe torches, there beyng redy made, to burn in the tymes of the said burying and Monethes Mind: and also that they do purvay for .iiii. tapers of .iii. lb evry pece, to brenne about the corps and herse for the foresaid .ii. seasons, whiche torches and tapers to be bestowed as hereafter shalbe devised; which .iiij. tapers I will be holden at every tyme by foure poore men, to the whiche I will that to everyone of theym be geven fro their labours at either of the saide .ij. tymes. iiijd. to as many as been weddid men: and if any of them happen to be unmarried, than they to have but .iij.d. a pece, and in lyke maner I will that the torche berers be orderid." In another part of his will he says : " Also I will, that if I decesse at my tenemente of Halstedis, that myn executrice doo purvay ayenst my burying competent brede, ale, and chese, for all comers to the parishe Churche, and a-yenst the Moneths Mynde I will be or-deyned, at the said Churche, competent brede, ale, pieces of beffe and moton, and rost rybbys of beffe, as shallbe thought nedeful by the discrecion of myn Execut-trice, for all comers to the said obsequy, over and above brede, ale, and chese, for the comers unto the dirige over night. And furthermore I will that my said Execut-trice do purvay ayenst the said Moneths Mynde .xxiiij. peces of beffe and moton, and .xxiiij. treen platers and .xxiiij. treen sponys; the whiche peces of fleshe with the said platers and sponys, wᵗ. .xxiiij.d. of siluer, I will be geven unto .xxiiij. poore persones of the said parishe of Theydon Garnon, if wᵗⁱn that parishe so many may be founde : for lake whereof, I will the .xxiiij. peces of flesh and .ij.s. in money, wᵗ the foresaid platers and sponys be geven unto suche poore persones as may be found in the parisshes of Theydon at Mount, and Theydon Boys, after the dis-crecion of myn Executors ; and if my said Moneths Mynde fall in Lent, or upon a fysshe day, than I will that the said .xxiiij. peces of fleshe be altered unto saltfyshe or stokfyshe, unwatered, and unsodeyn, and

that every piece of beef or moton, salt-fyshe or stokfyshe, be well in value of a peny or a peny at the leest ; and that noo dyner be purveyed for at hom but for my household and kynnysfolke: and I will that my knyll be rongyn at my Moneths Mynde after the guyse of London. Also I will that myn Executrice doo assemble upon the said day of Moneths Mynde .xii. of the porest menys childern of the fore-said parishe, and after the masse is ended and other obseruances, the said childern to be ordered about my grave, and there knelyng, to say for my soule and all Cris-ten soules, 'De profundis,' as many of them as can, and the residue to say a Pater noster, and an Ave oonly ; to the which .xij. childern I will be geven .xiiij.d. that is to meane, to that childe that beginneth ' De profundis ' and saith the preces, ij.d. and to eueryche of the other j.d." Chronicle, new edit. Preface, 45.

In the " Churchwardens' Accounts of St. Mary at Hill, London, 17 & 19 Edw. IV.," are the following articles : " Pd. to Sir I. Philips for keepyng the Morrow Mass at 6 o'clock upon feryall days, each quarter v.s."

" To the Par. Priest to remember in the pulpit the soul of R. Bliet, who gave vjs. viijd. to the Church works, ij.d."

In the " Accounts of St. Margaret, Westminster," we read : " Item, at the Monyth Mynde of Lady Elizabeth Coun-tess of Oxford, for four tapers, viijd." Under the year 1531, is, " Item, for mette for the theff that stalle the Pyx. iiijd." And in 1532 : " Item, received for iiii. Torches of the black Guard. viijd." On these occasions the word " Mind " signi-fied Remembrance: and the expression a " Month's Mind," a " Year's Mind," &c. meant that on that day, month, or year after the party's decease, some solemn ser-vice for the good of his soul should be celebrated. Some of these month's minds appear to have been conducted with great solemnity and at a very considerable cost. Anne Barneys, in a letter to Cromwell. Lord Privy Seal, about 1536, speaks of one where there were as many as a hun-dred priests in attendance. The earliest printed discourse of this character is that delivered by Bishop Fisher on Margaret, Countess of Richmond and Derby in 1509, which came from the press of Wynkyn de Worde in the same year.

Moon, The.—The moon, the ancient object of idolatrous worship, has in late times composed an article in the creed of popular superstition. The ancient Druids had their superstitious rites at the changes of the moon. Even down to quite recent times the nature and influ-ence of this planet and its rank in the cosmic system were very imperfectly known, even to scientific persons of all countries.

"The superstitions of our own countrymen," remarks Jamieson, "and of the Swedes on this head, equally confirm the account given by Cæsar concerning the ancient Germans, the forefathers of both. 'As it was the custom with them,' he says, 'that their matrons, by the use of lots and prophecies, should declare, whether they should join in battle or not, they said that the Germans could not be victorious, if they should engage before the full moon.' *Commen.* lib. i., c. 50. They reckoned new or full moon the most auspicious season for entering on any business. The Swedes do not carry this farther than they did." "Coeunt," says Tacitus, "certis diebus, quum, aut inchoatur Luna, aut impletur. Nam agendis rebus hoc auspicatissimum initium credunt."

Northbrooke, in his "Treatise against Dicing," 1577, makes St. Augustine observe: "It is better that women should picke woole or spinne vpon the Sabbaoth day, than that they should daunce impudently and filthily all the day long vpon the dayes of the new moone." Which seems to point to certain orgies of the early Christians on these occasions.

In the ballad of Sir Patrick Spens is the following stanza:

"I saw the new moon, late yestreen,
  Wi' the auld moon in her arm;
And if we gang to sea, master,
  I fear we'll come to harm."

Jamieson says that in Scotland, it is considered as an almost infallible presage of bad weather, if the moon lies fair on her back, or when the horns are pointed towards the Zenith. It is a similar prognostic, when the new moon appears with the old moon in her arms, or in other words, when that part of the moon which is covered with the shadow of the earth is seen through it. A Brugh, or hazy circle round the moon, is accounted a certain prognostic of rain. If the circle be wide, and at some distance from the body of that luminary, it is believed that the rain will be delayed for some time; if it be close, and as it were adhering to the disk of the moon, rain is expected very soon. *Dict.* v. Moon. Bailey tells us that the common people, in some counties of England, are accustomed at the prime of the moon, to say: "It is a fine moon, God bless her"; which some imagine to proceed from a blind zeal, retained from the ancient Irish who worshipped the moon, or from a custom in Scotland, (particularly in the Highlands), where the women make a curtesy to the new moon: and some English women still retain a touch of this gentil-

ism, who getting up upon, and sitting astride on a gate or stile, the first night of the new moon, say:

"All hail to the Moon, all hail to thee,
I prithee, good Moon, declare to me,
This night, who my husband shall be."

Aubrey gives it thus: "At the first appearance of the new moon after New Year's Day (some say any other new moon is as good), go out in the evening and stand over the spars of a gate or stile, looking on the moon, and say:

"All hail to the moon, all hail to thee,
I prithee, good moon, reveal to me
This night, who my husband (wife)
  must be."

You must presently after go to bed. I knew two gentlewomen that did this when they were young maids, and they had dreams of those that married them. In Yorkshire they kneel on a ground-fast stone." "Miscellanies," ed. 1857 p. 132-3.

Jamieson has quoted these words as used in Scotland, in a different form, from the Rev. J. Nichol's "Poems," vol. i. p. 31, 32, and cited the following note by the author: "As soon as you see the first new moon of the new year, go to a place where you can set your feet upon a stone naturally fixed in the earth, and lean your back against a tree; and in that posture hail or address the moon in the words of the poem. If ever you are to be married, you will then see an apparition, exactly resembling the future partner of your joys and sorrows." In one of his less known works Defoe has a chapter on omens, in which he says: "To see a new moon the first time after her change, on the right hand, or directly before you, betokens the utmost good fortune that month, as to have her on your left, or behind you, so that in turning your head back you happen to see her, foreshows the worst: as also, they say, to be without gold in your pocket at that time, is of very bad consequence." *Memoirs of Duncan Campbel*, 1732, p. 62. Turning a piece of money, and wishing, on the first sight of the new moon, is still a common practice and article of belief; but the planet must not be seen through glass.

Sir E. Sherburne, in his Notes to the *Medea of Seneca*, 1648, p. 105, says: "Of the beating of kettles, basons, and other brazen vessells used by the antients when the moon was eclipsed (which they did to drown the charmes of witches, that the moon might not heare them, and so be drawne from her sphaere as they supposed), I shall not need to speake, being a thing so generally knowne, a custom continued among the Turks at this day: yet I cannot but adde, and wonder at, what Joseph Scaliger, in his Annotations upon

Manilius, reports out of Bonincontrius, an antient commentator upon the same poet: who affirmes that in a towne of Italy where he lived, (within these two centuries of yeares), he saw the same peece of Paganisme acted upon the like occasion. But the Romans followed an exactly similar practice at the lunar eclipses and one of our own earlier writers, who was, however, a mere compiler, states that they were accustomed also to throw firebrands into the air, and carry about lighted torches, with a view to restore the moon's lustre. This author informs us, that the Spartans conferred on their Ephori the power of deposing the king, if when, according to custom, they had invited him to behold the stars on some bright (but moonless) night, and a star was seen to shoot, because, says the writer quite gravely, this shewed that the king had offended the gods. "So did Lysander," says he, "depose King Leonidas." Lloyd's *Stratagems of Jerusalem*, 1602, pp. 286-7.

At Melbourne, in Australia, if not elsewhere, it is a belief that fish caught in the full of the moon, and afterwards left exposed to its rays, becomes poisonous. But perhaps this phenomenon is really referable to climate and atmosphere. Some early (eleventh century) sun and moon weather portents are given in *Reliquiæ Antiquæ*, 1841, p. 15. Braithwaite, speaking of a Xantippean, says: "A burre about the mone is not half so certaine a presage of a tempest, as her brow is of a storme." *Whimzies*, 1631, 173. The hornedness of the new moon is still faintly considered by the vulgar as an omen with regard to the weather. They say on that occasion, the new moon looks sharp. In Dekker's "Match me in London," act i., the king says: "My Lord, doe you see this change i' th' moone, sharp hornes doe threaten windy weather." The ancients also chiefly regarded the age of the moon in felling their timber: their rule was to fell in the wane, or four days after the new moon, or sometimes in the last quarter. Pliny advises it to be in the very moment of the change, which happening to be in the last day of the winter solstice, the timber, he says, will be incorruptible. Melton tells us that, "St. Augustine in his 'Enchiridion' sayth, that it is a great offence for any man to observe the time and course of the moone, when they plant any trees or sowe any corne; for he sayth, none puts any trust in them but they that worship them: believing there is some divine power in them, according to those things they believe concerning the nativities of men." *Astrologaster*, 1620, p. 56. In "Tusser's Husbandry," under February, are the following lines:

"Sowe peason and beans in the wane of the moone,
Who soweth them sooner, he soweth too soone:
That they, with the planet, may rest and rise,
And flourish with bearing, most plentiful wise."

On which is the following note in "Tusser Redivivus," 1744, p. 16: "Peas and beans, sown during the increase, do run more to hawn and straw, and during the declension more to cod, according to the common consent of countrymen. And I must own I have experienced it, but I will not aver it so that it is not liable to exceptions."

An early authority also recommends us to "Kill swine in or neer the full of the moon, and the flesh will the better prove in boiling." And, again: "Kill fat swine for bacon (the better to keep their fat in boiling) about the full moon." Also, "Shear sheep at the moon's increase: fell hand timber from the full to the change. Fell frith, copice, and fuel at the first quarter. Lib or geld cattle, the moon in Aries, Sagittarius, or in Capricorn." *Husbandman's Practice*, 1664, 108. Stevenson tells us that "horses and mares must be put together in the increase of the moone, for foales got in the wane are not accounted strong and healthfull." *Twelve Moneths*, 1661, 19. Our ancestors seem to have been of opinion that fruit should be gathered, and cattle gelded, in the wane of the moon, "because in that season bodies have lesse humour and heat, by which an innated putrefaction is wont to make them faulty and unsound." *Curiosities, or, The Cabinet of Nature*, 1637, 231.

This planet, as Dr. Johnson tells us, has great influence in vulgar philosophy. In his memory, he observes, it was the precept annually given in one of the English almanacks, to kill hogs when the moon was increasing, and the bacon would prove the better in boiling. It is said, that, "to the influence of the moon is owing the increase and decrease of the marrow and brain in animals; that she frets away stones, governs the cold and heat, the rain and wind. Did we make observations, we should find that the temperature of the air hath so little sympathy with the new or full moon, that we may count as many months of dry as wet weather, when the return of the moon was wet, and contrariwise; so true is it, that the changes of the weather are subject to no rule obvious to us. 'Twere easy to shew, that the reason of the thing is directly against the popular opinion." Bayley's *Dict.* quoted in *Gents. Mag.*, September, 1734. A work already quoted tells us that it used to be thought "Good to purge with electuaries, the moon in Cancer. With pills, the moon in Pisces. With potions, the moon in Virgo. Good to take vomits, the moon being in Taurus, Virgo, or the latter part of Sagittarius. To purge the head by sneezing, the moon being in Cancer, Leo, or Virgo. To stop Fluxes and Rheumes, the moone being in Taurus, Virgo, or Capricorne. To bathe when the moone is in Cancer, Libra, Aquarius, or Pisces. To cut the hair off the head or beard, when the moon is in Libra, Sagittarius, Aquarius, or Pisces. Briefe observations of husbandry. Set, sow seeds, graft, and plant, the moone being in Taurus, Virgo, or in Capricorn. And all kind of corne in Cancer. Graft in March at the moone's increase, she being in Taurus or Capricorne." *Husbandman's Practice*, 1664, p. 116.

Werenfels, in his "Dissertation upon Superstition," speaking of a superstitious man, says: "He will not commit his seed to the earth when the soil, but when the moon requires it. He will have his hair cut when the moon is either in Leo, that his locks may stare like the lion's shag; or in Aries, that they may curl like a Ram's horn. Whatever he would have to grow, he sets about it when she is in her increase; but for what he would have made less, he chuses her wane. When the moon is in Taurus he never can be persuaded to take physick, lest that animal, which chews its cud, should make him cast it up again. If at any time he has a mind to be admitted into the presence of a prince, he will wait till the moon is in conjunction with the sun; for 'tis then the society of an inferior with a superior is salutary and successfull." *Engl. Transl.*, 1748, p. 6. Lord Northampton, in his "Defensative," 1583, observes: "They forbidde us, when the mone is in a fixed signe, to put on a newe garment; why so? because it is lyke that it wyll be too longe in wearing, a small faulte about this towne, where garments seldome last till they be payd for. But theyr meaning is, that the garment shall continue long, in respect of any strength or goodnes in the stuffe; but by the duraunce or disease of him, that hath neyther leysure nor liberty to weare it."

In a copy of the second edition of Holinshed, 1586, a contemporary owner, Thomas Hayward, has noted on a flyleaf: "At night y⁰ moone being at y⁰ full and about som 3 ours high did ascend up right into y⁰ heavens wᵗʰ a very swift course till yᵗ came to y⁰ hight of 6 hours high, & there stoode. The first beholder heereof was Mr. Robert Tailor of Hull Alderman, who seeing the same in his garden, and fearing to be deceaved went and tooke y⁰ moone by y⁰ topp of an house, by wᶜʰ he more perfectly perceaved the swiftnes thereof. . . . Y⁰ new yers day I came to Hull in y⁰ morning, and he tould me of yᵗ." Shakespear tells us in *Richard II.*, ii., 4:

"——— Meteors fright the fixed stars of Heaven :
The pale-fac'd moon looks bloody on the earth,
And lean-look'd prophets whisper fearful change :
These signs forerun the death or fall of kings."

Lodge notices a curious lunar superstition : "When the moone appeareth in the Spring time, the one horne spotted, and hidden with a blacke and great cloud, from the first day of his apparition to the fourth day after, it is some signe of tempests and troubles in the aire the Sommer after." *Wits Miserie*, 1596, p. 44. In "The Freiris of Berwik," attributed to Dunbar, is the following passage, seeming to shew that to swear by the moon, was one of the old forms of adjuration :

"Quhen Symone saw it appinuit on this wyis,
He had grit wondir ; and sweris be the mone,
That Freir Robert weill his dett had done."

Dunbar's *Works*, 1834, ii., 16. In "The Witch of Edmonton," 1658, p. 14, young Banks observes: "When the moon's in the full, then wit's in the wane." The notion that the moon is made of green cheese is noticed in the very early play of *Jack Juggler*. Butler touches on the subject of lunar superstitions; speaking of his Conjuror, he tells us :

"But with the moon was more familiar
Than e'er was Almanack well willer ;
Her secrets understood so clear,
That some believ'd he had been there ;
Knew when she was in fittest mood,
For cutting corns, or letting blood ;
When for anointing scabs or itches,
Or to the bum applying leeches ;
When sows and bitches may be spav'd,
And in what sign best sider's made ;
Whether the wane be, or increase,
Best to set garlick or sow pease :
Who first found out the Man i' th' moon,
That to the ancients was unknown.

*   *   *   *   *

He made an instrument to know
If the moon shine at full or no :
That wou'd as soon as e'er she shone, straight
Whether 'twere day or night, demonstrate :
Tell what her d'metre t'an inch is,

And prove that she is not made of
    green-cheese.
It would demonstrate that the man in
    The moon's a Sea Mediterranean;
And that it is no dog nor bitch,
That stands behind him at his breech;
But a huge Caspian Sea, or lake
With arms, which men for legs mistake;
How large a gulf his tail composes,
And what a goodly bay his nose is;
How many German leagues by th' scale
Cape-Snout's from Promontory Tail."

Hudibras, ed. 1694, pp. 338-9. To an inquiry in the "British Apollo," 1710, No.
x :—

"Pray tell your Querist if he may
Rely on what the vulgar say,
That when the moon's in her increase,
If corns be cut they'll grow apace;
But if you always do take care,
After the full your corns to pare,
They do insensibly decay,
And will in time wear quite away,
If this be true, pray let me know,
And give the reason why 'tis so.'"

It is answered:

"The moon no more regards your corns,
Than cits do one another's horns:
Diversions better Phœbe knows,
Than to consider your gall'd toes."

It appears that among the common
people in Scotland in the 18th century, "the moon in the increase, full
growth, and in her wane, were
the emblems of a rising, flourishing,
and declining fortune." "At the
last period of her revolution," the narrative quoted proceeds to state, "they
carefully avoid to engage in any business
of importance; but the first and middle
they seize with avidity, presaging the
most auspicious issue to their undertakings. Poor Martinus Scriblerus never
more anxiously watched the blowing of the
west wind to secure an heir to his genius,
than the love-sick swain and his nymph
for the coming of the new moon to be
noosed together in matrimony. Should
the planet happen to be at the height of
her splendour when the ceremony is performed, their future life will be a scene
of festivity, and all its paths strewed over
with rose-buds of delight. But when her
tapering horns are turned towards the
north, passion becomes frost-bound, and
seldom thaws till the genial season again
approaches. From the moon they not only
draw prognostications of the weather,
but according to their creed also discover
future events. There they are dimly pour-
trayed, and ingenious allusion never fails
in explanation. The veneration paid to this
planet, and the opinion of its influences,
are obvious from the meaning still affixed
to some words of the Gaelic language. In

Druidic mythology, when the circle of the
moon was complete, Fortune then promised to be the most propitious. Agreeably to this idea, rath, which signifies in
Gaelic a wheel or circle, is transferred to
signify fortune. They say 'ata rath air,'
he is fortunate. The wane, when the
circle is diminishing, and consequently
unlucky, they call mi-rath. Of one that
is unfortunate, they say, 'at a mi-rath
air.'" *Stat. Acc.*, i., 47. From the
same source we learn that "A cave in the
neighbourhood of Dunskey ought also to
be mentioned, on account of the great
veneration in which it is held (1791) by
the people. At the change of the moon
(which is still considered with superstitious reverence), it is usual to bring,
even from a great distance, infirm
persons, and particularly ricketty children, whom they often supposed bewitched, to bathe in a stream that pours
from the hill, and then dry them in a
cave." vii., 560. Shaw informs us that
at the full moon in March the inhabitants cut withes of the mistletoe or
ivy, make circles of them, keep them all
the year, and pretend to cure hectics and
other troubles by them. Johnson, in his
"Journey to the Hebrides," tells us, they
expect better crops of grain, by sowing
their seed in the moon's increase. *Account of Elgin and Moray*, appended to
Pennants *Tour in Scotland*. Martin,
speaking of Skie, says: "The natives are
very much dispos'd to observe the influence of the moon on human bodies, and
for that cause they never dig their peats
but in the decrease; for they observe that
if they are cut in the increase; they continue still moist and never burn clear, nor
are they without smoak, but the contrary
is daily observed of peats cut in the decrease. They make up their earthern
dykes in the decrease only, for such as are
made at the increase are still observed to
fall." *W. I. of Scotl.*, p. 174.

On the continent, there is the
testimony of Kirchmaier (or Naogeorgus) to shew that ideas, similar to
those cherished in Great Britain and
Ireland, were entertained on this
subject. They consulted the moon,
before they bled, cut their hair, pared
their nails, put their children to nurse,
took physic, or manured their fields.
Popish Kingdom, by Googe, 1570., p. 44.

Mungo Park, in his "Travels in Africa,"
speaking of the Mandingoe tribe of Indians, says: "On the first appearance of
a new moon, they view it as newly created,
and say a short prayer: this seems to be
the only visible adoration those negroes,
who are not Mahometans, offer to the
Deity. This prayer is pronounced in a
whisper, the person holding up his hands
before his face; at the conclusion they spit

upon their hands and rub them over their faces. They think it very unlucky to begin a journey, or any other work of consequence, in the last quarter of the moon. An eclipse, whether of sun or moon, is supposed to be effected by witch-craft. The stars are very little regarded; and the whole study of astronomy they view as dealing in magic. If they are asked for what reason they pray to the new moon, they answer, because their fathers did so before them." He tells us, in another place, "When the Mahometan Feast of Rhamadan was ended, the priests assembled to watch for the appearance of the new moon, but the evening being cloudy, they were for some time disappointed; on a sudden, this delightful object shewed her sharp horns from behind a cloud, and was welcomed with the clapping of hands, beating of drums, firing of muskets, and other marks of rejoicing."

Moon-Calf.—Among the preposterous inventions of fancy in ancient superstition occurs "The Moon-Calf": an inanimate shapeless mass, supposed by Pliny to be engendered of woman only. *Nat. Hist.*, x., 64. Drayton has devoted a poem to the subject, inserted among his miscellaneous pieces, 1627.

Moon-Wort.—Coles tells us: "It is said, yea and believed by many, that moon-wort will open the locks wherewith dwelling-houses are made fast, if it be put into the key-hole; as also that it will loosen the locks, fetters, and shoes from those horses' feet that goe on the places where it groweth; and of this opinion was Master Culpeper, who, though he railed against superstition in others, yet had enough of it himselfe, as may appear by his story of the Earl of Essex his horses, which being drawn up in a body, many of them lost their shoos upon White Downe in Devonshire, neer Tiverton, because moonwort grows upon heaths." *Introd. to the Knowledge of Plants*, 1656, p. 71. Turner was confident, that tho' moonwort "be the moons herb, yet it is neither smith, farrier, nor picklock." *British Physician*, 1687, p. 209. Wither alludes to the supposed virtues of the moonwort:

' There is a herb, some say, whose ver-
tue's such
It in the pasture, only with a touch,
Unshooes the new-shod steed."
—*Abuses Stript and Whipt*, 1613.

Mop.—Plot, speaking of the Statutes for hiring servants, says "in his "History of Oxfordshire," that at Banbury they called them the Mop. He says that at Bloxham the carters stood with their whips in one place, and the shepherds with their crooks in another; but the maids, as far as he could observe, stood promiscu-

ously. He adds that this custom seems as old as our Saviour, and refers to Matth. xx. 3. Eden tells us in a note : "In Gloucestershire, Oxfordshire, Wiltshire, and Berkshire, servants continue to attend the Mopp or Statute, as it is called (i.e., Michaelmas Fair) in order to be hired for a year. Each person has a badge, or external mark, expressive of his occupation. A carter exhibits a piece of whip-cord tied to his hat: a cow-herd has a lock of cow-hair in his: and the dairy-maid has the same descriptive mark attached to her breast. So in the North of England, at the Spring hiring-term, the servants to be hired, who are almost always persons to be employed in husbandry, are to be distinguished from others, who attend the market, by their wearing a large posie or bouquet of flowers at their breasts; which is no unapt emblem of their calling. Even in London, brick-layers and other house-labourers carry their respective implements to the places where they stand for hire: for which purpose they assemble in great numbers in Cheapside and at Charing-Cross, every morning, at five or six o'clock. So, in old Rome there were particular spots in which servants applied for hire. 'In Tusco vico, ibi sunt Homines qui ipsi se venditent.' Plauti *Curculio*, act iv." *State of the Poor*, 1797, i., 32.

The Michaelmas Hiring Fair took place at High Wycombe in 1903. The market-place was, as usual, the rendezvous of the farm-servants. The shepherds were distinguished, as a rule, by the tufts of wool they wear in their caps, the cowmen by a decoration of hair, and the ploughmen by their knotted whip cord. As soon as a bargain is struck the hired men and maidens display knots of bright coloured ribbons, and the rest of the day is spent among the swings and roundabouts. The present year's experience betrayed a decline in the interest shown and in the attendance. *Daily Mail*, Sept. 28-9, 1903.

More Sacks to the Mill.—This is called "an infant play" in *Love's Labour Lost*, written before 1598,, iv. 3. A writer in the *Gentleman's Magazine* for February, 1773, brackets it with *Hot Cockles*, with which it assuredly has nothing in common. My friend Mr. A. G. Greenhill, of Emmanuel, Cambridge, writes to me: "At Christ's Hospital in my time a game was played, called *Bring the Basket*. Sides having been chosen, one side went in and formed a line of backs, whereupon the other side had to leap, while a formula was repeated. If successful the second side went in again; but if not, it became their turn to form a line of backs. Sometimes, of course, the backs broke down, with the other boys on the top, all in confusion, on which the cry was raised : ' Sacks on the mill.' The game was discouraged by the masters, because it was necessarily injurious to the boys' clothes." There used to be a somewhat similar diversion, known as Hicocolorum, in which the line of backs was formed by the first boy placing himself against a fence or wall, the second leaning upon his chest, and the third placing his head between the second one's legs, and so on, till a line was made, which it was the aim of the opposing side to break. The formula here was Hicocolorum ! Jig, jig, jig !

Morris Dance. — The Morris Dance, in which bells are gingled, or staves or swords clashed, was learned, says Dr. Johnson, by the Moors, and was probably a kind of Pyrrhick or military dance. "Morisco," says Blount, "(Span.) a Moor; also a dance, so called, wherein there were usually five men, and a boy dressed in a girl's habit, whom they called the Maid Marian, or perhaps, Morian, from the Italian Morione, a head-piece, because her head was wont to be gaily trimmed up. Common people call it a Morris Dance." See the last edit. of Nares' "Glossary," and Halliwell's 'Archaic Dictionary," ad vocem. The derivation of Morris from Morisco quasi Moor is very doubtful, but no better etymology has yet been proposed.

In the Privy Purse Expenses of Henry VII., under 1494, is an entry under January 2, "For playing of the Mourice daunce, £2"; and under February 4, 1502, occurs a second payment for a similar purpose of £1 13s. 4d., which appears to be significant of its performance irrespectively of the season. But of course these exhibitions were before the King. In the third volume of the Shakespear Society's Papers, are some very interesting extracts from the papers of Richard Gibson, supposed to have been yeoman tailor to Henry VIII., relating to dramatic and other entertainments at Court in the very commencement of that prince's reign. Under the date of 1510-11, Gibson gives an account of a "Morryshe Dance," by the King's henchmen, who came out of an artificial hill, on the top of which was "a goldyn stoke, branchyd with roses and pomgarnats crowned." This was devised by Sir Henry Guildford. In Coates's "History of Reading," we have : —

"A.D. 1557, Item. payd to the mynstrels and the hobby horse uppon May Day, 3s.— Item. payed to the Morrys Daunsers and the Mynstrelles, mete and drink at Whitsontide, 3s. 4d.—Payed to them the Sonday after May Day, 20d.—Pᵈ to the Painter for painting of their cotes, 2s. 8d.—

Pᵈ to the Painter for 2 dz. of Lyvereyes, 20d." In the Churchwardens' and Chamberlain's books of Kingston-on-Thames are several particulars illustrative of this part of the subject. They are printed entire in Lysons' " Environs," vol. i. p. 226. The bells for the dancers are also charged in the accounts of St. Mary-at-Hill, London, (34 Eliz.) and St. Helen's in Abingdon, Berks. Morrice-dancing, with bells on the legs, continued to be common in and after Brand's time, in Oxfordshire and the adjacent counties, on May Day, Holy Thursday, and Whitsun Ales, attended by the fool (? Tom the Piper), or, as he is generally called, the Squire, and also a lord and lady. As to the Fool and Bessy, they have probably been derived to us from the ancient festival of Fools, held on New Year's Day. Bess was a common generic term for a female Tom-a-Bedlam. Waldron mentions seeing a company of Morris-dancers from Abington at Richmond in Surrey, in the summer of 1783. They appeared to be making a kind of annual circuit. In " Plaine Percivall the Peace-maker of England," mention is made of a "stranger, which seeing a quintessence (beside the Foole and the Maid Marian) of all the picked youth, strained out of a wholeendship, footing the Morris about a Maypole, and he not hearing the minstrelsie for the fidling, the tune for the sound, nor the pipe for the noise of the tabor, bluntly demaunded if they were not all beside themselves, that they so lip'd and skip'd without an occasion." In Pasquil and Marforius, 1589, the same author turns to his own account the May-games and the morris-dance, and applies them figuratively to some of the incidents and actors in the Martin-Marprelate controversy. Shakespear makes mention of an English Whitson Morrice Dance, in the following speech of the Dauphin in Hen. V. : —

> "No, with no more, than if we heard
> that England
> Were busied with a Whitson Morrice
> Dance."

" The English were famed," says Grey, in his " Notes on Shakespear, "for these and such like diversions; and even the old, as well as young persons, formerly followed them ; a remarkable instance of which is given by Sir William Temple." Among the Huth ballads is one entitled " Good Fellowes must go learne to Dance." It is of some merit, and has a share of that sparkling style, which distinguishes the versification of Suckling. The guests at an approaching wedding are the supposed speakers in the following passage :

"A bande of belles, in bauderycke wise,
  Would decke vs in our kynde a;
A shurte after the Moryce guyse,
  To flounce it in the wynde a.
A wyffler for to make the waye,
  And Maye brought in withall a,
Is brauer then the sunne, I saye,
  And passeth round or brall a."

Nash, who wrote nothing probably after
1600, describes in his "Summers Last
Will and Testament," printed in that
year, the fool as going round and collecting the money from the crowd. At an
earlier date we hear of a ladle suspended
from the beast's mouth, as a receptacle
for public contributions. In Nash's play
three clowns and three maids, while they
dance, sing the following lines in chorus:

"Trip and goe, heave and hoe,
  Up and downe, to and fro,
From the towne, to the grove,
Two and two, let us rove,
A Maying, a playing:
Love hath no gainsaying:
So merrily trip and goe."

The author of *Friar Bacons Prophesie*,
1604, recalling better times, says in his
poem:

"The Taber and the Pipe,
  The Bagpipe and the Crowde,
When oates and rye were ripe,
  Began to be alowde.
But till the harvest all was in,
  The Moris Dance did not begin."

But now, he adds further on:

"——Moris dances doe begin
  Before the harvest halfe be in."

The following description of a Morrice
Dance occurs in Rablet's "Cobbes Prophecies," 1614:

'It was my hap of late, by chance,
To meet a country morris dance,
When, cheefest of them all, the foole
Plaied with a ladle and a toole;
When every younger shak't his bells
Till sweating feet gave fohing smells;
And fine Maide Marian, with her smoile,
Shew'd how a rascall plaid the roile:
But, when the hobby-horse did wihy,
Then all the wenches gave a tihy:
But when they gan to shake their boxe,
And not a goose could catch a foxe,
The piper then put up his pipes,
And all the woodcocks look't like snipes,
And therewith fell a show'ry streame,"
                                &c., &c.

There is another in Cotgrave's "English
Treasury of Wit and Language," 1655:

"How they become the morris, with
  whose bells
They ring all in to Whitson ales, and
  sweat

Through twenty scarfs and napkins till
  the hobby horse
Tire, and the Maid Marian, resolv'd to
  jelly,
Be kept for spoon meat."

We have an allusion to the morris dancer
in the preface to the Candid and Ingenious Reader prefixed to "Mythomistes,"
circâ 1625, by Henry Reynolds: "Yet
such helpes, as if nature have not before-
hand in his byrth, given a poet, all such
forced art will come behind as lame to the
businesse, and deficient, as the best taught
countrey morris dauncer, with all his bells
and napkins, will ill deserve to be, in an
Inne of Courte at Christmas, tearmed the
thing they call a fine reveller." In his
"London and the countrey Carbona-
doed," 1632, Lupton says, relative to the
landlady at an ale-house: "Shee is merry,
and half-made (mad) upon Shrove-tuesday, May-daies, Feast-dayes, and Morris-
dances." Stevenson, in "The Twelve
Moneths," 1661, p. 17, speaking of April,
tells us: "The youth of the country make
ready for the Morris-dance, and the merry
milk-maid supplies them with ribbands
her true love had given her." The abhorrence of the Puritans to this diversion
in toto is depicted in Beaumont and
Fletcher's "Women pleased."

Walpole, or rather Vertue, in his "Catalogue of Engravers," under Peter Stent,
has described two paintings at Lord Fitz-
william's (rather coarsely and poorly executed) by Vinckenboom, about the end of
the reign of James I., in one of which a
morris-dance is introduced, consisting of
seven figures, viz., a fool, a hobby horse,
a piper, a Maid Marian, and three dancers. A reduced copy is given by Douce
from a tracing by Grose.

In Old Change, according to the
"History of Sign-Boards," 1867, there
was a sign called "The Three Morris
Dancers," in the time of Charles
II. See, for fuller particulars of this
subject, Douce's "Dissertation on the
ancient English Morris Dance," at
the end of his "Illustrations of Shakespear," 1807.

Mortuaries.—The payment of mortuaries is of great antiquity. It was anciently done by leading or driving a horse
or cow, &c. before the corpse of the deceased at the funeral. It was considered
as a gift left by a man at his death, by
way of recompense for all failures in the
payment of tithes and oblations, and
called a corse present. It is mentioned
in the National Council of Ensham about
the year 1006. Mortuaries were called
by our Saxon ancestors Soul shot
or payment. "Offeringes at Buri-
alles" are condemned in a list of "Grosse
Poyntes of Poperie, evident to all Men,"

in "A Parte of a Register," &c. (circâ 1593).

It was on mortuaries, and on an annual poll-tax of three hens, which he received from the population of a particular district that the Bishop of Olivolo, one of the old Venetian Sees, almost wholly relied for his income; and on the former account he was jocularly called the Bishop of the Dead. Hazlitt's *Venetian Republic*, 1900, ii., 384.

Most in Three Throws.—This amusement is cited in the dedication to Lilly of *Pantagruel's Prognostication*, about 1645; but we are left to conjecture its nature.

Mote Bell, Folk. — Ruffhead, speaking of the folc-mote comitatus, or shire-mote, and the folc-mote civitatis vel burgi, or burg-mote, says: "Besides these annual meetings, if any sudden contingency happened, it was the duty of the aldermen of cities and boroughs to ring the bell called in English Mot-bell, in order to bring together the people to the Burghmote," &c. *Preface to the Statutes at large.* See Tomlins *Law Dict.*, 1835, v. *Mote-Bell.* The Mot-Bell is mentioned in the laws of Edward the Confessor.

Mothering.—In former days, when the Roman Catholic was the established religion, it was the custom for people to visit their Mother Church on Mid-Lent Sunday, and to make their offerings at the high altar. Cowel, in his "Interpreter," 1607, observes that the now remaining practice of Mothering, or going to visit parents upon Mid-Lent Sunday, is really owing to that good old custom. Nay, it seems to be called Mothering from the respect so paid to the Mother Church, when the epistle for the day was, with some allusion, Galat. iv. 21, "Jerusalem Mater omnium,"; which epistle for Mid-Lent Sunday we still retain, though we have forgotten the occasion of it. Herrick has the following:

TO DIANEME.

A Ceremonie in Glocester.

"I'le to thee a Simnell bring,
'Gainst thou go'st a mothering ;
So that, when she blesseth thee,
Half that blessing thou'lt give me."

In the "Gentleman's Magazine" for February, 1784, p. 98, Nichols tells us, that whilst he was an apprentice, the custom was to visit his mother (who was a native of Nottinghamshire) "on Midlent Sunday (thence called Mothering Sunday) for a regale of excellent furmety." Another writer in the same volume, p. 343, says, I happened to reside last year near Chepstow, in Monmouthshire; and there, for the first time, heard of Mothering Sunday. My inquires into the origin and meaning of it were fruitless; but the practice thereabouts was, for all servants and apprentices, on Midlent Sunday, to visit their parents, and make them a present of money, a trinket, or some nice eatable; and they are all anxious not to fail in this custom." A correspondent in the volume for 1783, p. 578, expresses an opinion that Furmety or Mothering Sunday was "one of the things which probably refer simply to the idea of feasting or mortification according to the season and occasion." In Macaulay's time, Mothering Sunday met with a scrupulous observance at Claybrook. "Hist. and Antiq. of Claybrook," 1791, p. 128. At Leckford, near Stockbridge, Hants, this is called Wafering Sunday, from the wafer-cake impressed with an iron bearing an impression like a seal, offered by young people to their mothers on this occasion. The iron has two stamps; three locked hearts surmounted by a cross enclosed within a circle, and an anchor with foliate ornaments on either side. Two or three of these utensils, which were made red-hot over a charcoal fire, seem to suffice for the village, which employs a person named a waferer to do the work. *Antiquary* for May, 1893.

Mother Night.—A writer (Beckwith) in the "Gentleman's Magazine" for 1784, p. 97, observes that the night of the winter solstice was called by our ancestors "Mother Night," as they reckoned the beginning of their years from thence.

Mount-Cent.—See *Cent-Foot* and Nares, 1859, in v. In the Dumb Knight, 1608 (Hazlitt's Dodsley, x, 186), Philocles calls it *Mount-Saint*, and founds a compliment on it; but the queen corrects him and explains that the true name is *mount-cent.* The passage in the drama perhaps affords the best notion of the game. It has been supposed to be the same as picquet. In a facetious publication of the 17th c., Mars is introduced playing at cent with Venus. *Rodamontate ò Bravate Spagnole*, 1693, p. 71, part of *The Eloquent Master of Languages*, 1693.

Mourning.—Gough gives us numerous references to the classics to prove that the colour of mourning garments has, in most instances, been black from the earliest antiquity. *Sep. Mon.*, ii., Introd. xx. Polydore Vergil has a passage to this effect : "Plutarch writeth that the women in their mournyng laied a parte all purple, golde, and sumptuous apparell, and were clothed bothe they and their kinsfolk in white apparel, like as then the dead body was wrapped in white clothes. The white coloure was thought fittest for the ded, because it is clere, pure, and sincer, and leaste defiled. Of this ceremonie, as I take it, the French Quenes toke occasion, after the death of their housebandes the Kynges, to weare onely white cloth-yng, and if there bee any suche wid-dowe, she is commonly called the White Quene." Dupré tells us that the ancient Romans employed certain persons, named Designatores, clothed in black, to invite people to funerals, and to carry the coffin. There are persons in our days who wear the same clothing, and serve the same office. The Romans, saith Marolles, had in their ceremonies lictors, dressed in black, who did the office of our mourners. *Conformity*, p. 181. A writer in the "Gentleman's Magazine" for January, 1781, says: "We read in the Antiquities of Greece and Rome, that the branches of the Cypress and Yew were the usual sig-nals to denote a house in mourning. Gough, speaking of the signs of death in houses among the ancients, notices branches of pine and cypress on the autho-rity of Euripides, Suetonius and Virgil. He says, in a note, "Will it be thought a far-fetcht conjecture that yew trees in church yards supply the place of cyprus round tombs, where Ovid, Trist. III. xiii. 21, says they were placed. Comp. *Flowers on Graves, Funeral Customs*, &c. Duran-dus mentions black as anciently in use at funerals, which St. Cyprian seems to have inveighed against as the indication of sor-row on an event which to the Christian was a matter of joy. *De Ritibus*, 225. Cyprian's words are: "Cum sciamus fra-tres nostros accersione dominica de Seculo liberatos, non amitti sed præmitti, non sunt nobis hic accipiendæ atræ vestes, quando illi ibi indumenta alba jam sump-serint." It is stated that "Black is the fittest emblem of that sorrow and grief the mind is supposed to be clouded with; and, as Death is the privation of Life, and black a privation of Light, 'tis very probable this colour has been chosen to denote sadness, upon that account; and accordingly this colour has, for mourning, been preferred by most people throughout Europe. The Syrians, Cappadocians, and Armenians use sky-colour, to denote the place they wish the dead to be in, i.e., the Heavens; the Egyptians yellow, or fillemot, to show that as herbs being faded become yellow, so death is the end of human hope: and the Ethiopians grey, because it resembles the colour of the Earth, which receives the dead." Dun-ton's *Athenian Oracle Suppl.*, 301. Yel-low is the usual mourning colour in some countries, as much as white and black are in Europe. White and black not being colours at all in strictness, may be con-sidered as occupying the same neutral position: but, as Brand observes, the former is used only at the obse-quies of unmarried persons (and not always then) and very young children. Crimson would have been a much more suitable colour. The Bretons formerly employed yellow for this purpose, and even now, in Lower Brittany, saffron is recognised. Granger tells us, "It is re-corded that Anne Boleyn wore yellow mourning for Catherine of Arragon." For his authority he refers to Walpole's "Anecdotes of Painting." The same cir-cumstance is found in Hall's "Chron-icle," with the addition of Henry's wear-ing white mourning for Anne Boleyn. But in the time of the Stuarts purple was regarded as royal mourning. Pepys's *Diary*, September 16, 1660, and Note.

In the sixteenth century at Venice both scarlet and violet are found in use at the obsequies of a Doge; but the head of the eldest son of the deceased was draped in black. Hazlitt's *Venetian Republic*, 1900, ii., 175. Violet was the colour em-ployed at Rome in 1903 at the demise of His Holiness Leo XIII.

We read in Gough's Camden: "When a person is at the point of death, just before he expires, certain women mourners, standing in the cross-ways, spread their hands, and call him with cries adapted to the purpose, and endeavour to stop the departing soul, reminding it of the advantages it enjoys in goods, wives, person, reputation, kin-dred, friends, and horses: asking why it will go, and where, and to whom, and up-braiding it with ingratitude, and lastly, complaining that the departing spirit will be transformed into those forms which appear at night and in the dark: and after it has quitted the body, they bewail it with howlings and clapping of hands. They follow the funeral with such a noise, that one would think there was an end both of living and dead. The most violent in these lamentations are the nurses, daughters, and mistresses. They make as much lamentation for those slain in battle as for those who die in their beds, though they esteem it the easiest death to die fighting or robbing; but they vent every reproach against their enemies, and che-rish a lasting deadly hatred against all their kindred." Braithwaite, speaking of the death of "a zealous brother," says: "Some mourners hee hath of his owne, who howle not so much that hee should leave them, as that nothing is left them." *Whimzies*, 1631, p. 207.

In England it was formerly the fashion to mourn a year for very near relations. Thus Pope:

"Grieve for an hour perhaps, then mourn a year."

A writer of the early part of last cen-tury remarked a practice of the common people in some localities of tying a dirty cloth about their heads when they appear as chief mourners at a funeral. Pennant, in his "Tour in Scotland," 1769, remarks a singular custom in many parts of North Britain, of painting, on the doors and window-shutters, white tadpole-like figures, on a black ground, designed to express the tears of the country for the loss of any person of distinction. Nothing seems wanting to render this mode of expressing sorrow completely ridiculous, but the subjoining of a "N.B. These are tears." I saw a door that led into a family vault in Kelso Churchyard in 1785, which was painted over in the above manner with very large ones. In the 18th century, a writer from Galston, co. Ayr, informs us that it was usual "for even the women to attend funerals in the village, dressed in black or red cloaks." *Stat. Acc. of Scotland*, ii., 80. Women, and even ladies, sometimes follow the dead, especially (in the former case) among the poor, and in the latter, where the deceased is a child. At the obsequies of a person of high rank, it often happens that, where the funeral takes place (as indeed it usually does) in the country, one or two of the nearest female relatives claim the right of accompanying the remains. The same thing is occasionally witnessed in large towns, and among the middle classes I believe the custom is growing more and more common. Some curious particulars on this subject may be seen in Pegge's *Curialia*, 1818, pp. 314-16.

Mournival or **Murnival.**—A term of the game of gleek—four cards of a sort. Comp. Nares, *Glossary*, 1859, in v.

Mourre.—See *Cinque*.

Mouseear or **Scorpion-Grass.** —(Myosotis). Lupton, in his third book of "Notable Things," quoting Mizaldus, says: "Mousear, any manner of way ministered to horses, brings this help unto them, that they cannot be hurt, while the smith is shooing of them, therfore it is called of many, herba clavorum, the herb of nails." Edit. 1660, lib. 3, p. 53.

Mowing.—We learn from Bridges, that : "Within the Liberty of Warkworth is Ashe Meadow, divided amongst the neighbouring parishes, and famed for the following customs observed in the mowing of it. The meadow is divided into fifteen portions, answering to fifteen lots, which are pieces of wood cut off from an arrow, and marked according to the landmarks in the field. To each lot are allowed eight mowers, amounting to one hundred and twenty in the whole. On the Saturday sevennight after Midsummer Day, these portions are laid out by six persons, of whom two are chosen from Warkworth, two from Overthorp, one from Grimsbury

and one from Nethercote. These are called. Field-men, and have an entertainment provided for them upon the day of laying out the meadow, at the appointment of the Lord of the Manor. As soon as the meadow is measured, the man who provides the feast, attended by the Hay-ward of Warkworth, brings into the field three gallons of ale. After this the meadow is run, as they term it, or trod, to distinguish the lots ; and, when this is over, the Hay-ward brings into the field a rump of beef, six penny loaves, and three gallons of ale, and is allowed a certain portion of hay in return, though not of equal value with his provision. This hay-ward, and the Master of the feast, have the name of crocus-men. In running the field each man hath a boy allowed to assist him. On Monday morning lots are drawn, consisting some of eight swaths and others of four. Of these the first and last carry the garlands. The two first lots are of four swaths, and whilst these are mowing the mowers go double ; and, as soon as these are finished, the following orders are read aloud : 'Oyez, Oyez, Oyez, I charge you, under God, in his Majesty's name, that you keep the King's peace in the Lord of the Manor's behalf, according to the Orders and Customs of this meadow. No man or men shall go before the two garlands ; if you do you shall pay your penny, or deliver your scythe at the first demand, and this so often as you shall transgress. No man, nor men, shall mow above eight swaths over their lots, before they lay down their scythes and go to breakfast. No man, or men, shall mow any farther than Monks-holm-Brook, but leave their scythes there, and go to dinner ; according to the custom and manner of this Manor. God save the King !' The dinner, provided by the Lord of the Manor's tenant, consists of three cheese-cakes, three cakes, and a new milk-cheese. The cakes and cheese-cakes are of the size of a winnowing-sieve ; and the person who brings them is to have three gallons of ale. The master of the feast is paid in hay, and is farther allowed to turn all his cows into the meadow on Saturday morning till eleven o'clock ; that by this means giving the more milk the cakes may be made the bigger. Other like customs are observed in the mowing of other meadows in this parish." *Northamptonshire*, i., 219. See *Harvest*.

Muffin Bell.—The itinerant vendor of muffins and crumpets still haunts some of the outlying parts of London, and carries a bell to announce his approach. His basket is borne on his head. The usage goes back to a time when these delectable comestibles were not merely manufactured only by a few firms, but were not generally sold by the bakers. The trade remains a special and limited one; but the bell and its owner have become, like the church bell in the universality of clocks and watches, an anachronism.

Muffling.—See *Newcastle-on-Tyne*.

Mumble a Sparrow. — Grose mentions "Mumble a Sparrow: a cruel sport practiced at wakes and fairs in the following manner: a cock-sparrow, whose wings are clipped, is put into the crown of a hat; a man, having his arms tied behind him, attempts to bite off the sparrow's head, but is generally obliged to desist by the many pecks and pinches he receives from the enraged bird."

Mumchance.—An early game of chance played with money and dice, as we perceive from a passage in Cavendish's *Life of Wolsey;* but the exact particulars do not seem to be farther known. In the later authorities cited by Nares there is no explanation; in one from Decker's *Belman,* 1608, cards are mentioned; and we are told that the name was owing to the necessary silence to be observed. Doubtless the parties engaged, when heavy stakes were on, held their peace through suspense. The issue, it appears from Cavendish, who describes the Cardinal himself taking part in a turn, depended on the cast of the dice. In 1597 was published a tract entitled *Mihil Mumchance, his Discoverie of the Art of Cheating in false Dice play;* no doubt, in this as in other amusements of the kind a good deal of trickery prevailed.

Mumming.—Mumming is a Christmas sport, which consists in changing clothes between men and women who, when dressed in each other's habits, go from one neighbour's house to another, partaking of Christmas cheer, and making merry with them in disguise. Mumming is supposed to have been originally instituted in imitation of the Sigillaria, or festival days, added to the ancient Saturnalia, and condemned by the Synod of Trullus (Thurles), where it was decreed that the days called the Calends should be entirely stripped of their ceremonies, and that the faithful should no longer observe them, that the public dancings of women should cease, as being the occasion of much harm and ruin, and as being invented and observed in honour of the gods of the heathens, and therefore quite averse to the Christian life. They therefore decreed that no man should be clothed with a woman's garment, nor any woman with a man's. The same prohibition was published by the Council which met at Constantinople in 690-1, in its 62nd Canon. "The disguisyng and mummyng that is used in Christemas tyme," Langley observes in his synopsis of Polydore Virgil, "in the Northe partes came out of the feastes of Pallas, that were done with visars and painted visages, named Quinqatria of the Romaynes." Aubanus, speaking of mumming in Germany, says, that in the ancient Saturnalia there were frequent and luxurious feastings amongst friends: presents were mutually sent, and changes of dress made: that Christians have adopted the same customs, which continue to be used from the Nativity to the Epiphany: that exchanges of dress too, as of old among the Romans, are common, and neighbours by mutual invitations visit each other in the manner which the Germans call mummery. He adds that, as the heathens had their Saturnalia in December, their Sigillaria in January, and the Lupercalia and Bacchanalia in February, so, amongst Christians, these three months are devoted to feastings and revellings of every kind. Ihre speaks of the sort of mummery practiced in his time and before by the youth, who put on the forms of rams, and in that shape ran about molesting passengers and others. He seems disposed to identify this custom with that described by other writers, in which a stag, instead of a ram, used to be counterfeited in the same way. Bishop Faustinus in his sermon for the Kalends of January, asks whether any sensible person can credit, that people in their right minds could be found so silly as to put on the likeness of a deer, while others dressed themselves in the hides of cattle, others wore the heads of beasts, and transformed themselves so that they ceased to look like human beings. This was not peculiar to the Continent, but appears to have been practiced among us formerly on more than one of the merry-makings ingrafted on the original holy feasts of the early Christian Church. "Glossarium Suio-Gothicum," 1769, v. Jul.; Du Cange "Gloss." Art. Pelota.

Dr. Johnson was disposed to look on these extravagances as a probable vestige of the Festival of Fools. It appears from Henry ("History of Britain," vol. iv. p. 602) that "in the year 1348, eighty tunics of buckram, forty-two visors, and a great variety of other whimsical dresses, were provided for the disguising at court at the feast of Christmas." Stow has preserved an account of a remarkable mummery made in 1377 by the citizens of London for the amusement of the son of the Black Prince:

"On the Sunday before Candlemas, in the night, one hundred and thirty citizens, disguised, and well horsed, in a mummerie, with sound of trumpets, sackbuts, cornets, shalmes and other minstrels, and innumerable torch-lights of waxe, rode to Kennington, beside Lambeth, where the young Prince remayned with his mother. In the first rank did ride forty-eight in likeness and habit of esquires, two and two together, clothed in red coats, and gowns of say, or sandall, with comely visors on their faces. After them came forty-eight knights, in the same livery. Then followed one richly arrayed, like an emperour: and after him some distance, one stately tyred, like a pope, whom followed twenty-four cardinals; and, after them, eight or ten with black visors, not amiable, as if they had been legates from some forrain princes. These maskers, after they had entered the mannor of Kennington, alighted from their horses, and enter'd the hall on foot: which done, the Prince, his mother, and the Lords, came out of the chamber into the hall, whom the mummers did salute; shewing, by a paire of dice upon the table, their desire to play with the young prince, which they so handled, that the Prince did alwaies winne when he cast them. Then the mummers set to the Prince three jewels, one after another; which were, a boule of gold, a cup of gold, and a ring of gold, which the Prince wanne at three casts. Then they set to the Princes Mother, the Duke, the Earles, and other lords, to every one a ring of gold, when they did also win. After which they were feasted, and the musick sounded, the Prince and lords daunced on the one part with the mummers, which did also dance; which jollitie being ended, they were again made to drink, and then departed in order as they came." "The like," he says, "was to King Henry the Fourth, in the second year of his reign, hee then keeping his Christmas at Eltham; twelve aldermen of London and their sonnes rode a mnmming, and had great thanks." *Survey*, 1603, p. 97. We read of another mumming in Henry IV.'s time in Fabyan: "In whiche passe tyme the Dukys of Amnarle, of Surrey, and of Excetyr, with the Erlys of Salesbury and of Gloucetyr, with other of their affynyte, made provysion for a dysguysynge or a mummynge, to be shewyd to the Kynge upon Twelfethe Nyght, and the tyme was nere at hande. and all thynge redy for the same. Upon the sayd Twelfthe Day, came secretlye unto the Kynge the Duke of Amnarle, and shewyd to hym, that he, wyth the other Lordys aforenamyd, were appoynted to sle hym in the tyme of the fore sayd disguysynge." So that this mumming, it should seem, had like to have proved a very serious jest. *Chronicle*, 1516, fol. 169. In the "Paston Letters," in a letter dated Dec. 24th, 1484, we read that Lady Morley, on account of the death of her lord, July 23, directing what sports were to be used in her house at Christmas, ordered that "there were none disguisings, nor harping, nor luting, nor singing; nor none loud disports; but playing at the tables, and chess, and cards; such disports she gave her folks leave to play, and none other."

Northbrooke observes: "In the reign of King Henrie the eyght (An. 3. H. VIII.) it was ordeyned, that if anye persons did disguise themselues in apparel, and couer their faces with visors, gathering a companye togither, naming themselues mummers, which vse to come to the dwellingplaces of men of honour, and other substantiall persons, whereupon murders, felonie, rape, and other great hurts and inconueniencies haue aforetime growen and hereafter bee like to come, by the colour thereof, if the said disorder should continue not reformed, &c.: that then they shoulde be arrested by the King's liege people as vagabondes, and bee committed to the gaole without bayle or mainprise, for the space of three monethes, and to fine at the King's pleasure: and euery one that keepeth anye visors in his house, to forfeyte xxs." *Treatise against Dicing* 1577, repr. 1843. In Lodge's *Wits Miserie*, 1596, is the following passage: "I thinke in no time Jerome had better cause to crie out on pride then in this, for painting, now-a-daies, is growne to such a custome, that from the swartfaste deuil in the kitchin to the fairest damsel in the cittie, the most part looke like wizards for a Momerie, rather then Christians trained in sobrietie." In the interlude of the "Marriage of Wit and Wisdom," Idleness says:

> "—Now I have never a crose to blesse me,
>   Now I go a-mumming,
> Like a poore pennilesse spirit,
>   Without pipe or druming!"

In a former passage, Snatch says:

> "Where I lay last night, I stole away a sheete:
> We will take this and tie it to his hed,
> And soe we will blind him;
> And sirra, I charge you, when you here Any body comming,
> If they aske you any question, say you goo A-mumming."

The following is from Aubrey's "Collections for North Wilts," 1678: "Heretofore noblemen and gentlemen of fair estates had their heralds, who wore their coat of arms at Christmas, and at other solemn times, and cried largesse thrice. . . . . In days of yore lords and gentlemen lived in the country like petty kings. . . . . They always eat in Gothick halls, at the high table or oreille (oriel). . . . . Here in the hall, the mumming and loaf-stealing, and other Christmas sports, were performed." Edit. 1859, 40. In "Round about our Coal Fire," (circâ 1730) I find the following: "Then comes mumming and masquerading, when the squire's wardrobe is ransacked for dresses of all kinds. Corks are burnt to black the faces of the fair, or make deputy mustacios, and every one in the family, except the squire himself, must be transformed." At Tiverton, in Devon, a custom, probably dating from 1660, prevailed formerly of forming a procession of young men, dressed in the old fashion and armed with swords, for the purpose of levying black-mail on the inhabitants. It was headed by a sort of Merry-Andrew, called Master Oliver, who was pelted by the boys, the latter taking care not to let him catch them. There was a feast in the evening. Mr. Brand once saw in a printing office at Newcastle-upon-Tyne several carols for this season: for the Nativity, St. Stephen's Day, Childermas Day, &c., with Alexander and the King of Egypt, a mock play, usually acted about this time, by mummers. The conclusion of this bombastic play is in my Collection of Proverbs, 1882:

"Bounce, Buckram, velvet's dear;
Christmas comes but once a year:
And when it comes, it brings good cheer:
But when it's gone, it's never the near."

"Bounce, Buckram," &c., seems to intimate an inability on the part of the bouncers or mummers to afford velvet and their adoption of the cheaper material. Shakespear may have had the latter in his mind when he attired in buckram the imaginary antagonists of Falstaff (Henry IV. part 1, ii, 4). Brand's reflections that follow are equally new and excellent: the "carpe diem" of Horace is included in them, and, if I mistake not, the good advice is seldom thrown away. Subjoined is a Somersetshire mummer's song:

"Here comes I, liddle man Jan,
With my zword in my han!
If you don't all do,
As you be told by I,
I'll zend you all to York,
Vor to make apple-pie."

Mr. Halliwell, "Illustrations of Early English Literature," 1849, has printed "A Christmas Play, Performed by the Derbyshire Mummers," which does not appear to contain anything worth extracting. A version of this, said to be current in Worcestershire, may be found in "Notes and Queries," 2nd S. xi., 271. It is to be apprehended, however, that the old rural practice is degenerating into a piece of doggerel recitative supplied by metropolitan caterers.

Johnson tells us in his "Journey to the Western Islands," that a gentleman informed him of what he (Johnson) considered to be an odd game: At New Year's Eve, in the hall or castle of the laird, where at festal seasons there may be supposed a very numerous company, one man dresses himself in a cow's hide, upon which other men beat with sticks. He runs with all this noise round the house, which all the company quits in a counterfeited fright: the door is then shut. At New Year's Eve, there is no great pleasure to be had out of doors in the Hebrides. They are sure soon to recover from their terror enough to solicit for re-admission: which, for the honour of poetry, is not to be obtained but by repeating a verse, with which those that are knowing and provident take care to be furnished. The learned traveller tells us that they who played at this odd game, gave no account of the origin of it, and that he described it as it might perhaps be used in other places, where the reason of it is not yet forgotten.

Muscadel.—It is difficult to know whether the following passage from Fletcher's Drama of the "Pilgrim," 1621, is to be interpreted literally—I should presume not:

"*Alphonso.* Away with him!
Fling him i' th' hay-mow,—let him lie a-mellowing;
He stinks of Muscadel like an English Christmas."

Musical Chairs.—A drawing-room amusement, where one of the company performs on the piano, and, a double row of chairs having been placed in a line, back to back, the rest make the circuit, till the pianist abruptly comes to a stop, and the humour or fun consists in the number of players exceeding that of chairs by one or two, so that there must always be one or two out, when the scramble for seats, on the conclusion of the music, takes place.

Muss.—Rabelais mentions a Muss among Gargantua's Games. Book i. cap. 22. And in another place, book iii. cap. 40, it is facetiously suggested that it owes its name to Muschus, the inventor thereof, and it is said to be honest, healthful, ancient, and lawful. In Shakespear's *Antony and Cleopatra*, it is thus mentioned:

Ant. ——"When I cry'd, Ho!
Like boys unto a Muss, Kings would start forth,
And cry, your Will!"

It also occurs in Jonson's *Magnetic Lady*, iv., 3.

My Sow has Pigged. — Taylor the Water-poet refers to this game of cards in his "Motto," 1621; it is thus spoken of in "Poor Robin's Almanac" for 1734: "The lawyers play at beggar my neighbour; the new-marry'd couples play at put; the doctors and surgeons at thrust out rotten, but if they eat with a man that is so eat up with the pox that he is all compos'd of that sort of metal, they thrust out all together; the farmers play at My Sow's pigg'd; the schoolmasters play at questions and commands; and because every man ought to mind his business, he that plays most at all sorts of gaming, commonly at last plays a game at hide and seek, and cares not to leave off till he has got the rubbers." Mr. Halliwell says: "The following distich is used in this game:

'Higgory, diggory, digg'd,
My sow has pigg'd.'"

—*Popular Rhymes and Nursery Tales* 1849, p. 114. Comp. p. 90 *suprâ.*

Mysteries. — For notices of the existing collections, see Hazlitt's *Bibliographical Manual of Old English Plays,* 1892, p. 274. Pennant draws attention to the notices by Clarke in his Letters on Spain of dramatic performances there in comparatively modern times analogous to the English Mysteries. *Tours in Wales,* 1810, i., 194. In Quaritch's Catalogue for 1892 was the MS. of the *Towneley Mysteries,* printed for the Surtees Society, and wanting 24 leaves, with an interesting note. This series corresponds most closely with the York one.

Nails. — There was anciently a species of divination called onychomancy, or onymancy, performed by the nails of an unpolluted boy. Vestiges of this are still retained. Sir Thomas Browne admits that "Conjectures of prevalent humours may be collected from the spots in our nails," but rejects the sundry divinations vulgarly raised upon them: such as "that spots on the top of the nails signify things past, in the middle things present, and, at the bottom, events to come. That white specks presage our felicity, blue ones our misfortunes; that those in the nail of the thumb have significations of honour; of the fore-finger riches." Burton tells us, that a black spot appearing on the nails is a bad omen. Burton, giving in his *Astrologaster,* 1620, a catalogue of many superstitious ceremonies, tells us: "That to have yellow speckles on the nailes of ones hand is a greate signe of death." He observes that, "when the palme of the right hand itcheth, it is a shrewd sign he shall receive money"; which remains a belief among some people. In an old play, we read:

"When yellow spots do on your hands appear,
Be certain then you of a corse shall hear."

A publication of the beginning of the last century, referring to the gifts on the finger-nails states: "Those little spots are from white glittering particles which are mixed with red blood, and happen to remain there some time. The reason of their being called gifts, is as wise a one as those of letters, winding-sheets, &c., in a candle." *British Apollo,* 1708, i., No. 17. Comp. *Cornish Folk-lore.* The set and statary times, says Browne, of paring nails and cuting of hair is thought by many a point of consideration, which is perhaps but the continuation of an ancient superstition. To the Romans it was piacular to pare their nails upon the Nundinœ, observed every ninth day, and they avoided the operation on certain days of the week, according to that line of Ausonius:

"Ungues Mercurio, Barbam Jove, Cypride Crines,"

The celebrated Countess of Dorset, Pembroke, and Montgomery, according to her *Day Book,* 1676, cited by Southey, was accustomed to pare the nails of her hands and feet, and burn them in the fire afterwards. She notes on one occasion doing so about six in the morning in bed, and casting the parings into the fire when she rose. In the neighbourhood of Bottesford Moors, it is said that the children's nails are bitten off, and not pared, till they have passed the first twelvemonth; for otherwise it is thought that the child will grow up to be a thief! But the practice of biting the nails of infants is itself widely diffused, and though no special significance may be attached to it in general, the infringement of the rule is thought to be a certain forerunner of bad luck. A poor woman in Dorsetshire, some years ago, said that she always pared her children's nails over the leaves of the family Bible, to bring them up to be honest! To cut the nails upon a Friday or a Sunday, is accounted unlucky amongst the common people in many places, both here and abroad, except among the Jews, who usually select the former, the day preceding their own Sabbath. Addison's *Present State of the Jews,* 129. Holiday deprecates the omen, "that you may never pare your nailes upon a Friday." Lodge says, speaking of Curiositie: Nor will "he paire his nailes White Munday to be fortunate in his love." *Wits Miserie,* 1596, p. 12. In Tomkis's "Albumazar," 1615, we read:

"He puls you not a haire, nor paires a naile,
Nor stirs a foote, without due figuring The horoscope."

Names.—Among the Greeks it was an ancient custom to refer misfortunes to the signification of proper names. The Scholiast upon Sophocles observes that this ludicrous habit of analyzing the proper names of persons, and deriving ominous inferences from their different significations in their state of analysis, appears to have prevailed among the Grecian poets of the first reputation. Shakespear, he adds, was much addicted to it. He instances: "How is't with aged Gaunt?" *Richard II.*, ii., 1.

Names in all countries and ages have been principally derived from natal localities, callings, and personal aspects. Modern countries have resorted in considerable measure to classical, scriptural, or hagiological prototypes.

Nantwich.—Pennant, in his "Tour from Chester to London," p. 30, tells us, that "on Ascension Day, the old inhabitants of Nantwich piously sang a hymn of thanksgiving for the blessing of the brine. A very ancient pit, called the old Brine, was also held in great veneration, and till within these few years was annually, on that festival, bedecked with boughs, flowers, and garlands, and was encircled by a jovial band of young people, celebrating the day with song and dance."

Nativities.—Strype says, under the year 1570: "And because the welfare of the nation did so much depend upon the Queen's marriage, it seems some were employed secretly by calculating her nativity to inquire into her marriage. For which art even Secretary Cecil himself had some opinion. I have met among his papers with such a judgement made, written all with his own hand." *Annals of the Reformation*, ii., 16. There are even at this day persons who pretend to cast nativities, and to foretell the destinies of those who think proper to consult them. A man resided some years ago in Blackfriars, who made some remarkably lucky guesses, and had a considerable circle of believers.

Nativity of the Virgin.—(Sept. 8). Howell, in a letter without date, but about 1655, to Lord Dorchester, observes, that the writers hostile to the memory of Queen Elizabeth taxed her, among other matters, for suffering "the nativity of the Virgin Mary in September to be turned to the celebration of her own birthday, &c." But comp. *St. Elizabeth's Day.*

Neck.—Moulin says: "If the neck of any one grows stiff, or the muscles of the head are twisted awry, it is a portent that that person will die by the neck."—*Vates*, p. 218.

In the "Voyageur de Paris," quoted in a MS. note by Douce, the origin of necklaces is traced to the idea inculcated on the young girls of France by the old nurses that a small neck was a token of continence. Vol. iii., 223.

Neck-Verse.—The beginning of the 51st Psalm used to bear this name from the fact that in all capital cases, within benefit of clergy, the prisoner, by repeating his neck-verse, saved his neck or life. Lodge, speaking of an intelligencer, says: "hee will give a shroud wound with his tongue, that may bring a' man to his neck-verse." *Wits Miserie*, 1596, sign. N 3 verso. A story, which appears to be alluded to in the play of *Gammer Gurton's Needle*, written about 1566, is told in *Pasquil's Jests*, 1604, relevant to this old practice. It is of a man condemned to death at the Oxford Assizes, and being prompted by "a scholar" to the neck-verse, as the man himself could not read, at a certain place the scholar whispered him to take away his thumb, which prevented him from seeing the print, and the convict, misapprehending, repeated, "Take away thy thumb," upon which the judge ordered his removal. But when he was on the ladder, and just ready to be hanged, he cried, "Have at you daisy yonder!" and leapt off the cart. In Brathwaite's "Whimzies," 1631, p. 69, in the character of a jaylor the following passage: "If any of his more happy prisoners be admitted to his clergy, and by helpe of a compassionate prompter, hacke out his Necke-Verse, hee has a cold iron in store, if he be hot; but a hot iron if hee be cold. If his pulse (I mean his purse) bee hot, his fist may cry fizze, but want his impression: but if his pulse be cold, the poore beggarly knave must have his literal expression." The following explanation must be received *cum grano*:

"When Popery long since with tenets of nonsense
  And ignorance fill'd the land,
And Latin alone to Church-men was known,
  And reading a legible hand:

This privilege then, to save learned men,
  Was granted 'em by Holy Church,
While villains, whose crimes were lesser nine times,
  Were certainly left in the lurch.

If a monk had been taken for stealing of bacon,
  For burglary, murder, or rape:
If he could but rehearse, (well prompt) his Neck Verse
  He never could fail to escape.

When the world grew more wise, and with open eyes
  Were able to see through the mist,

'Twas thought 's just to save a Laity-
    Knave,
    As well as a rascally priest."

—*British Apollo*, 1710, No. 72. Sir Walter Scott notices the neck-verse as a cant
term formerly used by the marauders on
the Border :

   "Letter nor line know I never a one,
   Wer't my Neck-Verse at Hairibee."

—*Lay of the Last Minstrel*, Canto i. p.
24. A note adds, "Haribee, the place of
executing the Border marauders at Carlisle."

Newcastle-on-Tyne. — It was
an ancient custom for the mayor, aldermen, and sheriff of Newcastle-upon-Tyne,
accompanied with great numbers of the
burgesses, to go every year, at the feasts
of Easter and Whitsuntide, to a place
without the walls called the Forth, a little
Mall, where everybody walks, as they do
in St. James's Park, with the mace, sword
and cap of maintenance carried before
them. The young people of the town
still assemble there on these holidays, at
Easter particularly, play at hand-ball,
dance, &c., but are no longer countenanced in their innocent festivity by the
presence of their governors who, no
doubt, in ancient times, as the Bishops did
with their inferior clergy, used to unbend
the brow of authority, and partake with
their happy and contented people the
seemingly puerile pleasures of the festal
season.

Two annual fairs held on the Town
Moor were called Lammas and St.
Luke's Fairs, from the days on which they
begin. Bourne, in his history of that
town, tells us, that the tolls, booths, stal-
lage, pickage, and courts of pie-powder
(dusty foot) to each of these fairs, were
reckoned communibus annis, at twelve
pounds, in the time of Oliver Cromwell.
The records of the monasteries there would
doubtless have furnished some particulars
relative to the institution and ancient
customs of the fairs at that place. Bourne
says, the custom of the passing bell itself
was held to be popish and superstitious
during the Grand Rebellion, for in a vestry book belonging to the Chapel of All
Saints, it is observable that the tolling
of the bell is not mentioned in the parish
from the year 1643 till 1655, when the
church by this and such like means having been brought in dilapidation through
want of money, it was at a Vestry, held
January 21, that year, ordered to be
tolled again. A bell, usually called the
thief and reever bell, proclaims the two
annual fairs. A bell is rung at six every
morning, except Sundays and holidays,
with a view, it should seem, of calling up
the artizans to their daily employment;
it was formerly rung at four. The in-

habitants retain also a vestige of the old
Norman curfew at eight in the evening.
The bells there are muffled on the 30th of
January every year—the anniversary
of the death of Charles I. Their
sound is by this means peculiarly
plaintive. The inhabitants of that town
were particularly loyal during the parliamentary wars in the grand rebellion,
which may account for the use of this custom, which probably began at the Restoration.

The tolling of the great bell of
St. Nicholas' Church here has been
from ancient times a signal for the burgesses to convene on gild-days, or on the
days of electing magistrates. It begins
at nine o'clock in the morning, and with
little or no intermission continues to toll
till three o'clock, when they begin to elect
the mayor, &c. Its beginning so early
was doubtless intended to call together
the several companies to their respective
meeting-houses, in order to choose the
former and latter electors, &c. A popular notion prevails that it is for the old
mayor's dying, as they call his going out
of office : the tolling, as it were, of his passing bell. On Pancake Day, St. Nicho-
las's Bell tolled at noon ; shops were immediately closed ; all kinds of business
ceased ; and a carnival ensued, lasting
during the rest of the day. Bourne tells us
that it was a custom with several religious families to use prayers, as for a soul
departing, at the tolling of the Passing
Bell. It is stated in Brand's "History
of Newcastle," that the Mayor used to
keep his fool to entertain him and his
friends, as elsewhere, with his pleasantries. It appears from an Order of the
Common Council, dated 15th May, 1657,
that the scholars of the public grammar
school there, and other schools in the
town, were invited to attend the magistrates on Ascension Day, when the
magistrates, river jury, &c., of the
corporation, according to an ancient custom, make their annual procession by
water in their barges, visiting the bounds
of their jurisdiction on the river, to prevent encroachments. Chearful libations
are offered on the occasion to the genius
of our wealthy flood, which Milton calls
the "coaly Tyne" :

   "The sable stores on whose majestic
     strand
    More tribute yield than Tagus' golden
     sand."

In the Painted Hall at Greenwich Hospital, the Genius of the Tyne is represented pouring forth his coal in great
abundance. There is the Severn with her
lampreys, and the Humber with her pigs
of lead, which, with the Thames and Tyne
compose the four great rivers of England.

In the Ordinary of the Company of Cooks here, dated 1575, I find the following clause: "And alsoe that the said Felloship of Cookes shall yearlie of theire owne cost and charge mainteigne and keep the bone-fires, according to the auntient custome of the said towne on the Sand-hill; that is to say, one bone-fire on the Even of the Feast of the Nativitie of St. John Baptist, commonly called Midsomer Even, and the other on the Even of the Feast of St. Peter the Apostle, if it shall please the Maior and Aldermen of the said towne for the time being to have the same bone-fires." In the Ordinary of the Butchers' Company, dated 1621, is the following clause: Item, That noe one brother of the said Fellowship shall hereafter buy or seeke any licence of any person whatsoever to kill flesh within the town of Newcastle in the Lent season, without the general consent of the Fellowship, upon payne for every such defaute to the use aforesaide, £5." They are enjoined, it is observable, in this charter to hold their head meeting-day on Ash-Wednesday. They have since altered it to the preceding Wednesday.

It is said in a MS. Life of Alderman Barnes, of Newcastle, about 1680: 'His chief recreation was cock-fighting, and which long after he was not able to say whether it did not at least border upon what was criminal, he is said to have been the champion of the cock-pit. One cock particularly he had, called 'Spang (?Span) Counter,' which came off victor in a great many battles *a la main;* but the sparks of Streatlem Castle killed it out of mere envy: so there was an end of Spang Counter and of his master's sport of cocking ever after."

Brand speaks of having been more than once disturbed early on May morning at Newcastle-upon-Tyne by the noise of a song, which a woman sang about the streets who had several garlands in her hand, and which, if he mistook not, she sold to any that were superstitious enough to buy them:

"Rise up, maidens! fy for shame!
For I've been four lang miles from hame:
I've been gathering my garlands gay:
Rise up, fair maids, and take in your May."

There was an ancient usage here after the Assizes, arising out of the long period during which the journey from Newcastle to the next point, Carlisle, was rendered dangerous by the unsettled state of the Border. The Mayor, addressing the Judge, congratulated him on the completion of his labours, and as his farther course lay through a country much infested by the Scots, offered to his acceptance a Jacobus or 20s. gold piece of James I., wherewith to purchase a dagger to defend himself. But we have here probably the second or modified form of the custom, which may have at the outset extended to the provision of an armed escort. The selection of a Jacobus seems to date the introduction of the altered arrangement, and where there are two judges on circuit, it is said to be the practice to give one a Jacobus and the other a Carolus or piece of the same value of the next reign. In 1902, at the November Assizes, the Mayor, Sir William Stephenson, presented Mr. Justice Channell with the Jacobus as usual, and his lordship assured him, that he should keep the old coin as a memento.

New Year.—"Alle that take hede to dysmal dayes, or use nyce observvaunces in the newe moone, or in the new yere, as setting of mete or drynke, by nighte on the benche, to fede Alholde or Gobelyn."— "Dives and Pauper," 1493. There is a proverb current in the North:

"At New Year's tide,
The days lengthen a cock's stride."

Comp. Hazlitt's *Proverbs,* 1882, p. 83. In Westmoreland and Cumberland, "early on the morning of the first of January, the Fæx Populi assemble together, carrying stangs and baskets. Any inhabitant, stranger, or whoever joins not this ruffian tribe in sacrificing to their favourite

BLACKTHORN GLOBE.

saint-day, if unfortunate enough to be met by any of the band, is immediately mounted across the stang (if a woman, she is basketed), and carried, shoulder height, to the nearest public-house, where the payment of sixpence immediately liberates the prisoner." "None, though ever so industriously inclined, are permitted to follow their respective avocations on that day." *Gent. Mag.,* 1791, p. 1169. A strange custom still lingers in out-of-the-way country places in Herefordshire. On New Year's Day, very early in the morning, the farm boys go out and cut branches of the blackthorn, which they weave into a kind of globe of thorns. Then a large fire of straw is made in the farmyard, in which the globe of thorns is slightly burnt, while all the inmates of the farm stand, hand-in-hand, in a circle round the fire, shouting, in monotonous voice, the words "Old Cider," prolonging each syllable to its utmost extent. When the globe of thorns is slightly charred it is taken indoors and hung up in the kitchen, when it brings good luck for the rest of the year. No one seems to know the origin of the superstition, though probably the words "old cider" are a corruption of some much older words, probably an invocation to a heathen deity. Old people say that in their youth the practice was general in all country places in Herefordshire, and it was a pretty sight on New Year's morning to see the fires burning all over the neighbourhood. Another custom still in use is to take a particular kind of cake, and on New Year's morning to bring a cow into the farmyard and place the cake on her head. The cow walks forward, tosses her head, and the cake falls, and the prosperity of the New Year is foretold from the direction of its fall. *Daily Graphic,* January 1, 1898. The globular form is given to fruit trees at the present day in the neighbourhood of Paris. A cherry-tree so trained is figured in the *Royal Magazine* for September, 1903.

Christie says: "The new year of the Persians was opened with agricultural ceremonies (as is also the case with the Chinese at the present day)." He adds: "The Athenians (says Plutarch) celebrated three sacred ploughings." "The Chinese ploughing took place on the first day of their solar new year, (the same ceremony is practised in Tunquin, Cochin China, and Siam), which, however, happened at an earlier season than with the Greeks, viz., when the sun entered the 15th degree of Aquarius; but the difference of season need not be objected to, since we have observed that similar rites were adopted by the antient Persians, the beginning of whose year differed again from that of the Greeks and Chinese: but all these ceremonies may be presumed to have sprung from the same source. The Grecian ploughing was perhaps at first but a civil institution, although a mystical meaning was afterwards attached to it." *Inquiry into the Ancient Greek Game,* 1801, p. 136.

New Year's Day.—"It seems it was a custom at Rome, upon New Year's Day, for all tradesmen to work a little in their business by way of omen; for luck's sake, as we say, that they might have constant business all the year after." Massey's Notes on Ovid's *Fasti,* p. 14. Prynne, in his "Histriomastix," 1633, did not fail to detect a close correspondence between the practices on New Year's Day in his time and the ancient pagan festivals, and alluded to the prohibition published against the latter by the Catholic Church, as a hint to the English government that it should "go and do likewise." In "Vox Graculi," 1623, p. 49, is the following, under January:

This month you drink no wine commixt with dregs;
Eate capons, and fat hens, with dumpling legs.

"The first day of January being raw, colde, and comfortlesse to such as have lost their money at dice at one of the Temples overnight, strange apparitions are like to be seen: Marchpanes marching betwixt Leaden-hall and the little Conduit in Cheape, in such aboundance that an hundred good fellowes may sooner starve then catch a corner, or a comfit to sweeten their mouthes. It is also to be feared, that through frailty, if a slip be made on the messenger's default that carries them, for non-delivery at the place appointed; that unless the said messenger be not the more inward with is mistris, his master will give him rib-rost for his New Yeares Gift the next morning. This day shall be given many more gifts then shall be asked for; and apples, egges, and orenges, shall be lifted to a lofty rate; when a pome-water bestucke with a few rotten cloves, shall be more worth than the honesty of an hypocrite; and halfe a dozen of egges of more estimation than the vowes of a strumpet. Poets this day shall get mightily by their pamphlets. for an hundred of elaborate lines shall be lesse esteemed in London, then an hundred of Walfleet oysters at Cambridge."

"The King of light, father of aged time,
Hath brought about that day which is the prime
To the slow gliding months, when every eye
Wears symptoms of a sober jollity;
And every hand is ready to present
Some service in a real compliment.
Whilst some in golden letters write their love,
Some speak affection by a ring or glove,
Or pins and points (for ev'n the peasant may,
After his ruder fashion, be as gay
As the brisk courtly Sir), and thinks that he
Cannot, without gross absurdity,
Be this day frugal, and not spare his friend
Some gift, to shew his love finds not an end
With the deceased year."
—Poole's *English Parnassus,* 1657.

Hutchinson, speaking of the parish of Muncaster, under the head of "Ancient Custom," informs us: "On the eve of the New Year, the children go from house to house, singing a ditty which craves the bounty 'they were wont to have in old King Edward's days.'" *History of Cumberland*, i., 570. There is no tradition whence this custom rose; the donation is two-pence, or a pye at every house. The following passage from Lockhart's *Life of Scott*, under 1819, seems to be worth a place here: "In the next of these letters (one to Joanna Baillie), Scott alludes among other things to a scene of innocent pleasure, which I often witnessed afterwards. The whole of the ancient ceremonial of the daft days, as they are called in Scotland, obtained respect at Abbotsford. He said it was uncanny, and would certainly have felt it very uncomfortable, not to welcome the new year in the midst of his family and a few old friends, with the immemorial libation of a het pint." And it seems from the "Popish Kingdome" of Naogeorgus, that in Germany during the New Year's week debtors were left unmolested, and people kept high revelry "according to the auncient guise of heathen people vaine, and wished each other a happy new year." See *Jews.*

New Year's Day, Scotland.— The keen loyalty with which New Year's Day is observed in Edinburgh itself, to the present moment, was quite recently illustrated (1904) by the complete absence, on the arrival at Waverley Station of the London express, of porters and cabs, and a noble lord found it necessary to make his way to his hotel in a milk-cart.

New Year's Eve.—The Nidderdale people still adhere to the practice of running round the house on this anniversary. Comp. Lucas's *Studies in Nidderdale.*

New Year's Gifts.—As the vulgar, says Bourne, are always very careful to end the old year well, so they are no less solicitous of making a good beginning of the new one. The old one is ended with a hearty compotation. The new one is opened with the custom of sending presents, which are termed New Year's Gifts, to friends and acquaintances. He resolves both customs into superstitions as being observed that the succeeding year ought to be prosperous and successful. Stillingfleet says, that among the Saxons of the Northern nations the Feast of the New Year was kept with more than ordinary jollity: thence, as Olaus Wormius and Scheffer observe, they reckoned their age by so many Iolas; and Snorro Sturleson describes this New Year's Feast, just as Buchanan sets out the British

Saturnalia, as an occasion for feasting and sending New Year's Gifts to one another. *Orig. Brit.* page 343.

In the "Monthly Miscellany" for December 1692, there is an Essay on New Year's Gifts, which states, that "the ancient Druids, with great ceremonies, used to scrape off from the outside of oaks the misleden, which they consecrated to their great Tutates, and then distributed it to the people thro' the Gauls, on account of the great virtues which they attributed to it; whence New Year's Gifts are still called in some parts of France *Guy-l' an-neuf.* Our English nobility, every New Year's tide, still send to the King a purse with gold in it. Reason may be joined to custom to justify the practice; for as presages are drawn from the first things which are met on the beginning of a day, week or year, none can be more pleasing than of those things that are given us. We rejoice with our friends after having escaped the dangers that attend every year, and congratulate each other for the future by presents and wishes for the happy continuance of that course, which the ancients called *Strenarum Commercium.* And as formerly men used to renew their hospitalities by presents called *Xenia*, a name proper enough for our New Year's Gifts, they may be said to serve to renew friendship, which is one of the greatest gifts imparted by Heaven to men: and they, who have always assigned some day to those things which they thought good, have also judged it proper to solemnize the Festival of Gifts, and to show how much they esteemed it, in token of happiness, made it begin the year. The value of the thing given, or, if it is a thing of small worth, its novelty, or the excellency of the work, and the place where it is given, makes it the more acceptable, but above all, the time of giving it, which makes some presents pass for a mark of civility on the beginning of the year, that would appear unsuitable in another season." Henry III. according to Matt. Paris, appears to have extorted Gifts from his subjects. Matt. Paris, an. 1249, p. 757, ed. 1640.

A list of the New Year's Gifts distributed by Henry VI. in 1437 is printed in "Excerpta Historica," 1833. The practice of presenting New Year's Gifts to Royalty was sufficiently familiar in Henry VIIth's time, and his queen used, it seems, invariably to reciprocate by making a donation as nearly equal as possible to the value received in each case. Perhaps the most splendid New Year's Gifts ever made in early time were those which Wolsey presented to Henry VIII. One of these was a gold

cup, richly chased and engraved, of the value of £117 17s. 6d. From a MS. cited by Brand, it was usual, it seems, in the time of Edward VI. to give *rewards* on New Year's Day to those who had presented gifts previously to his Highness, and this practice continued at least till the time of Elizabeth, of whom it must be said that, if she took from her subjects, she was very liberal, so far as *estrennes* were concerned, in returning them "in reward" a full equivalent. Nichols, in his Preface to her Majesty's "Progresses" observes : "The only remains of this custom at Court now is that the two chaplains in waiting, on New Year's Day, have each a crown-piece laid under their plates at dinner. An Orange stuck with cloves appears to have been a New Year's Gift. So Ben Jonson, in his "Christmas His Masque :" "He has an Orange and rosemary, but not a clove to stick in it." The use of the orange stuck with cloves may be ascertained from "The Seconde Booke of Notable Things," by Thomas Lupton (1579) :—
"Wyne wyll be pleasant in taste and flavour, if an orenge or a lymon (stickt round about with cloves) be hanged within the vessel that it touch not the wyne : and so the wyne wyll be preserved from foystiness and evyll savor." In "Witt's Recreations," 1640, as republished in 1817, is a descriptive poem "On a Brede of divers colours, woven by four Maids of Honour and presented to the Queen on New Year's Day last." The queen, no doubt, was Henrietta-Maria. From a passage in Bishop Hall's "Satires," 1598 (Book v. Sat. 1) it should seem that the usual New Year's Gift of tenantry in the country to their landlords, was a capon : and this is corroborated in "A Lecture to the People," 1644 :

"Ye used in the former days to fall
　Prostrate unto your landlord in his hall,
When with low legs, and in an humble
　guise.
Ye offer'd up a Capon-sacrifice
Unto his worship at a New Year's
　Tide."

From a reference in Stephens's "Characters," 1615, p. 283 "Like an inscription with a fat goose against New Year's Tide," it may either be inferred that such a thing was a customary present or dish at this season. Overbury, in his Characters, speaking of "a Timist," says, that "his New Yeares Gifts are ready at Alhalomas, and the Sute he meant to meditate before them." In 1647, an anonymous writer, in addressing his tract, concerning "Motives grounded upon the word of God," to the Civic authorities of London, set forth that he presented these instead of heathenish and superstitious New Year's Gifts. It was customary, it seems, for the bailiffs

of Malden to send on the first of the year to the King's Vice-Admiral of Essex a present of oysters and wild fowl. Sir John Bramston notices the arrival of the gift on New Year's Day, March 26, 1688, in his "Autobiography," printed for the Camden Society in 1845.

In Brand's time it was still usual in Northumberland for persons to ask for a New Year's Gift on that day. Dr. Moresin tells us that in Scotland it was in his time the custom to send New Year's Gifts on New Year's Eve, but that on New Year's Day, they wished each other a happy day, and asked a New Year's Gift. *Papatus*, p. 1078. Buchanan once sent to Mary Queen of Scots a quatrain, in which he begged her Majesty to accept his very good wishes in earnest of anything more substantial, and concluded with, "Et quod abest opta tu mihi, da quod adest."

It appears that the modern practice of *Estrennes* in France is derived from the ancient usage of strena or presents made similarly on New Year's Day among friends with expressions of good wishes for the new season just commencing. The strena were given by relatives to each other. According to Le Bœuf, these presents had become popular in that country in the twelfth century. *Divers Ecrits*, i. 307. A fair is held at Paris on the Boulevards for fifteen days, commencing with the Jour de l'An, for the sale of playthings and sweatmeats.

Naogeorgus (Thomas Kirchmaier) is cited by Hospinian, as telling us, that it was usual in his time for friends to present each other with New Year's Gift; for the husband to give one to his wife ; parents to their children ; and masters to their servants, etc. ; a custom derived to the Christian world from the times of Gentilism. The superstition condemned in this by the ancient fathers, lay in the idea of these gifts being considered as omens of success for the ensuing year.

New Year's Water.—The children at Tenby used to come round, singing a pretty song, and carrying water, which they thus designated, to sprinkle over householders—presumably for good luck.

Nicholas' Clerks, St.—Comp. *Boy-Bishop* suprâ. The bad repute of the processions of youths, headed by the Episcopus Puerorum on Holy Innocents' Day and during Childermas, is supposed to have gained for them this bye-name, and it was eventually extended to depredators in general. In Bale's "Yet a course at the Romyshe Foxe," 1542, signat. D 4, the author enumerates some "auncyent rytes and lawdable ceremonyes of holy

Churche," then, it should seem, laid aside, with the following censure on the Bishop: "than ought my lorde also to suffre the same selfe ponnyshment, for not *goynge abought with Saynt Nycolas clarkes*," &c. Which passage appears to lend some countenance to the theory that the expression in italics originally signified nothing more than those who conducted the Service, but when Bale wrote, the festival of the Boy-Bishop had grown sufficiently scandalous to be made the subject of a prohibitory statute (33 Henry VIII.).

In the first part of "Henry IV." act ii. scene 1, highwaymen are called St. Nicholas's Clerks. In a tract which appeared in 1652, it is said of the Knights of the Blade, that they were "commonly called Hectors, or St. Nicholas' Clerkes." They were also called St. Nicholas' Knights. In "Plaine Percevall, the Peace-Maker of England," we read, p. 1: "He was a tender-harted fellow, though his luck were but hard, which hasting to take up a quarrell by the highway side, between a brace of St. Nicholas clargiemen, was so curteously imbraced on both parties, that he tendered his purse for their truce."

Nicholas's Day, St.—(Dec. 6). St. Nicholas was born in Patara, in Lycia, and, from a layman, was made Bishop of Myra. He died on the 8th of the ides of December, 343. In the "Festyvall," 1511, there is the following: "It is sayed of his fader, hyght Epiphanius, and his moder Joanna, &c. and when he was born, &c. they made him Christin, and called him Nycholas, that is a mannes name; but he kepeth the name of the child, for he chose to kepe vertues, meknes, and simpleness; he fasted Wednesday and Friday; these days he would souke but ones of the day, and therwyth held him plesed. Thus he lyved all his lyf in vertues with this childes name, and therefore children doe him worship before all other Saints, &c." In a MS. of the "Lives of the Saints," which Mr. Brand had, there was the following couplet upon St. Nicholas:

"Y^e furst day y^t was ybore, he gan to
  be good and clene,
For he ne wolde Wednesday ne Friday
  never more souke but ene."

So the "Golden Legend:" "He wolde not take the brest ne the pappe, but ones on the Wednesday, and ones on the Frydaye." The Roman Calendar has the following observations on St. Nicholas's Day: "Nicholas Bishop; School Holidays; the Kings go to church, with presents and great shew: the antient custom of poets in schools related to the boys; the kings feasts in schools." Douce observes: "The true reason why this saint was chosen to be the patron of scholars, may be

gathered from the following story in his life, composed in French verse by Maistre Wace, chaplain to Henry the Second: . . . 'Three scholars were on their way to school (I shall not make a long story of it), their host murdered them in the night, and hid their bodies; their . . . . he preserved. Saint Nicholas was informed of it by God Almighty, and according to his pleasure went to the place. He demanded the scholars of the host, who was not able to conceal them, and therefore showed them to him. Saint Nicholas by his prayers restored the souls to their bodies. Because he conferred such honours on scholars, they at this day celebrate a festival." The Rev. W. Cole says: "This, I suppose, sufficiently explains the naked children and tub, the well-known emblems of St. Nicholas."

It appears that the master of Wye School, founded by Archbishop Kempe in 1447, was to teach all the scholars, both rich and poor, the art of grammar gratis, unless a present was voluntarily made, and except "consuetam Gallorum et denariorum Sancti Nicolai gratuitam oblationem," the usual offering of cocks and pence at the Feast of St. Nicholas. It is said that at schools, the boys, when at play, if they wish to escape from their pursuers (as at Touch He), exclaim Nic'las, which at once disarms the youngster who, for the moment, is giving chase, or as the case may be. But the more usual formula is *Fain Play.*

As early as 1233 the Parish Clerks of London were incorporated under the style of the Fraternity of St. Nicholas, and certain property at Bishopsgate, mentioned in 27 Henry VI., is described as having formerly belonged to this brotherhood. Why such a body identified itself with the saint, seems really uncertain. Hazlitt's *Livery Companies*, 1892, p. 123.

There is a short series of miracles, ascribed to this personage in Mr. Wright's volume of *Early Mysteries*, 1838. The affiliation of marvels and prodigies cost the mediæval romancist even less than it does his successors in this class of literary invention.

In the "Mornyng Remembrance, or Moneths Mind of Margaret Countess of Richmond and Derby," by Bishop Fisher, 1509, it is said that "she praied to S. Nicholas the patron and helper of all true maydens," when nine years old, about the choice of a husband, and that the saint appeared in a vision and announced the Earl of Richmond. Comp. *St. Catherine.* Of the two London Fraternities of Haberdashers one was under the protection of St. Nicholas. Hazlitt's *Livery Companies*, 1892, p. 115.

There is a festival or ceremony observed in Italy (called Zopata, from a Spanish word signifying a shoe) in the courts of certain princes on St. Nicholas' Day, wherein persons hide presents in the shoes and slippers of those they do honour to, in such a manner as may surprise them on the morrow when they come to dress. This, it is repeated, is done in imitation of the practice of St. Nicholas, who used in the night time to throw purses in at the windows of poor maids, to be marriage portions for them. Brady notices a custom prevalent (he says) in Italy and parts of France among the nuns of placing a silk stocking with a piece of silver in it at the door of the abbess's chamber. In the paper the girls commend themselves to Great St. Nicholas of her chamber; and when, the next day, each stocking was filled with sweetmeats and other trifles, it was the saint who had put them there! There is no end of St. Nicholas's patronship. He was also the mariners' saint. In the "Vitæ Sanctorum," by Lippeloo and Gras, 1603, we read, that St. Nicholas preserved from a storm the ship in which he sailed to the Holy Land; and also certain mariners, who in a storm invoked his aid; to whom, though at a distance and still living, he appeared in person and saved them. In an ancient *fabliau* occurs the passage:—

"Esb aïz fut tut li plus sages.
Si plaissa la tourmente toz,
Ne valeit gueres li plus proz.
Rompent cordes, despescent tref,
Fruissent cheveil, desclot la nef,
Donc comencent tuit a crier,
Deu e ses sainz a reclamier.
Mult se cleiment cheitif e las,
Sovent crient: Saint Nicholas,
Socour nus, Saint Nicholas, sire,
Se tiels es cum oomes dire !
A tant uns hom lor aparut
Qui en la nief od els estut,
Et itant at a els parlié :
Je sui que m'avez appelé
Isnel le pas l'orez cessa,
E saint Nicholas s'en ala."

Maistre Waces St. Nicholas, von N. Delius, 1850, pp. 9-10.

Hospinian says, the invocation of St. Nicholas by sailors took its rise from the legendary accounts of Vincentius and Mantuanus. St. Nicholas is the present patron of those who lead a sea-faring life (as Neptune was of old), and his churches generally stand within sight of the sea, and are plentifully stocked with pious moveables. (Hospinian, "De Orig. Fest. Christ." p. 153). St. Nicholas's Church at Liverpool was close to the water, and was the earliest one built there. Armstrong, in his "History of Minorca," speaking of Ciudadella, says, "Near the entrance of the harbour stands a chapel dedicated to St. Nicholas,

to which the sailors resort that have suffered shipwreck, to return thanks for their preservation, and to hang up votive pictures (representing the danger they have escaped) in gratitude to the saint for the protection he vouchsafed them, and in accomplishment of the vows they made in the height of the storm. This custom, which is in use at present throughout the Roman Catholic world, is taken from the old Romans, who had it, among a great number of other superstitions, from the Greeks; for we are told that Bion the philosopher was shown several of these votive pictures hung up in a temple of Neptune near the seaside."

This personage, in connection with his maritime influence and celebrity, became the patron Saint of Great Yarmouth, and he appears on the corporate seal, ascribed to the 13th century, seated on a throne, holding a pastoral staff in his hand, and supported on either side by angels : there is the inscription : "O Pastor Vere Tibi Subjectis Miserere " and on the reverse side is a ship with the legend : *Sig: Comunit: De: Gernemutha.* Walford's *Pleasant days in Pleasant Places,* 1878, p. 165.

Nicholas's Eve, St.—(Dec. 5). Henry Machyn, in his "Diary" under 1556, observes : "The v. day of Desember was Sant Necolas evyn, and Sant Necolas whentt a-brod in most partt in London syngyng after the olde fassyon, and was reseyvyd with mony good pepulle in-to ther howses, and had myche good chere as ever they had, in mony plasses." Hospinian (who is followed by Naogeorgus and our Hone) tells us, that in many places it was the custom for parents, on the vigil of St. Nicholas, to convey secretly presents of various kinds to their little sons and daughters, who observed a fast on the occasion, and who were taught to believe that they owed them to the kindness of St. Nicholas and his train, who, going up and down among the towns and villages, came in at the windows, though they were shut, and distributed them. This custom, he says, originated from the legendary account of that Saint's having given portions to three daughters of a poor citizen, whose necessities had driven him to an intention of prostituting them, and this he effected by throwing a purse filled with money privately at night, in at the father's bedchamber window, to enable him to portion them out honestly.

"Saint Nicholas money used to give to maydens secretlie,
Who, that he still may use his wonted liberalitie,
The mothers all their children on the Eve do cause to fast,

And, when they every one at night in
    senselesse sleepe are cast,
Both Apples, Nuttes, and Peares they
    bring, and other things beside,
As caps, and shooes, and petticotes,
    which secretly they hide,
And in the morning found, they say,
    that this St. Nicholas brought :
Thus tender mindes to worship Saints
    and wicked things are taught."

The Popish Kingdome, 1570. See *Martinmas.*

Night Courtship.—A North-Country usage which has fallen into disuse.
See Halliwell in v. and the authority there
quoted.

Nightmare.—See *Ephialtes.*

Nine Holes.—A rural game. See
Nares, *Glossary*, ed. 1859, in v. I find the
following in Herrick :

    Upon Raspe. *Epig.*

"Raspe playes at Nine-holes; and 'tis
    known he gets
Many a teaster by his game, and bets :
But of his gettings there's but little
    sign ;
When one hole wastes more than he gets
    by nine."

Nine Men's Morris.—Mr. Tollett
writes : "In Cotgrave, under the article
Merelles, is the following explanation :
'Le Ieu des Merelles. The boyish game
called Merils, or five-penny morris : played
here most commonly with stones, but in
France with pawnes, or men made on
purpose, and tearmed merelles.' These
might originally have been black, and
hence called morris or merelles, as we yet
term a black cherry a morello, and a small
black cherry a merry, perhaps from
Maurus a Moor, or rather from Morum a
Mulberry." An account of this game is
given by Douce. "This game was sometimes called the Nine Men's Merrils, from
merelles or mereaux, an ancient French
word for jettons, or counters, with which
it was played. The other term, morris,
is probably a corruption suggested by the
sort of dance which, in the progress of the
game, the counters performed. In the
French merelles each party had three
counters only, which were to be placed in
a line in order to win the game. It appears to have been the tremerel mentioned in old fabliaux." *Illustr. of
Shakes.* i, 184. Le Grand, *Fabliaux,* ii, 208.
"Dr. Hyde thinks the morris, or merrils,
was known during the time that the Normans continued in possession of England,
and that the name was afterwards corrupted into three men's morals, or nine
men's morals. If this be true, the conversion of morrals into morris, a term so
very familiar to the country-people, was

extremely natural. The doctor adds, that
it was likewise called nine-penny or nine-
pin Miracle, three-penny morris, five-
penny morris, nine-penny morris, or
three-pin, five-pin and nine-pin morris,
all corruptions of three-pin, &c. merels."
The following is the account of this game
given by Dr. Farmer in a note to Shakespeare's *Mid. Night Dream,* ii, 2 :

    "The nine men's morris is fill'd up with
    mud."

"In that part of Warwickshire where
Shakespeare was educated, and the neighbouring parts of Northamptonshire, the
shepherds and other boys dig up the turf
with their knives to represent a sort of
imperfect chess-board. It consists of a
square, sometimes only a foot diameter,
sometimes three or four yards. Within
this is another square, every side of which
is parallel to the external square; and
these squares are joined by lines drawn
from each corner of both squares, and the
middle of each line. One party, or player,
has wooden pegs, the other stones, which
they move in such a manner as to take
up each other's men, as they are called,
and the area of the inner square is called
the pound, in which the men taken up are
impounded. These figures are by the
country people called nine men's morris,
or merrils; and are so called because each
party has nine men. These figures are
always cut upon the green turf, or leys,
as they are called, or upon the grass at
the end of ploughed lands, and in rainy
seasons never fail to be choaked up with
mud." Alchorne remarks : "nine men's
morris is a game still played by the shepherds, cow-keepers, &c. in the midland
counties, as follows : A figure (of squares,
one within another,) is made on the ground
by cutting out the turf : and two persons
each take nine stones, which they place by
turns in the angles, and afterwards move
alternately, as at chess or draughts. He
who can play three in a straight line may
then take off any one of his adversary's,
where he pleases, till one, having lost all
his men, loses the game."

Miss Baker, in her "Northamptonshire
Glossary," 1854, notices the Shepherd's
hey, race, ring, or run (as it is variously
called), a sport enjoyed by the lower classes
annually at Boughton-Green Fair, four
miles from Northampton. "A green-
sward circle," the writer says, "of considerable size, has been sunk about a foot
below the surface of the green, as far back
as memory can trace. A mazy path,
rather more than a foot in width, is formed
within by a trench, three or four inches
wide, cut on one side of it; and the trial
of skill consists in running the maze from
the outside to the small circle in a given
time, without crossing the boundaries of

the path." Some years ago at Saffron-Walden, there were the remains of a ground which had been cut in the turf for this purpose; but the marks of the morris-dancers' knives were scarcely discernible.

A writer in Willis's "Current Notes" for November, 1853, has the following account of the game: "There can be but little doubt that it is the same game as that commonly known in the South of England under the name of moriners or mariners. It is played by two persons with nine men each on a figure . . . generally on a board with the lines cut in it, and holes at the angles for pegs by way of men. The players take turns to 'pitch' their men, that is, to place them in the holes in such a way as to get, if possible, three in a line, or 'row.'" After they are all pitched, the players move alternately, the one whose turn it is shifting any one of his men to the next hole (if unoccupied) from the one it is then on, along a line. Whenever either player succeeds in making a 'row' of his own men, whether during the pitching or subsequent play, he is entitled to take off any one of his adversary's, which is not protected by being in a row, and the game is lost by the person whose number of men is first reduced by this process below three." Douce adds: "The jeu de merelles was also a table-game. A representation of two monkies engaged at this amusement may be seen in a German edition of Petrarch ' de Remedio utriusque Fortunæ,' b. i. ch. 26. The cuts to this book were done in 1520."

Nine Pins or **Skittles.**—Urquhart of Cromarty observes: "They may likewise be said to use their king as the players at nine pins do the middle kyle, which they call the king, at whose fall alone they aim, the sooner to obtain the gaining of their prize." *Discovery of a most exquisite Jewel*, 1657, p. 237, &c.

In 1684, during the great frost, the Master and Upper Wardens of the Founders' Gild played at nine pins on the Thames. Poor Robin, in his Almanack for 1695, in his observations on the spring quarter, says: "In this quarter are very much practised the commendable exercises of nine-pins, pigeon-holes, stool-ball, and barley-break, by reason Easter holydays, Whitson holydays, and May Day, do fall in this quarter."

" Ladies for pleasure now resort
Unto Hide Park-and Totnam Court;
People to Moorfields flock in sholes,
At nine-pins and at pigeon-holes.
The country lasses pastime make
At stool-ball and at barley-break;

And young men they pass time away
At wrestling and at foot-ball play.
And every one, in their own way,
As merry are as birds in May."

But in the Almanac for 1707 the game is introduced under the name of skittles: Copenhagen House, Islington, was noted for " Dutch Pins." Formerly, more than at present perhaps, nine-pins (with bowls) was the favourite amusement at suburban and riverside places of resort for oarsmen and holiday folk. Comp. *Games* suprâ. In the United States they play with ten pins, and term the game accordingly. Ten-pins is noted in Rowlands's *Letting of Humors Blood*, printed before 1600. But see *The Art of Playing at Skittles*, by A. Jones, 1773.

Speaking of this game, as it is now played at the Star near Aldgate, both in the form of thirty-one-up in the daytime by mere amateurs for amusement and in that of regular sport at night, the *Daily Graphic* of June 11, 1897, says: The skittle-alley is a long barn-like place which looks as if in a previous state of existence it might have been a back yard, and it has benches at one end. Upon the benches sit the experts and critics of the game, and upon the table in front of them are measures — pint measures — for refreshment. If you go in during the daytime it will be to find a game of a more or less desultory nature going on. "These yere," observes the landlord nodding towards the eight or ten skittlers, " ain't in a manner o' speakin' what you might call players: and they ain't as you might say playin' skittles, its thirty-one up as they're a playin', a sort of a rambling game, but it livens 'em up. There's a laugh attached to it—if you understand me, sir." But at night, as the landlord explains, there is a very different scene in the little alley. The gaslights flare and the place is thick with tobacco; a continual clamour partly begotten of beer, but more directly due to emulation, fills the place, and most of the players who are not playing are discussing their own chances with great emphasis. The emphasis is sometimes directed to description of the handicapper who has allowed them less start than they ought to have.

The skittle handicaps are conducted with the greatest strictness, and sometimes last over weeks, since there are a large number of competitors, and between good players a match " five up," whch is the usual length of a handicap game, often takes a long time. But the East-Ender takes his amusement, especially in the way of skittles, leisurely; he likes to eke it out as far as it will go. There are, as everybody knows, nine pins in the skittle diamond, each of them twenty-four inches apart. The player who bowls the cheese at them, usually after running up the narrow path leading to the diamond, hurls it from a distance of six feet at the pins, and so as to ensure that he shall not approach closer, a line of putty is placed across the path to show the impress of boots. The way of scoring is as follows. If the first player knocks down all the nine-pins then he is said to "set" the other player "one"—which is to say that the other player must knock all the pins down in two "goes." If the first player knocks down eight pins, so that he himself requires two "goes" to clear the lot, then he is said to "set two," which is to say that his opponent must knock all the pins down in three "goes" or else lose a point. As good players habitually knock down eight or nine, and eight is practically as good a "go" as nine, it will be understood that there are a large number of skittles. Seven or eight ties are by no means uncommon between good and well-matched players, and perhaps in a game of "five up" one might see a score of ties before the contest was decided. The excitement when, after two or three weeks of this sort of thing, the final heats are approaching, is very pronounced; it overflows from the skittle alley into the bar, and sometimes is a source of considerable anxiety to the neighbours in the little side street." The rules of the game are framed and glazed in the bar.

Noah's Ark.—A dark cloud of considerable length, broad in the centre, and tapering toward the extremities, in a manner which produces a real or supposed resemblance to the ark. It prognosticates heavy rains. The Scots, however, appear to draw a distinction between the different directions in which Noah's ark is seen; if it extends from S. to N., it portends fair weather: if from E. to W., wind and rain. Rain, it may be here added, is held to be foreshadowed by the appearance of what is called the Weather-Gall, or second rainbow. In the Cleveland country this is not called Noah's ark, apparently, but *Noeship*, merely another form, however, of the same term, as Noe is in early English the almost invariable shape in which the patriarch's name occurs.

Noddy.—An old game at cards, supposed to be the same as cribbage. See Halliwell in v. and *Cards* suprâ.

Nog Money.—In Scotland, upon the last day of the old year, the children go about from door to door asking for bread and cheese, which they call nog-money, in these words:

" Get up, gude-wife, and binno sweir,
 (i.e. be not lazy)
And deal your cakes and cheese, while
 you are here ;

For the time will come when ye'll be dead,
And neither need your cheese nor bread."

Noontide.—Mr. Johnson says, noontide "signifies three in the afternoon, according to our present account: and this practice, I conceive, continued down to the Reformation. In King Withfred's time, the Lord's day did not begin till sunset on the Saturday. Three in the afternoon was hora nona in the Latin account, and therefore called noon: how it came afterwards to signifie mid-day, I can but guess. The monks by their rules could not eat their dinner till they had said their noon-song, which was a service regularly to be said at three o'clock: but they probably anticipated their devotions and their dinner, by saying their noon song immediately after their mid-day song, and presently falling on. I wish they had never been guilty of a worse fraud than this. But it may fairly be supposed, that when mid-day became the time of dining and saying noon song, it was for this reason called noon by the monks, who were the masters of the language during the dark ages. In the 'Shepherd's Almanack' noon is mid-day; high noon, three." *Const.* Part 1, Anno 958, 5.

Nose.—It is still a rural or vulgar superstition, that a child born with a blue vein on the side of its nose is destined to be drowned. The bleeding of the nose was formerly treated as a bad portent. In the *History of Thomas of Reading*, by T. Deloney, printed before 1600, when the hero of the romance is on his way to the Crane Inn at Colebrook, where the host used to murder his guests by means of a false floor in the bedroom over the kitchen, and a boiling cauldron below, we are told that "his nose burst out suddenly a-bleeding," as he drew near to the town. The author has collected together nearly all the harbingers of evil known in his day in the narrative of circumstances which preceded the murder.

In Bodenham's *Belvedere*, 1600, p. 147, we have the following simile from one of our old poets:

" As suddaine bleeding argues ill ensuing,
So suddaine ceasing is fell Feares renewing."

Lancelot Gobbo, in the "Merchant of Venice," 1600, says, "I will not say you shall see a masque; but if you do, then it was not for nothing that my nose fell a-bleeding on Black-Monday last at six o'clock i' the morning," on which Steevens observes, that from a passage in Lodge's

"Rosalynde," 1590, it appears that some superstitious belief was annexed to the accident of bleeding at the nose : "—as he stoode gazing, his nose on a sodaine bledde, which made him conjecture that it was some friend of his." Again in Webster's "Dutchess of Malfy," 1623, act ii. sc. 2:

> "How superstitiously we mind our evils?
> The throwing down salt, or crossing of a hare,
> Bleeding at nose, the stumbling of a horse,
> Or singing of a creket, are of power
> To daunt whole man in us."

And a little farther on :

> "*Ant.* My nose bleeds.
> One that were superstitious would (ac)count
> This ominous, when it merely comes by chance."

Wither introduces this subject into his *Abuses*, 1613:

> For worthlesse matters some are wondrous sad,
> Whom if I call not vaine I must terme mad.
> If that their noses bleed some certaine drops,
> And then againe upon the suddaine stops,
> Or, if the babling foule we call a jay,
> A squirrell, or a hare, but crosse their way,
> Or, if the salt fall towards them at table,
> Or any such like superstitious bable,
> Their mirth is spoil'd because they hold it true
> That some mischance must thereupon ensue."

The nose falling a bleeding appears by the following passage to have been a sign of love : " Did my nose ever bleed when I was in your company? and, poore wench, just as she spake this, to shew her true heart, her nose fell a bleeding." Brathwaite's *Boulster Lecture*, 1640, p. 130.

Melton observes : "That when a man's nose bleeds but a drop or two, it is a sign of ill lucke ; that when a man's nose bleeds one drop, and at the left nostril, it is a sign of good lucke, but, on the right, ill." Grose says, a drop of blood from the nose commonly foretells death, or a very severe fit of sickness ; three drops are still more ominous. Burton says that "to bleed three drops at the nose is an ill omen," *Anatomy*, 1621, p. 214. In which he is followed by Keuchenius in an epigram, which explains the matter by the principle of uneven numbers (especially three and its multiples) being agreeable both to gods and men. *Crepundia*, p. 214. "That

your nose may never bleed only three drops at a time, is found among the omens deprecated in Holiday's "Marriage of the Arts," 1618.

In the Adventures of Master F.I., which may perhaps be a piece of his own personal history, Gascoigne describes a charm to check bleeding at the nose : "Hee (Ferdinando) layde his hande on hir temples, and priuily rounding hir in hir eare, desired hir to commaunde a hazell sticke and a knyfe: the whiche beyng brought, hee deliuered vnto hir, saying on this wise : Mistresse, I will speake certaine woordes in secrete to my selfe, and doe require no more, but when you heare me saie openly this worde *Amen*, that you with this knyfe will make a nicke vppon this hazell sticke : and when you haue made fiue nickes, commaunde mee also to cease." Works by Hazlitt, i. 422-3. It is added that this remedy was found effectual. In verses prefixed by A. W. to Gascoigne's Posies, 1575, it is said by the writer that the flower pimpernel (of which there is more than one variety) was considered of utility and virtue in this respect.

The following charm has been preserved, to stop bleeding at the nose and all other hæmorrhages in the country :

> "In the blood of Adam Sin was taken,
> In the blood of Christ it was all to shaken,
> And by the same blood I do thee charge,
> That the blood of (naming the party) run no longer at large."
> —*Athenian Oracle*, i, 158.

This physical symptom has long been reduced to a common-place level by the general belief and knowledge that it is a mere effort of nature, in the majority of instances, to counteract an excess of blood to the brain. It is extremely common in the young ; but in later life it has been observed that the hemorrhage often ceases, or occurs much less frequently. I have heard the itching of the nose interpreted into the expectation of seeing a stranger. So in the "Honest Whore," by Decker and Middleton, 1604, Bellafront says : "We shall ha guests to day, I lay my little maidenhead, my nose itches so." Works, 1840, iii, 36. The reply made by her servant Roger further informs us that the biting of fleas was a token of the same kind. Melton observes in his *Astrologaster*, 1620, that "when a man's nose itcheth, it is a signe he shall drink wine," and that "if your lips itch, you shall kisse some body."

Not or **Knot.**—This is a game played in Gloucestershire between two sides, each of whom is armed with bats, and endeavours to drive a ball in opposite directions. It is apt to become a violent and dangerous amuesment. Comp. *Shinty*.

Nottingham. "In Nottingham," says Deering, upon some old authority, which he does not specify, " by an antient custom, they keep yearly a general watch every midsummer eve at night, to which every inhabitant of any ability sets forth a man, as well voluntaries as those who are charged with arms, with such munition as they have; some pikes, some muskets, calivers, or other guns, some partisans, holberts, and such as have armour send their servants in their armour. The number of these are yearly almost two hundred, who at sun-setting meet on the Row, the most open part of the town, where the Mayor's Serjeant at Mace gives them an oath, the tenor whereof followeth, in these words : ' You shall well and truly keep this town till to-morrow at the sun-rising ; you shall come into no house without license, or cause reasonable. Of all manner of casualties, of fire, of crying of children, you shall due warning make to the parties, as the case shall require you. You shall due search make of all manner of affrays, bloudsheds, outcrys, and of all other thngs that be suspected,' &c. Which done, they all march in orderly array through the principal parts of the town, and then they are sorted into several companies, and designed to several parts of the town, where they are to keep the watch until the sun dismiss them in the morning. In this business the fashion is for every watchman to wear a garland, made in the fashion of a crown imperial, bedeck'd with flowers of various kinds, some natural, some artificial, bought and kept for that purpose, and also ribbans, jewels, and, for the better garnishing thereof, the townsmen use the day before to ransack the gardens of all the gentlemen within six or seven miles about Nottingham, besides what the town itself affords them, their greatest ambition being to outdo one another in the bravery of their garlands. This custom is now quite left off. It used to be kept in this town even so lately as the reign of King Charles I."

Novem Quinque.—This is mentioned as a game at cards or dice in the "English Courtier and the Countrey Gentleman," 1586. Comp. Nares, 1859, in v.

Numbers.—In Bell's MS. Discourse on Witchcraft I find the following passage : "Are there not some, who cure by observing numbers, after the example of Balaam, who used Magiam Geometricam ? Numb. xxiii. 4. ' Build me here seven altars, and prepare me seven oxen and seven rams,' &c. There are some witches who enjoin the sick to dipp their shirt seven times in south running water. Elisha sends Naaman to wash in Jordan seven times. Elijah, on the top of Carmel, sends his servant seven times to look out for rain. When Jericho was taken, they compassed the city seven times." Vallancey tells us, "in unenlightened times we find persons of the brightest characters tainted with superstition. St. Irenæus says, ' there must be four gospels and no more, from the four winds and four corners of the earth ;' and St. Austin, to prove that Christ was to have twelve apostles, uses a very singular argument, for, says he, ' The Gospel was to be preached in the four corners of the world in the name of the Trinity, and three times four makes twelve.' " *Collect.* ii, 12-13, *Note.*

The predilection for odd numbers is very ancient, and is mentioned by Virgil in his eighth Eclogue, where many spells and charms, still practised, are recorded : but notwithstanding these opinions in favour of odd numbers, the number thirteen is considered as extremely ominous, it being held that when thirteen persons meet in a room, one of them will die within a year. It has been suggested that the ancient popular superstition that it is unlucky to make one in a company of thirteen persons, may probably have arisen from the paschal supper. We can none of us forget that succeeded that repast, at which thirteen persons are said to have been present.

"Aut quemcumque Superorum, juxta Pythagoreos, qui ternarium numerum perfectum summo Deo assignant, a quo initium, et medium, et finis est: aut revera Hecaten dicit, cujus triplex potestas esse perhibetur : unde est tria Virginis Ora Dianæ. Quamvis omnium prope Deorum potestas triplici Signo ostendatur, ut Jovis trifidum Fulmen, Neptuni Tridens, Plutonis Canis triceps. Apollo idem Sol, idem Liber, vel quod omnia ternario Numero continentur, ut Parcæ, Furiæ, Hercules etiam trinoctio conceptus. Musæ ternæ : aut impari quemadmodumcumque : nam septem chordæ, septem planetæ, septem dies nominibus Deorum, septem Stellæ in Septentrione, et multa his similia : et impar numerus immortalis, quia dividi integer non potest, par numerus mortalis, quia dividi potest ; licet Varro dicat Pythagoreos putare imparem Numerum habere finem, parem esse infinitum ; ideo medendi causa multarumque rerum impares servari." Servius in P. Virgil. Eclog. viii. ed. Varior. See also Censorinus de Die Natali, 1695, p. 121, and Macrob. lib. i. Saturnal. cap. xiii ; Solin. cap. iii.

Fuller relates the following anecdote : " A covetous courtier complained to King Edward the sixt of Christ Colledge in Cambridge, that it was a superstitious foundation, consisting of a master and twelve fellowes, in imitation of Christ and his twelve apostles. He advised the King also to take away one or two fellowships, so to discompose that superstitious number. Oh no, (said the King) I have a better way than that, to mar their conceit, I will add a thirteenth fellowship unto them; which he did accordingly, and so it remaineth unto this day." *Mixt Contemplations*, 1660, part 2, p. 53.

This number was also supposed to be ominous in consequence of its agreement with that which attended the witches' meetings or sabbaths. Hence it was called the *Devil's dozen*, and afterwards the *Baker's*. Comp. Nares, *Glossary*, 1859, v. *Baker's Dozen*. Massinger, in *A New Way to pay Old Debts*, 1633, where Greedy says to Sir Giles Overreach:

"There are a dozen of woodcocks—"

the latter replies:

Make thyself thirteen, the Baker's dozen—"

In the "Gentleman's Magazine" for July, 1796, is an account of a dinner party consisting of thirteen, and of a maiden lady's observation, that as none of her married friends were likely to make an addition to the number, she was sure that one of the company would die within the twelvemonth. It is worthy of note that our own superstition respecting the number thirteen at a dinner-table is equally entertained by the Basques. The same may be said of the spilling of salt, knives crossed, the screech of the owl, or the barking of dogs, as presages of death, the commencement of any task on a Friday, and many of our notions about witchcraft and sorcery. But M. Michel's chapter on the superstitions of the "Pays Basque" should be read as a whole.

It is said of William Marquis Berkeley, who was born in 1426, that "This Lord William closeth the second Septenary Number from Harding the Dane, as much differing from his last ancestors, as the Lord Thomas, the first septenary lord, did from his six former forefathers. I will not be superstitiously opinionated of the misteries of numbers, though it bee of longe standing amongst many learned men; neither will I positively affirm, that the number six is fatall to weomen, and the numbers of seaven and nine to men. Or, that those numbers have, (as many have written,) magnam in tota rerum natura potestatem, great power in kingdoms and comon wealths, in families, ages of bodies, sickness, health, wealth, losse, &c.: Or, with Seneca and others: Septimus quisque Annus, &c. Each seaventh year is remarkable with men, as the sixth is with weomen. Or, as divines teach: that in the numbers of Seaven there is a misticall perfection which our under-

standinge cannot attaine unto: and that Nature herself is observant of this number." Fosbrooke's *Berkeley MSS.*, 1821, p. 156. His marginal references are as follow: "Philo-Judæus de Legis Alleg. lib. i. Hippocrates. Bodin. de Republicâ, lib. iv. cap. 2. See the Practice of Piety, fol. 418. 410. Censorinus de Die Natali, cap. 12. Seneca. Varro apud Gellium, lib. iii. Bucholcer, Jerom in Amos, 5."

An anonymous author, speaking of Heylin's "fatal Observation of the Letter H." says: "A sudden conceit darted into my thoughts (from the remembrance of former reading,) that such kings of England, as were the second of any name, proved very unfortunate princes:" and he proceeds, in confirmation of this hypothesis, to write the lives of the above kings. *Numerus Infaustus*, 1689, Pref. Mr. Roberts, in his "History of Lyme Regis," records an instance of the still prevailing belief in the peculiar power or faculty of a seventh son, as well as of the seventh son of a seventh son (without any intermediate female children). The former is, or was very recently, supposed to be able to cure ordinary diseases by the touch, but to the latter was reserved the higher gift of touching for the king's evil. In the diary of Walter Yonge, under date of 1606-7, it is said, that a seventh son was to be seen in London at that time, who healed the deaf, the blind, and the lame; but the imposture was exposed by the Bishop of London, who brought persons to the alleged miracle-worker, and satisfied all rational witnesses that the whole affair was a hoax and a falsehood.

Lemnius observes: "Augustus Cæsar, as Gellius saith, was glad and hoped that he was to live long, because he had passed his sixty-third year. For olde men seldome passe that year, but they are in danger of their lives, and I have observed in the Low Countries almost infinite examples thereof. Now there are two years, the seventh and ninth, that commonly bring great changes in a man's life and great dangers; wherefore sixty-three, that containes both these numbers multiplied together, comes not without heaps of dangers, for nine times seven, or seven times nine, are sixty-three. And thereupon that is called the climatericall year, because beginning from seven, it doth as it were by steps finish a man's life." The writer seems to have been of opinion that the septennial renewal of leases is referable to this origin. *Occult Miracles of Nature*, 1658, p. 142.

Werenfels, speaking of a superstitious man, says: "Upon passing the climaterick year, he is as much rejoiced as if he had escaped out of the paws of death.

When he is sick, he will never swallow the pills he is ordered to take, in equal number." *Dissertation on Superstition*, 1746, p. 7. In setting a hen, says Grose, the good women hold it an indispensable rule to put an odd number of eggs. All sorts of remedies are directed to be taken, three, seven, or nine times. Salutes with cannon consist of an odd number. A royal salute is thrice seven, or twenty-one guns. Even leases are usually made out of seven, fourteen, or twenty-one years. At games of chance or skill with cards, odd numbers are likewise much in favour, as, for instance, at vingt-et-un, picquet, ecarté, &c. In Ravenscroft's *Mamamouchi*, 1675, one of the characters, Trickmore, habited as a physician, says: "Let the number of his bleedings and purgations be odd, Numero Deus impare gaudet."

Flecknoe describes "One who troubles herself with every thing," as follows: "She is perpetually haunted with a panick fear of 'Oh what will become of us!' &c. and the stories of apparitions in the air, and prognosticks of extraordinary accidents to happen in the year 66, (when perhaps 'tis nothing but the extraordinary gingle of numbers,) makes her almost out of her wits agen." *Enigmatical Characters*, 1665, p. 109. Gaule classes with vain observations and superstitious ominations, "to collect or predict men's manners and fortunes by their names, or the anagram upon the name, or the allusion to the name, or the numbers in the name," &c. *Magastromancers posed*, p. 181. Sir Thomas Browne writes, "that Fluctus decumanus, or the tenth wave, is greater or more dangerous than any other, some no doubt will be offended if we deny: and hereby we shall seem to contradict antiquity: for, answerable unto the literal and common acceptation, the same is averred by many writers, and plainly described by Ovid:

" 'Qui venit hic fluctus, fluctus supereminet omnes
Posterior nono est, undecimoque prior.'

which, notwithstanding, is evidently false ; nor can it be made out by observation either upon the shore or on the ocean, as we have with diligence explored in both. And surely in vain we expect a regularity in the waves of the sea, or in the particular motions thereof, as we may in its general reciprocations, whose causes are constant and effects therefore correspondent. Whereas its fluctuations are but motions subservient: which winds, storms, shores, shelves, and every interjacency irregulates." "Of affinity hereto is that conceit of ovum decumanum, so called because the tenth egg is bigger than any other, according to the reason alleged by

Festus, 'Decumana ova dicuntur, quia ovum decimum majus nascitur.' For the honour we bear unto the clergy, we cannot but wish this true: but herein will be found no more verity than the other." He adds: "The conceit is numeral."

Nuptial Usages—Marriage,

(i) *the time of year.* In the "Roman Calendar," several days are marked as unfit for marriages, "Nuptiæ non fiunt," i.e. "Feb. 11, Jun. 2, Nov. 2, Dec. 1." On the 16th of September, it is noted, "Tobiæ sacrum. Nuptiarum Ceremoniæ a Nuptiis deductæ, videlicet de Ense, de Pisce, de Pompa, et de Pedibus lavandis." On the 24th of January, the vigil of St. Paul's Day, there is this singular restriction, "Viri cum Uxoribus non cubant." "Tempus quoque Nuptiarum celebrandarum" (says Stuckius) "certum a veteribus definitum et constitutum esse invenio. Concilii Ilerdensis, xxxiii. 9, 4. Et in Decreto Ivonis lib. 6, non oportet a Septuagesima usque in Octavam Paschæ, et tribus Hebdomadibus ante Festivitatem S. Joannis Baptistæ, et ab adventu Domini usque post Epiphaniam, nuptias celebrare. Quod si factum fuerit, separentur." *Antiquitat. Conviv.* p. 72. See also the formula in the append. to Hearne's "Hist. and Antiq. of Glastonbury," p. 309. In an almanack for the year 1559, by Lewis Vaughan, "made for the merydian of Gloucestre," are noted as follow: "the tymes of weddinges when it begynneth and endeth." "Jan. 14. Weding begin. Jan. 21. Weddinge goth out. April 3. Wedding begyn. April 29. Weddinge goeth out. May 22. Wedding begyn." And in another almanack for 1655, by Andrew Waterman, mariner, we have pointed out to us, in the last page, the following days as "good to marry, or contract a wife, (for then women will be fond and loving,) viz. January 2, 4, 11, 19, and 21. Feb. 1, 3, 10, 19, 21. March 3, 5, 12, 20, 23. April 2, 4, 12, 20, and 22. May 2, 4, 12, 20, 23. June 1, 3, 11, 19, 21. July 1, 3, 19, 19, 21, 31. August 2, 11, 18, 20, 30. Sept. 1, 9, 16, 18, 28. Octob. 1, 8, 15, 17, 27, 29. Nov. 5, 11, 13, 22, 25. Dec. 1, 8, 10, 19, 23, 29."

The month of May is generally considered as an unlucky one for the celebration of marriage. This is an idea, which has been transmitted to us by our ancestors, and was borrowed by them from the ancients. Thus Ovid, in his "Fasti," lib. v.:

"Nec viduæ tædis eadem, nec virginis apta

Tempora. Quæ nupsit, non diuturna fuit.

Hac quoque de causâ (si te proverbia tangunt),

Mense malas Maio nubere vulgus ait."

Our rustics retain to this day many superstitious notions concerning the times of the year when it is accounted lucky or otherwise to marry. It has been remarked that none are ever married on Childermas Day : for whatever cause, this is a black day in the calendar of impatient lovers. Randle Holme, too, tells us : "Innocence Day on what day of the week soever it lights upon, that day of the week is by astronomers taken to be a cross day all the year through." *Acad. of Armoury*, lib. 3, c. 3. The following proverb marks another ancient conceit on this head :

"Who marries between the sickle and
  the scythe,
Will never thrive."

(ii) *the hour*. The canonical hours for marriage fixed by the Church, unless dispensed with by special licence, are between eight o'clock in the morning and noon. They usually take place between eight and one in the afternoon. The Church imposes sacred rules or canons, and you are not to violate them, unless you pay for doing so. It is a mere question of cash.

In the arrangements for the marriage of Catherine of Arragon to Arthur, Prince of Wales, in 1501, the following passage occurs : "Item, that the maryage take begynnynge somewhat before ix at the clocke." *Traduction and mariage of the princesse*, (1502) A 4 vᵒ. In connection with the hour is the season of the year, for which there has never been any fixed rule, the event depending on the rank of the parties and in the case of the working classes and persons in employments on the occurrence of holidays. Comp. *Lucky and Unlucky Days*. It is said that there was formerly a custom in Edinburgh for a bride, meeting the King on foot in the street to kiss him ; but even in the 15th century James IV. of Scotland is found resisting this privilege.

(iii) *the place*. Vallancey informs us that the antient Etruscans always were married in the streets, before the door of the house, which was thrown open at the conclusion of the ceremony ; but it is scarcely safe, perhaps, to draw analogies between the practice of a people living in so different a climate from our own, and under such different conditions. "Collectanea," No. xiii. p. 67. As for the early Italians, in some of their republics it appears to have been usual to hear suits at law in the porch of the house ; but in the Lombard architecture of the middle ages the porch enjoyed a prominence, which among us it never possessed. All the ancient missals mention at the beginning of the nuptial ceremony, the placing of the man and woman before the door of the church, and direct, towards the conclusion, that here they shall enter the church as far as the step of the altar. "Missale ad Usum Sarum," 1555. See also the formula in the appendix to Hearne's "Hist. and Antiq. of Glastonb.," p. 309. Chaucer alludes to this custom in his "Wife of Bath" thus :

"She was a worthy woman all her live,
Husbands at the Church dore had she
    five."

In a collection of prints, illustrating ancient customs (which Brand saw) in the library of Douce, there was one that represented a marriage solemnizing at the church door. In a MS. cited in the "History of Shrewsbury," 1779, it is observed that "the pride of the clergy and the bigotry of the laity were such, that both rich and poor were married at the church doors." By the parliamentry reformation of marriage and other rites under King Edward the Sixth, the man and woman were first permitted to come into the body or middle of the church, standing no longer as formerly at the door : yet (from the superscription of Herrick's poem called "The Entertainment, or Porch-verse, at the marriage of Mr. Hen. Northly," &c.) one would be tempted to think that this custom had survived the Reformation. In Fletcher's "Scornful Lady," 1616, the lady says :

"Were my feet in the door ; were 'I
  John' said ;—
If John should boast a favour done by
  me,
I would not wed that year."

The celebration of the religious ceremony at the church-door might satisfy the clergy ; but it did not confirm the bond, unless an entry was made in the civil register. Otherwise one might have supposed that the man and woman were not deemed fit to enter the building, till their union had been fully solemnized.

Selden asserts that no where else, but before the face of, and at the door of the church, could the marriage-dower have been lawfully assigned ; which may derive support from the following passage : "Robert Fitz Roger, in the 6th Ed. I. entered into an engagement with Robert de Tybetot, to marry, within a limited time, John his son and heir, to Hawisia, the daughter of the said Robert de Tybetot, to endow her at the church-door on her wedding-day with lands amounting to the value of one hundred pounds per annum." *Uxor Hebraica* (Opera, tom. iii. p. 680). "Neque alibi quam in facie Ecclesiæ, et ad ostium Ecclesiæ atque ante desponsationem in initio Contractus (ut Juris Consultus nostri veteres aiunt) sic fundi dos legitimè assignari potuit."

(iv.) *the Service.* In a manuscript missal of the date of Richard II's reign, formerly the property of University College in Oxford, in the marriage ceremony, the man says : " Ich M. take the N. to my weddid wyf, to haven and to holden, for fayrere for fouler, for bettur for wors, for richer for porer, in seknesse and in helthe, fro thys tyme forward, till dethe us departe, if holichirche will it orden, and therto iche plight the my treuthe :" and on giving the ring (as in the Sarum book, edit. 1554, fol. 43) : " With this ring I the wedde and this gold and silver ich the gebe and with my bodi I the worschepe, and with all my worldly catelle [chatells] I the honoure." The woman says : " Iche N. take the M. to my weddid husbond, to haven and to holden, for fayrer for fouler, for better for wors, for richer for poorer, in seknesse and in helthe, to be bonlich and buxum in bed and at burde, tyl deth us departe, fro thys tyme forward, and if holichirche it wol orden, & therto Iche plight my truthe."

At the private marriage of Sir William Plumpton about 1451 to Joan Wintringham at Knaresborough the bridegroom, taking the bride with his right hand, repeated after the vicar : " Here I take the Jeannett to my weddid wife to hold and to have, att bed and att bord, for farer or lather, for better for warse, in sicknesse and in hele, to dede us depart, and thereto I plight the my trouth," which the bride repeated *mutatis mutandis,* after which the vicar said in a low voice the mass of the Holy Trinity. Sir William was dressed in a garment of green checkery and his wife in a red one. *Plumpton Correspondence,* 1839, lxxvii.

The variations of these missals on this head are observable. The Hereford Missal makes the man say : " I N . undersyng the N. for my wedde wyf, for betere for worse, for richer for porer, yn sekenes & in helthe, tyl deth us departe as holy church hath ordeyned, and therto Y plyght the my trowthe." The woman says : " I N. undersynge the N. &c. to be buxom to the tyl deth us departe," &c. In the Sarum Manual there is this remarkable variation in the woman's speech : " to be bonere and buxum in bedde and at borde," &c. Bonaire and buxum are explained in the margin by " meek and obedient." In the York Manual the woman engages to be " buxom " to her husband, and the man takes her " for fairer for fouler, for better for warse," &c. The so-called Bangor use varies, again, from those just cited, but substantially agrees with the texts of the Sarum and York Manuals. The Irish servicebook was probably compiled from the English.

There are three points to be noted in the foregoing extracts from these Rituals : that the Order of Matrimony is in English ; that the man seems to tender by way of symbol, when he gives the ring, *Gold and Silver,* and that the parties severally *undersign* themselves or rather put their names or marks as an evidence of the contract. The preservation of registers in churches for this purpose dates only from about 1538 ; the expression *undersign* occurs only in the later printed books : it is still in use as a synonym for subscribe.

It is observable that the joining together of the right hands in the marriage ceremony is noticed by Alexander ab Alexandro, *(Gen. Dies,* ii, 5). See also Quintus Curtius, lib. 1.

In Friar Bacons Prophesie, 1604, the father is made to give away his daughter. At one time he also performed the civil ceremony of marriage.

In England, during the time of the Commonwealth, justices of peace were empowered to marry people. A jeu d'esprit on this subject may be found in Flecknoe's " Diarium," 1656, p. 83, " On the Justice of Peace's making marriages, and the crying of them in the market." In the parish registers of Uxbridge, Middlesex, is a copy of one of the registrations of marriages, when the jurisdiction of the Church had been suspended :—

PUBLICATIONS.	MARRIAGES.
1653.	1653.
A contract of matrimony between Robert Flood and Elizabeth Howard, both of ye parish of Hillingdon in the County of Midd, was published in ye same Parish Church of Hillingdon on three severall Lords daies, viz., the 25th of December, ye 1st of January, and ye 8th of January, in ye year, 1653, at the close of the morning exercise, according to an Act of Parliament in that case provided.	Robert Flood and Elizabeth Howard, both of the parish of Hillingdon, were married this 9th day of January before mee, John Baldwin, Esq., Justice of the Peace, according to an Act of Parliament in that case made and provided. Jo. BALDWIN.

In the fifteenth century there seems to have been a prevalent superstition that prayers offered to the Holy Roods at Bermondsey Abbey and at the north door of St. Paul's by maidens desirous of obtaining a good husband were likely to prove effectual, for we find a young lady of the

Paston family in Norfolk recommended during her stay in London in 1465 to take this step. *Paston Letters*, ed. Gairdner, ii, 233. Stephens, in his character of "a plaine country bride," says: "She takes it by tradition from her fellow-gossips, that she must weepe shoures upon her marriage day: though by the vertue of mustard and onions, if she cannot naturally dissemble."

In Leap years it is yet the fashion to suppose that on the extra day (29th) of February women may propose marriage to the other sex, and in 1904 a good deal of correspondence occurred on the subject in the press.

A strange conception formerly prevailed that, if a man married a woman stripped of her clothing, her chemise (for propriety's sake) excepted, he was not answerable for her debts contracted before the ceremony. Numerous illustrations of this fallacy occur in *Notes and Queries* and elsewhere; the subjoined examples may suffice; they are taken from *N. & Q.* for 1876:—"An extraordinary method was adopted by a brewer's servant in February, 1723, to prevent his liability for the payment of the debts of a Mrs Brittain, whom he intended to marry. The lady made her appearance at the door of St. Clement Danes habited in her shift; hence her enamorato conveyed the modest fair to a neighbouring apothecary's, where she was completely equipped with cloathing purchased by him; and in these Mrs. Brittain changed her name at the church."—Malcolm's *Anecdotes of London*, p. 233.

"A few days ago a handsome, well-dressed young woman came to a church in Whitehaven to be married to a man, who was attending there with the clergyman. When she had advanced a little into the church, a nymph, her bride-maid, began to undress her, and by degrees stript her to her shift; thus was she led blooming and unadorned to the altar, where the marriage ceremony was performed. It seems this droll wedding was occasioned by an embarrassment, in the affairs of the intended husband, upon which account the girl was advised to do this, that he might be entitled to no other marriage portion than her smock."—*Annual Register*, 1766, Chronicle, p. 106. Nathan Alder married Widow Hibbert with only a smock on (for the same reason), at the old church in the parish of Ashton-under Lyne, on March 7, 1771. "At Ashton Church, in Lancashire, a short time ago, a woman was persuaded, that if she went to church naked, her intended husband would not be burthened with her debts, and she actually went as a bride like mother Eve, but to the honour of the clergyman, he refused the damsel the honours of wedlock."—*Chester Courant*, June 24, 1800. "In Lincolnshire, between 1838 and 1844, a woman was married enveloped in a sheet. And not many years back a similar marriage took place; the clergyman, finding nothing in the rubric about the woman's dress,. thought he could not refuse to marry her in her chemise only."

The manners and fashions of the higher classes in England and France in the thirteenth century were sufficiently in harmony to render it justifiable to introduce a notice of the ceremonies attendant on the marriage of Blonde of Oxford with Jean de Dammartin in the cognominal romance, which does not enter into the historical side of the subject and the intimate connection of the Dammartin family with the mediæval countship of Boulogne. We are there told that at short notice thirty minstrels, a hundred knights, and two hundred ladies came to the feast. The bride wore a gown of cloth of gold and a mantle of which the tassels were worth fourteen marks. Her hair was beautifully dressed, and hanging down to her girdle. A gold chaplet held it together, and on her temples a clasp, than which the king did not possess a richer. At her girdle hung a purse of unequalled beauty set in gold and precious stones, with pearls as large as peas, it was estimated at 100 livres. After the service the knights led the bride to the hall, where dinner was laid, and the banquet was followed by a performance of minstrelsy. In the evening the proceedings were brought to a close by supper and dancing. Next day there was a second dinner, and then the guests took their leave. *Romance of Blonde of Oxford and Jean de Dammartin*, edited from an unique MS. by Le Roux de Lincy, 1858; Hazlitt's *Coins of Europe*, 1893, p. 396.

A curious notice, from its early date, presents itself of a middle-class marriage in the Eastern counties in 1448 in a letter from Margaret Paston to her husband, where the writer says:—"Kateryn Walsaw xal be weddyd on the Monday nexst after Trinyte Sonday, as it is told me, to the galaunte with the grete chene; and there is purvayd for her meche gode aray of gwnys, gyrdelys, and atyrys, and meche other gode aray, and he hathe purcheysyd a gret purcheys of V. mark be yer to yevyn her to her joynture."

At the nuptials of Margaret, sister of Edward IV. of England, to Charles le Temeraire Duke of Burgundy, in 1468, the Lord Mayor of London, on the entry of the Princess into Cheap, presented her with a pair of rich basins, in each of which were a hundred pounds [livres?] of gold. The embarkation of the bride at Margate, on her departure, presents the earliest notice I have found of that now celebrated watering-place. "The Fryedaye next after the Nativite of Sainct John the Baptist she shipped at Margate, and ther she toke leve of the Kinge and departid." When she landed at Sluys, in Holland, she was received with great honour, and the contemporary narrative states that "thei gave unto my ladie xii marke of golde, the whiche is in valewe twoo hundrithe pounde of Englishe monneye." *Archæologia*, xxxi, 327-8. This great lady is known as having been the patroness of William Caxton, and her English origin explains the interest, which she evinced in his typographical labours.

At the marriage of Philip and Mary at Winchester, July 25th, 1555, the second course of dishes was claimed, as of custom, by the bearer. One of these, Edward Underhill, in the extant narrative of his inprisonment, etc., 1553-5, has left the following account: "The second course at the marriage of a king is given unto the bearers: I mean the meat, but not the dishes, for they were of gold. It was my chance to carry a great pasty of red deer in a great charger, very delicately baked, which, for the weight thereof, divers refused. The which pasty I sent unto London, to my wife and her brother."

Machyn describes in his "Diary," under December 1556, a wedding-supper, which was given at Henley-upon-Thames, for Master Venor and his wife at which he and some other neighbours were present; "and as we whet at soper," says he, "and or whe had supt, ther cam a xij wessells with maydens syngyng with ther wessells, and after cam the cheyff wyffes syngyng with ther wessells; and the gentyll-woman had hordenyd a grett tabull of bankett, dyssys of spyssys and frut, as marmelad, gynbred (gingerbread), gele, comfett," &c. The grandeur, with which the nuptials of Alderman White were celebrated, in 1558, appears to have been somewhat unusual, for after the ceremony, according to Machyn, there was a masque, with splendid dresses and appointments, and much dancing. Machyn notices a still more magnificent affair which was witnessed at the nuptials of a citizen in 1562; every luxury which could be procured for money was there, and there were three masques: one in cloth of gold, another of Friars, and a third of Nuns, and at the conclusion the friars and nuns danced together—a diversion which would not have been sanctioned in the previous reign. The celebrated Thomas Becon preached the wedding-sermon on that occasion. These masques at citizens' nuptials about this time appear to have been in imitation of the splendid pageants

on scriptural and other subjects introduced long before into the marriage-ceremonials of our kings and nobility. Brand himself notices the masque, which was represented at the nuptials of Sir Philip Herbert, in the time of James I., and evidently supposed it to be a custom peculiar to people of rank.

In the thirty-sixth volume of "Archæologia" will be found an account of the sumptuous and costly wedding of Richard Polsted, Esq., of Albury, to Elizabeth, daughter of William More, Esq., of Loseley, near Guildford, in 1567, with a list of all the marriage presents and their senders. Mr. Secretary Cecil, afterward Lord Burleigh, gave a doe. There is a very curious letter from Fleetwood, Recorder of London, to Lord Burghley, July 18th, 1583, on the subject of a clandestine and illegal marriage-ceremony, which had just then recently occurred. He tells the story as follows: "Abraham of Abraham, a gentilman of a hundred pound land in com(itatu) Lanc(astriæ) put his dawghter and heire unto my lady Gerrard of the Brenne. Sir Thomas and my lady being here in London, one Dwelles, a fenser nere Cicell howse, and his wiff, by indirect meanes, being of kyn to the girle, dyd invite all my lady's children and gentilwomen unto a breakfast. They cam thether, and at theire commyng the yowthes and servingmen were caried up to the ffens skolle. My lady's dowghters and gentilwomen must nedes play at the cardes, will they nill they. The girle Abraham, by the wiff of the howse, was conveyghed in to a chamber, and shut the dowre after her and there left her. The girle found in the chamber iiij. or v. tall men. She knew theym not. And ymediatlie the girle fell into a great ffeare seyng them to compasse her about. Then began an old priest to read upon a booke, his words she understood not, saving these words, 'I Henry take the Suzane to my wedded wiff.' This done they charged the wenche never to discover this to any body lyving, and so sent her downe to her fellowes."

In MS. Lansdowne, 33, is preserved an account of the expenses at the wedding of Mr. William Wentworth, son of Lord Wentworth, and Elizabeth Cecil, daughter of the Lord Treasurer Burleigh. The affair was unusually sumptuous, and lasted three days. A curious letter on the subject of the lady's fortune and jointure is printed by Ellis in his Third Series.

Mr. Halliwell, in a note upon the marriage of the Princess Elizabeth to the Elector Frederick of Bohemia, in 1613, in his edition of the "Autobiography of Sir Simonds D'Ewes," 1845, describes the wedding-ceremonial, quoting Wilson's

"Life and Reign of James I." "Her vestments were white, the emblem of innocency; her hair dishevelled, hanging down her back at length, an ornament of virginity; a crown of pure gold upon her head, the cognizance of majesty . . . . . her train supported by twelve young ladies in white garments, so adorned with jewels, that her passage looked like a milky way. She was led to church by her brother Prince Charles and the Earl of Northampton." Mead, in one of his letters to Sir Martin Stuteville, giving an account of the accession and marriage of Charles I. says: "I saw one of the pieces of money flung about at the marriage. On one side is Cupid, holding in one hand lillies, in the other roses. The motto, Fundit Amor Lilia mixta Rosis. On the other side, the picture of the King and Queene with this, Carolus Mag. et Henrietta Maria Rex et Regina Magnæ Britanniæ." These were *jetons*, however, not coins. They occasionally occur.

In an indenture of 1496 in relation to the prospective marriage of the heir of Sir Robert Plumpton to Isabel Babthorpe, cousin and heir to Dame Isabel Hastings, it is stipulated that Sir Roger shall defray the cost of the "array" of his son and of the meat and drink to be expended at the ceremony, while the bride's uncle Babthorpe shall pay for her outfit. This was the case of an English family in Yorkshire of good standing. *Plumpton Correspondence*, 1839, p. C.

At the marriages of the Anglo-Saxons, the parties were attended to church by music. In "The Christen State of Matrimony," 1543, p. 48, we read as follows: "Early in the mornyng the weddyng people begynne to exceed in superfluous eatyng and drinkyng, wherof they spytte untyll the halfe sermon be done, and when they come to the preachynge, they are halfe droncke, some all together. Therefore regard they neyther the prechynge nor prayer, but stond there only because of the custome. Such folkes also do come to the church with all manner of pompe and pride, and gorgiousnes of rayment and jewels. They come with a great noyse of harpes, lutes, kyttes, Basens, and drommes, wherwyth they trouble the whole church and hyndre them in matters pertayninge to God. And even as they come to the churche, so go they from the churche agayne, lyght, nyce, in shameful pompe and vaine wantonesse." The following is from Veron: "I knewe a priest (this is a true tale that I tell you, and no lye) whiche when any of his parishioners should be maryd, woulde take his backepype, and go fetche theym to the churche, playnge sweetelye afore them, and then would he laye his instrument handsomely upon the aultare, tyll he had maryed them and sayd masse. Which thyng being done, he would gentillye bringe them home agayne with backe-pype. Was not this priest a true ministrell, thynke ye? for he dyd not conterfayt the ministrell, but was one in dede." *Hunting of Purgatory to Death*, 1561, fol. 51v°.

In Deloney's "History of Jack of Newbury," 1597, speaking of his marriage and the bride's going to church, the writer observes, "There was a noise of musicians that play'd all the way before her." Dame Sibil Turfe, a character in Jonson's "Tale of a Tub," is introduced reproaching her husband as follows: "A clod you shall be called, to let no music go afore your child to church, to chear her heart up!" and Scriben, seconding the good old dame's rebuke, adds: "She's ith' right, sir; for your wedding dinner is starved without music."

Griffith has the following on marriage feasts: "Some cannot be merry without a noise of fidlers, who scrape acquaintance at the first sight; nor sing, unlesse the divell himselfe come in for a part, and the ditty be made in hell," &c. He has before said: "We joy indeed at weddings; but how? Some please themselves in breaking broad, I had almost said bawdy jests." *Bethel*, 1634, p. 279. In the same work, speaking of his bride, it is said, that "after her came the chiefest maidens of the country, some bearing bridecakes, and some garlands, made of wheat finely gilded, and so passed to the church. She was led to church between two sweet boys, with bridelaces and rosemary tied about their silken sleeves; the one was Sir Thomas Parry, the other Sir Francis Hungerford." In later times it was among the offices of the bride maids to lead the bridegroom to church, as it was the duty of the bridegroom's men to conduct the bride thither. It is stated in the account of the marriage ceremonials of Sir Philip Herbert and the Lady Susan, performed at Whitehall in the reign of James I., that "the Prince and the Duke of Holstein led the bride to church."

In an Epithalamium by Christopher Brooke in the second edition of England's Helicon, 1614, we read:

"Forth, honour'd groome; behold, not farre behind,
Your willing bride, led by two strengthlesse boyes."

Marked in the margin opposite, "Going to church—bride boyes." This has not been overlooked in the "Collier's Wedding:"

"Two lusty lads, well drest and strong,
Step'd out to lead the bride along:
And two young maids, of equal size,
As soon the bridegroom's hands surprize."

It appears from a passage in Stephens's "Character of a plaine Countrey Bride," that the bride gave also, or wore, or carried, on this occasion, "gilt rases of ginger." "Guilt rases of ginger, rosemary, and ribbands. She will therefore bestow a livery, though she receive no wages."

In 1561, one of the officials at the Queen's Bench was put in the pillory for coming to several gentlemen and ladies, and presenting them with nosegays, alleging that he was going to be married. This episode rests on the authority of Machyn the Diarist; but unluckily the passage where it is related is imperfect in the MS. In Hacket's "Marriage Present," a wedding sermon, the author introduces among flowers used on this occasion, prim-roses, maidens-blushes, and violets. Herrick plays upon the names of flowers selected for this purpose. In "Vox Graculi," 1623, "Lady Ver, or the Spring," is called "The nose-gay giver to weddings."

With regard to nosegays, called by the vulgar in the North of England and elsewhere pretty generally, posies, Stephens in his "Essayes," 1615, has a remarkable passage in his character of A plaine Country Bridegroom. "He shews," says he, "neere affinity betwixt marriage and hanging: and to that purpose he provides a great nosegay, and shakes hands with every one he meets, as if he were now preparing for a condemned man's voyage." Nosegays occur in "The Collier's Wedding."

It seems to have been customary at ordinary weddings in the time of Elizabeth for the party, on their return from church, to have an entertainment like our breakfast, when the bride was placed in the centre by herself, in the seat of honour; but afterward, when the gifts were presented to the newly-made couple, the man and his wife were seated side by side. I collect so much from the "Jeste of the Wife Lapped in Morelles Skin" circâ 1570, where there is this description of the latter part of the ceremony:

"The father and mother fyrst began
To order them in this wise:
The brydegrome was set by the brydes syde than,
After the countrey guise.
Then the father the fyrst present brought,
And presented them there richly, in fay,
With deeds of his land in a boxe well wrought,
And made them his heyres for aye—"

Speaking of wedding entertainments, Griffith, in his *Bethel*, 1636, says: "Some drink healths so long till they loose it,

and being more heathenish in this than was Ahasuerus at his feast, they urge their companions to drinke by measure, out of measure."

Evelyn, under Dec. 5, 1683, relates that at the wedding to her fifth husband of a Mistress Castle, daughter of a broom-man, whose wife sold kitchen stuff in Kent Street, but who, growing rich, became Sheriff of Surrey, and a fellow-magistrate with the diarist, there were present the Lord Mayor and civic dignitaries, Lord Chief Justice Jefferies, and other personages of distinction, and Evelyn himself, and that the party was exceedingly merry. "These great men," says he, "spent the rest of the afternoon, till eleven at night, in drinking healths, taking tobacco, and talking much beneath the gravity of Judges—" Comp. *Wedding Dinner.* "In most parts of Essex it is a common custom, we read, when poor people marry, to make a kind of Dog-hanging or Money-gathering, which they call a Wedding-Dinner, to which they invite tag and rag, all that will come: where, after dinner, upon summons of the fidler, who setteth forth his voice like a town-crier, a table being set forth, and the bride set simpering at the upper end of it: the bridegroom standing by with a white sheet athwart his shoulders, whilst the people march up to the bride, present their money and wheel about. After this offering is over, then is a pair of gloves laid upon the table, most monstrously bedaubed about with ribbon, which by way of auction is set to sale, at who gives most, and he whose hap it is to have them, shall withall have a kiss of the bride." *History of Sr Billy of Billericay, & his Squire Ricardo* (a very admirable parody on Don Quixote,) chap. ix.

What is sometimes termed a Serenade in Shakespear's *Cymbeline*, commencing, "Hark! Hark! the lark" appears to have been intended for a *Reveille matin* to a bride. In 1557-8, William Pickering obtained licence to print a ballad entitled "A Ryse and Wake." This was evidently a bride's good morrow, and perhaps the prototype of the composition found in the Roxburghe collection, and inserted in Collier's "Roxburgh Ballads," 1847. In Munday's "John A Kent and John A Cumber," is a passage which happily illustrates this portion of the subject. It is where Turnop and his companions serenade Marian and Sidanen, and afterward do the same to the two bridegrooms. Tom Tabrer says: "Well, then tune, all; for it drawes toward day: and if we wake not the bryde, why, then, it is woorth nothing." In Carleton's account of the nuptials of Sir Philip Herbert, it is stated that "they were lodged in the Council

Chamber, where the King gave them a reveille matin before they were up."

According to Donne's "Epithalamium," at the marriage of the Princess Elizabeth of England and Frederic of Bohemia, 1613, there was a particular hour, at which it was usual to wake the bride :

"Othres neer you shall whisperinge
    speake,
And wagers lay at whose side day will
    breake,
And win by obseruinge then whose hand
    it is,
That opens first a curtain, hers or his :
This wilbe try'd to morrow after nyne,
Till wch howre we thy day enlarge, O
    Valentine."

This extract is from an early MS. copy of the "Epithalamium," now before me. It is contained in a MS. volume of poems by Donne and others, of which I gave some notice in "Notes and Queries," 4th ser. ii. Pepys thought it very mean on the part of the Penns not to have music the morning after the wedding to wake up the newly married couple. *Diary*, 16 Feb. 1666-7.

Of such a reveille matin, as used on the marriages of respectable merchants of London in his time, Hogarth has left us a curious representation in one of his prints of the "Idle and industrious Apprentice." So, in the "Comforts of Wooing:" "Next morning, come the fidlers, and scrape him a wicked reveillez. The drums rattle, the shaumes tote, the trumpets sound tan ta ra ra ra, and the whole street rings with the benedictions and good wishes of fidlers, drummers, pipers, and trumpetters. You may safely say now the wedding's proclaimed." Misson, speaking of the reveillez on the morning after a wedding, says: "If the drums and fiddles have notice of it, they will be sure to be with them by day-break, making a horrid racket, till they have got the pence." Gay, in his "Trivia," has censured the use of the drum in this concert.

Northbrooke says : "In the councell of Laoditia (holden in the year of our Lorde God 364, vnder Pope Liberius) it was decreed thus: It is not meete for Christian men to dance at their mariages. Let them dyne and suppe grauely, giuing thanks vnto God for the benefite of marriages. Let the clergie aryse and go their wayes, when the players on their instruments (which serue for dauncing) doe begynne to playe, least by their presence they shoulde seeme to allowe that wantonesse." *Treatise against Dicing,* &c. 1577, repr. 122.

In Scott's "Mock-Marriage," a comedy, 1696, p. 50, it is said : "You are not so merry as men in your condition should be ; What ! a couple of weddings and not a dance." So, in the ballad called "The Winchester Wedding :"

"And now they had din'd, advancing
    Into the midst of the hall,
The fidlers struck up for dancing,
    And Jeremy led up the brawl.
Sucky, that danc'd with the cushion,"
    &c.

The usual custom now is to throw slippers after the bride and bridegroom, when they go away after the breakfast. In 1875 the writer threw one into the carriage of his sister-in-law Mrs. Ormrod of Pen-y-lan, Ruabon.

It is frequently the habit, at the commoner sort of weddings, to fling a handful of rice in the same manner, when the couple quits the house, and at St. Peter's Church, Brighton, some rice was lately thrown after the pair at the church-door, which is not so customary. In 1903 we find the vicar of Long Sutton, Lincolnshire, setting up public notices to check such a practice, as well as that of throwing *confetti.*

The custom of demanding toll of a bridal party was as recently as 1901 the subject of magisterial inquiry at Bingley, in Yorkshire, when a labourer was summoned for street obstruction. While a wedding party were on their way in a vehicle, defendant attached a rope to a lamp-post, and then crossed the road and held the rope to stop the carriage. When he had done that, he went to the window and received something from those inside. Some of the wedding party were not at all satisfied with the performance. The Chairman said the defendant was following out an old custom, and had no intention of doing any harm ; but the practice could not be allowed.

Coles in his *English Dictionary* speaks of Ball-money as given by a bride to her old play-fellows. Halliwell states that in the North a party attends at the church-gates to receive this as a right : but it might be equally distributed as a sign of the girl no longer requiring her former recreations. Brockett thought that the money was intended for the purchase of a football. In Normandy it was customary, as the Abbé de la Rue told Brand, for the bride to throw a ball over the church for the bachelors and married men to scramble for, and that they then danced together ; but in giving this information the abbé should have added, that the practice was probably confined to the low-pitched primitive structures, of which we yet possess numerous examples, especially in Kent and Essex, and which would alone render such a feat possible.

There was an ancient superstition that

for a bride to have good fortune it was necessary at her marriage that she should enter the house under two drawn swords placed in a manner of a St. Andrew's Cross. She was not to step over the threshold in entering the bridegroom's house, but was to be lifted over by her nearest relations. She was also to knit her fillets to the door-posts, and anoint the sides, to avert the mischievous fascinations of witches. Previous to this, too, she was to put on a yellow veil. In Braithwaite's "Boulster Lecture," 1640, p. 280, mention occurs of an ancient custom, "when at any time a couple were married, the soale of the bridegroom's shoe was to be laid upon the bride's head, implying with what subjection she should serve her husband." Grose tells us of a singular superstition: *i.e.* that if in a family, the youngest daughter should chance to be married before her older sisters, they must all dance at her wedding without shoes: this will counteract their ill luck, and procure them husbands. Pliny mentions that in his time the circos, a sort of tame hawk, was accounted a lucky omen at weddings. For the sun to shine upon the bride was the same. In Herrick's "Hesperides," p. 258, are ten short songs, or rather choral gratulations, entitled "Connubii Flores, or the Well Wishes at Weddings."

The subsequent I find in Northbrooke's "Treatise" 1577: "In olde time we reade that there was vsually caried before the mayde when she shoulde be maried and come to dwell in her husbandes house, a distaffe charged with Flaxe, and a spyndle hanging at it, to the intente shee might bee myndefull to lyue by hir labour."

The Romish rituals give the form of blessing the nuptial bed. This ceremonial is illustrated by an engraving in the ancient romance of Melusine, where it is said that "they went and led Raymond in to the pavilion, and soon he was brought to bed. And then came there the Bishop that had spoused them, and did hallow their bed, and after that every each one took his leave and the curtains were drawn about the bed." In the Durham Ritual is the office, *In thalamo*, which appears to be applicable to this occasion. Surtees Society ed. 1840, p. 111. From some lines by Herrick quoted under *Torches* we infer that the woman was conducted to her chamber with lights. It was an invariable rule for the men always to depart the room till the bride was undressed by her maids and put to bed. We learn from "Articles ordained by King Henry VII. for the Regulation of his Household," that this ceremony was observed at the marriage of a princess. "All men at her coming to

be voided, except woemen, till she be brought to her bedd: and the man, both: he sitting in his bedd, in his shirte, with a gowne cast about him. Then the bishoppe with the chaplaines to come in and blesse the bedde: then every man to avoide without any drinke, save the twoe estates, if they liste priviely."

In the "British Apollo," before quoted, No. 133, is the following query: "Why is the custom observed for the bride to be placed in a bed next the left hand of her husband, seeing it is a general use in England for men to give their wives the right hand when they walk together? *A.* Because it looks more modest for a lady to accept the honour her husband does her as an act of generosity at his hands, than to take it as her right, since the bride goes to bed first."

In a letter from Carleton to Winwood, of Jan. 1604-5, among other notices relating to marriages at court, is "At night there was casting off the bride's left hose, and many other pretty sorceries." It was similarly a custom among the noble Germans at weddings for the bride, when she was conducted to the bride-chamber, to take off her shoe, and throw it among the bystanders, which every one strove to catch, and whoever got it, thought it an omen that they themselves would shortly be happily married. Misson, writing about 1697, observes: "The bride maids carry the bride into the bed-chamber, where they undress her, and lay her in the bed. They must throw away and lose all the pins. Woe be to the bride if a single one is left about her; nothing will go right. Woe also to the bride-maids if they keep one of them, for they will not be married before Whitsontide." Or as we read in a book of the following century: "till the Easter following at soonest." A singular instance of tantalizing, however incredible it may seem, was most certainly practised by our ancestors on this festive occasion, *i.e.* sewing up the bride in one of the sheets. Herrick, in his Nuptial Song on Sir Clipesby Crew and his lady, is express to this purpose:

"But since it must be done, dispatch
  and sowe
Up in a sheet your bride, and what if
  so," &c.

It is mentioned too in the account of the marriage of Sir Philip Herbert: "At night there was sewing into the sheet."

There was an occasional waggery among some of the young fellows of the party in the shape of tying a bell under the marriage-bed. This was also a French usage, and in the *Contes D'Ouville,* i, 3, we read: "Il oult une risée de jeunes hommes qui s'etoient expres cachez aupres de son lit, comme on a coutume de faire en pareilles occasions," as if they stayed behind in hiding to listen.

Among the Anglo-Saxons next morning the whole company came into the chamber of the new married couple, before they arose, to hear the husband declare the morning's gift, when his relations became sureties to the wife's relations for the performance of such promises as were made by the husband. This was the ancient pin-money, and became the separate property of the wife alone. Owen explains that word as "signifying a garment or cloke with a veil, presented by the husband to his bride on the morning after marriage: and, in a wider sense the settlement he has made on her of goods and chattels adequate to her rank. In more modern times there is a custom similar to this in Prussia. There the husband may (is obliged if he has found her a virgin,) present to his bride the Morgengabe or gift on the morrow after marriage, even though he should have married a widow."

Nuptial Usages in Scotland, &c.—There is an ostensible survival in Huntley, Aberdeenshire, of a usage repeatedly mentioned as an act of hospitality or devotion in the Hebrew Scriptures. In 1903, on the eve of an intended marriage here between two persons of respectable position, the bridegroom being son of the Provost of the town, his feet were washed by his friends, and the bride's would have undergone the same ceremony, had not her health precluded it. These particulars transpired in the course of legal proceedings for breach of promise.

In the "Statistical Account of Scotland," parish of Gargunnock, co. Stirling, we read: "It is seldom there are social meetings. Marriages, baptisms, funerals, and the conclusion of the harvest, are almost the only occasion of feasting. Marriages usually happen in April and November. The month of May is cautiously avoided. A principal tenant's son or daughter has a crowd of attendants at marriage, and the entertainment lasts for two days at the expence of the parties. The company at large pay for the musick."

In Scotland there is said to have been formerly, and within living remembrance, a recognised custom that if a man and a woman were domiciled together, and he addressed her as his wife, she became entitled to claim matrimonial rights; or that even if he addressed her as wife, and she assented by a curtsey or otherwise it was allowed binding. There is an anecdote of a celebrated judge lately on the bench, who ran a risk of realizing the experience in his early career, and lost no time in crossing the border.

In the "Statistical Account of Scotland," the minister of Logierait in Perthshire says: "Immediately before the celebration of the marriage ceremony, every knot about the bride and bridegroom (garters, shoe-strings, strings of petticoats, &c.) is carefully loosened. After leaving the church, the whole company walk round it, keeping the church walls always upon the right hand. The bridegroom, however, first retires one way with some young men to tie the knots that were loosened about him; while the young married woman, in the same manner, retires somewhere else to adjust the disorder of her dress."

At the marriage of Miss Harvey to Sir Patrick Playfair, November 18, 1903, one of the bridesmaids wore for luck green stockings. Blue hats and feathers are sometimes provided for them in deference to the old rhyme:

"Something old and something new,
    Something borrowed and something blue."

A case quite recently occurred at Berwick, where a youthful bride absconded on the wedding day, and where the night before the bridegroom calling at her home, where she then was, and asking to see her, was refused by her mother on the plea that it was unlucky.

In "Observations on a Monthes Journey into France," (a MS. *circá* 1626, by an Oxford graduate,) is the following passage: "A scholler of the University never disfurnished so many of his friendes to provide for his jorney, as they (the French) doe neighbours, to adorne their weddings. At my beinge at Pontoise, I sawe Mistres Bryde returne from the church. The day before shee had beene somewhat of the condition of a kitchen wench, but now so tricked up with scarves, rings and crossegarters, that you never sawe a Whitsun-lady better rigged. I should much have applauded the fellowes fortune, if he could have maryed the cloathes; but (God be mercifull to hym) he is chayned to the wench; much joy may they have together, most peerlesse couple,

Hymen Hymenæi, Hymen, Hymen, O
    Hymenæe!

The match was now knytt up amongst them. I would have a French man marie none but a French woman."

In a volume published more than a century since, it is said: "'Tis worthy of remark that something like the antient custom of strewing the threshold of a new married couple with flowers and greens, is, at this day, practised in Holland. Among the festoons and foliage, the laurel was always most conspicuous: this denoted, no doubt, that the wedding day is a day of triumph." "Hymen, or an accurate Description of the Ceremonies used in Marriage in every Nation of the World," 1760, p. 39.

Mr Brand heard a gentleman say that he was told by Lord Macartney, that on the day previous to the marriage of the Duke of York (by proxy) to the Princess of Prussia, a whole heap of potsherds was formed at her Royal Highness's door, by persons coming and throwing them against it with considerable violence, a custom which obtains in Prussia, with all ranks, on the day before a virgin is married; and that during this singular species of battery the Princess, every now and then, came and peeped out at the door.

Mungo Park in his "Travels into the Interior of Africa," describes a wedding among the Moors, p. 135: "April 10, in the evening, the Tabala or large drum was beat, to announce a wedding. A great number of people of both sexes assembled. A woman was beating the drum, and the other women joining at times in chorus, by setting up a shrill scream. Mr. Park soon retired, and having been asleep in his hut, was awakened by an old woman, who said she had brought him a present from the bride. She had a wooden bowl in her hand; and before Mr. Park was recovered from his surprize, discharged the contents full in his face. Finding it to be the same sort of holy water with which a Hottentot priest is said to sprinkle a new-married couple, he supposed it to be a mischievous frolic, but was informed it was a nuptial benediction from the bride's own person, and which on such occasions is always received by the young, unmarried Moors, as a mark of distinguished favour. Such being the face, Mr. Park wiped his face, and sent his acknowledgments to the lady. The wedding-drum continued to beat, and the women to sing all night. About nine in the morning the bride was brought in state from her mother's tent, attended by a number of women, who carried her tent, (a present from the husband,) some bearing up the poles, others holding by the strings, and marched singing until they came to the place appointed for her residence, where they pitched the tent. The husband followed with a number of men, leading four bullocks, which they tied to the tent-strings, and having killed another and distributed the beef among the people, the ceremony closed."

The same traveller has left an account of the barbarous cruelty which, at that time was exercised at Color, a large town in the interior of Africa, upon women who had been convicted of infidelity. See *Bride, Garters, Gloves, Manx, Nuts, Orkney, Wedding, etc.*

Nurspell or **Nor-Spiel.**—A boys' game in Lincolnshire, somewhat similar to trap-ball. See *Trap-Ball* infrâ, and Halliwell in v.

Nutmeg, Gilt.—A gift at Christmas. It appears to be the *Gift* Nutmeg mentioned in *Love's Labor's Lost*, 1598. But Jonson in *Christmas His Masque* calls it rightly. See Nares in v.

Nuts.—In the marriage ceremonies amongst the ancient Romans, the bridegroom threw nuts about the room for the boys to scramble. The epithalamiums in the classics prove this. It was a token that the party scattering them was now leaving childish diversions. See Erasmus on the proverb, "Nuces relinquere." Adag., 1606, col. 1356.

"——Postquam te talos aule Nucesque
Ferre sinu laxo, donare et ludere vidi."

The Roman boys had some sport or other with nuts, to which Horace refers. Nuts have not been excluded from the catalogue of superstitions under papal Rome. Thus, on the 10th of August, in the Romish Calendar, I find it observed that some religious use was made of them, and that they were in great estimation.

Hutchinson observes that, in divining with nuts, "if the nuts lie still and burn together, it prognosticates a happy marriage or a hopeful love; if, on the contrary, they bounce and fly asunder, the sign is unpropitious." *Northumberland*, ii, 18. Burns describes the Allhallows Even ceremony of "burning the nuts," which had also been noticed by Pennant. "They name," says Burns, "the lad and lass to each particular nut, as they lay them in the fire, and accordingly as they burn quietly together, or start from beside one another, the course and issue of the courtship will be." Poems, 1787, p. 55 *et seqq.* A similar superstition reigns in Ireland. This custom is beautifully described by Gay in his "Spells:"

"Two hazel nuts I threw into the flame,
And to each nut I gave a sweet-heart's
    name :
This with the loudest bounce me sore
    amaz'd,
That in a flame of brightest colour
    blaz'd ;
As blaz'd the nut, so may thy passion
    grow,
For 'twas thy nut that did so brightly
    glow !"

Macaulay mentions that in Minorca in the earlier part of the eighteenth century, a custom as old as Theocritus and Virgil was kept up i.e. the ceremony of throwing nuts and almonds at weddings, that the boys might scramble for them. Virgil says: "Spargete, Marite, nuces." *Hist. of Claybrook*, 1791, p. 130.

Oak-Apple Day.—"May the 29th," says the author of the "Festa Anglo-Romana," 1678, "is celebrated upon a double account: first in commemoration of the birth of our sovereign King Charles the Second, the princely son of his royal father Charles the First of happy memory, and Mary the daughter of Henry the Fourth, the French king, who was born the 29th day of May 1630; and also, by Act of Parliament, 12 Car. II. by the passionate desires of the people, in memory of his most happy Restoration."

"A bow-shoot from Boscobel-house," says Stukeley, "just by a horse-track passing through the wood, stood the Royal Oak, into which the king and his companion, Colonel Carlos, climbed by means of the hen-roost ladder, when they judg'd it no longer safe to stay in the house; the family reaching them victuals with the nut hook. The tree is now enclosed in with a brick wall, the inside whereof is covered with lawrel, of which we may say, as Ovid did of that before the Augustan palace, 'mediamque tuebere quercum.' Close by its side grows a young thriving plant from one of its acorns." He adds, "Over the door of the inclosure, I took this inscription in marble: Felicissimam arborem quam in asylum potentissimi Regis Caroli II. Deus O. M. per quem reges regnant hic crescere voluit, tam in perpetuam rei tantæ memoriam, quam specimen firmæ in reges fidei, muro cinctam posteris commendant Basilius et Jana Fitzherbert. Quercus amica Jovi."

On the 29th of May, the anniversary of the Restoration of Charles II., it was long customary, especially in the North of England, for the common people to wear in their hats the leaves of the oak, which were sometimes covered on the occasion with leaf-gold. This was done in commemoration of the marvellous escape of that monarch from those that were in pursuit of him, who passed under the very oak tree in which he had secreted himself, after the decisive battle of Worcester. It was also the custom to decorate the monument of Richard Penderell in the church-yard of St. Giles-in-the-Fields, London, on the 29th of May, with oak branches." The boys at Newcastle-upon-Tyne had formerly a taunting rhyme on this occasion, with which they used to insult such persons as they met on this day who had not oak leaves in their hats:—

> "Royal Oak,
> The Whigs to provoke."

There was a retort courteous by others, who contemptuously wore plane-tree leaves, which is of the same homely sort of stuff:—

> "Plane-tree leaves;
> The Church-folk are thieves."

In Brand's MSS. Collections there was a note to the following effect: "Two soldiers were whipped almost to death, and turned out of the service, for wearing boughs in their hats on the 29th of May, 1716." Comp. Halliwell in v.

Oaths.—Mr. Tyler has devoted a volume to this subject; but I do not find, that he has entered much at large into the question in some of its more curious aspects. It is a branch of the present inquiry, which Brand himself completely overlooked. Tomlins, in his "Law Dictionary," 1835, has a useful paper on this matter, and Mr. Hampton, in his "Origines Patriciæ," 1846, quoting the Swedish saga of "Beowulf" in its Anglo-Saxon paraphrase, has some interesting remarks on the ancient Saxon or Northern usage of swearing fealty on the sword, which was called the Wapentake (weapon-touching), a term now only understood in its topographical acceptation. A passage in the "Honest Whore," 1604, the joint production of Decker and Middleton, illustrates the taking of bread and salt preparatorily to swearing, in accordance with the custom which seems to have prevailed on the continent, if not in England: "He took bread and salt by this light, that he would never open his lips." Middleton's Works, 1840, iii, 103.

Oaths were formerly administered, not on the Bible or Testament, but on the Book of Sequences or Tropery, corruptly *Toper*, or on the Primer, as we perceive in a letter from Sir Geoffrey Boleyn about 1460 to John Paston, where he says that the late Sir John Fastolfe in his place at Southwark, "by his othe made on his primer ther, grauntted and promitted to me to have the maner of Gunton—"

Mr. Fergusson in his *Rude Stone Monuments*, 1872, draws attention to the archaic usage or rite of swearing the oath to Wodin by two persons joining their hands through the hole in the ring Stone of Stennis, Orkney, whence we perceive the sacred attribute conferred on such remains by the popular idea as to the origin of their diversion from their perfect form.

The hand on certain Bohemian and Anglo-Saxon coins has been judged to be a symbol of the Deity. To hold up the hand before superiors seems to be a practice susceptible of a twofold explanation: as a guarantee that the party held no weapon and as an appeal for clemency. In the famous ballad-poem of *Adam Bel*, 1536, the outlaws lift their hands on entering the royal presence; in the Scotish courts it has always been usual to admit this act as an affirmation, the judge and the witness both standing; and the elevation of the hand has been lately allowed in England as a substitute for kissing the book. Hazlitt's *Popular Poetry of Scotland*, &c. 1895, ii, 111.

Warton has thrown together some of the most remarkable oaths in the "Canterbury Tales" of Chaucer: "The Host swears by my father's soul, by the precious corpus madrian, by St. Paul's bell, by God's bones, by Christ's nails and blood, by St. Damian, by St. Runian, and by Corpus Domini: Sir Thopas, by ale and bread: Arcites, by my pan (or head): Theseus, by mighty Mars the red. The carpenter's wife, by St. Thomas of Kent: The smith, by Christ's foot: The Cambridge scholar, by my father's kin, by my crown, for God's benes or benison, and by St. Cuthbert: Sir John of Boundis, by Saint Martin: Gamelyn the cook, by God's book, and by my halse (or neck): Gamelyn's brother, by St. Richere and by Christis ore: A Frankeleyn, by Saint James of Galicia: A porter, by God's beard: The maister outlawe, by the good rood: The man of law, Depardeux: The merchant, by St. Thomas of Inde: The Somnour, by God's arms two: The rioter, by God's digne bones: The host, again, by your father's kin, by arms, blood and bones: The monk, by my porthose (or breviary) and by God and St. Martin."

"Be the Rode of Chester," is an asseveration used by Langland in his Alliterative Poem on the Deposition of Richard II., written, it seems, at the end of the fourteenth or beginning of the fifteenth century. In "Ralph Roister Doister," Roister Doister exclaims: "By the Armes of Caleys, it is none of myne." At that time Calais was in the hands of the English, who retained it till 5 Mary. In the same play, we find, "by the crosse of my sword," "by cots precious potsticke," and other forms, some unusual and a few fantastic. There are also some eccentric and scarce forms of adjuration in "The Marriage of Wit and Wisdom," an old interlude, such as "By the brains of a black-pudding," and "By the guts of a crab-louse." In Heywood's "Edward IV." 1600, Hobs the tanner swears "by the meg-holly" and "by the mousefoot;" also, "by my holdame," "Gods blue baulkin," "by my feckins." In the same play, the Widow Norton is made to use (jocosely) the expression—"Clubs and clouted shoes!" interjectionally.

The statute 3 James I., against profane swearing, while it led to evasions even more profane than the original oaths, seems to have made fashionable a series of whimsical and innocuous asseverations, such as those we find in Heywood's "Fayre Mayde of the Exchange," 1607:

"*Bow.* By this hand, thou shalt go with me.

Crip. By this leg, I will not.

Bow. A lame oath! never stand to that.

Crip. By this crutch, but I will."

In "Mery Tales and Quicke Answeres," 1567, there is this: "Cockes armes (quod the bayllye), my poursse is pycked, and my moneye is gone." Cockes armes is of course a corruption of God's arms—God's charity or love; Browne, in his "Pastorals," 1614, calls it a dunghill oath:

"With that the miller laughing brush'd his cloathes,
And swore by cocke and other dung-hill oathes."

Skelton used the expression in his interlude entitled "Magnificence," printed probably in 1530. In his "Christian Admonitions against Cursing and Swearing," 1629, a broadside, Taylor the water-poet denounces the system of profane swearing, which in his time had come to a rank growth in England, and to which John Bunyan admits that he was long prone. But Richard Whitford, a brother of Sion, who wrote a century before Taylor, makes the same charge against his countrymen in his "Werke for Householders," 1530.

In the "Statistical Account of Scotland," vol. x., p. 413, "Parish of Tiry, in Argyleshire," we read: "The common people still retain some Roman Catholic sayings, prayers, and oaths, as expletives: such as 'Dias Muire let:' i.e. God and Mary be with you; 'Air Muire,' swearing by Mary, &c." In Brittany also they say Dame instead of Dieu, referring of course to the Virgin or Our Lady.

Obit.—See Nares and Halliwell in v. Numerous instances are cited in the present volume of money left for the performance of obits. Among the Paston Letters are two documents of 1444 and 1447 relative to the grant of lands for the performance of obituary service or prayers, called *certeynes*. Edit. Gairdner, i, 52, 66. Funds were bequeathed by members of the municipal Gilds of London for the celebration of obits in the place of worship frequented by the deceased and his brethren, the latter attending on the appointed day. Hazlitt's *Livery Companies*, 1892, *passim*. In the Privy Purse Expenses of Henry VII. under 1493 is an item: "To a preste that kepeth King Harry, 3s. 4d."—which is supposed to import a memorial service for Henry VI. *Excerpta Historica*, 1833, p. 92.

Obit Sunday was duly observed at Windsor on September 27, this year (1903). At the morning service the clergy, military knights, and choir walked in procession through the nave and entered the choir by the carved folding doors underneath the organ gallery. Bishop Barry delivered an interesting statement as to the royal founders and other benefactors. The Dean of Windsor also preached a special sermon. *Daily Mail*, Sept. 28, 1903.

Under the will of Richard King of Wisbeach, 1504, the testator gave and bequeathed the Falcon Petty Cury, Cambridge, to the Prior and Convent of Barnwell, partly on condition that a yearly obit was kept at Barnwell for his and his friend's souls. *Antiquary* for October, 1903. By an indenture between John Fisher, Bishop of Rochester, Christ's College, Cambridge, and St. John's College, Cambridge, detail Feb. 22, 1525, an obit used to be celebrated annually for the Bishop on the 3rd. February.

Old Ball.—In Lancashire the hobbyhorse is known as Old Ball; but this invention, which is, in the county named, more especially destined to Pace-egging time, or Easter, does not by any means exactly correspond with the genuine hobby-horse of Elizabethan days, but seems to be rather a provincial outgrowth from it.

Old Boots.—A popular name for the Devil.

Old Coles.—A correspondent of the *Athenæum* many years since, writing from Lower Wick, near Worcester, says: "I well remember that, in my juvenile days, old people used to speak of a spectre that formerly appeared in the parish of Leigh, in this county, whom they called Old Coles; and said that he frequently used, at the dead of night, to ride as swift as the wind down that part of the public road between Bransford and Brocamin, called Leigh Walk, in a coach drawn by four horses, with fire flying out of their nostrils, and that they invariably dashed right over the great barn at Leigh Court, and then on into the River Teme. It was likewise said that this perturbed spirit was at length *laid* in a neighbouring pool by twelve parsons, at dead of night, by the light of an inch of candle; and as he was not to rise again until the candle was quite burnt out, it was therefore thrown into the pool, and, to make all sure, the pool was filled up—

'And peaceful after slept Old Coles's shade.'

Now, as this legend belongs to ghost instead of fairy lore, and as the scene of action was not in a reputed fairy locality, I therefore did not notice it in my little work "On the Ignis Fatuus; or Will-o'-the- Wisp and the Fairies;" but it appears to be of kin to those mentioned by your correspondent.

"Upon my lately considering the tenor of this legend, I was led to think that 'Old Coles' must have been a person of some quality, and it induced me to look into Nash's History of Worcestershire, hoping it might throw some light upon the subject. Therein, in his account of Leigh (vol. ii. p. 73), the author says: 'This ancient lordship of the abbots of Pershore falling by the dissolution of monasteries into the king's hands, remained there till Elizabeth's time. The tenants of the house and demesne, both under the abbot and under the king and queen, were the Colles, of which family was Mr. Edward (Edmund) Colles, a grave and learned justice of this shire, who purchased the inheritance of this manor, Dec. 19, 1606: whose son and heir, Mr. Edmund Colles. (ob. 20 Sept. 1615) succeeded him, lived in the time of Mr. Habingdon, and being loaded with debts (which like a snowball from Malvern Hill gathered increase), thought fit to sell it to Sir Walter Devereux, Bart.' The Colleses were also possessed of the manor of Suckley which included those of Alfrick and Lusley. There is a farm called Colles Place (vulgo Coles Place, or Cold Place), in Lusley,—' which is mentioned in a ledger of the Priory of Malvern, in the reign of Henry III. as belonging to the family of Colles'—see Nash, vol. ii. p. 400,—which adjoins Leigh; and it shared the same fate, as appears by Nash's History, vol. ii. p. 397, as follows: "The manor of Suckley remained in the name of Hungerford till it passed by purchase from them to Mr. Edmund Colles, of Leigh, in the reign of Elizabeth. He left it to his son, Mr. William Colles, whose heir, Mr. Edmund Colles, sold it to Sir Walter Devereux, knight and baronet.' Now, it is not improbable that the legend may have referred to the unfortunate Edmund Colles, the second son who, having lost his patrimony, and perhaps died in distress, his spirit may have been supposed to haunt Leigh Court, which was the seat of his joys in prosperity and the object of his regrets in adversity." See Allies' *Antiquities of Worcestershire*, 1856, p. 452. But for a reason which will be, perhaps, made apparent by a reference to the 2nd edition of my *Proverbs*, 1882, pp. 315-16, I do not place much reliance, or any at all, on the theory propounded in Allies.

In the Comedy of Look About You, 1600, there is an allusion to Old Cole, where it appears to be used as a sort of common nick-name or by-word:

Rob. Ah, old Cole, now look about: you are catcht.

And in the Stationers' Registers, under date of January 25, 1636-7, occurs The History of Old Cole of Reading, as if it were some well-known popular tale or legend. Now, does it not appear very probable that this Old Cole was the same as the famous hero of romance, Thomas Cole, of Reading, whose real or supposed history and eventual murder at Colebrook by the host and hostess of the Crane Inn, Master and Mistress Jarman—of whom the latter might have supplied Shakespear with a hint for Lady Macbeth—are so entertainingly related by Deloney? A book which became extremely popular, and of which indeed the earliest impressions have perished, would naturally have diffused itself far beyond the topographical limits which the writer has assigned to it: nor can we be quite assured that the employment of the term "Old Cole" in a tract of 1592, as I have mentioned in my Proverbs, 1882, p. 315, did not originate in the same person, whose reputation was of course the ground for making him the subject of a book.

Old Harry.—One of the popular names of the Devil.

Old Nick.—Old Nick is the vulgar name of the evil being in the North of England, and is a name of great antiquity. There is a great deal of learning concerning it in Olaus Wormius. We borrowed it from the title of an evil genius among the ancient Danes. They say he has often appeared on the sea and on deep rivers in the shape of a sea monster, presaging immediate shipwreck and drowning to seamen. Junii *Etymolog.* v. *Nick.*

A writer in the "Gentleman's Magazine" for March, 1777, says, "Nobody has accounted for the Devil's having the name of Old Nick. Keysler mentions a Deity of the Waters worshipped by the antient Germans and Danes under the name of Nocca, or Nicken, styled in the Edda Nikur, which he derives from the German Nugen, answering to the Latin necare. Wormius says, the redness in the faces of drowned persons was ascribed to this Deity's sucking their blood out of their nostrils. *Mon. Dan.* p. 17. Wasthovius calls him Neccus, and quotes, from a Belgo-Gallic Dictionary, *Neccar,* Spiritus aquaticus, and *Necce* necare. *Pref. ad vitas Sanct.* and *Antiq. Suio-Goth.* 17. The Islandic Dictionary in Hickes renders Nikur *bellua aquatica. Thesaurus,* iii, 85. Lastly, Rudbekius mentions a notion prevalent among his countrymen, that Neckur, who governed the sea, assumed the form of various animals, or of a horseman, or of a man in a boat. He supposes him the same with Odin. *Atlantis,* part 1, c. 7. But the above authorities are sufficient to evince that he was the Northern Neptune, or some subordinate sea-god of a noxious disposition. It is not unlikely but the name of this evil spirit might, as Christianity prevailed in these Northern nations, be transferred to the Father of Evil."

This name, so familiar to our ears now-a-days, is derived with most probability from the nickers, or water-fairies, who were considered apparently by some of our old etymologists as equivalent to the sirens of classical fiction. Nicker is no longer preserved either as a separate designation, or in any other form, except in this sense so widely distinct from its original meaning. But examples of a similar kind, where the monks have borrowed from the fairy-mythology the nomenclature for another class of invisible powers, are not unfrequent. The authors of "Lancashire Folk-Lore," 1867, notice that "the Danish vikings called the Scandinavian sea-god Hold Nickar, which in time degenerated into the ludicrous expression, Old Nick;" but this statement is scarcely accurate. What immediately follows in the same work is more to the purpose. Nor should it be overlooked that, in the "History of Reynard the Fox," translated into English in 1481, from a Flemish original, the wolf calls the offspring of the marmoset (simia caudata) "nyckers." This is a remarkable piece of testimony, assuming (which is not by any means perfectly clear) that Old Nick is derived from this source.

For an account of the mischievous spirit "Nick," whose name and attributes are forgotten, except in connection with the ceremonies of Nickynan-night, and the Harvest festival,—vide report of the Royal Institute of Cornwall for 1842.

Old Scratch (which a writer in the "Athenæum," No. 983, derives from the *antiquus hostis* of the Fathers, and the Auld Ane, i.e. the Old One, are also names appropriated to the same evil being by the vulgar in the North. The epithet *old* to so many of his titles is of course employed and understood in a secondary or conventional sense.

Old Shock.—See Hunt's *Romances of the West of England,* ii, 59.

Ombre or **Hombre.**—A game at cards, of Spanish origin, similar to *primero,* on which it is said to be an improvement. It seems to have been played with four counters. An account of it, described on the title as "written at the request of divers Honourable Persons," was published in 1660; it is here called a royal game. A third type was known as *Quadrille;* but of ombre itself there was more than one variety, according to the *Compleat Gamester,* 1721; it is of a specially interesting character, because it seems to have been of great antiquity in Spain, and, as its name implies, is significant of national life and manners. Mr.

John Piggot has cited the following passage from Taylor's *History of Playing Cards*:—" The Italians have been the inventors of almost all the games of pure chance; the Spaniards, on the contrary, affect none but those of a dignified character. Their national game—ombre, 'the game of man,' a modification of the earlier game of primero—is of all modern games that which most resembles the ancient tarot. We may conclude, therefore, that it is the earliest of existing games, and upon that assumption, that the Spaniards were the earliest card players." Comp. *Quadrille:* Halliwell's *Arch. Dict.* in v.: Hazlitt's *Bibl. Coll.* i, 310, and Suppl. to *Coins of Europe*, 1897, v. Sardinia. In old houses there used to be tables with pools for playing ombre.

Omens.—The word omen is well known to signify a sign, good or bad, or a prognostic. It may be defined to be that indication of something future, which we get as it were by accident, and without our seeking for. A superstitious regard to omens seems anciently to have made very considerable additions to the common load of human infelicity. They are now pretty generally disregarded, and the wiser among us look back with perfect security and indifference on those trivial and truly ridiculous accidents which alternately afforded matter of joy and sorrow to our ancestors.

" L. Paullus, Consul iterum, cum ei, bellum ut cum Rege Perse gereret, obtigisset: ut ea ipsa die domum ad vesperum rediit, filiolam suam Tertiam, quæ tum erat admodum parva, osculans animadvertit tristiculam: quid est, inquit, mea Tertia? quid tristis es? Mi pater, inquit, Persa periit. Tum ille arctius Puellam complexus, *accipio*, inquit, *mea filia*, omen: erat autem mortuus catellus eo nomine." Cicero *de Divinat.* lib. i. sect. 46.

Gibbon speaking of the wars of the Emperor Maurice against the Avars, A.D. 595, tells us, that on setting out, " he (the Emperor) solicited without success a miraculous answer to his nocturnal prayers. His mind was confounded by the death of a favourite horse, the encounter of a wild boar, a storm of wind and rain, and the birth of a monstrous child—"

Omens appear to have been so numerous that we must despair of ever being able to recover them all: and to evince that in all ages men have been self-tormentors, the bad omens fill a catalogue infinitely more extensive than that of the good.

Llodowick Lloyd, in his *Stratagems of Jerusalem*, 1602, has collected some scattered notices of the belief in this class of manifestations among the ancients:

" Themistocles was assured of victory over King Xerxes and his huge army by crowing of a cocke, going to the Battle at Artemisium, the day before battell began, who having obtained so great a victory, gave a cocke in his ensigne ever after." . . . . " The first king of Rome, Romulus, builded his kingdom by flying of fowles and soothsaying. So Numa Pompil. was chosen second king of Rome by flying of fowles. So Tarquinius Priscus: an eagle took his cappe from his head and fled up on high to the skies, and after descended, and let his cappe fall on his head againe, signifying thereby that he should be king of Rome." . . . . " The Arabians, Carians, Phrygians, and Cilicians, do most religiously observe the chirping and flying of birds, assuring themselves good and bad events in their warres." . . . . " So superstitious grew the gentils, with such abhominable idolatry, that in Persia by a cock, in Egypt by a bull, in Æthiope by a dog, they tooke soothsaying; in Beotia by a beech tree, in Epyre by an Oake, in Delos by a dragon, in Lycia by a wolfe, in Ammon by a ramme, they receive their oracles, as their warrant to commence any warre, to enter any battell, or to attempt any enterprize."

Warkworth, who was a contemporary, describes three curious portents (as they were then regarded) which occurred in the thirteenth year of the reign of Edward IV. One was the foul and troubled state of the streams in various places, among others, at Hungervale, seven miles from Dudley, " that whenne," he proceeds, " it betokenethe batayle it rennys foule and trouble watere; and whenne betokenythe durthe or pestylence, it rennyth as clere as any watere, but this yere it renne ryght troubled and foule watere. Also ther is a pytte in Kente, in Langley Parke: ayens any batayle he will be drye, and it rayne nevere so myche; and if ther be no batayle towarde, he wille be fulle of watere, be it nevyre so drye a wethyre, and this yere he is drye. Also this same yere, ther was a voyce cryenge in the heyre, ' Bowes, Bowes,' whiche was herde of al menne; and many other dyverse tokenes have be schewede in Englonde this yere, for amendynge of mennys lyvynge."

Edward IV., at the battle of Mortimer's-Cross, is traditionally reported to have seen three suns, which blended immediately afterwards into one, and to this phenomenon is said to be due the addition of the sun to his cognizance. This is alluded to by Shakespear in the " Third Part of Henry the Sixth." At the accesion of Queen Elizabeth, in November, 1558, a storm burst over London, with thunder and lightning, and Sir John Hayward, in his Annals of the first four years of this reign, observes: "Likewise the spire of Allhallows church, in Bread Streete, being then of stone, was smitten about ten foote beneath the topp, from which place a stone was strucke that slew a dogg and overthrew a man with whom the dogg played. The accident was at that time esteemed prodigious by some whose affections rann with a bias, onely because it ensued soe greate actiones of change." In the November of 1623, while a priest named Drury was preaching to an audience in a room in the Blackfriars, the floor gave way, and several persons were killed. This casualty became well-known as the Fatal Vesper. In a copy of a contemporary account of the calamity, a MS. note says: "I am informed by the worshipful M. Thomas Smith of Bow Lane that besides those persons here recited was one Mr. Walsted of Oxfordshire, gentleman, who coming vp to London w^h a resolute purpose to disherite his eldest sonne who was a protestant, was drawne vnto this exercise, and there perished, before hee had effected what hee had determined to do." Walter Yonge, Esq. M.P. for Honiton in the time of James I., carefully notes down in his Diary, published by the Camden Society, all the portents and omens he witnessed or could hear of. There are several recorded by him as happening in one year—1607. It is said by Sir Simonds D'Ewes, that the silver bowl given by Sir Jervis Elvis, one of the accomplices in the Overbury murder, to St. John's College, Cambridge, fell down on the day of his execution at Tower Hill.

Aubrey, in his "Remains of Gentilism and Judaism," notices several portents which happened before changes of government in his time. At Sir Thomas Trenchard's, at Lichet in Dorset, on the first day of the sitting of the Parliament, 1641, while the family were at dinner, the sceptre fell out of the king's hand, in plaister, in the hall. At his majesty's trial, the head of his cane fell off. And before Cromwell's death, a great whale came to Greenwich. He notices the tearing of the canopy at James II.'s coronation, in returning from the Abbey: adding, "'twas of cloth of gold, and my strength I am confident could not have rent it, and it was not a windy day." Hickes, in a letter to Charlett (Jan. 23, 1710-11) also mentions "the omens that happened at the Coronation of James II., which," says he, "I saw: viz. the tottering of the crown upon his head: the broken canopy over it; and the rent flag hanging upon the White Tower when I came home from the Coronation. It was torn by the wind at the same time the signal was given

to the Tower that he was crowned. I put no great stress upon these omens, but I cannot despise them; most of them, I believe, come by chance, but some from superior intellectual agents, especially those which regard the fates of kings and nations."

Nash, speaking of the plague in London, says: "The vulgar menialty conclude therefore it is like to increase, because a hearnshaw, a whole afternoon together, sate on the top of Saint Peters Church in Cornehill. They talk of an oxe that told the bell at Wolwitch, and how from an oxe he transformed himselfe to an old man, and from an old man to an infant, and from an infant to a young man. Strange prophetical reports (as touching the sicknes) they mutter he gave out, when in truth they are nought els but cleanly coined lies, which some pleasant sportive wits have devised to gull them most grossely." *Christ's Tears over Jerusalem*, 1593, ed. 1613, p. 185.

Rats gnawing the hangings of a room, says Grose, is reckoned the forerunner of a death in the family. It was looked upon as a bad omen, if either a rat or mouse, gnawed one's clothes. This, however, was an idea derived from the classical ages. Cicero, in his Second Book on Divination, ridicules the propensity of his contemporaries to regard the gnawing of any thing by mice as a portent. For, he says, "before the Marsian war, because the Lanuvian mice ate the shields, the augurs held it to be a very great omen. As though indeed it signified ought, whether mice had eaten shields or sieves (cribra)—;" and Delrio, in his "Disquisitions on Magic," introduces, aptly enough, the anecdote related of Cato who, when told by some one that the mice had eaten his shoes, replied that that was no harbinger, but that the wonder would have been, if the mice had been eaten by the shoes. The same rejoinder has been put into the mouth of a more modern celebrity.

A writer in the "Athenian Oracle" asserts that he "knew a family never without one cricket before some one dyed out of it; another, that an unknown voice always called the person that was to die; another, that had something like a wand struck upon the walls; and another, where some bough always falls off a particular tree a little before death." He adds, inconsistently enough, "But ordinarily such talk is nonsense, and depends more upon fancy than any thing else." In the same work, we read of "its being a common thing that before a king or some great man dies, or is beheaded, &c., his picture or image suffers some considerable damage, as falling from the place where it hung, the string breaking by some strange invisible touch." Gay mentions, among rustic omens, the wether's bell and the lambkin; as also bees:

"———The weather's bell
Before the drooping flock toll'd forth
    her knell."

* * *

" The lambkin, which her wonted ten-
    dance bred,
Drop'd on the plain that fatal instant
    dead."

* * *

" Swarm'd on a rotten stick the bees
    I spy'd,
Which erst I saw when Goody Dobson
    dy'd."

I recollect nothing at present which seems to have been derived into modern superstition from the ancient mode of deducing omens from the inside of animals, unless it be that concerning the Merry Thought, thus noticed by the " Spectator:" " I have seen a man in love turn pale and lose his appetite upon the plucking of a Merry Thought."

In *Dives and Pauper*, 1493, ch. 46, it is said: " Some man hadde levyr to mete with a froude or a frogge in the way than with a knight or a squier, or with any man of religion, or of Holy Churche, for than they say and leve that they shal have gold. For sumtyme after the metyng of a frogge or a tode they have resceyved golde—wele I wote that they resseyve golde of men or of wymen, but nat of frogges ne of todes, but it be of the Devel in lyknesse of a frogge or a tode—these labourers, delvers, and dykers, that moost mete with frogges and todes, been fulle pore comonly and but men paye them their hyre, they have lytel or nought."

Willsford informs us that " Trefoile or Clavergrasse, against stormy and tempestuous weather, will seem rough, and the leaves of it stare and rise up, as if it were afraid of an assault. Tezils, or Fuller's Thistle, being gathered and hanged up in the house where the air may come freely to it, upon the alteration of cold and windy weather, will grow smoother, and against rain will close up his prickles. Heliotropes and marigolds do not only presage stormy weather, by closing or contracting together their leaves, but turn towards the sun's rays all the day, and in the evening shut up shop. Pine-apples hanging up in the house, where they freely may enjoy the air. will close themselves against wet and cold weather, and open against hot and dry times. The leaves of trees and plants in general will shake and tremble against a tempest more than ordinary. All tender buds, blossoms, and delicate flowers, against the incursion of a storm, do con-

tract and withdraw themselves within their husks and leaves, whereby each may preserve itself from the injury of the weather. Leaves in the wind, or down floating upon the water, are signs of tempests. In Autumn, (some say,) in the gall or oak-apple, one of these three things will be found (if cut in pieces,) : a flie, denoting want; a worm, plenty; but, if a spider, mortality." *Nature's Secrets*, 1658, p. 136, 144. Lupton has remarked, on the authority of Mizaldus: " If you take an oak-apple from an oak tree, and open the same, you shall find a little worm therein, which if it doth flye away, it signifieth wars; if it creeps, it betokens scarceness of corn : if it run about, then it foreshews the plague. This is the countryman's astrology, which they have long observed for truth. The leaves of an elm tree, or of a peach tree, falling before their time, do foreshew or betoken a murrain or death of cattle." *Notable Things*, ed. 1660, p. 52.

Elsewhere we find : " The fly in the oak-apple is explained as denoting war; the spider, pestilence; the small worm, plenty." *Suppl. to Ath. Oracle*, 476. Willsford adds that " The broom having plenty of blossoms, or the walnut tree, is a sign of a fruitful year of corn," and that " great store of nuts and almonds presage a plentiful year of corn, " especially filberds." " When roses and violets flourish in Autumn " he says, " it is an evil sign of an ensuing plague the year following, or some pestiferous disease." To rise on the right side was accounted lucky. So Claudio, in Fletcher's *Women Pleased*, says to Soto, who has been shot, but is not severely hurt : " You rose of your right side, and said your prayers too: you had been paid else." Dyce's *B. and F.* vii. 19. So in Marston's *What you Will*, 1607 : " you rise on your right side to-day, marry ": and again, in the *Dumb Knight*, by Lewis Machin, 1608, iv, 1, Alphonso says :

" Sure I said my prayers, ris'd on my
    right side,
Wash'd hands and eyes, put on my
    girdle last,
Sure I met no splea-footed baker,
No hare did cross me, nor no bearded
    witch,
Nor other ominous sign—"

It was considered unfortunate, on the contrary, to rise on the left side (or, as we still indeed say sometimes, to get out at the wrong side of the bed), and also to p . . . on a nettle, if we must trust a passage in the interlude of the " Marriage of Wit and Wisdom," and a second in Elderton's ballad of " Lenten Stuffe," 1570.

Many persons consider it unlucky to pass under a ladder, as it may prevent you from being married that year, to commence any work or even journey on a Friday, to see the new moon for the first time through glass, to cross steel, and so forth. It is thought to be a bad omen, if a lover sends his mistress a lock of his hair, and she accepts it, or to present a knife or pair of scissors to a friend, without taking a halfpenny or some such trifle in exchange. It is considered a sure sign by many persons that there will be another death very shortly in the family, when a corpse is limp or flabby, and there is always consequently a certain feeling of security, when the body of a deceased person is stiff. We gather that in the ages of chivalry it was thought unlucky to meet with a priest, if a man were going forth to war or to a tournament. Gaule adds, "So much the rather if it be early in the morning." Defoe observes: "Some will defer going abroad, tho' call'd by business of the greatest consequence, if on going out, they are met by a person who has the misfortune to squint. This turns them immediately back, and perhaps, by delaying till another time what requires an immediate despatch, the affair goes wrong, and the omen is indeed fulfilled, which, but for the superstition of the observer, would have been of no effect." *Duncan Campbel*, 1732, p. 61. Melton says: "That it is a very unfortunate thing for a man to meete early in the morning an ill-favoured man or woman, a rough-footed hen, a shag-haird dog, or a black cat." *Astrologaster*, 1620, 46. By the following simile from *Belvidere*, 1600, p. 160, it should seem that our ancestors considered "Heaviness" as an omen of some impending evil:

" As heaviness foretels some harme at hand,
So minds disturb'd presage ensuing ills."

In connection with this part of the subject, Brand quoted (not quite correctly) the annexed passage from Middleton's "Games at Chess." 1624. Works, ed. 1840, vol. iv. p. 370.

" *White Queen's Pawn.*—A sudden fear invades me, a faint trembling,
Under this omen,
As is oft felt the panting of a turtle
Under a stroking hand.
" *Black Queen's Pawn.*—That bodes good luck still.
Sign you shall change state speedily;
For that trembling
Is always the first symptom of a bride."

Shakespear, in *Richard III.*, 1597, makes Lord Hastings say that he might have avoided committal to the Tower, had he attended to the forewarning given by his palfrey which stumbled thrice, and started, when it looked on the Tower.

In Lincoln and the vicinity, the following lines used to be current:

" Take out, then take in,
Bad luck will begin;
Take in, then take out,
Good luck comes about."

Which bears upon a superstitious belief prevailing in that part of the country that it is a bad omen for the ensuing year, if anything, even the merest trifle, is removed from a house, till some article has been brought into it. Shaw, the historian of Moray, tells us that the ancient Scots much regarded omens in their expeditions: an armed man meeting them was a good omen: if a woman bare-foot crossed the road before them, they seized her and fetched blood from her forehead : if a deer, fox, hare, or any beast of game appeared, and they did not kill it, it was an unlucky omen. The minister of Applecross, Co. Ross, writing about 1795, observes: "The fabulous Boece records a tradition prevailing in his time, viz., that if a young woman should walk over the grave of Vanora, she shall entail on herself perpetual sterility." *Stat. Acc.* iii, 379. In the 18th century, at Forghen, in Banffshire, there were many believers in omens. *Stat. Acc.* xiv, 541.

"Omens and Prognostications of Things," says Bourne, "are still in the mouths of all, though only observed by the vulgar. In country places especially they are in great repute, and are the directors of several actions of life, being looked upon as presages of things future, or the determiners of present good or evil." He specifies several, and derives them with the greatest probability from the heathens, whose observations of these he deduces also from the practice of the Jews, with whom it was a custom to ask signs. He concludes all such observations at present to be sinful and diabolical. *Antiq. Vulg.* p. 70.

Gay ridicules these superstitious ideas:

" Why are those tears? why droops your head?
Is then your other husband dead?
Or does a worse disgrace betide?
Hath no one since his death apply'd?
Alas! you know the cause too well.
The salt is spilt, to me it fell,
Then to contribute to my loss,
My knife and fork were laid across,
On Fryday too! the day I dread!
Would I were safe at home in bed!
Last night, (I vow to Heav'n 'tis true,)
Bounce from the fire a coffin flew.

Next post some fatal news shall tell !
God send my Cornish friends be well !

* * *

That raven on your left-hand oak
(Curse on his ill-betiding croak,)
Bodes me no good. No more she said,
When poor blind Ball, with stumbling
 tread,
Fell prone ; o'erturn'd the pannier lay,
And her mas'd eggs bestrew'd the way.
She, sprawling in the yellow road,
Rail'd, swore and curst. Thou croaking
 toad,
A murrain take thy whoreson throat !
I knew misfortune in the note.
 Dame, quoth the raven, spare your
  oaths,
Unclench your fist, and wipe your
 cloathes ;
But why on me those curses thrown?
Goody, the fault was all your own ;
For had you laid this brittle ware
On Dun, the old sure-footed mare,
Though all the Ravens of the Hundred
With croaking had your tongue out-
 thunder'd,
Sure-footed Dun had kept his legs,
And you, good woman, sav'd your
 eggs."

Molinæus (*Vates*, p. 218) refers to the belief of the ancient Germans in omens derived from the neighing and whinnying of horses, as described by Tacitus, and in his own time, it was thought disastrous if, on leaving one's house very early in the morning, one encountered first either a black man or a lame man.

Filippo Maria Visconti, Duke of Milan (1421-47), considered it a bad omen if he accidentally put his right foot into his left shoe, and Dr. Schliemann, the Greek archæologist, was persuaded by an old woman always to put on his left stocking first. Hazlitt's *Venetian Republic*, 1900, ii, 88.

The following superstitions among the Malabrians are related in Phillips's Account of them, 1717 : " It is interpreted as a very bad sign if a blind man, a Bramin, or a washerwoman, meets one in the way : as also when one meets a man with an empty panel, or when one sees an oil mill, or if a man meets us with his head uncovered, or when one hears a weeping voice, or sees a fox crossing the way, or a dog running on his right hand, or when a poor man meets us in our way, or when a cat crosses our way : moreover when any earthen pot maker or widow meets us, we interpret it in the worst sense : when one sprains his foot, falls on his head, or is called back : presently the Professors of Prognostication are con-

sulted, and they turn to the proper chapter for such a sign, and give the interpretation of it."

One and Thirty, or Whip-her-Jenny.—The game of cards so called. When Nares published his Glossary in 1822, it was still played, but chiefly among children. The great object of the expert player was to get the ace at the bottom, which counting eleven went a good way toward winning the game. Chatto (*Facts and Speculations*, 1848, p. 115) states that it was a favourite game both in Spain and Ireland. The following reference to it is made in Taylor's " Wit and Mirth," 1629 : " An unhappy boy, that kept his fathers sheepe in the country, did vse to carry a paire of cards in his pocket, and meeting with boyes as good as himself, would fall to cards at the Cambrian game of whip-her-ginny, or English one and thirty ; at which sport hee would some dayes lose a sheepe or two." The fact of the ace, as above noticed, reckoning as eleven, bespeaks it a sort of vingt-et-un. Comp. Halliwell in v.

Onion-pennies.—Roman coins so called in Kennett's time at Silchester, supposed from a giant named Oniona, a legendary inhabitant of the city.

Onions.—Burton speaks of " Cromnysmantia," a kind of divination with onions laid on the altar at Christmas Eve, practised by girls, to know when they shall be married, and how many husbands they shall have. *Anatomy*, 1621, ed. 1660, p. 538. " With the introduction of the Protestant Faith," says an early writer, " were introduced your Gallegascones, your Scabilonians, your St. Thomas Onions, your ruffes, your cuffes, and a thousand such new-devised Luciferian Trinkets." *Quatron of Catholike Religion*, by Tho. Hyll, 1600, p. 86. In a tract of later date is the following passage : " *Macq.* Some convenient well scituated stall wherein to sit and sell time, rue, and rosemary, apples, garlike, and Saint Thomas onyons, will be a fit palace for me to practice pennance in." *Dialogue between Mistris Macquerella, &c.* 1650, p. 4. This appears from Naogeorgus to have been a German custom on St. Valentine's Day :—

" In these same dayes young wanton
 gyrles, that meete for marriage bee,
Doe search to know the names of them
 that shall their husbandes bee.
Four onyons, five, or eight they take,
 and make in every one
Such names as they do fansie most,
 and best do think upon.

Thus neere the chimney them they set,
    and that same onyon than,
That firste doth sproute, doth surely
    beare the name of their good man."

Popish Kingdom, by Googe, 1570, fol. 44.

Open-Tide.—The interval between
Epiphany and Ash Wednesday. See
Halliwell in v. where it is stated that
in some places the time after harvest is
or was so termed.

Oratio Prevaricatoria.—See
Hazlitt's edit. of Randolph, 1875, p. 671.

Ordeals.—Strutt, in his "Description of the Ordeals under the Saxons,"
tells us, that the second kind of Ordeal
by water, was, "to thrust the accused
into a deep water, where, if he struggled
in the least to keep himself on the surface,
he was accounted guilty; but if he remained on the top of the water without
motion, he was acquitted with honour.
Hence," he observes, "without doubt came
the long-continued custom of swimming
people suspected of witchcraft. There are
also," he further says, "the faint traces
of these ancient customs in another superstitious method of proving a witch. It
was done by weighing the suspected party
against the church Bible, which if they
outweighed, they were innocent; but, on
the contrary, if the Bible proved the
heaviest, they were instantly condemned."

This mode of discovery was not limited
to cases of witchcraft. It was also anciently employed for the detection of
theft, as appears by two forms in the
"Durham Ritual:" "Exorcismus Aquæ
ad Furtum Requirendum," and "Ad Furtum Requirendum Benedictio Aquæ."
The ordeal consisted in the repetition of
the first of these forms, and the dipping of
one of the hands of the suspected thief
in the water. If the liquid remained un-
changed, the man's innocence was established; but if it boiled or effervesced, he
was held guilty; and the *benedictio* followed, to still the water again. The
same service-book includes the form to be
used in cases of ordeal by fire, which was
not unsimilar. It seems to be pretty
clearly shown, that both were specimens
of that system of gross imposture, of which
the Romish Church has, from very early
times, been the patroness and promoter.
In Chambers's "Book of Days," an account will be found of the methods in
which the "fiery ordeal," at any rate,
was managed; it amounted to little more
than a juggler's trick. For an account
of the ancient ordeal by cold water, see
Dugdale, "Orig. Juridiciales," p. 87.

In the thirty-second volume of "Archæologia," Mr. William Sidney Gibson
observes, in reference to this subject: "In
the Book of Numbers we find the ordi-

nance applicable to the water of benediction, which discovered the innocence
or guilt of women suspected of adultery:
but he might have added, that in the
same Book (v. 18) Joseph the master-
carpenter or builder is subjected to a
similar ordeal as a test of his commission
of a certain crime under the Jewish law.
In the 'Antigone' of Sophocles, a person
whom Creon suspects of a misdemeanor
declares himself ready to handle hot iron
and to walk over fire, in order to manifest his innocence. . . . . The ordeal
trial prevailed among the Hindoos perhaps
to a greater extent than in any other
nation. It existed in France from before the time of Charlemagne (who
approved this mode of investigation) down
to the eleventh century. Grotius com-
municates many instances of water ordeal
in Bithynia, Sardinia, and other countries, and it was practised for centuries
by our Anglo-Saxon ancestors in common
with other nations of Teutonic origin."

In the *Nibelungenlied* (a compilation
from earlier legendary sources) the murderer of Siegfried is detected by making
all those, who might have been guilty of
the crime, pass in succession the bier on
which the body of the hero was laid, and
when the turn of the actual assassin came,
drops of blood, it is related, trickled from
the corpse.

Ork or **Orc** (Lat. *Orca*).—A fabulous
marine animal, by some identified with
the *narwhal*. See Nares' *Glossary*, 1859,
in v.

Orkneys.—In Orkney, formerly, the
commoner people went round on New
Year's Eve, and paid each other visits,
singing this and other verses:

"This night it is guid New'r E'en's
    night,
We're a' here Queen Mary's men;
And we're come here to crave our right,
And that's before our Lady!"

The Orcadians used to consider it unpropitious to marry in the wane of the
moon, or to kill cattle at that time, or to
turn their boat in opposition to the sun's
course. In the Statistical Account of
Scotland, the minister of South Ronaldsay and Burray, Orkney, says; "No couple
chuses to marry except with a growing
moon, and some even wish for a flowing
tide." They have a charm also whereby
they try if persons be in a decay or not,
and if they will die thereof, which they
call "casting of the heart." Gough says:
"Funeral ceremonies in Orkney are much
the same as in Scotland. The corpse is
laid out after being stretcht on a board
till it is coffined for burial. I know not
for what reason they lock up all the cats
of the house, and cover all the looking

glasses as soon as any person dies; nor can they give any solid reason." *Sepulchral Monuments*, ii, Introd. ccv. It by no means seems difficult to assign a reason for locking up the cats on the occasion; it is obviously to prevent their making any depredations upon the corpse, which it is known they would attempt to do if not prevented.

In a part of the parish of Sandwick, Orkney, every family that has a herd of swine, kills a sow on the 17th day of December, and thence it is called Sow-day. There is no tradition as to the origin of this practice. These cattle are usually bought at a kind of cow fair or mart at this time. *Mart for market* occurs in the Laws of David I. of Scotland in the Regiam Majestatem, 1609, p. 243. Two or more of the poorer sort of rustic families still join to purchase a cow, &c. for slaughter at this time, called always in Northumberland a mart; the entrails of which, after having been filled with a kind of pudding meat, consisting of blood, suet, groats, &c. are formed into little sausage links, boiled and sent about as presents. They are called black-puddings from their colour. Butler mentions the black pudding in his "Hudibras," speaking of the religious scruples of some of the fanatics of his time. "Several other charms also they have, about their marriage, when their cow is calfing, when churning their milk, or when brewing, or when their children are sick, by taking them to a Smith, (without premonishing him,) who hath had a Smith to his father, and a Smith to his grandfather. They have a charm whereby they stop excessive bleeding in any, whatever way they come by it, whether by or without external violence. The name of the patient being sent to the charmer, he saith over some words, (which I heard,) upon which the blood instantly stoppeth, though the bleeding patient were at the greatest distance from the charmer. Yea, upon the saying of these words, the blood will stop in the bleeding throats of oxen and sheep, to the astonishment of spectators. Which account we had from the ministers of the country." Brand's *Descr. of Orkney*, 1701, pp. 61-2.

He says, "When the beasts, as oxen, sheep, horses, &c. are sick, they sprinkle them with a water made up by them, which they call Fore-spoken water; wherewith likewise they sprinkle their boats, when they succeed and prosper not in their fishing. And especially on Hallow Even they used to sein or sign their boats, and put a cross of tar upon them, which my informer hath often seen. Their houses also some use then to sein."

Martin mentions a singular harvest superstition: speaking of the Orkneys, he says, "There is one day in harvest on which the vulgar abstain from work, because of an ancient and foolish tradition, that if they do their work the ridges will bleed." Brand also mentions this in his "Description," 1701. Speaking of St. Tredwell's Loch, he says, "It is held by the people as medicinal; whereupon many diseased and infirm people resort to it, some saying that thereby they have got good. Yet I hear that when they have done all that is usual for them to do; as going about the Loch, washing their bodies or any part thereof, leaving something at the Loch, as old clouts and the like, &c. it is but in few in whom the effect of healing is produced. As for this Loch's appearing like blood, before any disaster befal the Royal Family, as some do report, we could find no ground to believe any such thing." *Descr. of Orkney*, 1701, p. 56. He adds: "Evil spirits, also called fairies, are frequently seen in several of the Isles dancing and making merry, and sometimes seen in armour. Also I had the account of the wild sentiments of some of the people concerning them; but with such I shall not detain my reader." *Ibid.*, 1701, 63.

It is to be presumed that so late as 1795 the persecution of supposed witches was not yet entirely laid aside in the Orkneys. The minister of South Ronaldsay and Burray reported under that date: "The existence of fairies and witches is seriously believed by some, who, in order to protect themselves from their attacks, draw imaginary circles, and place knives in the walls of houses. The worst consequence of this superstitious belief is, that when a person loses a horse or cow, it sometimes happens that a poor woman in the neighbourhood is blamed, and knocked in some part of the head, above the breath, until the blood appears. But in these parishes there are many decent, honest, and sensible persons who laugh at such absurdities, and treat them with deserved contempt." *St. Acc.* xv. 311. In the same authority (xvi., 460) we read: "Parish of Sandwick, Orkney." "The people do no work on the 3rd day of March, in commemoration of the day on which the Church of Sandwick was consecrated; and as the Church was dedicated to St. Peter, they also abstain from working for themselves on St. Peter's Day (29th of June); but they will work for another person who employs them."

In the same work (xviii., 652) we are told "St. Serf was considered as the tutelar saint of this place, in honour of whom there was an annual procession on his day, viz., 1st July, early in the morning of which, all the inhabitants, men and women, young and old, assembled and carried green branches through the town, decking the publick places with flowers, and spent the rest of the day in festivity. (The church was dedicated not only to the Virgin Mary, but also to St. Serf.) The procession is still continued, though the day is changed from the Saint's Day to the King's [George III.] Birth Day."

Orphanage and **Orphanage Money.**—See *Extracts from the Remembrancia*, 1878, pp. 292-320.

Orpine.—In Dodoen's Herball we read: "The people of the countrey delight much to set orpyne in pots and shelles on Midsummer Even, or upon timber, slattes, or trenchers, dawbed with clay, and so to set or hang it up in their houses, where as it remayneth greene a long season and groweth, if it be sometimes oversprinkled with water. It floureth most commonly in August." The common name for orpine-plants was Midsummer Men.

Gerarde says of orpine: "This plant is very full of life. The stalks set only in clay, continue greene a long time, if they be now and then watered, they also grow." p. 519, edit. 1633. On the 22nd of January, 1801, a small gold ring, weighing eleven pennyweights, seventeen grains and a half, was exhibited to the Society of Antiquaries by John Topham, Esq. It had been found by the Rev. Dr. Bacon, of Wakefield, in a ploughed field near Cawood, in Yorkshire, and had for a device two orpine plants joined by a true-love knot, with this motto above: "Ma fiance velt;" i.e. my sweetheart wills, or is desirous. The stalks of the plant were bent to each other, in token that the parties represented by them were to come together in marriage. The motto under the ring was, "Joye l'amour feu." From the form of the letters it appeared to have been a ring of the fifteenth century.

Spenser thus mentions orpine:

"Cool violets, and orpine growing still."

It is alluded to in "The Cottage Girl," a poem "written on Midsummer Eve, 1786."

The orpine plant occurs among the following love divinations on Midsummer Eve, preserved in the "Connoisseur," No. 56: "I and my two sisters tried the dumb-cake together; you must know, two must make it, two bake it, two break it, and the third put it under each of their pillows (but you must not speak a word all the time,) and then you will dream of the man you are to have. This we did: and to be sure I did nothing all night but dream of Mr. Blossom." "The same night, exactly at twelve o'clock, I sowed hemp-seed in our back-yard, and said to myself,

'Hemp-seed I sow, hemp-seed I hoe,
And he that is my true-love come after me and mow.'

Will you believe me? I looked back, and saw him behind me, as plain as eyes could see him. After that, I took a clean shift and wetted it, and turned it wrong-side out, and hung it to the fire upon the back of a chair; and very likely my sweetheart would have come and turned it right again (for I heard his step) but I was frightened, and could not help speaking, which broke the charm. I likewise stuck up two Midsummer Men, one for myself and one for him. Now, if his had died away, we should never have come together, but I assure you his blowed and turned to mine. Our maid Betty tells me, that if I go backwards, without speaking a word, into the garden upon Midsummer Eve, and gather a rose, and keep it in a clean sheet of paper, without looking at it till Christmas Day, it will be as fresh as in June; and if I then stick it in my bosom, he that is to be my husband will come and take it out." Hannah More's heroine, Sally Evans, would never go to bed (this was in 1800) on Midsummer Eve without having some of the Midsummer Men in her room, as the bending of the leaves to the right or to the left, would never fail to tell her whether her lover was true or false.

Ositha's Day, St.—(Oct. 7). St. Ositha, queen and martyr according to Nicolas, and merely virgin according to the "Book of Days," is referred to the latter half of the eighth century. Aubrey, who collected his "Remains of Gentilism and Judaism" about 1678, observes: "In those dayes" (meaning in the earlier Christian ages), "when they went to bed, they did rake up the fire, and make a ✠ in the ashes, and pray to God and St. Sythe to deliver them from fire and from water, and from all misadventure."

Ossulston.—A stone attributed to the Romans, still existing at the north-east angle of Hyde Park, when Rocque published his map about 1740. Hence came the name of the Hundred, which continues to include the whole of London, and to extend to Brentford.

Ostriches.—Ross says:—"Dr. Browne (i.e. Sir Thomas) denies that ostriches eat and digest iron for these reasons: (Book iii. c. 22.) Because Aristotle and Oppian are silent in this singularity. 2. Pliny speaketh of its wonderful digestion. 3. Ælian mentions not iron. 4. Leo Africanus speaks diminutively. 5. Fernelius extenuates it, and Riolanus denies it. 6. Albertus Magnus refutes it. 7. Aldrovandus saw an ostrich swallow iron, which excluded it again undigested.

"*Answ.* Aristotle's, Oppian's, and Ælian's silence are of no force; for arguments, taken from a negative authority, were never held of any validity. Many things are omitted by them, which yet are true. It is sufficient that we have eyewitnesses to confirm the truth. As for Pliny, he saith plainly that it concocteth whatsoever it eateth. Now the Doctor acknowledgeth it eats iron: ergo, according to Pliny, it concocts iron. Africandus tells us that it devours iron. And Fernelius is so far from extenuating the matter, that he plainly affirms it, and shews, that this concoction is performed by the nature of its whole essence. As for Riolanus, his denial without ground we regard not. Albertus Magnus speaks not of iron, but of stones which it swallows, and excludes again without nutriment. As for Aldrovandus, I deny not but he might see one ostrich, which excluded his iron undigested; but one swallow makes no summer."

The theory that the ostrich can digest iron and stone proves fatal to those few specimens, which reach this country, as ignorant boys and even adults yet persist in throwing halfpence to them.

Sir Hugh Platt reminds us that the true *Aqua vitæ* cannot be made without that which the philosophers call the Stomack of the Ostrich. He proceeds to explain what this mysterious compound, known only to the initiated few, is. *Flora's Paradise*, 1608, p. 10.

Oswald's Eve, St.—(Aug. 4). St. Oswald, King of Northumberland, and martyr, is remembered at present chiefly by the story of his arm, which is related in the "Book of Days." To fast on St. Oswald's Eve, the 4th of August, is mentioned in the "Plumpton Correspondence," under the date of 1499, as a sure remedy against the plague. In a letter to Sir Robert Plumpton, Robert Leventhorpe says: "I wold advise your mastership, my lady, and all your household many (meny or meyny), from henceforth to make promyse, and keepe yt, to fast the even of St. Oswald, kyng and marter yerely; and that promise truly entended to be performed, I trust verely ye shalbe no more vexed with that sicknes."

Warton mentions that an anonymous Latin author of the 13th century left behind him an account of the Life and Miracles of St. Oswald. A great house of Augustinian or Black Canons was settled, before the Dissolution, at Nostel, not very far from Wakefield, co. York, and was under the patronage of St. Oswald. It had a cell at Woodkirk. "St. Oswalde," says Aubrey (1678), "was slayne

by Penda, on the great downe east of Marshfield in Gloucestershire, as you ride to Castle-Combe, from whence it is called St. Oswaldes downe. In these partes, nay, as far as Auburne-Chase (and perhaps a greate deale further), when they pent their sheep in the fold, they did pray to God and St. Oswald to bring the sheep safe to the fold, and in the morning they did pray to God and Saint Oswald to bring them safe from the fold. The countryfolk call St. Oswald St. Twasole."

His fame on the continent was also extensive. We find him the patron saint of churches and his name in the legends of coins.

Ouph, Ouphes.—A name for *elf, elves*, in the *Merry Wives of Windsor*, v, Sc. 5, where Anne Page, as the Fairy Queen, directs her attendant fairies to "strew good luck on every sacred room," &c.

Outlawry.—See Tomlins' *Law Dictionary*, 1835, in v. for an elaborate paper on this subject. The two main kinds were political and civil.

Outrope.—In a tract by Dekker, *A Knight's Conjuring*, 1607, a spendthrift refers to the extortions of his father for his sake by defrauding young wiseacres of their estates, and paying them partly in goods, which, had they been offered at the drum or at an out-rop, would have brought nothing approaching their estimated price. See *Extracts from Remembrancia*, 1878, p. 289 and Note; Halliwell, *Arch. Dict. v. Outrope.*

Ouvre la Bourse.—See *Cards.*

Over-Clover or **Warner.**—A boy's game. See Halliwell in v.v.

Ovum Angulnum.—See *Druid's Egg.*

Owl.—The ancients held owls in the utmost abhorrence. Pliny characterizes the bird as the "funeral owl and monster of the night"; and Ovid, Lucan, and Claudian bestow on him similar epithets. According to Virgil, it was an owl which foretold the death of Dido. Alexander ab Alexandro is emphatic in his condemnation of this inauspicious creature. Geniales Dies, v. 13: Grey's *Notes on Shakespear*, ii, 175. Rome once underwent a lustration because one of them strayed into the Capitol; and even Pennant assures us, that the appearance of the eagle owl in cities was regarded as ominous of evil. *Zoology*, i, 202. The Romans, however, appear to have viewed all owls, and not the screech-owl alone, as a bad portent. Molinœus describes the cry of the latter species as ominous, and all our English minor authorities adopt the same idea, merely copying from each other. Ross, "Arcana Microcosmi,"

Appendix, p. 218; Moresini "Papatus," p. 21; Mason's "Anatomie of Sorcerie," 1612, p. 85; Willsford's "Nature's Secrets," 1658, p. 134; Gaule's "Mag-astromancers Posed," &c. p. 181.

Ross informs us that "Lampridius and Marcellinus, among other prodigies, which presaged the death of Valentinian the Emperor, mention an owle which sate upon the top of the house where he used to bathe, and could not thence be driven away with stones. Julius Obsequens (in his 'Book of Prodigies,' c. 85), shewes that a little before the death of Commodus Antoninus the Emperor, an owle was observed to sit upon the top of his chamber, both at Rome and at Lanuvium. Xiphilinus, speaking of the prodigies that went before the death of Augustus, says, that the owl sung upon the top of the Curia. He shews also that the Actian war was presignified by the flying of owls into the Temple of Concord.

"Solaque culminibus ferali carmine bubo
Sæpe queri, et longas in fletum ducere voces."
—Virgil, *Æneid*, lib. iv. l. 462.

In Bartholomæus *De Proprietatibus Rerum*, ed. 1536, fol. 166 vᵒ. the author observes touching owls: "Diuynours telle that they betokyn euyll: for if the owle be seen in a citie, it signifyeth distruccion and waste, as Isidore sayth. The cryenge of the owle by nyght tokeneth deathe, as Diuinours coniecte and deme." This omen occurs in the "Assemblé of Foules:"

"The jelous swan ayanst hys deth that singeth,
The oule eke, that of deth the bode bringeth."

Again, in Spenser:

"The rueful Strich still wayting on the Beere,
The whistler shril, that whoso heares doth die."

Butler alludes to this ancient sentiment:

"The Roman Senate, when within
The city walls an owl was seen,
Did cause their clergy with lustrations
(Our Synod calls humiliations,)
The round fac'd prodigy t' avert
From doing town and country hurt."

In "Hamlet," 1603, Ophelia says: "Well, God 'ield you! They say the owl was a baker's daughter." Douce was the first to point out that this probably referred to the legend that a baker's daughter, who refused to give bread to Christ, was transformed by the Saviour into an owl. But none of our antiquaries has, I believe, mentioned that in Cornwall the legend is familiar, and of old date.

Hazlitt's *Proverbs*, 1882, p. 394. Again, in *Julius Cæsar*, Shakespear has the following passage:

"And yesterday the bird of night did sit
Even at noon-day upon the market place
Houting and shrieking."

Rowlands in his *Knave of Spades and Diamonds* (1613) gives an account of "The Country Cunning man:"

"Wise Gosling did but heare the scrich owle crie,
But told his wife, and straight a pigge did die.
Another time (after that scurvie owle)
When Ball his dog at twelve a clocke did howle;
He jogd his wife, and, Ill lucke, Madge, did say,
And fox by morning stole a goose away."

Marston in *Antonio and Mellida*, 1602, says:

"'Tis yet dead night, yet all the earth is cloucht
In the dull leaden hand of snoring sleepe:
No breath disturbs the quiet of the aire,
No spirit moves upon the breast of earth,
Save howling dogs, night crowes, and screeching owles,
Save meager ghosts, Piero, and blacke thoughts."

In "The Gentleman's Verses before he killed himselfe," inserted in "Wit Restored," 1658, the supposed writer says:

"——Methinks the owles
Prodigious summons strikes me, and she houles
My epicedium, with whose tragick quill
Ile pencill in this map my haplesse ill."

See Poole's "English Parnassus," 1657, v. Omens, for several passages from old English authors on this subject. The "Spectator" affirms that a screech owl at midnight has alarmed a family more than a band of robbers; and, as Grose tells us, a screech owl flapping its wings against the windows of a sick person's chamber, or screeching at them, portends that some one of the family shall shortly die. Speaking of the tawny owl, Pennant observes: "This is what we call the screech owl, to which the folly of superstition had given the power of presaging death by its cries." *Zoology*, i, 208.

In the 18th century, this superstition still flourished in undiminished vigour, and it cannot be said even now to be by any means extinct. In the year 1542, at Herbipolis or Würzburg in Franconia, this unlucky bird by its screeching songs affrighted the citizens a long time together, and immediately followed a great plague, war, and other calamities. Ross, writing in 1652, tells us: "About twenty years ago I did observe that in the house where I lodged, an owl, groaning in the window, presaged the death of two eminent persons who died there shortly after."

Oyentia, Oyer, or **Oyez.**—See *Cry.*

Pack-and-Penny Day.—The last day of the fair, when the goods are packed and paid for, is known in the West of England as Pack-an-Penny Day. At least, it was so in Jennings' time—about 1825.

Padfoot.—Not very dissimilar, apparently, from the barguest or boggart, is the pad-foot or supernatural sheep, or at least, animal of a somewhat similar description, the existence of which obtains credit in the Leeds district. It evidently belongs to the same type of superstition, and possesses analogous characteristics. A fuller account of the pad-foot may be found in the "Dialect of Leeds," 1862.

Paganalia.—See *Christmas Box.*

Pales, Worship of.—See *St. John the Baptist (Vigil of).*

Palfrey-Money.—A payment formerly due from the free and customary tenants of the manor of Wimbledon on each change of the lord, and amounting to £6 13s. 4d. It seems from entries in the Court Rolls of the manor under George I. that time was occasionally given for the satisfaction of this claim, which dated back at least to 33 Henry VI.

Pall and Underbearers.—Something, instead of the Pall used at present to cover the coffin, appears from Durandus to have been of great antiquity. *Rationale,* p. 225. The same writer informs us, in many quotations from the ancient Christian writers, that those of the highest order of clergy thought it no reproach to their dignity in ancient times to carry the bier, and that at the funeral of Paula bishops were what in modern language we call underbearers. How different an idea of this office prevails in our times! Durandus seems to say that the corpse was originally borne shoulder-high. *Ibid.,* p. 227.

In the *Irish Hudibras,* 1689, describing the burial of an Irish piper, the author tells us that the bier, through which the wattles were visible, was "overcast with a white velvet," probably meaning a blanket.

At the obsequies of Catherine of Arragon, the divorced wife of King Henry VIII., four knights bore the canopy, six knights supported the pall, and six barons or other noblemen were appointed to assist. The paper communicated from an original MS. in the Chapter House, Westminster, to the sixteenth volume of "Archæologia," contains very explicit particulars respecting this ceremony, the furniture of the funeral-car, the number of mourners, their dress, the etiquette to be observed on the occasion, and other interesting details. Walton, speaking of Herbert's ordination, tells us: "at which time the reverend Dr. Humphrey Henchman, now Lord Bishop of London, tells me, he laid his hand on Mr. Herbert's head, and (alas!) within less than three years, leant his shoulder to carry his dear friend to his grave." *Life of Mr. George Herbert,* 1670, p. 70.

Misson says: "The parish has always three or four mortuary cloths of different prices (the handsomest is hired out at five or six crowns), to furnish those who are at the charge of the interment. These cloths, which they call palls, are some of black velvet, others of cloth with an edge of white linen or silk a foot broad or thereabouts. For a bachelor or maid, or for a woman that dies in childbed, the pall is white. This is spread over the coffin, and is so broad that the six or eight men in black clothes that carry the body upon their shoulders, are quite hid beneath it to their waist; and the corners and sides of it hang down low enough to be borne by those (six friends, men or women, according to the occasion) who, according to custom, are invited for that purpose. They generally give black or white gloves, and black crape hatbands, to those that carry the pall; sometimes also white silk scarves." *Travels in England* (about 1697), by Ozell, 91.

Undertakers now provide the palls. For men, black silk scarves are sometimes given, sometimes they are of black satin. The more particular relatives and friends are usually selected to bear the pall, which practically consists in holding the tassels, not, as formerly, in contributing to carry the burden.

Pall Mall, Pell-Mell, or **Pale Maille.**—In Erondel's "French Garden," 1605, (Edit. 1621, sign. N 5 *verso*) in a dialogue, the lady says, "If one had paille-mails, it were good to play in this alley, for it is of a reasonable good length, straight, and even." And a note in the margin informs us: "A paille-mal is a wooden hammer set to the end of a long staffe to strike a boule with, at which game noblemen and gentlemen in France doe play much." Chamberlayne (*Angliæ Notitia,* 1676, p. 25,) spells it pelmel. It appears that in 1628 there was a place called *Palmail* in the neighbourhood of La.

Grainge Batelière at Paris. Fournier, *Paris Demoli*, 1855, p. 240.

My friend, Mr. H. B. Wheatley, kindly drew up for me some part of the following description; and he has since, in the third volume of the Antiquary, published a more elaborate paper, to which I must refer the reader. Pall Mall (*Italian*, palamaglio; *French*, palemaille) was a popular game in the sixteenth and seventeenth centuries, and few large towns were without a mall or prepared ground where it could be played. It was introduced into England in the reign of James I. who names it among other exercises as suited for his son Henry, who was afterwards Prince of Wales. *Basilikon Doron*, lib. 3.

Unfortunately no rules of the game have come down to us, so that we cannot tell how many players were required, or how many strokes were allowed before the ball passed successfully under one of the hoops, but from old dictionaries and drawings we are able to gather the following particulars: A long alley was prepared for the game by being made smooth, and then surrounded by a low wooden border, which was so marked as to show the position of the balls. Each player had a mallet and a round box-wood ball, and his object was to drive his ball through a high and narrow hoop called "The Pass," of which there were two, one at each end of the mall. Force and skill were both required in the player, who had to make the ball skate along the ground with great speed, and yet be careful that he did not strike it in such a manner as to raise it from the ground.

In the reigns of James I. and Charles I., pall-mall was played in a portion of St. James's Fields, adjoining the Park, and the site is still called Pall Mall. Charles II. was particularly fond of the game, and at his Restoration, as several houses were built and others planned in the old Pall-Mall, he had one of the avenues in St. James's Park prepared for a new Mall. It was one man's business to keep the place in perfect order, and as a part of his duty was to cover the ground with powdered cockle-shells, he was called the cockle-strewer. Pepys, in his *Diary*, May 15, 1663, reports a conversation with the Mall-Keeper, who explained to him how the ground was made for the game, but added that in dry weather the materials became dusty, and impeded the ball. Waller, in his poem on St. James's Park, thus describes with glowing terms the dexterity of Charles II. in the game:

" Here a well-polished mall gives us the
   joy,
To see our prince his matchless force
   imploy.

   .   .   .   .   .

No sooner has he touch'd the flying ball,
But 'tis already more than half the
   mall :
And such a fury from his arm has got
As from a smoking culverin t'were
   shot."

Kip, in his large view of St. James's Park, 1710, introduces players at this sport. Frequenters of Manchester are acquainted with a very narrow thoroughfare in that city called Pall-Mall after the London locality.

In the eighteenth century the game used to be played on the Campo S. Giacomo dell' Orio at Venice. Hazlitt's *Venetian Republic*, 1900, ii, 793.

Palming Dice.—One of the methods of cheating with dice. See a good account in Nares in v.

Palmistry.—See *Chiromancy*.

Palm Sunday.—This is called Palm Sunday, because on that day the boughs of yew-trees, or of the sallow, used to be carried in procession, in imitation of the palm-boughs which the Jews strewed in the way of Christ when he went up to Jerusalem. In "Fuller's Church History," p. 225, we read that "bearing of palms on Palm Sunday is in memory of the receiving of Christ into Hierusalem a little before his death, and that we may have the same desire to receive him into our hearts."

The palm-tree was common in Judea, and planted, no doubt, every where by the way-sides. Sprigs of other trees are still used as a substitute for palms in Roman Catholic countries. The Consecration Prayer seems to leave a latitude for the species of palm used instead of the real palm. In the "Gentleman's Magazine" for March, 1780, appears the ensuing extract from the English "Golden Legend," first printed in 1483 : " but for encheson that we haue non Olyue that berith grene leef, algate therfore we take ewe instede of palme and olyue, and beren about in processyon." Another writer in that Magazine for July, 1783, remarking on the same usage, inquires, "May we refer the branches (as well as the palms on Palm Sunday) to this, 'And they cut down branches and strewed them in the way'?"

In "Dives and Pauper," 1493, cap. iv. on the first commandment, we read : "On Palme Sondaye at procession the priest drawith up the veyle before the rode, and falleth down to the ground with all the people, and saith thrice, Ave Rex Noster, Hayle be thou our King.—He speketh not to the image that the carpenter hath made, and the peinter painted, but if the priest be a fole, for that stock or stone was never king; but he speakethe to hym that died on the crosse for us all, to him that is Kynge of all thynge."

"The Festyvall," 1511, fol. 28, speaking of the Jews strewing palm-branches before Christ, says: " And thus we take palme and floures in the processyon as they dyde, and go in processyon knelynge to the crosse in the worshyp and mynde of hym that was done on the crosse, worshyppynge and welcomynge hym with songe into the chyrche, as the people dyde our Lord into the cyte of Jherusalem. It is called Palme Sondaye for bycause the palme betokeneth vyctory, wherfore all Crysten people sholde bere palme in processyon, in tokennynge that he hath foughten wth the fende our enemye, and hath the vyctory of hym."

In the "Durham Ritual," the expression is: "hos palmarum cæterarumque frondium ramos." In the Sarum Missal, 1555, the forms of consecration of sprigs of flowers are also given.

Stow, in his " Survey," tells us, "that in the week before Easter, had ye great shewes made for the fetching in of a twisted tree or with, as they termed it, out of the wood into the King's house, and the like into every man's house of honour or worship." This must also have been a substitute for the palm. Coles, in his " Adam in Eden," says : " The (willow) blossoms come forth before any leaves appear, and are in their most flourishing estate usually before Easter, divers gathering them to deck up their houses on Palm Sunday, and therefore the said flowers are called palme." It is still customary with our boys, both in the South and North of England, to go out and gather slips with the willow-flowers or buds at this time. These seem to have been selected as substitutes for the real palm, because they are the only things, at this season, which can be easily come at, in which the power of vegetation can be discovered.

In the "Statistical Account of Scotland," vol. xv. p. 45, Parish of Lanark, we read of "a gala kept by the boys of the Grammar-school, beyond all memory, in regard to date, on the Saturday before Palm Sunday. They then parade the streets with a palm, or its substitute, a large tree of the willow kind, Salix caprea, in blossom, ornamented with daffodils, mezereon, and box-tree. This day is called Palm Saturday; and the custom is certainly a Popish relic of very ancient standing."

In Wales (and doubtless elsewhere) they commonly employ on this festival, in lieu of palm, what is popularly called goose and goslings. It flowers early, especially in mild seasons. But doubtless the palm, or palm-twig, which we see in the list of plants in our early vocabularies, is the sallow.

It is even yet a common practice in the neighbourhood of London. The young people go a palming; and the sallow is sold in London streets for the whole week preceding Palm Sunday. In the North, it is called "going a palmsoning or palmsning."

Newton, in his "Herball for the Bible," 1587, p. 206, after mentioning that the box-tree and the palm were often confounded together, adds: "This error grew (as I thinke) at the first for that the common people in some countries use to decke their church with the boughes and branches thereof on the Sunday next afore Easter, commonly called Palme Sunday; for at that time of the yeare all other trees, for the most part, are not blowen or bloomed."

In Germany, according to Naogeorgus, in his "Popish Kingdome," they were accustomed to substitute willow for palm and olive. In MS. Sloane, 2478, of the fourteenth century, are some lines on Palm Sunday.

" Nou ȝee that bereth to day ȝour palme,
Wel autȝe ȝe queme fuch a qualm,
   to Crift ȝour herte al ȝyve ;
As dude the chyldren of tholde lawe,
ȝyf ȝe hym lovede, ȝe fcholde wel vawe
   boe by tyme fchryve.

Lewede, that bereth palm an honde,
That nuteth what palm ys tonderftonde,
   anon ichulle ȝou telle ;
Hit is a tokne that alle and fome
That buth y-fchryve, habbeth overcome
   alle the develes of helle.

ȝyf eny habbeth braunches y-broȝt,
And buth un-fchryve, har boft nys noȝt
   aȝee the fend to fyȝte ;
Hy maketh ham holy as y were,
Vort hy boe fchryve hy fchulleth boe fkere
   of loem of hevene lyȝte."

The Church of Rome has given the following account of her ceremonies on this day : "The blessed Sacrament reverently carried, as if it were Christ, upon the ass, with strawing of bushes and flowers, bearing of palms, setting out boughs, spreading and hanging up the richest clothes, &c. all done in a very goodly ceremony to the honour of Christ, and the memory of his triumph upon this day." In the "Doctrine of the Masse Booke," 1554, we have : " When the Gospel is ended, let ther follow the halowyng of flouers and braunches by the priest, being araied with a redde cope, upon the thyrde step of the altere, turning him toward the South: the palmes, with the floures, being first laied aside upon the altere for the clerkes, and for the other upon the steppe of the altere on the south syde." Prayers: "I conjure the, thou creature of flouers and braunches, in the name of God the Father Almighty, and in the name of Jesu Christ hys sonne our Lord, and in the vertue of the Holy Gost. Therefore be thou rooted out and displaced from this creature of flouers and braunches, al thou strength of the adversary, al thou host of the Divell, and al thou power of the enemy, even every assault of Divels, that thou overtake not the foote steps of them that haste unto the grace of God. Thorow him that shal come to judge the quicke and the deade and the world by fyre. Amen."

"Almightye eternal God, who at the pouring out of the floude diddest declare to thy servaunt Noe by the mouthe of a dove, bearing an olive-braunch, that peace was restored agayne upon earth, we humblye beseche the that thy truthe may ✠ sanctifie this creature of flouers and branches, and slips of palmes, or bowes of trees, which we offer before the presence of thy glory; that the devoute people bearing them in their handes, may meryte to optayne the grace of thy benediccion. Thorowe Christe," &c.

There follow other prayers, in which occur these passages: After the flowers and branches are sprinkled with holy water—"Blesse ✠ and sanctifie ✠ these braunches of palmes, and other trees and flouers"—concluding with this rubrick: "So whan these thinges are finished, let the palmes immediately be distributed."

Fulke and others, on the part of the Protestants, and others have considered all this in a different light from the Rhemists. "Your Palm-Sunday Procession," says Fulke, "was horrible idolatry, and abusing the Lord's Institution, who ordained his Supper to be eaten and drunken, not to be carried about in procession like a heathenish idol: but it is pretty sport that you make the priests that carry this idol to supply the room of the ass on which Christ did ride. Thus you turn the holy mystery of Christ's riding to Jerusalem to a May-game and pagent-play."

In "A Dialogue, or familiar Talke, betwene two neighbours, concernyng the chyefest ceremonyes that were, by the mighti power of gods most holie pure worde suppressed in Englande, and nowe for our unworthines set up agayne by the bishoppes, the Impes of Antichrist, &c. 1554," it appears that crosses of palme were, in the papal times, carried about in the purse, and placed upon doors. These crosses were made on Palme Sunday, in Passion time, of hallowed palm. See signat. D. iii.-iv. "But tell me, Nicholas, hath not thy wyfe a crosse of palme aboute her? *Nich.* Yes, in her purse."

In "A short Description of Antichrist," &c. is the following: "They also, upon Palmes Sonday, lifte up a cloth, and say, hayle our kynge! to a rood made of a wooden blocke," fol. 26. At fol. 8 is noted the popish "hallowinge of Palme Stickes." "Upon Palme Sondaye they play the foles sadely, drawynge after them an asse in a rope, when they be not moche distante from the woden asse that they drawe." *Pylegremage of pure Devotyon, newly translatyd into Englishe,* 1551.

The ceremony of bearing palms on Palm Sunday was retained in England after some others had dropped, and was one of those which Henry VIII. in 1536 declared were not to be contemned and cast away. In an original Proclamation, printed and dated 26th February 30 Henry VIII. occurs the followng clause: "On Palme Sonday it shall be declared that bearing of palmes renueth the memorie of the receivinge of Christe in lyke maner into Jerusalem before his deathe." A similar interpretation of this ceremony to that given in the above occurs in Bishop Bonner's "Injunctions," 1555, signat. A 2. "To cary their palmes discreatlye," is among the Roman Catholic customs censured by Bale in his "Declaration of Bonners Articles," 1554, signat. D, and (D 2 verso) "to conjure palmes." Jeremy Collier mentions that the practice continued in 2 Edward VI. But in "Articles to be enquired of within the Archdeaconry of Yorke, by the churche wardens and sworne men, A.D. 163—" (any year till 1640), I find the following, alluding, it should seem, both to this day and Holy Thursday.— "Whether there be any superstitious use of crosses with towels, palmes, metwands, or other memories of idolaters." "I once knew a foolish, cockbrained priest," says Newton, in his "Herbal for the Bible," p. 207, "which ministered to a certaine yoong man the ashes of boxe, being (forsooth) hallowed on Palme Sunday, according to the superstitious order and doctrine of the Romish Church, which ashes he mingled with their unholie holie water, using to the same a kinde of fantasticall, or rather fanaticall, doltish, and ridiculous exorcisme; which woorthy, worshipful medicine (as he persuaded the standers by) had vertue to drive away any ague, and to kill the worms. Well, it so fell out, that the ague, indeed, was driven away; but, God knoweth, with the death of the poore yoong man. And no marvell. For the leaves of boxe be deleterious, poisonous, deadlie, and to the bodie of man very noisome, dangerous, and pestilent."

It may be worth mentioning that the Field of Towton, near Tadcaster, where the last battle was fought between the two Roses in 1461, is sometimes known as "Palm-Sunday Field."

In an anonymous contemporary narrative of the Restoration of King Edward IV. in 1471, printed for the Camden Society in 1838, there is an account, rather too long to transcribe, of a happy portent which befell the King at Daventry, on Palm Sunday, while the royal party was attending Divine service in the parish church. It appears that Edward, during his misfortunes had vowed, the first time that he beheld, on his return to his kingdom, an image of St. Anne, to pay his devotions to it, and make an oblation. There chanced to be a small alabaster figure of the Saint just above the spot where the monarch himself was kneeling, attached to a pillar, and it was enclosed and hidden from view in a wooden case, according to the usual practice, which was that the image should not be visible from Ash-Wednesday to the morning of Easter-Sunday. But on the present occasion, the case enshrining the figure of St. Anne miraculously opened of its own accord, and then closed again spontaneously, and then once more opened, and remained so, in the sight of the whole congregation. This was pronounced to be an omen of good fortune in store for King Edward, and his majesty, before leaving the church, gave a handsome donation to God and our holy lady St. Anne. In the presence of the King at this place in 1471, one seems to perceive a possibility of fixing the date of the ballad celebrating his adventure with the Barker or Tanner of Tamworth.

In the Churchwardens' Accounts of St. Mary at Hill in the city of London, from the 17th to the 19th year of King Edw. IV., I find the following entry: "Box and palm on Palm Sunday, 12d." And, ibid. among the annual church disbursements, the subsequent: "Palm, box, cakes, and flowers, Palm Sunday Eve, 8d." Ibid. 1486: "Item, for flowrs, oblëyes, and for box and palme ayenst Palm Sondaye, 6d." Ibid. 1493: "For settyng up the frame over the porch on Palme Sonday Eve, 6d." Ibid. 1531: "Paid for the hire of the rayment for the prophets, 12d., and of clothes of aras, 1s. 4d. for Palm Sunday." In Coates's "History of Reading," p. 216, Churchwardens' Accounts of St. Laurence Parish, 1505: "It. payed to the Clerk for syngyng of the passion on Palme Sunday, in ale, 1d." P. 217. 1509. "It. payed for a q'rt of bastard, for the singers of the pashyon on Palme Sondaye, iiijd." P. 221. 1541. "Payd to Loreman for playing the p'phett (prophet) on Palme Sonday, iiijd."

In Lysons' "Environs," among his extracts from the Churchwardens' and Chamberlains' Accounts of Kingston upon Thames, occurs the following: "1. Hen. VIII. For ale upon Palm Sonday on syngyng of the passion £0. 0s. 1d." In Churchwardens' Accompts, of St. Martin Outwich, London, occurs under 1510-11: "First, paid for palme, box-floures, and cakes, iiijd." Under 1525: "Paid for palme on Palme Sunday, ijd." "Paid for kaks, flowers and yow, ijd."

Among Dr. Griffith's "Extracts from the old Books of St. Andrew Hubbard's parish," Brand found: 1524-5. "To James Walker, for making clene the churchyard ag'st Palm Sonday, 1d." Ibid. "On Palm Sonday, for palm, cakes, and flowrs, 6d. ob." 1526-7. "The here of the angel on Palme Sonday, 8d." "Clothes at the Tow'r on Palme Sonday, 6d." 1535-7. "For brede, wyn and oyle, on Palm Sonday, 6d. "A preest and chylde that playde a messenger, 8d." 1538-40. "Rec'd in the Church of the Players, 1s." "P'd for syngyng bread, 2d." "For the aungel, 4d."

There is a strange allusion to the observances of Palm Sunday in the "Demaundes Joyous," 1511: "*Demaunde.* What daye in the yere ben the flyes moost aferde? *Reply.* That is on Palme Sonday, whan they se euery body haue an handeful of palme in theyr hande, they wene it is to kyll theym with."

At Caistor Church, in Lincolnshire, a deputy from Broughton comes on Palm Sunday morning, and places himself in the north porch, at or about the commencement of the first lesson for the day. He has in his hand a gad-whip, which he cracks thrice in front of the porch entrance (as it is alleged, in remembrance of Peter's denial of Jesus): he then wraps the thong round the stock, places some rods of mountain-ash length-wise upon it, and binds the whole with a bit of whipcord. Next he attaches to the whip-stock a purse containing two shillings; and, this done, he walks in and stands before the reading desk till the second lesson commences; he then approaches still nearer, till he can wave the purse over the minister's head; when he has completed this part of the ceremony, he kneels down on a cushion put for him, and holds the purse over the clergyman till the lesson is finished. After the conclusion of the service he takes the whip and purse to the adjacent hamlet of Undon, and leaves it at the manor-house. The whip is renewed yearly, and by this jocular tenure certain property in Broughton parish is held." The gad-whip is a Lincolnshire measure of ten feet. The whip is made of mountain-ash, or any other wood, and is wrapt round, half-way down, with white leather; the thong, which is very large, is also of white leather. Originally in lieu of the shillings, thirty pennies were usual, as to the significance of which see Hazlitt's Blount, 1874, p. 45.

The country folk meet every Palm Sunday on Silbury Hill, Wiltshire, an artificial mound covering an area of more than five acres, and celebrate the anniversary with cakes, figs, sugar, and water fetched from the Kennet. Fosbrooke's *Encyclopædia*, 1843, p. 551.

"Upon Palm Sunday," says Carew, in his survey of Cornwall," p. 144, "at our Lady Nant's Well, at Little Colan, idle-headed seekers resorted, with a palm crosse in one hand and a offering in the other. The offering fell to the priest's share, the cross they threw into the well, which, if it swamme, the party should outlive that yeare; if it sunk, a short ensuing death was boded, and, perhaps, not altogether untruly, while a foolish conceyt of this halsenyng might the sooner help it onwards." A correspondent of "Notes and Queries" observes that "the farmers and labourers of this immediate neighbourhood (Winchester) have a common idea that, from whatever quarter the wind blows for the most part on Palm Sunday, it will continue to blow from the same quarter for the most part during the ensuing summer." In Gloucestershire there is a curious notion that if flowers are sown on Palm Sunday the seeds will become double. The Winter portion of many of the Romish service-book ends with Palm Sunday.

There was a superstition in Germany, according to Naogeorgus, that boughs of the palm (as they were called) possessed the property of protecting the holders against storms and thunder. The Russians (of the Greek Church) have a very solemn procession on Palm Sunday.

Pancake-Bell.—This is rung on the morning of Shrove Tuesday, as a rule, in many parts (Newcastle-on-Tyne, York, Wrexham, &c.) to give notice, that it is time to get the frying pans ready. The sexton generally expects a small fee for his trouble. At York, according to a tract quoted by Brand, the apprentices, &c. exercised the privilege of going into the Cathedral at noon on Shrove Tuesday, and ringing the pancake bell. Dr. Lake, Bishop of Chichester, when he was translated to York, endeavoured to put a stop to the practice, and the attempt nearly cost him his life. "A Vindication of the Letter out of the North, concerning Bishop Lake's Declaration of his dying in the belief of the Doctrine of Passive Obedience, &c."

Pancakes.—Fosbrooke, in his "British Monarchism," ii. 127, mentions that pancakes or crum-cakes, as they were called, were eaten at Barking Nunnery before the dissolution, and no doubt the custom was universal. It was usual to have them after cock-threshing on Shrove-Tuesday. Selden, with his usual acuteness, saw in the practice of eating of fritters, a vestige of "church works."

Shakespear, in "All's Well that ends Well," alludes to this well-known custom. It appears from Rowley and Middleton's "World tossed at Tennis," 1620, that batter was used on Shrove-Tuesday at that time, no doubt for the purpose of making pancakes. In Gayton's "Festivous Notes upon Don Quixote," p. 99, speaking of Sancho Panza's having converted a cassock into a wallet, he observes: "It were serviceable after this greasie use for nothing but to preach at a carnivale on Shrove-Tuesday, and to tosse pancakes in after the exercise." Poor Robin, in his "Almanack for 1677," in his observation on February, says, there will be "a full sea of pancakes and fritters about the 26th and 27th days," i.e. Shrove-Tuesday fell on the 27th—with these lines:

"Pancakes are eat by greedy gut,
And Hob and Madge run for the slut."

In Goldsmith's day, eating pancakes was commonly practised among the country people, as he incidentally mentions (if any authority were wanted for such a thing) in his "Vicar of Wakefield."

A learned foreigner thought that our taste for cock-throwing must proceed from temporary insanity, the result of eating pancakes.—Note to "Veillè a la Campagne, or the Simnel, a Tale," 1745, p. 16. The custom of frying pancakes (in turning of which in the pan there is usually a good deal of pleasantry in the kitchen), is still retained in many families of the better sort throughout the kingdom.

Brand notes: "She that is noted for lying a-bed long, or any other miscarriage, hath the first pancake presented to her at Shrovetide or after cock-threshing, which most commonly falls to the dog's share at last, for no one will own it their due." This latter part of the note is to illustrate the following lines:

"Maids, fritters and pancakes ynow see ye make,
Let slut have one pancake for company sake."

"Tossing the pancake" is a custom too ancient and too popular at Westminster School to be forgotten on Shrove Tuesday, and the traditions of the institution were accordingly duly observed. Shortly after twelve o'clock a small procession, headed by one of the Abbey vergers carrying a silver wand, and in which the cook, arrayed in white, holding in his right hand a large frying-pan containing a newly made pancake, was a prominent figure, left the kitchen and advanced to the door of the great school. Knocking thrice, according to time-honoured custom, the inquiry was made, "Who demands admittance," when the reply was given, "The cook." The bar which separates the upper from the lower school had in the mean time been drawn out, and all the boys were congregated behind the barrier. On admission the cook and his attendants advanced midway up the hall, and the former, whirling the frying-pan three times round his head, dexterously hurled the pancake amid the crowd of expectant youngsters, who scrambled for its possession. Master Guy Simonds, son of Captain Simonds, chief officer of the Metropolitan Fire Brigade, had the good fortune to secure the largest piece, and immediately ran off to the Deanery to claim the usual reward of a guinea. The cook became entitled to a similar sum. *Daily Telegraph*, 27 Feb. 1895.

From "The Westmorland Dialect," by A. Walker, 8vo. 1790, it appears that cock-fighting and casting pancakes are still practiced on Shrove-Tuesday in that country. Thus p. 31: "Whaar ther wor tae be cock-feightin, for it war Pankeak-Tuesday." And p. 35: "We met sum lads an lasses gangin to kest their pankeaks." A correspondent of "Notes and Queries," writing from Hedon (?Heden in Kent), observes: "All the apprentices in the town, whose indentures terminate before the return of the day, assemble in the belfry of the church, at eleven o'clock, and in turn toll the tenor bell for an hour; at the sound of which all the housewives in the parish commence frying pancakes. The sexton, who is present, receives a small fee from each lad." 2nd Series, v, 391.

A kind of Pancake Feast, preceding Lent, was used in the Greek Church, whence we may probably have borrowed it with Pasche Eggs and other such like ceremonies. "The Russes," as Hakluyt tells us, "begin their Lent always eight weeks before Easter; the first week they eat eggs, milk, cheese, and butter, and make great cheer with pancakes and such other things."

Pargettor.—The artificer of decorated plaister-work. See Fairholt's *Dictionary of Terms in Art*, p. 329, and Hazlitt's *Livery Companies*, 1892, p. 590.

Parish Top.—A top bought for public exercise in a parish. See Nares in **v**. Otherwise known as *a town-top*, under which name it occurs in old plays.

Parkers of Browsholms.—This family formerly enjoyed the distinction of being hereditary bowbearers of Bowland Forest under the Dukes of Buccleugh, and possessed a valuable library long since dispersed. See Hazlitt's *Shakespear: Himself and his Work*, 2nd ed. 1903, p. 171. In the old ballad poem of *Adam Bel*, 1536, William of Cloudesby, on being pardoned, is made bowbearer to the King:—

" I gyue the xviii. pens a daye,
And my bowe shalt thou bere,
And ouer all the north countree
I make the chefe rydere."

Parochial Perambulations—Bourne cites Spelman as deriving this custom from the times of the heathens, and that it is an imitation of the feast called Terminalia, which was dedicated to the God Terminus, whom they considered as the guardian of fields and landmarks, and the keeper-up of friendship and peace among men. The primitive custom used by Christians on this occasion was, for the people to accompany the bishop or some of the clergy into the fields, where litanies were made, and the mercy of God implored, that he would avert the evils of plague and pestilence, that he would send them good and seasonable weather, and give them in due season the fruits of the earth.

The word *Parochia* or Parish anciently signified what we now call the Diocese of a bishop. In the early ages of the Christian Church, as kings founded cathedrals, so great men founded parochial churches for the conversion of themselves and their dependants: the bounds of the parochial division being commonly the same with those of the founder's jurisdiction. Some foundations of this kind were as early as the time of Justinian the Emperor. Before the reign of Edward the Confessor, the parochial divisions in this kingdom were so far advanced, that every person might be traced to the parish to which he belonged. This appears by the canons published in the time of Edgar and Canute. The distinction of the parishes as they now stand appears to have been settled before the Norman Conquest. In "Domesday Book" the parishes agree very near to the modern division. Camden tells us that this kingdom was first divided into parishes by Honorius, Archbishop of Canterbury, A.D. 636, and counts two thousand nine hundred and eighty-four parishes. The Lateran Council made some such division as this. It compelled every man to pay tithes to his parish-priest. Men before that time payed them to whom they pleased; but, without being sarcastical, one might observe, that since then it has happened that few, if they could be excused from doing it, would care to pay them at all.

In the Injunctions made in the reign of Queen Elizabeth, it is ordered "that the curate, at certain and convenient places, shall admonish the people to give thanks to God, in the beholding of God's benefits, for the increase and abundance of his fruits, saying the 103rd Psalm, &c. At which time the minister shall inculcate these, or such sentences,—'Cursed be he which translateth the bounds and doles of his neighbours,' or such orders of prayers as shall be hereafter."

In the Churchwardens' Accounts of St. Margaret's Westminster, under various years, are several entries of moneys paid on account of spiced bread, wine, ale, beer, fish, &c. for the Ascension Eve ceremony, including the Perambulation. The following is curious:

"1556.

"Item, paid for bread, wine, ale, and beer, upon the Ascension-Even and Day, against my Lord Abbott and his Covent cam in procession, and for strewing herbs the samme day, 7s. 1d." Lysons, in his "Environs," has quoted other entries from the Churchwardens' Accounts of St. Mary at Hill, London, under 1682:

	£	s.	d.
"For fruit on Perambulation Day	1	0	0
For points for two yeres . . .	2	10	0"

The following extracts are from the Churchwardens' Books of Chelsea:

"1670. Spent at the Perambu-			
lation Dinner	3	10	0
Given to the boys that were whipt	0	4	0
Paid for poynts for the boys .	0	2	0"

The whipping or bumping of the boys was a general custom, not always limited to them, in order, as it was said, to impress the confines on the memory.

In many manors a party, who are more usually on horseback than a-foot, proceed annually round the property, beating the bounds; the crosses or other marks indicative of the limits of the estate, are, where it has become necessary, unturfed or unearthed for the occasion; and at each halting point, one of the visitants is bumped smartly against the boundary-stone, or placed head downwards against it, or made to undergo any penalty of the kind, which occurs at the moment, under the facetious pretext of impressing the exact position on his mind. The man who is most nimble, or has the best horse,

stands the best chance of escape; but as a rule everybody gets his share. A gentleman well remembered returning black and blue from such an expedition; in his case two or three sharp strokes with a riding whip across the shoulders had been administered to guard against forgetfulness. On the same occasion the clergyman of the parish, whose brother was afterwards a bishop, was taken off his horse, and literally laid upright on his hat; but no other violence was offered, out of respect to his cloth.

Heath, in his "History of the Scilly Islands," tells us: "At Exeter, in Devon, the boys have an annual custom of damming-up the channel in the streets, at going the bounds of the several parishes in the city, and of splashing the water upon people passing by." "Neighbours as well as strangers are forced to compound hostilities, by giving the boys of each parish money to pass without ducking: each parish asserting its prerogative in this respect." Wither writes:—

"That ev'ry man might keep his owne possessions,
Our fathers us'd, in reverent processions,
With zealous prayers, and with praise-full cheere,
To walke their parish-limits once a yeare;
And well knowne markes (which sacrilegious hands
Now cut or breake) so bord'red out their lands,
That ev'ry one distinctly knew his owne;
And many brawles, now rife, were then unknowne."

Emblems, 1635, p. 161.

In Michael Wodde's "Dialogue," 1554, signat. D 8, we read: "What say ye to procession in Gang-daies, when Sir John saith a Gospel to our corne fieldes. *Oliver.* As for your Latine Gospels read to the corne, I am sure the corne understandeth as much as you, and therefore hath as much profit by them as ye have, that is to sai, none at al." What is related on this head in the life of Richard Hooker, is extremely interesting: "He would by no means omit the customary time of procession, persuading all, both rich and poor, if they desired the preservation of love and their parish rights and liberties, to accompany him in his perambulation: and most did so: in which perambulation he would usually express more pleasant discourse than at other times, and would then always drop some loving and facetious observations, to be remembered against the next year, especially by the boys and young people: still inclining them, and all his present parishioners, to meekness, and mutual kindnesses and love; because love thinks not evil, but covers a multitude of infirmities." In Herbert's "Country Parson," 1652, p. 157, we are told: "The countrey parson is a lover of old customs, if they be good and harmlesse. Particularly he loves procession, and maintains it, because there are contained therein four manifest advantages. First, a blessing of God for the fruits of the field. 2. Justice in the preservation of the bounds. 3. Charitie in loving, walking, and neighbourly accompanying one another, with reconciling of differences at that time, if there be any. 4. Mercie, in relieving the poor by a liberal distribution and largess, which at that time is or ought to be used. Wherefore he exacts of all to be present at the perambulation, and those that withdraw and sever themselves from it he mislikes, and reproves as uncharitable and un-neighbourly; and, if they will not reforme, presents them."

Aubrey, in his "Remaines of Gentilisme and Judaisme," says: "In Cheshire, in Mr. N. Kent's grandmother's time, when they went in perambulation, they did blesse the springs, i.e. they did read a Ghospell at them, and did believe the water was the better:" to this account in the MS. is added in pencil: "On Rogation days the Gospels were read in the cornfields here in England untill the Civill Warrs." In the parish of St. James, Westminster, at a vestry held in 1687, the expences of the Perambulation of Boundaries were limited to £10, and comprised bread, cheese, beer, and farthings and points for the boys.

On Lord Derby's Westmoreland estate the ancient custom—observed only once in a century—of walking the boundary took place in 1902. Halts were made along the 16 miles of route, and sports held, consisting of wrestling, tugs-of-war, &c., and at various points a barrel of ale and bread and cheese was provided. At the close the party, numbering several hundreds, adjourned to the hall, where a bullock had been roasted whole, and there were more sports.

At Oxford, at this time, the little crosses cut in the stones of buildings, to denote the division of the parishes, are whitened with chalk. Great numbers of boys, with peeled willow rods in their hands, accompany the minister in the procession. See *Gospel Oak* and *Wolverhampton.*

Googe in his version of "Naogeorgus," 1570, says:

"Now comes the day wherein they gad
    abrode, with crosse in their hande,
To boundes of every field, and round
    about their neighbours lande."

And he insinuates that they sometimes ate and drunk so plentifully that they forgot the great business of the day, and left the cross behind them.

Parsley.—Coles tells us that "Parsley was bestowed upon those that overcame in the Grecian games, in token of victory." So also Bartholomeus, "De proprietatibus Rerum," lib. xvii. fol. 249, "De Apio. Somtyme victours had garlondes of it, as Isidore sayth Libro xvii. Hercules made hym fyrste garlondes of this herbe." It is similarly introduced in Greene's "Second part of Conny-catching," 1592, sign. B 4 verso. At Islip, in Oxfordshire, the transplantation of parsley is considered inauspicious.

Parsloes, Essex.—See *Headless Steeds of Haddon.*

Pasch Eggs.—Comp. a good note in Nares, *Glossary,* 1859, in v.

Passage.—A game at dice, described by Nares and Halliwell. Supposed to be the same as the French *passe-dix.* But an earlier authority than the two writers above named cite for this amusement is the interlude of the *World and the Child,* 1522, where we read:

"Yea, and we shall be right welcome,
    I dare well say,
In East Cheap for to dine;
And then we will with Lombards at
    passage play,
And at the Pope's Head sweet wine
    assay—"

Shakespear: Himself and his work, by W. C. Hazlitt, 1903, p. 148; Hazlitt's Dodsley, xi, 431.

Passamezzo, Passing-Measure, or **Passa-measure.**—A slow dance, often mentioned by early writers. See Halliwell in v.

Passing, Saucing, or **Soul Bell.**—The ceremony of tolling a bell on this occasion was not only not as ancient as the use of bells, but the latter were originally employed for secular as well as ecclesiastical purposes, having been during centuries substitutes for clocks. It was only at a comparatively later date that they came into use as signals to convene the people to their public devotions. It has more probably been an after-invention of superstition. Thus praying for the dying was added to praying for the dead.

Wheatley, in his "Illustration of the Book of Common Prayer," 1741, apologizes for our retaining this ceremony: "Our Church," says he, "in imitation of the saints in former ages, calls on the minister and others, who are at hand, to assist their brother in his last extremity. In order to this she directs that when any one is passing out of this life, a bell should be tolled," &c. It is called from thence the Passing Bell. C. xxii, sect. 6.

"The Passing Bell," says Grose, "was antiently rung for two purposes: one to bespeak the prayers of all good Christians, for a soul just departing; the other, to drive away the evil spirits who stood at the bed's foot, and about the house, ready to seize their prey, or at least to molest and terrify the soul in its passage: but by the ringing of that bell (for Durandus informs us evil spirits are much afraid of bells,) they were kept aloof; and the soul, like a hunted hare, gained the start, or had what is by sportsmen called law. Hence, perhaps, exclusive of the additional labour was occasioned the high price demanded for tolling the greatest bell of the church; for that, being louder, the evil spirits must go farther off, to be clear of its sound, by which the poor Soul got so much more the start of them: besides, being heard farther off, it would likewise procure the dying man a greater number of prayers. This dislike of spirits to bells is mentioned in the Golden Legend."

Douce was inclined to think that the passing bell was originally intended to drive away any demon that might seek to take possession of the soul of the deceased. In the cuts to those *Horæ* which contain the Service of the Dead, several devils are waiting for this purpose in the chamber of the dying man, to whom the priest is administering extreme unction. He adds: "It is to hoped that this ridiculous custom will never be revived, which has most probably been the cause of sending many a good soul to the other world before its time: nor can the practice of tolling bells for the dead be defended upon any principle of common sense, prayers for the dead being contrary to the Articles of our Religion." In Catholic times here it has been customary to toll the Passing Bell at all hours of the night as well as by day: as the subsequent extract from the Churchwardens' Account for the parish of Wolchurch, 1526, proves: "Item. the clerke to have for tollynge of the passynge belle, for manne, womanne, or childes, if it be in the day, iiijd. Item. if it be in the night, for the same viijd." Bede contends that this bell, contrary to the present custom, should be tolled before the person's departure, that good men might give him their prayers, adding, that, if they do no good to the departing sinner, they at least evince the disinterested charity of the person that prefers them. Lib. iv., C. 23. Durandus says in his *Rationale*: "Aliquo moriente Campanæ debent pulsari, ut Populus hoc audiens oret pro illo."

The peal of the church-bell, prescribed by the Canonists, was thought indispensable to the translation of the soul of a dead person, and as an unbaptized infant could not receive this rite, the parents were haunted by the fear, that the soul of the departed would not quit the body.

It is scarcely necessary to remind the reader of the almost invariable craving which persons *in articulo mortis* manifest for abundance of fresh air, and for a place near the open window. The motive is obvious enough, and can have no affinity with the custom which prevailed very widely at one time of throwing the window and door open, immediately after death, that the liberated soul might properly pass. In an old English Homily for Trinity Sunday, occurs: "The fourme of the Trinity, was founded in manne, that was Adam our forefadir, of earth oon personne, and Eve of Adam the secunde persone: and of them both was the third persone. At the deth of a manne three bellis shulde be ronge, as his knyll, in worcheppe of the Trinetee, and for a womanne, who was the secunde persone of the Trinetee, two bellis should be rungen."

In "The Sheepheards description of Loue," by Sir W. Raleigh, in "Englands Helicon," 1600, are the following lines, in which the Passing Bell is termed the Sauncing Bell:

"*Melibeus.* Sheepheard, whats Loue, I pray thee tell?
Faustus. It is that fountaine, and that well,
Where pleasure and repentance dwell.
It is perhaps that sauncing bell,
That toles all into heauen or hell,
And this is Loue as I heard tell."

In *The Meeting of Gallants at an Ordinary,* 1604, it is called the Saunce Bell, where Signior Stramazoon says: "Stoote, the mad butchir, squeakes shriller then the Saunce Bell at Westminster." As for the title of "Soul Bell," as that bell is sometimes called, which they toll after a person's breath is out, if they mean by it that it is a call upon us to pray for the soul of the deceased person, I know not how the Church of England can be defended against the charge of those who, in this instance, would seem to tax us with praying for the dead. See Bishop Hall's "Apology against the Brownists." "We call them," says the Bishop, ibid. p. 568, "Soul Bells, for that they signify the departure of the soul, not for that they help the passage of the soul."—*Bourne.*

The following is a description of a Funeral or Dead Peale: "It being customary not only in this City of London, upon the death of any person that is a member of any of the honourable Societies of Ringers therein, (but likewise in most countries and towns in England, not only upon the death of a ringer, but likewise of any young man or woman,) at the funeral of every such person to ring a peal; which peal ought to be different from those for mirth and recreation, (as the musick at the funeral of any master of musick or the ceremony at the funeral of any person belonging to military discipline) and may be performed two different ways: the one is by ringing the bells round at a set pull, thereby keeping them up so as to delay their striking, that there may be the distance of three notes at least, (according to the true compass of ringing upon other occasions,) between bell and bell; and having gone round one whole pull every bell, (except the tenor,) to set and stand; whilst the tenor rings one pull in the same compass as before; and this is to be done whilst the person deceased is bringing to the ground; and after he is interred, to ring a short peal of round ringing, or changes in true time and compass, and so conclude. The other way is call'd buffeting the bells, that is, by tying pieces of leather, old hat, or any other thing that is pretty thick, round the ball of the clapper of each bell, and then by ringing them as before is shewn, they make a most doleful and mournful sound: concluding with a short peal after the funeral is over, (the clappers being clear as at other times:) which way of buffeting is most practis'd in this City of London." *Campanologia*, 1753, p. 200.

The following clause in the "Advertisements for due Order," &c. 1565, is much to our purpose: "Item, that when anye Christian bodie is in passing, that the bell be tolled, and that the curate be speciallie called for to comforte the sicke person; and after the time of his passinge, to ringe no more but one shorte peale; and one before the buriall, and another short peale after the buriall." I find the following in the York Articles (any year till 1640): "Whether doth your clark or sexton, when any one is passing out of this life, neglect to toll a bell, having notice thereof: or, the party being dead, doth he suffer any more ringing than one short peale, and, before his burial one, and after the same another?" Inquiry is also directed to be made, "whether at the death of any there be any superstitious ringing?" In the Chichester Articles of Enquiry, 1638, under the head of Visitation of the sicke and persons at the point of death, we read: "In the meane-time is there a passing-bell tolled, that they who are within the hearing of it may be moved in their private devotions to recommend the state of the departing soule into the hands of their Redeemer, a duty which all Christians are bound to, out of

a fellow-feeling of their common mortality." I find the following in the Worcester Articles of Visitation, 1662: "Doth the parish clerk or sexton take care to admonish the living, by tolling of a passing-bell of any that are dying, thereby to meditate of their own deaths, and to commend the other's weak condition to the mercy of God?" In similar Articles for the Diocese of St. David in the same year, I read as follows: "Doth the parish clerk, or sexton, when any person is passing out of this life, upon notice being given him thereof, toll a bell, as hath been accustomed, that the neighbours may thereby be warned to recommend the dying person to the grace and favour of God?"

Among the many objections of the Brownists, it is laid to the charge of the Church of England, that though we deny the doctrine of Purgatory and teach the contrary, yet how well our practice suits with it may be considered in our ringing of hallowed bells for the soul. Pennant says: that in the 18th century the Passing Bell was punctually sounded. "I mention this," he says, "because idle niceties have, in great towns, often caused the disuse. It originated before the Reformation, to give notice to the priest to do the last duty of extreme unction to the departing person, in case he had no other admonition. The canon (67) allows one short peal after death, one other before the funeral, and one other after the funeral. The second is still in use, and is a single bell solemnly tolled. The third is a merry peal, rung at the request of the relations; as if, Scythian like, they rejoiced at the escape of the departed out of this troublesome world.

Bede, speaking of the death of the Abbess of St. Hilda, tells us, that one of the sisters of a distant monastery, as she was weeping, thought she heard the well-known sound of that bell which called them to prayers, when any of them had departed this life. The abbess had no sooner heard this, than she raised all the sisters and called them into the church, where she exhorted them to pray fervently, and sing a requiem for the soul of their mother. Lib. iv, C. 23.

In Hooper's "Funeral Oration," 1549, occurs this singular passage: "Theyr remedyes be folyshe and to be mocked at, as the ryngynge of belles, to ease the payne of the dead wythe other:" as if the purpose of tolling the Passing Bell has been intended to give an easy passage to the dying person. The following passage is from Vernon: "If they shoulde tolle theyr belles (as they did in good Kynge Edwardes dayes) when any bodye is drawing to his ende and departinge out of this worlde, for to cause all menne to praye unto God for him, that of his accustomed goodnesse and mercye, he should vouch-safe to receave him unto his mercye, forgevinge him all his sinnes: Their ring-inge shuld have better appearance and should be more conformable to the aun-ciente Catholicke Churche." *Hunting of Purgatory to Death*, 1561, fol. 60.

In Birrel's "Diary," is the following curious entry: "1566. The 25 of October, vord came to the toune of Edinburghe, frome the Queine, yᵗ her Majestie wes deadly seike, and desyrit yᵉ bells to be runge, and all yᵉ peopill to resort to yᵉ kirk to pray for her, for she wes so seike that none lipned her life." *Fragm. of Scotish History*, 1796. There is, as may be supposed, no want of literary allusions to the present topic.

There is a passage in Shakespear's "Henry the Fourth," 1600, which proves that our poet has not been a more accurate observer of nature than of the manners and customs of his time:

" And his tongue
Sounds ever after as a sullen bell
Remember'd knolling a departing friend."

In Heywood's "Rape of Lucrece," first printed in 1608, Valerius says: "Nay if he be dying, as I could wish he were, I'le ring out his funerall peale, and this it is:

" Come lift and harke,
The bell doth towle,
For some but now
Departing soule.
And was not that
Some ominous fowle,
The batt, the night-
Crow, or screech-owle.
To these I heare
The wild wolfe howle
In this black night
That seems to skowle.
All these my black-
Booke shall in-rowle.
For hark, still, still,
The bell doth towle,
For some but now
Departing sowle."

Fuller writes: " Hearing a Passing-Bell, I prayed that the sick man might have, through Christ, a safe voyage to his long home. Afterwards I understood that the party was dead some hours before; and, it seems in some places of London, the tolling of the bell is but a preface of course to the ringing it out. Bells are better silent than thus telling lyes. What is this but giving a safe alarme to men's devotions, to make them to be ready armed with their prayers for the assistance of such who have already fought the good fight, yea and gotten the conquest? Not to say that men's charity herein may be

suspected of superstition in praying for the dead." *Good thoughts in Worse Times*, 1647, p. 2. Zouch says: " The Soul-bell was tolled before the departure of a person out of life, as a signal for good men to offer up ther prayers for the dying. Hence the abuse commenced of praying for the dead. He is citing Donne's Letter to Wotton in verse:

" And thicken on you now, as prayers ascend
To Heaven on troops at a good man's Passing Bell."

—Walton's Lives, 1790, p. 144.

" Ring out your belles, let mourning shewes be spread,
For Loue is dead."

—*Englands Helicon*, 1600.

" Make me a straine speake groaning like a bell,
That towles departing soules."

—Marston's *Works*, 1633, sign. D 5 verso.

" Hark, hark! what noise is this; a Passing Bell,
That doth our own fate in an others tell."

Sparke's *Scintillula Altaris*, 1652.

There is a proverb:

" When thou dost hear a toll or knell,
Then think upon thy Passing Bell."
Comp. *Capon-Bell*.

In Copley's " Wits, Fits, and Fancies," 1595, we find that the Passing Bell was antiently rung while the person was dying. " A gentleman lying very sicke abed, heard a Passing Bell ring out, and said unto his physition, tell me Maister Doctor, is yonder musicke for my dancing?" Again, concerning " The ringing out at the burial," is this anecdote: " A rich churle and a begger were buried, at one time, in the same church-yard, and the belles rung out amaine for the miser: Now, the wise-acre his son and executor, to the end of the worlde might not thinke that all that ringing was for the begger, but for his father, hyred a trumpetter to stand all the ringing-while in the belfrie, and betweene every peale to sound his trumpet, and proclaime aloude and say: Sirres, this next peale is not for R. but for Maister N. his father."

Distinction of rank was preserved in the North of England in the tolling of the Soul Bell. A high fee annexed excludes the common people and appropriates to the death of persons of consequence the tolling of the great bell in each church on this occasion. There, too, a bell is tolled, and sometimes chimes are rung, a little before the burial, and while they are conducting the corpse to church. They chime or ring, too, at some places, while the grave is filling up. This was noted by Durandus. In England in the 17th century, a fee of 20/- was charged for ringing either a forenoon or afternoon peal; this took place at the deaths of Edmund Shakespear the actor, the poet's brother, in 1607, and of Laurence Fletcher the actor in 1608: W. C. Hazlitt's *Shakespear: Himself and his Work*, 1903, p. 49. There seems to be nothing intended at present by tolling the Passing Bell, but to inform the neighbourhood of any person's interment.

At Hadleigh, in Suffolk, as late at all events as 1878, this bell was rung twelve hours after death, and at the conclusion there were nine knells for a male and six for a female. The charge made by the authorities of the church varied according to the fee paid; for the Union Bell, proclaiming the exit of a pauper, it was only 3/-. Walford's *Pleasant Days in Pleasant Places*, 1878, p. 36.

Passion Dock.—In the North of England, they make a herb-pudding, composed, among other ingredients, of the passion-dock, on Good Friday, and it is considered an indispensable feature. Unless the custom arose from a desire to perpetuate the recollection of the Passion in every possible way, it is difficult to assign an origin to it.

Passion Play.—For the performances of this nature in England in early times, see Hazlitt's Warton, 1871, ii, 232-3, and for Italian prototypes in 1298, &c. *ibid.* 229. See also his *Manual of Old English Plays*, 1892, p. 175.

In the *Daily News* of April 2, 1870, appeared the following paragraph: In the course of next summer the celebrated miracle play, the *Passion*, the last relic of those religious representations from which the dramatic literatures of all the modern nations of Europe are supposed to have sprung, will again be performed in the Bavarian village of Ober-Ammergau. The parish vowed to undertake the representation in 1633, in order to escape the plague, and the piece was first performed *ex voto* in the following year. It was repeated every ten years till 1674, and then again in 1680, from which time till the present it has been played every decennium. There can be no doubt that the play itself is older than 1633, and though some slight changes have been made it has remained essentially unaltered.

Passion Sunday.—Rites, peculiar, it should seem, to Good Friday, were used on this day, which the Church of Rome called therefore Passion Sunday.

Passion or Carling Sunday might often happen on this day. Easter always fell between the 21st of March and the 25th of April. I know not why these rites were confined in the calendar to the 12th of March, as the moveable feast and fasts are not noted there. Perhaps Passion Sunday might fall on the 12th of March, the year the calendar was written or printed in. However that be, one cannot doubt of their having belonged to what Durandus calls Passion Sunday.

In Randal Holmes' "Academy of Armory and Blazon," 1688, p. 130, I find the following: "Carle Sunday is the second Sunday before Easter, or the fifth Sunday from Shrove Tuesday." Marshal, in his "Observations on the Saxon Gospels," elucidates the old name (Care) of this Sunday in Lent. He tells us that "the Friday on which Christ was crucified is called, in German, both Gute Freytag and Carr Fryetag." That the word Karr signifies a satisfaction for a fine or penalty; and that Care, or Carr Sunday, was not unknown to the English in his time, at least to such as lived among old people in the country.

The "Popish Kingdom" of Naogeorgus, as translated by Googe, 1570, has the following summary for Care or Passion Sunday:

" Now comes the Sunday forth, of this
            same great and holy fast:
Here doth the Pope the shriven blesse,
            absoluing them at last
From all their sinnes; and of the Jewes
            the law he doth allow,
As if the power of God had not sufficient
            bene till now:
Or that the law of Moyses here were
            still of force and might,
In these same happie dayes, when Christ
            doth raigne with heavenly light.
The boyes with ropes of straw doth frame
            an vgly monster here,
And call him death, whom from the
            towne, with prowd and solemne
            chere,
To hilles and valleyes they conuey, and
            villages thereby,
From whence they stragling doe returne,
            well beaten commonly.
Thus children also beare, with speares,
            their cracknelles round about,
And two they haue, whereof the one is
            called sommer stout,
Apparalde all in greene, and drest in
            youthfull fine arraye;
The other Winter, clad in mosse, with
            heare all hoare and graye:
These two togither fight, of which the
            palme doth Sommer get.
From hence to meate they go, and all
            with wine their wistles wet.
The other toyes that in this time of holly
            fastes appeare,
I loth to tell, nor order like, is used
            every wheare."

Patrick's Day, St.—St. Patrick is mentioned in the "Prophecy of St. Berchan," A.D. 1094-7 :

"Erin shall not be without a wise one
After Bridget and Patrick of great
    deeds."

This is Mr. Skene's translation of the original Irish in his edition of the "Chronicles of the Picts and Scots," 1867. He has there also given extracts from Joceline's Life (1185), and from what is generally known as the " Vita Tripartita." There are several later biographies.

The shamrock is said to be worn by the Irish, upon the anniversary of this saint, for the following reason. When the saint preached the gospel to the pagan Irish, he illustrated the doctrine of the Trinity by showing them a trefoil, or three-leaved grass with one stalk, which operating to their conviction, the shamrock, which is a bundle of this grass, was ever afterwards worn upon this Saint's anniversary to commemorate the event. Spenser, in his " View of the State of Ireland," 1596, speaking of "these late warres of Mounster," before " a most rich and plentifull countrey, full of corne and cattle," says, the inhabitants were reduced to such distress that, " if they found a plot of watercresses or shamrocks there, they flocked as to a feast for the time."

Jones tells us that " St. Patrick, the Apostle of Ireland, is said to be the son of Calphurnius and Concha. He was born in Pembrokeshire (or rather Carnarvonshire) about the year 373. His original Welsh name was Maenwyn, and his ecclesiastical name of Patricius was given him by Pope Celestine, when he consecrated him a bishop, and sent him missioner into Ireland, to convert the Irish, in 433. When St. Patrick landed near Wicklow, the inhabitants were ready to stone him for attempting an innovation in the religion of their ancestors. He requested to be heard, and explained unto them that God is an omnipotent, sacred spirit, who created heaven and earth, and that the Trinity is contained in the Unity: but they were reluctant to give credit to his words. St. Patrick, therefore, plucked a trefoil from the ground, and expostulated with the Hibernians : Is it not as possible for the Father, Son, and Holy Ghost, as for these three leaves to grow upon a single stalk. Then the Irish were immediately convinced of their error, and were solemnly baptised by St. Patrick." The British Druids and Bards had an extraordinary veneration for the number three.

" Between May Day and harvest," observes Sir H. Piers, " butter, new cheese and curds, and shamrocks, are the food of the meaner sort all this season." Shirley's play of " St. Patrick for Ireland," 1640, merely relates the first landing of the Saint in Ireland and the introduction of Christianity into that country. A second part was announced, but does not seem to have been produced.

Mr. Thomas Wright, in 1844, devoted to the singular subject of St. Patrick's Purgatory a small octavo volume ; and it will be unnecessary therefore to dwell upon it at any length here ; but it may be mentioned that an ancient French fabliau exists, founded on this tradition, and is inserted in Le Grand's Collection, from which it was transferred to a little volume, published in 1786, under the title of "Tales of the Twelfth and Thirteenth Centuries." An early English metrical version, called " Owain Miles," is preserved in the Auchinleck MS., and was printed (with a few other pieces from the same source) in 1837. The account which Henry Jones, Bishop of Clogher, gives of this place in his tract of 1647, conveys a poor idea of its condition and character. He describes it as " a beggarly hole."

Perhaps one of the most complete summaries of the St. Patrick's Purgatory literature is that given by Turnbull in his Introduction to the *Visions of Tundale*, 88, 1843. But comp. Hazlitt's *Handbook*, 432, 447, 616, and *Bibl. Coll.* i, 323, 402. ii, 606, iii, 305, iv, 79, 180. About 1495 one Wilhelm von Horneck printed at Memmingen and addressed to the Duke of Würtemburg a poem *De Purgatorio diui Patricij.* A copy is in the Huth library.

In " Overbury's Characters," when describing a foot-man, he says, " 'Tis impossible to draw his picture to the life, cause a man must take it as he's running : only this, horses are usually let bloud on St. Steven's Day : on St. Patrick's he takes rent, and is drencht for all the yeare after." M. Salverte, in his work on the " Occult Sciences," 1843, quotes Gervase of Tilbury, for the legend that to do homage to a saint revered in Ireland (St. Patrick) the fish rise from the sea on the day of his festival, pass in procession before his altar, and then disappear. M. Salverte accounts for this superstition by supposing that it originated in the annual shoals of herring, mackerel, and tunny on the coast in the spring, in the neighbourhood of the church dedicated to the Saint. But this hypothesis in not extremely plausible.

The usages in London associated with this anniversary are yet maintained. The following is from the *Globe* newspaper of March 17, 1897 :—

" To-day being St. Patrick's Day, the band of the Coldstream Guards, which did duty with the detachment of the regiment mounting the Queen's Guard in London, played a choice selection of Irish music in the courtyard of St. James's Palace in the morning during the ceremony of changing the guard. Earlier in the day the drummers and fifers of the Grenadier Guards at Chelsea Barracks played a number of Irish airs. Sprigs of real and artificial shamrock were worn extensively by the Irish resident in Westminster, Chelsea, and other parts of London, and in many instances the day was observed as a holiday by the labourers at the gas works and other large places of business. A number of Irishmen attended the early services at the Catholic chapels, and in accordance with the Truce of St. Patrick, instituted by the late Cardinal Manning, have pledged themselves to abstain from intoxicating liquors for the day, to prevent the riotous scenes prevalent years ago on their national holiday. The day was celebrated by the military at Dublin, Aldershot, and other stations, in the usual way."

Paul's Church, St.—The then well-known profanations of St. Paul's Church are thus enumerated by Pilkington: "The south alley for vsurye and Poperye, the north for Simony and the Horse faire in the middest for all kinds of bargains, metinges, brawlinges, murthers, conspiracies, and the font for ordinary paimentes of money, are so well knowen to all menne as the begger knowes his dishe." *Burnynge of Paules*, 1563, sign. G 5. This is illustrated by the writers of the next reign and of the Civil War period; see the tract entitled: *The Meeting of Gallants at an Ordinarie, or, the Walkes in Powles*, 1604. The Puritan soldiers, according to the pamphleteers, spared no pains to shew their contempt for the place.

In Dekker's "Dead Tearme," 1607, signat. D 4, St. Paul's Steeple is introduced as describing the company walking in the body of the church, and among other things, the writer says: "What layinge of heads is there together and sifting of the brains, still and anon, as it growes towards eleven of the clocke, (even amongst those that wear guilt rapiers by their sides,) where for that noone they may shift from Duke Humfrey, and bee furnished with a dinner, at some meaner man's table." Afterwards he observes: "What byting of the thumbs to beget quarrels:" adding that, "at one time, in one and the same ranke, yea, foote by foote, and elbow by elbow, shall you see walking, the knight, the gull, the gallant, the upstart, the gentleman, the clowne, the captain, the appel-squire, the lawyer, the usurer, the cittizen, the bankerout, the scholler, the beggar, the doctor, the ideot, the ruffian, the cheater, the puritan, the cut-throat, the hye men, the low-men, the true man, and the thiefe: of all trades and professions some, of all countryes some. Thus whilest devotion kneeles at her prayers, doth profanation walke under her nose in contempt of religion." Comp. *Duke Humphrey.*

Paul's Day, St.—(Jan. 25). In the Roman Calendar it is called Dies Ægyptiacus (an unlucky day.) But no explanation seems ever to have been offered of the origin of this opinion or feeling, and the same may be said of the statement which follows. Hospinian tells us that it is a critical day with the vulgar, indicating, if it be clear, abundance of fruits; if windy, foretelling wars; if cloudy, the pestilence; if rainy or snowy, it prognosticates dearness and scarcity: according to the old Latin verses, thus translated in Bourne:

"If St. Paul's Day be fair and clear,
It doth betide a happy year;
If blustering winds do blow aloft,
Then wars will trouble our realm full
    oft;
And if it chance to snow or rain,
Then will be dear all sorts of grain."

Willsford, in his "Nature's Secrets," p. 145, gives the verses as follows:

"If St. Paul's Day be fair and clear,
It does betide a happy year;
But if it chance to snow or rain,
Then will be dear all kinds of grain:
If clouds or mists do dark the skie,
Great store of birds and beasts shall die;
And if the winds do fly aloft,
Then wars shall vex the kingdome oft."

Machyn the Diarist notices the annual procession to St. Paul's on January 25, 1557-8. "There was," says he, "a goodly procession at St. Paul's. There was a priest of every parryche of the dyosses of Londun, with a cope, and the bishop of Londun wayreng ys myter; and after cam a fat buck, and ys hed with the hornes borne a-pone a baner-pole, and xl hornes blohyng a-for the boke and be-hynd." This custom originated in 1375 under circumstances which are fully detailed in the "Book of Days."

Knight in his *Life of Erasmus*, 1726, notices this custom of bringing in procession into the church the head of a deer, fixed on the top of a long spear or pole, "with the whole company blowing Hunters Horns in a sort of hideous manner; and with this rude pomp they go up to the High Altar, and offer it there. You would think them all the mad Votaries of Diana." In relation to this usage it is best to refer to the tenure of the land at Westlee in Essex, as the offering seems to have been connected with the grant made to Sir William Le Baud by the canons of St. Paul's, 3 Edward I.

Paul's Evil, St.—A name given to the falling sickness.

Paul's Pitcher-Day.—(Jan. 24). This is a red letter day, as the late Mr. Couch of Bodmin pointed out, among the Cornish tinners. His words are these:—"The first red-letter day in the tinner's calendar is Paul's Pitcher-day, or the eve of Paul's Tide (January 24th). It is marked by a very curious and inexplicable custom, not only among tin-streamers, but also in the mixed mining and agricultural town and neighbourhood of Bodmin, and among the sea-faring population of Padstow. The tinner's mode of observing it is as follows:—On the day before the Feast of St. Paul, a water-pitcher is set up at a convenient distance, and pelted with stones until entirely demolished. The men then leave their work, and adjourn into a neighbouring ale-house, where a new pitcher, bought to replace the old one, is successively filled and emptied, and the evening is given up to merriment and misrule. On inquiry whether some dim notion of the origin and meaning of this custom remained among those who still keep it up, I find it generally held to be an ancient festival intended to celebrate the day when tin was first turned into metal,—in fact, the discovery of smelting. It is the occasion of a revel, in which, as an old streamer observes, there is an open rebellion against the water-drinking system which is enforced upon them whilst at work."

The custom of observing Paul's Pitcher Night, is probably half-forgotten even in Cornwall at the present time, where many of the ancient provincial usages have been suffered to die out; but Mr. Couch found it in full vigour so recently as 1859. The boys of Bodmin parade the town with pitchers, and into every house where the door can be opened, or has been inadvertently left so, they hurl a "Paul's pitcher." Punishing the youngsters is very much like the story of Mrs. Glasse and the hare: first *catch* them. The urchins cry, as they throw the pitcher:

"Paul's eve,
And here's a heave."

The origin of the practice has not been stated; it is doubtful whether it will ever be discovered. The author of the foregoing distich does not seem to have possessed a very poetical or musical ear.

Paul's Stump, St.—In Bagford's day (1714), a post near Billingsgate was known as St. Paul's Stump, and it was an usage which had grown obsolete even at that time, for the porters who plied there

to invite every passenger to kiss the post, whereupon, if he complied, they gave him a name, and he was to choose one of them for his godfather; but upon his refusal, he was bumped against the post. Leland's "Collectanea," ed. 1770, p. lxxvi.

Pax.—A tablet or disc of wood, metal, ivory, or glass used in the service of the church both in England and abroad as a means of passing the kiss of peace from the priest (representing Christ) to the congregation. The pax occurs in the English ritual as far back as the 13th century. *Antiquary*, July, 1897. Comp. *Nuptial Usages.*

Pax-cake.—A cake distributed in former times on Palm Sunday at Lellock Church, Hampshire.

Pearie.—Jamieson defines pearie, "that instrument of play used by boys in Scotland, which in England is called a peg-top." It seems to have been named from its exact resemblance to a pear. The humming-top of England is in Scotland denominated a French pearie, probably as having been originally imported from France. In Boyer's Dictionary, "faire une école" is rendered "to be pegged."

Peascod Wooing.—Grose tells us that a "scalding of peas is a custom in the North of boiling the common grey peas in the shell, and eating them with butter and salt, first shelling them. A bean, shell and all, is put into one of the pea-pods; whoever gets this bean is to be first married." If a young woman, while she is shelling peas, meets with a pod of nine, the first young man who crosses the threshold afterwards is to be her husband.

In the "Whitby Glossary," quoted by Atkinson, this is called pea-scalding, and is described as "a kind of popular festivity, at which green peas scalded, or slightly boiled with their pods on, are the main dish. Being set on the table in the midst of the party, each person dips his peascod in a common cup of butter and salt, made fluid by the heat of the steaming mass, and extracts the peas by the agency of his teeth." Heywood, in his "Fayr Mayde of the Exchange," 1607, introduces a scene in front of the Cripple of Fanchurch's shop, and makes one of the characters say:

"Now for my true loves handkercher!
these flowers
Are pretty toys, are very pretty toys.
Oh, but methinks the peascod would do better,
The peascod and the blossom wonderful!
.   .   .   .
But here's the question—whether my love, or no,

Will seem content? Ay, there the game
    doth go;
And yet I'll pawn my head he will ap-
    plaud
The peascod and the flow'r, my pretty
    choice.
For what is he, loving a thing in heart,
Loves not the counterfeit, tho' made by
    Art?"

Perhaps this is the oldest allusion to the belief of our ancestors, that the divination by the peascod was an infallible criterion in love affairs. Browne, in his "Pastorals," 1614, says:

"The peascod greene, oft with no little
    toyle,
He'd seek for in the fattest fertil'st
    soile,
And rend it from the stalke to bring it
    to her,
And in her bosom for acceptance wooe
    her."

In "As You Like It," Touchstone has these observations put into his mouth: "I remember, when I was in love, I broke my sword upon a stone, and bid him take that for coming anight to Jane Smile: and I remember the kissing of her batlet, and the cow's dugs that her pretty chopp'd hands had milk'd; and I remember the wooing of a peascod instead of her; from whom I took two cods, and giving her them again, said, with weeping tears, wear these for my sake." This superstition is also illustrated by Gay, in his "Pastorals;" and there are still persons who put faith in its efficacy. In the North of England and in Scotland, it is, or was, a custom to rub with peastraw a girl to whom her lover had not been true. In Devonshire there is a proverb:

"Winter time for shoeing:
Peascod time for wooing."

Peeping Tom of Coventry.—See Halliwell in v. and *Warwick Castle and its Earls*, by Lady Warwick, 1903, ch. iv. The story of Peeping Tom appears to have been an aftergrowth from the original Godiva legend.

Peg-fiched. — A West-country game. See Halliwell in v.

Peg in the Ring.—A mode of playing at top. See Halliwell in v.

Pelican.—Philip de Thaun, in his Anglo-Norman Bestiary, circa 1120, introduces the common fallacy respecting the pelican, as follows: "Of such a nature it is, when it comes to its young birds, and they are great and handsome, and it will fondle them, cover them with its wings: the little birds are fierce, take to pecking it—desire to eat it, and pick out its two eyes; then it pecks, and takes them, and slays them with torment; and thereupon leaves them—leaves them lying dead—then returns on the third day, is grieved to find them dead, and makes such lamentation, when it sees its little birds dead that with its beak it strikes its body that the blood issues forth; the blood goes dropping, and falls on its young birds—the blood has such quality, that by it they come to life——." Wright's *Popular Treatises on Science*, 1841, pp. 115-6. In *A Short Relation of the River Nile*, 1669, where the writer (Sir Peter Wyche) has been speaking of the Bird of Paradise, he proceeds to say: "The Pelican has better credit, (called by Quevedo the self-disciplining bird,) and hath been discovered in the land of Angola, where some were taken. I have seen two. Some will have a scar in the breast, from a wound of her own making there, to feed (as is reported) her young with her own bloud, an action which ordinarily suggests devout fancies." There seems to be here a vestige of a common morbid phenomenon in maternity.

Penny and Halfpenny Rents. —A form of tenure not uncommon in feudal times, the latter far rarer, however. In 1426-7, 5 Henry VI., Sir John Assheton acquired the manor of Ashton-under-Lyne at the rent of a penny a year.

Penny Hop.—A country club of dancers or a ball among the lower classes, where each person pays a penny to the fiddler. Institutions of this class, slightly varied, still exist even in the suburbs of London, the place of amusement being a loft or an empty chamber of some kind.

Penny-lattice-house.—An old term for a very low ale-house.

Penny-Prick.—For a notice of this game with counters I may refer to the notes to "The English Courtier and the Country Gentleman," 1586, which was reprinted in the *Roxburgh Library*, 1868, and which is a new title to *Civil and Uncivil Life*, 1579.

Penny Wedding.—In the "Statistical Account of Scotland," parish of Drainy, Co. Elgin, we are told, "a Penny Wedding is when the expence of the marriage entertainment is not defrayed by the young couple, or their relations, but by a club among the guests. Two hundred people, of both sexes, will sometimes be convened on an occasion of this kind." In the same work under 1799, the Editor observes "the scene which involved every amusement and every joy of an idle and illiterate age, was the penny bridal. When a pair were contracted, they for a stipulated consideration bespoke their wedding at a certain tavern, and then ranged the country in every direction to solicit guests. One, two, and even three hundred would have convened on these occasions, to make merry at their own expence for two or more days. This scene of feasting, drinking, dancing, wooing, fighting, &c. was always enjoyed with the highest relish, and, until obliterated by a similar scene, furnished ample materials for rural mirth and rural scandal. But now the penny bridal is reprobated as an index of want of money and of want of taste."

Again, it is said: "Marriages in this place are generally conducted in the Parish of Avock, Co. Ross, in the style of penny weddings. Little other fare is provided except bread, ale, and whisky. The relatives, who assemble in the morning, are entertained with a dram and a drink gratis. But, after the ceremony is performed, every man pays for his drink. The neighbours then convene in great numbers. A fiddler or two, with perhaps a boy to scrape on an old violoncello, are engaged. A barn is allotted for the dancing, and a house for drinking. And thus they make merry for two or three days, till Saturday night. On the Sabbath, after returning from church, the married couple give a sort of dinner or entertainment to the present friends on both sides. So that these weddings, on the whole, bring little gain or loss to the parties."

Penryn, Co. of Cornwall.—At this borough town, formerly also known as Permorin, the mayor has the right, said to be unique, of electing a churchwarden.

Pension.—The meeting of the Ancients at Gray's Inn. See Halliwell in v.

Pentacle.—A figure of three triangles intersected, and formerly used as a charm. See Halliwell in v.

Pepper Cakes.—In Yorkshire (Cleveland) the children eat, at the Christmas season, according to Mr. Atkinson, "a kind of gingerbread baked in large and thick cakes, or flat loaves," called pepper-cakes. They are also usual at the birth of a child. "One of these cakes," says Mr. A., "is provided and a cheese; the latter is on a large platter, or dish, and the pepper-cake upon it. The cutting of the Christmas cheese is done by the master of the house on Christmas Eve, and is a ceremony not to be lightly omitted. All comers to the house are invited to partake of the pepper-cake and Christmas cheese." *Cleveland Glossary,* 1868, in v.

Perilous Days.—In the "Book of Knowledge," which includes the *Practica Rusticorum,* I find the following "Account of the perillous dayes of every month." "In the change of every moon be two dayes, in the which what thing soever is

begun, late or never, it shall come to no good end, and the dayes be full perillous for many things. In January, when the moon is three or four dayes old. In February, 5 or 7. In March, 6 or 7. In April, 5 or 8. May, 8 or 9. June, 5 or 15. July, 3 or 13. August, 8 or 13. September, 8 or 13. October, 5 or 12. November, 5 or 9. In December, 3 or 13. "Astronomers say, that six dayes in the year are perillous of death : and therefore they forbid men to let blood on them, or take any drink : that is to say, January the 3d, July the 1st, October the 2d, the last of April, August the first, the last day going out of December. These six dayes with great diligence ought to be kept, but namely the latter three, for all the veins are then full. For then, whether man or beast be knit in them within seven dayes, or certainly within fourteen dayes, he shall die. And if they take any drinks within fifteene dayes, they shall die ; and, if they eat any goose in these three dayes, within forty dayes they shall die ; and, if any child be born in these three latter dayes, they shall die a wicked death.

"Astronomers and astrologers say, that in the beginning of March, the seventh night, or the fourteenth day, let thee bloud of the right arm ; and in the beginning of April, the eleventh day, of the left arm ; and in the end of May, third or fifth day, on whether arm thou wilt ; and thus, of all that year, thou shalt orderly be kept from the fever, the falling gout, the sister gout, and losse of thy sight."

"The superstitious," remarks Brockett, in his "North-Country Glossary," 1846, "will neither borrow nor lend on any of these days, lest the article should be employed for evil purposes."

Persona.—By one of the Constitutions of Clarendon, 10 Henry II. A.D. 1165, where the clergy is laid under subjection to the secular power, it is enacted that all archbishops and bishops, "et universæ personæ regni qui de rege tenent in capite," are liable to serve the Crown as other Barons. Parry's *Parliaments and Councils of England,* 1839, p. 13. Here the word *persona* seems to be equivalent to the modern parson, and the form *person* was long employed, the same being a representative before God of the congregation. In 1207, 8 John, the King requires the Bishops and Abbots to permit the Personæ and beneficed clergy to grant him a certain part of their income. *Ibid.* 2. In 1236 we find the expression *ecclesiasticæ personæ. Ibid.* 31.

Peter.—A choice kind of Malaga wine, popularly known as *Peter-see-me,* a corruption of *Pedro-Ximenes.*

Peter ad Vincula, St.—The Chapel in the Tower of London so called, where so many historical personages have been interred. With the exception of the Church of S. Pietro in Vincoli at Rome, it is said to be the sole example of such a dedication. D. C. Bell, *Notices*, 1877, p. 3. In a parliament held at Westminster, July 25, 1337, an inhabitant of Bodmin is commanded to attend there on Friday, the Feast of St. Peter ad Vincula (Aug. 1). Parry's *Parliaments and Councils of England*, 1839, p. 105.

Peter and Paul's, St., Eve and Day.—(June 28-9). In 14 Edward IV., 1474-5, it is recorded that "this yere was a grete watche upon seint Petres nyght, the kyng beyng in the Chepe; and there fill affrey bitwixt men of his household and the constablis; wherfore the kyng was gretely displeasid with the constablis."—A curious entry shewing that Edward had come personally and perhaps *incognito* into the City to see the Midsummer bonfires. *A Chronicle of London*, 1827, p. 145. Kethe, in his Blandford Sermon, 1570, speaks of the Midsummer rites, more usually performed on St. John's Eve, being also practised in popish times on the eve of SS. Peter and Paul the Apostles; and Brand himself was informed that about half a century prior (or about 1750) on this anniversary the Northumbrians carried some kind of firebrands about the fields of their villages. They made encroachments, on these occasions, upon the bonefires of the neighbouring towns, of which they took away some of the ashes by force: this they called "carrying off the flower (probably the flour) of the wake." But in fact these fires are, or were very recently, still usual both in the West and North of England on this festival instead of St. John's Eve; and a correspondent of the *Antiquary* for 1881 draws attention to the Cornish practice of waving torches over the head.

Fishermen were supposed to be under the special guardianship of St. Peter. In "Piers of Fulham," we have:

"But in stede of sturgen or lamprons, He drawyth vp a gurnerd or gogeons: Kodlynes, konger, or suche queyse fysche, As wolwyche roches that be not worth a rische. Suche fortune often with fischers falle, Thoghe they to Petyr bothe pray and calle."

See *Midsummer Watch*.

Peterborough Bridge Fair. —Peterborough Bridge Fair, which dates back to the days of the abbots, was duly proclaimed in 1901 on October 1. At noon a procession of the town council, headed by the mayor's sergeant and javelin men, marched to the bridge which divides Northamptonshire from Huntingdonshire, and there the fair was solemnly proclaimed, to be held "as well in Northamptonshire as in Huntingdonshire to-day, to-morrow, and the day afterwards." All persons were charged "to conduct themselves soberly and civilly, and pay all just dues and demands." The civic officials then adjourned to the Fair fields, where the words of the charter were repeated, and amid a pandemonium of steam organs and much chaff from the show people the fair was declared open. According to custom, the mayor afterwards entertained the authorities to a sausage and champagne luncheon.

Petting Stone. — Hutchinson, speaking of a cross near the ruins of the church in Holy Island, says: It is "now called the Petting Stone. Whenever a marriage is solemnized at the church, after the ceremony, the bride is to step upon it; and if she cannot stride to the end thereof, it is said the marriage will prove unfortunate." The etymology there given is too ridiculous to be remembered: it is called *petting*, lest the bride should take pet with her supper. *Hist. of Durham*, i, 32.

Philosopher's Game. — See Nares, *Glossary*, 1859, in v.

Phœbe.—The name of an old dance. See Halliwell in v.

Phœnix.—Philip de Thaun, in his Anglo-Norman twelfth-century Bestiary, says: "Phœnix is a bird, which is very elegant and handsome; it is found in Arabia, and is shaped like a swan; no man can seek so far as to find another on the earth; it is only one in the world, and is all purple; it lives five hundred years and more, Isidore says so (*ceo dit Ysidorus*). When it perceives age coming on, it goes and collects twigs, and precious spice of good odour; as leaves it takes them, and spreads itself upon them: by the sun's ray it takes the pure fire (of the heaven); voluntarily it spreads its wings over them; these it burns of its own will, and is reduced to powder. By the fire of the spice, by the good ointment—of the heat and humour the powder takes sweetness, and such is its nature, as the writing says, on the third day it comes to life again." Wright's *Popular Treatises on Science*, 1841, p. 113. This seems a curious parallel with the Christian legend of the Resurrection.

Browne tells us: "that there is but one Phœnix in the world, which, after many hundred years burns herself, and from the ashes thereof riseth up another, is a conceit not new or altogether popular, but of great antiquity; not only delivered by humane authors, but frequently expressed by holy writers; by Cyril, Epiphanius and others, by Ambrose in his Hexameron, and Tertullian in his Poem de Judicio Domini, and in his excellent Tract de Resurrectione Carnis; all which notwithstanding we cannot presume the existence of this animal, nor dare we affirm there is any Phœnix in Nature. For first there wants herein the definitive confirmator and text of things uncertain, that is, the sense of man. For though many writers have much enlarged thereon, there is not any ocular describer, or such as presumeth to confirm it upon aspection; and therefore Herodotus, that led the story unto the Greeks, plainly saith, he never attained the sight of any, but only the picture." The learned author proceeds to make Herodotus himself confess that the account seems to him improbable, Tacitus and Pliny also expressing very strong doubts on the subject. Some, he says, refer to some other rare bird, the Bird of Paradise, &c. He finds the passage in Psalms, "Vir justus ut Phœnix florebit," a mistake arising from the Greek word Phœnix, which signifies also a palm tree. By the same equivoque he explains the passage in Job where it is mentioned. In a word the unity, long life, and generation of this ideal bird are all against the existence of it.

The following passage is curious: "The third note is, that our life is but short; the rauen, the Phenix, the hart, lion, and the elephant, fulfill their hundreds, but man dyeth, when he thinketh yet his sun riseth——." *Plaine Mans Pilgrimage*, by W. Webster, 1610, p. 43.

When the Ashmolean Museum was still at Lambeth, in September, 1657, Evelyn visited it, and was shown, among other curiosities, *a feather from the wing of the phœnix.*

Phosphorus.—See *Haggs.*

Physiognomy.—Agrippa observes that "Physiognomy, taking Nature for her guide, upon an inspection, and well observing the outward parts of the body, presumes to conjecture by probable tokens at the qualities of the mind and fortune of the person: making one man to be Saturnal, another a Jovist, this man to be born under Mars, another under Sol, some under Venus, some under Mercury, some under Luna: and from the habits of the body collects their horoscopes, gliding, by little and little, from affections to astrological causes, upon which foundations they erect what idle structures they themselves please:" and he adds concerning metoposcopie, a species of physiognomy: "Metoposcopie, to know all things from the sole observation of the forehead, prying even into the very beginnings, progress, and end of a man's life, with a most acute judgement and learned ex-

perience; making herself to be like a foster-child of astrology." *Vanity of Arts and Sciences*, ed. 1676, p. 100.

"Physiognomy," says Gaule, "following from the inspection of the whole body, presumeth it can by probable signs attain to know, what are the affections of body and mind, and what a man's fortune shall be; so far forth as it pronounces him Saturnal or Jovial: and him Martial or Solar: another Venerial, Mercurial, or Lunar: and collecting their horoscopes from the habitude of the body, and from affections transcending, as they say, by little and little, unto causes, namely astrological; out of which they afterwards trifle as they list. Metoposcopy, out of a sagacious ingenie and learned experience, boasts herself to forsent all the beginnings, the progresses, and the ends of men, out of the sole inspection of the forehead: making herself also to be the pupil of astrologie." He concludes: "We need no other reason to impugne the error of all these Arts, than this self-same, namely, that they are void of all reason." *Mag-Astromancer Posed.*

Indagine in his *Palmistry and Physiognomy* records sundry divinations, too absurd to be transcribed (I refer the modern devotees of Lavater to the work itself) on "upright brows"—"Brows hanging over"—"playing with the bries"—"narrow foreheads"—"faces plain and flat"—"lean faces"—"sad faces"—"sharp noses"—"ape-like noses"—"thick nostrils"—"slender and thin lips"—"big mouths," &c., &c.

Some faint vestiges of these fooleries may still be traced in our villages, in the observations of rustic old women. To this head may be referred the observation somewhere to be met with, I think in one of our dramatic pieces, on a rascally-looking fellow: "There's Tyburn in his face without benefit of clergy."

Shakespear in Macbeth, i, 4, makes Duncan speak of the "mind's construction in the face," and doubts whether there was such an art. But the opinion of the moderns cannot be said to be much in favour of this so-called science: nor has it derived additional credit or weight from the rather weak and shallow arguments of Spurzheim and his allies, the *bumpologists*.

Piccadilly.—Originally a species of ruff, which became fashionable both for men and women in the time of James I. and appears on the engraved portraits of many celebrated characters of that time, although the ruff had been not uncommon in the preceding reign. The name appears to have subsequently attached itself to a tavern and tennis-court in the portion of the thoroughfare now so-called, on

which buildings were first erected. In the
"Honestie of this age," by Barnaby Rich,
1614, p. 25, is the following allusion to the
article of dress : "But he that some forty
or fifty yeares sithens should have asked
a pickadilly, I wonder who could have
understood him, or could have told what a
pickadilly had been, fish or flesh." But
Flecknoe in his Epigrams, 1665, intends
the resort above mentioned :

"And their lands to coyn they distil ye,
And then with the money
You see how they run ye
To loose it at Piccadilly."

Pick.—In the "Gentleman's Magazine" for January, 1791, are several
queries on cards. The writer informs us
that "the common people in a great part
of Yorkshire invariably call diamonds
picks. This I take," he says, "to be from
the French word piques, spades : but cannot account for its being corruptly applied
by them to the other suit." The true
reason, however, is to be gathered from
the resemblance the diamond bears to a
mill-pick, as fusils are sometimes called
in heraldry.

Picrous Day.—The late Mr. Couch
of Bodmin says: "The second Thursday
before Christmas-day is Picrous Day, still
kept, but with no other distinctive ceremonies than a supper and much merry-
making. The owner of the tin-stream
contributes towards this festivity a
shilling for each man. I would ask particular attention to the tradition that says
that this feast is intended to commemorate the discovery of tin by a man
named ' Picrous.' It would be interesting
to know from other correspondents,
whether such a belief is held by tinners
in other districts. My first impression
was that the day might take its name
from the circumstance of a pie forming
the *pièce de résistance* of the supper ; but
this explanation is not allowed by tinners,
nor sanctioned by the usages of the feast.
What truth there may be in this tradition
of the first tinner Picrous, it is now too
late to discover ; but the notion is worth
recording. It has occurred to me,
whether, from some similarity between the
names (not a close one, I admit), the
honour of Picrous may not have been
transferred to St. Piran, usually reputed
to be the patron-saint of tinners. Many
more violent transformations than this
mark the adaptation of heathen customs
to Christian times. Polwhele says : ' The
tinners of the country hold some holidays
peculiar to themselves, which may be
traced up to the days of saintly superstition. The Jew-whydn, or White Thursday before Christmas, and St. Piran's
Day, are deemed sacred in the mining

districts.' (' Hist. of C.' vol. i. p. 132,
note.) In the Blackmoor district, I have
never seen the slightest recognition of St.
Piran, who seems to have been, like St.
Keyne, 'no holy saint ;' and his connection
with tinning, as given by Polwhele, has
always been received here as a novel piece
of information. The Feast of St. Piran is
on the 5th of March : to which the nearest
of our holidays is *Friday in Lide*
(March)."

Pie Powder, Court of.—Courts
were granted at fairs, to take notice of all
manner of causes and disorders committed
upon the place called pie-powder, because
justice was done to any injured person,
before the dust of the fair was off his
feet. Babbington, in his *Observations on
the Sciences*, 1773, observes that "in the
Burrow Laws of Scotland an alien merchant is called *Pied puldreaux*, and likewise *ane Farand-man* . . . . The
Court of Pipowder is therefore to determine disputes between those who resort
to fairs and these kinds of pedlars, who
generally attend them. *Pied Puldreaux*
in old French signifies a pedlar, who gets
his livelihood by vending his goods where
he can, without any fixed residence." Or
rather perhaps, the Court of Pie Powder
means the Court of Pedlars. See the subsequent evidences : "Gif ane stranger mer-
chand travelland throw the realme, havand
na land, nor residence, nor dwelling within
the schirefdome, bot vaigand fra ane place
to ane other, quha therefore is called Pied
Puldreux, or dustifute," &c. Regiam
Majestatem, 1609. So chap. cxl. *ibid.*
"Anend ane Fairand-man or Dustifute."
So again in the table, *ibid.* "Dustiefute
(ane pedder) or cremar, quha hes na certaine dwelling-place, quhere he may dicht
the dust from his feet," &c. Barrington
erroneously interpreted "ane farandman"
as a man who frequents fairs, whereas he
was what we now term a traveller.

Pigeon-Holes. — This game probably resembled the variety of bagatelle
called bridge. From repeated entries in
the Chapel-Warden's Accounts of Brentford, 1620-43, we are left to judge that the
early game was played with a pair of holes
only. It seems to have been a favourite
pastime at Whitsuntide. In *The Brothers
of the Blade*, 1641, Corporal Dammee says
to Serjeant Slice-man : "Thou hadst
better turne tapster, or if (being a gentleman) thou scornst to be subject to the
imperious check and command of every
sordid mechanick, I would wish thee to
haunt bowling-allyes, and frequent gam-
ing-houses, where you may live all day
long upon the rooke on the Bankside, or
to play at nine-pins or pidgeon-holes in
Lincolnes-Inne fields."

"There was," says Mr. Halliwell, "a

machine with arches for the balls to run through," as in fact in the modern game, if people choose to play it so. Poor Robin for 1738 refers to pigeon-holes: "In this quarter the commendable exercise of nine-pins, pigeon-holes, stool-ball, and barley-break are much practiced, by reason Easter-holidays, Whitsun-holidays, and May-day fall in this quarter; besides the landlords holiday, which makes more mirth than any of the holidays aforesaid." He mentions it again in 1740. See Lysons, *Env. of London*, 1st. ed. ii, 55, and comp. *Troule-in-Madame and Whitsuntide*.

Pigeons.—Sir John Bramston in his *Autobiography*, mentions a boy's sport, which was in vogue in Essex, if not else-where, in the time of the early Stuarts. He says that, greatly to the annoyance of the owners, the country lads (himself in-cluded) used to catch their pigeons in the winter in an ingenious trap or, as he calls it, a thrap, "with corne under a dore, which wee tooke off the hinges and propt it with a stick, to which we fastened a line, which wee putt through a latice in a lower rome, where one held the line, and we were out of sight; and when the pidgeons were under the dore, we gave a pull, and the stick comeing away, the dore fell on the pidgeons, soe we culled at a pull a dosen or more at a fall, and soe wee did often."

Pepys the Diarist, under 27 January, 1667-8, notices a very different employ-ment of this bird: "Comes news from Kate Joyce that, if I would see her hus-band alive, I must come presently. So I to him, and find his breath rattled in his throat; and they did lay pigeons to his feet, and all despair of him." Joyce had tried to drown himself, and when they recovered him, they held him head down-ward, to let the water out.

Pig Running.—See Halliwell in v.

Pigs.—It is a common belief in Lincolnshire, that when pigs are taken from the sow, they must be drawn back-wards, if they are expected to do well: the sow will then go to the boar before Saturday night: and that they are not to be killed when the moon is on the wane, for that if they are, the bacon when cooked, will waste away. Some country people still slit the ears of their pigs to prevent them from being be-witched.

Steevens, in the *Gentleman's Magazine* for March, 1755 refers to an expression much used by the vulgar, wherein the sense and words are equally obscure: *An't please the pigs*. Pigs is perhaps a cor-ruption of pyx, the vessel in which the Host is kept in Roman Catholic Countries. The expression therefore means no more than Deo volente, or as it is translated into modern English, "God willing."

Pilliwinks or **Pyrewinks.**—The following is from Cowel's "Interpreter, 1607:" "Johannes Masham et Thomas Bote de Bury, die Lunæ proxime ante Festum Apostolorum Symonis et Judæ, anno regni Henrici Quarti post Conques-tum tertio, malitia et conspiratione inter eos inde præhabitis, quendam Robertum Smyth de Bury ceperunt infra predictam villam, et ipsum infra domum dicti Johannis Masham in ferro posuerunt, et cum cordis ligaverunt, et *super pollices ipsius Roberti quoddam instrumentum vocatum* Pryewinkes *ita strictè et durè posuerunt, quod Sanguis exivit de digitis illius*." Ex. Cartular. Abbatiæ Sancti Edmundi, MS. fol. 341. This was a form of torture at one time applied to witches in Scotland.

Pillory.—See Nares, Glos. 1859, in v. and Hazlitt's *Proverbs*, 1882, p. 149, where it is questioned whether the popular ex-pressions, "from pillar to post" and "from post to pillory" do not equally signify "from whipping-post to pillory," and Douce's "Illustrations of Shakes-peare," vol. i. p. 146.

"At Pavia a singular custom prevails,
To protect the poor debtor from bailiffs and jails:
He discharges his score without paying a jot,
By seating himself on a stone, *sans culotte.*
There solemnly swearing, as honest men ought,
That he's poorer than Job, when re-duced to a groat:
Yet this naked truth with such stigma disgraces,
That the rogue, as on Nettles sits, making wry faces."

—Epistles addressed to Rob. Jephson, Esq., 1794, p. 46. Besides the familiar mode of punishment, there was the usual

FINGER PILLORY.

and perhaps even more painful one of enclosing one or more fingers of the victim in a machine, which is figured in Wright's *Archæological Album*, 1845, p. 111, from an original in the Church of Ashby-de-la-Zouch, Leicestershire. This form resembles the stocks.

In mediæval London keepers of brothels, men or women, procurers and procuresses, adultresses and their paramours, priests found in the company of women of bad character, and common courtezans, were conducted to the pillory, escorted by the minstrels or city waits—a sort of official Skimmington. An excellent account of the pillory from ancient times in its various forms and stages of development may be found in Fosbrooke, *Encyclopædia*, 1843, p. 345. There is slight doubt that the original Greek type was a pillar, to which the culprit was secured.

PILLORY.

Piment.—A beverage formerly much in vogue. See Halliwell in v.

Pin-Drinking.—There was a custom which was called pin-drinking, or nick the pin, and which is thus explained in Cocker's Dictionary: "An old way of drinking exactly to a pin in the midst of a wooden cup, which being somewhat difficult, occasioned much drunkenness: so a law was made that priests, monks, and friars, should not drink to or at the pins." It is certainly difficult to say what law this was, unless it has been confounded with that of King Edgar. I find the custom differently alluded to in "Gazophylacium Anglicanum," 1689, where the expression "He is on a merry pin," is said to have arisen " from a way of drinking in a cup in which a pin was stuck, and he that could drink to the pin, i.e. neither under nor over it, was to have the wager."

"Such great drinkers," says Strutt, "were the Danes, (who were in England in the time of Edgar,) and so much did their bad examples prevail with the English, that he, by the advice of Dunstan, archbishop of Canterbury, put down many ale-houses, suffering only one to be in a village, or small town : and he also further ordained that gold or silver pins or nails should be fastened into the drinking cups and horns, at stated distances, that no one for shame's sake might drink beyond these or oblige his fellow to do so." See *Drinking Usages* and *Supernaculum*.

Pin, To Give the.—This was a custom which, in Brockett's time (1825) had become obsolete. See his *North Country Glossary in v.*

Pins and Points.—In the *History of Tom Thumb*, 1630, this form of juvenile speculation is coupled with counters and cherry-stones :

> Then, like a lustie gallant he
> Adventured forth to goe
> With other children in the streets,
> His pretty trickes to show.
> Where he for counters, pins and points,
> And cherry-stones did play,
> Till he amongst those gamesters young
> Had lost his stock away.

Boys, in the time of Elizabeth and her successor, used this medium for their amusement. The author of the poem puts into the hands of Tom the toys of his own young contemporaries.

Pious Uses of Early Secular Works and Undertakings.—See Jusserand, *Les Anglais au moyen âge*, 1884, ch. 1. The writer refers to the dedication to saints of the ancient bridge-chapels.

Piper, Tom the. — There is a curious passage about this character in the Morris-Dance, in a tract by Breton: " In the parish of Saint Asse, at the signe of the Hobbi-horse, Maid Marian and the Foole fell together by the eares with the Piper ; so that, had not the good-man of the Pewter Candlesticke set in for the Morris-dance, the May-game had beene quite spoyled : but when the game had gone round, and their braines were well warmed, their legges grew so nimble that their heeles went higher then their heads : but in all this cold sweate, while lusty guts and his best beloued were casting sheepeseyes at a Cods head, Hue and Cry came suddenly thorow the streete The Foxe hath killed a tame goose. At the sudden noise whereof the multitude were so scared, that all the morris-dancers were divided, and the Foole ran home to your towne." *Post with a Packet of Mad Letters,* 1602, un-dated ed. p. 58.

Among Lysons' extracts there is one entry which shows that the piper was sent (probably to make collections) round the country. Tollett says, to prove No. 9 to be Tom the Piper, Steevens has very happily quoted these lines from Drayton's "Idea," 1593:

"Myself above Tom Piper to advance, Who so bestirs him in the Morris Dance For penny wage."

His tabour, tabour-stick, and pipe, attest his profession; the feather in his cap, his sword, and the lower flap of his stomacher, may denote him to be a squire-minstrel, or a minstrel of the superior order. In Urry's "Chaucer," 1721, it is said: "Min-strels used a red hat." Tom Piper's bon-net is red, faced, or turned up with yellow, his doublet blue, the sleeves blue, turned up with yellow, something like red muf-fettees at his wrists, over his doublet is a red garment, like a short cloak with arm-holes and with a yellow cape, his hose red, and garnished across and perpendicularly on the thighs, with a narrow yellow lace. His shoes are brown.

Pitchering.—In Craven, there is a custom known as pitchering. The author of the "Dialect of Craven," 1828, de-scribes it thus: "One of the young inmates of the family takes a small pitcher and half fills it with water; he then goes, attended by his companions, and present-ing it to the lover, demands a present in money. If he (the lover) is disposed to give any thing, he drops his con-tribution into the pitcher, and they retire without further molestation. He is thus made a free-man and can quietly pay his visits in future, without being subject to any similar exaction. But, if after re-peated demands, the lover refuse to pay his contribution, he is either saluted with the contents of the pitcher, or a general row ensues, in which the water is spilled, and the pitcher is broken."

Pitching-pence.—A payment for-merly made at fairs on every bag of corn, &c.

Pixy.—Brand thought pixy to be a corruption of puckes—a plausible idea enough but without any philological authority. Neither Nares, nor Halliwell, nor Wedgwood, however, suggests any better or other derivation. Puck itself is simply A. S. *pouke,* a spirit; the pouke

in "Piers Plowman," &c. stands for the Devil.

There is a well known South of England proverb: "The good horse must smell to a pixy;" which means, that an intelligent animal ought to be able to discern the approach of a bog or marshy piece of ground, by the pixy or *ignis fatuus* visible above it. Hazlitt's *Proverbs,* 1882, p. 384. This seems to identify the pixy of Devon-shire and Cornwall with the will-o'-the-wisp, and is one more step towards the reduction to a dead scientific level of our superstitions and traditions founded on the old fairy mythology. There is much in common between will-o-the-wisp and Robin Goodfellow; but neither of these fanciful embodiments appears to have been familiar to the early Devonians and Cornu-bians, who applied to all preternatural beings this generic term pixy or spirit. The pixies of Cornwall and Devon seem to have a good deal in common with Robin. A valuable contributor to "Notes and Queries," who uses the initials H. G. T. sent to that periodical some curious par-ticulars, which tally very much with the attributes given to Robin in the "Mad Pranks," &c. 1628, and elsewhere. See *Cornish Pixies* suprâ.

Plaisterer.—See Hazlitt's *Livery Companies,* 1892. p. 590, where the trade is traced back to 1317: but it most pro-bably existed much earlier.

Planetary Houses.—Lodge thus glances at the superstitious "follower of the planetary houses:"—"And he is so busie in finding out the houses of the planets, that at last he is either faine to house himselfe in an hospitall, or take up his inne in a prison. . . . His name is Curiositie, who not content with the studies of profite and the practise of commendable sciences, setteth his mind wholie on astrologie, negromancie, and magicke. This Divel prefers an Ephi-merides before a Bible; and his Ptolemey and Hali before Ambrose, golden Chriso-stome, or S. Augustine: promise him a familier, and he will take a flie in a box for good paiment. . . . He will shew you the Devill in a christal, calculate the nativitie of his gelding, talke of nothing but gold and silver, elixir, calcination, augmentation, citrination, commentation, and swearing to enrich the world in a month, he is not able to buy himself a new cloake in a whole year. Such a divell I knewe in my daies, that having sold all his land in England to the benefite of the coosener, went to Antwerpe with protes-tation to enrich Monsieur the King's brother of France, le feu Roy Harie I meane; and missing his purpose, died miserably in spight at Hermes in Flush-ing. . . . He (Despair) persuades the merchant not to traffique, because it is given him in his nativity to have loss by sea; and not to lend, least he never receive again." *Wits Miserie*, 1596, pp. 11-12, 95.

Gaule asks, "Where is the source and root of the superstition of vain observation, and the more superstitious ominations thereupon to be found, save in those arts and speculations that teach to observe creatures, images, figures, signes, and accidents, for constellational; and, (as they call them,) second stars; and so to ominate and presage upon them, either as touching themselves, or others? as, namely, to observe dayes for lucky or unlucky, either to travail, sail, fight, build, marry, plant, sow, buy, sell, or begin any businesse in." *Mag-astromancers posed*, p. 181.

Werenfels says, speaking of a superstitious man: "He will be more afraid of the constellation-fires, than the flame of his next neighbour's house. He will not open a vein till he has asked leave of the planets. He will avoid the sea whenever Mars is in the middle of heaven, lest that warrior God should stir up pirates against him. In Taurus he will plant his trees, that this sign, which the astrologers are pleased to call fix'd, may fasten them deeper in the earth. . . . . He will make use of no herbs but such as are gathered in the planetary hour. Against any sort of misfortune he will arm himself with a ring, to which he has fixed the benevolent aspect of the stars, and the lucky hour that was just at the instant of flying away, but which, by a wonderful nimbleness, he has seized and detained." *Dissert. on Superstitions*, 1747, p. 6.

Plays on Sundays.—Plays appear to have been acted publicly and at Court on Sundays and holidays, but rather by sufferance than in conformity with law. The Corporation of London viewed dramatic exhibitions on the Sabbath and on holy feast-days with an especially unfavourable eye. Measures were continually taken for suppression of these amusements; but the offenders probably found them sufficiently lucrative to induce them to run the risk of evading the orders of the Common or Privy Council.

The performance of masques at Court was not unusual during the reigns of Elizabeth and James I. The presentation of Davenant's *Britannia Triumphans* on a Sunday in 1637 made a great stir, owing to the growth of Puritanism. The author of the *Stage Condemned*, 1689, thought this circumstance very remarkable, not being perhaps aware, how common the practice had formerly been.

Pledging.—The word pledge is, according to Blount, derived from the

French "pleige," a surety or gage. Howell, in a very excellent and long letter to the Earl of Clare about 1650, observes: "The word pleiger is also to drink after one is drunk to; whereas the first true sense of the word was, that if the party drunk to was not disposed to drink himself, he would put another for a pledge to do it for him, else the party who began would take it ill."

To pledge, in the sense of to gage or bind, does not seem to have always been understood in this sense, however, if we are to interpret as a security handed to the lender of money by the debtor the following passage in an ancient English poem, of which a fragment, (all that is known) is printed by Maitland in his Account of the Early Books at Lambeth:

"Syr he sayd be saynte Edmounde
Me they owe three pounde
And od two shyllynge
A stycke I haue to wytnes
. . . .
Of hasyll I wene it is
I haue no other thynge—"

In the tale of "King Edward and the Shepherd," printed by Hartshorne, 1829, in his "Ancient Metrical Tales," the pledging words employed are passilodion and berafrynde, which are evidently of the same burlesque character as the conjuring phrases introduced into the "King and the Hermit," and, at a later period, into Marlowe's "Faustus," written before 1593. See also the "Fabliaux" of M. Le Grand, tom. i. p. 119, and his "Histoire de la Vie privée des François," tom. iii. p. 270. The custom of pledging is to be found in the ancient romance of "Ogier le Danois," where Charlemagne pledges himself for Ogier. See Tressan, "Corps d'Extraits des Romans de Chevalerie," tom. ii. p. 77.

In Nash's "Pierce Pennilesse," 1592, we read: "You do me the disgrace, if you doo not pledge me as much as I drinke to you." John Heywood has the following line:

"I drinke (Quoth she,) Quoth he, I will not pledge."

Works, edit. 1598, sign F 4. Overbury, in his "Characters," speaking of a serving-man, says: "He never drinks but double, for he must be pledged; nor commonly without some short sentence nothing to the purpose: and seldom abstains till he comes to a thirst." Another old writer has the following passage: "Truely I thinke hereupon comes the name of good fellow, quasi goad fellow, because he forceth and goads his fellowes forward to be drunke with his persuasive termes as I drunke to you pray pledge me, you dishonour me, you disgrace mee, and with such like words, doth urge his consorts forward to be drunke, as oxen being prickt with goads, are compel'd and forced to draw the maine."

There is a remarkable passage in one of the sermons of Samuel Ward of Ipswich, 1627: "My Saviour began to mee in a bitter cup, and shall I not pledge him;" i.e. drink the same. Feltham, describing a Dutch feast, tells us: "At those times it goes hard with a stranger, all in curtesie will be drinking to him, and all that do so he must pledge: till he doth, the fill'd cups circle round his trencher, from whence they are not taken away till emptyed." *Brief Character of the Low Countries*, 1654, p. 57.

Plat gives a recipe to prevent drunkenness, "for the help of such modest drinkers, as only in company are drawn, or rather forced to pledge in full bolls such quaffing companions as they would be loth to offend, and will require reason at their hands, as they term it." *Jewel-House of Art and Nature*, 1594, p. 59.

Heywood informs us that "Divers authors report of Alexander, that, carousing one day with twenty persons in his company, hee dranke healths to every man round, and pledged them severally againe: and as he was to rise, Calisthenes the Sophist coming into the banquetting house, the king offered him a deepe quaffing-bowle, which he modestly refused, for which, being taxed by one there present, hee said aloud, I desire not, Oh Alexander, to receive a pledge from thee, by taking which I shall be presently inforced to inquire for a physition." *Philocothonista*, 1635, p. 12.

Plough, Fool.—In "Dives and Pauper," 1493, among superstitions censured we find the following: "ledyng of the ploughe aboute the fire as for gode begynnynge of the yere, that they shulde fare the better alle the yere followyng." In Bale's "Yet a Course at the Romyshe Foxe," 1542, the author declares: "than ought my lorde (Bonner) to suffre the same selfe ponnyshment for not sensing the plowghnes on Plowgh Mondaye."

Plough Light.—There was a light in many churches called the plow light, maintained by old and young persons who were husbandmen, before some image: who on Plough Monday had a feast, and went about with a plough, and some dancers to support it. Blomefield's *Norfolk*, iv, 207. This pageant or dance, as used at present, seems a composition made up of the gleaning of several obsolete customs, followed anciently, here and elsewhere, on this and the like festive occasions.

Plough-Monday. — The Monday after Twelfth Day (as Coles tells us) was

anciently called Plough Monday, when our Northern ploughmen begged plough-money to drink. In Tusser's "Husbandry," 1580, under the account of the Ploughman's Feast Days are the following lines:

"Plough Munday, next after that Twelf-tide is past,
Bids out with the Plough; the worst husband is last:
If Plowman get hatchet, or whip to the skrene,
Maids loseth their cocke, if no water be seen:"

which are thus explained in Hilman's "Tusser Redivivus," 1710: "After Christmas (which formerly, during the twelve days, was a time of very little work) every gentleman feasted the farmers, and every farmer their servants and task men. Plough Monday puts them in mind of their business. In the morning the men and the maid servants strive who shall show their diligence in rising earliest. If the ploughman can get his whip, his plough-staff, hatchet, or anything that he wants in the field, by the fire-side, before the maid hath got her kettle on, then the maid loseth her Shrove-tide cock, and it wholly belongs to the men. Thus did our forefathers strive to allure youth to their duty, and provided them innocent mirth as well as labour. On this Plough Monday they have a good supper and some strong drink." Coles tells us: "in some places, if the ploughman (after that day's work) come with his whip to the kitchen hatch, and cry 'cock in pot' before the maid can cry 'cock on the dunghill,' he gains a cock for Shrove-Tuesday."

In Tusser we find the ploughman's feasting days or holidays thus enumerated: 1. Plough Monday. 2. Shrove Tuesday, when, after confession, he is suffered "to thresh the fat hen." 3. Sheep-shearing, with wafers and cakes. 4. Wake Day, or the vigil of the church saint of the village, with flawns or pancakes. 5. Harvest-home, with a goose. 6. Seed-cake, a festival kept at the end of Wheat-sowing, when he is to be feasted with seed-cakes, pasties, and furmenty pot. No. 1 is peculiar to Leicestershire; 2, to Essex and Suffolk; 3, to Northampton; 4, to Leicestershire; 6, to Essex and Suffolk. We learn further from Tusser, that ploughmen were accustomed to have roast meat twice a week; viz. Sundays and Thursdays, at night. See edit. 1597, p. 137.

In a marginal note to Roiley's "Poetical Relation of the Gleanings of the Idiotismes and Absurdities of Miles Corbet Esquire," 1646, p. 6, we are told that the

Monday after Twelfth Day is called "Plowlick Monday by the husbandmen in Norfolk, because on that day they doe first begin to plough." In the "British Apollo," 1710, number 92, the following explanation occurs: "Plough Monday is a country phrase, and only used by peasants, because they generally used to meet together at some neighbourhood over a cup of ale, and feast themselves, as well to wish themselves a plentiful harvest from the great corn sown (as they called wheat and rye) as also to wish a God-speed to the plough as soon as they begin to break the ground to sow barley and other corn, which they at that time make a holiday to themselves as a finishing stroke after Christmas, which is their master's holyday time, as prentices in many places make it the same, appropriated by consent to revel amongst themselves."

Pegge, in the "Gentleman's Magazine" for December, 1762, informs us: "On this day the young men yoke themselves and draw a plough about with musick, and one or two persons in antic dresses, like Jack-Puddings, go from house to house to gather money to drink. If you refuse them they plough up your dunghill. We call them in Derbyshire the Plough Bullocks." Macaulay says: "On Plow-Monday I have taken notice of an annual display of morris-dancers at Claybrook, who come from the neighbouring villages of Sapcote and Sharnford." *Hist. of Claybrook*, 1791, p. 128.

In the Churchwardens' Accounts of St. Margaret's, Westminster, 1494, is the following: "Item of the Brotherhood of Rynsyvale for the plowgere £0 4s. 0d." In similar accounts for Wigtoft, Lincolnshire, 1575, is "Receid of Wyll^m. Clarke & John Waytt, of the plougadrin £1 0s. 0d." There is a custom in this neighbourhood of the ploughmen parading on Plow Monday; but what little they collect is applied wholly to feasting themselves. They put themselves in grotesque habits, with ribands, &c. It appears that the "sign," on which the plough used on these occasions stood, was charged to the parish sixteenpence or thereabouts in the reign of Edward VI. In the Churchwardens' Accounts of Heybridge near Malden, Essex, is the following account, "Item receyved of the gadryng of the white plowe £0 1s. 3d." To which this note is affixed: "Q. does this mean Plough Monday: on which the country people come and dance and make a gathering as on May-Day?"

There is a long and elaborate account in the "Book of Days" of this rustic festival, and in "Notes and Queries" for May 19, 1860, Cuthbert Bede alludes to the custom as then kept up in Hunting-donshire. It is still customary for the Lord Mayor of London to entertain the officers of the Corporation at a banquet on Plough Monday.

In a recent London newspaper occurred the subjoined paragraph: Yesterday, in accordance with an annual custom on Plough Monday (being the Monday following the Feast of the Epiphany), a Court of Wardmote was held at the Guildhall, the Lord Mayor presiding. The results of the election of members of the Court of Common Council and ward officers on St. Thomas's-day last were officially reported to the court, and the ward beadles attended and made the usual declarations on re-appointment. With that the proceedings, which were of a formal character throughout, ended. In the evening the Lord Mayor and Lady Mayoress entertained the members of their household, several of the Corporation officials, and a few private friends, at dinner at the Mansion-house. The guests numbered about 30. The dinner was served in the Venetian Parlour.

Among the ancients the "Compitalia were feasts instituted, some say, by Tarquinius Priscus, in the month of January, and celebrated by servants alone, when their plowing was over." Sheridan's Persius, edit. 1739, p. 67, note.

Pluck a Crow or Goose, to.— In the *Towneley Mysteries*, ed. 1836. p. 15, the phrase is: "to pulle a crawe." The subsequent occurs in Heywood:

"He loveth well sheeps flesh, that wets his bred in the wull
If he leave it not, we have a crow to pull."

A jealous wife is speaking concerning certain liberties which her husband is always taking with her maid. *Works*, ed. 1598, sign. G 4. Howell has in a similar sense: "I have a goose to pluck with you." Comp. Hazlitt's *Proverbs*, 1882, p. 443.

Pluckbuffet.—A sport with bows and arrows, where the archer, who missed the garland or white, received a buffet on his head on being plucked. It is mentioned in the Robin Hood ballads. See Hazlitt's *Tales and Legends*, 1892, p. 321.

Plum Porridge. — Both plum-porridge and Christmas pies are noticed in the following passage in Needham's "History of the Rebellion," 1661 :—

"All plums the prophet's sons defy,
And spice-broths are too hot;
Treason's in a December pye,
And death within the pot.
Christmas, farewell; thy days I fear
And merry days are done:
So they may keep feasts all the year,
Our Saviour shall have none.

Gone are those golden days of yore,
When Christmas was a high day:
Whose sports we now shall see no more;
'Tis turn'd into Good Friday."

Mr. Brand notes: I dined at the Chaplain's table at St. James's on Christmas Day, 1801, and partook of the first thing served up and eaten on that festival at table, i.e. a tureen of rich luscious plum-porridge. I do not know that the custom is anywhere else retained.

One of the adventures of Bamfylde Moore Carew was to cry *Plumb-Pudding, hot Plumb-Pudding, piping-hot, smoaking-hot, hot Plumb-Pudding,* up and down the streets of Bristol in female attire in the midst of the press-gang, the members of which bought his commodities. *Life and Adventures,* 1745, p. 52-3.

Plymouth Fishing Feast.—This was held in 1903 with the accustomed ceremonies at the Burrator reservoir, in the Dartmoor hills, which is famed for its trout. The mayor and corporation and a number of guests, having arrived at this spot, observed the ancient custom of toasting the memory of Francis Drake, who, three centuries ago, first brought the water into Plymouth. The mayor first drank to the pious memory of Sir Francis in a goblet of pure water from the reservoir, and then passed the vessel round. Afterward another goblet, filled with wine, was presented to the mayor, who drank to the toast: "May the descendants of him who brought us water never want wine."

Polichinello or **Punchinello.**—The original of the modern *Punch and Judy.* The exhibition is supposed to be of Italian origin and to have had a political or historical significance. It seems to be first mentioned as a licensed institution in London in 1666, when the parochial authorities of St. Martin's in the Fields received from Punchinello the Italian puppet-player for his booth at Charing Cross £2 12s. 6d., which bespeaks a lucrative enterprize. But Pepys saw the show in Moorfields August 22, same year: April 8, 1667, he does not mention where: and August 31, 1668, at Bartholomew Fair. Brewer's *Dict. of Phrase and Fable,* art. *Punch;* Hazlitt's *Manual of Old Plays,* 1892, p. 187: and Pepys under dates mentioned. On the top of the large room built by Sir Samuel Morland in his garden at Vauxhall was a Punchinello, holding a dial.

Polo.—A form of quintain practised in Persia and other eastern countries as far back as the 11th century. In the *Field* newspaper for 1872-3 and 1885 appeared some interesting archæological notices of it, and in the number for Oct.

17, 1885, Mr. E. H. Parry furnished the subjoined extract from the Travels of the three Sherleys about 1610 in Persia: "Before the house there was a very fair place to the quantity of some ten acres of ground, made very plain; so the king went down, and when he had taken his horse the drums and trumpets sounded. There were twelve horsemen in all with the king, so they divided themselves, six on the one side and six on the other, having in their hands long rods of wood, about the thickness of a man's finger, and at one end of the rods a piece of wood nailed on like unto a hammer. After they were divided and turned face to face, there came one into the middle, and threw a wooden ball between both the companies, and having goals made at either end of the plain, they begun their sport, striking the ball with their rods from one end to the other, in the fashion of our football play here in England; and even when the king had gotten the ball before him, the drums and trumpets would play one alarm, and many times the king would come to Sir Antony to the window, and ask him how he did like the sport."

The game is at present regularly played at Barn Elms, Surrey, by the members of the Ranelagh Club.

Water-polo seems to have been known and exercised at Venice in the thirteenth century, and the arsenal subsequently kept two large rafts or pontoons for this purpose to be delivered to the urban authorities from time to time, and then returned into store.

Pompey, the Black Dog.—For a brief account of this nursery phantom in some parts of the country, the reader may be referred to Hazlitt's *Proverbs,* 1882, p. 331.

Poor Boxes.—Aubrey, in his Natural History of Wiltshire, ed. 1847, observes: "Mr. A. Wood assures me that there were no almshouses, at least they were very scarce, before the Reformation; that over against Christ Church, Oxon, is one of the ancientest. In every church was a poor man's box, but I never remembered the use of it; nay, there was one at great inns, as I remembered it was before the wars. These were the days when England was famous for the grey goose quills." Comp. *Thrift-Box.*

In the time of the Commonwealth there was in the Houses of Parliament a poor-box, into which members put their fines for offences against the rules or against decorum, among the latter being that of climbing over the benches. Parry's *Parliaments and Councils of England,* 1839, under years 1640-61.

Pope Lady.—It is remarkable enough that at St. Albans, as recently as 1861, a correspondent of "Notes and Queries," purchased a "pope lady," a bun made in the form of a woman, and sold on the morning of the New Year.

Pope Julius's Game.—This was a game, at which four, and possibly more, persons could play. It is mentioned in the Privy Purse Expenses of Henry VIII. and apparently nowhere else: therefore the precise nature of the game cannot be determined. It seems to have been unknown to Strutt, Brand, Douce, Nares and all other antiquaries. In the King's Expenses for 1532 are four references to money lost at it by Henry; the earliest is in these terms: "Itm the xx daye November delive'd to the king grace at Stone whiche his grace loste at pope Julius game to my lady marques, m. Bryan, and maister Weston . . . . xiili. vis. viijd." So that, at any rate, it was a costly novelty; and during the same month "the king's grace" lost upwards of £30 more at this diversion. We do not hear of him playing any more; but that may arise from the absence of accounts. The pope alluded to would be probably Julius II. of the Della Rovere family of Urbino.

Popinjay.—In a letter to Henry VIII. from Lord Mountjoy, Captain of Tournay, in 1514, it is stated that there was an annual custom on the 2nd of March of shooting at the popinjay by a fraternity of St. George and that for the current year the provost or mayor of Tournay had acted as his deputy. The provost hit the mark and "soo," writes his lordship, "is yoʳ grace king of the popyngay for this yere." But he adds that if the king's representative should succeed a second time, Henry would become Emperor of the same, "Wherunto ther longgithe many gret roialties." This ceremony or sport was, no doubt, an artificial parrot. *Excerpta Historica*, 1833, p. 286.

Porpentine.—i.q. porcupine. See Nares, 1859, in v.

Portents.—The following is a passage in Stubbes' "Anatomie of Abuses," 1583. He is relating the dreadful end of a swearer in Lincolnshire: "At the last the people perceiving his ende to approche, caused the bell to tolle; who hearing the bell toll for him rushed up in his bed very vehemently." Howell, in a letter to Sir Kenelm Digby, dated 1640, implies that a turnip cut in the shape of a death's-head with a candle, was regarded by women and children as an evil portent. Defoe observes: "Nothing is more contrary to good sense than imagining every thing we see and hear is a prognostick either of good or evil, except it be the belief that nothing is so." *Memoirs of Duncan Campbel*, 1732, p. 60. He testi-

fies to the belief which in his day people entertained in "men on horseback, mountains, ships, forests, and other fine things in the air," as foreshadowing future events. Defoe mentions that, "Others again, by having caught cold, feel a certain noise in their heads, which seems to them like the sound of distant bells, and fancy themselves warned of some great misfortune." Grose says that "A person being suddenly taken with a shivering, is a sign that some one has just then walked over the spot of their future grave. Probably all persons are not subject to this sensation, otherwise the inhabitants of those parishes whose burial grounds lie in the common foot-path would live in one continued fit of shaking." Johnson, in his "Tour to the Hebrides," says, that Macaulay was induced to leave out of his "History of St. Kilda," a passage stating that the inhabitants were apt at the approach of a stranger, to catch cold. See *Divinations, Omens*, &c.

Another description of portents is that, which is described by Holinshed in connection with the historical murder of Arden or Ardern of Faversham in 1551-2: "This one thing seemeth strange and notable touching maister Arden, that in the place where he was layd being dead, all the proportion of his body might be seene two years after and more, as playne as could be: for the grasse did not growe where his body hadde touched, but betweene his legges, betweene his armes and about the holownes of his necke, and round about his body; and where his legges, armes, head, or any part of his body had touched, no grasse growed at all that time ; so that many strangers came in the meane time beside the Townesmen to see the print of his body there on the ground in that field . . ."

Portions, Wedding.—There are two instances in the "Privy Purse Expenses of the Princess Mary," under April, 1537, and April, 1538-9, of the princess contributing to the wedding-portions of poor girls. The earlier entry runs thus: "It'm geven to a pore maydenes mariage by my ladies grace at the request of Mr. Tyrrell . . . vijs. vjd." In the second case, Mary gave only 3s. 4d.

In the "Second Part of Queen Elizabeths Troubles," by T. Heywood, 1606, the author introduces Lady Ramsey, saying:

"——I have known old Hobson
Sit with his neighbour Gunter, a good man,
In Christs Church, morn by morn, to watch poor couples
That come there to be married, and to be

Their common fathers, and give them
    in the church,
And some few angels for a dower to
    boot."

Morant, speaking of Great Yeldham in
Hinckford Hundred, Essex, says: "A
house near the church was antiently used
and appropriated for dressing a dinner
for poor folks when married: and had all
utensils and furniture convenient for that
purpose. It hath since been converted
into a school." Again, speaking of
Matching in Harlow Half-Hundred, he
says: "A house close to the church yard,
said to be built by one . . . . . . Chimney,
was designed for the entertainment of
poor people on their wedding day. It
seems to be very antient but ruinous."

Posies.—These were invented for
rings, handkerchiefs, &c., and collections
of them were printed in the first half
of the 17th century. They are also to be
found inscribed on early knives, whence
the mottoes are described by Shakespear
as "cutler's poetry." Those engraved on
rings were adapted to the requirements
or fancies of lovers or friends. They
present themselves on rings given by men
to their mistresses and by the latter to
the objects of their preference. An early
garland of the kind above specified furnishes in its descriptive title the range of
these amatory compliments. The most
ancient impression which has fallen under
my notice is one of 1642:—

Cupids posies
For Bracelets, handkerchers, and rings,
With scarves, gloves, and other things.
Written by Cupid on a day,
When Cupid gave me leave to play.
The lover sheweth his intent
By gifts that are with posies sent.

Hazlitt's *Handbook*, 1867, p. 134, and
Bibl. Coll. 1903, p. 93.

A very curious case occurred of a ring
used by a Venetian gentleman of the
Pesaro family to seal a letter to a lady
of his acquaintance in 1796, with the posy,
Je ne change qu'en mourant, being lately
recovered in London, whither the owner
retired on the fall of the old Republic.
It had doubtless changed hands many
times. Hazlitt's *Venetian Republic*,
1900, ii, 324. See *Nuptial Usages* and
Rings.

Posset or **Caudle.**—Among the
Anglo-Saxons, as Strutt informs us, at
night the bride was by the women attendants placed in the marriage-bed, and
the bridegroom in the same manner conducted by the men, where having both,
with all who were present, drunk the
marriage health, the company retired.
Skinner derives the word from the French

poser, residere, to settle; because, when
the milk breaks, the cheesy parts, being
heavier, subside. "Nobis proprie desig-
nat Lac calidum infuso vino cerevisiâ, &c.
coagulatum."—See Junii *Etymol. in
verbo.*

In the evening of the wedding-day, just
before the company retired, the sack-
posset was eaten. Of this posset the
bride and bridegroom were always to
taste first. It is mentioned too among the
bridal rites in the "History of Jack of
Newbury" 1597, where we are told "the
sack-posset must be eaten." In "The
Fifteen Comforts of Marriage," p. 60, it
is called "an antient custom of the English matrons, who believe that sack will
make a man lusty, and sugar will make
him kind." The custom of eating a posset
at going to bed seems to have prevailed
generally among our ancestors. The
Tobacconist, in a book of Characters
printed in 1640, says: "And at my going
to bed, this is my posset." *The Wandering
Jew*, p. 20. Herrick has not overlooked
the posset in his "Hesperides," p. 253:
nor is it omitted in the "Collier's Wedding."

Misson says: "The posset is a kind
of cawdle, a portion made up of milk,
wine, yolks of eggs, sugar, cinnamon, nutmeg, &c." He adds: "They never fail
to bring them another sack posset next
morning." In the story of the *Curst
Wife lapt in Morels Skin* (about 1575) the
caudle is brought by the mother in the
morning. Montaigne in his Essay *Of the
Force of Imagination*, speaks of the
caudle as having in his time been administered to the bridegroom, not prior to
the retirement of the guests, but in the
course of the night. He observes in relation to a friend: "For I would do him
the office of a friend, and if needs were.
would not spare a miracle it was in my
power to do, provided he would engage to
me upon his honour to keep it to himself:
and only when they came to bring him his
caudle, if matters had not gone well
with him, to give me such a sign, and leave
the rest to me."

Even as late as 1811, Charles Lamb, in
a letter to William Hazlitt on the birth of
my father, says: "Sorry we are not
within caudle-shot."

Post and Pair.—This game is mentioned in the following passage from the
play of Nobody and Somebody (1606):

Sico(phant). Now sir, as you haue
    compast all the dice,
So I for cards. These for the game at
    maw,
All saving one, are cut next vnder that,
Lay me the ace of harts, then cut the
    cards,

O your fellow must needs haue it in his
　　first tricke.
Clow. I'le teach you a trick for this
　　yfaith.
Sicop. These for Premero cut vpon the
　　sides,
As the other on the ends.
Clow. Marke the end of all this.
Sicop. These are for post and paire,
　　these for saunt.
These for new cut.
　　　　　　　　—Sign. G 3 *verso.*

It is thus noticed in "Scogin's Jests,"
ed.1626: "On a certaine time, Scogin went
to his scholler, the aforesaid parson, to
dine with him on a Sunday; and this
aforesaid priest or parson all the night
before had been at cards playing at the
post."

In Nares' Glossary, 1859, the game
is described. According to Earle, in his
"Micro-cosmographie," 1628, it could be
played with a dozen counters.

Pot-Walloper.—The *Antiquary* for
May, 1896, records the death of the last
of the pot-wallopers of the borough of
Pontefract. This term implies a person,
who acquired the parliamentary franchise
by virtue of the possession of a free-hold
hearth, on which he could boil his pot.
It was prior to the Reform Bill of 1832,
and required a six months' continuous
residence as a qualification. The vessel
itself was a tripod and was suspended
by a chain from an iron bar suspended
in the chimney. Comp. Timbs, *Historic
Ninepins,* 1869, p. 255.

Pound or **Pin.**—An enclosed (usually square) fence used in villages and
parishes for the detention of stray cattle.
There was usually a *pound-keeper* or *pinner,* sometimes called a *pinder;* the *pinder*
of Wakefield has acquired exceptional
celebrity in connection with the Robin
Hood cycle of ballads, though really his
period is in all probability much later.
But the duties of pinner or pound-keeper
necessitated the employment of strong
and courageous fellows acquainted with
the whole neighbourhood. Even in the
metropolitan area pounds are still to be
seen on Putney and Wimbledon Commons,
and that on Barnes Common has only
disappeared quite recently, the strays
going to the Greenyard. It was the scene
of a *jeu d'esprit* between Foote and
Quin, which survives in an epigrammatic
copy of verses.

Prayers.—Cassalion has this taunt
against the Protestants: "Though," says
he, "the English now deny that prayers
are of any service to the dead, yet I could
meet with no other account of this ceremony than that it was a custom of the

old Church of England, i.e. the Church of
Rome." *De Vet. Sac. Christ. Rit.* p. 241.
Customary prayers for the dead in the
15th and 16th centuries appear to have
been the *pater noster, Ave, Credo,* and
De Profundis. Plumpton Corrrespon-
dence, 1839, p. 75. Priests offered to
obtain pardon for souls for 32755 years
in consideration of five *paternosters,* five
Ave Marias, and a *Credo.* See Hazlitt's
Bibl. Collections, 1903, p. 194, and his
*Ourselves in relation to a Deity and a
Church,* 1897, p. 167. There is a broadside from the press of Caxton containing
Death-bed Prayers. Prayers were formerly offered or solicited for the builders
of bridges. Sir Thomas Winnington
possessed a brass plate found in the
foundations of the old bridge over the
Teme at Stanford, Worcestershire, desiring prayers for Humphrey Pakynton
Esquire of Stanford, who defrayed the
charges for erecting this structure in the
first year of Edward VI.

Presterjohn.—A form given by the
Christian nationalities in the middle ages
to the name of a real or supposed King
of Ethiopia or Abyssinia, whom they pretended to have converted to Christianity.
The real name was probably *Ung Khan*
or *Khan Ung,* and it has been even
doubted whether this appellation was not
borne by more than one ruler, like
those of Pharaoh in Egypt and Arsaces in
Parthia.

Pretty Money.—New money put
by, and saved in a stocking or bag; the
amount is not limited, but it is usually
trifling, and seldom exceeds a few pounds.
East Anglia. In Sussex they call it
pocket-pieces.

Prevaricator.—The name of an
annually chosen officer at Cambridge, who
delivered before the assembled university
an address in Latin, in which he was left
at liberty to offer tolerably free and
humorous criticisms on the authorities.
Randolph the poet was Prevaricator for
1632, and his Oration was first printed in
my edition of his Works, 1875. I do not
think that any text was previously known
of these Saturnalian addresses.

Pricking at the Belt or Girdle,
or **Fast and Loose.**—A cheating
game, of which the following is a description: "A leathern belt is made up
into a number of intricate folds, and
placed edgewise upon a table. One of the
folds is made to resemble the middle of
the girdle, so that whoever shall thrust a
skewer into it would think he held it fast
to the table: whereas, when he has so
done, the person with whom he plays may
take hold of both ends and draw it away."
It appears to have been a game much
practised by the gipsies in the time of

Shakespear. Hazlitt's Dodsley, xiii, 174. It is still in vogue.

Pricking in Civic Elections.— The annual choice of the Sheriffs of London by this method is sufficiently familiar. But some of the City Gilds have been accustomed to resort in certain cases to the same process, the persons entitled to vote pricking on paper with a pin. See Hazlitt's *Livery Companies*, 1892, p. 464.

Pricking in the Old Hat.—It appears from a communication by Mr. W. Kelly to "Current Notes" for June, 1854, that the Chamberlain's Accounts for the Borough of Leicester for 1749-50 have the following entry : " Paid for prosecuting one Richardson, and others by (for?) pricking at a game called Pricking in the Old Hat, 6s. 10d." Unless this amusement resembled the preceding, and was an outgrowth from it, I cannot undertake a solution of the mystery involved in this registration.

Primero.—See an excellent account of it in Nares, *Glossary*, 1859, in v. and comp. *Quinola*.

Prince d'Amour.—See *Christmas Prince*.

Prince of Purpoole or **Portypool.**—See *Christmas Prince*.

Prison Bars or Base.—In the Dictionary of Johannes de Garlandia, written in the early part of the thirteenth century, under the enumeration of requisites for the house of a respectable person, we meet, oddly enough, with *barri*, which are thus explained to us : " Barri sunt genus ludi, Gallicè barres ;" and the editor, in a note, adds : " Possibly the game still called bars or prison-base, well-known to schoolboys." Comp. *Pulling off Hats* infrâ.

The game of " the country base " is mentioned in the " Faëry Queene," 1590, and by Shakespear in " Cymbeline." Also in Chettle's tragedy of " Hoffman," 1631 :

" I'll run a little course
At base, or barley-brake."

Again, in Brome's " Antipodes," 1640 :
" My men can run at base."

Again, in the thirtieth song of Drayton's " Polyolbion :"

" At hood-wink, barley-brake, at tick, or prison base."

Comp. Nares, *Glossary*, 1859, in v. In Southern Italy they have a children's sport, called *Bomba*, which resembles this, and which is familiar to English ears as the *sobriquet* of Ferdinand II. King of the Two Sicilies.

Prophecies.—It appears from a letter written in February, 1485-6, by Thomas Betanson to Sir Robert Plumpton, that prophesying was in that year felony. The writer says : " Also it is in actt, that all maner of profcyces is mayd felony." There does not seem to be any other record of this, as no such statute is on the parliament-roll ; but in the present imperfect state of the latter, such an omission is easily to be accounted for. We read that : " A.D. 1560. A skinner of Southwark was set on the pillory ; with a paper over his head, shewing the cause, viz. for sundry practices of great falsehood, and much untruth : and all set forth under the colour of southsaying." Stow's *Survey*, 1720, lib. i, p. 257.

Lloyd in his *Stratagems of Jerusalem*, 1602, p. 290, observes under this head : " Aristander the soothsayer, in the battell at Arbela, being the last against Darius, was seen on horsebacke hard by Alexander, apparelled all in white, and a crowne of golde upon his head, encouraging Alexander, by the flight of an eagle, the victory should be his over Darius. Both the Greekes, the Romaines, and the Lacedemonians, had theyr soothsayers hard by them in their warres."

In connection with this subject, the following communication from a correspondent of the *Pall Mall Gazette* (April, 1879) may be cited :—" It seems that the labouring classes in Mid-Somerset, like most other rural districts in England, hold or held sacred certain supposed prophecies of Mother Shipton, whose topographical knowledge, if we are to believe all that is said of her, must have been little less marvellous than her insight into the future. Of these prophecies the most widely believed in had reference to the fate of Ham Hill, a large stone quarry in the neighbourhood of Yeovil, and a prominent feature of the landscape for miles around. It was to the effect that at twelve o'clock on Good Friday of 1879, Ham Hill should suddenly be swallowed up by an earthquake, and that at the same time Yeovil should be visited by a tremendous flood. With such real anxiety was last Friday looked forward to, in consequence, that people actually left the locality with their families and went to stay with their friends in other parts of the country until the dreaded " visitation " should be over ; others, whose faith was less robust, nevertheless thought it advisable to remove their pots and pans from the shelves of their cupboards and stow away their clocks and looking-glasses in places where they were not likely to be shattered by the shock of the earthquake : others, again, suspended gardening operations for a day or two, thinking it mere waste to commit good seed to earth that was likely to behave so treacherously. On the morning of Good Friday itself large numbers of people—many of them from a distance—flocked to the spot, or as near to the spot as they dared venture, to await, half incredulous and half in terror, the stroke of twelve and the fulfilment of the prophecy. When, however, the appointed hour had passed, and Ham Hill still stood unabashed, they began to look sheepishly into each other's faces and to move away. At present in Mid-Somerset Mother Shipton and her prophecies are somewhat at a discount."

Mr. Goodrich-Frier (*Outer Isles*, 1902) has collected some curious notices of the faith in seers and prophecy in the Hebrides within a measurable period of time.

Propping. — A marriage custom, perhaps, peculiar to Northamptonshire. It is confined to marriages where the parties are well-known, or people of station, and consists "in placing pieces of timber or poles round the house and against the door of the newly-married couple." Baker adds: "An action, in connection with this curious practice, was tried at Northampton Assizes in 1842. At the marriage of a gentleman at Bugbrook, some of the villagers propped his house; and he being annoyed at the proceedings, fired from a window, and wounded the plaintiff, since which time the practice has been discontinued in that village, but is partially observed in some others (1854)."

Pterodactyl.—A huge flying reptile of prehistoric times, which may have given rise to the fabulous dragon of the middle ages.

Pudding, Christmas. — It is thought to be lucky to stir one's neighbours' puddings, and some women even now will go some distance to do so. I have understood that the Irish set their Christmas pudding on the fire at midnight on Christmas-Eve, and let it boil till the following mid-day.

Pudding-pieing.—In Kent, they go a pudding-pieing on Easter day, the pudding-pie being a sort of cheese-cake or custard, with a raised crust and currants sprinkled over. Cherry beer is commonly drunk with these delicacies by the young folks.

Puddining.—An ancient offering on the first visit of a young child to the house of a neighbour. See Halliwell in v.

Pulling off Hats.—At a Parliament held 6 Edward III., March 16, 1332, a Proclamation was ordered to be made, among other matters, against children playing any games, including (Prison) Bars and Pulling off Hats, in the Palace at Westminster during the sitting of Parliament. Parry's *Parliaments and Councils*, 1839, p. 97.

Pulver Wednesday.—See *Ash Wednesday*.

Punchinello.—Comp. *Polichinello*.

Purification of the Virgin.—See *Mary of Nazareth*.

Push-Ball. — A modern American form of football, of course eclipsing the European prototype. The ball used is a rubber bladder, which, when inflated, measures 6ft. 3in. in diameter. This sport is played at Harvard University, and its invention is ascribed to Mr. M. G. Crane, of Newton, Massachusetts.

Push-Pin.—"This," observes Strutt, "is a very silly sport, being nothing more than simply pushing one pin across another." Where Strutt obtained his information, I do not know; but from a coarse allusion in the Epigrams of Richard Middleton, of York, 1608, and from the way in which it is introduced into Fuller's *Gnomologia*, 1732, it might be supposed to have been of a somewhat different nature.

Put.—This is a game at cards, and is thus referred to in "The Riddle," a copy of verses inserted in "Rump Songs," 1662 :

"Shall's have a game at put, to passe
   away the time,
Expect no foul play, though I do play
   the Knave,
I have a King at hand, yea that I have ;
Cards, be ye true, then the game is
   mine."

Put is referred to in Speed's *Batt upon Batt*, 1694, where a dexterous player is said to "always have three trays in hand," and where it is numbered among the Christmas amusements. It appears to have been an amusement of the lower orders more particularly in the time of Queen Anne. Chatto's *Facts and Speculations*, 1848, p. 166.

Nabbes, in his *Springs glory*, a Masque, 1639, introduces a dialogue between Christmas, "personated by an old reverend gentleman in a furr'd gowne and cappe, &c.," and Shrovetide, "a fat cooke with a frying-pan, &c.," and enumerates certain games played at the former season, including *Put* :—

"*Christmas.* Thou get children?
Shrovetide. Yes more than Christmas, and better too: for thine are all unthrifts, whores, or murderers. Thy sonne *In and in* undid many a citizen. Thou hast a Daughter called *my Ladyes hole*, a filthy black slut she is; and *Put* is common in

every Bawdy house. 'Tis thought *Noddy* was none of thine own getting, but an aldermans, that in exchange cuckolded thee, when thou wast a Courtier."

Puttuck or **Pothook.**—A stout steel bar fastened by a collar to the neck of an offender. A correspondent of *Current Notes*, where (December, 1854, p. 101) an illustration of the object and its use is given, observes : " From older individuals than myself I learn that fifty or sixty years since they have seen it in use in the workhouse at Harleston."

Pyx Chapel. — This apartment, hitherto jealously guarded by double entrance doors, openable only by means of seven keys, each kept by a different official, has now been taken under the charge of the Office of Works, and is to be thrown open to public inspection, electric light being installed. The chapel, situated in the dark cloisters of Westminster Abbey, contains several objects of interest, and has been during centuries the repository of the standards and assays employed in the national coinage. The periodical Trial of the Pyx was a mysterious operation, of which very few outside those privileged to attend it had any knowledge. But the new arrangements will render the locality and matter more familiar.

Quaaltagh.—See *First Foot.*

Quadrille.—A game at cards allied to *primero, ombre,* &c. Counters were used, which in the first instance were put into a pool—a pool of quadrille being, like a rubber of whist, a succession of games. Only forty cards were used. I think the threes, fours, and fives were thrown out. There were four players. The three great cards or matadores were Spadille, the ace of spades ; Manille, according to the trump, the two of spades or clubs, or the seven of hearts or diamonds ; Basto, the ace of clubs. The trump was decided by " asking leave," the first hand having the prior right. If another said " preference," meaning hearts for the trump, the first gave way. The partner was decided by one of the players " accepting." If the first would not yield to " preference," he might "call a king"—i.e. naming a king, and giving some worthless card in exchange, for which he paid a fine, and then playing independent of the partner ; but if another said " I will play alone," all yielded to him. If the name of the trump made all the ten tricks, it was a " voice," if only five it was a " basto," if only four it was " codille," or basted off the board. When hearts or diamonds were trumps the ace was called Punto, and ranked above the

king ; if not, below him and the queen and knave.—*Notes and Queries.*

Quails.—It appears that the Romans used quails as well as cocks for fighting. Douce, (*Illustr. of Shakesp.* 1807, ii, 87) informs us, " Quail combats were well known among the ancients, and especially at Athens. Julius Pollux relates that a circle was made, in which the birds were placed, and he whose quail was driven out of the circle lost the stake, which was sometimes money, and occasionally the quails themselves. Another practice was to produce one of these birds, which being first smitten or filliped with the middle finger, a feather was then plucked from its head : if the quail bore this operation without flinching, his master gained the stake, but lost it if he ran away.

The Chinese have been always extremely fond of quail-fighting, as appears from most of the accounts of that people, and particularly in Mr. Bell's excellent relation of his ' Travels in China,' where the reader will find much curious matter on the subject. See Vol. i. p. 424, 8vo. edit. We are told by Mr. Marsden that " the Sumatrans likewise use these birds in the manner of game cocks." This account is accompanied by a copy from an elegant Chinese miniature painting, representing some ladies engaged at this amusement. Cocks and quails, fitted for the purpose of engaging one another to the last gasp for diversion, are frequently compared in the Roman writers, and with much propriety, to gladiators. Hence Pliny's expression " Gallorum, seu Gladiatorum ;" and that of Columella, " rixosarum Avium Lanistæ," Lanista being the proper term for the Master of the Gladiators.

Queen or **Lady of May.** — See *Maid Marian.*

Questions and Commands.— In " Round About Our Coal Fire (about 1730), this is named and explained :— " The time of the year being cold and frosty, the diversions are within doors, either in exercise or by the fire-side. Dancing is one of the chief exercises : or else there is a match at blindman's-buff, or puss in the corner. The next game is " Questions and Commands," when the commander may oblige his subject to answer any lawful question, and make the same obey him instantly, under the penalty of being smutted, or paying such forfeit as may be laid on the aggressor. Most of the other diversions are cards and dice."

Quince.—The following remarkable passage occurs in "The Praise of Musick," 1586 : " I come to mariages, wherein as our ancestors, (I do willingly harp upon this string, that our younger wits may know that they stand under correction of elder judgements,) did fondly and with a kind of doting maintaine many rites and ceremonies, some whereof were either shadowes or abodements of a pleasant life to come, as the eating of a Quince peare, to be a preparative of sweete and delightfull dayes between the maried persons."

A present of quinces, from a husband to his bride, is noticed as part of the wedding entertainment at an English marriage in 1725. The correspondent of "Notes and Queries," who commented on this usage (if such it was), observes, that it is apt to remind one of the ancient Greek custom, that the married couple should eat a quince together. There is no explicit statement, however, or even suggestion in the record, from which this gentleman quotes, that the ceremony was actually observed on the occasion to which he refers.

Quinola.—The term at primero for a chief card.

Quintain or **Quintal.**—This was a Roman amusement, but was also practised in the East, whence probably the Romans derived their knowledge of it, and in India.

The quintain seems indeed to have been practised by most nations in Europe. See Menage, "Dict." in v.; Le Grand, "Fabl." tom. ii. p. 214; Ducange and Spelman, "Glos.;" Matt. Paris, ed. 1640, Glos.;" Dugdale's "Warwicksh." p. 166; Cowell's "Interpr." in v.; Plot's "Oxfordsh." p. 200-1; and "Archæol." vol. i. p. 305. A description of the military quintain may be seen in Pluvinel ("L'Instruction du Roy sur l'exercise de monter à cheval," p. 217). and a singular specimen of the sport occurs in Tressani ("Corps d'Extraits de Romans," tom. ii. p. 30). Comp. *Polo.*

We know that the game or exercise was well known to Fitzstephen and Matthew Paris, the latter of whom expressly alludes to it under the year 1253 by the name of Quintena. This was in the time of Henry III., subsequently to the date at which Fitzstephen flourished and wrote, the latter having died, as it is supposed, in or about 1191. The treatment and details evidently varied according to circumstances, and there were two distinct kinds of sport, the land and the water quintain.

Running at the Quintain was a ludicrous kind of tilting at the ring, generally performed by peasants to divert their lord, and was thus done:—A strong post was set upright in the ground, about the height of a man on horseback, having on the top a pivot, which ran through a long horizontal beam, unequally divided, and at the least stroke revolving freely about its centre, somewhat in the nature of a turnstile. On the upright post the head and body of a figure of an unarmed man was fixed. The horizontal beam represented his arms; the shortest hand had a target, nearly covering the whole body, except a small spot on the breast, marked with a heart or ring, and at the end of the target was a wooden sword, a cudgel, or a bag of wet sand. At this figure peasants armed with poles for lances, and mounted on sorry jades of horses, ran full tilt, attempting to strike the heart or ring. These holes were of such a length, that if they struck the shield instead of the heart or ring, the short arm of the lever retiring, brought round that armed with a cudgel or sand-bag at such a distance and with such velocity, as commonly to meet and dismount the awkward assailant.

Stow tells us that the amusement was followed by the citizens of London in winter as well as in summer, namely, at Christmas. "I have seen," says he, "a quintain set upon Cornhill by the Leaden Hall, where the attendants of the lords of merry disports have run and made great pastime." So early as 1253, 38 Henry III., some of the king's servants came down to the city from Westminster, where the Court was, and there was a tumult, as the intruders insulted the Londoners, who were entitled to the name of Barons, and the royal party fell on them, and beat them, and over and above that the King amerced the city in 1000 marks. *Survey,* 1720, Book 1, p. 249. The water quintain was in vogue, it may be inferred, at Easter, and the other variety in the Christmas holidays.

Fitzstephen says of the water-quintain: "At Easter the diversion is prosecuted on the water; a target is strongly fastened to a trunk or mast fixed in the middle of the river, and a youngster standing upright in the stern of a boat, made to move as fast as the current and oars can carry it, is to strike the target with his lance, and if in hitting it he breaks his lance, and keeps his place in the boat, he gains his point, and triumphs; but if it happens the lance is not shivered by the force of the blow, he is of course tumbled into the water, and away goes his vessel without him. However, a couple of boats full of young men are placed, one on each side of the target, so as to be ready to take up the unsuccessful adventurer, the moment he emerges from the stream and comes fairly to the surface. The bridge and the balconies on the banks are filled with spectators, whose business is to laugh." *Descr. of London*, 1772, pp. 48-9.

Henry, referring to the land game, thus describes it: "A strong post was fixed in the ground, with a piece of wood, which turned upon a spindle, on the top of it. At one end of this piece of wood a bag of sand was suspended, and at the other end a board was nailed. Against this board they tilted with spears, which made the pins of wood turn quickly on the spindle, and the bag of sand strike the riders on the back with great force, if they did not make their escape by the fleetness of their horses. *Hist. of Great Britain*, iii, 594. He refers to Strype's Stow, 1720, i, 249, where the woodcut probably assisted his account. This may apply to the first half of the 18th century.

The quintain is introduced into the prose history of Merlin. In the account of the tournament at Logres, it is said: "After mete was the quyntayne reysed, and ther at bourded the yonge batchelers." It does not exactly appear what kind of quintain is here intended, but it was probably the Pel, of which a description may be read in Strutt. Something of this sort seems intended in the burlesque account of the marriage of Tybbe the Reve's daughter, in the "Tournament of Tottenham," written probably in the fourteenth century. In Strype's "Annals," anno 1575, among the various sports, &c. used to entertain Queen Elizabeth at Kenilworth Castle, he tells us, "That afternoon (as the relater expresseth it) in honour of this Kenilworth Castle, and of God and St. Kenelme, (whose day by the kalendar this was,) was a solemn country bridal, with running at Quintin."

A modification of the game appears in a missal in the Douce Collection, in which a person is represented balancing himself upon a pole laid across two stools. At the end of the pole is a lighted candle, from which he is endeavouring to light another in his hand at the risk of tumbling into a bucket of water placed under him.

It appears from Bishop Kennett, that the quintain was anciently a customary sport at weddings. He says it was used in his time at Blackthorne and at Deddington, in Oxfordshire. *Gloss. to P. A.* and Blount says: "It is a game or sport still in request at marriages, in some parts of this nation, especially in Shropshire: the manner now corruptly thus:—a quintain, buttress, or thick plank of wood is set fast in the ground of the high-way, where the bride and bridegroom are to pass; and poles are provided; with which the young men run a tilt on horseback, and he that breaks most poles, and shews most activity, wins

the garland." But he may be presumed to refer to the period anterior to the Civil War. *Glossographia*, 1656, in v.

Owen's description of the quintain as played at weddings seems to indicate a much milder diversion than that form of it usually practised. He says: "A pole is fixt in the ground, with sticks set about it, which the bridegroom and his company take up, and try their strength and activity in breaking them upon the pole." *Welsh Dict.* v. *Quintan.*

The quintain was one of the sports practised by the Cornish men in July on Halgaver Moor, near Bodmin. The method of playing at it as described in a newspaper of 1789 is exactly correspondent with that employed by our countrymen in Stow's time and in Fitzstephen's. "On Off'ham Green," says Hasted, "there stands a quintain, a thing now rarely to be met with, being a machine much used in former times by youth, as well to try their own activity, as the swiftness of their horses in running at it. (He gives an engraving of it.) The cross-piece of it is broad at one end, and pierced full of holes; and a bag of sand is hung at the other, and swings round on being moved with any blow. The pastime was for the youth on horseback to run at it as fast as possible, and hit the broad part in his career with much force. He that by chance hit it not at all, was treated with loud peals of derision; and he who did hit it, made the best use of his swiftness, lest he should have a sound blow on his neck from the bag of sand, which instantly swang round from the other end of the quintain. The great design of this sport was to try the agility of the horse and man, and to break the board, which, whoever did, he was accounted chief of the day's sport. It stands opposite the dwelling house of the estate, which is bound to keep it up." The same author speaking of Bobbing parish, says: "there was formerly a quintin in this parish, there being still a field in it, called from thence the Quintin-Field." *Hist. of Kent*, folio. ed ii, 224, 639. The quintain at Off'ham Green was still there in 1899.

This pastime, somewhat diversified, was in the 17th century practised by the Flemings at their wakes or festivals. In some cases one arm presented a ring, while the other held the club or sand-bag; in others the revolving arms were placed vertically, the lower shewing the ring, while the upper supported a vessel full of water, whereby the want of dexterity in the tilter was punished with a bath. Representations of this exercise may be seen among the prints after Wouverman, who died in 1668. Grose's *Antiquities*, iv.

Quoits.—In the Statute of Labourers, 1541, all labourers, artificers, and other workmen are prohibited under penalties from playing at certain games (coyting included) except at Christmas, and then in their master's house or presence. Antony Wood is our authority for the statement that Arthur Dee, Dr. Dee's son, played with quoits of gold, which his father had made by transmutation at Prague in Bohemia. Thorne's *Environs of London*, 1876, ii, 442. See *Cockall*. Among the Sikhs, Captain Mundy found the quoit in use as a weapon in war.

Races. — The earliest apparent notices of horse-races are in two very ancient French metrical romances mentioned by Wright. *Domestic Manners and Sentiments*, 1862, p. 318. But the present writer does not follow this authority in supposing that, while such an usage is specified, it was not carried out in practice; for in fact horse-races were familiar to the Greeks, and are described by Fitzstephen, who flourished in the time of Henry II. *Account of London*, 1772, p. 38. In the beginning of the 17th c. races were held both in Surrey and in Yorkshire, where the prize to have been able to the winner appears to have been a silver bell in Camden's day, and in or about 1618 we find Newmarket already a favourite resort of the King and Court. Hazlitt's *Venetian Republic*, 1900, ii, 240. During the reign of Charles I. Hyde Park was a favourite ground for this diversion, and in Shirley's play of *Hyde Park*, 1637, occur the names of several famous horses, which ran at that date, including Bay Tarrall, "that won the cup at Newmarket." Hazlitt's *Manual of Old Plays*, 1892, p. 112. In *Cyuile and Vncyuile Life*, 1579, Valentine, one of the interlocutors, says of gentlemen : "For though they refuse not for company & conversation to hauke & hunte, yet is our most continuall exercise eyther studie or ridinge of great & seruiceable horses—."

In Hinde's "Life of John Bruen," 1641, p. 104, the author recommends "unto many of our gentlemen, and to many of inferior rank, that they would make an exchange of their foot races and horse races," &c.

In 1654 and 1658 horse-races were suspended for six and eight months respectively by proclamation. Hazlitt's *Bibl. Coll.*, 1903, p. 90-1.

In the time of Charles II. a horse-race used to be periodically held at Leith under official or municipal sanction, and an extant broadside with the date 168 . , the last numeral being left blank to be supplied in MS. contains the rules observable on the occasion by those engaged or concerned. Hazlitt's *Bibl. Coll. & Notes*, 1903, p. 222. Comp. *To Bear the Bell and Horses.*

Misson, writing about 1698, says : "The English nobility take great delight in horse-races. The most famous are usually at Newmarket; and there you are sure to see a great many persons of the first quality, and almost all the gentlemen of the neighbourhood. It is pretty common for them to lay wagers of two thousand pounds sterling upon one race. I have seen a horse, that after having run twenty miles in fifty-five minutes, upon ground less even than that where the races are run at Newmarket, and won the wager for his master, would have been able to run a-new without taking breath, if he that had lost durst have ventured again. There are also races run by men." *Travels in England*, p. 231.

Raffling.—See *Rifling.*

Ragman.—An ancient game, which is supposed to have been played in the following manner:—a series of poetical characters were written in stanzas on a long roll of parchment or paper, and a seal was fastened with a string to each description. The roll was then folded up, and placed on the table, at which the company sat, and each then selected a character by touching a seal. No one could even foresee what character he or she would have, till the roll was opened. See farther in *Plumpton Correspondence*, 1839, p. 168, Wright's *Anecdota Literaria*, 1844, p. 81, and Hazlitt's *Popular Poetry*, i, 68, where it should have been perhaps rather stated that the term, as applied to this amusement, was a secondary sense. The antiquity of this sport is apparently testified by the *sobriquet* of *Ragman Roll* applied to the deed with the seals of the Scotish chiefs given by them as a token of their fealty to Edward I. But the term was in general use in the fourteenth century for a roll of any kind, with seals attached. Hence perhaps we gain the conventional term *rigmarole*. and the editor of the *Plumpton Correspondence* thinks that *Bully rook* in the *M. W. of W.* should be *Bully rag.*

Rags at Wells.—See *Blessing of Clouts.*

Rain.—See *Weather Omens.*

Rainbow.—The rainbow may be included among barometrical indicators. It is still a common saw :

> "The rainbow in the morning
> Is the shepherd's warning;
> The rainbow at night,
> Is the shepherd's delight."

Which is a belief entertained by the French, and (as M. Michel shews) by the inhabitants of the Basque country. The Cornish people have this version:

"A rainbow in the morn,
Put your hook in the corn;
A rainbow at eve,
Put your head in the sheave."

A curious and valuable assemblage of notices in reference to the rainbow, and its supposed influence and character in various countries, may be found in *Melusine* for April, 1884, and the notions of the Romans on the subject in *Miscellanea Virgiliana*, by a Graduate of Cambridge, (Donaldson), 1825, p. 39. The lunar rainbow differs from the solar one, is sometimes destitute of iridescence, and is rarer or more rarely visible.

Raphael, St.—Lydgate, in his *Vertue of the Masse*, says:

"—Raphaell by recorde of Thobye
Shall be your leche and your medycyne."

Hazlitt's *Fugitive Tracts*, 1875, i, sign. c 3.

Rapier-Dance.—See Halliwell in v.

Rats and Mice.—St. Gertrude was supposed to poison all rats and mice, so that none of these vermin were ever known to gnaw any Friars' cheese or bacon. Melton's *Astrologaster*, 1620, p. 19.

Rats Rhymed to Death.—For a superstition on this subject, see Nares, ed. 1859, in v. The term formed the title to a collection of ballads printed in 1660 in ridicule of the Rump Parliament. Sir W. Temple seems to have traced the idea to a Runic source.

Rattle. — Cornelius Scriblerus remarks: "I heartily wish a diligent search may be made after the true Crepitaculum, or rattle of the ancients, for that (as Archytas Terentinus was of opinion,) kept the children from breaking earthenware. The China cups in these days are not at all the safer for the modern rattles: which is an evident proof how far their Crepitacula exceeded ours."

Martial mentions this in the 54th Epigram of Book iv, under both its Roman names, crepitaculum being the more usual. See St. John's *Manners and Customs of Ancient Greece*, 1842, i, 145.

Rattlesnake.—Waterton the naturalist, in his exploration of Pernambuco and its neighbourhood in 1816, relates an interesting account of the peculiar fascination of this creature. In some tangled undergrowth in an abandoned orange orchard the writer distinguished an object, which he took to be a pale green grasshopper, near which six or seven black birds, with a white spot between the shoulders were hovering and crying. Waterton waited, till the grasshopper was

near enough to secure without injury or trouble, when the object raised itself, and it proved to be the head of a large rattlesnake. If Waterton had attempted to attack or seize it, the serpent would have sprung at him; but he stood still, and it glided away, and when it had gone, the birds did the same. The spell, as it were, was broken; the rattle was no longer audible.

Raven.—Bartholomeus says: "And as divinours mene the raven hath a maner virtue of meanyng and tokenynge of divination. And therefore, among nations, the raven among foules was halowed to Apollo, as Mercius saythe." *De Propr. Rerum*, ed. 1536, fol. 168.

Macaulay tells us: "The truly philosophical manner in which the great Latin Poet has accounted for the joyful croakings of the raven species, upon a favourable chaunge of weather, will in my apprehension point out at the same time the true natural causes of that spirit of divination, with regard to storms of wind, rain, or snow, by which the sea-gull, tulmer, cormorant, heron, crow, plover, and other birds are actuated sometimes before the change comes on. Of inspired birds, ravens were accounted the most prophetical. Accordingly, in the language of that district (St. Kilda), to have the foresight of a raven, is to this day a proverbial expression, denoting a preternatural sagacity in predicting fortuitous events. In Greece and Italy, ravens were sacred to Apollo, the great patron of augurs, and were called companions and attendants of that God." *Hist. of St. Kilda*, 165, 174, 176.

Ross informs us that "by ravens both publick and private calamities and death have been portended. Jovianus Pontanus relates two terrible skirmishes between the ravens and the kites in the fields lying between Beneventum and Apicium, which prognosticated a great battle that was to be fought in those fields. Nicetas speaks of a skirmish between the crowes and ravens, presignifying the irruption of the Scythians into Thracia." He adds: "Private men have been forewarned of their death by ravens, I have not only heard and read, but have likewise observed divers times. A late example I have of a young gentleman, Mr. Draper, my intimate friend, who about five or six years ago (1646) being then in the flower of his age, had on a sudden one or two ravens in his chamber, which had been quarrelling upon the top of the chimney; these they apprehended as messengers of his death, and so they were; for he died shortly after. Cicero was forewarned by the noise and fluttering of ravens about him, that his end was near. He that employed a raven to be the feeder of Elias, may employ the same bird as a messenger of death to others. We read in histories of a crow in Trajan's time that in the Capitol spoke in Greek All things shall be well." *Arcana Microcosmi*, pp. 219-20 of appendix.

Pennant says that " a vulgar respect is paid to the raven, as being the bird appointed by heaven to feed the prophet Elijah, when he fled from the rage of Ahab." *Zoology*, i, 219. Spenser speaks of

"The hoarse night raven, trompe of doleful dreere."

In " Othello," we have :

"—O, it comes o'er my memory
As doth the raven o'er th' infected house,
Boding to all."

So again elsewhere :

" The raven rook'd her on the chimney's top,
And chattering pies in dismal discord sang."

And in the second part of " Antonio and Mellida," 1602 :

" Now croaks the toad, and night crowes screech aloud,
Fluttering 'bout casements of departing soules,
Now gapes the graves, and through their yawnes let loose
Imprison'd spirits to revisit earth."

Moresin includes the croaking of ravens among omens. Hall, in his "Characters," 1608, tells us that if the superstitious man hears the raven croak from the next roof, he at once makes his will.

Raw Head and Bloody Bones.

—Among the objects to terrify children in former times we must not forget "Raw Head and bloody Bones," who twice occurs in Butler's " Hudibras :"

" Turns meek and secret sneaking ones
To raw-heads fierce and bloody bones."
And again :
" Made children with your tones to run for't,
As bad as Bloody-bones or Lunsford."

This was the Colonel Lunsford who was attached to the Earl of Bedford's force during part of the Civil War.

Reapers, The.

A child's game performed by two circles of small school-children of both sexes, holding hands, and singing, and at a stage in the chant disengaging hands again, and dancing round. The amusement is followed on Friday afternoons at Barnes, and at the international Folk-Lore Conference at Mercers'

Hall, a selection from this village-school attended, and went through the sport. Some other of the games described in Mrs. Gomme's volume are also played at Barnes.

Relics.

—In the " Privy Purse Expenses of Henry VIII." under 1530-1, are two entries of sums paid " in reward " to persons who brought " relick water " to the King. It does not seem to be very intelligible what was meant by this. Hone, in his " Every-day Book," enumerates a list of relics in which occur : " A tear which our Lord shed over Lazarus ; it was preserved by an angel, who gave it in a phial to Mary Magdalene," and a " phial of the sweat of St. Michael, when he contended with Satan." But perhaps the water offered to Henry's acceptance was merely holy water, additionally consecrated by the immersion of certain relics in it. The first entry in the book of Expenses stands thus : " Itm the same daye (18 Aug. 1530,) to Roger for bringing a glasse of relike water fro Wyndesor to hampton-courte . . . . xii*d*.;" and on the 22nd of July, 1531, the Abbot of Westminster received 20*s*. for bringing relic water to the King at Chertsey.

A note in Nichols's Leicestershire informs us that " upon the dissolution of the monasteries at Leicester, a multitude of false miracles and superstitious relicks were detected. Amongst the rest, Our Ladies Girdle shewn in several places and her milk in eight ; the penknife of St. Thomas of Canterbury, and a piece of his shirt, much reverenced by big-bellied women."

Relic Sunday.

—The third Sunday after Midsummer day. Old letters occur dated on this anniversary. It was the occasion, when holy relics in the churches and other ecclesiastical institutions were exhibited for worship or public curiosity.

Remarriage.

—Under the Saxon and Longobardic laws, says Sir H. Ellis in his " Original Letters Illustrative of English History," 1825, the custom was equally enforced of a widow not marrying again till a year had elapsed from the death of her first husband. He adds : " The notice of a forfeiture of property on this account occurs once in the " Domes-day Survey." In a letter of Edward the IV. in 1477 to Dr. Leigh, his ambassador in Scotland, relating to the proposed Scotish intermarriages, the king says : " Forsomoch also as aftre the old usaiges of this our royaume noon estat ne person honnorable communeth of mariage within the yere of their doole, we therffor as yit can not convenientely speke in this matier." The following passage is from Braithwaite's " Boulster Lecture," 1640 : — " Marry another, before those flowers that stuck his corpse be withered."

The passage in Shakespear's *Hamlet* very powerfully bears on this matter:—

"*Hor.* My lord, I came to see your father's funeral.

Ham. I pray thee, do not mock me, fellow-student : I think it was to my mother's wedding.

Hor. Indeed, my lord, it follow'd hard upon.

Ham. Thrift, thrift, Horatio ! the funeral bak'd meats

Did coldly furnish forth the marriage tables."

—Act 1, sc. 2.

Remember the Grotto.—Parties of children still occasionally go about in September with an oyster-shell in their hands, and beg money of the passers-by for the construction of an imaginary grotto. See farther in *Hone* and *Chambers.* The custom is almost extinct.

Remora or **Echeneïs.** — Montaigne enters at some length into the belief of the ancients in the power of this fish to stay the progress of ships. "Many are of opinion," he says, "that in the great and last naval engagement that Antony lost to Augustus, his admiral galley was stayed in the middle of her course by the little fish the Latins call *Remora,* by reason of the property she has of staying all sorts of vessels, to which she fastens herself. And the Emperor Caligula, sailing with a great navy upon the coast of Romania, his galley alone was suddenly stayed by the same fish, which he caused to be taken, fastened as it was to the keel of his ship, very angry that such a little animal could resist at once the sea, the wind, and the force of all his oars, by being merely fastened by the beak to his galley (nor is it a shell-fish), and was, moreover, not without great reason astonished that, being brought to him in the long boat, it had no longer the strength it had in the water." *Essays,* ed. Hazlitt, 1902, ii, 303.

Sir Thomas Browne doubts whether the story of the remora that it stays ships under sail be not unreasonably amplified. But Ross cites Scaliger as saying that this is as possible as for the loadstone to draw iron : for neither the resting of the one, nor moving of the other, proceeds from an apparent, but an occult virtue : for as in the one there is an hid principle of motion, so there is in the other a secret principle of quiescence. Browne's namesake, the pastoral poet, alludes to this strange legendary agent and power. Hazlitt's edit. ii, 306.

A correspondent of the *Penny Magazine* for August, 1840, narrates his personal observation of the habit of this creature, which he describes as the Sucking-fish, and is from four to five inches in length, firmly adhering to a shark, which had been caught, and instantly to the side of a bucket of water, when it had with considerable difficulty been detached from its first position.

Rent Dinner or **Supper.**—This is, generally speaking, an allowance made to each tenant in proportion to the amounts paid by him to his landlord. Three shillings is perhaps a minimum. In the accounts of the Court of Chancery, as much as £150 are somtimes charged for a single entertainment, and occasionally the items under the head of liquor are very extravagant.

Requiem.—Originally and usually a religious observance, but in a secondary sense or by poetical licence a secular tribute. The annual commemoration at Magdalen, Oxford, on May-Day morning was in its inception a requiem service for Henry VII. In North's "Forest of Varieties," 1645, at p. 80, is preserved the following Requiem at the entertainment of Lady Rich, who died August 24th, 1638 :

"Who 'ere you are, patron subordinate, Unto this House of Prayer, and doe extend

Your eare and care to what we pray and lend :

May this place stand for ever consecrate :

And may this ground and you propitious be

To this once powerful, now potential dust,

Concredited to your fraternal trust, Till friends, souls, bodies meet eternally.

And thou her tutelary angel, who Wer't happy guardian to so faire a charge,

O leave not now part of thy care at large,

But tender it as thou wer't wont to do.

Time, common father, join with mother-earth,

And though you all confound, and she convert,

Favour this relique of divine desert, Deposited for a ne're dying birth.

Saint, Church, Earth, Angel, Time, prove truly kind

As she to you, to this bequest consign'd."

Rex Fabarum at Merton College, Oxford.—See *Christmas Prince.*

Ribbands.—I know not whether the following passage is to be referred to this, or is given only as describing the bridegroom's awkwardness in supping broth.

Stephens, speaking of a plain country bridegroom, says: "Although he points out his bravery with ribbands, yet he hath no vaine glory; for he contemnes fine cloathes with dropping pottage in his bosome." *Essays*, 1615.

It is particularly stated by Lady Fanshawe in her account of the marriage of Charles II. and Catherine of Braganza, at which Sir Richard Fanshawe was a special guest, that the bride's ribbons were cut into pieces, and distributed among the company. See a good note in Pepys, ed. 1858, i, 12.

We see in another, under date of January 17, 1667-8, that at the marriage of Princess Anna of Prussia with Prince Frederic of Hesse the Ober-hofmeister distributed to the gentlemen present small pieces of ribband, on which the initials of the bride were embroidered, and the writer adds that this was a modified form of cutting up the bride's garter. "Formerly," he observes, "it was the custom for a Prussian Princess, immediately on leaving the company, to take her garter from her knee, and send it to the king, who tied one half of it round his own sword-knot, and sent the remainder as the most attractive present he could offer to a neighbouring and chivalrous monarch."

In the "Gentleman's Magazine" for October, 1733, are "Verses sent by a young lady, lately married, to a quondam lover, inclosing a green ribbon noozed:

"Dear D.
In Betty lost, consider what you lose,
And, for the bridal knot, accept this nooze;
The healing ribbon, dextrously apply'd,
Will make you bear the loss of such a bride."

Mr. Atkinson, in his "Cleveland Glossary," 1868, says, after describing the race to the bride-door for the ribbon, which usually, as he observes, went to the "winner's sweetheart:" "From a MS. I have been permitted to make use of, it appears that much or all of what is thus described is still 'practiced at St. Helen's, Auckland, and other villages in Durham, only the handkerchief (or ribbon) is supposed to be a delicate substitute for the bride's garter, which used to be taken off as she knelt at the altar.'"

It appears that the "Running for the Ribbon" still prevails, and Mr. Atkinson speaks of a tradition that the practice used to be to run from the gate of the church to the bride's house, and for the first to have the privilege not only of receiving the garter (before the ribbon or handkerchief was substituted), but of removing it with his own hands from the lady's leg.

This was sometimes, as it may be conceived, accomplished only by main force: and it is to be suspected indeed, that so coarse a usage was at all times very rare among the more educated classes. The same kind of contest is called in Westmoreland "Riding for the Ribbon." In "The Westmoreland Dialect," 1790, a country wedding is described with no little humour. The clergyman is represented as chiding the parties for not coming before him nine months sooner. The ceremony being over, we are told that "Awe raaid haam fearful wele, an the youngans raaid for th' ribband, me cusen Betty banged awth lads and gat it for sure."

In a Scotish ballad, called *Lady Mary Ann*, speaking of a young lad, it is said:

We'll sew a green ribbon round about
　　　his hat,
And that will let them ken he's to marry
　　　yet."

Mackay's *Ballads of Scotland*, 1861, p. 197. This seems to denote that a ribband was also an indication of the unmarried state. In former times lovers brought home from the fairs ribbands for their mistresses; but this gift would be rather to import an engagement. See *Fairings*. But from a passage from Pepys (Nov. 1, 1665) it is to be inferred that a ribband on the hat was usual on birthdays, as Lord Brouncker going with the Diarist and others to Mrs. Williams' lodgings, they all had a green ribband tied in their hats, it being my Lord's birthday. Comp. *May-day, Nuptial Usages, and Riding*.

Rice.—There is a common fallacy among sailors, that the regular use of rice as an article of food is conducive to blindness. This idea is said to proceed from the general use of rice by the Mahometans, and the prevalence among them of ophthalmia. The vulgar byename for rice on board ship is strike-me-blind.

Richard Cœur-de-Lion. — Gibbon, speaking of our Richard Plantagenet, Cœur de Lion, says: "the memory of this lion-hearted prince, at the distance of sixty years, was celebrated in proverbial sayings by the grandsons of the Turks and Saracens against whom he had fought: his tremendous name was employed by the Syrian mothers to silence their infants: and if a horse suddenly started from the way, his rider was wont to exclaim, Dost thou think King Richard is in that bush?" So in Richard Smith's *Life of Viscountess Montague*, 1627, we hear that *Talbot comes!* was an expression used long after the Anglo-Gallic wars, to terrify the French children, and still their cries. *Life of V. M.* trans. by C. F. 1627, sign. A 1 *verso*. The same is related of

Narses the Greek general and of others. Comp. *Barguest.*

A mass for the repose of the soul of Richard was formerly celebrated in Rouen Cathedral on the 6th of April, the anniversary of his death, in consideration of 300 measures or muids of wine left by him to the canons, and leviable on his estate at Rouen, as an indemnity for their losses through the French King. *Penny Magazine* for October, 1838.

Rich, Lady Diana.—See *Second Sight.*

Richard, St.—Aubrey, in his "Remains of Gentilism and Judaism," says: "This custome (the blessing of brine springs) is yearly observed at Droitwich in Worcestershire, where, on the day of St. Richard, (the patron or tutelar saint of that well, i.e. Salt Well) they keepe holyday, and dresse the well with green boughs and flowers. One yeare, sc[ilicet] a° [16]46, in the Presbyterian time, it was discontinued in the civil warres; and after that the springe shranke up, or dried up for some time; so afterwards they revived their annual custom, (notwithstanding the power of the parliament and soldiers), and the salt water returned again and still continues. This St. Richard was a person of great estate in these parts; and a briske young fellow that would ride over hedge and ditch, and at length became a very devout man, and after his decease was canonized for a saint. . . . The day of the solemnization of the feast and dressing this well is the ninth day after Whitsunday."

It is mentioned that the unexpected and miraculous recovery of a young child, over whom the wheel of a vehicle had passed in the street of Winterbourne Earls, near Salisbury, was ascribed at the time (A.D. 1278) to this canonized Bishop of Chichester. The person who drove over the boy is called a carter; but that term, like cart, was formerly understood in a wider and different sense. *Sussex Arch. Coll.* i, 1178.

Richmond.—Brand mentions that Douce had a curious print, entitled, "An exact Representation of the humorous Procession of the Richmond Wedding of Abram Kendrick and Mary Westurn 17. ." Two grenadiers go first, then the flag with a crown on it is carried after them: four men with handbells follow: then two men, one carrying a block-head, having a hat and wig on it, and a pair of horns, the other bearing a ladle: the pipe and tabor, hautboy, and fiddle: then the bridegroom in a chair, and attendants with hollyhock flowers; and afterwards the bride with her attendants carrying also hollyhock flowers.

Bride maids and bride men close the procession.

Riding.—In the early part of the present century, the Riding for the Broose, a form of Winning the Kail, was still kept up in North Britain. The Glossary to Burns, 1787, describes *Broose* (a word which has the same meaning with "Kail,") to be "a race at country weddings, who shall first reach the bridegroom's house on returning from church." The meaning of words is every where most strangely corrupted. Broose was originally, I take it for granted, the name of the prize on the above occasion, and not of the race itself: for whoever first reaches the house to bring home the good news, wins the "Kail," i.e. a smoking prize of spice broth, which stands ready prepared to reward the victor in this singular kind of race. Malkin says: "Ill may it befal the traveller, who has the misfortune of meeting a Welsh wedding on the road. He would be inclined to suppose that he had fallen in with a company of lunatics escaped from their confinement. It is the custom of the whole party who are invited, both men and women, to ride full speed to the church-porch; and the person who arrives there first has some privilege or distinction at the marriage feast. To this important object all inferior considerations give way; whether the safety of his majesty's subjects, who are not going to be married, or their own, be incessantly endangered by boisterous, unskilful, and contentious jockeyship. The natives, who are acquainted with the custom, and warned against the cavalcade by its vociferous approach, turn aside at respectful distance: but the stranger will be fortunate if he escapes being overthrown by an onset, the occasion of which puts out of sight that urbanity so generally characteristic of the people." *Tour in S. Wales* (Glamorganshire), p. 67.

Macaulay says: "A custom formerly prevailed in this parish and neighbourhood, of Riding for the Bride-Cake, which took place when the bride was brought home to her new habitation. A pole was erected in front of the house, three or four yards high, with the cake stuck upon the top of it. On the instant that the bride set out from her old habitation, a company of young men started off on horseback; and he who was fortunate enough to reach the pole first, and knock down the cake with his stick, had the honour of receiving it from the hands of a damsel on the point of a wooden sword: and with this trophy he returned in triumph to meet the bride and her attendants, who, upon their arrival in the village, were met by a party, whose office it was to adorn their horses' heads with garlands, and to present the bride with a posy. The last ceremony of this sort that took place in the parish of Claybrook was between sixty and seventy years ago, and was witnessed by a person now living in the parish. Sometimes the Bride Cake was tried for by persons on foot, and then it was called, ' throwing the quintal,' which was performed with heavy bars of iron; thus affording a trial of muscular strength as well as of gallantry." This was written in 1791.

A respectable clergyman informed Brand, that riding in a narrow lane near Macclesfield in Cheshire, in the summer of 1799, he was suddenly overtaken (and indeed they had well nigh rode over him) by a nuptial party at full speed, who before they put up at an inn in the town, described several circles round the market-place, or rode, as it were, several rings. Comp. *Bodmin Riding*, and *Langholme*.

All these *Riding* customs seem to refer back to a period of intertribal life, when wives and other property were *lifted* from adjoining communities on the Sabine principle and were continued, as was so often the case, as a sport, when they had been superseded as a necessity.

Riding at the Ring.—In the "Statistical Account of Scotland," Parish of Dunkeld, Perthshire, we have an account of a diversion with this name. "To prevent that intemperance," the writer says, "to which social meetings in such situations are sometimes prone, they spend the evening in some public competition of dexterity or skill. Of these, Riding at the Ring (an amusement of antient and warlike origin,) is the chief. Two perpendicular posts are erected on this occasion, with a cross-beam, from which is suspended a small ring: the competitors are on horseback, each having a pointed rod in his hand; and he who, at full gallop, passing betwixt the posts, carries away the ring on his rod, gains the prize." vol. xx., p. 433. Comp. *Races*.

Rifling or **Raffling.**—It is thus mentioned (without being described) in a letter from the Common Serjeant of London to Sir W. Cecil, Sept. 4, 1569 : "—At my nowe comynge thither (to Westminster) Mr Staunton and others of th' inhabitants of the said cytie (of Westminster) gave me to understande that there was a great disorder in or near Long Acre, by reason of certain games that were proclaymed there to be exercised, wheare indede theare was none used but one onlie game, called riflinge, by which they said diverse persons weare spoyled and utterlie undon. Wherupon I comaunded Mr Cobbrande the highe constable of the saide cytie and lyberties (taking with hym suche number of petit constables and others as to his discression sholde seme mete, and sendinge before worde to the constable of Sᵗ Gyles in the feildes to mete hym theare) to goe thither, and not onlie to apprehende all persones that sholde be founde theare usinge the same game, but also them that kepte the same games . . . . . Wherupon the keper of the same games was broughte before me, but none of them that played theare : and yet one of my owne servants, whom I sent pryvylie thither for that purpose, did see that game of ryflinge in use there at that tyme." Lysons *Env. of London*, 1st. ed. ii, 55.

Rifling is mentioned in the *Nomenclator of Junius*, 1585. Comp. Halliwell in v. *Raffling* is from *raff*, a gathering of people, not necessarily at first in a contemptuous sense.

In the Brentford Accounts for the Whitsuntide Ale, 1624, among the sports, by which money was made, occurs *Rifling*, which produced £2.

Ring.—Misson, speaking of Hyde Park, " at the end of one of the suburbs of London," says : " Here the people of fashion take the diversion of the ring. In a pretty high place, which lies very open, they have surrounded a circumference of two or three hundred paces diameter with a sorry kind of ballustrade, or rather with poles placed upon stakes, but three foot from the ground ; and the coaches drive round and round this. When they have turn'd for some time round one way, they face about and turn t'other : so rowls the world."

Ringers.—At South Brent, Devonshire, the annual custom is still observed of calling on new bell-ringers to sign the Ringer's Book, and of electing a Lord Chief. *Daily Mail*, November 7, 1903. There seem to have been throughout the country Honorable Societies of Ringers, at whose obsequies special observances were appointed.

Rings. — Swinburne writes : " The first inventor of the ring, as is reported, was one Prometheus." But he adds : " The workman which made it was Tubal-Cain : and Tubal-Cain, by the counsel of our first parent Adam, (as my author tells me) gave it unto his son to this end, that therewith he should espouse a wife, like as Abraham delivered unto his servant bracelets and ear-rings of gold. The form of the ring being circular, that is round and without end, importeth thus much, that their mutual love and hearty affection should roundly flow from the one to the other as in a circle, and that continually and for ever." *Tr. on Spousals*, p. 207. He quotes Alberic de Rosa *Dict.* v. *Annulus*.

He adds: "I do observe, that in former ages it was not tolerated to single or married persons to wear rings, unless they were judges, doctors, or senators, or such like honourable persons: so that being destitute of such dignity, it was a note of vanity, lasciviousness, and pride, for them to presume to wear a ring, whereby we may collect how greatly they did honour and reverence the sacred estate of wedlock in times past, in permitting the parties affianced to be adorned with the honourable ornament of the ring."

In 1477 the newly married Margery Paston sends her absent husband a ring with the image of St. Margaret as a remembrance, till he returns. *Paston Letters*, iii, 215.

Some very interesting remarks and information on this subject occur in Beloe's *Aulus Gellius*, ii, 216-17. The class of ring set with an intaglio or cameo was formerly general. In a fine three-quarter portait of Shakespear, Œtatis Suœ 47. A° 1611, engraved from an original picture in 1846, he wears one with a small medallion on his thumb.

Rings, Betrothal.—The usage of lovers wearing on holidays the rings given to them by their mistresses, may seem to be partly borne out by Chaucer, although the reference occurs in a poem which was little more than a paraphrase of Boccaccio's Filostrato. In the second book of Troilus and Cressida the poet makes Troilus and Cressida exchange rings, "of wych," he adds, "I cannot telle no scripture;" that is, I cannot say what were the posies.

On the site of the battle of Wakefield, where Richard Duke of York fell in 1460, a gold ring was long afterward found, and passed into the hands of Ralph Thoresby. It had the motto: *Pour bon Amour*, with the effigies of the three saints, and was supposed to have belonged to the Duke.

In the *Merchant of Venice*, Nerissa gives Gratiano

"—a hoop of gold, a paltry ring . . .
whose posy was
For all the world, like cutler's poetry
Upon a knife, 'Love me, and leave me
    not'"

and Gratiano has given it away, just as it turns out presently, that Bassanio has done with that which he received from Portia.

In Davison's "Poetical Rapsody," 1602, occurs a beautiful sonnet, "Upon sending his mistresse a gold ring, with this poesie, *Pure and Endlesse.*" In the poem of "The Milkmaids," printed in "Wit Restor'd," 1658, the milkmaids are represented as wearing jet-rings, with posies—*Yours more then his owne.* Wood-

ward, in his Poems, 1730, has the following lines:

"*To Phœbe, presenting her with a ring,*
    "Accept, fair maid, this earnest of my
        love,
    Be this the type, let this my passion
        prove:
    Thus may our joy in endless circles run,
    Fresh as the light, and restless as the
        sun:
    Thus may our lives be one perpetual
        round,
    Nor care nor sorrow ever shall be
        found."

The rings presented by a mistress to her lover may be supposed to have been worn only on special occasions, for in *England's Helicon*, 1600, we have:

    "My songs they be of Cinthia's prayse
    I weare her rings on holly-days."

It was a prevailing superstition, that the holder of a ring, given by a lover to his mistress, or the reverse, could detect inconstancy by the loss of lustre in the stones. In the ballad of *Hynd Horn*, the lady presents the ring to Horn before his departure on a voyage:—

    "He's left the land, and he's gone to
        the sea,
    An he's stayed there seven years and
        a day.
    Seven lang years he has been on the sea,
    And Hynd Horn has looked how his ring
        maybe.
    But when he looked this ring upon,
    The diamonds were both pale and
        wan—"

The hero returns home at once, only in time to save his sweetheart from marrying some one else.

In the old lace-making days in Buckinghamshire it was not unusual for lads to give their mistresses a set of bobbins attached to a button from their dress, instead of an engagement-ring.

It clearly appears from the Paston Letter that it was a custom for a third party to be entrusted with the betrothal or engagement ring, and to carry it about his person, waiting in succession on certain ladies selected beforehand; this was, where the alliance was almost purely a matter of business or expediency. And we learn from the same source, that an engagement once contracted could not be dissolved without a papal dispensation, which was extremely troublesome and costly. The Italian proctor mentioned in the case of Sir John Paston about 1473, that the expenses would be 1000 ducats, which was taken to mean 100 or at most 200. A friend, writing to Paston, informed him that this kind of transaction was of almost daily occurrence at Rome—

"Papa hoc facit hodiernis diebus multo-ciens." *P. L. ed.* Gairdner, iii, 101.

Rings, Cramp and other Physical.—At Coventry in 1802 and at Hackney in 1894 were found gold inscribed rings intended to protect the wearers against cramp and other diseases. In that dug up at Hackney, besides the Latin motto allusive to the Five Wounds of Christ, were figures of the Crucifixion, Virgin and child, &c. *Antiquary* for November, 1894. Comp. *Cramp-Rings* suprâ.

In Cartwright's Ordinary, apparently written in 1634, the Antiquary betrothes the widow Potluck with his biggest cramp-ring. The following extract of a letter from Sir Christopher Hatton to Sir Thomas Smith, dated Sept. 11, 158—, was read before the Society of Antiquaries by Dr. Morell on the 12th of November, 1772: "I am likewise bold to recommend my most humble duty to our dear Mistress (Queen Elizabeth) by this letter and ring, which hath the virtue to expell infectious airs, and is (as it telleth me) to be worn betwixt the sweet duggs, the chaste nest of pure constancy. I trust, sir, when the virtue is known, it shall not be refused for the value." *Minute Book of the Soc. of Antiq.*, Nov. 12, 1772. The letter, which was copied from one of the Harl. MSS., relates to an epidemical disorder, at that time very alarming. "Mr. Wright presented an engraving from a sardonyx, which formerly belonged to the Monastery of St. Alban's: the use of it, we are told, was to procure early births to labouring women, by being laid, in the time of travail, *inter mammas.*"—*Ibid.* March 11, 1773.

Rings, Enchanted or **Magical.**—See Wright's *Domestic Manners*, 1862, p. 268-9. These are features in European as well as Oriental fiction, the idea having perhaps originated in the East.

Rings, Funeral. — See *Funeral Customs.* It may here be added that under his will, 1637, Sir Henry Wotton, Provost of Eton, left to each fellow of the College a plain gold ring enamelled black, except the verge, with this motto within: *Amor unit omnia. Reliquiæ Wottonianæ*, 1672, e 3.

Rings, Garter or George.—Gold rings, sometimes made garter-wise, and with the same motto as belongs to the order, and presented by a new knight to his relations. These objects are occasionally found with the figure of a knight or horseman slaying a dragon, but whether St. George or St. Michael, is doubtful. *Reliquiæ Hearnianæ*, ed. 1869, i, 172.

Rings, Gimmal.—A joint ring (Lat. *Gemellus*) anciently a common token among betrothed lovers, and such rings

we find from existing specimens to have been in use among the Jews. *Miscellanea Graphica*, 1857, Plate x; *Archæologia*, xiv, 7; Nares, 1859, in v. The following remarkable passage is to be found in Greene's "*Menaphon*, 1589," sign. k 4 b: "'Twas a good world when such simplicitie was used, sayes the olde women of our time, when a ring of a rush would tye as much love together as a gimmon of gold."

In the play of *Lingua*, 1607, ii, 4, Anamnestes (Memory's page) is described as having, amongst other things, "a gimmal ring, *with one link hanging.*" Herrick mentions this as a love token. Morgan in his *Sphere of Gentry*, 1661, mentions three triple gimbal rings as borne by a family of the name of Hawberke, in the county of Leicester. In Dryden's "Don Sebastian," 1690, one of these rings is worn by Sebastian's father: the other by Almeyda's mother, as pledges of love. Sebastian pulls off his, which has been put on his finger by his dying father: Almeyda does the same with hers, which had been given her by her mother at parting: and Alvarez unscrews both the rings, and fits one half to the other.

Rings or **Pieces, Sacrament.**—In Berkshire there is a popular superstition that a ring made from a piece of silver collected at the communion, is a cure for convulsions and fits of every kind. It should seem that that collected on Easter Sunday is peculiarly efficacious. *Gents. Mag.*, for May and July, 1794. It is recorded that that silver ring will cure fits, which is made of five sixpences, collected from five different bachelors, to be conveyed by the hand of a bachelor to a smith that is a bachelor. None of the persons who gave the sixpences are to know for what purpose, or to whom, they gave them. A similar superstition is still, or was at least very recently, entertained (with trifling differences in the particulars) in Yorkshire, Gloucestershire, and East Anglia. In the former, thirty pennies collected from thirty different people, who were to be kept in ignorance of the object for which the money was asked, are exchanged for a half-crown of sacrament-money, and out of the latter is made a ring, which the patient wears till he is cured. The Gloucestershire belief is almost identical, and an instance has been known in which a man has worn this ring for three or four years in perfect reliance on its ultimate virtue, and has at last died with it on his fifth finger. In Cleveland, co. York, this is called the sacrament-piece, and Mr. Atkinson speaks of the thirty penny-pieces being drilled, and a ribbon passed through them, so as to form a kind of necklace, which is worn by the patient or believer as a charm against epilepsy. The necklace here was supposed to have the same property as the ring before described.

One may trace the same crafty motive for this superstition, as in the money given upon touching for the king's evil. It is stated that in Devonshire there is a similar custom: the materials, however, are different; the ring must be made of three nails, or screws which have been used to fasten a coffin, and must be dug out of the churchyard." *Gents. Mag.* 1794, p. 889.

Rings, Rush.—A custom extremely hurtful to the interests of morality appears anciently to have prevailed both in England and other countries, of marrying with a rush ring; chiefly practised, however, by designing men, for the purpose of debauching their mistresses, who sometimes were so infatuated as to believe that this mock ceremony was a real marriage. This abuse was strictly prohibited by the Constitutions of Richard, Bishop of Salisbury, in 1217. It seems, however, that this description of rings was in a manner countenanced by the authorities in civil contracts in France, where the contracting parties had been imprudent, and it was thought desirable to cover the shame of the families concerned. Douce refers Shakespear's expression. "Tib's rush for Tom's forefinger," which has so long puzzled the commentators, to this custom. In Quarles' "Shepheards Oracles," 1646, p. 63, is the following passage:

"The musick of the oaten reeds perswades
Their hearts to mirth—
And whilst they sport and dance, the love-sick swains
Compose rush-rings and myrtleberry chains,
And stuck with glorious king-cups and their bonnets
Adorn'd with lawrell-slips, chaunt their love-sonnets,
To stir the fires and to encrease the flames.
In the cold hearts of their beloved dames."

Comp. *Troth-Plight.*

Rings, Serjeants'.—It used to be customary for the serjeants-at-law, upon creation, to present to the judges a ring, with a posy or motto. The late Mr. Commissioner Fonblanque was present, when the subject of the posy for one of these rings happened to be in discussion, and was asked, what was his opinion of *To Wit?* "Yes," he playfully and wittily replied, "that would do very well:—but you should turn it into Latin—*Scilicet!*"

Prynne, by his will made in 1669, bequeathed, among other things, to his dear sister, Katherine Clerke, his "best serjeant's ring." "Wills from Doctors' Commons," 1863, p. 125.

Rings, Sheriffs'.—At Chester, out of certain charitable funds, it was a former practice to present the mayor with 40/- and the sheriff with 30/-. for the purchase of rings; but subsequently this grant was discontinued, and the ring for the sheriff was then provided by private subscription. *Antiquary*, February, 1897.

Rings, Signet.—The signet-ring was often employed as a medium of communication and a token, where the owner desired to transmit verbal instructions of important bearing by a messenger.

The authority of Joseph was symbolized by the one, which Thothmes IV. called Pharaoh took from his own finger, and placed on that of the son of Jacob; and these ornaments and emblems, fifteen hundred years prior to the birth of Christ, are found with the Cross as part of the legend.

When Cranmer leaves Henry VIII. to go before the Council, the King delivers to the prelate his ring as a protection, and, again, John Penri the chief mover in the Martin Marprelate business obtains access to Sir Richard Knightley's house at Fawsley as the bearer of Sir Richard's ring. Arber's *Introd. to Martin Marprelate Controversy*, 1879, 127; Hazlitt's *Shakespear's Library*, Part 1, vol. iv, p. 109; Idem, *Popular Poetry of Scotland*, 1895, ii, 104. In his *Domestic Manners and Sentiments in England during the Middle Ages*, 1862, pp. 266-8, Mr. Wright introduces several interesting particulars and illustrations of this subject.

Rings, Wedding.—Among the customs used at marriages, those of the ring and bride-cake seem of the most remote antiquity. Confarreation and the ring were used anciently as binding ceremonies by the heathens, in making agreements, grants, &c. whence they have doubtless been derived to the most solemn of our engagements. Columbiere, speaking of rings, says: "The hieroglyphic of the ring is very various. Some of the antients made it to denote servitude, alledging that the bridegroom was to give it to his bride, to denote to her that she is to be subject to him, which Pythagoras seemed to confirm, when he prohibited wearing a streight ring, that is, not to submit to over-rigid servitude." It appears from Aulus Gellius, that the ancient Greeks and most of the Romans wore the ring "in eo digito qui est in manu sinistra minimo proximus." He adds, on the authority of Appian, that a small nerve runs from this finger to the heart; and that therefore it was honoured with the office of bearing the ring, on account of its connexion with that master mover of the vital functions. *Noctes,* x, 10. Macrobius assigns the same reason, but also quotes the opinion of Ateius Capito, that the right hand was exempt from this office, because it was much more used than the left, and therefore the precious stones of the rings were liable to be broken : and that the finger of the left hand was selected, which was the least used. "Saturnal." lib. vii. c. 13. For the ring having been used by the Romans at their marriages, consult Juvenal, Sat. vi. v. 27.

Lemnius tells us, speaking of the ring-finger that "a small branch of the arterie, and not of the nerves, as Gellius thought, is stretched forth from the heart unto this finger, the motion whereof you shall perceive evidently in women with child and wearied in travel, and all effects of the heart, by the touch of your fore finger. I use to raise such as are fallen in a swoon by pinching this joynt, and by rubbing the ring of gold with a little saffron, for by this a restoring force that is in it, passeth to the heart, and refresheth the fountain of life, unto which this finger is join'd : wherefore it deserved that honour above the rest, and antiquity thought fit to compasse it about with gold. Also the worth of this finger that it receives from the heart, procured thus much, that the old physitians, from whence also it hath the name of *medicus,* would mingle their medicaments and potions with this finger, for no vemon can stick upon the very outmost part of it, but it will offend a man, and communicate itself to his heart."

The supposed heathen origin of our marriage ring had well nigh caused the abolition of it, during the time of the Commonwealth. In the Hereford, York, and Salisbury missals, the ring is directed to be put first upon the thumb, afterwards upon the second, then on the third, and lastly on the fourth finger, where it is to remain, "quia in illo digito est quedam vena procedens usque ad Cor"—an opinion exploded by modern anatomy. It is very observable that none of the above missals mentions the hand, whether right or left, upon which the ring is to be put. This has been noticed by Selden in his "Uxor Hebraica."

The "Hereford Missal" inquires: "Quæro quæ est ratio ista, quare Annulus ponatur in quarto digito cum pollice computato, quam in secundo vel tercio? Isidorus dicit quod quædam vena extendit se a digito illo usque ad Cor, et dat intelligere unitatem et perfectionem Amoris." The same rubric occurs in the "Sarum Missal :"—"ibique (sponsus) dimittat annulum, quia in medico est quædam vena procedens usque ad cor—" But the "Sarum Missal" lays down with

unmistakable precision the mode in which the husband shall take the ring from the minister—with the three first fingers of the right hand, and while he repeats after the minister, "With this ring I thee wed," &c. he is directed to hold his wife's right hand in his own left (manu sua sinistra tenens dexteram sponsœ). This may rather favour the notion that the ring was placed on the woman's *left* hand. Comp. Halliwell's *Archaic Dictionary,* 1860, in v.

The "British Apollo" affords, at all events, an utilitarian argument in favour of the fourth finger of the left hand. It says : "There is nothing more in this, than that the custom was handed down to the present age from the practice of our ancestors, who found the left hand more convenient for such ornaments than the right, in that it's ever less employed, for the same reason they choose the fourth finger, which is not less used than either of the rest, but is more capable of preserving a ring from bruises, having this one quality peculiar to itself, that it cannot be extended but in company with some other finger, whereas the rest may be singly stretched to their full length and streightness."

Of the popish hallowing of this ring the following form occurs in "The Doctrine of the Masse Booke," 1554. "The halowing of the womans ring at wedding. 'Thou Maker and Conserver of mankinde, gever of spiritual grace and graunter of eternal salvation, Lord, send thy ✠ blessing upon this ring,' (Here the Protestant translator observes in the margin, 'Is not here wise geare?') that she which shall weare it, maye be armed wyth the vertue of heavenly defence, and that it maye profit her to eternall salvation. thorowe Christ, &c.

'A Prayer.

✠'Halow thou Lord this ring which we blesse in thy holye name : that what woman soever shall weare it, may stand fast in thy peace, and continue in thy wyl, and live and grow and waxe old in thy love, and be multiplied into that length of daies, thorow our Lord, &c.' 'Then let holy water be sprinkled upon the ryng.'"

There seems to be no proof that in our ancient ceremony at marriages the man received as well as gave the ring : nor do I think the custom at all exemplified by the quotation from Lupton's first book of "Notable Things." The expression is equivocal, and "his maryage ring," I should think, means no more than the ring used at his marriage, that which he gave and which his wife received : at least we are not warranted to interpret it at present any otherwise, till some passage can actually be adduced from the ancient manuscript rituals to evince that there ever did at marriages take place such "Interchangement of rings," a custom which however certainly formed one of the most prominent features of the ancient betrothing ceremony. Yet concession must be made that the bridegroom appears to have had a ring given him as well as the bride in the Diocese of Bordeaux in France.

I observe in the will of Anne Barett, of Bury St. Edmunds, made in 1504, a curious provision, by which the testatrix bequeathed to Our Lady of Walsingham, her "corall bedys of thrys fyfty, and my maryeng ryng, w^h all thyngys hangyng theron." I do not understand this allusion thoroughly; but I suppose that it may have some reference to charms at that time worn suspended from the wedding-ring. *Bury Wills and Inventories,* 1850, p. 95. In the will of William Lenthall, the celebrated Speaker of the House of Commons, made in 1662, the testator desires that his son will wear his mother's wedding-ring about his arm, in remembrance of her. I presume he meant, tied to the arm by a ribbon. *Wills from Doctors' Commons,* 1863, p. 18.

Lady Fanshawe, in her *Memoirs,* mentions that she was married with her mother's wedding-ring, which her father gave her for the purpose. Her words are: "None was at our wedding but my dear father, who, at my mother's desire, gave me her wedding-ring, with which I was married . . ."

The loss of the wedding-ring was considered an evil portent even in the time of Charles I. In the "Autobiography of Sir John Bramston," under the date of 1631, where he describes the voyage over from Dublin to Holyhead, with his father and new step-mother, there is an account of the latter dropping her wedding-ring into the sea, near the shore, as they were riding on horseback along the beach. The writer says : "As shee (his step-mother) rode over the sands behind me, and pulling off her glove, her wedding-ringe fell off, and sunck instantly. She caused her man to alight ; she sate still behind me, and kept her eye on the place. Directed her man, but he not guessing well, she leaped off, saying she would not stirr without her ringe, it beinge the most vnfortunate thinge that could befall any one to loose the weddinge ringe." The ring was at last, after great search and trouble, recovered.

Many married women are so rigid, not to say superstitious, in their notions concerning their wedding rings, that neither when they wash their hands, nor at any other time, will they take it off from their finger, extending, it should seem, the expression of "till death us do part" even to this golden circlet, the token and pledge of matrimony. This feeling still remains very prevalent among all classes. There is an old proverb on the subject of wedding rings, which has no doubt been many a time quoted for the purpose of encouraging and hastening the consent of a diffident or timorous mistress :

"As your wedding-ring wears,
You'll wear off your cares."

Rings appear to have been given away formerly at weddings. In Wood's "Athenæ," we read in the account of the famous philosopher of Queen Elizabeth's days, Edward Kelley, "Kelley, who was openly profuse beyond the modest limits of a sober philosopher, did give away in gold-wire rings, (or rings twisted with three gold-wires,) at the marriage of one of his maid-servants, to the value of 4000*l*." This was in 1589 at Trebona.

Not only is the religious service supererogatory, but the ring is not essential, and forms no part of the ceremony under the Act 6 & 7 Will. IV. cap. 85. The sole original object of the ring was a confirmation of betrothal. A registrar may not sanction the use of the ring : this is expressly laid down in 19 & 20 Vict. c. 119. A bridegroom in Herefordshire produced on one occasion the symbol, and was requested to put it back into his pocket, as it was a mere graft on the service in the Church.

Ripon.—In commemoration of the return of St. Wilfred, patron-saint of Ripon, from Rome to Ripon in the seventh century, an annual procession round the city, preceded by the Royal Volunteer Band, takes place on the 29th July. The central figure is an effigy of the saint arrayed in his pontificals and carrying in his hand a crozier. On the Sunday the Mayor and Corporation attend divine service in their robes of office at the cathedral. *Antiquary,* 1882, p. 129. *Riponiensis* in the *Gentleman's Magazine* for 1790, says : "I think the day before *Holy Thursday* all the clergy, attended by the singing men and boys of the choir, perambulate the town in their canonicals, singing Hymns : and the Blue-Coat Charity boys follow, singing, with green boughs in their hands."

On Christmas Eve, the grocers used in 1790 to send each of their customers a pound, or half a pound, of currants and raisins to make a Christmas pudding, the chandlers, large mold candles and the coopers logs of wood, generally called Yule clogs, which were always used on this anniversary : but should the log be so large as not to be all burned that night, the remains are kept till Old Christmas Eve. *Gentl. Mag.* vol. lx. p. 719.

On Christmas Day, the singing boys came into the collegiate church with large baskets full of red apples, with a sprig of rosemary stuck in each, which they presented to all the congregation, and generally had a return made them of 2*d.* 4*d.* or 6*d.* according to the quality of the lady or gentlman.

At nine o'clock every evening, a man used to blow a large horn at the market cross and then at the mayor's door.

The Sunday before Candlemas Day, the collegiate church used to be one continued blaze of light all the afternoon by an immense number of candles. Some years ago no traveller could pass the town on Easter Day without being stopped, and having his spurs taken away, unless redeemed by a little money, which was the only way to have your buckles returned. On the eve of All Saints, the good women made a cake for every one in the family: so this was generally called Cake Night.

Robin Goodfellow. — In Mr. Wright's paper "On Friar Rush and the Frolicsome Elves," inserted among his collected Essays, 1846, he has noticed a trace of our Robin in a MS. of the thirteenth century. There is a story there given, which shews that he was known to our forefathers as early as the reign of Richard Lion-Heart, perhaps, and was then understood to possess the characteristics with which Shakespear and Jonson invested him three centuries later.

Gervase of Tilbury describes two spirits, of whom one had attributes not unsimilar, according to him, to those of Robin Goodfellow. They were called, he tells us, Portuni and Grant. The Portuni were of diminutive proportions, but "senili vulta, facie corrugatâ." He goes on to say: "If any thing should be to be carried on in the house, or any kind of laborious work to be done, they join themselves to the work, and expedite it with more than human facility. It is natural to these that they may be obsequious, and may not be hurtful. But one little mode, as it were, they have of hurting: for when, among the ambiguous shades of night, the English occasionally ride alone, the portune sometimes gets up behind him unseen; and when he has accompanied him, going on a very long time, at length, the bridle being seized, he leads him up to the hand in the mud, in which, while infixed, he wallows, the portune, departing, sets up a laugh; and so, in this way, derides human simplicity."

Robin Goodfellow, alias Pucke, alias Hobgoblin, says Percy, in the creed of ancient superstition was a kind of merry sprite whose character and achievements are recorded in the ballad, commencing

"From Oberon, in fairy land—"

which is printed at length in the present writer's *Fairy Tales,* &c. 1875, and is usually ascribed to Jonson's pen. There were several printed editions of it as a broadside; but Mr. Collier had an early MS. copy, in which Jonson's initials are appended. This may be regarded as a certain, but not as a conclusive, proof of his authorship. The earliest allusion to him by name which has occurred to me is in one of the Paston Papers under the date of 1489, where the Northern Rebels' proclamation is said to be "in the name of Mayster Hobbe Hyrste, Robyn Godfelaws brodyr he is, as I trow."

It was a proverbial saying, to judge from a passage in Harman's "Caveat for comen Cursetors," 1567, "Robin Goodfellow has been with you to-night," in allusion to a person who has been visited by some annoyance or misadventure. Reginald Scot gives an account of this frolicksome spirit: "Your grandames maids were wont to set a bowl of milk for him, for his pains in grinding malt and mustard, and sweeping the house at midnight—this white bread, and bread and milk, was his standing fee." *Discovery,* 1584, p. 66. In Rowlands' "More Knaves Yet," first printed before or in 1600, is the following passage of "Ghoasts and Goblins.":

"In old wives daies, that in old time
    did live
(To those odd tales much credit men
    did give)
Great store of goblins, fairies, bugs,
    night-mares,
Urchins, and elves, to many a house
    repaires.
Yea, far more sprites did haunt in divers
    places
Then there be women now weare devils
    faces.
Amongst the rest was a goodfellow devil
So cal'd in kindnes, cause he did no
    evill,
Knowne by the name of Robin (as we
    heare),
And that his eyes as broad as sawcers
    weare,
Who came by nights and would make
    kitchens cleane,
And in the bed bepinch a lazy queane.
Was much in mils about the grinding
    meal
(And sure I take it taught the miller
    steale):
Amongst the cream-bowles and milke-
    pans would be,
And with the country wenches, who
    but he

To wash their dishes for some fresh
 cheese-hire,
Or set their pots and kettles 'bout the
 fire.
'Twas a mad Robin that did divers
 pranckes,
For which with some good cheare they
 gave him thankes,
And that was all the kindness he expected,
With gaine (it seems) he was not much
 infected."

Harsnet thus speaks of him: "And if
that the bowle of curds and creame were
not duly set out for Robin Goodfellow, the
frier, and Sisle the dairy-maid, why then
either the pottage was burnt the next day
in the pot, or the cheeses would not curdle,
or the butter would not come, or the ale
in the fat never would have good head.
But, if a Peeter-penny, or an housle-egge
were behind, or a patch of tythe unpaid,
then 'ware of bull-beggars, sprites, &c."
*Declaration of Egregious Popish Impos-
tures,* 1603, ch. 20. He is mentioned by
Cartwright in the *Ordinary,* written about
1634, as a spirit particularly fond of dis-
concerting and disturbing domestic peace
and economy. Shakespear has also given
us a description of Robin Goodfellow, in
"A Midsummer-Nights Dream," 1600:

"Either I mistake your shape and
 making quite,
Or else you are that shrewd and knavish
 sprite,
Call'd Robin Good-fellow: are you
 not he,
That frights the maidens of the vil-
 lagery;
Skims milk; and sometimes labours in
 the quern,
And bootless makes the breathless housewife churn;
And sometimes makes the drink to bear
 no barm:
Misleads night-wanderers, laughing at
 their harm?
Those that hobgoblins call you, and
 sweet Puck,
You do their work, and they shall have
 good luck."

The *Merry Pranks,* 1628, declares:

"'Tis not your garments new or old
That Robin loves; I feele no cold.
Had you left me milke or creame,
You should have had a pleasing
 dreame."

In *Apothegmes of King James,* 1658,
p. 139, is a passage seeming to shew that
persons of the first distinction were anciently no strangers to the characters of
fairies. "Sir Fulk Greenvil had much
and private accesse to Queen Elizabeth,
which he used honourably, and did many
men good. Yet he would say merrily of
himself, that he was like Robin Good-

fellow, for when the maides spilt the milk-
pannes, or kept any racket, they would
lay it upon Robin, so what tales the ladies
about the Queen told her, or other bad
offices that they did, they would put it
upon him." Mr. Cooper, in a very interesting note to his "Sussex Vocabulary," 1853, observes, "A belief in the
freaks of Puck, Robin Goodfellow, and
their 'ryght merrie colleagues,' was
formerly very prevalent in Sussex, particularly on the Southdowns, where the
hag-tracks or pharirings were considered
positive proofs of their existence." Mr.
Blencoe, quoted by the same writer, adduces, in proof of the deep root of this
superstition, the numerous forms which
bear names connected with Puck, such as
Pookyde, Pookbourne, Pook-hole, Pook-
croft; but I regard this etymology as very
questionable. The French *Gobelin,* from
which we get our goblin, possesses many of
the attributes of Robin, and may be considered as his counterpart in France.

Robin Hood.—The romantic legend
about Maid Marian and Robin Hood
having been of noble birth, she daughter
of Lord Fitzwater, and he Earl of Huntingdon, is no longer credited, nor is it
probably of any great antiquity. Hazlitt's
Tales and Legends, 1892, p. 241 *et seqq.,*
where will be found an Essay on the
subject written on new lines, and em-
bodying the latest information. Latimer,
in his sixth sermon before Edward the
Sixth, mentions Robin Hood's Day, kept
by country people in memory of him, and
in a passage too well known to bear
quotation, tells us how he, the preacher,
"was fayne to giue place to Robin Hoodes
men." Machyn the Diarist says, 1559:
"The xxiiij day of June, ther was a May-
game . . . with a gyant and drumes
and gunes, and the ix wordes (worthies)
with spechys, and a goodly pagant with a
quen c . . . . and dyvers odur. with
spechys; and then sant Gorge and the
dragon, the mores dansse, and after Robyn
Hode and lytyll John, and M. Marian,
and frere Tuke, and they had spechys rond
a-bowt London."

In Coates's "History of Reading," p.
214, in the Churchwardens' Accounts of
St. Lawrence Parish, under 1499, is the
following article: "It. rec. of the gaderyng
of Robyn-hod. xixs." In similar Accounts
for St. Helen's, Abingdon, under 1566, we
find eighteen pence charged for setting up
Robin Hood's bower. Brathwaite, in his
"Strappado for the Divell," 1615, says:

——"As for his blond,
He says he can deriv't from Robin Hood
And his May-Marian, and I thinke he
 may,
For's mother plaid May-Marian t'other
 day."

In Dalrymple's Extracts from the "Book of the Universal Kirk," 1576, Robin Hood is styled King of May. We read, in Skene's "Regiam Majestatem," 1609 : "Gif anie provest, baillie, counsell, or communitie, chuse Robert Hude, litell John, Abbat of Unreason, Queens of Maii, the chusers sall tyne their friedome for five yeares ; and sall bee punished at the King's will : and the accepter of sic ane office, salbe banished furth of the realme." And under " pecuniall crimes,"—" all persons, quha a landwort, or within burgh, chuses Robert Hude, sall pay ten pounds, and sall be warded induring the Kings pleasure." Comp. *Maid Marian, May Games,* &c.

Robin Redbreast.—The " Guardian," No. 61, speaking of the common notion that it is ominous or unlucky to destroy some sorts of birds, as swallows and martins, observes that this opinion might possibly rise from the confidence these birds seem to put in us by building under our roofs ; so that it is a kind of violation of the laws of hospitality to murder them. Of the robin redbreast it is commonly said, that if he finds the dead body of any rational creature, he will cover the face at least, if not the whole body, with moss. An allusion probably to the old ballad of the *Cruel Uncle* or the *Babes in the Wood.* Shakespear (*Cymbeline,* iv, 4.) embodies this notion in the lines :

" The ruddock would
With charitable bill, (O bill fore shaming
Those rich-left heirs that let their
    fathers lie
Without a monument !) bring thee all
    this :
Yea, and furr'd moss besides, when
    flowers are none
To winter-ground thy corse."

Again, in the song from Webster's "White Divel," 1612 :

" Call for the robin redbreast and the
    wren,
Since o'er shady groves they hover,
And with leaves and flow'rs do cover
The friendless bodies of unburied men."

The office of covering the dead is likewise ascribed to the ruddock or robin by Drayton in " The Owl," 1604 :

" Cov'ring with moss the dead's un-
    closed eye,
The little red-breast teaches charitie."

Antony Stafford in his *Niobe,* 1611, describes him as sitting like a coroner on a murdered man in his red livery, and " playing the sorry tailor to make him a mossy raiment." Herrick has a picturesque passage, where he speaks of the robin coming to cover the motionless body

of Amaryllis ; and in another of those delightful small Anacreontic epigrams, with which his book abounds, the same author invites the bird to become his sexton, when he is no more. In the " West Country Damosel's Complaint," a ballad of the time of Charles or James I., the lover says, in allusion to his dead mistress :

" Come, come you gentle red-breast now,
And prepare for us a tomb,
Whilst unto cruel Death I bow,
And sing like a swan my doom."

Thomson, in his " Winter," mentions the familiarity of this bird. Pope would have us believe that, in his time, the respect for robin redbreast was on the decline ; but it is scarcely probable that it was so. Thomas Park the antiquary noticed that in some districts it was considered unlucky to keep, as well as to kill, a robin. The latter idea only is alluded to in the proverbs :

" The robin and the wren
Are God Almighty's cock and hen,"

and

" He that hurts robin or wren,
Will never prosper, boy nor man."

Now-a-days, the robin is more familiarly known to children, perhaps, by the nursery ballad of " Cock Robin." It is said of the young birds, when they are just fledged in the spring, that they have left off their red waistcoats, not having yet got the red breast, by which they are distinguished in winter.

Roc, The.—A huge and almost prehistoric bird, mentioned in the *Arabian Nights,* as something or somebody connected with the genie, who waited on Aladdin's wonderful lamp. No perfect specimen even of the egg is said to have been found, till a fossil one was washed ashore on the coast of Madagascar after a violent storm in 1893. The following is taken from the *Globe* newspaper :—Some months ago there was a sudden and violent storm along the coast of Madagascar. For a couple of days the big waves of the Mozambique Channel swept the sandy shores of the great African island, and then they subsided as suddenly as they had arisen, and the morning that followed was all that a sub-tropical morning could be, with a sea like burnished glass and not enough wind on the rippling waters to wreck a cockle-shell. Taking advantage of the calm, some beachmen put off in their fishing skiffs, and whether they had good or bad sport as far as the fish were concerned, the story does not relate : but one thing they found which never before came to any fisherman's basket. They were busy with their boats and lines when one of them saw something round and white shining in the sun in the distance, just as Sinbad saw an identical object from the palm tree in the desert island, where his comrades had deserted him. They rowed up to it, and there floating on the water was a great ivory sphere as big as a small barrel, the only perfect egg of the long extinct roc in the world! It had undoubtedly been washed out of the sand banks by the previous storm, and the scientific ornithological mind trembles to think what might have happened as that splendid dripping egg-shell from the mythical past was hauled into the little skiff and set rolling about on the bottom with no appreciation of its value among the splashing crimson mullet and brown sea-cod of a degenerate age. But fate was kind to learning on that soft African morning. The Hovas were neither too hasty, too hungry, nor too curious. They did not row ashore and spread the bread and butter of expectation while the great egg slowly roasted on a sacrilegious sea-weed fire: they did not even crack it with a handy thwart to see how far incubation had proceeded during a few thousand years with the embryo Prince of Djins inside, but they carried the awkward trophy of unknown origin back to their huts for which civilization owes them deathless thanks, and there it remained until a lucky traveller hit upon the trophy and secured it for the wonder of a sceptical and over prosaic modern world.

If we conclude, as undoubtedly we may, that the egg came from some old beach destroyed by the waves, then it is not difficult to imagine how it got there. We even get a little help from authentic history, for on very old Portuguese maps the ocean to the south of Madagascar is marked as " Psittacorum regio "—the region of giant birds, and Marco Polo, who was more accurate, we may perhaps be pardoned for saying, than some other recent travellers who have followed in his footsteps, declares " the island Magaster," is the spot where " Rukhs " are found, but he adds suggestively that it was not their proper home, for they only " made their appearance there at a certain season from the south." Putting these passages side by side, it is just possible for us to imagine a distant post-glacial spring, some little time before Tamatave was built, no doubt, and when Antananarivo was still leafy jungle, then as the African April dawned on the great island and the green rice-grass began to make impenetrable breast-high wildernesses of the sandy flats along the sea-shore we can perhaps vaguely picture the breeding rocs arriving at their nesting grounds—vast overpowering birds " with the bodies of cart-horses and the wings of dragons." Madagascar must

have been a truly interesting country when those stupendous flights were darkening the southern sky, and to the speculative naturalist—provided he could have got a safe point of observation, we can hardly imagine anything more fascinating than to have been able to watch the love gambols of these huge birds and the Titan combats of the males !

Temple, in his *Modern Peru*, shot a condor, which measured 40 feet outside the spread wings, and it was suggested that this might be the *roc* of antiquity and of the Aladdin story. The creature is not often mentioned in our early writers : but Sir John Suckling, in his *Cantilena Politica-Jocunda*, expresses a wish that he could obtain one to present to the young French king, and speaks of it as delineated on the map :

> "O, that I e'er might have the hap
> To get the bird within the map
> 'Tis called the Indian Roc !
> I'd give it him, and look to be
> As great as wise as Luisne,"
> Or else I had hard luck."

—Works, by Hazlitt, 1892, i, 81.

Roch's or Roche's, St., Day.

—(August 16.) Whitaker thinks that St. Roche or Rocke's Day was celebrated as a general harvest home.

Among the Churchwardens' Accounts of St. Michael Spurrier-Gate, York, printed by Nichols, 1797, I find : " 1518. Paid for writing of St. Royke Masse, 0*l*. 0*s*. 9*d*." Pegge, by whom the extract was communicated to Nichols, thought that " the writing probably means making a new copy of the music appropriated to the day." In the " Conflict of Conscience," 1581, by N. Woodes, this saint is mentioned as the one to whom prayers should be offered up against disease, plague and pestilence.

In Overbury's "Character of the Franklin," he says : " He allowes of honest pastime, and thinkes not the bones of the dead any thing bruised, or the worse of it, though the country lasses dance in the church-yard after even-song. Rock Monday, and the wake in summer, shrovings, the wakefull ketches on Christmas eve, the hoky, or seed cake, these he yeerely keepes, yet holds them no reliques of popery." Warner, in his " Albions England," mentions Rock Monday :

> " Rock and Plow Monday gams sal gang
>   with saint feasts and kirk fights : "

And again :

> " I'le duly keepe for thy delight Rock-
>   Monday, and the wake,
> Have shrovings, Christmas gambols,
>   with the hokie and seed cake."

Rogation Days.

—By the Canons of Cuthbert, Archbishop of Canterbury,

made at Cloveshoo, in the year 747, it was ordered that litanies, that is, rogations, should be observed by the clergy and all the people, with great reverence, on the seventh of the calends of May, according to the rites of the Church of Rome, which terms this the greater Litany, and also, according to the customs of our forefathers, on the three days before the Ascension of our Lord, with fastings, &c.

The litanies or rogations then used gave the name of Rogation Week to this time. They occur as early as the 550th year of the Christian era, when they were first observed by Mamertius Bishop of Vienne, on account of the frequent earthquakes that happened, and the incursions of wild beasts, which laid in ruins and depopulated the city. Blount tells us that Rogation week (otherwise days of perambulation,) is always the next but one before Whitsuntide; and so called, because on Monday, Tuesday, and Wednesday of that week, rogations and litanies were used; and fasting, or, at least abstinence, then enjoined by the Church to all persons, not only for a devout preparative to the feast of Christ's glorious Ascension, and the descent of the Holy Ghost shortly after, but also to request and supplicate the blessing of God upon the fruits of the earth. And, in this respect, the solemnization of matrimony is forbidden, from the first day of the said week till Trinity Sunday. The Dutch call it *Cruys-week*, Cross-week, and it is so called in some parts of England, because of old, (as still among the Roman Catholicks,) when the priests went in procession this week, the cross was carried before them. In the Inns of Court, he adds, it is called Grass-week, because the commons of that week consist much of salads, hard eggs, and green sauce upon some of the days. The feasts of the old Romans, called Robigalia and Ambarvalia (quod victum arva ambiret) did in their way somewhat resemble these institutions, and were kept in May in honour of Robigus.

Rogation Week, in the Northern parts of England, is still called Gang Week, from *to gang*, which in the North signifies to go. The word also occurs in the rubric to John, c. 17, in the Saxon Gospels: and the custom is noticed in the Laws of Alfred, c. 16, and in those of Athelstan, c. 13. Ascension Day, emphatically termed Holy Thursday with us, is designated in the same manner by King Alfred. Gangdays are classed under certain "Idolatries maintained by the Church of England," in "The Cobler's Book." In one of the "Merie Tales of Skelton," perhaps the

work of Doctor Andrew Borde, and first composed about 1550, if not earlier, the writer rather curiously makes Skelton say to a cobler, "Neybour, you be a tall man, and in the kynges warres you must bere a standard: a standard, said the cobler, what a thing is that? Skelton saide, it is a great banner, such a one as thou doest use to beare in Rogacyon Weeke." Johnson the botanist speaking of the birch tree, says: "It serveth well to the decking up of houses and banquetting-rooms, for places of pleasure, and for beautifying of streets in the Crosse or Gang Week, and such like."

In Lysons' "Environs," vol. i. p. 309, amongst his extracts from the Churchwardens' Accounts of Lambeth, I find the following relative to our present subject:

	£	s.	d.
"1516. Paid for dyinge of buckram for the Lett'y cloathes .	0	0	8
—— For paynting the Lett'y cloathes	0	0	8
—— For lynynge of the Lett'y cloathes	0	0	4

probably for the processions in which they chanted the Litany on Rogation Day."

It appears from a homily inserted in the "Epistles and Gospelles," that the custom had, in Henry VIIIth's time, grown into considerable abuse. The preacher complains: "Alacke, for pitie! these solemne and accustomable processions and supplications be nowe growen into a right foule and detestable abuse, so that the moost parte of men and women do come forth rather to set out and shew themselves, and to passe the time with vayne and unprofitable tales and mery fables, than to make generall supplications and prayers to God, for theyr lackes and necessities. I wyll not speake of the rage and furour of these uplandish processions and gangynges about, which be spent in ryotyng and in belychere. Furthermore, the Banners and Badges of the Crosse be so unreverently handled and abused, that it is merveyle God destroye us not in one daye. In these Rogation Days, if it is to be asked of God, and prayed for, that God of his goodnes wyll defende and save the corne in the felde, and that he wyll vouchsave to pourge the ayer. For this cause be certaine Gospels red in the wide felde amonges the corne and grasse, that by the vertue and operation of Gods word, the power of the wicked spirites, which kepe in the air and infecte the same (whence come pestilences and the other kyndes of diseases and syknesses), may be layde downe, and the aier made pure and cleane, to th' intent the corne may remaine unharmed, and not infected of the sayd hurteful spirites, but serve us for our use and bodely sustenaunce."

In 1903, at Ufford in Suffolk, the blessing of the crops was observed with due religious solemnity.

By "Advertisements partly for due order in the publique Administration of Common Prayers, &c. the 25th day of January (7 Eliz.) signat. B 1. it was directed, 'that, in the Rogation Daies of Procession, they singe or saye in Englishe the two Psalms beginnyng ' Benedic Anima mea,' &c. withe the Letanye & suffrages thereunto, withe one homelye of thankesgevyng to God, alreadie devised and divided into foure partes, without addition of any superstitious ceremonyes heretofore used." To gadde in procession is among the customs censured by John Bale, in his "Declaration of Bonner's Articles," 1554, signat. D 3. It appears from Kethe's Sermon at Blandford Forum, 1570, p. 20. that in Rogation Week the Catholicks had their " Gospelles at superstitious crosses, deck'd like idols." Plott tells us that at Stanlake, in Oxfordshire, the minister of the parish, in his procession in Rogation Week, reads the Gospel at a barrel's head, in the cellar of the Chequer Inn, in that town, where some say there was formerly an hermitage, others that there was anciently a cross, at which they read a gospel in former times; over which the house, and particularly the cellar, being built, they are forced to continue the custom in manner as above.

In the "Tryall of a Mans owne selfe," by Thomas Newton, 1586, he inquires, under "Sinnes externall and outward," against the first commandment, whether the parish clergyman " have patiently winked at, and quietly suffered, any rites wherein hath been apparent superstition—as gadding and raunging about with procession." In a later authority we have: "Doth your minister or curate, in Rogation Dayes, go in perambulation about your parish, saying and using the Psalms and Suffrages by law appointed, as viz. Psalm 103 and 104, the Letany and Suffrages, together with the Homily, set out for that end and purpose? Doth he admonish the people to give thanks to God, if they see any likely hopes of plenty, and to call upon him for his mercy, if there be any fear of scarcity: and do you, the churchwardens, assist him in it?"— *Articles of Inquiry within the Archdeaconry of Middlesex*, 1662. In similar "Articles for the Archdeaconry of Northumberland," 1662, the following occurs : "Doth your parson or vicar observe the three Rogation Dayes?" In others for the Diocese of Chichester, 1637, is the subsequent: "Doth your minister yerely in Rogation Weeke, for the knowing and

distinguishing of the bounds of parishes, and for obtaining God's blessing upon the fruites of the ground, walke the perambulation, and say, or sing, in English the Gospells, Epistles, Letanie, and other devout prayers; together with the 103d and 104th Psalmes?"

"It was customary" says Hawkins ("Hist. of Music," vol. ii. p. 112) "at the commencement of the procession, to distribute to each a willow wand, and at the end thereof a handful of points, which were looked on by them as honorary rewards, long after they ceased to be useful, and were called tags."

At Leighton Buzzard, on Rogation Monday, agreeably to the will of Mr. Edward Wilkes, a London merchant who died in 1646, the trustees of his almshouses and other benefactions met in 1896, and, accompanied by the town-crier and a band of boys carrying green boughs, beat the boundaries. The will of the founder was read and beer and plum rolls were distributed. In the evening there was a dinner. A remarkable feature in the perambulation was, and is, that while the will is read, one of the boys has to stand on his head. *Antiquary*, xxxii, 163. Herrick sings:

"————————Dearest, bury me
Under that holy-oke, or gospel tree:
Where (though thou see'st not) thou
    may'st think upon
Me, when thou yeerly go'st procession."

Roncesvalles, Brotherhood of.—See *Plough Monday*.

Rood of Grace, The.—"The Rood," as Fuller ("Hist. of Waltham Abbey," pp. 17) observes, "when perfectly made, and with all the appurtenances thereof, had not only the image of our Saviour extended upon it, but the figures of the Virgin Mary and St. John, one on each side : in allusion to John xix. 26. 'Christ on the Cross saw his mother and the disciple whom he loved standing by.' "

Such was the representation denominated the Rood, usually placed over the screen which divided the nave from the chancel of our churches. To our ancestors, we are told, it conveyed a full type of the Christian Church. The nave representing the church militant, and the chancel the church triumphant, denoting that all who would go from the one to the other, must pass under the Rood, that is, carry the Cross, and suffer affliction.

Geffrey Chamber, one of Cromwell's visitors at the Reformation, found in the monastery at Boxley "the Rood of Grace," as it was called, an object, he writes to his employer, of great veneration ; and in fact, Henry VIII. himself, at the commencement of his reign, had been repeatedly a votary there. Chamber thus exposes, in a letter he wrote about 1536 to Cromwell, the miserable system of imposture:—" I founde," says he, "in the image of the Roode callede the Roode of Grace, the whiche heretofore hath beene hadd in great veneracion of people, certen ingynes and olde wyer, wyth olde roton stykkes in the backe of the same, that dyd cause the eyes of the same to move and stere in the hede thereof lyke unto a lyvelye thyng; and also the nether tippe in lyke wise to move as thoughe itt shulde speke; whiche, so famed, was not a little straunge to me and other that was present at the pluckyng down of the same." It will be recollected that, in 1538, Fisher, Bishop of Rochester, exhibited a representation of this rood from the pulpit at Paul's Cross. This latter circumstance is mentioned in a contemporary diary:— "M. Gressham, mayir. On Saynt Mathies day thapostulle, the xxiiij. day of February, Sonday, did the Bishop of Rochester preche at Polles Cros, and had standyng afore hym alle his sermon tyme the pictur of the Roode of Grace in Kent, that had byn many yeris in the abbey of Boxley in Kent and was gretely sought with pilgryms, and when he had made an ende of his sermon, the pictor was toorn alle to peces." "Diary of a Londoner," temp. Hen. VII. and VIII. in "Reliq. Antiq." ii. 34.

Rope.—In Brand's day, the rope which remained after a man had been cut down, was an object of eager competition, he tells us, being regarded as of virtue in attacks of headache. But, in a tract printed in 1725, it is stated that at Bristol the same thing was thought to be a remedy for the ague. *Life of Nicholas Mooney, a notorious highwayman executed at Bristol, April 24, 1752,* p. 30.

Rope-Dancing. — See Nichols' "Progresses of Queen Elizabeth," vol. i. "Her Majesty," says Rowland White, in the Sidney Papers, "this day appoints a Frenchman to doe feates upon a rope in the Conduit Court." Andrews' Continuation of Henry's History, 1796, p. 532.

Rope-Pulling at Ludlow.—This has been a custom time out of mind. A newspaper for 1846 furnishes the following details of it as then observed: "The annual and time-out-of-mind custom of rope-pulling was duly observed last week. A little before four o'clock, the Mayor, accompanied by a numerous party of gentlemen, proceeded towards the market-hall out of one of the centre windows of which was suspended the focus of attraction, viz. the ornamental rope. Many thousand people of all degrees were here assembled, the majority of them prepared for the tug of war; and precisely as the

chimes told four, the Mayor and assistants gradually lowered the grand object of contention, amidst the deafening cheers of the multitude. The struggle then commenced in earnest, which, after the greatest exertion, ended in favour of the Corve-street Ward. As is always the case, the defeated party went round collecting subscriptions to purchase the leviathan rope from the successful possessors; which being accomplished, another fierce and manly struggle through the town ensued, and this time victory declared in favour of the Broad-street Ward. The approaching shades of night only put an end to the sports, and we are happy to add that not any accident occurred to mar the pleasures of the day."

Rose.—It is observable that it was anciently a fashion to stick a rose in the ear. At Kirtling, in Cambridgeshire, (at one time) the magnificent residence of the Norths, there used to be a juvenile portrait, (supposed to be one of Queen Elizabeth,) with a red rose sticking in her ear. In the queen's case, it might be significant of her historical descent. A rose is a symbol on some of the coins of the reign. In *Lingua,* 1607, act ii, sc. i, Appetitus says: "Crown me no crowns but Bacchus' Crown of Roses."

Evelyn, under June 15, 1670, relates that when he and others were dining at Goring House, "Lord Stafford, one of the guests, rose from table, because there were roses stuck about the fruit when the dessert was put on the table, such an antipathy, it seems, he had to them, as once Lady Sellenger also had, and to that degree that, as Sir Kenelm Digby tells me, laying but a rose upon her cheeks, when she was asleep, it raised a blister—" The Diarist admonishes us, however, that Sir Kenelm "was a teller of strange things."

Rose Acre.—See *Churchyards.*

Rosemary.—Coles, in his "Adam in Eden," speaking of rosemary, says: "The garden rosemary is called rosemarinum coronarium, the rather because women have been accustomed to make crowns and garlands thereof." The same author confirms the observation of rosemary, that it "strengthens the senses and memory."

Parkinson remarks:—"Rosemary is almost of as great use as bayes—as well for civill as physical purposes: for civil uses, as all doe know, at weddings, funerals, &c. to bestow among friends." *Paradisus Terrestris,* 1629, 598.

In Hacket's "Marriage Present," 1607, he thus expatiates on the use of rosemary, at this time. "The last of the flowers is the rosemary (rosemarinus, the rosemary is for married men) the which by name, nature, and continued use, man challengeth as properly belonging to himselfe. It overtoppeth all the flowers in the garden, boasting man's rule. It helpeth the braine, strengtheneth the memorie, and is very medicinable for the head. Another property of the rosemary is, it affects the hart. Let this Ros Marinus, this flower of men, ensigne of your wisdome, love and loyaltie, be carried not only in your hands, but in your heads and harts." Hacket adds: "Smell sweet, O ye flowers in your native sweetness: be not gilded with the idle arte of man." Both rosemary and bays appear to have been gilded on these occasions.

The presentation of a rosemary-branch seems to have been held equivalent to a wish for the long life and health of the recipient. In Tottels Miscellany, 1557, are some lines " Of a rosemary braunche sente:"

"Suche grene to me as you haue sent,
Such grene to you I sende agayn:
A flow'ring hart that wyll not feint,
For drede or hope of loss or gaine:—"

In one of the Diurnals is the following passage: "Nov. 28.—That afternoon Master Prin and Master Burton came into London, being met and accompanied with many thousands of horse and foot, and rode with rosemary and bayes in their hands and hats; which is generally esteemed the greatest affront that ever was given to the Courts of Justice in England." "A perfect Diurnal of that memorable Parliament begun at Westminister, &c. Nov. 3rd, 1640."

In "The Passage of our most drad Soueraigne Lady Quene Elyzabeth through the citie of London, &c." 1558, sign. D 3, is the following passage: "How many nosegayes did her grace receyve at poore womens hands? How oftentimes stayed she her chariot when she saw any simple body offer to speake to her Grace? A braunch of rosemary given to her Grace, with a supplication, by a poor woman about Fleet Bridge, was seene in her chariot till her Grace came to Westminster."

In an account of a wedding, in 1560, "of three sisters together," we read: "fine flowers and rosemary were strewed for them coming home: and so to the father's house, where was a great dinner prepared for his said three bride-daughters, with their bridegrooms and company." In the year 1562, July 20, a wedding at St. Olaves, "a daughter of Mr. Nicolls (who seems to have been the Bridge Master) was married to one Mr. Coke." "At the celebration whereof were present, my Lord Mayor, and all the Aldermen, with many ladies, &c. and Mr. Bacon, an eminent divine, preached a wedding sermon. Then all the company went home to the Bridge House to dinner: where was a good cheer as ever was known, with all manner of musick and dancing all the remainder of the day: and at night a goodly supper; and then followed a masque till midnight. The next day the wedding was kept at the Bridge House, with great cheer: and after supper came in masquers. One was in cloth of gold. The next masque consisted of friars, and the third of nuns. And after. they danced by times: and lastly, the friars and nuns danced together." Strype's Stow, 1754, i, 259.

We read in the account of the marriage of Jack of Newbury (1597), where speaking of the bride's being led to church, it is added by the writer that "there was a fair bride cup, of silver gilt, carried before her, wherein was a goodly branch of rosemary, gilded very fair, and hung about with silken ribbands of all colours."

Rosemary was used alike at weddings and at funerals. The former was commonly dipped in scented water. In Dekker's "Wonderful Yeare," 1603, signat. E 2 verso, speaking of a bride, who died of the plague on her wedding day, he says: "Here is a strange alteration, for the rosemary that was washt in sweet water to set out the bridall, is now wet in teares to furnish her buriall." Herrick's lines equally celebrate the double function:

"The rosemarie branch.
"Grow for two ends, it matters not at all,
Be't for my bridall or my buriall."

Hesperides, 1648, p. 131. In Fletcher's "Scornful Lady," 1616, it is asked:

"Were the rosemary branches dipped?"

Stephens in his *Essays and Characters,* 1615, says: "He is the finest fellow in the parish, and hee that misinterprets my definition, deserves no rosemary nor rosewater." He adds: "He must favour of gallantry a little: though he perfume the table with rose-cake: or appropriate Bonelace and Coventry-blew:" and is passing witty in describing the following trait of our bridegroom's clownish civility: "He hath heraldry enough to place every man by his armes." In Rowley's "Faire Quarrel," 1617, act. v. sc. 1, we read:

"*Phis.* Your maister is to be married to-day?
"*Trim.* Else all this rosemary is lost."

In Barrey's "Ram Alley," 1611, sign. F 4, is the following allusion to this old custom:

"Know, varlet, I will be wed this morning;
Thou shalt not be there, nor once be grac'd
With a piece of rosemary."

Hazlitt's Dodsley, x, 342. In the "Elder Brother," 1637, act iii. sc. 3, in a scene immediately before a wedding:

"*Lew.* Pray take a peece of rosemary.
Mir. I'll wear it but for the lady's sake, and none of yours.''

In the first scene of Fletcher's "Woman's Prize," the stage direction is: "Enter Moroso, Sophocles, and Tranio, with rosemary as from a wedding." So in the "Pilgrim," by Fletcher, 1621;

"*Alph.* Well, well, since wedding will come after wooing,
Give me some rosemary, and letts be going.''

We gather from Jonson's "Tale of a Tub," that it was customary for the bride maids, on the bridegroom's first appearance in the morning, to present him with a bunch of rosemary, bound with ribbons. "Look, an' the wenches ha' not found un out, and do present un with a van of rosemary and bays enough to vill a bowpott, or trim the head of my best vore horse: we shall all ha' bride-laces, or points, I zee." Similarly to this, in the "Marrow of Complements," 1655, a rustic lover tells his mistress that, at their wedding "Wee'l have rosemary and bayes to vill a bow-pot, and with the zame Ile trim that vorehead of my best-vore horse." In the "Knight of the Burning Pestle," 1613, act v. sc. 1, we read: "I will have no great store of company at the wedding, a couple of neighbours, and their wives, and we will have a capon in stewed broth, with marrow, and a good piece of beef stuck with rosemary." So late as 1698, the old country use appears to have been kept up, of decking the bridal bed with sprigs of rosemary: it is not however mentioned as being general. *Lex Forcia*, 1698, p. 17.

It appears that at the funeral of Robert Lockier, (who was shot for mutiny April 27th or 28th, 1649, the manner of which was most remarkable, considering the person to be in no higher quality than a private trooper, for the late king had not half so many to attend his remains) the corpse was adorned with bundles of rosemary on each side, one half of each was stained in blood, and the sword of the deceased with them." *Perfect Diurnal*, April 30-May 7, 1649.

"I saw a beggar put into an open coffin, with an abundance of bay leaves, rosemary, sweet briar, and floures, who was a drunken rogue, and his wife worse, yet she cried at the putting of him in."— *Letter of a Private Christian to the Lady Consideration*, 1655, p. 5.

Many instances of the use of rosemary at funerals are to be collected from old writers. In the second part of Dekker's "Honest Whore," 1630, signat. c 2 verso, is the following passage: "My windingsheete was taken out of lavender to be stucke with rosemary." In Shirley's "Wedding," 1633, signat. G 4 verso, scene "A table set forth with two tapers: servants placing ewe, bayes, and rosemary," &c. A writer in the "British Apollo," 1708, is of opinion that the use of rosemary at funerals proceeded in the first instance from its supposed properties as a disinfectant. Misson says, when the funeral procession is ready to set out, "they nail up the coffin, and a servant presents the company with sprigs of rosemary: every one takes a sprig and carries it in his hand till the body is put into the grave, at which time they all throw in their sprigs after it." *Travels*, p. 91. In Hogarth's "Harlot's Progress," at the prostitute's funeral, there are sprigs of rosemary, and Gay, in his "Pastorals," has this passage:

"To shew their love, the neighbours far and near
Follow'd with wistful look the damsel's bier:
Sprigg'd rosemary the lads and lasses bore,
While dismally the parson walk'd before.''

Rose of Jericho.—Sir Thomas Browne tells us: "The Rose of Jericho, that flourishes every year just about Christmas Eve, is famous in Christian reports. Bellonius tells us it is only a monastical imposture. There is a peculiarity in this plant; though it be dry, yet, on imbibing moisture, it dilates its leaves and explicates its flowers, contracted and seemingly dried up: which is to be effected not only in the plant yet growing, but also in some measure may be effected in that which is brought exsuccous and dry unto us: which quality being observed, the subtlety of contrivers did commonly play this shew upon the eve of our Saviour's Nativity: when by drying the plant again, it closed the next day, referring unto the opening and closing of the womb of Mary. Walsingham has the following passage: "In multis locis Angliæ Salices in Januario flores protulerunt, Rosis in quantitate et colore persimiles." *Historia Brevis*, 1574, p. 119.

Cotgrave in his Dictionary, 1650, has: "Rose of the mount of Jericho, of Jerusalem, or our Ladies rose, Rose de nostre Dame, rose de Jerico, rose de pienne." Herrick, in his "Good Wishes for the Duke of York," printed in his *Hesperides*, 1648, expresses this complimentary wish:

> "May his pretty dukeship grow
> Like t' a rose of Jericho:
> Sweeter far then ever yet
> Showers or sun-shines co'ld beget."

Rose, Under the.—The vulgar saying "Under the rose," is stated to have taken its rise from convivial entertainments, where it was an ancient custom to wear chaplets of roses about the head, on which occasions, when persons desired to confine their words to the company present, that they "might go no farther," they commonly said "they are spoken under the rose." Nazianzen, according to Sir Thomas Browne, seems to imply, in the following verses, that the rose, from a natural property, has been made the symbol of silence:

> "Utque latet Rosa verna suo putamine
>   clausa,
> Sic Os vincla ferat, validisque arctetur
>   habenis,
> Indicatque suis prolixa silentia labris."

Lemnius and others have traced this saying to another origin. The rose, say they, was the flower of Venus, which Cupid consecrated to Harpocrates, the God of Silence; and it was therefore the emblem of it, to conceal the mysteries of Venus. Newton says: "I will heere adde a common countrey custome that is used to be done with the rose. When pleasaunt and merry companions doe friendly meete together to make goode cheere, as soone as their feast or banket is ended, they give faithfull promise mutually one to another, that whatsoever hath been merrily spoken by any in that assembly, should be wrapped up in silence, and not to be carried out of the doores. For the assurance and performance whereof, the tearme whch they use, that all things there saide must be taken as spoken under the rose. Whereupon they use in their parlours and dining roomes to hang roses over their tables, to put the companie in memorie of secrecie, and not rashly or indiscreetly to clatter and blab out what they heare. Likewise, if they chaunce to shew any tricks of wanton, unshamefast, immodest or irreverent behaviour either by word or deed, they protesting that all was spoken under the rose, do give a strait charge and pass a Covenant of Silence and Secrecy with the hearers, that the same shall not be blowne abroad, nor tatled in the streetes among any others." *Herbal for the Bible*, 1587, 123-3.

So Peacham: "In many places as well in England as in the Low Countries, they have over their tables a rose painted, and what is spoken under the rose must not be revealed. The reason is this; the rose being sacred to Venus, whose amorous and stolen sports, that they might never be revealed, her sonne Cupid would needes dedicate to Harpocrates the God of Silence." *Truth of our Times*, 1638, p. 173. A correspondent of Notes and Queries" observes that, at Lullingstone Castle, in Kent, there is a representation of a rose nearly two feet in diameter, with the following inscription round it:

> "Kentish true blue,
> Take this as a token,
> That what is said here,
> Under the rose is spoken."

The Germans have hence a custom of describing a rose in the ceiling over the table. The rose is a very usual central ornament for modern reception rooms. How to interpret an allusion by Randolph in regard to a Maid of Honour seen by him in Somerset House Garden under peculiar conditions, I hardly know. He says :—

> "and as she goes,
> She views the situation of each rose—"
> Works, by Hazlitt, 1875, ii, 662.

Rostrum.—The familiar term now applied to the auctioneer's elevated seat at the head of the table, when a public sale is conducted. The name doubtless arose from the original projection of the desk in the form of a prow or beak of a vessel, and may be taken to be of comparatively modern origin, since auctions were long held in a different manner. The plural *Rostra*, however, was used to signify the stage in the Roman Forum from which speakers addressed their audiences, and which owed that designation to its embellishment with the beaks of ships taken in a war. Smith's *Dict. of Greek and Roman Antiq.*, 1856, v. *Rostra.* Comp. *Auctions.*

Rough Music.—See Halliwell in v. and comp. *Skimmington.*

Rounders.—This sport, which has fallen into comparative disuse of late years, was formerly a very popular schoolboy's amusement. It was played with a ball and a short, stout stick, a species of apology for a bat, and was of the same genus as cricket, but less aspiring and not so hazardous; it was chiefly confined to the younger lads, who still lacked the necessary skill and strength for the more ambitious game.

It is possible that this is the game which, under the name of rownes (rounds) is mentioned in the "English Courtier and the Country Gentleman," 1586.

Routing Well.—Comp. *Drumming Well.* One in the parish of Inveresk, Mid-Lothian, was said in the 18th century to predict a storm, when its rumbling noise was heard.

Rowan-Tree.—In the song of "The Laidley Worm," we read :

> " The spells were vain ; the hag returnes
> To the Queen in sorrowful mood,
> Crying that witches have no power
> Where there is a rowan-tree wood !"

Northumberland Garland, p. 63.

Rue.—Rue was hung about the neck, as an amulet against witchcraft, in tum esse tradit Aristoteles."—Wierus de Aristotle's time. " Rutam fascini Amule-Præstigiis Dæmonum, lib. v. cap. xxi. col. 584. Shakespear has this passage: "There's rue for you, and here's some for me. We may call it herb-grace o' Sundays." Rue was called herb of grace by the country people, and probably for the reason assigned by Warburton, that it was used on Sundays by the Romanists in their exorcisms. *Hamlet*, iv, 5. White Kennet, in a letter of June 19, 1716, mentions that the Jacobites on the 7th had bought rue and thyme.

Ruff or **Colchester Trump.**—There appears by a passage in Heath's "House of Correction," 1619, to have been an ancient game called ruffe : "A swaggerer is one that plays at ruffe, from whence he tooke the denomination of a ruffyn," &c. *English Courtier*, &c. 1586, H 3 *verso*. Heywood, in "A Woman Kilde with Kindnesse," 1607, mentions double ruff.

Rule.—The governing body at Clifford's Inn, while it remained an independent autonomous institution.

Rumbald.—Hasted, referring to Folkstone, says, "there was a singular custom used of long time by the fishermen of this place. They chose eight of the largest and best whitings out of every boat, when they came home from that fishery, and sold them apart from the rest, and out of the money arising from them they made a feast every Christmas Eve, which they called a rumbald. The master of each boat provided this feast for his own company. These whitings, which are of a very large size, and are sold all round the country, as far as Canterbury, are called rumbald whitings. This custom (which is now left off, though many of the inhabitants still meet socially on a Christmas Eve, and call it Rumbald Night), might have been antiently instituted in honour of St. Rumbald, and at first designed as an offering to him for his protection during the fishery." *Hist. of Kent*, folio ed. iii, 380.

Run a Tye, To.—" To May Day sports may be referred the singular bequest of Sir Dudley Diggs, knt., (says Hasted)

who by his last will, dated in 1638, left the sum of 20*l*. to be paid yearly to two young men and two maids, who, on May 19th, yearly, should run a tye, at Old Wives Lees in Chilham, and prevail ; the money to be paid out of the profits of the land of this part of the manor of Selgrave, which escheated to him after the death of Lady Clive. These lands, being in three pieces, lie in the parishes of Preston and Faversham, and contain about forty acres, and are commonly called the Running Lands. Two young men and two young maids run at Old Wives Lees in Chilham, yearly, on May 1st, and the same number at Sheldwich Lees, on the Monday following, by way of trial, and the two which prevail at each of those places run for the 10*l*. at Old Wives Lees, as above mentioned, on May 19." A great concourse of the neighbouring gentry and inhabitants constantly assemble there on this occasion. *Hist. of Kent*, folio ed. ii, 787.

Running for the Smock.—This was an annual performance at Gooseberry Fair, held at the beginning of August in Spa Fields. Two young girls, stripped to their smocks, ran 100 yards on the turf, and a Holland chemise decorated with ribbons was the reward of the winner of the race. But the same sport was generally prevalent in the North of England in former times.

At this fair there were stalls furnished with gooseberry fool and booths, where tea was served for threepence.

Run the Figure of Eight, To.—This sport is still followed by boys, and is alluded to by Shakespear in his "Midsummer Night's Dream" in the line :

> "And the quaint mazes in the wanton green."

The Figure of Eight is also a favourite feature in Skating.

Run the Hoop, To.—An ancient marine custom. Four or more boys, having their left hands tied fast to an iron hoop, and each of them a rope, called a nettle, in their right, being naked to the waist, wait the signal to begin ; this being made by a stroke with a cat of nine tails, given by the boatswain to one of the boys, he strikes the boy before him, and every one does the same. At first the blows are but gently administered ; but each, irritated by the strokes from the boy behind him, at length lays it on in earnest. This was anciently practised when the ship was wind-bound.

Rush-Bearing.—It appears that in ancient times the parishioners brought rushes at the Feast of Dedication, wherewith to strew the church, and from that circumstance the festivity itself has obtained the name of Rush-bearing, which occurs for a country wake in a Glossary to the Lancashire dialect. Braithwaite, describing a zealous brother, tells us: "He denounceth an heauie woe upon all wakes, summerings, and rush-bearings, preferring that Act whereby pipers were made rogues, by Act of Parliament, before any in all the Acts and Monuments."—*Whimzies*, 1631, p. 197. In the same work, p. 19 (Second Part), speaking of a peddlar the author says: "A countrey rush-bearing, or Morrice-Pastorall, is his festivall: if ever hee aspire to plum-porridge, that is the day. Here the guga-girles gingle it with his neat nifles." So, also, in Braithwaite's "Boulster Lecture," 1640, p. 78, we find: "Such an one as not a Rush-bearer or May-morrish in all that parish could subsist without him."

In 1875, in the Lake country, rushbearing was still continued on successive Sundays in the season at Grasmere, Ambleside, and Warcop. The subjoined written notice was attached to one of the entrances to Grasmere churchyard:—"The rush-bearing notices for 1875.—Mr. Dawson will give his gratuities of 6*d*. only to such bearers who are attending the parochial day, infant, and Sunday schools during the present school quarter. Rush-bearing standards for dressing by ladies will be received at the school by Mr. Fuller, only between the hours of four and six on Thursday next, after which no standard will be taken. The number of standards so received for dressing at the school will be limited to fifty, that is, to the fifty first brought to the school; all beyond this number will be refused, as the ladies cannot undertake a larger number." "All rush-bearings must be on the churchyard wall not later than six o'clock on Saturday the 17th inst.—July 10, 1875." The following hymn was long in use at Grasmere on this occasion:—

"HYMN FOR THE RUSH-BEARERS.
Our fathers to the house of God,
As yet a building rude,
Bore offerings from the flowery sod,
And fragrant rushes strew'd.
May we, their children, ne'er forget
The pious lesson given,
But honour still, together met,
The Lord of earth and heaven.
Sing we the good Creator's praise,
Who gives us sun and showers
To cheer our hearts with fruitful days,
And deck our world with flowers.
These, of the great Redeemer's grace,
Bright emblems here are seen;
He makes to smell the desert place
With flowers and rushes green.
All glory to the Father be,
All glory to the Son,
All glory, Holy Ghost, to Thee,
While endless ages run. Amen."

The communication to *Notes and Queries* (Aug. 28, 1875), from which the above extracts are derived adds:—Saturday evening was still very warm and bright, and from half-past five to six o'clock groups of nicely dressed little children were wending their way towards the parish church, which is situated at a curve of the road in the little scattered town of Grasmere; some of the children came as spectators, but most of them carried very beautiful ornaments made of rushes and flowers, the rushes to give the form, and the flowers the decoration. The rush-bearings were from two to five feet in height; many of them were crosses of various designs, usually the cross with a circle, as the circle gives strength to the rush arms. Those which were not crosses were of a variety of forms, some of them like the iron finials which are seen on the roofs of buildings. They were all mounted on small squares of wood, like those on which stuffed birds are set. The wall of the churchyard has a broad coping, and is about four feet high next the road, and two to three feet high at the inside. The Grasmere rush-bearing was a very interesting and pretty ceremony, and one that might, with advantage in many ways, be introduced into those villages where it is unknown, if for no other reason than that it pleases the children, gives them something pleasant to look forward to, and something pleasant to do.

In the West Country the girls make these crosses and cast them on the smooth surface of a pool or well. If they float, it is an augury of happy love; if they sink, it portends early death.

Rushes.—In Newton's "Herball for the Bible," 1587, is the following passage: "Sedge and rushes with the which many in the country do use in summer time to strawe their parlors and churches, as well for colleness as for pleasant smell." Chambers, and indeed all apartments usually inhabited, were formerly strewed in this manner. As our ancestors rarely washed their floors, disguises of uncleanliness became necessary things. It appears that the English stage was strewed with rushes. The practice in private houses is noticed by Dr. Johnson from Caius "de Ephemera Britannica."

In the Churchwardens' Accounts of St. Mary-at-Hill, London, 1493, we have "for 3 berden rushes for the new pews, 3*d*." In the same, 1504, occurs "Paid for 2 berden ryshes for the strewyng the newe pewes, 3*d*." In Accounts for the parish of St. Margaret's, Westminster, under 1544, is the following item: "Paid for rushes against the Dedication Day, which is always the first Sunday of October, 1*s*. 5*d*." In those of St. Laurence

Parish, Reading, for 1602, quoted by Coates, we have: "Paid for flowers and rushes for the churche when the Queene was in town, xx*d*."

Hentzner, in his "Itinerary," speaking of Queen Elizabeth's presence-chamber at Greenwich, says, "The floor, after the English fashion, was strewed with hay." Copley, in his "Wits, Fits, and Fancies," 1595, has a story to this purpose. Bridges, in his "Northamptonshire," vol. i. p. 187, speaking of the parish of Middleton Chenduit, says: "It is a custom here to strew the church in summer with hay gathered from six or seven swaths in Ashmeadow, which have been given for this purpose. The rector finds straw in winter." Hazlitt's *Blount*, 1874, p. 219. For farther particulars on this subject the reader may be referred to Mr. Alfred Barton's monograph, 4°, 1891.

Sack.—A dry Spanish wine, apparently from the German *sac*, Fr. *sec*. See Nares, 1859, in v. Sack was a very common drink in and after Shakespear's time at Stratford and elsewhere. It is mentioned by Gascoigne in his *Delicate Diet*, 1576, among the other wines then in vogue. According to a ballad of the time of James I. it seems to have been sold for eighteen pence the quart.

Sack-Posset.—See *Posset*.

Sacrifice.—The theory of it among primitive communities was the propitiation of the supposed author or authors of increase from season to season by the surrender of a share or of a choice portion of the produce of the earth and of live stock to a god. It appears to survive only in the tithes still exacted by the Church to enable it to maintain its offices of ministry and intercession. It evolved from this principle and idea that God Himself offered up His most precious possession to purify and redeem mankind instead of exercising His presumptive power of dispensing with any such mediatory process.

Saddler's Well.—In a tract of 1684 it is thus described: "The New Well at Islington is a certain spring in the middle of a garden, belonging to the Musick House, built by Mr. Sadler, on the North side of the great cistern that receives the New River water near Islington, the water whereof was before the Reformation, very much famed for several extraordinary cures performed thereby, and was therefore accounted sacred, and called Holy-Well. The priests belonging to the Priory of Clerkenwell using to attend there, made the people believe that the virtues of the waters proceeded from the efficacy of their prayers. But upon the Reformation the well was stopt up. . . ." The narrative, which is cur-

ious enough, goes on to tell us how an acquaintance of Sadler discovered the well again, the properties of the water, which was somewhat like Tonbridge, and how it was to be used.

Saddling the Spit.—It appears that, in the parish of St. Clement Danes "There was formerly a good custom of Saddling the Spit, which, for reasons well known at Westminster, is now laid aside: so that wives, whose husbands are seafaring persons, or who are otherwise absent from them, have lodged here ever since very quietly."

Sagittary.—A fabulous creature introduced into mediæval romance by Guido di Colonna. A centaur. Comp. Nares, 1859, in v.

Sailors' and Marine Superstitions. — "Innumerable," says Reginald Scot, "are the reports of accidents unto such as frequent the seas, as fishermen and sailors, who discourse of noises, flashes, shadows, ecchoes, and other visible appearances, nightly seen and heard upon the surface of the water." *Discovery*, ed. 1665, p. 53. Bishop Hall ridicules the superstition of sailors among the Romanists, who, in passing by St. Michael's Grecian promontory Malla, used to ply him with their best devotions, that he would hold still his wings from resting too hard upon their sails.

Sailors have various puerile apprehensions of it being ominous to whistle on shipboard, to drown a cat, to carry a corpse in their vessel, &c. It seems that the objection to whistling proceeds, or at least proceeded formerly, from a notion which prevailed that by so doing they mocked the devil, the stirrer up of winds and storms. In "A Helpe to Discourse," the latter idea is properly confuted: "The shippe is as insensible of the living as of the dead, and as the living made it goe the faster, so the dead made it not goe the slower, for the dead are no Rhemoras to alter the course of her passage, though some there be that thinke so, and that, by a kind of mournful sympathy." Comp. Remora.

The common sailors account it very unlucky to lose a water-bucket or a mop. Children are deemed lucky to a ship. The author of *A New Catalogue of Vulgar Errors*, 1767, remarks: "I look upon our sailors to care as little what becomes of themselves as any set of people under the sun, and yet no people are so much terrified at the thoughts of an apparition. Their sea songs are full of them; they firmly believe their existence: and honest Jack Tar shall be more frightened at a glimmering of the moon upon the tackling of the ship, than he would be if a Frenchman was to clap a blunderbuss to his head. I was told a story by an officer in the Navy, which may not be foreign to the purpose. About half a dozen of the sailors on board a man of war, took it into their heads that there was a ghost in the ship; and being asked by the captain what reason they had to apprehend any such thing, they told him they were sure of it, for they smelt him. The captain first laughed at them and called them a parcel of lubbers, and advised them not to entertain any such silly notions as these, but mind their work. It passed on very well for a day or two; but one night, being in another ghost-smelling humour, they all came to the captain and told him that they were quite certain there was a ghost, and he was somewhere behind the small beer-barrels. The captain, quite enraged at their folly, was determined they should have something to be frightened at in earnest: and so ordered the boatswain's mate to give them all a dozen of lashes with a cat o' nine tails, by which means the ship was entirely cleared of ghosts during the remainder of the voyage. However, when the barrels were removed, some time after, they found a dead rat, or some such thing, which was concluded by the rest of the crew to be the ghost which had smelt a little before." Our author accounts for this philosophically: "A great deal may be said in favour of men troubled with the scurvy, the concomitants of which disorder are, generally, faintings and the hip, and horrors without any grounds for them."

The prejudice that the presence of a dead body upon shipboard is fatal to the vessel, we find noticed in Twyne's *Pattern of Painful Adventures*, first printed about 1576: "Howbeit in the hotest of the sorowe the gouernour of the ship came vnto Apollonius, saying: My lord, pluck vp your heart, and be of good cheere, and consider I pray you that the ship may not abide to carrie the dead carkas, and therefore commaud it to be cast into the sea. . ." But the belief has always been strong, and may still survive. We find it in the ballad of "Bonnie Annie," and Coleridge, in our own time, has introduced it into his "Rime of the Ancient Mariner,"—a poem in which the author's German sympathies are powerfully present. Mr. Kinloch informs us, that "when a ship became unmanageable, lots were cast to discover the person who occasioned the disaster, and the man on whom the lot fell was condemned." Pennant says, that "the appearance of the dolphin and the porpesse are far from being esteemed favourable omens by the seamen, for their boundings, springs, and frolicks in the water, are held to be sure signs of an approaching gale." *Zoology*, iii, 67. See *Castor and Pollux* and *Lucky and Unlucky Days*, &c.

Petronius Arbiter notices a very singular marine superstition; it is that no person in a ship must pare his nails or cut his hair, except in a storm. "Audio enim non licere cuiquam mortalium in nave neque ungues neque capillos deponere, nisi quum pelago ventus irascitur." Petron. 369, edit. Mich. Hadrianid. Juvenal, Sat. xii. l. 81, says:—

"Tuti stagna sinus. Gaudent ibi vertice raso
Garrula securi narrare pericula nautæ."

Saint Cross.—Near Winchester. This *hospitium* for men and women, apart from its other benefactions, is bound on demand by ringing at the gates to supply to every traveller a piece of bread and a cup or glass of ale. The quality is not stipulated.

Saint-Graal.—See *Graal*.

Saints' Days.—A writer in "Current Notes" for December, 1857, judiciously observes respecting those saints, who are merely commemorated: "It is a fact hitherto almost unnoticed, that these Saints' Days now considered as distinctive badges of Romanism continued to retain their appropriated stations in our popular Protestant English Almanac, until the alteration of the style in 1752, when they were discontinued."

Salamander.—It is rather difficult to account for the absurd and barbarous superstition about this beautiful and harmless creature, as is not even an inhabitant of the tropics, and does not evince any fondness for warmth.

"There is a vulgar error," says Vaughan, "that a salamander lives in the fire. Yet both Galen and Dioscorides refute this opinion: and Mathiolus in his Commentaries upon Dioscorides, a very famous physician, affirms of them, that by casting of many a salamander into the fire for tryal, he found it false. The same Experiment is likewise avouched by Joubertus." *Brief Natural History*, p. 91. "Should a glass-house fire be kept up without extinction, for a longer term than seven years, there was a theory that a salamander would be generated in the cinders. This very rational idea is much more generally credited than wise men would readily believe." — Andrews' *Anecdotes*, edit. 1790, p. 359. What *wise men* would be apt to believe it!

Sallinger's or **St. Leger's Round.**—An old dance and tune. See Nares, 1859, in v.

Salt.—Selden observes of salt, that it "was vsed in all sacrifices by expresse commandement of the true God, the Salt of the Couenant in holy writ, the religion of the salt, set first, and last taken away, as a symbole of perpetual-friendship, that in Homer Πασσέ δ' Αλος Θείοιο, (he sprinkled it with divine salt) the title of αγνιτης (the cleanser,) giuen it by Lycophron, and passages of the oceans medicinable epithets because of his salt-nesse, you shall see apparant and apt testimonie" of its having had a most respected and divinely honoured name. *Notes on the Polyolbion.*

"Salt," says Seward, "was equally used in the sacrifices both by Jews and pagans. But the use of salt in baptism was taken from the Gentile idolatry, and not from the Jewish sacrifices. Salt, as an emblem of preservation, was ordered by the Law of Moses to be strewed on all flesh that was offered in sacrifice. But among the pagans it was not only made use of as an adjunct, or necessary concomitant of the sacrifice, but was offered itself as a propitiation. Thus in the *Ferialia* or offerings to the *Dii Manes*, when no animal was slain:

' Parva petunt Manes, Pietas pro divite grata est
Munere; non avidos Styx habet una Deos.
Tegula porrectis satis est velata Coronis,
Et parcæ fruges, parvaque Mica Salis.'

'The Manes' rights expences small supply,
The richest sacrifice is piety.
With vernal garlands a small tile exalt
A little flour and little grain of salt.'

"That the flour and salt were both designed as propitiary offerings to redeem them from the vengeance of the Stygian or Infernal Gods, may be proved from a like custom in the Lemuria, another Festival to the same Deities . . . "It is plain, therefore, that the salt in the former ceremony was offered as a redemption, which property the Papists impiously ascribe to it still; and the parva mica, a little grain, is the very thing put into the child's mouth at present." Further on, he writes: "Then he, the priest, exorcises and expells the impure spirits from the salt, which stands by him in a little silver box; and putting a bit of it into the mouth of the person to be baptized, he says: 'Receive the salt of wisdom, and may it be a propitiation to thee for eternal life.'" *Conformity between Popery and Paganism*, p. 53.

Pennant, in his "Tours in Wales," tells us that "A tune called Gosteg yr Halen, or the prelude of the salt, was always played whenever the salt seller was placed before King Arthur's knights at his Round Table." In Lord Fairfax's "Orders for the Servants of his Household at Denton," after the Civil Wars, I find, "For the chamber let the best fashioned and apparell'd servants attend above the salt, the rest below." *Antiq. Repertory*, 1808, iv, 310.

In Scotland, it was a common practice in the end of the 18th century to "put a small quantity of salt into the first milk of a cow, after calving, that is given any person to drink." "This was done," it is added, "with a view to prevent skaith, if it should happen that any person is not canny." *Stat. Acc.* xvi, 121, Killearn, Co. Stirling, Anno 1795.

In a little volume (a translation from the French) published in the time of Charles II., we meet with what is still a not uncommon sentiment, the reluctance to be helped to salt. The writer, who of course merely expresses the French view of the subject, although it is common to other countries, observes: "Some are so exact, they think it uncivil to help any body that sits by them, either with salt or with brains; but in my judgement that is but a ridiculous scruple, and if your neighbour desires you to furnish him, you must either take some out with your knife, and lay it upon his plate; or, if they be more than one, present them with the salt, that they may furnish themselves." *Rules of Civility*, 1685, p. 34. On the other hand, Stuckius tells us that the Muscovites thought that a prince could not shew a greater mark of affection than by sending to him salt from his own table. *Convivial Antiquities*, p. 17. Comp. *Nantwich*.

Mungo Park, in his "Travels," tells us: "It would appear strange to an European to see a child suck a piece of rock-salt as if it were sugar: this is frequent in Africa: but the poorer sort of inhabitants are so rarely indulged with this precious article, that to say, 'A man eats salt with his victuals,' is to say he is a rich man." It is this kind, which they leave about in English deer-parks for the animals to lick.

Salt-Eel.—A game similar to *Hide and seek*. See Halliwell in v.

Salt, Falling of.—It has been observed by Bailey, on the falling of salt, that it proceeds from the ancient opinion that salt was incorruptible: it had therefore been made the symbol of friendship: and if it fell, usually the persons between whom it happened, thought their friendship would not be of long duration. Hall, in his "Characters," 1608, makes it a characteristic of his Superstitious man, to look pale and red if the salt fall towards him," and not to be at his ease "till one of the waiters have poured wine on his hands." The last-mentioned idea is perhaps traceable from the opinion which we find diffused widely among the Lydians and other nations of antiquity, who held that the pouring of wine upon the ground or upon their clothes, accompanied by prayer, was more efficacious as an augury than the flight of birds.

Gaule tells us: "I have read it in an orthodox Divine, that he knew a young gentleman who, by chance, spilling the salt on the table, some that sate with him said merrily to him, that it was an ill omen, and wish'd him take heed to himselfe that day: of which the young man was so superstitiously credulous, that it would not go out of his mind: and going abroad that day, got a wound of which he died not long after." *Mag-Astromancers Posed*, 320. Grose says on this subject, "to scatter salt, by overturning the vessel in which it is contained, is very unlucky, and portends quarrelling with a friend or fracture of a bone, sprain, or other bodily misfortune. Indeed this may in some measure be averted by throwing a small quantity of it over one's head. It is also unlucky to help another person to salt. To whom the ill luck is to happen does not seem to be settled." This notion about the spilling of salt and wine is mentioned by Scot, in his "Discoverie of Witchcraft," 1584, by Gaule ("Mag-Astro-Mancers posed," &c. pp. 181 and 320, as above), and by Melton ("Astrologaster," 1620, p. 45). But none of these writers it would seem, shared the belief. In Brand's time, as now, the omen was thought to be averted by throwing a little of the spilled salt over the shoulder.

Pennant tells us : "The dread of spilling salt is a known superstition among us and the Germans, being reckoned a presage of some future calamity, and particularly that it foreboded domestic feuds, to avert which, it is customary to fling some salt over the shoulder into the fire, in a manner truly classical." Both Greeks and Romans mixed salt with their sacrificial cakes : in their lustrations also they made use of salt and water, which gave rise in after-times to the superstition of holy water. *Journey from Chester to London*, p. 31, Home's *Demonologie*, p. 58.

"I have two friends of either sex,
    which do
Eat little salt or none, yet are friends
    to,
Of both which persons I can truly tell,
They are of patience most invincible,

Whom out of temper no mischance at all
Can put, no, if towards them the salt
    should fall."
        Gayton's *Art of Longevity*, 1659.

In the "British Apollo," 1708, it is said :
"Wee'l tell you the reason
Why spilling of salt
Is esteem'd such a fault,
Because it doth ev'ry thing season.
Th' antiques did opine
'Twas of friendship a sign,
So serv'd it to guests in decorum :
And thought love decay'd
When the negligent maid
Let the salt-cellar tumble before them."

  "Mollivit aversos Penates
  Farre pio et saliente mica."
        Horat. lib. iii. Od. 23.
  "Salinum Eversum.
"Prodige, subverso casu leviore Salino,
Si malè venturum conjicis Omen : adest.
        Idem.
"Deliras insulse ; salem sapientia servat :
Omen ab Ingenio desipiente malum.
        Idem.
"Perde Animam temulente, cades ; sic auguror Omen ;
Non est in toto Corpore mica Salis."
        Keuchenii *Crepundia*, 1662.

Salt in Funeral Rites.—It was customary in Brand's day in some parts of Northumberland, to set a pewter plate, containing a little salt, upon the corpse. Comp. *Funeral Customs*. The Devil abhors salt, says Moresin, which is the emblem of eternity and immortality. It is not liable to putrefaction itself, and it preserves things that are seasoned with it from decay. Considered in reference to this symbolical explication, how beautiful is that expression : "Ye are the salt of the earth !" *Papatus*, 1594, p. 154. Scot, in his "Discoverie," 1584, cites Bodin, as telling us that "the devil loveth no salt in his meat, for that is a sign of eternity. and used by God's commandment in all sacrifices."

Douce says, the custom of putting a plate of salt upon corpses is still retained in many parts of England, and particularly in Leicestershire, but it is not done for the reason here given. The pewter plate and salt are laid on the corpse with an intent to hinder air from getting into the bowels and swelling up the belly, so as to occasion either a bursting, or, at least, a difficulty in closing the coffin. *Gents. Mag.* lx, 603, 760. Comp. Nares, *Glossary*, 1859, v., *Salt* and *Irish Superstitions* and *Weather Omens*.

Salt-Silver.—See *Martinmas*.

Sanctuaries.—It is said that even assassins were secure from the arm of the law by the payment of five pounds, if they could reach unmolested the principal gate of Chirk Castle in Denbighshire. A privilege, of course, enjoyable only by rich persons. This was a survival of the were-gelt. Besides this place of refuge, there were at various periods of our history, others both in London and the provinces. See *Alsatia*. Sir H. Ellis notices, especially, that the site of Paris Garden was originally "a sanctuary ground of the great House of St. John at Clerkenwell. Ellis's *Orig. Letters*, 3rd. S., i, 147. Among the provincial sanctuaries, may be mentioned that at Coots, near Loughborough, in Leicestershire, which is particularly referred to in a letter from the Marquis of Dorset to his nephew Thomas Arundel, Feb. 19, 1528-9, printed by Ellis. There was another at Beaulieu, Hants.

In the 16th volume of "Archæologia" is a list of persons who sought sanctuary at Beverley, in the reigns of Edward IV., Henry VII., and Henry VIII., printed from Harl. MS. 4292. To these, of course, we have to add the sanctuary in the cloisters of Westminster, to which the poet Skelton fled, to shield himself from the retribution of Wolsey.

The ground round Holyrood House, Edinburgh, down to quite recent days, retained the ancient right of securing the residents within certain limits from arrest for civil process, but did not protect criminal delinquents.

Sanctus, Black.—A burlesque hymn founded on that of the Romish service. See Nares, 1859, in v. The composition of parodies of this class seems to have been not unusual; we have some of the *Gude and Godlie Ballades*, too, set to popular secular airs, 1578. Comp. *Burlesque*.

Sargon.—A fish, supposed to be the *sparus* of Linnæus, and our gilt-head. It was anciently supposed to have an extraordinary affection for goats, and to leap for joy when they approached the sea. See *Nares*, 1859, in v. for the popular superstition, which does not seem to have been rationally explained.

Saturday.—The numerous notices, which succeed, of the religious observance of this day, more especially the later part, point of course in some measure to its treatment as a sort of vigil, but, at the same time, we appear to discern a lengthened wavering of sentiment between the Sabbath of the Jews and that of the Gentiles. Many still regard Sunday, not as the seventh day or day of rest, but as the first one, or opening of the week.

Wheatley tells us, that in the East, the Church thought fit to indulge the humour of the Judaizing Christians so far, as to observe the Saturday as a Festival Day of Devotion and thereon to meet for the exercise of religious duties, as is plain from several passages of the ancients. "Illustr. of the Common Prayer," 1741, p. 191. King Edgar, A.D. 958, made an Ecclesiastical law that the Sabbath or Sunday should be observed on Saturday at noon, till the light should appear on Monday morning.

It appears by a Council of William, King of Scotland, A.D. 1203, that it was then determined that Saturday, after the twelfth hour, should be kept holy. Hence, without doubt, was derived the original custom of spending a part of Saturday afternoon without servile labour. Robert of Brunne, in his *Handlyng Sinne*, (A.D. 1303), treating of the Saturday half holyday, and how it was once especially kept holy in England in honour of the Virgin, tells his hearer:

> "ȝif þou make karol or play,
> þou halewyſt nat þyn halyday . . ."

Also, if he gave a prize for a wrestling-match:

> "ȝyf þou ever ſettyſt ſwerde eyþer ryng
> Fur to gadyr a wraſtlyng,
> þe halyday þou holdeſt noghte
> When ſwyche bobaunce for þe ys wroghte."

Further, to give a prize to get all the girls together, and see which is the prettiest, is extremely wrong:

> "ȝyf þou ever yn felde, eyþer in toune,
> Dedyſt flowre gerlande or coroune
> To make wommen to gadyr þere,
> To ſe whyche þat feyrer were ;—
> þys ys aȝens þe commandement,
> And þe halyday for þe ys ſhent :
> Hyt ys a gaderyng for lecherye,
> And ful grete pryde, and hertè hye."

Ed. Furnivall, p. 33. A striking instance of this is recorded by Moresin : "Et videre contigit Anno 1582 Lugduni in vigiliis natalium Domini, depræhensos in stupro duos post missam saltare hora inter duodecimam et primam noctis, cum præter unum aut aliud altaris lumen nullum esset in Templo reliquum, &c."—*Papatus*, p. 177.

In 1332, at a Provincial Council, held by Archbishop Mepham, at Mayfield, after complaint made, that instead of fasting upon the vigils, they ran out to all the excesses of riot, &c. it was appointed, among many other things relative to holy-days, that, "The solemnity for Sunday should begin upon Saturday in the evening and not before, to prevent the misconstruction of keeping a Judaical Sabbath."

The Hallowing of Saturday afternoon is thus accounted for in "Dives and Pauper," 1493: "The thridde Precepte,

xiv. chap. *Dives.* How longe owyth the haliday to be kept and halowyd? *Pauper.* From even to even. Nathelesse summe begynne sonner to halow after that the feestis, and after use of the cuntré. But that men use in Saturdaies and vigilies to ryng holy at midday compellith nat men anon to halowe, but warnythe them of the haliday folowynge, that they shulde thynke thereon and spede theym, and so dispose hem and their occupacions that they might halowe in due tyme."

The following curious extract is from a MS. volume of Homilies, in the Episcopal Library at Durham: "It is written in the liffe of seynt * * * * * that he was bisi on Ester Day before none that he made one to shave him or the sunne went doune. And the fiend aspied that, and gadirid up his heeris; and whan this holi man sawe it, he conjured him and badde him tell him whi he did so. Thane said he, bycause yᵘ didest no reverence to the Sundaie, and therfore this heris wolle I kepe unto yᵉ day of Dome in reproffe of the. Thane he left of all his shavyng and toke the heris of the fiend, and made to brene hem in his owne hand for penaunce, whiche him thought he was worthé to suffre: and bode unshaven unto Monday. This is saide in reproffe of hem that worchen at afternone on Saturdayes." "Dies Sabbathi ab ipsa diei Saturni hora postmeridiana tertia, usque in lunaris diei diluculum festus agitator," &c.—Selden, *Analect. Angl.* lib. ii. cap. 6.

In Bale's "Yet a course at the Romyshe Foxe," is the following "Processyon upon Saturdayes at Even-songe."— "Your holye Father Agapitus, popett of Rome, fyrst dreamed it out and enacted it for a lawdable ceremonye of your whoryshe Churche. But I marvele sore that ye observe yt upon Saturdayes at nyght at Even-songe he commaundynge yt to bee observed upon the Sondayes, in the mornynge betwixt holie water makynge and high masse. . . Moch is Saturnus beholden unto yow (whyche is one of the olde goddes) to garnyshe the goyng out of hys daye with so holye an observacyon. Joye yt ys of your lyfe as to remember your olde fryndes. Doubtlesse yt ys a fyne myrye pageant, and yow worthye to be called a Saturnyane for it." In "Articles for the Sexton of Faversham," 22 Hen. VIII. I find: "Item, the said sexton, or his deputy, every Saturday, Saint's even, and principal feasts, shall ring noon with as many bells as shall be convenient to the Saturday, saint's even, and principal feasts," &c.

In a sermon by Henry Mason, parson of St. Andrew Undershaft, is the following, which should seem to prove that at that time Saturday afternoon was kept holy by some even in the metropolis. "For better keeping of which (the Seventh) Day, Moses commanded the Jews (Exod. xvi. 23) that the day before the Sabbath they should bake what they had to bake; and seeth what they had to seeth; that so they might have no businesse of their own to do, when they were to keepe God's holy day. And from thence it was that the Jews called the sixth day of the week, the preparation of the Sabbath. Matt. xxvii. 62, and Luke xxiii. 54. ——" answerably whereunto, and (as I take it) in imitation thereof, the Christian Church hath beene accustomed to keepe Saterday half holy-day, that in the afternoon they might ridd by-businesses out of the way, and by the evening service might prepare their mindes for the Lord's Day then ensuing. Which custome and usage of God's people, as I will not presse it upon any man's conscience as a necessarie dutie; so every man will grant mee, that God's people, as well Christian as Jewish, have thought a time of preparation most fit for the well observing of God's holy day."

I find the following homely rhymes upon the several days of the week in "Divers Crab-tree Lectures," 1639, p. 126:

" You know that Munday is Sundayes brother;
Tuesday is such another;
Wednesday you must go to church and pray;
Thursday is half-holiday;
On Friday it is too late to begin to spin;
The Saturday is half-holiday agen."

Bourne observes, that in his time it was usual in country villages, where the politeness of the age had made no great conquest, to pay a greater deference to Saturday afternoon than to any other of the working days of the week. The first idea of this cessation from labour at that time was, that every one might attend evening prayers as a kind of preparation for the ensuing Sabbath. The eve of the Jewish Sabbath is called the Preparation, Moses having taught that people to remember the Sabbath over night. With regard to Saturday afternoons, perhaps men who live by manual labour, and have families to support by it, cannot spend them better than in following the several callings in which they have employed themselves on the preceding days of the week. For industry will be no bad preparation for the Sabbath. Considered in a political view, much harm has been done by that prodigal waste of days, very falsely called Holy Days in the Church of Rome. They have, however well intended, greatly favoured the cause of vice and dissipation, without doing any essential service to that of rational religion. Complaints appear to have been made in almost every synod and council of the licentiousness introduced by the keeping of vigils. Nor will the philosopher wonder at this, for it has its foundation in the nature of things.

It is curious enough that we have returned to an observance of Saturday afternoon, not as a religious fast or vigil, but as a period of relaxation and amusement for our workers. But the observation of Sundays draws also to an end.

Saucing-Bell.—See *Passing-Bell.*

Saunt.—In *Lingua*, 1607 (Hazlitt's *Dodsley*, ix. 387), Anamnestes says: "As for Memory, he's a false-hearted fellow : he always deceives them ; they respect not him, except it be to play a game at chests, primero, saunt, maw, or such like." Compare *Cent-Foot.*

Scales.—Rice, in his "Inuectiue againste Vices taken for Vertue," 1579, mentions this twice, but gives no farther explanation.

Scatter Mice, To.—It is a common expression, when a lady pays visits to her neighbours after her confinement, to say, that she comes to scatter her mice ; the origin of the phrase is not so clear ; but the meaning is, that the person whom she thus visits is thought to be so placed in a fair way of being the next to fall into a similar predicament.

Scholars. — Among the ancient Romans, the Quinquatria, on the 20th of March, were the holidays both of masters and scholars, on which occasion the scholars presented their masters with the Minervalia, and the masters distributed among the boys ears of corn. It appears that Gregory the Great, as well as St. Nicholas, was the patron of scholars, and that on his day boys were called, and in many places, in Hospinian's time, still continued to be called, to the school with certain songs, substituting one in the place of St. Gregory to act as bishop on the occasion with his companions of the sacred order. Presents were added, to induce the boys to love their schools. This custom is stated to have descended from the heathens to the Christians. Comp. *Boy-Bishop.*

Scholastica's Day, St.—(Feb. 10). The legend of this saint occurs among the hagiology in the Vernon MS. at Oxford, written before 1400. In the 12th Henry VI. (1433-5) it is related that "also this same yere was a gret frost and a strong lastyng more than xj. wokes, for it dured fro seynt Kateryne even unto seynt Scolastyce day the virgyne in

Feverer." *A Chronicle of London*, 1827, p. 120.

The annual custom on this day at Oxford is thus described in Gutch's "Collectanea Curiosa," 1781, from a paper by Dr. Wallis "on the Privileges, &c., of the University of Oxford." "By an instrument under the City Seal, 15 May, 31 Edward III. (1357) in part of compensation for the great outrage of the townsmen on the scholars, 29 Edward III (1354) they are to pay to the University an hundred marks yearly. But . . . . for such year one, wherein the Mayor and 62 Commoners procure a mass at St. Mary's Church, on Saint Scholastica's Day, and thereat offer each of them a penny at least, for the souls of scholars and others slain in the great conflict. Which mass (by the orders 27 Eliz.) is commuted into a sermon or communion with such oblation, and to the use of the University. Of late the use hath been to have only the Litany and the Oblation."

School-Games. — See Mrs. Gomme's well-known volume and a paper on *Old Berkshire School-Games* in *Antiquary*, xxvii, 192. It may be generally observed, that the same sport is followed at different times under varied designations.

Scolding-Cart.—This was somewhat similar to the cucking-stool, but was always furnished with wheels, the latter only occasionally so. Comp. *Skimmington.*

Scorpion.—It was popularly believed in former times that an oil might be extracted from this creature, capable of healing a wound occasioned by its sting on homœopathic principles. Such an idea was even entertained by Sir Kenelm Digby and Dr. Moffatt or Moufet.

Scorton Arrow.—The 229th annual archery contest for this trophy was held in 1902 at Settle, Yorkshire. The Rev. C. Hutton Coates, a member of the Toxophilites, was the winner.

Scotch and English.—Hutton, in his "History of the Roman Wall," after an account of the incessant irruptions upon each other's lands between the inhabitants of the English and Scotish borders, in ancient times, and before the union of the two kingdoms, observes, "The lively impression, however, of former scenes did not wear out with the practice ; for the children of this day, upon the English border, keep up the remembrance by a common play called Scotch and English or the Raid, i.e. Inroad :" 1804, p. 104. "The boys of the village chuse two captains out of their body, each nominates, alternately, one out of the little tribe. They then divide into two parties, strip, and deposit their clothes, called wad, in two heaps, each upon their own ground, which is divided by a stone, as a boundary between the two kingdoms. Each then invades the other's territories : the English crying ' Here's a leap into thy land, dry-bellied Scot.' He who can plunders the other side. If one is caught in the enemies' jurisdiction, he becomes a prisoner, and cannot be released except by his own party. Thus one side will some-times take all the men and property of the other."

This seems to be the same game with that described by Jamieson, in his " Ety-mological Dictionary," *v.* Wadds. In the Glossary to Sibbald's " Chronicle of Scotish Poetry," Wadds is defined " A youthful amusement, wherein much use is made of pledges." Wad, a pledge, says Jamieson, is the same with the vadium of lower Latinity.

Scotch Hoppers. — In " Poor Robin's Almanack for 1677," in his verses to the reader, on the back of the title-page, our star-gazer professes to show

" The time when school-boys should play at scotch-hoppers."

The same periodical for 1707 says : " Law-yers and physitians have little to do this month, and therefore they may (if they will) play at scotch-hoppers. Some men put their hands into peoples pockets open, and extract it clutch'd, of that beware. But counsel without a cure is a body without a soul." And again, in 1740 : " The fifth house tells ye when it is the most convenient time for an old man to play at scotch-hoppers amongst the boys."

Scottering. — An old harvest cus-tom among boys. See Halliwell in *v.*

Scottles. — A boy's game in Suffolk. See Halliwell in *v.*

Scrambling for Nuts, &c. — To scramble for nuts seems, from a passage in Drayton's " Nimphidia," 1627, to have been a pastime with our ancestors. It is still a favourite one among schoolboys, who are not particular as to the kind of fruit, nuts or apples. This amusement used to consist in the present Editor's boyhood in the boys standing at the top of a lawn, so as to take an even start, and the master with a supply of apples or other fruit (more generally apples) throw-ing them up the grassplot, his pupils at a given signal running in pursuit.

Scratch-Cradle. — A game for-merly played by children with threads which they alternately extended and shortened, repeating the word *Criss-Row*, in the form of a manger and a cradle. The more correct name is *Cratch-Cradle*,

referring to the manger and cradle of Jesus Christ.

Scrolls. — The carriage about the person of a scroll containing passages from the Bible was, and yet is, considered a protection or charm. Quite recently a Jewish woman let out on hire at 25/- a year a talisman of this kind, engrossed in the Yeddish dialect. *Daily Mail*, July 21, 1903.

Scurran-meggy. — A game played with a top called a *sc.-top* in Cumberland in the 18th century. *Halliwell.*

Sea-weed. — See *Weather-Omens.*

Second Sight. — Rowland tells us : " The magick of the Druids, or one part of it, seems to have remained among the Britains even after their con-version to Christianity, and is called Taish in Scotland ; which is a way of predicting by a sort of vision they call second sight : and I take it to be a relick of Druidism, particularly from a noted story related by Vopiscus, of the Emperor Dioclesian, who when a private soldier in Gallia, on his removing thence reckoning with his hostess, who was a Druid woman, she told him he was too penurious, and did not bear in him the noble soul of a soldier ; on his reply that his pay was small, she, looking stedfastly on him, said, that he needed not be so sparing of his money, for after he should kill a boar, she confidently pronounced, he would be Emperor of Rome, which he took as a compliment from her ; but, seeing her serious in her affirmation, the words she spoke stuck upon him, and he was after much de-lighted in hunting and killing boars, often saying when he saw many made Emperors and his own fortune not much mending, I kill the boars, but 'tis others that eat the flesh. Yet it happen'd that many years after, one Arrius Aper, father in law of the Emperor Numerianus, grasping for the Empire, traiterously slew him, for which fact being apprehended by the soldiers and brought before Dioclesian, who being then become a prime Comman-der in the army, they left the traytor to his disposal, who, asking his name, and being told that he was called Aper, *i.e.* a boar, without further pause, he sheathed his sword in his bowels, saying Et hunc Aprum cum cæteris, i.e. " Even this boar also to the rest :" which done, the soldiers, commending it as a quick, extraordinary act of justice, without further deliberation saluted him by the name of Emperor. I bring this story here in view, as not im-proper on this hint, nor unuseful to be observed, because it gives fair evidence of the antiquity of the second sight, and withal shews that it descended from the antient Druids, as being one part of the diabolical magick they are charg'd with: and, upon their dispersion into the territories of Denmark and Swedeland, continued there in the most heathenish parts to this day, as is set forth (by Defoe) in the story of the late Duncan Campbel." *Mona Antiqua*, 140.

Aubrey tells us how Lady Diana Rich, daughter to the Earl of Holland, saw her own apparition in the garden at Holland House, Kensington, about a month before she died of the small-pox. *Miscellanies*, 1857, p. 89. See also Sir Walter Scott's *Minstrelsy*, clxvi. There are on this point other curious particulars in Aubrey's "Miscellanies." But the belief long survived Aubrey's day. Throughout the whole of Scotland this article of the popular creed long remained unimpaired, and even now a diligent explorer of the more remote parts of the Highlands, not to say of the other districts of North Britain and of some less frequented localities in England, Wales, and Ireland, especially the two latter, would infallibly meet with examples of a lingering faith in second sight. Attention may be directed to a series of letters written by or to Pepys the diarist and others, educated Englishmen of high standing, among the Pepys correspondence, and belonging to the year 1699-1701. Among the Lowland Scots, Johnson seems to have thought, that in his time (1780) this sort of superstition was dying out; but I am hardly disposed to accept the Doctor in the present case as a conclusive authority. He met with a minister, he tells us, who came to Skye with a foregone resolution not to give credit to it. "We should have had little claim," says Dr. Johnson, writing about 1780, "to the praise of curiosity, if we had not endeavoured with particular attention to examine the question of second sight. Of an opinion received for centuries by a whole nation, and supposed to be confirmed through its whole descent by a series of successive facts, it is desirable that the truth should be established, or the fallacy detected. The second sight is an impression made either by the mind upon the eye, or by the eye upon the mind, by which things distant or future are perceived, and seem as if they were present. A man on a journey, far from home, falls from his horse; another, who is perhaps at work about the house, sees him bleeding on the ground, commonly with a landscape of the place where the accident befalls him. Another seer, driving home his cattle, or wandering in idleness, or musing in the sun-shine, is suddenly surprised by the appearance of a bridal ceremony, or funeral procession, and counts the mourners or attendants, of whom, if he knows them, he relates the names, if he knows them not he can describe the dresses. Things distant are seen at the instant when they happen. Of things future I know not that there is any rule for determining the time between the sight and the event.

"This receptive faculty, for power it cannot be called, is neither voluntary nor constant. The appearances have no dependence upon choice: they cannot be summoned, detained or recalled. The impression is sudden, and the effect often painful. By the term second sight seems to be meant a mode of seeing superadded to that which Nature generally bestows. In the north it is called taich; which signifies likewise a spectre or a vision. I know not, nor is it likely that the Highlanders ever examined, whether by taich, used for second sight, they mean the power of seeing or the thing seen."

Dr. Johnson adds: "A gentleman told me, that when he had once gone far from his own island, one of his labouring servants predicted his return, and described the livery of his attendant, which he had never worn at home; and which had been, without any previous design, occasionally given him . . . . The second sight is only wonderful because it is rare, for, considered in itself, it involves no more difficulty than dreams or perhaps than the regular exercises of the cogitative faculty; a general opinion of communicative impulses, or visionary representations, has prevailed in all ages and all nations; . . . the second sight of the Hebrides implies only the local frequency of a power which is nowhere totally unknown; and where we are unable to decide by antecedent reason, we must be content to yield to the force of testimony. . . . . To talk with any of these seers is not easy. There is one living in Sky, with whom we would have gladly conversed; but he was very gross and ignorant, and knew no English. The proportion in these countries of the poor to the rich is such, that, if we suppose the quality to be accidental, it can rarely happen to a man of education: and yet on such men it has sometimes fallen. There is now a second sighted gentleman in the Highlands, who complains of the terrors to which he is exposed. The foresight of the seers is not always prescience: they are impressed with images of which the event only shows them the meaning. They tell what they have seen to others, who are at that time not more knowing than themselves, but may become at last very adequate witnesses, by comparing the narrative with its verification." He concludes with observing: "I never could advance my curiosity to conviction; but came away, at last, only willing to believe."

In his "Ode on the popular Superstitions of the Highlands of Scotland." Collins touches upon this subject. The Shetlanders are very credulous under this head, and are strong believers in second sight. A story was related to me by the late Sir Robert Hamilton, upward of 40 years ago, of a boat's crew that left Lerwick on a rough day, and after being absent some time, were seen (as it was given out) to return to land, and go to their respective homes. The next morning the bodies of the men were washed up! But the credit still enjoyed by this superstition is very wide and deep-rooted even at the present day, and the anecdotes which are current about it, are certainly in some cases very remarkable.

Seed-Cake.—In Brathwaite's "Lancashire Lovers," 1640, p. 19, the rustic lover entices his mistress to marriage with promise of many rural pleasures, among which occurs, "Wee will han a seed-cake at Fastens:" and in Overbury's "Characters," 1638, under the character of a Franklin, we find enumerated the several country sports, amongst which occurs "the hoky or seed cake." "I have been told," says Miss Baker, writing in 1854, "that some fifty years ago, it was customary on All Souls' Day, for people (in Northamptonshire) to send seed cakes to their various friends, which were called soul-cakes; and as this was the period when wheat-sowing usually ended, it is probable both these observances (alluding to the seed-cake given to ploughmen after the wheat-sowing) have the self-same origin." They are probably identical with the Shropshire *Soul-Cake.*

See-Saw.—Gay describes the well-known sport of see-saw thus:

"Across the fallen oak the plank I laid,
And myself pois'd against the tott'ring maid;
High leap'd the plank, adown Buxoma fell," &c.

Douce seems to have thought that this was identical with the old game of Riding the Wild Mare, which is referred to in the "Knight of the Burning Pestle," written in 1610 or 1611: "Sweetheart, i' faith, I'll have Ralph come and do some of his gambols. He'll ride the wild mare, gentlemen, 'twould do your hearts good to see him."

This is still a popular game, and is carried out on an improved plan.

Selling of Pears or How Many Plums for a Penny?—The name of an old game, supposed to be analogous to the ancient *Chytrinda.* See St. John's

Manners and Customs of Ancient Greece, 1842, i, 152. This was a boy's sport; one for girls, called the *Tortoise,* is supposed to have been similar, but is not known in any English analogue.

Sepulchral Monuments.—See Fosbroke's *Encyclopædia,* 1843, ch. xi, and comp. *Cremation, Funeral Customs,* &c. Since Fosbroke's time much has been discovered and some matters set in a new light by the researches of Fergusson and Pitt-Rivers, as well as by the excavations, which have been undertaken by learned societies everywhere, and by the more exhaustive or correct conclusions thus rendered possible.

Serf, St.—See *Orkneys.*

Serpents.—The belief in augury and divination by the motions of serpents, seems from the account left to us by Cicero, to have flourished among the Romans, but to have been in modified regard by the better-informed. Speaking of the death of Gracchus, he says, that the severity of his disease was rather the cause of it, than a serpent's venom; but after all, he adds, the ill-luck of the augur was not so great, but that occasionally things will fall out by chance as he foretold. *De Divinatione,* lib. ii, sect. 28. Ross says that he had heard of battles between land and water serpents being treated as premonitory of misfortunes to men; and he intimates the same thing of emmets, as exemplified in a great combat between two swarms of these creatures prior to certain battles recorded in history between the Venetians and Lombards, and between the armies of Liege and Burgundy.

In the *Daily News* for Nov. 30, 1869, appeared the subjoined paragraph: A curious picture of Arab life has just been exhibited before the Court of Assizes at Constantina, in Algeria. A native, named Ben-Kemmari, was accused of mutilating his wife by cutting off her nose and upper lip in a fit of jealousy. The mother of the victim said that to cure her son-in-law of his jealousy she had consulted a much venerated Marabout, who had given her as a charm for her daughter a serpent's head wrapped up in hemp leaves, which was to be placed in the folds of the husband's turban. The woman appealed to the public present to prove that by this method she would have cured the man of his suspicions, and several Arabs at once took off their head gear and triumphantly showed the same talisman, while a native officer of the court, without being consulted, called out to the judge, "Yes, I have also a serpent's head; it gives strength to the man and fidelity to the woman."

Pepys was assured by a Mr. Templer that in Lancashire there were serpents, which grew to a great size, and which fed upon larks, which they caught by lying immediately below the bird, and ejecting poison on it, "which," says the Diarist, "is very strange." Feb. 4, 1661-2. In her *Letters from the United States, &c.* 1856, the Hon. Amelia Murray reports, as something which she had heard and credited, that in Louisiana there was a snake, which milked cows, and called a cow, which it had once milked, to be operated upon again, with a note resembling that of its calf!

Serra or **Serre.**—See *Fabulous Creatures.*

Set.—Game at whist and at tennis.

Set-a-Foot.—(A slight variety of *Scotch and English* and of analogous character to *Tom Tiddler* and *I'm the King of the Castle*), survived the Union a hundred years, and was played at during the early years of the present century. It consisted of a heroic contention, imbued with all the nationality of still older days. The signal for the war was chaunted as by bards—

"Set-a-foot on Scotish ground,
English, if ye dare."

And forthwith the two bodies of eight, ten, twelve, or even more schoolboys were arranged on either side, the one representing the Scotch and the other the English forces: and, be it said in honour of these representations, they fought for the victory of their accepted cause as earnestly as if the battle was real:

"No slackness was there found,
And many a gallant schoolfellow
Lay panting on the ground."

The field was thus ordered. The green sward, divided by any slight natural hollow, was chosen, if possible; if not, a conventional line was drawn, and the combatants confronted each other across the imaginary border. In a heap, perhaps a hundred or two hundred yards behind each, was piled a booty of hats, coats, vests, and other clothing and chattels, which stood in the stead of property to be harried or cattle to be lifted. The game was played by raids to seize and carry off these deposits; as whenever the store was exhausted, the nationality was beaten. The races and the struggles to achieve this victory were full of excitement. Sometimes one, swift of foot, would rush alone into the exploit: sometimes two or three, to distract the adversary, without leaving their own side defenceless, or exposed to inroad. Then the chase; the escape of the invader with his plunder; or being obliged to throw it down for personal safety; or being captured, and sent back with it, there to stand, chapfallen

and taunted, until one of his comrades could run in and touch him; when his restoration to the ranks was the result, though perhaps his ransomer was made prisoner in his stead. And so the war was carried on, so long as a rag was left to the pillager; and it was a sight to see occasionally, near the close, the awful condition of the losing side of the combatants. Almost every stitch of raiment was gradually devoted to the exigencies of the battle, and deposit after deposit was harried till every article, shoes, stockings, braces, &c. was "won away," and many of their discomfited wearers at last succumbed to their fate with nothing to cover their nakedness but trousers and shirt. I am not sure that even the last was not sometimes staked on the issue, so enthusiastic was set-a-foot. *Notes and Queries*, Aug. 1, 1858.

Seven Brothers, Festival of the.—(July 10). In *A Chronicle of London*, under 13 Henry IV. (1411-12), we find: "And prynce Henry lay at the bysshopes inne of Dorham fro the seid day of his comynge to towne unto the Moneday nest after the feste of Septem fratrum." These appear to have been brothers, who suffered martyrdom at the same time.

Seven Whistlers, The.—This superstition seems to be peculiar to Leicestershire. The seven whistlers are seven birds, whose voices warn the colliers in that locality of impending danger; and it is said that formerly, at least, no one would descend a pit if he heard the seven whistlers, whose prophetic notes no miner could disregard. Cases had been known in which men who had descended the pits, after this admonition, lost their lives. The belief in these supernatural songsters has expired, perhaps; yet scores of human beings perish yearly in our mines. *Current Notes* for April, 1855.

Shaftesbury. — "Shaftesbury is pleasantly situated on a hill, but has no water, except what the inhabitants fetch at a quarter of a mile's distance from the manour of Gillingham, to the lord of which they pay a yearly ceremony of acknowledgement, on the Monday before Holy Thursday. They dress up a garland very richly, calling it the Prize Besom, and carry it to the Manour-house, attended by a calf's-head and a pair of gloves, which are presented to the lord. This done, the Prize Besom is returned again with the same pomp, and taken to pieces: just like a milk-maid's garland on May Day, being made up of all the plate that can be got together among the housekeepers." —*Dodsley's Travels of Tom Thumb*, p. 16.

Shaking of the Sheets.—An old country dance. See Nares, 1859, in v.

Shaking the Smock.—In Killigrew's *Parson's Wedding*, 1664 (Hazlitt's *Dodsley*, xiv. 500), Wanton asks Wild to let her shake her smock over him, before he goes into the widow's chamber, for luck's sake.

Shark.—Couch of Polperro says: "The common opinion that sharks are compelled to turn on their backs, in order to seize their prey, has arisen from a mistaken view of this action," namely, the habit and necessity of bringing round the mouth in a direction enabling the serrated teeth to act as a circular saw in severing a bulky or tough substance. *Illustrations of Instinct*, 1847, p. 56-7. This may be perhaps regarded as a distinction without a difference.

Sharp Tuesday.—See *Shrove-Tuesday*.

Sharping-Corn.—Corn given to the smith at Christmas by the farmers for sharpening their tools or implements, generally half a bushel for each ploughland. *Blount* quoted by Halliwell in v. Coles mentions the same thing.

Sheep-Shearing.—Aubanus tells us, that the pastoral life was anciently accounted an honourable one, particularly among the Jews and the Romans. Mention occurs in the Old Testament of the festive entertainments of the former on this occasion, particularly in the second Book of Samuel, where Absalom the King's son was master of the feast. Varro may be consulted for the manner of celebrating this feast among the latter. In England, particularly in the Southern parts, for these festivities are not so common in the North, on the day they begin to shear their sheep, they provide a plentiful dinner for the shearers and their friends who visit them on the occasion : a table, also, if the weather permit, is spread in the open village for the young people and children. The washing and shearing of sheep is attended with great mirth and festivity. Indeed, the value of the covering of this very useful animal must always have made the shearing-time, in all pastoral countries, a kind of Harvest home. *Antiq. Conviv.* 62. In Tusser's "Husbandry," 1580, under "The Ploughman's Feast Days," are the following lines :

"Sheep Shearing.

"Wife, make us a dinner, spare flesh neither corne,
Make wafers and cakes, for our sheepe must be shorne,
At sheep shearing, neighbours none other things crave,
But good cheere and welcome like neighbours to have."

The expense attending these festivities appears to have afforded matter of complaint. Thus in "Questions of profitable and pleasant Concernings, &c. 1594 :" "If it be a Sheep Shearing Feast, Master Baily can entertaine you with his Bill of Reckonings to his Maister of three Sheapherds Wages, spent on fresh cates, besides spices and saffron pottage." In Brathwaite's "Lancashire Lovers," 1640, Camillus the clown, courting Doriclea, tells her : "We will have a lustie cheese-cake at our Sheepe Wash." There is a beautiful description of this festivity in Dyer's "Fleece," at the end of the first book, and in Thomson's "Seasons (Summer)."

Sheffield Knives or **Thwittles.** —Chaucer's "Miller of Trumpington" is represented as wearing a Sheffield knife :

"A Sheffield thwitel bare he in his hose :"

and it is observable that all the portraits of Chaucer give him a knife hanging at his breast. In the "Witch of Edmonton," 1658, Somerton says : "But see, the bridegroom and bride comes : the new pair of Sheffield knives fitted both to one sheath."

Shere, Chare, or **Maundy Thursday.**—Shere Thursday is the Thursday before Easter, and is so called "for that in old fathers days the people would that day shere theyr hedes and clypp theyr berdes, and pool theyr heedes, and so make them honest ayenst Easter day." It was also called Maundy Thursday. A writer in the "Gentleman's Magazine" for July 1799, says : "Maundy Thursday, called by Collier Shier Thursday, Cotgrave calls by a word of the same sound and import, Sheere Thursday." See Collier's "Eccles. Hist." vol. ii. p. 97. In Lydgate's Vertue of the Masse it is said :

So as thyn heed hath a precellence,
Aboue all membres in comparyson,
So cryst Ihesu of magnyfycence,
Thrugh his dyuyne dysposycyon
Sette the masse for shorte conclusyon,
As on shyrethursdaye the gospell ye maye rede,
For a prerogatyfe aboute euery orayson,
To helpe all them that to hym call at nede.

Fosbroke mentions as in use at Barking Nunnery, "Russeaulx (a kind of allowance of corn) in Lent, and to bake with eels on Sheer Thursday :" also, "stubbe eels and shafte eels baked for Sheer Thursday." Comp. *Maundy Thursday.*

Sheriffs or **Shire-reeves.**—On the 12th November, the morrow of St. Martin, the sheriffs for England and Wales are still (1904) nominated in the Court of Exchequer, where the Chancellor of the Exchequer, the Chief Justice of England, and others, attend to hear objections, and so forth, and ultimately make a selection of three persons for each county, from whom the sovereign is called upon to choose the future sheriffs. The chancellor and his colleagues, preparatively to the ceremony, take an oath in Norman-French to act with justice and impartiality.

In the "Gentleman's Magazine" for October, 1804, appeared the following communication from Mr. Nichols:

"*Monday, October 1st.* 1804.

"This day the lord mayor and aldermen proceeded from Guildhall, and the two sheriffs with their respective companies from Stationers' Hall, and having embarked on the Thames, his lordship in the city barge, and the sheriffs in the Stationers' barge, went in aquatic state to Palace Yard. They proceeded to the Court of Exchequer, where, after the usual salutations to the bench (the cursitor baron, Francis Maseres, Esq. presiding), the recorder presented the two sheriffs; the several writs were then read, and the sheriffs and the senior under-sheriff took the usual oaths. The whole of the numerous company then again embarked in their barges, and returned to Blackfriars Bridge, where the state carriages were in waiting. Thence they proceeded to Stationers' Hall, where a most elegant entertainment was given by Mr. Sheriff Domville." Sir H. Ellis has observed elsewhere that "the ceremony on this occasion, in the Court of Exchequer, which vulgar error supposed to be an unmeaning farce, is solemn and impressive; nor have the new sheriffs the least connection either with chopping of sticks, or counting of hobnails."

Shetland Isles about 1725.—

A curious picture of the social and religious condition of this outlying portion of North Britain, illustrative of the survival down to comparatively modern times of fairly archaic ideas and usages, is presented by a communication to the *Scotsman*, abstracted from the *Globe* newspaper of Feb. 24, 1903. Some of the particulars deserve to be transcribed:—At the beginning of the eighteenth century the social and religious condition of Shetland left much to be desired; and in the hope of bringing about an improvement, memorials were drawn up in the different parishes about the year 1725, and presented to the "Stewart and Justiciar-Depute," setting forth the low condition of the people, and praying that the Magistrate would take the same under his most serious consideration, and "not only cause the good laws against profane-

ness and immorality to be put into vigorous execution, but also to make Acts agreeable thereunto, and adapted to the particular circumstances of the country for the suppressing of sin, and promoting of piety and virtue, by inflicting condign punishment upon all transgressors."

The question of Sabbath observance (then as now) seems to have been very clamant, for it was the first to receive attention. No one was to be allowed to travel by land or sea on Sunday on any secular business, nor to engage in any work or recreation under a penalty of four pounds Scots (3/4) for the first offence, and double that amount for the second—in addition to which the transgressor had to "satisfy the kirk for the scandal." If the fines were not forthcoming, the Sabbath-breaker was to be "punished in his person." Further, any one wilfully staying away from church was liable to a fine of twenty shillings Scots (1/8) for each offence, failing which he had to undergo the aforesaid punishment in his person. Profane swearers and liars were liable to a fine of twenty shillings Scots for each offence; drunkards, half-a-crown; those who were found giving or selling drink to an intoxicated person, a like sum; scolds and disturbers of the peace, three pounds: and if fining did not have the desired effect, the inevitable corporal punishment was resorted to. Professional beggars were very sharply dealt with, it being decreed that anyone convicted of said offence should be "put in firmance, to be punished with the stocks or juggs"; while on the other hand, to give ear to the plaint of a beggar was to lay oneself open to a fine of ten pounds Scots. The question of the relationship of master and servant also seems to have been a vexed one in those days, for special attention was given to it. Disobedience or insolent servants were liable to receive "punishment in their persons," with the forfeiture of six months' wages. No householder was allowed to keep more servants than he actually required, nor to "entertain in his family idle persons capable of work."

The abject and friendless poor who were unfit for work were provided for in a somewhat novel fashion. The fines obtained for breaches of the law were put into what was known as the "Poors' Box," and out of this fund each pauper received a sum with which to buy clothes; while for their maintenance they had to look to certain householders in the parish to which they belonged. The kirk session nominated the houses in which the paupers were to be lodged and fed, and each of these groups of houses was known as a "quarter," while "quarter-wife" was a female pauper moving from one house to another at stated intervals. The pauper usually stayed in each house one night for every merk of land owned or rented by the householder. This somewhat arbitrary method of supporting the poor seems to have been tolerated by the people with a fairly good grace. The "quarter" system was still in vogue in some parts of the country about the middle of the 19th century. No man was allowed to take unto himself a wife unless he had "forty pounds Scots of free gear to set up house upon, or some lawful trade whereby he could subsist; nor such as could not read." Those old enactments were gradually superseded by the laws governing the rest of Scotland; but the office of "Ranselman" survived (in a less arbitrary form) for well-nigh half a century.

Shewri While.—This name used to be applied to a supposed evil spirit of the female sex, which haunted one of the hills in Monmouthshire, and molested and misled any traveller who happened to have occasion to pass that way. She was accustomed, when she saw anyone who had missed his road over the mountain, to greet him with "Whoo-whoop," and to beckon him from a distance to follow her; she would then lead her dupe a long dance, and end by bringing him back to the starting place. This superstition appears to have died out.

Shick-Shack Day.—A term employed in Surrey for Royal Oak Day, the 29th of May. A correspondent of *Notes and Queries* stated that he had heard the name associated with an obscure tradition of a king, who had escaped from his enemies by means of a hollow oak-tree (the owl legend being also remembered).

Shinty.—This is a game played during the winter and at Christmas in the Highlands of Scotland with a wooden ball, each of the players being provided with a curved stick. It appears to be similar to golf. An account of it, with an engraving, is given in the *Penny Magazine* for January 31, 1835. It may be that our colloquialism shindy is derived from this game. A Shinty match is mentioned in the *Gentleman's Magazine* for February, 1795.

The sport, a rather boisterous one, appears to have been a favourite amusement of the Highland labourers and tenants, and to have been encouraged by the laird. Jamieson regards it as analogous to the English Hackie (or Hockey), and Grose is inclined to identify it with the Gloucestershire *Not*, a game played with a knotted ball.

Shitten or **Shut-in Saturday.**—The Saturday in Passion Week. Forby, in his "Vocabulary," 1830, says that it should be pronounced Shutten, or Shut in Saturday; it is the day on which our Saviour was laid in the sepulchre.

Shoe-Omens.—The casual putting the left shoe on the right foot, or the right on the left, was thought anciently to be the forerunner of some unlucky accident. Scot, in his "Discovery," tells us: "He that receiveth a mischance, will consider whether he put not on his shirt the wrong side outwards, or his left shoe on his right foot."

Two early English writers advert to this portent, but in terms of incredulity, if not of derision, and one of them (Gaule) adds, that it was deemed "inauspicious to burst the shoe-latchet." Mason's Anatomie of Sorcerie, 1612, 90, and Gaule, *Mag-astromancers*, 181. Thus Butler, in his "Hudibras," writes, on the authority of Pliny:

"Augustus having b'oversight
Put on his left shoe 'fore his right,
Had like to have been slain that day,
By soldiers mutin'yng for pay."

Similar to this, says Grose, is putting on one stocking with the wrong side outward, without design: though changing it alters the luck.

Filippo-Maria Visconti, Duke of Milan, who died in 1447, was, in common with the majority of his contemporaries, a firm believer in astrology and divination. . . . To a more sceptical generation, some of his superstitious foibles cannot fail to present a ludicrous and contemptible aspect. . . . He viewed it as a circumstance of sinister omen, if his right foot was accidentally put into his left shoe. Hazlitt's *Venetian Republic*, 1900, ii, 88.

It is accounted lucky by the vulgar to throw an old shoe after a person when they wish him to succeed in what he is going about. John Heywood refers to this usage, doubtless of considerable antiquity even in his time, in his "Works," first printed in 1546:

"I will streight weie anker, and hoyse vp sayle,
And thytherward hye me in haste lyke a snayle,
And home agayne hytherward quicke as a bee,
Now for good luck, caste an olde shoe after mee."

Grose, citing Jonson, saying "Would I had Kemp's shoes to throw after you," observes, throwing an old shoe or shoes after anyone going on an important business, is by the vulgar deemed lucky. Jonson was probably alluding to Kemp's famous exploit, related in the "Nine Daies Wonder," 1600. Gayton has the following passage: " An incantation upon the horse, for want of nailing his old shoes at the door of his house when he came forth: or because, nor the old woman, nor the barber, nor his niece, nor the curate designed him the security of an old shooe after him." *Festivous Notes,* 1654, p. 104.

I find the following in " The Ravens Almanacke," 1609: " But at his shutting in of shop, could have bene content to have had all his neighbours have throwne his olde shooes after him when hee went home, in signe of good lucke." In Ben Jonson's " Masque of Gypsies " we find this superstition mentioned:

> *Gypsie.* " Hurle after an old shoe,
> I'le be merry what ere I doe—"

Again, in the " Honest Man's Fortune (1613)," Mallicorn says:

> " Captain, your shoes are old; pray put 'em off,
> And let one fling 'em after us—"
> Beaumont and Fletcher by Dyce, iii, 426.

This is a common practice at weddings, when the married couple are setting out on their honeymoon. Mr. Hallen gives a curious charm from the Clackmannan Kirk Session records: " 1633, Jan. 6.— Compeirit Janet White and declarit that Girsell Tamsone being in hir childill (childbed) sent hir to hir husband, Jhon Wallace, to bring his left foote shooe to drink out off, using it as a remedie to cuir hir. Sicklyke compeirit James Drysdall, and confirmit the same, declairing that he after the shooe was (. . . . ?) to him againe he sained it upon the fire and put the catt into it, saying, All my wyffes sicknes be upon the catt. . . . The Session thinking it a sort of sorcerie, ordaint hir to cum after Sermon before the pulpit and crave God's pardon . . . and to pay in penaltie fortie shilling." *Antiquary* for August, 1889.

In the " Witch of Edmonton," 1658, Old Carter tells his daughter and her sweetheart : " Your marriage-money shall be receiv'd before your Wedding Shooes can be pulled on. Blessing on you both." So in Dekker's " Match me in London " : " I thinke your Wedding Shoes have not beene oft unty'd." Down answers, "Some three times."

Shoeing the Colt.—The exaction of a fine or treat from a new comer into any office—a form of footing.

Shoeing the Wild Mare.—From scattered notices in several old works, I collect that this was a diversion among our ancestors, more particularly intended for the young, and that the Wild Mare was simply a youth so called, who was allowed a certain start, and who was pur-

sued by his companions, with the object of being shoed, if he did not succeed in outstripping them. The only allusion pure and simple to this pastime is, I believe, in Breton's " Fantasticks," 1626, where he speaks of a youth " shewing their agility in shooing the Wild Mare;" but in Skelton's " Elynour Rumming," and in the " Frere and the Boye," occur references to what must have been a popular air or ballad founded on the game, and Ravenscroft, in his " Melismata," 1611, has a passage mentioning Away the Mare (just as it is mentioned in the two earlier places):

> " Heigh ho, away the mare,
> Let vs set aside all care."

Herrick, in his " New Yeares Gift Sent to Sir Simeon Steward," seems, however, to set the matter at rest, and to show that the conjecture as to the character of the sport, just hazarded, is likely to be correct:

> ——" but here a jolly
> Verse crown'd with yvie and with holly;
> That tels of winters tales and mirth,
> That milk-maids make about the hearth,
> Of Christmas sports, the wassel-boule,
> That tost up after Fox-i'-th' hole, ;
> Of Blind-man-buffe, and of the care
> That young men have to shooe the mare."

Of course, the nursery game mentioned by Mr. Halliwell is entirely different from this adult pastime. The former appears to be known in Denmark; it is played with the toes. There is more than one version in our own language; the following is printed by Mr. Halliwell :

> " Shoe the colt, shoe !
> Shoe the wild mare !
> Put a sack on her back,
> See if she'll bear.
> If she'll bear,
> We'll give her some grains;
> If she won't bear,
> We'll dash out her brains."

Popular Rhymes and Nursery Tales, 1849, p. 101.

Shoes.—The celebrated Thomas Coryat, when he started on his second travels in 1612, hung up in the church of his native place, Odcombe, the shoes in which he is said to have walked from Venice, and they remained there, it is understood, till the beginning of the 18th century. It appears to have been a custom among the Chinese for an official, on relinquishing his duties, to suspend his shoes in a conspicuous place by way of suggestion to those coming after him, that they should walk in his footsteps.

Shooting the Black Lad.—An ancient and long-standing usage at Ashton-under-Lyne on the 16th of April, in commemoration of Sir Ralph of Ashton, Vice-Constable of England in the reign of Richard III. and the holder of a penny-rent here. See Hazlitt's *Proverbs*, 1882, p. 361, for farther particulars.

Shove-Groat.—See a good account in Nares, *Glossary*, 1859, in v. See also Halliwell in v. *Shovel-Board.* A writer in Willis's " Current Notes " for April, 1853, says: " In the 13th year of Henry VIII. the Benchers of the Temple made an order ' that none of the Society within this house shall exercise the play of shoffe-grotte or slyp-grotte upon pain of six-shillings and eightpence.' " This game was otherwise called shove-halfpenny: the mode of playing it is explained in " Current Notes " for June, 1853; and in the number for July, 1853, is a long paper, well worth reading on the subject.

This is one of the amusements prohibited by the statute 33 Henry VIII. A Shove-Groat shilling is mentioned in the *Second Part of Henry IV.* 1600. In Saxony, long before that time, they had a sort of silver coin or counter known as a *spielgroschen.* Shove-Groat was also called *Slide-groat, Slide-Thrift,* and *Slip-Thrift.* In the Diary of Philip Henslowe the manager, edited by Collier, is the following curious entry: " Lent unto John Pallmer, the 8 of July, 1599, when he playd a shove groat at the cort. Redy mony, v^s,

> Mr. Griffen, at the hachette,
> Mi. Drayton,
> Harry Chettelle."

These three names were perhaps added as witnesses. Comp. *Up, Jenkins.*

This game is cited as *Slip-Thrift* and *Short-Thrift*, as if it were a costly recreation, by Richard Rice in his *Invective*, 1579. He says, that man was made in God's image, and that his gifts might not die with him his Creator sent him into Paradise. " What to dooe there?" inquires our author. " To bowle, or to plaie at dise, or cardes, penipricke, or slipthrift?" He tells us elsewhere that the game was played with pased-groats. Rice also mentions short-thrift, perhaps another form of it. Slipthrift is referred to in the " English Courtier and the Countrey Gentleman," 1586.

Shreving Pew.—That where the worshipper knelt to confess at Shrovetide. In the Churchwardens' Accounts of St. Mary at Hill, in the City of London, A.D. 1493, is the following article: " For a mat for the Shreving Pewe, iij d."

Shrew-Mouse. — Pliny, in the Eighth Book of his " Natural History," says that among the Romans the cry of the shrew-mouse was regarded as an augury of evil, and Moulin quotes Valerius Maximus for the same piece of folk-lore.

Shrovetide, or Confession Time.—From v. *scrivan* to shrieve, prior to the English Reformation, was a period of penitential observance preparatory to Easter; but at a later date was partly converted into a sort of holiday and carnival with the incidence of collops, pancakes, &c. and a variety of sports. These details are mentioned under their respective heads. In the North of England, Shrove Tuesday is called Fastens E'en, the succeeding day being Ash Wednesday, the first day of the Lenten Fast. I observe that the late Mr. Hunter in his " Hallamshire Glossary," 1829, notices the term Fasten-Tuesday as the name under which Shrove Tuesday, though only in strictness a vigil, is known in that district of Yorkshire. It is called Fasguntide by Blount in his " Glossographia," 1681, a word interpreted by Forby fasting-time. It is no longer known, although Mr. Halliwell, in his " Dictionary of Archaisms," 1847, seems to quote it as a current provincialism in the Eastern shires.

Shrove-tide plainly signifies the time of confessing sins, as the Saxon word Shrive, or Shrift, means *Confession.* This season has been anciently set apart by the Church of Rome for a time of shriving or confessing sins. This seemingly no bad preparative for the austerities that were to follow in Lent, was, for whatever reason, laid aside at the Reformation.

The luxury and intemperance that usually prevailed at this season were vestiges of the Romish carnival, which Moresin derives from the time of Gentilism, introducing Aubanus as describing it thus: " Men eat and drink and abandon themselves to every kind of sportive foolery, as if resolved to have their fill of pleasure before they were to die, and as it were forego every sort of delight." Thus also Selden : "What the Church debars us one day, she gives us leave to take out in another—first there is a Carnival and then a Lent." Langley, in his " Abridgment of Polydore Virgil," observes: " This furnishyng of our bellies with delicates, that we use on Fastingham Tuiesday, what tyme some eate tyl they be enforsed to forbeare all again, sprong of Bacchus Feastes, that were celebrated in Rome with great joy and deliciouse fare."

Taylor, the Water Poet, in his " Jacke-a-Lent," 1620, gives the following account of Shrove Tuesday: " Shrove Tuesday, at whose entrance in the morning all the whole kingdom is inquiet, but by that time the clocke strikes eleven, which (by the help of a knavish sexton) is commonly before nine, then there is a bell rung cal'd the Pancake-bell, the sound whereof makes thousands of people distract'd, and forgetful either of manners or humanitie; then there is a thing called wheaten floure, which the cookes do mingle with water, egges, spice, and other tragical, magicall inchantments, and then they put it by little and little into a frying-pan of boiling suet, where it makes a confused dismall hissing (like the Lernean Snakes in the reeds of Acheron, Stix, or Phlegeton), untill at last, by the skill of the cooke, it is transformed into the forme of a Flip-Jack, cal'd a pancake, which ominous incantation the ignorant people doe devoure very greedily." I know not well what he means by the following: "Then Tim Tatters (a most opulent villaine), with an ensigne made of a piece of a baker's mawkin fix't upon a broome-staffe, he displaies his dreadful colours, and calling the ragged regiment together, makes an illiterate oration, stuff't with most plentiful want of discretion."

"Here must enter that wadling, stradling, bursten-gutted Carnifex of all Christendome, vulgarly enstiled Shrove Tuesday, but, more pertinently, sole Monarch of the Mouth, high Steward to the Stomach, chiefe Ganimede to the Guts, prime peere of the Pullets, first Favourite to the Frying-pans, greatest Bashann to the Batterbowles, Protector of the Pancakes, first Founder of the Fritters, Baron of Bacon-flitch, Earle of Eggebaskets, &c. This corpulent commander of these chollericke things called cookes, will shew himselfe to be but of ignoble education; for by his manners you may find him better fed than taught whenever he comes."—*Vox Graculi*, 1623.

Bishop Hall, in his "Triumphs of Rome," thus describes the Jovial Carneval: "Every man cries Sciolta, letting himself loose to the maddest of merriments, marching wildly up and down in all forms of disguises; each man striving to outgo other in strange pranks of humorous debauchedness, in which even those of the holy order are wont to be allowed their share; for howsoever it was by some sullen authority forbidden to clerks, and votaries of any kind, to go masked and misguised in those seemingly abusive solemnities, yet more favourable construction hath offered to make them believe that it was chiefly for their sakes, for the refreshment of their sadder and more restrained spirits, that this free and lawless Festivity was taken up."—P. 19.

Overbury, in his "Characters," speaking of a "Franklin," says, that among the ceremonies which he annually observes and that without considering them as reliques

of Popery, are "Shrovings." Among the "Records of the City of Norwich," mention is made of one John Gladman, "who was ever, and at thys our is a man of sad disposition, and trewe and feythfull to God and to the Kyng, of disporte as hath ben acustomed in ony cite or burgh thorowe alle this reame, on Tuesday in the last ende of Cristemesse (1440,) vizt. Fastyngonge Tuesday, made a disport with hys neyghbours, havyng his hors trappyd with tynnfoyle and other nyse disgisy things, coronned as Kyng of Crestemesse, in tokyn that seson should end with the twelve monethes of the yere, aforn hym went yche moneth disguysed after the seson requiryd, and Lenton clad in whyte and red heryngs skinns and his hors trappyd with oystershells after him, in token that sadnesse shuld folowe and an holy tyme, and so rode in divers stretis of the cite with other people with hym disguysed, makyng myrth, disportes, and plays, &c." Blomefield's *Norfolk*, 1745, ii, 111. In the "Northumberland Household Book," 1512, it appears "that the clergy and officers of Lord Percy's Chapel performed a play before his Lordship upon Shrowftewesday at night," p. 345; it was not an unusual occasion for such spectacles.

The subsequent passage in Hall's "Virgidemiæ," 1598, seems to imply that a hen was a usual present at Shrove-tide: as also a pair of gloves at Easter.

"For Easter Gloves, or for a Shroftide hen,
Which brought to give, he takes to sell again."
—*Book* iv. *Sat.* 5, p. 42.

In the "Life of Antony à Wood," p. 46, are some curious particulars relating to indignities shown at that time, 1647, to freshmen at Oxford on Shrove-Tuesday. A brass pot full of cawdle was made by the cook at the freshman's charge, and set before the fire in the College-hall. "Afterwards every freshman, according to seniority, was to pluck off his gowne and band, and, if possibly, to make himself look like a scoundrell. This done, they were conducted each after the other to the high table, and there made to stand on a forme placed thereon; from whence they were to speak their speech with an audible voice to the company: which, if well done, the person that spoke it was to have a cup of cawdle, and no salted drinke; if indifferently, some cawdle and some salted drink; but if dull, nothing was given to him but salted drink, or salt put in College beere, with tucks to boot. Afterwards when they were to be admitted into the Fraternity, the Senior Cook was to administer to them an oath over an old shoe, part of which runs thus : ' Item tu jurabis, quod Penniless Bench non visitabis,' &c. After which spoken with gravity, the freshman kissed the shoe, put on his gowne and band, and took his place among the Seniors." The Editor observes, p. 50 : " The custom described above was not, it is probable, peculiar to Merton College. Perhaps it was once general, as striking traces of it may be found in many societies in Oxford, and in some a very near resemblance of it has been kept up till within these few years." Comp. *Hens*, where it is shown that they, as well as cocks, were formerly threshed at Shrovetide.

" To tuck, was to set the nail of their thumb to their chin, just under the lippe, and by the help of their other fingers under the chin, they would give him a mark, which sometimes would produce blood."
—*Wood.*

At Brasenose College on this anniversary it is usual for the butler to present a copy of verses. A collection of these was printed in 1857.

Hearne, in his *Diary*, 1724-5, writes : " At Sunningwell, near Abingdon in Berks, they have a custom (which I suppose was formerly in other places, tho' I do not know of any else where it is now) every Shrove Tuesday, at night, in the dusk of the evening, for the boys and girls to say these verses about the village—

Beef and bacon's
Out of season,
I want a pan
To parch my peason ;

which they repeat several times, and then throw stones at all people's doors, which makes the people generally to shut up their doors that evening."

Canon Bowles informed Brand, that in the neighbourhood of Salisbury, in Wiltshire, the boys go about before Shrovetide, singing these rhymes :

"Shrove Tide is nigh at hand,
And I am coming a shroving ;
Pray, Dame, something,
An apple or a dumpling,
Or a piece of truckle cheese
Of your own making,
Or a piece of pancake."

It may not be improper to insert here a rhyme, which a gentleman in the Isle of Wight heard sung by some young boys in chorus on Shrove Tuesday, 1855 ; he communicated it to " Notes and Queries."

" Shroving, shroving, I am come to
shroving—
White bread and apple pie,
My mouth is very dry ;
I wish I were well a-wet,
As I could sing for a nut.

Shroving, shroving, I am come to
shroving.
A piece of bread, a piece of cheese,
A piece of your fat bacon,
Dough nuts, and pancakes,
All of your own making.
Shroving, shroving, I am come to
shroving."

An odd practice seems to prevail in some parts of Somersetshire, and also in Devonshire and Dorsetshire, on Shrove Tuesday, which is locally nick-named Sharp Tuesday. The youngsters go about after dusk, and throw stones against people's doors, by what is considered by them an indefeasible right. They at the same time sing in chorus :

" I be come a shrovin
Vor a little pankiak ;
A bit o' bread o' your baikin,
Or a little truckle cheese o' your maikin,
If you'll gi' me a little I'll ax no more,
If you don't gi' me nothin, I'll rottle
your door."

It appears that in Staffordshire, this day is known as Goodish (or rather Gooding) Tuesday, a term of which the signification has only been conjectured. In Oxfordshire, the following versions have been met with :

" Knick, knock, the pan's hot,
And we be come a shroving :
A bit of bread, a bit of cheese,
A bit of barley dumpling.
That's better than nothing,
Open the door and let us in,
For we be come a pancaking."

Or,

" Pit a pat, the pan is hot,
We are come a shroving ;
A little bit of bread and cheese
Is better than nothing.
The pan is hot, the pan is cold ;
Is the fat in the pan nine days old?"

In Dekker's " Seven Deadly Sins of London," 4to. 1606, p. 35, is this passage : " They presently (like prentices upon Shrove-Tuesday) take the lawe into their owne handes and do what they list." And it appears from contemporary writers that this day was a holiday, time immemorial, for apprentices and working people. See Dodsley's " Old plays," Hazlitt's edit. xi, 195-6, 436-7.

Heath, in his " Account of the Scilly Islands," has the following passage : " On a Shrove Tuesday in each year, after the throwing at cocks is over, the boys in this island have a custom of throwing stones in the evening against the doors of the dwellers' houses ; a privilege they claim time immemorial, and put in practice without controul, for finishing the day's sport. I could never learn from whence this custom took its rise, but am informed that the same custom is now used in several provinces of Spain, as well as in some parts of Cornwall. The terms demanded by the boys are pancakes, or money to capitulate."

The apprentices, whose particular holiday this day is now esteemed, and who are on several accounts so much interested in the observation thereof, ought, with that watchful jealousy of their ancient rights and liberties (typified so happily on this occasion by pudding and play), as becomes young Englishmen, to guard against every infringement of its ceremonies, so as to transmit them entire and unadulterated to posterity. In the time of Elizabeth and her successor, the day was one on which great licence was used, and riotous scenes were too frequent. See the second part of Dekker's "Honest Whore," 1630, and Nabbes's "Totenham Court," 1638, where one of the characters says, "If I doe, I have lesse mercie then prentices at Shrovetide." This may refer to the cockthreshing on this day. Comp. *Pancakes.*

Among the sports of Shrove Tuesday, cock-fighting and throwing at cocks appear almost everywhere to have prevailed. Rivett, in his Reply to Smirke, 1676, has the following curious passage: "It was Shrove-Tuesday with them, and, not having yet forgot their boys-play, they had set up the cock, and would have been content some of them to have ventur'd their coffee-farthings, yea their Easterpence by advance, to have a fling at him."

It is a remarkable thing that the difficulty of suppressing cockfighting remains to be overcome. One reason probably is that influential and (supposed to be) educated English gentlemen take an interest in its continuance.

"Shrove-Tide," says Warton, "was formerly a season of extraordinary sport and feasting. In the Romish Church there was antiently a feast immediately preceding Lent, which lasted many days, called 'Carniscapium.'" See Carpentier in v. Supp. Lat. Gloss. Du Cange, tom. i. p. 381. In some cities of France an officer was annually chosen, called Le Prince d'Amoreux, who presided over the sports of the youth for six days before Ash-Wednesday. Ibid. v. "Amoratus," p. 195; and v. "Cardinalis," p. 818. Also v. "Spinetum," tom. iii. p. 848. Some traces of these festivities still remain in our Universites. Carpentier, under the year 1355, mentions a petition of the scholars to the master of the School of Ramera, to give them a cock, which they asserted the said master owed them upon Shrove Tuesday, to throw sticks at according to the usual custom, for their sport and entertainment.

At Paris the approach of the season of self-denial is similarly commemorated and compensated by revelry and licence, and in 1897 the anniversary of the *Bœuf Gras* was celebrated with all the customary honours.

From Lavaterus it should seem that anciently in Helvetia fires were lighted up at Shrove-tide. "And as the young men in Helvetia, who with their fire-brand, which they light at the bone-fires at Shrof-tide," &c. *Of Ghosts and of Spirits Walking by Night,* 1572, p. 51. "Among the Finns no fire or candle may be kindled on the eve of Shrove-Tuesday."—Douce. See *Cock-Fighting, Cock-Thrashing, Cock-penny, Pancakes,* &c.

Shuffle or **Shovel Board.**—This was very recently played. Pepys mentions that he had a turn at it at Hackney in 1664. Douce, about eighty years ago, heard a man ask another to go into an ale-house in the Broad Sanctuary, Westminster, to play at it. In Isaak Walton's time, a shovel board was probably to be found in every public house. A correspondent of "Current Notes," writing from New York in 1852, thus describes this game: "It is played on a table or board about 40 feet long and 18 inches wide. It is made of clean white pine without knots, and fine sand is sifted all over, to enable the players to shovel their pieces along. On each side of the board there are narrow troughs or gutters, to catch the pieces if they fly off, which they frequently do. The game is played by two persons, who have each four pieces, numbered 1 to 4. The pieces are of brass, exactly the size and form of half-pound flat weights. A line is marked across the board, about half a foot from the farther extremity, and the art is to discharge the piece from the hand with just sufficient force to go beyond the line, which counts so many; but if the piece lies half off and half on the farther end, it counts double. But to do that requires great skill and long practice. The players play off their pieces alternately, and the chief effort is to knock the antagonist's piece from the table."

There was formerly at the Falcon Inn at Stratford-on-Avon a board of this description, on which Shakespear is alleged to have played. There is no authority for such an idea, but the board is preserved in the Birthplace Museum. In the Instructions of Sir John Wynn of Gwydyr about 1610 to his chaplain he tells him that if he (Sir John) should play at bowls or shovel-board, and there should be no strangers, he would like of his company." Pennant's *Tours in Wales,* 1810, iii, 404.

Shuggy-Shew.—See *Swing.*

Shuttlecock.—See *Battledore.*

Signet, Royal.—In the Robin Hood episode (Hazlitt's *Tales and Legends,* 1892, p. 319), where the disguised King takes from his pocket the broad signet on alleged behalf of his royal master, the outlaw at once bends his knee to it.

In *Adam Bel,* 1536, where Cloudesly is in Carlisle, about to be executed, his two comrades, Bel and Clym, knock at the town gate; and when the porter comes, they shew him what they pretend to be the king's seal, which procures their admission:

"The porter had ween'd it had been so,
And lightly did off his hood:
'Welcome be my lord's seal,' said he;
'For that shall ye come in.'"

Fox, in his *Book of Martyrs,* who is followed by the writer of the fifth act of *Henry VIII.,* relates how, in view of the summons of Cranmer before the Council, Henry sent for him, and in case the Council would not listen to him, delivered him his signet, which he was to exhibit as a token to them that they were discharged from their deliberation upon his matter. It is a graphic and affecting passage— more so in the prose book than in the drama; and again in the ballad-poem of *Robin Hood and Queen Katherine,* the royal page sent to the outlaw by the queen, says to Robin:

"She bids you post to fair London court,
Not fearing anything;
For there shall be a little sport,
And she hath sent you her ring."

The effect of which delivery is to satisfy the bold archer that he may go in safety with such a passport. So, in the *Blind Beggar of Bethnal Green,* by John Day, 1659, Old Strowd, desiring that £100 should be sent him, forwards his ring to the holder of the money as a token.

These were outward and visible symbols intelligible to most persons in an illiterate age, when a written warrant or order would have proved useless. A similar custom and idea prevailed among the ancient Greeks. In the Deipnosophistæ of Athenæus, xiii, 49, a lover of Lais the courtezan signifies his wish to see her by sending her his seal; but she declines, because it is of clay.

Signs, Tavern.—See *Tavern Signs.*

Silver Games.—Humphrey Roberts, of King's Langley, in his "Complaint for Reformation," 1572, says: "I may speake of one notable abuse, whiche among yᵉ rest is so much practised, yᵗ it is made in a maner lawfull called a siluer game. These siluer games are becom such snares, & as it wer baits to catch men: yᵗ it seemeth vnto me Sathan to (*sic*) becom a coning goldsmyth." Roberts, in a description which occupies several pages, proceeds to draw a picture of the profanation of the Sundays by these silver games, and the desertion of the churches. The exact nature of the game so designated he does not, however, disclose, but leaves us to conjecture that they were amusements of a more or less frivolous character, chiefly confined to the country, for he draws a distinction between them and the "vayne deuices and fond exercises" of great towns and cities, such as bull-baiting, and "many such vnfruitefull pastimes, tendyng to no comodytie for yᵉ commonwealth: for which purpose Parysh Garden is a place."

In *Green's Tu Quoque,* by John Cook, 1614, we have a passage in which "the silver game" is mentioned as something to do with success in a lovesuit. Lysons quotes two entries relating to Brentford under 1629: "Received of Robert Bicklye for the use of our games . . . 2/;" and, "Of the said Robert Bicklye for a silver bar which was lost at Elyng . . . 3/6." Hazlitt's *Dodsley,* xi, 249. Lysons, in an extract from a "Chapel-Warden's Account of 1634," notices a payment of 11*s.* 8*d.* "for the silver games," but omits to explain what they were.

Simnels.—Simnel is from the Latin *Simila,* the finest part of the flour. By statute 51 Hen. III. Simnel bread (*panis similageneus*) was to weigh two shillings less than Wastell bread. I owe these two items of information to Pegge's "Curialia," 1818, where several other curious circumstances connected with this very ancient usage are brought together.

A writer in the "Gentleman's Magazine" for July, 1783, speaking of cross buns, saffron cakes, or symnels in Passion Week, observes that "these being formerly at least, unleavened, may have a retrospect to the unleavened bread of the Jews, in the same manner as lamb at Easter to the Paschal Lamb." Simnels are still commonly used in Lancashire at Easter; they are identical, I believe, with the Semeslins of which Hutchinson, in his "History," speaks as in use in the North. It is, in fact, a species of plum-cake. At Bury, in Lancashire, on Mid Lent Sunday, which is there called Simblin (Simnel) Sunday, simnel cakes are sold openly in the shops, which are only closed during the services.

Simon and Jude Day, SS.— (Oct. 28). In the Runic Calendar St. Simon and St. Jude's Day was marked by a ship, on account of them having been fishermen. This seems to have been the day on which votaries came formerly to

Glastonbury to offer to Joseph of Arimathea. In the metrical " Life of Joseph," 1520, sign. A 5, it is said, that two young women, in the " xviii. yere of henry our kyng," were mortally sick of the pestilence, and were thought to be beyond cure, but

" Theyr prayer makyng to ioseph of
        aramathye
So began to recouer & brought theyr
        offryng
On Symons day & Iude vnto Glastonbury."

We learn from Holinshed that, in 1536, when a battle was appointed to have been fought upon this day between the king's troops and the rebels in Yorkshire, so great a quantity of rain fell upon the eve thereof, as to prevent the battle from taking place. It appears that this day was accounted rainy as well as St. Swithin's, from the following passage in the " Roaring Girl :" " As well as I know 'twill rain upon Simon and Jude's Day." And again : " Now a continual Simon and Jude's rain beat all your feathers as flat down as pancakes."

On this day the Lord Mayor of London was formerly elected ; his inauguration and the show took place on the 29th October. The following charm belongs to this day : " Take an apple, pare it whole, and take the paring in your right hand, and standing in the middle of the room, say the following verse :

' St. Simon and Jude, on you I intrude,
By this parting I hold to discover,
Without any delay, to tell me this day
The first letter of my own true lover.'

Turn three times round, and cast the paring over your left shoulder, and it will form the first letter of your future husband's surname, but if the paring break into many pieces, so that no letter is discernible, you will never marry ; take the pips of the same apple, put them into spring water and drink them."

" Festa dies Judæ prohibet te incedere
        nude,
Sed vult ut Corpus vestibus omne tegas.
Festa dies Judæ cum transiit atque
        Simonis
In Foribus nobis esse putatur Hiems.
Simonis Judæ post Festum væ tibi nude
Tunc inflant Genti mala gaudia veste
        carenti."
        Buchleri *Sententiæ Rythmicæ.*

Sin Eaters.—" Within the memory of our fathers," remarks Bagford, " in Shropshire, in those villages adjoyning to Wales, when a person dyed, there was notice given to an old sire, (for so they called him), who presently repaired to the place where the deceased lay, and stood before the door of the house, when some of the family came out and furnished him with a cricket, on which he sat down facing the door. Then they gave him a groat, which he put in his pocket ; a crust of bread, which he eat ; and a full bowle of ale, which he drunk off at a draught. After this, he got up from the cricket and pronounced, with a composed gesture, the ease and rest of the soul departed, for which he would pawn his own soul. This I had from the ingenious John Aubrey, Esq. who made a collection of curious observations, which I have seen. and is now remaining in the hands of Mr. Churchill the bookseller. How can a man think otherwise of this, than that it proceeded from the ancient heathens?" Leland's *Collect.* lxxxvi.

" In the county of Hereford," says Aubrey, " was an old custome at funeralls to hire poor people, who were to take upon them the sinnes of the party deceased. One of them, (he was a long, leane, ugly, lamentable poor raskal,) I remember lived in a cottage on Rosse highway. The manner was, that when the corpse was brought out of the house, and layd on the biere, a loafe of bread was brought out, and delivered to the sinne eater, over the corps, as also a mazar bowle, of maple, full of beer, (which he was to drink up,) and sixpence in money : in consideration whereof he took upon him, *ipso facto*, all the sinnes of the defunct, and freed him or her from walking after they were dead. This custome alludes, methinks, something to the scapegoat in the old lawe, Levit. chap. xvi. v. 21, 22, ' And Aaron shall lay both his hands on the head of the live goate, and confesse over him all the iniquities of the Children of Israel, and all their transgressions in all their sins, putting them upon the head of the goat, and shall send him away by the hand of a fit man into the Wilderness. And the goat shall bear upon him all their iniquities into a land not inhabited : and he shall let the goat goe into the Wilderness.'

" This custome, (though rarely used in our dayes) yet by some people was observed even in the strictest time of the Presbyterian Government, as at Dynder ; (*volens nolens* the parson of the parish,) the kindred of a woman deceased there had this ceremonie punctually performed, according to her will : and, also, the like was done at the City of Hereford in those times, where a woman kept, many yeares before her death, a mazard bowle for the sinne-eater ; and the like in other places in this countie : as also in Brecon." " At Llanggors where Mr. Gwyn the Minister about 1640 could not hinder the performance of this ancient custom. I believe it was heretofore used all over Wales." In another page Aubrey says: "A.D. 1686. This custom is used to this day in North Wales:" where milk seems to have been the substitute for beer.

Bishop Kennet in whose possession Aubrey's MS. appears to have been, has added this note:—"It seems a remainder of this custom which lately obtained at Amersden, (Ambrosden) in the county of Oxford, where at the burial of every corpse one cake and one flaggon of ale, just after the interment, were brought to the minister in the church porch."

Singin' E'en.—Jamieson informs us that Singin-E'en is the appellation given in the county of Fife to the last night of the year.

Sixes and Sevens.—A writer in the "Gentleman's Magazine" enquires after the origin of the phrase "I found everything at sixes and sevens, as the old woman left her house." A very good note on this subject may be found in *Notes and Queries*, 1st. S. 111, 425-6.

Skating.—More properly, *secatting*, from the A. S. verb, *to cut*. See, for an account of this amusement, which in some countries forms a business as a habitual method of locomotion, Nares, *Gloss*. in v.

Skimmington.—"To ride," or "riding Skimmington," is, according to Grose, a ludicrous cavalcade in ridicule of a man beaten by his wife: it consists of a man riding behind a woman with his face to the horse's tail, holding a distaff in his hand, at which he seems to work, the woman all the while beating him with a ladle: a smock displayed on a staff is carried before them, as an emblematical standard, denoting female superiority: they are accompanied by what is called rough music, that is, frying-pans, bull's-horns, marrow-bones and cleavers, &c. a procession admirably described by Butler in his "Hudibras."

From one passage of Machyn's "Diary," under 1562-3, it would seem that scolds were occasionally made, as a punishment, to ride in a cart through the streets, with a distaff in their hands. In the Notes to this Diary, 1848, Mr. Nichols describes a curious penalty (curious from its indirectness) imposed in the presence of a member of the Camden Society on a termagant. "About 1790 one of the members of the Camden Society," he tells us, "witnessed a procession of villagers on their way to the house of a neighbouring farmer, in the parish of Hurst (Berkshire,) who was said to have beaten his wife. The serenaders, consisting of persons of all ages and denominations, were well supplied with kettles, tin cans, cover-lids, hand-bells,

pokers and tongs, and cows' horns, and drawing up in front of the farm, commenced a most horrible din, showing at least that the ceremony was known by the name of rough music? After some time, the party quietly dispersed, apparently quite satisfied with the measure of punishment inflicted by them on the delinquent." The passage in Machyn himself, on which Mr. Nichols's illustration was founded, is as follows: "The xxij day of Feybruary (1562-3,) was Shroyff-monday, at Charyng crosse ther was a man cared of iiij men, and a-for hym a bagpipe playng, a sha[w]me and a drum playhyng, and a xx lynkes bornyng a-bowtt hym, because ys next neybors wyff ded bett here hosband; ther for yt is ordered that ys next naybor shall ryd a-bowtt the plase."

In Lupton's "Too good to be true," 1580, p. 50, *Siuqila* or *Aliquis* says: "In some places with us, if a woman beat her husband, the man that dwelleth next unto hir shall ride on a cowlstaffe; and there is al the punishment she is like to have." *Omen* observes: "That is rather an uncomly custome than a good order, for he that is in faintnesse, is undecently used, and the unruly offendor is executed thereby. If this be all the punishment your wives have that beate their simple husbandes, it is rather a boldning than a discouraging of some bolde and shamelesse dames, to beate their simple husbandes, to make their next neyghbors (whom they spite) to ride on a cowle staffe, rather rejoicing and flearing at the riding of their neighbours, than sorrowing or repenting for beating of their husbands."

In "Divers Crab-tree Lectures," &c. 1639, a cut representing a woman beating her husband with a ladle, is called "Skimmington and her husband." This cut is repeated in a chapter, entitled "Skimmington's Lecture to her husband, which is the errand scold," with some verses wherein occur the following pithy lines:

"But all shall not serve thee,
For have at thy pate,
My ladle of the crab-tree
Shall teach thee to cogge and to prate."

Pepys in his *Diary*, June 10th, 1667, writes: "Down to Greenwich, where I find the street full of people, there being a great riding there to-day for a man, the constable of the town, whose wife beat him."

Misson says: "I have sometimes met in the streets of London a woman carrying a figure of straw representing a man, crown'd with very ample horns, preceded by a drum, and followed by a mob, making a most grating noise with tongs, gridirons, frying-pans, and sauce-pans. I asked what was the meaning of all this; they told me that a woman had given her husband a sound beating, for accusing her of making him a cuckold, and that upon such occasions some kind neighbour of the poor innocent injur'd creature generally performed this ceremony." The following passage is taken from King's "Miscellany Poems:"

> "When the young people ride the Skimmington,
> There is a general trembling in the town,
> Not only he for whom the person rides
> Suffers, but they sweep other doors besides;
> And by that hieroglyphic does appear
> That the good woman is the master there."

Hence seemingly it was part of the ceremony to sweep before the door of the person whom they intended to satirize—and if they stopped at any other door and swept there too, it was a pretty broad hint that there were more skimmingtons, *i.e.* shrews, in the town than one. In the print of "a Skimmington," engraved by Hogarth, for "Hudibras," we observe a tailor's wife employed in this manner to denote her own, but, as she thinks, her husband's infamy.

In *Hymen*, 1760, is the following account of a skimmington, "There is another custom in England, which is very extraordinary; a woman carries something in the shape of a man, crowned with a huge pair of horns: a drum goes before and a vast crowd follows, making a strange music with tongs, gridirons, and kettles. This burlesque ceremony was the invention of a woman, who thereby vindicated the character of a neighbour of hers, who had stoutly beaten her husband for being so saucy as to accuse his wife of being unfaithful to his bed. The figure with horns requires no explanation; it is obvious to every body that it represents the husband."

The following curious paper was read before the Society of Antiquaries, January 23, 1806: "This is to certifie that Dorothy Awseter, the wife of Francis Awseter, of Southall, in the p^sh of Hesse, in the countie of Midd, is a turbulent woman continually in contencon with her neighbours and continually comencing suits in lawe without any just cause at all, haunting alehouses, and continually breeding quarrels there. And upon all occasions full of provoking speeches and uncivill language. Witness our hands, the 21st of Feb., anno dom. 1659. Signed, Jane Awseter, widow; Robert Awseter, Mari Allonsoun, Catherine Mede, Wm. Stafford, Ann Stafford, Thom. Awsiter, and Susan Awsiter."

In one of George Houfnagle's "Views in Seville," dated 1593, is a curious representation of riding the stang, or "skimmington," as then practised in that country. The patient cuckold rides on a mule, handshackled, and having on an amazing large pair of antlers, which are twisted about with herbs, with four little flags at the top, and three bells. The vixen rides on another mule, and seems to be belabouring her husband with a crabbed stick; her face is entirely covered with her long hair. Behind her, on foot, follows a trumpeter, holding in his left hand a trumpet, and in his right a bastinado, or large strap, seemingly of leather, with which he beats her as they go along. The passengers, or spectators, are each holding up at them two fingers like snail's horns. In the reference, this procession is styled in Spanish "Execution de Justitia de los Cornudos patientes." A somewhat similar chastizement was inflicted in Spain on those married people who disgrace themselves; the wife, by infidelity, and the husband by collusion and derivation of profit from her shame. Comp. *Pillory* and *Stang*.

Skittles.—Comp. *Nine Pins*.

Slam. — In "Witts Recreations," 1640, is the epigram:

> "*On Tuck.*
> At post and pair, or slam, Tom Tuck would play,
> This Christmasse, but his want wherewith, says nay."

Slappaty Pouch. — See Davis, *Suppl. Glossary*, 1881, p. 597.

Slide. ⎰
Slip. ⎱ **Thrift.**—See *Shove-Groat*.

Smock Race.—The smock race, run by young girls in their chemises only, was formerly usual on Ascension Day in the North of England. The prize was a fine Holland smock or chemise. The sport, not a very delicate one, is described in the "Poetical Miscellanies," published by Steele, 1714.

Smock-Turning. — There is a charm known at Whitby, and in the Cleveland country generally, as well as in other parts, as smock-turning. The women and lasses of Whitby put their shifts on inside out, to secure, as they fancy, a successful voyage for their husbands or sweethearts, and a fair wind. The usage seems originally to have had a more recondite meaning, and to have been connected with the almost universal creed in witchcraft and the power to dissolve or weaken spells by various methods, some of them (to our modern apprehension) not very obvious. But, certainly, if a farmer could believe that his ox was secured from preternatural influences by firing a shot over him from tail to head, there was no reason why the poor folk at Whitby should not indulge in their smock-turning superstition which, of course, proceeded on the common inverting theory. Comp. *Irish Superstitions.*

Smoke Money.—This was for the candles at the Purification. In Lysons's "Environs," vol. i, p. 310, among his curious extracts from the Churchwardens' Accounts at Lambeth, I find the following :

"1519. Paid for Smoke Money at Seynt Mary Eves, 0. 2. 6."

This occurs again in 1521 :

"Paid by my Lord of Winchesters scribe for Smoke Money, 0. 2. 6."

Comp. *Candlemas.*

Snails.—Snails were used in love divinations : they were set to crawl on the hearth, and were thought to mark in the ashes the initials of the lover's name. On the subject of these divinations there is a most curious passage in the third Idyl of Theocritus.

Snake-rings.—See *Druids' Eggs.*

Snakes.—Nares, Glossary, 1859, in v. points out the old-fashioned error as to the seat of the poison in the forked tongue of the snake instead of in the teeth or fangs. The bite of the snake was also wrongly supposed to produce a painless death, as in Shakespear's *Antony and Cleopatra*, where the creature is described as a *worm*. Cleopatra, however, killed herself with an asp—a *genus* at present unknown to us.

Bishop Hall's "Superstitious Man" thought it unlucky to let a snake go alive. A snake-catcher in the New Forest, who lived there on sufferance all his life, had an impediment in his utterance, which the local folk ascribed to his parcel-snake mouth. Hazlitt's *Tales and Legends*, 1892, p. 265. Comp *Serpents.*

Snap-dragon.—See Halliwell in v.

Sneezing.—Sneezing has been held ominous from times of the most remote antiquity. Eustathius upon Homer has long ago observed, that sneezing to the left was unlucky, but prosperous to the right.

"She spoke : Telemachus then sneez'd aloud ;
Constrain'd, his nostrils eccho'd through the crowd.
The smiling Queen the happy omen blest :
So may these impious fall, by Fate opprest."—*Odyss.* b. xviii.

Xenophon having ended a speech to his soldiers with these words : viz. "We have many reasons to hope for preservation ;"

they were scarce uttered when a soldier sneezed : the whole army took the omen, and at once paid adoration to the gods. Then Xenophon, resuming his discourse, proceeded : "Since, my fellow-soldiers, at the mention of your preservation, Jupiter has sent this omen," &c.

Aristotle has a problem, "Why sneezing from noon to midnight was good, but from night to noon unlucky." St. Austin tells us that "the antients were wont to go to bed again, if they sneezed while they put on their shoe." The Rabbinical account of sneezing is very singular. It is, that "sneezing was a mortal sign even from the first man, until it was taken off by the special supplication of Jacob. From whence as a thankful acknowledgment, this salutation first began and was after continued by the expression of Tobim Chaiim, or vita bona, by standers by upon all occasions of sneezing."

Apuleius mentions sneezing ; as does Pliny also in his problem, "cur sternutantes salutantur." The latter says that to sneeze to the right was deemed fortunate, to the left or near a place of burial, the contrary.

The custom of blessing persons when they sneeze has without doubt been derived to the Christian world, where it generally prevails, from the times of heathenism. Bartholinus cites Pliny, Aristotle, and others to shew that the ancients regarded sneezing as an omen, and the blessing customarily bestowed upon the sneezer as a deprecation of evil likely to arise.

It is said that Tiberius the Emperor, otherwise a very sour man, would perform this rite most punctually to others, and expect the same from others to himself. Petronius Arbiter, too, describes it. Cœlius Rhodoginus has an example of it among the Greeks in the time of Cyrus the younger, namely, where one of the Greeks, while they were consulting about their retreat, sneezed, whereupon all the others saluted upon Jupiter Soter, and it occurs as an omen in the eighteenth Idyllium of Theocritus, where he refers to a portent of this kind occuring to Menelaus prior to his marriage with Helen of Troy. So also in the seventh "Idyllium," l. 96. In the Greek Anthology it is alluded to in an epigram. *Antholog. Gr. ex recens.* Brunckii, 1794, iii, 95.

It is said that sneezing (with irritation of the nostrils) was regarded as a sign that a man's wife would have a happy confinement, and that sneezing at the commencement of a repast was of especially good augury : but if the phenomenon was delayed till the entertainment was half-finished, the omen was, on the contrary, unlucky. The writer exemplifies this by the case of Telemachus, whose sneezing foreboded calamity to the suitors of Penelope. The act should be repeated twice or thrice; but according to Scot, if the same person sneezes twice every night for three nights together, it prognosticates a death in the house, or some severe calamity, or a great piece of good luck—a rather wide range of contingencies! An English author enumerates among portents sneezing at meat. Gaule's *Mag-astromancers Posed,* p. 181.

Rosse says: "Prometheus was the first that wisht well to the sneezer, when the man, which he had made of clay, fell into a fit of sternutation, upon the approach of that celestial fire which he stole from the sun. This gave original to that custome among Gentiles in saluting the sneezer. They used also to worship the head in sternutation, as being a divine part and seat of the senses and cogitation." *App. to Arcana Microcosmi.* p. 292. Plutarch mentions that, when Themistocles sacrificed in his galley before the battle with Xerxes, and one of the assistants upon the right hand sneezed, Euphrantides, the soothsayer, presaged the victory of the Greeks and the overthrow of the Persians. This habit is referred to in the *Golden Legend,* 1483, and before the date of that work in English by John of Salisbury, in his *Nugæ Curialium,* where he says: "Rusticanum et fortè Ofelli Proverbium est—Qui Somniis et Auguriis credit, nunquam fore securum. Ego Sententiam et verissimam et fidelissimam puto. Quid enim refert ad consequentiam rerum, si quis semel aut amplius sternutaverit? Quid si oscitaverit? His mens nugis incauta seducitur, sed fidelis nequaquam acquiescit."

Sir Thomas Browne on the authority of Hippocrates says, that "sneezing cures the hiccup, is profitable to parturient women, in lethargies, apoplexies, catalepsies. It is bad and pernicious in diseases of the chest, in the beginning of catarrhs, in new and tender conceptions, for then it endangers abortion." "Sneezing being properly a motion of the brain suddenly expelling through the nostrils what is offensive to it, it cannot but afford some evidence of its vigour, and therefore, saith Aristotle, they that hear it προσκυνουσιν ως ιερον honour it as something sacred and a sign of sanity in the diviner part, and this he illustrates from the practice of physicians, who in persons near death use sternutatories (medicines to provoke sneezing,) when if the faculty arise, and sternutation ensues, they conceive hopes of life, and with gratulation receive the signs of safety." He adds: "Some

finding, depending it, effects to ensue; others ascribing hereto as a cause, what perhaps but casually or inconnexedly succeeded; they might proceed into forms of speeches, felicitating the good and deprecating the evil to follow." Browne supposes that the ground of this ancient custom was the opinion the ancients held of sternutation, which they generally conceived to be a good sign or a bad, and so upon this motion accordingly used a "Salve" or Ζευ σωσον, as a gratulation from the one, and a deprecation from the other. In Horman's "Vulgaria," 1519, we read: "Two or three neses be holsom: one is a shrewd token."

Howell records a proverb: "He hath sneezed thrice; turn him out of the hospital," but it is very questionable whether this is not one of those sayings which the ingenious author devised, by his own confession, for the benefit of posterity.

Our forefathers drew omens even from the times of sneezing. To sneeze on Monday, was dangerous; on Tuesday, signified kissing a stranger; on Wednesday, a letter; on Thursday, "something better;" on Friday, sorrow in store; on Saturday, the sight of one's sweetheart on Sunday. The next quotation is ironical:

"When you sneeze, strait turne your-
    selfe unto your neibours face:
As for my part, wherein to sneeze, I
    know no fitter place;
It is an order, when you sneeze, good
    men will pray for you:
Marke him that doth so, for I thinke
    he is your friend most true.
And that your friend may know who
    sneezes, and may for you pray,
Be sure you not forget to sneeze full in
    his face alway.
But when you hear'st another sneeze,
    although he be thy father,
Say not God bless him, but choak up,
    or some such matter, rather."

The *Schoole of Slovenrie,* by R. F. 1605, p. 6.

Hall, in his "Characters," 1608, mentions that the superstitious man of his day would have regarded it as a mark of neglect if his friends did not uncover when he sneezed. In Portugal, says Brand himself, it would be considered a great breach of good manners to omit it. The custom of blessing sneezers the Spaniards found among the natives of the New world at the period of the conquest of Florida by Fernando de Soto in 1542. Salutation of sneezers by removal of the hat is described in a French work of the 17th century as an article of etiquette.

Hanway, in his "Travels into Persia," tells us that sneezing is held a happy omen among the Persians, especially when repeated often. It is received at this day in the remotest parts of Africa. So we read in Codignus, that upon a sneeze of the Emperor of Monomotapa, there passed acclamations through the city. And as remarkable an example there is of the same custom in the remotest parts of the East, in the Travels of Pinto. The Siamese wish long life to persons sneezing: for they believe that one of the judges of hell keeps a register wherein the duration of men's lives is written, and that when he opens his register and looks upon any particular leaf, all those whose names happen to be entered in such leaf never fail to sneeze immediately. This appears to be a trace of the Rabbinical theory already referred to. There are some superstitions relating to sneezing mentioned in the notes to the variorum edition of Minucius Felix, p. 243. See also "Chevræana," tom. i. p. 170, and Beloe's Herodotus, vol. iii. p. 105.

The following notes on this subject were communicated to Brand by the Rev. Stephen Weston, B.D., F.S.A :

"Περὶ κληδονισμῷ πταρμικῷ, De Ominatione sternutaria.

"Sternutationem pro Dæmonio habuit Socrates. Τὸν πταρμὸν θεὸν ἡγούμεθα, Ariſtot. in Problem. Πταρμὸς ἐκ δεξιῶν, Victoriæ ſignum. Plutarch in Themiſt. *ut ſuprâ*, unde lepide Ariſtophanes in Equitibus

ταῦτα φροντίζοντί μοι
Ἐκ δεξιᾶς ἀπέπαρδε καταπύγων ἀνήρ·
Κἀγὼ προσεκυσα.—Ιππεις. v. 635.

"Sternutantibus apprecabantur antiqui ſolenne illud Ζευ σῶσον, unde Epigr. Ammiani in hominem cum pravo naſo, *i.e.* longiſſimo.—'When he ſneezes he never cries God ſave, becauſe his Ear is ſo far from his noſe that he cannot hear himſelf ſneeze,' vid. Rhodig. de Ammiano, l. xvii. c. 11. 'Ουδὲ λέγει Ζεῦ σῶσον, etc." Ariſtot. "Problem." ſect. xxxiii. p. 9.

Meridianæ Sternutationes fauſtæ—matutinæ infelices. Plin. l. xxviii. c. 2, de caus. Sternut. Aureus argutum ſternuit, omen Amor. Propert. 2, 234
Odyſſ. Hom. ρ. v. 541.—μέγ ἔπταρεν—ubi vid. Schol.
Catullus Epigr. 45.—Dextram ſternuit ad probationem.—S. W."

Solstice.—The term usually applied to the periods of the year in June and December, when the Sun is at the turning-point in its course. It is at these seasons that men have usually celebrated, as we see, certain festivals of a quasi-religious complexion. Comp. *Mother Night.*

Songle.—A handful of leased corn, after it has been tied up. See Halliwell in v.

Sops in Wine.—i.q. *pinks* or *gilliflowers*. See Nares, ed. 1859, in v. The most probable explanation of the term is that pinks were used to flavour wine, and Nares adduces a mention of *July-flower* wine. Lysons, in his account of Wilsdon or Willesdon Parish, tells us of an "Inventory of the Goods and Ornaments belonging to Wilsdon Church about 1547," in which occur "two masers were appointed to remayne in the church for to drynk yn at brideales." The pieces of cake or wafers, that appear to have been immersed in the wine on this occasion, were properly called sops, and doubtless gave name to the flower termed "sops in wine." *Environs*, 1st ed. iii, 624. Comp. *Sussex Archæol. Coll.* xiv, 135.

Sorcery.—The difference between a conjurer, a witch, and an enchanter, according to Minsheu, is as follows:— "The conjurer seemeth by praiers and invocations of God's powerful names, to compel the divell to say or doe what he commandeth him. The witch dealeth rather by a friendly and voluntarie conference or agreement between him and her and the divell or familiar, to have his or her turn served, in lieu or stead of blood or other gift offered unto him, especially of his or her soule. And both these differ from inchanters or sorcerers, because the former two have personal conference with the divell, and the other meddles but with medicines and ceremonial formes of words called charmes, without apparition." "These sorcerers, or magicians do not always employ their art to do mischief: but, on the contrary, frequently exert it to cure diseases inflicted by witches, to discover thieves, recover stolen goods, to foretell future events and the state of absent friends."

A sorcerer or magician, says Grose, differs from a witch in this: a witch derives all her power from a compact with the devil: a sorcerer commands him and the infernal spirits by his skill in powerful charms and invocations, and also soothes and entices them by fumigations. For the devils are observed to have delicate nostrils, abominating and flying some kinds of stinks: witness the flight of the evil spirit into the remote parts of Egypt, driven by the smell of a fish's liver burned by Tobit. They are also found to be peculiarly fond of certain perfumes: insomuch that Lilly informs us that one Evans, having raised a spirit at the request of Lord Bothwell and Sir Kenelm Digby, and forgotten a fumigation, the spirit, vexed at the disappointment, snatched him out from his circle and carried him from his house in the Minories into a field near Battersea Causeway.

Mason ridicules "Inchanters and charmers—they, which by using of certaine conceited words, characters, circles, amulets, and such like vaine and wicked trumpery (by God's permission) doe worke great marvailes: as namely in causing of sicknesse, as also in curing diseases in men's bodies. And likewise binding some, that they cannot use their naturall powers and faculties; as we see in night-spells, Insomuch as some of them doe take in hand to bind the devil himselfe by their inchantments." *Anatomie of Sorcery*, 1612. In the Sarum Articles of Inquiry, 1614, is the following: "67. Item, whether you have any conjurers, charmers, calcours, witches, or fortune-tellers, who they are, and who do resort unto them for counsell?"

A similar demand occurs in the "York Articles of Inquiry" (any year till 1640): "Whether there be any man or woman in your parish that useth witch-craft, sorcery, charmes, or unlawfull prayer, or invocations in Latine or English, or otherwise, upon any Christian body or beast, or any that resorteth to the same for counsell or helpe."

The legend of the *Friar and the Boy*, which the Editor has inserted in his *Popular Poetry*, 1864-6, seems to have come to us immediately from the French; but it is probably of German origin. The enchanted pipe occurs in *Friar Bacon*. *The Cuckolds' Dance* is another supernatural narrative printed in the same collection, with a critical preface.

In the Tale of the Basyn, where the priest rises in the night and lays hold of the enchanted basin, the latter remains immovably attached to his hands:

"His handys fro the basin myzt he not twyn.
Alas, seid Sir John, how shall I now begynne?
Here is sum wychcrafte.
Faste the basin con he holde,
And all his body tremeld for colde;
Leuer then a c. pounde he wolde
That hit were him rafte."

But the spell is eventually dissolved by the parson of the parish, who arrives on the spot with the husband; the basin fell from them; and they all fled for shame. The inference from the presentment of the priest and the parson as the bad and good genius of the piece perhaps is, that the story in its existing form was composed about the epoch of the Reformation. Hazlitt's *Popular Poetry*, iii. 50.

At the trial of the Countess of Somerset, in 1616, for her complicity in the Overbury murder, it is said that proofs were brought forward, in order to attach greater odium to her, of her having used magical spells and other unlawful arts to gain her purposes. It also exhibited the spirit of the age, that Mrs. Turner, another of the confederates, was accused of having employed sorceries to draw Sir Arthur Mainwaring to her bed.

Pepys records under July 31. 1665, a case mentioned to him as having occurred at Bordeaux of the now familiar artifice, at first thought to be supernatural, of lifting a body from the ground, where the lungs of the latter, as well as those of the persons lifting it are inflated with air. The words of the charm or spell communicated to Pepys were:

"Voyci un Corps mort,
Royde comme un Baston,
Froid comme Marbre,
Leger come un Esprit.
Levons le au nom de Jesus Christ."

But it had long been a well understood piece of natural magic abroad, especially at Venice. *Diary*, ed. 1858, ii, 273, and the long and interesting note.

On the 2nd of February, 1903, a wood-dealer was sent to prison at Botsham sessions, Cambridgeshire, for having administered to his horses a concoction formed of wash purchased from the village blacksmith, some nails, parings of hoof, and a pennyworth of pins, over which he pronounced an incantation, and then dosed the animals with the strange fluid, with the result that one of them died. They had evinced a reluctance to work, which the prisoner ascribed to sorcery. Still more recently a case occurred at Bishop Stortford in Essex of a staunch belief in the efficacy for malignant purposes of the hair cut from the nape of the neck of the intended victim, with parings of his nails, and other ingredients, mixed with water which were to be corked up in a bottle, and placed on the fire at night. The person desirous of exercising an evil influence wished, as the bottle burst from the heat, that sickness might fall on his supposed enemy, and the nearer to midnight the wish was expressed, the likelier it was thought to be realized. These modern instances are painfully curious.

Andrews, speaking of the death of the Earl of Angus in 1588, tells us, as a proof of the blind superstition of the age "he died, (says a venerable author) of sorcery and incantation." "A wizard, after the physicians had pronounced him to be under the power of witchcraft, made offer to cure him, saying, (as the manner of these wizards is) that he had received wrong. But the stout and pious Earl declared that his life was not so dear unto him, as that, for the continuance of some years, he would be beholden to any of the devil's instruments, and died." *Cont. of Henry*, 4th ed. 194.

A writer of the 18th century, referring to Lochcarron, Rosshire, says: "There is one opinion which many of them entertain, and which indeed is not peculiar to this parish alone, that a popish priest can cast out devils and cure madness, and that the Presbyterian clergy have no such power. A person might as well advise a mob to pay no attention to a Merry Andrew, as to desire many ignorant people to stay from the (popish) priest." *Stat. Acc.* xiii, 557.

But perhaps one of the most curious incidents in the history of sorcery in any country is the statute which passed into law at Venice in 1410, for prohibiting the domestic serfs of both sexes from employing the mysteries of the black-art as a means of gaining the affections of their masters. Hazlitt's *Hist. of the Venetian Republic*, 1860, vol. iv p. 330. Every nation has its peculiar cast of superstition. In the early folk-lore of Venice, we must not be surprised to find a large belief in the influence, for good or evil, of spirits who controlled the water and the winds.

Sortes or **Lots.**—This is a species of divination performed by opening the works of Virgil, &c., and remarking the lines which shall be covered with your thumb the instant the leaves are opened; by which, if they can be interpreted in any respect to relate to you, they are accounted prophetic. This custom appears to have been of very ancient date, and was tried with Homer's poems as well as Virgil's. They who applied to this kind of oracle were said to try the *Sortes Homericæ* or *Sortes Virgilianæ*.

Ferrand in his *Erotomania*, 1640, p. 177 mentions the "kinde of divination by the opening of a booke at all adventures: and this was called the Valentinian Chance, and by some, Sortes Virgilianæ: of which the Emperor Adrian was wont to make very much use." Home (*Demonologie*, 1650, p. 81) says: "For sorcery, properly so called, viz. divination by lotts, it is too much apparent how it abounds. For lusory lots the State groans under the losse by them, to the ruine of many men and families; as the churches lament under the sins by them: and for other lots, by sieves, books, &c. they abound as witchery, &c. abounds."

Welwood says in his *Memoirs*, 1718, that Charles I. and Lord Falkland, being in the Bodleian Library, made this experiment of their future fortunes, and met with passages equally ominous to each. Aubrey, however, in his "Remains of Gentilism" (*circa* 1670), tells the story of consulting the Virgilian lots differently. He says:—"In December 1648, King Charles the first being in great trouble, and prisoner at Caersbrooke, or to be brought to London to his triall, Charles Prince of Wales, being then at Paris, and

in profound sorrow for his father, Mr. Abraham Cowley went to wayte on him. His highnesse asked him whether he would play at cards, to divert his sad thoughts. Mr. Cowley replied he did not care to play at cards, but if his highnesse pleased he would use Sortes Virgilianæ: Mr. Cowley alwaies had a Virgil in his pocket. The Prince accepted the proposal, and prickt a pinne in the fourth booke of the Æneid at this place:

" At bello audacis populi vexatus et armis,
Finibus extorris, complexu avulsus Iüli,
Auxilium imploret, videatque indigna suorum
Funera ; nec, quum se sub leges pacis iniquæ
Tradiderit : regno aut optatâ luce fruatur :
Sed cadat ante diem, mediâque inhumatus arenâ."

Æneid, lib. iv. l. 615.

The Prince understood not Latin well, and desired Mr. Cowley to translate the verses; which he did admirably well."

" 'But vex'd with rebels and a stubborn race,
His country banish'd and his son's embrace,
Some foreign prince for fruitless succours try
And see his friends ingloriously die:
Nor, when he shall to faithless terms submit,
His throne enjoy, nor comfortable light,
But, immature, a shameful death receive
And in the ground the unbury'd body leave.'

—Dryden's *Miscellanies*," vi.

Johnson, in his "Life of Cowley," suspects that great poet to have been tinctured with this superstition, and to have consulted the Virgilian lots on the great occasion of the Scottish Treaty, and that he gave credit to the answer of the oracle. Allan Ramsay has these lines:

" Waes me, for baith I canna get,
To ane by law we're stented;
Then I'll draw cuts, and take my fate,
And be with ane contented."

Poems, 1721, p. 81. In the Glossary he explains "Cuts. lots. These cuts are usually made of straws unequally cut, which one hides between his finger and thumb, while another draws his fate."

Soul-Bell.—See *Passing-Bell.*

Soul-Cakes or **Soul-Mass Cakes.**—Sir Henry Ellis points out that, in Aubrey's time, in Shropshire, there was set upon the board on All Souls'

Day a high heap of Soul-cakes, lying one upon another, like the picture of the shew-bread in the old Bibles. They were about the bigness of twopenny cakes, and every visitant that day took one. Comp. *Hallowmas* and *Seed-Cakes*.

Souls, Three.— For this metaphysical survival of the peripatetic school of philosophy see Nares, *Glossary*, 1859, in v.

Southwark or **St. Margaret's Fair.**—A correspondent of *Notes and Queries* tells us it was established by the charter granted by King Edward IV. to the city of London on Nov. 9, 1462. It was appointed to be held on September 7, 8, and 9, and was attended by the usual Court of Piepowder for the hearing of pleas and the issue of process connected with matters arising in the fair. The site, which was on St. Margaret's Hill, near the present Town Hall, is indicated by the circumstance that when, in 1743, the fair was partially suppressed, and the stall-keepers in consequence discontinued their customary gratuity to the debtors in the Marshalsea, the latter threw over their prison walls a quantity of stones and rubbish, which lighted among the booths in the fair. On this occasion one life seems even to have been lost. Subsequently the site was removed to the Mint in Southwark, and the proceedings were finally suppressed in 1763, not without some difficulty, for Mr. Rendle says (quoting the *Annual Register*) :—" After many futile attempts the High Constable with 100 petty constables went to Suffolk Place (Mint district), and pulled the booths down."

Mr. Halliwell, in his notes to "Ludus Coventriæ," 1841, has quoted an extract from a showman's bill of the seventeenth century, preserved in Harl. MS., 5931, where it states that, " At Crawley's show at the Golden Lion, near St. George's Church, during the time of Southwark-Fair, will be presented the whole story of the old creation of the world, or Paradice Lost, yet newly reviv'd with the addition of Noah's flood." Two of these pieces are no longer known ; but in 1662 George Bayley was licenced to exhibit a show called *Noah's Flood ;* and probably the *Creation of the World* was the same as the spectacle exhibited at Bartholomew's Fair, and alluded to under the title of *The World's Creation* in *Wit and Drollery,* 1682. See Hazlitt's *Manual of Old Plays,* 1892, pp. 54, 167.

Gay, in his fable of the "Two Monkeys," thus describes Southwark Fair :

" The tumbler whirles the flip-flap round,
With sommersets he shakes the ground ;
The cord beneath the dancer springs ;

Aloft in air the vaulter swings,
Distorted now, now prone depends,
Now through his twisted arms ascends ;
The croud in wonder and delight,
With clapping hands applaud the sight."

Sow.—Grose tells us, " If going on a journey on business a sow cross the road, you will probably meet with a disappointment, if not a bodily accident, before you return home. To avert this, you must endeavour to prevent her crossing you : and if that cannot be done, you must ride round on fresh ground : if the sow is with her litter of pigs, it is lucky, and denotes a successful journey." It should seem that swine appearing in sight, in travelling, was an omen of good luck.

Sow-Day.—See *Orkneys.*

Sowens.—Eden, in his " State of the Poor," vol. i. p. 300, in a note, tells us : " Robert Burns, the Ayrshire ploughman, mentions sowens as part of the rural feast which concludes the merriment of his countrymen on Hallow-e'en. Sowens, with butter instead of milk, is not only the Hallow-e'en supper, but the Christmas and New-year's-day's breakfast, in many parts of Scotland." The Burns here mentioned was the same, whom we now regard as a Poet, as well as a Ploughman.

Span-Counter.—This is mentioned as a youthful sport in " The First part of King Henry VI." 1594 : "*Cade.* But doest thou heare Stafford tell the King, that for his fathers sake, in whose time boyes plaide at spanne-counter with French Crownes, I am content that hee shall be king as long as he liues." This occurs with a difference in Henry VI. Part ii, Act. iv, sc. 2, as the play is now printed ; yet in either case the stakes seem impossibly high for youthful gamesters.

Mr. Halliwell-Phillipps notices a passage in Dr. Forman's *Diary,* where it is said that Forman used to play at this about 1570, with his companion and bedfellow, Henry Gird. Strutt says that this is like marbles,—except that counters are used in it. Comp. Nares, *Gl.* 1859, 819.

Speech of Animals, Birds, and Flowers.—The theory of a language intelligible among what are usually regarded as dumb or inarticulate creatures or things is of great antiquity, and was known to the Greek dramatists from the so-called Æsopian apologues, as it became to the modern poets of different countries, who have used the common privilege of interpreting the vocal utterances of animals and birds and the supposed significance of floral types. In Baldwin's *Beware the Cat,* originally printed before 1570, the author makes his feline hero betray the secrets of Popish priests and the abuses prevalent in Society, and the Argument before the book acquaints us, that the King's Players were then rehearsing a play of *Esop's Crow*, where the majority of the actors were birds. Hazlitt's *Prefaces, Dedications and Epistles*, 1874, pp. 69-75. At a much later date—in 1655—Thomas Fuller produced his *Speech of Birds* and of *Flowers;* and the *Language of Flowers* is a familiar work of popular reference. The poets have used this theory.

Spells.—Cotta very sensibly observes: "If there be any good or use unto the health by spels, they have that prerogative by accident, and by the power and vertue of fancie. If fancie then be the foundation whereupon buildeth the good of spels, spels must needs be as fancies are, uncertaine and vaine : so must also, by consequence, be their use and helpe, and no lesse all they that trust unto them." He elsewhere asks: "How can religion or reason suffer men that are not voyd of both, to give such impious credite unto an insignificant and senselesse mumbling of idle words, contrary to reason, without president of any truly wise or learned, and justly suspected of all sensible men?" citing Fernel. "De Abd. Rer. Causis:" "Scripta, Verba, Annuli, Characteres, Signa, nihil valent ad profligandos morbos, si nulla superior Potestas divina vel Magica accesserit." *Discoverie*, 1612, p. 50. Comp. *Sorcery, Witchcraft, &c.*

Spelly-Coat.—Allan Ramsay explains Spelly Coat to be "one of those frightful spectres the ignorant people are terrified at, and tell us strange stories of; that they are clothed with a coat of shells, which make a horrid ratling ; that they'll be sure to destroy one, if he gets not a running water between him and it. It dares not meddle with a woman with child." *Poems*, 1721, p. 227.

Spice.—Fr. *espèce*, a jot, bit, small portion, or least mixture. Thus Caxton, in the *Mirror of the World*, cap. i, has: "Gods bounte is all pure without ony espece of Evyll." *Gentl. Mag.*, September, 1767.

Spider.—It is vulgarly thought unlucky to kill spiders. It would be ridiculous to suppose that this has been invented to support the Scotish proverb that "Dirt bodes Luck:" it is however certain that this notion serves, in many instances, among the vulgar as an apology for the laziness of housewives in not destroying their cobwebs. It has rather been transmitted from the magicians of ancient Rome, by whom, according to Pliny's "Natural History," presages and prognostications were made from their manner of weaving their webs.

Defoe tells us that, in his time, it was deemed a sign that a man would receive money, if a little spider, or money-spider fell upon his clothes (*Duncan Campbel*, 1752, 60.) ; and Park, in a MS. note to his copy of Bourne and Brand, mentions the same belief as existing in the last century. Gilbert White explains the real nature of the gossamer as follows : "Strange and superstitious as the notions about the gossamer were formerly, no body in these days doubts but that they are the real production of small spiders, which swarm in the fields in fine weather in Autumn, and have the power of shooting out webs from their tails, so as to render themselves buoyant, and lighter than air." *Selborne*, p. 91.

Spinny-Wye.—Is the name of a game among children at Newcastle-upon-Tyne. I suspect this is nearly the same with "Hide and Seek." "I spye, is the usual exclamation at a childish game called 'Hie, spy, hie.'"

Spirits.—Comp. *Ghosts, Magic, Sorcery*, &c. In "The unfained Retractation of Fraunces Cox, which he uttered at the pillery in Chepesyde and elsewhere, accordyng to the Counsels commaundement, Anno 1561, 25th June," he says, "that from a child he began to practise the most divelish and supersticious knowledge of necromancie and invocations of sprites, and curious astrology. He now utterly renounces and forsakes all such divelish sciences, wherein the name of God is most horribly abused, and society or pact with wicked spirits most detestably practised, as necromancie, geomancie, and that curious part of astrology wherein is contained the calculating of nativities or casting of nativities, with all other the like magikes."

Spirits that give disturbance by knocking are no novelties. Thus Osborne, speaking of unhappy marriages, says : "It must needs render their sleepe unquiet, that have one of those cadds or familiars still knocking over their pillow." *Advice to a Son*, 1656, p. 36. Moresin traces to its origin the popular superstition, relative to the coming again, as it is commonly called, or walking of spirits, and speaks of it as an idea which the Roman Catholics borrowed from the heathen Romans. He quotes Manilius, Ovid (in his "Metamorphoses"), and Alexander ab Alexandro. *Papatus*, 1594, p. 11. From the subsequent passage in "Hamlet" the walking of spirits seems to have been enjoined by way of penance:

"I am thy father's spirit,
Doom'd for a certain term to walk the night;
And for the day confin'd to fast in fires

Till the foul crimes done in my days of
Nature
Are burnt and purg'd away."

The following was communicated to Mr.
Brand by a gentleman, to whom it had
been related by a sea captain of the port
of Newcastle upon Tyne. "His cook,"
he said, "chanced to die on their passage
homeward. This honest fellow, having
had one of his legs a little shorter than
the other, used to walk in that way which
our vulgar idiom calls 'with an up and
down.' A few nights after his body had
been committed to the deep, our captain
was alarmed by his mate with an account
that the cook was walking before the ship,
and that all hands were upon deck to see
him. The captain, after an oath or two
for having been disturbed, ordered them
to let him alone, and try which, the ship
or he, should get first to Newcastle. But,
turning out on further importunity, he
honestly confessed that he had like to have
caught the contagion, and on seeing something move in a way so familiar to that
which an old friend used, and withal having a cap on so like that which he was wont
to wear, verily thought there was more in
the report than he was at first willing to
believe. A general panic diffused itself.
He ordered the ship to be steered towards
the object, but not a man would move the
helm! Compelled to do this himself, he
found, on a nearer approach, that the
ridiculous cause of all their terror was
part of a main top, the remains of some
wreck, floating before them. Unless he
had ventured to make this near approach
to the supposed ghost, the tale of the walking cook had long been in the mouths, and
excited the fears of many honest and very
brave fellows in the Wapping of Newcastle upon Tyne."

Ramsay mentions, as common in Scotland, the vulgar notion that a ghost will
not be laid to rest till some priest speak
to it, and get account of what disturbs it:

"For well we wat it is his ghaist
Wow, wad some folk that can do't best
Speak til't, and hear what it confest:
To send a wand'ring Saul to rest
'Tis a good deed
Amang the dead."

Poems, 1721, p. 27. Dr. Johnson, in his
description of the Buller of Buchan, in
Scotland, pleasantly tells us: "If I had
any malice against a walking spirit, instead of laying him in the Red Sea, I
would condemn him to reside in the Bullar
of Buchan."

Mr. Jasper Wood, who was Vicar of
Bodmin, in Cornwall, from 1679 to 1716,
and whose monument is still to be seen
in the churchyard, laboured for many
years of his life under the impression
that he was haunted by evil spirits, who
laid him under the power of witchcraft.
An account of this extraordinary case was
published at Exeter in 1700, and is reprinted in Sir John Maclean's *History of
the Deanery of Trigg Minor*, 1873. A
copy of the original, two folio leaves, is
in the British Museum. Hazlitt's *Bibl.
Coll.* i, 467. There is a passage in the
"Spectator," where he introduces the
girls in his neighbourhood, and his landlady's daughters, telling stories of spirits
and apparitions; how they stood pale as
ashes, at the foot of the bed, and walked
over churchyards by moonlight: of their
being conjured to the Red Sea, &c. He
observes that "one spirit raised another,
and, at the end of every story, the whole
company closed their ranks and crowded
about the fire."

Martin, speaking of the Western Islands
of Scotland, says: "There were spirits
also that appeared in the shape of women,
horses, swine, catts, and some like fiery
balls, which would follow men in the
fields: but there have been but few instances of these for forty years past.

"These spirits used to form sounds in
the air, resembling those of a harp, pipe,
crowing of a cock, and of the grinding of
querns: and sometimes they thrice heard
voices in the air by night, singing Irish
songs: the words of which songs some of
my acquaintance still retain. One of
them resembled the voice of a woman who
had died some time before, and the song
related to her state in the other world.
These accounts I had from persons of as
great integrity as any are in the world."
Home, in his *Douglas*, writes:

"In such a place as this, at such an
hour,
If ancestry can be in aught believ'd,
Descending spirits have convers'd with
man,
And told the secrets of the world unknown."

In the "Museum Tradescantianum," 1660,
p. 42, we find an "Indian Conjurer's
Rattle, wherewith he calls up spirits."

The aborigines of Australia, when can-
nibalism prevailed, removing the rete
museorum below the cuticle of the scalded
carcass of a captive or settler found that
the body of the victim became white, and
hence formed the notion that Europeans
were their own dead relatives returned
from the other world. Inman's *Ancient
Faiths*, 1876, p. 72.

Spitting.—Spittle among the ancients was esteemed a charm against all
kinds of fascination: so Theocritus (in
Creech's translation:)

Thrice on my breast I spit to guard me
   safe
From fascinating charms.

And thus Persius upon the custom of
nurses spitting upon children :

  See how old Beldams expiations make ;
  To atone the gods the bantling up they
    take ;
  His lips are wet with lustral spittle,
    thus
  They think to make the gods pro-
    pitious.

Delrio mentions that some think the passage in Tibullus is to be referred to this.
Disq. Magicæ, p. 391 : —

  Hunc puer, hunc Juvenis, turba circum-
    stetit arcta,
  Despuit in molles, et sibi quisque sinus.
           Eleg. lib. 1, *Eleg.* 2.

This custom of nurses of lustrating the
children by spittle," says Seward,
"was one of the ceremonies used on
the Dies Nominalis, the day the child
was named : so that there can be
no doubt of the Papists deriving
this custom from the heathen nurses
and grand-mothers. They have indeed
christened it, as it were, by flinging in
some scriptural expressions ; but then they
have carried it to a more filthy extravagance by daubing it on the nostrils of
adults as well as of children."

Sheridan, the translator of Persius, remarks : " Plutarch and Macrobius make
the days of lustration of infants thus :
' The 8th day for girls, and the 9th for
boys. Gregory Nazianzen calls this festival 'Ονομαστήρια because upon one of
those days the child was named. The old
grandmother or aunt moved around in a
circle, and rubbed the child's forehead
with spittle, and that with her middle
finger, to preserve it from witchcraft. It
is to this foolish custom St. Athanasius
alludes, when he calls the heresy of Montanus and Priscilla γραῶν πτυσματα."

Spitting, according to Pliny, was superstitiously observed in averting witchcraft
and in giving a shrewder blow to an
enemy. Its virtue in the former respect
is mentioned as an old superstition by
Alexander ab Alexandro. The following
is in " Plaine Percevall the Peace Maker
of England " (circâ 1589), signat. D 2 :—
" Nay no further Martin thou maist spit
in that hole, for I'll come no more there."
Browne in his *Pastorals*, 1613-14, describes
a scene at the forge, where the smith is
shoeing the horses brought to him, spitting
in his hand as a preliminary ceremonial :

  As when a smith and's man (lame vul-
    can fellowes)

  Call'd from the anuile or the puffing
    bellowes,
  To clap a well-wrought shooe (for more
    then pay)
  Vpon a stubborne nagge of Galloway ;
  Or vnback'd Iennet, or a Flaunders
    mare,
  That at the forge stand snuffing of the
    ayre ;
  The swarthy smith spits in his buck-
    thorne fist,
  And bids his man bring out the fiue-fold
    twist.

—Hazlitt's ed. p. 140.

In a very curious tract, it is said : " One
of his (Nim's) guardians (being fortified
with an old charm) marches cross-legged,
spitting three times, East, South, West,
and afterwards prefers his vallor to a
catechising office. In the name of God,
quoth he, what art thou? whence dost
thou come ?" &c., seeing something that
he supposed to be a ghost. *Life of a
Satyrical Pvppy, called Nim*, 1657.

Pope Pius IX. (1846-78) was said to have
the evil eye, and when he blessed people,
some would avert their faces, and spit,
to avoid the spell.

The boys in the North of England used
to have a custom amongst themselves of
spitting their faith (or, as they call it,
"their saul'), when required to make asseverations in matters which they thought
of consequence. In combinations of the
colliers, &c., about Newcastle-upon-Tyne
for the purpose of raising their wages,
they are said to spit upon a stone together,
by way of cementing their confederacy.
Hence the popular saying, when persons
are of the same party, or agree in sentiment, that " they spit upon the same
stone."

Levinus Lemnius tells us : " Divers experiments shew what power and quality
there is in man's fasting spittle, when he
hath neither eat nor drunk before the use
of it : for it cures all tetters, itch, scabs,
pushes, and creeping sores : and if venomous little beasts have fastened on any
part of the body, as hornets, beetles, toads,
spiders, and such like, that by their
venome cause tumours and great pains
and inflammations, do but rub the places
with fasting spittle, and all those effects
will be gone and dispersed. Since the
qualities and effects of spittle come from
the humours, (for out of them it is drawn
by the faculty of Nature, as fire draws
distilled water from hearbs) the reason
may be easily understood why spittle
should do such strange things, and destroy
some creatures." *Secret Miracles of
Nature*, 1658, p. 164. But this idea had
been advanced by Pliny. Sir Thomas
Browne leaves it undecided whether the

fasting spittle of man be poison unto snakes and vipers, as experience hath made us doubt. A namesake of this writer, speaking of lust, says, " Fewell also must bee withdrawne from this fire, fasting spittle must kill this serpent." Browne's *Map of the Microcosme*, 1642, sign. B 8 *verso*.

In Pennant's time, it seems that the Welsh used commonly to spit at the name of the devil, and smite their breasts at that of Judas. In North Wales, and very probably elsewhere, it is very usual among all classes of people to spit after smelling a bad odour, in order to prevent infection or other consequences. Brand thought that the practice among boxers of spitting on their hands before commencing operations had its origin in this idea; but the supposition appears problematical enough. Inexperienced and undisciplined oarsmen follow the same custom, under the erroneous impression that it relieves the rising blisters; and indeed it is common among all classes in the lower ranks of society, as a fancied mode of securing a tighter grasp of an object. Fishwomen generally spit upon their hansel for good luck. Grose mentions this as a common practice among the lower class of hucksters, pedlars, and dealers in fruit or fish, on receiving the price of the first goods they sell. Of the handsel Misson observes as follows: " A woman that goes much to market told me t'other day, that the butcher women of London, those that sell fowls, butter, eggs, &c., and in general most trades-people, have a particular esteem for what they call a handsel; that is to say, the first money they receive in the morning; they kiss it, spit upon it, and put it in a pocket by itself." To spit upon cattle was considered a safeguard against witchcraft; and in Scotland formerly it was the practice, before a newly-dropped calf received any nourishment, to put a piece of cow-dung into its mouth as a preservative against malignant influences. *Stat. Acc.* xvi. 122, Parish of Killearn, co. Stirling.

Delrio, who portrays the manners and ideas of the continent, mentions that upon those hairs which come out of the head in combing, they spit thrice before they throw them away. *Disq. Mag.* lib. vi, c. 2.

It is related by the Arabians that when Hassan the grandson of Mahomet was born, he spit in his mouth. Mungo Park, in his Travels, speaking of the Mandingoes, says: " A child is named when it is seven or eight days old. The ceremony commences by shaving the infant's head. The priest after a prayer in which he solicits the blessing of God upon the child and all the company, whispers a few sentences in the child's ear, and spits three times in his face, after which, pronouncing his name aloud, he returns the child to his mother." Mungo Park notices that the negroes spat three times on a stone laid on the ground as a security for a prosperous journey.

Splayed Bitch.—It was formerly a superstition that certain persons had the power of transforming themselves into animals, particularly hares, and that nothing could catch such except a splayed bitch.

Spook.—A spectre, originally a Dutch word; it occurs in connection with an incident in the history of the Plumptons. *Plumpton Correspondence*, 1839.

Sports.—Many of the diversions practised by our forefathers and foremothers and handed down to us with greater fidelity, perhaps, than any other sort of heirloom, were current among the nations of antiquity; and it may be useful to suggest to the modern English reader that he should collate what he finds in this and other cognate sources of information with the third chapter of Mr. St. John's *Manners and Customs of Ancient Greece*, 1842. Comp. *Games*.

Spurn-Point. — This sport, which seems to have been a description of ninepins, is thus referred to in a ballad of the " Common Cries of London," by W. Turner, published about 1600 :

" Come, let us leave this boyes play,
    And idle prittle prat,
And let us go to nine holes,
    To spurn-point, or to cat."

Randolph also mentions it in his *Conceited Pedler*, 1630.

Squailing or **Squoiling.** — Cock-throwing. See Halliwell in v.

Squirrel-Hunting.—A Derbyshire custom among men and boys, the Monday after the first Sunday in November, when the wakes are held. See Halliwell in v.

Stalbotes or **Stabotes.**—Fisher-boats, apparently those plying or working within the liberties of the Tower of London, which in 1354 were charged with a yearly payment in aid of the maintenance of the Chapel in the Tower. Bell, *Notices*, 1877, p. 3.

Stalking - horse. — A real or fictitious horse used to screen a fowler from the game. See Halliwell in v.

Standing at the Creed.—This originally formed a sort of adjunct or outgrowth of the practice of standing up at certain portions of the religious service, sword in hand, to be prepared to defend the cause of the true faith. It is related in *A Help to Discourse*, first printed in

1619, that " It is a custom in Poland, that when in the churches the Gospel is reading, the nobility and gentry of that country draw out their swords, to signify that they are ready to defend the same, if any dare to oppugn it."

An old writer, speaking of a proud woman, says : " Shee likes standing at the Creed, not because the Church commands it, but because her gay cloathes are more spectable." Browne's *Map of the Microcosme*, 1642, H 2. And in the *Times Anatomised*, 1647, by Thomas Ford, is the following : " Like that notorious pickpocket, that whilst (according to the custome) every one held up their hands at rehearsing the Creed, he by a device had a false hand, which he held up like the rest, whilst his true one was safe in other mens pockets."

Stang.—There used formerly to be a kind of ignominious procession, in the North of England, called " Riding the Stang," when, as the Glossary to Douglas's Virgil (1710) informs us, one is made to ride on a pole for his neighbour's wife's fault.

The word stang, says Ray, is still used in some colleges in Cambridge : to stang scholars in Christmas-time being to cause them to ride on a colt-staff or pole for missing chapel. It is derived from the Islandic *staung*, hasta. " Staung Eboracensibus est Lignum ablongum. Contus bajulorum."—*Hickes.*

Callendar observes, says Jamieson in his Dictionary, that, in the North, riding the stang, " is a mark of the highest infamy." " The person," he subjoins, " who has been thus treated, seldom recovers his honour in the opinion of his neighbours. When they cannot lay hold of the culprit himself, they put some young fellow on the stang, or pole, who proclaims that it is not on his own account that he is thus treated, but on that of another person, whom he names." " I am informed," Jamieson adds, " that in Lothian, and perhaps in other counties, the man who had debauched his neighbour's wife was formerly forced to ride the stang."

In Ramsay's Poems, 1721, a note says : " The riding of the stang on a woman that hath beat her husband, is, as I have described it, by one's riding up on a string, or a long piece of wood, carried by two others on their shoulders, where, like a herauld, he proclaims the woman's name, and the manner of her unnatural action."

Here we have evidently the remains of a very ancient custom, doubtless derived from Scandinavia. Seren gives *stong-hesten* as signifying the rod or roddle-horse. The Goths were wont to erect what they called Nidstaeng, or the pole of infamy,

with the most dire imprecations against the person who was thought to deserve this punishment; Isl. Nidstog. He who was subjected to this dishonour was called Niding, to which the English word infamous most nearly corresponds; for he could not make oath in any cause. The celebrated Islandic bard, Egill Skallagrim, having performed this tremendous ceremony at the expense of Eric Bloddox, King of Norway, who, as he supposed, had highly injured him, Eric soon after became hated by all, and was obliged to fly from his dominions. The form of imprecation is quoted by Callendar.

There is the following passage on this subject in the " Costume of Yorkshire," 1814, where a plate illustrates the "Riding of the Stang :" " This ancient provincial custom is still occasionally observed in some parts of Yorkshire, though by no means so frequently as it was formerly. It is no doubt intended to expose and ridicule any violent quarrel between man and wife, and more particularly in instances where the pusillanimous husband has suffered himself to be beaten by his virago of a partner. A case of this description is here represented, and a party of boys, assuming the office of public censors, are riding the stang. This is a pole, supported on the shoulders of two or more of the lads, across which one of them is mounted, beating an old kettle or pan with a stick. He at the same time repeats a speech, or what they term a nominy, which, for the sake of detailing the whole ceremony, is here subjoined :

' With a ran, tan, tan,
On my old tin can,
Mrs.——and her good man.
She bang'd him, she bang'd him,
For spending a penny when he stood in
    need.
She up with a three-footed stool ;
She struck him so hard, and she cut so
    deep,
Till the blood run down like a new stuck
    sheep !' "

This custom (even in Brand's time,) was growing into disuse, for at the assizes at Durham, in 1793, " Thomas Jameson, Matthew Marrington, Geo. Ball, Jos. Rowntree, Simon Emmerson, Robert Parkin, and Frances Wardell, for violently assaulting Nicholas Lowes, of Bishop Wearmouth, and carrying him on a stang, were sentenced to be imprisoned two years in Durham Goal, and find sureties for their good behaviour for three years." In Gloucestershire and elsewhere in England this was called " a Skimmington," q.v.

See farther particulars of the stang in Wright and Fairholt's *Archæological Album*, 1845, p. 54-6.

Statute of Merchants.—The Statute "De Mercatoribus" passed 11 Edward I. at Acton Burnel in a parliament held at Shrewsbury. Parry, 52.

Stealy-Clothes.—A boy's game. See Halliwell in v.

Stephen's Day, St.—(Dec. 26). In the "Gentleman's Magazine" for May, 1811, it is said to have been customary to distribute goose-pies (*i.e.* Christmas pasties made with goose), on St. Stephen's Day, among the poorer people in parts of Yorkshire, and of those which were baked for this occasion to reserve one till Candlemas. In "Notes and Queries" for Dec. 1859, Mr. J. Gough Nichols printed a curious letter from Robert Heyricke, Alderman of Leicester, to Sir William Heyricke, of Wood-street, London, his brother, and uncle of the poet, dated from Leicester, 2 Jan. 1614-15. Here the writer refers to the custom of holding up hands and spoons at a Christmas merry-making in remembrance of those who were absent. His words are: "And the same day (St. Stephen's Day) we were busy wth hollding up hands and spoones to yow, owt of porredge and pyes, to the remembraunce of yowre g[t] lyberality of frute and spice, which God send yow long lyffe to contynew, for of that day we have not myssed anny St. Steven this 47 yeare to have as many gas[tes] as my howse woolld holld, I thank God for yt." In a letter written on the following St. Stephen's-day (Dec. 26, 1615) the worthy alderman again touches on this now forgotten usage of holding up the hands and spoons for friends at a distance.

Bishop Hall says: "On St. Stephen's Day blessings are implored upon pastures." There is a proverb, which is expressive of the great doings, as we say, or good eating at this festive time:

"Blessed be St. Stephen
There's no fast upon his even."

I take it to have been nothing more than one of those meaningless jingles, which occur in old charms and superstitious rhymes, which is mentioned by Aubrey under this head. He observes: "When the bread was put into the oven, they prayed to God and Saint Stephen to send them a just batch and an even."

Among the Finns, upon St. Stephen's Day, a piece of money or a bit of silver must be thrown into the trough out of which the horses drink, by every one that wishes to prosper. Comp. *Blood-Portents.*

Steward of the Royal Household.—On the deposition of Edward II. in 1327 Sir Thomas Blount, holder of this office, broke his staff, whereby his functions determined, and *ipso facto* all

members of the household were discharged. This formality may have been usual under similar circumstances; but, so far as I am aware, it is not on record. Green states that it was customary at the demise of the Crown. *History of the English People*, 1881, i, 392.

Stirrup-Cup.—The drink offered to a guest departing on horseback from a house. Comp. *Bridling Cast.*

Stirrup-Verse.—In "Batt upon Batt," by John Speed, 1694, we find a notice of what is called Stirrup Verse at the grave, p. 12:

"Must Megg, the wife of Batt, aged eightie
Deceas'd November thirteenth, seventy three.
Be cast, like common dust, into the pit,
Without one line of monumental wit?
One death's head distich, or mortality-staff
With sense enough for church-yard epitaph?
No stirrup-verse at grave before she go?
Batt does not use to part at tavern so."

Stir-up Sunday.—From the commencing words of the Collect for the day, the twenty-first Sunday after Trinity is called by schoolboys and girls by this name. It is the last Sunday usually before the holidays. The young folks occasionally indulge in the following rather profane parody:

"Stir up, we beseech thee,
The pudding in the pot,
And when we get home,
We'll eat it all hot!"

Stobball-Play.—See Halliwell in v.

Stocking, Flinging the.—In the "British Apollo," it is said, that this ceremony arose from a desire on the part of the company to impress on the wedded couple that "ill or well, the act was all their own." In a "Sing-Song on Clarinda's Wedding," is an account of this ceremony:

"This clutter ore, Clarinda lay
Half-bedded, like the peeping day
Behind Olimpus' cap:
Whiles at her head each twitt'ring girle
The fatal stocking quick did whirle
To know the lucky hap."

Fletcher's *Ex Otio Negotium*, 1656, p. 230.

So in "Folly in Print," 1667, in the description of a wedding, we read:

"But still the stockings are to throw,
Some threw too high, and some too low,
There's none could hit the mark," &c.

Flinging the Stocking is thus mentioned in a scarce old book, "The sack posset must be eaten and the stocking flung, to see who can first hit the bridegroom on the nose." *West Country Clothier Undone by a Peacock*, p. 65.

In the "Progress of Matrimony," 1733, is another description:

"Then come all the younger folk in,
With ceremony throw the stocking;
Backward o'er head in turn they toss'd
  it,
Till in sack-posset they had lost it,
Th' intent of flinging thus the hose,
Is to hit him or her o' the nose;
Who hits the mark thus o'er left
  shoulder,
Must married be, ere twelve months
  older.
Deucalion thus and Pyrrha threw
Behind them stones, whence Mankind
  grew!"

Again, in "The Country Wedding," 1735:

"Bid the lasses and lads to the merry
  brown bowl,
While rashers of bacon shall smoke on
  the coal:
Then Roger and Bridget, and Robin and
  Nan,
Hit 'em each on the nose with the hose
  if you can."

In the "Fifteen Comforts of Marriage," p. 60, the custom is represented a little differently. "One of the young ladies, instead of throwing the stocking at the bride, flings it full in the bason (which held the sack posset.)" So, in a little volume printed in the 18th century: "The men take the bride's stockings, and the women those of the bridegroom: they then seat themselves at the bed's feet, and throw the stockings over their heads, and whenever one hits the owner of them, it is looked upon as an omen that the person will be married in a short time; and though this ceremony is looked upon as mere play and foolery, new marriages are often occasioned by such accidents."

Throwing the stocking has not been omitted in "The Collier's Wedding."

"The stocking thrown, the company
  gone,
And Tom and Jenny both alone."

Misson, in his Travels, tells us of this custom, that the young men took the bride's stocking, and the girls those of the bridegroom: each of whom, sitting at the foot of the bed, threw the stocking over their heads, endeavouring to make it fall upon that of the bride, or her spouse: if the bridegroom's stockings, thrown by the girls, fell upon the bridegroom's head, it was a sign that they themselves would soon be married: and a similar prognostic was taken from the falling of the bride's stocking, thrown by the young men.

Stocks.—Comp. Halliwell in v. The oldest representation of the stocks is engraved by Strutt (vol. ii., plate 1) from an illumination in a twelfth-century MS. of the Psalter in the library of Trinity College, Cambridge. Mr. Wright, in his *Archæological Album* (p. 102), gives a cut copied from Camille Bonnard's work on the costume of the thirteenth, fourteenth, and fifteenth centuries, who took it from a miniature in a MS. of Livy, supposed to have been executed about the year 1380, now in the Ambrosian Library, Milan. This cut I now reproduce. The

offender, it will be seen, is confined only by the right leg, and though a chair is placed behind him, it does not appear that he could possibly sit down. The other figure is evidently a spectator mocking and insulting him.—*Antiquary*, July 1885.

It is stated that in 4 Henry IV. (1410-11) the stocks between Cornhill and the Poultry were commenced, and that the structure was completed in the year following. *A Chronicle of London*, 1827, p. 93. They were usually known as the Poultry Stocks, and preserved their old position down to the time of Elizabeth.

The stocks are the "enchanted wooden post" of *Hudibras*, where the prisoner rejoices in the inability of the authorities to put his mind in the same ignoble durance. In Germany, according to a carving in soapstone by Dürer, a padlock on the lips was sometimes an additional penalty, perhaps in the case of a scold. *Country Life*, 1897, p. 611.

A gardener named Jackson, who was in the employment of a relative of the Editor, mentioned that, when he was a boy about 1835, he was put into the stocks at Putney in Surrey. They used to be kept, he said, in the churchyard. Wright quotes a passage from the *Leeds Mercury* of April 14, 1860, informing us that a notorious Sunday gambler, one John Gambles of Stanningley, was sentenced to sit in the stocks six hours, but escaped and on returning to the locality underwent the punishment. *Dom. Manners and Sentiments*, 1862, p. 343. The present writer observed stocks in Cornwall in one or two outlying places as late as 1865.

Country Life above cited engraves representations of the stocks at Odiham in Hampshire and Ufford in Northamptonshire, and refers to others still or very recently existing at Wallingford, Newbury, and Beverley.

Stonehenge.—See *Stones post.*

Stone, London.—"London Stone," says King, " preserved with such reverential care through so many ages, and now having its top incased within another stone, in Cannon Street, was plainly deemed a record of the highest antiquity, of some still more important kind; though we are at present unacquainted with the original intent and purport for which it was placed. It is fixed, at present, close under the south wall of St. Swithin's Church; but was formerly a little nearer the chancel, facing the same place; which seems to prove its having had some more antient and peculiar designation than that of having been a Roman milliary; even if it ever were used for that purpose afterwards. It was fixed deep in the ground; and is mentioned so early as the time of Ethelstan, King of the West Saxons, without any particular reference to its having been considered as a Roman Milliary stone." *Munimenta Antiqua*, i, 117.

It appears that Sir Christopher Wren, in consideration of the depth and largeness of its foundation, was convinced that it must have been some more considerable monument than a miliary stone. *Parentalia*, p. 265. In the time of Queen Elizabeth the Stone was made a sort of bill-posting medium. In *Pasquil and Marforius*, 1589, sign. D. 3 *verso*, we read: " Set up this bill at London Stone. Let it be doone sollemnly, with drom and trumpet, and looke you advance my cullours on the top of the steeple right over against it." Also: " If it please them these dark winter nights, to sticke uppe their papers uppon London Stone." There are some curious observations with regard to this stone in the " Gentleman's Magazine," vol. xlii., p. 126. See also Pennant's " London," p. 4.

Stones.—In the semi-mythical narrative of Geoffrey of Monmouth, who followed the yet more legendary and dubious Gildas, and who is more or less copied by Gaimar, Wace, and the Gaulish Lazamon, we are informed that under the advice of Merlin the successor of Vortigern, Aurelius Ambrosius, sent a ship to Ireland, where on a mountain called Killaraus, supposed to be the Curragh of Kildare, there were certain wonderful stones, which were of mystical character and of medicinal virtue. It is farther pretended that these were shipped to England, and placed on Salisbury Plain, where the remains of them yet exist. The place of worship or burial thus formed had and has parallels elsewhere in England, in the Isles of Scotland, in Brittany, &c., and the form seems to follow that in vogue among the ancient Jews. The treasure thus acquired was beneficial in a variety of aspects. They were capable of healing those who bathed in the water impregnated with them, of curing wounds, and so forth; and we learn that the original name of Stonehenge was Ælinge or the Place of the Sick.

The whole of this account is nothing more than a fabulous tradition; the sole noticeable point seems to be that the materials employed in erecting the monument are not uniform and are (perhaps designedly) unhewn, but of different sorts of sandstone and greenstone as if the structure had been of gradual formation, down to the sixth century, when it was probably completed. At the same time, there is an indication that a certain amount of faith was at some remote epoch reposed in these stones, and such a superstition may have tended to influence their removal from their original positions and partial disappearance. I do not know what amount of reliance is to be placed on the idea that our Saxon rulers, after their conversion to Christianity gradually conceded the ancient pagan burial places for use as Christian cemeteries, and on my theory that Stonehenge was one of these converted places, the locality having been originally a place of sacrifice to idols and of interment of the dead. The origin and antiquity of Stonehenge and similar remains form a question of great difficulty, which even Fergusson does not profess to have settled. Yet that writer and other modern authorities on the subject have done much to dissipate the errors and absurdities of their predecessors. *Rude Stone Monuments*, 1872, *passim*. See also Wright's *Wanderings of an Antiquary*, 1854, p. 191 *et seqq.*

Stones in Scotland and the Islands.—Of the Stone of Scone, King observes: " The famous Stone of Scone, formerly in Scotland, on which the Kings of England and Scotland are still crowned, though now removed to Westminster, and inclosed in a chair of wood, is yet well known to have been an antient Stone of Record, and most solemn designation, even long before it was first placed at Scone." *Mun. Ant.* i, 118. Buchanan tells us it formerly stood in Argyleshire; and that King Kenneth, in the ninth century, transferred it thence to Scone, and inclosed it in a wooden chair. It was believed by some to have been that which Jacob used for a pillow, and to have travelled into Scotland from Ireland and from Spain. But, whatever may be thought of such a tradition, it is clear enough that before the time of Kenneth, that is before 834, it had been placed simply and plainly as a stone of great import and of great notoriety in Argyleshire, and on account of the reverence paid to it was removed by Kenneth. A curious investigation of the history of this stone may be seen in the "Gentleman's Magazine," vol. ii, p. 452; vol. iii, p. 23.

Monsieur Jorevin, who was in England in the time of Charles II., saw it, and thus describes it: "Jacob's Stone, whereon he rested his head when he had the vision of the angels ascending and descending from heaven to earth on a long ladder. This stone is like marble, of a bluish colour, it may be about a foot and a half in breadth, and is enclosed in a chair, on which the Kings of England are seated at their Coronation; wherefore to do honour to strangers who come to see it, they cause them to sit down on it." *Antiq. Repertory*, iv, 565.

"There is a large stone about nine or ten feet high, and four broad, placed upright in a plain, in the isle of North Ronaldshay; but no tradition is preserved concerning it, whether erected in memory of any signal event, or for the purpose of administering justice, or for religious worship. The writer of this (the parish priest) has seen fifty of the inhabitants assembled there, on the first day of the year, and dancing with moon-light, with no other music than their own singing." *Statist. Acc. of Scotland*, vol. vii. p. 486. Vallancey says: "In the Highlands of Scotland a large chrystal, of a figure somewhat oval, was kept by the priests to work charms by; water poured upon it at this day, is given to cattle against diseases: these stones are now preserved by the oldest and most superstitious in the country (Shawe). They were once common in Ireland." *Collectanea*, xiii, 17. In the "Statistical Account of Scotland," we read: "The inhabitants can now laugh at the superstition and credulity of their ancestors, who, it is said, could swallow down the absurd nonsense of 'a Boon to Shearers,' *i.e.* reapers, being turned into large grey stones, on account of their

kemping, *i.e.* striving. These stones, about twenty years ago, after being blasted with gunpowder, were used in building the farm-houses then erecting near the spot, which had formerly been part of a common." xii, 303, par. of Mourwald, co. Dumfries. This and the following extracts refer to the close of the 18th century.

Again, the Minister of Unst in Shetland says: "A custom formerly prevailed for persons to throw three stones, as a tribute to the source of the salubrious waters, when they first approach a copious spring, called Yelaburn, or Hiclaburn (the Burn of Health 'in that neighbourhood.') A considerable pile has thus been raised. But the reputation of the spring begins to decline, and the superstitious offering is now no longer so religiously paid." v. 185.

Speaking of Fladda Chuan, Martin says: "there is a chapel in the Isle, dedicated to St. Columban. It has an altar in the East end, and, therein, a blue stone of a round form on it, which is always moist. It is an ordinary custom, when any of the fishermen are detained in this Isle by contrary winds, to wash the blue stone with water all round, expecting thereby to procure a favourable wind." "And so great is the regard they have for this stone, that they swear decisive oaths upon it." *Western Islands of Scotland*, 166.

The same author, referring to Iona, says: "There is a stone erected here, concerning which the credulous natives say, that whoever reaches out his arm along the stone three times in the name of the Father, Son, and Holy Ghost, shall never err in steering the helm of a vessel." Speaking (*ibid.* p. 59) of the Island Borera, he says: "There is a stone in form of a cross, in the Row, opposite to St. Mary's Church, about five foot high: the natives call it the Water-Cross, for the antient inhabitants had a custom of erecting this sort of cross to procure rain, and when they had got enough, they laid it flat on the ground; but this custom is now disused." Again, in reference to Arran, he mentions a green stone, much like a globe in figure, about the bigness of a goose-egg, which for its intrinsic value had been carefully transmitted to posterity for several ages. "The virtue of it is to remove stitches in the side, by laying it close to the place affected. They say if the patient does not outlive the distemper, the stone removes out of the bed of its own accord, and *è contra*. The natives use this stone for swearing decisive oaths upon it. The credulous vulgar believe that if this stone is cast among the front of an enemy, they will all run away. The custody of it is the peculiar privilege of a family called Clan-Chattons, alias Mack-Intosh. (*Ibid.* p. 225.)"

Holinshed, speaking of the death of King John, says: " And when the King suspected them (the pears) to be poisoned indeed, by reason that such pretious stones as he had about him cast foorth a certeine sweat, as it were bewraieing the poison," &c. *Chronicle*, ed. 1587, ii, 336. Comp. *Turquoise*. Borlase tells us: " Another relick of these Druid fancies and incantations is doubtless the custom of sleeping on stones, on a particular night, in order to be cured of lameness." *Antiq. of Cornwall*, 138. The term *Druid* or *Druidical* has long since met with qualified acceptance among antiquaries. The Celts of Gaul and Britain had their priests, and they may have been known as Druids; but not only has the term been too freely applied, but the functions of these persons has been undoubtedly misunderstood and exaggerated.

The custom of laying flat stones in our churches and church-yards over the graves of the better sort of persons, on which are inscribed epitaphs containing the name, age, character, &c. of the deceased, has been transmitted from very ancient times, as appears from the writings of Cicero "de Legibus," xi.

Some useful information on this topic may be found in Fosbroke's *Encyclopædia*, 1843, ch. xvi.

Stones, Holed and Magical.— Mr. Fergusson (*Rude Stone Monuments*, 1872, pp. 161, 366, &c.) has entered into some particulars on this very curious and still rather obscure subject. There seem to have been two distinct classes of such monuments: those where the perforations were due to natural causes (action of water, &c.) and those where they were executed with tools, like the sculptures found on so many ancient remains. Mr. Lukis has engraved two or three examples in his *Notes on the Prehistoric Remains of the Channel Islands*, 1887. See *Antiquary*, xxxii, 335, 363, where some representations of stones with perforations in them, many of ancient date, and found in barrows or graves, are given. The custom appears to have been common to all parts of the world, and these objects were doubtless treated as amulets. Shells were also employed: and all kinds of human utensils occur with this familiar feature—even an executioner's axe. Comp. *King's Evil, Amulets, Charms* and *Stones*.

The larger of these archæological objects could not have been pierced from the same motive as coins, for suspension round the neck or from a chain: they were doubtless so treated on symbolical and religious grounds.

Creeping through Tolmen, or perforated stones, was a Celtic ceremony, and is also practiced in the East Indies. Borlase mentions a stone in the parish of Marden through which many persons have crept for pains in their backs and limbs, and many children have been drawn for the rickets. Two brass pins, he adds, were carefully laid across each other on the top edge of this stone for oracular purposes. *Nat. Hist. of Cornwall*, p. 179. Brockett says: " Holy-stones, or holed-stones, are hung on the heads of horses as a charm against diseases—such as sweat in their stalls are supposed to be cured by the application. I have also seen them suspended from the tester of a bed, as well as placed behind the door of a dwelling-house, attached to a key—to prevent injury from witches." But these stones were only efficacious when the hole was natural, that is, water-worn or the fruit of some other analogous agency.

A correspondent of "Notes and Queries" in 1851, says: " I recently observed a large stone, having a natural hole through it, suspended inside a Suffolk farmer's cow-house. Upon enquiring of a labourer, I was informed this was intended as a preventative of night-mare in the cattle. My informant (who evidently placed great faith in its efficacy), added that a similar stone suspended in a bed-room, or a knife or steel laid under the foot of the bed, was of equal service to the sleeper, and that he had himself frequently made use of this charm."

Stone, To Mark with a White. —Has been understood, from classical times as an expression for commemorating any piece of good fortune or any lucky day. Catullus, *Carmina*, lxviii, 147. It is still occasionally heard. But, on the other hand, the resting-place of the guillotine at La Roquette, near Paris, was, till its recent disappearance for improvements, marked with five white stones.

Stool-Ball.— This was a game at ball, no longer known, where the balls, according to Dr. Johnson, were driven from stool to stool. Poor Robin introduces it into his Almanack for 1740, so that Johnson may have been well acquainted with its character, supposing it to have been much played then:

" Now milk-maids pails are deckt with flowers,
And men begin to drink in bowers,
The mackarels come up in shoals,
To fill the mouths of hungry souls:
Sweet sillabubs, and lip-lov'd tansey,
For William is prepared by Nancy.
Much time is wasted now away,
At pigeon-holes and nine-pin play,
Whilst hob-nail Dick, and simp'ring Frances

Trip it away in country dances;
At stool-ball and at barley-break,
Wherewith they harmless pastime
make."

It is mentioned in the "Ordinary Visitation for the Archdeaconry of Suffolk for 1638," and in *Totenham Court*, by T. Nabbes, published in the same year, Stickwell says: "At stoole ball I have a North-west stripling shall deale with ever a boy in the Strand." In Lewis's "English Presbyterian Eloquence," he says, that the Puritans were not allowed to play even at stool-ball for a Tansey. The following is in Bold's "Wit a Sporting," 1657, p. 74.

> "*Stool Ball.*
>
> At stool ball, Lucia, let us play
> For sugar, cakes, and wine;
> Or for a Tansey let us pay,
> The loss be thine or mine.
> If thou, my dear, a winner be
> At trundling of the ball,
> The wager thou shalt have, and me,
> And my misfortunes all."

Poor Robin, in his Almanack for 1677, in his "Observations on Easter Monday and Tuesday," says:

> "Young men and maids,
> Now very brisk,
> At barley-break and
> Stool-ball frisk."

Stool of Repentance.—A writer in the *Gentleman's Magazine* for 1732 says: The Stool of Repentance is an ecclesiastical engine of popish extraction, for the punishment of fornication and other immoralities, whereby the delinquent publicly takes shame to himself, and receives a solemn reprimand from the Minister of the Parish." Blount finds it called "le Goging Stole." He says it was in use even in the Saxon time, when it was called Scealfing-ʃtole, and described to be "Cathedra in qua rixosæ mulieres sedentes aquis demergebantur." It was a punishment inflicted also antiently upon brewers and bakers transgressing the law. We seem here to have a type of the *Cucking Stool*, q.v.

Stop-Ball.—This game is mentioned, but not described, in the *Gentleman's Companion*, 1676, p. 136.

Stot or **Great Tuesday.**—This is the first Tuesday after the 27th of October. "On this day," observes the author of the "Dialect of Craven," 1828. "a fair is held at Settle (on the Ribble, sixty miles from York.) for the sale (I suppose as the name implies) of stots or bullocks, &c. It is very probable, that this fair is alluded to in Henry Lord Clifford's 'Household Book,' in 1510: 'Sold It[em] of lames of John Scotte yow-fflocke this yere, besides the tythe xi ᶜˣ ; yᵉ of ix score lames drawen and selled for viᵈ. a pece som payable at the grete Tewsday next.'"

Stow-Green Fair.—Presumably the fair held at Stowmarket, Suffolk, to which the first Earl of Bristol refers in his Diary under 1692:—"June 17. For the chest of drawers bought at Stow-Green Fair, £1. 17. 6."

Stranger.—A person belonging to another parish. So the poet Messinger is described in the register of St. Saviour's Southwark, in March, 1638-9 under this appellation for the reason given, and similarly John Aubrey the antiquary in that of St. Mary Magdalen, Oxford, in 1697. Aubrey's *Miscellanies*, 1857, xiv.

Stranger.—A fungous parcel about the wick of a candle, so called, because it was supposed to denote the arrival of one from that quarter nearest the object. The name is also given to a piece of floating leaf in a tea-cup. Among the Greeks this description of omens was judged by the manner in which the flame ascended.

Stratford-on-Avon Runaway Mop.—Stratford-on Avon still has what is called a "runaway" mop or fair, the object of which is to enable those who were engaged at the first mop, and who have run away from their situations, to be re-engaged. Domestic and farm servants claim this privilege according to custom, if they are dissatisfied with their situations, and, on the other hand, employers exercise the right of summary dismissal within the prescribed time. It is, however, a declining custom. Three pigs were roasted whole in the streets at the last, which was recorded.

Streeking.—Anglo-Saxon ʃtɾecan, *extendere*. A streeking board is that on which they stretch out and compose the limbs of the dead body, sometimes called a straightening board. See Durandus "Rationale," pp. 224-5. Durandus gives a pretty exact account of some of the ceremonies used at laying out the body, as they were in the last century, and are, for the most part, still practised in the North of England, where the laying out is called streeking. He mentions the closing of the eyes and lips, the decent washing, dressing, and wrapping up in a winding sheet or linen shroud: of which shroud Prudentius in his "Hymnus ad Exequias Defuncti" thus speaks in Beaumont's translation:

> "The custome is to spread abroad
> White linens, grac'd with splendour
> pure."

In Copley's "Wits, Fits, and Fancies," 1595, is the following, alluding to the practice of laying out, or streeking the body: "One said to a little child, whose father died that morning, and was layd out in a coffin in the kitchen, Alas! my prety child, thy father is now in heaven: the child answered, Nay, that he is not: for he is yet in the kitchen."

Strickler.—Holme observes: "The strickler is a thing that goes along with the measure, which is a straight board with a staffe fixed in the side, to draw over corn in measureing, that it exceed not the height of the measure. Which measureing is termed Wood and Wood." *Academy of Armory*, 1688, p. 337.

Shaw, speaking of some provincialisms of the south of Staffordshire respecting measures, quantities, &c. &c. says: "Strike is now the same thing with bushel, though formerly two strikes were reckoned to a bushel; for, the old custom having been to measure up grain in a half-bushel measure, each time of striking off was deemed a strike, and thus two strikes made one bushel; but this is now become obsolete, bushel measures being in use; or if a half bushel be used, it is deemed a half-strike: at present therefore strike and bushel are synonymous terms. The grosser articles are heaped; but grain is stricken off with the strait edge of a strip of board, called a strickless: this level measure of grain is here provincially termed strike and strickless." *Staffordshire*, ii, part 1, p. 207.

Stroke-bias. — A Kentish sport. See Halliwell in v.

Stroking.—See an account of Mr. Valentine Greatrakes' stroking for different disorders, in the "Gent. Mag." for Jan. 1779, and comp. Hazlitt's *Bibl. Coll.* i, 190, ii, 257. This stroking seems to have been the prototype of our modern massage.

Stumbling.—Cicero (*De Divinatione*, ii, 40) has adverted to this superstition, and Moulin (*Vates*, p. 218) declares (as usual, without assigning any reason) that it is ominous to stumble at the threshold. Bishop Hall's "Superstitious Man," if he stumbled at the threshold, "feared a mischief," and Gaule pronounces that it was bad luck to stumble at the outset of any undertaking. *Magastromancers Posed*, p. 181.

"That you may never stumble at your going out in the morning, is found among the omens deprecated in Barten Holiday's "Marriage of the Arts," 1618, sign. E *verso*. Melton classes among omens a man stumbling in the morning as soon as he goes out of doors, and a horse stumbling on the highway. *Astrologaster*, 1620, p. 43. The superstition that it was unfortunate to stumble at a grave is noticed by Shakespear:

"How oft to-night
Have my old feet stumbled at graves."

and by Braithwaite in his Character of a Jealous Man among his Whimzies, 1631. The idea is by no means extinct.

We gather from Congreve's "Love for Love," where in the character of Old Foresight he so forcibly and wittily satirizes superstition, that to stumble in going down stairs is held to be a bad omen. It is lucky, says Grose, to tumble up stairs; probably this is a jocular observation, meaning it was lucky the party did not tumble down stairs.

Poor Robin ridicules the superstitious charms to avert ill luck in stumbling: "All those, who walking the streets, stumble in a stick or stone, and when they are past it, turn back again to spurn or kick the stone they stumble at, are liable to turn students in Goatam College; and upon admittance to have a coat put upon him, with a cap, a bauble, and other ornaments belonging to his degree." *Almanack* for 1695.

Sturbridge Fair.—This is also known as St. Audry's Fair, and it is said that the word tawdry takes its origin from the flimsy goods which were offered for sale at this place—an etymology for which I am not going to vouch any more than for that which explains Stourbridge itself to signify St. Audry's Bridge. In a satirical pamphlet, published in 1700, it is called *Stir-Bitch Fair*, a name which, apart from any double meaning, may be a development from the corrupt form *Styrr-bygge*, which occurs in a historical document as early as 1558. In An Historical Account of Sturbridge, Bury, and other Fairs, printed at Cambridge about 1750, it is said, on the authority of Fuller, that a Kendal clothier casually wetted his cloth in the Stur on the east of Cambridge, on his way to London, and offered it at Sturbridge for sale, obtaining for it even in its damaged state a good price. This circumstance drew others to the spot, and constituted the foundation of what became the greatest fair in England, and the Kendal men long exercised the right of choosing one of their number to be chief factor, before whom a sword was carried in mock solemnity down to the time of the Civil War.

Evelyn mentions that, when in August, 1654, he was on the roof of King's College, Cambridge, he could descry the folks preparing to set up their tents and booths at the fair.

The fair used to be kept near the little brook Sture in a large cornfield, half a mile east of Barnwell, extending from the river Cam towards the road for about half a mile square between Chesterton and Cambridge. The booths were placed in rows, like streets, and were known as Cheapside, &c. and were filled with coffee-houses, taverns, eating-houses, music houses, &c. The company was of course most miscellaneous, and included itinerant players and women of ill-repute. Some goods were brought from Atherston Fair, and sold here for the supply of Essex, Suffolk, and Norfolk. *England's Gazetteer*, 1751, in v.

The field on which the Fair was held, was to be cleared of its crop by the 24th of August, or the builders of the booths were at liberty to trample it under foot, and if the booths and other erections were not removed by Old Michaelmas Day at noon, the farmer could enter, and destroy whatever he found in the way of obstacles to his operations.

"The shops or booths," it is said in the *Account*, "are built in regular rows like streets, having each their name: as Garlick Row, Ironmongers Row, Cook Row, and Booksellers Row; this last has been for several years past deserted by men eminent in that trade. This area was formerly divided into many streets, which were called Cornhill, Cheapside, the Poultry, . . ." *Historical Account*, pp. 20-1. Places of business of every imaginable sort were to be found, and coffee-houses, restaurants, exhibitions of curiosities and wonders, rope-dancers, conjurers, and even six or seven brick houses, where refreshments of a superior kind were provided. There was also a dramatic entertainment licensed only for the time of the fair. At the south end of Garlick Row was the Duddery, occupying a space of 240 to 300 feet, and dedicated to the use of woollen-drapers, wholesale tailors, slopsellers, &c. and hereabouts divine service was held twice a day on the Sundays during the fair by the minister of Barnwell. The goods on sale at Sturbridge were chiefly conveyed on pack-horses in early days, and often from great distances, and during the English occupation of parts of France, in the reign of Henry V. and VI. numbers of French tradespeople came over here, and sold their commodities.

It is said that Richard, Duke of York, who fell at Wakefield, once spent a day at Sturbridge Fair, where a tent of cloth of gold was erected for him and his retinue, and a band of music furnished; but at Bury Fair the princess Mary, sister of Henry VIII., was to be seen every year, and had a tent similarly provided for her, and after her marriage to the Duke of Suffolk, the latter made Bury the scene of a yearly tilt, in which he and his noble friends took part.

The *Historical Account* informs us that Richard III. sent in 1484 two agents to Sturbridge Fair to ascertain from the traders, how the inhabitants of their respective counties stood affected to him; they purchased a vast quantity of goods, and praised their employer as a most desirable sovereign for a commercial people.

The Cry was proclaimed at Sturbridge before the commencement of each year's fair; this recited all the conditions on which the fair was held, and enumerated the various regulations in force for its management, and for the keeping of the king's or queen's peace. The document, as it used to be read, is printed at length in Gutch's "Collectanea Curiosa."

The University of Cambridge enjoyed certain vested interests in Sturbridge Fair from an early date. In the draft of a paper prepared in 1589 by the government of Queen Elizabeth with a view to the renewal of this and other rights held by the town and university by prescription, there are some interesting particulars, which it is unnecessary to reproduce here, since they are given at length in the "Egerton Papers."

In the accounts of the priories of Maxtoke in Warwickshire, and of Bicester in Oxfordshire, in the time of Henry IV., the monks appear to have laid in yearly stores of various, yet common necessaries, at the Fair of Sturbridge, in Cambridgeshire, at least one hundred miles distant from either monastery.

At Sturbridge Fair the authorities at Bene't or Corpus Christi College in the fourteenth century are found laying in their stock of cloth for the common livery or *liberatura* of the fellows, which was always to be uniform in colour and pattern, and also for the dress of the College servants. *History of C. C. C. Cambridge*, by Stokes, 1898, p. 16-17. But although Cambridge was largely supplied with goods of all kinds either hence or at Midsummer Fair, the store of salt fish for winter use was laid in from Lynn Mart or Ely Fair. Clark's *Cambridge*, 1890, p. 112. Of course housekeepers took advantage of this as well as of the other great fairs to lay in their stocks of keeping provisions. Tusser says:—

"At Bartholomew tide, or at Sturbridge fair,
Buy that is needful thy house to repair";

but he also suggests that some local farmers acquired with a commercial view or sent their own produce to the fair:—

"Then sell to thy profit both butter and cheese,
Who buyeth it sooner the more he shall leese."

In the old tale of the *Miller of Abingdon*, founded on the Reeve's Tale of Chaucer, we see how the miller's servant had to go overnight in order to execute some commission at the fair for his mistress; if this was not Sturbridge Fair, it was another in the vicinity. Proceedings commenced, perhaps, at an earlier hour in those days, and the first comers were the first served.

Bale mentions " the bakers boyes crye, betwixte hys two bread panners in Sturbridge fayre : by and beare awaye, steale and runne awaye," &c. There is an allusion to the Fair in *Pasquil's Jests*, 1604.

At Stourbridge Fair, book auctions were anciently held. Dixon, in his " Canidia, or the Witches," 1683, says :

" A fire licking a child's hair
Was to be seen at Sturbridge fair,
With a lambent flame, all over a sweating mare."

And the same writer also speaks of—

" Women-dancers, puppet-players
At Bartholomew and Sturbridge fairs."

" Expositas latè Cami Flumina merces,
Divitiasque loci, vicosque, hominumque labores,
Sparsaque per virides passim magalia campos."

—*Nundinæ Sturbrigienses*, 1709. A haberdasher was in the writer's time residing at Cambridge, who had in his possession a licence to hold a booth there. Some notices of Stourbridge or Sturbridge and Bartholomew Fairs may be seen in *Old English Jest-Books*, 1864, especially in the *Pleasant Conceits of Old Hobson*, 1607, where some of the amusements of both these institutions are illustrated. See an interesting account of Stourbridge fair in Mr. Thorold Rogers's " History of Agriculture and Prices in England," 1866, vol. i. p. 141-4, and the Notes to the Dialect Society's ed. of Tusser's *Husbandry*, pp. 295-6.

Sugar and Water Sunday.— In some parts of the North of England it has been a custom from time immemorial for lads and lasses of the neighbouring villages to collect together at springs or rivers on some Sunday in May, to drink sugar and water, where the lasses give the treat ; this is called Sugar and Water Sunday. They afterwards adjourn to the public-house, and the lads return the compliment in cakes, ale, punch, &c. A vast concourse of both sexes assembles for the above purpose at the Giant's Cave, near Eden Hall, in Cumberland, on the third Sunday in May. *Gentl. Mag.* lxi, 991.

Suit and Service.— See Tomlins, *Law Dict.* 1835, v. *Suit.* In 1602 Shakespear bought a cottage and garden in Chapel Lane, but, owing to his absence from Stratford, as suit and service were due to the lady of the manor, possession was reserved till his next visit to his native place. Fleay, *Chronicle History*, 1886, p. 146. What a spectacle to have been with our eyes privileged to behold !

Summer Bird or **Cuckold.—** The expression occurs in the " Schole House of Women," 1541 :

" And all to the end some other knave
Shall dub her husband a summer bird—"

In the " Sack-full of Newes," 1640, in one of the tales, it is said : " So the poore man was cruelly beaten, and made a summers bird nevertheless."

Summerings.— The generic term applied to the sports and ceremonies observed by our ancestors at Midsummer, on St. John's Eve, &c. See Nares, 1859, in v.

Summer Solstice. — See *St. John's Eve*, and *Solstice*.

Sun and Moon.— See Halliwell in v. The Dictionary of Thomas Thomas, however, which that gentleman quotes in an edition of 1644, first appeared in 1587.

Sun-burned.— Where in *Much Ado about Nothing*, 1600, ii, 1, Beatrice speaks of being sun-burned, she evidently does so in contradistinction to going into the world, or settling in life, and the Rev. Joseph Hunter has, I consider, most satisfactorily explained the phrase by pointing out that in the earlier rituals of the Church there was a passage forming part of the office for Churching of Women, " So that the sun shall not burn thee by day, nor the moon by night,"—one now omitted. A woman, who was *sun-burned*, was, according to this view, one unmarried —perhaps not in hope of meeting with a husband. Hunter's *New Illustrations of Shakespear*, 1845, i, 251. The expression is occasionally found in a playful or jocular sense, applied to a widow or widower, who was said to lie under the disadvantage of being *son-burned*. Comp. my *Shakespear: Himself and his Work*, 1903, p. 258.

Sun, Dancing of the, on Easter Day.— The custom of rising on Easter morning, to see the sun dance, had not escaped the notice of Sir Thomas Browne, who observes : " We shall not, I hope, disparage the Resurrection of our Redeemer, if we say that the sun doth not dance on Easter Day : and though we would willingly assent unto any sympathetical exultation, yet we cannot conceive therein any more than a tropical expression. Whether any such motion there was in that day wherein Christ arised, Scripture hath not revealed, which hath been punctual in other records concerning solary miracles ; and the Areopagite that was amazed at the eclipse, took no notice of this : and, if metaphorical expressions go so far, we may be bold to affirm, not only that one sun danced, but two arose that day; that light appeared at his nativity, and darkness at his death, and yet a light at both; for even that darkness was a light unto the Gentiles, illuminated by that obscurity. That 'twas the first time the sun set above the horizon. That, although there were darkness above the earth, yet there was light beneath, nor dare we say that hell was dark if he were in it."

Breton, in his "Fantasticks," 1626, seems almost to refer seriously to this delusion, where he says of Easter Sunday : "I conclude it is a day of much delightfulnesse : the Sunnes dancing day, and the Earth's holy-day." This popular notion is alluded to in Suckling's Ballad :

"But, Dick, she dances such a way !
No sun upon an Easter Day
Is half so fine a sight."

I have heard of it when a boy, and cannot positively say from remembrance, (says Brand) whether I have not seen tried, an ingenious method of making an artificial sun-dance on Easter Sunday. A vessel full of water was set out in the open air, in which the selected sun seemed to dance, from the tremulous motion of the water. This will remind the classical scholar of a beautiful simile in the "Loves of Medea and Jason," in the "Argonautics" of Apollonius Rhodius, where it is aptly applied to the wavering reflections of a love-sick maiden :

Ἠελίου ὡς τίς τε δόμοις ἐνὶ πάλλεται αἴγλη
Ὕδατος ἐξανιοῦσα, τὸ δὴ νέον ἠὲ λέβητι
Ἠέ που ἐν γαυλῷ κέχυται· ἡ δ' ἔνθα καὶ ἔνθα
Ὠκείῃ στροφάλιγγι· τινάσσεται ἀΐσσουσα·
*Ὡς δὲ &c.—Argonaut. Γ l. 756.

Ed. R. F. P. Brunck, 8vo. Argent. 1780.

"Reflected from the sun's far cooler ray,
As quiv'ring beams from tossing water play
(Pour'd by some maid into her beechen bowl),
And ceaseless vibrate as the swellings roll,
So heav'd the passions, &c."—J. B.

Sun Worship. — That the Caledonians paid a superstitious respect to the sun, as was the practice among many other nations, is evident, not only by the sacrifice at Baltein, but upon many other occasions. When a Highlander went to bathe, or to drink waters out of a consecrated fountain, he must always approach by going round the place from East to West on the South side, in imitation of the apparent diurnal motion of the sun. This is called in Gaelic going round the right or the lucky way. The opposite course is the wrong, or the un-

lucky way. And if a person's meat or drink were to affect the wind-pipe, or come against his breath, they would instantly cry out deisheal ! which is an ejaculation, praying that it might go by the right way.

The Greenlanders at this day keep a Sun Feast at the winter solstice, about Dec. 22, to rejoice at the return of the sun, and the expected renewal of the hunting season, &c. which custom they may possibly have learnt of the Norwegian colony formerly settled in Greenland. Crantz, *Hist. of Greenland,* i, 176. See *St. John's Eve.*

Sunday after Marriage in N. Wales.—"In North Wales," says Pennant, "on the Sunday after marriage, the company who were at it, come to church, *i.e.* the friends and relations of the party make the most splendid appearance, disturb the church, and strive who shall place the bride and groom in the most honourable seat. After service is over, the men, with fidlers before them, go into the alehouses in the town."

Sunday Hirings in Northumberland &c.—Preparatorily to, and during the harvest in many agricultural districts large numbers of labourers, chiefly Irish, who had performed the journey as far as possible on foot, were in the habit of presenting themselves for employment, and concluded arrangements with the farmers on Sundays, perhaps to be in readiness for the next morning and week. The persons so engaged were of the lowest class, except such (*Cottiers*), as came from the West of Ireland, who were accustomed about a century or less ago to migrate annually to England in search of work, and also availed themselves of this Sunday usage. The process generally lasted from 2 to 6 or 7 p.m. *Penny Magazine* for July, 1838.

Sunday, Saint. — This saint is jocularly introduced into the interlude of the *Pardoner and the Frere,* 1533, attributed (perhaps wrongly) to John Heywood. The blessed arm of Sweet Saint Sunday is one of the charms against diseases, etc., cited by the worthy Pardoner. Mr. Edward Peacock of Bottesford Manor, informs the writer :—In the "Churchwardens' Account Book of Louth, Lincolnshire, the following entry occurs under the year 1535, "For a hooke of yron to sainct sonday pycture 1*d.*" It has been suggested that Saint Sunday is the English form of Saint Dominic. Unless proof can be given of this, we may dismiss it as an unlikely conjecture. The Louth churchwardens' accounts have never been published, though some extracts have seen the light, transcribed by a gentleman who could read old handwriting very imperfectly. I have every intention of publishing the earlier years in full, and of giving copious extracts from those of a more recent time. I transcribed them for that purpose several years ago. Whenever the book appears, I shall endeavour to give all that is known about Saint Sunday in a note on the passage I quote.

There was in the middle of the seventeenth century a gate at Drogheda called "Saint Sunday's." Oliver Cromwell, in his letter to William Lenthall, the Speaker of the Long Parliament, dated from Dublin, 17th of September, 1649, says, "About 100 of them (the Royalists) possessed St. Peter's church-steeple; some the west gate, and others a strong round tower next the gate called St. Sundays."—*Carlyle's Cromwell*. ed. 1865, vol. ii. p. 53.

Supernaculum.—Brand observes that to drink supernaculum was an ancient custom not only in England, but also in several other parts of Europe, of emptying the cup or glass, and then pouring the drop or two that remained at the bottom upon the person's nail that drank it, to show that he was no flincher. "To make a pearl on your nail" was a proverb derived hence; see *De Supernaculo Anglorum*, 1746, p. 8, Hazlitt's *Proverbs*, 1882, in v., and *Notes and Queries*, 4th S. i, 460, 559.

But in a narrative of the visit of a King of Spain to Petworth House in Sussex about 1703, it is said: "He, the King, eat and drank very heartily, but tasted no liquors but his own, which were the small drink—water discoloured by the infusion of cinnamon, and the strong red and white Tyrol wine. When he called for either of them, his taster, who is always one of the lords of his bedchamber, brings the liquor in a little bottle, and covers it, or rather hides it with a salver, upon which he pours out what he tastes, near as much as what we call a supernaculum." *Sussex Arch. Coll.* xiv, 15.

The Chinese are said to have a custom somewhat similar to our old supernaculum. When anyone's health is proposed, they empty their glasses and then tap them in concert with or against the thumb-nail.

Supernatural Lore. — This is classifiable into 1. Primitive Popular Beliefs; 2. Real Incidents overlaid or distorted by credulity and ignorance; 3. Legends or myths utilized for literary purposes in romance and the drama. The entries within the covers of the present volume relative to these topics are too numerous to recite; among them are: Apparitions, Charms, Divination, Fairies, Ghosts, Omens, Ordeals, Witchcraft.

Superstition.—In connection with the early belief in supernatural agencies, which the church has naturally fostered,

I allude to the tales of enchantment which exist in our language, and also to two or three burlesques on these tales, which were composed at a remote date. Among the latter, "The Friar and the Boy," the "Tournament of Tottenham," and the "Tale of the Basin," may be mentioned as holding a conspicuous position both on account of their curiosity and their intrinsic merit.

Robert of Brunne, in his comment on the first commandment, in his "Handlyng Synne," A.D. 1303, has a section against witchcraft and belief in omens and dreams. He first denounces necromancy, doing sacrifice to the devil, and trying to raise the devil to discover things hidden. Then he tells people that it is also witchcraft to make a child look in a sword, a basin, in "thumbe" or crystal; to believe in the pie's chattering: it is no truth, but false believing:

> "Many beleuyn yn þe pye :
> Whan ſhe comp lowe or hye,
> Cheteryng, and hap no reſte,
> þan ſey þey we ſhul haue geſte.
> Manyon trowyn on here wyles ;
> And many tymes þe pye hem gylys."

He next warns his hearers against believing in good or ill luck from the people they meet when going out to buy or borrow. If they don't speed well, they curse the people they met; but this is the enticement of the devil. Hansel, too, is all nonsense: Robert believes it not, and never will:

> "For many hauyn glade honcel at þe morw
> And to hem, or euyn, comp mochyl sorw ;
> And manyon hauyn yn þe day grete noy,
> And ȝyt or euyn comp to hem mochyl ioye."

He goes on to protest against belief in dreams "for many be nat but gleteryng glemys;" discusses the six kinds of dreams; denounces witchcraft again, and tells a curious tale of a witch and her cow-sucking bag. Lastly he, like Bishop Pecock in his "Repressor," more than a hundred years later, protests against belief in the three sisters who come before a child is born, and shape its destiny to evil or to good.

Henry, speaking of our manners between A.D. 1399 and 1485, says: "There was not a man then in England who entertained the least doubt of the reality of sorcery, necromancy, and other diabolical arts." *Hist. of Gr. Britain*, iv, 542.

Newton of Cheshire enumerates quite a number of points, in the form of interrogatories, which were thought to be by more than possibility matters of practice or opinion in the Elizabethan era. His list is edifying; but I have space only for a couple of examples within my immediate subject:—"*Apothecarie* or *oyle maker:* Whether they haue superstitiouslie obserued or stayed for choyse dayes or houres, or any other ceremonious rytes in gathering his herbes or other simples for the making of his drouges and receiptes.

"*Caruers, grauers, painters* and *image-makers.* Whether in the making, grauing or painting of any Image or picture eyther of man or other creature, they haue shewed all the skill and cunning that possibly they could, hoping thereby to bringe men in loue with their worke piece, and so to worship it." *Trve Tryall and Examination of a man's own self*, 1586, pp. 39, 42.

The following is from Copley's "Wits, Fits, and Fancies," 1595: "A plaine country vicar perswaded his parishioners in all their troubles and adversities, to call vpon God, and thus he said: There is (dearly beloued) a certaine familiar beast amongst you called a hog, see you not how towards a storme or tempest it crieth euermore, ourgh, ourgh? So must you likewise in all your eminent troubles and dangers, say to yourselues, Lourghd, Lourghd, helpe me."

Bishop Hall, in his Characters, 1608, speaking of the superstitious man, observes that "Old wives and starres are his counsellors: his night-spell is his guard, and charms his physicians. He wears paracelsian characters for the tooth ache; and a little hollowed wax is his antidote for all evils." Among the ancient Britons, the generality of diseases were attempted to be cured by charms and incantations.

Melton classes among superstitions the idea, "That tooth-aches, agues, cramps, and fevers, and many other diseases, may be healed by mumbling a few strange words over the head of the diseased." *Astrologaster*, 1620, p. 45.

The "Spectator," accounting for the rise and progress of ancient superstition, tells us, our forefathers looked upon nature with more reverence and horror, before the world was enlightened by learning and philosophy, and loved to astonish themselves with the apprehensions of witchcraft, prodigies, charms, and enchantments. There was not a village in England that had not a ghost in it. The churchyards were all haunted. Every common had a circle of fairies belonging to it, and there was scarce a shepherd to be met with who had not seen a spirit. Hence Gay:

—"Those tales of vulgar spirites,
Which frighten'd boys relate on winter nights,

How cleanly milkmaids meet the fairy train,
How headless horses drag the clinking chain:
Night-roaming ghosts by saucer eye-balls known,
The common spectres of each country town."

In Kirkwall and St. Ola, in Scotland, it seems that the inhabitants in the 18th century were accustomed to "make vows to this or the other favourite saint, at whose church or chapel in the place they lodge a piece of money, as a reward for their protection; and they imagine that if any person steals, or carries off that money, he will instantly fall into the same danger from which they, by their pious offering, had been so lately delivered." *Stat. Acc.* vii, 500.

In Eriskay, Hebrides, the fishermen still refuse to wear clothes dyed with the lichen or crottle found on the rocks, although it is used in other cases. They say that it comes from the rocks, and will go back there. Goodrich-Freer, *Outer Isles*, 1902, p. 203.

Speaking of popular notions and what he terms "an old wife's dreams," Montaigne writes:—Where one scale is totally empty, I let the other waver under old wives' dreams; and I think myself excusable, if I prefer the odd number; Thursday rather than Friday; if I had rather be the twelfth or fourteenth than the thirteenth at table; if I had rather, on a journey, see a hare run by me than cross my way, and rather give my man my left foot than my right, when he comes to put on my stockings. *Essays*, ed. by W. C. Hazlitt, 1902, iv, 35.

In the Adriatic provinces there seems to be a lingering custom of deprecating envy toward a child, who may be met by a stranger, and to whom the latter says: "Non gli noccia l'invidia." Hon. Margaret Collier, *Our Home by the Adriatic*, 1886, p. 57.

Susceptor.—A godfather or godmother. "I had given me the name of my grandfather, my mother's father, who, together with a sister of Sir Thomas Evelyn of Long Ditton, and Mr. Comber, a near relation of my mother, were my susceptors." Evelyn's *Diary*, ed. 1862, i, 4.

Swan, The.—"Ad vada Meandri concinit albus olor."—*Ovid.* It is said "that swans, a little before their death, sing most sweetly, of which, notwithstanding, Pliny thus speaks: 'Swans are said to sing sweetly before their death, but falsely, as I take it, being led so to think by some experiments.' *Nat. Hist.* x. 23. Ælian ridicules this belief properly enough; 'That swans are skilful in singing is now rife in every man's mouth, but, for myself, I never heard them sing, and perchance no man else;' and Scaliger to the like purpose writes: 'Touching the sweet singing of the swan, which with Greece, the mother of lies, you dare to publish, I cite you to Lucian's Tribunal, there to set abroach some new stuff.'" Ælian, lib. x. c 14. Vaughan's *Brief Nat. History*, p. 88; Scaliger's *Exercitationes*, 23. See also Browne's Works by Hazlitt, *Glossary*, v. *Swan*.

In Varchi's "Blazon of Jealousie," 1615, Tofte, the translator, tells in a note a very different story of a swan. "The tale of the swan about Windsor, finding a strange cocke with his mate, and how farre he swam after the other to kill it, and then, returning backe, slew his hen also, (this being a certaine truth, & not many yeers done vpon this our Thames) is so well knowne to many gentlemen, and to most watermen of this riuer, as it were needlesse to vse any more words about the same."

Lord Northampton tells us, "It chaunceth sometimes to thunder about that time and season of the yeare when swannes hatch their young; and yet no doubt it is a paradox of simple men to thinke that a swanne cannot hatch without a cracke of thunder." *Defensative*, 1583, Tt 2 verso. The swans, which are in the habit of visiting the Scotish lakes used to be regarded by the farmers as prognosticators of the weather. *Stat. Acc.* x. 14. Par. of Wick, Caithness.

Swan-upping (corruptly hopping,) is described and illustrated by Hone in his "Every-Day Book," and some papers on the subject will be found in Mr. Kempe's "Loseley MSS." 1836. Several books, according to a letter printed in the latter volume, were at one time extant, containing orders under this head, and Hone has inserted a reprint of one of these in his entertaining Miscellany. Swan-upping was, among our ancestors, a very favourite sport, not unattended by risk; for the birds seldom submitted to the process without a struggle, which occasionally cost the captor a ducking. The *Swan with Two Nicks*, a tavern sign, has been corrupted into the *Swan with Two Necks*. Comp. *General Index* to Hazlitt's *Bibl. Coll.* in v. and *B. C.* 4th Series, in v.

Swarff-money. — See Hazlitt's Blount, 1874, p. 202 for a Warwickshire memorial custom connected with this, which was presumably only the black money or *derniers noirs* of foreign origin, which long circulated in England, and were at length forbidden. Tomlins (*Law Dict.* 1835 in v.) thought the term a corruption of *warth* or guard money, which seems scarcely tenable.

Swines' Grease.—Langley, in his summary of Polydore Vergil, (first printed in 1546) observes: "The bryde anoynted the poostes of the doores with swynes grease, because she thought by that meanes to dryve awaye all misfortune." Pennant, in his "Tour in Scotland," observed a similar class of superstition.

Swing.—See *Meritot*.

Swithin, St., Translation of. —(July 15). The Rev. John Earle, in an "Essay on the Life and Times of St. Swithin," 1861, observes: "Swithun, Bishop of Winchester, architect, statesman; during life a chief man in his nation, and after death installed as a saint in the calendar, has dwindled into a myth. Swithun had been 108 years in his humble grave, when he was the cause of a holy-day in Wessex. A grand assembly of men and women of all degrees, met at Winchester, on the 15th of July, 971, to convey Swithun's stone coffin from without the north side to within the east end of the church." This was the pious work of Ethelwold, Swithun's follower in the episcopate, and the old church of St. Peter and St. Paul at Winchester thenceforth till the time of Henry VIII. was called St. Swithin's. In Henry's reign its name was again changed, and it became the Church of the Holy Trinity. Even Mr. Earle admits that there is no contemporary authority for the life of this saint, and that the earliest record concerning him dates no further back than a century subsequent to his death.

The oldest calendar containing St. Swithin's name appears to be an Anglo-Saxon one attached to a missal in the public library at Rouen, and assigned by Mr. Earle to the beginning of the eleventh century. Here the 2nd July is marked as the deposition of the saint, and July 15th as his translation. Blount tells us that St. Swithin was called the weeping St. Swithin, for that, about his feast, Præsepe and Aselli, rainy constellations, arise cosmically, and commonly cause rain.

There is an absurd superstition, that "If it rain on St. Swithin's Day, there will be rain more or less for forty-five succeeding days." In Jonson's "Every Man out of his Humour," 1600, there is an allusion to St. Swithin: "O, here's St. Swithin, the fifteenth day; variable weather, for the most part rain; good: for the most part rain. Why, it should rain fourty days after, now, more or less: it was a rule held afore I was able to hold a plough, and yet here are two days no rain; ha! it makes me muse." In "Poor Robin's Almanack," for 1697, there is a reference to the common superstition about the consequences of a rainy St. Swithin's Day. Poor Robin relates the Popish legends about the saint, but observes at the conclusion that it is better to make hay while the sun doth shine, than to believe—

"Tales and lies
Which idle monks and friars devise."

"If on Swithin's Feast the welkin lours,
And ev'ry pent-house streams with hasty show'rs,
Twice twenty day shall clouds their fleeces drain,
And wash the pavements with incessant rain."

—*Gay's Trivia.*

"July, to whom the dog-star in her train,
St. James gives oisters, and St. Swithin rain."

Churchill.

"St. Swithin's Day if thou dost rain,
For forty days it will remain :
St. Swithin's Day if thou be fair,
For forty days 'twill rain na mair."

Old Proverb.

July the 4th, the "Translation of St. Martin," according to the following lines, used to be considered equally ominous :

"Martini magni translatio in pluviam det,
Quadraginta dies continuere solet."

And St. Vitus's Day seems to have enjoyed a similar reputation at one time. The same superstition prevails in France respecting St. Medard's Day (June 8). The French likewise regard the day of SS. Gervais et Portais (June 19), and in Belgium and Germany similar notions seem to prevail with an equally good foundation.

In the "Daily News," of July 16, 1868, occurred the following paragraph : "The fallacy of the popular notion respecting the forty days' rain, that is supposed to follow a rainy St. Swithin's day has been demonstrated by observations taken at Greenwich, during a period of 20 years, which show that the greatest number of rainy days, after St. Swithin's day, have taken place when the 15th of July was dry. In 1845, when the day was fine, there were 26 days out of the alloted 40 ; in 1848 there were 31 ; and in 1860, 29 ; and both for the public health and the country's good it is hoped that the result of 1868 may prove the reverse to the old adage."

In 1897, after a somewhat prolonged drought, a deluge of rain fell on the 19th July, and on the following day there was a second heavy fall. Some rain occurred on the 21st. But it is remarkable that in 1885 a great drought followed St. Swithin's Day, although rain fell upon the day itself.

In the Churchwardens' Accounts of Horley, Surrey, under 1505-6, is the following entry, which implies a gathering on this saint's day or account :

"Itm. Saintt Swithine farthyngs the said 2 zeres, 3s. 8d."

From the Churchwardens' Accounts of Kingston-upon-Thames, 23 Henry VII., it seems that all householders keeping a "brode gate," were charged fourpence on account of St. Swithin, and that the same amount was levied under this head on such as owned one tenement.

The belief in the impropriety of gathering the apples before they had been christened by St. Swithin is very general, and is still strongly cherished. A servant of one of the editor's friends was horror-stricken very lately at the bare proposition to pick the fruit before the saint had performed the baptismal ceremony. The christening of apples is supposed to affect the flavour of the fruit. In Somersetshire and Wiltshire, or some parts of them, that day indeed is known as Apple Christening Day.

Granger, "Biog. Hist. of Engl.," vol. iii, p. 54, quotes the following passage from Birkenhead's "Assembly Man," 1663 : "As many sisters flock to him as at Paris on St. Margaret's Day, when all come to church that are or hope to be with child that year."

Sword Dance.—Wallis tells us, that the Saltatio armata of the Roman Militia on their Festival Armilustrium, celebrated on the 19th of October, was in his time still practised by the country people in this neighbourhood, on the annual Festivity of Christmas, the Yule-tide of the Druids. "Young men march from village to village, and from house to house, with music before them, dressed in an antic attire, and before the vestibulum or entrance of every house entertain the family with the Motus incompositus, the antic Dance, or Chorus Armatus, with sword or spears in their hands, erect and shining. This they call the sword dance. For their pains they are presented with a small gratuity in money, more or less, according to every householder's ability : their gratitude is expressed by firing a gun. One of the company is distinguished from the rest by a more antic dress ; a fox's skin generally serving him for a covering and ornament to his head, the tail hanging down his back. This droll figure is their chief or leader. He does not mingle in the dance." *Hist. of Northumb.* ii, 28.

Henry, in his "History of Britain," says, "The Germans, and probably the Gauls and Britons, had a kind of martial dance which was exhibited at every entertainment. This was performed by certain young men, who, by long practice, had acquired the art of dancing amongst the sharp points of swords and spears, with such wonderful agility and gracefulness, that they gained great applause to themselves, and gave great delight to the spectators."

I find a curious and very minute description of the Sword Dance in Olaus Magnus. He tells us that the Northern Goths and Swedes have a sport wherein they exercise their youth, consisting of a dance with swords in the following manner: first, with their swords sheathed and erect in their hands, they dance in a triple round: then with their drawn swords held erect as before: afterwards, extending them from hand to hand, they lay hold of each other's hilts and points, and while they are wheeling more moderately round and hanging their order, throw themselves into the figure of a hexagon, which they call a rose: but, presently raising and drawing back their swords, they undo that figure, in order to form with them a four-square rose, that they may rebound over the head of each other. Lastly, they dance rapidly backwards, and vehemently rattling the sides of their swords together, conclude their sport. Pipes or songs (sometimes both) direct the measure, which at first is slow, but increasing afterward, becomes a very quick one towards the conclusion.

Douce had a very old cut representing the Sword Dance, which was still "performed (sixty years ago) by the morris-dancers in the vicinage of Lincoln." T. Park's note in a copy of Bourne and Brand's "Popular Antiquities," p. 176. This may have been about 1740.

Moresin (*Papatus*, 1594, p. 160) speaks of having seen a dance so named *without swords*, and it is still occasionally so practised.

In a drama played by a set of "Plow-Boys or Morris-Dancers," in their ribbon dresses, with swords, October 20, 1779, at Revesby Abbey, Lincolnshire, the assumed characters of the piece are different from those of the more regular morris, and they were accompanied by two men from Kirtley without any particular dresses, who sang the song of Landlord and Tenant. The Dramatis personæ were; *Men*, The Fool and his five sons, Pickle Herring, Blue Breeches, Pepper Breeches, Ginger Breeches, and John Allspice: *Woman*, Cicely: with a fidler or master music man. In the play itself the hobby horse is not omitted:

"We are come over the mire and moss;
We dance an hobby horse;
A dragon you shall see,
And a wild worm for to flee.
Still we are all brave jovial boys,
And take delight in Christmas toys."

A writer in the "Gentleman's Magazine" for May 1811, tells us that in the North Riding of Yorkshire the Sword Dance is performed from St. Stephen's Day till New Year's Day. The dancers usually consist of six youths dressed in white with ribbands, attended by a fidler, a youth with the name of 'Bessey,' and also by one who personates a doctor. They travel from village to village. One of the six youths acts the part of king in a kind of farce which consists chiefly of singing and dancing, when the Bessey interferes while they are making a hexagon with their swords, and is killed.

Mr. Fallow, in the *Antiquary* for May, 1895, has a paper, which tends to confirm what has gone before, and to shew that the Yorkshire Sword-Dancers, a distinct usage from the Mummers, were still in vogue at least in 1880. Attention may be especially drawn to the illustrations derived from photographs taken from a group in the neighbourhood of Leeds at the period mentioned.

Mr. Brand was a frequent spectator of this dance, which in his time was performed with few or no alterations in Northumberland and the adjoining counties: one difference however was observable in the Northern Sword Dancers, that when the swords were formed into a figure, they laid them down upon the ground and danced round them. Comp. Lucas, *Studies in Nidderdale*, p. 45, and *Hobby Horse* and *Morris Dance* suprâ.

We are to conclude that, in some places where the pageant was retained, the dancers ploughed up the soil before any house where they received no reward for their pains. *Vocab. Utriusque Juris a Scot. J. C.* v. *Aratrum.*

Sycham Lamp.—See *Will o' the Wisp.*

Tables or **Backgammon.**—To the Romans the game was familiar under the name of *Duodecim Scripta*, and there is a bronze mirror extant, on the back of which a youth and maiden are represented playing at it, she saying, according to a legend at her side *Devincam te*, and he replying, *Opcinor*. It had been known to the Greeks (Smith's *Dict. of Gr. and R. Antiq.* 1856, v. *Latrunculi*) but was probably introduced from Italy, where it was common in the thirteenth century. Robert of Brunne in 1303 denounces play at chess and tables, first, by men generally on holy-days at the tavern, which he calls "the devylys knyfe," (it slays thee, either soul or life):

> "ȝyf þou euere wyþ iogeloure,
> Wyþ hafadoure or wyþ rotoure,
> Hauntyſt tauerne, or were to any pere
> To playe at þe ches or at þe tablere,
> Specially before þe noun
> Whan Goddys feruyſe owþ to be doun :
> Hyt ys aȝens þe comaundement
> And holy cherches afent."

Secondly, by the rich slothful man at home :

> "ȝyf hyt be nat þan redy, hys dyner,
> Take furþe þe cheffe or þe tabler ;
> So ſhal he pley tyl hyt be none
> And Goddys feruyſe be al done."

—*Handlyng Synne,* ed. Furnivall, ii, 1040-7, at 4307-10.

Barnes derives this word from the Welsh *Back-cammawn* or the Little Fight, and supposes it to have been somewhat similar to the ancient *Gwdra. Notes on Ancient Britain,* 1858, p. 19. As early as 1508, backgammon was also known as *Irish* or the *Irish* game. Barclay in his free English version of the *Ship of Fools,* says :

> "On suche chaunce nowe fortune throwes her dice,
> That though one knowe but the yrishe game,
> Yet would he haue a gentlemans name—"

Hazlitt's Warton, 1871, iii, 193-4.

But Howell, in a letter to Master G. Stone, in 1635, says : "When you have learnt Baggamon, you must not forget Irish, which is a serious and solid game." Whence one might conclude the two to vary. Arden of Faversham was playing at tables, when he was assassinated at a preconcerted signal; this memorable tragedy, of which a rough representation occurs on the title of an edition of the well-known drama on the subject and on that of a ballad in the Roxburghe collection, was enacted in 1551 on St. Valentine's day at about 7 in the evening; and a full account of it may be found in Holinshed. The cut shews the table, on which the game was in course of being played, and the draught - board. The drama in question was performed before 1592.

Latimer, in his sixth sermon before Edward VI., 1549, says : "He maye go where he wyll for any house he shall haue to dwell vpon. or any glebe lande to kepe hospitalitie withal, but he must take vp a chamber in an alehouse, and . there sit and plaie at the tables all the day. A goodlye curate."

In the Privy Purse Expenses of Henry VII. under 1496 occurs a payment for what appears to be a set of counters and the case to hold them : "March 1. For tablemen and the case, 8s. 8d." Comp. *Tick-Tack.*

Taffies.—The practice to which Pepys refers in his Diary for 1667, was very common at one time, and till very lately bakers made gingerbread Welshmen, called taffies, on St. David's Day, which were made to represent a man skewered : "In Mark Lane I, also observe (it being St. David's Day) the picture of a man dressed like a Welshman, hanging by the neck, upon one of the poles that stand out at the top of one of the merchants' houses in full proportion, and very handsomely done, which is one of the oddest sights I have seen a good while."

Tag. — The *Gentleman's Magazine* for 1738 tells us that "in Queen Mary's reign, Tag was all the play : where the lad saves himself by the touching of cold iron—by this it was intended to shew the severity of the Church of Rome. In later times this play has been altered amongst children of quality, by touching of gold instead of iron."

Tails.—Mr. Baring-Gould, in his "Curious Myths of the Middle Ages" 1866, says, "I well remember having it impressed upon me by a Devonshire nurse, as a little child, that all Cornishmen were born with tails; and it was long before I could overcome the prejudice thus early implanted in my breast against my Cornubian neighbours." Mr. Gould reminds us, that the same idea has been connected with Devonshire and Kent.

Talc, Oil of.—A cosmetic formerly employed in the same way as *ceruse.* See a long and good account in Nares, *Gl.* 1859, in v. The word and thing appear to belong to alchemy.

Talisman.—See *Charms.* In a newspaper of August 26, 1903 was a case of a thief who carried on his person the scale of a fish, and who said that it was his talisman.

Tamans.—Vallancey tells us that in Ireland conjurers are called Tamans. "I know," says he, "a farmer's wife in the County of Waterford, that lost a parcel of linen. She travelled three days journey to a taman, in the County of Tipperary : he consulted his black book, and assured her she would recover the goods. The robbery was proclaimed at the chapel, offering a reward, and the linen was recovered. It was not the money, but the taman that recovered it." Comp. *Irish Superstitions.*

Tangrogo.—"The cavern of Tangrogo," notices Mr. Williams, "was formerly believed to be enchanted, and to contain hidden treasures, guarded by a great dog of a supernatural species, kept there by the Three Fairy Sisters, whose footmarks were always to be seen in the mud of a small lodgment of water within the mouth of the cavern." This cavern is in the commote of Isdulas in Denbighshire. *Denbigh and its Lordship*, 1860, p. 224.

Tankard-bearer.—The carrier of water to houses in London from the several conduits, before other sources of supply existed.

Tansey.—Tansay, says Selden, in his "Table Talk," was taken from the bitter herbs in use among the Jews at this season. Our meats and sports, says he, much of them have relation to church work. Our tansies at Easter have reference to the bitter herbs; though at the same time 'twas always the fashion for a man to have a gammon of bacon, to show himself to be no Jew.

Johnson, in his edition of Gerard's "Herball," fol. Lond. 1633, p. 65, speaking of tansie, says, "In the spring time are made with leaves hereof newly sprung up, and with eggs, cakes or tansies, which be pleasant in taste, and good for the stomache; for, if any bad humours cleave thereunto, it doth perfectly concoct them and scowre them downwards." In Coles' "Adam in Eden," 1657, our author speaking of the medicinal virtues of tansey, ch. ccxlix. says, that their special property was to remove the phlegm which had been engendered by the constant fish-diet during Lent. They are so called, says he, from the herb tansey. In an old Christmas carol, in the Douce Collection, there is this passage :

"Soone at Easter cometh Alleluja,
    With butter, cheese, and a tansey."
Comp. *Stool-ball.*

Tan-we or **Tan-wed.**—One of the fiery apparitions peculiar to Wales, is what is called the Tan-we or Tan-wed. This appeareth, says Mr. Davis, to our seeming in the lower region of the air, straight and long, not much unlike a glaive, mours or shoots directly and level, (as who shall say I'll hit) but far more slowly than falling stars. It lighteneth all the air and ground where it passeth, lasteth three or four miles or more, for aught is known, because no man seeth the rising or beginning of it; and when it falls to the ground, it sparkleth and lighteth all about. These commonly announce the death or decease of freeholders by falling on their lands; and you shall scarce bury any such with us, says Mr. Davis, be he but a lord of a house and garden,

but you shall find some one at his burial that hath seen this fire fall on some part of his lands. Sometimes these appearances have been seen by the persons whose death they foretold : two instances of which Mr. Davis records as having happened in his own family. The *Cambrian Register*, 1796, p. 431, (but these superstitions remain pretty much the same now) observes : "it is a very commonly-received opinion that within the diocese of St. David's, a short space before death, a light is seen proceeding from the house, and sometimes, as has been asserted, from the very bed where the sick person lies, and pursues its way to the church where he or she is to be interred, precisely in the same track in which the funeral is afterwards to follow. This light is called Canwyll Corpt, or the Corpse Candle."

Tappie-tousie. — Of this sport among children Jamieson gives the following account : "One, taking hold of another by the forelock of his hair, says to him, 'Tappie, tappie tousie, will ye be my man?' If the other answers in the affirmative, the first says, 'Come to me then, come to me then;' giving him a smart pull towards him by the lock which he holds in his hand. If the one who is asked answers in the negative, the other gives him a push backward, saying, 'Gae fra me then, gae fra me then.' "The literal meanings of the terms is obvious. The person asked is called Tappie-tousie, q. dishevelled head, from tap and tousie. It may be observed, however, that the Suio-Gothic tap signifies a lock or tuft of hair. *Haertapp, floccus capillorum*—Ihre, *Gloss.* 857.

"But the thing that principally deserves our attention is the meaning of this play. Like some other childish sports, it evidently retains a singular vestige of very ancient manners. It indeed represents the mode in which one received another as his bondman. 'The thride kind of nativitie, or bondage, is quhen ane frie man, to the end he may have the menteinance of ane great and potent man, randers himself to be his bond-man in his court, be the haire of his forehead; and gif he thereafter withdrawes himselfe, and flees away fra his maister, or denyes to him his nativitie : his maister may prove him to be his bond-man, be ane assise, before the Justice; challengand him, that he, sic ane day, sic ane yeare, compeirid in his court, and there yeilded himselfe to him to be his slave and bond-man. And quhen any man is adjudged and decerned to be native or bond-man to any maister; the maister may take him be the nose, and reduce him to his former slaverie.'

"This form, of rendering one's self by the hair of the head, seems to have had a religious origin. The heathenish rite of consecrating the hair, or shaving the head, was early adopted among Christians, either as an act of pretended devotion, or when a person dedicated himself to some particular saint, or entered into any religious order. Hence it seems to have been adopted as a civil token of servitude. Thus those who entered into the monastic life, were said *capillos ponere*, and *per capillos se tradere*. In the fifth century Clovis committed himself to St. Germer by the hair of his head. *Vita S. Germer*, ap. Carpentier *Gloss.* v. *Capilli*. Those who thus devoted themselves were called the servants of God, or of any particular saint.

"This then being used as a symbol of servitude, we perceive the reason why it came to be viewed as so great an indignity to be laid hold of by the hair. He who did so claimed the person as his property. Therefore, to seize, or to drag one by the hair, *comprehendere*, or *trahere per capillos*, was accounted an offence equal to that of charging another with a falsehood, and even with striking him. The offender, according to the Frisic laws, was fined in two shillings; according to those of Burgundy, also, in two; but if both hands were employed, in four. *Leg. Fris.* ap. *Lindenbrog*, tit. xxii, 864; *Leg. Burgund.* tit. v. 8. 4. According to the law of Saxony, the fine amounted to an hundred and twenty shillings. *Le. Sax.* ibid. cap. i, s. 7. Some other statutes made it punishable by death." *Ducange*, 243.

Tarans.—In Scotland, children dying unbaptized (called Tarans) were supposed to wander in woods and solitudes, lamenting their hard fate, and were said to be often seen. In the north of England it is thought very unlucky to go over their graves. It is vulgarly called going over "unchristened ground."

Tarantula.—Pepys was induced by "a great traveller," Mr. Temple, to believe that there were places where, in the harvest-time, fiddlers attend in the field, in case of any of the men being stung by this spider, to play their instruments by way of antidote or protection. *Diary*, Feb. 4, 1661-2.

Task.—In Ross-shire, it appears that the term Task was applied to supposed apparitions. A writer of the 18th century, speaking of the parish of Applecross in that county, says: "The ghosts of the dying, called Tasks, are said to be heard, their cry being a repetition of the moans of the sick. Some assume the sagacity of distinguishing the voice of their departed friends. The corps follows the track led by the tasks to the place of interment: and the early or late completion of the prediction is made to depend on the period of the night at which the task is heard." This was in 1792.

Taunton.—The Rev. Prebendary Askwith stated at the Easter vestry for the parish of St. Mary Magdalene at Taunton in 1902 that the vestry had been regularly held at eleven o'clock in the morning of Easter Tuesday ever since the time of Queen Elizabeth. The meeting is also by ancient prescriptive right held without any notice being given. Another peculiarity is that there are three churchwardens, all of whom are elected by the parishioners, the vicar having no power of appointment. Prebendary Askwith said he was informed by his legal advisers that if the slightest deviation were made in the method of procedure, such as the giving of public notice of the meeting, the ancient prescriptive right might be lost, and the proceedings would have to be conducted in accordance with modern law.

Taverns (Tabernœ) and Ordinaries.—In an account by an Italian of London in 1669 (*Antiquary*, 1 August, 1884) we read: The houses which are known by the name of inns are for the most part most noble, and are all superbly furnished, so that persons of high quality, as well women as men, do not make the smallest scruple of going to them. There are also a great quantity of "ordinaries," which in France would be called *bons traiteurs*, —that is to say, people who provide dinners and suppers,—some kept by Englishmen and some by Frenchmen, where the first gentlemen of the Court go in the morning with the same frequency that the gentlemen of Florence go to the inns in the evening, to flee from subjection, and to enjoy liberty.

"The difference between taverns and ordinaries is that people generally go to the first to drink—not that you cannot sometimes eat in the former, or that you may never drink in the latter, but that is out of the ordinary way, and in such a case the hosts are out of their element; the matter of fact is that both the one and the other are very dear.

"There are an infinite number of beer shops, where every sort of drink in the country is sold: of these I have counted as many as thirty-two kinds. These places are not very extravagant, and they are nearly always to be found full, downstairs crowded with the rabble, and upstairs with every condition of men, from artisans to gentlemen. They differ in this point from the taverns—namely, that in those they drink Spanish wine, which here they call sack, wines of the Canaries, Malaga, and Bourdeaux, Muscat, and other valuable foreign wines, whilst in the beershops there is nothing but ale, cock-ale, Butter ale, Lambeth ale, and the like. "There are other more common and cheaper "ordinaries," where they serve lackeys and other poor people. They eat very coarsely, however, in these places, and do not drink any wine. For 12 *soldi* you may have three dishes, all of which consist of beef, veal, mutton, or lamb, according to the season."

There were, from a very remote date, in all parts of London, including East Cheap and the riverside, innumerable houses of entertainment of all ranks or pretentions. We meet in a decree of 1633 with regulations for the management of ordinaries, tavern-keepers, and petty ostryes (Fr. *osteriés*). A usual tariff for a dinner at one of the better houses seems in the reign of Elizabeth and her successor to have been sixpence, equal to three shillings of our current money; and this charge probably embraced some sort of wine. The practice of frequenting taverns, both on the part of individuals seeking their meals, of parties of friends dining or drinking together, and of officials and public bodies meeting to transact business, was formerly universal alike in England and on the Continent. Among the Paston Letters is a lawyer's account in which items occur for wine consumed at the Cardinal's Hat. In the Elizabethan age men foregathered, not at each other's houses, but at the hostelry, where they met with suitable accommodation and perfect freedom. Shakespear saw his friends at London and at Stratford in this way. Hazlitt's *Shakespear: Himself and his Work*, 1903, p. 50. And similarly Jonson and all that circle. Abroad it was, and to a greater extent than in England remains, the same. Jean le Houx speaks of taking his wine or his cyder "a l' hostel." *Vaux de Vire*, by Muirhead, 1875. And the present writer has dwelled in his Shakespear monograph also on the intimate association of the tavern with the theatre in old times—a legacy from the ancients, and a feature of contemporary London life.

Comp. *Tavern-Signs*, Hazlitt's *Bibl. Coll.* v.v. *Almshouses, Maltworms, Rowlands, Taylor,* &c; Wright's *Domestic Manners and Sentiments*, 1862; Riley's *Memorials*, 1868; and Hazlitt's *Old Cookery Books*, 1886, and *Livery Companies*, 1892, where many important particulars occur.

Pepys notes under Sept. 23, 1662:— "Sir G. Carteret told me how in most cabaretts in France they have writ upon the walls in fair letters to be read, ' Dieu te regarde,' as a good lesson to be in every man's mind, and have also in Holland their poors' box, in both which places, at the making all contracts and bargains, they give so much, which they call ' God's penny.' " The Diarist mentions the latter circumstance under May 18, 1660, when he was in Holland.

Tavern Signs.—The Checquers, a common sign of a public-house, was originally intended, I should suppose, for a kind of draught-board, called tables, and showed that there that game might be played. From their colour which was red, and the familiarity to a lettuce, it was corruptly called the Red Lettuce, which word is frequently used by ancient writers to signify an ale-house. Thus in "The Drunkard's Prospective," &c. by Joseph Rigbie, 1656, p. 6:

> "The Tap-house fits them for a jaile,
> The jaile to th' gibbet sends them without faile,
> For those that through a lattice sang of late
> You oft find crying through an iron grate."

In confirmation of the above hypothesis I subjoin a curious passage from Gayton : " Mine host's policy for the drawing guests to his house and keeping them when he had them, is farre more ingenious than our duller ways of billiards, kettle pins, noddy boards, tables, truncks, shovel boards, fox and geese, or the like. He taught his bullies to drink (more Romano) according to the number of letters on the errant ladies name:

> ' Clodia sex Cyathis, septem Justina bibatur :'

the pledge so followed in Dulcinea del Toboso would make a house quickly turn round."

It was related to Mr. Brand " by a very noble personage " that the chequers represented the arms of the ancient Earls of Warenne and Surrey, who enjoyed the right of licensing taverns at an early date. But the kind of design or decoration, which we find here, was familiar to the inhabitants of Pompeii, and was probably known even in this country long before the earldom of Warenne and Surrey rose into existence. It seems to have derived its name from the abacus or table (so called) which was employed in the calculations connected with the public accounts, and thence became the common sign of the money-changers (including such innkeepers as followed the vocation concurrently with their own.). See a view of the left hand street of Pompeii (No. 9), presented by Sir William Hamilton, (together with several others, equally curious,) to the Society of Antiquaries.

" In London," says Steevens, " we have

still the sign of the Bull and Gate, which exhibits an odd combination of images. It was originally (as I learn from the title-page of an old play) the Bullongne Gate, *i.e.* one of the Gates of Bullogne : designed perhaps as a compliment to Henry VIII. who took that place in 1544. The Bullogne Mouth, now the Bull and Mouth, had probably the same origin, *i.e.* the mouth of the harbour of Bullogne." To these may be added the Bell and Savage, i.e. the "Belle Sauvage," who was once to be shown there ; the Goat and Boots is said to be corrupted from *God Encompasseth* us, &c.

"Henry VIII. having taken the town of Bulogne, in France, the gates of which he brought to Hardes, in Kent, where they are still remaining, the flatterers of that reign highly magnified this action, which, Portobello-like, became a popular subject for signs, and the Port or Harbour of Bullogne, called Bullogne Mouth, was accordingly set up at a noted inn in Holborn."—*Antiq. Repert.* ed. 1807, vol. ii. p. 396.

By the following passage in Braithwaite's "Whimzies," 1631, it should seem that signs in ale-houses succeeded birchpoles. The author is describing a painter. "Hee bestowes his pencile on an aged peece of decayed canvas in a sooty alehouse, where Mother-Red-cap must be set out in her colours. Here hee and his barmy hostesse draw both together, but not in like nature : she in ale, he in oyle : but her commoditie goes better downe, which he meanes to have his full share of, when his worke is done. If she aspire to the conceite of a signe, and desire to have her birch-pole pulled downe, hee will supply her with one."

In Flecknoe's "Characters," 1658, speaking "of your fanatick reformers," he observes, " As for the signs, they have pretty well begun their reformation already, changing the sign of the salutation of the Angel and our Lady, into the Souldier and Citizen, and the Katherine Wheel into the Cat and Wheel ; so as there only wants their making the Dragon to kill St. George, and the Devil to tweak St. Dunstan by the nose, to make the reformation compleat. Such ridiculous work they make of their Reformation, and so zealous are they against all mirth and jollity, as they would pluck down the sign of the Cat and Fiddle too, if it durst but play so loud as they might hear it." Ed. 1665, p. 84. There is a letter in the "Gentleman's Magazine" for September, 1770, on the Original of Signs denoting Trades.

Sir Thomas Browne is of opinion that the human faces described in alehouse signs, in coats of arms, &c. for the sun and moon, are reliques of paganism, and that these visages originally implied Apollo and Diana. Butler asks a shrewd question on this head, which I do not remember to have seen solved :

"Tell me but what's the nat'ral cause,
Why on a sign no painter draws
The full moon ever, but the half?"

Hudibras, p. 12, c. iii. In a tract cited these expressions occur :

"Going still nearer London, I did come
In a little space of time to Newington.
Now as I past along I cast my eye on
The signs of Cock and Pie, and Bull and
Lion."

"Poor Robin's Perambulation," 1678. Compare the "British Apollo," 1710 :

"I'm amaz'd at the signs,
As I pass through the town :
To see the odd mixture,
A Magpye and Crown,
The Whale and the Crow,
The Razor and Hen,
The Leg and sev'n Stars,
The Bible and Swan,
The Ax and the Bottle,
The Tun and the Lute,
The Eagle and Child,
The Shovel and Boot."

In a poem, written about the same time, we read :

"Without, there hangs a noble sign,
Where golden grapes in image shine—
To crown the bush, a little punch
Gut Bacchus dangling of a bunch,
Sits loftily enthron'd upon
What's called (in minature) a tun."
Compleat Vintner, 1720, pp. 36, 38.

In Scotland a wisp of straw upon a pole is, or was heretofore the indication of an ale house. The phrase occurs in Dunbar's "Testament of Andro Kennedy." See Larwood and Hotten's *History of Sign-Boards*, 1866, for fuller particulars; but an enlarged and revised edition is a *desideratum*.

Tennis.—An evolution from *handball* or *jeu de paume*. See an interesting paper by Mr. Andrew Hibbert in the *Antiquary*. In the *Privy Purse Expenses of Henry VII.* 1493-1505, there are several entries relating to tennis :—" May 13, 1494. To a Spanyard the tenes pleyer, £4.

July 6.—To Hugh Denes for balls at the paume play, 1/-.

March 29, 1495. For the Kinges losse at the paune [paume] play, 7/8.

July 5, 1496. To the new pleyer at tenes, £4.

August 30, 1497. To Jakes Haute [Jacques Haut] for the tenes playe, £10."

Our next King, his son, was fond of this sport, and charges appear in his privy expenses for tennis-coats, tennis-drawers and tennis-slippers. Referring to him in 1519, the Venetian ambassador, who knew him intimately, says in his Report to the Senate, that he was extremely fond of tennis, at which game it is the prettiest thing to see him play, his fair skin glowing through a shirt of the finest texture. His elder brother Arthur had also been partial to the same sport, and the shirt, which he wore, was made of long lawn embroidered with blue silk round the collar and wrists.

In James the First's *Basilikon Doron*, 1599, he recommends this sport, which he calls *the caitch* or *tennise* as a suitable one for his son Henry, and as the latter was at this time only about six years of age, it is easy to understand what he means by advising him to use it and other field sports moderately, "not making a craft of them."

His son Charles, when Prince, is said to have been addicted to the same amusement, as well as to bowls (as elsewhere mentioned), and to have occasionally played for a watch of Edward East's make, popularly known as an *Edwardus East*. Hazlitt's *Livery Companies*, 1892, p. 425.

Pepys mentions a visit to the tennis-court in September, 1667, to see a match between Prince Rupert and one Captain Cooke against Bab May and the elder Chichley, where the King was and Court; and "it seems," says he, "they are the best players at tennis in the nation."

In the *Patterne of Painfull Adventures* by Lawrence Twyne (1576), King Altistrates of Pentapolis is represented playing at tennis, and Prince Apollonius is said to serve him skilfully with the ball. In 1620, Middleton published his *Courtly Masque; the Device called the World tost at Tennis.*

Day, in the *Parliament of Bees*, 1641, character 7, has the following passage:

Par. Suppose all kingdomes in the world were bals,
And thou stood'st with a racket 'twixt foure walls,
To tosse *ad placitum:* how wouldst thou play?
Acol. Why, as with bals, bandy 'em all away;
They gone, play twice as many of the score.

In Howlet's *School of Recreation*, 1684, occurs a copy of verses entitled "The Tennis Court."

The game of hand-tennis, or fives, was a favourite recreation of Hazlitt the essayist and critic; and he has left an entertain-

ing paper upon it, and upon the great expert of that day, Cavanagh.

In the 18th century, Copenhagen House, Islington, was a famous resort of fives-players, while it was kept by Mr. and Mrs. Tomes. Mrs. Tomes claimed to have made the first fives-ball ever thrown up against Copenhagen House; this was in 1779. It was a sport, with which the landlady, a Shropshire woman, had been familiar in her own county. *Clubs and Club Life in London*, by J. Timbs, 1872, p. 462.

An Italian resident in London in 1669 (*Antiquary*, August, 1884), says:—Before the fire there were six different tennis courts, all built in the French fashion. Now there are only four, two having been burnt. The finest is that belonging to the king, just opposite the palace, with which there is communication by a gallery over an arch. The king has a bedroom there to change his clothes in, the window of which, guarded by an iron grating, looks upon the game. They generally play there three times a week, in the morning, in vests suited to the purpose.

In James Street, Haymarket, there existed till 1866 the ancient Tennis Court, which is mentioned by writers of the period of the Restoration, and which had an inscription on the side looking to the street, commemorative of its origin and antiquity.

Lawn-tennis has become a fashionable and popular variety, in which a court, chalked out on a plot of turf, 78 feet by 36 feet, with inner courts, alleys, and a net, does duty for the original one with its four enclosing walls, where rackets, fives, and handball were formerly played. Comp. *Troco.*

We hear casually of this pastime as being in vogue in France in 1316, in which year Louis X., having played at it in the Bois de Vincennes, caught a chill, which is supposed to have been the cause of his death. According to a received tradition, on which a ballad was founded, the invasion of France by Henry V. of England was provoked by the transmission of a load of tennis-balls in lieu of the tribute demanded.

In 1572 Charles IX. of France divided his time during the massacre of St. Bartholomew between playing at tennis and firing from the palace windows at the Huguenots.

There is an incidental allusion to the game, as played in France in the 16th and 17th centuries in one of the *Vaux de Vire* of Jean le Houx, where he is describing a drinking bout under the similitude of a set at tennis; and it seems that in the time of Le Houx, who died in 1616, fifteen and a bisque amounted to a sort of double odds. *Vaux de Vire*, edit. Muirhead, pp. lx. and 189.

In Italy it was equally in vogue in the fifteenth century. We learn that Ludovico Il Moro, Duke of Milan, was passionately addicted to it, and during his last days in confinement at Loches in Touraine he beguiled his time, when his treatment had been made less rigorous, between tennis and cards. Hazlitt's *Venetian Republic*, 1900, ii, 138.

Ten-Pounding. — Forby has an account of a Suffolk custom : " A custom exists among harvest-men in Suffolk, which is called Ten-pounding. In most reaps there is a set of rules agreed upon amongst the reapers before harvest, by which they are to be governed during its continuance. The object of these rules is usually to prevent or punish loss of time by laziness, drunkenness, &c. ; and to correct swearing, lying, or quarrelling amongst themselves ; or any other kind of misbehaviour which might slacken the exertions, or break the harmony of the reap. One of the modes of punishment directed by these rules, is called ten-pounding, and it is executed in the following manner : Upon a breach of any of the rules, a sort of drum-head court-martial is held upon the delinquent ; and if he is found guilty is instantly seized, and thrown down flat on his back. Some of the party keep his head down, and confine his arms ; whilst others turn up his legs in the air, so as to exhibit his posteriors. The person who is to inflict the punishment then takes a shoe, and with the heel of it (studded as it usually is with hob-nails) gives him the prescribed number of blows upon his breech, according to the sentence. The rest of the party sit by, with their hats off, to see that the executioner does his duty ; and if he fails in this, he undergoes the same punishment. It sometimes happens, that, from the prevailing use of highlows, a shoe is not to be found among the company. In this case, the hardest and heaviest hand of the reap is selected for the instrument of correction, and, when it is laid on with hearty good will, it is not inferior to the shoe. The origin of the term ten-pounding is not known ; but it has nothing to do with the number of blows inflicted." *Vocab. of East Anglia*, 1830, v. *Ten-Pounding*.

Tenterden, Kent.—There is a custom at Tenterden, in Kent, a borough-town, of which I scarcely know the origin, but which, I understand, is observed every Sunday. Two men, one carrying a gold mace, the other a silver one, and both quaintly attired in the old style, precede the Mayor of Tenterden into church, escort his worship to his pew, and at the conclusion of the service, repeat the ceremony by conducting him back to his carriage. It may not be improper to add, that in the parish of St. Stephen, Hackington, in the same county, it was formerly usual for every person to pay twopence to the minister as an offering at the Communion, and a penny towards the purchase of wine for the Sacrament.

Tenth Wave, &c.—See *Numbers.*

Terræ Filius.—The Oxonian counterpart of the Cambridge Prevaricator, q.v.

Tharf Cake.—This term is in Langland's *Piers Ploughman* (about 1350), where it appears to be used for unleavened bread. A correspondent of *Notes and Queries*, writes :—It does not appear, however, to be generally known that the expression is still in use in the Northern Counties, where it has probably maintained its ground from the time of the Danish Conquest. An old friend, who was born and bred in Northumberland, to which county her family belongs, informs me that it has been a familiar thing to her all her life. " In Northumberland," she writes, " it is, or was, customary to use only home-baked bread, raised with yeast and made in large loaves, which required several hours to bake. But if the family were in more immediate want of bread, a piece of dough was taken and made into a cake, and baked quickly on a gridle or in an oven, and this was the Theorf, or, as we pronounced it, Tharf, cake. I do not know if the word was in general use, but my mother, who used very old words at times, always pronounced it so."

I have been struck by the difference of practice above noticed between the north and south sides of the border, bread being invariably supplied by professional bakers on the Scotch side, whilst English families as generally bake at home. So much was this the case that, living far from a town, and wishing to make our household bread at home, we some years ago engaged the services of a Northumbrian girl, as being familiar with the custom.

Theophany.—L'Estrange, in his " Alliance of Divine Offices," p. 135, says : " The celebration of Christmas is as old as the time of Gregory Nazianzen, and his great intimate St. Basil, having each an excellent homily upon it ; the latter of whom says : ' We name this festival the Theophany.' "

Thing Done, A.—A social game of the Elizabethan time, somewhat similar to the more modern *Consequences.* See Nares, ed. 1859 in v. and the Notes to Jonson's *Cynthia's Revels.*

Thirteen.—See *Numbers.*

Thomas's Day, St.—See *Gooding.*

Thraw.—The Scots thought formerly, and may do so still, that to die with what they call a thraw, that is, in pain and contortion, was an indication of having lived an ill life. Leyden, writing in 1801, observes: "To die with a thraw is reckoned an obvious indication of a bad conscience. When a person was secretly murdered, it was formerly believed that if the corpse were watched with certain mysterious ceremonies, the death-thraws would be reversed on its visage, and it would denounce the perpetrators and circumstances of the murder. The following verse occurs in a ballad, of which I have heard some fragments. A lady is murdered by her lover: her seven brothers watch the corpse: it proceeds:

'Twas at the middle o' the night,
The cock began to craw;
And at the middle o' the night,
The corpse began to thraw.'"

Glossary to the Complaint of Scotland,
1801, p. 188.

Thread-my-Needle.—This was a children's game. A certain number stood in a row with joined hands, and ran between each other, without letting go their hold. Poor Robin has it in his Almanac for 1738: "The summer quarter follows spring as close as girls do one another, when playing at thread-my-needle, they tread upon each other's heels." See Halliwell in v.

Three Kings of Cologne.—Of these Magi or sages (vulgarly called the three Kings of Cologne), the first named Melchior, an aged man with a long beard, offered gold: the second, Jasper, a beardless youth, offered frankincense: the third, Balthasar, a black or moor, with a large spreading beard, offered myrrh: according to this distich:

"Tres Reges Regi Regum tria dona
ferebant;
Myrrham Homini, Uncto Aurum, Thura
dedere Deo."

Festa Anglo-Romana, p. 7.

The dedication of "The Bee-hive of the Romish Church," compiled, rather than translated, by George Gilpin the elder, 1579, concludes thus: "Datum in our Musæo the 5 of January, being the even of the three Kings of Collen, at which time all good Catholiks make merry and crie, 'The King drinkes.' In anno 1569. Isaac Rabbolence, of Loven." Selden, in his "Table Talk," p. 20, says, "Our chusing kings and queens on Twelfth-Night has reference to the three Kings; (but is not this, after all, a little doubtful?)"

The "lyf of the three Kynges of Coluyn" was one of the early books printed at Westminster by Wynkyn de Worde, and in Fleet street in 1511, 1526, and 1530. Hazlitt's *Handbook,* 1867, p. 116. In the Chester Mysteries, the play of the "Three Kings" was allotted to the Corporation of Vintners. Comp. *King-Game.*

The following "Charm, or Protection," was "found in a linen purse of Jackson, the murderer and smuggler, who died (a Roman Catholic) in Chichester Goal, Feb. 1749. He was struck with such horror on being measured for his irons, that he soon after expired.

"Ye three holy Kings,
Gaspar, Melchior, Balthasar,
Pray for us now and the hour of death.

"These papers have touch'd the three heads of the holy Kings at Cologne. They are to preserve travellers from accidents on the road, head-achs, falling sickness, fevers, witchcraft, all kinds of mischief, and sudden death."—*Gent. Mag.* for Feb. 1749.

Thrift-Box.—Comp. *Barbers.* Douce had a curious Dutch mezzotinto, representing "June," engraved by J. Cole of Amsterdam, from a design by C. Dasart. There was a young figure (I think a boy dressed in girl's cloaths) with a garland of flowers about her head; two rows, seemingly of beads, hung round her neck, and so loosely as to come round a kind of box, which she held with both hands, perhaps to solicit money. She had long hair flowing down her back and over her shoulders. A woman was represented bawling near her, holding in her right hand a bough of some plant or tree, pointing out the girl to the notice of the spectators with her left. She had a thrift-box hung before her. Another woman held the girl's train with her right hand, and laid her left on her shoulder. She too appeared to be bawling. The girl herself looked modestly down to the ground. Something like pieces of money hung in loose festoons on her petticoat.

Thumb.—Among the Close Rolls of King John, is a letter, dated 14 May, 1208, to the Justiciary of Ireland, respecting the promised surrender to the Earl of Pembroke of the Castle of Dunmas, in which is mentioned a recognized usage of taking a person by the thumb or arm in token of agreement. *Excerpta Historica,* 1833, p. 401.

In "Orpheus Caledonius," 1733, is inserted a song with the title, "There's my Thumb," and the last stanza runs:

"Dearest maid, nay, do not fly me,
Let your pride no more deny me:
Never doubt your faithful Willie;
There's my thumb, I'll ne'er beguile ye."

Scott has borrowed this idea of substituting the thumb for the fingers, where Rob Roy addresses exactly the same words to Baillie Nicol Jarvie.

It may be permissible to draw attention to the apparent existence of a similar custom observed among the Romans, whose very word *polliccor* seems to be derived from *Pollex* in its substantive meaning.

The practice of placing the wedding-ring on the bride's thumb is mentioned and reprehended by Butler:

"Others were for abolishing
That Tool of Matrimony, a ring,
With which th' unsanctifi'd bridegroom
Is married only to a thumb."

"Hudibras," 1678, Part iii. c. 2, ed. 1694, p. 100.

In reference to the ring formerly worn by women as an emblem of widowhood on the thumb, the following passage from the "Spectator" may be worth giving: "It is common enough among ordinary people, for a stale virgin to set up a shop in a place, where she is not known; where the large thumb ring, supposed to be given her by her husband, quickly recommends her to some wealthy neighbour, who takes a liking to the jolly widow, that would have overlooked the venerable spinster."

The ceremony long adhered to by the scholars in Queen's College at Oxford, who waited upon the fellows placing their thumbs upon the table; which, as I have been informed, still continues in some parts of Germany, whilst the superior drinks the health of the inferior, arose from an ancient distrust of good faith on the part of dependents. The suspicion that men formerly had of attempts upon their lives on such occasions is well known, from the common account with regard to the origin of pledging.

Tom Brown, in his *Letters from the Dead to the Living*, ii, 178, mentions a parson, who had forgotten even to drink over his right thumb. The "British Apollo," 1708, says:—

"When mortals, with wine,
Make their faces to shine,
'Tis to look like Apollo in luster;
And, circulatory,
To follow his glory,
Which over the left thumb they must, Sir."

In "The Winchester Wedding," is another allusion:

"Then Phillip began her health,
And turn'd a beer-glass on his thumb;
But Jenkins was reckon'd for drinking
The best in Christendom."

On the passage in "Macbeth (act. ii. sc. 1):"

"By the pricking of my thumbes
Something wicked this way comes."

Steevens observes, "It is a very ancient superstition that all sudden pains of the body, and other sensations which could not naturally be accounted for, were presages of somewhat that was shortly to happen. Hence Mr. Upton has explained a passage in the 'Miles Gloriosus' of Plautus ": "Timeo quod rerum gesserim hic, ita dorsus totus prurit."

Among the French, formerly, to bite the thumb-nail and to draw the nail from betwixt the teeth scornfully was regarded as a serious insult and mode of contempt. *Rules of Civility*, 1685, p. 44. Winstanley says: "The Italians, when they intend to scoff or disgrace one, use to put their thumb between two of their fingers, and say 'Ecco, la fico;' which is counted a disgrace answerable to our English custom of making horns to the man whom we suspect to be a cuckold." Comp. *Cuckoldom*.

Thumb-ring.—A plain gold ring formerly worn by aldermen and others on the thumb. Comp. *Rings*.

Thunder and Lightning.—See *Weather*.

Tickle-me-quickly. — A game mentioned in Taylor the Water-Poet's *Motto*, 1622.

Tick-Tack.—This may probably be the same as *tric-trac*, the game, at which Machiavelli describes himself about 1513, in a letter to a friend, as playing with some common men during his temporary retirement from public life.

This game at tables is the same as the later *trick-snack*, says Mr. H. B. Wheatley. "Dict. of Reduplicated Words," p. 87. His first quotation is from Bullein's "Dialogue," 1573: "In this lande I did see an ape plaie at ticke-tacke, and after at Irishe on the tables, with one of that lande." The game is also mentioned (with others) in "The English Courtier and the Countrey Gentleman," 1586: "In fowle weather, we send for some honest neighbours, if happely wee bee without wiues, alone at home (as seldome we are) and with them we play at dice, and cardes, sorting our selues accordinge to the number of players, and their skill, some in ticktacke, some lurche, some to Irish game, or dublets." Shakespear has a game of tick-tack in "Measure for Measure," act. 1. sc. iii.

In Hall's "Horæ Vacivæ," 1646, are the following observations on the game of tick-tack. "Tick-tack sets a man's intentions on their guard. Errors in this and war can be but once amended." For tick-track, Mr. Wheatley ("Dict." p. 93) quotes Shadwell's "True Widow," 1679, Urquhart's "Rabelais," p. 74 (ed. 1750), and "Memoirs of P. H. Bruce," p. 65. But see Halliwell, v. *Tick-Tack.*

Tid, Mid, Misera.—See *Carlings.*

Tindle or **Tinley.**—In the "Gentleman's Magazine," for November 1784, it is stated that "at the village of Findern, in Derbyshire, the boys and girls go every year in the evening of the 2nd of November (All Souls' Day) to the adjoining common, and light up a number of small fires amongst the furze growing there, and call them by the name of Tindles. Upon enquiring into the origin of this custom amongst the inhabitants of the place, they supposed it to be a relique of popery, and that the professed design of it, when first instituted, was to light souls out of purgatory. But, as the commons have been enclosed there very lately, that has most probably put an end to the custom, for want of the wonted materials."

The ceremony of bearing blazing straw round people's grounds on All Souls' Eve, which was formerly usual in certain parts of this country among the Roman Catholics, and was called a Tinley, is referred to the same cause by a writer in the Magazine for 1788.

Tipcat.—One of the four charges which Bunyan brought against himself was that in his youth he was addicted to playing at tip-cat. "In the middle of a game at tip cat he paused," one of his biographers informs us, "and stood staring wildly upwards with his stick in his hand." He had heard a supernatural warning voice.

This is commonly called *Cat.*

Tithe-Ale.—"About eighteen miles south of Grantham we pass by a noble seat, and see Boston at a distance. Here we came to a parish, of which the parson hath tithe ale." Evelyn's *Diary,* August 20, 1654.

Toadstone.—Pennant, speaking of the toad, with the Roman fables concerning it, adds: "In after-times superstition gave it preternatural powers, and made it a principal ingredient in the incantations of nocturnal hags:

'Toad that under the cold stone
Days and nights has thirty-one
Swelter'd venom sleeping got,
Boil thou first ith' charmed pot.'

"We know by the poet that this was intended for a design of the first consideration, that of raising and bringing before the eyes of Macbeth a hateful sight of the prosperity of Banquo's line. This shews the mighty powers attributed to this animal by the dealers in the magic art. But the powers our poet endues it with are far superior to those that Gesner ascribes to it. Shakespear's witches used

it to disturb the dead: Gesner's only to still the living."

In the same volume, speaking of the wolf fish teeth, Pennant observes: "These and other grinding teeth are often found fossil, and in that state called Bufonites, or Toad stones: they were formerly much esteemed for their imaginary virtues, and were set in gold, and worn as rings."

"We may add here," he continues, "another superstition in respect to the toad. It was believed by some old writers to have a stone in its head, fraught with great virtues, medical and magical. It was distinguished by the name of the reptile, and called the Toad Stone, Bufonites, Crepandine, Krottenstein; but all its fancied powers vanished on the discovery of its being nothing but the fossile tooth of the sea-wolf, or some other flat-toothed fish, not unfrequent in our island, as well as several other countries." *Zoology,* 1776, iii, 15.

Dr. Bell pointed out that in Fenton's *Certaine Secrete Wonders of Nature,* 1569, there is this passage: "There is found in the heades of old and great toades a stone, which they call borax, or stolon: it is most commonly found in the head of a hee toade, of power to repulse poisons, and that it is a soveraigne medicine for the stone." *Shakespear's Puck.* ii, 39. To this toadstone Shakespear alludes in the following beautiful simile:

"Sweet are the uses of adversity,
Which, like the toad, ugly and venomous,
Wears yet a precious jewel in its head."

Steevens in his note upon this place says, that Lupton, in his first book of "Notable Things," 1579, bears testimony to the virtues of the toad stone called Crapaudina. In his seventh book he instructs how to procure it, and afterwards tells us: "You shall knowe whether the Tode Stone be the ryght and perfect stone or not. Holde the stone before a tode, so that he may see it; and, if it be a right and true stone, the tode will leape towarde it, and make as though he would snatch it. He envieth so much that man should have that stone."

The toad is made to bear a part in the traditional narrative of the death of King John at Swinestead Abbey. In the St. Albans Chronicle, first printed there in 1483, a monk declares that he will give the King such a drink, that all England should be glad thereof; and the same monk went into a garden, and found a toad, which he put into a cup, and pricked it in many places, so that the venom came forth, and then he filled the vessel with good ale, of which he drank, and handed it to the King, who did likewise, and both died soon after. A modern naturalist appears to think that this creature really secretes a fluid, which it is able to discharge in self-defence. Figuier, *Reptiles and Birds* (1869), p. 30.

Mr. Brand cited Gesner to shew that witches were supposed to be able to deprive men of the faculty of generation by means of toads.

Toast.—A drinking phrase. Comp. *Healths* and *Pledging*. In Fulwell's "Like will to like, quoth the Deuill to the Collier," 1568," is a song beginning

"Troll the bole, and drink to me, and troll the bole again-a,
And put a browne tost in the pot, for Philip Flemmings brain-a."

The word occurs in Wither:

"Will he will drinke, yet but a draught at most
That must be spiced with a nut-browne tost."

Abuses Stript and Whipt, 1613, p. 174. In drinking toasts, the ladies have a modest custom of excusing themselves, thus elegantly described by Goldsmith in his "Deserted Village:"

"Nor the coy maid, half willing to be prest,
Shall kiss the cup to pass it to the rest."

From these passages it should seem that the saying "Who gives a toast?" is synonymous with "Whose turn is it to take up this cup and propose a health?" It was the practice to put toast into ale with nutmeg and sugar. This appears from "Wine, Beere, Ale, and Tobacco, contending for superiority," 1630, of which a later edition has a frontispiece, representing three women and a man playing with three dice.

Our custom of toasting, or drinking healths, Prynne, in his "Healthes Sicknesse," inveighs against in language most strongly tinctured with enthusiastic fury. This extraordinary man concludes his "Address to the Christian Reader" thus: "The unfained well-wisher of thy spiritual and corporal, though the oppugner of thy pocular and pot-emptying health, William Prynne." In the "Cheimonopegnion, or a Winter Song," by Raphael Thorius, the following passages occur:

"Cast wood upon the fire, thy loyns gird round
With warmer clothes, and let the tosts abound
In close array, embattel'd on the hearth."

So again:

"And tell their hard adventures by the fire,

While their friends hear, and hear, and more desire,
And all the time the crackling chestnuts roast,
And each man hath his cup, and each his toast."

When the lady in "Hudibras" is endeavouring to pursuade her lover to whip himself for her sake, she uses the following words, which intimate a different origin for the custom of toasting :

It is an easier way to make
Love by, than that which many take,
Who would not rather suffer whipping,
Than swallow toasts of bits of ribbin?"

"'Twas usual then the banquet to prolong,
By musick's charm, and some delightful song :
Where every youth in pleasing accents strove
To tell the stratagems and cares of love.
How some successful were, how others crost :
Then to the sparkling glass would give his toast:
Whose bloom did most in his opinion shine,
To relish both the musick and the wine."
                    King's *Art of Cookery.*

Hearne tells me that his friend Mr. King of Hertfordshire, though a godson of George I., used to drink to *Betty of Hearts*, whom Hearne understood or suspected to be James the Third's queen, or, as other's might put it, the consort of the Pretender. *Diary*, 1724, ed. 1869, ii, 209. The Jacobite traditions had one curious survival, which is believed to be not even yet discarded. At dinners to royal personages in Great Britain finger-glasses are advisedly omitted, because the secret friends of the Stuarts used to pass their wine-glasses over them allusively to the exiles across the water.

Pennant mentions that the master of the household was from ancient times toasted in water as "the Top Beam of the Great Hall." At the Scotish complimentary dinners they usually drink the healths, one foot on the chair and one on the table. Comp. *Healths.*

In the "Tatler," No. 24, is an account of the origin of the word toast, in its present sense, stating that it had its rise from an accident at Bath in the reign of Charles II. : "It happened that on a publick day a celebrated beauty of those times was in the Cross Bath, and one of the crowd of her admirers took a glass of water in which the fair one stood, and drank her health to the company. There was in the place a gay fellow, half fuddled, who offered to jump in, and swore, though he liked not the liquor, he would have the toast. He was opposed in his resolution; yet this whim gave foundation to the present honour which is done to the lady we mention in our liquor, who has ever since been called a toast."

Tobacco.—A foreign weed, which has made so many Englishmen, especially of the common sort, become its votaries, must not be omitted in our catalogue of popular antiquities. It is said to have been first brought into England by Captain (afterwards Sir Richard) Grinvil and Sir Francis Drake about the year 1586.

James I. who was a great opponent of the devil, and even wrote a book on Demonology, made a formidable attack also upon this "Invention of Satan," in "A Counterblaste to Tobacco," 1604. His majesty in the course of his work informs us, "that some of the gentry of the land bestowed (at that time) three, some four hundred pounds a yeere upon this precious stink!" An incredible sum, especially when we consider the value of money in his time. They could not surely have been sterling, but Scotish pounds.

He concludes this bitter blast of his, his sulphureous invective against this transmarine weed, with the following peroration: "Have you not reason then to be ashamed and to forbear this filthy novelty, so basely grounded, so foolishly received, and so grossly mistaken in the right use thereof! In your abuse thereof sinning against God, harming yourselves both in persons and goods, and taking also thereby (look to it ye that take snuff in profusion!) the marks and notes of vanity upon you; by the custom thereof making yourselves to be wondered at by all foreign civil nations, and by all strangers that come among you, to be scorned and contemned; a custom loathsome to the eye, hateful to the nose, harmful to the brain, dangerous to the lungs, and in the black stinking fume thereof, nearest resembling the horrible Stygian smoke of the pit that is bottomless."

If even this small specimen of our learned monarch's oratory, which seems well adapted to the understandings of old women, does not prevail upon them all to break in pieces their tobacco-pipes and forego smoking, it will perhaps be impossible to say what can. The subject, as his majesty well observes, is smoke, and no doubt many of his readers will think the arguments of our royal author no more than the fumes of an idle brain, and it may be added, too, of an empty head. The King "professed that were he to invite the devil to a dinner, he should have these three dishes: 1. a pig: 2. a poll of ling and mustard; and 3. a pipe of tobacco for digesture." *Apothegms*, 1658, p. 4.

An ironical encomium on, and serious invective against tobacco occurs in Burton: "Tobacco, divine, rare, superexcellent tobacco, which goes farre beyond all their panaceas, potable gold, and philosophers' stones, a sovereign remedy to all diseases. A good vomit, I confesse, a vertuous herbe, if it be well qualified, opportunely taken, and medicinally used, but as it is commonly used by most men, which take it as tinkers do ale, 'tis a plague, a mischiefe, a violent purger of goods, lands, health, hellish devilish and damnd tobacco, the ruine and overthrow of body and soule." *A. of M.* 1621, p. 452.

An account of a Buckinghamshire parson (the Rev. W. Breedon, minister at Thornton) who abandoned himself to the use of tobacco, may be found in Lilly's "History of his Life and Times."

Several of our early writers and also of our later (Charles Lamb included) have devoted themselves to the praise of the Indian weed:

A Tobacconist.

"All dainty meats I do defie,
Which feed men fat as swine:
He is a frugal man indeed
That on a leaf can dine.
He needs no napkin for his hands
His fingers ends to wipe,
That keep his kitchen in a box,
And roast meat in a pipe."

Witts Recreations.

"Hail, Indian plant, to antient times unknown,
A modern truly thou, of all our own;
If through the tube thy vertues be convey'd
The old man's solace, and the student's aid!
Thou dear concomitant of nappy ale,
Thou sweet prolonger of a harmless tale;
Or if, when pulveriz'd in smart rappee,
Thou'lt reach Sir Fopling's brain, if brain there be;
He shines in dedications, poems, plays,
Soars in pindaricks, and asserts the bays;
Thus dost thou every taste and genius hit,
In smoak, thou'rt wisdom; and in snuff thou'rt wit."

The London Medley, 1731, p. 8.

"Little tube of mighty pow'r,
Charmer of an idle hour,
Object of my warm desire,
Lip of wax and eye of fire:
And thy snowy taper waist,
With my finger gently brac'd;
And thy pretty swelling crest,
With my little stopper prest," &c.

Hawkins Browne.

Tom.—The name of the Knave of trumps in the old game of Gleek. See Nares in v. and *ibid.* Tib, Tiddy, &c. and Cotgrave's *Wit's Interpreter*, 1655, to which he particularly refers.

Tom of Bedlam.—See Halliwell in v.

Tom the Piper.—See *Piper*.

Tom Thumb.—Tom Thumb, the offspring given by Merlin the enchanter to the childless ploughman, was a spirit as much as Robin Goodfellow was one, and in the "Life and Death of Tom Thumbe," 1630, he is in fact so described, for Merlin resolved:—

"No blood nor bones in him should be, in shape and being such,
That men should heare him speake, but not
his wandering shadow touçh."

This seems a singularly curious allusion, as if he was a superhuman creature, casting no shadow, yet the writer of the chapbook scarcely maintains consistency, (What writers of chapbooks do?) in the string of inventions, which constitutes the subject matter of this quaint and engaging little booklet. In modern literature there is the tale of Peter Schlemihl; but he was an ordinary mortal, who sold his shadow to the Devil.

In the accepted story in an English dress (for that in Grimm varies) Tom, like Puck and Ariel, manifested himself, during his terrestrial sojourn, to all those about him, and did not even possess the gift of invisibility conferred on Shakespear's two spirits. But he differed from them in returning to Fairyland, where he is at the present moment, although King Arthur caused him to be interred with royal honours, and erected over his remains a splendid mausoleum (it is related) of grey marble.

Tom Tidler's Ground.—There used to be a schoolboy's game so called, when I was a child. One boy represented Tom Tidler (an advocate of absolute and undivided monarchy), and several others made it their object to invade his territory, a small piece of ground, chalked round or otherwise distinguished, crying, "I am on Tom Tidler's ground, picking up gold and silver!" Tom Tidler's part consisted in endeavouring to catch the marauders. There was, perhaps, some origin for this sport which can no longer be traced.

Tom Tidler seems to have been a person of some celebrity in the beginning of the 18th century at least, for Mr. Halliwell notices a rhyme entitled "Tom Tidler's on the Friar's ground," as occurring in a ballad published about 1720. This relic

is parallel with "*I am the King of the Castle*," &c.

Tooth-ache.—Some charms for curing the toothache are printed in the first volume of *Reliquiæ Antiquæ*, 1841.

Top.—The following mention of whipping the top occurs in Persius's third satire:

"Neu quis callidior buxum torquere flagello."

Thus also in Virgil's seventh Æneid:

"As young striplings whip the top for sport,
On the smooth pavement of an empty court;
The wooden engine whirls and flies about,
Admir'd with clamours of the beardless rout.
They lash aloud, each other they provoke,
And lend their little souls at ev'ry stroke."

Dionysius Cato recommends the top as a harmless amusement in contrast to dice-play, in which there was hazard and speculation. "*Trocho lude*," he says, "aleas fuge," which the "Luytel Caton" in the Vernon MS. ab. 1375, A.D., translates "Take a *toppe*, ʒif þou wold pleye, and not as þe hasardrye" (leaf 310, col. 1)

In a mutilated and fragmentary window at Thornhill Church, near Dewsbury, is a representation of a female holding a child on each arm, while two others are playing at her feet. One of them has a top spinning on the ground, and I think a whip raised in his right hand. The glass is of the latter part of the fifteenth century, and is supposed to represent the Blessed Virgin and St. Joseph, our Saviour, and his foster brother St. James.

In Sir Thomas More's "Workes," 1557, are some allegorical verses on the ages of man, in which childhood is represented as a boy whipping a top. The boy is made to say:

"A toppe can I set, and dryue in its kynde."

Playing with tops is found among the illuminations of Mr. Ive's Missal. Under the rules drawn up for Harrow School in 1590 by John Lyon the founder, the amusements were limited to driving a top, tossing a hand-ball, running, and shooting. Sir H. Ellis, *History of St. Leonard, Shoreditch*, 1798, p. 169. Comp. *Pearie*.

It is curious that on the title page of "Times Whirligig," by Humphrey Willis, 1647, is a woodcut, illustrating the title, of a committee-man balancing himself on a top.

Poor Robin, in his Almanack for 1677, tells us, in "The Fanatick's Chronology," it was then "1804 years since the first invention of town-tops." In the *Fifteen Comforts of Marriage*, p. 143, we read: "Another tells 'em of a project he has to make town tops spin without an eel-skin, as if he bore malice to the schoolboys."

"The whirling top they whip,
And drive her giddy till she fall asleep."
—*Dryden.* Lemnius remarks: "Young youth do merrily exercise themselves in whipping top, and to make it run swiftly about, that it cannot be seen, and will deceive the sight, and that in winter to catch themselves a heat." *Occult Miracles of Nature*, 1658, 369. Cornelius Scriblerus says: "I would not have Martin as yet to scourge a top, till I am better informed whether the Trochus which was recommended by Cato be really our present top, or rather the hoop which the boys drive with a stick."

It is said in some of the Voyages, I think it is in Hawkesworth's, that the top is well known among the Indians, some of whom pointed to our sailors, who seemed to wonder at seeing it amongst them, that in order to make it spin they should lash it with a whip.

To sleep like a town top is a proverbial expression. The more usual expression at present is to sleep like a top. A top is said to sleep when it turns round with great velocity, and makes a smooth humming noise. The following custom is now laid aside; a large top was formerly kept in every village, to be whipped in frosty weather, that the peasants might be kept warm by exercise, and out of mischief, while they could not work.

Torches.—Originally primitive appliances formed of cordage steeped in tow, whence comes the word *funeral* from Lat. *funis*, a rope. But they gradually acquired a more elegant and convenient shape, and were charged with wax or with a mixture of wax and resin.

At ancient Roman weddings the manner was that two children should lead the bride, and a third bear before her a torch of white thorn, in honour of Ceres. I have seen foreign prints of marriages, where torches were represented as carried in the procession. Gough, speaking of funeral torches, says: "The use of torches was however retained alike in the day-time, as was the case at weddings; (*Sepulchral Monuments*, ii. Introd.) whence Propertius beautifully,

"Viximus insignes inter utramque facem:"

which is illustrated by Ovid;

"Et face pro thalami fax mihi mortis adest;"

Swinburne has the following remark: "At

their (the gipsies') weddings they carry torches, and have Paranymphs to give the bride away, with many other unusual rites." *Journey through Calabria*, p. 304. Ovid speaking of February, a month set apart for Parentalia or funeral anniversaries, and therefore not proper for marriage, writes:

"Conde tuas, Hymenæe, faces, et ab ignibus atris
Aufer, habent alias mœsta sepulchra faces."

According to Sir Thomas Browne, "The Romans admitted but five torches in their nuptial solemnities." *Garden of Cyrus*, p. 91.

"Deductio sequitur in Domum, nec sine Facibus, et Sponsa Matri Sponsi traditur. Quamprimum vero Sponsa Cubiculum ingreditur, Maritus pede suo Uxoris pedem tangit statimque ambo recluduntur."—Selden's *Uxor Hebraica* (Opera, tom. iii. p. 686).

"The Nuptial Torch," (says the author of "Hymen, &c. an Account of the Marriage Ceremonies of different Nations," p. 149) "used by the Greeks and Romans, has a striking conformity to the flambeaux of the Japanese. The most considerable difference is, that amongst the Romans, this torch was carried before the bride by one of her virgin attendants; and among the Greeks, that office was performed by the bride's mother." In the Greek Church the bridegroom and bride enter the church with lighted wax tapers in their hands; torches are used at Turkish marriages.

The custom of using torches and lights at funerals, or in funeral processions, appears to have been of long standing. Durandus *de Ritibus*, 228. Gregory tells us that "the funeral tapers, however thought of by some, are of harmelesse import. Their meaning is to shew, that the departed soules are not quite put out, but, having walked here as the Children of Light, are now gone to walk before God in the light of the living." *Posthuma*, 1649, 112; Gough's *Sep. Mon.* ii. Introd. vii.

Strutt tells us the burning of torches was very honourable. To have a great many was a special mark of esteem in the person who made the funeral to the deceased. By the will of William de Montacute, Earl of Salisbury, executed April 29, 1397, "Twenty-four poor people, cloathed in black gowns and red hoods, are ordered to attend the funeral, each carrying a lighted torch of eight pounds weight;" and from the account given by Stow of Sir John Gresham's funeral in 1556, it appears that he "had four dozen of great staff torches and a dozen of great long torches." *Manners and Customs*, ii, 108.

The following is an extract from the "Will of Thomas Windsor, Esq.," 1479: "Item, I will that I have brennyng at my burying and funeral service, four tapers and twenty-two torches of wax, every taper to conteyn the weight of ten pounds, and every torch sixteen pounds, which I will that twenty - four very poor men, and well disposed, shall hold as well at the tyme of my burying as at my Moneths Minde. Item, I will that after my Moneths Minde be done, the said four tapers be delivered to the churchwardens, &c. And that there be a hundred children within the age of sixteen years to be at my Moneths Minde, to say for my soul. That against my Moneths Minde, the candles bren before the rude in the Parish Church. Also that at my Moneths Minde my executors provide twenty priests to singe Placebo, Dirige, &c." *Gentl. Mag.* 1793, lxiii, 1191.

It was pretended at the time, as appears from a letter addressed to Secretary Cromwell, by a Frenchman, that on the day before the execution of Anne Boleyn, the tapers round the tomb of Katherine of Arragon "kendeld of them selfs," and that after matins, at *Deo Gratias*, "the said tapers quenched of them selfs."

In the Churchwardens' Accounts of St. Margaret's, Westminster, under 1460-1 is the following article : "Item rec' de Joh'e Braddyns die sepultur' Robti Thorp gen' p. iiii. Tor'. vj*s*. viij*d*." on which Pegge observes : "Little was done in these ages of gross Popery without lights. These torches cost 1*s*. 8*d*. apiece ; but we find them of various prices, according, as we may suppose, to their size. The churchwardens appear to have provided them, and consequently they were an article of profit to the church." The Editor adds : "These torches, it is conceived, were made of wax, which in ordinary cases were let out by the church, and charged to the party according to the consumption at the moment. This appears in the York Churchwardens' Accompts, where wax is charged." Nichols's *Illustr.* 1797, p. 243.

Ibid A.D. 1519 : "Item, Mr. Hall, the curate, for iv. torches, and for the best lights, at the buryal of Mr. Henry Vued, my Lord Cardinal's servant, vj*s*. vj*d*." In the Churchwardens' Accounts of St. Lawrence parish, Reading, are the following articles : "A.D. 1502. It. rec. of wast of torchis at the berying of sir John Hide, vicar of Sonyng, ij*s*. vj*d*." A.D. 1503. rec. for wast of torchye at the burying of John Long, maist' of the Gram' Scole, vj*s*. viij*d*." "A.D. 1504. It. rec. of the same Margaret," (late the wife of Thomas Platt,) "for wast of torchis at the yer mind of the seid Thomas, xx*d*."

Torches were constantly employed at convivial entertainments, in public processions by night, during parliamentary or official sittings under grave emergencies, and as an habitual method of locomotion in towns after dusk. Charles VI. of France narrowly escaped death through a contact with the lighted flambeaux held by attendants in the saloon, where festivities were being celebrated. During the anxious deliberations on the Carmagnola business about 1430 the Great Council of Venice sat by torchlight ; at the inauguration of a dogaressa in 1597 the 300 gilt baskets holding the superb confectionery provided for the occasion were carried round the Piazza in the same way ; and in the latter part of the 17th century torches were used at sea to throw light on the movements of fleets. These appliances seem to have been charged with a blend of wax and resin for the sake of durability. Hazlitt's *Venetian Republic*, 1900, ii, 76-7, *et alibi*.

Vernon says : "If the Christians should bury their dead in the nighte time, or if they should burne their bodies, as the Painims did, they might well use torches as well as the Painims without any just reprehension and blame." He observes (a little farther on) : "Moreover it is not to be doubted but that the auncient byshops and ministers of the Church did bryng in this manner bearinge of torches, and of singinge in funerals, not for the intent and purpose that the Painmes did use it, nor yet for to confirme their superstitious abuses and errours, but rather for to abolishe them. For they did see that it was an hard thing to pluck those old and inveterate customes from the hartes of them that had been nouselled in them from their youth. They did foresee that if they had burid their dead without som honest ceremonies, as the worlde did then take them, it had bene yet more harde to put away those olde rotten errors from them that were altogether wedded unto them." Our author tells us : "Chrisostome, likening the deade whome they followed with burnynge torches unto wrestlers and runners, had a respect unto the customes and fashions of Grekeland, beyng a Greeke himcelfe, among whiche there was a certain kind of running, after this maner. The firste did beare a torche, being lighted, in his hand, which being weary, he did deliver unto him that followeth next after him. He againe, that had received the torche, if he chaunced to be wery, did the like : and so all the residue that followeth in order ;" hence "among the Grekes and Latines to geve the lampe or torche unto another, hath beene taken for to put other in his place, after that one is werye and hath perfourmed his course." He concludes: "This may very well be applyed unto them, that departe out of this world." *Hunting of Purgatory,* 1561, fol. 40, 45, 47. Again, at folio 151, he says: "Singinge, bearinge of lightes, and other like ceremonies as were used in their buringes and funeralles, were ordeyned, or rather permitted and suffred by y⁰ auncient bishoppes and pastours, for to abolish, put downe, and dryve awai the superstition and ydolatri yᵗ the heathen and paynymes used about their dead: and not for anye opinion yᵗ they had, yᵗ such thinges could profite the soules departed, as it doth manifestly appear by their owne writings."

Herrick has a copy of verses illustrative of this subject:

"*Upon a Maid that dyed the Day she was married.*

"That morne which saw me made a bride,
The ev'ning witnes that I dy'd.
Those holy lights, wherewith they guide
Unto the bed the bashful bride,
Serv'd but as tapers for to burne
And light my reliques to their urne.
This epitaph, which here you see,
Supply'd the Epithalamie."

The following is the epitaph of the great Budè at St. Genevieve, Paris:

"Que n'a-ton plus en torches dependu,
Suivant la mode accoutumée en Sainte?
Afin qu'il soit par l'obscur entendu
Que des François la lumiere est eteinte."

Toss-Pot.—The following passage shews plainly the etymology of "Tosspot:" it is extracted from "The Schoolemaster, or Teacher of Table Philosophie," 1576, Book iv. chap. 35. "Of merry Jests of Preaching Friars:" "A certaine frier tossing the pot, and drinking very often at the table, was reprehended by the Priour," &c.

Totemism.—An apparent survival of the Pythagorean doctrine concerning animals, with certain modifications. The modern authorities seem to establish its universality. The ancient theory of metempsychosis was corrupted into a superstition, that if an ancestor, or the member of a clan was changed into a particular creature, beast, bird, or fish, all beings to come of that genus were to be held sacred; and it even appears that the name of the tribe or community was bestowed on them. See Laing's *Human Origins,* 1897, pp. 185-6, where, and elsewhere in the same author's admirable writings, the theories of Totemism and Animism are explained and discussed. In its more rudimentary or archaic stage the former seems to have extended to inanimate objects.

Touch.—This is a childish or schoolboy's game. Several play at it. One boy endeavours to touch one of his playmates, and they do their best to escape him. The moment he succeeds, he exclaims, Touch, or Touch he; the boy touched is obliged to take his place, and the game begins over again.

A variety is called *Touch Wood,* where the difference is that, by laying a hand or finger on anything of that material, the player is exempt from the consequences of being touched.

Touch-pieces.—See *King's Evil.*

Town-Husband. — See Halliwell in v.

Trade and Labour Songs.—See a reference in *Antiquary,* October, 1885, p. 150. In 1841 Charles Mackay edited for the Percy Society a Collection of Songs and Ballads on this subject belonging to the 14th, 15th, and 16th centuries.

Transfiguration-Day.—(August 6). The anniversary, or supposed one, of the change in Christ's personality witnessed by Peter, James, and John, A.D. 32 on Mount Tabor. The festival was instituted by pope Calixtus II. in 1455, and in or about 1490 Caxton printed the service used in our churches on this occasion on the eighth day before the Ides of August. Hazlitt's *Bibl. Coll. and Notes,* i, 425; ii, 602, where a later impression by Pynson, apparently in 1499, is noticed. *Plumpton Correspondence,* p. 130.

Transformation. — See *Splayed Bitch* and *Werwolf.* The metamorphosis of human and other creatures into new and strange shapes constitutes of course the groundwork of Ovid's production, and was agreeable to the Greek philosophy, as well as to the Pythagorean theory of transmigration, as we find beautiful youths and maidens converted into birds and flowers. Keightley, in his *Mythology of Ancient Greece and Italy,* did excellent service in illustrating the subject more scientifically than his predecessors.

Transubstantiation. — In a Compendious Buik of Godly Sanges, &c., printed before 1578, is the following passage, which has been intended, no doubt, as an argument against transubstantiation:

"Giue God be tranfubftantiall
In breid with *Hoc eſt corpus meum,*
Quhy war ȝe ſa vnnaturall
As tak him in ȝour teith, and fla him?"

In Heath's "Epigrammes," 1610, I find the following:

"*In Transubstantiatores.*

The cannibals eate men with greedinesse;
And transubstantiators do no lesse:

No lesse? Nay more; and that farre
    more by ods;
Those eat man's flesh, these ravine upon
    Gods."

Pleasantries at the expence of this ancient
ritualistic observance are numerous in
every literature. In *Doctor Double Ale*
(about 1550), we have:

    "For yet I deny nat
    The masses priuat,
    Nor yet forsake
    That I of a cake
    My maker may make—"

Hazlitt's *Pop. Poetry*, iii, 317.

**Transylvanian Supersti-
tions.**—See *Nineteenth Century*, July,
1885.

Trap-Ball or Trap-Bat. — Mr.
Atkinson observes: "The probability is
that the game is a lineal descendant from
the ball-play of the old Danes, or North-
men and Icelanders. The game is called
Spell and Knor, and the word Spell has
come to be understood as the designation
of the peculiar kind of trap used in it.
But surely 'Spell and Knor' is a corruption of 'Spell a' Knor' i.e. the play
at ball. The object of the game is to exceed one's competitors in the distance to
which the ball is driven. On the liberation
of the spring of the trap or spell, the
ball, previously whitened all over with
chalk, is struck in mid-air with the tribbit-
stick, and the place at which it falls, being
noted by the lockers-out, the distance
from the trap is measured in spaces of
twenty yards each, or scores. There is
one day in the year—Shrove Tuesday—
when it is customarily practiced, not quite
exclusively. The tribbit-stick is elsewhere
called primstick, gelstick, buckstick, trib-
bit, trevit, &c." *Cleveland Glossary*,
1868, pp. 299, 542.

Spell and Norr (or Nurr) is not peculiar,
however, to the North, for in the "Worcestershire Chronicle" for September,
1847, we read: "Before the commons were
taken in, the children of the poor had
ample space wherein to recreate themselves at cricket, nurr, or any other
diversion; but now they were driven from
every green spot, and in Bromsgrove here,
the nailor boys, from the force of circumstances, have taken possession of the
turn-pike-road to play the before-mentioned games, to the serious inconvenience
of the passengers, one of whom, a woman,
was yesterday knocked down by a nurr,
which struck her on the head. Surely it
would be an act of humanity on the part
of those who have been most benefited by
the inclosing of the common to afford the
children of the poor of this parish a small
space of ground for the purposes of health
and amusement."

Tray-Trip. — Grose says (I think
erroneously) this was an ancient game,
like Scotish Hop, played on a pavement,
marked out with chalk into different com-
partments. It is mentioned without any
explanation of its precise nature, further
than that it was a popular game with cards
or dice, or both, in the "English Courtier
and the Cuntrey Gentleman," 1586; and
in the Percy MS. "Loose Songs," p. 68,
we find "fful oft shee and I within the
buttery played att tray-trippe of a dye."
See note to Mayne's *City Match*, 1639, act
2, in Hazlitt's Dodsley. Mr. Thomas
Wright, in his "Provincial Dictionary,"
notes trip-trap as a game peculiar to the
North of England, also called trip—the
same, no doubt, as our tray-trip. Comp.
Nares, 1859, p. 896, and *Tribet post.*

Treacle, or rather **Triacle,
Water.**—A supposed universal antidote
and specific, made in various ways, and
originally, of course, unconnected with
treacle; Gr. Θηριακα. See receipts for
making this water in Nares, *Gl.* in v.

In Newbery's *Dives Pragmaticus*, 1563,
sign B 2 *verso*, he says:

    "I haue fine Triacle of Genes, the
      plague to preuent
    Fyne waters fine oyles, of odour ex-
      cellent."

Tree-Geese.—See *Barnacles.*

Tree-Lore.—Grose tells us, that if a
tree of any kind is split—and weak,
ricketty, or ruptured children drawn
through it, and afterwards the tree is
bound together, so as to make it unite,
as the tree heals and grows together, so
will the child acquire strength. Sir John
Cullum, who saw this operation twice performed, thus describes it: "For this
purpose a young ash was each time
selected, and split longitudinally, about
five feet: the fissure was kept wide open
by my gardener; whilst the friend of the
child, having first stripped him naked,
passed him twice through it, almost head
foremost. As soon as the operation was
performed, the wounded tree was bound
up with a pack-thread; and as the bark
healed, the child was to recover. The first
of the young patients was to be cured of
the ricketts, the second of a rupture."
This is a very ancient and extensive piece
of superstition.

Grose refers to the vulgar opinion
"concerning the power of ash trees to
repel other maladies or evils, such as
shrew-mice, the stopping one of which
animals alive into a hole bored in an ash
is imagined an infallible preventative of
their ravages in lands."

In a Scotish statistical report of 1796,
it is said of Newparish: "There is a
quick thorn of a very antique appearance,

for which the people have a superstitious veneration. They have a mortal dread to lop off or cut any part of it, and affirm with a religious horror, that some persons, who had the temerity to hurt it, were afterwards severely punished for their sacrilege." *Stat. Acc.* iii, 609.

In the "Gentleman's Magazine" for October 1804, is given an engraving of an ash tree, growing by the side of Shirley-street, (the road leading from Hockly House to Birmingham,) at the edge of Shirley-heath in Solihull Parish. The upper part of a gap formed by the chizzel has closed, but the lower remains open. The tree is healthy and flourishing. Thomas Chillingworth, son of the owner of an adjoining farm, now (1804) about thirty-four years of age, was, when an infant of a year old, passed through a similar tree, now perfectly sound, which he preserves with so much care that he will not suffer a single branch to be touched, for it is believed the life of the patient depends on the life of the tree (a suggestion of hamadryadism): and the moment that it is cut down, be the patient ever so distant, the rupture returns, and a mortification ensues. It is not however uncommon for persons to survive for a time the felling of the tree. In one case the rupture suddenly returned, and mortification followed. These trees are left to close of themselves, or are closed with nails. The wood-cutters very frequently meet with the latter. One felled on Bunnan's Farm was found full of nails. This belief is so prevalent in this part of the country, that instances of trees that have been employed in the cure are very common. The like notions obtain credit in some parts of Essex. In a previous part of the same volume it is stated that this ash tree stands "close to the cottage of Henry Rowe, whose infant son Thomas Rowe was drawn through the trunk or body of it in the year 1791. to cure him of a rupture, the tree being then split open for the purpose of passing the child through it. The boy is now thirteen years and six months old: I have this day, June 10, 1804, seen the ash tree and Thomas Rowe, as well as his father Henry Rowe, from whom I have received the above account; and he superstitiously believes that his son Thomas was cured of the rupture, by being drawn through the cleft in the said ash tree and by nothing else."

Among tree-superstitions must be ranked what Armstrong says : " The vine excepted, the Minorquins never prune a tree, thinking it irreligious in some degree to presume to direct its growth ; and if you express your wonder that they forbear this usual practice, and inform them of the advantages that attend it in other countries, their answer is ever ready : God knows best how a tree should grow." *Hist. of Minorca*, p. 191.

Tregeagle and Dosmare Pool.—(Communicated by the late T. Q. Couch, Esq. to the Editor). A little to the north of St. Neot's Church, in East Cornwall, is a melancholy moor bordered by rough granite tors. The rude cottages, scattered sparsely over the landscape, are such shapeless heaps of unhewn granite that, at a distance, and when not sending up their wreaths of smoke they give little more evidence of human neighbourhood than the wonderfully poised piles which crest the hills around. On this bleak marsh is a lonely mountain tarn filled by the drainage of the moors, and having until of late years no visible outlet or inlet :

" Dosmery poole amid the moores
On top stands of a hill ;
More than a mile about, no streames
It empt, nor any fill."

So says or sings Carew, who gives what is still the belief of the country side, that it ebbs and flows with the sea, and so deep is it, that a fagot once thrown in was sucked down by a central whirlpool, and after passing among the bases of the hills, was taken up in Fowey harbour. It avails little that some matter-of-fact persons have, by actual experiment of sounding, sought to destroy this old and well-established fact. No finer picture of savage desolation can be imagined than this spot, in some of its aspects, presents. On a lowering November day, when the gusts are driving the rain-clouds across this desert, and soughing among the rushes and bent grass, and when the low of the half-wild herds is mingled with the plaintive whistle of the curlew, it looks like a bit of primitive barrenness, untouched save by the wild workings of the elements. It will be expected that a spot so weird and wild will not be without its grim and awful story ; accordingly we find it especially associated with the deeds of giant Tregeagle. When travelling over this neighbourhood, some few years ago, I gleaned, from oral tradition and written record, all that was known of his story, and as it well illustrates the influences at work to modify and debase popular fable, I have thought that my notes might be worthy of a place in the Reports of this Society. It will be well first to give the ordinary and current book-versions of the legend. Michell's *History of St. Neot's*, p. 58.

Tregeagle was steward to John, Earl of Radnor, of Llanhydrock. He was a very wicked man, who by craft and cruelty became very rich and powerful. Neither pity nor remorse checked him in his avarice; indeed, some say that the curse of blood rested on his ill-gotten gains. With all this, however, riches flowed in too slowly for his longings, so, for present advantage, he entered into a compact with the Evil-one, whereby for a certain time his wealth and influence became unbounded, and his greed and tyranny growing with his means, he did such deeds as made him the bye-word of after generations. In the midst of his enjoyment of his power the Devil claimed the forfeited soul. As the price of the unholy bargain he finds no rest, but is bound to the fulfilment of some endless task, such as the baling of this ever-filling pool with a limpet-shell, varied by his binding the shifting sands of the northern coasts in bundles with bands of the same material. Every now and then he is disturbed in his hopeless labour by the persecution of the insatiable fiend, from whom he flies over morland and hill tracked by the remorseless hunter and his hell-hounds, and finds respite only when he can get a temporary shelter in the chapel of St. Michael on Roche rock. The howls of the harassed Tregeagle are often heard by the belated hind, and "he roars like the great Tregeagle" is the common exclamation of the Cornish mother of her screaming child.

Another story, still more terrible, is related of him. Some time after Tregeagle had disappeared from amongst men a tenant of the Earl was sued by the new steward for arrears of rent. The sum, it seems, had really been paid, but Tregeagle had not given credit for it in his books. At the trial, the supposed debtor contrived by glamour to raise the spirit of Tregeagle and present him as a witness in the court, and by the evidence produced the plaintiff was nonsuited. "On retiring from the bar this singular witness was left behind in court; the defendant being requested by some gentlemen of the long robe to take him away, he sternly replied, that, as he had been at the pains of bringing the evidence, those who complained might take the trouble to remove him." The spirit of Tregeagle was with difficulty exorcised, and, "as perpetual rest was deemed impossible, some work of extreme difficulty was thought necessary to furnish his spirit with employment," and his task was the lading Dosmery pool with a limpet-shell and trussing the northern sands with ropes of the same. Hitchins and Drew's *Hist. of Cornwall*, i, 71.

The story, of which the book version is here given, presents many points of interest, and has an important bearing upon the historic value of legend in general, and the mode in which it becomes altered and vitiated. In looking into the history of this fable, I may remark, that, because Carew, in his "Survey" (temp. Eliz.), and Hals, in his "Parochial History" (temp. 1736), made no mention of Tregeagle, we are not to conclude that such a story did not exist in one of its earlier versions. Little trust is, in these matters, to be placed in negative evidence, as it is only until lately that our popular tales have been looked upon but as "unconsidered trifles." The circumstance that Tregeagle is stated to have been steward to John, Earl of Radnor, permits us to fix the date of the legend, or rather of its earliest modification. Robartes of Llanhydrock was made Earl of Radnor by Charles II. in 1679, and Tonkin, in his description of the parish of St. Allen, gives some particulars respecting the Tregeagle connecting them with this nobleman, and offering some curious confirmation of this strange story. He tells us that Sir Richard Roberts, afterwards Lord Roberts, possessed the manor of Bosvellick towards the latter part of Queen Elizabeth's reign, and that John Roberts his son, first Earl of Radnor, "was nursed here by Mrs. Tregeagle, the daughter of Degory Polwhele, Esq. and wife of John Tregeagle, Gent., who held a lease of the estate from Sir Richard Roberts. And this was the rise of the Tregeagles, for John Tregeagle their son, being fosterbrother to the said Earl, was afterwards by him made his chief steward, and brought forward in the world." A John Tregeagle, probably the same, was sheriff of Cornwall in 1695, and twice represented Bossiney in Parliament. The fall of the Tregeagles was as rapid as their rise, for Hals says that the sons by ill-conduct wasted and sold their lands, temp. George II. It may be asked, Is there any warrant for the blot on the escutcheon of Tregeagle —any circumstance to show that his name is justly sent down to posterity with the brand of infamy and mark of blood upon it? It is a remarkable fact that the scandal-loving Hals makes no mention of tyranny or crime in connection with Tregeagle, which it is probable he would have done, had there been any great occasion, since the very completion of the publication of his History was prevented by the free way in which he handled the private history of many of our county families, and the subsequent withdrawal of their patronage. The modern legend may, however, be held as bearing some evidence that John Tregeagle was, at least, a harsh and arbitrary man, and there is one authority which represents him as cruel and severe. We find, from an interesting narrative, communicated by

Moses Pitt to Dr. Fowler, Bishop of Gloucester, and reprinted in C. S. Gilbert's *Survey of Cornwall*, that there lived in the 17th century, in the parish of St. Teath, a woman, Ann Jeffries, who was under the delusion that she was visited and fed by fairies, who conferred on her the power of curing diseases. This was so generally believed that multitudes of sick people repaired to her from all parts, from Land's-end, and even from London. The writer relates that John Tregeagle, Esq., Justice of Peace, and steward to John Earl of Radnor, apprehended Ann by warrant as an imposter, and sent her to Bodmin gaol, "and ordered the prison-keeper that she should be kept without victuals, and she was so kept, and yet she lived, and that without complaining." On her dismissal Tregeagle continued his severity to the deluded or deluding girl, and even kept her a prisoner in his own house without meat, for the purpose of testing the truth of her statement that she was fed by fairies.

Popular fable is liable to modification by the changing circumstances of man, and the varying aspects of external nature; but even then the process is slow, and the additions generally in keeping with the original plan. It is fortunate that the interpolations of books are not easily admitted into the oral version of those stories. There is no doubt that this tale, which our late Cornish histories would bring down to a date scarcely exceeding a hundred and fifty years, is really very old, but overlaid and disfigured by the accretions of succeeding ages. The additions are, however, not without their value, for they are as regular and definite as a geological section, each modification clearly indicating the age to which it belongs. With the plain country people this man of rents and leases, growing from the unscrupulous pettifogger to the overbearing *parvenu*, is a spirit grim, shadowy, and gigantic, doomed to be the sport of some spirit more powerful than himself, by whom he is bound to some interminable and purposeless labour.

The antiquity of Tregeagle, as well as his giant proportions, may be illustrated by many instances in Cornwall, where there are so many remarkable natural objects to be accounted for in the popular mythology. Near Penare point, on the southern shore, are scattered huge blocks of quartz which tradition says were hurled there by the great Tregeagle from the opposite coast. Rocks and dark caverns are frequently associated with his name. The first germ of this legend may be British as is the name: at all events those acquainted with European folk-lore will readily recognize the Scandinavian element, and see its affinity with the Wuthend Heer of Germany and the other forms which have resulted from amalgamation with pre-existing or subsequent traditions. In our own country various are its shapes. The Cornish peasant who startles at the far-off wailing of Tregeagle, herein proves his kinship with the Westmoreland hind, who

"——oftentimes will start,
For overhead are sweeping Gabriel's
    hounds,
Doom'd, with their impious lord, the
    flying hart
To chase for ever on aërial grounds."

The monkish additions are seen in the sanctuary which is afforded to the harassed spirit by St. Michael of Roche, and the dread which the pursuing fiend has of the holy rock and its chapel. It is a strange coincidence that, in much later times, John Tregeagle, the unjust and unpitying steward, should have happed upon a tradition so capable, with a little adaptation, of perpetuating the memory of his misdeeds to all ages.

Trenchmore.—A lively tune in triple time, to which in Elizabethan days they danced in a rough and boisterous fashion. See Nares, *Gl.* in v. The word acquired a secondary meaning, as we perceive in Breton's *Wit's Trenchmour*, 1597.

Tribet.—A children's game in Lancashire, said to be part of a form of *trap*. See Halliwell in v. and *Tray Trip* suprà.

Tric-trac.—See *Tick-Tack*.

Trinity Sunday.—In a letter from Mr. E. G. to Aubrey, dated Ascension Day, 1682, is an account of Newnton in North Wiltshire; where, to perpetuate the memory of the donation of a common to that place, by King Athelstan, and of a house for the hayward, the following ceremonies were appointed: "Upon every Trinity Sunday, the parishioners being come to the door of the hayward's house, the door was struck thrice in honour of the Holy Trinity; then they entered. The bell was rung; after which, silence being ordered, they read their prayers aforesaid. Then was a ghirland of flowers (about the year 1660 one was killed striving to take away the ghirland) made upon an hoop, brought forth by a maid of the town upon her neck; and a young man (a batchelor) of another parish, first saluted her three times, in honour of the Trinity, in respect of God the Father. Then she puts the ghirland upon his neck, and kisses him three times, in honour of the Trinity, particularly God the Son. Then he puts the ghirland on her neck again, and kisses her three times, in respect of the Holy Trinity, and particularly the Holy Ghost.

Then he takes the ghirland from her neck, and by the custom must give her a penny at least, which, as fancy leads, is now exceeded, as 2*s.* 6*d.*, or &c.

"The method of giving this ghirland is from house to house annually, till it comes round. In the evening every commoner sends his supper up to this house, which is called the Eale House; and having before laid in there equally a stock of malt which was brewed in the house, they sup together, and what was left was given to the poor."

Pennant observes: "In Wales, on Thursday after Trinity Sunday, which they call Dudd son Duw, or Dydd gwyl duw, on the eve before, they strew a sort of fern before their doors, called Red yn Mair." This is at Caerwis.

Trinity Sunday Even. — In Lysons' "Environs," i, 310, among his curious extracts from the Churchwardens' Accounts at Lambeth, are the following: 1519. Item, for garlonds and drynke for the chylderne on Trenyte Even 6*d.*

——To Spryngwell and Smyth for syngyng with the procession on Trenete Sonday Even, 12*d.*

——Item, for four onssys of garnesyng rebonds, at 9*d.* the once, 3*s.*

Trinoda Necessitas.—See Tomlins, *Law Dict.*, 1835, in v.

Trip or **Trip-trap.**—A game played in the North of England with a *trip-stick*. See Halliwell in v.

Tripos.—The person who made the disputation on Ash Wednesday at Queen's College, Cambridge, and was otherwise known as Bachelor of the Stool. See Pepys's *Diary*, Feb. 26, 1659-60. The Tripos appears to have stood in the same relation to the lesser *Comitia* as the *Prevaricator* to the University itself and the Oxonian *Terræ Filius.* Pepys says that Fuller, who came to see him, 23 Sept. 1664, was Cambridge Prevaricator in his time. See Randolph's Poems, ed. Hazlitt, p. 670, for the text of the address delivered in 1632 by the poet—perhaps the only relic of the kind, which survives.

Troco.—A game similar to lawn-tennis, formerly played with balls and cues, iron rings being fixed on the grassplot. At Bramshill, in Hampshire, celebrated by Browne in the dedication of the *Shepherd's Pipe,* 1614, there used to be the *Troco* Terrace devoted to this amusement.

Troth-Plight. — In Whitford's "Werke for Householders," &c. (first printed before 1530) is the following caution on the aboue subject: "The ghostly ennemy doth deceyue many persones by the pretence & colour of matrymony in pryuate & secrete contractes.. For many men whan they can nat obteyne theyr vnclene desyre of the woman, wyll promyse maryage and thervpon make a contracte promyse & gyue fayth and trouth eche vnto other, sayenge 'Here I take the Margery vnto my wyfe, & therto I plyght the my trouth.' And she agayne vnto him in lyke maner. And after that done, they suppose they maye lawfully vse theyr vnclene behauyour, and somtyme the acte and dede dothe folowe, vnto the greate offence of god & their owne soules. It is a great ieopardy therfore to make any suche contractes, epecyally amonge them selfe secretely alone without recordes, whiche must be two at the least." *Edit.* 1533, sign. e 3.

Among the Interrogatories for the Doctrine and Manners of Mynisters, &c. early in the reign of Elizabeth No. 28, is "Whether they have exhorted yong folke to absteyne from privy contracts, and not to marry without the consent of such their parents and fryends as have auctority over them; or no." Swinburne on "Spousals," p. 10, says: "Some spousals are contracted by signs, as the giving and receiving a ring, others by word."

Mr. Halliwell-Phillipps, in his *Outlines of the Life of Shakespear*, 1883, has shown that the great poet had a precontract with his wife, a matter of common occurrence in those days. The parties plighted their faith to each other before two or more witnesses, and considered themselves practically united in wedlock. The lady seems to have usually received as a token a bent or crooked sixpence, but sometimes, as we shall see, the money was broken between them. Mr. Phillipps cites a case in which the lover presented his mistress with a pair of gloves, two oranges, two handkerchiefs, and a red silk girdle, and this was in the same year (1582) in which Shakespear was engaged to Anne Hathaway. But this question is more fully illustrated and discussed in the present writer's monograph on Shakespear, 1903, in connection with a volume entitled: *The Lawes Resolutions of Women's Rights,* 1632.

In Field's "A Woman's a Weather-Cock," 1612, Scudmore, Act ii, sc. 1, tells the priest who is going to marry his mistress to Count Fredericke,

"She is contracted, sir, nay married
Unto another man, though it want forme:
And such strange passages and mutuall vowes,
'Twould make your short haire start through your blacke cap
Should you but heare it."

In Brathwaite's "Whimzies," 1631, the author has the following passage: can it allude to the custom of interchanging betrothing rings? "St. Martin's Rings and counterfeit bracelets are commodities of infinite consequence. They will passe for current at a May pole, and purchase a favor from their May-Marian." Comp. *Rush-Rings.* St. Martin's Rings were something similar.

It was anciently very customary, among the common sort of people, to break a piece of gold or silver in token of a verbal contract of marriage and promises of love: one half whereof was kept by the woman, while the other part remained with the man. This is referred to in "Bateman's Tragedy": "Long they dwelt not on this theme, before they fell to that of love, renewing their vows of eternal love and constancy that nothing but death should be able to separate them: and, to bind it, he broke a piece of gold, giving her the one half, and keeping the other himself: and then with tears and tender kisses they parted." And again, in the "Exeter Garland":

"A ring of pure gold she from her finger took,
And just in the middle the same then she broke :
Quoth she, as a token of love you this take,
And this as a pledge I will keep for your sake."

The Dialogue between Kitty and Filbert in the "What d'ye call it," by Gay, is much to our purpose:

"Yet, Justices, permit us, ere we part,
To break this ninepence as you've broke our heart."

"*Filbert* (breaking the ninepence)—As this divides, thus are we torn in twain.

"*Kitty* (joining the pieces)—And as this meets, thus may we meet again."

In Codrington's "Second Part of Youth's Behaviour," 1664, p. 33, is the following very remarkable passage: "It is too often seen that young gentlewomen by gifts are courted to interchange, and to return the courtesie: rings indeed and ribbands are but trifles, but believe me, that they are not trifles that are aimed at in such exchanges: let them therefore be counselled that they neither give nor receive any thing that afterwards may procure their shame, &c."

Brand remarks: "strong traces of this remain in our villages in many parts of the kingdom. I have been more than once assured from credible authority on Portland Island that something very like it is still practised there very generally, where the inhabitants seldom or never intermarry with any on the main-land, and where the young women, selecting lovers of the same place (but with what previous rites, ceremonies, or engagements, I could never learn), account it no disgrace to allow them every favour, and that too from the fullest confidence of being made wives, the moment such consequences of their stolen embraces begin to be too visible to be any longer concealed."

As to the resumption of troth-plight see Introduction to Sir Walter Scott's *Pirate.* "The antient Frenchmen" observes Sir W. Vaughan, 1600, "had a ceremonie, that when they would marrie, the bridegroom should pare his nayles and send them unto his new wife: which done, they lived together afterwards as man and wife." *Golden Grove,* 1608, O 2. *verso.*

Troule-in-Madame, Trol-my-Dames, or **Trunks.**—This word or term is a corruption of *Trou Madame,* and the game corresponds to *Pigeon-Holes.* The form *Trol-my-Dames* occurs in the *Winter's Tale.* The sport is alluded to in "The Christmas Prince," 1607:

"Why say you not that Munday will bee drunke,
Keeps all vnruly wakes, & playes at trunkes."

It is also referred to in Halliwell's "Dictionary," and in "Poor Robin" for 1715: "After dinner (for you must not have too long intermissions) to your sack again, typire, topire, and tropire, and for recreations to such liquor, billiards, kettle-pins, noddy-boards, tables, trunks, shovel-boards, fox and geese, and those two excellent games at cards, one and thirty, and drive knaves out of town."

True-Love-Knot.—A knot, among the ancient Northern Nations, seems to have been the symbol of love, faith, and friendship, pointing out the indissoluble tie of affection and duty. Thus the ancient Runic inscriptions, as we gather from Hickes's "Thesaurus," are in the form of a knot. Hence, among the Northern English and Scots, who still retain, in a great measure, the language and manners of the ancient Danes, that curious kind of knot, a mutual present between the lover and his mistress, which, being considered as the emblem of plighted fidelity, is therefore called a True-love Knot: a name which is not derived, as one would naturally suppose it to be, from the words "True" and "Love," but from the Danish verb "Trulofa," fidem do, I plight my troth, or faith. Thus we read, in the Islandic Gospels, the following passage in the first chapter of St. Matthew, which confirms, beyond a doubt, the sense here given: "til einrar Meyar er truofad var einum Manne," &c. *i.e.* to a virgin espoused, that is, who was promised, or had engaged herself to a man, &c. and Isidorus appears to have been clearly of opinion that this bond was binding and indissoluble. Hickes *Gram. Island,* p. 4; Selden's *Uxor Hebraica* (Opera, iii, 670).

Browne, in his "Vulgar Errors," says: "The True-Lover's Knot is much magnified, and still retains in presents of love among us; which, though in all points it doth not make out, had, perhaps, its origin from Nodus Herculanus, or that which was called Hercules his Knot, resembling the snaky combination of the Caduceus, or Rod of Hermes, and in which form the Zone or woollen girdle of the bride was fastened, as Turnebus observes in his "Adversaria." I find the following passage in the "Merry Devil of Edmonton," 1608:

"With pardon, Sir, that name is quite undon,
This True-Love-Knot cancelles both maide and nun."

In "Paradoxical Assertions and Philosophical Problems," by R. H. 1664, p. 19, we read: "I shall appeal to any Enamoreto but newly married, whether he took not more pleasure in weaving innocent True-love Knots than in untying the virgin zone, or knitting that more than Gordian Knot, which none but that invincible Alexander, Death, can untye?"

Gay, in his pastoral called the "Spell," thus beautifully describes the rustic manner of knitting the true-love knot:

"As Lubberkin once slept beneath a tree,
I twitch'd his dangling garter from his knee;
He wist not when the hempen string I drew;
Now mine I quickly doff of inkle blue;
Together fast I tie the garters twain,
And, while I knit the knot, repeat this strain—
Three times a True-Love's Knot I tye secure:
Firm be the knot, firm may his love endure."

Another species of knot divination is given in the "Connoisseur," No. 56, "Whenever I go to lye in a strange bed, I always tye my garter nine times round the bed-post, and knit nine knots in it, and say to myself:

'This knot I knit, this knot I tye,
To see my love as he goes by,
In his apparel'd array, as he walks in every day.'"

Ozell says: "The favour was a large knot of ribbands, of several colours, gold, silver, carnation, and white. This is worn upon the hat for some weeks." He adds elsewhere: "It is ridiculous to go to a wedding without new cloaths. If you are in mourning, you throw it off for some days, unless you are in mourning for some near relation that is very lately dead." Note to his translation of *Misson*, p. 350-1. Hence, evidently, the bride favours or top-knots at marriages, which have been considered as emblems of the ties of duty and affection between the bride and her spouse, have been derived. Misson elsewhere says: "Autrefois en France on donnoit des livrees de Noces; quelque Noeud de Ruban que les Conviez portoient attaché sur le bras: mais cela ne se pratique plus que parmi les paisans. En Angleterre on le fait encore chez les plus grands Seigneurs. Ces Rubans s'appellent des Faveurs," &c.

Trulis.—A Scotish game mentioned in the Bannatyne MS. 1568, as play at the Trulis. *Trouil* is a spindle. Mr. Brand supposed this pastime to resemble *T totum.*

Trump.—i.q. *Ruff.* a game at cards similar to the modern *Whist,* but formerly played by six, as well as four, persons.

Trunk.—A boys' plaything similar to the modern pea-shooter.

Trunket.—A game played with short sticks. Somewhat resembling cricket, and perhaps the germ of that game. See Halliwell in v.

Trunks. — i.q. *Troll-Madame* or *Troule-in-Madame.*

Turning Cat in Pan.—Pegge supposes turning "Cat in Pan" a corruption of turning cate, the old word for cake, in pan. *Gents. Mag.* xxiv. 67. It is added elsewhere: "When the lower side is made brown in the frying-pan, the cake is turned the other side downwards." John Heywood has the following line:

"Thus may ye see to turne the Cat in the Pan."

"Workes," ed. 1598, sign. H 3. See also "Gent. Mag." vol. xxiv. p. 212; vol. liii. p. 928; vol. lxxxii. pp. 228, 308, 429, 627.

Turning the Cup over.—A Sussex Harvest custom. See *Sussex Arch. Coll.* xiv, 187.

Turquoise. — Of the turquoise, Fenton, in his *Secret Wonders of Nature,* 1569, (chiefly from Pliny) says: "The Turkeys doth move when there is any peril prepared to him that weareth it." The turquoise (by Nicols in his *Lapidary*) is likewise said to take away all enmity, and to reconcile man and wife. Other superstitious qualities are imputed to it, all of which were either monitory or preservative to the wearer. Comp. Nares, *Glossary,* 1859, in v. The turquoise is not really a stone at all.

Tutbury.—See *Bull-Baiting.*

Twelfth Day.—This day, which is well known to be called the Twelfth, from its being the twelfth in number from the

Nativity, is called also the Feast of the Epiphany, from a Greek word signifying manifestation, from our Lord having been on that day made manifest to the Gentiles. This, as Bourne observes, is one of the greatest of the twelve, and of more jovial observation for the visiting of friends, and Christmas gambols. But Old Twelfth Day was on the 12th January or the 12th day of the New Year.

The customs of this day, various in different countries, yet agree in the same end, that is, to do honour to the Eastern Magi, who are supposed to have been of royal dignity. In the Roman calendar, I find an observation on the fifth day of January, the eve or vigil of the Epiphany, "Kings created or elected by beans." The sixth is called "The Festival of Kings," with this additional remark, that this ceremony of electing kings was continued with feasting for many days."

A writer in the "Gentleman's Magazine," for December, 1764, thinks the practice of choosing king and queen on Twelfth Night owes its origin to the custom among the Romans, which they took from the Grecians, of casting dice who should be the *Rex Convivii;* or as Horace calls him, the *Arbiter Bibendi.* Whoever threw the lucky cast, which they termed *Venus* or *Basilicus,* gave laws for the night. In the same manner the lucky clown, who out of the several divisions of a plum-cake draws the king, thereby becomes sovereign of the company: and the poor clod-pole, to whose lot the knave falls, is as unfortunate as the Roman, whose hard fate it was to throw the *damnosum Caniculum.* See also Alexander ab Alexandro, ii, 22.

The following extract from Collier's "Ecclesiastical History," vol. i. p. 163. seems to account in a satisfactory manner for the name of Twelfth Day. "In the days of King Alfred, a law was made with relation to holidays, by virtue of which the twelve days after the Nativity of our Saviour were made Festivals."

In England Twelfth Day and Night were not unusual occasions for theatrical exhibitions and pageants. Hazlitt's *Manual of Old Plays,* 1892, *passim.* An unique broadside Bill or Advertisement announces the performance of a tilting match about 1590 at Westminster, in which one Callophisus challenged all comers in vindication of his mistress. This event had been signified by way of device "before the Queen on the previous Twelfth Night. But Shakespear's drama so-called was performed at the Middle Temple at Candlemas, 1602. Robert May, in his *Accomplished Cook,* 1660-71-85. supplies us with some very curious particulars of the "Triumphs and Trophies to be used at

festival time, as Twelfth Day, &c." These are found extracted in the *Gentleman's Magazine* for 1815.

Evelyn notes under January 6, 1661-2: "This evening, according to custom, his Majesty opened the revels of that night by throwing the dice himself in the privy-chamber, where was a table set on purpose, and lost his £100. (The year before he won £1500.) The ladies also played very deep. I came away when the Duke of Ormond had won about £1000, and left them still at passage, cards, &c." At other tables, both there and at the Groom-porter's, the writer beheld evidence of passion and folly, which he deemed deplorable and scandalous.

In "Vox Graculi," 1623, p. 52, speaking of the sixth of January, the writer tells us, "This day, about the houres of 5, 6, 7, 8, 9, and 10; yea in some places till midnight well nigh, will be such a massacre of spice-bread, that, ere the next day at noone, a two-penny brown loafe will set twenty poore folkes teeth on edge. Which hungry humour will hold so violent, that a number of good fellowes will not refuse to give a statute marchant of all the lands and goods they enjoy, for halfe-a-crownes worth of two-penny pasties. On this night much masking in the Strand, Cheapside, Holburne, or Fleet-Street."

It appears from Herrick's "Hesperides," in a poem, entitled "Twelfe Night, or King and Queene," that the Twelfth Cake was formerly full of plums, and with a bean and a pea: the former whoever got, was to be king; whoever the latter, was to be queen. And at p. 271 of the same work, which is in everybody's hands, there is a farther illustration of this portion of the subject. See also in "Queen Elizabeth's Progresses," vol. ii. "Speeches to the Queen at Sudley," p. 8.

It may rather seem to belong to religious than popular customs to mention, on the authority of the "Gentleman's Magazine," for January, 1731, p. 25, that at the Chapel-Royal at St. James's, on Twelfth Day that year, "the King and the Prince made the offerings at the altar of gold, frankincense, and myrrh, according to custom. At night their Majesties, &c. played at hazard, for the benefit of the groom-porter." The same thing is stated by Walpole in a letter to George Montagu, Jan. 9, 1752.

In Gloucestershire there is a custom on Twelfth Day, of having twelve small fires made, and one large one, in many parishes in that county, in honour of the day. At Pauntley, on the borders of Gloucestershire and Worcestershire, and thereabouts, there is a superstition, that the smut in wheat may be prevented in the following manner. On the eve of Twelfth Day, all the farm-servants assemble in one of the fields belonging to their respective employers, whose wheat has been sown, and at the end of twelve lands, they make twelve fires with straw in a row; one of these is made larger than the others; and round it they drink to their master's health and to a good harvest. On going home, they are treated to a repast of cakes soaked in cyder.

The same is done in Herefordshire under the name of wassailing, as follows: At the approach of the evening on the vigil of the Twelfth Day, the farmers, with their friends and servants, meet together, and about six o'clock walk out to a field where wheat is growing. In the highest part of the ground, twelve small fires, and one large one, are lighted up. The attendants, headed by the master of the family, pledge the company in old cyder, which circulates freely on these occasions. A circle is formed round the large fire, when a general shout and hallooing take place, which you hear answered from all the adjacent villages and fields. Sometimes fifty or sixty of these fires may be all seen at once. This being finished, the company return home, where the good housewife and her maids are preparing a good supper. A large cake is always provided, with a hole in the middle. After supper, the company all attend the bailiff (or head of the oxen) to the wain-house, where the following particulars are observed: The master, at the head of his friends, fills the cup (generally of strong ale), and stands opposite the first or finest of the oxen. He then pledges him in a curious toast: the company follow his example with all the other oxen, addressing each by his name. This being finished, the large cake is produced, and with much ceremony put on the horn of the first ox, through the hole above-mentioned. The ox is then tickled, to make him toss his head: if he throw the cake behind, then it is the mistress's perquisite; if before (in what is termed the boosy), the bailiff himself claims the prize. The company then return to the house, the doors of which they find locked, nor will they be opened till some joyous songs are sung. On their gaining admittance, a scene of mirth and jollity ensues, which lasts the greatest part of the night.

Formerly it was customary in Devonshire on this night to drink hot cyder and eat cakes, and after the company had partaken of this entertainment to their satisfaction, they proceeded into the orchard, where they offered a portion to the apple-trees and pear-trees by laying a piece of cake on a bough of each, and pouring over it a libation of hot cyder.

The men who happened to be present then fired a salute, and the women and girls sang in chorus: .

> "Bear blue, apples and pears enou',
> Barn fulls, bag fulls, sack fulls. Hurrah! Hurrah! Hurrah!'"

There are several versions of the subjoined song; but that here given is current in Devonshire on Twelfth Day:

> "Apple-tree, apple-tree,
> Bear apples for me:
> Hats full, laps full,
> Sacks full, caps full:
> Apple-tree, apple-tree,
> Bear apples for me."

In the South-hams of Devonshire, on the Eve of the Epiphany, the farmer attended by his workmen, with a large pitcher of cyder, goes to the orchard, and there, encircling one of the best bearing trees, they drink the following toast three several times:

> "Here's to thee, old apple-tree,
> Whence thou may'st bud, and whence thou may'st blow!
> And whence thou may'st bear apples enow!
> Hats full! caps full!
> Bushel—bushel—sacks full,
> And my pockets full too! Huzza!"

This done, they return to the house, the doors of which they are sure to find bolted by the females, who, be the weather what it may, are inexorable to all entreaties to open them till some one has guessed at what is on the spit, which is generally some nice little thing difficult to be hit on, and is the reward of him who first names it. The doors are then thrown open, and the lucky clodpole receives the tit-bit as his recompense. Some are so superstitious as to believe that if they neglect this custom, the trees will bear no apples that year.

On the Eve of Twelfth Day, as a Cornish man informed Mr. Brand, on the edge of St. Stephen's Down, October 28, 1790, it is the custom for the Devonshire people to go after supper into the orchard, with a large milk-pan full of cyder, having roasted apples pressed into it. Out of this each person in company takes what is called a clayen cup, *i.e.* an earthenware cup full of liquor, and standing under each of the more fruitful apple-trees, passing by those that are not good bearers, he addresses it in the following words:

> "Health to thee, good apple-tree,
> Well to bear, pocket-fulls, hat-fulls,
> Peck-fulls, bushel-bag-fulls!"

And then drinking up part of the contents, he throws the rest, with the fragments of the roasted apples, at the tree. At each cup the company set up a shout. Pennant, in his account of this custom, says, "that after they have drank a chearful glass to their master's health, success to the future harvest, &c. then returning home, they feast on cakes made of carraways, &c. soak'd in cyder, which they claim as a reward for their past labours in sowing the grain. This," he observes, "seems to resemble a custom of the antient Danes, who in their addresses to their rural deities, emptied on every invocation a cup in honour of them."—*Pennant's Tour in Scotland*, edit. 8vo. Chester, 1771, p. 91. Comp. *Apple-Howling* and references. Moresin observes, that our ceremony of choosing a king on the Epiphany, or Feast of the Three Kings, is practised among the Romanists about the same time of the year; and that he is called the Bean King, from the lot. *Papatus*, 1594, p. 143.

From a description given in an old writer, we gather that the materials of the Twelfth Cake were in his time (1620) flour, honey, ginger, and pepper. One was made for every family. The maker thrust in, at random, a small coin as she was kneading it. When it was baked, it was divided into as many parts as there were persons in the family. It was distributed, and each had his share. Portions of it also were assigned to Christ, the Virgin, and the three Magi, which were given away in alms. Whoever found the piece of coin in his share was saluted by all as king, and being placed on a seat or throne, was thrice lifted aloft with joyful acclamations. He held a piece of chalk in his right hand, and each time he was lifted up, made a cross on the ceiling. These crosses were thought to prevent many evils, and were much revered. Aubanus, *Mores, Leges, et Ritus Omnium Gent.* 1620, p. 266.

Mr. Brand adds an account of the more modern practice from the "Universal Magazine," for 1774. After tea a cake is produced, and two bowls, containing the fortunate chances for the different sexes. The host fills up the tickets, and the whole company, except the King and Queen, are to be ministers of state, maids of honour, or ladies of the bed-chamber. Often the host and hostess, more by design perhaps than by accident, become King and Queen. According to Twelfth day law each party is to support his character till midnight. In France, while that country had a Court and King, one of the courtiers was chosen king, and the other nobles attended on this day at an entertainment. The Bean King was for the nonce supreme. At the end of the year 1792, the Council-general of the Commons at Paris passed an arrêt, in consequence of which "La Fête

de Rois" (Twelfth Day) was thenceforth to be called "La Fête de Sans-Culottes." It was called an anti-civic feast, which made every priest that kept it a Royalist.

This custom is practised no where that I know of at present in the North of England, though still very prevalent in the South.

In Germany they observed nearly the same rites in cities and academies, where the students and citizens chose one of their own number for King, providing a banquet on the occasion.

Twickenham.—There was an ancient custom at Twickenham of dividing two great cakes in the church upon Easter Day among the young people; but, it being looked upon as a superstitious relic, it was ordered by Parliament, 1645, that the parishioners should forbear that custom, and, instead thereof, buy loaves of bread for the poor of the parish with the money that should have bought the cakes. It appears that the sum of £1 per annum is still charged upon the vicarage for the purpose of buying penny loaves for poor children on the Thursday after Easter. Within the memory of man they were thrown from the church-steeple to be scrambled for; a custom which prevailed (even in Brand's time) at Paddington.

Tying the Point.—A nuptial custom, of which an account may be found in Scot's *Discovery*, 1584, and elsewhere.

Tyree, Hebrides.—They still relieve the monotony of the long winter evenings by meeting at a particular house, and holding what is termed a ceilidh, at which stories are narrated, usually narratives connected with old local superstitions. Goodrich-Freer, *Outer Isles*, 1902, p. 65.

Unconsecrated Ground. — Arnot, speaking of St. Leonard Hill, says, "In a Northern part of it," (he mentioned before that part of it was the Quakers' burying ground,) "Children who had died without receiving baptism, and men who have fallen by their own hand, use to be interred." *Hist. of Edinburgh*, p. 252. This reminds us of Virgil:—

> "Infantumque Animæ flentes in limine
>   primo:
> Quos dulcis Vitæ exsortis; et ab ubere
>   raptos,
> Abstulit atra dies, et funere mersit
>   acerbo.—
> Proxima deinde tenent mæsti loca, qui
>   sibi letum
> Insontes peperere manu, lucemque
>   perosi
> Projecere Animas."—*Æneid*, vi. 427.

There is a story of Louis XIV. of France who, when the ecclesiastics refused Christian burial to a great theatrical performer, inquired how far down the consecration extended, and on being told, six feet, directed them to make a grave seven feet deep. The question is slowly losing its acuteness or virulence, and some day it will be settled by an universal system of cremation. Louis the Great was here a little before his time.

Uncovering the Head in Church. — An early, but unknown authority reprobates a custom then prevalent for the audience to sit in churches with their hats on. "Thine own children (the writer says) even glory in their shame, when not as masters, but as scholars, not as teachers, but as disciples, they sit covered at their most solemn holy meetings, without difference of place, degree, age, season, or any personal relation whatsoever. Although we have known some, and those not a few, who have presumed to sit covered in the presence of God at such a time as this; but when a great person hath come into the assembly, have honoured him with the uncovering of the head, as though civill respect towards a mortall prince were to be expressed by more evident signs of submission from the outward man than religious worship towards the immortal God."

He tells us, however, that they were uncovered when they sang the Psalms: "When the minister prayeth or praiseth God in the words of the Psalmist, as he frequently doth; at which time every one almost is vailed, who, notwithstanding, presently condemn themselves in this very thing which they allow, forasmuch as they all uncover the head when the same Psalmes are sung by them, only changed into meeter, and that perchance for the worse." Our author concludes by observing, properly enough, that "we cannot imagine lesse, than that this covering of the head in the congregation, where infirmity or sickness doth not plead for it, tendeth to the dishonour of Jesus Christ, whose servants we profess ourselves to be, especially at this time, and to the contempt of his messenger representing the office and person of Christ before our eyes." *Englands Faithful Reprover and Monitour*, 1653, pp. 48, 50. So, in "A Character of England," 1659, p. 13: "I have beheld a whole congregation sitting on their * * * * with their hats on, at the reading of the Psalms, and yet bareheaded when they sing them."

The Society of Friends followed the Jews in the practice of wearing their head-gear in church, which women have always done; it is part of the early and long conflict between Judaism and Christianism, to which we have referred under Saturday.

Uncumber, St.—Michael Woode, in his "Dialogue between two Neighbours," 1554, says: "if a wife were weary of her husband, she offered otes at poules at

London to St. Uncumber." St. Uncumber is not even mentioned by Hone, the Book of Days, or the Anniversary Calendar. Sir H. Nicolas, in his "Chronology of History," has also overlooked him. Perhaps it was some jocose name, or a pleasantry to which the key is lost.

In John Heywood's play of *The Four P.P.*, about 1540, the palmer, recounting his wanderings, says:

Then at the Rhodes also I was;
And round about to Amias.
At St. Uncumber and St. Trunnion;
At St. Botolph and St. Anne of Buxton.

Unicorn.—This fiction is probably not earlier than the Crusades, or perhaps than the date of Sir John Mandeville's return from his travels, when a variety of strange stories began to circulate in reference to the marvels to be seen in distant regions. Mandeville, unlike Marco Polo, who had preceded him, was a man of private fortune, who travelled for his pleasure, and he seems, instead of limiting himself to what he actually saw or heard, as Herodotus so wisely did, to have copied matter out of other books.

The original word *Rem*, translated Unicorn in our version of the Book of Job, xxxix. 9, is by Jerome, Montanus, and Aquila, rendered Rhinoceros : in the Septuagint, Monoceros. There was formerly a feeling, almost amounting to certainty, even among scientific persons, that the one-horned rhinoceros was the unicorn of fable; but this idea can hardly be said to have maintained its ground; and, indeed, a few years since, an animal was said to have been discovered much more closely approximating in form and appearance to the mythical unicorn. The fabulous animal of heraldry, so called, is nothing more than a horse with the horn of the pristis, or sword fish, stuck in his forehead.

The earliest mentions of this fabulous creature I have met with hitherto are in the Anglo-Norman *Bestiary* of Philip de Thaun, ascribed to the reign of Henry I., where occurs the notion of the danger from the creature to any one, who was not a pure virgin, and, again, in the "Ancren Riwle," a manual of monastic life, composed in what is termed (for want of a better name) *semi*-Saxon, during the thirteenth century. Both are anterior to Mandeville. In the *Riwle* we find, adopting for the convenienme of the general reader Mr. Morton's translation, merely an incidental allusion :— "An angry woman is a she-wolf, and an angry man is a wolf, or a lion, or an unicorn." A good account of this legendary beast is to be seen in the *Archæological Album*, 1845, with an illustration here reproduced.

In an inventory taken by direction of Cromwell, Vicar-General, in or about 1536, of the Church of St. Swithin's, Winchester, appear the two following items: "One pastoral staf of an unicorns horn," "One rectors staf of unicorns horn." Rhinoceros horn was probably the real substance in these cases, and in all of them perhaps we are to recognize the "unicorns' horns of unusual size," which an Italian visitor to England about 1500 tells us that he saw in certain monasteries.

Coryat observes in his *Traveller for the English Wits*, 1616, that he saw two unicorns in the menagerie at the Court of the Great Mogul, and he states that

from the attacks of poison is symbolized in the device of the Alviano family of Orvieto, where one of these fabulous creatures, encompassed by reptiles, purifies the water of a fountain by the immersion of its horn, the motto being *Venena Pello.*

The ancient Italian house of Borromeo adopted the cognizance of an unicorn looking toward the sun. Mrs. Bury Palliser, *Historic Devices*, 1870, pp. 20, 47. At the feet of the effigy of Thomas Chaucer in Ewelme Church, Oxfordshire, is the unusual cognizance of an unicorn couchant.

This legend is to be found in many places. Northbrooke quoted it in his

UNICORN.

they had been obtained in Bengal. He supplies a rough illustration of one, which resembles a horse with a single horn projecting from its forehead. An unicorn's horn, sent by a King of Persia, was among the treasures preserved at St. Denis, near Paris, when Evelyn the Diarist was there in 1643. Evelyn noticed two unicorns' horns in the Treasury of St. Mark at Venice about the same time, and about 1670 Lassels describes a well within the precincts of the Arsenal, of which the water was safeguarded from poison by two pieces of unicorns' horns at the bottom. *Voyage of Italy*, ed. 1686, part 2, p. 247. The notion of the unicorn protecting man

"Treatise against Da[u]ncing, &c. (1577)," ed. 1843, p. 110. In the "History of Sign-boards," edit. 1866, it is said: "The qualities attributed to the unicorn caused this animal to be used as a sign both by chemists and goldsmiths. It was believed that the only way to capture it was to leave a handsome young virgin in one of the places where it resorted. As soon as the animal had perceived her, he would come and lie quietly down beside her, resting his head in her lap, and fall asleep, in which state he might be surprised by the hunters who watched for him. This laying his head in the lap of a virgin" (of which there is a representation in Plate

16) "made the first Christians choose the unicorn as the type of Christ born from the Virgin Mary."

Possibly this was why the Scots placed it on one of their gold coins where an unicorn holds the shield, and thence it found its way to England. The hackneyed rhyme arising out of the association of the lion and the unicorn in the royal arms of England is so well known that its repetition seems almost ridiculous :

"The lion and the unicorn,
Fighting for the crown,
The lion chased the unicorn
All round the town."

William Browne refers to this whimsical legend when he writes :

"Rather the stately vnicorne
Would in his breast enraged scorne,
That maids committed to his charge
By any beast in forrest large
Should so be wronged—"
Works by Hazlitt, i, 56.

Unlawful Games.—In 1608 an ordinance of the Founders' Gild of London forbad apprentices to play at bowls, and bet at cards, dice, tables, shovelboard, and other unlawful games. See *Remembrancia*, pp. 16-19.

Up Jenkins or **Coddem.**—See *Shove-Groat.*

Uphalic Day.—(January 29). This, the close of the Yule festivity is annually celebrated at Lerwick, Shetland ; it is the 24th night after Christmas (old style). A considerable number of the inhabitants assemble at the Market Cross at 9 o'clock in the evening, dressed in various masquerading disguises, and there having torches provided, they form a procession, which marches through the streets of the town.

Up-se Frieze. — Which puzzled Brand, was the Friesland beer, which was commonly drunk in England in the seventeenth century. It is often mentioned in old plays and tracts. The following passage occurs in Rowlands's "Humors Ordinarie," (1600) :

"Tom is no more like thee then chalks like cheese
To pledge a health, or to drink up-se frieze :
Fill him a beaker, he will never flinch, &c."

Up-Sitting.—There was formerly, and until the early part of the last century at least, if not still, what was known as the Upsitting or Getting-up. Fletcher, in the "Woman Hater," 1607, makes Valore say to Gondarino :

"Farewell, my lord ; I was entreated
To invite your worship to a lady's up-sitting—"

which Cotgrave seems to have confounded with the churching itself, whereas it is rather the celebration of the mother's recovery from her lying-in.

Urine.—The following singular passage is in Greene's "Quip for an Vpstart Covrtier," 1592. "Questioning," says he, "why these women were so cholericke, he, like a skofling fellow, pointed to a bush of nettles : Mary (quoth hee) al these women that you heare brawling, frowning, and scolding thus, have severally p . . . on this bush of nettles ; and the vertue of them is to force a woman that waters them to be as peevish for the whole day, and as waspish as if shee had bene stung in the brow with a hornet."

Among Vicary's Receipts occur one which must have been introduced into the Materia Medica as a charm, viz. "Five spoonfuls of knave (male) child urine of an innocent (idiot)." *Treasure of Anatomy*, 1641, p. 234. Butler's description of Lilly under the name of Sidrophel is fraught with a great deal of his usual pleasantry :

"Quoth Ralph, not far from hence doth dwell
A cunning man, hight Sidrophel,
That deals in Destiny's dark counsels
And sage opinions of the moon sells ;
To whom all people, far and near,
On deep inportances repair ;
When brass and pewter apt to stray,
And linen slinks out of the way :
When geese and pullen are seduc'd,
And sows of sucking pigs are chows'd ;
When cattle feel indisposition,
And need th' opinion of physician ;
When murrain reigns in hogs or sheep,
And chickens languish of the pip ;
When yeast and outward means do fail
And have no pow'r to work on ale ;
When butter does refuse to come,
And love proves cross and humoursome ;
To him with questions, and with urine
They for discov'ry flock, or curing."

Hartlib tells us : "In Holland they as carefully preserve the cowes urine, as the dung to enrich their land : old urine is excellent for the Roots of trees. . . . I know a woman who lived five miles south of Canterbury, who saveth in a pail, all the droppings of the houses, I meane the urine, and when the pail is full, sprinckleth it on her meadow," and with such good results that her neighbours took her to be a witch. *Legacie*, 1651, p. 47. The magical divination which we find so humourously described in Butler's "Hudibras," is affirmed by Monsieur Le Blanc in his Travels to be used in the East Indies :

"Your modern Indian magician
Makes but a hole in th' earth to p——
in,
And straight resolves all questions by't,
And seldom fails to be i' the right."

In "Sylva, Or the Wood," p. 130, we read that "a few years ago, the women in labour used to drinke the urine of their husbands, who were all the while stationed, as I have seen the cows in St. James's Park, and straining themselves to give as much as they can." Pennant tells us, that the Highlanders, on New Year's Day, burn juniper before their cattle; and on the first Monday in every quarter, sprinkle them with urine. Comp. *Bishopping* and *Ireland*.

Urisk, Highland.—Scott, in his Notes to the "Lady of the Lake," describes this as "a figure between a goat and a man; in short, precisely, that of a Grecian satyr." This spirit or deity is not mentioned by Campbell in his *Popular Tales of the West Highlands*, 1860-2.

Ursula of Britain, St.—See on this legend a very excellent and exhaustive article in Chambers's *Encyclopædia*, in v. Brewer, *Dict. of Phrase and Fable*, 3rd ed. pp. 925, 938, may be also consulted. The legend was long commemorated on the money of Cologne, which bore on one side a representation of St. Ursula and her companions, and a 6-ducat piece in gold has this story on one side and the Adoration of the Magi on the other. The original name of the husband of St. Ursula is said to have been Holofernes. See Hazlitt's *Coins of Europe*, Suppl. 1897, p. 28, and *Shakespear: Himself and his Work*, by same, 1903, p. 108.

Utas.—See Nares, 1859, in v. In a letter of July 6, 1453, from Margaret Paston to her son John Paston, the writer concludes: "Wretyn at Norwych, on the Utas day of Peter and Powll." Of the two festivals or commemorations of St. Agnes one was kept on the 21st, and the other on the 28th: but they were independent events. A letter from Sir John Paston to his brother in 1472 is dated "the Twysday next aftyr Seynt Agnet the fyrst." Compare *Agnes* suprâ.

Valentine's Day, St.—(Feb. 14). This saint is held to have been an Elder of the Church, beheaded in the reign of Claudius. If Bishop Hall may be believed, he was a man of singular chastity of life. I have searched the legend of St. Valentine, but think there is no occurrence in his life that could have given rise to this ceremony. I find in the Roman Calendar the following observation only under this date:—

"Manes nocte vagari creduntur."

Butler, in his "Lives of the Saints,"

says that the custom originated among the Romans, and that, on the Feast of Februata Juno (Feb. 13), boys drew the names of girls in order to be able to divine who should be their mistress, and that, this pagan usage giving offence to the Christian priesthood, the names of saints were substituted on the slips of paper for those of sweethearts. Butler mentions, as one of the most strenuous opponents of Valentines, St. Francis of Sales. Other writers and authorities concur in recognizing in the anniversary a trace of the Roman and Italian Lupercalia, and one suggests that it arose from the ancient idea that birds choose their mates at this date. Elson, *Shakespeare in Music*, 1901, 238.

Grose explains Valentine to mean the first woman seen by a man, or man seen by a woman, on St. Valentine's Day. It is a ceremony," says Bourne, "never omitted among the vulgar, to draw lots, which they term Valentines, on the eve before Valentine Day. The names of a select numbers of one sex are, by an equal number of the other, put into some vessel; and after that every one draws a name, which for the present is called their Valentine, and is looked upon as a good omen of their being man and wife afterwards. *Antiquitates Vulgares*, chap. xx. Chaucer seems to allude to the usage in the following passage:—

"Nature, the Vicare of the Almightie Lord,
That hote, colde, hevie, light, moist, and drie,
Hath knit by even number of accord
In easie voice, began to speak and say,
Foules, take hede of my sentence I pray,
And for your own ease in fordring of your need
As fast as I may speak I will me speed.
Ye know well how on St. Valentine's Day,
By my statute and through my governaunce,
Ye doe chese your makes, and after flie away
With hem as I pricke you with pleasaunce."

Lydgate, in a poem written by him in praise of Queen Catherine, consort to Henry V. writes:—

"Seynte Valentine, of custome yeere by yeere
Men have an usaunce in this religioun
To loke and serche Cupides Kalendare,
And chose theyr choyse, by grete affeccioun;
Such as ben prike with Cupides mocioun,
Takyng theyre choyse as theyr sort doth falle:
But I love oon whiche excellith alle."

The same author wrote a set of verses, entitled, "Chusing Loves on S. Valentines Day," and among Gower's "Balades," first printed in 1818, a French Valentine written by him (Gower) appears.

In the Paston Letters under 1477, Dame Elizabeth Drews, writing to John Paston, reminds him, in reference to his suit for her daughter Margery, that the ensuing Friday will be St. Valentine's Day, and that he had best come over to their house on Thursday night, and stay till Monday, and Margery herself, in two letters to Paston, terms him in each instance her right well-beloved Valentine, almost as if that were then a recognized synonym for a sweetheart.

Some poems on this theme are in the volume said to have been written by Charles Duke of Orleans in England, during his imprisonment. But those productions in English, attributed to the Duke, were more probably translated by some anonymous person.

In the D'Ewes Correspondence there is a letter from William Boswell, Jesus College, Cambridge, to Sir William Waldegrave, dated May 18, 1608, in which the writer says:

"About a quarter of a yeare since, Mr. Clapton was, amongst other fellowes and gentlemen of our colledge, drawne by paper lotts, to be Valentine to one of Dr. Duports daughters: which being tould unto Mr. Clapton, he came presently, and asked mee what he should doe: I resolved him as the other company did; which afterwards giving gloves unto their Valentines, wee also bought a paire, costing 2s. 6d., and bestowed them uppon her." There is a curious entry in Walter Yonge's Diary under 1621-2, on this subject. It appears that this year somebody sent a Valentine to the daughter of Sir John Crofte, purporting to come from the King, and a silly report circulated thereupon, that the lady was married to James.

In Lord North's "Forest of Varieties," 1645, p. 61, in a letter to his brother, he says, "A lady of wit and qualitie, whom you well knew, would never put herself to the chance of a Valentine, saying that shee would never couple herself, but by choyce. The custome and charge of Valentines is not ill left, with many other such costly and idle customes, which by a tacit generall consent wee lay down as obsolete." Herrick speaks of the practice of divining by rosebuds the name of the man whom a girl should have for her Valentine, and says that, once married, she must give up choosing Valentines, as well as going a-Maying.

In Shipman's "Carolina," p. 135, is a copy of verses entitled, "The Rescue," 1672. To Mrs. D. C., whose name being left after drawing Valentines and cast into the fire, was snatcht out. In "Poor Robin's Almanack," for 1676, that facetious observer of our old customs tells us, opposite to St. Valentine's Day in February:

> "Now Andrew, Antho-
> ny, and William,
> For Valentines draw
> Prue, Kate, Jilian."

In the same for 1757 we have:—

> "This month bright Phœbus enters
> Pisces,
> The maids will have good store of kisses,
> For always when the fun comes there,
> Valentine's Day is drawing near,
> And both the men and maids incline
> To chuse them each a Valentine;
> And if a man gets one he loves,
> He gives her first a pair of gloves;
> And, by the way, remember this,
> To seal the favour with a kiss.
>
> This kiss begets more love, and then
> That love begets a kiss again,
> Until this trade the man doth catch,
> And then he doth propose the match,
> The woman's willing, tho' she's shy,
> She gives the man this soft reply,
> 'I'll not resolve one thing or other,
> Until I first consult my mother.'
> When she says so, 'tis half a grant,
> And may be taken for consent."

Pepys of course is not silent here. Under 14 Feb. 1665-6, Mr. Hill the musician calls on him, and he thinks that Hill has come to be Mrs. Pepys's Valentine; but he finds it is not to be so. In the following year, however, he carried Mrs. Pierce and Knipp, and his wife, to the New Exchange, and to his Valentine, Mrs. Pierce aforesaid, he gave a dozen pairs of gloves and a pair of silk stockings, and to Knipp *for company*, although Mrs. Pepys had laid out on her the day before 20/-, six pairs of gloves. This was what the excellent Diarist thought a judicious enjoyment of life, while a man was capable of doing so. Under 16 Feb. 1666-7, the Diarist tells us: "I find that Mrs. Pierce's little girl is my Valentine, she having drawn me; which I was not sorry for, easing me of something more than I must have given to others. But here I do first observe the fashion of drawing of mottos as well as names: so that Pierce, who drew my wife, did draw also a motto, and this girl drew another for me. What mine was, I have forgot; but my wife's was, 'Most constant and most fair.'" Under April 26, 1667, there is an entry illustrative of the costliness of Valentines in certain cases, the famous Mrs. Stewart receiving from the Duke of York and Lord Mandeville on successive occasions jewels worth £800 and £300.

In the " British Apollo " we find :—

Question. " In chusing Valentines (according to custom) is not the party chusing (be it man or woman) to make a present to the party chosen?

Answer. We think it more proper to say, drawing of Valentines, since the most customary way is for each to take his or her lot. And chance cannot be termed choice. According to this method, the obligations are equal, and therefore it was formerly the custom mutually to present, but now it is customary only for the gentlemen."

We find the following curious species of divination in the Connoisseur, as practised on Valentine's Day or Eve. " Last Friday was Valentine Day, and the night before I got five bay-leaves, and pinned four of them to the four corners of my pillow, and the fifth to the middle ; and then, if I dreamt of my sweet-heart, Betty said we should be married before the year was out. But to make it more sure, I boiled an egg hard, and took out the yolk, and filled it with salt ; and when I went to bed, eat it, shell and all, without speaking or drinking after it. We also wrote our lovers' names upon bits of paper, and rolled up in clay, and put them into water : and the first that rose up was to be our Valentine. Would you think it, Mr. Blossom was my man? I lay a-bed and shut my eyes all the morning, till he came to our house : for I would not have seen another man before him for all the world."

The children in Norfolk *catch* Valentines, as they term it, by being the first to say, " Goodmorrow, Valentine," to any one whom they think likely to make them a present. But they must do this before the sun rises, or they are entitled to nothing, because they are sun-burnt. There is, or was, an usage in Oxfordshire, for children to go about, and levy a toll of pence from the benevolent, where the formula is a little longer :

" Good morrow, Valentine,
First 'tis yours, then 'tis mine,
So please give me a Valentine."

An enterprising perfumer endeavoured in 1868 to impart to the ancient usage a somewhat novel character, and had on sale a large assortment of boxes containing articles of millinery, singing birds, scents, and so on, in lieu of the simple letter with its enshrined mottoes, device, or cartoon, which satisfied the taste of the last generation. So we improve upon our ancestors and, so to speak, trend out old customs ; for, whatever may be the gain here in elegance and costly effect, the simple rites of the original festival of St. Valentine are seriously tampered with, and we are not sure whether there may not be a few still living who will regard this daring innovator with an unfriendly eye.

Goldsmith, in his " Vicar of Wakefield," speaks of rustics sending True-love Knots on Valentine morning. Moresin relates that it was usual in his time (1594) in Scotland for people to exchange presents on St. Valentine's Day, and that elsewhere men made gifts to women on this festival, and women afterwards (*alio tempore*) made a suitable return. Pennant, in his " Tour in Scotland," tells us, that in February young persons draw Valentines and from thence collect their future fortune in the nuptial state.

Bourne adds, " There is a rural tradition, that on this day every bird chooses its mate," and concludes that perhaps the youthful part of the world hath first practiced this custom, so common at this season. Herrick, in his "Hesperides," draws a comparison between the supposed coupling of birds on this day and the choice of Valentines. In the old ballad of " The Two Valentines," a very familiar proverb is reproduced with a variation, as follows :—

" There is an old proverb,
That birds of a feather
Upon St. Valentine's Day
Will meet together."

Gay has left us a poetical description of some rural ceremonies used on the morning of this day :

" Last Valentine, the day when birds of kind
Their paramours with mutual chirpings find,
I early rose, just at the break of day,
Before the sun had chased the stars away :
A-field I went, amid the morning dew,
To milk my kine (for so should housewives do),
Thee first I spied, and the first swain we see,
In spite of fortune, shall our true love be."

A spring 10-days' fair was held at Faversham in Kent in early times and down to the end of the 18th century, and was known as St. Valentine's Fair. In the play of *Arden of Faversham*, 1592, founded on a murder committed there in 1550-1, the crime was to have been perpetrated during this festival, and purports in the local records to have taken place on the evening of the 15th. As this was Sunday, and the parties were playing at tables or backgammon, and Arden himself had just previously been out on business ; it seems far more probable that the tragedy occurred on the Saturday or Monday. One alleged cause of Arden's (or rather Ardern's) unpopularity was that, whereas this fair had been usually held partly in the town and partly in the Abbey precincts, he caused it for his advantage, as the Abbey land belonged to him, to be wholly kept there.

There is an account of the manner in which St. Valentine's Day was anciently observed in France, in Goujet *Bibliothèque Françoise*, tom. ix. p. 266. Comp. *Onions*.

Vampire.—As early as the twelfth century, a belief in the existence and noxious power of vampires was entertained in this country. It probably came to us from Germany and the north; but the ancient Greeks had a similar superstition. The vampire was supposed to be a wicked man, whose remains, though buried with the customary forms, did not suffer dissolution. Mr. Wright, in his "Essays," 1846, has given an account of this article of faith. He says: "His body did not undergo the same process of dissolution as other corpses, but the skin became dry and distended like the parchment of a drum; and the man's spirit, or some demon, entered into it, and at night the dead man left his grave and walked about the streets, and knocked at people's doors, and always called by name some person in the house. If the person who was named answered, he was sure to die on the following day. Hence, from caution, it became a custom that no one answered to his name at night until it had been called twice, for the burrulaca (vampire) never called the same person a second time in one night. But, as Mr. Wright points out, the vampire also pursued his wanderings occasionally in the daytime.

The reduction of the vampire to normal matter of fact is not part of the present design. But the reader may refer to Waterton's *Wanderings*, ed. 1903, pp. 8, 127, 213-14.

Vaudeville.—At present understood of a musical drama or one interspersed with songs, but originally a term applied to a certain type of poetry produced in Lower Normandy under the name of *Vaux de Vire*, from the river Vire and the hill known as Les Vaux. An advocate of the place, Jean le Houx, who died in 1616, made a large collection of these *chansons*, of which there are numerous modern editions, the best being perhaps that published by Mr. Muirhead in 1875 with an English translation.

Vavasour.—An early proper name, but originally a person, who held his lands in fealty.

Vervain.—Borlase, speaking of the Druids, says: "They are excessively fond of the Vervaine, they use it in casting lots, and foretelling events." "It was to be gathered at the rise of the Dog-Star." *Antiq. of Cornwall*, p. 91. The following occurs in Aubrey's "Miscellanies," p. 147:

Vervain and Dill
Hinder witches from their will."

If a man gather vervaine the first day of the new moon, before sun rising, and drinke the juice thereof, it will make him to avoid lust for seven yeares.—Coles, *Introd. to the Knowledge of Plants*, 1656, p. 69. Pulverized vervain in wine, taken on Midsummer-day, was considered a sure specific against liver complaint by the Saxon leeches. See *Charms* and *King's Evil*.

Vincent's Day, St.—(Jan. 22). Douce's MSS. Notes say, "Vincenti festo si Sol radiet memor esto:" thus Englishised by Abraham Fleming:

"Remember on St Vincent's Day,
If that the sun his beams display."

See Scot's *Disc. of Witchcraft*, book xi. c. 15.

Vingt-et-un.—See *One-and-Thirty*.

Virginity.—In the earliest ages of Christianity, virginity was honoured, out of deference most likely to the Virgin Mother, with almost divine adoration, and there is but little doubt but that the origin of nunneries is closely connected with that of the virgin garland.

A writer in the "Antiquarian Repertory" says: "that in this nation, as well as others, by the abundant zeal of our ancestors virginity was held in great estimation: insomuch that those who died in that state were rewarded at their death with a garland or crown on their heads, denoting their triumphant victory over the lusts of the flesh. Nay, this honour was extended even to a widow who had never enjoyed but one husband. These garlands, or crowns, were most artificially wrought in filagree work, with gold and silver wire, in resemblance of myrtle, with which plant the funebrial garlands of the antients were always composed, whose leaves were fastened to hoops of larger iron wire, and they were lined with cloth of silver."

"Besides these crowns, the antients had also their depository garlands, the use of which continued till of late years, and may perhaps still in some parts of England. These garlands, at the funerals of the deceased, were carried solemnly before the corpse by two maids, and afterwards hung up in some conspicuous place within the church, and were made in the following manner: viz. the lower rim or circlet was a broad hoop of wood, whereunto was fixed at the sides thereof part of two other hoops, crossing each other at the top at right angles, which formed the upper part, being about one-third longer than the width. These hoops were wholly covered with artificial flowers of paper, dyed horn, and silk, and more or less beautiful according to the skill or ingenuity of the performer. In the vacancy of the inside from the top hung white paper cut in form of gloves, whereon was written the deceased's name, age, &c., together with long strips of various coloured papers or ribbons: these were many times intermixed with gilded or painted empty shells of blown eggs, as farther ornaments, or it may be as emblems of bubbles, or the bitterness of this life: while other garlands had only a solitary hour-glass hanging therein, as a more significant symbol of mortality." iv, 239.

In the Papal times in England sometimes the form of a last testament ran thus: "Commendo Animam meam Deo, beatæ Mariæ, et omnibus Sanctis." I saw in the churches of Wolsingham and Stanhope, Durham, specimens of those garlands: the form of a woman's glove, cut in white paper, hung in the centre of each of them. Douce saw a similar instance in the church at Bolton in Craven, in 1783. At Skipton, too, the like custom still prevailed in Brand's time. In 1794, Sir H. Ellis states that he saw garlands of white paper hanging up in a church no farther from the metropolis than Paul's Cray in Kent.

It was the custom in many country churches to hang a garland of flowers over the seats of deceased virgins, in token, says Bourne, of esteem and love, and as an emblem of their reward in the heavenly church. It was usual in the primitive Christian Church to place crowns of flowers at the heads of deceased virgins: for this we have the authority of Damascenus, Gregory of Nysse, St. Jerome, and St. Austin.

It appears that on June 4th, 1747, a letter was read by the Secretary to the Society of Antiquaries "from Mr. Edward Steel of Bromley, concerning the custom of burying the dead, especially batchelors and maidens, with garlands of flowers, &c. used formerly in several parts of this kingdom." Dr. Lort observed in August, 1785, that "At Grey's-foot Church, between Wrexham and Chester, were garlands, or rather shields, fixed against the pillars, finely decorated with artificial flowers and cut gilt paper." In Yorkshire, it seems to have been usual, when a virgin died in a village, one, nearest to her in size, and age, and resemblance, carried the garland before the corpse in the funeral procession, which was afterwards hung up in the church. This was sometimes composed entirely of white paper, and at others the flowers, &c. cut out upon it were coloured.

There appeared in the "Morning Chronicle" for Sept. 25th, 1792, an elegiac ode by Miss Seward, whereto in reference to Eyam in Derbyshire the following note was subjoined: "The antient custom of

hanging a garland of white roses made of writing paper, and a pair of white gloves, over the pew of the unmarried villagers who die in the flower of their age, prevails to this day in the village of Eyam, and in most other villages and little towns in the Peak." At Ashford in the same county from the beams of the north aisle used very recently to hang five funeral garlands of white paper cut into flowers, which were once carried before the funeral procession at the burial of virgins, and afterwards replaced in their positions.

Nichols, speaking of Waltham in Framland Hundred, says: "In this church, under every arch, a garland is suspended: one of which is customarily placed there whenever any young unmarried woman dies." *Leicestershire*, ii, part 1, 382.

These are mentioned in the "Dialect of Craven," 1828, as common ornaments of the churches in that deanery. They are "made of flowers, or of variegated coloured paper, fastened to small sticks, crossing each other at the top, and fixed at the bottom by a similar hoop, which was also covered with paper. From the top were suspended two papers, cut in the form of gloves, on which the name and age of the deceased virgin were written. One of these votive garlands was solemnly borne before the corpse by two girls, who placed it on the coffin in the church during the service. Thence it was conveyed in the same manner to the grave, and afterwards was carefully deposited on the screen dividing the quoir from the nave either as an emblem of virgin purity, or of the guilt and uncertainty of human life."

"In the case of an unmarried female," says the author of the "Cleveland Glossary," 1868, "the custom, until recently, was to carry a garland, composed of two circular hoops crossing each other, dressed with white paper cut into flowers or leaves, or in the form of a wreath of particoloured ribbons, having a white glove in the centre inscribed with the name, or initials, and age of the deceased. This garland was laid on the coffin during its passage from the church to the grave, and afterwards, at least in some cases, suspended from the ceiling of the church. In the chancels at Hinderwell and Robin Hood's Bay some of these garlands were still in being only a few years since."

In "The Life and lamented Death of Mrs. Susannah Perwich," 1661, we have the rites of a virgin lady's funeral minutely described: "The herse, covered with velvet, was carried by six servant maidens of the family, all in white. The sheet was held up by six of those gentlewomen in the school that had most acquaintance with her, in mourning habit, with white scarfs and gloves. A rich costly garland of gumwork, adorned with banners and scutcheons, was borne immediately before the herse by two proper young ladies, that entirely loved her. Her father and mother, with other near relations and their children, followed next the herse, in due order, all in mourning: the kindred next to them, after whom came the whole school of gentlewomen, and then persons of chief rank from the neighbourhood and from the City of London, all in white gloves, both men, women, children, and servants, having been first served with wine. The herse being set down (in Hackney Church) with the garland upon it, the Rev. Dr. Spurstow preached her Funeral Sermon. This done, the rich coffin, anointed with sweet odors, was put down into the grave in the middle alley of the said church," &c. Her father, it seems, then kept the long famous boarding school for young ladies at Hackney, of which there is so curious an account by William Blake, housekeeper there about this time.

There is a passage in Shakespear's "Hamlet," act v. sc. 1:

"Yet here she is allow'd her virgin crants,"

Reed's "Shakesp." 1803, vol. xviii. p. 336. "Krans, *Sertum* Isl. & Belg. id. Germ. *krantz*. Helvigius natum putat a κορωνίς, alii a *cranium*; Watchterus a C B. *crwnn*, rotundus, quum circulari figurâ caput ambiat."—Ihre. *Gloss. Suio-Goth.* tom. i. p. 1156.

In "Syr Gyles Goosecappe Knight," a comedy, 1606, sign. A 4 *verso*, a different test is, of course jocularly, proposed:

"*Will.* Ile answere for her, because I know her ladyship to be a perfect maide indeede.

Bullaker. How canst thou know that?

Will. Passing perfectly, I warrant ye.

Iacke. By measuring her necke twice, and trying if it will come about hir fore-head, and slyp ouer her nose."

There is still a common saying, that twice round the wrist (in a woman) once round the neck, and twice round the neck once round the waist.

I do not observe that any of our writers on popular antiquities has noticed the indication of virginity, which Browne mentions as apparently a matter of cur-rent belief in this country at the time he wrote his "Pastorals:"

"There is a weed vpon whose head growes Downe:
Sow-thistle 'tis ycleep'd, whose downy wreath,
If any one can blow off at a breath,
We deeme her for a maid—"

In a satirical publication entitled *The*

Horn Exalted, 1661, an Italian is made to say: "Our garlands in the winter, and at virgins' funerals, are they not made of horns?"

There was an old superstition that a virgin might procure the pardon of a criminal at the very gallows. Thus, in *Arden of Faversham*, 1592, Michael says:

"——and Susan, being a maide,
May begge me from the gallows of the Shreife."

In Captain Marryat's *Masterman Ready* a woman belonging to a savage tribe, saves one of the characters from a cruel death by offering at the place of execution to marry him.

Virgins of Cologne, Eleven Thousand.—This is a familiar story to all English visitors to the cathedral; and their bones are shown—actually the bones of animals. *Eleven thousand* is taken to be a misreading for *two*. The myth is connected with the legendary history of St. Ursula of Britain, and the ship freighted with the virgins, it must have been a miraculously large one, and the *Adoration of the Magi* or Three Kings of Cologne, constitute favourite types on the reverses of the money formerly struck by the prince-bishops.

Vitus, St. — (June 15). On St. Vitus's Day, the Skinners' Company, accompanied by girls strewing herbs in their path, and by the blue-coat boys placed by their patronage on the foun-dation of Christ's Hospital, march in procession from Dowgate-Hill, where their hall is, to St. Antholin's Church, in Wat-ling Street, to hear service. The origin of this custom does not seem to be known: but it is ancient. In Buchlerus is a pas-sage which seems to prove that St. Vitus's Day was (almost) equally famous for rain with St. Swithin's. Googe says:

"The nexte is Vitus sodde in oyle,
before whose ymage faire
Both men and women bringing hennes
for offring do repaire:
The cause whereof I doe not know, I thinke, for some disease
Which he is thought to drive away from such as him do please."

Perhaps this is what is called *St. Vitus's Dance*, a form of paralysis, but which is now supposed to have no connection with the saint. The name of St. Vitus does not occur in the Roman Calendar. See Davis, *Suppl. Glossary*, 1881, p. 564.

Wads.—See *Scotch and English.*

Wad-Shooting.—In the "Statisti-cal Account of Scotland, parish of Kirk-den, Angus, it is said, "Christmas is held as a great festival in this neighbourhood." On that day, "the servant is free from his master, and goes about visiting his friends and acquaintance. The poorest must have beef or mutton on the table, and what they call a dinner with their friends. Many amuse themselves with various diversions, particularly with shooting for prizes, called here Wad-shooting; and many do but little business all the Christmas week; the evening of almost every day being spent in amusement." In the same work, the inhabitants are said to "have no pastimes or holidays, excepting dancing on Christmas and New Year's Day."

Waez or **Wayz Goose.**—In "Notes and Queries," for August 4, 1866, this term is explained to signify a stubble-goose, which is mentioned by Chaucer in the *Cook's Prologue*. In the "Calendrier Belge," 1862, is an account of the goose-feast held at Waes, in Brabant, which may suggest a different etymology. At present the Wayz Goose is the annual celebration of a day's holiday among printers and their staffs, and if the custom had any peculiar connection, at the outset, with the goose, it seems to have lost such connection. I view, personally, the etymology introduced by the writer in "Notes and Queries" with some share of distrust, as I am rather of an opinion that the ancient practice of holding a grand goose-feast annually at Waes, in Brabant, at Martinmas, is more likely to have given rise to our English phrase. The intercourse between this kingdom and the Low Countries was, in former times, so regular and large, that many usages were apt to undergo transplantation, and the art of printing may be only one among several obligations we lie under to the Dutch and Flemings. The printer's Wayz Goose, in modern days, has no fixed season, but is usually held in July. There is a passage in "The Scolehouse of Women," 1541, in which the way goose is mentioned: but what the author meant precisely by the term, in this case, it appears somewhat difficult to decide:

"—And yet the rib, as I suppose,
That God did take out of the man,
A dog vp caught, and a way gose
Eat it clene—."

Wafering Sunday.—Otherwise known as *Mothering Sunday*, Midlent Sunday. See *Mothering Sunday*.

Wafers.—Wafers and hippocras were customary at weddings and funerals alike. This sort of refection is mentioned in the "Account of the Coronation of Richard III." 1483, printed in "Excerpta Historica," 1833.

In the Churchwardens' Accounts of St. Lawrence's Parish, Reading, 1561, is the following entry: "Bryde-Past. It. re-ceyved of John Radleye, vis. viijd." A note says: "Probably the wafers, which, together with sweet wine, were given after the solemnization of the marriage." See the "Account of the Ceremony of the Marriage between the Elector Frederick and Elizabeth, eldest daughter of James I. on St. Valentine's Day, 1613-14." in Leland. So, at the marriage of Queen Mary and Philip of Spain in Winchester Cathedral, 1554, "Wyne and sopes were hallowed."

In the *Antiquary* for February, 1899, in a paper by Mr. H. P. Feasey on a Pair of Wafer-Irons, was a representation of the article which was used for making or baking this confection, whether for ordinary use or for the service of the Church.

By the following extract from the Obituary of Richard Smyth, wafers appear to have been then used at funeral entertainments: "1671-2, January 2. Mr. Cornelius Bee, bookseller in Little Britain, died *hora* xi° *ante merid*. his 2 eldest daughters Mᶦˢ Norwood and Mᶦˢ Fletcher, widdows, executrixes; buried Jan. 4 at Great St. Bartholomew's wᵗʰout a sermon, wᵗʰout wine or waffers, only gloves and rosemary, &c." Comp. *Christening*.

Waff.—See *Wraith*.

Waits.—Waits, who were originally watchmen, are constantly mentioned in the old chronicles and romances. They seem to have grown into common use as musicians on festive occasions, and are often found in combination with haut-boys. The itinerant players, who are at present known under the same designation, are very degenerate representatives of those whom even our grandfathers knew, and the old custom of serenading people in their sleep (or rather out of it) for a week or fortnight preceding Christmas, with a view to a subsequent gratuity, has almost gone out of fashion, so far as the great towns are concerned.

The duty prescribed to the ancient wait in the Black Book of Edward IV., 1478, was to pipe the watch nightly, from Michaelmas till Maundy Thursday, four times within the Court, and in summer nights three times, and to make good cheer. He was to eat in the hall with the minstrels, and was to receive for his supper half a loaf and half a gallon of ale; in summer, two candles and half a bushel of coals; in winter, half a loaf, half a gallon of ale, four candles, half a bushel of coals; and moreover, during actual attendance in Court, fourpence halfpenny a day, or, if he was not thought worth so much (which was left to the discretion of the Steward and Treasurer) threepence only. He was entitled to his livery, like the minstrels; and during sickness, an extra allowance of food might be given to him.

Part of his duty was to secure all doors,

and to guard against thieves, fire, and other dangers, and to attend at the making of Knights of the Bath. This personage was a *Yeoman* wait, and under him was a *Groom* Wait. Pegge's *Curialia*, 1818, p. 101-2. Some curious additional information on this subject may be read in Chappell's *Popular Music*, 49, 547.

Edward IV., as it appears from his "Black Book," 1478, kept thirteen minstrels and a wait in his household. Of the former, one was a verger or chief, "that directeth them all in festival days," says Pegge, "to their stations, to blowings and pipings to such offices as must be warned to prepare for the King and his household, at meats and suppers, to be the more ready in all services; and all these sitting in the hall together, whereof some use trumpets, some shawms, and small pipes, and some are strange-men coming to this court at five feasts of the year, and then to take their wages of household after four pence halfpenny a day, if they be present in Court; and then they to avoid the next day after the feasts be done." Two of the regular minstrels were to attend the king, when he went on horseback, and sometimes his majesty had two of the "strange" minstrels likewise in waiting. These officials were entitled to receive, besides their board (including four gallons of ale among them every evening) their clothing, or twenty shillings a-year in money instead. There is this curious passage a little further on: "The King woll not for his worship that his minstrels be too presumptuous, nor too familiar, to ask any rewards of the Lords of his land, remembering the example of King Henry the Second, who forbad his minstrels and gleemen, so long as they were in his service, from asking any gratuity at the hands of any one, inasmuch as the Kings nobles, out of the affection they bore to his person, would rather give what they had to the poor."

The provision just quoted exhibits a remarkable change in the character of the jongleurs of Edward's time, and the state of the profession, from the lofty privileges and almost unbridled license enjoyed by the ancient troubadours in all parts of Western Europe, especially in the country, which was the cradle of the Provençal poetry and literature.

In the Privy Purse Expenses of Henry VIII. under 1532 are the two ensuing entries:—

"Itm the xi daye (of October) paied to the waytes of Caunterbury in rewarde . . . . vijs. vjd."

"Itm the xix daye (of November) paied to the waytes at Caunterbery in rewarde . . . . xviijs. viijd."

In 1582 we find Robert Dudley, Earl of Leicester, writing to the Lord Mayor and Aldermen of London, to request that his servant might be admitted to a vacant place in the City Waits. *Extracts from the Remembrancia*, 1878, p. 275.

In a small volume published about 1830 there is an account of the Dustmen and Harp Waits of Pentonville, who favoured the locality with performances on the harp and violin, and distributed a circular announcing their merits, and their intention of paying a call at houses later on in the expectation of a farther diffusion of those favours which had enlivened their houses and cheered their hearts for a series of years. They described themselves in this document as "Wandering Melodists and Christmas Waits," and expressed a hope that their sprightly notes of melody, awaking sweet Echo on the dull Ear of Night, had stolen on the gentle slumbers of their patrons, and had again lulled them to repose with the soothing candanza of the Lullaby. Martyndale, *Familiar Analysis of the Calendar*, (1831), p. 269.

Miss Baker says, writing in 1854: "The Corporation of Northampton, within the remembrance of my informant, had a band of musicians, called the corporation waits, who used to meet the judges at the entrance into the town at the time of the assizes. They were four in number, attired in long black gowns, two playing on violins, one on the hautboy, and the other on a whip and dub, or tabor and pipe."

Wake, Lady of the.—The Lady of the Wake is described in "Witts Recreations" (1640), in a poem, perhaps by Herrick:

"Feele how my temples ake
For the lady of the wake;
Her lips are as soft as a medlar,
With her posies and her points,
And the ribbon on her joynts,
The device of the fields and the pedlar."
—Works by Hazlitt, Appendix, No. 111.

Wake-Meat.—Among some Middle English Glosses in *Reliquiæ Antiquæ*, 1841, occurs "obsonium, wake-mete," apparently the entertainment usually provided at a wake.

Wakes.—Called also Feasts of Dedication, Revellings, Rush-bearings, and in the North of England, Hoppings.

The true etymology of *Wake* is, I believe, given in an extract from a metrical Life of St. John in Dugdale's "Warwickshire," quoted by Strutt:—"And ye shal understond & know how the Evyns were first found in old time. In the begynning of holy Churche, it was so that the pepul cam to the Chirche with candellys brennyng and wold wake and coome with light toward to the Chirche in their devocions; and after they fell to lecherie and songs, daunces, harping, piping, and also to glotony and sinne, and so turned the holinesse to cursydness: wherfore holy Faders ordenned the pepul to leve that Waking and to fast the Evyn. But hit is called Vigilia, that is waking in English, and it is called Evyn, for at evyn they were wont to come to Chirche." Wake is mentioned in the same sense in the "Promptorium Parvulorum."

Speght, in his "Glossary to Chaucer," says: "It was the manner in times past upon festival evens called Vigiliæ, for parishioners to meet in their church houses or church yards, and there to have a drinking fit for the time. Here they used to end many quarrels between neighbour and neighbour. Hither came the wives in comely manner: and they which were of the better sort had their mantles carried with them, as well for shew as to keep them from cold at the table. These mantles, also, many did use in the church at morrow-masses and other times." As early as the time of King Edgar, according to Wheloc's edition of Bede, quoted by Brand, great licence prevailed at these wakes, and Edgar's 28th Canon directs the observance of order and decorum. An instance is recorded under that reign of certain merchants from Ireland having come over to attend the wake at Barnwell or Beorna-wyll, near Cambridge, and having been robbed by a priest belonging to the place, which at that time was a large open area devoted to the annual celebration of sports on the Feast of the Nativity of St. John the Baptist, and in the centre of which was a spring, whence the plain and the Abbey derived their name (Beorna-wyll i.e. *Well of the Youths*). Wright's *Domestic Manners*, 1862, pp. 67, 78. Comp. *Sturbridge Fair*.

In the "Ancren Riwle" (13th century), there is a curious allusion to the case of a lady who was nearly dying unshriven, because she refused to confess, till the last moment, that she had once lent a garment to another woman to go to a wake. In Tusser's "Husbandry" are the following lines:

"*The Wake-Day.*
"Fil oven ful of flawnes, Ginnie passe not for sleepe,
To-morrow thy father his wake day will keepe:
Then every wanton may danse at her will
Both Tomkin with Tomlin, and Jankin with Gil."

Great numbers attending at these wakes, by degrees less devotion and reverence were observed, till, at length, from hawkers and pedlars coming thither to sell their petty wares, the merchants came also and set up stalls and booths in the churchyards: and not only those, says Spelman,

who lived in the parish to which the church belonged resorted thither, but others also, from all the neighbouring towns and villages; and the greater the reputation of the saint, the greater were the numbers that flocked together on this occasion. The holding of these fairs on Sundays was justly found fault with by the clergy. The Abbot of Ely, in John's reign, inveighed much against so flagrant a profanation of the Sabbath; but this irreligious custom was not entirely abolished till the reign of Henry VI., a period in our history when a good deal of opposition to profane amusements was offered by the Puritan party. It was to pacify this growing feeling that Henry consented temporarily to the suppression of markets and fairs on Sundays and holy days, in the 23rd year of his reign.

Ellis, in the second series of his "Original Letters," 1827, has printed extracts from Lansdowne MS. 111., one of which may here fitly be introduced. "In Wales, upon the Sundays and holidays, the multitude of all sorts of men, women, and children of every parish do use to meet in sundry places, either on some hill or on the side of some mountain, where their harpers and crowthers sing them songs of the doings of their ancestors; namely, of their wars against the kings of this realme, and the English nation, &c. Here also do they spend their time in hearing some part of the lives of Thalaassyn, [Taliesin], Marlin, Beno, Rybbye, Jermin, and such other the intended prophets and saints of that country."

Stubbes gives us the manner in his time of keeping of wakes and feasts in England. "This is their order therein. Euery town, parish, and village, some at one part of the yere, some at the other (but so that euery one keepe his proper daie assigned and appropriate to it self which they call their wake daie) vseth to make great preparation and prouision for goode cheare. To the which all their freendes and kinsfolkes farre and nere are inuited." He adds that there are such doings at them, "in so muche as the poore men that beare the charges of these feastes and wakesses are the poorer and keepe the worser houses a long tyme after. And no maruaile, for many spend more at one of these wakesses then in the whole yere besides." *Anatomie of Abuses*, ed. 1584, p. 96. Stubbes has been already mentioned as a Puritan: and consequently one who did not duly distinguish between the institution itself and the degenerate abuse of it. Northbrooke says: "Also their daunces were spirituall, religious, and godly, not after our hoppings and leapings, and intermingling men with women, &c. (dauncing every one for his part), but soberly, grauely," &c. Also, "What good doth all that daucing of yong women holding vpon mennes armes, that they may hop the higher?" *Treatise against Dicing*, 1577, repr. 1843, pp. 157, 166.

Hall, in his "Triumphs of Rome," alludes as follows to these convivial entertainments : "What should I speak of our merry wakes and May games and Christmas triumphs, which you have once seen here and may see still in those under the Roman dition : in all which put together, you may well say no Greek can be merrier than they."—*Triumph of Pleasure*, p. 23. A contributor to the "Antiquarian Repertory" has preserved a part of an old song which used to be sung in the North at wakes as well as at Christmas. Ed. 1807, iv, 453.

"They hate the laurell, which is the reason they have no poets amongst them ; so as if there be any that seeme to have a smatch in that generous science, he arrives no higher than the style of a ballet, wherein they have a reasonable facultie ; especially at a wake, when they assemble themselves together at a towne-greene, for then they sing their ballets, and lay out such throats as the country fidlers cannot be heard."—*A Strange Metamorphosis of Man*, &c. 1634. In the old ballad of "Sack for my Money (*circâ* 1630)" we have :

"The country blades with their own maids,
    At every merry meetings,
For ale and cakes at their town wakes,
    Which they did give their sweetings,
Upon their friend a crown will spend
    In sack that is so trusty."

Herrick says :—

Come Anthea let us two
Go to feast, as others do.
Tarts and custards, creams and cakes,
Are the junketts still at wakes :
Unto which the tribes resort,
Where the businesse is the sport.
Morris-dancers thou shalt see,
Marian too in pagentrie :
And a mimick to devise
Many grinning properties.
Players there will be, and those,
Base in action as in clothes ;
Yet with strutting they will please
The incurious villages.
Near the dying of the day,
There will be a cudgell-play,
When a coxcomb will be broke,
Ere a good word can be spoke,
But the anger ends all here,
Drencht in ale, or drown'd in beere.
Happy rusticks, best content
With the cheapest merriment :
And possesse no other feare
Then to want the wake next yeare."

Hinde, speaking of popish and profane wakes at Tarum, says :—"Popery and profannes, two sisters in evil, had con-

sented and conspired in this parish, as in many other places, together to advance their idols against the Arke of God, and to celebrate their solemne feastes of their Popish saints, as being the Dii Tutelares, the speciall patrons and protectors of their church and the parish, by their wakes and vigils, kept in commemoration and honour of them, in all riot and excesse of eating and drinking, dalliance and dancing, sporting and gaming, and other abominable impieties and idolateries." *Life of Bruen*, 1641, p. 89.

Macaulay observes that there is a wake the Sunday next after St. Peter, to whom the Church is dedicated ; adding : "the people of this neighbourhood are much attached to the celebration of wakes ; and on the annual return of those festivals, the cousins assemble from all quarters, fill the church on Sunday, and celebrate Monday with feasting, with musick, and with dancing. The spirit of old English hospitality is conspicuous among the farmers on those occasions ; but with the lower sort of people, especially in manufacturing villages, the return of the wake never fails to produce a week at least of idleness, intoxication, and riot ; these and other abuses, by which these festivals are so grossly perverted from the original end of their institution, render it highly desirable to all the friends of order, of decency, and of religion, that they were totally suppressed." "History of Claybrook." 1791. p. 93. Sir H. Ellis refers us to Nichols' Leicestershire, vol. iv. p. 131. Comp. *Dedication-Feasts, Fairs, Lich-Wake, Rush-Bearing*, &c.

Waking the Well.—It has been conjectured that the ancient usage of Waking the Well led by insensible degrees to the institution of the fair, because the assemblages of persons for this purpose created trading centres, and under the sanction of religion a new phase of commercial life arose and flourished. I will leave this hypothesis for the present unexamined : but the reader may refer to what has just been said about Wakes.

The following is a copy of an ancient ballad, printed in "Reliquiæ Antiquæ," from a MS. at Cambridge, entitled : I have forsworne hit whil I life to wake the welle :

"The last tyme I the wel woke,
Syr John caught me with a croke ;
He made me to swere be bel and boke
    I shuld not telle.

ʒet he did me a wel wors turne,
He leyde my hed agayne the burne,
He gafe my maydenehed a spurne,
    And rose my kelle.

Sir John came to cur hows to play,
Fro evensong tyme til light of the day

We made as mery as flowres in May;
    I was begylede.
Sir John he came to our hows,
He made hit wondur copious:
He seyd that I was gracious
    To beyre a childe.

I go with childe, wel I wot,
I schrew the fadur that hit gate,
Withowtene he fynde hit mylke and
    pape
    A long while ey."

For some additional details on this subject, the reader may refer to Willis's " Current Notes," for December, 1855, and Borlase's "Natural Hist. of Cornwall," p. 31. Comp. also *Holy Wells* suprà.

Walsingham, Our Lady of.—Under the will of Isabel, Countess of Warwick, 1439, the testatrix enumerates a series of bequests to various objects, and says, among other matters: " Also I woll the tablett with the Image of our lady with a glasse to for hit be offered to our lady of Walsingham . . . " Which illustrates the wide diffusion of the faith in this shrine.

Among the Paston Letters is one from Margaret Paston to her husband who was ill in London, dated from Oxnead, 28th September, 1443, from which I shall quote the following passage, as it illustrates a very curious superstition of the time: " My moder," says the writer, " be hestyd a nodyr ymmage of wax of the weytte of yow to oyer Lady of Walsyngham, and sche sent iiij. nobelys to the iiij. Orderys of Frerys at Norweche to pray for yow, and I have be hestyd to gou on pylgreymmays to Walsingham,and to Sent Levenardys for yow. . ." In a letter of about the same date from Justice Yelverton to John Paston, the extraordinary prestige of this shrine in the district is strongly exemplified. Comp. Hazlitt's *Dodsley*, i, 335, his *Proverbs*, 1882, p. 450, and his *Fugitive Tracts*, 1875, 1st Series, where from the piece entitled *The Foundation of the Chapel of Walsingham* (circâ 1495) we perceive that this building was constructed on the model of that at Nazareth by the immediate instrumentality of Our Lady.

In the account of Walsingham Chapel, Norfolk, in Moore's " Monastic Remains," I find the following: " The Wishing Wells still remain—two circular stone pits filled with water, inclosed with a square wall, where the pilgrims used to kneel and throw in a piece of gold, whilst they prayed for the accomplishment of their wishes."

" To swear Walsingham" was an ancient form of saying, " to swear by our Lady of Walsingham."

Other, and for Londoners nearer, places of resort were Barking and Willesden. All these institutions seem cognate to the Breton Pardons, which the French government has lately abolished. In the *Scholehouse of Women*, first printed about 1540, we read:

  " On pilgremage then must they go
  To Wilsdon, Barking, or to some hallowes—"

—Hazlitt's *Popular Poetry*, 1864-6, iv, 117.

Henry VIII. once walked barefoot hither, it is reported, from Balsham to present a necklace to the Virgin, before his grace had formed the scheme of despoiling all these Romish institutions. When Erasmus was at Walsingham, there were two chapels, one for Our Lady and the other for her Son. The image of the Virgin was at the Dissolution committed to the flames.

Wandering Jew.—This is a vulgar error of considerable antiquity. Percy tells us that it obtained full credit in this part of the world, before the year 1228, as we learn from Matthew Paris. In that year it seems there came an Armenian archbishop into England to visit the shrines and relics preserved in our churches, who being entertained at the monastery of St. Albans, was asked several questions relating to his country, &c. Among the rest, a monk who sat near him inquired " if he had ever seen or heard of the famous person named Joseph, that was so much talked of, who was present at our Lord's crucifixion and conversed with him, and who was still alive in confirmation of the Christian faith." The archbishop answered that the fact was true; and afterwards one of his train, who was well known to be a servant of the abbot's, interpreting his master's words, told them in French that his lord knew the person they spoke of very well: that he dined at his table but a little while before he left the East: that he had been Pontius Pilate's porter, by name Cartaphilus, who, when they were dragging Jesus out of the door of the judgment hall, struck him with his fist on the back, saying, " Go faster, Jesus, go faster; why dost thou linger?" Upon which Jesus looked at him with a frown and said, " I, indeed, am going; but thou shalt tarry till I come." Soon after he was converted and baptized by the name of Joseph. He lives for ever, but at the end of every hundred years falls into an incurable illness, and at length into a fit of ecstasy, out of which when he recovers, he returns to the same state of youth he was in when Jesus suffered, being then about thirty years of age. He remembers all the circumstances of the death and resurrection of Christ, the saints that rose with him, the composing of the Apostle's Creed, their preaching and dispersion, and is himself a very grave and holy person. This is the substance of

Matthew Paris's account, who was himself a monk of St. Albans, and was living at the time when this Armenian archbishop made the above relation. Since his time several impostors have appeared at intervals under the name and character of the Wandering Jew.

Brand himself remembered to have seen one of these impostors in the last century in the north of England, who made a very hermit-like appearance, and went up and down the streets of Newcastle with a long train of boys at his heels, muttering "Poor John alone, alone! poor John alone!" Brand thought he pronounced his name in a manner singularly plaintive. Sir William Musgrave had a portrait with his name below, *Poor Joe alone*, which corresponds with the former account.

Warden-pie.—A pie made of Warden pears or *poires dc garde*. See Nares, *Gloss.* 1859, in v. and Hazlitt's *Gleanings in Old Garden Literature*, 1887, p. 140-1.

Wards and Liveries, Court of. —See Nares, *Gloss.* 1859, in v. and Sir James Ley's treatise on the subject, 8°, 1642.

Ware, Great Bed of.— See Nares, ed. 1859, in v.

Warpell-Way.—See *Whorpell Way.*

Warts. — "For warts," says Sir Thomas Browne, "we rub our hands before the moon, and commit any maculated part to the touch of the dead. Old women were always famous for curing warts; they were so in Lucian's time." (*Opera, p.* 272). But warts, on the other hand, seem in certain cases to have been considered lucky, for in *Syr Gyles Goosccuppe, Knight*, a play, 1606, Lord Momford is made to say: "The creses here are excellent good: the proportion of the chin good; the little aptnes of it to sticke out; good. And the wart aboue it most exceedingly good."

Misson observes that "when Englishmen, *i.e.* the common people, have warts or moles on their faces, they are very careful of the great hairs that grow out of those excrescences: and several have told me that they look upon those hairs as tokens of good luck." *Travels in England*, p. 338. Grose says, "To cure warts, steal a piece of beef from a butcher's shop and rub your warts with it: then throw it down the necessary-house, or bury it: and as the beef rots, your warts will decay."

See more superstitions relating to warts in Turner "On the Diseases of the Skin," and in La Forest, "L'Art de soigner les Pieds," p. 75.

Washing the bride's and bridegroom's feet before marriage.— See *Nuptial Usages in Scotland.*

Wassail.—There was an ancient custom, which is yet retained in many places, on New Year's Eve: young women went about with a wassail bowl of spiced ale, dressed up with garlands and ribbons, and with some sort of verses that were sung by them as they went from door to door. Wassail is derived from the Anglo-Saxon **Væ þæl**, be in health. It were unnecessary to add, that they accepted little presents on the occasion from the houses at which they stopped to pay this annual congratulation.

Wassail originally signified a salutation, but afterwards grew to signify revelry, excess. It appears from Thomas de la Moore (Vita Edw. II.) and Havillan (in "Architren." lib. 2), that was-haile and drinc-heil were the usual ancient phrases for quaffing among the English.

Ben Jonson personifies Wassel as "a neat sempster and songster, her page bearing a brown bowl, drest with ribbands and rosemary, before her." "I see a custome in some parts among us: I mean the yearely was-haile in the country on the vigil of the new yeare, which I conjecture was a usuall ceremony among the Saxons before Hengist, as a note of health-wishing, which was express among other nations in that form of the health of their mistresses and friends. 'Bene vos, bene vos, bene te, bene me, bene nostram etiam Stephanium [στεφάνιον] in Plautus, and infinite other testimonies of that nature (in him, Martiall, Ovid, Horace, and such more), agreeing nearly with the fashion now used: we calling it a health, as they did also in direct terms; which, with an idol called Heil, antiently worshipt at Cerne in Dorsetshire, by the English Saxons, in name expresses both the ceremony of drinking and the new years acclamation, whereto in some parts of this kingdom is joyned also solemnity of drinking out of a cup, ritually composed, deckt, and filled with country liquor," &c.—*Selden's Notes on Drayton's Polyolb.* song 9.

In his "Table-Talk," he says: "The Pope in sending relicks to princes, does as wenches do by their wassails at New Years tide; they present you with a cup, and you must drink of a slabby stuff, but the meaning is, You must give them moneys, ten times more than it is worth." From Wither's *Christmas Carol* it seems that the girls went about in the streets with these bowls, and sang carols, no doubt, with the same view.

We read in the "Glossary to the Exmoor Dialect:" "Watsail, a drinking song, sung on Twelfth Day Eve, throwing toast to the apple-trees, in order to have a fruitful year, which seems to be a relic of the heathen sacrifice to Pomona."

"The Wassel Bowl," says Warton (edit.

of Milton's Poems, 1785, p. 51) "is Shakespear's Gossips' Bowl in the 'Mid-summer Night's Dream,' act. i. sc. 1." See "The Beggar's Bush," act iv. sc. 4, and Polwhele's "Old English Gentleman," p. 137. In the "Antiquarian Repertory" is a wood-cut of a large oak beam, the ancient support of a chimney-piece, on which is carved a large bowl, with this inscription on one side, "Wass-heil."

The ingenious remarker on this re-presentation observes, that it is the figure of the old Wassel-Bowl, so much the de-light of our hardy ancestors, who on the vigil of the new year never failed to as-semble round the glowing hearth with their chearful neighbours, and then in the spicy wassel-bowl (which testified the good-ness of their hearts) drowned every former animosity, an example worthy modern imitation. Wassel was the word, wassel every guest returned as he took the circ-ling goblet from his friend, whilst song and civil mirth brought in the infant year.

This seems to have been done in some places upon Christmas Eve; for in Her-rick's "Hesperides," p. 311, I find it among the Christmas Eve ceremonies. Sir Thomas Ackland, Bart. informed Mr. Brand at Werington, October 24th, 1790, that this was done in his neighbourhood on Christmas Eve. See also "Gent. Mag." 1791, p. 116. "Archæol." vol. xi. p. 420.

Macaulay, in his "History of Clay-brook," 1791, p. 131, observes : "Old John Payne and his wife, natives of this parish, are well known from having perambulated the Hundred of Guthlaxton many years, during the season of Christmas, with a fine gew-gaw which they call a wassail, and which they exhibit from house to house, with the accompaniment of a duet. I apprehend that the practice of wassail-ing will die with this aged pair. We are by no means so tenacious of old usages and diversions in this country, as they are in many parts of the world."

At these times the fare in other respects was better than usual, and, in particular, a finer kind of bread was provided, which was, on that account, called wassel-bread. Lowth, in his "Life of William of Wyke-ham," derives this name from the wastel-lum or vessel in which he supposes the bread to have been made. See Milner, *ut supra*, p. 421. To this account may be added what the author of the "Dialect of Craven" says: "A ring was frequently put into the wassail-bowl, which was dived for by the young people. He who obtained the ring was to be married first."

In the Collection of Ordinances for the Royal Household we have some account of the ceremony of wasselling, as it was prac-tised at Court, on Twelfth Night, in the reign of Henry the Seventh. From these we learn that the ancient custom of pledg-ing each other out of the same cup had now given place to the more elegant prac-tice of each person having his cup, and that "When the steward came in at the doore with the wassel, he was to crie three tymes, Wassel, wassel, wassel; and then the chappell (the boys of the King's Chapel) were to answere with a songe." *Archæologia*, x, 423.

"The kyng to morrow schal ete here,
He and alle hys men,
Ever one of us and one of them,
To geder schal sitte at the mete,
And when they haue almost y-ete,
I wole say wassayle to the kyng,
And sle hym with oute any le[s]yng—"
    Old Chronicle, quoted by Warton.

Bale in his play of "Kynge Johan," has a sort of burlesque on the wassail song :

"Wassayle, wassayle out of the milke payle,
Wassayle, wassayle, as whyte as my nayle,
Wassayle, wassayle, in snowe, froste, and hayle,
Wassayle, wassayle, with partriche and rayle,
Wassayle, wassayle, that much doth avayle,
Wassayle, wassayle, that never wyll fayle."

In "How the Goode wif Thaught hir Daughter " we have, among other admoni-tions :

"Sitte thou nought to longe on nyghtis by the cuppe,
And cry wasseile and drynkeheil for then our sires thrifte is vppe—"

In Ritson's "Antient Songs," 1790, p. 304, is given "A Carrol for a Wassel Bowl, to be sung upon Twelfth Day at night—to the tune of "Gallants, come away;" from "New Christmas Carols: being fit also to be sung at Easter, Whit-sontide, and other festival days in the year;" no date, 12mo. b. l. in the Bod-leian, among Wood's books.

A wassailer's song on New Year's Eve, as it was sung in Gloucestershire in the 18th century, was communicated to Brand by Lysons. See it printed in the Percy Society volume, 1846; but its genuineness has been doubted.

The word *wassail* was in certain parts of the country corrupted into *vessel*, and it was usual to carry about the *vessel-cup* at Christmas, and sing carols, with a view to collect money. This was done in 1813, and perhaps later, at Holderness and in other parts of Yorkshire. The cup was sometimes accompanied by an image of Christ and roasted apples.

Wassail Candle.—A large candle used at any feast.

Wassailing.—See my edition of Blount's *Tenures*, 1874, v. *Hereford*.

Wat.—A species of apparition known in Buckinghamshire by the name of "the Wat," was said to haunt prisons. The night before the arrival of the judges at the assizes it made its appearance like a little flame, and by every felon to whom it became visible was accounted a most fatal omen. The moment the unhappy wretch saw this, he thought that all was over with him, and resigned himself to the gallows.

Watch.—Comp. *Bellman* and *Waits.* Shakespear in his *Much Ado about Nothing*, iii, 3, and *Hamlet*, i, 1, has introduced two types of watch. The former is a provincial and comic sketch. The latter approaches more nearly to the feudal or military character and to the original *wait.* The early London functionary included in his duties that of noting the progress of the hours. Dekker made the Bellman of London a vehicle for two of his entertaining publications, the *Bellman of London* and *Lanthorne and Candlelight*, 1608. The bellman seems to have carried a lantern and to have been accompanied by a dog. In one of the earliest entries in his *Diary*, Jan. 16, 1659-60, Pepys records the fact of the bellman going his round, as he was staying up later than usual, and calling out, "past one of the clock, and a cold, frosty, windy morning."

This institution, prior to the appearance of the police, was almost universal in some shape or under some name or other.

Watkin's Ale.—In one of the Huth Ballads, printed together in 1867, is an Elizabethan one on this subject, where a lover offers his mistress the particular kind of ale, of which the designation is figurative.

Wayland Smith.—A very ancient and famous Scandinavian legend, existing in a variety of forms, and apparently transmitted to England by the Saxons, who had a version of it very similar to that associated with the sepulchral monument at the foot of White Horse Hill, Uffington, Berkshire, where, as at Osnabrück, an invisible smith shoed horses left on the spot with a piece of money for his fee. This Saxon type has very little in common beyond the name with the Swedish original myth. Scott has in his *Kenilworth* utilized the Berkshire tradition. Lysons, *M. B. Berkshire*, 215. All this Smith-lore seems to have arisen from the anxiety of early mechanics to conceal their art from motives of interest of more than one kind.

Mr. Halliwell, in his preface to the romance of "Torrent of Portugal," 1842, remarks: "Wayland Smith is said to have taken up his abode in the valley of the White Horse (in Berkshire), in the midst of a number of upright, but rude and mis-shapen stones. There he is said to shoe all horses brought thither, provided a piece of money be left upon one of the stones."

See Singer's little monograph on this story (adapted chiefly, with additions, from a publication in 1833 by MM. Depping and Michel), 1847, where the reader will find many references to information, and a large assemblage of interesting particulars, for which there is no space here.

Weapon-Salve.—In 1631, William Foster published a treatise called *Hoplo-Crisma Spongvs; or, A Sponge to wipe away the Weapon Salve*, wherein he sought to prove that this alleged remedy was magical and unlawful—he might have added, futile and imaginary.

Werenfels says :—"If the superstitious person be wounded by any chance, he applies the salve, not to the wound, but what is more effectual, to the weapon by which he received it. By a new kind of art, he will transplant his disease, like a scion, and graft it into what tree he pleases. The fever he will not drive away by medicines, but what is a more certain remedy, having pared his nails, and tied them to a cray-fish, he will turn his back, and as Deucalion did the stones from which a new progeny of men arose, throw them behind him into the next river." *Diss. on Superstitions*, p. 8.

Weapon-Shawing.—The minister of Kincardine says : "Nigh to the church there is an alley, walled in, and terminating in a large semi-circle, appropriated to that antient military exercise and discipline known by the name of Weaponshawing." *Stat. Acc. of Scotl.* iii, 512.

Wear the Willow, To.—To wear the willow long implied a man's being forsaken by his mistress. In Field's "A Woman is a Weathercock," act i. sc. 1. on a marriage going to be solemnized, Count Frederick says: "My bride will never be readie, I thinke : heer are the other sisters." Pennant observes : "Looke you, my lorde; thereas Lucida weares the willow-garland for you, and will so go to church, I hear." As Lucida enters with a willow garland, she says :

"But since my sister he hath made his choise,
This wreath of willow, that begirts my browes,
Shall never leave to be my ornament
Till he be dead, or I be married to him."

Macaulay, the historian of Claybrook, observes : "The only custom now remaining at weddings, that tends to recall a classical image to the mind, is that of sending to a disappointed lover a garland made of willow, variously ornamented; accompanied sometimes with a pair of gloves, a white handherchief, and a smelling bottle."

Take the following from Bold's "Wit a Sporting," 1657:

> "*The Willow Garland.*
>
> A willow garland thou didst send
> Perfum'd last day to me,
> Which did but only this portend:
> I was forsook by thee.
> Since it is so, I'le tell thee what,
> To-morrow thou shalt see
> Me weare the willow, after that
> To dye upon the tree."

Herrick bears similar testimony in his "Verses to the Willow Tree," and indeed the illustrations of this subject are innumerable. Comp. *Columbine.*

Weasel.—The meeting of a weasel is a bad omen. Defoe had heard of persons who credited this; possibly he did so himself. He adds: "I have known people who have been put into such terrible apprehensions of death by the squeaking of a weazel, as have been very near bringing on them the fate they dreaded." *Mem. of Mr. Duncan Campbel*, 1732, p. 60. See Congreve's *Love for Love.*

Weather.—An early English author tells us: "Thunders in the morning signifie wynde: about noone, rayne; in the evening, great tempest. Somme wryte (their ground I see not) that Sondayes thundre should brynge the death of learned men, judges, and others; Mondayes thondre, the death of women; Tuesdayes thundre, plentie of graine; Wednesdays thundre, the death of harlottes, and other blodshede; Thursdays thundre, plentie of shepe and corne; Fridaies thundre, the slaughter of a great man, and other horrible murders; Saturdayes thundre, a generall pestilent plague and great deathe. Some have observed evil weather to folow when watry foules leave the sea, desiring lande: the foules of the lande flying hyghe: The crying of fowles about waters making a great noyse with their wynges: also the sees swellyng with uncustomed waves: if beastes eate gredely: if they lycke their hooves: if they sodaynlye move here and there, makyng a noyse, brethyng up to the ayre with open nostrels: rayne foloweth. Also the busy heving of moules; the appering, or coming out of wormes: hennes resorting to the perche or reste, covered with dust; declare rayne. The ample working of the spinnar in the ayre; the ant busied with her egges: the bees in fayre weather not farre wanderyng: the continuall pratyng of the crowe, chiefly twyse or thryse quycke calling, shew tempest. Whan the crowe or raven gapeth against the sunne,

in summer, heate foloweth. If they busy themselves in proyning or washyng, and that in wynter, loke for raine. The uncustomed noise of pultry, the noise of swine, or pecokes, declare the same. The swalowe flying and beating the water, the chirping of the sparrow in the morning, signifie rayne. Raine sodainly dried up; woody coveringes strayter than of custome; Belles harde further then commonly; the wallowyng of dogges: the alteration of the cocke crowing; all declare rainy weather. I leave these, wanting the good grounde of the rest." Leonard Digges, *Prognostication*, 1556, fol. 6 *verso*.

See Hearne's edition of Robert of Avesbury's History of Edward III. p. 266. In the Roman Calendar I find an observation on the 13th December, "That on this day prognostications of the months were drawn for the whole year."

> "Prognostica mensium per totum annum."

In "The Shepherd's Almanack" for 1676, among the observations on the month of January, we find the following: "Some say that if on the 12th of January the sun shines, it foreshews much wind. Others predict by St. Paul's Day; saying, if it rain or snow, indifferent; if misty, it predicts great dearth; if it thunder, great winds, and death of people that year." Lodge, in his "Wits Miserie," 1596, glances at the superstitions of St. Paul's and St. Peter's Day, p. 12, "And by S. Peter and S. Paule the fool rideth him."

Bishop Hall, in his "Characters of Virtues and Vices," 1608, speaking of the superstitious man, observes that "Saint Paules Day and Saint Swithines, with the Twelve, are his oracles, which he dares believe against the almanacke." Gay, in his "Trivia," repeats the superstition, concluding with a moral:

> "Let no such vulgar tales debase thy mind,
> Nor Paul, nor Swithin, rule the clouds and wind."

Stevenson gives the following superstition: "They say, so many dayes old the moon is on Michaelmas Day, so many floods after."

Cuthbert Bede, in "Notes and Queries" for February 10, 1866, says that a Huntingdonshire cottager said to him on the preceding 25th January: "We shall have a fine spring, Sir. There is an old proverb that says: If Paul's Day is fine, it will be a fine spring." The cottager referred to the adage:

> "If St. Paul be fair and clear,
> Then betides a happy year."

Now, perhaps, this may be the true reason, why St. Paul's Day used to be the time, from which the weather, &c. were computed. "There is a general tradition," says Sir Thomas Browne, "in most parts of Europe, that inferreth the coldnesse of succeeding winter from the shining of the sun on Candlemas Day, according to the proverbiall distich:

"Si Sol splendescat Mariâ purificante,
Major erit glacies post festum quam
    fuit ante."
Vulgar Errors, 1646, p. 289.

The minister of Kirkmichael, in Banfshire, tells us, "the appearance of the three first days of winter is observed in verses thus translated from the Gaelic: 'Dark, lurid, and stormy, the first three days of winter; whoever would despair of the cattle, I would not till summer.'"

In Lloyd's "Stratagems of Jerusalem," 1602, p. 286, we read: "The Thracians, when it thunders, take their bowes and arrowes, and shoote up to the cloudes against the thunder, imagining by their shooting to drive the thunders away. Cabrias, the Generall of Athens, being ready to strike a battell on sea, it suddenly lightened, which so terrified the soldiers that they were unwilling to fight, untill Cabrias said, that now the time is to fight, when Jupiter himself, with his lightening, doth shewe a signe that he is readie to go before us. So Epaminondas, at his going to battell it suddenly lightened that it so amazed his souldiers that Epaminondas comforted them and saide, 'Lumen hoc Numina ostendunt,' by these lightenings the gods shew us that we shall have victories. In Rome, the Dictator, the Consul, the Prætor, and other magistrates were to be removed from their offices, if the soothsayer saw any occasion by lightning, thundering, by removing of starres, by flying of fowles, by intrailes of beasts, by eclipse of the sun and moone, Pau. Æmilius, Consul and Generall of the Romanes in Macedonia, at what time he sacrific'd unto the Gods in the city of Amphipolis, it lightened, whereby he was perswaded it pretended the overthrow of the kingdom of Macedonia, and his great victory and tryumph of the same at Rome."

Leigh, speaking of Tiberius Cæsar, says: "He feared thunder exceedingly, and when the aire or weather was any thing troubled, he ever carried a chaplet or wreath of lawrell about his neck, because that, (as Pliny reporteth,) is never blasted with lightning." The same author mentions a similar charm. "He was so much afraid of thunder and lightning, that he ever carried about with him for a preservative remedy a seale skinne or of a sea-calfe, which, as Pliny writeth, checketh all lightninge. Tonitrua et Fulgura paulo infirmius expavescebat, ut semper et ubique pellem, Vituli marini circumferret, pro remedio." *Observations on the Twelve Cæsars*, 1647, p. 63.

Sheridan ("Notes on Persius," Sat. ii. v. *Bidental*) says: "It was a custom whenever a person fell by thunder, there to let him lie, and to fence in the place; to sacrifice a sheep and erect an altar there," edit. 1739, p. 33.

Massey remarks: "The left hand thunder was accounted a happy omen by the Romans, but by the Greeks and barbarians it was thought otherwise: so inconsistent are superstitious observations." Notes to Ovid's *Fasti*, p. 90; Cicero *De Divinatione*, lib. ii, c. 39. It appears from the following passage in Greene's Penelope's Web, 1587, that wearing a bay leaf was a charm against thunder: "He which weareth the bay-leafe is priviledged from the prejudice of thunder." So, in Webster's "White Devil," 1612, Cornelia says:

——"Reach the bays:
I'll tie a garland here about his head,
'Twill keep my boy from lightning."

In *A Strange Metamorphosis of Man*, 1634, it is observed, that the bay is "so privileged by nature, that even thunder and lightning are here even taxed of partiality, and will not touch him for respects sake, as a sacred thing." In a similar sense we find a quotation from one of the early poets:

"As thunder nor fierce lightning harmes
    the bay,
So no extremitie hath power on fame."
Bodenham's *Belvedere*, 1600, p. 90.

Lodge remarks: "You beare the feather of a phœnix in your bosome against all wethers and thunders, laurell to escape lightning," &c. Diogenes in his Singularitie, 1591, p. 2.

Bishop King alludes to the superstitious idea of laurel being a defensative against thunder.

"I see that wreath, which doth the
    wearer arme
'Gainst the quick strokes of thunder, is
    no charme
To keepe off death's pale dart: for
    (Johnson) then,
Thou had'st been number'd still with
    living men;
Times sythe had feard thy lawrell to
    invade,
Nor thee this subject of our sorrow
    made."
—*Jonsonus Virbius*, 1638.

Wiilsford says: "Thunder and lighting in winter in hot countryes is usual, and hath the same effects; but in those northern climates it is held ominous, portending factions, tumults, and bloody wars, and a thing seldome seen, according to the old adage, 'Winters thunder is the sommers wonder.'" *Nature's Secrets*, 113. "Some say, thunder on Shrove-Tuesday fortelleth wind, store of fruit, and plenty. Others affirm, that so much as the sun shineth that day, the like will shine every day in Lent."

Willsford furnishes the following catalogue of portents: "Beasts eating greedily, and more than they used to do, prenotes foul weather; and all small cattel, that seeme to rejoyce with playing and sporting themselves, foreshews rain. Oxen and all kinds of neat, if you do at any time observe them to hold up their heads, and snuffle in the air, or lick their hooves, or their bodies against the hair, expect then rainy weather. Asses or mules, rubbing often their ears, or braying much more than usually they are accustomed, presages rain. Hogs crying and running unquietly up and down, with hay or litter in their mouths, foreshews a storm to be near at hand. Moles plying their works, in undermining the earth, foreshews rain: but if they do forsake their trenches and creep above ground in summer time, it is a sign of hot weather; but when on a suddain they doe forsake the valleys and low grounds, it foreshews a flood neer at hand; but their coming into meddows presages fair weather, and for certain no floods. The little sable beast (called a flea) if much thirsting after blood, it argues rain. The lamentable croakings of frogs more than ordinary, does denote rainy weather. Glow-worms, snayles, and all such creatures, do appear most against fair weather; but if worms come out of the earth much in the day-time, it is a presage of wet weather; but in the summer evenings it foreshews dewy nights, and hot days to follow." *Nature's Secrets*, 1658, p. 130.

The *Husbandman's Practice*, 1664, informs us: Ducks and drakes shaking and fluttering their wings when they rise; young horses rubbing their backs against the ground; sheep bleating, playing, or skipping wantonly; swine being seen to carry bottles of hay or straw to any place and hide them; oxen licking themselves against the hair; the sparking of a lamp or candle; the falling of soot down a chimney more than ordinary; frogs croaking; swallows flying low, &c. &c. Coles says: "If the down flyeth off colt's-foot, dandelyon, and thistles, when there is no winde, it is a signe of rain." *Introd. to the Knowl. of Plants*, 1656, p. 28. As regards the duck, the proverb: "Like a dying duck in a thunder storm" is supposed to

allude to the inability of this bird, though an aquatic one, to endure heavy rain.

Hogs pricking up their ears we find described as a rainy omen. An old author explains this as follows: "Some say that a hog is most dull and of a melancholy nature: and so by reason doth foresee the raine that commeth: and in time of raine indeed I have observed that most cattell doe pricke up their eares: as for example an asse will, when he perceiveth a storme or raine or hail doth follow." *Curiosities, or the Cabinet of Nature*, 1637, p. 262. Decker has a passage:

> " Beasts licking 'gainst the hayre
> Foreshew some storme, and I fore-see some snare."
> —*Match me in London*, 1631, act iv.

From the following simile in *Belvedere*, 1600, p. 153, it should seem that our ancestors held some how or other the hedge-hog to be a prognosticator of the weather:

> " As hedge-hogs doe fore-see ensuing stormes,
> So wise men are for fortune still prepared."

The disposition of sheep to put their feet into the hedge as for shelter has been thought to be a sign of approaching rain. This animal is apt to suffer in that part from the wet.

Willsford tells us: "Porpaises, or sea hogs, when observed to sport and chase one another about ships, expect then some stormy weather." In Ravenscroft's *Canterbury Guests*, p. 24, we read: "My heart begins to leap, and play like a porpice before a storm." "Dolphines," Willsford continues, "in fair and calm weather persuing one another as one of their waterish pastimes, foreshews wind, and from that part whence they fetch their frisks; but if they play thus when the seas are rough and troubled, it is a sign of fair and calm weather to ensue. Cuttles, with their many legs swimming on the top of the water, and striving to be above the waves, do presage a storm. Sea-urchins thrusting themselves into the mud, or striving to cover their bodies with sand, foreshews a storm. Cockles, and most shell-fish, are observed against a tempest to have gravel sticking hard into their shells, as a providence of Nature to stay or poise themselves, and to help weigh them down, if raised from the bottome by surges. Fishes in general, both in salt and fresh waters, are observed to sport most, and bite more eagerly, against rain than at any other time."

Sir Thomas Browne notices as a common opinion in his day (I suspect that he shared it himself) the belief, "that a king-fisher, hanged by the bill, sheweth us what quarter the wind is, by an occult and secret propriety, converting the breast to that point of the horizon from whence the wind doth blow." He speaks of this as "very strange, introducing natural weathercocks, and extending magnetical positions as far as animal natures: a conceit supported chiefly by present practice, yet not made out by reason or experience." Wild notices the swarming of kingfishers as a portent of fair weather. *Iter Boreale*, 1660, p. 19.

Willsford also writes: "The cock, if he crows in the day time very much, or at sun-setting, or when he is at roost at unusual hours, as at 9 or 10, expect some change of weather, and that suddenly, but from fair to foul, or the contrary: but when the hen crows, good men expect a storm within doors and without. If the hens or chickins in the morning come late from their roosts, (as if they were constrained by hunger,) it presages much rainy weather." He adds, respecting the halcyon, that the breeding time of that bird, the fortnight before the winter solstice, "shews a quiet and tranquil time." Again: "Bees, in fair weather, not wandering far from their hives, presages the approach of some stormy weather . . . wasps, hornets, and gnats biting more sorely then they used to do, is a sign of rainy weather."

The Romans observed that, in anticipation of bad weather, ants ran about uneasily, carrying their eggs backwards and forwards. Donaldson's *Miscellanea Virgiliana*, 1825, p. 39.

It is thought that from the movements of the herd of Cashmere goats in Windsor Great Park the coming weather may be augured. If it is going to rain, they remain at headquarters: but if they anticipate fair weather, they freely wander over the park.

The idea that prognostications of rain may be drawn from spider's webs is mentioned by Pliny, and seems to be countenanced by Bartholomæus: "Also he (Pliny) saythe, spynners (spiders) ben tokens of divynation and of knowing what wether shal fal, for oft by weders that shal fal, some spin and weve higher or lower. Also he saythe, that multytute of spynners is token of mouche reyne."

Willsford tells us: "Spiders creep out of their holes and narrow receptacles against wind or rain: Minerva having made them sensible of an approaching storm." He adds: "The commonwealth of emmets, when busied with their eggs, and in ordering their state affairs at home, it presages a storm at hand, or some foul weather; but when Nature seems to stupifie their little bodies, and disposes

them to rest, causing them to withdraw into their caverns least their industry should engage them by the inconveniency of the season, expect then some foul and winterly weather." *Nature's Secrets*, 1658, p. 131.

There is a vulgar opinion, that the character of the coming summer may be prognosticated by the appearance of the larva of the cicada. If the larva should lie in the froth or cuckoo-spit (as it is commonly called) with the head of the insect upwards, it would portend a dry summer, if downwards, a wet one.

It used to be thought that the cutting of the fern was accompanied by rain; and there is a story somewhere of the country people, in the time of Charles I., being served with a warning not to touch their bracken, because his Majesty intended a journey, and desired dry weather. A piece of sea-weed, suspended from the wall, or elsewhere, is still held to be a very good barometer. At the approach of rain, it becomes moist and limp. The reason of this phenomenon is that the salt resident in the weed follows the normal tendency to grow dry or moist according to the temperature.

Willsford tells us: "Salt extracted out of the earth, water, or any mineral, hath these properties to foreshew the weather; for, if well kept, in fair weather it will be dry, and apt to dissolve against wet into its proper element; on boards that it hath lain upon, and got into the pores of the wood, it will be dry in fair and serene weather, but when the air inclines to wet, it will dissolve; and that you shall see by the board venting its brackish tears: and salt sellers will have a dew hang upon them; and those made of mettal look dim against rainy weather." *Nature's Secrets*, 139.

Knap-weeds are popularly supposed, like sea-weed, to prognosticate changes in the weather, but in a different fashion. The calix, which does not wither when the flower blooms, closes round the seed-vessels, and forms a hard globular substance; in dry weather this calix expands, but at the approach of rain it shuts up again.

There is nothing superstitious in prognostications of weather from aches and corns. "Aches and corns," says Bacon, "do engrieve (afflict) either towards rain or frost: the one makes the humours to abound more, and the other makes them sharper." Thus also Butler:

"As old sinners have all points
O' th' compass in their bones and joints;
Can by their pangs and aches find
All turns and changes of the wind,
And better than by Napier's bones,
Feel in their own the age of moones."

In a passage of Gay's first Pastoral are some curious rural omens of the weather. He mentions pricking corns as a sign of rain, and the flight of swallows as one of fair weather: as with us, the more than usually disagreeable odour of the sewers and the reeking of stone walls or buildings were regarded in this writer's time as indications of wet, and he implies the same of the creaking of the shopkeepers' signs and the stockings suspended from the hosiers' poles "flying from side to side with the slackened gale." Bishop Hall seems to refer to the well-understood weather portent indicated by Gay, where he says:

"So brekes he like a marble towards raine."

Hasted, speaking of nailbourns or temporary land springs, which are not unusual in Kent, in the parts eastward of Sittingborne, says, that "their time of breaking forth, or continuance of running, is very uncertain : but whenever they do break forth, it is held by the common people as the forerunner of scarcity and dearness of corn and victuals. Sometimes they break out for one, or perhaps two successive years, and at others, with two, three, or more years intervention, and their running continues sometimes only for a few months, and at others for three or four years." *Hist. of Kent*, folio ed. 111, 333.

M. Michel observes that the Basques still believe in the efficiency of an immersion of some holy relic, accompanied by prayers, as a charm to produce rain ; and in certain parts of Mexico cattle are sacrificed at rain-making feasts instituted to propitiate the gods, when the British used, at least till lately, to content themselves more economically with appealing through his Grace the Primate. *Journal of the R. Geogr. Society*, Feb. 1903, p. 131.

Naogeorgus reproves the propensity of the Germans of his time to rely on "sky omens," astrology, and the words of "blind astronomers." *Regnum Papisticum*, by Googe, 1570, 44. Moresin reckons among omens "the hornedness of the moon, the shooting of the stars, and the cloudy rising of the sun."

Schenkius says, "It is a custom in many parts of Germany to drag the images of St. Paul and St. Urban to the river, if on the day of their feast (January 25) it happens to be foul weather." In Hazlitt's *Proverbs*, 1882, will be found a large body of matter connected with weather lore.

Weathercock.—Vanes on the tops of steeples were anciently (as pointed out by Du Cange) made in the form of a cock (called hence weathercocks), and put up,

in papal times, to remind the clergy of watchfulness.

Gramaye shews that the manner of adorning the tops of steeples with a cross and a cock, is derived from the Goths, who bore that as their warlike ensign. Peter Le Neve's Communication to the Society of Antiquaries (Minute Book, Jan. 29, 1723-4.).

In "A Help to Discourse," first printed in 1619, the cock on the top of steeples is explained to signify that we should thereby "remember our sinnes, and with Peter seeke and obtaine mercy : as though without this dumbe cocke, which many will not hearken to, untill he crow, the Scriptures were not a sufficient larum." A writer, dating Wisbeach, May 7, in the "St. James's Chronicle," June 10th, 1777, says, that "the intention of the original cock-vane was derived from the cock's crowing when St. Peter had denied his Lord, meaning by this device to forbid all schism in the Church, which might arise among her members by their departing from her communion, and denying the established principles of her faith. But though this invention was, in all probability, of popish original, and a man who often changes his opinion is known by the appellation of a weather-cock, I would hint to the advocates for that unreformed church, that neither this intention, nor the antiquity of this little device, can afford any matter for religious argument."

Wedding Cake.—See *Bride, Marriage, Nuptial Usages, &c.*

Wedding Favours.—See *Favours* and Pepys, Feb. 20 and 22, 1666-7. The Diarist and others went to Sir W. Pen's house after his daughter's wedding, and had favours given to them, which they put into their hats. These are still usual, but are confined to servants in attendance.

Wedding-Presents.—Among the entries in the "Privy Purse Expenses of Henry VII." are several denoting that Henry was in the habit of making "offerings" at the weddings of people whom he liked, or who were in his service. This does not, I think, necessarily imply that the king was present on all these occasions ; but that he adopted that plan of paying a compliment to the wedded pair.

Sir W. Vaughan of Merioneth observes : "The marriage day being come, (in some shires of England,) the invited ghests do assemble together, and at the very instant of the marriage, doe cast their presents (which they bestowe upon the new-married folkes) into a bason, dish, or cup, which standeth upon the table in the church, ready prepared for that purpose. But this custome is onely put in use amongst them which stand in need." *Golden Grove*, 1600, ed. 1608, sign. O 4.

In a letter from William Wilson the actor to Edward Alleyn, founder of Dulwich College, written in 1617, there is a mention of the approaching marriage of the writer at St. Saviour's Southwark, which took place November 2 in the year named, and the expression of a hope, that his fellow-players at the Fortune will make offerings at the church or privately to Wilson "of their own good nature." *Athenæum*, Sept. 19, 1903. Possibly there was, as in the quotations from Vaughan, some receptacle specially allotted at St. Saviour's for these gifts on the part of friends; and both passages point to a pecuniary donation.

An odd, but very acceptable present is noticed in the acounts of Mrs. Joyce Jeffries, of Hereford, under 1647, as made by her to a bride: "September 5. Paid the butcher for a fatt weather to present this bridewoeman at her wedding day, 6s. 6d."—*Archæol.* vol. 37, p. 221.

It appears from Allan Ramsay's "Poems," 1721, p. 120, that it was a fashion in Scotland for the friends to assemble in the new-married couple's house, before they had risen out of the bed, and to throw them their several presents upon the bed-clothes:

"As fou's the house cou'd pang,
To see the young fouk or they raise,
Gossips came in ding dang,
And wi' a soss aboon the claiths,
Ilk ane their gifts down flang," &c.

Here a note informs us, "They commonly throw their gifts of household furniture above the bed-cloaths where the young folks are lying." One gives twelve horn spoons; another a pair of tongs, &c.

As regards gifts by a suitor to a woman made before marriage, in the case of Robinson v. Cumming in 1742 it seems to have been deemed by Lord Hardwicke that a distinction existed between presents offered by "an adventurer," when in the event of a miscarriage of the matter a return could not be enforced, especially if the lady was a person of superior fortune, and such as might be received from a party, who had approached her with a view to marriage, and had had reasonable expectation of success, under which circumstances his lordship held that the articles were reclaimable. To come to a conclusion on such lines strikes a layman as attended by difficulty.

Wedding Psalm.—In the "Monthly Magazine" for 1798, p. 417, we read: "It is customary, in country churches, when a couple has been newly married, for the singers to chaunt, on the following Sunday, a particular Psalm, thence called the Wedding Psalm, in which are these words, 'Oh well is thee, and happy shalt thou be.'"

Wedding Ring. — Comp. *Ring.* Hutchinson tells us, that "a syllabub is prepared for the May Feast, which is made of warm milk from the cow, sweet cake and wine: and a kind of divination is practised, by fishing with a ladle for a wedding ring, which is dropped into it, for the purpose of prognosticating who shall be first married."

Wedding Sermon.—A wedding sermon was anciently preached at almost every marriage of persons of any consequence. A few of them are valuable as illustrations of manners; but an overwhelming majority exceedingly foolish and dull.

Weeping-Cross. — Originally a station, where penitents offered up their tears as a mark of contrition and sacrifice, but subsequently employed in a secondary and figurative sense. Comp. Nares, ed. 1859, in v. and Hazlitt's *Proverbs*, 1882, p. 187.

Welsh Main.—Pegge describes the Welsh Main, in order to expose the cruelty of it, and supposes it peculiar to this kingdom, known neither in China, nor in Persia, nor in Malacca, nor among the savage tribes of America. Suppose, says he, sixteen pairs of cocks; of these the sixteen conquerors are pitted the second time—the eight conquerors of these are pitted a third time—the four of these a fourth time—and lastly, the two conquerors of these are pitted a fifth time—as if it had been necessary to improve upon the inherent cruelty of the stupid and detestable sports, spurs were introduced, and were at one time in general use. See *Cock-Fighting.*

Wembdon, Somersetshire.—Collinson mentions a well in the parish of Wembdon, called St John's Well, to which in 1464 "an immense concourse of people resorted: and that many who had for years laboured under various bodily diseases, and had found no benefit from physick and physicians, were, by use of these waters (after paying their due offerings,) restored to their pristine health." *Somersetshire*, iii, 104.

Wenlock, Salop.—The practice, which prevailed at one time at Wenlock in Shropshire, of going in procession to the extreme limits of the franchise, with a man who was dressed in a grotesque fashion, and was called a bailiff, and all the other incidence of municipal pomp, seems to have been allied to the perambulations in Rogation Week. The members of the procession, consisting of men and boys, were mounted and armed with wooden swords, which they wore on the right side; they called at all the private houses on the way, and demanded refreshment. On their return, they proceeded to the Guildhall, where the town clerk read aloud a parody upon a charter, in which were these lines:

"We go from Bickbury, and Badger,
    to Stoke on the Clee,
To Monkhopton, Round Acton, and so
    return we."

Werwolf.—An account of this remarkable superstition, which was well known to the antients, or at least was familiar in the time of Pliny, who refutes it, is given in Sir Frederic Madden's Introduction to the romance of "William and the Werwolf," a translation from the French "Roman de Guillaume de Palerme," and in Mr. Thomas Wright's "Essays on the Superstitions of the Middle Ages," 1846. The werwolf, or *loup-garou*, as the French call it, is simply a man transformed, as a penance, into a wolf, and doomed to remain in that shape for a term of three or seven years. He wanders about by night, and can only obtain restoration to the human form before the allotted time by the stroke of a key and effusion of blood. Blood-letting is the usual mode, it may be observed, of breaking this kind of spell. Sir Frederic Madden remarks : "This term (werwolf) has the same meaning, and is compounded of the same elements, as the λυκ-ανθρωπος of the Greeks. From the high antiquity of the tradition respecting were-wolves, and its having been current among the Celtic as well as Gothic nations, we find the expression in most of the dialects formed from each of the parent languages, and all corresponding to the signification above affixed of *man-wolf*, *i.e.* a wolf partaking of the nature of man, or, in other words, a man changed, by magical art, into the temporary form of a wolf." In William Baldwin's tract entitled, "Beware the Cat," first printed in 1561, if not before, there is a passage which appears to indicate a somewhat varying form of the same strange belief. It is as follows : "There is also in Ireland one nacion whereof some one man and woman are at euery seuen yeeres end turned into wulues, and so continew in the woods the space of seuen yeers ; and if they happen to liue out the time, they return to their own form again and other twain are turned for the like time into the same shape ; which is penance (as they say) enioyned that stock by Saint Patrick for some wickednes of their ancestors ; and that this is true witnessed a man whom I left aliue in Ireland, who had performed this seuen yeeres penance, whose wife was slain while she was a wulf in her last yeer."

The author of a passage in the "Flyting betwixt Montgomery and Polwart," 1629 (but written long before), seems to have formed a somewhat indistinct notion of the werwolf, where he speaks of wor wolves and wilde cates in the same line.

"There is a Polish story of a witch who made a girdle of human skin, and laid it across the threshold of a door, where a marriage feast was being held. On the bridal pair stepping across the girdle they were transformed into wolves. Three years after, the witch sought them out, and cast over them dresses of fur with the hair turned outward, whereupon they recovered their human forms."—*Curious Myths of the Middle Ages*, by S. Baring-Gould, 1866, p. 143.

Another form of the word is *Garwolf*, and in Brittany the same legend or fiction is found to have existed under the name of *Bisclaveret*, a story on which is included among the *Lays* of Marie de France.

There seems some cognate idea in a German tract of the earlier part of the 16th c. entitled *Hochstratus Ovans*, where one of the interlocutors is Edwardus Leus, who is said "ex homine commutatus nuper in Canem." Hazlitt's *Coll. and Notes*, 1903, p. 185.

Comp. Scot's *Discovery of Witchcraft*, ed. 1651, pp. 69-70, an excellent account in Nares, *Glossary*, 1859, in v., and Mr. Baring-Gould's *Book of Werewolves*, 1865.

Westminster School.—Something like the Eton Montem festivities appear to have been kept up in Westminster School after the Reformation, as we may gather from the following passage in the funeral sermon of Bishop Duppa, preached at the Abbey Church of Westminster, April 24th, 1662, p. 34 : "Here (*i.e.* in Westminster School) he had the greatest dignity which the school could afford put upon him, to be the Pædonomus at Christmas, Lord of his fellow scholars : which title was a pledge and presage that, from a lord in jeast, he should, in his riper age, become one in earnest."

A writer in the "Gentleman's Magazine" for 1790, p. 256, says that at Westminster School, upon Shrove Tuesday, the Under Clerk of the College enters the school, and preceded by the Beadle and other officers, throws a large pancake over the bar, whch divides the upper from the under school. A gentleman who was formerly one of the masters of that school confirmed the anecdote to Brand, with this alteration, that the cook of the seminary brought it into the school, and threw it over the curtain which separated the forms of the upper from those of the under scholars. This still (1903) takes place.

Wetting the Block.—A custom among shoemakers. See Halliwell in v.

Wheat, Parboiled.—Chandler, in his "Travels" tells us, that he was at a funeral entertainment amongst the modern Greeks, where, with other singular rites, "two followed carrying on their heads each a great dish of parboiled wheat. These were deposited over the body." There is "a practice of the Greek Church, not yet out of use, to set boyled corne before the singers of those holy hymnes, which use to be said at their commemorations of the dead, or those which are asleep in Christ. And that which the rite would have, is, to signifye the resurrection of the body. Thou foole! that which thou soweth is not quickened except it dye."—*Gregorii Opuscula*, 1650, p. 128.

Whetstone.—See Nares, *Glossary*, 1859, in v. Collier's *Bibl. Account*, 1865, ii, 512, and Hazlitt's *Handbook*, 1867, p. 650. In Riley's *Memorials*, 1868, there are many entries of the award of the whetstone, accompanied by the pillory; it was a punishment for lying. In a case, which occurred in the City in 1364 one John de Hakford was sentenced to come out of Newgate without hood and girdle, barefoot and unshod, with a whetstone hung by a chain from his neck, and lying on his breast, it being marked with the words *A false liar;* he proceeded in this way to the pillory with trumpets before him, and this was to be repeated four times during his year's inprisonment.

Whichenovre, co. Stafford.—An usage, similar to that at Dunmow, Essex, existed at Whichenovre in Staffordshire, with the addition of a present of corn. At Whichenovre a less rigorous oath was exacted. The following is the form which held 10 Edw. III. and which was sworn on a book laid above the flitch. In that year Sir Philip de Somerville was Lord of the manor: "Here ye, Sir Philippe de Somervile, Lord of Whichenovre, maynteyner and gyver of this baconne; that I A. sithe I wedded B my wife, and sythe I hadd hyr in my kepyng, and at my wylle by a yere and a day, after our mariage, I wold not have chaunged for none other, farer ne fowler, rycher ne pourer, ne for none other descended of greater lynage, slepyng ne waking, at noo tyme. And yf the seyd B. were sole, and I sole, I would take her to be my wyfe, before all the wymen of the worlde, of what condiciones soever they be, good or evylle, as helpe me God ond hys seyntys: and this flesh and all fleshes." Plot's *Staffordshire*, p. 44, and see a letter from Horace Walpole to Lady Aylesbury, Aug. 23, 1760, in Cunningham's ed. iii, 333.

Whiffler.—Comp. Nares, ed. 1859, in v. and Hazlitt's *Livery Companies*, 1892, p. 309, where a whiffler is delineated.
These functionaries played on a whiffle or pipe, whence their name. They usually formed part of the old Lord Mayor's Show. But in *Old Meg of Herefordshire for a Maid Maryan*, 1609, the term is applied to the performers in a morris-dance.

Whigmeleerie.—Jameson notices Whigmeleerie as the name of a ridiculous game which was occasionally used in Angus at a drinking club. A pin was stuck in the centre of a circle, from which there were as many radii as there were persons in the company, with the name of each person at the radius opposite to him. On the pin an index was placed, and moved round by every one in his turn; and at whatsoever person's radius it stopped, he was obliged to drink off his glass. Whigmeleeries are "whims, fancies, crotchets."

Whip-her-Jenny.—A game similar to *One and Thirty*.

Whip the Cat.—See Halliwell in v.

Whip the Cock, To.—See *Cock-thrashing*.

Whip-Dog-Day.—See *St. Luke's Day*.

Whip-top, or **Top and Scourge.**—An early game both here and abroad. In a Flemish *Book of Hours* of the 15th century, in the Huth Collection, one of the decorations represents two children playing at it.

Whirligig, The.—See *Penny Magazine* for 1837, p. 340, where an illustration of this contrivance for chastizing camp-followers, &c. may be seen. Grose includes it in his *Military Antiquities*.

Whirlin Sunday.—A writer in the "Gentleman's Magazine" for 1789, p. 491, tells us that "in several villages in the vicinity of Wisbech, in the Isle of Ely, the fifth Sunday in Lent has been, time immemorial, commemorated by the name of Whirlin Sunday, when cakes are made by almost every family, and are called, from the day, Whirlin Cakes."

Whist.—This game, which is supposed to be of English origin, and to have succeeded Quadrille, as the latter had replaced Ombre, is mentioned in Farquhar's *Beaux' Stratagem*. Chatto (*Facts and Speculations*, 1848, p. 161) says that it was originally played with swabbers, which are described as probably so termed, because they entitled the holders of certain cards to a share in the profits of the game. Whist, or Whick, as it was long called, was during a considerable period a popular, rather than a fashionable, recreation, and does not seem to have come into favour among the upper classes till the end of the eighteenth century, when Daines Barrington speaks of it (1787) as prevailing not only in England, but on the Continent. Comp. *Trump*.

Whistles.—In "The Pedlar's Lamentation," an early ballad, whistles are mentioned as children's toys:

" Exchange then a groat for some pretty
    toy,
 Come, buy this fine whistle for your
    little boy—"

Cornelius Scriblerus is made to observe: " Play was invented as a remedy against hunger. It is therefore wisely contrived by Nature, that children as they have the keenest appetites, are most addicted to plays." " To speak first of the whistle, as it is the first of all play-things. I will have it exactly to correspond with the ancient fistula, and accordingly to be composed *septem paribus disjuncta cicutis*."

White and Black.—In 2 and 3 Philip and Mary (1555), c. ix. an act of Parliament was passed " to make voyde dyvers lycences of houses wherin unlawfull games bee used." Here we find mention of some diversion described as" White & Blacke, Making & Marring," apparently independent of the recreations previously enumerated, such as bowling, tennis, dice-play, and so forth. *Statutes of the Realm*, 2 and 3 P. and M. (Record Com. ed.)

White Bread Meadow.—A custom in connection with the letting of a piece of land at Bourne known as " the White Bread Meadow " was still observed in 1902. The land was let by auction, and at each bid a boy was started to run to a given public-house, the land being let to the person whose bid had not been challenged, when the last boy returned. The money—in this case amounting to £5 7s. 6d.—was partly spent in a bread and cheese and onion supper at a public-house, and the remainder in loaves of bread, delivered to every house in a certain district of the town.

White Horse, Berkshire.—One of a group of monuments distributed over the country, and probably the most celebrated. It is an area of 371 feet in length, acording to Lysons (*M. B. Berkshire*, 215), on the downs near Uppington Castle, over which the turf periodically grows, and which was long every third year the scene of a ceremony well known as the *Scouring of the White Horse* or, in other words, the removal of the turf from the underlying chalk so as to leave the mythical figure visible.

White Lady.—In the family of Gould of Law-Trenchard, in Devonshire, was a White Lady, who is described as flitting at full moon through the long avenue, "sparkling like the spray of a waterfall, as she passes from shadow into light." A second tradition of similar character belongs to Salmesbury Hall between Blackburn and Preston which was formerly said to be haunted by a white apparition, supposed to be the daughter of Sir John Southworth, who was seen to traverse the gallery and corridors, and pass into the garden, where she met her lover, with whom her union had been forbidden. Harland and Wilkinson, *Lancashire Legends*, 1873, p. 264.

White Mary.—" In North Wales," as Pennant informs us, " when they bless another, they are very apt to join to the blessing of God, the blessing of white Mary," evidently alluding to the Virgin Mary.

White Paternoster.—A charm, which seems to have been in use in England and in other parts of Europe from a very early period in lieu of a prayer, and to have been a popular institution nowhere recognised by the church. It has been thought that the term *white* here used is analogous in its signification or import to the idea of mysterious sanctity attached to white objects such as disembodied spirits or souls redeemed from perdition. Comp. *Whiteness*, and see *Charms, Cramp, Leg Charms, Love Charms*, &c. suprà. In the *Antiquary* for March, 1904, E. C. Vansittart has a very interesting paper on this rather obscure subject, and the writer quotes allusions from Chaucer's *Miller's Tale* and several continental sources, drawing attention to the fact that the white paternoster is akin to the familiar rhyme elsewhere printed. " Matthew, Mark, Luke, and John, &c."

Whiteness.—The idea of connecting whiteness with purity of spirit seems to exist in the legendary account of the letiche, a white animal, which is only visible by night, and represents the soul of an unbaptized infant, which may have been supposed to undergo some such purgatorial process, before its reception into grace. The presentment of the spirits of those who have died contrite, or who have expiated their worldly offences otherwise, in the likeness of children in white raiment with glory round them is a common incident in mediæval English fiction. There is a story to the effect in the *Ancren Riwle*.

The readers of our old English romances are probably in no need of being reminded that, towards the close of " Sir Isumbras," the battle which would have been otherwise lost, is decided favourably by the unexpected appearance of three personages " clad in angels wede," one riding on a leopard, a second on a lion, and a third on a unicorn. They discover themselves, after the rout of the Saracens, to be the sons of Sir Isumbras.

In the pleasing story of the *Childe of Bristowe*, where the child's father, a pitiless usurer, has been sent to eternal punishment for his misdeeds, the son strives by acts of benevolence and piety, to procure his parent's delivery from the torments of hell. After a certain time, the boy summons his father's spirit to appear before him in the chamber where the wicked usurer died, and it comes with lightning and thunder, "brennyng as glede," and "The devel be the nekke gan him lede in a brennyng cheyne." The second time, the usurer's ghost presents itself in the room:

> "And as he sate in his prayere,
> The spiret before hym gan appere,
> Right as he dud before,
> Save the cheyn away was caught;
> Blak he was, but he brent noght."

The child's atonement had wrought this; but the process was still incomplete. He had other sacrifices to make, other hardships to endure, other works to accomplish. In fact, the mystical number three is made in the present legend, as in so many others, a necessary agent in the working out of a miraculous interposition. Finally, the usurer's soul is redeemed from perdition, and the last interval between it and its saviour is thus portrayed:

> "When he knelid and prayed long,
> Hym thoght he herd the myriest song
> That any erthly man myght here:
> After the song he sawe a light,
> As thow a thousand torches bright,
> It shone so faire and clere,
> In that light, so faire lemand,
> A naked child in angel hand
> Before him did appere.
> And seid: Sone, blessid thu be,
> And alle that ever shale come of the;
> That ever thu goten were.
> Fader, he seid, ful wel is me,
> In that plite that y now se,
> Y have, that ye be save.
> Sone, he seid, y go to blisse,
> God almighti quyte the this,
> Thi good ageyn to have."

Comp. *White Lady.*

Whitening of Houses.

Pennant, noticing the whitening of houses, says: "This custom, which we observed to be so universally followed from the time we entered Glamorganshire, made me curious enough to enquire into its origin, which it owes entirely to superstition. The good people think that by means of this general whitening they shut the door of their houses against the devil." *Tour through S. Wales*, p. 28.

Whit Monday.

This is the Bank Holiday, and the cart-horse parade takes place.

Whitsun Ales.

For the church ale, says Carew, "two men of the parish are yerely chosen by their last foregoers to be wardens, who, dividing the task, make collection among the parishioners of whatsoever provision it pleaseth them voluntarily to bestow. This they employ in brewing, baking, and other acates, against Whitsontide; upon which holydays the neighbours meet at the church house, and there merily feed on their owne victuals, contributing some petty portion to the stock, which, by many smalls, groweth to a meetly greatnes: for there is entertayned a kind of emulation between these wardens, who by his graciousness in gathering, and good husbandry in expending, can best advance the churches profit. Besides the neighbour parishes at those times lovingly visit one another, and this way frankly spend their money together. The afternoones are consumed in such exercises as olde and yong folke (having leysure) doe accustomably weare out the time. . . . When the feast is ended, the wardens yeeld in their account to the parishioners; and such money as exceedeth the disbursment is layd up in store, to defray any extraordinary charges arising in the parish, or imposed on them for the good of the countrey or the princes service: neither of which commonly gripe so much, but that somewhat still remayneth to cover the purses bottom."

At p. 8 of "A serious Dissuasive against Whitsun Ales," 1736, written by a Gloucestershire clergyman, we read: "These sports are attended usually with ludicrous gestures, and acts of foolery and buffoonery—but children's play, and what therefore grown up persons should be ashamed of." Comp. *Ale.*

In the introduction to his "Natural History of North Wilts," Aubrey gives the following curious account of Whitsun Ales: "There were no rates for the poor in my grandfather's days; but for Kingston St. Michael (no small parish) the church-ale of Whitsuntide did the business. In every parish is (or was) a church house, to which belonged spits, crocks, &c. utensils for dressing provision. Here the housekeepers met and were merry, and gave their charity. The young people were there too, and had dancing, bowling, shooting at butts, &c., the ancients sitting gravely by, and looking on. All things were civil, and without scandal." Browne of Tavistock says:

> "*Willy.* By my booke this is a tale
> Would befit our Whitson-ale:
> Better cannot be I wist,
> Descant on it he that list.

And full gladly giue I wold
The best cosset in my fold,
And a mazor for a fee,
If this song thou'lt teachen me.
'Tis so quaint and fine a lay,
That vpon our reuell day,
If I sung it, I might chance
(For my paines) be tooke to dance
With our Lady of the May."
  The Shepherd's Pipe, 1614, sign. C 6.

Whitsun-Ale, Lord and Lady of the.—A writer in the "Antiquarian Repertory" described a custom prevalent at Whitsuntide in the Cotswold country. But the account given presents no distinctive characteristics. "Two persons," says the narrator, "are chosen previous to the meeting to be Lord and Lady of the Yule (Ale?) who dress as suitably as they can to the characters they assume. A large empty barn, or some such building, is provided for the Lord's hall, and fitted up with seats to accommodate the company. Here they assemble to dance and regale in the best manner their circumstances and the place will afford. Each young fellow treats his girl with a ribbon or favour; the Lord and Lady honour the hall with their presence, attended by the steward, sword-bearer, purse-bearer, and mace-bearer, with their several badges or ensigns of office. They have likewise a page or train-bearer, and a jester drest in party-coloured jacket, whose ribaldry and gesticulation contribute not a little to the entertainment of the company. The Lord's music, consisting generally of a pipe and tabor, is employed to conduct the dance." Description of Sculptures on the outside of St. John's Church, Cirencester, in Carter's "Antient Sculpture," &c. vol. ii. p. 10. See Rudder's "Gloucestershire," 1779, pp. 23, 24 (for the supposed origin of these ales).

Elsewhere we see that the Lady of the Ale was awarded in 1621 at Brentford a gratuity of five shillings.

Whitsunday.—John Squire, Vicar of St. Leonard, Shoreditch, 1587-1653, is good enough to tell us that the day was so named on four grounds: from the time of year, from the custom of the time, from the mercy of God to man, from the mercy of man to man. 1. The time, he says, is *tempus albi solis*, when the season was attended by greatest sunshine: 2. the custom of the time was, that this was *Dominica in Albis;* they used *albis vestibus post baptismum;* 3. The mercy of God to man was shown by the Holy Ghost coming down on man this day; 4. the mercy of man consisted in the gift of white loaves to the poor. But the use of white vestments was, no doubt, the true and sole origin of the expression.

In a monument in the church at Lydington, co. Rutland, to Helen, wife of Robert Hardy, 1486, it is said that the lady died on *Wissonday* in that year. Wright's *Rutland*, 1684, p. 81.

Whitsun Even.—Among the ancient church disbursements of St. Mary at Hill, London, I find the following entry: "Garlands, Whitsunday, iijd." Sometimes also the subsequent: "Water for the funt on Whitsun Eve, id." This is explained by the following extract from Strutt: "Among many various ceremonies, I find that they had one called, 'the font hallowing,' which was performed on Easter Even and Whitsunday Eve; and, says an old homilist, 'in the begynnyng of holy chirch, all the children weren kept to be crystened on thys even, at the font hallowyng; but now, for enchesone that in so long abydynge they might dye without crystendome, therefore, holi chirch ordeyneth to crysten at all tymes of the yeare; save eyght dayes before these evenys, the chylde shalle abyde till the font hallowing, if it may savely for perill of death, and ells not.'"

Whitsuntide.—In Poor Robin's Almanack for 1677, in June, opposite Whitsunday and Holidays, we read:

At Islington A fair they hold, Where cakes and ale Are to be sold.   At Highgate and At Holloway, The like is kept Here every day.   At Totnam Court And Kentish Town, And all those places Up and down."

In the "Country-mans Counsellor," (which is a part of "A help to Discourse," first printed in 1619,) 1627, is the following note: "Likewise it is observed, that, if the sunne shine on Easter Day, it shines on Whitsunday likewise." "In some parts of England, they call it the lamb-playing, which they look for as soon as the sun rises in some clear spring or water, and is nothing but the pretty reflection it makes from the water, which they may find at any time, if the sun rises clear, and they themselves early, and unprejudiced with fancy."—*Athenian Oracle*, vol. ii. p. 348. Naogeorgus says:

"On Whitsunday whyte pigeons tame
    in strings from heauen flie,
And one that framed is of wood still
    hangeth in the skie.
Thou seest how they with idols play,
    and teach the people to;
None otherwise then little gyrles with
    pvppets vse to do."

A superstitious notion appears anciently to have prevailed in England, that "whatsoever one did ask of God upon Whitsunday morning, at the instant when the sun arose and play'd, God would grant it him." Arise Evans says, "I went up a hill to see the sun arise betimes on Whitsunday morning," and saw it at its rising "skip, play, dance, and turn about like a wheel."

In the Churchwardens' Accounts of St. Mary's parish, Reading, we find the following: "A.D. 1557. Item, payed to the morrys daunsers and the mynstrelles, mete and drink at Whytsontide, iijs. iiijd." Parish of St. Laurence, "A.D. 1502. It. payed to Will'm Stayn' for makyng up of the maydens ban' cloth, viijd." "A.D. 1504. It. payed for bred and ale spent to the use of the church at Whitsontyd, ijs. vjd. ob. It. for wyne at the same tyme, xiiijd." "A.D. 1505. It. rec. of the maydens gaderyng at Whitsontyde by the tre at the church dore, the Kyng play at Whitsuntide, xxxvjs. viijd." Comp. *King-Game.*

"At a vestry held at Brentford in 1621, several articles were agreed upon with regard to the management of the parish stock by the chapel-wardens. The preamble stated that the inhabitants had for many years been accustomed to have meetings at Whitsontide, in their church-house and other places there, in friendly manner to eat and drink together, and liberally to spend their monies, to the end neighbourly society might be maintained; and also a common stock raised for the repairs of the church, maintaining of orphans, placing poor children in service, and defraying other charges." In the Accompts for the Whitsontide Ale, 1624, the gains are thus discriminated:

	£	s.	d.
Imprimis, cleared by the pigeon holes	4	19	0
————by hocking . . .	7	3	7
————by riffeling	2	0	0
————by victualling . . .	8	0	2
	22	2	9

The hocking occurs almost every year till 1640, when it appears to have been dropt. It was collected at Whitsuntide:

1618. Gained with hocking at Whitsuntide . . . . . . £16 12s. 3d.

The other games were continued two years later. Lysons' "Environs," vol. ii. p. 55. In p. 54, are the following extracts from the Chapel Warden's Account Books:

	£	s.	d.
1620. Paid for 6 boules . .	0	0	8
———— for 6 tynn tokens	0	0	6
———— for a pair of pigeon holes	0	1	6
1621. Paid to her that was Lady at Whitsontide, by consent	0	5	0
— Good wife Ansell, for the pigeon holes . . .	0	1	6

	£	s.	d.
— Paid for the games . .	1	1	0
1629. Received of Robert Bicklye, for the use of our games	0	2	0
— Of the said R. B. for a silver bar which was lost at Elyng . . .	0	3	6
1634. Paid for the silver games	0	11	8
1643. Paid to Thomas Powell, for pigeon holes . . .	0	2	0

The following occur in the Churchwardens' Books at Chiswick:

1622. Cleared at Whitsuntide	5	0	0
— Paid for making a newe of pigeing holes . . .	0	2	6

Ibid. vol. ii. p. 221.

They have a custom at Whitsuntide at Lichfield, it appears from Mr. Fienne's MSS., quoted by Southey, on Monday and Tuesday, called the Green Bower Feast, by which they hold their charter. The sheriff and bailiff assist at the ceremony of dressing up babies with garlands and greens, and carry them in procession through all the streets; and then they assemble themselves at the market-place, and go in a procession through the great street to a hill beyond the town, where is a large green bower made, in which they have their feast. Many smaller bowers are made round for company, and for booths to sell sweetmeats, etc.

At Ensham in Oxfordshire, in the Whitsun season, the townspeople were allowed to cut down and carry away as much timber as they could lay in the abbey-yard, the churchwardens making the first chop on the trees. As much as they could carry out, in spite of the opposition of the servants, they were to keep for the reparation of the church. By this service they kept the right of commonage. Hazlitt's edit. of Blount's *Tenures*, 1874, p. 116.

Whitsun-Tuesday.—By his will in 1729 Thomas Fairchild, of Shoreditch, gardener, left £25 for a sermon on this day in the afternoon on "the wonderful Works of God in the Creation" or on "the Certainty of the Resurrection of the Dead, proved by the certain Changes of the Mineral and Vegetable Parts of the Creation." Ellis, *St. Leonard Shoreditch*, 1798, p. 277. The benefaction was subsequently (1733) increased to £171 by his nephew and others. *Ibid:*, pp. 286-7.

Whittle-gate.—A curious custom formerly prevalent in Cumberland in the case of poor schoolmasters. See Halliwell in v.

"Crossthwaite church, in the Vale of Keswick, in Cumberland, have five chapels belonging to it. The minister's stipend is £5 per annum, and goose-grass, or the right of commoning his geese; a whittlegait, or the valuable privilege of using his knife for a week at a time at any table in the parish; and lastly a hardened sark, or a shirt of coarse linen." —*Park*. In Northumberland a species of coarse linen is called Harn.—*Brand*.

Whooping-cough. — The "Worcester Journal," in one of its issues for 1845, had this astounding item : " A party from this city, being on a visit to a friend who lived at a village about four miles distant, had occasion to go into the cottage of a poor woman, who had a child afflicted with the whooping-cough. In reply to some inquiries as to her treatment of the child, the mother pointed to its neck, on which was a string fastened, having nine knots tied in it. The poor woman stated that it was the stay-lace of the child's godmother which, if applied exactly in that manner round about the neck, would be sure to charm away the most troublesome cough ! Thus it may be seen that, with all the educational efforts of the present day, the monster superstition still lurks here and there in his caves and secret places."

And in a Monmouthshire paper of the same period there was a second recipe of an equally philosophical and enlightened character. " A few days since an unusual circumstance was observed at Pillgwenlly, which caused no small degree of astonishment to one or two enlightened beholders. A patient ass stood near a house, and a family of not much more rational animals were grouped round it. A father was passing his little son under the donkey, and lifting him over its back a certain number of times, with as much solemnity and precision as if engaged in the performance of a sacred duty. This done, the father took a piece of bread, cut from an untasted loaf, which he offered the animal to bite at. Nothing loath, the Jerusalem pony laid hold of the bread with his teeth, and instantly the father severed the outer portion of the slice from that in the donkey's mouth. He next clipped off some hairs from the neck of the animal, which he cut up into minute particles, and then mixed them with the bread which he had crumbled. This very tasty food was then offered to the boy who had been passed round the donkey so mysteriously, and the little fellow having eaten thereof, the donkey was removed by his owners. The father, his son, and other members of his family were moving off, when a bystander inquired what all these 'goings on' had been adopted for? The father stared at the ignorance of the inquirer, and then in a half contemptuous, half condescending tone, informed him that 'it was to cure his poor son's hooping-cough, to be sure !' Extraordinary as this may appear, in days when the school-master is so much in request, it is nevertheless true."

Whores, Punishment of.—It was a custom in England to cut the sinews of the legs and thighs of whores, that is, to hamstring them. " Meretrices et impudicas mulieres subnervare." Jacob, *Law Dict.* v. *Subnervare*. This statement is to be received with allowance. It was rather an occasional punishment. Comp. Hazlitt's edit. of Blount's *Tenures*, 1874, p. 433, and *Bawdry* supra. In *A Chronicle of London*, 1089-1483, 4°, 1827, and in Riley's *Memorials*, 1868, are entries illustrative of this subject and of the dress to be worn by women of bad repute within the civic jurisdiction. The most plausible solution of the metamorphosis of the *meretrix* into the courtezan is that such folks were apt to be of lax morality, and to be thrown in the way of temptation. Several of our eminent lawyers, to their cost, married their laundresses.

Whorpell or **Warpell-way.**—A foot and perhaps bridle path between common fields, which it seems from entries in manorial records to have been usual from time to time to lay out and define. The term occurs in Surrey, Sussex, Norfolk, &c. In the first-named county there are examples at Putney, Mortlake, and Wimbledon. In Putney the actual Cooper's Arms Lane was formerly known as the Warpell-way, and is so marked on old plans. Halliwell explains *warps* to mean "distinct pieces of ploughed land separated by the furrows," and states that the word is current in East Sussex and Kent. See *Notes and Queries*. April 6, 1889. A second track towards the Ridgeway at Wimbledon similarly bore the name. The thoroughfare in Putney partly preserves the ancient nomenclature in *Warpole Road*.

Whuppity Scoorie.—The ancient custom at Lanark of Whuppity Scoorie, the origin and meaning of which are lost, has just been celebrated, and watched by a crowd of adults. The town bell is rung nightly at six o'clock from March to September and then lies dumb for six months. On the first night of the ringing all the young folk congregate at the cross, and after parading three times round the parish church the Lanark lads meet the New Lanark boys in a free fight, in which the only legitimate weapons are their caps tied at the end of pieces of string. *Daily Mail*, March, 4, 1903.

Widowhood.—It seems to have been a practice of very high antiquity for widows of station not to remarry within a twelvemonth of the decease of the first husband. In a letter to Dr. Alexander

Legh, his representative at the Court of the King of Scots, written in 1477, Edward IV. reminds him that he has come to no decision respecting the proposed second nuptials of the Duchess of Burgundy and the Duke of Albany on this account—" forsomoch as aftre the old usaiges of this our Royaume noon estat ne person honourable commeth of mariage within the yere of their doole."—Ellis's *Original Letters,* 1st Series, i, 17. Where the tenants of the crown *in capite* left widows, the latter had to assign their dowers to the sovereign, and to become his or her wards, and might not marry again without the royal consent. *Ibid.* 2nd S. i, 89.

Wife.—The superstition that a wife is a marketable commodity, was entertained, to his misfortune, by one Parson Cheken, or Chicken, in the reign of Queen Mary, for in his " Diary," Henry Machyn notes under the year 1553: "The xxiiij of November, dyd ryd in a cart Cheken, parson of Sant Necolas Coldabbay, round abowt London, for he sold ys wyff to a bowcher."

This superstition still prevails among the lowest of our vulgar, that a man may lawfully sell his wife to another, provided he deliver her over with a halter about her neck. It is painful to observe, that instances of this frequently occur in our newspapers; but is becoming of more and more rare occurrence, and may be securely regarded as one of those vestiges of barbarous ignorance which are fast dying out from among us. Yet in the *Daily Telegraph* newspaper for January 18, 1868, there is the following extract: "The *Blackburn Standard* reports that on Saturday afternoon last a mechanic, named Thomas Harland, sold his wife to another man, named Lomax, for the sum of 20s., and all parties being agreeable to the bargain, Mrs. Harland has been transferred to her new husband. The following agreement has been drawn up and signed by the parties : 'Blackburn, Jan. 11, 1868: This is to certify to all whom it may concern, that I, Thomas Harland, of Blackburn, do relinquish all my conjugal rights to my wife, Sarah Ellen Harland, in favour of Henry Lomax, for the sum of 1l. sterling. As witness our hands, &c., Thomas Harland ; witness, Philip Thomas and George Swarbrick." Harland has since announced that he will not be answerable for any debts his late wife may contract."

Wigan and Lancashire Sports.—At Wigan there was formerly for the purpose of general athletic exercises and amusements a properly prepared course of three miles, on part of the site of which lay the Wigan Cricket Ground 20 years ago. The names of the competitors had to be given in to the town bailiff, and 5s. deposited as entrance fee for the chief race for a plate of £10 value. The sports lasted for several days. They were publicly advertised during every market day for over a month before, with the hope of inviting distant competitors. These races for footmen afterwards gave place to horse races on the same ground; but there are no races at Wigan now. *Globe,* Jan. 15, 1904. Racecourses and other large open areas in the vicinity of towns, while land was less valuable, were not unfrequent or unusual.

Wild Mare.—An old name for the game of *see-saw.*

Wilfrid, St.—See *Ripon.*

Will o' the Wisp or **Kit with the Canstick (Candlestick).**—Wisp, in the name of this phenomenon, implies a little twist of straw, a kind of straw torch. Thus Junius in verbo: " Frisiis ' wispien,' etiamnum est ardentes straminis fasciculos in altum tollere." These names have undoubtedly been derived from its appearance, as if Will, Jack, or Kit, or some country fellows, were going about with lighted straw torches in their hands. In the West of England, the will-o'-wisp is known under this name, and also under that of Joan-in-the-Wad. In the vulgar dialect of Newcastle-upon-Tyne, it has been corrupted into weeze.

In Warwickshire, mab-led (pronounced mob-led) signifies led astray by a will-o'-the-wisp. This was the Mab of fairy-lore. It had the title also of " Gyl burnt-Tayle or Gillion a burnt Taile." So in Gayton's " Festivous Notes upon Don Quixot," 1654, p. 268, we find " An *Ignis fatuus,* an exhalation and Gillion a burnt traile, or will with the wispe." Also in p. 97, " Will with the wispe, or Gyl burnt tayle."

It is called also a Sylham lamp. Thus we find in Gough: " In the low grounds at Sylham, just by Wingfield in Suffolk, are the Ignes fatui, commonly called Sylham lamps, the terror and destruction of travellers and even of the inhabitants, who are frequently misled by them." Reginald Scot, before he mentions " Kit with the Kanstick," has the words " Sylens," which, I have no doubt, is a corruption of the above Sylham.

This appearance, called in Latin *ignis fatuus,* has long composed an article in the catalogue of popular superstitions. Clowns, however, are not the only persons who have been misled by it, for as the subsequent account of it will evince, it has hitherto eluded the most diligent pursuit of our writers of natural history.

Thomas White defines it to be a certain

viscous substance, reflecting light in the dark, evaporated out of a fat earth, and flying in the air. It commonly haunts church-yards, privies and fens, because it is begotten out of fatness: it flies about rivers, hedges, &c. because in those places there is a certain flux of air. It follows one that follows it, because the air does so. *Peripatetical Institutions*, 1656, p. 148. "The Scotish Encyclopædia" defines it to be "a kind of light, supposed to be of an electric nature, appearing frequently in mines, marshy places, and near stagnating waters." The account adds: "It was formerly thought, and is still by the superstitious believed, to have something ominous in its nature, and to presage death and other misfortunes. There have been instances of people being decoyed by these lights into marshy places, where they have perished; whence the names of Ignis fatuus, Will with a Wisp, and Jack with a Lanthorn, as if this appearance was an evil spirit, which took delight in doing mischief of that kind."

Willsford says: "The lowest meteor in the air is the burning candle, or as some call it, Ignis fatuus. This is a hot and moist vapour, which striving to ascend, is repulsed by the cold, and fired by Antiperistasis, moves close by the earth, carried along with the vapours which feed it, keeping in low and moist places. The light is of an exceeding pale colour, very unwholesome to meet withal, by reason of the evil vapours it attracts unto it, which nourishes the pallide flame, and will often ascend (as those exhalations do,) and as suddenly fall again, from whence the name is derived." He adds: "These pallid fires appear but at some times of the year, and that in certain places: and in those parts where they are most usual, they are not commonly seen, but as forerunners of sultry heat in sommer, and wet in the winter: they are usually observed to appear in open weather." *Nature's Secrets*, 1658, pp. 56, 120.

Gregory writes much to the same effect: "Hujusmodi flammulas Philosophi ad Meteora traducunt, causantes Exhalationem ad infimam Aëris regionem elevatam, ibique per Antiperistasin accensam (Garatum leges) quæ dum ascendere nititur, frigore mediæ Regionis depellitur, et apparet quasi saltans loca decliviora quærens, unde et ad Aquas sequentem ducit, sæpe etiam in magnis Tempestatibus aut velis affigitur aut præcedit vel sequitur. Meteorol. fol. 50. Stellulas istas sic a philosophis fabrefactas, ne non sibi aliisve quid altum sapere videantur, vocaverunt Ignes fatuos." *Ibid.*

The ignis fatuus is said to have been observed to stand still as well as to move, and sometimes to seem fixed on the surface of the water. This phenomenon is supposed to be chiefly seen in summer nights, frequenting meadows, marshes, and other moist places. It is often found also flying along rivers and hedges, as if it met there with a stream of air to direct it.

Sir Isaac Newton calls it a vapour shining without heat, and says that there is the same difference between this vapour and flame, as between rotten wood shining without heat, and burning coals of fire. Some have supposed, among whom were Willoughby and Ray, that the ignis fatuus is nothing more than some nocturnal flying insect. Bradley thought it to be a group of such. Derham, on the other hand, thought this phenomenon was composed of fixed vapours. In favour of Ray's hypothesis, we are informed that the Ignes fatui give proof as it were of sense by avoiding objects: that they often go in a direction contrary to the wind, that they often seem extinct, and then shine again: that their passing along a few feet above the ground or surface of the water agrees with the motion of some insect in quest of prey: as does also their settling on a sudden, as well as their rising again immediately. Some indeed have affirmed that Ignes fatui are never seen but in salt marshes, or other boggy places. On the other hand, it is proved that they have been seen flying over fields, heaths, and other dry places.

What follows from *A Help to Discourse*, 1638, is a curious sample of the old ideas vulgarly prevalent under the present head: "Q. What fire is that which sometimes followes and sometimes flyeth away? —A. An Ignis fatuus, or a walking fire (one whereof keepes his station this time near Windsor) the pace of which is caused principally by the motion of the ayre enforcing it." Should this be considered as not very satisfactory, what will be thought of the subsequent explanation from the *Cabinet of Nature*, 1637? : "Q. What is the cause of the Ignis fatuus, that either goes before or follows a man in the night?— A. It is caused of a great and well compacted exhalation, and being kindled, it stands in the aire, and by the man's motion the ayre is moved, and the fire by the ayre, and so goes before or follows man: and these kinds of fires or meteors are bred near execution places, or church yards, or great kitchens, where viscous and slimy matters and vapours abound in great quantity."

Widely different are the sentiments of Pennant on this subject: speaking of the winter gull, he says, that "it frequents, during winter, the moist meadows in the inland parts of England, remote from the sea. The gelatinous substance known by the name of star-shot, or star jelly, owes its origin to this bird, or some of the kind, being nothing but the half digested remains of earthworms, on which these birds feed and often discharge from their stomachs." *Zoology*, ii, 538. He refers to Morton's "Natural History of Northampton."

The mystery and difficulty attendant on the solution of this appearance under a variety of conditions are simply due to the former ignorance prevailing even among the majority of learned persons of chemical laws and principles. The phosphorescence observed on the fur of animals is no longer ascribed to supernatural causes.

The Cambridge men find it possible, when they are on the river, to ignite the phosphoric weed, which floats on the surface of the water; and throughout the fen-country the will o' the wisp is a familiar phenomenon, beginning perhaps to be better understood.

One of the popular attributes of the ignis fatuus, as has been already noticed, is the love of mischief in leading men astray in dark nights, which in Drayton's "Nymphydia" is given to the Fairy Puck:

"Of purpose to deceive us:
And leading us makes us to stray
Long winter nights out of the way,
And when we stick in mire or clay,
  He doth with laughter leave us."

Hentzner, who was in England in 1598, tells us, that returning from Canterbury to Dover, "there were a great many Jack-w'-a-Lanthorns, so that we were quite seized with horror and amazement." Edit. 1757, p. 101. Elsewhere it is remarked: "No, it may be conjectured that some Ignis fatuus, or a fire drake, some William with a wispe, or some gloworme illumination did inlighten and guide them." *A Personall Treaty with his Majesty*, 1648, p. 81.

We gather from Boreman's *Description of a Great Variety of Animals*, &c. vol. ii. that a respectable person in Hertfordshire, presuming upon the knowledge of the grounds about his house, was tempted one dark night to follow one of these lights, which he saw flying over a piece of fallow ground. It led him over a ploughed field, flying and twisting about from place to place—sometimes it would suddenly disappear, and as suddenly appear again. It once made directly to a hedge; when it came near, it mounted over, and he lost sight after a full hour's chase. On his return home he saw it again, but was already too much fatigued to think of renewing the pursuit.

At Astley, seven miles from Worcester, three gentlemen once saw one of these appearances in a garden about nine o'clock in a dark night. At first they imagined it to be some country fellow with a lanthorn, till approaching within about six yards, it suddenly disappeared. It became visible again in a dry field, thirty or forty yards off. It disappeared as suddenly a second time, and was seen again a hundred yards off. Whether it passed over the hedge, or went through it, could not be observed, for it disappeared as it passed from field to field. At another time, when one approached within ten or twelve yards, it seemed to pack off as if in a fright. Hutchinson, speaking, in the parish of Whitbeck, of a lake on the estate of R. Gibson, Esq., at Barfield, observes: "Here, and in the adjoining morasses, is much of that inflammable air which forms the lucid vapour vulgarly called Will with the wisp, frequently seen in the summer evenings." *Cumberland*, 1552.

The expression in the "Tempest," act iv. sc. 1, "Played the Jack with us" is explained by Johnson, "he has played Jack with a lanthern, he has led us about like an Ignis fatuus, by which travellers are decoyed into the mire."

Milton's "Frier's Lantern" in L'Allegro, is the Jack and lantern, says Warton, which led people in the night into marshes and waters.

There are innumerable literary references to the present superstition, some of no weight or interest, some merely figurative—but I may append a selection: Thus in Langland's "Piers Plowman," written about 1350,

"—That alle that herde that horn
Helde hir noses after
And wisshed it hadde been wexed
With a wispe of firses."

Will-with-a-wisp occurs in Fletcher's drama of "The Captain," written about 1613. In "The Vow-breaker," 1636, act. ii. sc. 1, we read: "Ghosts, hobgoblins, Will with a wispe, or Dicke a Tuesday." In Glapthorne's "Albertus Wallenstein," 1640, we find:

"Your wild irregular lust which like
    those fire-drakes
Misguiding nighted travellers, will lead
    you
Forth from the fair path," &c.
        ——"A wand'ring fire
Compact of unctuous vapour, which the
    night
Condenses, and the cold environs round
Kindled through agitation to a flame,
Which oft, they say, some evil spirit
    attends,
Hovering and blazing with delusive
    light,

Misleads th' amaz'd night-wand'rer
  from his way
To bogs and mires, and oft through
  pond and pool,
There swallow'd up and lost, from suc-
  cour far."
  —*Milton's Par. Lost*, book ix. l. 634.

"How Will a' Wisp misleads night-
  faring clowns,
O'er hills, and sinking bogs, and path-
  less downs."
  —*Gay.*

"Sæpe autem, dum Tecta petunt, vesti-
  gia fallit
Materiâ pingui exoriens erraticus Ignis;
(Quem densant Tenebræ, circumdant
  Frigora, donec
Sæpe agitando rapit spatiosam in
  fomite flammam).
Ille per aërios fallaci lumine campos
Cursitat, erroresque vagos seducit in
  altum
Nocte silente Lacum, alit sparsas per
  prata paludes."
—*Woodward's "Rusticæ Nundinæ,"*
(*Poems*, 1730, p. 139.).

"Ah homely swains! your homeward
  steps ne'er lose;
Let not dank Will mislead you on the
  heath,
Dancing in mirky night, o'er fen and
  lake
He glows to draw you downward to
  your death,
In his bewitch'd, low, marshy, willow
  brake!
What though far off, from some dark
  dell espied,
His glimmering mazes cheer th' excur-
  sive sight,
Yet turn, ye wand'rers, turn your steps
  aside,
Nor trust the guidance of that faithless
  light."
Collins, *Ode on the Superstitions of the
Highlands*, 1788.

Lady Bradshaigh, writing to Richardson, the novelist, in relation to their meeting in the Park, when he did not recognise
her, remarks: "I . . . had an opportunity
of surveying you unobserved, your eyes
being engaged amongst the multitude,
looking, as I knew, for a certain gill o'
the wisp, who, I have a notion, escaped
being known by you."

Mr. Thomas Wright, in his series of
papers on the "Superstitions, &c. of the
Middle Ages," 1846, notices the fifollets or
feux-follets, which were regarded with the
same awe and mysterious terror in France
as our ignis fatuus, and similarly looked
upon as malignant spirits haunting
marshes and bogs.

In Italy two kinds of these lights are
said to have been discovered; one, in the
mountains, the other in the plains: they
are called by the common people cularsi,
because they look upon them as birds, the
belly and other parts of which are resplendent like the pyraustæ, or fire-flies.

In an account by Ignatio Somis of the
preservation and deliverance of three
women, buried thirty-seven days in the
ruins of a stable, by a heavy fall of snow
from the mountains, at the village of
Borgomoletto, in Italy, 1755, it is stated
that on the melting of the snow, &c., when
the unhappy prisoners "seemed for the
first time to perceive some glimpse of
light, the appearance of it scared Anne
and Margaret to the last degree, as they
took it for a forerunner of death, and
thought it was occasioned by the dead
bodies; for it is a common opinion with
the peasants, that those wandering wild-
fires which one frequently sees in the open
country, are a sure presage of death to
the persons constantly attended by them,
whichever way they turn themselves, and
they accordingly call them death-fires."
Comp. *Elf-Fire* and *Castor and Pollux.*

Willesden.—See *Walsingham.*

Wind.—Pomponius Mela, who wrote
in the reign of the Emperor Claudius,
mentions a set of priestesses in the Island
of Sena, or the Ile des Saints, on the coast
of Gaul, who were thought to have the
quality of troubling the sea and raising
the winds by their enchantments, being,
however, subservient only to sea-faring
people, and only to such of them as come
on purpose to consult them.

The power of confining and bestowing
is attributed to Eolus in the "Odyssey."
Calypso, in other places of the same work,
is supposed to have been able to confer
favourable winds.

The winds have had their properties assigned to them in our weather folk-lore:

"When the wind is in the east,
'Tis neither good for man nor beast;
When the wind is in the north,
The skilful fisher goes not forth;
When the wind is in the south,
It blows the bait in the fishes' mouth;
When the wind is in the west,
Then it is at the very best."

In Sinclair's "Statistical Account of
Scotland," the minister of Kirkmichael,
in the county of Banff, tells us: "On the
first night of January, they observe, with
anxious attention, the disposition of the
atmosphere. As it is calm or boisterous;
as the wind blows from the S. or the
N.; from the E. or the W., they prognosticate the nature of the weather till
the conclusion of the year. The first night
of the new year, when the wind blows from
the west, they call dàr-na coille, the night
of the fecundation of the trees; and from

this circumstance has been derived the name of that night in the Gaelic language. Their faith in the above signs is couched in verses (thus translated) : "The wind of the S. will be productive of heat and fertility ; the wind of the W. of milk and fish ; the wind from the N. of cold and storm ; the wind from the E. of fruit on the trees." xii, 458.

Martin (*W. Isl. of Scotland*, 166) says that it was an ancient custom among the Islanders to hang a he-goat to the boat's mast, hoping thereby to procure a favourable wind.

The Laplanders, says Scheffer, have a cord tied with knots for the raising of the wind ; they, as Ziegler relates it, tie their magical knots in this cord : when they untie the first, there blows a favourable gale of wind ; when the second, a brisker ; when the third, the sea and wind grow mighty, stormy, and tempestuous. This, he adds, that we have reported concerning the Laplanders, does not in fact belong to them, but to the Finlanders of Norway, because no other writers mention it, and because the Laplanders live in an inland country. However, the method of telling winds is this : "They deliver a small rope with three knots upon it, with this caution, that when they loose the first they shall have a good wind ; if the second, a stronger ; if the third, such a storm will arise that they can neither see how to direct the ship and avoid rocks, or so much as stand upon the decks, or handle the tackling."

Windsor Hill.—Sir Hugh Platt mentions a curious circumstance relative to pears in this locality. "Trees that beare earlie," he says, "or often in the yeare, as pear-trees vpon Windsor-hill, which beare three times in a yeare ; these, though they be removed to as rich, or richer ground, yet they doe seldom beare so early, or so often, except the soile bee of the same hot nature, & haue the like advantages of situation, and other circumstances, with those of Windsore. And therfore commonly, the second fruite of that peare-tree beeing remooued, doth seldome ripen in other places." This information Platt had from his correspondent Mr. Andrew Hill. The pear intended is probably the Windsor pear. *Flora's Paradise*, 1608, p. 140.

Wine in the Church at Marriage.—This custom is enjoined in the Hereford Missal. "Post Missam, Panis, et Vinum, vel aliud bonum potabile in Vasculo proferatur, et gustent in nomine Domini, Sacerdote primò sic dicente : ' Dominus vobiscum.' "

By the Sarum Missal it is directed that the sops immersed in this wine, as well as the liquor itself, and the cup that contained it, should be blessed by the priest : — " Benedicatur Panis et Vinum vel aliud quid potabile in Vasculo, et gustent in nomine Domini Sacerdote dicente, Dominus vobiscum.' The form of Benediction ran thus : " Benedic Domine panem istum et hunc potum et hoc vasculum, sicut benedixisti quinque panes in Deserto et sex hydrias in Chanaan Galileæ, ut sint sani et sobrii atque immaculati omnes gustantes ex iis," &c.

The beverage used on this occasion was to be drunk by the bride and bridegroom and the rest of the company. This was as important a ceremony as the *Confarreatio* elsewhere referred to and explained. "Certe et in Græcorum ritibus, Compotatio est in Ecclesia nuptialis, quæ Confarreationis vicem videtur præstare." —Seldeni *Uxor Hebraica*, Opera, tom, iii, p. 668.

In the articles ordained by Henry VII. for the regulation of his household, "Article for the Marriage of a Princess," we read : "Then pottes of ypocrice to bee ready, and to be put into the cupps with soppe, and to be borne to the estates ; and to take a soppe and a drinke," &c. In Dekker's "Satiro-Mastix," 1602, we read : "And when we are at church bring out the wine and cakes." Farmer has adduced a line in an old canzonet on a wedding, set to music by Morley, 1606 : "Sops in wine, spice cakes are a-dealing."

The allusions to this custom in our old plays are very numerous ; as in Shakespear's "Taming of the Shrew," where Gremio calls for wine, gives a health, and having quaffed off the muscadel, throws the sops in the sexton's face. In the beginning of Armin's "History of the Two Maids of Moreclacke," 1609, the serving-man, who is perfuming the door, says : "The Muscadine stays for the bride at church." Again, in Fletcher's "Scornful Lady," act i. sc. 1, there is an allusion to the hippocras and cakes. In Jonson's "Magnetic Lady," the wine drunk on this occasion is called "a knitting cup." In the "Compleat Vintner," &c. a poem, 1720, p. 17, the writer says :—

"What priest can join two lovers hands,
But wine must seal the marriage-bands ?

*   *   *   *   *

As if celestial wine was thought
Essential to the sacred knot,
And that each bridegroom and his bride
Believ'd they were not firmly ty'd,
Till Bacchus, with his bleeding tun,
Had finish'd what the priest begun."

The present usage is followed by the modern Russians.

Winifred's Well, St. — In the "Travels of Tom Thumb" by Robert Dodsley, we read : "A man would be inexcusable that should come into North

Wales and would not visit Holywell or St. Winifride's Well, and hear attentively all the stories that are told about it. It is indeed a natural wonder, though we believe nothing of the virgin and her rape; for I never felt a colder spring, nor saw any one that affords such a quantity of water. It forms alone a considerable brook which is immediately able to drive a mill."

Pennant, in his account of this well, says: "After the death of that saint, the waters were almost as sanative as those of the Pool of Bethesda: all infirmities incident to the human body met with relief: the votive crutches, the barrows, and other proofs of cures, to this moment remain as evidences pendent over the well. The resort of pilgrims of late years to these fontanalia has considerably decreased. In the summer, still a few are to be seen in the water in deep devotion up to their chins for hours, sending up their prayers, or performing a number of evolutions round the polygonal well, or threading the arch between well and well a prescribed number of times." Elsewhere he adds: "The bathing well at Whiteford is an oblong, 38 feet by 16, with steps for the descent of the fair sex, or of invalids. Near the steps, two feet beneath the water, is a large stone, called the wishing-stone. It receives many a kiss from the faithful, who are supposed never to fail in experiencing the completion of their desires, provided the wish is delivered with full devotion and confidence. On the outside of the great well, close to the road, is a small spring, once famed for the cure of weak eyes. The patient made an offering to the nymph of the spring of a crooked pin, and sent up at the same time a certain ejaculation, by way of charm: but the charm is forgotten, and the efficacy of the waters lost. The well is common."

Lilly relates that in 1635 Sir George Peckham, Knt. died in St. Winifred's Well, "having continued so long mumbling his paternosters and *Sancta Winifreda ora pro me*, that the cold struck into his body, and after his coming forth of that well he never spoke more." *Hist. of his Life and Times*, 32.

An account of a miracle pretended to have been wrought at this well will be found in a pamphlet entitled, "Authentic Documents relating to the miraculous Cure of Winefrid White, of Wolverhampton, at Winefrid's Well, alias Holywell, in Flintshire, on the 28th of June, 1805; with observations thereon, by the R. R. J—M." 1806.

Winlaton Hopping.—The *Newcastle Daily Chronicle* of May 21, 1889, contained the subjoined description of this festival: "There was stir, excitement, and hilarity at Winlaton yesterday. The occasion was the annual hopping, and the old-fashioned Front Street, with its cottage buildings, small shops, and somewhat twisted thoroughfare, was for the nonce the locality in which some thousands of holiday-keepers passed their time. Winlaton hopping is one of the oldest social gatherings that northern records can show. It is probably the oldest fixture of the kind in the district. There are some, however, who can remember when the annual gathering was a different affair to what it is now. It has always been on the Monday and Tuesday following the 14th of May, and it has always been preceded by what is known as "Hopping Sunday." Every house was first of all almost turned inside out, previous to being put into apple-pie order for the reception of visitors. When the Sunday came, with the regularity of clock work there came with it all the absent Winlatonians from a distance, with hearty greetings to their friends and relatives, to eat of the veal and ham and new cabbage which formed the universal dish of the village on that particular day, and to join in the revels of the two or three days and nights succeeding. This custom is still to some extent followed in the village; but it is slowly but surely dying out. Winlaton at that period might almost have been described as the abode of Vulcan. There were smithies to be found at every quarter of it, and the spot on which the biggest show-ground was situate yesterday was only thirty or forty years ago a pond, on the margin of which there was situate a band of blacksmiths' shops, from which the loud clang of the hammer was heard, and out of which dust-begrimed, stalwart forms issued as regularly as meal-time came. At the high end of the village—where the Drill Hall now stands—and in some of the back streets, smithies in tolerably large numbers were once to be found.

The old-fashioned hopping does not embrace many attractions. There were a good many small stalls, with their loads of sweet stuffs and spice, but the only showman who used to put up an appearance was old Tommy Elliott, an itinerant exhibitor, with his peep-show containing views of Earl Grey's Monument, Grey Street, and other places in Newcastle. The views were excellent, the places represented had not long been built by Grainger, and Tommy did a roaring trade. He was popular in the village; he either took coppers or brass buttons for a peep at his wonderful collection, and "females and boys under 12 years of age," as is the custom with some exhibitions now, were not debarred from sharing in the entertainment. Then the poets honoured the hopping with their verse. There were two songs upon it which have survived from among the rest, regarding one of which—written a good many years ago by John Leonard, of Gateshead, Mr. Allan, in his Tyneside Collection, says it is worthy of a place beside "Swalwell Hopping," as being descriptive of the customs of our country visitors. The rhymester dilates in this song on the mirth in the village, the recreation at Tench's hotel, and a score of scenes that were enacted over and over again in the main street. Tench's hotel would at that time occupy the site now held by the Highlander Inn.

During the last year or two the Hopping has swelled to proportions that have drawn to the village thousands from the neighbouring places. This year's hopping actually commenced on Saturday, but yesterday was regarded, strictly speaking, as the opening day. In the town generally the amusements were of a modernized and commonplace type. But at the upper end of Front Street it was more on the old-fashioned style; for the stalls, with their pyramids of candy and spice, and the shooting galleries and the swings were principally of the kind our forefathers used to see fifty or sixty years ago.

"We talk neither about politics nor religion as to-day happens," remarked a Winlaton man in the street, and really it looked like it, for the street was filled with a merry crowd all day, and at night the people in their hundreds were mounting the steep from Blaydon to Winlaton, and from several other directions were pouring into the village. The hopping, in accordance with usual custom, will be continued to-day, and there may possibly be something in the nature of a wind-up to-morrow. The romping fun and rowdyism that marked the hopping of a long since departed time are now conspicuous by their absence, and visitors will now find only healthful recreation, abundance of mirth, and innocent pleasure. The hopping, like the crowds, is well conducted, and if this could be managed at other places, no one would have cause to regret the revival in the old class of public entertainment that seems at many parts of the North of England to have set in.

Winning the Kail.—In Scotland termed Broose, in Westmoreland called Riding for the Ribbon. The race from the church to the bride's door used to be formerly on horseback, and was called "Riding the bruse;" and he who reached the goal first, won the bruse, a species of spice-broth, otherwise called kail.—Atkinson's *Cleveland Glossary*, 1868. This

is mentioned under the present title in "The Collier's Wedding":

"Four rustic fellows wait the while
To kiss the bride at the church-stile:
Then vig'rous mount their felter'd steeds—
—To scourge them going, head and tail,
To win what country call 'the kail.'"
See *Riding.*

Winwaloe's Day, St.—(March 3). The name of the saint is variously spelled, Winwalli, Winwolano, Vinwoley, Walovay, etc., and it appears that he was Abbot of Tauracune in Brittany. A section of a modern work is devoted to the district of St. Winwaloe, in Cornwall, of which he was the patron saint, and which derived its name from him. *Churches and Antiquities of Cury and Gunwalloe*, by A. H. Cummings, 1875, pp. 116-32, 182-7.

An account of this British saint is given by Butler. There is no doubt that the name was pronounced at a very early date, Winnaloe, and that even abbreviated into Winnol. The stormy weather, which is usual at this season, is known in some districts as Winnol-weather. In Forby's time (he died in 1825), some remains still existed of the priory or cell of St. Winwaloe at Wereham, in Norfolk, at which place a celebrated horse-fair (subsequently, for the sake of convenience, removed to Downham market) used to be held on the anniversary-day.

Wise Men and Women.—Cotta says: "This kinde is not obscure, at this day swarming in this kingdom, whereof no man can be ignorant, who lusteth to observe the uncontrouled liberty and licence of open and ordinary resort in all places unto wise-men and wise-women, so vulgarly termed for their reputed knowledge concerning such diseased persons as are supposed to be bewitched." *Tryall of Witchcraft*, 1616, 60. The same author elsewhere says: "the mention of witchcraft doth now occasion the remembrance in the next place of a sort of practitioners whom our custome and country doth call wise men and wise women, reputed a kind of good and honest harmless witches or wizards, who by good words, by hallowed herbes, and salves, and other superstitious ceremonies, promise to allay and calme divels, practises of other witches, and the forces of many diseases." *Short Discoverie of Unobserved Dangers*, 1612, p. 71.

Wishing Wells.—See *Walsingham.*

Witch.—A term applied to a man in *Gesta Romanorum*, edit. Madden, 1838, p. 456, and in Wicliff's New Testament.

Witch is from Anglo-Saxon *wicca*. In Low Latin, the word *veijus* stands for a sorcerer. It is now exclusively applied to the female sex. In the "Promptorium

Parvulorum," "wytche" is apparently a synonym for ephialtes or the night-mare.

Witchcraft.—Witchcraft is defined by Scot to be, "in estimation of the vulgar people, a supernatural work between a corporal old woman and a spiritual devil:" but, he adds, speaking of his own sentiments on the subject, "it is, in truth, a cozening art, wherein the name of God is abused, prophaned, and blasphemed, and his power attributed to a vile creature." *Discovery*, 1584, ed. 1665, 284. Perkins, in his *Discourse of Witchcraft*, 1608, defines witchcraft to be an art serving for the working of wonders by the assistance of the devil, so far as God will permit. Delrio defines it to be an art in which, by the power of the contract entered into with the devil, some wonders are wrought, which pass the common understanding of men. Witchcraft, in modern estimation, is a kind of sorcery (especially in women), in which it is ridiculously supposed that an old woman, by entering into a contract with the devil, is enabled in many instances to change the course of nature, to raise winds, perform actions that require more than human strength, and to afflict those that offend her with the sharpest pains.

Gibbon, speaking of the laws of the Lombards, A.D. 643, tells us: "The ignorance of the Lombards, in the state of paganism or Christianity, gives implicit credit to the malice and mischief of witchcraft : but the judges of the seventeenth century might have been instructed and confounded by the wisdom of Rotharis, who derides the absurd superstition, and protects the wretched victims of popular or judicial cruelty." He adds in a note: "See 'Leges Rotharis,' No. 379, 47. Striga is used as the name of witch. It is of the purest classical origin (Horat. 'Epod.' v. 20, Petron. c. 134), and from the words of Petronius (quæ Striges comederunt nervos tuos?) it may be inferred that the prejudice was of Italian rather than barbaric extraction." There is the passage in Ovid :

"Nocte volant, puerosque petunt nutricis egentes ;
Et vitiant cunis corpora rapta suis.
Carpere dicuntur lactentia viscera rostris ;
Et plenum poto sanguine guttur habent."

—*Fasti*, lib. iv. l. 135.

It seems very reasonable to suppose with Mr. Gomme that the germ of much of the belief in witchcraft and fairy-lore is to be sought in the ancient habit of isolation by certain persons or groups of persons belonging to communities and the consequent superstition, which was apt to grow up respecting them and their nature, where there was an absence of all education and culture, and everything was judged by the dictates of instinct and self-protection. *Folk-Lore Society, Presidential Address*, 1894, p. 55. It may be added that necromancy was apparently imputed in remote times to the cave-dwellers, whose resorts were particularly inaccessible, and who in some cases pursued callings beyond the vulgar comprehension. *Torrent of Portugal*, a Romance, ed. Halliwell, 1842, viii.

One of the most curious, if not earliest, examples of a belief in witchcraft is connected with the interview in the Isle of Thanet between Ethelbert, King of Kent, and St. Augustine in the open air, which was purposely so arranged, lest, had it taken place under a roof, the strangers might have practised some unlawful arts on the King. For this anecdote there is the authority of Bede.

In the legendary story of Hereward the Saxon appears the wise woman of Brandon, near Ely, who from a scaffold erected in the fen before the walls, delivered an anathema against Hereward and his ally the Abbot of Ely, and it is related that, ere the witch could pronounce her malediction the third time, the scaffold was set on fire by the Saxons, and the woman burned or killed. Hazlitt's *Tales and Legends*, 1892, pp. 188-90.

The destruction of innumerable objects of antiquity was, it has been surmised, partly due to a belief that they were the work of enchantment, and that the spell could only be broken by their disappearance. The bronzes and sculptures, which we at present so greatly covet, were regarded by the priest-ridden people as dangerous idols. Wright's *Wanderings of an Antiquary*, 1854, p. 52.

A passage in one of the "Towneley Mysteries" points to a very curious, yet very common superstition in this, as well as in other countries, in former times—the power of evil spirits to produce deformity upon a child at its birth. The hour of midnight was looked upon by our forefathers as the season when this species of sorcery was generally accomplished. The passage referred to above is as follows :

"*Tercius Pastor.* I know him by the eere marke : that is a good tokyn.
Mak. I telle you, syrs, hark : hys noys was broken.
Sythen told me a clerk, that he was forspokyn.
Primus Pastor. This is a false work. I wold fayn be wrokyn :
Gett wepyn

Uxor. He was takyn with an elfe:
I saw it myself.
When the clok stroke twelf,
    Was he forshapyn."

In Grafton's "Chronicle," it is laid to
the charge (among others) of Roger
Bolingbroke, a cunning necromancer, and
Margery Jordane, the cunning witch of
Eye, that they at the request of Eleanor,
Duchess of Gloucester, had devised an
image of wax representing the King
(Henry VI.) which by their sorcery by
little and little consumed: intending
thereby in conclusion to waste and destroy
the king's person. Shakespear mentions
this in the second part of Henry VI. act
i. sc. 4. But a more particular account
of the matter may be found in *A Chronicle
of London* under 20 Henry VI. (1441-2),
where the penance imposed on the duchess
and the punishment of her accomplices are
described. "In this yere my lady of
Gloucestre hadde confessyd here wichecraft, as it is aforeseid she was yoyned be
alle the spriualte assent to penaunce," and
the duchess came from Westminster to
London and landed at Temple Bridge from
her barge, and there she took a taper of
wax weighing two pounds in her hand, and
went through Fleet Street barefoot and
hoodless to St. Paul's, where she offered
up her taper at the high altar. On the
Wednesday following she came again by
barge to the Swan in Thames Street,
whence she proceeded barefoot through
Bridge street and Gracechurch street to
Leadenhall and St. Mary Cree. On Friday
she disembarked at Queenhithe, and
walked to Cheapside and St. Michael's
Cornhill. And on each of these occasions
she was met at the landing place by the
Mayor, Sheriffs, and Crafts of London.
The duchess was interned at Chester for
life.

A document, purporting to be the confession of Bernard de Vignolles, dated
from Rouen, March 14, 1495-6, charges
Sir John Kendal, Grand Prior of the
Order of St. John of Jerusalem at Rhodes,
Sir John Tong his nephew, a knight of
that order, and others, of a treasonable
design to compass the death of Henry VII.
by necromancy, with a view to the establishment on the throne of Perkin Warbeck.
Plumpton Correspondence, 1839, p. 120,
Note.

See Servius on the 8th Eclogue of
Virgil; Theocritus, Idyl. ii. p. 22; Ovid
says:

"Devovet absentes, simulacraque cerea
    figit
Et miserum tenues in jecur urget acus."
    —*Heroid. Ep.* vi. l. 91.

The following is from "The First Part

of the Contention between the Houses of
Lancaster and Yorke," 1594:

"*Elinor.* What sir Iohn Hum, what
newes with you?

Sir John. Iesus preserue your Maiestie.

Elinor. My Maiestie. Why man I am
but grace.

Sir Iohn. I, but by the grace of God and
Hums aduise, your graces state shall be
aduaunst ere long.

Elinor. What hast thou conferd with
Margery Iordaine the cunning witch of
Ely, with Roger Bullingbrooke and the
rest, and will they vndertake to do me
good?

Sir Iohn. I haue Madame, and they haue
promised me to raise a spirite from depth
of vnder ground, that shall tell your grace
all questions you demand."

The foregoing appeared, on the whole,
to be too curious an illustration to be
overlooked. Further on in the drama
Bolingbrooke invokes the spirit, and a
scene occurs, rather too lengthy for transcription, where Bolingbroke interrogates
it. The whole can be read in my Shakespear's Library. This is farther illustrated
by a passage in one of Daniel's Sonnets
printed with Sydney's "Astrophel," 1591:

"The slie inchanter, when to work his
    will
And secret wrong on some forspoken
    wight,
Frames Waxe, in forme to represent
    aright
The poore unwitting wretch he meanes
    to kill,
And prickes the image, fram'd by
    magicks skill,
Whereby to vex the partie day and
    night."

And by another in Constable's "Diana,"
1594:

"Witches which some murther do in-
    tend
    Doe make a picture and doe shoote
        at it;
    And in that part where they the pic-
        ture hit,
The parties self doth languish to his
    end."

Andrews tells us, speaking of Ferdinando,
Earl of Derby, who in the reign of Queen
Elizabeth died by poison, "The credulity
of the age attributed his death to witchcraft. The disease was odd, and operated
as a perpetual emetic, and a waxen image,
with hair like that of the unfortunate
Earl, found in his chamber, reduced every
suspicion to certainty." *Cont. of Henry*,
4° ed. p. 98, and *Gentl. Mag.* for 1751, p.
269. The Earl died April 16, 1594.

In "The First Part of Edward IV." by
T. Heywood, 1600, the Duchess of York is
made to say to Edward her son:

"O Edward, Edward! Fly, and leave
this place,
Wherein, poor silly king, thou art enchanted.
This is her dam of Bedfords work, her
mother,
That hath bewitched thee, Edward, my
poor child."

The scene where Richard accuses Hastings
of conspiring with others to bewitch him
occurs in the "True Tragedie of Richard
the Third," 1594. But in the "True
Tragedie of Richard Duke of York," 1595,
Richard is made to impute his deformity
to natural causes.

Stow prints a form of oath taken by one
of the parties to a wager of battle in
connection with the title to some land in
the Isle of Harty, adjoining Sheppey, in
Kent, in 1571, and it runs thus: "This
heare, you justices, that I haue this day
neither eate, drunke, nor haue upon me
either bone, stone, ne glasse, or any in-
chantment, sorcerie, or witchcraft, where-
through the power of the word of God
might be inleased or diminished, and the
diuels power increased: . . ." *Annals*,
1615, p. 669.

It appears from Strype's *Annals*, sub
anno 1589, that "one Mrs. Dier had
practised conjuration against the Queen,
to work some mischief to her Majesty:
for which she was brought into question:
and accordingly her words and doings
were sent to Popham the Queen's attorney
and Egerton her solicitor by Walsingham
the secretary and Sir Thomas Heneage
her vice chamberlain, for their judgement,
whose opinion was that Mrs. Dier was not
within the compass of the statute touching
witchcraft, for that she did no act, and
spake certain lewd speeches tending to
that purpose but neither set figure nor
made pictures." Sub anno 1578, Strype
says: "Whether it were the effect of
magic, or proceeded from some natural
cause, but the Queen was in some part of
this year under excessive anguish by pains
of her teeth: insomuch that she took no
rest for divers nights, and endured very
great torment night and day."

King James tells us that "the devil
teacheth how to make pictures of wax or
clay, that, by roasting thereof, the persons that they bear the name of may be
continually melted, or dried away by continual sickness." *Demonology*, p. 2, c. 5.

The faith in waxen images long survived, for Blagrave, who wrote about 1675,
observes that "the way which the witches
usually take for to afflict man or beast in
this kind, is, as I conceive, done by image
or model, made in the likeness of that
man or beast they intend to work mischief
upon, and by the subtilty of the devil
made at such hours and times when it shall
work most powerfully upon them by thorn,
pin, or needle, pricked into that limb or
member of the body afflicted." *Astrological Practice of Physic*, p. 98. Coles says
that witches "take likewise the roots of
mandrake, according to some, or as I
rather suppose the roots of briony, which
simple folke take for the true mandrake,
and make thereof an ugly image, by which
they represent the person on whom they
intend to exercise their witchcraft." He
tells us elsewhere: "Some plants have
roots with a number of threds, like beards,
as mandrakes, whereof witches and im-
posters make an ugly image, giving it the
form of the face at the top of the root,
and leave those strings to make a broad
beard down to the feet." *Art of Simpling*,
26, 66.

In ancient times even the pleasures of
the chase were checked by the superstitions
concerning witchcraft. Thus Reginald
Scot says: "That never hunters nor their
dogs may be bewitched, they cleave an
oaken branch, and both they and their
dogs pass over it." Ed. 1665, p. 152.

On March 11, 1618-19, Margaret and
Philip Flower, daughters of Joane Flower,
were executed at Lincoln for the supposed
crime of bewitching Henry Lord Roos,
eldest son of Francis Manners, Earl of
Rutland, and causing his death; also, for
most barbarously torturing by a strange
sickness Francis, second son of the said
Earl, and Lady Katherine, his daughter;
and also, for preventing, by their diabolical arts, the said Earl and his countess
from having any more children. An account was printed of this affair in 1619.
Walter Yonge, M.P. for Honiton, in his
"Diary" under 1606, notices a case of
witchcraft, which occurred in the family
of Dr. Holland, rector of Exeter College,
in Oxford. He says: "This year there
was a gentlewoman and near kinswoman
to Doctor Holland's wife, rector of Exon
College in Oxford, strangely possessed and
bewitched, so that in her fits she cast out of
her nose and mouth pins in great abundance, and did divers other things very
strange to be reported."

At Cambridge in 1620, while the crusade
against witchcraft was in full vigour, they
had a separate place of confinement for
this class of offender, called the Witches'
Gaol, which was separated by a partition
from the felons' gaol in the Jew's House
given to the town in 1224 by Henry III.
Atkinson and Clarke's *Cambridge*, 1897,
p. 93.

There is a relation printed in 1643 of a
witch, who was taken by the Parliament's
forces, as she was standing on a small
plank, and so sailing over the river at
Newbury. Hazlitt's *Coll. and Notes*,
1903, p. 28.

Bewitched persons were said to fall frequently into violent fits and vomit needles, pins, stones, nails, stubbs, wool, and straw. This was an artifice of the medical profession, which Jorden exposes in the "Suffocation of the Mother," &c. 1603, p. 24, where he says: "Another policie Marcellus Donatus tells us of, which a physition used towardes the Countesse of Mantua, who being in that disease which we call melancholia Hypochondriaca, did verily believe that she was bewitched, and was cured by conveying of nayles, needles, feathers, and such like things into her close-stoole when she took physicke, making her believe that they came out of her bodie."

It is related in the " Life of Lord Keeper Guildford," p. 131, that when his lordship was upon the circuit at Taunton Dean, he detected an imposture and conspiracy against an old man charged with having bewitched a girl of thirteen years of age, who, during pretended convulsions, took crooked pins into her mouth and spit them afterwards into bye-standers' hands. Comp. *Hogarth Moralized*, and *Medley.*

Heath tells us, "Some few of the inhabitants of the Scilly Islands imagine, (but mostly old women,) that women with child and the first born are exempted from the power of witchcraft." *Hist. of Scilly Islands*, p. 120.

In "Macbeth," act iii. sc. i., Shakespear expresses a current belief at the period that a witch, assuming the form of an animal with a tail, was unable to compass the caudine appendage, in the passage:

"*First Witch.* —In a seive I'll thither sail,
And, like a rat without a tail,
I'll do, I'll do, I'll do."

Steevens seems to have thought that this was simply because there was no part of a woman correspondent to the tail in a rat or other animal.

Jonson, in his " Masque of Queenes," 1609, introduces the following description of the witches' meeting: "These witches, with a kind of hollow and infernall musique, came forth from thence. First one, then two, and three, and more, till theyr number encreased to eleuen : all differently attired : some wth ratts on theyr heads : some on their shoulders : others wth oyntment-potts at theyr girdles ; all with spindells, timbrells, rattles, or other veneficall instruments, making a confused noyse, wth strange gestures. . . . . These eleuen witches beginning to daunce (w[ch] is an usual ceremony at theyr convents, or meetings, where, sometimes, also, they are vizarded and masqu'd), &c."

Bacon tells us that " the ointment that witches use, is reported to be made of the fat of children digged out of their graves : of the juices of smallage, wolf-bane, and cinque-foil, mingled with the meal of fine wheat : but I suppose the soporiferous medicines are likest to do it, which are hen-bane, hemlock, mandrake, moon-shade, or rather night-shade, tobacco, opium, saffron, poplar-leaves," &c.

Scot prescribes the subsequent charm against witchcraft. "To unbewitch the bewitched, you must spit in the pot where you have made water. Otherwise spit into the shoe of your right foot before you put it on : and that Vairus faith, is good and wholesome to do, before you go into any dangerous place." *Discovery*, ed. 1665, 152.

Witchcraft Abroad. — A remarkable piece of romantic fiction appeared in 1609, founded, it is to be presumed, on some Spanish legend, under the title of *The Famous and renowned History of Morindos a King of Spaine : Who maryed Miracola a Spanish Witch ; and of their seauen daughters, rightly surnamed Ladies with bleeding hearts : their births, their liues, and their deathes. A History most wonderfull, strange, and pleasant to the reader.*

It is well known that "the wife of Marshal d'Ancre was apprehended, imprisoned, and beheaded for a witch, upon a surmise that she had enchanted the Queen of France to doat upon her husband : and they say, the young King's picture was found in her closet, in virgin wax, with one leg melted away. When asked by her judges what spells she had made use of to gain so powerful an ascendancy over the Queen, she replied, 'that ascendancy only which strong minds ever gain over weak ones."

It was in 1634 that the famous Urban Grandier was, at the instigation of Cardinal Richelieu whom he had satirized, tried and condemned to the stake, for exercising the black art on some nuns of Loudun in the Viennois, who were supposed to be possessed.

An early number of the " Gentleman's Magazine " supplies the following story : " A man at a village near Mortagne in France had been long ill of a distemper, which puzzled the physicians : his wife believed he was bewitched, and consulted a pretended conjurer, who shewed her the wizard (her husband's uncle) in a glass of water, and told her, that to oblige him to withdraw the charm, they must beat him and burn the soles of his feet. On her return she sent for the uncle, and with the assistance of her relations beat him unmercifully, and burnt the soles of his feet, and the crown of his head in such a manner, that in two days after he died. The woman and her accomplices were seized. She owned the fact, and said if it was to do again, she would do it. This happened in December last. * * * * * * The Tournelle condemned the woman to be hanged for the above fact, but the account adds, that "great interest was making to get her sentence commuted, the fact proceeding from conjugal affection." *Gents. Mag.* January and August, 1731.

Sir H. Ellis was the first, I believe, to notice that Aubrey, in his "Remains of Gentilism," refers to the meeting of witches on May-day Eve, on a mountain called the Blocks-berg, in the Hartz range in Germany, to dance and feast there; adding, that the people to guard themselves against their malignant influence, stick at their doors a particular thorn— the white thorn elsewhere mentioned.

The following is from the "Gentleman's Magazine" for 1775 : "Nov. 15. Nine old women were burnt at Kalisk, in Poland, charged with having bewitched and rendered unfruitful the lands belonging to a gentleman in that Palatinate."

The following is from the "Gentleman's Magazine" for January, 1731. "Of Credulity in Witchcraft" : "From Burlington to Pensilvania 'tis advised, that the owners of several cattel believing them to be bewitched, caused some suspected men and women to be taken up, and trials to be made for detecting 'em. Above three hundred people assembled near the Governour's House, and a pair of scales being erected, the suspected persons were each weighed against a great Bible : but, all of them vastly outweighing it, the accused were then tied head and feet together, and put into a river, on supposition, that if they swam they must be guilty. This they offered to undergo, in case the accusers should be served in the like manner : which being done, they all swam very buoyant and cleared the accused. A like transaction happened at Frome in Somersetshire in September last, published in the 'Daily Journal,' Jan. 15, relating that a child of one Wheeler, being seized with strange fits, the mother was advised by a cunning man to hang a bottle of the child's water, mixed with some of its hair, close stop'd, over the fire, that the witch would thereupon come and break it; it does not mention the success; but a poor old woman in the neighbourhood was taken up, and the old trial by water-ordeal reviv'd. They dragg'd her, shiv'ring with an ague, out of her house, set her astride on the pommel of a saddle, and carried her about two miles to a mill-pond, stript off her upper cloaths, tied her legs, and

with a rope about her middle threw her in, two hundred spectators aiding and abetting the riot. They affirm she swam like a cork, tho' forced several times under the water ; and no wonder, for when they strained the line, the ends thereof being held on each side of the pond, she must of necessity rise ; but by haling and often plunging, she drank water enough, and when almost spent, they poured in brandy to revive her, drew her to a stable, threw her on some litter in her wet cloaths, where in an hour after she expired. The Coroner upon her inquest could make no discovery of the ring-leaders : altho' above forty persons assisted in the fact, yet none of them could be persuaded to accuse his neighbour : so that they were able to charge only three of them with manslaughter."

See also Keysler, "De Mulieribus Fatidicis," *ad calcem* "Antiq. Select. p. 371 ; Mallet's "Northern Antiquities," transl. by Percy, vol. i. ; "Notes to the Edda," vol. ii. ; Henry's "Hist. of Gr. Brit." 4to. ed. (Andrews' Contin. pp. 35, 196-8, 207, 303, 374) ; Gyffard's "Discourse of Witches," &c. 1587 ; "An Endeavour towards a Defence of the Being of Witches and Apparitions," by a F.R.S., 1666 ; and Hutchinson's "Essay," 1718, cap. 2. Among foreign publications, "De Lamiis et Phitonicis Mulieribus, ad illustrissimum Principem Dominum Sigismundum Archiducem Austrie Tractatus pulcherrimus," (1489,) "Compendium Maleficarum," 1626, "Tractatus duo singulares de examine Sagarum super Aquam frigidam projectarum," 1686, and "Specimen Juridicum de nefando Lamiarum cum Diabolo Coitu," per J. Hen. Pott, 1689. Comp. *Amulets, Charms, Divination, Spells, Spirits, Sorcery,* &c. suprâ, the General Index to Hazlitt's *Bibl. Coll.* 1893, and his *Proverbs,* 1882.

The present entry might be almost interminably extended, if one were to multiply examples from all available sources, and include all the points of view from which the human species has looked at this question, and the diversity of methods for guarding against the evil or danger. The Siamese lets off fireworks at his New Year's festival, and makes a stupendous uproar, to frighten away witches, and the natives of Barotseland will not approach too close to the Victoria Falls, because they regard them as the work and abode of supernatural spirits.

Witchcraft in Cornwall, 1853.—(From the Notes of the late T. Q. Couch of Bodmin). The notion that mysterious contracts are formed between evil spirits and wicked men is a very old and wide spread one, though with us it has become obsolete. In the present day such a bargain is but rarely suspected, and but few are found hardy enough to declare that they are parties to so unholy a transaction. There are, however, even now occasional instances of persons who do not scruple to declare that they have bartered their future well-being for present power and advantage. A poor unhappy fellow, but lately dead, pretended, in vulgar parlance, to have "sold himself to the devil," and was consequently looked on by his neighbours as a miracle of impiety. Not that he was actively vicious; for if he had supernatural powers of ill-doing, he was never known to use them to the detriment of others, except indeed when the depth of his potations had not left him cash enough to pay the reckoning. He was then accustomed to hold his hat up the chimney, and demand money, which was promptly showered down into it. The coin so obtained the landlord invariably refused, with a shudder, and was glad to get quit of him on these terms.

The faculty of witchcraft is thought to be hereditary, and on this account alone many really good-natured persons are kept aloof from by their neighbours, and rendered miserable by being the object of all manner of unkind suspicions. They are studiously shunned, or, when communication with them cannot be avoided, their ill-wish is deprecated by a slavish deference. If met on the highway care is taken to pass them on the right hand.

For some inexplicable reason the power of witchcraft is most frequently delegated to females. These witches are supposed to have the power of changing their shape and resuming it at will. An old woman, who was ugly, lame, and cross-tempered, in fact the very ideal of a witch, is said to have met with her lameness in the following way. A hare of very large size, remarkably fleet of foot, and very wily, was occasionally met with in various parts of the parish, and though it had been frequently pursued, had always wearied or baffled the hounds. It had been fired at times without number, and according to our best shots had carried off incredible quantities of lead. At length it came to be conferred as something more than an ordinary hare. On a certain day it crossed the path of two or three determined sportsmen, who followed it for many miles, and fired several rounds at it with the usual want of success. Before relinquishing the chase, one of the party suggested the trial of silver bullets, and accordingly silver coins were beat into slugs for the purpose. The hare was again seen, fired at, and this time wounded, but not so effectually as to prevent its running round the brow of a hill and disappearing among the rocks. The sportsmen searched eagerly, but vainly for it; the hare was however nowhere to be seen; but crouched under a shelving rock was old Molly, panting and flushed as if from a hard chase. From that day forward she was noticed to have a limp in her gait.

The toad and the black cat are among the most usual attendants of the witch, or rather the forms which her imps most commonly assume. The appearance of a toad on the door-step is taken for a certain sign that the house is under malign influence, and the poor animal is put to some frightfully barbarous death.

The most common results of the witch's malice, or, as it is termed, "the ill-wish," are, misfortunes in business, diseases of an obstinate and deadly character in the family or among the cattle. The cow refuses "to give down" her milk, the butter is spoilt, or the household tormented by incredible quantities of those animalcules said by Sir Hugh Evans to be "familiar to man, and to signify love." There are a hundred ways in which the evil influence may be manifested.

When witchcraft is suspected, the person "overlooked" has immediate recourse to the conjurer, the very bad representation of the astrologer of a former age. The conjurer is an important character in a Cornish village. He is resorted to by despairing lovers: he counsels those under the evil eye, and discloses the whereabouts of stolen goods. His answers, too, are given with true oracular ambiguity. "Own horn eat own corn," was his reply to a person who consulted him about the disappearance of various little household articles. When appealed to in cases of suspected witchcraft, the certainty of weird influence is proved beyond doubt, and the first letter of the witch's name, or a description of her person, is given, or even, it is said, her bodily presence depicted on a mirror. The certainty of the ill-wish being thus established, and the person of the witch fixed on, the remembrance of some past "difference" or quarrel places the matter beyond doubt.

One of the various methods of dissolving spells is now resorted to. It is a belief that the power for evil ceases the moment blood is drawn from the witch, and our newspapers not unfrequently record instances of assault, when the intention was in this way to break the witch's spell. When an ox or other animal has died in consequence of the ill-wish, it is usual to take out the heart, stick it over with nails and pins, and roast it before the fire until they have one by one dropped from it, during which process the witch is supposed to be suffering in mysterious sympathy with the roasting heart. There are many stories told of how the wicked woman has been, by these means, driven to confess, and to loose the family from the spell.

The wiser method of prevention is very often taken, and the house, with all its contains, is protected from harm by nailing a horse-shoe over the centre of the doorway. No evil spirit can come in its neighbourhood, and it has the power of rendering all ill-wishes harmless to those who are under its guard. There are few farmhouses without it, and scarcely a vessel or boat puts to sea without its horse-shoe nailed to the mast or bowsprit. Another preventative of great fame is the mountain ash or care tree. Comp. *Horseshoe.*

Besides the witch and conjurer, we have yet another and a more pleasing character to mention. The charmer is generally an elderly female, supposed to be gifted with supernatural power, which she exercises for good. By her incantations and ceremonies she stops blood, and cures inflamed eyes and erysipelas (*vulgò* wildfire). I know but little of her doings, and have heard only one of her many charms, which is good for an inflammation, and runs thus :—

"There were two angels came from the east,
One brought fire, the other frost :
Out fire !—in frost !"

(Here follows the name of the Trinity.) It seemed necessary to give an account of this—the most debasing of all our superstitions, in order to render the subject of our popular antiquities complete. For the sake of lessening, in some degree, the feeling of humiliation which the contemplation of this subject must bring, I append, as an encouraging contrast, the following interesting and original letter, containing an account of a case tried at Exeter, where the witch was, in open court, gravely put to the ordeal of the creed and Lord's prayer. The letter is dated September ye 14th, 1696, and was addressed to the Bishop of Exeter by Archdeacon Blackburne.

" My most Hon^d. Lord.

" Y^r Lordship was pleas'd to command me by Mustion to attend the tryal of ye witch, and give you some account of it : It was thus.—

" Elizabeth Homer, alias Turner, was arraigned on several inditements for mourthering Alice the daughter of Thomas and Elizabeth Bovet, and for pining and lameing Sarah and Mary daughters of ye same Thomas and Elizabeth Bovet.

" The evidence given wch was anything material was thus :—

" Thomas Bovet the father swears that Alice the youngest of ye three daughters being about four years old was taken very ill in her belly & that physitians cou'd see no natural cause of her illness and y^t she died in 5 days. That Mary was so taken likewise. Her body strangely distorted and her legs twisted like the screw of a gun ; that she would often goe w^h her eyes shut into the fire and say that Bett Homer drove her in, continued thus above 7 weeks. She was about 10 years old.

" That Sarah 9 years old was taken after ye same manner, complaining of being scratch'd in bed by a cat wch she said was Bett Homer whom she describ'd exactly in the apparel she had on, tho' the child had not seen her in 6 months before.

" That after their imprisonment they were both tormented by pinching and biting, al ye time crying out stil on Bett Homer, at present the prints of pinches and marks of teeth appearing on their arms and cheeks, (this point attested also by Justice Anchestor who was wth the children at the time.) that they would vomit pins and stones ; 2 crooked pins came away in Sarah's water. Sarah cry'd out the witch had put a pin into her, the print of one appeared just under the skin, and at last it came out upon her middle finger ; cry'd out of being struck by ye witch wth a stick the mark of which stroke appear'd at the time upon her ankle. Sarah said that Bett Homer told her how she kill'd Alice by squeezing her breath out of her body, and that she had a teat on her left shoulder which was suck't by toads.

" Elizabeth Bovet the mother depos'd in like manner concerning Alice who continued ill 5 days and so dy'd crying out, why doe you kill me ? That Sarah and Mary were taken ill alternately not able to say their prayers, saying they were threaten'd by the witch if they should doe it to be served by her as Alice was, and that she made 'em swear and curse. That they were both of late very hungry, and being asked why they were so, they said the head of Bett Homer came off of her body and went into their belly which wou'd when they laid so appear to be prodigiously swell'd and the swelling abate all of a sudden when they said it was gone out of 'em again.

" That Sarah walk't up a wall 9 foot high 4 or 5 times backwards and forwards her face and forepart of her body parallel to the ceeling of ye room saying at the time that Bett Homer carry'd her up.

" The children were also produced in court who gave the same account sensibly enough, Mary adding further that she saw Bett Homer in her ful shape playing with a toad in a basin and leaving it suck her at a nipple between her breast and shoulder.

"Alice Osborn swore that she threaten'd her upon refusing her some barm; she afterwards found a vessel, after she had wash'd it for brewing, fill'd full of drink which they threw away, and then brewing and filling y⁰ vessel wᵗʰ drink in 4 or 5 days neither she nor her husband having drawn any she found it quite empty, and as dry as if no drink had ever been in it. That Bett Homer threaten'd her husband saying, Thou hast children as well as others, and if I come home again I'll mind some of 'em.

"John Fursey depos'd to his seeing her three nights together upon a large down in the same place as if rising out of the ground.

"Margaret Armiger deposed that on y⁰ Saturday before the tryal when the witch was in prison she met her in the country at about 20 foot distance from her.

"Mary Stephens deposes she took a red hot nail, and drove it into the witches left foot-step upon which she went lame and being search'd her leg and foot appear'd to be red and fiery, that she continued so 4 or 5 days when she pull'd up the nail again and then the witch was well. This is what was most material against her.

"The witch deny'd all and shew'd her shoulder bare in court, when there appear'd nothing but a kind of mole or wart, as it seem'd to me. She said the Lord's Prayer, stopping a little at Forgive us our trespasses, but recover'd and went on, and she repeated the Creed without a fault.

"My Lord Chief Justice by his questions and manner of summing up the evidence seem'd to me to believe nothing of witchery at all, and to disbelieve the fact of walking up the wall which was sworn by the mother. The jury brought her in not guilty. * * * * * *

"My Lord
Yʳ Lps
most oblig'd and
most obedient humble servᵗ
Blackburne."

See *Life of the Right Hon. Francis Blackburne*, by Edward Blackburne, 8⁰, 1874.

Witchcraft in Ireland. — See *Ireland*.

Witchcraft in Scotland. — Andrews, speaking of the profligate Bothwell, says, in a note: "It seems strange that an author so respectable as Mr. Guthrie should allow any discredit to the asseverations in a will in which the testator affirms, 'that, as he had from his youth addicted himself much to the art of enchantment at Paris and elsewhere, he had bewitched the Queen (Mary) to fall in love

with him," &c. &c. *Cont. of Henry's Hist. of Britain,* &c., p. 178.

In the "Flyting betwixt Montgomery and Polwart," 1629, (but written about fifty years before), there is a graphic description of "thir venerable virgines, whom the world call witches," which is curious, as being the production of a Scotish pen, and illustrating the notions on the subject then entertained in that country.

Spottiswood, cited by Andrews in his Continuation of Henry says: "In the North" (of Britain) there were "matronlike witches and ignorant witches." It was to one of the superior sort that Satan, being pressed to kill James the Sixth, thus excused himself in French, "Il est homme de Dieu."

From the "News from Scotland declaring the Damnable Life and Death of Dr. Fian," 1591, it appears that, having tortured in vain a suspected witch with "the pilliwinckes upon her fingers, which is a grievous torture, and binding or wrenching her head with a cord or rope, which is a most cruel torture also, they, upon search, found the enemy's mark to be in her forecrag, or forepart of her throat, and then she confessed all." Dr. Fian was by the king's command consigned on this occasion "to the horrid torment of the boots," and afterwards strangled and burnt on the Castle-hill, Edinburgh, on a Saturday in the end of January, 1591-2.

In the Diary of Robert Birrell is inserted some curious memorials of persons suffering death for witchcraft in Scotland. "1591, 25 of Junii, Euphane M'Kalzen ves brunt for vitchcrafte. 1592. The last of Februarii, Richard Grahame wes brunt at ye Crosse of Edinburghe, for vitchcrafte and sorcery. 1593. The 19 of May, Katherine Muirhead brunt for vichcrafte, quha confest sundrie poynts therof. 1603. The 21 of Julii, James Reid brunt for consulting and useing with Sathan and witches, and quha wes notably knawin to be ane counsellor with witches. 1605. July 24th day, Henrie Lowrie brunt on the Castle Hill, for witchcraft done and committed be him in Kyle, in the parochin." *Fragm. of Scotish History,* 1798.

Ramsay, in his "Gentle Shepherd," has made great use of this superstition. He introduces a clown telling the powers of a witch in the following words:

"She can o'ercast the night, and cloud
  the moon,
And mak the deils obedient to her crune.
At midnight hours o'er the kirkyards
  she raves,
And howks unchristen'd weans out of
  their graves:
Boils up their livers in a warlock's pow,
Rins withershins about the hemlock's
  low;

And seven times does her pray'rs back-
    ward pray,
Till Plotcok comes with lumps of Lap-
    land clay,
Mixt with the venom of black taids and
    snakes;
Of this unsonsy pictures aft she makes
Of ony ane she hates; and gars expire
With slaw and racking pains afore a
    fire:
Stuck fou of prines, the divelish pictures
    melt;
The pain by fowk they represent is felt.''

Afterwards he describes the ridiculous
opinions of the country people, who never
fail to surmise that the commonest natural
effects are produced from supernatural
causes.

" When last the wind made glaud a
    roofless barn;
When last the burn bore down my
    mither's yarn;
When brawny elf-shot never mair came
    hame;
When Tibby kirnd, and there nae butter
    came;
When Bessy Freetock's chuffy-cheeked
    wean
To a fairy turn'd, and could nae stand
    its lane;
When Wattie wander'd ae night thro'
    the shaw,
And tint himsel amaist amang the snaw;
When Mungo's mare stood still and swat
    with fright,
When he brought East the howdy under
    night;
When Bawsy shot to dead upon the
    green,
And Sarah tint a snood was nae mair
    seen;
You, Lucky, gat the wyte of aw fell out,
And ilka ane here dreads you round
    about.'' &c.

The register shows that, in the
parish of Auchterhouse, co. Forfar, a fast
was observed, July 9, 1646, partly " because of the pregnant scandal of witches
and charmers within this part of the land,
we are to supplicate the Lord therefore.''
The registers also contain the following
entries to the present purpose: " 6
Januare, 1650. On that day the minister
desired the Session to make search every
ane in their own quarter gave they knew of
any witches or charmers in the paroch,
and delate them to the next Session.''
" July 18, 1652. Janet Fife made her
public repentance before the pulpit, for
learning M. Robertson to charm her child;
and whereas M. Robertson should have
done the like, it pleased the Lord before
that time to call upon her by death.''

The reservoir for the Gairie Mills, at Kir-
riemuir, in the same county, was formed
out of a circular pond, commonly called
the Witch-Pool. The books of Mid-Calder,
co. Edinburgh, confirm the statements
that witches used to be burned.

The minister of Kirkmichael, Banffshire, writing about 1795, says: " In this
county, the 12th of May is one of the
witches' festivals. On the morning of that
day, they are frequently seen dancing on
the surface of the water of Avon, brushing
the dews of the lawn, and milking cows in
their fold. Any uncommon sickness is
generally attributed to their demoniacal
practices. They make fields barren or
fertile, raise or still whirlwinds, give or
take away milk at pleasure. The force
of their incantations is not to be resisted,
and extends even to the moon in the midst
of her aërial career. It is the good fortune, however, of this country to be provided with an anti-conjurer that defeats
both them and their sable patron in their
combined efforts. His fame is widely
diffused, and wherever he goes, *crescit
eundo*. If the spouse is jealous of her
husband, the anti-conjurer is consulted to
restore the affections of his bewitched
heart. If a near connection lies confined
to the bed of sickness, it is in vain to
expect relief without the balsamick medicine of the anti-conjurer. If a person
happens to be deprived of his senses, the
deranged cells of the brains must be adjusted by the magic charms of the anti-
conjurer. If a farmer loses his cattle, the
houses must be purified with water
sprinkled by him. In searching for the
latent mischief, this gentleman never fails
to find little parcels of heterogeneous ingredients lurking in the walls, consisting
of the legs of mice and the wings of bats;
all the work of the witches. Few things
seem too arduous for his abilities; and
though, like Paracelsus. he has not as yet
boasted of having discovered the Philosopher's Stone; yet by the power of his
occult science he still attracts a little of
their gold from the pockets where it
lodges and in this way makes a shift to
acquire subsistence for himself and
family.'' *Stat. Acc.* xii, 465.

The minister of a Perthshire parish
records that he had known "An instance
in churning butter, in which the cream,
after more than ordinary labour, cast up
only one pound of butter, instead of four,
which it ought. By standing a little while
to cool, and having the labour repeated
over again, it cast up the other three
pounds of butter.'' This was about 1795.
Stat. Acc. xviii, 123, xix, 354.

To the " Statistical Account,'' vol. v.
pp. 240. 254; vol. vii. p. 280; vol. viii, p.
177; vol. ix. p. 74; vol. xii. p. 197; vol.

xiv. p. 372: vol. xviii. p. 57: vol. xx. 194, 242, we are indebted for the following particulars:—" The History of the Bargarran Witches, in the parish of Erskine, is well known to the curious. As late as the end of the 17th century a woman was burnt for witchcraft at Sandyford, near the village, and the bones of the unfortunate victim were lately found at the place." In 1698, the Session, after a long examination of witnesses, referred the case of Marion Lillie, of Spott, East Lothian, for imprecations and supposed witchcraft to the presbytery, who referred her for trial to the civil magistrate. The said Marion was generally called the Rigwoody Witch. In October, 1705, many witches were burnt on the top of Spott loan. In the parish of East Monkland, Lanark, upon a rising ground there was in the last century still to be seen an upright granite stone, where, it was said, in former times they burnt those imaginary criminals called witches.

Tradition long continued to preserve the memory of the spot in the lands belonging to the town of Newburgh, co. Fife, on which more than one unfortunate victim fell a sacrifice to the superstition of former times, intent on punishing the crime of witchcraft. " The humane provisions of the legislature," (it is said by the writer of this account,) " joined to the superior knowledge which has, of late years, prevaded all ranks of men in society, bid fair to prevent the return of a phrenzy, which actuated our forefathers universally and with fatal violence." In 1653, the minister of Newburgh put in against Katherine Key the following points, on which inquiry seemed to him desirable:—"1. That being refused milk—the kow gave nothing but red blood; and being sent for to sie the kow, she clapped (stroked) the kow, and said the kow will be weill and thereafter the kow becam weill. 2. (A similar charge.). 3. That the minister and his wife, having ane purpose to take ane child of theirs from the said Katherine, which she had in nursing, the child would suck none woman's breast, being only one quarter old; but, being brought again to the said Katherine, presently sucked her breast. 4. That thereafter the child was spayned (weaned), she came to sie the child and wold have the bairne (child) in her arms, and thereafter the bairne murned and gratt (weeped fore) in the night, and almost the day tyme; also that nothing could stay her, untill she died. Nevertheless, before her coming to see her and her embracing of hir, took as weill with the spaining and rested as weill as any bairne cold doe. 5. That she is of ane evill brutte and fame, and so

was her mother before her." The event is not recorded.

In Kircaldy, co. Fife, it is said in the *Stat. Account:* " A man and his wife were burned in 1633 for the supposed crime of witchcraft. The following items of execution expenses are equally shocking and curious :

	£	s.	d.
" For ten loads of coals to burn them . . .	3	6	8 Scots.
For a tar barrel . . .	0	14	0
For towes	0	6	0
For harden to be jumps to them	0	3	10
For making of them .	0	0	8."

We are told that the boundary-line of the parishes of Dyke and Moy, co. Elgin and Forres, where the boundary crosses the heath called the Hardmoor, there lies somewhere a solitary spot of classic ground renowned for the Thane of Glammis's interview with the wayward or weird sisters in " Macbeth." Elsewhere it is added: " In Macbeth's time, witchcraft was very prevalent in Scotland, and two of the most famous witches in the kingdom lived on each hand of Macbeth, one at Collace, the other not far from Dunsinnan House, at a place called the Cape. Macbeth applied to them for advice, and by their counsel built a lofty castle upon the top of an adjoining hill, since called Dunsinnan. The moor where the witches met which is in the parish of St. Martin's, is yet pointed out by the country people, and there is a stone still preserved, which is called the Witches Stone."

Pennant tells us that the last instance of the frantic executions for witchcraft, of which so much has been already said, in the North of Scotland, was in June, 1727, as that in the South was at Paisley in 1696, where among others, a woman, young and handsome, suffered, and with a reply to her inquiring friends worthy a Roman matron, being asked why she did not make a better defence on her tryal, answered, " My persecutors have destroyed my honor, and my life is not now worth the pains of defending." The last instance of national credulity on this head was the story of the Witches of Thurso, who tormenting for a long time an honest fellow under the usual form of cats, at last provoked him so, that one night he put them to flight with his broad sword, and cut off the leg of one less nimble than the rest; on his taking it up, to his amazement he found it belonged to a female of his own species, and next morning discovered the owner, an old hag, with only the companion leg to this. " Tour in Scotland," p. 145.

In the " Statistical Account of Scotland," parish of Loth, co. Sutherland, it is stated that the unhappy woman here alluded to was burnt at Dornoch, and that "the common people entertain strong prejudices against her relations to this day." In Pennant's time there was still shown, he says, "a deep and wide hollow, beneath Calton Hill, the place where those imaginary criminals, witches and sorcerers, were burnt in less enlightened times." There is a Scotish proverb—"Ye breed of the witches, ye can do nae good to your sel." See Extracts from the Scotish Kirk and Session Records in *Antiquary,* August, 1889.

But these narratives of almost obsolete superstitions must never be thought a reflection on this country as long as any memory remains of the Tring case in 1751 (see below), or of that ridiculous imposture in the capital itself, in 1762, of the Cock-lane ghost, which found credit with all ranks of people.

In the Highlands of Scotland the housewives used within memory to tie a piece of red worsted round their cows' tails on sending them out in the spring to grass, to guard them against evil spirits. *N. and Q.* 1st. S. iv, 380-1.

In his *National Tales and Legends,* 1892, the present Editor has a considerable division assigned to supernatural stories.

Witchcraft in the Isle of Man.—See *Manx.*

Witchcraft, Statutes on.—The

witch statutes in our English code of laws were enacted in the 33rd year of Henry VIII. the 1st of James and the 9th of George II. By the 33rd Hen. VIII. c. viii. the law adjudged all witchcraft and sorcery to be felony without benefit of clergy. By 1 Jac. I. c. xii. it was ordered that all persons invoking any evil spirits, or consulting, covenanting with, entertaining, employing, feeding, or rewarding any evil spirit: or taking up dead bodies from their graves to be used in any witchcraft, sorcery, charm, or enchantment, or killing or otherwise hurting any person by such infernal arts, should be guilty of felony without benefit of clergy, or suffer death. And if any person should attempt by sorcery, to discover hidden treasure, or to restore stolen goods, or to provoke unlawful love, or to hurt any man or beast, though the same were not effected, he or she should suffer imprisonment and pillory for the first offence, and death for the second.

By Stat. 9 Geo. II. c. v. it was enacted that no prosecution should in future be carried on against any person for conjuration, witchcraft, sorcery, or enchantment. But the misdemeanor of persons pretending to use witchcraft, tell fortunes, or to discover stolen goods by skill in the

occult sciences was for many years afterwards punished with a year's imprisonment, and standing four times in the pillory. Thus the witch act, a disgrace to the code of English laws, was not repealed till 1736.

Witches.—The following passage is

from Scot : " No one endued with common sense but will deny that the elements are obedient to witches and at their commandment, or that they may, at their pleasure, send rain, hail, tempests, thunder, lightning; when she, being but an old doting woman, casteth a flint-stone over her left shoulder, towards the west, or hurleth a little sea-sand up into the element, or wetteth a broom-sprig in water, and sprinkleth the same in the air ; or diggeth a pit in the earth, and putting water therein, stirreth it about with her finger ; or boileth hog's bristles, or layeth sticks across upon a bank, where never a drop of water is: or buryeth sage till it be rotten: all which things are confessed by witches, and affirmed by writers to be the means that witches use, to move extraordinary tempests and rain." *Discovery,* ed. 1665, p. 33.

Bacon's reflections on witches in the tenth century of his "Natural History" form a fine contrast to the narrow and bigoted ideas of the royal author of "Demonology." "Men," he says "may not too rashly beleeve the confession of witches, nor yet the evidence against them, for the witches themselves are imaginative, and believe sometimes they do that which they do not : and people are credulous in that point, and ready to impute accidents and natural operations to witchcraft. It is worthy the observing, that both in antient and late times, (as in the Thessalian witches and the meetings of witches that have been recorded by so many late confessions,) the great wonders which they tell, of carrying in the aire, transforming themselves into other bodies, &c. are still reported to be wrought not by incantations or ceremonies, but by ointments and anointing themselves all over. This may justly move a man to think that these fables are the effects of imagination ; for it is certain that ointments do all, (if they be laid on any thing thick,) by stopping of the pores, shut in the vapours, and send them to the head extremely. And for the particular ingredients of those magical ointments, it is like they are opiate and soporiferous ; for anointing of the forehead, neck, feet, back-bone, we know is used for procuring dead sleeps. And if any man say that this effect would be better done by inward potions; answer may be made, that the medicines which go to the ointments are so strong, that if they were used inwards they would kill those that use them : and therefore they work potently though outwards."

Cotta follows on the same side : "Neither can I beleeve (I speake with reverence unto graver judgements) that the forced coming of men and women to the burning of bewitched cattell, or to the burning of the dung or urine of such as are bewitched, or floating of bodies above the water, or the like, are any trial of a witch." *Short Discovery*, p. 54.

It appears, on the contrary, from Strype's "Annals" under 1558, that even such a churchman as Bishop Jewel, preaching before the Queen, said : "It may please your grace to understand that witches and sorcerers within these few last years are marvelously increased within your graces realm. Your graces subjects pine away, even unto the death, their colour fadeth, their flesh rotteth, their speech is benumbed, their senses are bereft. I pray God they never practise further then upon the subject." "This," Strype adds, "I make no doubt was the occasion of bringing in a bill, the next Parliament, for making enchantments and witchcraft felony." One of the Bishop's strong expressions is, "These eyes have seen most evident and manifest marks of their wickedness."

It is to the eternal honour of Sir Matthew Hale, who flourished in the still bigoted and intolerant reign of Charles II., that in the case of an old woman, who was brought before him as a witch, he discharged her, and furthermore observed that whether, in returning home, she walked on her feet or rode through the air, was immaterial to the Court.

Roger North remarks : "It is seldom that a poor old wretch is brought to trial for witchcraft, but there is at the heels of her a popular rage that does little less than demand her to be put to death ; and if a judge is so clear and open as to declare against that impious vulgar opinion, that the devil himself has power to torment and kill innocent children, or that he is pleased to divert himself with the good people's cheese, butter, pigs, and geese, and the like errors of the ignorant and foolish rabble ; the countrymen (the triers) cry 'this judge hath no religion, for he doth not believe witches,' and so, to shew that they have some, hang the poor wretches." *Life of Lord Keeper Guilford*, p. 129 ; *Pandemonium, or, The Devil's Cloyster*, 1684, and *Peck's Desiderata Curiosa*, ii, 47.

Warner says, "It would be a curious speculation to trace the origin and progress of that mode of thinking among the Northern nations, which gave the faculty of divination to females in antient ages,

and the gift of witchcraft to them in more modern times." *Hampshire*, 1793, elsewhere cited.

Henry mentions Pomponius Mela, as describing a Druidical nunnery, which, he says, was situated in an island in the British sea, and contained nine of these venerable vestals, who pretended that they could raise storms and tempests by their incantations, could cure the most incurable diseases ; could transform themselves into all kinds of animals, and foresee future events. *H. of Gt. Britain*, 48 ed. i, 90.

King James's reason, in his "Dæmonology," why there are or were twenty women given to witchcraft for one man, is curious. "The reason is easy," as this sagacious monarch thinks, "for as that sex is frailer than men is, so it is easier to be entrapped in these grosse snares of the divell, as was over well proved to be true, by the serpent's deceiving Eva at the beginning, which makes him the homelier with that sexe sensine." His Majesty in this work quaintly calls the devil "God's Ape and Hangman."

According to the popular belief on this subject, there are three sorts of witches : the first kind can hurt but not help, and are with singular propriety called the Black Witches. The second kind, very properly called White Ones, have gifts directly opposite to those of the former ; they can help but not hurt. By the following lines of Dryden, however, the white witch seems to have a strong hankering after mischief :

"At least as little honest as he could,
  And like white witches mischievously
        good."

The third species, as a mixture of white and black, are styled the Grey Witches ; for they can both help and hurt. Thus the end and effect of witchcraft seems to be sometimes good and sometimes the direct contrary. In the first case the sick are healed, thieves are bewrayed, and true men come to their goods. In the second, men, women, children, or animals, as also grass, trees, or corn, &c., are hurt.

Gaule, as cited before, says : "According to the vulgar conceit, distinction is usually made between the white and the black witch, the good and the bad witch. The bad witch they are wont to call him or her that workes malefice or mischiefe to the bodies of men or beasts : the good witch they count him or her that helps to reveale, prevent, or remove the same."

A writer in the *Graphic* in December, 1882, observes : Witches are much more common in the West of England than they were in the realms of Cetewayo, who "smelt them out," or in those of Saul, who did much the same thing. The rural people are as credulous as the parishioners of Coverley, in the *Spectator's* time, when the Coverley witch possessed a cat known to have spoken several times during her life. A Plymouth witch has lately caused a good deal of discomfort (though not by causing a storm) to a seafaring young man. He set sail with a smack owner of Brixham, as a member of the crew, but his health suffered in his maritime adventure, and a physician advised him that he was in danger of losing his eyesight. The master of the smack bade the young mariner consult a white witch at Plymouth, and the sufferer took this advice. The white witch boldly declared that not the invalid but the whole smack was under a spell, and suffering from the wiles of sorcerers. More abject superstition could not be found on the African Gold Coast, or in the Andaman Islands. The master and the lad now visited the witch together, but the spell could not be removed. The youth, who had "moved Acheron" before tryng ordinary means of cure, now went into an infirmary, and recovered not only his health, but wages from his too spiritually-minded master. But none the less the witch will continue to drive her magic wheel, and a roaring trade, in Plymouth.

Perkins, in his *Discourse of Witchcraft*, 1608, says: "It were a thousand times better for the land, if all witches, but specially the Blessing Witch, might suffer death. Men doe commonly hate and spit at the damnifying sorcerer, as unworthie to live among them, whereas they flie unto the other in necessitie, they depend upon him as their god, and by this meanes thousands are carried away to their finall confusion. Death therefore is the just and deserved portion of the Good Witch."

According to Gaule "In every place and parish, every old woman with a wrinkled face, a furr'd brow, a hairy lip, a gobber tooth, a squint eye, a squeaking voice, a scolding tongue, having a rugged coate on her back, a skull-cap on her head, a spindle in her hand, a dog or cat by her side, is not only suspected but pronounced for a witch. Every new disease, notable accident, miracle of nature, rarity of art, nay and strange work or just judgement of God, is by them accounted for no other but an act or effect of witchcraft." He adds: "Some say the devill was the first witch when he plaid the impostor with our first parents, possessing the serpent as his impe to their delusion (Gen. 3), and it is whispered that our grandame Eve was a little guilty of such kind of society." *Select Cases of Conscience*, 1646, p. 410.

The mode of becoming a witch, Grose, apprises us, is as follows: a decrepit,

superannuated old woman is tempted by a man in black to sign a contract to become his both soul and body. On the conclusion of the agreement he gives her a piece of money, and causes her to write her name and make her mark on a slip of parchment with her own blood. Sometimes, also, on this occasion, the witch uses the ceremony of putting one hand to the sole of her foot, and the other to the crown of her head. On departing, he delivers to her an imp or familiar. The familiar, in the shape of a cat or kitten, a mole or miller-fly, or some other insect or animal, sucks her blood through teats in different parts of her body. There is a great variety of the names of these imps or familiars. In making these bargains, it is said, there was sometimes a great deal of haggling. The sum given to bind the bargain was sometimes a groat, at other times half-a-crown.

In "The Witch of Edmonton," 1658, act ii. sc. 1, the witch Elizabeth Sawyer is introduced gathering sticks, with this soliloquy:

—"Why should the envious world
Throw their scandalous malice upon me,
'Cause I am poor, deform'd, and ignorant,
And like a bow buckl'd and bent together,
By some more strong in mischief than myself?
Must I for that be made a common sink,
For all the filth and rubbish of men's tongues
To fall and run into? Some call me witch;
And being ignorant of myself, they go
About to teach me how to be one: urging
That my bad tongue (by their own usage made so)
Forespeaks their cattle, doth bewitch their corn,
Themselves, their servants, and their babes at nurse.
This they enforce upon me: and in part
Make me to credit it."

In "The Wandering Jew Telling Fortunes to English Men," 1640, is "The Witches Fortune. A witch is the devills otter-hound, living both on land and sea, and doing mischiefe in either; she kills more beasts than a licensed butcher in Lent, yet is nere the fatter; shees but a dry nurse for the flesh, yet gives suck to the spirit. A witch rides many times poast on hellish businesses, yet if a ladder do but stop her, shee'll be hang'd ere shee goes any further," &c.

In vexing the parties troubled, witches are visible to them only; sometimes such parties act on the defensive against them, striking at them with a knife, &c.

Sometimes witches content themselves with a revenge less than mortal, causing the objects of their hatred to swallow pins, crooked nails, dirt, cinders, and trash of all sorts : or by drying up their cows and killing their oxen ; or by preventing butter from coming in the churn : or beer from working. Sometimes, to vex squires, justices, and country-parsons, fond of hunting, they change themselves into hares, and elude the speed of the fleetest dogs.

King James says that "Witches can raise stormes and tempests in the aire, either upon sea or land." Comp. *Wind*. By the severe laws once in force against witchcraft, to the disgrace of humanity, great numbers of innocent persons, distressed with poverty and age, were brought to violent and untimely ends.

It used to be the practice for the witch, when she came for her trial, to walk backward, and the judge is cautioned in an official document to make many crosses at the time of her approach to the Bar.

The method taken by persons to keep those who were suspected of witchcraft awake, when guarded, was "to pierce their flesh with pins, needles, awls, or other sharp pointed instruments. To rescue them from that oppression which sleep imposed on their almost exhausted nature, they sometimes used irons heated to a state of redness."

Witches' Broom. — The popular notion about witches riding on broomsticks through the air seems to be associated with the nursery rhyme, who was supposed to have ascended in a basket to brush the cobwebs from the sky with her broom. Halliwell's *Nursery Rhymes*, 6th ed. p. 145.

Dr. A. H. Reginald Buller, of Birmingham University, has been investigating the subject of "witches' brooms," which are very plentiful on trees about Birmingham, and used to be thought to be the "brooms" on which witches made their midnight rides in the air. The brooms are very thick, tangled masses of birch-twigs, which look like birds' nests, and give the affected trees a very striking appearance, particularly in winter, when there are no leaves to hide them. Dr. Buller explains them as being caused by extemely small mites, which can only be seen with the aid of the microscope. The mites attack the buds, and the twigs do not mature properly, and their ends die off. In consequence of this the lower buds on the twigs, which, under ordinary circumstances, would never develop into branches, shoot out. This process is re-peated year by year, and gradually leads to the formation of the brooms. *Daily Mail*, Nov. 25, 1903.

Scot, speaking of the vulgar opinion of witches flying, observes that "the devil teacheth them to make ointment of the bowels and members of children, whereby they ride in the air and accomplish all their desires. After burial they steal them out of their graves and seeth them in a cauldron, till the flesh be made potable, of which they make an ointment, by which they ride in the air." *Discovery*, ed. 1665, book 3, c. 1. Wierus exposes the folly of this opinion in his book "De Præstigiis Dæmonum, proving it to be a diabolical illusion, and to be acted only in a dream. It is exposed as such by Oldham :

> "As men in sleep, though motionless
>   they lie,
> Fledg'd by a dream, believe they mount
>   and flye :
> So witches some inchanted wand be-
>   stride,
> And think they through the airy regions
>   ride."

Sir Matthew Hale had the broom in his mind, when he remarked that an old woman brought before him could go away, and it did not signify whether she walked on the ground, or passed through the air.

Butler has the following on this subject :—

> "Or trip it o'er the water quicker
> Than witches when their staves they
>   liquor,
> As some report."

Witches, Literary Notices relative to.—In Jonson's "Masque of Queenes," 1609, which is in itself a perfect thesaurus of witch-lore, the principal witch is speaking :

> "A rusty blade, to wound mine arme,
> And as it drops, I'le speake a charme
> Shall cleave the ground, as low as lies
> Old shrunke-up chaòs."

The following passage is taken from Stephens's "Characters," 1615: "The torments therefore of hot iron and mercilesse scratching nayles, be long thought uppon and much threatened (by the females) before attempted. Meane time she tolerates defiance thorough the wrathfull spittle of matrons, in stead of fuell, or maintenance to her damnable intentions." He goes on—" Children cannot smile upon her without hazard of a perpetuall wry mouth : a very noble-mans request may be denied more safely than her petitions for butter-milke, and small beere ; and a great ladies or queenes name may be lesse doubtfully derided. Her prayers and amen be a charm and a curse: her contemplations and soules delight bee other men's mischiefe: her portion and sutors be her soule and a succubus: her highest adorations bee yew trees, dampish church-yards, and a fayre moon-light: her best preservatives be odde numbers and mightie Tetragramaton."

The subsequent occurs in Cotgrave's "Treasury of Wit and Language," p. 298;

"Thus witches
Possess'd, ev'n in their death deluded,
    say
They have been wolves and dogs, and
    sail'd in egge-shels
Over the sea, and rid on fiery dragons,
Pass'd in the air more than a thousand
    miles
All in a night: the enemy of mankind
So pow'rfull, but false and falsehood
    confident."

In the same work, p. 263, we read:

"Thou art a soldier,
Followest the great Duke, feed'st his
    victories,
As witches do their serviceable spirits,
Even with thy prodigal blood."

Witches' Marks, &c.—Various were the modes of trying witches. This was sometimes done by finding private marks on their bodies; at others by weighing the suspected wretch against the church Bible; by another method she was made to say the Lord's Prayer. Butler alludes to this trial:

"He that gets by heart must say her
The back way, like a witches prayer."

She was sometimes forced to weep, and was so detected, as a witch can shed no more than three tears, and those only from her left eye.

King James says: "They cannot even shed tears, though women in general are like the crocodile, ready to weep upon every light occasion."

Among the presumptions, whereby witches were condemned, was one specified in Scot's "Discovery," p. 15: "If she have any privy mark under her arm-pit, under her hair, under her lip, or *****, it is presumption sufficient for the judge to proceed and give sentence of death upon her": again, King James speaking of the helps that may be used in the trial of witches, says, "the one is—the finding of their marke and trying the insensibleness thereof."

Gaule also mentions "Some marks or tokens of tryall altogether unwarrantable; as proceeding from ignorance, humor, superstition. Such are 1. The old paganish sign, the witches' long eyes. 2. The tradition of the witches not weeping. 3. The witches making ill-favoured faces and mumbling. 4. To burn the thing bewitched, &c. (I am loath to speak out, lest I might teach these in reproving them). 5. The burning of the thatch of the witches' house, &c. 6. The heating of the horseshoe, &c. 7. The scalding water, &c. 8. The sticking of knives acrosse, &c. 9. The putting of such and such things under the threshold, and in the bed-straw, &c. 10. The sieve and the sheares, &c. 11. The casting the witch into the water with thumbes and toes tied across, &c. 12. The tying of knots," &c. *Select Cases*, 1646, p. 75.

There were other modes of trial: by the stool, and by shaving off every hair of the witch's body. Shakespear, in "Troilus and Cressida," 1609, act ii. sc. 1, says:

"Thou stool for a witch."

And Dr. Grey's "Notes" afford us this comment on the passage: "In one way of trying a witch they used to place her upon a chair or a stool, with her legs tied cross, that all the weight of her body might rest upon her seat; and by that means, after some time, the circulation of the blood would be much stopped and her sitting would be as painful as the wooden horse; and she must continue in this pain twenty-four hours, without either sleep or meat, within which time the imp would be sure and come and suck her; and it was no wonder, that when they were tried with such an ungodly trial, they would confess themselves many times guilty to free themselves from such torture." Hutchinson's *Essay on Witchcraft*, p. 63.

Witches were also detected by putting hair, parings of the nails, and urine of any person bewitched into a stone bottle, and hanging it up the chimney. Bold, in his *Wit a Sporting*, 1657, p. 76, says:—

A Charm to bring in the Witch.
To house the hag you must do this
Commix with meal a little ****.
Of him bewitch'd, then forthwith make
A little wafer, or a cake;
And this rarely bak'd will bring
The old hag in: no surer thing."

Swimming a witch was another kind of popular ordeal. By this method she was handled not less indecently than cruelly; for she was stripped naked and cross bound, the right thumb to the left toe, and the left thumb to the right toe. In this state she was cast into a pond or river, in which if guilty, it was thought impossible for her to sink. James I. sagaciously observes that "it appears that God hath appointed for a supernatural signe of the monstrous impietie of witches, that the water shall refuse to receive them in her bosom that have shaken off them the sacred water of baptism, and wilfully refused the benefit thereof."

Nash tells us, that "14 May 1660. Four persons accused of witchcraft were brought from Kidderminster to Worcester Goal, one Widow Robinson, and her two daughters, and a man. The eldest daughter was accused of saying that if they had not been taken, the king should never have come to England; and, though he now doth come, yet he shall not live long, but shall die as ill a death as they; and that they would have made corn like pepper. Many great charges against them, and little proved, they were put to the ducking in the river: they would not sink, but swam aloft. The man had five teats, the woman three and the eldest daughter one. When they went to search the woman, none were visible; one advised to lay them on their backs and keep open their mouths, and then they would appear: and so they presently appeared in sight."

The doctor adds, that "it is not many years since a poor woman, who happened to be very ugly, was almost drowned in the neighbourhood of Worcester, upon a supposition of witchcraft; and had not Mr. Lygon, a gentleman of singular humanity and influence, interfered in her behalf, she would certainly have been drowned, upon a presumption that a witch could not sink." It appears that in 1716, Mrs. Hicks, with her daughter aged nine years, was hanged in Huntingdon for witchcraft, for selling their souls to the devil, tormenting and destroying their neighbours, by making them vomit pins, raising a storm, so that a ship was almost lost by pulling off her stockings, and making a lather of soap. *Worcestershire*, ii., 38.

In the "Gentleman's Magazine" for February, 1759, we read: "One Susannah Haynokes, an elderly woman of Wingrove near Aylesbury, Bucks, was accused by a neighbour for bewitching her spinning wheel, so that she could not make it go round, and offered to make oath of it before a magistrate: on which the husband, in order to justify his wife, insisted upon her being tried by the church Bible, and that the accuser should be present: Accordingly she was conducted to the parish church, where she was stript of all her cloaths, to her shift and under coat, and weighed against the Bible: when, to the no small mortification of the accuser, she outweighed it, and was honourably acquitted of the charge."

In Bell's MS. "Discourse of Witchcraft," 1705, on the subject of witches' marks, I read as follows: "This mark is sometimes like a little teate, sometimes like a blewish spot; and I myself have seen it in the body of a confessing witch like a little powder-mark of a blea (blue) colour, somewhat hard, and withal insensible, so as it did not bleed when I pricked it." It seems from a passage in Beaumont and Fletcher's "Honest Man's Fortune (1613)," that a beard was considered a mark of a witch.

Other methods of detecting a witch were by burning the thatch of her house, or by burning any animal supposed to be bewitched by her, as a hog or ox; these, it was held, would enforce a witch to confess. In "The Witch of Edmonton," (Enter Old Banks and two or three countrymen), we read:

"*O. Banks.* My horse this morning runs most pitiously of the glaunders, whose nose yesternight was as clean as any man's here now coming from the barber's; and this I'll take my death upon't is long of this jadish witch, Mother Sawyer.

(Enter W. Hamlac, with thatch and a link.)

Haml. Burn the witch, the witch, the witch, the witch.

Omn. What hast got there?

Haml. A handful of thatch pluck'd off a hovel of hers; and they say when 'tis burning, if she be a witch, she'll come running in.

O. Banks. Fire it, fire it: I'll stand between thee and home for any danger. (As that burns, enter the witch.)

1 *Countryman.* This thatch is as good as a jury to prove she is a witch.

O. Banks. To prove her one, we no sooner set fire on the thatch of her house, but in she came running, as if the divel had sent her in a barrel of gunpowder; which trick as surely proves her a witch, as———"

Justice. Come, come; firing her thatch? Ridiculous: take heed, sirs, what you do: unless your proofs come better arm'd, instead of turning her into a witch, you'll prove yourselves starke fools."

Old Banks then relates to the Justice a most ridiculous instance of her power: "Having a dun cow tied up in my back side, let me go thither, or but cast mine eye at her, and if I should be hanged I cannot chuse, though it be ten times in an hour, but run to the cow, and taking up her tail, kiss (saving your worship's reverence) my cow behinde; that the whole town of Edmonton has been ready ****** with laughing me to scorn." As does a countryman another: "I'll be sworn, Mr. Carter, she bewitched Gammer Washbowl's sow, to cast her pigs a day before she would have farried; yet they were sent up to London, and sold for as good

Westminster dog-pigs, at Bartholomew
Fair, as ever great-belly'd ale-wife longed
for." Act iv. sc. 1.

Witches, Preservatives against.

—Mr. Brand transcribed from
his physical MS. dated 1475, the following
charm against witchcraft : " Here ys a
charme for wyked wych. In nomine
Patris, et Filii, et Spiritus Sancti, Amen.
Per Virtutem Domini sint Medicina mei
pia Crux ✠ et passio Christi ✠. Vulnera
quinque Domini sint Medicina mei ✠.
Virgo Maria mihi succurre, et defende ab
omni maligno Demonio, et ab omni maligno Spiritu : Amen. ✠ a ✠ g ✠ l ✠ a
✠ Tetragrammaton. ✠ Alpha. ✠ oo. ✠
primogenitus, ✠ vita, vita. ✠ sapiencia,
✠ Virtus, ✠ Jesus Nazarenus rex judeorum, ✠ fili Domini, miserere mei Amen.
✠ Marcus ✠ Matheus ✠ Lucas ✠
Johannes mihi succurrite et defendite
Amen. ✠ Omnipotens sempiterne Deus,
hunc N. famulum tuum hoc breve Scrip-
tum super se portantem prospere salve
dormiendo, vigilando, potando, et preci-
pue sompniando ab omni maligno
Demonio, eciam ab omni maligno spiritu
✠."

In his First Book of Notable Things
(1579), Lupton notes the statement of
Pliny "that men did fasten upon the
gates of their towns, the heads of wolves,
thereby to put away witchery, sorcery, or
enchantment ; which many hunters observe
or do at this day, but to what use they
know not." Ed. 1660, p. 52.

Scot tells us : "Against witches, in
some countries, they nail a wolf's head on
the door. Otherwise, they hang scilla
(which is either a root, or rather in this
place garlick,) in the roof of the house,
to keep away witches and spirits ; and so
they do Alicum also. Item, perfume made
of the gall of a black dog, and his blood,
besmeared on the posts and walls of the
house, driveth out of the doors both devils
and witches. Otherwise : the house where
herba betonica is sown, is free from all
mischiefs," &c. *Discovery*, ed. 1665, p.
151-2. The idea seems to be taken from
the Vates of Molinæus, p. 237, to which
the reader may be referred.

The same author says : "To be delivered
from witches they hang in their entries an
herb called pentaphyllon, cinquefoil, also
an olive branch : also frankincense, myrrh,
valerian, verven, palm, antirchmon, &c.,
also hay-thorn, otherwise white-thorn
gathered on May Day." *Discovery*, 1665,
p. 151.

Coles observes that "if one hang mistletoe about their neck, the witches can have
no power of him. The roots of angelica
doe likewise availe much in the same case,
if a man carry them about him, as Fuch-
sius saith." *Art of Soimpling*, p. 67.

Gaule, speaking of the preservatives
against witchcraft, mentions as in use
among the Papists, "the tolling of a
baptized bell, signing with the signe of
the crosse, sprinkling with holy water,
blessing of oyle, waxe, candles, salt, bread,
cheese, garments, weapons, &c. carrying
about saints' reliques with a thousand
superstitious fopperies ;" and then enumerates those which are used by men
of all religions : "1. In seeking to
a witch to be holpen against a witch.
2. In using a certaine or supposed charme,
against an uncertaine or suspected witchcraft. 3. In searching anxiously for the
witches signe or token left behinde her in
the house under the threshold, in the bed-
straw ; and to be sure to light upon it,
burning every odd ragge, bone, or feather
that is to be found. 4. In swearing, rayling, threatning, cursing, and banning the
witch ; as if this were a right way to bewitch the witch from bewitching. 5. In
banging and basting, scratching and
clawing, to draw blood of the witch. 6.
In daring and defying the witch out of
a carnal security and presumptuous
temerity." *Select Cases of Conscience*,
1646, p. 142.

"Ignorance," says Osborne, "reports
of witches that they are unable to hurt
till they have received an almes : which,
though ridiculous in itselfe, yet in this
sense is verified, that charity seldom goes
to the gate but it meets with ingratitude."
Advice to a Son, 1656, p. 94. In "The
Witch of Edmonton," 1658, young Banks
says : "Ungirt, unbless'd, says the proverb. But my girdle shall serve a riding
knit ; and a fig for all the witches in
Christendom."

It occurs also among the following ex-
perimental rules whereby to afflict witches,
causing the evil to return back upon them,
given by Blagrave in his *Astrological
Practice of Physic*, 1689: "1. One way
is by watching the suspected party when
they go into their house ; and then presently to take some of her thatch from
over the door, or a tile, if the house be
tyled : if it be thatch, you must wet and
sprinkle it over with the patient's water,
and likewise with white salt, then let it
burn or smoke through a trivet or the
frame of a skillet ; you must bury the
ashes that way which the suspected witch
liveth. 'Tis best done either at the change,
full, or quarters of the moon ; or otherwise, when the witches significator is in
square or opposition to the moon. But if
the witches house be tiled, then take a
tile from over the door, heat him red hot,
put salt into the patient's water, and
dash it upon the red hot tile, until it be
consumed, and let it smoak through a
trivet or frame of a skillet as aforesaid.

2. Another way is to get two new horse-shoes, heat one of them red-hot, and quench him in the patient's urine, then immediately nail him on the inside of the threshold of the door with three nails, the heel being upwards; then, having the patient's urine set it over the fire, and set a trivet over it, put into it three horse nails and a little white salt. Then heat the other horse-shoe red hot, and quench him several times in the urine, and so let it boil and waste until all be consumed; do this three times, and let it be near the change, full, or quarters of the moon; or let the moon be in square or opposition unto the witches significator. 3. Another way is to stop the urine of the patient close up in a bottle, and put into it three nails, pins, or needles, with a little white salt, keeping the urine always warm. If you let it remain long in the bottle, it will endanger the witches life; for I have found by experience, that they will be grievously tormented, making their water with great difficulty, if any at all, and the more if the moon be in Scorpio in square or opposition to his significator, when it's done. 4. Another way is either at the new, full, or quarters of the moon; but more especially, when the moon is in square or opposition to the planet, which doth personate the witch, let the patient blood, and while the blood is warm, put a little white salt into it, then let it burn and smoak through a trivet. I conceive this way doth more afflict the witch than any of the other three before mentioned." He adds, that sometimes the witches will rather endure the misery of the above torments than appear, " by reason country people oft times will fall upon them, and scratch and abuse them shrewdly." It was an article in the creed of popular superstition concerning witches to believe " that when they are in hold, they must leave their devil." See Holiday's " Marriage of the Arts," 1618. " Empescher qu'un Sorcier," says M. Thiers, " ne sorte du Logis ou il est, en mettant des Balais à la porte de ce logis." *Traité des Superstitions,* p. 331.

Other preventatives, according to the popular belief, are taking the wall of her in a town or street, and the right hand of her in a lane or field; while passing her, by clenching both hands, doubling the thumbs beneath the fingers; and also by saluting her with civil words before she speaks; but no presents of apples, eggs, or other things must be received from her on any account.

The superstition of holding the poker before the fire to drive away the witch has been already noticed. Whatever may be the reason, it is a certain fact that setting up a poker before a fire has a wonderful effect in causing it to burn, but if or no it affect a witch, is another question. Heath tells us, that " some few of the inhabitants of the Scilly Isles imagine (but mostly old women) that women with child, and the firstborn, are exempted from the power of witchcraft." *Scilly Islands,* p. 120.

Witches, The Tring.—In the " Gentleman's Magazine " for 1751 occur the following particulars: Tring, May 2, 1751. " A little before the defeat of the Scotch, in the late rebellion, an old woman named Ruth Osborne, came to one Butterfield, who then kept a dairy at Gubblecot, and begged for some butter-milk; but Butterfield told her with great brutality that he had not enough for his hogs; this provoked the old woman, who went away, telling him, that the Pretender would have him and his hogs too. Soon afterwards several of Butterfield's calves became distemper'd : upon which some ignorant people who had been told the story of the buttermilk, gave out that they were bewitched by old Mother Osborne : and Butterfield himself, who had now left his dairy, and taken the public-house by the brook of Gubblecot, having been lately, as he had been many years before at times, troubled with fits, mother Osborne was said to be the cause; he was persuaded that the doctors could do him no good, and was advised to send for an old woman out of Northamptonshire, who was famous for curing diseases that were produced by witchcraft. This sagacious person was accordingly sent for and came; she confirmed the ridiculous opinion that had been propagated of Butterfield's disorder, and ordered six men to watch his house day and night with staves, pitch-forks, and other weapons, at the same time hanging something about their necks which she said was a charm that would secure them from being bewitched themselves. However, these extraordinary proceedings produced no considerable effects, nor drew the attention of the place upon them, till some persons, in order to bring a large company together with a lucrative view, ordered by anonymous letters, that public notice should be given at Winslow, Leighton, and Hampstead, by the cryer, that witches were to be tried by ducking at Longmarston on the 22d of April. The consequences were as above related, except that no person has yet been committed on the Coroner's inquest except one Thomas Colley, chimney sweeper; but several of the ringleaders in the riot are known, some of whom live very remote, and no expence or diligence will be spared to bring them to justice." It appears, that Thomas Colley was executed, and afterwards hung in chains for the murder of the above Ruth Osborne.

Such, it should seem, was the folly and superstition of the crowd, that when they searched the workhouse for the supposed witch, they looked even into the salt-box, supposing she might have concealed herself within less space than would contain a cat. The deceased, being dragged into the water, and not sinking, Colley went into the pond, and turned her over several times with a stick. It appears that the deceased and her husband were wrapped in two different sheets; but her body, being pushed about by Colley, slipped out of the sheet, and was exposed naked.

It is some relief to read in the same periodical for July 1760: "Two persons concerned in ducking for witches all the poor old women in Glen and Burton Overy were sentenced to stand in the pillory at Leicester."

Witchfinder.—Some persons were supposed by the popular belief to have the faculty of distinguishing witches. These were called Witch-Finders. The old, the ignorant, and the indigent (says Granger), such as could neither plead their own cause, nor hire an advocate, were the miserable victims of this wretch's credulity, spleen, and avarice. He pretended to be a great critic in special marks, which were only moles, scorbutic spots, or warts, which frequently grow large and pendulous in old age, but were absurdly supposed to be teats to suckle imps. His ultimate method of proof was by tying together the thumbs and toes of the suspected person, about whose waist was fastened a cord, the ends of which were held on the banks of a river by two men, in whose power it was to strain or slacken it. Matthew Hopkins, one of the most celebrated witch-finders of his day, is supposed to have been alluded to by Butler in his well-known lines of "Hudibras":

" Has not this present Parliament,
A ledger to the devil sent,
Fully impower'd to treat about
Finding revolted witches out:
And has not he, within a year,
Hang'd three score of 'em in a shire?
Some only for not being drown'd,
And some for sitting above ground
Whole days and nights upon their breeches,
And feeling pain, were hang'd for witches;
Who after prov'd himself a witch,
And made a rod for his own breech."

See Granger's "Biographical History," 1775, vol. ii. p. 409. Compare also Grey's edit. of "Hudibras," vol. ii. pp. 11, 12, 13.

The experiment of swimming was tried upon Hopkins himself in his own way,

and he was, upon the event, condemned and, as it seems, executed as a wizard. Hopkins had hanged, in one year, no fewer than sixty reputed witches in his own county of Essex.

Howell, in a curious letter to Sir Edward Spencer, dated 20th February, 1647-8, says that within two years "three hundred witches were arraigned, and the major part executed, in Essex and Suffolk only." This was doubtless through Hopkins and other informers.

We have an account that in 1649 and 1650, "the magistrates of Newcastle upon Tyne sent into Scotland to agree with a Scotchman, who pretended knowledge to find out witches by pricking them with pins. They agreed to give him twenty shillings a-piece for all he could condemn, and bear his travelling expences. On his arrival the bellman was sent through the town to invite all persons that would bring in any complaint against any woman for a witch, that she might be sent for and tryed by the persons appointed. Thirty women were, on this, brought into the Town Hall and stripped, and then openly had pins thrust into their bodies, about twenty-seven of whom he found guilty. His mode was, in the sight of all the people to lay the body of the person suspected naked to the waist, and then he ran a pin into her thigh, and then suddenly let her coats fall, demanding whether she had nothing of his in her body, but did not bleed: the woman through fright and shame, being amazed, replied little, then he put his hand up her coats and pulled out the pin, setting her aside as a guilty person and child of the devil. By this sort of evidence, one wizard and fourteen witches were tried and convicted at the Assizes, and afterwards executed. Their names are recorded in the Parish Register of St. Andrew's." Gardiner's *England's Grievance*, 1656, p. 107, and Brand's *Newcastle*.

In "The Witch of Edmonton," 1658, p. 32, something of the kind may be intended, where Winifrid as a boy says:

"I'll be no Pander to him; and if I finde
Any loose Lubrick 'scapes in him, I'll watch him,
And, at my return, protest I'll shew you all."

Butler says, speaking of the Witch-Finder, that, of witches some be hanged

—" for puting knavish tricks
Upon green geese and turkey-chicks,
Or pigs, that, suddenly deceas't
Of griefs, unnat'ral as he guest."

Witch's Cat.—In an account of witchcraft, the cat, who is the *sine quâ*

non of a witch, deserves particular consideration. If I mistake not, this is a connection which has cost our domestic animal all that persecution with which it is, by idle boys at least, incessantly pursued. In ancient times the case was very different. These animals were anciently revered as emblems of the moon, and among the Egyptians were on that account so highly honoured as to receive sacrifices and devotions, had stately temples erected to their honour, and after death were embalmed. Large numbers of these feline mummies have been in our days exported to Europe, and utilized for practical purposes. It is said that in whatever house a cat dies, all the family shaved their eyebrows. No favourite lap-dog among the moderns has received such posthumous honours. Diodorus Siculus relates that, a Roman happening accidentally to kill a cat, the mob immediately gathered about the house where he was, and neither the entreaties of some principal men sent by the king, nor the fear of the Romans, with whom the Egyptians were then negotiating a peace, could save the man's life.

We are told that the devil gives the witches a beast about the bigness and shape of a young cat, which they call a carrier. What this carrier brings they must receive for the devil. These carriers fill themselves so full sometimes, that they are forced to spew by the way, which spewing is found in several gardens where colworts grow, and not far from the houses of those witches. It is of a yellow colour like gold, and is called "Butter of Witches." This is doubtless different from the substance which is called in Northumberland "Fairy Butter." *Relation of the Swedish Witches at the end of* Glanvill's *Sadducismus Triumphatus.*

In "News from Scotland: the damnable Life and Death of Dr. Fian," (1591,) "Agnis Thompson confessed, that at the time when his Majesty was in Denmark, she, being accompanied with the parties before specially named, took a cat and christened it, and afterwards bound to that cat the chiefest parts of a dead man, and several joints of his body; and that in the night following, the said cat was conveyed into the midst of the sea by all these witches sailing in their riddles or cieves, as is aforesaid, and so left the said cat right before the town of Leith in Scotland: this done, there did arise such a tempest in the sea as a greater hath not been seen: which tempest was the cause of the perishing of a boat or vessel coming over from the town of Brunt Island to the town of Leith, wherein were sundry jewels and rich gifts which should have been presented to the now Queen of Scotland, at her Majesty's coming to Leith. Again it is confessed that the said christened cat was the cause that the King's Majesty's ship, at his coming forth of Denmark, had a contrary wind to the rest of the ships then being in his company: which thing was most strange and true, as the King's Majesty acknowledgeth."

This Dr. Fian was "Register to the devil, and sundry times preached at North Baricke kirke to a number of notorious witches:" the very persons who in this work are said to have pretended to bewitch and drown his Majesty in the sea coming from Denmark.

Steevens, in his Notes on Shakespear, refers to Baldwin's "Beware the Cat," first published perhaps before 1561, for a statement that "it was permitted to a witch to take her a cattes body nine times." The following passage occurs in Dekker's "Strange Horse-Race," 1613: "When the grand helcat had gotten these two furies with nine lives." And in Marston's "Dutch Courtezan," we read:

"Why then thou hast nine lives like a
    cat."
—Workes, 1633, Bb 3.

In the description of the witch mause, in the "Gentle Shepherd," the following occurs:

——"And yonder's mause,
She and her cat sit beeking in her
    yard."

In Gay's fable of the "Old Woman and her Cats," one of these animals is introduced as upbraiding the witch as follows:

"'Tis infamy to serve a hag;
Cats are thought imps, her broom a
    nag;
And boys against our lives combine,
Because, 'tis said, your cats have nine."
See the *British Apollo*, 1708, ii, No. 1.

Warburton, on the passage in "Macbeth," "Thrice the brinded cat hath mew'd," observes, that, "A cat, from time immemorial, has been the agent and favourite of witches. This superstitious fancy is pagan and very ancient: and the original, perhaps, this: when Galinthia was changed into a cat by the fates, (says Antonius Liberalis, 'Metam.' c. xxix.) by witches, (says Pausanias in his 'Bæotics,') Hecate took pity of her and made her her priestess: in which office she continues to this day. Hecate herself, too, when Typhon forced all the gods and goddesses to hide themselves in animals, assumed the shape of a cat. So Ovid:

'Fele soror Phœbi latuit.''

There is a very curious extract from a file of informations, taken by some justices against a poor witch, preserved in the "Life of the Lord Keeper Guilford," which forcibly satirizes the folly of admitting such kind of evidence as was brought against them: "This informant saith he saw a cat leap in at her (the old woman's) window, when it was twilight: and this informant farther saith, that he verily believeth the said cat to be the devil: and more saith not." It may be observed upon this evidence, that to affect the poor culprit, he could not well have said less.

The witch's cat, accompanied by its mistress, is delineated on the title-page of a second issue in 1621 of the case of diabolical possession of the Earl of Rutland's family, originally published in 1619.

Hogarth, in his "Medley," represents with great spirit of satire a witch sucked by a cat, and flying on a broom-stick. It being said, as Trusler remarks, that the familiar with whom a witch converses, sucks her right breast, in shape of a little dun cat, as smooth as a mole, which, when it has sucked, the witch is in a kind of trance.

Witch's Cauldron.—This is thus described by Olaus Magnus: "Olla autem omnium Maleficarum commune solet esse Instrumentum, quo succos, herbas, vermes, et exta decoquant, atque ea venefica dape ignavos ad vota alliciunt, et instar bullientis Ollæ, Navium & Equitum aut Cursorum excitant Celeritatem."—Olai Magni *Gent. Septentr. Hist. Brevis*, p. 96.

On the title page of an early German tract we meet with a woodcut of the caldron, into which two witches throw a snake and a cock. Ulricus Molitor, *Tractatus perutilis de phitonicis mulieribus* (about 1490).

It is almost unnecessary to remind the reader of the scene in *Macbeth*. But the following from Middleton is very curious in the presence of the possibility that his play was older than Shakespear's:

"1 *Witch*.	Here's the blood of a bat.
Hec.	Put in that, O put in that.
2.	Here's Libbard's bane.
Hec.	Put in againe.
1.	The juice of toade, the oile of adder.
2.	Those will make the yonker madder.
Hec.	Put in : thers all, and rid the stench.
Firestone.	Nay here's three ounces of the red-hair'd wench.
All.	Round around, around, &c."

In the church at Frensham, on the borders of Surrey and Hampshire, was formerly, if it is not still, preserved what is traditionally termed "Mother Ludlam's Cauldron," a copper vessel standing on an iron tripod with three legs; it is engraved in Willis's *Current Notes* for October, 1851. Near Farnham is a cavern known as "Mother Ludlam's Hole," her supposed residence.

Witch's Dance.—Jonson, in the *Masque of Queenes*, 1609, describes the Witches' Dance: "At w^ch, wth a strange and sodayne musique, they fell into a magicall daunce full of preposterous change, and gesticulation, but most applying to theyr property : who, at theyr meetings, do all thinges contrary to the custome of men, dancing back to back, hip to hip, theyr handes joyn'd and making theyr circles backward, to the left hand, with strange phantastique motions of theyr heads and bodyes." These passages may be compared with scenes in Shakespear's "Macbeth," and Middleton's "Witch."

One plainly sees in *News from Scotland* above quoted the foundation stones of the "Royal Treatise on Dæmonology :" and it is said "these confessions made the King in a wonderful admiration," and he sent for one Geillis Duncane, who played a reel or dance before the witches, "who upon a small trump, called a Jew's Trump, did play the said dance before the King's Majesty: who, in respect to the strangeness of these matters, took great delight to be present at all their examinations." Who is there so incurious that would not wish to have seen the monarch of Great Britain entertaining himself with a supposed witches' performance on the Jew's-harp !

Witch's Sabbath.—The Sabbath of the witches is supposed to be held on a Saturday, when the devil is by some said to appear in the shape of a goat, about whom several dances and magic ceremonies are performed. Before the assembly breaks up, the witches are all said to have the honour of saluting Satan's posteriors. See King James's remarks on this subject in his "Dæmonology." Satan is reported to have been so much out of humour at some of these meetings. that, for his diversion, he would beat the witches black and blue with the spits and brooms, the vehicles of their transportation, and play them divers other unlucky tricks. They afterwards proceed at these assemblies to the grossest impurities and immoralities, and it may be added, blasphemies, as the devil sometimes preaches to them a mock sermon.

They afterwards open graves for the purpose of taking out joints of the fingers and toes of dead bodies. with some of the winding sheet, in order to prepare a powder for their magical purposes. Here also the devil distributes apples, dishes, spoons, or other trifles, to those witches who desire to torment any particular person to whom they must present them. Here also, for similar purposes, the devil baptizes waxen images.

The Sabbath of witches is a meeting to which the sisterhood, after having been anointed with certain magical ointments, provided by their infernal leader, are supposed to be carried through the air on brooms, coulstaves, spits, &c. At these meetings they have feastings, musick, and dancing, the devil himself condescending to play at them on the pipes or cittern.

Withersden, Co. Kent.—Hasted tells us that, "at Withersden is a well, which was once famous, being called St. Eustace's Well, taking its name from Eustachius, Abbot of Flai, who is mentioned by Matt. Paris, An. 1200, to have been a man of learning and sanctity, and to have come and preached at Wye, and to have blessed a fountain there, so that afterwards its waters were endowed by such miraculous power, that by it all diseases were cured." *Hist. of Kent.* folio ed. iii, 176.

Withold, St.—Supposed to be identical with St. Vitalis, of which name there were two saints, one who suffered martyrdom at Ravenna under Nero being probably the one here intended. See Nares, ed. 1859, in v.

Wives' Feast Day.—A name for Candlemas in the North of England.

Wizard.—See Nares, 1859, in v. A wizard, as distinguished from a witch, was a person, who had supernatural power or insight, but not necessarily for the purpose of inflicting injury. He was rather a conjurer. It was a term even applied to political quackery, as in a tract printed in 1652, entitled *The Wizard Unvisored.* A singularly curious story is related by Melton in his *Astrologaster,* 1620, of Henry Cuffe of Merton College, Oxford, who was hanged at Tyburn for his complicity in the Earl of Essex's plot in 1601. A wizard produced a pack of cards, out of which Cuffe drew at random three; they were three knaves; and the man bad him put them on the table with their faces downward. Then he told him to take them up one by one. On the first he then perceived a portrait of himself in full armour, surrounded by men with bills and halberds. On the second was the judge, who presided at his trial; and on the third there was a view of Tyburn with the executioner. This happened, it is said, twenty years prior to the actual occurrence.

Melton enumerates, as wizards at this time flourishing in London, the cunning man on the Bankside, Mother Broughton in Chick-lane, young Master Olive in Turnbull Street, the shag-haired wizard in Pepper-Alley, the chirurgeon with the bag-pipe cheek, Doctor Forman at Lambeth, and a man in Moorfields.

Wolf, The.—Turner, in the *Huntyng of the Romyshe Vuolfe (circa* 1554), sign. E 5, says: "The propertie of a wolfe is, that if a man se the wolfe after the wolfe se the man, that then a man shall not be dumme. But if the wolfe se the man, before the man se the wolfe, then is the man by the syght of the wolfe made dum, or at least so deafe, that he can scarcely speake." Randolph refers to the idea in the *Muses' Looking-Glass,* written before 1635.

Werenfels says: "When the superstitious person goes abroad, he is not so much afraid of the teeth, as the unexpected sight of a wolf, lest he should deprive him of his speech."

The following story is worth perpetuation as an evidence of the powerful instinct of this animal. It appears to hearken back to the Elizabethan period:—

It was credibly informed me by a friend of mine long resident in Ireland, of one that, travelling in an evening betwixt two townes in that country, some three miles distant, was there several times set upon by a wolfe, from whose jawes he by his sword so oft delivered himselfe. Approaching neare the towne where he was bent, he incountered a friend of his travayling all unarmed towards the towne from whence he came, unto whom (advising him of his peril and assault, accounting himselfe secure so neare the towne) he lent his sword. Now, having parted and divided themselves some little distance, this olde wolfe sets upon his new guest, who finding him armed with the other's weapon, presently leaves him, making after the other with all speede he might: overtook him, before he came to the towne, assaulted and slew him." *Philosopher's Banquet,* 1614, p. 201. Comp. *Preservatives against Witches.*

Wolverhampton.—"Many of the older inhabitants of Wolverhampton can well remember, remarks Shaw, when the sacrist, resident prebendaries, and members of the choir, assembled at morning prayers on Monday and Tuesday in Rogation week, with the charity children, bearing long poles clothed with all kinds of flowers then in season, and which were afterwards carried through the streets of the town with much solemnity, the clergy, singing men and boys, dressed in their sacred vestments, closing the procession, and chanting in a grave and appropriate melody, the Canticle, Benedicite, Omnia Opera, &c." "This ceremony, innocent at least, and not illaudable in itself, was of high antiquity, having probably its origin in the Roman offerings of the Primitiæ, from which (after being rendered conformable to our purer worship) it was adopted by the first Christians, and handed down, through a succession of ages, to modern times. The idea was, no doubt, that of returning thanks to God, by whose goodness the face of nature was renovated, and fresh means provided for the sustenance and comfort of his creatures. It was discontinued about 1765. The boundaries of the township and parish of Wolverhampton are in many points marked out by what are called gospel trees, from the custom of having the Gospel read under or near them by the clergyman attending the parochial perambulations. Those near the town were visited for the same purpose by the processioners before mentioned, and are still preserved with the strictest care and attention."

Shaw, speaking of Wolverhampton and the processioners there, says: "Another custom (now likewise discontinued) was the annual procession, on the 9th of July (the eve of the great fair), of men in antique armour, preceded by musicians playing the Fair-tune, and followed by the steward of the Deanery Manor, the peace-officers, and many of the principal inhabitants. Tradition says the ceremony originated at the time when Wolverhampton was a great emporium of wool, and resorted to by merchants of the staple from all parts of England. The necessity of an armed force to keep peace and order during the fair, (which is said to have lasted fourteen days, but the charter says only eight,) is not improbable. This custom of Walking the Fair (as it was called) with the armed procession, &c. was first omitted about the year 1789." *Staffordshire*, vol ii, part 1, p. 163.

Wooden Horse, The.—An obsolete military punishment chiefly adopted in the case of soldiers not accustomed to riding. It is described (with an illustration) in the *Penny Magazine* for 1837, p. 338-9, from the account given by Grose, in his *Military Antiquities*, and there is a reference to a characteristic passage in Scott's *Old Mortality*.

Woodroff.—This is used for garlands on St. Barnabas's Day (June 11). Loudon, quoted in Worcester's Dict., says that woodroff is "supposed to be a corruption of the word wood-rowell, the whorls of leaves, according to Turner, (who seems to be followed by Gerarde), representing certain kinds of 'rowelles of

spores.' The common name (adds Loudon, *ibid.*) of plants of the genus asperula."

Woollen Manufacture.—The Act for Burying in Woollen in 1678 created a good deal of dissatisfaction, and was intended to encourage the trade in that material. Misson, speaking of funerals in England, says: "There is an Act of Parliament which ordains that the dead shall be buried in a woollen stuff, which is a kind of a thin bays, which they call flannel; nor is it lawful to use the least needleful of thread or silk. This shift is always white; but there are different sorts of it as to fineness, and consequently of different prices. To make these dresses is a particular trade, and there are many that sell nothing else." The shirt, for a man "has commonly a sleeve purfled about the wrists, and the slit of the shirt, down the breast, done in the same manner. This should be at least half a foot longer than the body, that the feet of the deceased may be wrapped in it, as in a bag. Upon the head they put a cap, which they fasten with a very broad chin-cloth; with gloves on the hands, and a cravat round the neck, all of woollen. The women have a kind of head-dress with a fore-head cloth." He adds, "that the body may ly the softer, some put a lay of bran, about four inches thick, at the bottom of the coffin. The body is visited to see that it is buryed in flannel, and that nothing about it is sowed with thread."

In the Churchwardens' Accounts of Minchinhampton, co. Gloucester, for 1678, occurs this item: "Paid for a booke to enter yᵉ burialls in woolen, 2s." In 1730 Mrs. Oldfield the actress was nevertheless buried in Westminster Abbey in a Holland shift trimmed with lace and a Brussels lace headdress. Hazlitt's *Bibl. Coll.* iii, 271.

Woolward.—The abstinence from the use of linen next the person as a penance. See Halliwell in v.

Worm.—The name given by Shakespear to the asp, by which Cleopatra destroyed herself; but the original sense was *a serpent* or the mythical dragon.

Wotton or **Wootton, near Dorking.**—Under the will of Mr. Glanvill, one of the clerks of the Treasury, dated December 31, 1717, an annual payment of 40/- is made on the anniversary of his death to each of five poor boys, not exceeding 16 years of age, on the condition that with their hands on his grave-stone they shall repeat without book the Lord's Prayer, the Apostles' Creed, and the Ten Commandments, that they shall read the 15th chapter of the First Epistle of St. Paul to the Corinthians, and shall write two verses of it in a legible hand. And £30 more was to be paid out yearly in binding them as apprentices to some handicraft or husbandry, no one of them having more than £10 paid on his behalf. The boys were to be chosen out of the parish by the trustees, and if so many were not to be found there of the pres-cribed age, they might be taken from the parishes of Westcot, Abinger, Shere, Ash-ted, Epsom, or Cheam. *England's Gazet-teer*, 1751, v. *Wotton*. The custom was observed in 1904.

Wounds.—Comp. Nares, 1859, in v.

Wraith or Waff.—Pennant, in des-cribing the customs of the Highlanders, tells us that in certain places the death of people is supposed to be foretold by the cries and shrieks of benshi or the fairy's wife, uttered along the very path where the funeral is to pass, and what in Wales are called corpse candles are often imagined to appear and foretell mortality. In Carmarthen there is hardly any one that dies but some one or other sees his light or candle. There is a similar super-stition among the vulgar in Northumber-land. They call it seeing the waff or ghost of the person whose death it fore-tells.

Pinkerton, who wrote about the same time, says: "Tales of ghosts, brownies, fairies, witches, are the frequent enter-tainment of a winter's evening among the native peasantry of Kircudbright-shire. It is common among them to fancy that they see the wraiths of persons dying, which will be visible to one and not to others present with him. Sometimes the good and the bad angel of the person are seen contending in the shape of a white and a black dog. Only the ghosts of wicked persons are supposed to return to visit and disturb their old acquaintance. Within these last twenty years, it was hardly possible to meet with any person who had not seen many wraiths and ghosts in the course of his experience." *Heron's Journey*, 1792, ii, 227.

Jamieson seems to take a rather different view of the import of a wraith or waff: "The wraith of a living person," says he, "does not, as some have supposed, indicate that he shall die soon: although in all cases viewed as a premonition of the disembodied state. The season, in the natural day, at which the spectre makes its appearance, is understood as a certain presage of the time of the person's de-parture. If seen early in the morning, it forebodes that he shall live long, and even arrive at old age: if in the evening, it indicates that his death is at hand." *Etym. Dict.* in v.

Three hundred miners employed at the Glyncorrwg Colliery, near Port Talbot, Glamorganshire, refused to go to work in July, 1902, owing to a story having been

circulated by some of their number that last week the figure of a woman (wraith) waving a lighted lamp was seen in the workings, and that screams were heard. The men, who are of a superstitious class, insisted that the mine was haunted.

There is a very remarkable type of this class of superstition, and one without any parallel in our English folklore, in the Breton legend of the Orphan of Lannion, where a girl, who had been murdered, reappeared every night in the form of a light flickering round the cross, near which the tragedy had occurred, and at the very hour, until the time arrived, when she, had she been spared, would have died in the ordinary way, and the vision then gradu-ally attained a larger and more distinctly human shape, and was finally seen to ascend to heaven in the arms of an apparition in a luminous robe with wide stretched wings. Michel and Fournier, *Hotelleries*, 1859, p. 345.

Wrapped in his Mother's Smock.—I am of opinion that the vulgar saying, "Oh you are a lucky man; you were wrapped up in a part of your mother's smock," originated in the super-stition about the caul, q.v. In the "Athenian Oracle," speaking of this, the authors say: "We believe no such cor-respondences betwixt the actions of human life and that shirt."

Wrath or Wroth Silver.—Money paid on Martinmas morning (Nov. 11) by the parishes within the manor of Knight-low, Warwickshire, to the agent of the lord, the Duke of Buccleuch. See Hazlitt's Additions to Blount in *Antiquary*, Sept. 1885, for a more particular account of the usage and ceremony, and a very in-teresting and scholarly contribution by Mr. Gomme to the same organ for January, 1894.

Wren.—"The wren is called a trog-lodyte, as it is supposed, from the mode in which it constructs its nest, that is to say in the form of a cavern, with one very small and nar-row aperture through which the birds gain an entrance; but it does not appear that the wren's nest is narrower or more cavern-like than that of other small birds. It builds of various materials, and in various places." Yarrell's *British Birds*, 1843, ii, 166.

The following remarks occur in a paper read several years ago before the British Archæological Association: "The Greeks called both the wren and some kind of crested serpent (the cobra de capelho?) Βασιλίσκος (little king); while the Spaniards term the former reyzuelo, and the latter reyecillo, both diminutives of *rey* (king). The Latin *regulus* (the same) seems till recent times to have included

all kinds of wrens; and the following names from other tongues seem as generally applied; Italian *reatino* (little king), Swedish *kungs-fogel* (king's fowl); Danish, *fugle-konge* (fowl king). Moreover, some of the kingly names given to the wren apply better to the troglodyte or common wren, than to the regulus or golden-crest; such are the German *zaun-könig* (hedgeking), the Italian *re di siepe, di macchia* (king of the hedge, bush), the former being notoriously fond of sticking to his hedge, while the latter often sings on the top of a tree; the Dutch *winter-koninkje* (little winter-king) is applicable to both equally, if derived, as seems likely, from their singing in the winter. . . . .
Another Danish name for the common wren, elle-konge (the alder-king), (German, erlkönig), and that for the wagtail (*motacilla alba*, a kindred bird), elle-kongens datter (the alder-king's daughter), gives another glimpse of mythological allusion. The Swedes, I may add, also call the willow-wren (*motacilla trochilus*) sparf-kung; the Danse spurrekonge (sparrow-king.) . . .

An early French writer on ornithology observes (on the authority of Aristotle), that, though of such diminutive bulk, it harasses the eagle, who holds sway over all other birds. Belon, *De la Nature des Oyseaux*, 1555, p. 342. Pliny notices that in Egypt the wren was supposed to perform the offices of toothpick for the crocodile. *Nat. Hist.* viii, 25.

Vallancey speaking of this, the augur's favourite bird, says that "The Druids represented him as the king of all birds. The superstitious respect shown to this bird gave offence to our first Christian missionaries, and by their commands he is still hunted and killed by the peasants on Christmas Day, and on the following (St. Stephen's Day) he is carried about hung by the leg, in the centre of two hoops crossing each other at right angles, and a procession made in every village. of men, women and children, singing an Irish catch, importing him to be king of all birds. Hence the name of this bird in all the European languages, *Greek*, τρόχιλος, βασιλεύς; *Latin*, regulus; *French*, roytelet, berichot (or berchot); *Welsh*, bren, king; *Teutonic*, koning vogel, king bird; *Dutch*, konije, little king." *Collect.* xiii, 97.

Brand himself notes: "Mr. Gregory informed me, May 23, 1805, that in Ireland they still go out on St. Stephen's Day to hunt the wren." The same occurs in the Isle of Man, and in Surrey, and elsewhere. But the old religious cult is forgotten. Comp. *Manx* and *Robin Redbreast* suprâ.

It is singular enough that in France in the early part of the present century the same practice was observed. "While I was at Le Ciotat, near Marseilles," writes Sonnini, "the particulars of a singular ceremony were related to me,. which takes place every year at the beginning of Nivose (the latter end of December). A numerous body of men, armed with swords and pistols, set off in search of a very small bird which the ancients call troglodytes, (Motacella Troglodytes, L. Syst. Nat. edit. 13, Anglicè the common wren,) a denomination retained by Guenau de Montbeillard, in his 'Natural History of Birds.' When they have found it, a thing not difficult, because they always take care to have one ready, it is suspended on the middle of a pole, which two men carry on their shoulders, as if it were a heavy burthen. This whimsical procession parades round the town: the bird is weighed in a great pair of scales, and the company then sits down to table and makes merry." *Travels*, 1800, pp. 11-12.

The name which the French confer on the wren, Bœuf de Dieu, is in all likelihood, a purely whimsical denomination, for which it would be fruitless to seek or suggest a serious origin. In Egypt they term it, even more strangely and unaccountably, the polecat, or the father of the woodcock, the latter title originating, it is said, in the resemblance between the plumage of the two birds.

Wrestling.—This is not the proper place for entering into the nice distinctions between the various schools of wrestling in Cornwall, Cumberland, Nottinghamshire, &c. It is well known that the differences in practice are considerable. In 1303, Robert of Brunne notices the practice of giving a sword or ring as a prize for wrestling, but says it must not be done on a holyday:

" 3yf pou euer fettyſt fwerde eyper ryng
For to gadyr a wraſtlyng,
Þe holyday pou holdeſt noghte
Whan ſwyche bobaunce for pe ys wroghte.
Cuntek pere comyp, or owper bobaunce;
And ſum men ſlayn, or loſt purghe chaunce."
                    Handlyng Synne, l. 990-5..

He afterward warns men against getting up wrestlings in order to gain praise for it (l. 3690-2), and also (l. 8999) says that "karolles, wreastlynges, or somour games," are not to be held in the church or churchyard.

Myrc, too, warns his hearers against "schotnge, wrastelynge, and open play, and goynge to þe ale on holydaye" ("Instructions for Parish Priests," p. 31, l. 99718; Early Engl. Text Soc. 1868.)

Chaucer says of the miller, in the Prologue to the Canterbury Tales, "At:

wrastlynge he wolde bere awey the ram,"
—a change of prize from the sword and
ring noticed above.

In the Robin Hood story (Hazlitt's *Tales
and Legends*, 1892, p. 310), the Knight of
Utersdale, Sir Richard at-Lee, pleads to
Robin as an excuse for not having kept
his day in returning a loan made to him
by the outlaw, that he had been detained
at a wrestling at Wentbridge, where there
was an attempt to deprive a yeoman of
the prize won by him. These were, no
doubt, periodical institutions, especially
in the North of England. The prize in
this instance was a pair of gloves, a gold
ring, and a pipe of wine, and we may not
be wrong in assigning the incident to the
vicinity of the period, when the *Little
Gest* was written—about 1480—rather
than to the Robin Hood epoch itself.

In the "Tale of the Basyn," it is said
of the parson :

" He harpys and gytryns and syngs well
    ther-too,
He wrestels and lepis, and casts the ston
    also—"

In the "Governor," 1531, Sir T. Elyot
observes: "Wrastlyng is a verye good
exercise in the beginning of youth, so that
it bee with one that is equall in strength
or some what vnder, and that the place
be soft, that in falling their bodies be
not brused. There be diuers manners of
wrastlyngs: but the best, as wel for health
of body, as for exercise of strength, is,
when laying mutually their hands one
ouer an others neck, with the other hande
they holde fast each other by the arm,
and clasping their legs together, they in-
force themselues with strength and
agilytie, to throw downe each other, which
is also praised by Galen."

Again, in the " Maner of the tryumphe
at Caleys and Bullen (1532)" it is said :
" And that day there was a great wrastelynge bytwene englyshmen & frensshmen
before bothe yᵉ kynges/ the frensshe kyng
had none but preestes that wrasteled/
whiche were bygge men & stronge/ they
were bretherne/ but they had moost
falles." Browne, in the fifth song of
"Britannia's Pastorals," 1614, writes:

" As when the gallant youth which liue
    vpon
The western downes of louely Albion ;
Meeting, some festiuall to solemnize,
Choose out two, skil'd in wrastling
    exercise,
Who strongly, at the wrist or coller
    cling,
Whilst arme in arme the people make
    a ring."

On St. Bartholomew's Day, during the
fair, wrestling-matches appear to have
been held at Clerkenwell. Machyn the
diarist notes the attendance of the Lord
Mayor and other civic dignitaries at the
match held on the 24th August, 1559. It
seems that it was also customary to have
shooting-matches at or about the same
season in Finsbury-fields.

Heywood, in his "Apology for Actors,"
1612, quotes Stowe for the fact that a
play on the Creation was performed anciently by the skinners at Clerkenwell,
"in place whereof, in these latter daies,"
observes Heywood, "the wrastling and
such other pastimes haue bene kept, and
is still held about Bartholmew-tide." In
"Totenham Court," 1638, by T. Nabbes,
there is this passage : " *Stitchwell.* I have
a Cornish-lad that wrastles well, and hath
brought home rabbets every Bartholmew-
tide these five yeares."

The minister of Monquhitter reported
in 1799 : " People who are not regularly
and profitably employed, rejoice in a
holiday as the means of throwing off that
languor which oppresses the mind, and of
exerting their active powers. So it was
with our fathers. They frequently met
to exert their strength in wrestling, in
casting the hammer, and in throwing the
stone, their agility at foot-ball, and their
dexterity at coits and penny-stone."
Stat. Acc. xxi, 145.

Misson says " Wrestling is one of the
diversions of the English, especially in
the Northern Counties." *Travels*, p. 306,
and comp. Sir T. Parkins, *Inn Play*, 1727.

Wretch or **Wrath Cock.**—Comp.
Nares, 1859, in v.

Yatton, Co. Somerset.—Collinson, speaking of Yatton, Somersetshire,
says, that "John Lane of this parish,
gent. left half an acre of ground, called
the Groves, to the poor for ever, reserving
a quantity of the grass for strewing the
church on Whitsunday."

**Yawning for a Cheshire
Cheese.**—This was, as the "Spectator"
for September 25, 1711, tells us, a Christmas amusement in his time.

Year's Mind.—See *Month's Mind.*
"I shulde speake nothing," says Veron,
"in the mean season, of the costly feastes
and bankettes that are commonly made
unto the priestes (which come to suche
doinges from all partes, as ravens do to
a deade carkase,) in their buryinges,
moneths mindes and yeares myndes."
Hunting of Purgatory, 1561, fol. 36. A
few pages farther on he adds: "The auncient fathers, being veri desirous to move
their audience unto charitye and almose
dedes, did exhorte them to refresh
the poore and give almoses in the
funeralles, & yeares myndes of their
frends & kynnesfolkss, in stedde of

the bankettes that the paynymes & heathen were wont to make at suche doinges, and in stedde of the meates that they did bring to their sepulchres and graves." *Hunting of Purgatory*, 1561, fol. 106.

Yeoman-Fewterer.—The Keeper of the Dogs, an officer under the Huntsman, whose duty was to uncouple or tie up the animals, according to circumstances, to feed them, and to attend to them generally. Sometimes the term was simply *fewterer*.

Yew.—The yew is now become the funeral tree; and the same honours are paid to it by the poets of the present age, as the Cypress enjoyed from the bards of antiquity. Upon looking into Wotton's "Leges Wallicæ," 173)., p. 262, I find the following: "Taxus Sancti libram valet;" with the subsequent note. "Sancti. Sancto nempe alicui dicata, Dubritio v. gr. vel Teliao, quales apud Wallos in Cœmeteriis etiamnum frequentes visuntur." See Ducange, *Glos.* v. *Arbores Sacræ.*

The planting of yews in churchyards seems to derive its origin from ancient funeral rites: in which, Sir Thomas Browne conjectures, from its perpetual verdure, it was used as an emblem of the resurrection. A gentleman assured Brand that he remembered to have read in a Book of Churchwardens' Accounts in the possession of Mr. Littleton, of Bridgnorth, Salop, an account of a yew tree being ordered to be planted in the churchyard for reverence' sake.

The yew is called by Shakespear, in his "Richard the Second," 1597, the double fatal yew, because the leaves of the yew are poison, and the wood is employed for instruments of death. In Poole's "English Parnassus," 1657, the yew has the epithets of "warlick, dismal, fatal, mortal, venemous, unhappy, verdant, deadly, dreadful," annexed to it: these are all from old English poets. Chaucer, in his "Assemble of Foules," calls it "the shooter ewe." The yew tree is thus mentioned in "Loves Festivall at Lusts Funerall," at the end of Brathwaite's "Boulster Lecture," 1640:

"The screch oule frights us not, nor th' towling-bell
Summons our vading-startling ghosts to hell.
Tombs, forlorne charnels, unfrequented caves,
The fatall ewe, sad sociate to graves,
Present no figures to our dying eyes
'Cause vertue was our gole, her praise our prize."

In Gayton's "Art of Longevity," 1659, p 58, is the following passage alluding to

St. Paul's Churchyard having been turned into a herb market:

"The ewe, sad box, and cypress (solemn trees)
Once church-yard guests (till burial rites did cease)
Give place to sallads," &c.

Daines Barrington observes: "that trees in a church yard were often planted to skreen the church from the wind; that, low as churches were built at this time, the thick foliage of the yew answered this purpose better than any other tree. I have been informed, accordingly, that the yew trees in the church yard of Gyffin, near Conway, having been lately felled, the roof of the church hath suffered excessively."

A writer in the *Gentleman's Magazine*, for February, 1780, J. O. dislikes all the reasons assigned for planting yew trees in churchyards, except their gloomy aspect and their noxious quality. The first intended to add solemnity to the consecrated ground, the other to preserve it from the ravages of cattle. To countenance his first reason, he quotes Dryden, who calls the yew the mourner yew, and Virgil, who calls it the baneful yew; and to make it still more fitting for the place, adds the magic use which Shakespear makes of it in Macbeth:

"Liver of blaspheming Jew,
Gall of goats, and slips of yew
Sliver'd in the moon's eclipse."

He adds, "the great dramatist's opinion of its noxious properties is evident from Hecate's answer to the aërial spirit:

"With new fall'n dew,
From church yard yew,
I will but 'noint,
And then I'll mount." &c.

One may ask those who favour the opinion that yews were planted in churchyards for making bows, and as being there fenced from the cattle, are not all plantation grounds fenced from cattle? and whence is it that there are usually but one yew tree, or two at the most, in each churchyard?

Coles gives an account of "the leaves of yew trees poisoning a clergyman's cowes that eat them, who seeing some boyes breaking boughs from the yew tree in the churchyard, thought himselfe much injured. To prevent the like trespasses, he sent one presently to cut downe the tree and to bring it into his back yard." Two of the cows feeding upon the leaves, died in a few hours afterwards, and Coles remarks that the clergyman had a just reward.

In the "Gentleman's Magazine" for Dec., 1779, A. B. mentions the two reasons already assigned for the planting of yew trees in churchyards : but he considers the slow growth of these trees as an objection to the idea of their protecting the church from storms ; and the rarity of their occurrence (it being very uncommon to meet with more than one or two in the same place), an indication that they could not have been much cultivated for the purposes of archery. He adds, " I cannot find any statute or proclamation that directs the cultivation of the yew tree in any place whatever." By different extracts from our old statutes, he continues, " it appears that we depended principally upon imported bow-staves for our best bows ; which one would think needed not to have been the case, if our church yards had been well stocked with yew trees." " The English yew," moreover, " was of an inferior goodness ;" and that our brave countrymen were forced to have recourse to foreign materials appears from the Statute 12 Edward IV. (1472), by which the Venetian merchants with each butt of wine were required to present four good bowstaves gratuitously ; and this was, no doubt, then an established practice. Hazlitt's *Venetian Republic*, 1900, ii, 581. The following prices of purchase were settled in "An act of Bowyers," 8 Eliz. : " Bows meet for men's shooting, being outlandish yew of the best sort, not over the price of 6s. 8d. ; Bows meet for men's shooting, of the second sort, 3s. 4d. : bows for men, of a coarser sort, called livery bows, 2s. ; bows being English yew, 2s."

Gerarde, he says, "mentions their growing in church yards where they have been planted. Evelyn only says, that the propagation of them has been forborne since the use of bows has been laid aside."

On the statute 22 Edw. IV., ch. 4, which declares the price of a yew bow is not to exceed 3s. 4d., Barrington says : " I should imagine that the planting yews in church yards, being places fenced from cattle, arose, at least in many instances, from an attention to the material from which the best bows are made ; nor do we hear of such trees being planted in the church yards of other parts of Europe." It appears by 4 Hen. V. ch. 3. that the wood of which the best arrows were made was the ash. But from the act 6 Henry VIII. c. 13, it seems to be inferible that at that time bows were made of elm or any " other wode of easy pryce." There is a statute so late as the 8th Eliz. c. 10, which relates to bowyers, each of whom is always to have in his house fifty bows made of elm, witch, hazel, or ash. *Observations on the Statutes*, 191.

Grose observes that " Yew at length became so scarce (as I have hinted in a preceding note) that to prevent a too great consumption of it, bowyers were directed to make four bows of witch-hazle, ash or elm, to one of yew. And no person under seventeen, unless possessed of moveables worth forty marks, or the son of parents having an estate of ten pounds per annum, might shoot in a yew bow." *Military Antiquities*, i, 142. Drayton, in his " Polyolbion," says :

" All made of Spanish yew, their bows are wondrous strong."

On which there is this note : By 5 Edw. IV. ch. 4 (Irish Statutes), " every Englishman is obliged to have a bow in his house of his own length, either of yew, wych, hasel, ash, or awburn, probably alder."

The song in Shakespear's " Twelfth Night," act ii. sc. 4, commencing, " Come away, come away, death," mentions the custom of sticking yew in the shroud. There is another song in the " Maid's Tragedy," by Beaumont and Fletcher, 1619, beginning,

" Lay a garland on my hearse, Of the dismal yew."

which forms an appropriate illustration of this subject. A credible person, who was born and brought up in a village in Suffolk, informed Mr. Brand that when he was a boy, it was customary there to cut sprigs and boughs of yew trees to strew on the graves, &c., at rustic funerals.

Lysons notices several yew trees of enormous growth in the counties of Berks and Bucks ; particularly one at Wyrardisbury in the latter county, which, at six feet from the ground, measures thirty feet five inches in girth. There is a yew tree of vast bulk at Isley in Oxfordshire, supposed to be coëval with the church ; which is known to have been erected in the twelfth century. Others of great age may be seen in various parts of England. *Magna Brit.* i, 254, 578, 643, 681.

Warner speaking of Brockenhurst Church, Hants, says : " The church-yard exhibits two examples of enormous vegetation. A large oak, apparently coëval with the mound on which it grows, measuring five and twenty feet in girth ; and a straight majestic yew tree. On the latter, the axe has committed sad depredations ; despoiling it of five or six huge branches, a circumstance that doubtless has taken greatly from its antient dignity. Still, however, it is a noble tree, measuring in girth fifteen feet, and in height upwards of sixty. I should think it might lay claim to an antiquity, nearly equal to its venerable neighbour. The New Forest, and Brockenhurst in particular, being formerly so famous for the production of yews, it might be a matter of wonder that so few remained to the present day, did we not recollect that the old English Yeomanry were supplied from this tree with those excellent bows, which rendered them the best and most dreaded archers in Europe. This constant and universal demand for yew produced in time such a scarcity, that recourse was had to foreign countries for a supply: and the importation of them was enjoined by express acts of parliament passed for that purpose. *Remarks on S. W. Parts of Hampshire*, 1793, i, 95. Comp. also Stat. 13 Edw. I. c. 6. Edw. iv. c. 2; Rich. III. c. 2; and Henry VIII. c. 3.

Collinson, speaking of two very large yew trees in the churchyard of Ashill, observes in a note, that "our forefathers were particularly careful in preserving this funeral tree, whose branches it was usual for mourners to carry in solemn procession to the grave, and afterwards" (as has been already noticed) "to deposit therein under the bodies of their departed friends." *Somersetshire*, Hundr. of Abdick and Bulston, 13.

In a printed account of the parish of Burton (Preston Patrick) Westmoreland, we read: "Mr. Machel takes notice of a yew tree in the chapel yard, which he says was very old and decayed (1692); which shews, he observes, the antiquity of the chapel. The yew tree is there yet, which shews also the longevity of that species of wood. These yew trees in church and chapel yards seem to have been intended originally for the use of archery. But this only a matter of conjecture: Antiquity having not furnished any account (so far as we have been able to find) of the design of this kind of plantation." Nicholson and Burn, i, 242.

"Here," says Macpherson, in his Ossianic poems, which of course merely illustrate the old Scotish usage, speaking of two departed lovers, "rests their dust, Cuthullin! These lonely yews sprang from their tomb, and shade them from the storm!"

The parishioners of Fortingal, county Perth, reckoned among their curiosities in the 18th century a yew tree in the churchyard fifty-two feet in circumference, and the minister of Dunscore, co. Dumfries, reported in 1792, that in one corner of the churchyard there "grew a large yew tree, which was consumed in the heart. Three men have stood in it at once; but it was overturned by the wind this season."

It appears that in Lord Hopetoun's garden at Ormistoun Hall, there was a remarkable yew tree. About the twentieth part of an English acre was covered by it. The minister of the parish of Ormistoun thus described it in 1792: "the diameter of the ground overspread by its branches is fifty-three feet. Its trunk eleven feet in circumference. From the best information it cannot be under two hundred years old. It seems rather more probable to be between three hundred and four hundred years old." Again: "Two yew trees at Ballikinrain, Killearn, co. Stirling, at a distance like one tree, cover an area of eighteen yards diameter." And lastly: "There is a yew tree in the garden of Broich, Kippen, co. Perth and Stirling. The circumference of the circle overspread by the lower branches is a hundred and forty feet. It is supposed to be two hundred or three hundred years old." This was of course in the 18th century. *Stat. Acc.* ii, 453; iii, 144; iv, 172, xvi, iii; xxiii, 128.

Ymgambio.—See *Gwindy*.

Youling.—i.q. *Yuling*. Said to be an old Kentish custom in Rogation week. *Uling*, *Yuling*, *Youling*, *Yawling*, and *Howling*, appear to be mere variants. Comp. *Apple-Howling* suprâ.

Yule.—Bosworth (*Compend. A-S. and Engl. Dict.* 1876, v. *Geól*) makes the root *Gál*, merry, and defines Yule as the merry feast, and leads us to understand that our Anglo-Saxon forefathers had their Yule, their *ere* or *before* Yule, and their after Yule, corresponding to the later Christmas and New Year's holydays. Comp. *Whitsuntide* suprâ and Hazlitt's Blount, 1874, p. 89. The A-S. *Geól* appears to be cognate to the Sanscrit *Ywala*, the Sun.

Hearne, in his *Diary*, December 21, 1710, mentions the supposition that Yule may be derived from Ioulos, the name of the month in which our Christmas occurs with certain nations. In the earlier Scotish nomenclature it was treated as equivalent to the Latin *Julius*. An article on this subject, too long to transcribe, and scarcely capable of condensation, is in Mr. Atkinson's "Cleveland Glossary," 1868, p. 588.

"One of the principal feasts," it is said in the *Gentleman's Magazine for* 1784, "among the Northern nations was the *Juul*, afterwards called *Yule*, about the shortest day, which as Mr. Mallet observes, bore a great resemblance to the Roman *Saturnalia*, which primarily were limited to a single day. The writer just cited, following Bryant, identified Saturn with Noah. Comp. Keightley's *Mythology*, 1854, p. 466.

John Herolt, a Dominican, in a sermon on the Nativity, condemning those who made a bad use of this festival, mentions persons who spend the whole night in revelry, who practise divinations by salt and other (as he considered them) profane occupations:—

"Qui istam noctem in ludo consumpserunt. Item qui cumulos salis ponunt, et per hoc futura prognosticant. Item qui calceos per caput jactant; similiter qui arbores cingunt. Et significantur qui cum micis et fragmentis, qui tolluntur de mensa in vigilia natalis Christi sua sortilegia exercent."

Leland has the following:

"Yule att York, out of a cowcher belonging to the Cytty, per Carolum Fairfax, ar.

"The Sheriffs of York by the custome of the cytty, do use to ride betwixt Michalemas and Mydwynter, that is Youle, and for to make a proclamation throughout the citty, in forme following: 'O yes! We command of our liege lords behalf the King of England (that God save and keepe), that the peace of the King be well keeped and maynteyned within the citty and suburbs, by night and by day, &c. Also, that no common woman walke in the streets without a gray hood on her head, and a white wand in her hand, &c. Also the Sheriffes of the citty on St. Thomas Day the Apostle, before Youle, att tenne of the bell, shall come to All-hallow kirke on the pavement, and ther they shall heare a masse of St. Thomas in the high wheare (quire), and offer at the masse; and when the masse is done, they shall make a proclamation att the pillory of the Youle-Girth (in the forme that followes) by ther serjant: We commaund that the peace of our Lord the King be well keeped and mayntayned by night and by day, &c. (prout solebat in proclamatione prædicta vice-comitum in eorum equitatione.) Also that no manner of man make no congregations nor assemblyes (prout continetur in equitatione vice-comitum). Also that all manner of whores and thieves, dice players, carders, and all other unthrifty folke, be welcome to the towne, whether they come late or early, att the reverence of the high feast of Youle, till the twelve days be passed.' The proclamation made in forme aforesaid, the fower serjeants shall goe or ride (whether they will); and one of them shall have a horne of brasse, of the toll-bouth; and the other three serjeants shall every one of them have a horne, and so go forth to the fower barres of the citty, and blow the Youle-Girth. And the Sheriffes for that day use to go together, they and their wives, and ther officers, att the reverence of the high feast of Yole, on ther proper costs," &c. *Itinerary*, ed. 1770, iv., 182.

Blount tells us, that in Yorkshire and our other northern parts they had an old custom: After sermon or service on Christmas Day, the people would, even in the churches, cry Ule, Ule, as a token of rejoicing: and the common sort ran about the streets, singing

Ule, Ule, Ule, Ule,
Three puddings in a pule,
Crack nuts, and cry Ule.

Grose, in his "Provincial Glossary," tells us, that in "Farm-houses in the North, the servants lay by a large knotty block for their Christmas fire, and during the time it lasts they are entitled by custom to ale at their meals. In Gloucestershire, in the Cotswolds, they formerly had at Whitsuntide a festival called indifferently an *Ale* and a *Yule;* but it is to be suspected that the former name is the correct one. Comp. *Whitsuntide* suprâ.

I find the following curious passage in the "Scotch Presbyterian Eloquence Displayed," p. 98: "One preaching against the observation of Christmas, said in a Scotch jingle, 'Ye will say, sirs, good old Youl day; I tell you, good old Fool day. You will say it is a brave holiday; I tell you it is a brave belly-day.'" Swift, in his "Tale of a Tub," might have given this as an instance of Jack's tearing off the lace, and making a plain coat. There is a proverb:

"It is good to cry Ule at other men's costs."

The Scotish proverb, "A Yule feast may be quit at Pasche" is as much as to say, remarks Mr. Hislop ("Proverbs of Scotland," 1862, p. 36), "Some undertakings can conveniently be done at any time."

Wormius notices that even in his time the Icelanders dated the beginning of their year from Yule, in consequence of an ancient custom which the laws of their country obliged them to retain. They even reckoned a person's age by the Yules he had seen. Comp. *Christmas* and *Gule of August*, and see Lucas, *Studies in Nidderdale*, 42, et seqq.

Yule Dough.—The Yule-Dough, or Dow, was a kind of Baby, or little image of paste, which our bakers used formerly to bake at tl is season, and present to their customers, in the same manner as the Chandlers gave Christmas candles.

They are called Yule cakes in the county of Durham. I find in the Roman Calendar that at Rome, on the vigil of the Nativity, sweet meats were presented to the Fathers in the Vatican, and that all kinds of little images (no doubt of paste) were to be found at the confectioners' shops. There is the greatest probability that we have had hence both our Yule-doughs, plum-porridge, and mince-pies, the latter of which are still in common use at this season. The Yule-dough has perhaps been intended for an image of the child Jesus, with the Virgin Mary. It is now, If I mistake not, pretty generally laid aside, or at most retained only by children.

Yule Gifts or **Julklaps.**—Were so called from those who received them striking against the doors of the donors.

Yule Log or **Clog.**—Clog is properly a piece of wood, fastened about the legs of beasts, to keep them from running astray. In a secondary or figurative sense, it signifies a load, let, or hindrance. Thus also a truant-clog. Bailey supposes clog to come from log (which he derives from the Saxon lȝan to lie, because of its weight, it lies, as it were, immoveable), the trunk of a tree, or stump of wood for fuel. Block has the same signification. In the Supplement to the "Gentleman's Magazine" for 1790, the subsequent note upon the Yule-log occurs: "On the Yule-log see the 'Cyclops' of Euripides, Act i. sc. v. 10. 'Archæologia,' vol. vii. p. 360." Beckwith in the same miscellany for February, 1784, says: "That this rejoicing on Christmas Eve had its rise from the Juul, and was exchanged for it, is evident from a custom practised in the Northern Counties, of putting a large clog of wood on the fire this evening, which is still called the Yule-clog."

Christmas, says Blount, was called the Feast of Lights in the Western or Latin Church, because they used many lights or candles at the feast; or rather, because Christ, the light of all lights, that true light, came into the world. Hence the Christmas candle, and what was, perhaps, only a succedaneum, the Yule-block or clog, before candles were in general use. Thus a large coal is often set apart at present in the North for the same purpose, *i.e.* to make a great light on Yule or Christmas Eve. Lights, indeed, seem to have been used upon all festive occasions. Thus our illuminations, fireworks, &c. on the news of victories.

In the ancient times to which we would trace up the origin of these almost obsolete customs, blocks, logs, or clogs of dried wood might be easily procured and provided against this festive season. At that time of day it must have been in the power but of few to command candles or torches for making their annual illumination. However this may be, I am pretty confident that the Yule-block will be found, in its first use, to have been only a counterpart of the Midsummer fires, made within doors because of the cold weather at this winter solstice, as those in the hot season, at the summer one, are kindled in the open air.

Brand adds : "After a diligent and close study of Gebelin, the French Bryant, on this subject, one cannot fail, I think, of adopting this hypothesis, which is con-firmed by great probability, and many cogent, if not infallible proofs."

The size of these logs of wood, which were, in fact, great trees, may be collected hence: "that, in the time of the civil wars of the last century, Captain Hosier (I suppose of the Berwick family) burnt the house of Mr. Barker, of Haghmond Abbey, near Shrewsbury, by setting fire to the Yule-log." In his "Hesperides," 1648, Herrick tells us how the Yule-log of the new Christmas was wont to be lighted "with last year's brand."

Formerly, at Tibenham, in Norfolk, and doubtless elsewhere in the East of England, a piece of the Yule-log was reserved to light the log the following year. It was also customary, so long as the log continued to burn, to allow the farm servants to partake in common with their employers of the best cyder, which was tapped for the occasion, having lain a year or more in the wood to mature. *Current Notes* for August, 1856.

In Warmstrey's "Vindication of the Solemnity of the Nativity of Christ," 1648, is the following passage: "The blazes are foolish and vaine," (he means here, evidently, the Yule-clogs or logs,) "and not countenanced by the church."

"Now blocks to cleave
This time requires,
'Gainst Christmas for
To make good fires."
Poor Robin for 1677.

A clergyman of Devonshire informed Mr. Brand that the custom of burning the Christmas-block still continued in that county. This was in the 18th century, and I believe that the usage is still retained. Comp. *Kitchen Fire.* The habit of keeping the fire alight throughout the year may have had a superstitious origin. There is a Scotish proverb, "He's as bare as the birk at Yule E'en," which perhaps, alludes to this custom, the birk meaning a block of the birch-tree, stripped of its bark and dried against Yule Even. It is spoken of one who is exceedingly poor.

Thiers states, that it was the practice in France to light the log on Christmas Eve, and to burn it for a certain time every day till Twelfth Night. He ascribes singular virtues to this log which in France used, he seems to say, to be carefully preserved in the house under a bed, or in some other secure place, as a protection against thunder and fire during the rest of the year. It was also regarded as beneficial, when properly administered, in the cure of diseases in animals; it was dipped in the water-trough used for cows in calf, to expedite delivery, and its ashes, scattered over the land, kept the corn clear of blight. *Traité des Superstitions,* 1679, i, 323.